Communications in Computer and Information Science 1517

More information about this series at https://link.springer.com/bookseries/7899

Teddy Mantoro · Minho Lee ·
Media Anugerah Ayu · Kok Wai Wong ·
Achmad Nizar Hidayanto (Eds.)

Neural
Information Processing

28th International Conference, ICONIP 2021
Sanur, Bali, Indonesia, December 8–12, 2021
Proceedings, Part VI

 Springer

Editors
Teddy Mantoro (iD)
Sampoerna University
Jakarta, Indonesia

Media Anugerah Ayu (iD)
Sampoerna University
Jakarta, Indonesia

Achmad Nizar Hidayanto (iD)
Universitas Indonesia
Depok, Indonesia

Minho Lee (iD)
Kyungpook National University
Daegu, Korea (Republic of)

Kok Wai Wong (iD)
Murdoch University
Murdoch, WA, Australia

ISSN 1865-0929 ISSN 1865-0937 (electronic)
Communications in Computer and Information Science
ISBN 978-3-030-92309-9 ISBN 978-3-030-92310-5 (eBook)
https://doi.org/10.1007/978-3-030-92310-5

This Springer imprint is published by the registered company Springer Nature Switzerland AG
The registered company address is: Gewerbestrasse 11, 6330 Cham, Switzerland

Preface

Welcome to the proceedings of the 28th International Conference on Neural Information Processing (ICONIP 2021) of the Asia-Pacific Neural Network Society (APNNS), held virtually from Indonesia during December 8–12, 2021.

The mission of the Asia-Pacific Neural Network Society is to promote active interactions among researchers, scientists, and industry professionals who are working in neural networks and related fields in the Asia-Pacific region. APNNS has Governing Board Members from 13 countries/regions – Australia, China, Hong Kong, India, Japan, Malaysia, New Zealand, Singapore, South Korea, Qatar, Taiwan, Thailand, and Turkey. The society's flagship annual conference is the International Conference of Neural Information Processing (ICONIP).

The ICONIP conference aims to provide a leading international forum for researchers, scientists, and industry professionals who are working in neuroscience, neural networks, deep learning, and related fields to share their new ideas, progress, and achievements. Due to the current COVID-19 pandemic, ICONIP 2021, which was planned to be held in Bali, Indonesia, was organized as a fully virtual conference.

The conference had four main themes, i.e., "Theory and Algorithms," "Cognitive Neurosciences," "Human Centred Computing," and "Applications." The proceedings consist of two CCIS volumes, which are organized in topical sections according to the four main themes mentioned previously, along with the topics covered in three special sessions. Another topic is from a workshop on Artificial Intelligence and Cyber Security which was held together with ICONIP 2021. Thus, in total, eight different topics were accommodated at the conference. The topics were also the names of the 15-minute presentation sessions at ICONIP 2021. The eight topics in the conference were: Theory and Algorithms; Cognitive Neurosciences; Human Centred Computing; Applications; Artificial Intelligence and Cybersecurity; Advances in Deep and Shallow Machine Learning Algorithms for Biomedical Data and Imaging; Reliable, Robust, and Secure Machine Learning Algorithms; and Theory and Applications of Natural Computing Paradigms.

Our great appreciation goes to the Program Committee members and the reviewers who devoted their time and effort to our rigorous peer-review process. Their insightful reviews and timely feedback ensured the high quality of the papers accepted for publication. Enormous thanks are addressed to the Organizing Committee who has done every effort to make this conference a successful one. Finally, thank you to all the authors of papers, presenters, and participants at the conference. Your support and engagement made it all worthwhile.

December 2021

Teddy Mantoro
Minho Lee
Media A. Ayu
Kok Wai Wong
Achmad Nizar Hidayanto

Organization

Honorary Chairs

Jonathan Chan   King Mongkut's University of Technology Thonburi, Thailand

Lance Fung   Murdoch University, Australia

General Chairs

Teddy Mantoro   Sampoerna University, Indonesia

Minho Lee   Kyungpook National University, South Korea

Program Chairs

Media A. Ayu   Sampoerna University, Indonesia

Kok Wai Wong   Murdoch University, Australia

Achmad Nizar   Universitas Indonesia, Indonesia

Local Arrangements Chairs

Linawati   Universitas Udayana, Indonesia

W. G. Ariastina   Universitas Udayana, Indonesia

Finance Chairs

Kurnianingsih   Politeknik Negeri Semarang, Indonesia

Kazushi Ikeda   Nara Institute of Science and Technology, Japan

Special Sessions Chairs

Sunu Wibirama   Universitas Gadjah Mada, Indonesia

Paul Pang   Federation University Australia, Australia

Noor Akhmad Setiawan   Universitas Gadjah Mada, Indonesia

Tutorial Chairs

Suryono   Universitas Diponegoro, Indonesia

Muhammad Agni Catur Bhakti   Sampoerna University, Indonesia

Proceedings Chairs

Adi Wibowo   Universitas Diponegoro, Indonesia
Sung Bae Cho   Yonsei University, South Korea

Publicity Chairs

Dwiza Riana   Universitas Nusa Mandiri, Indonesia
M. Tanveer   Indian Institute of Technology, Indore, India

Program Committee

Abdulrazak Alhababi   Universiti Malaysia Sarawak, Malaysia
Abhijit Adhikary   Australian National University, Australia
Achmad Nizar Hidayanto   University of Indonesia, Indonesia
Adamu Abubakar Ibrahim   International Islamic University Malaysia, Malaysia
Adi Wibowo   Diponegoro University, Indonesia
Adnan Mahmood   Macquarie University, Australia
Afiyati Amaluddin   Mercu Buana University, Indonesia
Ahmed Alharbi   RMIT University, Australia
Akeem Olowolayemo   International Islamic University Malaysia, Malaysia
Akira Hirose   University of Tokyo, Japan
Aleksandra Nowak   Jagiellonian University, Poland
Ali Haidar   University of New South Wales, Australia
Ali Mehrabi   Western Sydney University, Australia
Al-Jadir   Murdoch University, Australia
Ana Flavia Reis   Federal Technological University of Paraná, Brazil
Anaissi Ali   University of Sydney, Australia
Andrew Beng Jin Teoh   Yonsei University, South Korea
Andrew Chiou   Central Queensland University, Australia
Aneesh Chivukula   University of Technology Sydney, Australia
Aneesh Krishna   Curtin University, Australia
Anna Zhu   Wuhan University of Technology, China
Anto Satriyo Nugroho   Agency for Assessment and Application of
                              Technology, Indonesia
Anupiya Nugaliyadde   Sri Lanka Institute of Information Technology,
                              Sri Lanka
Anwesha Law   Indian Statistical Institute, India
Aprinaldi Mantau   Kyushu Institute of Technology, Japan
Ari Wibisono   Universitas Indonesia, Indonesia
Arief Ramadhan   Bina Nusantara University, Indonesia
Arit Thammano   King Mongkut's Institute of Technology Ladkrabang,
                              Thailand
Arpit Garg   University of Adelaide, Australia
Aryal Sunil   Deakin University, Australia
Ashkan Farhangi   University of Central Florida, USA

Atul Negi	University of Hyderabad, India
Barawi Mohamad Hardyman	Universiti Malaysia Sarawak, Malaysia
Bayu Distiawan	Universitas Indonesia, Indonesia
Bharat Richhariya	IISc Bangalore, India
Bin Pan	Nankai University, China
Bingshu Wang	Northwestern Polytechnical University, Taicang, China
Bonaventure C. Molokwu	University of Windsor, Canada
Bo-Qun Ma	Ant Financial
Bunthit Watanapa	King Mongkut's University of Technology Thonburi, Thailand
Chang-Dong Wang	Sun Yat-sen University, China
Chattrakul Sombattheera	Mahasarakham University, Thailand
Chee Siong Teh	Universiti Malaysia Sarawak, Malaysia
Chen Wei Chén	Chongqing Jiaotong University, China
Chengwei Wu	Harbin Institute of Technology, China
Chern Hong Lim	Monash University, Australia
Chih-Chieh Hung	National Chung Hsing University, Taiwan
Chiranjibi Sitaula	Deakin University, Australia
Chi-Sing Leung	City University of Hong Kong, Hong Kong
Choo Jun Tan	Wawasan Open University, Malaysia
Christoph Bergmeir	Monash University, Australia
Christophe Guyeux	University of Franche-Comté, France
Chuan Chen	Sun Yat-sen University, China
Chuanqi Tan	BIT, China
Chu-Kiong Loo	University of Malaya, Malaysia
Chun Che Fung	Murdoch University, Australia
Colin Samplawski	University of Massachusetts Amherst, USA
Congbo Ma	University of Adelaide, Australia
Cuiyun Gao	Chinese University of Hong Kong, Hong Kong
Cutifa Safitri	Universiti Teknologi Malaysia, Malaysia
Daisuke Miyamoto	University of Tokyo, Japan
Dan Popescu	Politehnica University of Bucharest
David Bong	Universiti Malaysia Sarawak, Malaysia
David Iclanzan	Sapientia Hungarian Science University of Transylvania, Romania
Debasmit Das	IIT Roorkee, India
Dengya Zhu	Curtin University, Australia
Derwin Suhartono	Bina Nusantara University, Indonesia
Devi Fitrianah	Universitas Mercu Buana, Indonesia
Deyu Zhou	Southeast University, China
Dhimas Arief Dharmawan	Universitas Indonesia, Indonesia
Dianhui Wang	La Trobe University, Australia
Dini Handayani	Taylors University, Malaysia
Dipanjyoti Paul	Indian Institute of Technology, Patna, India
Dong Chen	Wuhan University, China

Donglin Bai	Shanghai Jiao Tong University, China
Dongrui Wu	Huazhong University of Science & Technology, China
Dugang Liu	Shenzhen University, China
Dwina Kuswardani	Institut Teknologi PLN, Indonesia
Dwiza Riana	Universitas Nusa Mandiri, Indonesia
Edmund Lai	Auckland University of Technology, New Zealand
Eiji Uchino	Yamaguchi University, Japan
Emanuele Principi	Università Politecnica delle Marche, Italy
Enmei Tu	Shanghai Jiao Tong University, China
Enna Hirata	Kobe University, Japan
Eri Sato-Shimokawara	Tokyo Metropolitan University, Japan
Fajri Koto	University of Melbourne, Australia
Fan Wu	Australian National University, Australia
Farhad Ahamed	Western Sydney University, Australia
Fei Jiang	Shanghai Jiao Tong University, China
Feidiao Yang	Microsoft, USA
Feng Wan	University of Macau, Macau
Fenty Eka Muzayyana Agustin	UIN Syarif Hidayatullah Jakarta, Indonesia
Ferda Ernawan	Universiti Malaysia Pahang, Malaysia
Ferdous Sohel	Murdoch University, Australia
Francisco J. Moreno-Barea	Universidad de Málaga, Spain
Fuad Jamour	University of California, Riverside, USA
Fuchun Sun	Tsinghua University, China
Fumiaki Saitoh	Chiba Institute of Technology, Japan
Gang Chen	Victoria University of Wellington, New Zealand
Gang Li	Deakin University, Australia
Gang Yang	Renmin University of China
Gao Junbin	Huazhong University of Science and Technology, China
George Cabral	Universidade Federal Rural de Pernambuco, Brazil
Gerald Schaefer	Loughborough University, UK
Gouhei Tanaka	University of Tokyo, Japan
Guanghui Wen	RMIT University, Australia
Guanjin Wang	Murdoch University, Australia
Guoqiang Zhong	Ocean University of China, China
Guoqing Chao	East China Normal University, China
Sangchul Hahn	Handong Global University, South Korea
Haiqin Yang	International Digital Economy Academy, China
Hakaru Tamukoh	Kyushu Institute of Technology, Japan
Hamid Karimi	Utah State University, USA
Hangyu Deng	Waseda University, Japan
Hao Liao	Shenzhen University, China
Haris Al Qodri Maarif	International Islamic University Malaysia, Malaysia
Haruhiko Nishimura	University of Hyogo, Japan
Hayaru Shouno	University of Electro-Communications, Japan

He Chen	Nankai University, China
He Huang	Soochow University, China
Hea Choon Ngo	Universiti Teknikal Malaysia Melaka, Malaysia
Heba El-Fiqi	UNSW Canberra, Australia
Heru Praptono	Bank Indonesia/Universitas Indonesia, Indonesia
Hideitsu Hino	Institute of Statistical Mathematics, Japan
Hidemasa Takao	University of Tokyo, Japan
Hiroaki Inoue	Kobe University, Japan
Hiroaki Kudo	Nagoya University, Japan
Hiromu Monai	Ochanomizu University, Japan
Hiroshi Sakamoto	Kyushu Institute of Technology, Japan
Hisashi Koga	University of Electro-Communications, Japan
Hiu-Hin Tam	City University of Hong Kong, Hong Kong
Hongbing Xia	Beijing Normal University, China
Hongtao Liu	Tianjin University, China
Hongtao Lu	Shanghai Jiao Tong University, China
Hua Zuo	University of Technology Sydney, Australia
Hualou Liang	Drexel University, USA
Huang Chaoran	University of New South Wales, Australia
Huang Shudong	Sichuan University, China
Huawen Liu	University of Texas at San Antonio, USA
Hui Xue	Southeast University, China
Hui Yan	Shanghai Jiao Tong University, China
Hyeyoung Park	Kyungpook National University, South Korea
Hyun-Chul Kim	Kyungpook National University, South Korea
Iksoo Shin	University of Science and Technology, South Korea
Indrabayu Indrabayu	Universitas Hasanuddin, Indonesia
Iqbal Gondal	RMIT University, Australia
Iuliana Georgescu	University of Bucharest, Romania
Iwan Syarif	PENS, Indonesia
J. Kokila	Indian Institute of Information Technology, Allahabad, India
J. Manuel Moreno	Universitat Politècnica de Catalunya, Spain
Jagdish C. Patra	Swinburne University of Technology, Australia
Jean-Francois Couchot	University of Franche-Comté, France
Jelita Asian	STKIP Surya, Indonesia
Jennifer C. Dela Cruz	Mapua University, Philippines
Jérémie Sublime	ISEP, France
Jiahuan Lei	Meituan, China
Jialiang Zhang	Alibaba, China
Jiaming Xu	Institute of Automation, Chinese Academy of Sciences
Jianbo Ning	University of Science and Technology Beijing, China
Jianyi Yang	Nankai University, China
Jiasen Wang	City University of Hong Kong, Hong Kong
Jiawei Fan	Australian National University, Australia
Jiawei Li	Tsinghua University, China

Jiaxin Li	Guangdong University of Technology, China
Jiaxuan Xie	Shanghai Jiao Tong University, China
Jichuan Zeng	Bytedance, China
Jie Shao	University of Science and Technology of China, China
Jie Zhang	Newcastle University, UK
Jiecong Lin	City University of Hong Kong, Hong Kong
Jin Hu	Chongqing Jiaotong University, China
Jin Kyu Kim	Facebook, USA
Jin Ren	Beijing University of Technology, China
Jin Shi	Nanjing University, China
Jinfu Yang	Beijing University of Technology, China
Jing Peng	South China Normal University, China
Jinghui Zhong	South China University of Technology, China
Jin-Tsong Jeng	National Formosa University, Taiwan
Jiri Sima	Institute of Computer Science, Czech Academy of Sciences, Czech Republic
Jo Plested	Australian National University, Australia
Joel Dabrowski	CSIRO, Australia
John Sum	National Chung Hsing University, China
Jolfaei Alireza	Federation University Australia, Australia
Jonathan Chan	King Mongkut's University of Technology Thonburi, Thailand
Jonathan Mojoo	Hiroshima University, Japan
Jose Alfredo Ferreira Costa	Federal University of Rio Grande do Norte, Brazil
Ju Lu	Shandong University, China
Jumana Abu-Khalaf	Edith Cowan University, Australia
Jun Li	Nanjing Normal University, China
Jun Shi	Guangzhou University, China
Junae Kim	DST Group, Australia
Junbin Gao	University of Sydney, Australia
Junjie Chen	Inner Mongolia Agricultural University, China
Junya Chen	Fudan University, China
Junyi Chen	City University of Hong Kong, Hong Kong
Junying Chen	South China University of Technology, China
Junyu Xuan	University of Technology, Sydney
Kah Ong Michael Goh	Multimedia University, Malaysia
Kaizhu Huang	Xi'an Jiaotong-Liverpool University, China
Kam Meng Goh	Tunku Abdul Rahman University College, Malaysia
Katsuhiro Honda	Osaka Prefecture University, Japan
Katsuyuki Hagiwara	Mie University, Japan
Kazushi Ikeda	Nara Institute of Science and Technology, Japan
Kazuteru Miyazaki	National Institution for Academic Degrees and Quality Enhancement of Higher Education, Japan
Kenji Doya	OIST, Japan
Kenji Watanabe	National Institute of Advanced Industrial Science and Technology, Japan

Kok Wai Wong	Murdoch University, Australia
Kitsuchart Pasupa	King Mongkut's Institute of Technology Ladkrabang, Thailand
Kittichai Lavangnananda	King Mongkut's University of Technology Thonburi, Thailand
Koutsakis Polychronis	Murdoch University, Australia
Kui Ding	Nanjing Normal University, China
Kun Zhang	Carnegie Mellon University, USA
Kuntpong Woraratpanya	King Mongkut's Institute of Technology Ladkrabang, Thailand
Kurnianingsih Kurnianingsih	Politeknik Negeri Semarang, Indonesia
Kusrini	Universitas AMIKOM Yogyakarta, Indonesia
Kyle Harrison	UNSW Canberra, Australia
Laga Hamid	Murdoch University, Australia
Lei Wang	Beihang University, China
Leonardo Franco	Universidad de Málaga, Spain
Li Guo	University of Macau, China
Li Yun	Nanjing University of Posts and Telecommunications, China
Libo Wang	Xiamen University of Technology, China
Lie Meng Pang	Southern University of Science and Technology, China
Liew Alan Wee-Chung	Griffith University, Australia
Lingzhi Hu	Beijing University of Technology, China
Linjing Liu	City University of Hong Kong, Hong Kong
Lisi Chen	Hong Kong Baptist University, Hong Kong
Long Cheng	Institute of Automation, Chinese Academy of Sciences, China
Lukman Hakim	Hiroshima University, Japan
M. Tanveer	Indian Institute of Technology, Indore, India
Ma Wanli	University of Canberra, Australia
Man Fai Leung	Hong Kong Metropolitan University, Hong Kong
Maram Mahmoud A. Monshi	Beijing Institute of Technology, China
Marcin Wozniak	Silesian University of Technology, Poland
Marco Anisetti	Università degli Studi di Milano, Italy
Maria Susan Anggreainy	Bina Nusantara University, Indonesia
Mark Abernethy	Murdoch University, Australia
Mark Elshaw	Coventry University, UK
Maruno Yuki	Kyoto Women's University, Japan
Masafumi Hagiwara	Keio University, Japan
Masataka Kawai	NRI SecureTechnologies, Ltd., Japan
Media Ayu	Sampoerna University, Indonesia
Mehdi Neshat	University of Adelaide, Australia
Meng Wang	Southeast University, China
Mengmeng Li	Zhengzhou University, China

Miaohua Zhang	Griffith University, Australia
Mingbo Zhao	Donghua University, China
Mingcong Deng	Tokyo University of Agriculture and Technology, Japan
Minghao Yang	Institute of Automation, Chinese Academy of Sciences, China
Minho Lee	Kyungpook National University, South Korea
Mofei Song	Southeast University, China
Mohammad Faizal Ahmad Fauzi	Multimedia University, Malaysia
Mohsen Marjani	Taylor's University, Malaysia
Mubasher Baig	National University of Computer and Emerging Sciences, Lahore, Pakistan
Muhammad Anwar Ma'Sum	Universitas Indonesia, Indonesia
Muhammad Asim Ali	Shaheed Zulfikar Ali Bhutto Institute of Science and Technology, Pakistan
Muhammad Fawad Akbar Khan	University of Engineering and Technology Peshawar, Pakistan
Muhammad Febrian Rachmadi	Universitas Indonesia, Indonesia
Muhammad Haris	Universitas Nusa Mandiri, Indonesia
Muhammad Haroon Shakeel	Lahore University of Management Sciences, Pakistan
Muhammad Hilman	Universitas Indonesia, Indonesia
Muhammad Ramzan	Saudi Electronic University, Saudi Arabia
Muideen Adegoke	City University of Hong Kong, Hong Kong
Mulin Chen	Northwestern Polytechnical University, China
Murtaza Taj	Lahore University of Management Sciences, Pakistan
Mutsumi Kimura	Ryukoku University, Japan
Naoki Masuyama	Osaka Prefecture University, Japan
Naoyuki Sato	Future University Hakodate, Japan
Nat Dilokthanakul	Vidyasirimedhi Institute of Science and Technology, Thailand
Nguyen Dang	University of Canberra, Australia
Nhi N. Y. Vo	University of Technology Sydney, Australia
Nick Nikzad	Griffith University, Australia
Ning Boda	Swinburne University of Technology, Australia
Nobuhiko Wagatsuma	Tokyo Denki University, Japan
Nobuhiko Yamaguchi	Saga University, Japan
Noor Akhmad Setiawan	Universitas Gadjah Mada, Indonesia
Norbert Jankowski	Nicolaus Copernicus University, Poland
Norikazu Takahashi	Okayama University, Japan
Noriyasu Homma	Tohoku University, Japan
Normaziah A. Aziz	International Islamic University Malaysia, Malaysia
Olarik Surinta	Mahasarakham University, Thailand

Olutomilayo Olayemi Petinrin	Kings University, Nigeria
Ooi Shih Yin	Multimedia University, Malaysia
Osamu Araki	Tokyo University of Science, Japan
Ozlem Faydasicok	Istanbul University, Turkey
Parisa Rastin	University of Lorraine, France
Paul S. Pang	Federation University Australia, Australia
Pedro Antonio Gutierrez	Universidad de Cordoba, Spain
Pengyu Sun	Microsoft
Piotr Duda	Institute of Computational Intelligence/Czestochowa University of Technology, Poland
Prabath Abeysekara	RMIT University, Australia
Pui Huang Leong	Tunku Abdul Rahman University College, Malaysia
Qian Li	Chinese Academy of Sciences, China
Qiang Xiao	Huazhong University of Science and Technology, China
Qiangfu Zhao	University of Aizu, Japan
Qianli Ma	South China University of Technology, China
Qing Xu	Tianjin University, China
Qing Zhang	Meituan, China
Qinglai Wei	Institute of Automation, Chinese Academy of Sciences, China
Qingrong Cheng	Fudan University, China
Qiufeng Wang	Xi'an Jiaotong-Liverpool University, China
Qiulei Dong	Institute of Automation, Chinese Academy of Sciences, China
Qiuye Wu	Guangdong University of Technology, China
Rafal Scherer	Częstochowa University of Technology, Poland
Rahmadya Handayanto	Universitas Islam 45 Bekasi, Indonesia
Rahmat Budiarto	Albaha University, Saudi Arabia
Raja Kumar	Taylor's University, Malaysia
Rammohan Mallipeddi	Kyungpook National University, South Korea
Rana Md Mashud	CSIRO, Australia
Rapeeporn Chamchong	Mahasarakham University, Thailand
Raphael Couturier	Université Bourgogne Franche-Comté, France
Ratchakoon Pruengkarn	Dhurakij Pundit University, Thailand
Reem Mohamed	Mansoura University, Egypt
Rhee Man Kil	Sungkyunkwan University, South Korea
Rim Haidar	University of Sydney, Australia
Rizal Fathoni Aji	Universitas Indonesia, Indonesia
Rukshima Dabare	Murdoch University, Australia
Ruting Cheng	University of Science and Technology Beijing, China
Ruxandra Liana Costea	Polytechnic University of Bucharest, Romania
Saaveethya Sivakumar	Curtin University Malaysia, Malaysia
Sabrina Fariza	Central Queensland University, Australia
Sahand Vahidnia	University of New South Wales, Australia

Saifur Rahaman	City University of Hong Kong, Hong Kong
Sajib Mistry	Curtin University, Australia
Sajib Saha	CSIRO, Australia
Sajid Anwar	Institute of Management Sciences Peshawar, Pakistan
Sakchai Muangsrinoon	Walailak University, Thailand
Salomon Michel	Université Bourgogne Franche-Comté, France
Sandeep Parameswaran	Myntra Designs Pvt. Ltd., India
Sangtae Ahn	Kyungpook National University, South Korea
Sang-Woo Ban	Dongguk University, South Korea
Sangwook Kim	Kobe University, Japan
Sanparith Marukatat	NECTEC, Thailand
Saptakatha Adak	Indian Institute of Technology, Madras, India
Seiichi Ozawa	Kobe University, Japan
Selvarajah Thuseethan	Sabaragamuwa University of Sri Lanka, Sri Lanka
Seong-Bae Park	Kyung Hee University, South Korea
Shan Zhong	Changshu Institute of Technology, China
Shankai Yan	National Institutes of Health, USA
Sheeraz Akram	University of Pittsburgh, USA
Shenglan Liu	Dalian University of Technology, China
Shenglin Zhao	Zhejiang University, China
Shing Chiang Tan	Multimedia University, Malaysia
Shixiong Zhang	Xidian University, China
Shreya Chawla	Australian National University, Australia
Shri Rai	Murdoch University, Australia
Shuchao Pang	Jilin University, China/Macquarie University, Australia
Shuichi Kurogi	Kyushu Institute of Technology, Japan
Siddharth Sachan	Australian National University, Australia
Sirui Li	Murdoch University, Australia
Sonali Agarwal	Indian Institute of Information Technology, Allahabad, India
Sonya Coleman	University of Ulster, UK
Stavros Ntalampiras	University of Milan, Italy
Su Lei	University of Science and Technology Beijing, China
Sung-Bae Cho	Yonsei University, South Korea
Sunu Wibirama	Universitas Gadjah Mada, Indonesia
Susumu Kuroyanagi	Nagoya Institute of Technology, Japan
Sutharshan Rajasegarar	Deakin University, Australia
Takako Hashimoto	Chiba University of Commerce, Japan
Takashi Omori	Tamagawa University, Japan
Tao Ban	National Institute of Information and Communications Technology, Japan
Tao Li	Peking University, China
Tao Xiang	Chongqing University, China
Teddy Mantoro	Sampoerna University, Indonesia
Tedjo Darmanto	STMIK AMIK Bandung, Indonesia
Teijiro Isokawa	University of Hyogo, Japan

Thanh Tam Nguyen	Leibniz University Hannover, Germany
Thanh Tung Khuat	University of Technology Sydney, Australia
Thaweesak Khongtuk	Rajamangala University of Technology Suvarnabhumi, Thailand
Tianlin Zhang	University of Chinese Academy of Sciences, China
Timothy McIntosh	Massey University, New Zealand
Toan Nguyen Thanh	Ho Chi Minh City University of Technology, Vietnam
Todsanai Chumwatana	Murdoch University, Australia
Tom Gedeon	Australian National University, Australia
Tomas Maul	University of Nottingham, Malaysia
Tomohiro Shibata	Kyushu Institute of Technology, Japan
Tomoyuki Kaneko	University of Tokyo, Japan
Toshiaki Omori	Kobe University, Japan
Toshiyuki Yamane	IBM, Japan
Uday Kiran	University of Tokyo, Japan
Udom Silparcha	King Mongkut's University of Technology Thonburi, Thailand
Umar Aditiawarman	Universitas Nusa Putra, Indonesia
Upeka Somaratne	Murdoch University, Australia
Usman Naseem	University of Sydney, Australia
Ven Jyn Kok	National University of Malaysia, Malaysia
Wachira Yangyuen	Rajamangala University of Technology Srivijaya, Thailand
Wai-Keung Fung	Robert Gordon University, UK
Wang Yaqing	Baidu Research, Hong Kong
Wang Yu-Kai	University of Technology Sydney, Australia
Wei Jin	Michigan State University, USA
Wei Yanling	TU Berlin, Germany
Weibin Wu	City University of Hong Kong, Hong Kong
Weifeng Liu	China University of Petroleum, China
Weijie Xiang	University of Science and Technology Beijing, China
Wei-Long Zheng	Massachusetts General Hospital, Harvard Medical School, USA
Weiqun Wang	Institute of Automation, Chinese Academy of Sciences, China
Wen Luo	Nanjing Normal University, China
Wen Yu	Cinvestav, Mexico
Weng Kin Lai	Tunku Abdul Rahman University College, Malaysia
Wenqiang Liu	Southwest Jiaotong University, China
Wentao Wang	Michigan State University, USA
Wenwei Gu	Chinese University of Hong Kong, Hong Kong
Wenxin Yu	Southwest University of Science and Technology, China
Widodo Budiharto	Bina Nusantara University, Indonesia
Wisnu Ananta Kusuma	Institut Pertanian Bogor, Indonesia
Worapat Paireekreng	Dhurakij Pundit University, Thailand

Yu Sang	PetroChina, China
Yu Xiaohan	Griffith University, Australia
Yu Zhou	Chongqing University, China
Yuan Ye	Xi'an Jiaotong University, China
Yuangang Pan	University of Technology Sydney, Australia
Yuchun Fang	Shanghai University, China
Yuhua Song	University of Science and Technology Beijing
Yunjun Gao	Zhejiang University, China
Zeyuan Wang	University of Sydney, Australia
Zhen Wang	University of Sydney, Australia
Zhengyang Feng	Shanghai Jiao Tong University, China
Zhenhua Wang	Zhejiang University of Technology, China
Zhenqian Wu	University of Electronic Science and Technology of China, China
Zhenyu Cui	University of Chinese Academy of Sciences, China
Zhenyue Qin	Australian National University, Australia
Zheyang Shen	Aalto University, Finland
Zhihong Cui	Shandong University, China
Zhijie Fang	Chinese Academy of Sciences, China
Zhipeng Li	Tsinghua University, China
Zhiri Tang	City University of Hong Kong, Hong Kong
Zhuangbin Chen	Chinese University of Hong Kong, Hong Kong
Zongying Liu	University of Malaya, Malaysia

Contents – Part VI

Human Centred Computing

Advances in Deep and Shallow Machine Learning Algorithms for Biomedical Data and Imaging

Theory and Applications of Natural Computing Paradigms

Applications

Cognitive Neurosciences

Scale-Aware Multi-stage Fusion Network for Crowd Counting

Qi Liu[1,2], Jun Sang[1,2(✉)], Fusen Wang[1,2], Li Yang[1,2], Xiaofeng Xia[1,2], and Nong Sang[3]

[1] Key Laboratory of Dependable Service Computing in Cyber Physical Society of Ministry of Education, Chongqing University, Chongqing 400044, China
[2] School of Big Data and Software Engineering, Chongqing University, Chongqing 401331, China
jsang@cqu.edu.cn
[3] School of Artificial Intelligence and Automation, Huazhong University of Science and Technology, Wuhan 430074, China

Abstract. Crowd counting has been widely researched and many hopeful results have been obtained recently. Due to the large-scale variation and complex background noise, accurate crowd counting is still very difficult. In this paper, we raise a simple but efficient network named SMFNet, which focuses on dealing with the above two problems of highly congested noisy scenes. SMFNet consists of two main components: multi-scale dilated convolution block (MDCB) for multi-scale features extraction and U-shape fusion structure (UFS) for multi-stage features fusion. MDCB can address the challenge of scale variation via capturing multi-scale features. UFS provides an effective structure that continuously combines outputs of different stages to achieve the capability of optimizing multi-scale features and increasing resistance to background noise. Compared with the existing methods, SMFNet achieves better performance in capturing effective and richer multi-scale features through progressively multi-stage fusion. To evaluate our method, we have demonstrated it on three popular crowd counting datasets (ShanghaiTech, UCF_CC_50, UCF-QNRF). Experimental results indicate that SMFNet can achieve state-of-the-art results on highly congested scenes datasets.

Keywords: Crowd counting · Multi-scale features · Multi-stage fusion

1 Introduction

Crowd counting has receiving considerable attention from researchers recently. With the development of deep learning on computer vision, many researchers have leveraged convolutional neural network based method to generate high-quality density map and perform accurate crowd counting [1–8]. Although these methods have achieved remarkable progress, the problem of accuracy degradation will still occur when applied to highly congested scene. And scale variation

Supported by National Natural Science Foundation of China (No. 61971073).

T. Mantoro et al. (Eds.): ICONIP 2021, CCIS 1517, pp. 3–11, 2021.
https://doi.org/10.1007/978-3-030-92310-5_1

is the major issue that seriously affects the quality of the estimated density maps. Recently, many CNN-based methods [1,2,9,10] with multi-column structure, multi-branch structure and multi-scale module like Inception [11] have been proposed to deal with scale variation problem. These modules adopt the filters of different sizes to capture variation in head sizes and show good improvements. However, there still exist some blatant shortcomings. The larger target in crowd scene is mainly extracted through kernels with large receptive fields (5×5, 7×7). And they can enhance the ability to capture large heads by adding more big kernels, but each additional large filter could significantly increase the number of training parameters.

In addition, these methods [1,2,9,10] mainly focus on catching the final scale diversity by stacking multi-scale features blocks directly, while ignoring different stages integration. As for crowd counting, shallow layer contains more low-level details [6] that guarantee the precise position of the people head, deep layer involves more high-level context that preserves more contextual information and overall looking of crowd region. Hence, it can be noticed that fusion of different layers may play an important role for better accuracy. Therefore, our method employs a novel multi-stage fusion for more robust crowd count.

Based on the above two points, we propose a novel Scale-aware Multi-stage Fusion Network called SMFNet, which better integrates the output of multiple stages in backend network, and achieves state-of-the-art crowd counting performance in highly congested noisy scenes. The structure of the proposed SMFNet is shown in Fig. 1. SMFNet is built upon the multi-scale dilated convolution block (MDCB) and U-shape fusion structure (UFS). MDCB is applied for multi-scale features extraction, which is constructed by different dilated convolutional layers stacked upon each other to strengthen the robustness for different heads sizes. To further enhance scale diversity captured by MDCB, we design the UFS to progressively optimize and enrich the extracted multi-scale features through merging different stages features together, while filtering low-level background noise that causes interference to density maps.

To summarize, the major contributions of our paper are as follows:

- We propose a multi-scale dilated convolution block (MDCB) to extract features at different scales to overcome scale diversity without involving extra computations.
- We propose an U-shape fusion structure (UFS) to progressively optimize and enrich extracted multi-scale features by concatenating and fusing features from multiple stages.
- We propose a novel SMFNet by integrating MDCB and UFS that achieves state-of-the-art performance in highly crowded scenes.

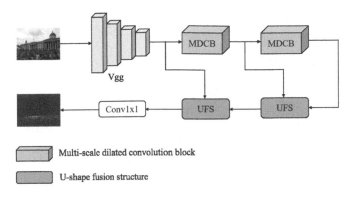

Fig. 1. The architecture of the Scare-aware Multi-stage Fusion Network (SMFNet).

2   Our Proposed Method

2.1   Multi-scale Feature Extraction

Following the previous methods [3, 4, 7, 8], we adopt the first ten layers of VGG-16 [12] as our backbone network, which can effectively capture the features of an input crowd image.

In CNN, different kernel sizes can capture feature at different scales [9]. Many previous CNN-based works [2, 9, 10] employ multiple filter sizes to adapt the changes in head sizes. However, these methods usually tend to utilize large kernels to extract large head, which could lead to an increase in training parameters when more big kernels are added. Inspired by [3, 12], dilated convolution kernel can expand the receptive field size without adding more parameters while keeping details of input image, and the stacking of more small kernels has better representation than directly adopting fewer large kernels. Hence, to tackle the challenge of scale diversity better, we all employ small kernels (1×1, 3×3) with different increasing dilation rates to capture features in various scales. Motived by the success of Inception structure [10] in image recognition domain, we design the multi-scale dilated convolution block (MDCB) as multi-scale feature extraction of SMFNet. An overview of MDCB is illustrated in Fig. 2.

To be specific, MDCB consists of a simple convolutional layer with 1×1 kernel size and dilation rate 1, and three convolutional layers with kernel sizes 3×3 and increasing dilation rates 1, 2, 3, which are equivalent to the filters of 1×1, 3×3, 5×5 and 7×7 respectively. The branch with filter size 1×1 is utilized to keep the feature scale from front layer to cover little targets, while others gradually increase receptive field sizes to capture large targets without involving extra parameters. This setting ensures that a smaller receptive field with different dilation rates can extract more information. Then, features from different branches in parallel are subsequently integrated by an Element-wise add operation together. Through the ablation experiments, we finally choose two cascaded multi-scale dilated convolution blocks to extract multi-scale features.

2.2   Multi-stage Feature Fusion

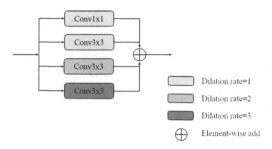

Fig. 2. Overview of multi-scale dilated convolution block (MDCB).

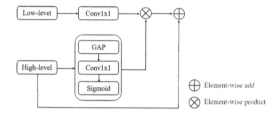

Fig. 3. Overview of the U-shape fusion structure (UFS).

Although the proposed MDCB provides scale variation, the hierarchical features between different blocks are not fully utilized. As discussion in first section, features from shallow layers can accurately locate the head position but preserve much low-level noise, while the features from the deep layers contain more contextual information. Hence, we improve the architecture by the proposed U-shape fusion structure (UFS), which could progressively optimize the extracted multi-scale features by concatenating and fusing adjacent stages features, while filtering low-level noise features that lead to error estimation. Compared with previous crowd counting methods based on multi-column, multi-branch or multi-scale module [1,2,9,10] that ignore taking advantage of the features from different layers, SMFNet achieves a more robust crowd counting performance through further multi-stage feature fusion.

The structure of U-shape fusion structure is presented in Fig. 3, which is used to combine features from adjacent layers in the network backend. Firstly, the feature maps from low-level layer could reduce the channels through a 1×1 convolution. The high-level feature maps through GAP (global average pooling) compute large-range context along the channel dimension, which captures the important channels while suppressing unnecessary channels. Then generated global contextual information is through a 1×1 convolution with Sigmoid activation function to calculate weight information, the value of which ranges from 0 to 1 that indicates regions the network focus on. Secondly, this computed weight information is adopted as guidance to weight low-level feature maps through

Table 1. Estimation errors on ShanghaiTech PartA, ShanghaiTech PartB, UCF_CC_50 and UCF-QNRF respectively.

Methods	PartA		PartB		UCF_CC_50		UCF-QNRF	
	MAE	RMSE	MAE	RMSE	MAE	RMSE	MAE	RMSE
MCNN [9]	110.2	173.2	26.4	41.3	337.6	509.1	227.0	426.0
SwitchCNN [10]	90.4	135.0	21.6	33.4	318.0	439.2	228.0	445.0
CSRNet [3]	68.2	115.0	10.6	16.0	266.1	397.5	–	–
SANet [2]	67.0	104.5	8.4	13.6	258.4	334.9	–	–
TEDNet [7]	64.2	109.1	8.2	12.8	257.1	363.5	113.0	188.0
DSPNet [15]	68.2	107.8	8.9	14.0	243.3	307.6	107.5	182.7
SCLNet [16]	67.9	103.0	9.1	14.2	258.9	326.2	110.0	182.5
ADCrowdNet [5]	63.2	98.9	**7.7**	12.9	266.4	358.0	–	–
HACNN [17]	62.9	**96.1**	8.1	13.4	256.2	348.4	118.1	180.4
CAN [8]	62.3	100.0	7.8	**12.2**	**212.2**	**243.7**	107.0	183.0
(SMFNet) Ours	**57.7**	**96.1**	8.8	14.7	239.6	337.4	**95.5**	**166.7**

Element-wise product operation to extract effective multi-scale features while filtering low-level features with noise. Finally, when the weighted low-level feature maps involve more multi-scale noise-free features, final feature maps can be generated by adding with high-level features maps to further boost multi-scale features. The computed final feature maps are adopted as the high-level feature maps for the next U-shaped fusion process.

3   Implementation Details

3.1   Ground Truth Generation

Similar to previous methods [3,4,7,10] of generating density map for ground truth, we employ a normalized Gaussian (which is normalized to 1) kernel to blur each head annotation. For ShanghaiTech [9] and UCF_CC_50 [13], the fixed kernel is adopted to generate density maps. Whereas the adaptive-geometry kernel is utilized for UCF-QNRF [14], because of large variation in crowd scene.

3.2   Loss Function

To reinforce the consistency of density levels in the global and local areas, we adopt Euclidean loss and multi-scale density level consistency loss proposed in [4]. Let L_e denote Euclidean loss, which can be defined as follows:

$$L_e = \frac{1}{N} \left\| G(X_i; \theta) - D_i^{GT} \right\|_2^2, \tag{1}$$

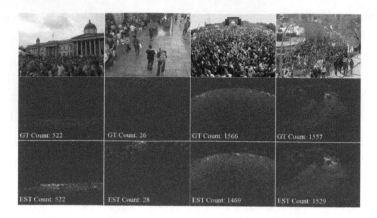

Fig. 4. Visualization of the estimated density maps generated by the proposed SMFNet and description of the counting results. From the first row to the third row represent the crowd images, corresponding ground truth maps and estimated density maps from ShanghaiTech PartA [9], ShanghaiTech PartB [9], UCF_CC_50 [13] and UCF-QNRF [14] datasets respectively.

where N is the number of images in the batch, $G(X_i; \theta)$ is the estimated density map for image X_i with parameter θ, D_i^{GT} is the ground truth for X_i. Let L_c denote multi-scale density level consistency loss, which can be defined as follows:

$$L_c = \frac{1}{N} \sum_{i=1}^{N} \sum_{j=1}^{S} \frac{1}{k_j^2} \left\| P_{ave}(G(X_i; \theta), k_j) - P_{ave}(D_i^{GT}, k_j) \right\|, \qquad (2)$$

where S is the number of scale levels, P_{ave} is average pooling with parameter k_j that is the output size of average pooling. Following the set of [4], we employ three output levels (1, 2, 4) of average pooling to estimate consistency of the density levels in global and local areas. Final objective function can be formulated as:

$$L = L_e + \alpha L_c, \qquad (3)$$

where α is the parameter that provides tradeoff between these two loss functions. For ShanghaiTech PartA [9] and UCF-QNRF [14], α is set as 1000, while 100 is applied for ShanghaiTech PartB [9] and UCF_CC_50 [13].

4   Experiments

4.1   Results and Comparison with State-of-the-Art

We perform experiments on three popular datasets and compare it with existing state-of-the-art crowd counting methods. The experimental results are listed in Table 1 for ShanghaiTech PartA [9], ShanghaiTech PartB [9], UCF_CC_50 [13] and UCF-QNRF [14] respectively.

Table 2. Estimation errors for distinct modules of our proposed SMFNet on Shang-haiTech PartA. The figure in parentheses represents the number of corresponding modules.

Combination of different modules	MAE	RMSE
Common Conv3x3(1,2)	62.9	102.9
MDCB(1)	61.3	101.4
MDCB(1,2)	59.2	98.8
MDCB(1,2,3)	60.8	101.7
Common Conv3x3(1,2) + UFS(1,2)	58.7	97.3
MDCB(1) + UFS(1)	59.5	96.5
MDCB(1,2) + UFS(1,2)	**57.7**	**96.1**
MDCB(1,2,3) + UFS(1,2,3)	60.4	97.2

For ShanghaiTech PartA, our model achieves the best result on MAE and comparable result on RMSE, and we get 7.3% MAE improvement compared with the state-of-the-art method CAN [8]. For ShanghaiTech PartB, ADCrowd-Net [5] achieves the best MAE 7.7 and CAN achieves [8] the best RMSE 12.2. On UCF_CC_50, SMFNet achieves 6% and 3% improvement for MAE and RMSE respectively compared with the third best approach HACNN [17]. On UCF-QNRF, SMFNet achieves the lowest results which delivers 10.2% lower MAE and 8.9% lower RMSE than state-of-the-art method CAN [8]. As for highly congested scenes like ShanghaiTech PartA and UCF-QNRF, it can be observed that the SMFNet outperforms all existing methods. Figure 4 shows several examples from testing set in ShanghaiTech PartA, ShanghaiTech PartB, UCF_CC_50 and UCF-QNRF datasets and proves the good performance of our proposed method SMFNet in counting people.

4.2 Ablation Experiments on ShanghaiTech PartA

Our network architecture consists of backbone network [12], multi-scale dilated convolution block (MDCB) and U-shape fusion structure (UFS). To demonstrate their effectiveness and find the number of blocks, we conduct experiments by gradually adding these components one by one. In addition, to make full use of the different stage features in network backend, the number of UFS is the same as the number of blocks. The experimental results are shown in Table 2.

In Table 2, we firstly adopt two common convolutional layers with 3x3 kernel size and a 1×1 convolution after backbone network as baseline model, where MAE is 62.9. After that, by only replacing the above two common convolutional layers with the proposed MDCB incrementally, the MAE decrease to 61.3, 59.2 and 60.8 respectively. Above experiments could illustrate that the features with different receptive fields caused by MDCB are beneficial to count crowd accurately.

To illustrate the effectiveness of U-shape fusion structure, we embed two proposed UFS to enrich the baseline model, the MAE can reach 58.7 that has decreased by 4.1 compared with the baseline. Moreover, when the UFS are gradually adding to above three networks with different number of MDCB, the MAE decrease to 59.5, 57.7 and 60.4 respectively. Obviously, it also can be noticed that when UFS is embedded between the various layers of backend network, all the results are improved. Hence, we can proof the validity of the U-shape fusion organization, which helps draw rich and effective multi-scale features by multistage fusion. According to experimental results, the combination of two MDCB and two UFS achieves the best performance, so we choose it as our model.

5   Conclusion

In this paper, we have proposed a novel Scale-aware Multi-stage Fusion Network called SMFNet for more robust crowd counting in the highly congested noisy scenes. To deal with scale diversity problem, we design a multi-scale dilated convolution block (MDCB) to capture different scales of features. To further optimize and enrich extracted multi-scale features, we put forward a U-shape fusion structure that progressively integrates features output by multiple stages, while filtering low-level noise features. Experimental results have indicated the effectiveness and robustness of our proposed SMFNet, which achieves the advanced counting performance on highly congested scenes datasets such as ShanghaiTech PartA and UCF-QNRF datasets, and comparable results on ShanghaiTech PartB and UCF_CC_50 datasets.

References

1. Sindagi, V.A., Patel, V.M.: Generating high-quality crowd density maps using contextual pyramid CNNs. In: ICCV, pp. 1861–1870 (2017)
2. Cao, X., Wang, Z., Zhao, Y., Su, F.: Scale aggregation network for accurate and efficient crowd counting. In: Ferrari, V., Hebert, M., Sminchisescu, C., Weiss, Y. (eds.) ECCV 2018, Part V. LNCS, vol. 11209, pp. 757–773. Springer, Cham (2018). https://doi.org/10.1007/978-3-030-01228-1_45
3. Li, Y., Zhang, X., Chen, D.: CSRNET: dilated convolutional neural networks for understanding the highly congested scenes. In: CVPR, pp. 1091–1100 (2018)
4. Dai, F., Liu, H., Ma, Y., Cao, J., Zhao, Q., Zhang, Y.: Dense scale network for crowd counting. arXiv preprint arXiv:1906.09707 (2019)
5. Liu, N., Long, Y., Zou, C., Niu, Q., Wu, H.: ADCrowdNet: an attention-injective deformable convolutional network for crowd understanding. In: CVPR, pp. 3225–3234 (2019)
6. Sindagi, V.A., Patel, V.M.: Multi-level bottom-top and top-bottom feature fusion for crowd counting. In: ICCV, pp. 1002–1012 (2019)
7. Jiang, X., Xiao, Z., Zhang, B., Zhen, X., Cao, X., Doermann, D.: Crowd counting and density estimation by trellis encoder-decoder networks. In: CVPR, pp. 6133–6142 (2019)
8. Liu, W., Salzmann, M., Fua, P.: Context-aware crowd counting. In: CVPR, pp. 5099–5108 (2019)
9. Zhang, Y., Zhou, D., Chen, S., Gao, S., Ma, Y.: Single-image crowd counting via multi-column convolutional neural network. In: CVPR, pp. 589–597, June 2016

10. Sam, D.B., Surya, S., Babu, R.V.: Switching convolutional neural network for crowd counting. In: CVPR, pp. 4031–4039 (2017)
11. Szegedy, C., et al.: Going deeper with convolutions. In: CVPR, June 2015
12. Simonyan, K., Zisserman, A.: Very deep convolutional networks for large-scale image recognition. In: ICLR (2015)
13. Idrees, H., Saleemi, I., Seibert, C., Shah, M.: Multi-source multi-scale counting in extremely dense crowd images. In: CVPR, pp. 2547–2554 (2013)
14. Idrees, H., Saleemi, I., Seibert, C., Shah, M.: Composition loss for counting, density map estimation and localization in dense crowds. In: ICCV, pp. 532–546 (2018)
15. Zeng, X., Wu, Y., Hu, S., Wang, R., Ye, Y.: DSPNet: deep scale purifier network for dense crowd counting. Expert Syst. Appl. **141**, 112977 (2020)
16. Wang, S., Lu, Y., Zhou, T., Di, H., Lu, L., Zhang, L.: SCLNet: spatial context learning network for congested crowd counting. Neurocomputing **404**, 227–239 (2020)
17. Sindagi, V.A., Patel, V.M.: HA-CCN: hierarchical attention-based crowd counting network. TIP **29**, 323–335 (2020)

Video Captioning with External Knowledge Assistance and Multi-feature Fusion

Jiao-Wei Miao, Huan Shao, Yi Ji, Ying Li, and Chun-Ping Liu[(✉)]

School of Computer Science and Technology, Soochow University, Suzhou, China
{20185227039,20185227043}@stu.suda.edu.cn, {jiyi,ingli,cpliu}@suda.edu.cn

Abstract. Video captioning aims to describe the main content of a given video in natural language, which has become a research hotspot because of its wide potential application prospect. Semantic information, as a priori knowledge, is often applied to improve the caption quality, but the scope of these semantic information is relatively small, resulting in insufficient coverage of video attributes. In this paper, we introduce external knowledge from ConceptNet to expand the semantic coverage, so that the model can refer to more semantic information. In addition, a multi-feature fusion is proposed to obtain more informative video features and higher quality semantic features. Experimental results on the MSVD and MSRVTT datasets show that the proposed method can greatly improve the caption diversity and model performance, surpass all previous models in all evaluation metrics, and achieve the new state-of-the-art results.

Keywords: Video captioning · Semantic information · Feature fusion

1 Introduction

Video captioning is an important and challenging task, which has great potential applications in many fields, such as video surveillance, video recommendation and so on. Inspired by the machine translation, the methods based on the encoder-decoder framework occupied the mainstream position in this field [2,6]. The encoder obtains all kinds of instructive information from the video and annotations, and the decoder generates accurate natural language caption according to the encoded information, bridging the gap between vision and language.

Semantic information can be regarded as a modality in the video to represent the existing attributes in the video, and can be utilized as a prior knowledge. Previous work [2] utilized semantic features to guide caption generation, but the semantic features used in the aforementioned model are based on some high-frequency semantic words selected manually. As videos in the wild contain a large number of scenes, objects and actions, the coverage of these semantic words is small, so the coverage of attributes in the video is insufficient.

In this work, we propose to introduce external knowledge from ConceptNet [5] to obtain more semantic words and to expand the semantic coverage, so that

---

J.-W. Miao and H. Shao—These authors contributed equally to this work.

© Springer Nature Switzerland AG 2021
T. Mantoro et al. (Eds.): ICONIP 2021, CCIS 1517, pp. 12–19, 2021.
https://doi.org/10.1007/978-3-030-92310-5_2

our model can refer to a wider range of semantic information when decoding, and improve the accuracy and diversity of caption. Specifically, for each semantic word, other words related to its meaning and relevance degrees are obtained from ConceptNet, and we design two extension methods to assign semantic values to the related words. Both of these extension methods rely on the original semantic value, higher quality original semantic features can make extension methods more effective. In view of this situation, a multi-feature fusion method is proposed to improve the interaction between static features and dynamic features of video, and higher quality semantic features can be obtained by feeding the fused video features into the semantic detection network. Experiments on two benchmark datasets show that our proposed semantic extension and multi-feature fusion method (SEMF) can achieve excellent results.

To summarize, the contributions of this work lie in two-fold:

- We propose to introduce more semantic words with the help of ConceptNet to expand the existing semantic scope, so that our model can refer to more semantic information.
- More instructive and informative video features can be obtained through our proposed multi-feature fusion method, and higher quality semantic features can be acquired through the fused features.

2   Related Work

With the rise of deep learning, various models using neural networks occupied the mainstream of video captioning. Wang *et al.* [9] developed a new way, with the help of part of speech information and grammatical structure to guide the model to produce accurate caption. Because there are similar semantic scenes in different videos, and the same words or phrases exist in the corresponding descriptions, Pei *et al.* [8] designed a memory structure to explore the relationship between words and visual context, so as to improve the understanding of words. According to Aafaq *et al.* [1], the feature extracted from convolution network is condensed by hierarchical short-time fourier transform, and the temporal information is integrated into encoded results.

Semantic information, as the embodiment of attributes, has been paid more and more attention in visual captioning tasks. In some works [2,3], semantic information is obtained by multi instance learning or multi-label classification, and then they are applied in decoder to assist captioning generation. However, in these models, the semantic scope is small, which leads to insufficient coverage of image or video attributes.

3   Model

Our model is based on the encoder-decoder framework, and the overall structure is shown in Fig. 1. The encoder is composed of two video feature extractors and a semantic detection network. The decoder integrates semantic information into the decoding process by levering a variant Network of LSTM.

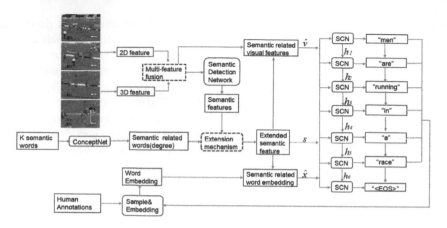

Fig. 1. Model overview. Our proposed components are displayed in two dotted boxes.

3.1 Visual Features and Semantic Features Extraction

The video feature of the i-th video is composed of static visual feature e_i and dynamic feature r_i, their concatenated result v_i is the overall feature of the video, where $e_i \in \mathbb{R}^{D_e}$, $r_i \in \mathbb{R}^{D_r}$, $v_i \in \mathbb{R}^{D_v}$, $Dv = De + Dr$. In the following part of multi-feature fusion, we design a more effective fusion method, which can obtain more informative video features.

In order to obtain the semantic information, we adopt the same way as baseline [2] and train the semantic detection network through video features and real semantic labels. First, we manually select the K meaningful words with high frequency from the training set and validation set as semantic words, including nouns, verbs, adjectives, etc. Labeling them as semantic words set $A = \{a_0, a_1, a_2, ..., a_{k-1}\}$, the real semantic labels of video are constructed by these words. Specifically, generate a K dimensional zero vector $\hat{s}_i$ for the i-th video, traverse all the annotations of the i-th video, if a semantic word a_j appears in the any annotation, then the corresponding element $\hat{s}_{ij}$ is set to 1, otherwise it is 0, and the final result $\hat{s}_i$ is the real semantic label of the i-th video. The input of the semantic detection network is the overall feature v_i of the video, and the output is the K dimensional semantic vector s_i, $s_i = [s_{i0}, s_{i1}, ..., s_{i,K-1}]$, where the value s_{ij} on the j-th dimension represents the probability that a_j is the video attribute, which is between [0, 1]. Specifically, $s_i = \sigma(f(v_i)) \in (0,1)^K$, where $f(\cdot)$ is a multilayer feed-forward neural network. They together with the loss function described in formula 1 constitute the semantic detection network.

$$L(s_i, \hat{s}_i) = \frac{1}{N} \sum_{i=0}^{N-1} \sum_{j=0}^{K-1} \hat{s}_{i,j} \log s_{i,j} + (1 - \hat{s}_{i,j}) \log(1 - s_{i,j}) \qquad (1)$$

3.2 Semantic Extension Mechanism

Due to the limited range of K semantic words based on manual selection, the coverage of video scene attributes is insufficient. As there is a semantic relationship between different words, the same meaning can be expressed by different words with similar semantics. In addition, when a certain semantic word belongs to the attributes of a certain video, other semantically related words are also likely to be the attribute words of the video. Based on the above assumptions, we extend the range of K selected semantic words with the help of ConceptNet. In ConceptNet [5], natural language words and phrases are connected to each other by edges with labels and weights. With this powerful tool, we can obtain the semantically related words and the relevance degree of each semantic word, as shown in Fig. 2. As to the semantic value of related words, the following two methods are designed, and they are named method a, method b respectively.

(a) The semantic value of the related words are the result of multiplication of semantic value of original selected semantic word and relevance degree value.
(b) The semantic value of the related words are the same as that of the original selected semantic word.

Through above two methods, the model can obtain more reference information in decoding. However, it is worth noting that related words with different relevance degree may bring different contributions to the model, and the related words with low relevance degree may introduce noise and lead to the performance degradation. We will analyze this in the later experimental part.

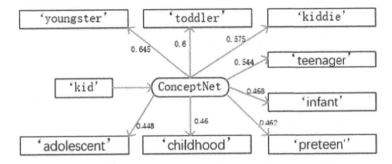

Fig. 2. The related words and relevance degrees can be obtained through ConceptNet.

3.3   Multi-feature Fusion

The above two methods of semantic extension all rely on the value of original semantic feature, and the latter depends on video features. Concatenate fusion can be seen as the separation of static features and dynamic features. This fusion method is sub-optimal for video features acquisition, because the video itself is composed of static scenes and dynamic changes, so we argue that the interactive fusion of static and dynamic features can improve the feature quality. We propose an interactive fusion method by element-wise multiplication as formula 2:

$$v_i = e_i \times r_i \qquad (2)$$

This method can make the features with high response value more prominent than those with low response value after fusion, and restrain the influence of low response value features on the model, further widens the gap between the two kinds features. This can be seen as a special "attention mechanism", because its function is similar to the "attention mechanism", which makes the original high weight features still have high weight after fusion.

4   Experiment

4.1   Datasets

MSVD [4] contains 1970 videos, of which 1200 are used for training, 100 for validation, and 670 for testing. We tokenize the captions from the training and validation datasets, 12952 words are obtained after remove the low-frequency words. MSRVTT [10] is a relatively large dataset, with a total of 10000 videos, of which 6513 videos are used for training, 497 for validation, 2970 for testing, and each video has 20 annotations. We tokenize the captions and filter low-frequency words, 13794 words are obtained. The rest of the words are represented by '<unk>' and the symbol of '<EOS>' is added to indicate the end of sentence.

4.2   Ablation Study

Analysis on Semantic Extension Mechanism. "MyBaseline" model utilizes different visual features and semantic features with baseline model [2], and it is abbreviated as "MB" in Table 1. Here, "MyBaseline (MB)" model utilizes concatenated features just like the baseline model. We apply two extension methods to "MyBaseline", and verify the impact of related words with different relevance degree on the performance of the model, the results are shown in Table 1.

Analysis on Multi-feature Fusion. The video features obtained by different fusion methods have different instructive value, and the more instructive video features can obtain higher quality semantic features. Experimental results using different features and semantics are compared in Table 2. The performance of model can be effectively improved with our proposed fusion method, which proves effectiveness of the proposed fusion method.

SEMF consists of semantic extension and multi-feature fusion. It can be seen from Table 3 that our model greatly improves the model performance and the diversity of caption. It is worth noting that, for the extension method b of MSRVTT dataset, when the related words with low relevance degree are extended, the model performance does not decline as sharply as the corresponding result in Table 1, which proves the effectiveness of the proposed fusion method.

Table 1. $B-4$, R,M and C are abbreviations of $BLEU-4$, $ROUGE_L$, $METEOR$ and $CIDEr$ respectively, which are used to evaluate the quality of captions, the same below. x in MB(x_y) represents the extension method and y represents the lowest relevance degree.

Dataset	Model	$B-4$	R	M	C	Model	$B-4$	R	M	C
MSVD	MB	60.1	77.4	40.3	114.9	MB	60.1	77.4	40.3	114.9
	MB(a_0.8)	60.6	78	40.5	117.3	MB(b_0.8)	60.8	77.7	40.5	117.2
	MB(a_0.7)	61.9	78.3	40.7	117.6	MB(b_0.7)	63	78.9	41.1	117.3
	MB(a_0.6)	63.9	79.1	41.6	121.9	MB(b_0.6)	63.2	79.1	41.7	121.4
	MB(a_0.5)	63.7	79.4	42	122.3	MB(b_0.5)	64.9	79.7	**42.6**	123.1
	MB(a_0.4)	65.1	79.8	**42.5**	124.1	MB(b_0.4)	64.7	79.8	42.2	124.1
	MB(a_0.265)	**65.3**	**79.8**	42.4	**124.3**	MB(b_0.265)	**65.2**	**79.9**	42.4	**127.4**
MSRVTT	MB	46.3	63.9	29.8	54	MB	46.3	63.9	29.8	54
	MB(a_0.8)	46.7	64	30	54.6	MB(b_0.8)	46.7	63.9	29.9	54.6
	MB(a_0.7)	47	64.2	30	55.3	MB(b_0.7)	47.1	**64.3**	**30**	**54.9**
	MB(a_0.6)	47.3	64.2	30	55.3	MB(b_0.6)	46.9	64	30	54.9
	MB(a_0.5)	47.4	64.2	30.1	55.1	MB(b_0.5)	**47.2**	64.1	29.9	54.3
	MB(a_0.4)	**47.5**	**64.3**	**30.1**	**55.3**	MB(b_0.4)	45.8	63.4	29.4	52.2
	MB(a_0.264)	47.2	64.1	30	54.3	MB(b_0.264)	43.7	62.8	28.8	49.6

Table 2. Mybaseline is built on concatenated features, and MyBaseline* is based on fusion features created by formula 2.

Dataset	Model	$B-4$	R	M	C
MSVD	MyBaseline	60.1	77.4	40.3	114.9
MSVD	MyBaseline*	61.1	78.2	41	116.6
MSRVTT	MyBaseline	46.2	63.8	29.8	53.9
MSRVTT	MyBaseline*	47.6	64.4	30.3	55.2

4.3   Comparison with Prior Work

We display the results of our model along with a few of existing relevant models in Table 4. Sibnet [6] utilized two branches to extract content features and semantic features respectively, and the obtained features are fused and then sent to the decoder. ORG-TRL [11] designed a new training method to integrate the knowledge of external language model into the current caption model to solve the problem of long tail distribution in annotations. STG-KD [7] exerted spatio-temporal graph network to capture the interactive information in the video.

Table 3. Results of semantic extension based on proposed multi-feature fusion.

Dataset	Model	B − 4	R	M	C	Model	B − 4	R	M	C
MSVD	MB*	61.1	78.2	41	116.6	MB*	61.1	78.2	41	116.6
	MB*(a_0.8)	62.9	79.1	41.2	120	MB*(b_0.8)	62.2	78.9	41.2	119.5
	MB*(a_0.7)	63.6	79.6	41.9	122.3	MB*(b_0.7)	64.2	79.9	42.3	124.5
	MB*(a_0.6)	65.3	80	42.7	124.6	MB*(b_0.6)	65.2	79.9	42.7	127.7
	MB*(a_0.5)	**66.8**	80.6	**43.5**	125.1	MB*(b_0.5)	66.1	80.6	43.4	125.6
	MB*(a_0.4)	66.6	**80.9**	43.4	**127.6**	MB*(b_0.4)	**66.5**	**80.9**	**43.7**	127.8
	MB*(a_0.265)	66.3	80.6	43.4	126.8	MB*(b_0.265)	66.2	80.9	43.1	**128.1**
MSRVTT	MB*	47.6	64.4	30.3	55.2	MB*	47.6	64.4	30.3	55.2
	MB*(a_0.8)	47.6	64.4	30.2	55.2	MB*(b_0.8)	47.7	64.4	30.2	55.6
	MB*(a_0.7)	47.8	64.7	30.4	56.3	MB*(b_0.7)	48.2	64.7	30.3	56.6
	MB*(a_0.6)	48.6	**65.1**	**30.6**	**56.5**	MB*(b_0.6)	48.6	64.9	30.5	56.6
	MB*(a_0.5)	48.5	64.8	30.5	56.2	MB*(b_0.5)	48.6	65	**30.5**	**56.9**
	MB*(a_0.4)	**48.9**	64.9	30.4	56.2	MB*(b_0.4)	**48.7**	**65.1**	30.5	56.6
	MB*(a_0.264)	48.7	64.9	30.3	55.7	MB*(b_0.264)	48.6	65	30.5	55.7

Table 4. Comparison result with existing models on the MSVD (the left part of the table) and MSRVTT (the right part of the table) dataset

Model	Year	B − 4	R	M	C	—	B − 4	R	M	C
SibNet [6]	2018	54.2	71.7	34.8	88.2	—	40.9	60.2	27.5	47.5
POS [9]	2019	53.9	72.1	34.9	91	—	41.3	62.1	28.7	53.4
MARN [8]	2019	48.6	71.9	35.1	92.2	—	40.4	60.7	28.1	47.1
GRU-EVE [1]	2019	47.9	71.5	35	78.1	—	38.3	60.7	28.4	48.1
STG-KD [7]	2020	52.2	73.9	36.9	93	—	40.5	60.9	28.3	47.1
ORG-TRL [11]	2020	54.3	73.9	36.4	95.2	—	43.6	62.1	28.8	50.9
SAM-SS (baseline) [2]	2020	61.8	76.8	37.8	103	—	43.8	62.4	28.9	51.4
SEMF (ours)	-	**66.5**	**80.9**	**43.7**	**127.8**	—	**48.6**	**65**	**30.5**	**56.9**

5 Conclusion

This paper focuses on the semantic information in video captioning. Our model obtains more reference semantics by introducing semantically related words from ConceptNet. In addition, a method of multi-feature fusion is proposed to obtain more instructive and informative video features, so as to obtain higher quality semantic features. Through the above two methods, the performance of the model and the diversity of caption are greatly improved. Extensive experimental results demonstrate the effectiveness of our proposed methods, and our model achieves results that are superior to the state-of-the-art models on two datasets.

Acknowledgment. Supported by National Natural Science Foundation of China Nos. 61972059, 61773272, 61602332; Natural Science Foundation of the Jiangsu Higher Education Institutions of China No. 19KJA230001, Key Laboratory of Symbolic Computation and Knowledge Engineering of Ministry of Education, Jilin University No. 93K172016K08; Postgraduate Research & Practice Innovation Program of Jiangsu Province SJCX20_1063; Project Funded by the Priority Academic Program Development of Jiangsu Higher Education Institutions (PAPD).

References

1. Aafaq, N., Akhtar, N., Liu, W., Gilani, S.Z., Mian, A.: Spatio-temporal dynamics and semantic attribute enriched visual encoding for video captioning. In: Proceedings of the IEEE/CVF Conference on Computer Vision and Pattern Recognition, pp. 12487–12496 (2019)
2. Chen, H., Lin, K., Maye, A., Li, J., Hu, X.: A semantics-assisted video captioning model trained with scheduled sampling. Front. Robot. AI **7**, 475767 (2020)
3. Fang, H., et al.: From captions to visual concepts and back. In: Proceedings of the IEEE Conference on Computer Vision and Pattern Recognition, pp. 1473–1482 (2015)
4. Guadarrama, S., et al.: YouTube2Text: recognizing and describing arbitrary activities using semantic hierarchies and zero-shot recognition. In: Proceedings of the IEEE International Conference on Computer Vision, pp. 2712–2719 (2013)
5. Liu, H., Singh, P.: ConceptNet-a practical commonsense reasoning tool-kit. BT Technol. J. **22**(4), 211–226 (2004). https://doi.org/10.1023/B:BTTJ.0000047600.45421.6d
6. Liu, S., Ren, Z., Yuan, J.: SibNet: sibling convolutional encoder for video captioning. In: Proceedings of the 2018 ACM on Multimedia Conference, pp. 1425–1434 (2018)
7. Pan, B., et al.: Spatio-temporal graph for video captioning with knowledge distillation. In: Proceedings of the IEEE/CVF Conference on Computer Vision and Pattern Recognition, pp. 10870–10879 (2020)
8. Pei, W., Zhang, J., Wang, X., Ke, L., Shen, X., Tai, Y.W.: Memory-attended recurrent network for video captioning. In: Proceedings of the IEEE/CVF Conference on Computer Vision and Pattern Recognition, pp. 8347–8356 (2019)
9. Wang, B., Ma, L., Zhang, W., Jiang, W., Wang, J., Liu, W.: Controllable video captioning with pos sequence guidance based on gated fusion network. In: Proceedings of the IEEE/CVF International Conference on Computer Vision, pp 2641–2650 (2019)
10. Xu, J., Mei, T., Yao, T., Rui, Y.: MSR-VTT: a large video description dataset for bridging video and language. In: Proceedings of the IEEE Conference on Computer Vision and Pattern Recognition, pp. 5288–5296 (2016)
11. Zhang, Z., et al.: Object relational graph with teacher-recommended learning for video captioning. In: Proceedings of the IEEE/CVF Conference on Computer Vision and Pattern Recognition, pp. 13278–13288 (2020)

A Novel Transfer-Learning Network for Image Inpainting

Hui Chen[1], Zhichao Zhang[2](✉), Jinsheng Deng[3], and Xiaoqing Yin[3]

[1] Science and Technology on Integrated Logistics Support Laboratory,
National University of Defense Technology, Changsha, China
[2] College of Computer, National University of Defense Technology, Zunyi, China
`zhangzhichao11@nudt.edu.cn`
[3] College of Advanced Interdisciplinary Studies,
National University of Defense Technology, Zunyi, China

Abstract. Image restoration techniques have developed rapidly in recent years. Some high-level vision tasks such as style transfer, automatic coloring, and large mask inpainting rely on deep learning methods to retrieve specific image attributes. However, due to the lack of a key remainder, the quality of image restoration remains at a low level. For instance, when the mask is large enough, traditional deep learning methods cannot imagine and fill a car on a bridge from a model. It is all dependent on the capacity of neural imagination. This is what an abstract neuron is good at. In this paper, we not only find specific neurons to guide semantic retrieval but also discover more neurons that serve as the indicator. In addition, we propose three principles to guarantee the leverage of reasonable visualization and coherent accuracy in terms of neuron guidance. A novel network called the Transfer-learning Network is designed to adopt the joint training strategy, multi-modal guided neurons, and multi-path attention edge algorithm for inpainting in a coarse-to-fine manner. This is the first time an extremely large mask is filled (35%–66%), guided by a high-level understanding of an image from abstract neuron reflection. Through ablation and combined experiments, the Transfer-learning Network validates that artificial neurons enhance the performance of joint training in multitasking vision problems. Therefore, this joint training framework meets the requirements of refining the background, i.e., removing meaningless noise more sharply and smartly between junior and advanced comprehensive vision tasks.

Keywords: Multi-modal neuron · High semantic guided training · Large mask inpainting · Deep learning

1 Introduction

Artificial neuron application is a new trend in computer vision tasks. In addition, multiple strategies in deep learning training methods have been adopted to generate high-performance models. In terms of the above insightful ideas, we explore to tackle image repairing and large mask inpainting aided by transfer

© Springer Nature Switzerland AG 2021
T. Mantoro et al. (Eds.): ICONIP 2021, CCIS 1517, pp. 20–27, 2021.
https://doi.org/10.1007/978-3-030-92310-5_3

learning. Furthermore, during the training process, specific neurons, which can reflect and imagine the missing part, are built and adopted to guide the final generative image restoration in image inpainting.

Therefore, considering an image that lacks a majority of the information, imagination is essential for reasonable intense image structure reconstruction, as illustrated in Fig. 1. Human neurons reflect specific people regardless of the information carrier. This means the human neurons are multimodal in video, image, voice, text, sketch, and so on. It also makes specific responses to the stimuli. Neurons are multimodal and highly abstracted in neural networks because of the similarity between the human brain and artificial intelligence in terms of how neurons are connected. These multimodal neurons can not only perceive fixed high-level semantic meanings but also hold the capacity to imagine some images or to explain text input. Although the concepts of explainable deep neural networks remain mysterious in mathematical reasoning and predictable science, the study reveals how neurons work in visual feature optimization. Therefore, in this paper, we make better guidance for image restoration areas using an entirely novel method. The insightful idea is that traditional deep learning methods cannot restore large mask regions in image inpainting. Not only the object structure or color but also the texture and the missing objects cannot be restored because the method cannot restore objects that do not exist in the entire picture. Therefore, experienced neurons are pretrained to predict the objects in the large missing regions. We call this network "Deep Transfer-learning Network." It is a high-level semantic image restoration method for large mask inpainting. The contributions of this study are as follows:

- We discover that some specific artificial neurons can guide the image inpainting with large semantic areas missing. These neurons are pretrained in an intensively constructed neural network, which is called Transfer-learning Network.
- Our training strategy is fine-tuned. The Transfer-learning Network is intensively reconstructed for joint training of multiple low- and high-level vision tasks, and transfer learning is also introduced to develop four semantic maps for the multi-neuron guidance of inpainting.

2 Related Work of Inpainting

Recent studies on image inpainting focus on deep learning methods that can handle large missing regions and generate high-quality images without noise and artifacts. These approaches can capture the intrinsic hierarchical representations automatically and comprehend the contextual features to execute image inpainting. Yang et al. [8] proposed a multi-task learning framework based on image structure knowledge. The main concept involved learning the features of the embedded structure and pyramid structure loss in the process of image inpainting. EdgeConnect [4] was employed by Kamyar et al., which can develop a two-stage adversarial model for image inpainting by introducing an edge generator. The edge generator generates approximate edges according to regular or irregular missing regions of an input image; subsequently, to fill the hole, the approximate edges are regarded as prior information. Ren et al. [5] proposed an effective two-stage network, StructureFlow, for image inpainting to reconstruct structures and generate textures. This method demonstrated that edge-preserved images play a significant role in image inpainting. A pyramidal architecture based on contexture information, called PENNet, was employed by Zeng et al. [12] for generating high-quality images. Moreover, Nakamura et al. [3] proposed a CNN for removing redundant or disliked text from input images.

3 Implement

3.1 Proposed Framework

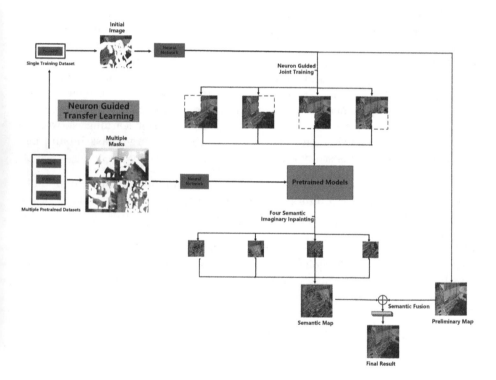

Fig. 1. Proposed network architecture and training strategy.

In this study, we propose the Transfer-learning Network to restore and refine images through joint training [6,9]. The framework of the Transfer-learning Network is shown in Fig. 1. The proposed Transfer-learning Network consists of three stages. The architecture and function of each stage are elaborated in the following sections.

In the first stage, efficient feature extraction is performed to obtain a trade-off shallow convolutional depth. Moreover, lightweight and propagating features are required in the case of vanishing gradients [1]. It takes blurry and masked images as input. The second stage involves feature extraction by attention modules. Inpainting is aided by multipath feature extraction in refinement fusion paths. In the third stage, we search the input feature, extract patches from the background, and fuse the patches into low dimensions from the background.

Computer vision tasks in deep learning have been developed over many years, and there are three branches in graphics analysis: low-level patch enhancement such as deblurring, deraining, and defogging; middle-level information extraction such as object detection, depth estimation, and object classification; high-level semantic completion such as style transfer, automatic coloring, and large mask inpainting.

Low-level vision tasks rely heavily on basic dataset information, and traditional methods work well on these computer vision tasks with the aid of mathematical statistics and kernel estimation. However, traditional mathematical approaches cannot extract multiple information effectively and flexibly owing to the dimensions of pixel attributes and a vast amount of data. Middle-level vision tasks can be easily solved by convolutional neural networks in deep learning. Diverse image features are extracted by convolutional layers. In addition, deep neural networks perform well in terms of speed and accuracy in complex vision tasks such as dense object detection. However, these tasks still cannot comprehend the actions of people in images, and therefore, some errors are confusing and unavoidable. These models still need evolve. High-level semantic vision tasks need more guided information rather than making a predictable inference. For instance, most deep inpainting methods fill a large mask aided by contextual patch information, without experienced guidance or the capacity of imagination.

3.2   Multipath Fusion with Progressive Weighted Training

Multiple datasets (VisDrone, COCO, DOTA, CityScape) were used to train an experienced model. Neurons guided the fusion of four semantic maps into one semantic map. The Places2 dataset was also trained by transfer learning to generate the preliminary map, as shown in Fig. 1. Then the semantic and preliminary middle results were fused into the final result. In multiple pretrained datasets, multi-modal neurons are abstracted into experienced counterparts that can respond to specific stimuli such as buildings and cars. Neurons guide image repair using high-level semantics, with the assistance of a model trained on numerous datasets (including edge detection and background attention). Inpainting with a large mask includes four steps: semantic reconstruction, structural reconstruction, background filling, and preprocessing. The training includes a mixed strategy of joint training, transfer learning, and multi-model learning. Finally, the synthesis loss function is defined as the sum of the adversarial loss function, scale loss function, edge generative loss, and L_2 loss (Fig. 2).

$$L_{final} = L_{adv} + L_{scale} + L_{edge} + L(\theta) \tag{1}$$

(a)   (b)   (c)   (d)   (e)   (f)

Fig. 2. Channel and spatial feature visualization map.

4   Experiments

4.1   Experimental Details

We conducted comparative experiments with deblur methods (deblurGAN [2], DMPHN [13]) and inpainting methods (CA [10], EC [4], LBAM [7], and RN [11]) on various datasets.

We implemented our deblur stage via TensorFlow. The model was trained with Adam ($\beta1 = 0.9, \beta2 = 0.999$). The input images were randomly cropped to 256×256. A batch size of 16 was used for training four NVIDIA RTX2080Ti GPUs of size 11 GB. At the beginning of each epoch, the learning rate was initialized as 10^{-4}; subsequently, it decayed by half every 10 epochs. We trained 170 epochs on VisDrone [15] and 150 epochs on Places2 [14] datasets. The Transfer-learning Network was designed for multitasking between deblurring and inpainting; it should be noted that the Transfer-learning Network can also be separated into two models for realizing plug and play.

4.2   Comparative Experiments

These results indicate that our methods can achieve state-of-the-art numerical performance, which can be attributed to the combination of the CNN-based method with sharper inpainting as well as end-to-end training. By contrast, other combined methods adopt a two-stage scheme and cannot be jointly trained. Our model can also be trained for arbitrary region completion. For textured and smooth regions, most approaches performed favorably. In addition, for structural regions, the proposed method was more effective in filling the cropped regions with attention and edge restoration. The network shows that multistage workflows have a promising visual effect in processing low-quality images for multitasking.

We removed background occlusions and characters; thus, the images restored via inpainting were sharp. The restored images exhibited vivid colors, sharp details, and robust restored structures. The results of comparative experiments

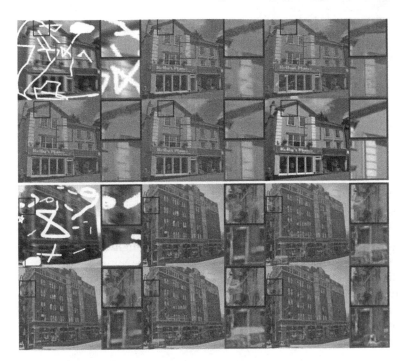

Fig. 3. The visual effect of comparative experiments.

demonstrated that the Transfer-learning Network enables higher flexibility than other restoration methods and can simultaneously solve multiple tasks, as shown in Fig. 3.

4.3 Ablation Experiments

The original inpainting benchmark is denoted as Transfer-learning Network1. Transfer-learning Network2 denotes the addition of a lightweight and residual process. Subsequently, we added the edge reconstruction and attention modules to the refinement path and denote it as Transfer-learning Network3. Transfer-learning Network4 denotes the joint training of deblurring and inpainting. Finally, we combined the above strategies and modules into Transfer-learning Network5. The results displayed in Table 1 summarize each part of the design that enhances the performance of image restoration in terms of their peak signal-to-noise ratios (PSNRs) and structural similarity indices (SSIMs).

The inputs were blurry and broken images. Transfer-learning Network1 performed the worst. Furthermore, the comparison results of Transfer-learning Network3 and Transfer-learning Network5 demonstrated the benefits of background refinement for inpainting. The comparison results of Transfer-learning Network2 and Transfer-learning Network3 indicate that multiscale contextual attention

Table 1. Ablation results on PSNR and SSIM on deblur datasets.

Ablation study	VisDrone (size = 256)	
	PSNR	SSIM
Transfer-learning Network1	35.76744	0.8539278
Transfer-learning Network2	35.95104	0.860545
Transfer-learning Network3	36.94918	0.830236
Transfer-learning Network4	37.95304	0.844492
Transfer-learning Network5	37.96030	0.852030

modules and edge generative prior enhance the repair grain and structure reconstruction. The comparison results of Transfer-learning Network1 and Transfer-learning Network2 indicate that the residual and lightweight performance of Transfer-learning Network2 is similar to Transfer-learning Network in terms of visual effect; however, Transfer-learning Network2 has a smaller model and runs faster during training.

Our method, aided by the loss weight scheduling technique, exhibited a dramatic downward trend and remained at approximately 9%. In addition, model accuracy improved from approximately 4% to 7%.

5   Conclusion

In this study, we validated three main features of artificial neurons: reflecting specific stimuli, attention edge mechanism, and capacity of abstraction. In addition, we designed the Transfer-learning Network, which realizes large mask inpainting with the aid of multi-modal neurons. We propose the Transfer-learning Network for deblurring and inpainting based on the principle of repairing images from coarse-to-fine layers. Based on this principle, first, the input was deblurred to extract sharp features. Next, the refined background patches were extracted and separated by the network into four scales. Each path predicted holes with masks using multipath contextual attention modules, aided by a coherency algorithm in a multiscale and iterative manner. Finally, the double features were fused in the final stage, and sharper predictions were sent into the discriminator.

The plug-and-play properties enhance network construction and flexibility for multitasking. The progressive weighted training strategy was slower than the general training process owing to the addition of ground truth images. In the future, several enhancements need to be proposed for attention modules to refine features and match patches more effectively and quickly. In addition, this network architecture could solve other restoration problems, such as dehazing and defogging, which are yet to be investigated.

References

1. He, K., Zhang, X., Ren, S., Sun, J.: Deep residual learning for image recognition. In: Proceedings of the IEEE Conference On Computer Vision and Pattern Recognition, pp. 770–778 (2016)
2. Kupyn, O., Budzan, V., Mykhailych, M., Mishkin, D., Matas, J.: DeblurGAN: blind motion deblurring using conditional adversarial networks. In: Proceedings of the IEEE Conference on Computer Vision and Pattern Recognition, pp. 8183–8192 (2018)
3. Nakamura, T., Zhu, A., Yanai, K., Uchida, S.: Scene text eraser. In: 2017 14th IAPR International Conference on Document Analysis and Recognition (ICDAR), vol. 1, pp. 832–837. IEEE (2017)
4. Nazeri, K., Ng, E., Joseph, T., Qureshi, F.Z., Ebrahimi, M.: Edgeconnect: Generative image inpainting with adversarial edge learning. arXiv preprint arXiv:1901.00212 (2019)
5. Ren, Y., Yu, X., Zhang, R., Li, T.H., Liu, S., Li, G.: StructureFlow: image inpainting via structure-aware appearance flow. In: Proceedings of the IEEE/CVF International Conference on Computer Vision, pp. 181–190 (2019)
6. Wei, H., Feng, L., Chen, X., An, B.: Combating noisy labels by agreement: a joint training method with co-regularization. In: Proceedings of the IEEE/CVF Conference on Computer Vision and Pattern Recognition, pp. 13726–13735 (2020)
7. Xie, C., et al.: Image inpainting with learnable bidirectional attention maps. In: Proceedings of the IEEE/CVF International Conference on Computer Vision, pp. 8858–8867 (2019)
8. Yang, J., Qi, Z., Shi, Y.: Learning to incorporate structure knowledge for image inpainting. In: Proceedings of the AAAI Conference on Artificial Intelligence, vol. 34, pp. 12605–12612 (2020)
9. Ye, X., et al.: Deep joint depth estimation and color correction from monocular underwater images based on unsupervised adaptation networks. IEEE Trans. Circuits Syst. Video Technol. **30**(11), 3995–4008 (2019)
10. Yu, J., Lin, Z., Yang, J., Shen, X., Lu, X., Huang, T.S.: Generative image inpainting with contextual attention. In: Proceedings of the IEEE Conference on Computer Vision and Pattern Recognition, pp. 5505–5514 (2018)
11. Yu, T., et al.: Region normalization for image inpainting. In: Proceedings of the AAAI Conference on Artificial Intelligence, vol. 34, pp. 12733–12740 (2020)
12. Zeng, Y., Fu, J., Chao, H., Guo, B.: Learning pyramid-context encoder network for high-quality image inpainting. In: Proceedings of the IEEE/CVF Conference on Computer Vision and Pattern Recognition, pp. 1486–1494 (2019)
13. Zhang, H., Dai, Y., Li, H., Koniusz, P.: Deep stacked hierarchical multi-patch network for image deblurring. In: Proceedings of the IEEE/CVF Conference on Computer Vision and Pattern Recognition, pp. 5978–5986 (2019)
14. Zhou, B., Lapedriza, A., Khosla, A., Oliva, A., Torralba, A.: Places: a 10 million image database for scene recognition. IEEE Trans. Pattern Anal. Mach. Intell. **40**(6), 1452–1464 (2017)
15. Zhu, P., et al.: VisDrone-VID2019: the vision meets drone object detection in video challenge results. In: Proceedings of the IEEE/CVF International Conference on Computer Vision Workshops (2019)

BPFNet: A Unified Framework for Bimodal Palmprint Alignment and Fusion

Zhaoqun Li[1], Xu Liang[2], Dandan Fan[3], Jinxing Li[2], and David Zhang[1,3(✉)]

[1] The Chinese University of Hong Kong (Shenzhen), Shenzhen, China
zhaoqunli@link.cuhk.edu.cn, davidzhang@cuhk.edu.cn
[2] Harbin Institute of Technology (Shenzhen), Harbin, China
[3] Shenzhen Institute of Artificial Intelligence and Robotics for Society,
Shenzhen, China

Abstract. Bimodal palmprint recognition use palm vein and palmprint images at the same time, which can achieve high accuracy and has intrinsic anti-falsification property. For bimodal palmprint recognition and verification, the ROI detection and ROI alignment of palmprint region-of-interest (ROI) are two crucial points for bimodal palmprint matching. Most existing plamprint ROI detection methods are based on keypoint detection algorithms, however the intrinsic difficulties lying in keypoint detection tasks make the results not accurate. Besides, in these methods the ROI alignment and feature fusion algorithms at image-level are not fully investigated. To improve the performance and bridge the gap, we propose our Bimodal Palmprint Fusion Network (BPFNet) which focuses on ROI localization, alignment and bimodal image fusion. BPFNet is an end-to-end deep learning framework which contains two parts: The detection network directly regresses the palmprint ROIs and conducts alignment by estimating translation. In the downstream, the fusion network conducts bimodal ROI image fusion leveraging a novel cross-modal selection scheme. To demonstrate the effectiveness of BPFNet, we implement experiments on two touchless palmprint datasets and the proposed framework achieves state-of-the-art performances.

Keywords: Biometric · Touchless palmprint recognition · Bimodal fusion

1 Introduction

As a representative technology in biometric, touchless palmprint recognition has drawn great attention to researchers recently due to its potential applications on person identification. A pioneer work of palmprint recognition is PalmCode [14] that uses orientation information as features for matching. After that, more and more coding based methods [6,7] emerge in this field. With the development of machine learning algorithms, researchers bend their effort for extracting high discriminative palmprint descriptor via leveraging local region information [10], collaborative representation [15], binary representation [2] and so on. Recently, convolutional neural network (CNN) has achieved tremendous success in palmprint related tasks such as palmprint alignment [11], hyperspectral palmprint

© Springer Nature Switzerland AG 2021
T. Mantoro et al. (Eds.): ICONIP 2021, CCIS 1517, pp. 28–36, 2021.
https://doi.org/10.1007/978-3-030-92310-5_4

verification [17] and palmprint ROI feature extraction [3]. Inspired by powerful metric learning techniques [1] in face recognition, [20] employ well-designed loss functions to enhance intra-class and inter-class distance distribution.

Among diverse application schemes, bimodal palmprint recognition takes advantage of palmprint and palm vein images simultaneously and achieves better performance. Compared to person identification using single palmprint, palmprint recognition with dual-camera could improve recognition accuracy by multi-model information fusion and has high anti-falsification property. In the bimodal palmprint recognition pipeline, palm detection and ROI extraction are essential prerequisites for feature extraction and have a large influence on the final performance. In [11], an end-to-end VGG based framework is proposed for joint palmprint alignment and identification. Nevertheless, the model size is huge which is not suitable for mobile or other real-time applications. [16] adopts a YOLOv3 based detector for palm detection while its keypoint detection strategy is not always stable and the model is not designed for multi-modal image fusion. Most existing works [11,16] fulfill ROI extraction by keypoint detection, however the task is not robust and generally more difficult compared to bounding box regression. In addition, most public bimodal datasets do not contain adequate camera information for ROI alignment, thus the alignment is restricted at image-level.

To address the above concerns, we aim to design a unified framework for efficient bimodal palmprint recognition. In this paper, we propose our BPFNet which conducts ROI localization, ROI alignment and bimodal image fusion tasks with an end-to-end fashion. In BPFNet, the detection network (DNet) directly regresses the rotated bounding box by point view and also predicts the image disparity, making it compatible with other annotation systems. After extracting the ROIs in a differentiable manner, the fusion network (FNet) refines the palmprint and palm vein ROI features, obtaining the final descriptor by a novel cross-modal selection mechanism. Finally, experimental results on CUHKSZ-v1 dataset and ablation studies demonstrate the superiority of our method. To summarize, the contribution of our paper is three-fold:

1. We propose a novel end-to-end deep learning framework fulfilling palm detection, ROI alignment, and bimodal feature fusion simultaneously, which can generate a high discriminative palmprint descriptor.
2. A novel ROI localization scheme is applied, which is also compatible with other datasets, achieving 90.65% IoU on CUHKSZ dataset.
3. We design a novel cross-modal selection module for bimodal image fusion, where the fusion is dominated by the palmprint feature and the selection is based on the correlation between image features.

2   Preliminaries

2.1   ROI Localization

The palmprint ROI is a rotated rectangle (generally a square) which is determined by keypoints on the hand image. Touchless palmprint datasets may have

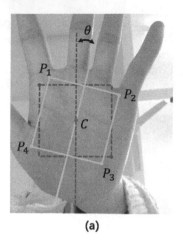 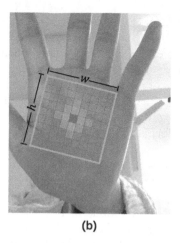

(a)   (b)

Fig. 1. Illustration of ROI localization and ground truth heat map. (a) The ground truth ROI (green box) can be regard as a rotated version of blue box, which could be represented as (x_c, y_c, w, h, θ). (b) The ground truth heat map is a gaussian distribution centered on palm center C. (Color figure online)

different annotation systems and the number of keypoints also varies. In order to generalize our detection algorithm, instead of detecting the key points, we regress the ROI with a rotated bounding box directly. Denote the center of ROI bounding box as $C(x_c, y_c)$, as shown in Fig. 1(a), the ground truth bounding box (green box) can be obtained by rotating a regular bounding box (blue box) around C by angle θ. Therefore we can represent the bounding box as (x_c, y_c, w, h, θ), where w and h denote its width and height. In our methods, we empoly the DNet to learn these parameters, which will be described in Sect. 3.1.

3   Method

3.1   Detection Network

Backbone. In our DNet, the front part is a ResNet18 network whose output stride is 64, following two deconvolution layers with batch normalization and ReLU activation. The output stride of the deconvolution layers is 2, so the final output stride is 16. Denote the backbone feature as $F \in \mathbb{R}^{H \times W \times C_B}$, where H, W are the height and width of the feature map. For the sake of memory usage, in BPFNet the backbone feature F is reused for bimodal fusion and palmprint recognition.

Four Heads Design. In our detection network, we have four heads on the top of the backbone feature F, namely *Center Head, Size Head, Rotation Head,* and *Disparity Head*, as shown in Fig. 2. Each head contains a Conv-ReLU-Conv subnet and generates a heat map whose shape is the same as F. The first three

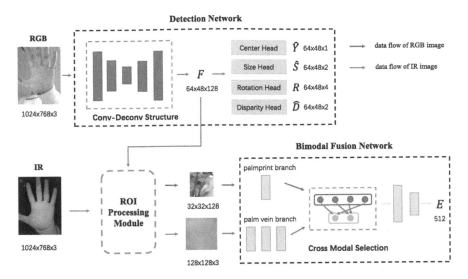

Fig. 2. The pipeline of BPFNet. The feature size is tagged with the format $H \times W \times C$. DNet generates palmprint feature F using a ResNet backbone and four heads are appended which are designed for ROI prediction and disparity estimation. The predicted parameter is then passed to ROI Processing Module for ROI extraction and alignment. The final palmprint descriptor E in FNet is generated by cross-modal selection.

heads are responsible for predicting the rotated bounding box and the last is to estimate the disparity between palmprint image and palm vein image.

For the palm center C, we compute a low-resolution equivalent $\tilde{C} = \lfloor \frac{C}{16} \rfloor$. Each pixel on the feature maps contains predicted values and the pixel on the palm center should have the most information about the palm. Let $\hat{Y} \in \mathbb{R}^{H \times W}$ be the output heat map of the Center Head, of which the palm center $(\tilde{x}_c, \tilde{y}_c)$ is expected to be 1 while other position should be 0. The ground truth heat map $Y \in \mathbb{R}^{H \times W}$ is further splat by a Gaussian kernel $Y_{xy} = \exp(-\frac{(x-\tilde{x}_c)^2+(y-\tilde{y}_c)^2}{2\sigma^2})$, where σ is an adaptive standard deviation depending on the box size [19]. The formation of Y is illustrated in Fig. 1(b) . We use pixel-wise logistic regression with focal loss [9] as the supervision signal for the palm center prediction:

$$L_c = -\sum_{xy} \begin{cases} (1-\hat{Y}_{xy})^\alpha \log(\hat{Y}_{xy}) & \text{if } Y_{xy} = 1 \\ (1-\hat{Y}_{xy})^\beta (\hat{Y}_{xy})^\alpha \log(1-\hat{Y}_{xy}) & \text{otherwise} \end{cases} \tag{1}$$

where α, β are hyperparamters to adjust the loss curve.

As to the Size Head and Disparity Head, we regress the target ground truth values $S = (w, h)$ and $D = (d_x, d_y)$ on the palm center $(\tilde{x}_c, \tilde{y}_c)$. The regression is supervised by L1 loss functions:

$$\begin{aligned} L_s &= |\hat{S}_{\tilde{x}_c \tilde{y}_c} - S| \\ L_d &= |\hat{D}_{\tilde{x}_c \tilde{y}_c} - D| \end{aligned} \tag{2}$$

where $\hat{S} \in \mathbb{R}^{H \times W \times 2}$ and $\hat{D} \in \mathbb{R}^{H \times W \times 2}$ denote the size prediction and disparity prediction feature maps.

Besides the above heads, we add a Rotation Head for inclination prediction. Since the direct regression for θ is relatively hard [12], we take a strategy that first judges whether the orientation is positive and then selects the output angular value. To be specific, each pixel in the feature map R outputs 4 scalars, where the first two logits are used to conduct orientation classification and the rest scalars are corresponding angular values. Suppose $R_{\tilde{x}_c \tilde{y}_c} = (l_1, l_2, \theta_1, \theta_2)$, the classification is trained with:

$$L_r = \sum_{i=1}^{2} softmax(l_i, c_i) + c_i |\theta_i - \theta| \qquad (3)$$

where $c_i = \mathbb{1}(\theta > 0)$ is the sign indicator.

3.2 ROI Processing Module

The four heads enable us to recover the rotated bounding box and extract the ROI on backbone feature F and palm vein image. In the ROI recovery, we pick the pixel in $\hat{Y}$ with maximum value as palm center, denoted as $(\hat{x}, \hat{y})$. Then the predicted bounding box is simply $(\hat{x}, \hat{y}, \hat{w}, \hat{h}, \hat{\theta})$. In our implementation, F is first rotated by angle θ which is realized by applying an affine transformation matrix. We then crop and resize the ROI using ROIAlign operator [4]. The whole process only involves matrix multiplication and pixel interpolation, which is fully differentiable. For the palm vein image, we first translate it by $(\hat{d}_x, \hat{d}_y)$ to align the hands. Next, the ROI extraction of the palm vein image is straightforward.

3.3 Bimodal Fusion Network

The whole FNet is composed of several ResBlocks [5] inserting a cross-modal selection module. Before the fusion process, we construct two light branches for preprocessing. In the palmprint branch, one ResBlock is used to convert F into fusion space. As the input of the palm vein branch is the ROI image, for the sake of balance, more blocks are added in the palm vein branch for feature extraction and downsampling. The two branches joint at our proposed cross-modal selection module, where the features have the same spatial dimension (H_f, W_f). After feature enhancement, two ResBlocks are added for further high-level feature extraction.

Cross-Modal Selection. The vascular distribution endows the palm vein image the ability of anti-counterfeit, while the palmprint image of one individual has more texture information and therefore is more distinctive. In this work we focus more on person identification and treat the bimodal images differently in the fusion process. Basically, the feature fusion should be guided by the palmprint feature. To accord the idea, we propose a selection scheme based on the channel correlation. Suppose $P \in \mathbb{R}^{C_1 \times H_f \times W_f}$, $V \in \mathbb{R}^{C_2 \times H_f \times W_f}$ are the palmprint feature and the palm vein feature respectively. The correlation $r \in \mathbb{R}^{C_1 \times C_2}$ between channels is defined as their cosine similariy $r_{ij} = \frac{<P_i | V_j>}{||P_i||_2 \cdot ||V_j||_2}$, where the subscripts $1 \leq i \leq C_1$, $1 \leq j \leq C_2$ are the channel numbers and $< \cdot | \cdot >$ denotes the inner product.

For each channel of palmprint feature P_i, it will select the k-th palm vein feature V_k which has maximum correlation to enhence its representation, *i.e.* $k = \max_j r_{ij}$. Denote the selected feature as $V_i^s (V_i^s = V_k)$, the fusion is the summation of two features: $P_i^f = P_i + V_i^s$.

3.4   Network Training

Following [8,16], we adopt arc-margin loss [1] on the top of the FNet to supervise the embedding E:

$$L_{arc} = - \log \frac{e^{s \cos(\eta_y + m)}}{e^{s \cos(\eta_y + m)} + \sum_{j=1, j \neq y}^{n} e^{s \cos(\eta_j + m)}} \quad (4)$$

where η is the angle between logit and weight in classification layer, y denotes the ground truth label and n is the number of classes. In Eq. (4), s and m are hyperparameters which represent scale and angular margin respectively. In this paper, we set $s = 32$ and $m = 0.5$. The whole network is supervised by the following loss:

$$L_{total} = L_c + \lambda_1 L_r + \lambda_2 (L_s + L_d) + \mu L_{arc} \quad (5)$$

where $\mu, \lambda_1, \lambda_2$ are trade-off loss weights. We set $\mu = 1, \lambda_1 = 0.1, \lambda_2 = 0.1$ in our experiments unless specified otherwise.

4   Experiments

4.1   Datasets and Metrics

We conduct experiments on the touchless palmprint benchmarks CUHKSZ-v1 and TongJi. CUHKSZ-v1 has 28,008 palm images from 1167 individuals and TongJi has 12000 images from 300 individuals. For each dataset, we follow the official train/test split, and each palm is regarded as one class.

Rank-1 accuracy and EER (Equal Error Rate) are used for evaluating palmprint verification performance. In the evaluation, we adopt a test-to-register protocol that considers the real application of palmprint verification. The protocol is widely used in previous works [3,11]. Under this protocol, four images are registered as enrollment and the remaining test images are matched to these images, where the minimum distance of four distances is used as matching distance.

Table 1. The performance comparison (%) of single RGB image input versus bimodal image input.

Methods	Test ROI	CUHKSZ		TongJi	
		Rank-1	EER	Rank-1	EER
RGB	Predicted	99.89	0.15	99.93	0.22
RGB + IR	Predicted	**100**	**0.11**	**100**	**0.03**
RGB	Ground truth	99.47	0.18	99.72	0.39
RGB + IR	Ground truth	99.68	0.14	99.97	0.05

Table 2. The performance comparison (%) on CUHKSZ dataset with ground truth ROI (GT ROI) or ROI extracted by BPFNet (Predicted ROI).

Methods	GT ROI		Predicted ROI	
	Rank-1	EER	Rank-1	EER
CompCode	99.83	0.32	96.67	2.88
OrdinalCode	99.79	0.42	95.23	3.39
LLDP$_3$	99.68	0.44	95.12	2.64
CR-CompCode	99.79	0.32	97.67	2.06
Resnet18	99.25	0.58	98.41	0.66
VGG11-bn	90.89	2.50	95.55	1.37
GoogLeNet	84.11	2.97	80.19	2.81
PalmNet	95.97	0.79	96.21	1.48
BPFNet$_{rgb}$	99.47	0.18	**99.89**	**0.15**

4.2 Implementation

The DNet (based on ResNet18) is pretrained on ImageNet and all the layers in FNet are initialized by a Gaussian distribution of mean value 0 and standard deviation 0.01. We use the stochastic gradient descent (SGD) algorithm with momentum 5e–4 to optimize the network. The batch size for the mini-batch is set to 64. The initial learning rate for the CNN is 1e–2, which is annealed down to 1e–4 following a cosine schedule without restart. The total training epochs are 100.

4.3 Bimodal Fusion

For showing the effect of the bimodal fusion scheme, as BPFNet is separable, we conduct palmprint recognition experiments using single RGB images as comparison. For eliminating the possible influence of the ROI bias, we also evaluate our model with ground truth ROIs. The experiment results are shown in Table 1. We can see that the palm vein image can improve the recognition performance.

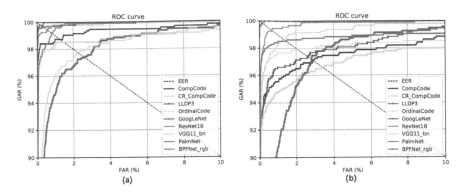

Fig. 3. The ROC curves obtained using the methods listed in Table 2. The figure shows the results of methods (a) with ground truth ROI as input and (b) with our extracted ROI as input.

4.4   Comparison with Other Methods

We compare our method with coding based methods including CompCode [7], OrdinalCode [18], LLDP [10], CR-CompCode [15] as well as deep learning method PalmNet [3] and several baselines. All deep learning baselines are trained with arc-margin loss. These methods use palmprint ROI images as input and do not involve palm vein image fusion. For a fair comparison, we report the performances of our model trained with only RGB images, denoted as BPFNet$_{rgb}$. Moreover, considering the possible influence of ROI bias, we compare both the performances using ROI extracted by BPFNet and the performances using ground truth ROI, as shown in Table 2. The corresponding ROC curves are plotted in Fig. 3.

5   Conclusion

In this paper, we propose a novel framework, named BPFNet, for bimodal palmprint recognition. In our method, the detection network directly regresses the rotated bounding box, which makes it compatible with other annotation systems. In the downstream, the fusion network conducts feature fusion using the proposed cross-modal selection. Finally, comprehensive experiments are carried out to demonstrate the superiority of our method.

Acknowledgement. This work is supported by Shenzhen Institute of Artificial Intelligence and Robotics for Society. The work is also supported in part by the NSFC under Grants 6217070450 and 62076086, Shenzhen Science and Technology Program (RCBS20200714114910193), Open Project Fund from Shenzhen Institute of Artificial Intelligence and Robotics for Society (AC01202005017).

References

1. Deng, J., Guo, J., Xue, N., Zafeiriou, S.: Arcface: additive angular margin loss for deep face recognition. In: CVPR, pp. 4690–4699 (2019)
2. Fei, L., Zhang, B., Xu, Y., Guo, Z., Wen, J., Jia, W.: Learning discriminant direction binary palmprint descriptor. IEEE Trans. Image Process. **28**(8), 3808–3820 (2019)
3. Genovese, A., Piuri, V., Plataniotis, K.N., Scotti, F.: Palmnet: gabor-pca convolutional networks for touchless palmprint recognition. IEEE Trans. Inf. Forensics Secu. **14**(12), 3160–3174 (2019)
4. He, K., Gkioxari, G., Dollar, P., Girshick, R.: Mask R-CNN. In: ICCV (2017)
5. He, K., Zhang, X., Ren, S., Sun, J.: Deep residual learning for image recognition. In: CVPR, pp. 770–778 (2016)
6. Jia, W., et al.: Palmprint recognition based on complete direction representation. IEEE Trans. Image Process. **26**(9), 4483–4498 (2017)
7. Kong, A.W., Zhang, D.: Competitive coding scheme for palmprint verification. In: Int. Conf. Pattern Recogn. **1**, 520–523 (2004)
8. Li, Z., Liang, X., Fan, D., Li, J., Jia, W., Zhang, D.: Touchless palmprint recognition based on 3D gabor template and block feature refinement. arXiv preprint (2021). arXiv:2103.02167
9. Lin, T.Y., Goyal, P., Girshick, R., He, K., Dollár, P.: Focal loss for dense object detection. In: ICCV, pp. 2980–2988 (2017)
10. Luo, Y.T., et al.: Local line directional pattern for palmprint recognition. Pattern Recogn. **50**, 26–44 (2016)
11. Matkowski, W.M., Chai, T., Kong, A.W.K.: Palmprint recognition in uncontrolled and uncooperative environment. IEEE Trans. Inf. Forensics Secur. **15**, 1601–1615 (2019)
12. Mousavian, A., Anguelov, D., Flynn, J., Kosecka, J.: 3D bounding box estimation using deep learning and geometry, In: CVPR (2017)
13. Xiao, B., Wu, H., Wei, Y.: Simple baselines for human pose estimation and tracking. In: ECCV, pp. 466–481 (2018)
14. Zhang, D., Kong, W.K., You, J., Wong, M.: Online palmprint identification. TPAMI **25**(9), 1041–1050 (2003)
15. Zhang, L., Li, L., Yang, A., Shen, Y., Yang, M.: Towards contactless palmprint recognition: a novel device, a new benchmark, and a collaborative representation based identification approach. Pattern Recogn. **69**, 199–212 (2017)
16. Zhang, Y., Zhang, L., Zhang, R., Li, S., Li, J., Huang, F.: Towards palmprint verification on smartphones. arXiv preprint (2020). arXiv:2003.13266
17. Zhao, S., Zhang, B., Chen, C.P.: Joint deep convolutional feature representation for hyperspectral palmprint recognition. Inf. Sci. **489**, 167–181 (2019)
18. Sun, Z., Tan, T., Wang, Y., Li, S.Z.: Ordinal palmprint represention for personal identification [representation read representation]. In: CVPR. vol. 1, pp. 279–284 (2005)
19. Zhou, X., Wang, D., Krähenbühl, P.: Objects as points. In: arXiv preprint (2019). arXiv:1904.07850
20. Zhu, J., Zhong, D., Luo, K.: Boosting unconstrained palmprint recognition with adversarial metric learning. IEEE Trans. Biometr. Behav. Ident. Sci. **2**(4), 388–398 (2020)

Cortical Coding of Surface Textures and Contour Shapes in the Intermediate-Level Visual Area V4

Itsuki Machida[1], Atsushi Kodama[1], Kouji Kimura[1], Motofumi Shishikura[1], Hiroshi Tamura[2,3], and Ko Sakai[1(✉)]

[1] Department of Computer Science, University of Tsukuba, Ibaraki 305-8573, Japan
`sakai@cs.tsukuba.ac.jp`
[2] Graduate School of Frontiers Biosciences, Osaka University, Osaka, Japan
[3] Center for Information and Neural Networks, Osaka, Japan

Abstract. Integration of multiple properties of an object is a fundamental function for object recognition. Surface texture and contour shape are thought to be crucial characteristics that contribute to the recognition. We investigated the cortical coding of surface and shape in monkey V4, with the focus on the integration of the two. To examine how V4 neurons code surface and shape; whether single neurons jointly code the two, or distinct groups of neurons independently code the two, we examined the activities of V4 neurons in response to natural image patches and their silhouette, wherein the former included both contour shape and surface properties, such as texture and color, but the latter included only contour shape. We analyzed the correlation between the spike counts responding to the natural and silhouette patches. The correlation coefficient across neurons was 0.56, suggesting partial joint-coding of surface and shape in V4. The modulation latency was 78 and 57 ms for the natural and silhouette patches. The dimension of the neural responses for the natural patches was approximately 30% greater than that for the silhouette patches. These results indicate more complicated computation and representation for the natural images compared to the silhouette images. These results suggest two sub-populations of neurons, one with joint-coding of surface and shape, and the other without.

Keywords: Computational neuroscience · Vison · Cortex · V4 · Electrophysiology

1 Introduction

Object recognition in machine vision has been greatly advanced with the emergence of Deep Convolutional Nets (CNN). One of major improvement in CNN compared to the traditional Neural Nets is auto-encoding wherein middle- to high-level image features are encoded within individual intermediate layers. This layered intermediate representation corresponds to the cortical representation in the mammalian visual system [1]. Throughout the hierarchical visual cortex,

© Springer Nature Switzerland AG 2021
T. Mantoro et al. (Eds.): ICONIP 2021, CCIS 1517, pp. 37–45, 2021.
https://doi.org/10.1007/978-3-030-92310-5_5

image features are extracted and represented by neurons; beginning from simple extraction of contour lines, continuing to the segregation of figure and ground (FG), and to the representation of object parts in medial-axis and 3D surfaces. It is expected that the investigation on the cortical coding greatly contributes to the understanding of the visual system and further to the evolution of machine vision. Physiological studies have suggested that an intermediate-level visual cortex, V4, is crucial for coding abstract and meaningful representation that leads to the formation of an object by integrating low-level local image features (often called "proto-object") [2]. We focused on monkey V4 and investigated the neural coding therein.

Integration of multiple properties of images is one of the most important function to realize the excellent performance in object recognition and scene under-standing. Particularly, the integration of contour shapes and surface properties such as pattern, texture, and color has been considered crucial. Because, natural scenes are composed of multiple surfaces with colors and textures, and the segregation of surfaces directly contribute to the determination of object shapes. Recent studies have suggested integrated representation along with the distinct representation of contour shapes and surfaces [3,4]. However, how V4 neurons treat and integrate shape and surface to construct an object has not been clarified.

Our recent study indicated that V4 neurons were crucial for the FG segregation that was essential for the correct integration of local features 5. We reported that V4 neurons showed FG-dependent responses to both natural and silhouette images wherein the former included both surface properties and contour shape but the latter included only contour shape [5]. However, the previous study did not examine differences in neural signals between those responding to natural and silhouette images. Further analyses are expected to clarify how surface and shape were represented and integrated in the intermediate stage of the visual cortex.

In the present study, we investigated neural coding of surface textures and contour shapes in V4 neurons, with a focus on the integration of the two. Specifically, we examined the neural activities in response to figure and ground during the presentation of natural images and their silhouette images. During the experiment, a set of local patches of the natural and silhouette images were presented to the animals, with the aim of excluding global and top-down. First, we computed the correlation between the responses to the natural image patches and that to the corresponding silhouette image patches, in order to clarify how much the neurons jointly responded to surface textures and contour shapes. Second, we examined whether the duration necessary for processing the natural and silhouette patches differed. Next, we performed dimensional analysis on the neural activities in response to the natural and silhouette patches. In short, the dimension represents the number of neurons that is needed for the representation of the stimuli given no redundancy among neurons [6]. The results of these analyses suggest two sub-populations of neurons in V4, one with joint-coding of surface and shape and the other without.

2 Physiological Data for Analyses

2.1 Experimental Procedure

Electrophysiological experiments were conducted at Cognitive Neuroscience Lab. at Osaka University [5] and the recorded data were provided for the present analyses. This section summarizes the essence of the experiment. The detailed preparations and procedures were described elsewhere 5.The neural activities of three hemispheres of two female macaque monkeys (Macaca fuscata) were provided. During experiment sessions, the monkeys were analgesized and immobilized. All animal experiments were performed in accordance with the guidelines of the National Institute of Health (1996) and the Japan Neuroscience Society, and were approved by the Osaka University Animal Experiment Committee (certification no: FBS-13–003). For recordings of the neural activity of V4 cells, 32-channel silicon probes with eight shafts were used. The neural signals were sorted to single-unit spiking activities off-line for each session.

2.2 Stimuli

Stimuli presented to the monkeys were comprised of two sets of small patches, which were generated from natural images included in Berkeley Segmentation Dataset (BSD) [7]. Example stimuli are shown in Fig. 1. These local patches were used to exclude top-down global influence. The first set consisted of natural image patches (natural patch-es). We chose 105 sub-regions (69×69 pixels) from the BSD that included the con-tours passing through the center of the patches. Because the distribution of contour curvatures is highly non-uniform in natural scenes, we controlled the distributions of the degree of convexity, closure, and symmetry of contours 8. The second set consist-ed of natural contours with one side filled with the preferred color of the cell (either white, black, red, green, yellow, or blue) and the other with the opposite color (silhouette patches). We also used mirrored images of the natural and silhouette patches. The colors were inverted in the mirror images so as to keep contrast polarity. In many cases, the CRF center of a cell was located on the figure and ground regions of the original and mirror (or mirror and original) patches, respectively. To obscure the boundary of stimulus and background, we attenuated contrast towards the periphery with a Gaussian. The assignment of FG regions within the patches were given psychophysically [5]. A single stimulus was shown for 200 ms followed by a blank of 200 ms.

2.3 Data Analysis

For the examination of responsiveness to stimuli, we compared the firing rates of isolated single units during the pre-stimulus period (-50-+50 ms after stimulus onset) with those of the stimulus period (50–250 ms after stimulus onset), for all stimuli, with t-tests. A value of $p < 0.05$ was used as the criterion for responsiveness. To estimate the retinotopic location and extent of the classical

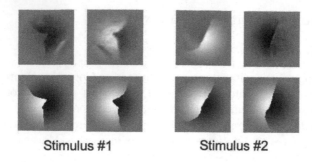

Stimulus #1   Stimulus #2

Fig. 1. Two example sets of stimulus patches. The top images are the original (left) and the mirror (right) patches (natural patches), and the bottom images are their silhouette patches. Images were mirrored with respect to the tangent of the contour passing through the patch center.

receptive fields (CRFs), we counted the number of spiking events in isolated single units during the presentations of the grating patches shown at different retinal positions. The center and extent of the CRFs were estimated from the mean spike count maps fitted by a two-dimensional Gaussian function. Based on the positional relation between the CRF center and the content of the image patch, we classified the patches for each cell into two categories: CRF center on the figure or on the ground. To examine the modulation of each cell by FG and contrast polarity, we performed a two-way repeated-measures analysis of variance (ANOVA). The isolated units with (1) the significant response to stimuli (2) their CRF centers located within the stimulus patch, and (3) the significant modulation to FG, were subjected to the present analyses.

3   Correlation Between the Responses to Natural and Silhouette Images

To clarify how much the neurons jointly responded to surface textures and contour shapes, we compared the neural responses to the natural image patches and that to the corresponding silhouette image patches. The peristimulus time histogram (PSTH) of an example neuron is shown in Fig. 2. This cell preferred figure compared to ground (responding to an object rather than to background), and evoked greater responses to the natural patches compared to the silhouette patches.

To extract the neural activities relevant to an object, we focused on the responses to figure, and thus the responses to ground were subtracted from the respons-es to figure. Specifically, we compared the response to the original (or mirror) patch where figure region was projected onto the CRF center and the response to the mirror (or original) patch where ground was projected:

$$\mathbf{F} - \mathbf{G} = \frac{1}{n} \sum_{i=1}^{n} (F_i - G_i) \Big/ \max \left(\frac{1}{n} \sum_{i=1}^{n} |F_i - G_i| \right), \tag{1}$$

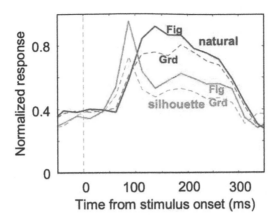

Fig. 2. PSTHs of an example cell across all natural (blue lines) and silhouette (orange) patches. The solid and dotted lines indicate the responses to figure and ground, respectively. (Color figure online)

where F and G represent the spike count for the figure and ground patches, i and n indicate the patch and the total number of them, respectively. We computed this F–G for the pairs of natural patches and that of silhouette patches, and then compared the two.

The distribution of the F–G responses to the natural and silhouette patches are shown in Fig. 3 for the population of cells. In this analysis, since figure and ground regions needed to be projected onto the CRF center in the original and mirror patches, respectively, the number of analyzed cells was limited to 47. We observe a wide variety of cells; some cells responded equally to the natural and silhouette, and some responded mostly to natural patches. A linear regression analysis showed the slope of 0.59, indicating that more cells responded frequently to the natural patches compared to the silhouette patches. Pearson's correlation coefficient was 0.56 ($p < 0.001$), indicating significant but weak- to medium-level correlation between the responses to the natural and silhouette patches. These results suggest a weak degree of joint coding as a population with a variety of cells with different degrees of joint coding.

4   Modulation Latency

To examine the difference/similarity between the neural processing for surface proper-ties and contour shapes, we compared modulation latencies for the natural and silhouette patches. The modulation latency is the time after stimulus onset when the activity differentiates between figure and ground. It is expected that the more complicated processing needs the longer computation time. We would expect a longer latency for the natural images than silhouette images. However, if truly joint coding takes place, it could take similar time with or without surface textures. The latency was deter-mined by the two-phase linear regression analysis [9] on a differential spike count histogram.

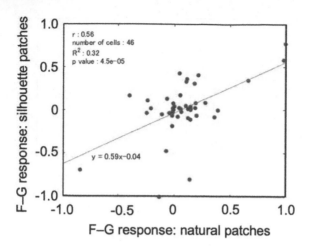

Fig. 3. The correlation between the F–G responses to the natural and silhouette patches. The blue dots indicate individual cells, and the red line indicates the regression.

The time courses of cells responding to natural and silhouette patches were shown in Fig. 4. The mean responses across cells for the preferred (figure or ground) and non-preferred (ground or figure) sides (thick red and blue lines, respectively) begin to diverge at 78 and 57 ms after the stimulus onset for the natural and silhouette patches, respectively. The modulation latency for the silhouette patches (57 ms) was consistent with the previous report (53 ms) using the same stimulus set but a different cell set [5]. The result indicates that the natural patches need 21 ms longer time for determining a figure (object) region. Since the response latency (time that the cells in V4 begin to respond to visual stimuli) was around 40 ms, the duration needed for processing contour shape was approximately 20 ms, and the addition of surface texture doubled the duration to approximately 40 ms. A shorter latency for silhouette images might be expected since the higher contrast tends to evoke the shorter latency. How-ever, the effect is rather small in V4 cells; approximately 10 ms for the change in 75% contrast [10]. The 20 ms difference in modulation latency suggests distinct processing for surface and shape, which would support partial or no joint coding for surface and shape.

5   Dimensional Analysis—Complexity in Neural Representation

To examine the difference between the processing of surface texture and contour shape, we estimated the dimension of the neural responses to the natural and silhouette patches. The dimension corresponds to the complexity of the neural representation in response to the stimulus set, given the independent responses across the cells. In short, the dimension corresponds to the number of cells that is

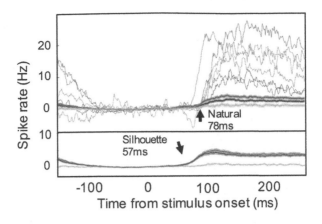

Fig. 4. The time course of the neural responses. (Top) The responses to the natural patches. Thin lines indicate example responses of individual cells. Thick red and blue lines indicate the mean responses to preferred and non-preferred sides (figure and ground), respectively, and a thick green line indicate the modulation responses (preferred minus non-preferred responses). The error shade indicates the standard error. (Bottom) The responses to the silhouette patches. (Color figure online)

needed for the representation of the stimulus set. Previous studies have reported that the dimension for the high-level visual cortex, IT, was approximately 70–110 [6]. The responses of 390 cells were analyzed in the present study.

We estimated the dimension based on principle component analysis that was applied to a $m \times n$ matrix which was composed of the activity of n cells in response to m stimuli. The significance of the estimated components were then evaluated by the parallel analysis method [6]. Specifically, the estimated eigen values were considered significant if they were greater than the eigen values generated from randomly shuffled data. It has been reported that the estimated dimension depends on the number of cells and stimuli [6]. We repeatedly performed bootstrap sampling within the range of the cells and stimuli (n=390 and m=210), and estimated the dimension for every n (1–390) and m (1–210). The number of resampling for each m and n was 20,000, and the mean across the resampling were defined as the dimension for that m and n.

The estimated dimensions for the stimulus set (m=210) are shown in Fig. 5. We observe that the dimension increases as the number of cells increases. To estimate the dimension at infinity, we fitted the dimensions with a nonlinear function [6],

$$y = a \left[1 - \left(\frac{b}{\exp(\frac{x^c}{d}) - 1 + b} \right)^e \right]^f \tag{2}$$

In the present study, we fixed the number of stimuli, and extrapolated with respect to the number of cells. The estimated dimension for the natural and silhouette patches were 19 and 14, respectively, indicating that neural processing for the natural patches was, in fact, more complicated than that for the

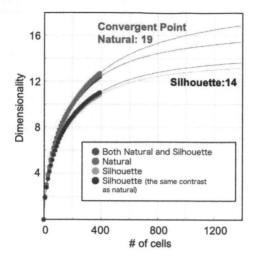

Fig. 5. The dimensionality as a function of the number of cells given the presented stimuli (210 patches). As the responses of more cells were taken into account, the dimensionality increased but converged at 14 and 19 for the silhouette and natural patches, respectively.

silhouette patches. These dimensions were derived solely from the neural activities; therefore, they represent the difficulty for the V4 cells in processing the stimuli. The present estimation was limited to the present stimulus set, and thus the dimensionality is likely underestimated [6]. With the extrapolation to the infinite number of stimuli, out preliminary estimation indicated that the dimensionality increased up to twofold. Although the result was rather noisy, the difference between the natural and silhouette patches was intact. The present result supports that the cortical representation of surface texture and contour shape would be different.

6   Conclusion and Discussion

We investigated the cortical coding of surface and shape in the intermediate-level visual area, V4, of monkeys. We analyzed the correlation between the spike counts responding to the natural and silhouette patches. The correlation coefficient was weak but significant, suggesting partial joint-coding of surface and shape in V4. To further investigate the neural coding for surface and shape, we analyzed the modulation latency and dimensionality. The duration needed for the natural images was almost doubled compared to that for the silhouette images. The dimension of the neural responses for the natural patches was approximately 30% greater than that for the silhouette patches. These results indicate more complicated computation and representation for the natural images, suggesting distinct processing for surface and shape. These results suggest two sub-populations of cells in V4, one with joint-coding of surface and shape, and the other without. The present analyses provided new evidence for under-standing neural coding in intermediate-level cortical processing. However, the present study was limited to single-cell analyses. Investigation into population coding would be inevitable. Our study was also limited to local image patches; the top-down influence, specifically, global features such as closure and knowledge, was intentionally excluded. Further investigations with global features are expected to advance the understanding of neural coding and cortical processing.

Acknowledgments. We appreciate Dr. Yukako Yamane with Okinawa Institute of Science and Technology for providing us the physiological data and discussions. This work was partially supported by Grant-in-aid from JSPS (KAKENHI 20H04487, 19H01111 A) and RIEC, Univ. Tohoku (H31/A12).

References

1. Bashivan, P., Kar, K., DiCarlo, J.J.: Neural population control via deep image syn-thesis. Science **364** (2019). https://doi.org/10.1126/science.aav9436
2. Mihalas, S., Dong, Y., von der Heydt, R., Niebur, E.: Mechanisms of perceptual organization provide auto-zoom and auto-localization for attention to objects. PNAS **18**, 7583–7588 (2011)
3. Sakai, K., Sakata, Y., Kurematsu, K.: Interaction of surface pattern and contour shape in the tilt after effects evoked by symmetry. Sci. Reports **11** (2021). https://doi.org/10.1038/s41598-021-87429-y
4. Sakai, K., Narushima, K., Aoki, N.: Facilitation of shape-from-shading perception by random textures. J. Opt. Soc. Am., A **23**, 1805–1813 (2006)
5. Yamane, Y., Kodama, A., Shishikura, M., Tamura, H., Sakai, K.: Population coding of figure and ground in natural image patches by V4 neurons. PloS one **15**, e0235128 (2020). https://doi.org/10.1371/journal.pone.0235128
6. Lehky, S.R., Kiani, R., Esteky, H., Tanaka, K.: Dimensionality of object representations in monkey inferotemporal cortex. Neural Comput. **26**, 2135–2162 (2014)
7. Fowlkes, C.C., Martin, D.R., Malik, J.: Local figure-ground cues are valid for natural images. J. Vision, **7**(2), 1–14 (2007)
8. Sakai, K., Matsuoka, S., Kurematsu, K., Hatori, Y.: Perceptual representation and ef-fectiveness of local figure-ground cues in natural contours. Front. Psychol. **6**, 1685 (2015). https://doi.org/10.3389/fpsyg.2015.01685
9. Sugihara, T., Qiu, F.T., von der Heydt, R.: The speed of context integration in the visual cortex. J. Neurophysiol. **106**, 374–385 (2011)
10. Lee, J., Williford, T., Maunsell, J.H.: Spatial attention and the latency of neuronal re-sponses in macaque area V4. J. Neurosci. **27**, 9632–9637 (2007)

Dynamical Characteristics of State Transition Defined by Neural Activity of Phase in Alzheimer's Disease

Sou Nobukawa[1,2]($\boxtimes$) (iD), Takashi Ikeda[3] (iD), Mitsuru Kikuchi[3,4], and Tetsuya Takahashi[3,5,6] (iD)

[1] Department of Computer Science, Chiba Institute of Technology, 2-17-1 Tsudanuma, Narashino, Chiba 275–0016, Japan
nobukawa@cs.it-chiba.ac.jp

[2] Department of Preventive Intervention for Psychiatric Disorders, National Institute of Mental Health, National Center of Neurology and Psychiatry, Tokyo, Japan

[3] Research Center for Child Mental Development, Kanazawa University, Ishikawa, Japan

[4] Department of Psychiatry and Behavioral Science, Kanazawa University, Ishikawa, Japan

[5] Department of Neuropsychiatry, University of Fukui, Fukui, Japan

[6] Uozu Shinkei Sanatorium, Toyama, Japan

Abstract. In recent findings of dynamical functional connectivity (dFC) as the degree of variability for functional connectivity, the dFC reflects the abilities and deficits in cognitive functions. Recently, we introduced the instantaneous phase difference between electroencephalography (EEG) signals (called the dynamical phase synchronization (DPS) approach) and succeeded in detecting moment-to-moment dFC dynamics. In this approach, neural interactions in whole-brain activity are decomposed into phase differences of pairwise brain regions. From the viewpoint of "emergence" in complex systems where interactions among several components produce additional functions, an integrated analysis of interactions in a whole-brain network without separating each interaction in pairwise brain regions might lead to new understanding of cognitive functions. Alzheimer's disease (AD) involves cognitive impairments due to the loss of multiple neural interactions and affects dFC. We hypothesized that instantaneous phase dynamics without decomposing to pairwise instantaneous phase differences would bring another dimension of understanding of alternations of dFC regarding cognitive impairment in AD. To prove this hypothesis, we introduced dynamic states based on instantaneous frequency distribution across the whole brain. Upon applying this method to EEG signals of healthy controls (HC) and subjects with AD, the results showed that the state of the occipital leading phase in the AD group was more difficult to maintain. Moreover, the degree of maintenance of this state has a relatively high correlation with cognitive function in AD. In conclusion, dynamic states based on whole-brain instantaneous frequency distribution might be an additional approach to reveal different aspects of dFC among the other approaches.

© Springer Nature Switzerland AG 2021
T. Mantoro et al. (Eds.): ICONIP 2021, CCIS 1517, pp. 46–54, 2021.
https://doi.org/10.1007/978-3-030-92310-5_6

Keywords: Alzheimer's disease · Cognitive functions · Dynamical functional connectivity · Electroencephalography

1   Introduction

Large accumulation studies on neural dynamics have shown that a wide range of spatial and temporal neural interactions, which are reflected as functional connectivity (FC) and phase amplitude coupling, achieve integration for neural processes of cognitive functions (reviewed in [14]). Moreover, recent findings of dynamical functional connectivity (dFC), defined by the degree of variability in the strength of FC, showed that dFC more precisely reflects the abilities and deficits of cognitive functions in pathological conditions, such as schizophrenia, Alzheimer's disease (AD), and autism spectrum disorder rather than FC (reviewed in [5]). The temporal variation of coherence among blood-oxygen-level-dependent (BOLD) signals of brain regions through sliding-time-window analysis have been utilized to evaluate dFC [1,10]. Subsequently, the combination of graph analysis and clustering methods against transitions of FC in the time window revealed temporospatial patterns of network dynamics of the whole brain [1,11].

In addition to studies on the dFC of BOLD signals, studies on the dFC of electroencephalography (EEG) and magnetoencephalography (MEG) have been conducted [2,3,21]. The application of dFC analysis to EEG/MEG signals has higher temporal resolution in comparison with BOLD signals; however, it is difficult to detect the dynamics of dFC with multiple temporal scales through the sliding-time-window process, including moment-to-moment dynamics in milliseconds [2,3,21]. To overcome this difficulty, our recent study introduced the instantaneous phase difference between EEG signals, and through multiple temporal scale complexity analysis of this phase difference, the proposed method (the dynamical phase synchronization (DPS) approach) succeeded in detecting the moment-to-moment dFC dynamics and alternation of the dFC of the frontal cortical network in aging [15]. In the DPS approach, neural interactions during whole-brain activity are decomposed into phase differences of pairwise brain regions [15]. From the viewpoint of "emergence" in complex systems, where interactions among several components induces additional functions and behaviors [20], the integrated analysis of interactions in a whole-brain network without separating each interaction into pairwise brain regions might lead to a greater understanding of cognitive functions.

AD involves cognitive impairments due to the loss of multiple neural interactions induced by progressive neuronal death, neurofibrillary tangles, and senile plaques in widespread brain regions [9]. The progression of AD leads to alterations in the temporal complexity of neural activity on multiple temporal scales [16,17]. Moreover, a recent study with dFC captured by a sliding time window reported alternation of network dynamics in AD [8,18,19].

In this context, we hypothesized that instantaneous phase dynamics without decomposing to pairwise instantaneous phase differences in the DPS approach [15] brings another dimension of understanding of alternations of dFC in AD and its relationship with cognitive impairment. In this study, to prove this hypothesis, we introduced dynamic states based on instantaneous frequency distribution across the whole brain and evaluated the dynamics of the state transitions as an expanding approach to the DPS approach in AD.

2   Materials and Methods

2.1   Subjects

We used 16 AD subjects who satisfied the National Institute of Neurological and Communicative Disorders and Stroke-Alzheimer's Disease and Related Disorders Association (NINCDS-ADRDA) criteria and were in a state before the onset of primary dementia in accordance with Diagnostic and Statistical Manual of Mental Disorders (4th edition; DSM-IV) criteria and sex- and age-matched healthy older subjects who were non-smokers and were not on medication [16,17]. In the healthy older (healthy control: HC) group, subjects with medical or neurological conditions involving epilepsy or head trauma in the past and with a history of alcohol or drug dependency were removed. In AD subjects, medications that affect the central nervous system were not administered, and the Functional Assessment Staging Test (FAST) and Mini-Mental State Examination (MMSE) were conducted. There were 3 subjects with mild AD (FAST 3), 7 with moderate AD (FAST 4), and 6 with mild dementia (FAST 5). The MMSE scores were distributed in the range of $10 - 26$ (average: 15.56). More detailed information on the subjects is shown in Table 1. Informed consent was obtained from all participants before conducting the study. The experimental protocol of this study was approved by the Ethics Committee of Kanazawa University and was carried out according to the Declaration of Helsinki.

Table 1. Physical characteristics of healthy older subjects (HC) and subjects with Alzheimer's disease (AD). MMSE, Mini-Mental State Examination.

	HC and AD subjects	p values	
Male/female	7/11	5/11	0.72
Age (year)	59.3 (5.3, 55−66)	57.5 (4.7, 43−64)	0.31
MMSE score	NA	15.5 (4.7, 10−26)	NA

2.2   EEG Recordings

For the EEG recording, 16 electrodes located at Fp1, Fp2, F3, F4, C3, C4, P3, P4, O1, O2, F7, F8, Fz, Pz, T5, and T6 according to the international 10–20 system electrode placement were used. EEG signals were measured using the binaural connection as a reference. During EEG measurement, the subjects sat in an electrically shielded and soundproof recording room, and the room illuminance was controlled. The EEG-4518 apparatus (Nihon Kohden, Tokyo, Japan) was used for EEG measurement. The EEG signal was recorded using a sampling frequency of 200 Hz and a bandpass filter of 2.0–60 Hz. Eye movements were traced utilizing bipolar electrocardiography (EOG). Each subject's EEG signal was measured for 10 to 15 min in a resting state with their eyes closed. In the recorded EEG signals, an artifact-free continuous 50-s (10000 data points) epoch was chosen for the state estimation process described in Sect. 2.3 for each subject.

2.3 Estimation Method for Dynamical State Based on Frequency Distribution

In this study, the states of brain activity were defined by utilizing the instantaneous frequency dynamics of EEG signals. The instantaneous frequency dynamics were estimated by the following process (overview in Fig. 1 (a)). The time-series of multichannel EEG signals were band-pass filtered for the frequency range [4 : 13] Hz. This frequency range was set to involve the dominant frequency component of the EEG activity in the HC and AD groups. Through the Hilbert transformation, the wrapped instantaneous phase $\theta(t)$ $(-\pi \leq \theta \leq \pi)$ was estimated. This instantaneous phase involves phase noise that causes a significantly large deviation from the instantaneous frequency range [4 : 13] Hz, known as phase slips [6]. Therefore, the median-filtered process for instantaneous frequency IF was applied. This estimation method was used for the DPS approach in our previous study [15].

In the state estimation process based on the instantaneous frequency $IF_i(t)$ (i: electrode location) (overview in Fig. 1 (b)), $IF_i(t)$ is transformed to the phase around the averaged phase among all electrodes as follows:

$$dIF_i = IF_i(t) - \overline{IF(t)}, \tag{1}$$

where $\overline{IF(t)}$ exhibits the averaged $IF_i(t)$ among all electrodes. Moreover, the standard deviation of $dIF_i(t)$ among all electrodes was normalized to 1.0 by a Z-scored process. The time-series of $dIF_i(t)$ of both the HC and AD groups were classified into k clusters using the k-means algorithm. Each cluster corresponds to dynamic states based on the 16 values of $dIF_i(t)$. The dynamic transition of these states is assumed to reflect moment-to-moment dFC in the whole brain network without separating each interaction in pairwise brain regions in the DPS approach. In this study, we used a cluster size of $k = 4$.

2.4 Statistical Analysis

To evaluate the dynamic characteristics of the transition of states based on $dIF_i(t)$, we assessed the transition probability among k states from time t [s] to $t + \Delta t$ [s], where Δt corresponds to sampling period $\Delta t = 0.005$ [s]. To assess

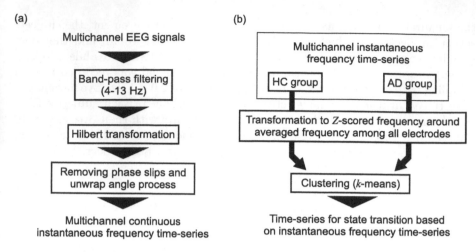

Fig. 1. (a) Estimation process for instantaneous frequency time-series of electroencephalography (EEG) signals. (b) Estimation process for state based on instantaneous frequency time-series of EEG signals.

differences in this transition probability between the AD and HC groups, t-tests were used. Benjamini-Hochberg false discovery (FDR) correction was applied to the t-score for multiple comparisons of the transition probability ($q < 0.05$) (16 p values: $k \times k$ state transitions).

3   Results

The mean $dIF_i(t)$ among subjects in the HC and AD groups in duration for each state (#1, #2, #3, and #4) are shown in Fig. 2. In both groups, the right (left) hemispheric leading phase and frontal (occipital) leading phase were confirmed as #1 (#2) and #3 (#4) states, respectively. Furthermore, we evaluated these transition probabilities among #1,#2,#3, and #4 states. Figure 3 shows the mean values of the state transition probabilities in the HC and AD groups and the t-value of the state transition probabilities between the AD and HC groups. As a result, the AD probability of states #4 to #4 is significantly smaller ($q < 0.05$) than that of the HC group. That is, it is difficult to maintain the state of the occipital leading phase in the AD group. We evaluated the relationship with cognitive function quantified by the MMSE score compared to the probability of states #4 to #4 in AD. As a result, a relatively high correlation (Pearson's correlation $\rho = 0.46$) was confirmed.

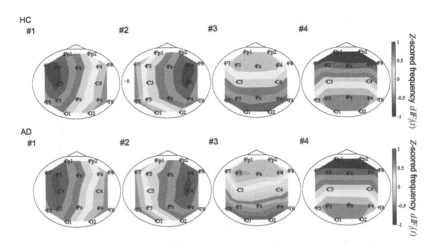

Fig. 2. Mean values of Z-scored frequency $dIF_i(t)$ among subjects in healthy control (upper part) and Alzheimer's disease (lower part) groups in duration for each state (#1, #2, #3, and #4). In both groups, right/left hemispheric and frontal/occipital region-specific phase leading was confirmed.

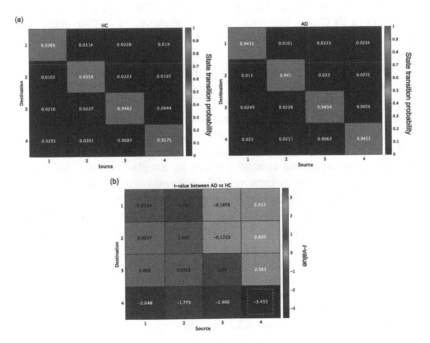

Fig. 3. (a) Mean values of the state transition probabilities in healthy control (HC) and Alzheimer's disease (AD) groups. (b) t value of the state transition probabilities between the AD and HC groups. A positive (negative) t value corresponds to a higher (lower) probability of AD compared to that for HC. The red dotted square indicates the t value satisfying the criteria of Benjamini-Hochberg false discovery (FDR) $q < 0.05$. The probability of AD of states #4 to #4 is significantly smaller ($q < 0.05$) than that of the HC group. (Color figure online)

4   Discussion and Conclusions

In this study, to reveal alternations of dynamic interactions in the whole brain network in AD and its relationship with cognitive impairment, we introduced an estimation method for dynamic states based on instantaneous frequency distribution in the whole brain. After applying this method to EEG signals of HC and AD subjects, it was found that the state of the occipital leading phase in the AD group was more difficult to maintain than in the HC group. Moreover, the degree of maintenance of this state, quantified by the state transition probability from #4 to #4, has a relatively high correlation with cognitive function in AD.

In previous studies of dFC in AD EEG signals, reductions in temporal variation of phase synchronization and changes in topological network features were reported [8, 18]. Escudero *et al.* showed that temporal variation in the clustering coefficient, degree centrality, and efficiency in the resting-state FC exhibit different characteristics in comparison with healthy older subjects [8]. Nunez *et al.* also showed that the temporal variation of dFC estimated by phase synchronization in AD EEG signals reduces in alpha and beta bands [18]. The difficulty in maintaining the state for the leading phase of the occipital region, as observed in Fig. 3, leads to a reduction in the diversity of dynamic states of phase distribution; consequently, this reduction might correlate with alternations of topological characteristics of dFC and the reduction of variability of dFC in AD.

Microstates, which are intermittently changing quasi-stable states reflecting brain activity state and cognitive processes [13], have been used for decades to evaluate dynamic state transition of whole brain activity through the classification of the spatial distribution of power [12, 22, 23]. A case with instantaneous amplitude distribution of EEG signals, instead of instantaneous frequency distribution as used in our proposed method, corresponds to this conventional microstate analysis. To compare with this case, we evaluated the state transition between the cases with instantaneous amplitude and frequency. As a result, although the topographies of classified states are similar in both cases, the time-series of state transition is significantly different (matching rate for similar topography appearing is less than 20% in the state transition time-series between both methods; data not shown). This implies that a state based on an instantaneous frequency reflects other aspects of the network dynamics of brain activity in comparison with a conventional microstate.

The limitations of this study need to be considered. A comparison between the proposed method for whole-brain dFC by whole-brain instantaneous frequency distribution and the method for instantaneous phase difference between pairwise brain regions typified as the DPS approach [15] must be compared to evaluate the advantage of the proposed method. Additionally, the use of different k cluster numbers to estimate the dynamic state based on phase distribution must be evaluated (in this study, $k = 4$ was fixed). Moreover, alternations in dFC have been observed in various psychiatric disorders [4, 7]. Therefore, alternations of dynamic states based on whole-brain frequency distribution might appear in these disorders; such disease-specific characteristics must be revealed. In future work, we will deal with these issues.

In conclusion, in this study, we introduced dynamic states based on whole-brain instantaneous frequency distribution that reflect cognitive impairment. Although several limitations remain, this approach, which significantly differs from the conventional microstate analysis and DPS approach, might become an additional approach to reveal different aspects of dFC.

Acknowledgment. This work of Sou Nobukawa was supported by a research grant from the Okawa Foundation and JSPS KAKENHI for Early-Career Scientists under Grant 18K18124.

References

1. Allen, E.A., Damaraju, E., Plis, S.M., Erhardt, E.B., Eichele, T., Calhoun, V.D.: Tracking whole-brain connectivity dynamics in the resting state. Cerebr. Cortex **24**(3), 663–676 (2014)

2. Betzel, R.F., Erickson, M.A., Abell, M., O'Donnell, B.F., Hetrick, W.P., Sporns, O.: Synchronization dynamics and evidence for a repertoire of network states in resting EEG. Front. Comput. Neurosci. **6** (2012)

3. Cabral, J., Kringelbach, M.L., Deco, G.: Functional connectivity dynamically evolves on multiple time-scales over a static structural connectome: models and mechanisms. NeuroImage **160**, 84–96 (2017)

4. Chen, H., Nomi, J.S., Uddin, L.Q., Duan, X., Chen, H.: Intrinsic functional connectivity variance and state-specific under-connectivity in autism. Human Brain Mapp. **38**(11), 5740–5755 (2017)

5. Cohen, J.R.: The behavioral and cognitive relevance of time-varying, dynamic changes in functional connectivity. NeuroImage **180**, 515–525 (2018)

6. Cohen, M.X.: Fluctuations in oscillation frequency control spike timing and coordinate neural networks. J. Neurosci. **34**(27), 8988–8998 (2014)

7. Dong, D., et al.: Reconfiguration of dynamic functional connectivity in sensory and perceptual system in schizophrenia. Cerebr. Cortex **29**(8), 3577–3589 (2019)

8. Escudero, J., Smith, K., Azami, H., Abásolo, D.: Inspection of short-time resting-state electroencephalogram functional networks in Alzheimer's disease. In: 2016 38th Annual International Conference of the IEEE Engineering in Medicine and Biology Society (EMBC), pp. 2810–2813. IEEE (2016)

9. Ewers, M., Sperling, R.A., Klunk, W.E., Weiner, M.W., Hampel, H.: Neuroimaging markers for the prediction and early diagnosis of Alzheimer's disease dementia. Trends Neurosci. **34**(8), 430–442 (2011)

10. Hansen, E.C., Battaglia, D., Spiegler, A., Deco, G., Jirsa, V.K.: Functional connectivity dynamics: modeling the switching behavior of the resting state. Neuroimage **105**, 525–535 (2015)

11. Kang, J., Pae, C., Park, H.J.: Graph-theoretical analysis for energy landscape reveals the organization of state transitions in the resting-state human cerebral cortex. PloS one **14**(9), e0222161 (2019)

12. Khanna, A., Pascual-Leone, A., Michel, C.M., Farzan, F.: Microstates in resting-state EEG: current status and future directions. Neurosci. Biobehav. Rev. **49**, 105–113 (2015)

13. Lehmann, D.: Multichannel topography of human alpha EEG fields. Electroencephal. Clin. Neurophysiol. **31**(5), 439–449 (1971)

14. Medaglia, J.D., Lynall, M.E., Bassett, D.S.: Cognitive network neuroscience. J. Cogn. Neurosci. **27**(8), 1471–1491 (2015)
15. Nobukawa, S., Kikuchi, M., Takahashi, T.: Changes in functional connectivity dynamics with aging: a dynamical phase synchronization approach. NeuroImage **188**, 357–368 (2019)
16. Nobukawa, S., et al.: Classification methods based on complexity and synchronization of electroencephalography signals in Alzheimer's disease. Front. Psychiatry **11** (2020)
17. Nobukawa, S., Yamanishi, T., Nishimura, H., Wada, Y., Kikuchi, M., Takahashi, T.: Atypical temporal-scale-specific fractal changes in Alzheimer's disease EEG and their relevance to cognitive decline. Cogn. Neurodyn. **13**(1), 1–11 (2019)
18. Núñez, P., et al.: Characterizing the fluctuations of dynamic resting-state electrophysiological functional connectivity: reduced neuronal coupling variability in mild cognitive impairment and dementia due to Alzheimer's disease. J. Neural Eng. **16**(5), 056030 (2019)
19. Schumacher, J., et al.: Dynamic functional connectivity changes in dementia with lewy bodies and Alzheimer's disease. NeuroImage Clin. **22**, 101812 (2019)
20. Sporns, O., Betzel, R.F.: Modular brain networks. Ann. Rev. Psychol. **67**, 613–640 (2016)
21. Tewarie, P., et al.: Tracking dynamic brain networks using high temporal resolution meg measures of functional connectivity. NeuroImage **200**, 38–50 (2019)
22. Van de Ville, D., Britz, J., Michel, C.M.: Eeg microstate sequences in healthy humans at rest reveal scale-free dynamics. Proceed. Nat. Acad. Sci., 201007841 (2010)
23. Zhang, K., et al.: Reliability of eeg microstate analysis at different electrode densities during propofol-induced transitions of brain states. NeuroImage **231**, 117861 (2021)

Robot Arm Control Using Reward-Modulated Hebbian Learning

Koutaro Minato[1] and Yuichi Katori[1,2]

[1] Future University Hakodate, 116-2 Kamedanakano-cho,
Hakodate, Hokkaido 041-8655, Japan
katori@fun.ac.jp
[2] The Institute of Industrial Science, The University of Tokyo,
4-6-1 Komaba Megro-ku, Tokyo 153-8605, Japan

Abstract. In recent years, soft robots with "softness" have been attracting much attention. Since soft robots have "softness", they are expected to be able to perform delicate tasks that only humans can do. On the other hand, it is challenging to control. Therefore, in this research, we focused on reservoir computing with a biologically inspired learning algorithm. Reward-modulated Hebbian learning, one of the reservoir computing frameworks, is based on Hebbian learning rules and rewards and allows us to train the network without explicit teacher signals. The rewards are provided depending on the predicted and actual state of the environment influenced by the exploratory noise. We demonstrate that our model successfully controls the robot arm so that the tip position of the arm draws a given target trajectory.

Keywords: Reward-modulated Hebbian learning · Soft robotics · Reservoir computing

1 Introduction

In recent years, new research aimed at "softness" has been appeared in different science and technology fields. Traditional robotics has pursued the traditional engineering values of speed, power, precision, and certainty. However, it cannot make the "soft" motions that living things do. Soft robots are composed of soft materials, which are inspired by animals (e.g., squid, starfish, worms) that do not have hard internal skeletons [1]. Soft robots carry many advantages associated with mechanical softness [2,3]. On the other hand, it is challenging to control soft robots compared to ordinary robots [4,5]. Also, when a soft robot makes motion, its body produces diverse and complex dynamics. These are often high-dimensional, non-linear, and depend on the history of past stimuli.

Reservoir computing(RC) [6] is a kind of recurrent neural network. RC is constructed with a randomly connected neural network (dynamical reservoir), and only readout connections are learned. It is also suitable for handling non-linear and those containing past information. However, most RC models rely on supervised learning rules. In many motor tasks, including generation and planning

© Springer Nature Switzerland AG 2021
T. Mantoro et al. (Eds.): ICONIP 2021, CCIS 1517, pp. 55–63, 2021.
https://doi.org/10.1007/978-3-030-92310-5_7

of motion, explicit teacher signal is not available. Reward-modulated Hebbian learning (RMHL) [7] is one of the frameworks of reservoir computing and is based on Hebbian learning rules and rewards obtained. This RMHL framework allows performing learning without using an explicit teacher signal.

In the present study, we addresses to control the complex dynamics of soft robots by using RMHL. We conduct an experiment using a robot arm of a 2-joint 6-muscle model of the forearm and upper arm, a muscle and skeletal system.

2   Methods

In the present study, we proposed the reservoir computing model for controlling the robot arm. The model is required to generate an appropriate control signal that causes tensions on muscles of the robot arm based on the given target time course of the tip of the arm. In the following subsections, we first explained the target of the control (robot arm), and then we describe the proposed model, including the network architecture and the network configuration procedure.

2.1   Robot Arm

The robot arm we use in the present study is a 2-joint, 6-muscle model of the forearm and upper arm, which is muscles and skeletal system (see Fig. 1)[8,9]. This robot arm was simulated using MuJoCo [10]. In this musculoskeletal system, muscles act as actuators that generate joint torque. In this model, the shoulder has a pair of monoarticular muscles and a pair of biarticular muscles for bending and stretching the shoulder. The elbow also has a pair of monoarticular muscles and a pair of biarticular muscles. This monoarticular muscle act only on one joint, and the biarticular muscles act on two joints.

In this robot arm model, each muscle is controlled with a control signal ranging from 0 to 1. 0 indicates that the muscle tension is 0, and 1 indicates that the muscle tension is maximum.

In this model, the robot arm is controlled using a feedback controller. The input signal to the feedback controller is based on the difference between the target angle of the robot arm joint and the actual angle of the robot arm joint. The output signal of the feedback controller is a control signal that causes tension on the muscles and moves the joint of the robot arm.

2.2   Network Architecture

The overall structure of the model used in the present research is shown in Fig. 2. The network model is composed of the reservoir and the feedback controller. The training of the reservoir is based on the concept of predictive coding [11], and the reward modulated Hebbian learning (RMHL). The reservoir generates the time cause of the target joint angle and predicts the time course of the tip position of the arm. Training of the connections from the reservoir to the output layer that generates the target joint angle is achived based on RMHL, while the training

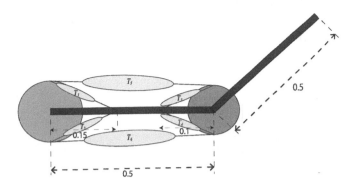

Fig. 1. Arm 2-joint 6-muscle model: Gray represents shoulder and elbow joints. Black represents forearm and upper arm. Red represents muscle. (Color figure online)

of the connection from the reservoir to the prediction layer is achieved by the FORCE algorithm [12]. The feedback controller generates the control signal for the muscles on the arm, and the controller is driven based on the differences between the target angle and the actual joint angles.

The reservoir is consisting of N sparsely and recurrently connected neurons. The firing rate of the neuron at time t is given by $r(t) = \tanh[x(t)]$. The dynamics of the internal state x of the network is given by

$$\tau \dot{x}(t) = -x(t) + W^{in}c(t) + W^{rec}r(t) + W^e e_{ya}(t), \tag{1}$$

where $e_{ya}(t) = y_t(t) - y_a(t)$, and $c(t)$ is the state of the context layer. This context information is passed from $c(t)$ to the reservoir. Also, the context information is converted by the converter and passed to the target time course $y_t(t)$, which is the tip position. $y_p(t)$ is the predicted tip position, and $y_a(t)$ is the actual tip position of the robot arm. τ is the time constant. $e_{ya}(t)$ is the difference between target teacher signal $y_t(t)$ and the actual tip position $y_a(t)$. W^{rec}, W^{in}, and W^e denote the synaptic weights for recurrent connection within the network, connections from context layer to the network, connections from $e_{ya}(t)$ to the reservoir, respectively. These synaptic weights are configured with the following procedure.

The recurrent connection is configured sparsely and randomly with the following procedure. Firstly, generate a matrix of $N_x \times N_x$ with a connection rate β^{rec}, where N_x is the number of neurons in the reservoir. The elements of this matrix W_0^{rec} are randomly set to a non-zero value of -1 or 1. Then, the spectral radius of this matrix ρ_0 is calculated. The synaptic connection of the recurrent connnection W^{rec} is given as $W^{rec} = \alpha_r W_0^{rec}/\rho_0$ with the coefficient of synaptic strength α_r. Note that the spectral radius of W^{rec} equals α_r.

The connection for the contextual input W^{in} and the error feedback W^e are configured with the following procedure. First, generate a matrix of $N_x \times 2$ and $N_x \times 2$ with a connection rate 0.1. The non-zero elements of these matrices W_0^{in} and W_0^e are set to, uniformly distributed random numbers from -1 to 1.

W^{in} is given as $W^{in} = \alpha_i W_0^{in}$ with the synaptic strength α_i. W^e is given as $W^e = \alpha_e W_0^e$ with the synaptic strength α_e.

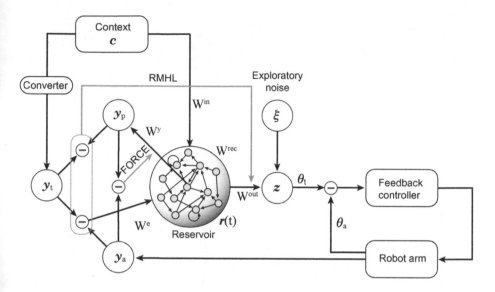

Fig. 2. Network architecture

The reservoir generate the target joint angle $\theta_t(t)$ in the output layer $z(t)$, and the output layer additionary receive the exploratory noise $\xi(t)$:

$$z(t) = W^{out}r(t) + \xi(t), \tag{2}$$

where W^{out} is the connections from the reservoir to the output layer $z(t)$. Here, we use the Ornstein-Uhrenbeck process as the exploratory noise. The Ornstein-Uhrenbeck process is the stochastic process given by the following stochastic differential equation

$$\dot{\xi}(t) = -\theta\xi(t) + \sigma\dot{W}(t), \tag{3}$$

where $W(t)$ presents the Wiener process, which has Gaussian increments, namely, the difference of the variable in a small-time step is normally distributed with a mean 0. Here, the exploratory noise is designed so that its amplitude is modulated with the e_{ya}: when the actual tip position $y_a(t)$ approaches the target tip position $y_t(t)$, the noise amplitude is decreased.

2.3   Reward-Modulated Hebbian Learning

The connection from the reservoir to the output layer is trained with reward-modulated Hebbian learning (RMHL). The reward is a scalar value utilized to modulate the Hebbian learning on the output connection that strengthens the connection between correlated neurons.

In the present study, the reward is configured based on the comparison between the prediction and the actual tip position of the robot arm. The reward is provided when the actual tip position is closer to the target tip position than the predicted tip position. The reward $R(t)$ is defined with the following equation.

$$R(t) = \begin{cases} -\tanh[e_{ya}(t) - e_{yp}(t)] & \text{if } e_{ya}(t) - e_{yp}(t) < 0, \\ 0 & \text{if } e_{ya}(t) - e_{yp}(t) > 0, \end{cases} \tag{4}$$

where $e_{yp}(t) = |\boldsymbol{y_t}(t) - \boldsymbol{y_p}(t)|$ is the difference between the target tip position $\boldsymbol{y_t}(t)$ and the predicted tip position $\boldsymbol{y_p}(t)$. The reward $R(t)$ is provided when the $e_{ya} < e_{yp}$, and the weight change on the output connection $W^{out}(t)$ is given by

$$\Delta W^{out}(t) = R(t)\boldsymbol{\xi}(t)\boldsymbol{r}(t). \tag{5}$$

2.4 FORCE Learning

The connections from the reservoir to the prediction layer is trained with the first order reduced and controlled error (FORCE) learning, which is one of the online learning algorithms. According to the FORCE learning algorithm, W^y is updated with the following equations.

$$W^y(t + \Delta t) = W^y(t) + (\boldsymbol{y_a}(t) - \boldsymbol{y_p}(t))P(t)^T \boldsymbol{r}(t)^T. \tag{6}$$

The training progress so that the difference between the predicted tip position $\boldsymbol{y_p}(t)$ and the actual tip position $\boldsymbol{y_a}(t)$ is reduced. Where P is the running estimate of the inverse correlation among the output of the neurons and is updated with the following equation:

$$P(t + \Delta t) = P(t) - \frac{P(t)\boldsymbol{r}(t)\boldsymbol{r}(t)^T P(t)}{1 + \boldsymbol{r}(t)^T P(t)\boldsymbol{r}(t)}. \tag{7}$$

The initial value of P is $P(0) = I/\alpha_f$, where the matrix I is the identity matrix and α_f is the regularalization parameter.

2.5 Feedback Controller

The feedback controller generates the control signal for the muscles on the arm, and the controller is driven based on the differences between the target angle and the actual joint angles. The feedback controller generates the control signal that causes tension on the muscles on the arm, based on the difference between the target joint angle $\boldsymbol{\theta_t}(t)$, which is the output of the reservoir, and the actual joint angle $\boldsymbol{\theta_a}(t)$. Based on the differences between the target and actual joint angle, the joint torque $\boldsymbol{F}(t)$ is determined using the proportional integral derivative (PID) control. The joint torque is given by

$$\boldsymbol{F}(t) = K_P(\boldsymbol{\theta_t}(t) - \boldsymbol{\theta_a}(t)) + K_I \int_0^t (\boldsymbol{\theta_t}(s) - \boldsymbol{\theta_a}(s))ds + K_D(\dot{\boldsymbol{\theta}}_t(t) - \dot{\boldsymbol{\theta}}_a(t)) \tag{8}$$

where, K_P, K_I, and K_D represent the gains of proportional control, integral control, and differential control, respectively.

The tension (control signal) of the robot arm can be obtained by using the pseudo-inverse matrix of matrix A and the joint torque [13]. The matrix A is determined by the moment arm of the robot arm. The moment arm A^T of the robot arm is determined as the follows based on the architecture of the robot arm shown in Fig. 1.

$$A^T = \begin{pmatrix} 0.15 & -0.15 & 0 & 0 & 0.5 & -0.5 \\ 0 & 0 & 0.1 & 0.1 & 0.5 & -0.5 \end{pmatrix} \tag{9}$$

The tension of the robot arm is given by

$$\left(T_1, T_2, T_3, T_4, T_5, T_6\right)^T = -(A^T)^{\#} F(t) \tag{10}$$

T_1 to T_6 are the tensions of muscles in the robot arm, which correspond to the muscles shown in Fig. 1. $(A^T)^{\#}$ is the pseudo inverse matrix of A^T. Since the value of the control signal is limited between 0 and 1, the tension is set to 0 if T_i is less than 0 and is set to 1 if T_i is more than 1.

The control signal from the feedback controller is sending to the robot arm, and the state of the robot arm is updated. The state of the robot arm can be obtained as actual joint angle $\theta_a(t)$ and as actual tip position of the arm $y_a(t)$.

The parameter values used in the present study are as follows. $N_x = 200$, $\tau = 0.2, \beta^{rec} = 0.1, \alpha_r = 0.8, \alpha_i = 0.1, \alpha_e = 0.1, \alpha_f = 0.1, \theta = 10, \sigma = 0.2, K_P = 4.0, K_I = 0.7, K_D = 0.3$.

3   Results

First, we evaluated the model with a task that requires the tip of the robot arm to draw a circle (see Fig. 3(A)). The experiment was performed in 5000 time-steps(25 s) per episode. In one episode, the target signal y_t goes around the circle in Fig. 3(A) about 12 times. The experiment is repeated for 30 episodes.

Also, after each episode, the tip of the robot arm returns to the coordinates (1,0), which is the outstretched position. Learning was done from episodes 1 to 29, and learning was turn off in episode 30.

In the first episode, the robot arm did not draw a circle well, but as the learning progress, the robot arm could draw the circle (Fig. 3(C)(D)).

Figure 3(E)(F) shows the time course of the joint angles and the tip position. Upper panels in Fig. 3(E)(F) shows the target and actual joint angles θ_t and θ_a in the first and last episodes, respectively. Light blue and blue curves indicate the target θ_t and the actual θ_a angle of the shoulder joint, respectively. Purple and red curves indicate the target θ_t and the actual θ_a angle of the elbow joint, respectively. Lower panels in Fig. 3(E)(F) shows the target, actual, and predicted tip position y_t, y_a, and y_p in the first and last episodes, respectively. Orange, red, and brown curves indicate y_t, y_a, and y_p of y coordinate respectively. Blue, green, and purple curves indicate y_t, y_a, and y_p of x coordinate respectively.

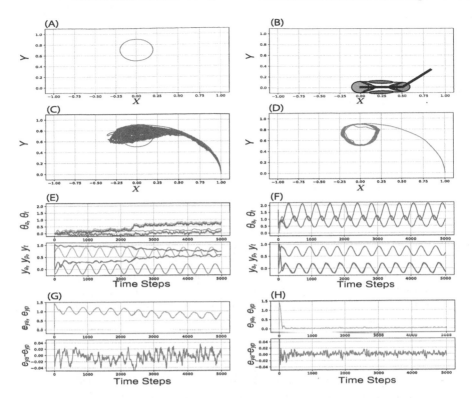

Fig. 3. (A) The circle that is required to be drawn by the arm tip. (B) The layout of the robot arm. The shoulder joint is fixed at the coordinates (0,0). (C): The orbits drawn by actual tip position y_a in the first ten episodes. (D): The orbits drawn by y_a in the last episode. (E) and (G): First episode. (F) and (H): Last episode. (Color figure online)

In the first episode, both joint angles exhibit slight fluctuation, and the tip position also fluctuates around the center of the target circle (Fig. 3 (E)). In the last episode, the orbit of the tip position roughly follows the target circle.

Figure 3(G)(H) shows the time courses of the differences in the actual, predicted, and target tip positions. Upper panels in Fig. 3(G) (H) shows the e_{ya} and e_{yp} in the first and last episodes. Blue curves represents e_{ya} and orange curves represents e_{yp}. Lower panels in Fig. 3(G) (H) shows the $e_{ya} - e_{yp}$ in the first and last episodes. The differences between the actual and the target tip position y_a and between the predicted and the target tip position y_p are larger in the early episodes, but after the learning, the differences are reduced. The difference $e_{ya} - e_{yp}$ is reflected to the reward value; if $e_{ya} - e_{yp}$ is negative, the reward is provided. The fluctuation of the difference $e_{ya} - e_{yp}$ is decreased as the learning progress. This indicates that the number of updates in W^{out} and amplitude of the exploratory noise become smaller as the learning progresses.

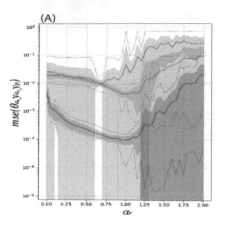
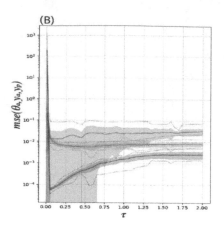

Fig. 4. The dependencies of the mean squared error (MSE) on the parameter values. (A) The dependencies of the MSEs on the strength of the recurrent connection α_r. (B) The dependencies of the MSEs on time constant of the reservoir τ. Red, orange, and green curves indicate the MSE of $\boldsymbol{\theta}_t$ and $\boldsymbol{\theta}_a$, the MSE of $\boldsymbol{y}_t$ and $\boldsymbol{y}_a$, and MSE of $\boldsymbol{y}_t$ and $\boldsymbol{y}_p$, respectively. The bold curve indicates the mean value, the thin curve indicates the minimum and maximum values, and the filled area indicates the standard deviation. (Color figure online)

Figure 4 shows the dependencies of the mean squeared error (MSE) of $\boldsymbol{\theta}_t$ and $\boldsymbol{\theta}_a$, MSE of $\boldsymbol{y}_t$ and $\boldsymbol{y}_a$, and MSE of $\boldsymbol{y}_t$ and $\boldsymbol{y}_p$ on the strength of the recurrent connection α_r and τ. The MSE between $\boldsymbol{\theta}_t$ and $\boldsymbol{\theta}_a$ is minimized around $\alpha_r = 0.8$. Also, when α_r exceeds 1, it starts to exhibit chaotic activity. Furthermore, the MSEs become small in the vicinity of 0.1 to 0.2 (Fig. 4(B)).

4   Conclusion

In the present study, we addressed controlling a robot arm with 2-joints and 6-muscles by the reservoir computing that generates the motor command (target joint angles) and predicts the state of the robot (tip position of the arm). We show that the model successfully controls the robot arm so that the tip position of the arm draws a given target trajectory.

This can be achieved by comparing the predicted arm motion with the actual arm motion. The actual arm motion is reflected in a realization of the exploratory noise. When the influence of the exploratory noise contributes to getting closer to the target motion than the predicted value, the learning progresses based on the realization of exploratory noise.

However, the actual orbit did not exactly match the target orbit, and there was a deviation. A possible reason for this deviation is that the feedback control does not perform completely redundant arm control. A possible solution to overcome the problem is to use an inverse static model and a model using a reverse dynamics model together with PID control [13]. In the future, by incorporating these approaches into the present model, we expect to establish a further advantageous model for soft robot control.

Acknowledgements. This paper is based on results obtained from a project, JPNP16007, commissioned by the New Energy and Industrial Technology Development Organization (NEDO) and is supported by JSPS KAKENHI Grant Number 21H05163, 20H04258, 20H00596, and JST CREST(JPMJCR18K2).

References

1. Sheoherd, R.F., et al.: Multigait soft robot. PNAS of USA **108**(51), 20400–20403 (2011)
2. Kim, S., Laschi, C., Trimmer, B.: Soft robotics: a bioinspired evolution in robotics. Trends Biotechnol. **31**, 287–294 (2013)
3. Trivedi, D., Rahn, C.D., Kier, W.M., Walker, I.D.: Soft robotics: biological inspiration, state of the art, and future research. Appl. Bionics Biomech. **5**(3), 99–117 (2008)
4. Li, T., et al.: From the octopus to soft robots control: an octopus inspired behavior control architecture for soft robots. Vie et Milieu, **61**, 211–217 (2012)
5. Nie, X., Song, B., Ge, Y., Chen, W.W., Weerasooriya, T.: Dynamic tensile of soft materials. Exp. Mach. **49**(4), 451–458 (2009)
6. Jaeger, H.: Tutorial on training recurrent neural networks, covering BPPT, RTRL, EKF and the "echo state networks" approach. GMD report, German Nation. Res. Center Inf. Technol. **159**, 1–46 (2002)
7. Hoezer, G.M., Legenstein, R., Maass, W.: Emergence of complex computational structures from chaotic neural networks through reward-modulated hebbian learning. Cerebr. Cortex **24**(3), 677–690 (2012)
8. Izawa, J., Kondo, T., Ito, K.: Biological robot arm motion through reinforcement learning. Proceed. 2002 IEEE Int. Conf. Robot. Autom., **4**, 3398–3403 (2002)
9. Kambara, H., Kim, K., Shin, D., Sato, M., Koike, Y.: Learning and generation of goal-directed arm reaching from scratch. Neural Netw. **22**(4), 348–361 (2009)
10. Todorov, E., Erez, T., Tassa, Y.: MuJoCo: a physics engine for model-based control. In: IEEE/RSJ International Conference on Intelligent Robots and Systems, pp. 5026–5033 (2012)
11. Katori, Y.: Network model for dynamics of perception with reservoir computing and predictive coding. In: Delgado-García, J.M., Pan, X., Sánchez-Campusano, R., Wang, R. (eds.) Advances in Cognitive Neurodynamics (VI). ACN, pp. 89–95. Springer, Singapore (2018). https://doi.org/10.1007/978-981-10-8854-4_11
12. Sussillo, D., Abbott, L.F.: Generating coherent patterns of activity from chaotic neural networks. Neuron, **63**(4), 554–557 (2009)
13. Katayama, M., Kawato, M.: Virtual trajectory and stiffness ellipse during multijoint arm movement predicted by neural inverse models. Biol. Cybern. **69**, 353–362 (1993)

Intermediate Sensitivity of Neural Activities Induces the Optimal Learning Speed in a Multiple-Timescale Neural Activity Model

Tomoki Kurikawa[✉] [iD]

Department of Physics, Kansai Medical University,
Shinmachi 2-5-1, Hirakata, Osaka, Japan
kurikawt@hirakata.kmu.ac.jp

Abstract. Collective dynamics of the neural population are involved in a variety of cognitive functions. How such neural dynamics are shaped through learning and how the learning performance is related to the property of the individual neurons are fundamental questions in neuroscience. Previous model studies answered these questions by using developing machine-learning techniques for training a recurrent neural network. However, these techniques are not biologically plausible. Does another type of learning method, for instance, a more biologically plausible learning method, shape the similar neural dynamics and the similar relation between the learning performance and the property of the individual neurons to those observed in the previous studies? In this study, we have used the recently proposed learning model with multiple timescales in the neural activity, which is more biologically plausible, and analyzed the neural dynamics and the relation regarding the sensitivity of neurons. As result, we have found that our model shapes similar neural dynamics and the relation. Further, the intermediate sensitivity of neurons that is optimal for the learning speed generates a variety of neural activity patterns in line with the experimental observations in the neural system. This result suggests that the neural system might develop the sensitivity of neural activities to optimize the learning speed through evolution.

Keywords: Delayed match to sample · Multiple timescale · Learning

1 Introduction

In neural systems, rich neural dynamics are ubiquitously observed. These dynamics are involved in a number of cognitive functions, such as, working memory [13] and decision-making [7]. How such dynamics perform the cognitive functions [1,11,13] and how collective dynamics of the neural population are related to the property of individual neurons [2,12,14] are crucial questions for understanding the information processing in the neural systems.

Delayed (non) match to sample task [1,11,13] is a fundamental task of cognitive functions. In this task, a sample stimulus is applied to an animal, followed

© Springer Nature Switzerland AG 2021
T. Mantoro et al. (Eds.): ICONIP 2021, CCIS 1517, pp. 64–72, 2021.
https://doi.org/10.1007/978-3-030-92310-5_8

by delayed period, and finally a test stimulus is presented. The animal must respond to the test stimuli depending on the sample stimulus. To perform this task, animals are required to retain information of the sample stimulus and to compare it with the test stimuli. By using a developed machine learning technique of training a recurrent neural network, a previous study [1] demonstrated that stable neural trajectories underlie the computation of this task.

In several studies [4,12,14], how the sensitivity of individual neurons is related to the learning performance is investigated. They demonstrated that intermediate sensitivity, around "edge of chaos", is optimal for the learning performance by using the machine learning methods.

Although these studies advance understanding of computation in the neural system, the used technique is not biologically plausible due to non-locality of required information: the global structure of connectivity is necessary. How more biologically learning shapes the neural dynamics for performing this task and how the learning performance is related to the parameters remain unclear. We developed more biologically plausible learning model in previous studies [5,6] with multiple timescales in the neural activities. By using this model, we have investigated what neural dynamics is shaped through learning process and the relation between the learning performance and the sensitivity of individual neurons in the present study. Further, we have examined the similarity between the neural activities in our model and those in experimentally observations [1].

2   Model

2.1   Neural Dynamics

Our model is based on a previous study [5,10] that showed that an RNN with multiple timescales enables the learning of sequential neural patterns including non-Markov sequences and a simple context-dependent working memory task. The model has two populations with different timescales connected to each other (Fig. 1A). One population comprises N fast neurons x, and the other comprises N slow neurons y. The fast population receives an external stimulus and generates a target response corresponding to the given input. These neurons evolve according to

$$\tau_x \dot{x}_i = \tanh\left(\beta_x I_i\right) - x_i, \tau_y \dot{y}_i = \tanh(\beta_y x_i) - y_i, \tag{1}$$

where $I_i = u_i + \tanh(r_i) + (\eta_\mu^\alpha)_i$, $u_i = \sum_{j \neq i}^N J_{ij}^X x_j$, and $r_i = \sum_{j \neq i}^N J_{ij}^{XY} y_j$. J_{ij}^X is a recurrent connection from the i to j-th neuron in the population of x and $\boldsymbol{J}^{XY}$ is a connection from the i-th neuron in the population of y to the j-th neuron in the population of x. The mean values of J^X and J^{XY} are set to zero with a variance equal to $1/N$. N, β_x, and β_y are set to $100, 2.0$, and 2.0, respectively, while the time scales of x and y, denoted as τ_x and τ_y, are set to 1 and 33, respectively. I_i is the i th element of an input pattern. As initial states of the fast and slow neurons, we set their activities to $0.01 \times \zeta$ and ζ is randomly generated according to the standard normal distribution.

2.2   Learning Process

In our model, only J^X is plastic and changes according to

$$\dot{J}_{ij}^X = \epsilon(\xi_i - x_i)(x_j - u_i J_{ij}^X)/N, \tag{2}$$

where ϵ is the learning speed, and it is set to 0.03. ξ_i is the i-th element of a target $\boldsymbol{\xi}$, which is an N-dimensional pattern. In previous studies [6, 8, 9], we demonstrated that a single population with a single timescale learns mappings between constant input and target patterns using this learning rule. In the current two-population model, there are two inputs for the fast sub-network—one is from an external input and the other is from the slow sub-network that stores previous information. Thus, the synaptic dynamics is able to modify the connection to generate a target pattern depending not only on the currently applied input but also on the preceding input, as shown in [10]. In the recent study [5], we demonstrated that this model performs a context-dependent task. In the present study, we show that the model enables a more complex task and relation between activities of individual neurons and collective neural dynamics.

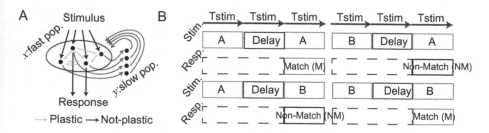

Fig. 1. A: Schematic of our model. B: Delayed match to sample task. T_{stim} denotes the stimulus duration.

2.3   Delayed Match to Sample Task

In this paper, we consider a delayed match to sample task 1B such as [1, 13], which is composed of two stimuli and two responses (Fig. 1B). Two stimuli A and B are applied to fast neurons in a network sequentially: the first stimulus (referred as sample stimulus) is applied, followed by the delay time (here, we apply the delay signal to the network). After the delay time, the second stimuli (referred as test stimulus) is applied. When these two stimuli are same, the network is supposed to generate a "match" response. Otherwise, it is supposed to generate a "non-match" response. Here, we denote match and non-match responses as M and NM, respectively. Thus, the network must maintain the sample stimulus and compare it with the test one to generate an adequate response. This task is a simple benchmark for basic cognitive functions: memorizing previous stimuli and comparing two stimuli.

The stimulus patterns are random N-bit binary patterns, each element of which corresponds to a neuron of x, with probabilities $P(X_i = \pm 1) = 1/2$, where X_i is the activity state of the i-th element of patterns $X = A$ and B. The target response patterns M and NM are assigned to a subset of the fast neurons (denoted as output neurons in the following), here $N/2$ neurons. Therefore, these response patterns are random $N/2$-bit binary ones which are determined probabilistic in the same way as in the stimulus patterns. Because the target patterns are assigned to only half of the fast neurons, the learning rule of the connection J_{ij}^X (Eq. (6)) that the target pattern is not assigned to i-th neuron cannot be defined. In this case, J_{ij}^X is not changed during the learning process. All elements of the delay signal D are -1. We apply the sample stimulus, the delay signal, and the test stimulus sequentially with duration time $T_{stim} = 40$, $T_{delay} = 20$, and $T_{stim} = 40$, respectively, as an external input η in Eq. 1, as illustrated in Fig. 1B. Now, the target patterns are defined only when the test stimulus is applied. Therefore, the learning process runs only upon the test stimulus; otherwise, only the neural dynamics run.

If the fast dynamics reach M (or NM), namely $\sum_i M_i x_i / N > 0.9$, a trial is completed, and the next trial starts. If the fast dynamics do not, the learning one target is terminated at the given time $t = T_{end}$. Here, T_{end} is set to $T_{stim} + T_{delay} + T_{stim} = 100$ We consider the four cases to be learned. As one learning epoch, four cases are learned once in random order. Every 10 learning epochs, success rate for all of the four cases are measured by examining 20 trials for each case. If the success rate is over 90%, the learning is completed.

3   Results

3.1   Neural Dynamics After Learning Process

Now, we present four success trials corresponding to the four cases (two sample stimuli by two test stimuli) in Fig. 2. The overlaps of activities of output neurons with response patterns M and NM are plotted in Figs. 2A–D. The network correctly recognizes the test stimuli and generates the adequate responses: When the stimulus A is applied after the application of A (case $A - A$, Fig. 2A), the overlap with M surges and reach to the criterion of the response in the presence of the test stimulus. Applying the stimulus B after A (case $A - B$, Fig. 2B), in contrast, the overlaps with NM surges. Note that the test stimulus A (or B) allows the network to generate the different responses, depending on the sample stimuli. Consequently, the sample stimulus is also likely to generate M and/or NM. Indeed, upon the sample stimulus A, activity pattern of output neurons approaches and departs from both of patterns M and NM. Approaching and departing from M and NM are often observed in another network after learning. This behavior causes the variability in neural trajectories across the difference in initial states. For instance, the value of the overlap in Fig. 2A at the beginning of the delay period is more different from that in Fig. 2C, comparing to the difference between the values of the overlaps at the beginning of the delay period in Figs. 2B and D (see also Fig. 2F). Such variability results in poorer performance of the cases $A - A$ and $A - B$ than that of the cases $B - A$ and $B - B$ as shown later.

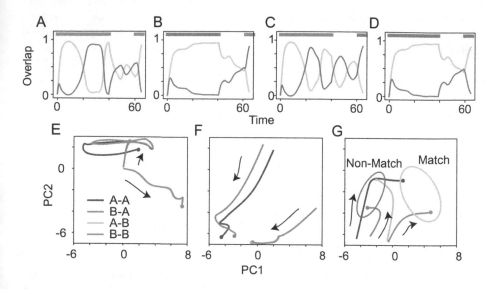

Fig. 2. A–D: Neural activities of output neurons in the fast group are plotted by taking the their overlap with M and NM patterns in cyan and red, respectively. The top purple and green bars in the panels indicate duration of application of stimuli A and B, respectively. E–G:Neural dynamics of all slow and fast neurons are plotted on two principal component spaces (E, F, and G: the dynamics in the presence of the sample stimuli, the delay period, and the test stimuli, respectively). The four trajectories represent neural dynamics under different cases. (Color figure online)

To see the neural dynamics of all fast and slow neurons, we analyzed neural dynamics by principal component (PC) analysis for all neurons. The neural dynamics are projected onto the 2D PC space upon the sample stimulus, the delay period, and the test stimulus in Figs. 2E–G. We exemplify typical neural dynamics by showing a single trail for each of four cases in different color. In the presence of the sample stimuli, neural trajectories are separated into two groups depending on the present stimuli. Following the sample stimuli, the delay signals are applied. Two groups of trajectories evolve with a decrease in the distance between them. Although the difference decreases, it still remains at the end of the delay period, and the information of the preceding stimuli is retained especially by virtue of the slow dynamics, as noted in [5]. Finally, applying the test stimuli to the network separates the four trajectories into the match and non-match areas depending on the sample and test stimuli.

To precisely evaluate the performance of this model, we measured the success rate for 30 realizations of networks. Each realization is generated from i.i.d probability distribution and trained by the same learning rule with different stimuli

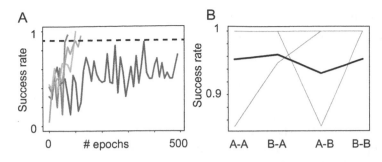

Fig. 3. A: Change in the success rate through learning process. Four different lines represent four different realizations of networks. The dotted line indicates the criterion of the learning. B: After learning, success rate for each case is shown for three networks (thin lines) and averaged success rate across 27 success networks is plotted (thick line).

and responses that are also generated from i.i.d probability distributions. We depict development in success rate throughout the learning for four networks that are randomly chosen out of 30 ones. One network does not achieve success rate $= 0.9$ within 500 learning epochs, defined as failure in the learning. Statistically, 27 networks out of 30 networks succeed learning in the learning. For 27 success networks, we plot the success rate for each case in Fig. 3B. On average, the success rate takes the high values, around 0.95 for all cases. To analyze in detail, we also plot the success rate for three networks for all cases. The success rate takes lower values for only one or two cases, while that for other cases takes nearly 1. The lower success-rate cases correspond to those in which the activity pattern of output neurons approaches and departs from M and NM in the presence of the sample stimulus, as shown above.

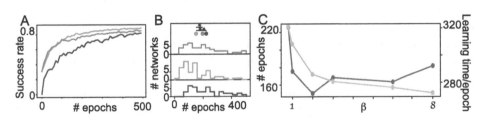

Fig. 4. A: Change in the success rate throughout the learning for $\beta = 0.8, 2$ and 8 in blue, red, and green, respectively. The success rates are obtained by averaging over 60 networks. B: Histograms of the number of epochs to finish learning process for $\beta = 0.8, 2$ and 8 in blue, red, and green, respectively. Circles in the top panel represent average number of epochs. C: Dependence of the number of epochs to finish learning process (blue, left tick) and learning time per epoch (red, right tick) on β. (Color figure online)

3.2 Dependence of the Sensitivity of Single Neurons

Next, we investigated how learning performance and collective activity of the population are related to the sensitivity of individual neurons. To this end, first, we analyzed the learning process for different β. The developments in the success rate averaged over 60 networks are shown throughout the learning for $\beta = 0.8, 2$ and 8 in Fig. 4A. The success rate for $\beta = 2$ increases most rapidly than those for other β. To validate statistically this trend, we applied Mann-Whitney U test to distributions of the number of learning epochs to complete the learning for different β (Fig. 4B). Each distribution is generated from 60 networks. As a result, the number of learning epochs for $\beta = 2$ is significantly smaller than those for $\beta = 0.8$ and 8 (p value $= 0.0007, 0.035$, respectively).

For systematic understanding the dependence of β, we examined the learning process for a variety of β (Fig. 4C). As β increases, the learning speed increases up to $\beta = 2$. Above $\beta = 2$, the learning speed decreases a little again, meaning that $\beta = 2$ is optimal *beta* regarding to the learning speed.

Why does such dependence in the learning occur? We measured the learning time for each learning step. The learning time decreases rapidly with the increase in β, as shown in Fig. 4C. For $\beta = 0.8$, the sensitivity of neurons is quite small, therefore, the large change in the connections is necessary for achieving the criterion to finish a learning step, resulting in the slower learning. In contrast, for $\beta = 2$ and 8, the neural activities change quickly with a small change in the connections, meaning that the learning speed is shorter. Generally, the longer time to learn one case disrupts the previously learned structure in the connectivity for the other cases. Thus it takes longer time for the network to simultaneously succeed for four cases.

3.3 Activities of Individual Neurons for Different β

Finally, we explored activities of individual neurons after the learning for different β. In previous study [1], it is observed that neurons show a variety of activities in performing the delayed sample to match task. For instance, persistent activities across an entire trial and transient activities are commonly observed. Are such neural activities observed in our model? Figure 5A shows activities of two fast neurons for four cases and for $\beta = 0.8$ as typical examples. The neural activities show static behavior in the presence of the sample stimulus, whereas the transient behaviors are not observed. For $\beta = 2$ and 8, in contrast, neural activities shows a variety of behaviors, as shown in Figs. 5B and C. Transient activities at the beginning and in the middle of the stimulus duration are often observed (top panel in Fig. 5B and panels in Fig. 5C) and the transition activities are also observed (bottom panel in Fig. 5B). These behaviors are similar to those observed experimentally [1].

4 Discussion

In this paper, we have developed the learning rule requiring only local information with multiple time scales in neural activity and examine the delayed

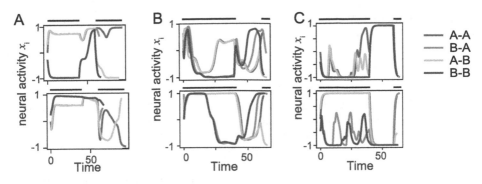

Fig. 5. Neural activities x_i of individual neurons for $\beta = 0.8, 2, 8$ in A, B, and C, respectively. Different panels show activities in different neurons. Different colors represent neural activities for different cases. Top black bars indicate duration of the application of the stimuli A or B.

match to sample task by this model. This model forms the neural trajectories that store the sample stimulus and converge to adequate states under the test stimulus depending on the sample one. The trajectory-based computation is previously proposed in [1] by using the machine learning method that is not biologically plausible. Our result suggests that the trajectory-based computation is ubiquitous independent of the learning methods.

How the property of individual neurons is related to the computational ability performed by neural dynamics of the neural population is one of the fundamental questions in the neuroscience [2, 4, 6, 12, 14]. Several studies [4, 12, 14] showed that intermediate sensitivity of individual neurons (β in our model) is optimal for learning performance. In these studies, the learning methods are based on the machine learning technique. We found that the learning speed is optimal for intermediate β with our learning model which is more biologically plausible. This result is in line with assertions in the previous studies. Further, our results show that, for the intermediate β, the activities of the individual neurons are more similar to the experimentally observed activities [1], comparing to those for the lower β. This suggests that the sensitivity of individual neurons is adjusted to train the neural population to perform the cognitive task with short time.

Similarity between the neural activities in models and experimental data is analyzed briefly in our model. Thus it has to be analyzed in detail for future work. For instance, the mixed selectivity is considered to be a critical property of neural activities for efficient computing in the neural system [3]. Further, although which neural behavior for $\beta = 2$ or $\beta = 8$ is more consistent to the experimentally observed one is an important question, difference between neural activities for intermediate β ($\beta = 2$), and those for higher β, ($\beta = 8$) is unclear. To answer this question, more quantitative data of neural activities during the task are necessary.

Acknowledgments. We thank Kunihiko Kaneko for fruitful discussion for our manuscript. This work was partly support by JSPS KAKENHI (no. 20H00123).

References

1. Chaisangmongkon, W., Swaminathan, S.K., Freedman, D.J., Wang, X.J.J.: Computing by robust transience: how the fronto-parietal network performs sequential. Category-based decisions. Neuron **93**(6), 1504–1517.e4 (2017)
2. Chialvo, D.R.: Emergent complex neural dynamics. Nat. Phys. **6**(10), 744–750 (2010)
3. Fusi, S., Miller, E.K., Rigotti, M.: Why neurons mix: high dimensionality for higher cognition. Curr. Opinion Neurobiol. **37**, 66–74 (2016)
4. Ghazizadeh, E., Ching, S.: Slow manifolds in recurrent networks encode working memory efficiently and robustly. arXiv preprint 2101.03163, January 2021
5. Kurikawa, T.: Transitions among metastable states underlie context-dependent working memories in a multiple timescale network. arXiv preprint 2104.10829, April 2021
6. Kurikawa, T., Barak, O., Kaneko, K.: Repeated sequential learning increases memory capacity via effective decorrelation in a recurrent neural network. Phys. Rev. Res. **2**(2), 023307 (2020)
7. Kurikawa, T., Haga, T., Handa, T., Harukuni, R., Fukai, T.: Neuronal stability in medial frontal cortex sets individual variability in decision-making. Nat. Neurosci. **21**(12), 1764–1773 (2018)
8. Kurikawa, T., Kaneko, K.: Embedding responses in spontaneous neural activity shaped through sequential learning. PLoS Comput. Biol. **9**(3), e1002943 (2013)
9. Kurikawa, T., Kaneko, K.: Dynamic organization of hierarchical memories. PLoS ONE **11**(9), e0162640 (2016)
10. Kurikawa, T., Kaneko, K.: Multiple-timescale neural networks: generation of context-dependent sequences and inference through autonomous bifurcations. arXiv preprint, p. 2006.03887, June 2020
11. Kurikawa, T., Mizuseki, K., Fukai, T.: Oscillation-driven memory encoding, maintenance, and recall in an EntorhinalHippocampal circuit model. Cerebral Cortex **31**(4), 2038–2057 (2021)
12. Orhan, A.E., Ma, W.J.: A diverse range of factors affect the nature of neural representations underlying short-term memory. Nat. Neurosci. **22**(2), 275–283 (2019)
13. Stokes, M.G., Kusunoki, M., Sigala, N., Nili, H., Gaffan, D., Duncan, J.: Dynamic coding for cognitive control in prefrontal cortex. Neuron **78**(2), 364–375 (2013)
14. Sussillo, D., Abbott, L.F.: Generating coherent patterns of activity from chaotic neural networks. Neuron **63**(4), 544–557 (2009)

A Region Descriptive Pre-training Approach with Self-attention Towards Visual Question Answering

Bisi Bode Kolawole[1](✉) and Minho Lee[2]

[1] School of Electrical and Electronics Engineering, Kyungpook National University, 80, Daehak-ro, Buk-go, Daegu, Republic of Korea
[2] Graduate School of Artificial Intelligence, Kyungpook National University, 80, Daehak-ro, Buk-go, Daegu, Republic of Korea

Abstract. Concatenation of text (question-answer) and image has been the bedrock of most visual language systems. Existing models concatenate the text (question-answer) and image inputs in a forced manner. In this paper, we introduce a region descriptive pre-training approach with self-attention towards VQA. The model is a new learning method that uses the image region descriptions combined with object labels to create a proper alignment between the text(question-answer) and the image inputs. We study the text associated with each image and discover that extracting the region descriptions from the image and using it during training greatly improves the model's performance. In this research work, we use the region description extracted from the images as a bridge to map the text and image inputs. The addition of region description makes our model perform better against some recent state-of-the-art models. Experiments demonstrated in this paper show that our model significantly outperforms most of these models.

Keywords: Visual question answering · Region descriptions · Object label · Pre-training

1 Introduction

Recently, proven learning networks in application domain such as Natural Language Processing (NLP) and Computer Vision (CV) are trained either by pre-training on a large-scale dataset or fine-tuning on the target dataset. Their pre-training and transfer learning methods follow naturally from their widespread use in both CV and NLP [8,20,21]. It has become a common practice due to its simplicity of usage and strong representation power on large public-available models trained on large-scale data sources. Through this, the pre-trained model provides useful information on specific target tasks. This information is considered essential for a clear understanding of visual language tasks, especially the relationship between the modalities.

The advent of Transformer models [14] brings about a leap in NLP. The attention mechanism in Transformers is efficient and flexible in aggregating and

© Springer Nature Switzerland AG 2021
T. Mantoro et al. (Eds.): ICONIP 2021, CCIS 1517, pp. 73–80, 2021.
https://doi.org/10.1007/978-3-030-92310-5_9

aligning word embedding features in sentences. Taking advantage of the flexibility of the Transformer model, models like UNITER [21], OSCAR [2], ViLBERT [3] were able to successfully adapt the Transform's BERT [7] model for visual language tasks.

Examining various state-of-the-art models [3,4,8,12,21] designed for visual language task shows that the key goal of these models is effectively aggregating the multimodal information in both visual language domains. Considering tasks like VQA (visual question answering), for the model to generate right answer, it will empower integrating language information from the text (question-answers) and aggregating their visual information from an input image, together with aligning the language with visual clues [20]. The lack of proper alignment information between the modalities makes alignment modeling weak supervised learning task, which is further complicated with oversampling and ambiguity [1,2].

In this paper, we present a region descriptive pre-training approach with self-attention towards visual question answering. The model captures useful relationship information between the image (visual) and the associated text (language) using the Transformer's self-attention mechanism. We explore region descriptions combined with the object labels to create a proper alignment between text and image information in a semantic space. The Transformer model [14] is the backbone of this model where the encoder part of the Transformer, BERT is used. Our main contribution is the introduction of region descriptions which we believe will further enhance the language understanding of the model and create proper alignments between the text and image features.

2   Related Work

It is well known that self-supervised learning relies solely on data for supervision, which applies to many visual-language tasks [14,21]. Pre-trainable language models like BERT [7], XLNet [16], and RoBERTa [19] have achieved remarkable results in various natural language tasks. Their task's capacity to be pre-trained over a huge language dataset, as well as the usage of Transformers for learning contextualized text representations, have been important to their success [14].

Pre-training generic models to address vision-language tasks such as VQA has recently attracted a lot of attention. Recent models use BERT to connect these two modalities by utilizing its Transformer-based structure with co-attention. Models such as VL-BERT [20] and VisualBERT [4] propose the use a single Transformer architecture to align both image and text. Other models like the ViLBERT [3] and the LXMERT [8] propose the use of different Transformers for both the text and image. A more or less similar architecture is VATT [18], VATT employs a single Transformer architecture to join three different modalities, which are video, audio and text. Despite the use of various Transformer architectures, the models were able to achieve a remarkable result.

Our concept of using object labels is inspired by [1,2], where object tags are used to facilitate learning alignments between two modalities (text and image). We believe our model can produce better results by introducing region descriptions with object labels, with this we hope to create a better learning alignment between the two modalities. We rely heavily on the self-attention mechanism of Transformers for creating a proper alignment between the modalities. Through various experiments, we have confident to show that our model performs better than others with the help of the region descriptions. Therefore, using a single-stream Transformer architecture with the help of region descriptions during pre-training differentiates our model from others.

3   Overview and Approach

3.1   Model Overview

Based on the current BERT modification, which includes the addition of new elements to support visual contents as well as a new form of visual feature embedding into the inputs, the idea behind our model follows the use of the Transformer self-attention mechanism to implicitly create a proper alignment between the elements of the input text, region descriptions with object labels and the image region features. The architecture is outlined in Fig. 1. The addition of the region descriptions makes the model capture the relationship context in the text and image, thereby creating a proper learning alignment. Since the self-attention mechanism of a Transformer model doesn't have a particular order, the position of the tokens together with the location of the region features are encoded as additional inputs.

We make use of Faster R-CNN when extracting the image features. Given an image with N regions of objects. We extract the image features $v´$ of each region N-dimensional vector ($N = 2048$) together with feature position r a R-dimensional vector ($R = 6$). Both the image features $v´$ and the feature positions r are concatenated and transformed into image region feature v using linear projection so that its vector dimension with the text embedding will be the same. We are able to obtain the region descriptions by studying the relationship between COCO images and their captions and by extracting the position information of the objects in the image. The extraction of the object position information was with a state-of-the-art captioning model [2,21]. We consider the relationship information between the object in the image an important factor, especially during training. Since the captions in the image describe the relationship of the objects in the image perfectly, we decide to use it as our region description (together with the extracted object position information) and combine it with the extracted object labels detected by the Faster R-CNN in the images. Using WordPiece, we tokenize the input sentences according to the BERT model. The subword token is obtained by adding the word embedding and the positional embedding. Finally, all embeddings are routed through the multi-layer Transformer network.

3.2   Pre-training Approach

The generic nature of our model enables its pre-training on large datasets with well designed pre-training tasks. We tend to focus more on VQA throughout

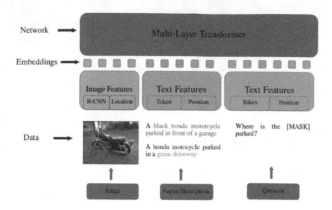

Fig. 1. The proposed architecture of our model, showing the input data (Image, region descriptions and question), the embeddings and the Transformer network.

this work. The pre-training corpus is built on existing visual language and text-only datasets such as COCO [10], Visual Genome [15], Conceptual Captions [16], flicker30k [16] etc. The total number of images in the set is 4.1 million. The whole corpus consist of 6 million texts, region descriptions with labels and images. Our pre-training objectives are similar to those of existing models such as BERT [7], OSCAR [2], and UNITER [21]. The two pre-training tasks that we exploit to incur loss in this work are as follows:

Masked Word Modeling (MWM). Our MWM is similar to BERT's MLM. The image region features are denoted as v. The region description with object labels is denoted as z while the words are as w. The region description with object labels and word tokens lies within the same semantic domain while the image regions lie within the visual domain. The discrete token sequence m (lets say $m \triangleq [w, z]$) are randomly masked with a probability of 15% and the masked ones m_i are replaced with a special token [MASK]. The goal is to minimize the negative log-likelihood of the masked words being predicted based on their surrounding word $\mathbf{m}_{\backslash i}$ and all image region v:

$$l_{MWM} = -\mathbb{E}_{(\mathbf{v},\mathbf{m})\sim D} \log p(m_i | \mathbf{m}_{\backslash i}, \mathbf{v}) \qquad (1)$$

Visual-Word Matching (VLM). For VLM, the encoder output which is the special token [CLS], represents the joint representation of both modalities. Firstly, we group the region description z with image representation v and denotes it as m'. During training, we mask out the image feature representations by replacing z with a probability of 50% with a different description sequence from the dataset. The encoder output, which is the joint representation of m' and w, is fed into a fully-connected layer. The sigmoid function then predicts the output score, 1 or 0 which means that the pair contains the original image feature representation or not respectively. We use s($\boldsymbol{m,w}$) to denote the output score. For optimization, we use binary cross-entropy as our loss function. The loss is defined as follows:

$$l_{VLM} = -\mathbb{E}_{(m',w)\sim D}[y log\, s(\boldsymbol{m'}, \boldsymbol{w}) + (1 - y)log(1 - s(\boldsymbol{m'},\boldsymbol{w}))] \qquad (2)$$

4 Experiments

4.1 Fine-Tuning for Downstream Visual Question Answering Task

In VQA, the input to the model is a question-answer pair with an image. The model is expected to predict the correct answer based on the question asked on a given image. We consider VQA to be a multi-classification problem in which the model selects an answer from a shared answer set. The VQA v2.0 dataset [5] is used in this experiment. This is a widely used dataset that contains an open-ended question about images. The images used in the dataset are gotten from MSCOCO image dataset [10]. The dataset is divided into three sections: train (444k questions with 83k images), validation (214k questions with 41k images), and test (448k questions with 81k images). A shared set of 3,129 answers are provided for the questions. Following [11], the model is expected to pick the corresponding answer from the shared set for each questions. During fine-tuning, we concatenate the text (question, regional description with object labels) and the image region features to form one input sequence. The [CLS] output is fed into a linear classifier. We use a binary cross-entropy loss to train the classifier. Each answer candidate is assigned a soft-target score based on its relevance to the 10 human responses. We consider AdamW as our optimizer and set the learning rate of $5e$-5 with weight decay of 0.01. At inference, we use the softmax function for the answer prediction.

Table 1. Comparing our model with other visual language models. The results for Test-Dev and Test-Std were both obtained on the VQA Evaluation server.

Method	(Test-Dev)				(Test-Std)			
	Overall	Yes/No	Number	Other	Overall	Yes/No	Number	Other
BAN [11]	–	–	–	–	70.4	85.6	53.7	60.7
DFAF [12]	70.22	86.09	53.32	60.49	70.34	–	–	–
ViLBERT [3]	70.55	–	–	–	70.9	–	–	–
VisualBERT [4]	70.80	–	–	–	71.1	–	–	–
LXMERT [8]	72.42	–	–	–	72.5	88.2	54.2	63.1
OSCAR$_B$ [2]	73.16	89.45	**56.70**	62.95	73.44	89.6	**56.73**	63.19
Ours	**73.55**	**90.10**	56.53	**63.26**	**73.76**	**90.22**	56.17	**63.46**

The experimental results are shown in Table 1. Pre-training the model with region descriptions improves the model's performance significantly. We compare our model's performance with other state-of-the-art models. According to the table, our model outperforms these models significantly. The use of region description during pre-training with the help of the transformer's self-attention mechanism is significant for the proper alignment of both modalities.

4.2   Implementation Details

Our model is implemented based on the Pytorch framework. We consider BERT-base as the Transformer backbone for the model. For faster training, we use the Nvidia Apex for distributed training. We run our pre-training and fine-tuning experiments on Nvidia GPUs. The model is pre-trained using similar configurations as BERT-base. The image region feature dimension is 2054, which is the concatenation of both image features and the feature position. The image features with the feature position are extracted with Faster-RCNN + ResNet 101. We use COCO caption for the region descriptions. We use four to six descriptions per image as shown in Fig. 2.

The bathroom is a mess with sport gear
A bathroom a toilet, a plant, a stand and several footwear on the floor
A bathroom with ski equipment laid out on the floor
A bathroom with a lot of toilet and ski boot

Four people wait to cross the street at an intersection
People looking at a stop light at the other side of the road
A group of people standing next to a crosswalk
A group of men walking across the street

Fig. 2. Example of images with their region descriptions. We are able to use 4 to 6 descriptions per image. We selected the descriptions that accurately describes the relationship between the objects in the image.

4.3   Qualitative Analysis

We visualize the attended part of an image using Gaussian blur. The purpose is to know the part of the image the model's self-attention mechanism is attending to on a given question input. We selected an image at random and asked different questions about it. As shown in Fig. 3, the model attends to the relevant part of the image and provides the correct answer. We tested the model on questions that require critical thinking, and each time it generates the right answers. This verifies the importance of pre-training with region descriptions as it creates better alignment and improves the language understanding of the model.

(a) Question: *What is he sitting on?* Answer: *couch*

(b) Question: *What emotions are the people depicting?* Answer: *happy*

(c) Question: *What colors are the cups?* Answer: *red*

Fig. 3. A randomly selected image showing the attended part of the model when generating the corresponding answers. The model's self-attention mechanism was able to focus on the most important part of the image when picking out the answer.

5 Conclusion

In this paper, we presented our model which is, a region descriptive pre-training approach with self-attention towards visual question answering. Our model uses region descriptions with object labels to proper align the two modalities in visual language tasks. We were able to achieve better performance with the help of the Transformer's self-attention mechanism. Our results show that the pre-training procedure employed eases the learning alignments between the two modalities better. We hope to expand our pre-training method to other visual language tasks in the future, making the model more generic.

Acknowledgment. This research was partly supported by the MSIT(Ministry of Science and ICT), Korea, under the ITRC(Information Technology Research Center) support program (IITP-2021-2020-0-01808) supervised by the IITP (Institute of Information & Communications Technology Planning & Evaluation)[50%] and the National Research Foundation of Korea(NRF) grant funded by the Korea government(MSIT) (No. 2021R1A2C3011169)[50%].

References

1. Anderson, P., et al.: Bottom-up and top-down attention for image captioning and visual question answering. In: CVPR (2018)
2. Li, X., et al.: OSCAR: object-semantics aligned pre-training for vision-language tasks. In: Vedaldi, A., Bischof, H., Brox, T., Frahm, J.-M. (eds.) ECCV 2020. LNCS, vol. 12375, pp. 121–137. Springer, Cham (2020). https://doi.org/10.1007/978-3-030-58577-8_8
3. Lu, J., Batra, D., Parikh, D., Lee, S.: ViLBERT: pretraining task-agnostic visiolinguistic representations for vision-and-language tasks. arXiv preprint arXiv:1908.02265

4. Li, L., Yatskar, M., Yin, D., Hsieh, C., Chang, K.: VISUALBERT: a simple and performant baseline for vision and language. arXiv preprint arXiv:1908.03557
5. Agrawal, A., et al.: VQA: visual question answering. arXiv:1906.08237
6. Yang, Z., Dai, Z., Yang, Y., Carbonell, J., Salakhutdinov, R., Le, Q.: XLNet: generalized autoregressive pretraining for language understanding. arXiv preprint arXiv:1906.08237 (2020)
7. Devlin, J., Chang, M., Lee, K., Toutanova, K.: BERT: pre-training of deep bidirectional transformers for language understanding, arXiv preprint (2019)
8. Tan, H., Bansal, M.: LXMERT.: learning cross-modality encoder representations from transformers. In: EMNLP (2019)
9. Ren, S., He, K., Girshick, R., Sun, J.: Faster R-CNN: towards real-time object detection with region proposal networks. arXiv preprint arXiv:1506.01497 (2016)
10. Lin, T., et al.: Microsoft COCO: common objects in context. arXiv preprint arXiv:1405.0312
11. Kim, J.-H., Jun, J., Zhang, B.-T.: Bilinear attention networks. In: NIPS (2018)
12. Gao, P., et al.: Dynamic fusion with intra- and inter-modality attention flow for visual question answering. arXiv preprint arXiv:1812.05252 (2019)
13. He, K., Zhang, X., Ren, S., Sun, J.: Deep residual learning for image recognition. arXiv preprint arXiv:1512.03385 (2015)
14. Vaswani, A., et al.: Attention Is All You Need. arXiv preprint: 1706.03762 (2017)
15. Krishna, R., et al.: Visual genome: connecting language and vision using crowd-sourced dense image annotations. arXiv preprint (2016)
16. Sharma, P., Ding, N., Goodman, S., Soricut, R.: Conceptual captions: a cleaned, hypernymed, image alt-text dataset for automatic image captioning. In: Annual Meeting of the Association for Computational Linguistics (2018)
17. Young, P., Lai, A., Hodosh, M., Hockenmaier, J.: From image descriptions to visual denotations: new similarity metrics for semantic inference over event descriptions. Trans. Assoc. Comput. Linguist. 2, 67–78 (2014)
18. Akbari, H., et al.: VATT: transformer for multimodal self-supervised learning from raw video, audio and text. arXiv preprint arXiv:2104.11178 (2021)
19. Liu, Y., et al.: RoBERTa: a robustly optimized BERT pretraining approach. arXiv preprint arXiv:1907.11692 (2019)
20. Su, W., et al.: VL-BERT: pre-training of generic visual-linguistic representations. In: ICLR (2020)
21. Yen-Chun, C., et al.: UNITER: UNiversal image-TExt representation learning. In: Vedaldi, A., Bischof, H., Brox, T., Frahm, J.-M. (eds.) ECCV 2020. LNCS, vol. 12375, pp. 104–120. Springer, Cham (2020). https://doi.org/10.1007/978-3-030-58577-8_7

Prediction of Inefficient BCI Users Based on Cognitive Skills and Personality Traits

Laura J. Hagedorn$^{(\boxtimes)}$, Nikki Leeuwis, and Maryam Alimardani

Tilburg University, 5037 AB Tilburg, The Netherlands

Abstract. BCI inefficiency is one of the major challenges of Motor Imagery Brain-Computer Interfaces (MI-BCI). Past research suggests that certain cognitive skills and personality traits correlate with MI-BCI real-time performance. Other studies have examined sensorimotor rhythm changes (known as μ suppression) as a valuable indicator of successful execution of the motor imagery task. This research aims to combine these insights by investigating whether cognitive factors and personality traits can predict a user's ability to modulate μ rhythms during a MI-BCI task. Data containing 55 subjects who completed a MI task was employed, and a stepwise linear regression model was implemented to select the most relevant features for μ suppression prediction. The most accurate model was based on: Spatial Ability, Visuospatial Memory, Autonomy, and Vividness of Visual Imagery. Further correlation analyses showed that a novice user's μ suppression during a MI-BCI task can be predicted based on their visuospatial memory, as measured by the Design Organization Test (DOT).

Keywords: Brain-Computer Interface (BCI) · Motor Imagery (MI) · BCI inefficiency · μ suppression · Cognitive factors · Personality · Visuospatial memory · Design Organization Test (DOT)

1 Introduction

Motor-Imagery Brain-Computer Interface (MI-BCI) systems allow users to control external devices by decoding brain activity that occurs with imagination of movement. MI-BCIs have been investigated in several applications ranging from communication and movement control to neuro-rehabilitation [5], but in contrast to their high potential, MI-BCIs are barely used outside laboratories because of the inconsistency of user performances [15,23]. It has been shown that around 15% to 30% of subjects are not able to control MI-BCI systems even after extensive training, which can lead to frustrating and costly procedures for users as well as researchers [23]. Well-defined prediction paradigms that identify inefficient users early on in research could help to avoid unnecessary training sessions or lead to the establishment of alternative training protocols for the low performers [23]. Therefore, MI-BCI performance prediction is of high interest to the BCI community.

© Springer Nature Switzerland AG 2021
T. Mantoro et al. (Eds.): ICONIP 2021, CCIS 1517, pp. 81–89, 2021.
https://doi.org/10.1007/978-3-030-92310-5_10

Several researchers have already investigated the impact of individual factors (e.g. gender, cognitive ability, etc.) as well as temporal factors (e.g. motivation, fatigue, etc.) on MI-BCI performance [4,9,15,17] and it has been established that users' performance is influenced by mental and psychological states [4,7,9]. For instance, Jeunet et al. [4] classified the learning style of participants, which requires a certain level of autonomy, as a crucial factor and reliable predictor of MI-BCI performance. Additionally, many researchers have found correlations between the cognitive skills and MI-BCI performance [4,9,17]. Jeunet et al. [4] reported strong correlations between MI-BCI performances and user's spatial ability as measured by a Mental Rotation Task (MRT) and Pacheco et al. [17] found correlations between spatial ability (as measured by Block Design Test and MRT) and the performance of 7 male users in a flexion vs. extension MI-BCI.

Leeuwis et al. [8,9] could not confirm the impact of spatial ability on MI-BCI performance, but they reported a significantly higher visuospatial memory in high aptitude BCI users. They concluded that visuospatial memory correlates positively with the users' performances, which was classified as a negative predictor by Jeunet et al. [4]. Because of these contradicting findings, spatial ability and visuospatial memory are reviewed in particular in this research.

The presented studies mainly rely on the user's online classification accuracy during the MI-BCI task, which is captured in the percentage of correctly recognized mental commands by a BCI classifier [11]. However, using this metric alone is problematic as BCI classifiers are usually initially calibrated, and then applied to classify the EEG signals in the following trials [11]. This means that the classifier parameters are not adapted to the subject's learning of the MI task, and hence the low BCI accuracy could be due to the system instead of the user [1].

To avoid this pitfall, it is suggested to rely on brain pattern changes in the sensorimotor cortex (the μ band) that are associated with movement imagery [13]. It has been shown that the μ waves are larger when a subject is at rest and are suppressed when the person generates, observes or imagines movement [6]. This pattern change is referred to as event-related (de)synchronization (ERD/ERS) (in short μ suppression) and is commonly used as a reliable measure for MI-BCI classifiers [3,19]. Therefore, our study focused on the research question: *Can cognitive skills and personality traits predict a user's ability to generate μ suppression in sensorimotor regions during motor imagery of left and right hands?* To answer this question, we used a dataset containing personality information, cognitive test results and EEG signals from 55 participants who completed a two-class MI-BCI experiment. The μ suppression values were computed and together with personality and cognitive factors they were used to train a stepwise linear regression model to select relevant factors that could predict a subject's MI task performance.

2   Methods

2.1   Experiment

2.1.1   Participants
The data employed in this research was collected by Leeuwis et al. [9]. EEG signals were collected form 55 participants ($36 females, 21 males, M_{age} =$ $20.71, SD_{age} = 3.52$) while they performed a two-class MI task. The participants were all right-handed and naïve to MI-BCI.

2.1.2   EEG Recording
The EEG signals were recorded via 16 electrodes distributed over the sensori-motor area according to the international 10–20 system (F3, Fz, F4, FC1, FC5, FC2, FC6, C3, Cz, C4, CP1, CP5, CP2, CP6, T7, T8). The g.Nautilus amplifier was used to amplify the recorded signals, and the sampling rate was 250 samples per second. To minimize the noise during recording, a bandpass filter from 0.5 30 Hz was applied.

2.1.3   MI Task and the BCI System
Details of the experimental procedure can be found in Leeuwis et al. [9]. After participants completed the demographic questionnaire and the cognitive tests, they were placed before a screen and the researcher positioned the EEG cap on their head. The researcher explained that the participant had to imagine squeezing their left or right hand following a cue on the screen without generating any physical movement or muscle tension. The BCI task was repeated in 4 runs, each including 40 MI trials (20 left and 20 right). Each trial took 8 s starting with a fixation cross, followed by a cue at second 3, which indicated the direction of the MI task, and finally the presentation of feedback associated with the task during the last 3.75 s (Fig. 1). The first run was used for calibration and did not provide feedback. In runs 2 to 4, the parameters of the classifier were adjusted according to the EEG data collected in the latest run to provide feedback to the subject.

2.1.4   Measurements
Several individual factors including demographics, personality traits and cognitive skills were measured before the participants performed the BCI task. These measurements included the following assessments: A demographic questionnaire, Affinity for Technological Scale (ATI), Mental Rotation Task (MRT), Design Organization Test (DOT), Five Factor Personality Inventory (FFPI), Vividness of Visual Imagery Quiz (VVIQ), and the Questionnaire for Current Motivation (QCM). For details about the measurements and the procedure, see [9].

2.2   Data Analysis

Data analysis was conducted in Python 3.9.1. This included the EEG pre-processing, μ suppression analysis and the implementation of the regression model.

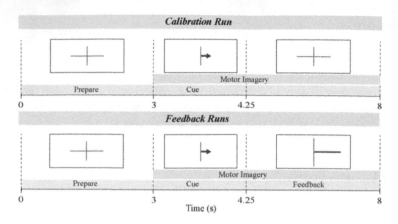

Fig. 1. The timeline of the MI task in one BCI trial. From [9].

2.2.1 EEG Pre-processing and μ Suppression Analysis

Similar to [10] and [18], μ rhythms were exclusively obtained from the EEG channels C3 and C4, as the μ suppression is the strongest in these areas [10]. Given that μ waves are constricted to the movement of the opposite upper limb, the brain activity at C4 was associated with the left-hand MI and activity at C3 with the right-hand MI. Once the signals from these channels were isolated, they were segmented into MI trials. In each trial, the first 3 s were extracted as the resting state, and the last 4 s were identified as the MI phase (Fig. 1). For each EEG segment (rest and MI), spectral density was estimated using Welch's periodogram [12] and the mean power over the μ frequency band (8-12Hz) was computed. Thereafter, the event-related (de-)synchronization for each trial was calculated using the following function [18]:

$$ERD/ERS = \frac{\mu - \gamma}{\gamma} \tag{1}$$

where μ represents the average power during the MI phase and γ is the average power during the rest period. This procedure was repeated for all participants separately for the left-hand (C4) and right-hand (C3) MI trials in all 4 runs. Finally, the resulted μ suppression for each participant in all trials was averaged and assigned as the participant's final μ suppression value. Once the final μ suppression values for all participants were calculated, outliers were detected by using the interquartile range technique, which detected and removed two outliers in the data.

2.2.2 Regression Model

Because of the large number of predictors that were investigated in this research, a stepwise linear regression algorithm was implemented. This model iterates through the predictor variables and only includes features that improve the model. Additionally, it repeatedly controls whether the significance level of earlier added features decreases and removes them through backward elimination if that is the case [20]. In the present research, the maximum number of features to be selected at one time was set to 4. The subsets of features were evaluated on their coefficient of determination (R^2), which is a commonly used measurement for the accuracy of predictive regression models, as it measures how well the predictions of a model fit the actual values [14].

2.2.3   Correlation Analysis

Following the identification of the most relevant features by the stepwise linear regression model, a correlation analysis was performed on the selected features separately. Pearson's r was calculated for normally distributed variables and Kendall's tau for variables with non-normal distribution. Differences of gender were checked with an independent t-test. The variables were checked for normality by applying the Shapiro-Wilk test and multicollinearity was tested with the Variance Inflation Factor (VIF) similar to Leeuwis et al. [9].

3   Results

Our results showed no significant differences between genders ($t(34) = -0.19, p = .8$) in terms of generated μ suppression, and neither did the age of the participants ($r_\tau = 0.028, p = .7$). The model that was able to predict μ suppression the most accurately was generated by: *Spatial Ability + Visuospatial Memory + Autonomy + VVIQ* ($R^2_{adj} = 0.128, p < .05$). Further correlation tests on the identified features in this model showed that Visuospatial Memory ($r(50) = .32, p = .02$) significantly correlated with μ suppression (Fig. 2).

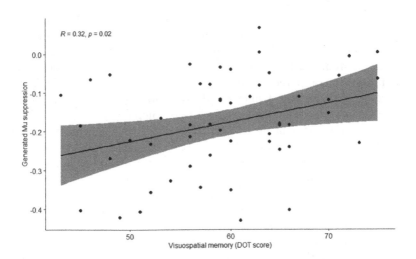

Fig. 2. Significant correlation was found between participants' Visuospatial Memory (DOT score) and μ suppression in a MI-BCI task.

However, no significant correlation was found between Spatial Ability (as measured by the MRT) ($r(50) = .008, p > .5$), Autonomy ($r(50) = 0.09, p < .5$), VVIQ ($r(50) = -.1, p < .5$) and the generated μ suppression.

Finally, the best performing model proposed by Leeuwis et al. [9] (Gender + Emotional Stability + Orderliness + VVIQ) was tested, but did not show significant results in prediction of μ suppression ($R^2_{adj} = -0.03804, p = 0.7$).

4   Discussion

The aim of this research was to investigate whether the cognitive skills and personality traits can be used as effective predictors of MI-BCI (in)efficiency among novice BCI users. Unlike previous studies that relied on the BCI classifier's online performance as a measure of the user's efficiency score [4,9,21], we used the subject's ability to produce μ suppression as an indicator of their MI task performance [18]. The μ band ERD/ERS of EEG signals at C3 and C4 during a left vs. right MI-BCI task were extracted from 55 participants, and after outlier removal, a stepwise linear regression algorithm was implemented to predict 53 participants' μ suppression based on their cognitive skills and personality traits. The best performing model obtained by our study identified four factors of Spatial Ability, Visuospatial Memory, Autonomy and Vividness of Visual Imagery as predictors of μ suppression. Among these, the only cognitive factor that demonstrated a significant correlation with μ suppression was Visuospatial Memory. Although the rest of features did not correlate with the generated μ suppression individually, their inclusion in the model supports the findings of previous researches [4,9].

Leeuwis et al. [8], as well as Pacheco et al. [17], found that high aptitude subjects performed better on the Design Organization Test (DOT) that was used to measure visuospatial memory. The current research found that Visuospatial Memory (measured by DOT) correlates negatively with the magnitude of μ suppression, which means that subjects that scored higher on the DOT generated more μ suppression compared to subjects with lower scores on the DOT. Similar outcomes were detected by Jeunet et al. [4] who used the Corsi Block Task to evaluate visuospatial short-term and working memory abilities and classified visuospatial memory as a negative predictor of MI-BCI performance. Further research is necessary to ascertain the role of visuospatial memory skills on MI and BCI performance and resolve the inconsistency that exists in these reports.

Additionally, past research reported relationships between spatial ability as measured by the Mental Rotation Test (MRT) and MI-BCI performance [4,17]. Although no prior study has investigated the μ rhythms with regard to spatial ability and BCI performance, it was expected that participants who scored higher on the MRT would also show a higher ability in generating μ suppression. This assumption was based on the establishment that spatial ability is intimately related to the concept of motor imagery [4,16]. However, this research did not validate this hypothesis, as there was no significant correlation between MRT scores and μ suppression.

Moreover, Jeunet et al. [4] concluded that MI-BCI performance is correlated with the users' ability to learn independently, which requires a certain level of autonomy. Leeuwis et al. [9] further confirmed personality dimension Autonomy as an effective predictor of MI-BCI performance. Although Autonomy, as an independent factor, was not significantly correlated with μ suppression, it was chosen as a relevant feature by the regression model, indicating that it significantly improved the performance of the model and can therefore be considered as a potential predictor for MI-BCI performance in the future research.

In the experiment conducted by Leeuwis et al. [9], high Vividness of Visual Imagery was a positive predictor of MI-BCI performance. Similarly, Touckovic and Osuagwu [24] reported a positive correlation between MI-BCI performance and vividness of imagery. The results of this study partially supported the impact of this factor on MI performance by reporting VVIQ as a predictor in the best performing model. However, further correlation analysis did not show a significant relationship between VVIQ and μ suppression. This result is consistent with the reports of Vasilyev et al. [22] who also did not find a correlation between vividness of imagery and μ-rhythm ERD, but observed a significant impact of kinaesthetically vivid images on subjects' cortical excitability. Future research should further investigate the role of this factor, as these reports remain inconclusive. Leeuwis et al. [9] proposed a linear regression model to predict users' MI-BCI performance using the classifier's online error rates. Their most accurate model was: Gender + Emotional Stability + Orderliness + VVIQ, but this model did not show significant prediction in the present study, although the same dataset was used. The only factor that was common between their model and our best performing model was Vividness of Visual Imagery. Gender, Emotional stability, and Orderliness did not correlate with μ suppression independently. This inconsistent finding calls for further research to fully understand the occurrence of the μ rhythms and its relationship with cognitive factors and MI-BCI performance.

Finally, some limitations of this study have to be mentioned. Although our data included a larger number of subjects than other similar studies [4,15], the data was imbalanced in terms of age and gender, which occurred due to convenience sampling [9]. Only young and healthy subjects participated in the study, which reduces the generalizability of our findings to other populations for which MI-BCI applications are more relevant (e.g. individuals with motor impairment). Although studies have shown no difference in MI-BCI training between healthy subjects and patients with motor disabilities [2], the outcome of our study should be validated with other populations, particularly motor impaired subjects. Future research should also focus on other cognitive profiles and psychological measures across a broad range of subjects in order to investigate the behaviour of the μ waves in relation to the MI task and BCI performance. This will encourage development of accurate models that can predict a user's (in)ability to operate a MI-BCI system as a step toward alleviation of the BCI inefficiency problem. Consequently, this will broaden the range of MI-BCI applications outside the laboratories and will support the implementation of reliable BCIs in clinical systems.

5 Conclusion

This study aimed to identify cognitive skills and personality traits to predict a BCI user's μ suppression during a MI task. A stepwise linear regression model was trained on the data to select relevant factors that could predict participants' μ rhythms. The most accurate model was based on three cognitive factors of Spatial Ability, Visuospatial Memory and Vividness of Visual Imagery and one personality trait, i.e. Autonomy. Correlation analyses for each predictor resulted in a significant correlation between Visuospatial Memory and μ suppression. Our findings confirm that an individual's personality and cognitive abilities can indeed predict MI-BCI performance. The outcome of this study will contribute to future MI-BCI research by providing a tool for identifying low BCI performers in an early stage of research or clinical treatment. This would ultimately save resources and facilitate adjusted user training for different groups of BCI users.

References

1. Alimardani, M., Nishio, S., Ishiguro, H.: Brain-computer interface and motor imagery training: the role of visual feedback and embodiment. In: Evolving BCI Therapy-Engaging Brain State Dynamics, vol. 2, p. 64 (2018)
2. de Castro-Cros, M., Sebastian-Romagosa, M., Rodríguez-Serrano, J., Opisso, E., Ochoa, M., Ortner, R., Guger, C., Tost, D.: Effects of gamification in BCI functional rehabilitation. Front. Neurosci. **14**, 882 (2020)
3. Friedrich, E.V., Scherer, R., Neuper, C.: Long-term evaluation of a 4-class imagery-based brain-computer interface. Clin. Neurophysiol. **124**(5), 916–927 (2013)
4. Jeunet, C., N'Kaoua, B., Subramanian, S., Hachet, M., Lotte, F.: Predicting mental imagery-based BCI performance from personality, cognitive profile and neurophysiological patterns. PLoS One **10**(12), e0143962 (2015)
5. Khan, M.A., Das, R., Iversen, H.K., Puthusserypady, S.: Review on motor imagery based BCI systems for upper limb post-stroke neurorehabilitation: from designing to application. Comput. Biol. Med. **123**, 103843 (2020)
6. Kübler, A., Mattia, D.: Brain-computer interface based solutions for end-users with severe communication disorders. In: The Neurology of Conciousness, pp. 217–240. Elsevier (2016)
7. Lee, M., Yoon, J.G., Lee, S.W.: Predicting motor imagery performance from resting-state EEG using dynamic causal modeling. Front. Hum. Neurosci. **14**, 321 (2020)
8. Leeuwis, N., Alimardani, M.: High aptitude motor-imagery BCI users have better visuospatial memory. In: 2020 IEEE International Conference on Systems, Man, and Cybernetics (SMC), pp. 1518–1523. IEEE (2020)
9. Leeuwis, N., Paas, A., Alimardani, M.: Vividness of visual imagery and personality impact motor-imagery brain computer interfaces. Front. Hum. Neurosci. **15**, 634748 (2021)
10. Lemm, S., Schafer, C., Curio, G.: BCI competition 2003-data set iii: probabilistic modeling of sensorimotor/spl mu/rhythms for classification of imaginary hand movements. IEEE Trans. Biomed. Eng. **51**(6), 1077–1080 (2004)
11. Lotte, F., Jeunet, C.: Online classification accuracy is a poor metric to study mental imagery-based BCI user learning: an experimental demonstration and new metrics. In: 7th International BCI Conference (2017)

12. Matinmikko, M., Sarvanko, H., Mustonen, M., Mammela, A.: Performance of spectrum sensing using Welch's periodogram in Rayleigh fading channel. In: 2009 4th International Conference on Cognitive Radio Oriented Wireless Networks and Communications, pp. 1–5. IEEE (2009)

13. Mensh, B., Werfel, J., Seung, H.: BCI competition 2003-data set IA: combining gamma-band power with slow cortical potentials to improve single-trial classification of electroencephalographic signals. IEEE Trans. Biomed. Eng. **51**(6), 1052–1056 (2004). https://doi.org/10.1109/TBME.2004.827081

14. Müller, A.C., Guido, S.: Introduction to machine learning with Python: a guide for data scientists. O'Reilly Media, Inc., Sebastopol (2016)

15. Nijboer, F., Birbaumer, N., Kubler, A.: The influence of psychological state and motivation on brain-computer interface performance in patients with amyotrophic lateral sclerosis-a longitudinal study. Front. Neurosci. **4**, 55 (2010)

16. Osuagwu, B.A., Vuckovic, A.: Similarities between explicit and implicit motor imagery in mental rotation of hands: an EEG study. Neuropsychologia **65**, 197–210 (2014)

17. Pacheco, K., Acuna, K., Carranza, E., Achanccaray, D., Andreu-Perez, J.: Performance predictors of motor imagery brain-computer interface based on spatial abilities for upper limb rehabilitation. In: 2017 39th Annual International Conference of the IEEE Engineering in Medicine and Biology Society (EMBC), pp. 1014–1017. IEEE (2017)

18. Penaloza, C.I., Alimardani, M., Nishio, S.: Android feedback-based training modulates sensorimotor rhythms during motor imagery. IEEE Trans. Neural Syst. Rehabil. Eng. **26**(3), 666–674 (2018). https://doi.org/10.1109/TNSRE.2018.2792481

19. Quintero-Rincón, A., Batatia, H., et al.: Mu-suppression detection in motor imagery electroencephalographic signals using the generalized extreme value distribution. In: 2020 International Joint Conference on Neural Networks (IJCNN), pp. 1–5. IEEE (2020)

20. Tanaka, K., Kurita, T., Meyer, F., Berthouze, L., Kawabe, T.: Stepwise feature selection by cross validation for eeg-based brain computer interface. In: The 2006 IEEE International Joint Conference on Neural Network Proceedings, pp. 4672–4677. IEEE (2006)

21. Tibrewal, N., Leeuwis, N., Alimardani, M.: The promise of deep learning for BCIs: classification of motor imagery EEG using convolutional neural network. bioRxiv (2021)

22. Vasilyev, A., Liburkina, S., Yakovlev, L., Perepelkina, O., Kaplan, A.: Assessing motor imagery in brain-computer interface training: psychological and neurophysiological correlates. Neuropsychologia **97**, 56–65 (2017)

23. Vidaurre, C., Blankertz, B.: Towards a cure for BCI illiteracy. Brain Topogr. **23**(2), 194–198 (2010)

24. Vuckovic, A., Osuagwu, B.A.: Using a motor imagery questionnaire to estimate the performance of a brain-computer interface based on object oriented motor imagery. Clin. Neurophysiol. **124**(8), 1586–1595 (2013)

Analysis of Topological Variability in Mouse Neuronal Populations Based on Fluorescence Microscopy Images

Margarita Zaleshina[1]([⊠]) [iD] and Alexander Zaleshin[2] [iD]

[1] Moscow Institute of Physics and Technology, Moscow, Russia
[2] Institute of Higher Nervous Activity and Neurophysiology, Moscow, Russia

Abstract. In this work, we processed sets of images obtained by light-sheet fluorescence microscopy method. We selected different cell groups and determined areas occupied by ensembles of cell groups in mouse brain tissue. Recognition of mouse neuronal populations was performed on the basis of visual properties of fluorescence-activated cells. In our study 60 fluorescence microscopy datasets obtained from 23 mice ex vivo were analyzed. Based on data from light-sheet microscopy datasets, we identified visual characteristics of elements in multi-page TIFF files, such as the density of surface fill and its distribution over the study area, the boundaries of distinct objects and object groups, and the boundaries between homogeneous areas. To identify topological properties, we performed operations such as contouring and segmentation, and identification of areas of interest. Individual elements in fluorescence microscopy records were selected based on their brightness in grayscale mode. Frequently occurring patterns formed by individual elements were classified and found in other sets of images: this way we built a training sample and classified the optogenetics data. The presence of training samples was tested for different types of fluorescence microscopy. We selected and constructed six sets of typical samples, with certain topological properties, on the basis of the density at the boundaries, the density inside the boundaries, and the shape type.

Keywords: Mouse brain · Optogenetics · Pattern recognition · Brain mapping

1 Introduction

The brain can be represented as a spatially distributed multi-scale and multi-level structure in which continuous dynamic processes occur. Neuroimaging techniques are applied to visualize internal characteristics of the brain based on electronic medical records, including the diagnosis of tumors or injuries. Radiologists and neurophysiologists process a series of brain images as two-dimensional slices and develop three-dimensional models based on tomography and microscopy data. With improvements in measuring equipment and increases in the accuracy of data processing, researchers receive data that were unclear when applying of previous methods, and therefore were excluded as noise.

© Springer Nature Switzerland AG 2021
T. Mantoro et al. (Eds.): ICONIP 2021, CCIS 1517, pp. 90–97, 2021.
https://doi.org/10.1007/978-3-030-92310-5_11

The identification of individual ensembles and the principles of their interaction, and the correlation of activity of ensembles, are considered by many authors. Segmentation of a large set of neurons involves grouping them into neural ensembles, which are usually formed as populations of cells with similar properties.

In this work we applied spatial data processing methods for pattern recognition and comparative analysis of fluorescence microscopy records. Based on the identified topological properties of the images, we performed operations such as contouring and segmentation, and identification of areas of interest. Next, we built a set of training samples and classified the data in optogenetics multi-page TIFF files.

2 Background and Related Works

2.1 Brain Imaging Components

Characteristic sizes of individual elements, distances between elements, and distribution of densities for groups of elements can be used to create typical training samples when processing of brain imaging components.

An analysis of spatially distributed brain structure and activity should include the following main components: choice of coordinate systems and scales; recognition and classification of experimental results; segmentation and calculation of connectivity of brain regions. It is noticeable that all images of the brain contain data that strongly differ from each other in size, i.e., in fact, such data belong to two different scales. In many studies, data at a different scale is very often cut out as "noise".

Figure 1 shows sparse and dense density distributions of elements in brain images.

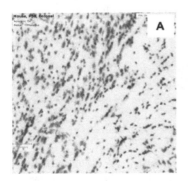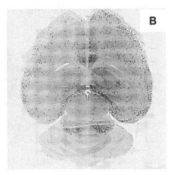

Fig. 1. A. Distribution of elements in mouse brain tissue (https://atlas.brain-map.org/atlas?atlas= 1#atlas=1&plate=100960224&structure=549&x=2811.40625&y=3496.265625&zoom=0&res olution=1.05&z=5) B. Distribution of elements in fluorescence microscopy (https://search.kg.ebr ains.eu/instances/Dataset/ebfe2271-8868-4cd9-8ecd-f293e3a95bd9)

Novel developments in biomedical physics support coverage of a wide range of spatio-temporal resolution and sensitivity [1]. A methodology for building computational models based on two-dimensional histological images usually uses visual characteristics to perform image filtering and segmentation, as well as to link neighboring slices [2]. To select neurons of various types, other approaches can also be used, including chemical and genetic ones, which make it possible to present a computational model in a visual form [3]. But many effects have not been considered in detail for cases of intermediate scales and borderline areas.

For individual slices, basic parameters can be calculated for further spatial data processing. At the scale of individual cells, the following spatial characteristics of cells can be used: sizes of individual cells, and distances between cells (including those normalized by cell size). At the scale of cell populations, the following spatial characteristics of areas can be used:

- density of cells inside the area sections, which is equal to the number of cells divided by the areal size of sections;
- coverage coefficient, which is equal to the area occupied by cells divided by total areal size (in sections, or in the total slice);
- density distribution for individual sections within the entire slice.

2.2 Stable Ensembles and Their Surroundings

Extended regions, which are defined as stable ensembles, are composed of elements with similar functional properties. Similar processes, long in time and space, ensure the formation of such dynamically stable large ensembles with a self-sustaining configuration of their parameters. Elements of stable ensembles, as a rule, remain in place for a long time.

However, not all areas that are distinct after segmentation can be attributed to stable ensembles. Usually a region that has the properties of both ensembles appears on the border between two ensembles. This border area is unstable in its temporal and spatial characteristics; its stable elements migrate from place to place over time.

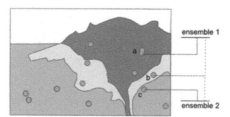

Fig. 2. Ensembles and their surroundings. The area of ensemble 1 (a) is shown in lilac, the intermediate area (b) is shown in beige, and the area of ensemble 2 (c) is shown in pear color. Elements of ensembles are shown in blue circles.

Figure 2 shows two ensembles and the boundary area between them. Elements of the boundary area have different functional properties.

3 Materials

As raw material, we used fluorescence microscopy datasets obtained from 23 mice *ex vivo*. Spatial analysis of the distribution of cells according to fluorescence microscopy datasets was performed based on data packages published in an open repository (https:// ebrains.eu). The data are all from male animals, on post-natal day 56. After perfusion-fixation, the brain was extracted and cleared using CLARITY/TDE [4]. These sets consisted of multi-page TIFF files. Each multi-page TIFF file included separate images - slices with dorsal or ventral projection of the whole volume brain. We used the Allen Mouse Common Coordinate Framework [5] to map data to spatial coordinates. Calculations were performed for the ranges of 10–100 nm. These ranges are typical for cells, ensembles, and agglomerations of cells [6].

Set 1 [7]: We studied whole-brain datasets from transgenic animals with different interneuron populations (parvalbumin, somatostatin, or vasoactive-intestinal peptide positive cells) which are labeled with fluorescent proteins. These datasets were obtained from 11 mice *ex vivo*. The data was represented in 48 multi-page TIFF files. Each multi-page TIFF included 288 slices with dorsal or ventral projections of the mouse brain. The data resolution is $10.4 \times 10.4 \times 10\,\mu$.

Set 2 [8]: We studied whole-brain datasets obtained using light-sheet microscopy in combination with tissue clearing. These datasets were obtained from 12 mice *ex vivo*. The data was represented in 14 multi-page TIFF files. Each multi-page TIFF included 800 slices with dorsal or ventral projections of the mice brain. The data resolution is $10 \times 10 \times 10\,\mu$.

4   Methods

Based on data from the light-sheet microscopy datasets, we identified the visual characteristics of elements in multi-page TIFF files, such as the density of surface fill and its distribution over the study area, the boundaries of distinct objects and object groups, and the boundaries between homogeneous areas. Individual elements were selected based on their brightness in grayscale mode. Frequently occurring patterns formed by individual elements were classified and found in other sets of images.

4.1   Step 1. Pre-calculation of Object Parameters

Operations: Selection of the boundaries of the individual elements and areas. Identification of characteristic dimensions of elements, characteristic distances between elements, and characteristic sizes of areas.

Input: single pages from multi-page TIFF files.

Output: *i)* selected elements (in the form of point objects) and areas (in the form of polygon objects) on pages (slices), *ii)* calculated typical sizes of elements and preliminary typical sizes of areas.

Individual "cell-like" elements were selected with the Extracts contour lines algorithm (see Sect. 4.5) by their characteristic sizes, distances between cells, and intensities of elements normalized to the background intensity. The interval between contour lines was set as 10 nm. A point was set at the location of the centroid of each identified cell. Long strips of noise were then cleared using a spatial query.

Based on a layer of individual cells, layers with the distribution of cells on the slices were built, and the density of distribution of elements on the slices was calculated.

Distinct homogeneous areas were selected using the calculation of the average density of the texture elements of the areas. Between selected areas with different textures, boundaries were constructed in the form of isolines. With the same applied average density parameters, typical "cell-agglomeration" objects were recognized as independent areal elements.

4.2 Step 2. Generalized Processing of Multi-page TIFF Files, Localization of Areas with Intense Activity

Operations: Generalized operations on all pages of multi-page TIFF files. Identification of characteristic distributions of density and intensity for zones.

Input: sets of multi-page TIFF files.

Output: summary layer with generalized zoning for each multi-page TIFF file (such a total output was done for each of the 48 + 12 sets of mice brain images).

The summary sheet generation and calculation of generalized indicators for all multi-page TIFF slices were performed using cell statistics (see Sect. 4.5).

The division of data into separate "intensity zones" was based on the following features:

– intensity of individual "cells" within a slice,
– boundaries of "intensity zones" (by intensity ranges) inside a slice,
– number and density of cells within the border of the "intensity zones".

Additional verification was performed using the Identifies segments tool (see Sect. 4.5). The result of segmentation is to obtain "slot areas", i.e. sets of points and areas, buffers which can be used for subsequent zonal operations.

4.3 Step 3. Calculation of Characteristics for Image Patterns

Operations: Calculation of ranges of values for selection of "samples" in images.

Input: zoned generalized layers.

Output: set of typical samples.

The selection of "samples" was based on the following features:

– shape and size of the "intensity zones",
– distribution of activity within "intensity zones", based on density of luminous elements,
– distribution of activity near the boundaries of "intensity zones",
– calculation of the "intensity zones" offset from slice to slice. As neighbors, sets of 20 slices were considered (this follows from the thickness of the slices and from the typical length).

4.4 Step 4. Classification with Calculated Training Data Features

Operations: Selection of "samples" according to the specified parameters in the images, and counting of "samples". Overlay of results on the atlas of the mouse brain [5], in order to determine into which zones "samples" most often fall.

Input: sets of typical samples.

Output: relation of samples to zones and to the coordinates of the mouse brain atlas.

The completed sets of samples, i.e. "ensembles-of-interest", make it possible to perform an analysis of activity, including:

- determining how the localization of a certain "sample" shifts from slice to slice within a single multi-page TIFF file,
- determining the location of a set of cells from a sample to the area of a specific structure of the mouse brain.

4.5 Applications for Spatial Analysis

In this work the data were processed using QGIS geoalgorithms (http://qgis.org); see Table 1 for details.

Table 1. Spatial data processing applications.

Plugin	Description
Extracts contour lines	Generate a vector contour from the input raster by joining points with the same parameters. Extracts contour lines from any GDAL-supported elevation raster
Nearest neighbor analysis	Performs nearest neighbor analysis for a point layer. The output tells how data are distributed (clustered, randomly or distributed)
Cell statistics	Computes per-cell statistics based on input raster layers and for each cell writes the resulting statistics to an output raster. At each cell location, the output value is defined as a function of all overlaid cell values of the input rasters
Heatmap	Creates a density (heatmap) raster of an input point vector layer using kernel density estimation The density is calculated based on the number of points in a location, with larger numbers of clustered points resulting in larger values
Identifies segments	i.segment - Identifies segments (objects) from imagery data
EnMAP-box classification	Classification with training data features

To create a reference layer, an image calculated as an average over a set of all slices was taken. Cell statistics were performed either on a set of all slices, or on a "test set" consisting of 20 slices. The reference layer parameter specifies an existing raster layer to use as a reference when creating the output raster.

5 Results

As a result of the calculations performed in Step 3, we selected and constructed six sets of typical samples for Set 1 and Set 2 with certain topological properties, on the basis of the density at the boundaries, the density inside the boundaries, and the shape type ("Areal Spot" or "MultiCurve"). The combined indicators typical for parameters of a certain type of area were revealed. The resulting Table 2 shows the ranges of parameters for configuring training samples.

Table 2. The ranges of parameters for configuring training samples ($p < .05$)

	Density inside (units per 100 square nanometers)	Boundary density (units per 100 square nanometers)	Linearity (as ratio of length to width)
Areal spot A	0.50 ± 0.05	0.60 ± 0.04	0.51 ± 0.05
Areal spot B	0.72 ± 0.07	0.59 ± 0.03	0.56 ± 0.05
Areal spot C	0.14 ± 0.01	0.44 ± 0.03	0.45 ± 0.05
Set of lines D	0.07 ± 0.02	n/a	0.18 ± 0.01
Set of lines E	0.10 ± 0.01	n/a	0.14 ± 0.01
Set of lines F	0.77 ± 0.05	n/a	0.07 ± 0.01

Using the methods of multi-factor analysis, it was found that the percent ratio differs significantly for different types of parameters considered in Table 2. All factors were checked in pairs against each other in the full record for the absence of dependence ($p < .05$).

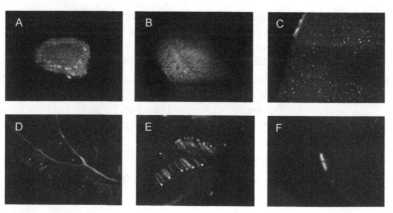

Fig. 3. Typical samples A – F in multi-page TIFF files (see text for details).

The patterns that are most consistently obtained are represented in Fig. 3: A – areal spot with high density at the boundaries, B – areal spot with high density inside the boundaries,

C – areal spot with low density inside the boundaries, D – fork lines, E – multiset of short lines, and F – single line.

6 Conclusion

In this work we demonstrated the usability of spatial data processing methods for pattern recognition and comparative analysis of fluorescence microscopy records. Geoinformation applications provide sets of options for processing topological properties of images, such as contouring and segmentation, identification of regions of interest, data classification, and training sample construction. We have shown that the application of the procedure for combining a group of cells into typical ensembles enriches the possibilities of brain image processing.

Such applied algorithms and methods can be used for data processing at an "intermediate scale" and in describing the specific characteristics of the distinctive regions formed near the borderlines of stable ensembles. In addition, for unstable ensembles, the effect of porosity of regions near borderlines can be shown.

Methods developed on the basis of the typical characteristics of structures, locations, and typical sizes of brain cells can be used in detection of different types of cells and their ensembles. Training samples can be applied to improve the accuracy of determining the spatial localization of elements in the brain.

References

1. Townsend, D., Cheng, Z., Georg, D., Drexler, W., Moser, E.: Grand challenges in biomedical physics. Front. Phys. **1** (2013)
2. Azevedo, L., Faustino, A.M.R., Tavares, J.M.R.S.: Segmentation and 3D reconstruction of animal tissues in histological images. In: Tavares, J.M.R.S., Natal Jorge, R.M. (eds.) Computational and Experimental Biomedical Sciences: Methods and Applications. LNCVB, vol. 21, pp. 193–207. Springer, Cham (2015). https://doi.org/10.1007/978-3-319-15799-3_14
3. Falcucci, R.M., Wertz, R., Green, J.L., Meucci, O., Salvino, J., Fontana, A.: Novel positive allosteric modulators of glutamate transport have neuroprotective properties in an in vitro excitotoxic model. ACS Chem. Neurosci. **10**, 3437–3453 (2019)
4. Costantini, I., Ghobril, J.-P., Di Giovanna, A.P., Mascaro, A., Silvestri, L., Müllenbroich, M.C., et al.: A versatile clearing agent for multi-modal brain imaging. Sci. Rep. **5**, 9808 (2015)
5. Wang, Q., Ding, S.-L., Li, Y., Royall, J., Feng, D., Lesnar, P., et al.: The Allen mouse brain common coordinate framework: a 3D reference atlas. Cell **181**, 936–953 (2020)
6. Bonsi, P., et al.: RGS9-2 rescues dopamine D2 receptor levels and signaling in DYT1 dystonia mouse models. EMBO Mol. Med. **11** (2019)
7. Silvestri, L., et al.: Whole brain images of selected neuronal types. Human Brain Project Neuroinform. Platform (2019). https://doi.org/10.25493/68S1-9R1
8. Silvestri, L., Di Giovanna, A.P., Mazzamuto, G.: Whole-brain images of different neuronal markers. Human Brain Project Neuroinform. Platform (2020). https://doi.org/10.25493/A0XN-XC1

Human Centred Computing

UED: A Unified Encoder Decoder Network for Visual Dialog

Cheng Chen and Xiaodong Gu[(⊠)] [ID]

Department of Electronic Engineering, Fudan University, Shanghai 200433, China
xdgu@fudan.edu.cn

Abstract. This paper addresses the problem of visual dialog, which aims to answer multi-round questions based on the dialog history and image content. This is a challenging task because a question may be answered in relations to any previous dialog and visual clues in image. Existing methods mainly focus on discriminative setting, which design various attention mechanisms to model interaction between answer candidates and multi-modal context. Despite having impressive results with attention based model for visual dialog, a universal encoder-decoder for both answer understanding and generation remains challenging. In this paper, we propose UED, a unified framework that exploits answer candidates to jointly train discriminative and generative tasks. UED is unified in that (1) it fully exploiting the interaction between different modalities to support answer ranking and generation in a single transformer based model, and (2) it uses the answers as anchors to facilitate both two settings. We evaluate the proposed UED on the VisDial dataset, where our model outperforms the state-of-the-art.

Keywords: Visual dialog · Cross modal learning · Encoder decoder network

1 Introduction

Visual dialog is recently introduced by Abhishek et al. [2]. Compared with visual question answering, it requires the agent to communicate with human about an image in multiple rounds.

Most of the current visual dialog model focus on modeling the interaction between answer candidates, current question, previous dialog history and image. Nevertheless, the answer candidates are invisible in generative setting, how to learn a unified model that can capture such interaction for both answer ranking and generation settings is a seldom explored territory.

In this work, we formulate the interaction of all entities in discriminative setting using a pretrained transformer. As shown in Fig. 1, in discriminative setting the agent infers whether the answer candidate is the correct one with the powerful representation yielded by fully attention of each entities. Inspired by the recent success of visual and language pretraining, transformer is employed

© Springer Nature Switzerland AG 2021
T. Mantoro et al. (Eds.): ICONIP 2021, CCIS 1517, pp. 101–109, 2021.
https://doi.org/10.1007/978-3-030-92310-5_12

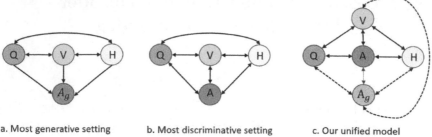

a. Most generative setting   b. Most discriminative setting   c. Our unified model

Fig. 1. Interaction flow direction illustration. Q: question, V: image, H: dialog history, A: answer candidates, A_g: generated answer.

as the encoding backbone as it has natural capability of capturing interaction between different entities from different modalities. As aforementioned, generative setting can only employ information contained in textual context and image to reconstruct the answer. As shown in Fig. 1, the interaction between generated answer and multi-modal context is unidirectional.

To leverage the discriminative clues in answer candidates for easing the difficulty of answer generation, we employ the answer candidates used in discriminative setting as anchor points to promote the bi-directional interaction between generated answer and other entities as shown in Fig. 1. Noted that, the attention flow from multi-modal to generated answer is explicit and the reverse attention is implicitly performed by anchor answer A. More specifically, a contrastive loss is devised to preserve the similarity of generated answer features and the target answer, while distinguishing other answer options. This also leads to the elegant view of how to bridge the discrepancy between discriminative and generative settings, and how to fully exploit the clues in answer candidates. The main contributions of this paper are as follows.

(1) We introduce a unified model for visual dialog, which processes all interactions between different entities for both discriminative and generative settings.
(2) The target answers is employed as anchor points to help both of the encoder and decoder for distinguishing the answer options with complex semantics. Compared to previous methods, the contrastive loss enables the bidirectional attention flow between all answer candidates and generated answer features to learn discriminative features for distinguishing the answers with complex semantics.
(3) Extensive experiments were performed on visual dialog benchmark [2], and the qualitative results indicate that our model obtains reliable improvement on both tasks by unified contrastive learning.

2   Proposed Method

2.1   Problem Formulation

We first formally describe the visual dialog problem. Given a question Q_t grounded on an image I at $t - th$ turn, as well as the previous dialog history formulated as $H_t = \{C; (Q1; A1), ..., (Q_{t-1}; A_{t-1})\}$ (where C denotes the caption sentence of the image), our task aims to predict the target answer A_t by ranking a list of 100 answer candidates $\{A_t^1, A_t^2..., A_t^{100}\}$ in discriminative setting or generate the required answer in generative setting.

2.2   Cross Modal Extractor Backbone

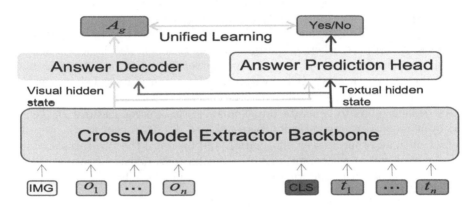

Fig. 2. The framework of our UED for unified generative and discriminative learning.

To jointly learn these the tasks in an end-to-end framework, ViLBERT [1] is adopted as the backbone network to extract cross modal features. ViLBERT is a two stream pretrained multi-modal network, which can jointly model visual and linguistic inputs by employing co-attention layers. Noted that, any pretrained multi-modal architecture can be adopted to our method. Following ViL-BERT, we embedded the visual and text sequence as $I = \{[IMG]O_1, ..., O_n\}$ and $D = \{[CLS]C[SEP]Q_1[SEP]A_1, ...Q_t[SEP]A_t[SEP]\}$, here I is object features extracted by Faster R-CNN. We feed the two sequences into ViLBERT and obtain output textual hidden state and visual hidden state as:

$$D_h, I_h = \text{ViLBERT}(D, I), \tag{1}$$

where $D_h = \{d_1, ..., d_t\}$ and $I_h = \{i_1, ..i_n\}$.

As ViLBERT contains multiple transformer blocks and cross attention blocks, the yielded feature D_h and I_h contains deep fused cross modal features.

2.3   Unified Learning of Two Tasks

Given the learned cross modal features D_h and I_h, we rank the answer candidates through the Next Sentence Prediction (NSP) loss.

The NSP loss is trained to predict 1 when the target answer A_t is appended, and 0 when a negative answer A_n sampled from other answer candidates is appended to it. To autoregressively generate an answer, we also train UED with the textual input with answer mask:

$$D_g = \{[CLS]C[SEP]Q_1[SEP]A_1, ...Q_t[SEP][MASK]\}, \qquad (2)$$

where the answer tokens is replaced by the special [MASK] token to make it blind to encoder. The hidden state yielded by ViLBERT D_g and I_h are fed to the decoder to generate the answer A_g.

To model the cross-impact and interaction between the two tasks, we enable the task-specific answer representations interact with each other via contrastive training. Specifically, the answer representations in discriminative setting is divided into two part, where the target answer representations A_p is regarded as positive query feature, and the negative answer representations together with all answer options in other dialog within a mini batch is regarded as negative key features $A_n = \{A_{n1}, ...A_{nn}\}$.

As decoder aims to generate target answer, the answer features A_g generated by it requires to semantically correspond to A_p. To encourage the decoder interact with all other answer information and optimize the two tasks simultaneously, we leverage the target answer as anchor and define a contrastive loss to transfer useful mutual information between two tasks. The contrastive loss is thus defined as:

$$L_c = \frac{exp(A_p \cdot A_g/\tau)}{\sum_{i=0}^{n-1} exp(A_p \cdot A_{ni}/\tau)}, \qquad (3)$$

where τ is a temperature parameter.

2.4   Visually Grounded Training Objectives

During the training of UED, We use two visually grounded training objectives masked language modeling (MLM) and next sentence prediction (NSP) to supervise the cross modal extractor backbone ViLBERT.

Similar to MLM in BERT, 10% tokens in textual input and 15% tokens in visual input are randomly masked out and replaced with a special token [MASK]. The model is required to recover them based not only on the surrounding tokens and the cross modal clues:

$$L_{mlm} = -E_{(D,I)\sim T}logP(W_m|D_{\backslash m}, I_{\backslash m}), \qquad (4)$$

where W_m is the masked tokens and T refers to the training set.

The NSP loss is implemented as:

$$L_{nsp} = -E_{(D,I)\sim T}logP(y|N(D,I)), \qquad (5)$$

where $y \in \{0,1\}$ serves as the supervision label, and $N()$ is the binary next sentence prediction head to predict the probability based on the dot product of [CLS] representation in text features and [IMG] representation in image features.

For the generative setting, the decoder is required to reconstruct the sequential target answer tokens depending on all the dialog context and input image. The loss is defined as maximum log-likelihood loss:

$$L_g = -E_{(D,I) \sim T} \log P(A|D_{\backslash A}, I), \tag{6}$$

The overall objective is expressed as:

$$L_{ued} = L_{mlm} + L_{nsp} + \alpha L_g + L_c, \tag{7}$$

where $\alpha = 0.05$ is the weighting parameter.

3   Experiments

3.1   Dataset

The VisDial v1.0 dataset is used in our experiments. It consists of 123,287 images in the training set, 2064 in the validation set, and 8,000 images in the testing set. Each image is associated with a caption sentence and 10 question answer pairs. For each round of question answer pair, 100 answer candidates are given.

3.2   Evaluation Metric

Following previous works [2,3], the ranking metrics like Recall@K (K = 1, 5, 10), Mean Reciprocal Rank (MRR), and Mean Rank is adopted. Since the 2018 VisDial challenge releases the dense annotations of each answer option's relevance degree, normalized discounted cumulative gain (NDCG) that penalizes the lowranked answer options with high relevance is also used.

3.3   Implementation Details

We use ViLBERT base as the backbone, which has 12 layers of transformer blocks with each block having a hidden state size of 768 and 12 attention heads. The decoder consists of 12 layers of transformer blocks, each block has hidden size of 1024 and 16 attention heads. The max text sequence length is 256. We train on 8 V100 GPUs with a batch size of 120 for 20 epochs. The Adam optimizer with initial learning rates of 2e-4 is adopted. A linear decay learning rate schedule with warm up is employed to train the model.

3.4   Comparison to State-of-the-Art Methods

We compare our method with recently published methods, including MN [2], FGA [3], CoAtt [4], HCIAE [5], ReDAN [6], LTMI [7], VDBERT [8], DAN [9], Synergistic [10], GNN [11]. Tables 1, and Table 2 summarize the results on the aforementioned benchmark. Follow previous works [2,4], comparison of the generative setting is performed on val split of the dataset. We select here MN, CoAtt, HCIAE, and ReDAN for comparison of generative setting, as their performances of both settings in all metrics are available in the literature. Among all evaluation metrics, our UED significantly outperforms other models, even including some ensemble variants such as Synergistic and ReDAN. Notably, our model significantly surpasses the state-of-arts by more than 1 points absolute improvements under the metrics Recall@1 in both discriminitive and generative settings. Moreover, the performance improvements under strict ranking metrics are more obvious (e.g., Recall@1, MRR).

As aforementioned, UED supports ranking the answer candidates and generating answer in a single pass, the two tasks are jointly trained by unified contrastive loss. As the results show, the generative setting surpasses the state of art by a large margin, which indicates the contrastive loss enables the decoder to perceive more discriminitive information from the rich answer candidates and our model is able to perform well in both task.

Table 1. Performance comparisons of discriminative setting on the test-std split of VisDial v1.0 dataset. The top 1 results are highlighted by **bold**.

Methods	R@1↑	R@5↑	R@10↑	NDCG↑	MRR↑	Mean↓
MN	40.98%	72.30%	83.30%	47.50	55.49	5.92
FGA	49.58%	80.97%	88.55%	52.10	63.70	4.51
GNN	47.33%	77.98%	87.83%	52.82	61.37	4.57
MN-Att	42.42%	74.00%	84.35%	49.58	56.90	5.59
ReDAN	42.45%	64.68%	75.68%	64.47	53.73	6.64
LTMI	50.20%	80.68%	90.35%	59.03	64.08	4.05
VDBERT	51.63%	82.23%	90.68%	59.96	65.44	3.90
DAN	49.63%	79.75%	89.35%	57.59	63.20	4.30
Synergistic	47.90%	80.43%	89.95%	57.32	62.20	4.17
Ours – UED	**51.73%**	**82.42%**	**91.13%**	**60.22**	**65.86**	**3.78**

Table 2. Performance comparisons of generative setting on the val-std split of VisDial v1.0 dataset. The top 1 results are highlighted by **bold**.

Methods	R@1 ↑	R@5↑	R@10↑	NDCG↑	MRR↑	Mean↓
MN	38.01%	57.49%	64.08%	56.99	47.83	18.76
CoAtt	40.09%	59.37%	65.92%	59.24	49.64	17.86
HCIAE	39.72%	58.23%	64.73%	59.70	49.07	18.43
ReDAN	40.27%	59.93%	66.78%	60.47	50.02	17.40
Ours – UED	**41.89%**	**61.07%**	**67.12%**	**61.21**	**51.11**	**17.12**

3.5   Ablation Studies

In this section, we perform ablation studies to evaluate the effects of different training settings. We first remove the decoder used for generative setting, and the results are shown in row 1. Comparing row 1 and row 4, it can be observed that training generative task brings improvements to ranking task.

In row 2, we vary the setting of decoder size. Specifically, a light decoder which has 8 layers of transformer blocks with each block having a hidden state size of 768 and 16 attention heads is adopted. The results shows that decoder size has little impact to the results. The reason is that decoder is not pretrained on large dataset.

The main characteristic of UED is the unified contrastive loss, which combines all answer candidates and generated answer to learn more useful clues. To study the impact of the contrastive loss alone, we train our UED without it and report the result in row 3. Comparing to the full model with contrastive loss (row 4), row 3 gets worse performance across the ranking metrics, which further verifies the effectiveness of contrastive loss. The full model UED gets highest results in all metrics.

Table 3. Ablation studies on the VisDial v1.0 dataset

Row	Methods	R@1↑	R@5↑	R@10↑	NDCG↑	MRR↑	Mean↓
1	UED-w/o-decoder	53.58%	83.86%	91.93%	60.02	64.79	3.83
2	UED-lidecoder	53.92%	84.08%	92.08%	60.86	64.97	3.81
3	UED-w/o-L_c	53.78%	83.98%	92.06%	60.02	64.88	3.88
4	**Ours – UED**	**54.08%**	**84.32%**	**92.31%**	**61.06**	**65.48**	**3.71**

3.6   Qualitative Result

We illustrate some qualitative examples of our UED in Fig. 3. Evidently, training with contrastive loss can produce more accurate result. Unified training of two tasks helps our model distinguish the target answer from the answers with similar semantics with the ground truth answer. It is very difficult for the model to predict the answer without proper reference to the visual information. As

Q1: Is there any person in the scene?
A1: Yes, there is one.
Q2: What is he doing?
A2: He is playing with the cat and dog. (GT)

1. He is playing with the cat.
2. He is playing with the cat and dog. (GT)
3. Not that i can see.
4. I cannot tell.

Base Model

1. He is playing with the cat and dog. (GT)
2. Not that i can see.
3. He is playing with the cat.
4. I cannot tell.

W/Unified Learning

Fig. 3. The effects of unified learning of two tasks in our UED.

our model exploits rich information from all answer candidates and generated answer. It performs better than the baseline.

4 Conclusion

In this paper, we study the problem of visual dialog. A unified transformer model UED that exploits the answers as anchor points to jointly train discriminitive and generative tasks. UED is capable of modeling all the interactions between all answer candidates and the generated answer to supervise the training of two tasks via simple unified contrastive learning. Moreover, it can rank or generate answers seamlessly in one single pass, and the training of two tasks is simultaneous. Experiments on visual dialog benchmark show the effectiveness of the proposed model, and more extensive ablation studies further confirm the correlation between two tasks and reveal that modeling the relations explicitly by employing answers as anchor points can improve their performance.

Acknowledgments. This work was supported in part by National Natural Science Foundation of China under grant 61771145.

References

1. Lu, J., Batra, D., Parikh, D., Lee, S.: ViLBERT: pretraining task-agnostic visiolinguistic representations for vision and-language tasks. In: 2019 Advance in Neural Information Processing Systems (NIPS), pp. 524–534. MIT Press, Vancouver, CA (2019)
2. Das, A., et al.: Visual dialog. In: Proceedings of the IEEE Conference on Computer Vision and Pattern Recognition, pp. 326–335. IEEE, Honolulu, HI (2017)
3. Schwartz, I., Yu, S., Hazan, T., Schwing, A.G.: Factor graph attention. In: Proceedings of the IEEE Conference on Computer Vision and Pattern Recognition, pp. 2039–2048. IEEE, Long Beach, CA (2019)
4. Wu, Q., Wang, P., Shen, C., Reid, I., van den Hengel, A.: Are you talking to me? Reasoned visual dialog generation through adversarial learning. In: Proceedings of the IEEE Conference on Computer Vision and Pattern Recognition, pp. 6106–6115. IEEE, Salt Lake City, Utah (2018)
5. Lu, J., Kannan, A., Yang, J., Parikh, D., Batra, D.: Best of both worlds: transferring knowledge from discriminative learning to a generative visual dialog model. In: Advances in Neural Information Processing Systems, pp. 314–324. MIT press, California, USA (2017)
6. Gan, Z., Cheng, Y., Kholy, A.E., Li, L., Liu, J., Gao, J.: Multi-step reasoning via recurrent dual attention for visual dialog. In: Proceedings of the Conference of the Association for Computational Linguistics, pp. 6463–6474. ACL, Florence, ITA (2019)
7. Nguyen, V.-Q., Suganuma, M., Okatani, T.: Efficient attention mechanism for visual dialog that can handle all the interactions between multiple inputs. In: Vedaldi, A., Bischof, H., Brox, T., Frahm, J.-M. (eds.) ECCV 2020. LNCS, vol. 12369, pp. 223–240. Springer, Cham (2020). https://doi.org/10.1007/978-3-030-58586-0_14

8. Wang, Y., Joty, S., Lyu, M.R., King, I., Xiong, C., Hoi, S.C.: VD-BERT: a unified vision and dialog transformer with BERT. In: 2020 ACL Conference on Empirical Methods in Natural Language Processing (EMNLP), pp. 3325–3338. ACL (2020)
9. Kang, G.C., Lim, J., Zhang, B.T.: Dual attention networks for visual reference resolution in visual dialog. In: Proceedings of the Conference on Empirical Methods in Natural Language Processing, pp. 2024–2033. ACL, Hong Kong (2019)
10. Guo, D., Xu, C., Tao, D.: Image-question-answer synergistic network for visual dialog. In: Proceedings of the IEEE Conference on Computer Vision and Pattern Recognition, pp. 10434–10443. IEEE, Long Beach, CA (2019)
11. Zheng, Z., Wang, W., Qi, S., Zhu, S.C.: Reasoning visual dialogs with structural and partial observations. In: Proceedings of the IEEE Conference on Computer Vision and Pattern Recognition, pp. 6669–6678. IEEE, Long Beach, CA (2019)

Exploring Effective Speech Representation via ASR for High-Quality End-to-End Multispeaker TTS

Dawei Liu[1], Longbiao Wang[1(✉)] ⓘ, Sheng Li[2(✉)] ⓘ, Haoyu Li[3],
Chenchen Ding[2], Ju Zhang[4], and Jianwu Dang[1,5] ⓘ

[1] Tianjin Key Laboratory of Cognitive Computing and Application,
College of Intelligence and Computing, Tianjin University, Tianjin, China
{daveliu,longbiao_wang}@tju.edu.cn
[2] National Institute of Information and Communications Technology, Kyoto, Japan
sheng.li@nict.go.jp
[3] National Institute of Informatics (NII), Tokyo, Japan
[4] Huiyan Technology (Tianjin) Co., Ltd., Tianjin, China
[5] Japan Advanced Institute of Science and Technology, Ishikawa, Japan

Abstract. The quality of multispeaker text-to-speech (TTS) is composed of speech naturalness and speaker similarity. The current multispeaker TTS based on speaker embeddings extracted by speaker verification (SV) or speaker recognition (SR) models has made significant progress in speaker similarity of synthesized speech. SV/SR tasks build the speaker space based on the differences between speakers in the training set and thus extract speaker embeddings that can improve speaker similarity; however, they deteriorate the naturalness of synthetic speech since such embeddings lost speech dynamics to some extent. Unlike SV/SR-based systems, the automatic speech recognition (ASR) encoder outputs contain relatively complete speech information, such as speaker information, timbre, and prosody. Therefore, we propose an ASR-based synthesis framework to extract speech embeddings using an ASR encoder to improve multispeaker TTS quality, especially for speech naturalness. To enable the ASR system to learn the speaker characteristics better, we explicitly feed the speaker-id to the training label. The experimental results show that the speech embeddings extracted by the proposed method have good speaker characteristics and beneficial acoustic information for speech naturalness. The proposed method significantly improves the naturalness and similarity of multispeaker TTS.

Keywords: Speech synthesis · End-to-end model · Speech embedding · Speech recognition

1 Introduction

In recent years, end-to-end speech synthesis [1–3] has achieved significant progress. An increasing number of researchers have started to explore how to

© Springer Nature Switzerland AG 2021
T. Mantoro et al. (Eds.): ICONIP 2021, CCIS 1517, pp. 110–118, 2021.
https://doi.org/10.1007/978-3-030-92310-5_13

synthesize high-quality speech using a small amount of target speakers' speech, just minutes or even seconds. The ultimate goal of multispeaker text-to-speech (TTS) tasks is to solve the above problem.

The most straightforward approach for multispeaker TTS is to fine-tune the pretrained model directly using target speakers' data [4,5], but it is limited by the size of the target speakers' data. Another practical approach is to use speaker embedding. Previous studies have trained speaker embedding networks jointly with the end-to-end TTS model [4,6]. This means that speaker embedding networks and the TTS model are trained on the same datasets. However, speaker embedding networks and the TTS model have different requirements for datasets: the former requires a vast number of speakers in the training data, whereas the latter requires high-quality training data for each speaker. Therefore, some researchers have proposed training the speaker embedding networks separately [7,8], and then, they can be trained on more data regardless of speech quality. Speaker verification or speaker recognition (SV/SR) systems are currently widely used to extract the speaker embedding for multispeaker TTS [7–9]. [8] extracted the d-vector from the SV system as the speaker embedding, and the model can synthesize unseen target speakers' speech with only seconds of reference audio. [7] investigated two state-of-the-art speaker embeddings (x-vector and learnable dictionary encoding) to obtain high-quality synthesized speech. [9] used the traditional SR network as the speaker encoder to extract the embedding for cross-lingual multispeaker TTS.

Although the current multispeaker TTS [7–9] mentioned above has made remarkable progress, it still has substantial room for improvement. First, the objective of SV/SR tasks is to discriminate the speakers. The speaker embeddings extracted by the SV/SR model can improve the speaker similarity in general but ignore the dynamic properties of speech. The lack of the dynamic information related with the speaker might damage the quality of multispeaker TTS. Second, the speaker embedding extraction methods are borrowed from SV/SR tasks, making the development of multispeaker TTS depend on SV/SR tasks. More novel and practical approaches should be explored.

Unlike the above drawbacks of using an SV/SR system, the speech representations extracted from automatic speech recognition (ASR) include relatively more complete speech information. In this study, (1) we propose novel speaker embeddings extracted from a transformer-based ASR system to improve the multispeaker TTS quality instead of using an SV/SR system. (2) This ASR system is specially trained since the ASR task eliminated the speaker's characteristics in the network. To compensate for the speaker information loss, we explicitly added the speaker-id to the label in training so that the system would preserve the speaker's characteristics. Experiments show the proposed method can effectively improve the naturalness of synthesized speech without any loss of similarity compared with the conventional SV-based method.

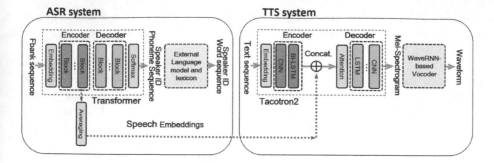

Fig. 1. Framework of our proposed model.

2 Exploring Effective Speech Representation via ASR for High-Quality End-to-End Multispeaker TTS

In this paper, we use ASR's encoder module to extract speech embeddings for multispeaker TTS. This approach avoids the problem encountered with speaker embeddings extracted by the SV/SR-based method that can only improve the speaker similarity but lack a positive influence on speech naturalness. Li et al. [10] used the TTS model to show that speaker information is relatively complete before the ASR decoder, but it decreases linearly as the layers of the encoder become deeper. This discovery indicates that although the ASR task eliminated the speaker characteristics, the ASR system still preserves them. In this paper, we explicitly feed the speaker-id to the label during transformer-based ASR model training so that we can more effectively preserve the speaker characteristics [11].

Although there have been existing works that integrate ASR and TTS models, our proposed method lies in none of these following categories. Recent studies have shown that jointly training ASR and TTS using cycle-consistency training [12] or autoencoders [13] can substantially improve ASR systems. [14] proposed a machine speech chain with semisupervised learning and improved ASR-TTS performance by training each other using only unpaired data. Tjandra et al.[15] used a SR model to let TTS synthesize unseen speakers' speech and further improve ASR.

The framework of the proposed method is shown in Fig. 1. The proposed system comprises two components: the transformer-based ASR model and the multispeaker TTS system based on Tacotron2 and the WaveRNN vocoder. We first train the Transformer-based ASR model, and then use it to extract speech embedding for multispeaker TTS. As described in Fig. 1, we extract 512-dimensional speech embeddings from the encoder of the transformer-based ASR model and concatenate these speech embedding to the outputs of the TTS encoder (512-dim); then, the augmented results (1024-dim) are input into the TTS attention module. The audio samples are available online[1].

---

[1] https://daveliuabc.github.io/multispeaker-demo/.

2.1 Transformer-Based End-to-End ASR Systems

We used the implementation of the transformer-based neural machine translation (NMT-Transformer) [16] in tensor2tensor[2] for all our experiments. The feature settings are the same as in our previous work [11].

We used 69 English phones[3] as the modeling unit. An external decoding process with lexicon and language models from LibriSpeech transcriptions is used to generate word-level recognition results. The speaker-id was explicitly added as the label during training [11,16]. We feed speaker-ids as the ground truth in training, and the combinations of speaker attributes (e.g., <SPK>) are inserted at the beginning of the label of the training utterances. The training labels are organized as "<SPK-1001> labels </S>". The network is trained to output them at the beginning of decoding automatically, so we do not have to prepare classifiers for these attributes.

2.2 Multispeaker TTS Systems

We based the end-to-end multispeaker TTS model architecture on Tacotron2 [3][4]. In multispeaker TTS, the input text sequences are converted to fixed-dimensional character embeddings, and then, the character embeddings pass through convolutional neural network (CNN) layers and the BLSTM layer to generate fixed-dimensional encoder outputs. We concatenate the embeddings extracted from the trained transformer-based ASR model with the fixed-dimensional output of the multispeaker TTS encoder and then input it to the location-sensitive attention module of the multispeaker TTS. The multispeaker TTS decoder can predict an 80-dimensional Mel-spectrogram. We used WaveRNN [17][5] as the multispeaker TTS vocoder, which converts the synthesized 80-dimensional Mel-spectrogram into time-domain waveforms.

3 Experimental Setup

3.1 Data Description

We trained the ASR model and the synthesizer of multispeaker TTS using 100 h of LibriSpeech [18] data (train-clean-100) and trained the vocoder using VCTK [19] datasets. All of them were trained separately. The LibriSpeech data (test-clean) were used to test the ASR model and multispeaker TTS.

---

[2] https://github.com/tensorflow/tensor2tensor.

[3] We train the phone-level ASR system to extract the phonetic posteriorgram (PPG) feature for TTS in the future.

[4] https://github.com/CorentinJ/Real-Time-Voice-Cloning.

[5] https://github.com/mkotha/WaveRNN.

3.2   ASR Models

Two ASR models required for embedding extraction were trained on the same LibriSpeech train-clean-100 but with different multitask training methods following [11,16]. These models and their performance on test-clean are as follows:

1. ASR_{ori}: trained using the original label. Rescored with an external trigram language model from all LibriSpeech transcripts, the WER% was approximately 9.0% after language model rescoring.
2. ASR_{spk}: trained using multitask training with the speaker-id and label. The WER% was approximately 9.0% after language model rescoring.

We randomly selected seven speakers from train-clean-100 and test-clean and randomly selected 30 voices for each speaker. We used ASR_{ori} and ASR_{spk} models to extract speech embeddings and used uniform manifold approximation and projection (UMAP) to visualize the extracted speech embeddings. The visualization results are shown in Fig. 2. Through visualization, it can be found that the proposed ASR_{spk} model can extract effective speaker information not only for seen speakers (train-clean-100) but also for the unseen speakers (test-clean). There were only 251 speakers in the training set (train-clean-100), so the speaker information contained in the unseen speaker's speech embeddings extracted using the ASR_{spk} model was encouraging.

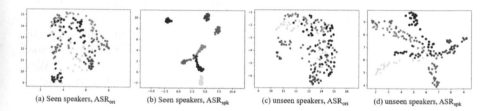

(a) Seen speakers, ASR_{ori} (b) Seen speakers, ASR_{spk} (c) unseen speakers, ASR_{ori} (d) unseen speakers, ASR_{spk}

Fig. 2. Different E2E ASR models' speech embedding distributions by UMAP on selected data (seen from the training set, unseen from the testing set).

3.3   Multispeaker TTS System

We trained the synthesizer and vocoder separately, and used the same synthesizer and vocoder in all the experiments. We trained the synthesizer based on the original LibriSpeech train-clean-100 datasets and embeddings from the above two models (ASR_{ori} and ASR_{spk}).

We trained the vocoder based on VCTK datasets. We refer to the TTS systems according to the different ASR embedding sources: **ASR_{ori}-TTS** and **ASR_{spk}-TTS**. Simultaneously, we trained the synthesis model in [8](See Footnote 4) on the original LibriSpeech train-clean-100 datasets as a baseline that was referred to **Baseline(replica [8])**. The speaker encoder of the model maps a sequence of Mel-spectrograms to a d-vector and uses a generalized end-to-end SV loss [20,21].

3.4   Evaluation Metrics

The evaluations for the multispeaker TTS task comprise subjective and objective evaluations. The subjective evaluation metrics use the mean opinion score (MOS) for naturalness and the differential MOS (DMOS) [22] score for similarity. As metrics for the objective evaluation, acc% is used for SV, which is the ratio of the number of testing pairs identified as the same speaker over the total number of testing pairs, and the word recognition error rate (WER%) for the ASR task. All experiments were conducted on public datasets.

Subjective Evaluation. The same 25 listeners provided the MOS and DMOS scores. The listeners come from a professional team, and all of them have been learning English for more than ten years, while nineteen of them have majored in English. They used headphones for listening tests. For the naturalness evaluation, all listeners completed 56 audio tasks. Additionally, for the similarity evaluation, all listeners completed 100 pairs of audio tasks. The definitions of MOS and DMOS are as follows:

1. The MOS evaluates the naturalness of synthesized speech and reference audio from the target speakers with rating scores from 1 to 5, where 1 is the poorest result to understand, and 5 is the best result, with 0.5-point increments for each level.
2. The DMOS is used to evaluate the similarity between synthesized audio and reference audio subjectively: 1 (from a different speaker, sure), 2 (from a different speaker, not sure), 3 (from the same speaker, not sure), and 4 (from the same speaker, sure).

Objective Evaluation. The value of acc% from the ResCNN-based SV system [23], which was trained on VoxCeleb2 datasets, was used to evaluate similarity as the objective evaluation of the multispeaker TTS task. Every model provided 90 pairs of audio for testing seen speakers and 200 pairs for testing unseen speakers.

4   Experimental Results

4.1   Subjective Evaluation

The experimental results are listed in Table 1. The embedding extracted by ASR contained relatively complete speech information, such as speaker information and timbre. Therefore, compared with the baseline (replica [8]), all the proposed systems (ASR_{ori}-TTS and ASR_{spk}-TTS) achieved significant improvement in naturalness, whereas the similarity did not decrease (at least for ASR_{ori}-TTS). In Table 1, the randomly selected reference audio sometimes contains plenty of prosody and emotion, leading to a slightly higher MOS score for the unseen speaker than for the seen speaker. The work in [8] obtained similar experimental results on the same dataset. The naturalness' improvement of synthesized speech leads to a DMOS score of unseen speakers that is slightly higher than that of seen speakers. Table 1 shows that ASR_{ori}-TTS has slightly better speaker similarity

Table 1. Naturalness and similarity for multispeaker TTS. (95% confidence interval)

	Naturalness (MOS)		Similarity (DMOS)	
	Seen	Unseen	Seen	Unseen
Ground truth	4.53 ± 0.26	4.51 ± 0.23	3.38 ± 0.29	3.58 ± 0.84
Baseline (replica [8])	2.60 ± 0.57	3.11 ± 0.31	1.89 ± 0.24	2.01 ± 0.29
ASR_{ori}-TTS	3.12 ± 0.52	3.47 ± 0.27	1.90 ± 0.21	2.10 ± 0.23
ASR_{spk}-TTS	3.57 ± 0.25	3.82 ± 0.25	1.96 ± 0.22	1.93 ± 0.28

Table 2. SV Performance (acc%) as the objective evaluation of multispeaker TTS.

	Seen	Unseen
Ground truth	100%	100%
Baseline (replica [8])	57.78%	18.00%
ASR_{ori}-TTS	65.56%	26.00%
ASR_{spk}-TTS	91.11%	52.00%

than the baseline (replica [8]). For ASR_{spk}-TTS, the seen speakers achieve a higher DMOS score. This result proves the effectiveness of explicitly feeding the speaker-id as the label during training. The DMOS score on unseen speakers obtained by ASR_{spk}-TTS may reflect the shortcoming where we did not give speaker information expected by the system.

4.2 Objective Evaluation

The experimental results are listed in Table 2. The experimental results show that the proposed ASR_{spk}-TTS model achieved the best results, effectively surpassing the baseline model (replica [8]) for both seen and unseen speakers. The low scores for the baseline (replica [8]) were caused by the small number of speakers in the training datasets, which caused the speaker encoder network of the baseline [8] to fail to learn useful speaker embedding. Although the proposed ASR_{spk}-TTS model achieved good results, there was still a gap between seen and unseen speakers. The reason is that there are only 251 speakers in the training set, which may have caused a problem in the proposed method's construction of the speaker embedding space. Moreover, the slight drop in similarity scores in the subjective evaluation in Table 1 may have been caused by this.

4.3 Further Analysis

The proposed ASR_{ori} and ASR_{spk} models almost achieved the best and second-best performance (highlighted in gray and light gray, respectively) on both objective and subjective tasks compared with the baseline (replica [8]). In Subsect. 3.2, we also noticed that the recognition performance of these two models is almost identical. As pointed out in previous work [10], speaker information is relatively complete before the ASR decoder, but the ASR task eliminated the speaker's characteristics in the network. To compensate for this fact, we explicitly added the speaker-id to the label in training so that the system would learn the speaker's characteristics. For this reason, the current task (extracting the speech embedding) can benefit from it. This is an interesting topic that merits an in-depth investigation in the future.

In real applications, TTS is integrated with ASR systems for complex tasks, such as speech-to-speech translation or dialogue systems, such as Amazon Alex, Microsoft Cortana, Apple Siri, and Google Translation. Inspired by this approach, the proposed method saves the development cost of training additional SV/SR systems on data containing many speakers.

The speech chain [24] and motor theory indicated that human speech production and perception functions evolve and develop together, sharing the same speech gestures in speech communication [25, 26]. ASR and TTS are the inverse tasks of each other, and this paper reveals a close relation between ASR and TTS, which can help us design the next generation of speech applications. Human can recognize linguistic information meanwhile can preserve the speaker information, vice versa. In the current situation, however, either ASR or SV/SR cannot replicate this function. This is a topic worth investigating in the future.

5   Conclusion

This paper proposed a novel method to extract more effective speech representations from a transformer-based ASR model to improve the naturalness and similarity of multispeaker TTS. Compared with the traditional method, the proposed method does not rely on an individual SV/SR system. To enable the ASR system to learn more speaker characteristics, we explicitly added the speaker-id to the training label. Experiments showed that the proposed method almost achieved the best performance on both objective and subjective tasks. Because TTS is always integrated with ASR systems for complex tasks, such as a multispeaker speech chain, the proposed method reduces the development cost caused by integrating an additional SV/SR model.

Acknowledgment. This work was supported in part by the National Natural Science Foundation of China under Grant 61771333, NICT International Funding, and JSPS KAKENHI Grant No. 21K17837. We thank Prof. Zhenhua Ling of the University of Science and Technology of China for useful discussions.

References

1. Arik, S., et al.: Deep voice: real-time neural text-to-speech. In: Proceedings of ICML, pp. 264–273 (2017)
2. Ren, Y., et al.: Fastspeech: fast, robust and controllable text to speech. In: Advances in Neural Information Processing Systems (2019)
3. Shen, J., et al.: Natural TTS synthesis by conditioning WaveNet on Mel spectrogram predictions. In: Proceedings of ICASSP, pp. 4779–4783 (2018)

4. Chen, Y., et al.: Sample efficient adaptive text-to-speech. In: Proceedings of ICLR (2019)

5. Kons, Z., et al.: High quality, lightweight and adaptable TTS using LPCNet. In: Proceedings of INTERSPEECH, pp. 176–180 (2019)

6. Nachmani, E., et al.: Fitting new speakers based on a short untranscribed sample. In: Proceedings of ICML, pp. 5932–5940 (2018)

7. Cooper, E., et al.: Zero-shot multi-speaker text-to-speech with state-of-the-art neural speaker embeddings. In: Proceedings of ICASSP, pp. 6184–6188 (2020)

8. Jia, Y., et al.: Transfer learning from speaker verification to multispeaker text-to-speech synthesis. In: Advances in Neural Information Processing Systems, pp. 4480–4490 (2018)

9. Chen, M., et al.: Cross-lingual, multi-speaker text-to-speech synthesis using neural speaker embedding. In: Proceedings of INTERSPEECH, pp. 2105–2109 (2019)

10. Li, C., et al.: What does a network layer hear? Analyzing hidden representations of end-to-end ASR through speech synthesis. In: Proceedings of ICASSP, pp. 6434–6438 (2020)

11. Li, S., et al.: Improving transformer-based speech recognition systems with compressed structure and speech attributes augmentation. In: Proceedings of INTERSPEECH, pp. 1408–1412 (2019)

12. Hori, T., et al.: Cycle-consistency training for end-to-end speech recognition. In: Proceedings of ICASSP, pp. 6271–6275 (2019)

13. Karita, S., et al.: Semi-supervised end-to-end speech recognition using text-to-speech and autoencoders. In: Proceedings of ICASSP, pp. 6166–6170 (2019)

14. Tjandra, A., et al.: Listening while speaking: speech chain by deep learning. In: Proceedings of ASRU, pp. 301–308 (2017)

15. Tjandra, A., et al.: Machine speech chain with one-shot speaker adaptation. In: Proceedings of INTERSPEECH, pp. 887–891 (2018)

16. Vaswani, A., et al.: Attention is all you need. CoRR abs/1706.03762 (2017)

17. Kalchbrenner, N., et al.: Efficient neural audio synthesis. In: Proceedings of ICML, pp. 3775–3784 (2018)

18. Panayotov, V., et al.: Librispeech: an ASR corpus based on public domain audio books. In: Proceedings of ICASSP, pp. 5206–5210 (2015)

19. Yamagishi, J., et al.: CSTR VCTK Corpus: English multi-speaker corpus for CSTR voice cloning toolkit (version 0.92) (2019). https://doi.org/10.7488/ds/2645

20. Wan, L., et al.: Generalized end-to-end loss for speaker verification. In: Proceedings of ICASSP, pp. 4879–4883 (2018)

21. Paul, D., et al.: Speaker conditional WaveRNN: towards universal neural vocoder for unseen speaker and recording conditions. In: Proceedings of INTERSPEECH (2020)

22. Lorenzo-Trueba, J., et al.: The voice conversion challenge 2018: Promoting development of parallel and nonparallel methods. In: Odyssey 2018 The Speaker and Language Recognition Workshop (2018)

23. Zhou, D., et al.: Dynamic margin softmax loss for speaker verification. In: Proceedings of INTERSPEECH (2020)

24. Denes, P., Pinson, E.: The Speech Chain, 2nd edn. Worth Publisher, New York (1993)

25. Kashino, M.: The motor theory of speech perception: its history, progress and perspective (Japanese). Acoust. Sci. Tech. 62(5), 391–396 (2006)

26. Liberman, A., Mattingly, I.: The motor theory of speech perception revised. Cognition 21, 1–36 (1985)

A SSA-Based Attention-BiLSTM Model for COVID-19 Prediction

Shuqi An, Shuyu Chen$^{(\boxtimes)}$, Xiaohan Yuan, Lu Yuwen, and Sha Mei

School of Big Data and Software Engineering, Chongqing University,
Chongqing, China
{shuqian,sychen,xhyuan,luyuwen,shamei}@cqu.edu.cn

Abstract. The Corona Virus Disease 2019 (COVID-19) has widely spread over the world and comes up with new challenges to the research community. Accurately predicting the number of new infections is essential for optimizing available resources and slowing the progression of such diseases. Long short-term memory network (LSTM) is a typical method for COVID-19 prediction in deep learning, but it is difficult to extract potentially important features in time series effectively. Thus, we proposed a Bidirectional LSTM (BiLSTM) model based on the attention mechanism (ATT) and used the Sparrow Search Algorithm (SSA) for parameter tuning, to predict the daily new cases of COVID-19. We capture the information in the past and future through the BiLSTM network and apply the attention mechanism to assign different weights to the hidden state of BiLSTM, enhance the ability of the model to learn vital information, and use the SSA to optimize the critical parameters of the model for matching the characteristics of COVID-19 data, enhance the interpretability of the model parameters. This study is based on daily confirmed cases collected from six countries: Egypt, Ireland, Iran, Japan, Russia, and the UK. The experimental results show that our proposed model has the best predictive performance among all the comparison models.

Keywords: COVID-19 · Attention mechanism · BiLSTM · Sparrow search algorithm

1 Introduction

In order to prevent and control this epidemic, people have introduced various modeling and prediction methods to predict the evolution of the infection cases, such as the Susceptible-Infected-Recovered (SIR) model [1], the Susceptible-Exposed-Infected-Removed (SEIR) model, and the Autoregressive Integrated Moving Average model (ARIMA) [2], to simulate the speed and route of the

Supported by National Natural Science Foundation of China (No. 61572090), Chongqing Science and Technology Project (No. cstc2018jscx-mszdX0109), and the Fundamental Research Funds for the Central Universities (No. 2020CDJYGRH-YJ04).

T. Mantoro et al. (Eds.): ICONIP 2021, CCIS 1517, pp. 119–126, 2021.
https://doi.org/10.1007/978-3-030-92310-5_14

spread of COVID-19 in the population. But the uncertainty of the transmission route of COVID-19 has led to limitations in traditional mathematical models. Deep learning can also predict the spread of infectious diseases, we use the deep learning model to train the data and find its intrinsic relationship to make time-series predictions. LSTM and ARIMA models were used to predict the total number of COVID-19 cases in multiple countries respectively [7], the experimental results have confirmed that the deep learning model has better results. A biologically heuristic LSTM model (LSTM-COVA) was proposed in [8], the author applied the LSTM-COVA model to predict daily new cases of COVID-19. A hybrid AI intelligent model is proposed in [4], which proposed an improved susceptible infected (ISI) model to predict the changes of the infection rate. To effectively extract potential features in the sequence, we combined the attention mechanism with the neural network. A multi-channel LSTM and attention mechanism is utilized in [5] to predict the number of Guangzhou flu infections. A multistage attention network was proposed in [9], which could capture the mutation information in a sequence to obtain a more accurate prediction. Like other neural network models, some parameters of the neural network model directly control the network model's topology. The sparrow search algorithm [6] in the swarm intelligence algorithm has the characteristics of fewer parameters to be adjusted and stronger optimization ability. It has been applied in many fields, therefore, we choose this algorithm to select the optimal parameters of our model to improve the prediction efficiency.

2   Methods and Models

2.1   LSTM and BiLSTM

The Recurrent Neural Network (RNN) network [10] can memory historical information and apply the information to the current output, so people often used RNN in time series prediction, but it cannot deal with long-term dependence effectively. Therefore, long and short-term memory (LSTM) introduces a gating mechanism to solve this problem. LSTM comprises three gates: input gate (i), forget gate (f), output gate (o).

$$f_t = \sigma(W_f[h_{t-1}, x_t] + b_f) \tag{1}$$

$$i_t = \sigma(W_f[h_{t-1}, x_t] + b_i) \tag{2}$$

$$C_t' = tanh(W_c[h_{t-1}, x_t] + b_c) \tag{3}$$

$$C_t = f_t * C_{t-1} + i_t * C_t' \tag{4}$$

$$O_t = \sigma(W_o[h_{t-1}, x_{t-1}] + b_o) \tag{5}$$

$$h_t = O_t * tanh(C_t) \tag{6}$$

$$y_t = W_y h_t + b_y \tag{7}$$

In the above equations from (1) to (7), i_t and C'_t together represent the input gate, while C_t and C_{t-1} denote the current and previous cell states, respectively. O_t and h_t together form the output gate, while the hidden layer h_t signifies the output through the output gate at the current time; W_f, W_i, W_c, W_o, and W_y respectively represent the weight matrix of the forget gate, input gate, current cell state, output gate, and output layer, while b_f, b_c, b_o, b_y represent their corresponding deviation vectors; $\sigma(x)$ and $\tanh(x)$ respectively represent the *Sigmoid* and *Tanh* activation functions.

Bi-directional Long and Short-term Memory network (BiLSTM) [3] applied in natural language processing firstly, it can capture the two-way semantic dependence. BiLSTM comprises two LSTM layers, the forward LSTM layer and the backward LSTM layer [11]. Therefore, compared to LSTM, it can learn both forward and backward information at the same time, it can solve the problem of the loss of prediction accuracy caused by random fluctuations in traditional time series prediction.

2.2 Attentional Mechanism

In the neural network model, the attention mechanism [12] is a resource allocation mechanism that can allocate computing resources into the tasks more critical. The attention mechanism selectively learns the intermediate results of the training model and then assigns different weights to these intermediate results to associate the output sequence with these intermediate results. Combine the attention mechanism with the neural network model can make the model focus on the important information in time series and reduce its attention to other useless information.

Figure 1(a) shows the structure of the attention mechanism, where x_t represents the input data, h_t denotes the output of the data after training by the neural network layer, α_t signifies the value of weight assigned by the attention mechanism to h_t. Figure 1(b) illustrates the structure of the ATT-BiLSTM model. In this model, x_t represents the input data, BiLSTM layer receives the data and performs bidirectional learning. The output vector h_t is trained by the BiLSTM network layer input to the attention layer, and calculate the probability corresponding to each eigenvector according to the weight distribution, and iterative to obtain a better weight parameter matrix. The output layer calculates the output Y through the fully connected layer.

2.3 Sparrow Search Algorithm

The sparrow search algorithm (SSA) is a relatively new swarm intelligence heuristic algorithm proposed in 2020 [6]. According to the biological characteristics of sparrows, we divide their populations into producers and scroungers. Producers can get food give priority during the search process, while scroungers search for food based on producers. Some of these sparrows act as scouts and

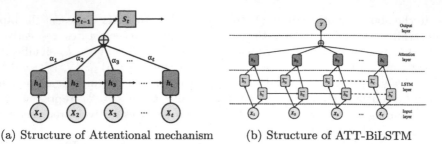

(a) Structure of Attentional mechanism   (b) Structure of ATT-BiLSTM

Fig. 1. Structure of Attentional mechanism and ATT-BiLSTM.

make warning signals when predators arrive. Producers and scroungers can transform dynamically to obtain better food sources. Based on these characteristics, we summarized the mathematical model of SSA:

Step 1: Initialize the parameters in the sparrow population. We define the initial location of sparrows as follows: $x_i = (x_{i1}, x_{i2}, ..., x_{iD})(i=1,2,..., pop)$, where pop represents the population size of sparrows.

Step 2: Update the location of producers by formula (8).

$$x_i^{g+1} = \begin{cases} x_i^g \cdot exp(\frac{-i}{\alpha \cdot g_{max}}), R < ST \\ x_i^g + Q \cdot L, R \geq ST \end{cases} \qquad (i = 1, 2, ...PN) \qquad (8)$$

where g represents the current iteration, α is a random value in the range of $(0,1]$, Q represents a random number that obeys normal distribution; L represents a one-dimensional matrix, $R \in [0,1]$ and $ST \in [0.5,1]$, where R and ST represent the alarm value and safety threshold respectively, PN represent the number of producers, g_{max} represents the maximum iterations.

Step 3: Calculate the location of scroungers by formula (9).

$$x_i^{g+1} = \begin{cases} Q \cdot exp(\frac{G_{worst}-x_i^g}{i^2}), i > pop/2 \\ S_{best} + |x_i^g - S_{best}| \cdot A^+ \cdot L, else \end{cases} \qquad (i = PN+1, PN+2, ..., pop) \qquad (9)$$

where G_{worst} represents the worst position of the sparrows, S_{best} denotes the current best location of the producers, $A^+ = A^T(AA^T)^{-1}$, where A signifies a one-dimensional matrix.

Step 4: Update the position of scouters by formula (10). Randomly select part of the sparrows in the population as scouting sparrows.

$$x_i^{g+1} = \begin{cases} G_{best} + \eta \cdot |x_i^g - G_{best}| & f(x_i^g) > f(G_{best}) \\ x_i^g + K \cdot (\frac{|x_i^g - G_{worst}|}{((f(x_i^g)-f(G_{worst}))+\sigma)}) & f(x_i^g) = f(G_{best}) \end{cases} \qquad (10)$$

Where G_{best} indicates the best position of the current population, σ stands for constant, η represents a random number, it obeys a normal distribution with a variance of 1 and a mean value of 0. Among them, K represents the controlling factor($K \in [-1, 1]$).

Step 5: Obtain the current positions of producers, scroungers, and scouters, and get the optimal fitness value of the population.

Step 6: Repeat the above steps until the tolerance ε or the maximum number of iterations g_{max} is satisfied, and then obtain the best fitness value f_{best} the optimal location X_{best}.

2.4 SSA-ATT-BiLSTM

We proposed the SSA-ATT-BiLSTM model to predict the daily new cases of COVID-19. We train all available information of the past and future through the BiLSTM network, then use the attention mechanism to assign different weights to the features of the model and select the optimal parameters for the model by SSA. That is, choose a set of hyperparameters to minimize the prediction error of ATT-BiLSTM. The SSA minimizes the mean square error between the expected and actual output of the ATT-BiLSTM network by obtaining the minimum value of the fitness function. First, we encoded the ATT-BiLSTM part of the model according to the parameters passed by SSA to obtain the hyperparameters such as the number of iterations, learning rate, hidden nodes, and batch size. Then we train the data of COVID-19, make predictions on the test set, and calculated the mean-square error between the actual and expected outputs, finally returned the mean square error to the SSA as the fitness value. SSA used the fitness value to initial the population and update the location of the producer, scrounger, and scouter by formula (8), formula (9), formula (10), respectively. Keep updating the population until met the termination condition. The optimal value of the optimization goal is obtained when reached the termination condition. Through this approach, we eventually obtained the optimized network hyperparameters. Finally, constructed the BiLSTM model with the optimal values of hyperparameters, then trained and predicted the network model through COVID-19 data.

3 Experiments

3.1 Experiment Data

We randomly selected six countries including Russia, Egypt, Ireland, Iran, Japan, and the UK to verify the prediction performance of our proposed model based on their daily confirmed data of COVID-19. The considered COVID-19 datasets are gathered from January 22, 2020, until March 2, 2021. We utilized 70% of the COVID-19 dataset as the training set and 30% as the testing set, dividing the dataset into 280-day training samples and 120-day testing samples. The dataset is publicized by the Center for Systems Science and Engineering (CSSE) at Johns Hopkins University [13].

3.2 Metrics

We chose four evaluation indexes of the regression algorithm, Root Mean-Squared Error (RMSE), Mean Absolute Percentage Error (MAPE), R-Square (R^2), and Mean Absolute Error (MAE) to evaluate the model objectively. The smaller the values of RMSE, MAPE, MAE, and MSE, the smaller the deviation between the model prediction result and the true value, the more accurate the result is; the closer the determination coefficient R^2 is to 1, the better the model predicts.

3.3 Comparison and Analysis of results

The network model is constructed at the TensorFlow 1.4.0 framework. The CPU of this experiment is i5-8265U, while the GPU is NVIDIA's GTX-1050. We used the Back Propagation Neural Network (BPNN) model [14], BiLSTM model, and BiLSTM-ATT model as comparative experiments models, these models used the Grid Search algorithm [15] for parameter tuning.

Figure 2 illustrates the prediction results of several different models in Egypt, Ireland, Iran, Japan, Russia, and the UK. The prediction period is 120 days from November 3, 2020, to March 2, 2021. Each image comprises the curve comparison between the predicted values of various methods and the corresponding actual data. Table 1 provides the evaluation index calculation results of each prediction model, to compare the prediction results of different models accurately. Our model attained the best R^2 values of 0.9696 and 0.9644 in Egypt and Russia, respectively. These prediction results signify that the BPNN model has the worst prediction effect among the models. Its predicted value is quite different from the actual values. In all six countries, the MAPE value of SSA-ATT-BLSTM is lower than ATT-BiLSTM, which shows that the tuning ability of SSA is better than the grid search algorithm, but the difference between the two is not apparent. The fundamental reason is that the two prediction models have the same unit structure. On the whole, comparing with other models, the value of R^2 of our model is closer to 1, and the values of evaluation indicators such as RMSE, MAPE, and MAE in our model is lower than other models, signifying that the prediction of the SSA-ATT-BiLSTM model is better than other models.

4 Results and Discussion

In this article, we propose an SSA-ATT-BiLSTM model to solve the problem of predicting daily new cases of COVID-19. The model used ATT to enhance the model's ability to capture the important features of COVID-19 data and use the SSA algorithm to optimize the parameters of the ATT-BiLSTM model. We randomly selected data from six different countries which severely affected by COVID-19, and use BPNN, BiLSTM, ATT-BiLSTM as comparison models, these models used the Grid Search algorithm to optimize their parameters. Comparing with these models, our model has better performance. Therefore, we can conclude that our model is applicable in many countries, and has broad application prospects in COVID-19 prediction research.

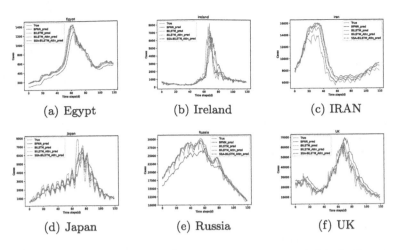

(a) Egypt   (b) Ireland   (c) IRAN

(d) Japan   (e) Russia   (f) UK

Fig. 2. Comparison of forecasting performance among our model and other models in six different countries.

Table 1. Comparison of prediction accuracy of different models in six countries

Country	Model	MAPE	RMSE	MAE	R^2
Egypt	BPNN	0.2095	147.6191	113.2855	0.7834
	BiLSTM	0.0766	78.887	52.0979	0.9381
	Attention-BiLSTM	0.0608	65.9437	41.7337	0.9567
	SSA-ATT-BiLSTM	**0.0502**	**55.3095**	**34.0384**	**0.9696**
Ireland	BPNN	0.2747	924.8108	437.1012	0.6772
	BiLSTM	0.237	751.9778	364.5325	0.7866
	Attention-BiLSTM	0.2401	736.2902	373.2303	0.7954
	SSA-ATT-BiLSTM	**0.2278**	**643.464**	**330.599**	**0.8437**
Iran	BPNN	0.1537	1690.367	1276.358	0.5916
	BiLSTM	0.1342	1546.155	1164.556	0.6583
	Attention-BiLSTM	0.0946	1207.241	879.9821	0.7917
	SSA-ATT-BiLSTM	**0.0729**	**920.37**	**664.869**	**0.8789**
Japan	BPNN	0.2184	878.9868	579.9561	0.7305
	BiLSTM	0.1461	609.6014	404.6344	0.8704
	Attention-BiLSTM	0.1411	572.7213	385.863	0.8856
	SSA-ATT-BiLSTM	**0.1351**	**543.989**	**354.273**	**0.9044**
Russia	BPNN	0.0682	2010.834	1577.55	0.8502
	BiLSTM	0.0501	1345.003	1060.743	0.9329
	Attention-BiLSTM	0.0401	1129.497	858.9894	0.9527
	SSA-ATT-BiLSTM	**0.0362**	**980.047**	**780.898**	**0.9644**
UK	BPNN	0.2949	8344.011	6538.767	0.6798
	BiLSTM	0.1791	5329.643	4104.531	0.8693
	Attention-BiLSTM	0.1441	4599.895	3383.99	0.9027
	SSA-ATT-BiLSTM	**0.1302**	**4395.52**	**3196.95**	**0.9111**

References

1. Kermack, W.O., Mckendrick, A.G.A.: A contribution to the mathematical theory of epidemics. Proc. R. Soc. Math. Phys. Eng. Sci. **115**(772), 700–721 (1927)
2. Hernandez-Matamoros, A., Fujita, H., Hayashi, T., Perez-Meana, H.: Forecasting of COVID19 per regions using ARIMA models and polynomial functions. Appl. Soft Comput. **96**, 106610 (2020)
3. Schuster, M., Paliwal, K.K.: Bidirectional recurrent neural networks. IEEE Trans. Sig. Process. **45**(11), 2673–2681 (1997)
4. Du, S., et al.: Predicting COVID-19 using hybrid AI model. IEEE Trans. Cybern. **50**(7), 2891–2904 (2020)
5. Zhu, X., et al.: Attention-based recurrent neural network for influenza epidemic prediction. BMC Bioinform. **20**(Suppl. 18), 575 (2019)
6. Xue, J., Shen, B.: A novel swarm intelligence optimization approach: sparrow search algorithm. Syst. Sci. Control Eng. **8**(1), 22–34 (2020). https://doi.org/10.1080/21642583.2019.1708830
7. Elsheikh, A.H., Saba, A.I., Elaziz, M.A., Lu, S., Shehabeldeen, T.A.: Deep learning-based forecasting model for COVID-19 outbreak in Saudi Arabia. Process Saf. Environ. Prot. **149**, 223–233 (2021)
8. Martínez-lvarez, F., et al.: Coronavirus optimization algorithm: a bioinspired meta-heuristic based on the COVID-19 propagation model. Big Data **8**(4), 308–322 (2020)
9. Hu, J., Zheng, W.: A deep learning model to effectively capture mutation information in multivariate time series prediction. Knowl.-Based Syst. **203**, 106139 (2020)
10. Lipton, Z.C., Berkowitz, J., Elkan, C.: A critical review of recurrent neural networks for sequence learning. In: Computer Science (2015)
11. Wang, S., Wang, X., Wang, S., Wang, D.: Bi-directional long short-term memory method based on attention mechanism and rolling update for short-term load forecasting. Int. J. Electr. Power Energy Syst. **109**, 470–479 (2019). https://doi.org/10.1016/j.ijepes.2019.02.022
12. Xu, K., et al.: Show, attend and tell: neural image caption generation with visual attention. In: Computer Science, pp. 2048–2057 (2015)
13. Johns Hopkins University: Center for systems science and engineering. https://github.com/CSSEGISandData/COVID-19. Accessed 2 Mar 2021
14. Rumelhart, D., Hinton, G.E., Williams, R.J.: Learning representations by back propagating errors. Nature **323**(6088), 533–536 (1986)
15. Lerman, P.M.: Fitting segmented regression models by grid search. J. R. Stat. Soc. Ser. C (Appl. Stat.) **29**(1), 77–84 (1980). http://www.jstor.org/stable/2346413

Explaining Neural Network Results by Sensitivity Analysis for Deception Detection

Xuecheng Zhang$^{(\boxtimes)}$ and Xuanying Zhu

The Australian National University, Canberra, Australia
{u6284513,xuanying.zhu}@anu.edu.au

Abstract. Previous researches show that people are only able to recognise deception with an accuracy of 54%. In this paper, using physiological signals from observers, we train a three-layer neural network, a long short-term memory (LSTM) and a multi-tasking learning neural network (MTL-NN). We demonstrate that examined models are able to identify deception with an accuracy up to 62%, surpassing the average accuracy of human deception detection. The superior deception recognition ability shows that these tools are capable of helping people discriminate against deception. Further, to improve the interpret-ability of neural networks, we extract rules from the trained models using sensitivity analysis. We find that the rule extraction methods using sensitivity analysis along with genetic algorithm (GA) based data reduction successfully explain all three neural network models. We hope the rule extraction methods can help to improve the interpret-ability of neural networks.

Keywords: Neural network explanation · Rule extraction · Sensitivity analysis · Genetic algorithm · LSTM · MTL

1 Introduction

Liars evoke abnormal physiological responses which can be recognised by observers. The higher galvanic skin response (GSR), enlarged pupil dilation (PD), and increased heart rate (HR) of liars may have a subtle influence on liars' behaviour, posture, or movement dynamics, which are visible to observers [6]. People being deceived are responsive to the overt cognitive and emotional messages of liars, obtaining similar physiological responses with the liars [15]. Utilising observers' physiological signals such as blood volume pulse (BVP), GSR, PD and skin temperature (ST), neural networks (NNs) and multitasking learning NNs (MTL-NNs) trained in [14,15] are able to estimate if a person's subjective belief in some information has been manipulated.

Aiming to explore whether presenters' subjective belief can be better estimated by observers' physiological signals using other techniques, we extend [14,15] by adding a long short-term-memory (LSTM) for prediction. Further, it is unknown how NN classifies inputs because these interactions are interpreted

© Springer Nature Switzerland AG 2021
T. Mantoro et al. (Eds.): ICONIP 2021, CCIS 1517, pp. 127–135, 2021.
https://doi.org/10.1007/978-3-030-92310-5_15

incomprehensibly as weight vectors. Rule extraction may be useful as it demonstrates the internal knowledge from the problem domain [1]. Therefore, the paper also aims to improve the interpret-ability of the NN using rule extraction.

In this paper, rule extraction is attempted by sensitivity analysis and we apply rule extraction to three trained models, including a three-layer NN, an LSTM and a MTL-NN. Sensitivity analysis has previously been applied to convolutional neural network [12], and NN [4,10], but to the best of our knowledge, none of the existing work has focused on the sensitivity analysis of MTL-NN. More importantly, as the input data is high-dimensional which may contain features that are useless for rule extraction, we use generic algorithm (GA) to remove unnecessary features for rule extraction. Finally, a decision tree is used as a baseline method for rule extraction.

We highlight the main contributions of this paper as below:

1. We extended previous work to include LSTM and validated that manipulation in subjective belief can be identified.
2. Due to the black-box nature of NN, we also explored several rule extraction methods for interpret-ability and showed that sensitivity analysis with GA as feature selection worked the best.

2   Dataset

We use a dataset from [15] which records data from 23 observers, each viewing 16 unique videos. In each video, one presenter presents some information and their subjective belief may have been manipulated. The labels are binary bits indicating manipulation of the presenter's belief. Four physiological signals from observers watching the videos are recorded, namely BVP, GSR, ST and PD.

Since the acquired signals range in different values, we first normalise each signal to the range from zero to one. We then remove noise from the signals by applying a Butterworth filter. Following [14], we extract 8 features from each of the four signals, including 1) *minimum*, 2) *maximum*, 3) *mean*, 4) *standard deviation*, 5) *variance*, 6) *root mean square*, 7) *means of the absolute values of the first difference* and 8) *means of the absolute values of the first difference* These features are used to train the three-layer NN and MTL-NN. For LSTM, the preprocessed time-series BVP, GSR, ST and PD are used as inputs.

3   Methods

We first train three models, including an LSTM, a MTL-NN and a three-layer NN. Once three models are trained, we apply several rule extraction methods on the trained models for interpret-ability. The rule extraction is attempted by 1) a decision tree as a baseline method, 2) local regression based sensitivity analysis, 3) local regression based sensitivity analysis with GA as feature reduction.

3.1   Classification

The first model is **LSTM**. As shown in Fig. 1a, the input layer contains a three-dimensional input including the batch size, input dimension, and time step of each input data. The input of LSTM contains time steps and features and the input shape is reshaped to (1,batch,119) where 119 equals to the length of the inputs. The learning rate and epoch are set to 0.0001 and 350 respectively due to the best performance among the validation set.

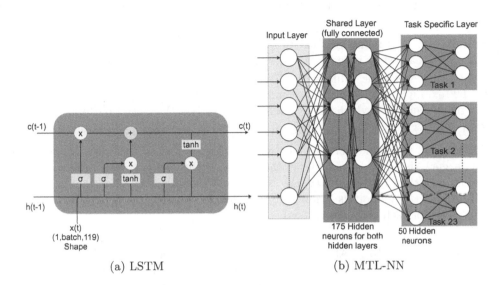

(a) LSTM   (b) MTL-NN

Fig. 1. The structure of LSTM and MTL-NN.

Following [14,15], we also implemented a **MTL-NN** and a **three-layer NN**. The learning rate and epoch are set to is 0.00001 and 400 respectively.

The whole dataset is split into a train set (80%) and a test set (20%). When training each model, a 12 cross-validation is performed on the train set to construct a *training* set (occupying 11/12 of the train set) and a *validation* set (1/12 of the train set). *Validation* set is used to tune hyper-parameters for each model, while performance on test data is reported in Sect. 4.

3.2   Rule Extraction

Rule extraction method deduces meaningful rules that leverage the interpretability of the NN. We apply rule extraction methods to generate rules based on the outputs of the NNs. The general idea of training is to generate IF-THEN-ELSE rules for each feature: IF $f(X) \geq \alpha$ THEN $Y = 1$ ELSE $Y = 0$ where α represents a boundary and X, Y represent inputs and outputs respectively [9]. With rule extraction, people can explicitly understand the effect of specific features on the result from rules.

Decision Tree (Baseline). The implemented decision tree uses CART algorithm [13]. It divides the current sample into two sub-samples, and each non-leaf node obtains two branches. As CART algorithm generates binary tree, only "True" or "False" can be made in every decision. The binary decision is similar to "IF-THEN rules" in rule extraction method. For this study, we use the decision trees as the baseline for rule extraction compared with sensitivity analysis.

After training the classifier (three-layer NN, LSTM or MTL-NN), 80% of the classifier outputs are used as labels to train the decision tree and 20% of the classifier outputs are used for testing the rules extracted by the decision tree.

Sensitivity Analysis. Sensitivity analysis aims to find the *boundary* of every feature for each class based on the derivative. According to IF-THEN-ELSE rule in Sect. 3.2, when the value of $A_i^{(p)}$ (where i stands for i^{th} feature and p stands for p^{th} example) is close to the boundary, a small permutation in it may change the output class C_j which leads to a large derivative. We use [5] to approximate $F(A_i^{(p)}) = \frac{\partial C_j}{\partial A_i^{(p)}}$ and find the maximum value of F as the *boundary* for each class. Afterwards, we define that the rule will be triggered when the value is smaller (or larger) than the boundary for each class. If the value of feature is smaller (or larger) than the boundary, the correspondent output class obtains a vote. When sensitivity analysis is finished, each feature possesses a unique boundary and rules for each class are created.

Genetic Algorithm. After performing sensitivity analysis, boundary of each feature is generated. Nevertheless, if a feature does not have much influence on the result, adding it to the knowledge may lead to a bad result. Therefore, GA is introduced to perform data reduction [11]. In this paper, GA aims to select the subset of features with the best explanation accuracy, i.e. the best prediction accuracy from the outputs generated by classifiers. The chromosome is encoded in binary with length of feature size indicating whether the particular feature is used or not. The reproduction method is *recombination with uniform crossover* and the cross rate and mutation are set to 0.8 and 0.003 respectively. After executing GA, the unsatisfied features can be eliminated, because the crossover and mutation can substitute deficit solutions with good solutions in population.

4   Results and Discussion

In this paper, we have two aims. The first aim is to compare the performance of the three-layer NN, LSTM and MTL-NN. To shrink the influence of imbalanced data, we use accuracy and F1 score. The results are shown in Table 1. The second aim is to introduce several rule extraction methods and compare their performances with decision tree classifier as a baseline. For sensitivity analysis based method, we obtain two rules (binary output) for each feature. Characteristic input method [7] which aims to categorise the input patterns based on classifier outputs is used to determine which rules should be applied to input patterns.

We define those input patterns which trigger deception as a characteristic ON pattern and non-deception as a characteristic OFF pattern. We compute the *Euclidean distance* of input pattern to each of the mean characteristic ON and characteristic OFF and choose the rule with the shortest distance. The class possessing the most votes is elected to be the output prediction. To evaluate the performance of rule extraction method, each method needs to predict the output of three different classifiers and reports the average accuracy over 10 runs and the average accuracy is obtained as shown in Table 2.

4.1   NN Effectiveness

As can be seen from Table 1, MTL-NN obtains the highest accuracy (62.0%). It demonstrates that when there are similarities in the data, we can use MTL-NN to train these groups separately but concurrently in the shared layer to obtain satisfactory results. The three-layer NN performs the worst, with an accuracy at the chance level. The mechanism of the general three-layer NN is insufficient to learn time series. Even though the three-layer NN has already undergone preprocessing, the performance of three-layer NN is not as superior as LSTM. It shows that LSTM is better at processing time-series compared to NN.

Comparing LSTM and MTL-NN, we can see although MTL-NN achieves the highest accuracy, its average F1 score is lower than that of LSTM and the difference is not statistically significant ($p > 0.05$, t-test). It may indicate that MTL-NN is more vulnerable to the imbalanced dataset, probably due to the complicated structure of MTL. Another reason for the lower F1 score of MTL is related to the loss function. The loss function, in this case, was calculated by the sum of the loss of each task. The setting of loss function may be problematic since the learning difficulty of independent tasks is different. The testing loss of 23 tasks among MTL-NN is depicted in Fig. 2. As seen, those tasks in the middle of Fig. 2 clearly converge nearly in 50 epochs, but the tasks depicted in green converge approximately in 300 epochs. The fixed weight setting may restrict MTL-NN and provide an unsatisfactory result. For future work, dynamic weight methods in MTL-NN should be explored. Gradient normalisation (GradNorm) [2] maintains the loss of each task at the same order of magnitude and each task obtains the similar learning rate. Also, dynamic task prioritization [8] concentrates on tasks that are burdensome to learn. These methods having dynamic weighting mechanism may enhance the performance of MTL-NN.

Table 1. Overall accuracy and F1 score of NN, LSTM and MTL-NN over 10 runs

NN method	Accuracy	Average F1 Score
Three-layer	50.7%	58.9%
LSTM	59.3%	**67.8%**
MTL	**62.0%**	66.0%

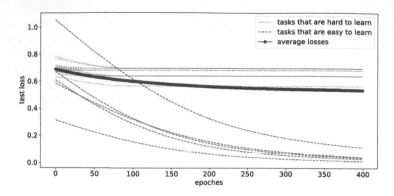

Fig. 2. Test loss of each individual task, and the average loss out of all tasks among MTL-NN

4.2   Rule Extraction Performance

As shown in Table 2, Sensitivity Analysis + GA performs the best for all examined NNs. Sensitivity analysis + GA based rule extraction method yields 89.1% of accuracy in predicting the outputs of the three-layer NN. Outputs of LSTM and MTL are harder to predict, with an accuracy of 82% and 64.2%, respectively. This may imply that the three-layer NN which has the simplest structure among the three examined models is easier to interpret than other models. Compared with sensitivity analysis without GA, the algorithm with GA is much more accurate, which improves the accuracy by around 10% in the result of LSTM and MTL-NN ($p < 0.05$ in both cases, t-test). That is to say, GA algorithm utilised as feature selection extracts the important features from the output of NN and subsequently, these features can be used for rule extraction.

Table 2. Different rule extraction method are performed on three-layer NN, LSTM, MTL-NN respectively and report the accuracy of NN output prediction after 10 experiments.

Rule extraction method	NN method		
	Three-layer NN	LSTM	MTL-NN
Decision tree	77.0%	81.6%	60.9%
Sensitivity analysis	86.4%	73.0%	54.3%
Sensitivity analysis + GA	**89.1%**	**82.0%**	**64.2%**

When sensitivity analysis is performed without GA, it obtains 86.4% accuracy in predicting outputs of the three-layer NN. This accuracy is higher than decision tree classifier (77.0%). However, the performance in rule extraction of the sophisticated models such as LSTM and MTL-NN is unacceptable, with the accuracy of MTL dropping to 54.3%. These results indicate that sensitivity analysis alone cannot correctly extract rules from complex NNs such as MTL. For future work, DeepRed proposed by Zilke et al. [16] could be used to extract rules for more complex NNs. DeepRed uses a divide-and-conquer method that extracts intermediate rules for each layer of a DNN [9], while sensitivity analysis only focuses on the impact of inputs on outputs. Therefore DeepRed might be an alternative to sensitivity analysis for rule extraction for complex NNs.

For MTL, all rule extraction methods perform ineffectively. Although sensitivity analysis + GA achieves the best accuracy for MTL at 64.2%, it does not statistically outperform decision tree ($p > 0.05$, t-test). Sensitivity analysis + GA is based on sensitivity analysis. The performance of sensitivity analysis + GA is restricted by sensitivity analysis. In addition, the structure of MTL model containing shared layers and task-specific layers is more complex than LSTM. Since the centers of characteristic ON and characteristic OFF in MTL are too close to each other, the applied Euclidean distance may not be effective to draw a clear boundary between two classes, thus leading to the worse performance on rule extraction. For future work, more experiments could be conducted on finding a more suitable method, for example, the Gaussian mixture model which classifies input patterns with a probability might be a solution.

5   Conclusion and Future Work

We live in a society surrounded with lies, yet it is difficult for individuals to tell the difference between real and manipulated information. The paper firstly utilises the three-layer NN, LSTM and MTL-NN to detect presenters' subjective beliefs using observers' physiological signals. As a result, LSTM and MTL-NN generate an acceptable accuracy surpassing human deception recognition. In this way, the NN can assist people in recognising dishonesty. Next, since people are unknown about the behaviour of hidden neurons in the well-trained NN, several methods have been attempted to extract rules from these three NN structures. Sensitivity Analysis with dimension reduction based on GA successfully explains the well-trained NN with the highest score among other tools.

The MTL-NN model trained in this paper uses fixed weights in the loss function. A good method of weighting should be dynamic, which can be adjusted according to the learning stages of different tasks, the learning difficulty, and even the learning effect. GradNorm [2] uses different weights to enable independent tasks to obtain the same learning rate. Dynamic task prioritization [8] hopes to offer more weighting value to the tasks that are burdensome to learn. These methods can be used for improving MTL-NN. In addition, since complex model may influence the performance, some other light model containing fewer parameters like GRU [3] can be used and compare with MTL-NN performance.

Moreover, this paper also introduces sensitivity analysis with GA to extract rules from the neural network. However, its performance on the complex NN like MTL-NN does not produce a decent result. One problem is that if the centers of characteristic ON and characteristic OFF are too close, the *euclidean distance* used to define rules is insufficient to draw a clear boundary between two classes.

Future work could experiment using the Gaussian mixture model to classify the new input with probability instead of directly giving the class label. Alternative to sensitivity analysis, another solution for rule extraction is to utilise DeepRED [16] purposed by Zilke et al. Future work could explore if DeepRED can be used to interpret complex NN models such as MTL-NN.

References

1. Andrews, R., Diederich, J., Tickle, A.B.: Survey and critique of techniques for extracting rules from trained artificial neural networks. Knowl.-Based Syst. 8(6), 373–389 (1995)
2. Chen, Z., Badrinarayanan, V., Lee, C.Y., Rabinovich, A.: Gradnorm: gradient normalization for adaptive loss balancing in deep multitask networks. In: International Conference on Machine Learning, pp. 794–803. PMLR (2018)
3. Cho, K., et al.: Learning phrase representations using rnn encoder-decoder for statistical machine translation. arXiv preprint arXiv:1406.1078 (2014)
4. Choi, J.Y., Choi, C.H.: Sensitivity analysis of multilayer perceptron with differentiable activation functions. IEEE Trans. Neural Netw. 3(1), 101–107 (1992)
5. Cleveland, W.S.: Robust locally weighted regression and smoothing scatterplots. J. Am. Stat. Assoc. 74(368), 829–836 (1979)
6. Elkins, A., Zafeiriou, S., Pantic, M., Burgoon, J.: Unobtrusive deception detection. In: The Oxford Handbook of Affective Computing, pp. 503–515. Oxford University Press (2014)
7. Gedeon, T., Turner, H.S.: Explaining student grades predicted by a neural network. In: Proceedings of 1993 International Conference on Neural Networks (IJCNN-93-Nagoya, Japan), vol. 1, pp. 609–612 (1993). https://doi.org/10.1109/IJCNN.1993.713989
8. Guo, M., Haque, A., Huang, D.-A., Yeung, S., Fei-Fei, L.: Dynamic task prioritization for multitask learning. In: Ferrari, V., Hebert, M., Sminchisescu, C., Weiss, Y. (eds.) ECCV 2018. LNCS, vol. 11220, pp. 282–299. Springer, Cham (2018). https://doi.org/10.1007/978-3-030-01270-0_17
9. Hailesilassie, T.: Rule extraction algorithm for deep neural networks: a review. arXiv preprint arXiv:1610.05267 (2016)
10. Hashem, S.: Sensitivity analysis for feedforward artificial neural networks with differentiable activation functions. In: [Proceedings 1992] IJCNN International Joint Conference on Neural Networks, vol. 1, pp. 419–424. IEEE (1992)
11. Mitchell, M.: An Introduction to Genetic Algorithms. MIT press, Cambridge (1998)
12. Rodner, E., Simon, M., Fisher, R.B., Denzler, J.: Fine-grained recognition in the noisy wild: sensitivity analysis of convolutional neural networks approaches. arXiv preprint arXiv:1610.06756 (2016)
13. Safavian, S.R., Landgrebe, D.: A survey of decision tree classifier methodology. IEEE Trans. Syst. Man Cybern. 21(3), 660–674 (1991)
14. Zhu, X., Gedeon, T., Caldwell, S., Jones, R., Gu, X.: Deceit detection: identification of presenter's subjective doubt using affective observation neural network analysis. In: 2020 IEEE International Conference on Systems, Man, and Cybernetics (SMC), pp. 3174–3181. IEEE (2020)

15. Zhu, X., Qin, Z., Gedeon, T., Jones, R., Hossain, M.Z., Caldwell, S.: Detecting the *Doubt Effect* and *Subjective Beliefs* using neural networks and observers' pupillary responses. In: Cheng, L., Leung, A.C.S., Ozawa, S. (eds.) ICONIP 2018. LNCS, vol. 11304, pp. 610–621. Springer, Cham (2018). https://doi.org/10.1007/978-3-030-04212-7_54
16. Zilke, J.R., Loza Mencía, E., Janssen, F.: DeepRED – rule extraction from deep neural networks. In: Calders, T., Ceci, M., Malerba, D. (eds.) DS 2016. LNCS (LNAI), vol. 9956, pp. 457–473. Springer, Cham (2016). https://doi.org/10.1007/978-3-319-46307-0_29

Stress Recognition with EEG Signals Using Explainable Neural Networks and a Genetic Algorithm for Feature Selection

Eric Pan$^{(\boxtimes)}$ and Jessica Sharmin Rahman

School of Computing, Australian National University, Canberra, Australia
{eric.pan,jessica.rahman}@anu.edu.au

Abstract. Stress is a natural human response to external conditions which have been studied for a long time. Since prolonged periods of stress can cause health deterioration, it is important for researchers to understand and improve its detection. This paper uses neural network techniques to classify whether an individual is stressed, based on signals from an electroencephalogram (EEG), a popular physiological sensor. We also overcome two prominent limitations of neural networks: low interpretability due to the complex nature of architectures, and hindrance to performance due to high data dimensionality. We resolve the first limitation with sensitivity analysis-based rule extraction, while the second limitation is addressed by feature selection via a genetic algorithm. Using summary statistics from the EEG, a simple Artificial Neural Network (ANN) is able to achieve 93.8% accuracy. The rules extracted are able to explain the ANN's behaviour to a good degree and thus improve interpretability. Adding feature selection with a genetic algorithm improves average accuracy achieved by the ANN to 95.4%.

Keywords: Stress detection · Artificial Neural Network · EEG · Rule extraction · Neural network explainability · Genetic algorithm

1 Introduction

1.1 Background

Stress exists for humans in all domains, whether it is work, study, or otherwise situations with external pressures. There are many other forms of stress, all of which depend on psychological factors and induce physiological responses [3]. It is imperative to have a method of measurement that can objectively quantify important symptoms or indicators of stress. This is especially the case where specialist psychologists are not available to exercise expert judgement and identify stress [4]. One tool for objective measure is the electroencephalogram (EEG). By successfully discovering patterns in EEG signals instrumental to stress recognition, our findings can provide stress researchers with more confidence on its efficacy in this domain.

© Springer Nature Switzerland AG 2021
T. Mantoro et al. (Eds.): ICONIP 2021, CCIS 1517, pp. 136–143, 2021.
https://doi.org/10.1007/978-3-030-92310-5_16

Artificial Neural Networks (ANNs) are good function approximators that also excel at simple classification tasks. Despite being able to achieve high performance and good results in terms of predictions and classifications, many domain experts are skeptical to use them to make highly crucial decisions that have significant ramifications if done wrong [7]. This is because the knowledge represented in the parameters of ANNs are difficult to interpret. Unless a human can logically interpret its actions in the context of the domain, experts cannot justify it as a decision-making tool. This is prevalent in domains with high ethical stakes or where explanations must be given to key stakeholders. This disadvantage has led to the development of algorithms which extract rules and behavior patterns from neural networks, which are easy for humans to understand [6].

Another prominent issue in the world of machine learning is high-dimensional data. A large number of features gives rise to the problem of data sparsity, and it becomes difficult for models to generalize and learn useful patterns. This issue is prevalent in tasks involving EEG data since there are so many channels [9]. Feature selection therefore becomes extremely important when working with high dimensional data.

1.2 EEG Signals

The EEG is a commonly used medical imaging technique which reads electrical activity from the surface of the scalp generated by the brain. These readings are human physiological features which undergo change when a person experiences different emotions, including stress [12]. Combined with high temporal resolution (large reading frequency) [12] makes the EEG an ideal tool for stress detection. The signals used in this paper come from a 14-channel headset. Each channel detects activity from a different part of the brain. These channels are: AF3, F7, F3, FC5, T7, P7, O1, O2, P8, T8, FC6, F4, F8, AF4. Such contact-based devices are common amongst studies involving physiological reactions, such as classifying emotions [1].

1.3 Proposed Task

We aim to perform a binary classification on stress. The goals of the paper are to demonstrate the merits of using wearable devices to learn about stress, to provide confidence that neural networks can be explained intuitively, and to show how the right kind of input processing can dramatically yield better results. We leverage the predictive ability of neural networks to do this, while deducing meaningful rules that compress the neural network's behavior into a digestible, explainable series of decisions. To select only the useful features, genetic algorithms (GA) are among the methods that can be configured freely with parameters to improve efficacy [10].

The experiment will be conducted in two phases. The first phase includes building the optimal ANN architecture for the EEG dataset, manually selecting features qualitatively, and then implementing the sensitivity analysis-based rule extraction for the network. The second part will be identical to the first except the optimal features are selected by the genetic algorithm. Their respective performances are compared. The rest of this paper is structured as follows. Section 2 describes the methods and techniques used in our study, including the dataset, architecture, rule extraction and feature selection. Section 3 presents the performance results of these techniques in identifying stress. Finally, Sect. 4 discusses future work and concludes the paper.

2   Methodology

2.1   Data Exploratory Analysis and Preprocessing

For this study, 25 undergraduate students wore EEG devices while watching a series of stressed and non-stressed films lasting around one minute. Stressed films had stressful content in the direction towards distress, fear and tension whereas the non-stressed films had content that created an illusion of meditation or soothing environments. There were three of each category of film. We note that stress can certainly be measured on a sliding scale, however in this experiment, the stimuli to induce stress has only two levels. For each of the 14 channels (described in Sect. 1.2), raw measurements were taken over time for each participant, forming time series data. The following summary statistics of the time series data were produced for each EEG channel: mean, min, max, sum, variance, standard deviation, interquartile range, skewness, root mean square, averages of first and second differences between consecutive signal amplitudes, Hjorth mobility parameter and Hurst exponent. The approximate entropy and fuzzy entropy measured randomness in signal fluctuations. Each observation contains a label of *calm* (1) or *stressed* (2) according to the category of film shown.

In the first phase of the experiment, features selection was done manually by identifying variables which are intuitively redundant. In the second phase of the experiment, we implemented a genetic algorithm to stochastically search for the optimal subset of features to be used by the ANN. We discuss this method in detail in Sect. 2.3.

2.2   Neural Network Design

The optimal model was found to be a three-layer fully connected neural network, with 196 input features corresponding to the EEG signals in the input layer, a first hidden layer with 3 neurons, a second hidden layer with 1 neuron, and finally two output neurons (calm/stressed) for binary classification. The weighted sum of each hidden neuron goes through a sigmoid activation function before being fed to the next layer.

The shallow feedforward ANN model was trained with the Adam optimizer and cross entropy loss function to penalize more heavily for misclassifying training examples and faster convergence. To avoid overfitting, 300 epochs of training were conducted. The learning rate was 0.01. The same neural network architecture (see Fig. 1) was used to evaluate the performance of different feature selections.

Fig. 1. The 3-layer ANN architecture selected.

2.3 Feature Selection with GA

To extend and improve on the approach in our first phase, we utilize a genetic algorithm for feature selection. Each individual in the population represented one subset of the available EEG features. Figure 2 shows how representing the inclusion/exclusion of the features as bit strings translates into a fully connected neural network.

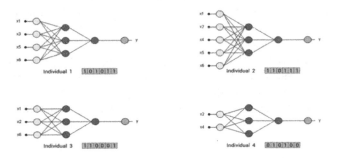

Fig. 2. ANN representation after feature selection with GA [11].

The population size of 20 was initialised randomly. We used an individual's average 5-fold testing accuracy as the measure of fitness, consistent with the performance measure in Sect. 2.6. The selection of the surviving individuals into the next generation was done with the proportional method – according to their relative fitness in the population.

Following selection, a new population was bred through crossover. Uniform crossover was used for this purpose. We chose uniform crossover because with so many available features, it's not feasible to manually pick justifiable crossover points. There are also no obvious contiguous regions in the EEG feature space. For additional exploration, the GA mutated the bit strings in the new generation with a small rate of 0.02 per attribute, giving an expected number of mutations of about 4. We also incorporated elitism which ensured that the population's best fitness is never decreasing and enabled the retention of good solutions. The proportion of elites to retain at each generation was 10%, which means the top 2 individuals were always directly put into the next generation, without mutation.

2.4   Sensitivity Analysis on Characteristic Patterns

One of the primary goals of this paper is to detect decision boundaries along input feature space, by identifying where there is a large rate of change in the output nodes with respect to the input nodes. It is theorized that where a small change in the value of an input causes the output to change from 0 to 1 or vice versa, it is likely to be the location of a decision boundary [7]. By searching for such decision boundaries in all input parameters, we produce simple rules to predict the output of the underlying ANN.

The fully-trained neural network is differentiated to find the gradients of the input features. For each output node (one for each class out of K), we calculated the gradient of input x for observation i. For each of the input features, a value z is found is where the absolute value of this gradient is largest. In Engelbrecht et al. [7], the decision boundary for each input feature is found by computing the gradient for every input pattern in the dataset, plotting a graph of the gradients and using a curve fitting algorithm to locate the peak gradient. The corresponding input value will then become the decision boundary. However, this is computationally expensive and thus, characteristic patterns are used to compress and represent the training set, as described in Gedeon et al. [5]. This reduces the number of gradients calculated.

Computing the gradient of each input for every pattern in the dataset was done over the characteristic patterns which represent the "typical" input pattern for each output class. Using the fully-trained ANN described in Sect. 2.2, each input was classified as *calm* or *stressed*. For each of these classes, a characteristic pattern (for example class k_1) was calculated as the arithmetical mean vector of all the relevant input patterns (all that the ANN classified as). For this EEG dataset, there are two characteristic patterns.

2.5   Rule Extraction

For each characteristic pattern, a gradient was calculated for each pair of output and input node. Only a set number of input variables with high gradients (in absolute value) were picked for each characteristic pattern to become rules. Since these will be the highest gradients, they are the most significant for determining the output and are most likely to be close to decision boundaries. Once a predetermined number of the highest gradients was selected, the corresponding inputs features become rules. A value on either side of each boundary was sampled to determine which class the ANN will predict if the input attribute were smaller/larger than the boundary value [7]. Thus, each characteristic pattern will have its own set of rules generated. In this paper, the number of rules extracted was 5. This allows the rules to have relatively high predictive power, while being interpretable. Too many rules would be hard for humans to make sense of.

When classifying a new input, it is first grouped into one of the characteristic patterns by Euclidean distance. Then the rules belonging to that characteristic pattern was run against the new input – giving a classification of *calm* or *stressed*.

For each characteristic pattern, the 5 rules were formed as the condition for an unseen input to be predicted as the class that isn't the characteristic class. We call these 5 rules the "rules against" the canonical class.

2.6 Performance Measure

As the provided EEG dataset is perfectly balanced, accuracy can be reliably used [8] as the evaluation measure. A train-test-validation split of the dataset was used to tune hyper parameters as well as give an unbiased evaluation of the chosen model. 20% of the data was used for the final evaluation, with the remaining 80% used to tune hyper parameters. Each neural network setting was evaluated with the average testing accuracy from the hold-out test sets during a 5-fold cross validation. Using rules extracted from the optimal ANN trained with all training data, predictions from these rules were compared to both the ANN outputs and the ground truth labels.

3 Results and Discussion

Overall, the ANN, rule extractions, and feature selection by GA all achieved a high level of performance, with the feature selection in phase two especially able to improve on previous results. We present the final results in Table 1.

Table 1. Final evaluation results – average final testing accuracy over 100 runs. The ANN results are not affected by the number of rules.

	Manual feature selection			GA feature selection		
	1 rule	5 rules	10 rules	1 rule	5 rules	10 rules
ANN against ground truth	–	93.8%	–	–	95.4%	–
Rules against ANN output	54.4%	85.0%	85.6%	57.1%	84.9%	90.3%
Rules against ground truth	54.5%	86.2%	87.5%	56.2%	86.3%	90.6%

3.1 Classification and Feature Selection Results

In the first phase of our study, the chosen 196-3-1-2 architecture with sigmoid activations achieved high cross-validation accuracy of 94.2%, and a final testing accuracy of 93.8% averaged over 100 runs. In the second phase, the fittest subset of features was selected according to the genetic algorithm. After 20 generations, 98 attributes out of the 210 available were retained. This is a very significant reduction in dimensionality by 53%. Using these features to train an ANN, we obtained 95.4% accuracy. This is an accuracy improvement of 1.6% compared to the testing performance of the ANN model without GA feature selection. Despite only using a small population of 20 and a low number of generations, the GA was able to eliminate over half of the input features as redundancies, achieving better generalization.

No previous research used this identical dataset therefore we couldn't conduct a direct comparison. However, there is related research experimenting on the same task of stress detection. One such paper is Irani et al. [2]. For this experiment, no physical sensors were used and instead, computer vision techniques are utilized. Accuracies of 60% and 82% are obtained using RGB and thermal modalities, respectively. Compared to the higher of the two (82%), the results of this paper using EEG sensors and rule extraction does outperform it.

3.2 Rule Extraction Results

Using the default setting of 5 rules, the average testing accuracy of the rules when compared to the output of the phase one ANN reached 85.0%. After adding GA feature selection, the rule accuracy vs ANN prediction was 84.9%. This is a good level of accuracy considering the simplification from a continuous function-approximating ANN to a discrete one and much reduced set of simple rules. The high accuracy is in large part due to the effectiveness of the use of characteristic patterns. The characteristic patterns themselves are an encapsulation of the ANN's behavior.

The rules are useful mostly for classifying outliers, as only exceptional conditions will allow it to predict against its typical class. This is an explanation for the testing accuracies against ground truth labels of 86.2% (manual) and 86.3% (GA), which are higher than the rules' accuracies against the ANN output. As the number of rules extracted increases, the classification accuracy improves. As this sets a higher threshold for a prediction to be made against the default characteristic class, the predictive behaviour approaches that of the underlying ANN. However, there is a tradeoff between accuracy performance and interpretability. Having too many rules is difficult for humans to understand.

4 Conclusion and Future Work

This paper presented a shallow neural network built on EEG signals as a classifier for human stress. Combined with a GA based feature selection and sensitivity analysis-based rule extractions, a smaller, more powerful and more interpretable neural network achieved up to 86.3% accuracy. The ANN model prior to rule extractions reached 93.8% and 95.4% accuracy with manual and GA feature selection, respectively. Our work highlights EEG data as a key component in stress recognition research. In conjunction with a simple neural network model, a person's stress level can be reliably recognized. We also resolved the high dimensionality issue of EEG by adding a genetic algorithm to identify the most relevant features to be incorporated into the ANN.

By introducing rule extraction, we add evidence that neural networks can be explainable and hence, support its wider usage even in sensitive domains. Experts can be confident deploying neural networks to solve problems, with rules as a "sense check" to provide an additional layer of assurance. Our paper further implements characteristic patterns for faster computation, but a possibility for future work would be extracting unconditional rules that do not rely on these characteristic patterns. This would require the sensitivity analysis to be performed over the entire training set. Such an approach could result in better decision boundaries and achieve a similar level of accuracy with fewer rules.

References

1. Rahman, J., Gedeon, T., Caldwell, S., Jones, R., Jin, Z.: Towards effective music therapy for mental health care using machine learning tools: human affective reasoning and music genres. J. Artif. Intell. Soft Comput. Res. **11**(1), 5–20 (2020)
2. Irani, R., Nasrollahi, K., Dhall, A., Moeslund, T., Gedeon, T.: Thermal superpixels for bimodal stress recognition. In: Sixth International Conference on Image Processing Theory, Tools and Applications (IPTA), Oulu, Finland, pp. 1–6 (2016)
3. Lupien, S., Maheu, F., Tu, M., Fiocco, A., Schramek, T.: The effects of stress and stress hormones on human cognition: implications for the field of brain and cognition. Brain Cogn. **65**(3), 209–237 (2007)
4. Saeed, S., Anwar, S., Khalid, H., Majid, M., Bagci, U.: EEG based classification of long-term stress using psychological labeling. Sensors (Basel, Switzerland) **20**(7), 1886 (2020)
5. Gedeon, T., Turner, H.: Explaining student grades predicted by a neural network. In: Proceedings of 1993 International Conference on Neural Networks (IJCNN-93-Nagoya, Japan), Nagoya, Japan, vol. 1, pp. 609–612 (1993)
6. Hailesilassie, T.: Rule extraction algorithm for deep neural networks: a review. Int. J. Comput. Sci. Inf. Secur. (IJCSIS) **14**(7), 371–381 (2016)
7. Mira, J., Sánchez-Andrés, J.V. (eds.): IWANN 1999. LNCS, vol. 1607. Springer, Heidelberg (1999). https://doi.org/10.1007/BFb0100465
8. Chawla, N., Japkowicz, N., Kotcz, A.: Editorial: special issue on learning from imbalanced data sets. SIGKDD Explor. Newsl. **6**, 1–6 (2004)
9. Erguzel, T., Ozekes, S., Tan, O., Gultekin, S.: Feature selection and classification of electroencephalographic signals: an artificial neural network and genetic algorithm based approach. Clin. EEG Neurosci. **46**, 321–326 (2014). https://doi.org/10.1177/1550059414523764
10. Babatunde, O., Armstrong, L., Leng, J., Diepeveen, D.: A genetic algorithm-based feature selection. Int. J. Electron. Commun. Comput. Eng. **5**, 889–905 (2014)
11. Gomez, F., Quesada, A., Lopez, R.: Genetic algorithms for feature selection. Neural Designer Data Science and Machine Learning Blog. https://www.neuraldesigner.com/blog/genetic_algorithms_for_feature_selection. Accessed 21 June 2021
12. Kalas, M., Momin, B.: Stress detection and reduction using EEG signals. In: International Conference on Electrical, Electronics, and Optimization Techniques (ICEEOT), pp. 471–475 (2016). https://doi.org/10.1109/ICEEOT.2016.7755604

BCI Speller on Smartphone Device
with Diminutive-Sized Visual Stimuli

Nuray Serkali(ID), Adai Shomanov(ID), Madina Kudaibergenova(ID),
and Min-Ho Lee(✉)(ID)

School of Engineering and Digital Sciences, Nazarbayev University,
Kabanbay Batyr Avenue 53, Nur-Sultan 010000, Kazakhstan
{nuray.serkali,adai.shomanov,madina.kudaibergenova,minho.lee}@nu.edu.kz

Abstract. In real-world BCI applications, small-sized and low-impact stimuli are more appropriate for smart devices. However, diminishing the stimuli intensity leads to a reduction of P300 amplitude, causing lower system performance. The purpose of this study is to propose a state-of-the-art BCI speller where diminutive (less than 1 mm) visual stimuli were implemented in a smartphone interface. To boost the task-relevant brain components, participants performed a certain mental task according to the given cue signs. Additionally, we applied a data-driven optimization approach to represent the user-specific spatial-temporal features. The results showed 96.8% of spelling accuracy with a maximum ITR of 31.6 [bits/min], which is comparable or even superior to conventional speller systems. Our study demonstrated the feasibility to create more reliable and practical BCI spelling systems in the future.

Keywords: BCI speller · Event related potential (ERP) · Late positive potential (LPP) · Sound imagery · Mental task

1 Introduction

Brain-computer interface (BCI) systems are a non-muscular communication opportunity for people with severe disabilities. BCI helps patients with neuromuscular disorders to project their intention by controlling external devices, such as personal computers, synthesizer for speech, and prostheses [1]. Due to its qualities as optimal price, easy utilization, and no risk, electroencephalography (EEG) is frequently used in researching brain activities [2].

Prior researches have noted that the quality of evoked potentials highly depend on the target stimulus's visual or auditory characteristics [3–5]. Therefore, the main idea of BCI performance improvement was to regularize the shape, color, or intensity of the stimuli (i.e. transferring familiar face pictures to stimulus [3,4], random stimulus [6], and color distinction [5]). These studies basically strengthened the existing visual or auditory stimulus by making them either

Supported by Faculty Development Competitive Research Grant Program (No. 080420FD1909) at Nazarbayev University.

T. Mantoro et al. (Eds.): ICONIP 2021, CCIS 1517, pp. 144–151, 2021.
https://doi.org/10.1007/978-3-030-92310-5_17

more intense or louder, which evoked stronger ERP response, and therefore, caused improvements in the performance.

Moreover, users cannot sit in front of a monitor for long time while doing stimuli tasks due to various factors and task complexities. Thus, in real-world smaller stimuli seem to be more practical. Xu et al. [7] introduced miniature asymmetric visual evoked potentials (aVEPs) to increase speller performance. In the subsequent research, placing unobtrusive visual stimuli outside of the fovea vision, then applying canonical pattern matching method has resulted in a satisfactory performance for classification of ERP components [8].

The aim of this research is to present the idea of diminishing the external properties of visual stimuli in BCI speller systems and maintaining the performance achieved in previous studies. We theorize that performing voluntary mental task could elicit endogenous ERP components, and this complementary synthesis of oddball signals might improve the performance. The mental task for the subjects was to imagine the high-pitch sound, that was played before the experiment, when the target character appeared on screen. Two mental tasks: passive concentration (PC) and active concentration (AC) were designated in order to devaricate the ERP responses.

The hardware setup of this study is a mobile phone screen - speller layout with diminutive visual stimuli (defined as a *dot-speller*), and the subjects were guided to perform the mental task while the target symbol was presented. The paradigms in this experiment were all implemented to present a more user-friendly BCI system which can minimize the unpreventable adverse impact of external stimuli (e.g., noisy visual/auditory stimuli). As a result, a high level cognitive neural activity ERP component that can decode the user's intention, a late positive potential (LPP), was observed.

2   Materials and Methods

2.1   Participants and Data Acquisition

14 healthy subjects (aged 25–33 years, 4 females, 5 BCI naive users) participated in this study. All participants are confirmed to have normal or corrected vision and be free of psychiatric or neurological disorders. During data acquisition, the subjects were sitting on a chair around 80 cm away from the visual stimulus.

EEG data was recorded via an ActiCap EEG amplifier (Brain Products, Germany) with 32 channels (Fp1-2, F3-4, Fz, F7-8, FC5-6, FC1-2, T7-8, C3-4, Cz, CP1-2, CP5-6, TP9-10, P3-4, P7-8, Pz, PO9-10, O1-2, and Oz). Electrodes with 10–20 system standard were used along with forehead grounded reference on nose (Ag/AgCl electrodes with a maximum impedance of 10 kΩ). The DC artifacts were removed from the data by applying a notch filter with 1 KHz and 60 Hz sampling rate. Finally, Butterworth filter (5th order) with parameters of 0.5 Hz and 30 Hz was used to filter out noise.

The subjects were fully informed of the experiment's objectives. Consent was taken from all subjects in written form. The experiment was revised and

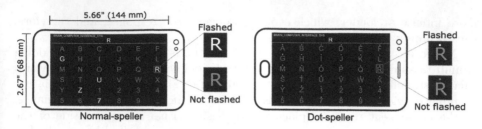

Fig. 1. Illustration of speller systems. Dot- and normal-speller systems were implemented in the smartphone layout

has the approval of the Institutional Review Board at Korea University [1040548-KUIRB-16-159-A-2].

2.2   Dot- and Normal-Speller Experiments

Two groups of mental states were introduced: AC and PC. In the PC condition, subjects were instructed to focus on the given stimuli without any certain mental task. In the AC condition users had an instruction to gaze at the target character and perform a sound imagery task, which was remembered (8 KHz frequency for 2 min) before the experiment. Basically, we validated the spelling performance of the different mental tasks within both dot- and normal-speller layouts.

A normal-speller [9] and a dot-speller were implemented in the smartphone environment. Both of the interface layouts were designed with 36 target visual stimuli ('A'–'Z', '1'–'9', '-'). Individual stimuli had equal positions on the screen by 6 rows and 6 columns. The stimuli were grey colored, and the background was black. The individual letters in the normal-speller were repetitively flashed. In the dot-speller tiny dots (less than 1 mm) were visually positioned on the top of individual letters, and these dot-symbols were flashed instead of the letter itself (see Fig. 1-(d)). Target and non-target trials ratio was 2:10. Note that our experimental approach (e.g., protocol, validation) to the speller experiments was designed based on well-established methods in related studies [3,4,10,11]. A sequence of 12 flashes (i.e. trials) was counted as a single iteration of flashed letters twice within rows and columns. There were overall 10 sequences with around 70 ms stimuli flash, and 150 ms ISI. The newly developed speller layout was presented in a smartphone (Galaxy 9, Samsung) environment with a 1440p OLED/5.8-inch panel using the screen capturing application.

The experimental procedures for spellers were identical. The training phase was conducted offline, and patients were instructed to spell the following phrase, 'BRAIN_COMPUTER_INTERFACE_SYS' (28 characters including spaces '-') according to the task. Therefore, 3360 trials (28 characters × 10 sequences × 12 flashes) were collected in each condition. Two classifiers were then constructed based on the training dataset: PC vs. NT and AC vs. NT. In the test phase, subjects had an instruction to spell 'U3RQJSMAUWES2QEF_KOREA UNIVERSITY' (32 characters) according to the given task. After presenting all the letters (i.e., the end of 10 sequences) in every attempt, online feedback was available for users (on top-left corner classifier showed the found target character). A total of 3840 trials (32 characters × 10 sequences × 12 flashes) were therefore collected in both conditions, and these test datasets were used to evaluate speller performance.

3   Data Analysis and Performance Evaluations

EEG data were first down-sampled 100 Hz, and then epochs were acquired by extracting individual trials in the interval of [−100 and 1000 ms] referencing the stimulus onset, after which baseline-correction was performed: subtraction of mean amplitudes in [−100 and 0] ms pre-stimulus time interval. Afterwards, ERP responses for *NT*, *PC* and *AC* were investigated in the individual setups (i.e., *normal-speller*, and *dot-speller*). In each session, all trials in the training and test phases were concatenated. The Grand Averaged ERP patterns were then evaluated across all subjects. Decoding accuracy and information transfer rates (ITRs) were calculated along with the individual sequences to evaluate the spelling performances [12]. Note that the training data were used to construct the classifier parameters, and the decoding accuracy was evaluated in the test dataset.

In the training phase, k intervals with a step length of 20 ms and an interval length of 100 ms were created. The mean amplitude features [1] in k time intervals were calculated from the ERP trials across all channels. The signed r-squared value [13] was applied to statistically investigate the differences in temporal ERP responses across all channels. A regularized linear discriminant analysis (RLDA) [14] classifier was generated from the selected feature set.

Commonly, for all experiments certain target stimuli were presented 10 times (i.e. 10 sequences), and decoding accuracy was calculated for individual sequence (e.g. the decoding accuracy of last sequence was computed by the taking the average of accumulated epochs of all 10 sequences). The speller layout had 36 classes (the chance level at 2.77%), and the classifier output $f(\mathbf{x}_i)$ was calculated from all the individual letters ($i = 1, ..., 36$). The estimated letter i, which has the highest classification score, was chosen as the desired target symbol. These decision functions were used to provide real-time feedback for the test phase in all individual experiments.

4   Results

4.1   ERP Responses

Typical P300 components [15] were observed in both the normal- and dot-speller experiments as these systems are designed within the oddball paradigm. Mean values for the peak amplitudes in the interval of 300–400 ms (i.e., P300) at the Cz electrode were 1.657 (±1.125)uV, 0.902 (±1.859)uV, 1.837 (±1.122)uV,

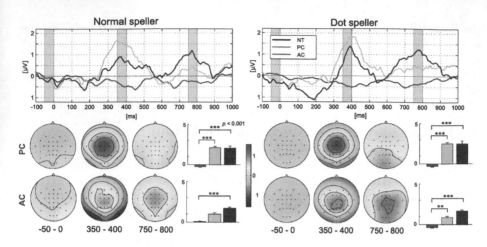

Fig. 2. Average ERP responses at electrode Cz. The scalp plots demonstrate the distribution of signal response for the three different conditions, i.e., *NT*, *PC*, and *AC* trials

and 1.394 (±2.639)uV for normal-passive, normal-active, dot-passive, and dot-active, respectively. The peak amplitude indicates that P300 components were more strongly evoked during passive concentration compared to active task.

Additionally, LPP was observed in the interval of 700–800 ms, and peak amplitudes mean values at the Cz electrode were 0.463 (±1.210) uV, 1.196 (±0.989) uV, 0.476 (±0.996) uV, and 1.244 (±1.105) uV for normal-passive, normal-active, dot-passive, and dot-active, respectively. Contrary to the P300 components, the LPPs were evoked by the active task in both speller systems (see Fig. 2).

4.2   Decoding Accuracy of Normal- and Dot-Speller

Figure 3 indicates the decoding accuracy for target and non-target discrimination in four conditions. Decoding accuracies were calculated from 1 to 10 sequences (x-axis) for individual users as well as the average speller performances. Results demonstrate that active tasks in both speller systems significantly outperformed passive tasks. Precisely, the average accuracies were 53.5%, 83.0%, 62.9%, and 88.8% after sequence four, and 76.3%, 94.1%, 78.1% and 96.8% after the 9th sequence for the normal-passive, normal-active, dot-passive, and dot-active conditions, respectively.

Paired t-tests indicate that active tasks ($p > 0.05$) have similar pattern with the passive tasks ($p > 0.05$) in both speller systems. The active tasks demonstrate higher performance than the passive task in sequences 2–6 and 2–8 for normal-speller and dot-speller respectively. The maximum ITRs were 13.5, 28.6, 18.3, and 31.6 [bits/min] for the normal-passive, normal-active, dot-passive, and dot-active conditions, respectively.

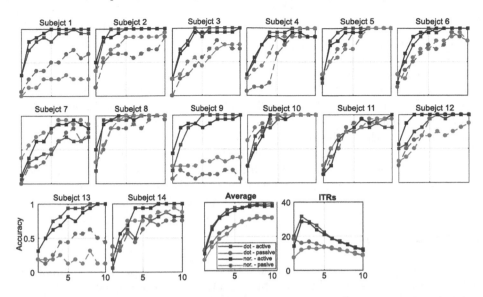

Fig. 3. Decoding accuracy for target and non-target discrimination in the four conditions. The figure indicates the decoding accuracy plots for 14 subjects and the averaged decoding accuracy across all subjects. In the last plot, ITR values for each of the sequences for the four conditions are presented. For each of the subjects, active task experiments produced much higher decoding accuracy than the passive tasks.

5   Discussion

This study aimed to investigate the practical perspective of real-world BCI applications as we studied the performance of a speller system, the application of which combines pixel-level visual stimuli and sound imagery stimuli (dot-speller). The proposed speller systems still rely upon their performance in an oddball paradigm, but with a focus on less obtrusive visual interface. To investigate the efficacy of small visual stimulation, we investigated the differences between a typical speller where the letters themselves were flashed and our novel dot-speller where 0.1 mm dots were flashed instead of the letters on a smartphone. Additionally, we examined the utility of active sound imagery tasks within this setup compared to passive gazing. Our results point to some important implications for future practical BCI interfaces.

Concerning the issue of intentional command, there were two significant intervals for discriminating AC and PC at 300–400 ms (P300) and 700–800 ms (LPP) intervals (see Fig. 2). Interestingly, the PC task showed a stronger P300 component compared to the AC, while the opposite result was found in the LPP. We propose that the LPP stems from the user's active mental task and could be a powerful feature compared to P300 component. While P300 response is the exogenous reaction to the oddball stimulus [9], passive attention can lead to false commands, whereas the active mental would be far more reliable in terms of intention.

Regarding the intention issue, Fig. 3 indicates that the active task significantly outperformed the passive attention task. The average spelling accuracies for the passive task were 76.3% and 78.1% in the normal- and dot-layout systems, respectively. This accuracy is lower than in previous studies where results have shown more than 90% accuracy [3,4,16,17]. This reduced performance is mainly due to our speller system being implemented on a smartphone interface. The indicative stimulus sizes were less than 0.8 cm for the normal-speller letters and only 0.1 mm for the dot-speller layout. As previously was found, smaller-sized and closer-positioned letters can reduce ERP responses, which in turn results in a decreased system performance [18]. Regardless of this shortcoming, the spelling accuracies for the active tasks were 94.1% and 96.8%. This result is comparable to or even outperforms many advanced spelling systems [4,5,16,17,19].

6   Conclusion

In this article, we proposed and tested a novel concept of lowering the impact of external stimuli (visual) while maintaining high classification accuracy by generating endogenous ERP components through a mental task (sound imagery) the user executes. The experiment was run and compared between four possible combinations of stimuli, which allowed us to study the impact of both external (normal- and dot-speller) and mental (passively attending and active concentrating) stimuli. As a result, executing a mental task improved the performance significantly, and the dot-speller showed higher accuracy than the traditional speller. The experiments were taken by healthy (normal or corrected vision) individuals, so further study should be conducted to find out the proposed feature's applicability for users with eye impairments. The feature proposed in this article demonstrates superior potential to create more reliable, user-friendly BCI spelling systems in the future.

References

1. Lee, M.H., et al.: EEG dataset and OpenBMI toolbox for three BCI paradigms: an investigation into BCI illiteracy. GigaScience 8(5), giz002 (2019)
2. Nicolas-Alonso, L.F., Gomez-Gil, J.: Brain-computer interfaces, a review. Sensors 12(2), 1211–1279 (2012)
3. Yeom, S.K., Fazli, S., Müller, K.R., Lee, S.W.: An efficient ERP-based brain-computer interface using random set presentation and face familiarity. PLoS ONE 9(11), e111157 (2014)
4. Li, Q., Liu, S., Li, J., Bai, O.: Use of a green familiar faces paradigm improves p300-speller brain-computer interface performance. PLoS ONE 10(6), 1–15 (2015). https://doi.org/10.1371/journal.pone.0130325
5. Li, Q., Lu, Z., Gao, N., Yang, J.: Optimizing the performance of the visual P300-speller through active mental tasks based on color distinction and modulation of task difficulty. Front. Hum. Neurosci. 13, 130 (2019)
6. Kubová, Z., Kremlacek, J., Szanyi, J., Chlubnová, J., Kuba, M.: Visual event-related potentials to moving stimuli: normative data. Physiol. Res. 51(2), 199–204 (2002)

7. Xu, M., Xiao, X., Wang, Y., Qi, H., Jung, T.P., Ming, D.: A brain-computer interface based on miniature-event-related potentials induced by very small lateral visual stimuli. IEEE Trans. Biomed. Eng. **65**(5), 1166–1175 (2018)
8. Xiao, X., Xu, M., Jin, J., Wang, Y., Jung, T.P., Ming, D.: Discriminative canonical pattern matching for single-trial classification of ERP components. IEEE Trans. Biomed. Eng. **67**(8), 2266–2275 (2019)
9. Farwell, L.A., Donchin, E.: Talking off the top of your head: toward a mental prosthesis utilizing event-related brain potentials. Electroencephalogr. clin. Neurophysiol. **70**(6), 510–523 (1988)
10. Lee, M.H., Williamson, J., Won, D.O., Fazli, S., Lee, S.W.: A high performance spelling system based on EEG-EOG signals with visual feedback. IEEE Trans. Neural Syst. Rehabil. Eng. **26**(7), 1443–1459 (2018)
11. Lee, M.H., et al.: OpenBMI: a real-time data analysis toolbox for brain-machine interfaces. In: 2016 IEEE International Conference on Systems, Man, and Cybernetics (SMC), pp. 001884–001887. IEEE (2016)
12. McFarland, D.J., Sarnacki, W.A., Wolpaw, J.R.: Brain-computer interface (BCI) operation: optimizing information transfer rates. Biol. Psychol. **63**(3), 237–251 (2003)
13. Blankertz, B., Lemm, S., Treder, M., Haufe, S., Müller, K.R.: Single-trial analysis and classification of ERP components: a tutorial. NeuroImage **56**(2), 814–825 (2011)
14. Friedman, J.H.: Regularized discriminant analysis. J. Am. Stat. Assoc. **84**(405), 165–175 (1989)
15. Bennington, J.Y., Polich, J.: Comparison of P300 from passive and active tasks for auditory and visual stimuli. Int. J. Psychophysiol. **34**(2), 171–177 (1999)
16. Jin, J., et al.: The changing face of P300 BCIs: a comparison of stimulus changes in a P300 BCI involving faces, emotion, and movement. PLoS ONE **7**(11), e49688 (2012)
17. Lu, Z., Li, Q., Gao, N., Yang, J.: The self-face paradigm improves the performance of the P300-speller system. Front. Comput. Neurosci. **13**, 93 (2019)
18. Cao, T., Wan, F., Wong, C.M., da Cruz, J.N., Hu, Y.: Objective evaluation of fatigue by EEG spectral analysis in steady-state visual evoked potential-based brain-computer interfaces. Biomed. Eng. Online **13**(1), 28 (2014)
19. Gu, Z., Chen, Z., Zhang, J., Zhang, X., Yu, Z.L.: An online interactive paradigm for P300 brain-computer interface speller. IEEE Trans. Neural Syst. Rehabil. Eng. **27**(2), 152–161 (2019)

Examining Transfer Learning with Neural Network and Bidirectional Neural Network on Thermal Imaging for Deception Recognition

Zishan Qin[1]([✉]), Xuanying Zhu[1], and Tom Gedeon[2]

[1] Australian National University, Canberra, Australia
{taylor.qin2,xuanying.zhu}@anu.edu.au
[2] Curtin University, Perth, Australia
tom.gedeon@curtin.edu.au

Abstract. Deception is a common feature in our daily life, which can be recognised by thermal imaging. Previous research has attempted to identify deception with causality features extracted from thermal images using the extended Granger causality (eGC) method. As the eGC transformation is complicated, in this paper we explore whether a transfer learning model trained on the eGC-transformed thermal deception dataset can be applied to the original thermal data to recognise deception. We explore two feature selection methods, namely linear discriminant analysis (LDA) and t-distributed random neighborhood embedding (t-SNE), and three classifiers, including a support vector machine (SVM), a feed forward neural network (NN) and a bidirectional neural network (BDNN). We find that using features selected by LDA, a transfer learning NN is able to recognise deception with an accuracy of 91.7% and an F1 score of 0.92. We believe this study helps foster a deeper understanding of eGC and provides a foundation for building transfer learning models for deception recognition.

Keywords: Bidirectional neural network · Extended granger causality · Transfer learning · Feature extraction · Linear discriminant analysis

1 Introduction

Deception is common in our global society, with 93% of people being involved in deception in their daily life [8]. Deception may result in harmless falsehoods, but it may also have disastrous effects and even endanger people's lives. Therefore, it would be helpful to assist people with detect deception.

Several attempts have been made on using thermal imaging to detect deception. This is because when people lie, the blood flowing in the facial area will increase, resulting in a fluctuation in the temperature which can be captured by thermal camera [17]. Using thermal imaging, Pavlidis et al. [16] were able to detect deception from the facial region of the liar with an accuracy of 83%. Warmelink et al. [22] applied thermal imaging to train a lie detection system in

© Springer Nature Switzerland AG 2021
T. Mantoro et al. (Eds.): ICONIP 2021, CCIS 1517, pp. 152–159, 2021.
https://doi.org/10.1007/978-3-030-92310-5_18

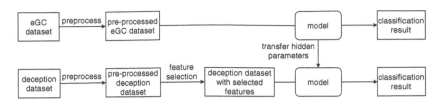

Fig. 1. General structure for our model

an airport scenario with an accuracy of greater than 60%. In [1], Abouelenien et al. extracted important features from thermal images and showed that their system could detect lies with an accuracy above 60%. Such recognition rate was enhanced to 87% in [5] where a support vector machine (SVM) was trained on causality features extracted from thermal images using an extended version of the Granger causality algorithm (eGC) [20].

Despite the high recognition rate achieved in [5], the procedure to convert thermal features using the eGC algorithm is complicated. In [11] transfer learning trained on a large complex dataset is effectively applied to a smaller dataset. Inspired from it, in this paper we explored whether a transfer learning model trained on the eGC-transformed thermal deception data can be applied to recognise deception with the original thermal deception data. To choose a suitable transfer learning model, we examined a Support Vector Machine (SVM), a feed-forward Neural Network (NN) and a Bidirectional Neural Network (BDNN). We hope the transfer learning model can deal with new thermal data which do not need to go through the complex eGC transformation.

A schematic graph of this study is summarised in Fig. 1. We highlight the main contributions of this paper as below.

- We validated the feasibility of deception recognition using transfer learning models trained on causality features extracted from thermal imaging and applied to original thermal imaging data. This alleviates the burden of training on the original dataset, the size of which is very large. Compared with the original dataset, the size of the eGC-transformed dataset is much smaller. Thus it is easier to train a good model on the eGC-transformed dataset, saving the amount of training time for models.
- We compared three classifiers, namely SVM, NN and BDNN, and two feature selection methods. We found that using features selected by linear discriminant analysis (LDA), a transfer learning NN is able to recognise deception with an accuracy of 91.7%. This can be used as a reference, aiding in choosing a more suitable classifier models for transfer learning in a similar setting.

2   Dataset

2.1   Description of the Datasets

The thermal deception dataset provided by [5] contains 480 thermal features for 31 participants collected in a mock crime scenario. Participants were either assigned to a deception group or a truth group. In the deception group, participants were instructed to steal an object which does not belong to them and were asked to deny the possession during an interview. In the truth group, participants did not conduct any theft and thus told the truth. During the interview, a thermal imaging camera was used to record the changes in facial temperature of each participant. The camera collected 480 features from five facial regions, including the perioral region, forehead, cheeks, perinasal region and chin.

[5] also provides an eGC thermal dataset, where the eGC transformation was conducted on the thermal deception dataset using Eq. (1). The relationship between every two features of the large dataset was extracted by eGC, which created 20 features for 31 participants' thermal videos, with five regions per face.

$$eGC_{Y \to X} = ln(\frac{var(W_j(t))}{var(W_j'(t))}) \tag{1}$$

Remark. This formula indicates the connectivity from Y to X. Assuming we try to predict the future terms of X based on the past data from X and Y, we can regard Y as the cause of X if the past term of Y would be useful for predicting the future term of X [3]. $W_j(t)$ and $W_j'(t)$ are the model residuals of X and Y.

2.2   Preprocessing of the Datasets

We first applied the Min-Max normalisation [15] on both the thermal dataset and the eGC dataset to improve NN's performance and to reduce the computational time during training. We then split the data in a 70:30 ratio to construct training and test data for both the original thermal dataset and the eGC dataset.

3   Methods

3.1   Feature Selection

To select features from the original thermal dataset which are used to train the transfer learning model, we examined two methods, including linear discriminant analysis (LDA) and t-distributed random neighborhood embedding (t-SNE).

LDA [21] is very commonly used in extracting features for classification tasks [9]. The goal of LDA is not only to maximize the distance between different classes, but also to minimize the differences within each class itself. This is a good choice because maximizing the distance between the means of each class can lead to better classification results when projecting the data into a low-dimensional space, due to the reduced overlap between different classes. LDA can have good results when the input data follows the Gaussian distribution, which is applicable since our original dataset has been normalized. LDA has been used to extract and select useful features for thermal imaging classification [9].

t-SNE is also a very useful method for feature selection in thermal imaging [4]. t-SNE [10] is a nonlinear dimensionality reduction technique that works by

Algorithm 1: BDNN
1) Forward Pass   for i = 1 to n: Forward pass for forward hidden layer. Store activations.   for i = n to 1: Forward pass for forward hidden layer. Store activations.   for i = 1 to n: Forward pass for output layer with activations from both hidden layers.   **2) Backward Pass**   for i = 1 to n: Backward pass for output layer. Store activations.   for i = n to 1: Backward pass for forward hidden layer with activations from output layer.   for i = 1 to n: Backward pass for backward hidden layer with activations from output layer.   **3) Update Weights**

minimizing the difference between a distribution consisting of pairwise probabilistic similarities of input features in the original high-dimensional space. The equivalent distribution is reduced into low-dimensional space, using gradient descent to minimize the Kullback–Leibler divergence, which measures the differences between two probability distributions. t-SNE has been applied in [4] to reduce feature dimensions for classification based on thermal imaging.

3.2   Classification Model

Support Vector Machine [6] finds the best separation hyperplane between classes by training cases placed at the edges of class descriptors, i.e. support vectors. Training cases outside the support vector are discarded. In this way, fewer training samples are used, so that a high classification accuracy can be achieved on a small training set. This property is advantageous for situations where the number of object samples is often smaller than the number of features. In this paper, we use SVM with polynomial kernel as our baseline model which has been found as the best performing classifier on the eGC dataset [5].

Neural Network is also examined as it is a non-linear model. A 'neuron' in a neural network is a mathematical function that collects and classifies information according to the other neurons connected to it. A neural network contains multiple layers of interconnected nodes. Each node is a perceptron. The perceptron feeds the signal generated by the multiple linear regression into an activation function, which may be non-linear [2].

Bidirectional Neural Network [13] connects two hidden layers in opposite directions to the same output. There is one input at each moment. The hidden layer has two nodes, one for forward pass and the other for backward propagation, and the output layer is determined by the values of these two nodes. This model should be applicable because this structure provides the output layer with complete past and future information for each point in the input sequence [18].

The implementation of BDNN is summarized as Algorithm 1. Note that in our implementation, we use different loss functions for forward and backward

Table 1. Hyper-parameters for the thermal dataset and the eGC dataset.

	Learning rate	Hidden node	Epoch number	Batch size
Thermal dataset	0.41	5	100	9
eGC dataset	0.01	5	100	14

pass. For forward pass, we use cross entropy loss function but for the backward pass, we use a loss function combining a Sigmoid layer and the binary cross entropy (BCE) loss in one single class, calculated by Eq. (2). This can take the benefit of the log-sum-exp trick for numerical stability [12].

$$l_n = -w_n[y_n log\sigma(x_n) + (1 - y_n)log(1 - \sigma(x_n))]$$ (2)

3.3 Transfer Learning

Transfer learning [14] is a technique where a NN is first trained on a problem, and then the hidden layers from the trained model are used as initialization for a new model trained on a new problem. The information from these hidden layers can be effectively used in the new problem, and a well-fitting model can be obtained early in the training. We call the previous problem as the *source domain* and the new problem as the *target domain*. Transfer learning aims to find an effective transfer method so that knowledge transferred from the source domain can assist training in the target domain. In this study, *source domain* is the eGC dataset, while *target domain* is the original thermal dataset. The transferred knowledge is the hidden layer of model trained on the eGC dataset.

Hyper-parameters were tuned on NN and BDNN both for the original thermal dataset and the eGC dataset. Different feature selection methods did not make differences to the hyper-parameters. We have designed simple experiments for the parameters and determined the parameters to be the ones with the highest test accuracy. The parameters are shown in the Table 1.

3.4 Evaluation Metrics

To evaluate the effectiveness of our models, we used two metrics, namely test accuracy and F-score. The accuracy metric is used to measure the percentage that the model makes a correct prediction. F-score is the harmonic mean of precision and recall, calculated as $F_1 = \frac{2}{recall^{-1} + precision^{-1}}$, where recall evaluates the relevant instances that were retrieved and specificity measures how well the model can identify true negatives. The efficiency of our models was measured by the amount of time (in ms) spent on training and testing for each model. All experiments were conducted on the Mac operating system with a core i3 processor and an 8 GB RAM.

4   Results and Discussion

We evaluated the classification of the deception thermal dataset from three perspectives: model, feature extraction method, and whether transfer learning is

Table 2. Mean accuracy and F1 of SVM, NN and BDNN with and without transfer learning.

	SVM				NN				BDNN			
	FF		SF		FF		SF		FF		SF	
	Acc	F1	Acc	F1	Acc	F1	Acc	F1	Acc	F1	Acc	F1
No TL	58.9 [5]	–	87.1 [5]	0.88 [5]	48.3	0.34	81.7	0.75	57.5	0.33	64.8	0.33
With TL	64.3	0.39	66.7	0.4	50	0.33	**91.7**	**0.92**	50.3	0.33	73.3	0.66

FF: Full Features, **SF**: Selected Features, **TL**:Transfer Learning, **Acc**:Accuracy,

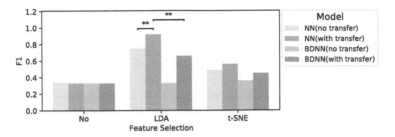

Fig. 2. F1 scores of NN and BDNN with and without transfer learning. The ** above certain pairs of bars show the result differences are significant ($p < 0.01$, t-test).

applied. For each case, we ran the model for 10 times and we calculated the average accuracy and F-score over 10 times as reported in Table 2.

As can be seen from Table 2, the highest classification performance was achieved by transfer learning NN trained with selected features, reaching an accuracy of 91.7% and an F1 score of 0.92. These results were higher than those obtained in [5] where SVM with selected features and no transfer learning was found to be the best performing model. The accuracy of transfer learning NN on selected features was 10% higher than the same model without transfer learning, demonstrating the effectiveness of transfer learning for NN. A similar enhancement was also found in BDNN, with the accuracy and F1 score increased by around 10% and 0.33 before and after transfer learning. However, the use of transfer learning was not effective on SVM, resulting in a significant drop in both accuracy and F1 score. As mentioned in [19], transfer learning may hinder performance when the sources of dataset are not similar. Therefore the decrease of results when transfer learning was applied for SVM may be due to the dissimilarity between the source eGC dataset and the target thermal dataset.

The statistical analyses were performed on the F1 score of each model using Student's t-test [7]. As shown in Fig. 2, both LDA and t-SNE were able to select features that achieve higher classification results. LDA was more effective, selecting features that achieve higher performance than t-SNE. With LDA, both transfer learning NN and BDNN achieved a significant enhancement in f1 score, by 0.59 and 0.33 respectively ($p < 0.01$ in both cases, t-test). This suggests that the LDA feature selection method can effectively enhance the performance on neural network based transfer learning models.

Table 3. Training time and testing time (in milliseconds) of SVM, NN and BDNN with and without transfer learning.

	SVM				NN				BDNN			
	FF		LDA		FF		LDA		FF		LDA	
	TrT	TeT	TrT	TeT	TrT	TeT	TrT	TeT	TrT	TeT	TrT	TeT
No TL	1.01	0.45	0.58	0.19	113.16	0.12	99.79	0.08	513.55	0.14	489.23	0.13
With TL	1.24	0.34	0.70	0.21	49.32	0.13	43.18	0.09	489.42	0.13	388.71	0.14

FF: Full Features, **TL**: Transfer Learning, **TrT**: Training Time, **TeT**: Testing Time.

Comparing the results of NN and BDNN with LDA and transfer learning, we could find that NN achieved a statistically better result than BDNN ($p < 0.01$, t-test), showing that NN with LDA and transfer learning is a better model for this task. Although the BDNN model performed less well, it can be applied to other classification tasks with more samples but fewer features. Thus, we can gain the advantage of the BDNN being able to explore future points in time.

To evaluate the efficiency of each model, we calculated the average training and testing time of each model over 10 runs as listed in Table 3. As seen, transfer learning accelerated training for NN and BDNN. LDA as a feature selection method further reduced the training time. The results show that transfer learning with appropriate feature selection could make the training faster.

5   Conclusion and Future Work

In this study we explored if a transfer learning model trained on the causality features extracted from a thermal deception dataset can be applied to the original thermal data to recognise deception. We found that features selected by LDA could help with positive transfer, with an average test accuracy of 91.7% achieved on NN and 73.30% on BDNN. However, when without feature selection, or when transfer learning was conducted on a SVM model, the model may overfit with the eGC dataset, resulting in a drop in the classification accuracy.

For future work, to prevent over-fitting for transfer learning models, several strategies such as dropout and regularization can be examined. Future work could also be expanded to explore whether the use of more complex neural networks such as residual neural networks is helpful in building an effective and efficient model for deception recognition.

References

1. Abouelenien, M., Pérez-Rosas, V., Mihalcea, R., Burzo, M.: Deception detection using a multimodal approach. In: Proceedings of the 16th International Conference on Multimodal Interaction, pp. 58–65 (2014)
2. Anand, R., Mehrotra, K.G., Mohan, C.K., Ranka, S.: An improved algorithm for neural network classification of imbalanced training sets. IEEE Trans. Neural Netw. 4(6), 962–969 (1993)

3. Bressler, S.L., Seth, A.K.: Wiener-granger causality: a well established methodology. Neuroimage **58**(2), 323–329 (2011)
4. Brzezinski, R.Y., et al.: Automated thermal imaging for the detection of fatty liver disease. Sci. Rep. **10**(1), 1–11 (2020)
5. Derakhshan, A., Mikaeili, M., Nasrabadi, A.M., Gedeon, T.: Network physiology of 'fight or flight' response in facial superficial blood vessels. Physiol. Meas. **40**(1), 014002 (2019)
6. Gold, C., Sollich, P.: Model selection for support vector machine classification. Neurocomputing **55**(1–2), 221–249 (2003)
7. Iyanda, A.R., Ninan, O.D., Ajayi, A.O., Anyabolu, O.G.: Predicting student academic performance in computer science courses: a comparison of neural network models. Int. J. Mod. Educ. Comput. Sci. **10**(6), 1–9 (2018)
8. Jacobsen, C., Fosgaard, T.R., Pascual-Ezama, D.: Why do we lie? A practical guide to the dishonesty literature. J. Econ. Surv. **32**(2), 357–387 (2018)
9. Kheiralipour, K., Ahmadi, H., Rajabipour, A., Rafiee, S., Javan-Nikkhah, M., Jayas, D.: Development of a new threshold based classification model for analyzing thermal imaging data to detect fungal infection of pistachio kernel. Agric. Res. **2**(2), 127–131 (2013)
10. Li, M.A., Luo, X.Y., Yang, J.F.: Extracting the nonlinear features of motor imagery EEG using parametric t-SNE. Neurocomputing **218**, 371–381 (2016)
11. Lin, Y.P., Jung, T.P.: Improving EEG-based emotion classification using conditional transfer learning. Front. Hum. Neurosci. **11**, 334 (2017)
12. Murphy, K.P., et al.: Naive Bayes classifiers. Univ. Br. Columbia **18**(60), 1–8 (2006)
13. Nejad, A.F., Gedeon, T.D.: Bidirectional neural networks and class prototypes. In: Proceedings of ICNN'95-International Conference on Neural Networks, vol. 3, pp. 1322–1327. IEEE (1995)
14. Pan, S.J., Yang, Q.: A survey on transfer learning. IEEE Trans. Knowl. Data Eng. **22**(10), 1345–1359 (2009)
15. Patro, S., Sahu, K.K.: Normalization: a preprocessing stage. arXiv preprint arXiv:1503.06462 (2015)
16. Pavlidis, I., Eberhardt, N.L., Levine, J.A.: Seeing through the face of deception. Nature **415**(6867), 35–35 (2002)
17. Pavlidis, I., Levine, J.: Thermal image analysis for polygraph testing. IEEE Eng. Med. Biol. Mag. **21**(6), 56–64 (2002)
18. Rakitianskaia, A., Bekker, E., Malan, K.M., Engelbrecht, A.: Analysis of error landscapes in multi-layered neural networks for classification. In: 2016 IEEE Congress on Evolutionary Computation (CEC), pp. 5270–5277. IEEE (2016)
19. Rosenstein, M.T., Marx, Z., Kaelbling, L.P., Dietterich, T.G.: To transfer or not to transfer. In: NIPS 2005 workshop on transfer learning, vol. 898, pp. 1–4 (2005)
20. Schiatti, L., Nollo, G., Rossato, G., Faes, L.: Extended granger causality: a new tool to identify the structure of physiological networks. Physiol. Meas. **36**(4), 827 (2015)
21. Song, F., Mei, D., Li, H.: Feature selection based on linear discriminant analysis. In: 2010 International Conference on Intelligent System Design and Engineering Application, vol. 1, pp. 746–749. IEEE (2010)
22. Warmelink, L., Vrij, A., Mann, S., Leal, S., Forrester, D., Fisher, R.P.: Thermal imaging as a lie detection tool at airports. Law Hum. Behav. **35**(1), 40–48 (2011)

Multi-scale Fusion Attention Network for Polyp Segmentation

Dongjin Huang$^{(\boxtimes)}$, Kaili Han, Yongjie Xi, and Wenqi Che

Shanghai Film Academy, Shanghai University, Shanghai, China
djhuang@shu.edu.cn

Abstract. Polyp segmentation is an essential step in the diagnosis and treatment of colorectal cancer. Due to the low contrast between the foreground and the background, the large difference in shape and size and the blurred boundary of the polyp, accurate polyp segmentation faces huge challenges. In this paper, we propose a Multi-scale Fusion Attention Network (MSFANet) for polyp segmentation. Firstly, we design the Gated Local Attention Module (GLAM) to connect the encoder and decoder to extract local features of polyps of different shapes and sizes. Secondly, the Positional Global Attention Module (PGAM) is constructed at the end of the encoder to capture the global dependency of context information. Finally, in the decoding stage, we present the Dilated Dense Connection (DDC) to enhance the transfer and reuse of features. Meanwhile, the Multi-scale Feature Fusion Attention Module (MFFAM) is designed to selectively aggregate multi-scale features and emphasize target features. In addition, we evaluate our MSFANet model on the public datasets Kvasir-SEG and EndoScene. Compared with other state-of-the-art methods, our model shows better segmentation results.

Keywords: Polyp segmentation · Deep learning · Attention mechanism · Multi-scale fusion

1 Introduction

Colorectal cancer (CRC) is the third most common cancer that threatens human life and health [1]. CRC screening and early diagnosis and treatment can effectively reduce the mortality of CRC. Colonoscopy is the first choice for the detection of polyps, but the process is time-consuming and the missed detection rate is high [2]. Therefore, accurate polyp segmentation is of important practical significance for the early detection of CRC.

In recent years, numerous convolutional neural networks have been applied to medical image segmentation. U-Net [3] proposes a high-precision medical image semantic segmentation model based on small samples, but it leads to redundant problem. UNet++ [4] has improved the structure of U-Net [3] for polyp segmentation, however it ignores the relationship between polyp regions and boundaries. For this problem, SFANet [5] constructs the structure of parallel decoders, but it is easy to overfit. Under the influence of SFANet [5], PraNet [6]

T. Mantoro et al. (Eds.): ICONIP 2021, CCIS 1517, pp. 160–167, 2021.
https://doi.org/10.1007/978-3-030-92310-5_19

designs a parallel reverse attention network for polyp segmentation. ACSNet [7] presents adaptive network for polyp segmentation, but it ignores the differences between local features and context dependencies. In short, though these models have obtained relatively good results, there are still many problems, such as incomplete segmentation of small polyp regions and boundaries.

In this paper, we propose a Multi-scale Fusion Attention Network (MSFANet) for polyp segmentation. We construct the Gated Local Attention Module (GLAM) to connect the encoder and decoder, which extracts local features and enhances the small polyp areas. The Positional Global Attention Module (PGAM) is placed at the end of the encoder to achieve the global context features. And the Dilated Dense Connection (DDC) is designed in the encoding stage to enhance feature propagation. Meanwhile, we present a Multi-scale Feature Fusion Attention Module (MFFAM) to selectively aggregate local features from GLAM, global features from PGAM, and features delivered by DDC and the previous decoder to capture polyp regions.

2   Method

Figure 1 shows the structure of the proposed MSFANet, which employs a basic encoder and decoder structure, and utilizes ResNet34 [8] as the encoder.

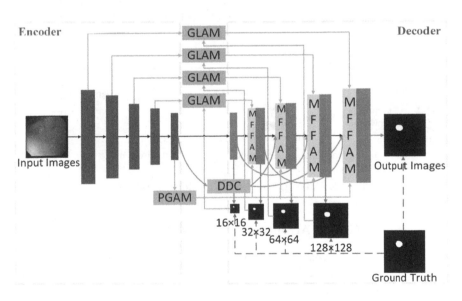

Fig. 1. An overview of the proposed MSFANet.

We construct GLAM to connect the encoder and decoder and achieve local features. At the end of the encoder, we propose PGAM to extract global context features. In the decoder, DDC is presented for feature reuse. At the same time, we design MFFAM to selectively integrate local features and global features to concentrate on segmentation target of different polyps.

2.1   Gated Local Attention Module (GLAM)

GLAM suppresses irrelevant areas in the input images while enhancing the local features that are useful for segmentation target. As shown in Fig. 2, the prediction feature determines the attention map. And we add gated attention [9] to concentrate the attention coefficients in local areas.

The attention map of the nth GLAM is expressed as $A_n \in \mathbb{R}^{1 \times H_n \times W_n}$. Attention A_n^m at position $m \in [1, 2, ..., H \times W]$ is calculated as:

$$A_n^m = 1 - \frac{|p_{n+1}^m - 0.5|}{0.5} \tag{1}$$

where, p_{n+1}^m is the value of the mth position of the p_{n+1} prediction feature. We take 0.5 as the threshold to improve the sensitivity of the current position to foreground pixels. And a_i^l and e_i are the feature vectors corresponding to the ith position of the lth layer of the attention map and the ith position of the encoder feature, respectively. Subsequently, we multiply a_i^l and e_i, and then add the result to the original feature. After that, we obtain the attention coefficient through ReLU and sigmoid function. At last, the feature map of the encoder is multiplied by attention coefficient to focus the attention on the target area.

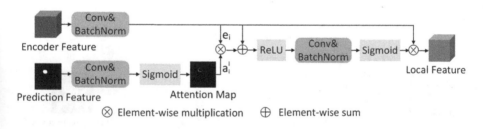

Fig. 2. Gated Local Attention Module (GLAM).

2.2   Positional Global Attention Module (PGAM)

Since the polyp area is relatively large compared to some fine structures (e.g., blood vessels), we design PGAM at the end of the encoding stage to obtain global features. In order to capture richer context dependencies on global features, a position attention module [10] is imported in PGAM.

The architecture of PGAM is exhibited in Fig. 3. Firstly, the feature map $F \in \mathbb{R}^{C \times W \times H}$ generated by the encoder is subjected to convolution to obtain three feature maps $\{F_1^p, F_2^p, F_3^p\} \in \mathbb{R}^{C \times (H \times W)}$. Secondly, we execute matrix multiplication on the transpose of F_1^p and F_2^p to gain the spatial attention map A^p. After that we perform matrix multiplication and sum to get the final position

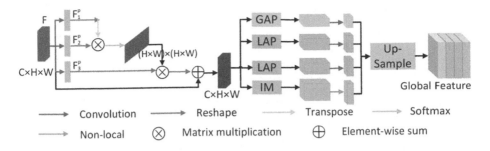

Fig. 3. Positional Global Attention Module (PGAM).

attention P. The position attention captures the spatial dependence between arbitrary positions of the global feature.

Subsequently, we use four branches of global average pooling (GAP), local average pooling (LAP) and identity mapping (IM) to extract global feature from the attention map P. Finally, we perform convolution, upsampling and concatenation on the four feature maps to achieve global features. Then global features will be input to each MFFAM and aggregate them into different features.

2.3 Dilated Dense Connection (DDC)

In order to ensure the reuse of information between different layers of the model and solve the problem of large memory usage, we construct DDC. As shown in Fig. 1, there are five layers of network in the decoding stage, and the input of each layer includes the union connection of the output of the upper layer and the previous layer with a gap from the upper layer.

2.4 Multi-scale Feature Fusion Attention Module (MFFAM)

In the decoder, MFFAM filters out irrelevant information transmitted by global features, gradually removes noise areas, and emphasizes local areas that are more related to the target region achieved from local features.

As shown in Fig. 4. In order to capture the dependency between any two channels, we leverage the channel attention module [10] to obtain channel attention C, which is similar in structure to the position attention module. Then we employ a non-local operation [11] on the channel attention C to heighten the long-range dependencies. Next, for feature maps of different sizes, we set them to the same size through upsampling, and then connect the features from GLAM, PGAM, DDC, and channel attention map C. Finally, the connected features are input to the Squeeze-and-Excitation module (SE) [12], so as to determine the most relevant feature to the segmentation target. In addition, we introduce edge contour information for supervision to improve the accuracy of result.

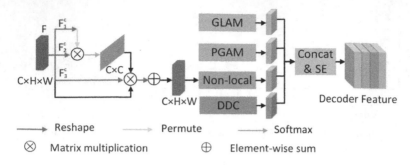

Fig. 4. Multi-scale Feature Fusion Attention Module (MFFAM).

3   Experiments

3.1   Datasets

In this study, we test our model on two commonly used polyp segmentation datasets: Kvasir-SEG [13] and EndoScene [14]. The Kvasir-SEG dataset is the largest and most challenging dataset recently released, which contains 1000 RGB polyp images from real colonoscopy videos. We divide the dataset into training set, validation set and testing set, with 600 images, 200 images, and 200 images respectively. The EndoScene dataset contains 912 images, each with at least one polyp region, and these images are from 44 video sequences of 36 subjects. The dataset is divided into 547 training set images, 183 validation set images and 182 testing set images. In the experiment, we adjust the image size to 384 × 288.

3.2   Implementation Details and Evaluation Metrics

We expand the training set through data augmentation, which includes random horizontal and vertical flips, rotations, zooms, and moves. We train 150 epochs and set the batchsize to 4. At the same time, we set the initial learning rate to 1e-3 and use a polynomial decay learning rate strategy to reduce it. And we leverage the SGD optimization algorithm to optimize the overall parameters.

We use "Recall", "Specificity", "Precision", "Dice Score", "Intersection-over-Union for Segmentation (IoUs)", "IoU for Background (IoUb)", "Mean IoU (mIoU)" and "Accuracy" to evaluate the performance results.

3.3   Results and Analysis

We compare our MSFANet with several representative polyp segmentation models, including UNet [3], UNet++ [4], SegNet [15], SFANet [5], PraNet [6] and ACSNet [7]. As shown in the result on the Kvasir-SEG in Table 1, MSFANet is higher than other methods in seven indicators. And *Recall* is only 0.18% lower than the highest value of ACSNet, while *Precision* is 0.64% higher, indicating that our MSFANet has a low missed detection rate and false detection rate.

Table 1. Comparison with other state-of-the-art methods on the Kvasir-SEG dataset.

Methods	Rec	Spec	Prec	Dice	IoUs	IoUb	mIoU	Acc
UNet [3]	88.07	96.79	82.67	82.71	73.57	93.02	83.30	94.49
UNet++ [4]	88.80	97.24	83.05	81.97	72.96	94.13	83.54	95.04
SgeNet [15]	88.08	98.24	90.46	86.91	80.01	94.67	87.34	95.75
SFANet [5]	89.29	97.59	86.84	85.86	78.16	94.08	86.12	95.36
PraNet [6]	91.50	98.39	92.22	90.48	84.74	95.84	90.29	96.80
ACSNet [7]	**92.64**	98.53	93.46	91.79	86.67	96.65	91.66	97.53
Ours	92.46	**98.55**	**94.10**	**92.25**	**87.19**	**96.66**	**91.92**	**97.58**

The result on the EndoScene is exhibited in Table 2, our model also acquires the best result. Although *Precision* is lower than other models, *Recall* and *Dice* are much higher than other methods, demonstrating that there is a great balance between *Recall* and *Precision*, which makes our network performance better.

Table 2. Comparison with other state-of-the-art methods and Ablation study on the EndoScene dataset (Bl = Baseline).

Methods	Rec	Spec	Prec	Dice	IoUs	IoUb	mIoU	Acc
UNet [3]	85.33	98.88	83.74	80.39	71.02	95.88	83.45	96.19
UNet++ [4]	79.39	99.20	85.89	77.60	69.04	95.66	82.35	95.69
SgeNet [15]	83.74	99.01	85.72	81.27	72.56	96.05	84.31	96.10
SFANet [5]	84.67	99.03	87.23	82.96	75.97	96.38	86.18	96.64
PraNet [6]	86.71	99.06	86.49	84.57	76.68	98.36	87.52	98.45
ACSNet [7]	89.98	98.46	86.32	86.39	78.93	98.03	88.48	98.12
Ours	**91.41**	**99.21**	86.79	**87.83**	**80.37**	**98.76**	**89.56**	**98.83**
Bl	87.71	98.70	86.07	85.15	76.61	98.17	87.39	98.28
Bl+GLA	88.60	99.00	86.01	85.26	77.64	98.41	88.02	98.48
Bl+GLA+PGA	89.69	98.81	86.53	85.72	78.30	98.39	88.35	98.48
Bl+GLA+PGA+DDC	89.50	98.86	**87.94**	86.26	79.28	98.44	88.86	98.53
Bl+GLA+PGA+DDC+MFFA	90.67	99.03	87.43	87.43	80.33	98.67	89.50	98.74

Figure 5 shows the qualitative results of comparative experiments. It can be seen that the segmentation result of MSFANet model is closest to the ground truth (GT). MSFANet can well cope with the challenges presented before. For polyps with low contrast (Fig. 5 the first and fourth rows), large polyps (Fig. 5 the second and fifth row), multiple polyps (Fig. 5 the third row), and small polyp (Fig. 5 the sixth row), our model has excellent processing results. These examples illustrate that our model can selectively aggregate multi-scale features to segment polyps, thereby greatly improving segmentation performance.

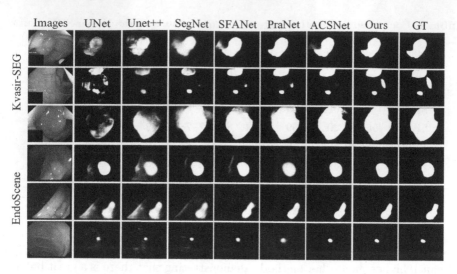

Fig. 5. Polyp segmentation results of different methods.

3.4 Ablation Study

In order to prove the effectiveness of the various modules in the MSFANet model and have a deeper understanding of our MSFANet, we execute ablation study using the EndoScene dataset. And we employ ResUNet [16] as the baseline and gradually add GLAM, PGAM, DDC and MFFAM modules.

The experimental result is shown in Table 2. When we gradually add each module to the network, the segmentation performance of the model will be improved to varying degrees. These results illustrate that the proposed GLAM, PGAM, DDC and MFFAM modules can improve the accuracy of segmentation.

4 Conclusion

In this paper, we propose a Multi-scale Fusion Attention Network (MSFANet) for automatic segmentation of polyps in colonoscopy images. We construct GLAM and PGAM to extract local features and global features respectively, then design DDC in the decoding stage to ensure the information reuse between different layers, and propose MFFAM to aggregate local and global multi-scale features. Compared with other state-of-the-art methods, our MSFANet model shows a superior segmentation performance. In future work, we will further improve our network model and consider applying the model to polyp detection.

References

1. Siegel, R., DeSantis, C., Jemal, A.: Colorectal cancer statistics, 2014. CA: Cancer J. Clin. **64**(2), 104–117 (2014)

2. Leufkens, A., Van Oijen, M., Vleggaar, F., Siersema, P.: Factors influencing the miss rate of polyps in a back-to-back colonoscopy study. Endoscopy **44**(05), 470–475 (2012)

3. Ronneberger, O., Fischer, P., Brox, T.: U-Net: convolutional networks for biomedical image segmentation. In: Navab, N., Hornegger, J., Wells, W.M., Frangi, A.F. (eds.) MICCAI 2015. LNCS, vol. 9351, pp. 234–241. Springer, Cham (2015). https://doi.org/10.1007/978-3-319-24574-4_28

4. Zhou, Z., Rahman Siddiquee, M.M., Tajbakhsh, N., Liang, J.: UNet++: a nested U-Net architecture for medical image segmentation. In: Stoyanov, D., et al. (eds.) DLMIA/ML-CDS 2018. LNCS, vol. 11045, pp. 3–11. Springer, Cham (2018). https://doi.org/10.1007/978-3-030-00889-5_1

5. Fang, Y., Chen, C., Yuan, Y., Tong, K.: Selective feature aggregation network with area-boundary constraints for polyp segmentation. In: Shen, D., et al. (eds.) MICCAI 2019. LNCS, vol. 11764, pp. 302–310. Springer, Cham (2019). https://doi.org/10.1007/978-3-030-32239-7_34

6. Fan, D.P., et al.: PraNet: parallel reverse attention network for polyp segmentation. In: Martel, A.L., et al. (eds.) MICCAI 2020. LNCS, vol. 12266, pp. 263–273. Springer, Cham (2020). https://doi.org/10.1007/978-3-030-59725-2_26

7. Zhang, R., Li, G., Li, Z., Cui, S., Qian, D., Yu, Y.: Adaptive context selection for polyp segmentation. In: Martel, A.L., et al. (eds.) MICCAI 2020. LNCS, vol. 12266, pp. 253–262. Springer, Cham (2020). https://doi.org/10.1007/978-3-030-59725-2_25

8. He, K., Zhang, X., Ren, S., Sun, J.: Deep residual learning for image recognition. In: Proceedings of the IEEE Conference on Computer Vision and Pattern Recognition, pp. 770–778 (2016)

9. Oktay, O., et al.: Attention U-Net: learning where to look for the pancreas. arXiv preprint arXiv:1804.03999 (2018)

10. Fu, J., et al.: Dual attention network for scene segmentation. In: Proceedings of the IEEE/CVF Conference on Computer Vision and Pattern Recognition, pp. 3146–3154 (2019)

11. Wang, X., Girshick, R., Gupta, A., He, K.: Non-local neural networks. In: Proceedings of the IEEE Conference on Computer Vision and Pattern Recognition, pp. 7794–7803 (2018)

12. Hu, J., Shen, L., Sun, G.: Squeeze-and-excitation networks. In: Proceedings of the IEEE Conference on Computer Vision and Pattern Recognition, pp. 7132–7141 (2018)

13. Jha, D., et al.: Kvasir-SEG: a segmented polyp dataset. In: Ro, Y.M., et al. (eds.) MMM 2020. LNCS, vol. 11962, pp. 451–462. Springer, Cham (2020). https://doi.org/10.1007/978-3-030-37734-2_37

14. Vázquez, D., et al.: A benchmark for endoluminal scene segmentation of colonoscopy images. J. Healthc. Eng. **2017** (2017)

15. Wickstrøm, K., Kampffmeyer, M., Jenssen, R.: Uncertainty and interpretability in convolutional neural networks for semantic segmentation of colorectal polyps. Med. Image Anal. **60**, 101619 (2020)

16. Xiao, X., Lian, S., Luo, Z., Li, S.: Weighted Res-UNet for high-quality retina vessel segmentation. In: 2018 9th International Conference on Information Technology in Medicine and Education (ITME), pp. 327–331. IEEE (2018)

A Fusion Framework to Enhance sEMG-Based Gesture Recognition Using TD and FD Features

Yao Luo[1,2], Tao Luo[1], Qianchen Xia[2,4(✉)], Huijiong Yan[2,3], Liang Xie[2], Ye Yan[2,3], and Erwei Yin[2,3]

[1] College of Intelligence and Computing, Tianjin University, Tianjin 300072, China
[2] Tianjin Artificial Intelligence Innovation Center, Tianjin 300450, China
xqc65@msn.com
[3] Defense Innovation Institute, Academy of Military Sciences, Beijing 100071, China
[4] Department of Industrial Engineering, Tsinghua University, Beijing 100084, China

Abstract. Gesture recognition based on surface electromyographic (sEMG) is one of the most critical technologies in the field of human–computer interactions(HCI). The previous sEMG-based gesture recognition frameworks have poor effect due to the inappropriate feature processing. In this paper, we propose a sEMG-based gesture recognition framework called TF-LSTMCNN(LSTM and CNN based on TD and FD features). We formulated the feature combination from time domain (TD) and frequency domain (FD) as the diversified feature representation, as well as an advanced feature representation learned from a fusion technique that integrates a variety of discriminative sEMG signal patterns. To generate diversity feature representations, we considered the redundancy and uniqueness among features and chose a combination of TD and FD features. The accuracy of the proposed method achieved 85.13%, and is 8.58% higher than SVM which showed higher performance in the machine learning (ML) methods.

Keywords: Feature fusion · sEMG · Text input · Hand gesture

1 Introduction

sEMG is a non-stationary bioelectric signal collected by the electrodes placed on the surface of skin [8], and represents the comprehensive superposition of action potential sequences in time and space. Moreover, sEMG reflects muscular movement (such as: muscular strength, joint torque, etc.) and is generated 30–150 earlier than the body movement [6]. From this aspect, it can be used as a real-time control signal of gesture recognition. As one of the most important forms of HCI, text input has high requirements on real-time performance. Traditional text input methods mainly rely on mechanical keyboard and mouse, which are bulky and inconvenient to carry. Therefore, sEMG-based gesture recognition for text input is of great significance.

© Springer Nature Switzerland AG 2021
T. Mantoro et al. (Eds.): ICONIP 2021, CCIS 1517, pp. 168–175, 2021.
https://doi.org/10.1007/978-3-030-92310-5_20

The information expressed by the single feature is not comprehensive enough to reflect the characteristics of the muscular movement, and the pivotal information may be lost. Usually, first-order discrete features are often combined into high-order features due to the correlation among features, which enrich the expressions of the motion information. The current researches on feature combination are mostly based on TD features [13,14] without consideration of the redundancy among TD features [4].

Researches based on sEMG pattern recognition have tend to use traditional ML classifiers. Many researches have shown that DL can perform better than traditional classification methods (e.g., SVM) in sEMG-based gesture recognition. LSTM is more appropriate to learn representation from the sequential features, while CNN is more suitable for the features with spatial information [7]. The existing DL studies on sEMG do not take into consideration of the compatibility among features and networks, as well as ignore the characteristics of data.

Considering the above problems, we proposed a feature fusion method based on TD and FD features. The main contributions of this article can be summarized as follows.

1) We represented the feature combination selected from which were combined by each of the six primary TD features with one classic FD feature in pairs, and it showed higher performance than either the single feature.
2) We proposed a sEMG-based TF-LSTMCNN network architecture for gesture recognition, which achieved higher gesture recognition accuracies than those traditional ML methods.

2   Related Works

The sEMG signal has problems such as non-stationarity [2,12], randomness [12], strong noises [3], information redundancy [9,15], and large dimensions. The features extracted from the original data through prior knowledge to optimized information improve the recognition accuracy. Therefore, in order to achieve a better sEMG-based gesture recognition performance, feature extraction can be performed on the original data.

Principally, there are two main types of sEMG feature: TD and FD features. Li et al. [10] extracted the MAV feature from the instantaneous sEMG signals in the high-density sEMG data set CapgMyo and normalized it for decoding. Chen et al. [5] extracted the RMS feature and used Two-step SVM to recognize the six movements of the upper limbs and perform real-time control. Although the single feature extraction method has low computational complexity (compared to multiple features) and high efficiency, the extracted information cannot describe sEMG in multiple dimensions and is so deficient that it has weak access to motion information and limited expressiveness.

With the rapid development of DL, Atzori et al. [1] discovered that the accuracy rate of the CNN model was the highest among the rates obtained from SVM, KNN, LDA and RF methods. Pan et al. [11] based on deep belief networks

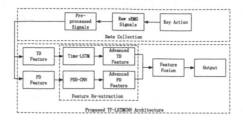

Fig. 1. Proposed TF-LSTMCNN framework

(DBN) to learn more representative features, and combined manual features with DBN features to obtain more robust recognition results. But it does not take into account the difference among feature sets and the redundancy. These DL methods based on sEMG all recognize the limitations of single feature, and multi-feature fusion methods for pattern recognition. However, the adaptability of features and networks is not considered, and a single network is used to process different types of features, resulting in less performance improvement.

3   Methods

The proposed TF-LSTMCNN network architecture is shown in Fig. 1. When an action is performed, the raw sEMG signals are collected. Preprocessing is applied on sEMG to reduce noise, and then TD features are put into Time-LSTM network (Sect. 3.1) because of its ability to capture temporal information. Relevantly, PSD (Power Spectral Density) features are fed locally into PSD-CNN network (Sect. 3.2) on account of their spatial information. Then, the advanced features extracted from the two networks are fed to the fusion network module (Sect. 3.3), and finally the classification information is obtained as the output.

3.1   Time-LSTM

The Time-LSTM network used in this research is composed of three layers of LSTM, as well as a layer of BN (Batch Normalization) and a Fully Connected (FC) layer. Among them, each layer of the LSTM is set with a drop-out rate of 0.05, the activation function of the FC layer is set to ReLU (Rectified Linear Unit), and the output of the FC is 2 × the number of classes. The Time-LSTM network structure is shown in Fig. 2(a).

3.2   PSD-CNN

The PSD feature plays an important role in the field of traditional FD signal analysis, and can represent the most primitive FD information. On the each channel, the PSD feature represents the transformation of the signal power with frequency in the unit band within the time length of the channel, and has a certain local correlation. CNN has better information capture ability for data with spatial information, so we used CNN to further analyze and re-extract PSD features. The proposed PSD-CNN module is mainly composed of two Conv layers, two Pool layers and a FC layer. The output of the final FC layer is 2 × the number of categories, as shown in Fig. 2(b).

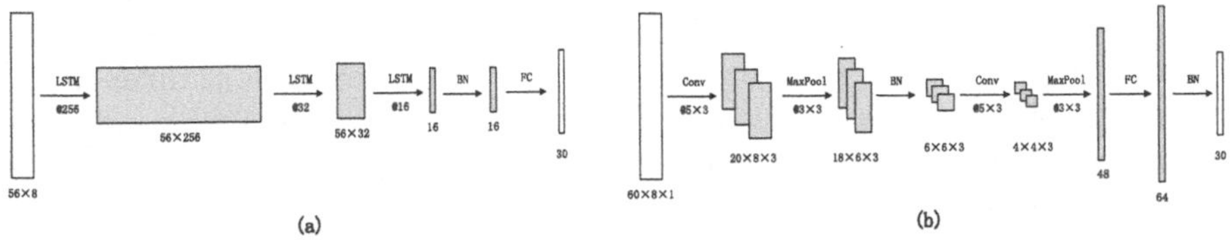

Fig. 2. (a)Proposed Time-LSTM network. (b)Proposed PSD-CNN network

3.3   Feature Fusion

There is redundancy and less specific information among TD features. Therefore, we applied the combination of TD and FD features for feature fusion, which not only avoids the redundancy among features but also obtains information in different dimensions. The two kinds of advanced information are expressions of two different levels and dimensions of sEMG signals. Based on this, we performed concatenate operation on these two kinds of advanced information representations, and used them as the input of the decision fusion layer. We adopted sliding window with length of 10 to extract TD features. We selected six classic TD features: RMS, IEMG, VAR, ZC, WL and MAV, then combined them with PSD as feature combinations, respectively. Feature combinations were trained on the proposed TF-LSTMCNN network, and the feature combination achieving highest accuracy would be selected as the final feature combination.

4   Experiments

4.1   Data Acquisition

10 healthy subjects (aged 23–27: 7 male and 3 female) participated in the experiments. The sEMG data were recorded by using 8 Ag/AgCl EMG electrodes, with a sampling rate 1000 Hz. Due to the symmetry of the left and right hands, only the right hand will be discussed below in this article. The standard typing method defines a total of 15 keys for the right hand excluding the thumb(we only studied the letter keys), for a total of 30 buttons. Before the experiments, participants were trained in standard typing to tap the corresponding keys proficiently according to the instructions. After each key action of the user, participants were asked to keep the finger to the initial state.

Each subject needed to do ten groups of experiments. In each group, the subjects performed 15 key action rounds in sequence with a 2s break among key action rounds, in which the subjects were asked to repeat the key action 10 times. After repeated demonstrations and experiments, the subjects could complete the reaction, start the action, and return to the initial state after the completion of the action within 1.6s. The experimental paradigm is shown in Fig. 3.

Each key action was repeated for 10 times in one group, and there were 15 kinds of actions, so a total of 1500 samples were collected for each subject in ten groups. We used 10-fold cross-validation to measure the performance of the proposed network architecture on the data of 10 subjects. The samples in the same round of 10 groups for each subject were considered as a fold and there were a total of 10 folds, of which 9 folds were used for training, and the remaining 1 fold was used for testing.

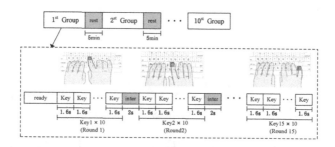

Fig. 3. Experimental paradigm design

4.2   Results

The experimental results for the fusion of six classical TD features and PSD feature using the TF-LSTMCNN network are shown in Fig. 4(a). It can be seen that the combination of MAV and PSD features has the highest accuracy, and the average accuracy of ten subjects is 85.14%, while that of the feature combination of ZC and PSD is the lowest, only 72.09%. The accuracy for feature combination of RMS, IEMG, VAR, WL with PSD is 84.5%, 85.07%, 82.85%, 82.8%, respectively.

The accuracy of ours is higher than either single sub-network. Time-LSTM sub-network and PSD-CNN sub-network achieve accuracy rates of 77.48% and 71.07% respectively, which proves that the feature combination of MAV and PSD can achieve greater classification effect. The accuracy of ours is higher than that of the two decision fusion methods. Score-sum fusion and score-max fusion achieve accuracy rates of 82.46% and 59.08% respectively, which proves that the fusion of the proposed network effectiveness, as shown in Fig. 4(b).

We also compared the proposed TF-LSTMCNN with traditional ML methods including SVM, RF, KNN, LDA, as shown in Fig. 4(c). Among them, the average recognition accuracies of SVM, RF, KNN, LDA and the TF-LSTMCNN in this article are 76.56%, 77.32%, 75.92%, 53.82% and 85.14% respectively. All the methods use the same feature combination of MAV and PSD. The recognition accuracy of TF-LSTMCNN in this article is much higher than that of the other ML methods, which proves the superiority of the proposed TF-LSTMCNN.

5   Discussion

The proposed TF-LSTMCNN architecture is verified on the test set, and the confusion matrix in Fig. 5 is obtained. It can be seen that the misjudgment rate of some actions is higher, which may be related to the key design in the standard typing method and the kinematics of the fingers of the human hand. There are two types of confusion in the confusion matrix: intra-finger confusion and inter-finger confusion.

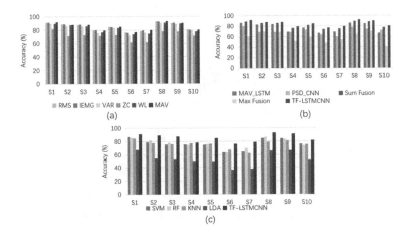

Fig. 4. The experimental results on different feature extraction methods and classifiers. (a) is the results of the six feature combinations. (b) is the comparison of the TF-LSTMCNN, its sub-network and two decision fusion methods. (c) is the comparison of the TF-LSTMCNN and ML methods.

There are the confusion of action 1–6 and the confusion of action 7–9 in the intra-finger confusion. This large-scale confusion is principally caused by the similarity of the activated muscular groups and force patterns among different actions of the same finger.

At the same time, in the intra-finger confusion, actions with similar serial numbers are more confusing, that is, they are confused in order. Take the right middle finger as an example, the buttons controlled by the right middle finger are "I", "K", and "," from top to bottom, corresponding to the middle finger moving one key distance up, middle finger in-place clicking, middle finger moving one key distance down, and the corresponding labels are 7, 8, 9. It is not difficult to conclude that the closer the serial numbers are, the more similar the actions are.

Action 1–6 are relatively more confusing, because the 6 category actions of the index finger are more difficult to categorize than the 3 category actions of other fingers. At the same time, the degree of distinction among actions is relatively small, and the movement patterns among actions are more similar.

The inter-finger confusion is mainly reflected in actions 10–15. These 6 actions are controlled by the little finger and the ring finger, while the little finger and the ring finger are synergistic and interfere with each other during actions. For example, there is confusion among action 10 and 13. These two key actions are moving one key distance up by the ring finger and the little finger respectively. In the process of large-scale movement, the movement of the little finger is likely to drive the ring finger to exert force.

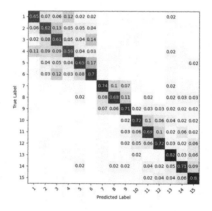

Fig. 5. The confusion matrix of the predicted results in the test set of 10 subjects.

6   Conclusion

In this paper, we presented a new TF-LSTMCNN framework that formulates a feature combination of two domains for the feature diversity and transformed them into an advanced feature fusion. To reduce the computational complexity and ensure the complementarity, the combination process performance was mainly depended on gesture recognition performance: the most discriminative feature combination representations were selected and subsequently used as the input of the proposed TF-LSTMCNN for gesture recognition. We also performed experiments to demonstrate the superiority of the proposed TF-LSTMCNN framework. The accuracy of the proposed method achieved 85.13%, and than of SVM which showed higher performance in ML methods are 8.58%.

Future work is mainly based on the study of FD feature extraction of sEMG signals. The PSD features of some subjects perform poorly in the PSD-CNN architecture, so further improvements to the PSD-CNN architecture may be needed.

References

1. Atzori, M., Cognolato, M., Muller, H.: Deep learning with convolutional neural networks applied to electromyography data: a resource for the classification of movements for prosthetic hands. Front Neurorobot. **10**, 9 (2016)
2. Bahador, A., Yousefi, M., Marashi, M., Bahador, O.: High accurate lightweight deep learning method for gesture recognition based on surface electromyography. Comput. Methods Programs Biomed. **195**, 105643 (2020)
3. Benatti, S., Montagna, F., Kartsch, V., Rahimi, A., Rossi, D., Benini, L.: Online learning and classification of emg-based gestures on a parallel ultra-low power platform using hyperdimensional computing. IEEE Trans. Biomed. Circ. Syst. **13**(3), 516–528 (2019)
4. Chen, H., Zhang, Y., Li, G., Fang, Y., Liu, H.: Surface electromyography feature extraction via convolutional neural network. Int. J. Mach. Learn. Cybernet. **11**(1), 185–196 (2019). https://doi.org/10.1007/s13042-019-00966-x
5. Chen, Y., Zhou, Y., Cheng, X., Mi, Y.: Upper limb motion recognition based on two-step svm classification method of surface emg. Int. J. Control Autom. **6**(3), 249–266 (2013)
6. Ding, Q.C., Xiong, A.B., Zhao, X.G., Han, J.D.: A review on researches and applications of semg-based motion intent recognition methods. Acta Automatica Sinica (2016)
7. Hu, R., Chen, X., Zhang, X., Chen, X.: Adaptive electrode calibration method based on muscle core activation regions and its application in myoelectric pattern recognition. IEEE Trans. Neural Syst. Rehabil. Eng. **29**, 11–20 (2020)
8. Yu, H., Wong, Y., Dai, Q., Kankanhalli, M., Geng, W., Li, X.: semg-based gesture recognition with embedded virtual hand poses adversarial learning. IEEE Access **7**, 104108–104120 (2019)
9. Jiang, S., et al.: Feasibility of wrist-worn, real-time hand, and surface gesture recognition via semg and imu sensing. IEEE Trans. Ind. Inform. **14**(8), 3376–3385 (2018)
10. Li, Y., Zhang, Q., Zeng, N., Chen, J., Zhang, Q.: Discrete hand motion intention decoding based on transient myoelectric signals. IEEE Access **7**, 81630–81639 (2019)
11. Pan, T.Y., Tsai, W.L., Chang, C.Y., Yeh, C.W., Hu, M.C.: A hierarchical hand gesture recognition framework for sports referee training-based emg and accelerometer sensors. IEEE Transactions on Cybernetics (2020)
12. Qi, J., Jiang, G., Li, G., Sun, Y., Tao, B.: Intelligent human-computer interaction based on surface emg gesture recognition. IEEE Access **7**, 61378–61387 (2019)
13. Song, W., et al.: Design of a flexible wearable smart semg recorder integrated gradient boosting decision tree based hand gesture recognition. IEEE Trans. Biomed. Circ. Syst. **13**(6), 1563–1574 (2019)
14. Wahid, M.F., Tafreshi, R., Langari, R.: A multi-window majority voting strategy to improve hand gesture recognition accuracies using electromyography signal. IEEE Trans. Neural Syst. Rehabil. Eng. **28**(2), 427–436 (2020)
15. Wu, J., Sun, L., Jafari, R.: A wearable system for recognizing american sign language in real-time using imu and surface emg sensors. IEEE J. Biomed. Health Inform. **20**(5), 1281–1290 (2016)

Label Aggregation for Crowdsourced Triplet Similarity Comparisons

Jiyi Li[1(✉)], Lucas Ryo Endo[2], and Hisashi Kashima[2]

[1] University of Yamanashi, Kofu, Japan
`jyli@yamanashi.ac.jp`
[2] Kyoto University, Kyoto, Japan
`{lucas,kashima}@ml.ist.i.kyoto-u.ac.jp`

Abstract. Organizing objects such as human ideas and designs based on their similarity relationships is important in data exploration and decision making. Because humans are better at relative judgments than absolute judgments, those similarity comparisons are often cast as triplet comparisons asking which of two given objects is more similar to another given object. Crowdsourcing is an effective way to collect such human judgments easily; however, how to aggregate the labels of crowdsourced triplet similarity comparisons for estimating similarity relations of all objects when there are only a smaller number of labels remains a challenge. In this work, we construct two novel real datasets for investigating this research topic. For the label aggregation approach, we propose a family of models to learn the object embeddings from crowdsourced triplet similarity comparisons by incorporating worker abilities and object difficulties. Because of the diverse properties of real datasets, we automatically search for the optimal model from all variants of the proposed model. The experimental results verified the effectiveness of our approach.

Keywords: Crowdsourcing · Label aggregation · Triplet similarity comparison

1 Introduction

Organizing various objects such as human ideas and designs based on their similarity relationships is an important first step in data exploration and decision making [7]. Crowdsourcing is widely used as an inexpensive and rapid way to collect data for pairwise similarity comparisons of objects (e.g., [4]), especially when feature representations or similarities of the objects are not readily available. Pairwise similarities among the objects are usually evaluated in terms of binary judgments indicating whether or not two objects are similar to each other. These pairwise similarity comparisons are aggregated to organize the objects into groups to elucidate the landscape of these objects for decision-making. However, there are at least two problems when using these crowdsourced pairwise similarity labels. First, it is often difficult for humans to make absolute judgments,

T. Mantoro et al. (Eds.): ICONIP 2021, CCIS 1517, pp. 176–185, 2021.
https://doi.org/10.1007/978-3-030-92310-5_21

especially when the judgments are subjective. Second, there are large differences in the abilities and label numbers among workers and difficulties among objects.

For the first problem, the threshold for distinguishing similarity and dissimilarity is difficult to determine. For such cases, judgments based on relative comparisons are more human-friendly. For example, a triplet similarity comparison can be described as "object a is more similar to object b than to object c" [3,10], and a quadruplet similarity comparison can be described as "objects a and b are more similar than objects c and d." [1,11]. Such relative comparisons can assist a model to better estimate the similarities among objects. In this paper, we focus on triplet similarity comparisons. One of the obstacles in conducting relative comparisons is that the total number of combinations of objects is huge. Given n objects, the number of triplets is $\mathcal{O}(n^3)$. A worker cannot label all triplets and can only evaluate a small subset. We need a method that can aggregate a small number of labels and estimate the similarity relations of all objects.

For the label aggregation methods, in the early years, one type of solutions is to learn the similarity matrix of objects, i.e., multi-dimensional scaling [10]. After that, another type of solutions is proposed that first learns the object embeddings from labeled triplets, i.e., stochastic triplet embeddings [3], based on the Gaussian kernel (STE) or Student-t kernel (tSTE), and then estimates the object similarities based on the embeddings. However, these existing approaches were not proposed for addressing the second problem. On the topic of label aggregation for *categorical labels* [5,6,12] and *pairwise preference comparison labels* [2] in the crowdsourcing context, researchers always incorporate worker abilities and/or object difficulties as the crucial factors in constructing the probabilistic models. In this paper, we propose a family of the stochastic triplet embedding models incorporating worker abilities and object difficulties to learn the object embeddings from *triplet similarity comparison labels*, namely, Crowdsourced (t-distributed) Stochastic Triplet Embeddings (Crowd-(t)STE). The performances of variants of the proposed model depend on the diverse properties of the real datasets; thus we also automatically search the optimal model with the best validation performance from all variants of our model.

The contributions of this paper are as follows: (1) Because there were no existing datasets available for investigating this research topic, we created two novel real datasets with the large-scale crowd labels available. (2) We propose an approach to solve the problems of the stochastic triplet embedding in the crowdsourcing context. (3) We propose a family of models by incorporating the worker ability and object difficulty by constructing diverse similarity kernels and loss objectives. There are 10 variants in total and we automatically search the optimal model.

2   Our Approach

2.1   Notations and Problem Definition

We denote the set of objects by $\mathcal{O} = \{o_i\}_{i=1}^n$. We assume that no feature representations of the objects are available. Our goal is to estimate the similarity relations among all objects. For this purpose, we learn the representations $\mathbf{X} = \{\mathbf{x}_i\}_{i=1}^n$ of the objects in a d-dimensional latent feature space, i.e., $\mathbf{x}_i \in \mathbb{R}^d$, by utilizing the triplet similarity comparisons of objects. We use crowdsourcing to collect the triplet similarity comparison labels. We denote the set of crowd workers by $\mathcal{A} = \{a_l\}_{l=1}^m$. For three given objects o_i, o_j, and o_k in $\mathcal{O}$, the triplet similarity comparison we consider is a type of questions that ask crowd workers to annotate the relations of pairwise similarities among them. More specifically, we ask a question that is "which object of o_j or o_k is more similar to the anchor object o_i?"; the candidate answers are either of "o_j" or "o_k". If a worker a_l annotates that o_i and o_j are more similar, then the triplet similarity label is $y_{ijk}^l = 1$; otherwise $y_{ijk}^l = 0$. The set of triplet similarity labels is defined as $\mathcal{Y} = \{y_{ijk}^l\}_{i,j,k,l}$ for the set of triplets $\mathcal{T} = \{(o_i, o_j, o_k)\}_{i,j,k}$. The set of labels given by worker a_l is denoted by $\mathcal{Y}^l$; the label set of a triplet is defined as $\mathcal{Y}_{ijk}$.

Since the total number of object triplets is cubic in the number of objects, it costs too much budget and time to collect the labels for all of the triplets. In addition, due to the diverse ability and diligence of crowd workers, the collected labels are more likely to be noisy. We thus must collect multiple labels for a triplet and aggregate them to obtain more reliable labels, which further increases the total number of collected labels. These facts motivate us to estimate more accurate similarities of all objects based on a smaller number of similarity comparison labels. We only use a subset of triplets and only use a subset of labels for each triplet in the training stage. The problem setting can be summarized as follows.

INPUTS: A set of objects $\mathcal{O}$, a set of crowd workers $\mathcal{A}$, and a subset of triplet similarity comparison labels $\mathcal{Y}_t \subset \mathcal{Y}$, with the subset $\mathcal{Y}_{ijk,t} \subset \mathcal{Y}_{ijk}$ for each triplet, for the subset of triplets $\mathcal{T}_t \subset \mathcal{T}$.

OUTPUTS: The object representations $\mathbf{X} = \{\mathbf{x}_i\}_{i=1}^n$. In addition, by some variants of the proposed model, we can also obtain the estimated object difficulty $\mathbf{H} = \{\mathbf{h}_i\}_{i=1}^n$, $\mathbf{h}_i \in \mathbb{R}^d$ and the estimated worker ability $\mathbf{W} = \{\mathbf{W}^l\}_{l=1}^m$, where the size of $\mathbf{W}^l$ depends on the variants of the model.

2.2   Label Aggregation for Triplet Similarity Comparisons

Given a triplet of objects (o_i, o_j, o_k), we define the probability that "object o_i is more similar to object o_j than to object o_k". In the existing general models of Stochastic Triplet Embedding (STE) [3], the probability is given as

$$p_{ijk} = \frac{\mathbf{K}(\mathbf{x}_i, \mathbf{x}_j)}{\mathbf{K}(\mathbf{x}_i, \mathbf{x}_j) + \mathbf{K}(\mathbf{x}_i, \mathbf{x}_k)}, \tag{1}$$

$$\mathbf{K}(\mathbf{x}_i, \mathbf{x}_j) = \exp\left(-(\mathbf{x}_i - \mathbf{x}_j)^\top (\mathbf{x}_i - \mathbf{x}_j)\right) \tag{2}$$

is a kernel function for measuring the similarity of two objects. The object embeddings can be learned by minimizing the cross-entropy loss function:

$$\mathcal{L} = - \sum_{(o_i, o_j, o_k) \in \mathcal{T}_t} \left(s_{ijk} \log p_{ijk} + (1 - s_{ijk}) \log(1 - p_{ijk}) \right) + \lambda_0 ||\mathbf{X}||_2^2, \quad (3)$$

$$s_{ijk} = \sum_{y_{ijk}^l \in \mathcal{Y}_{ijk,t}} \mathbb{1}(y_{ijk}^l = 1) / |\mathcal{Y}_{ijk,t}|, \quad (4)$$

where s_{ijk} is the normalized sum computed from y_{ijk}^l and indicates the proportion of answers saying o_i and o_j being more similar. $\mathbb{1}$ is an indicator function. λ_0 is a regularization hyperparameter. Then the estimated labels of triplet similarity comparisons of all objects can be computed by using the object embeddings. ven Der Maaten et al. [3] also proposed a t-distributed Stochastic Triplet Embedding (tSTE), which uses a heavy-tailed Student-t kernel with α degrees of freedom instead of the Gaussian kernel (2), expressed as

$$\mathbf{K}(\mathbf{x}_i, \mathbf{x}_j) = \left(1 + \frac{(\mathbf{x}_i - \mathbf{x}_j)^\top (\mathbf{x}_i - \mathbf{x}_j)}{\alpha} \right)^{-\frac{\alpha+1}{2}}. \quad (5)$$

2.3 Label Aggregation for Crowdsourced Triplet Similarity Comparisons

In the crowdsourcing context, there are large differences in the abilities among workers and difficulties among objects. Existing (t)STE methods do not consider them. We thus propose Crowd-(t)STE to solve this problem.

Worker Ability Modeling. The previously mentioned (t)STE model assumes that all crowd workers perform equally well. It does not distinguish the labels from different workers and utilizes the normalized sum (majority voting) of the labels in Eq. (4). However, in the crowdsourcing context, the ability and diligence of workers are diverse. We thus propose a model that incorporates worker abilities. We define an ability matrix $\mathbf{W}^l \in \mathbb{R}^{d' \times d'}$ for a worker a_l, and propose the probabilistic model and the two kernels as

$$p_{ijk}^l = \frac{\mathbf{K}(\mathbf{x}_i, \mathbf{x}_j, \mathbf{W}^l)}{\mathbf{K}(\mathbf{x}_i, \mathbf{x}_j, \mathbf{W}^l) + \mathbf{K}(\mathbf{x}_i, \mathbf{x}_k, \mathbf{W}^l)}, \quad (6)$$

$$\mathbf{K}(\mathbf{x}_i, \mathbf{x}_j, \mathbf{W}^l) = \exp\left(-(\mathbf{x}_i - \mathbf{x}_j)^\top \mathbf{W}^l (\mathbf{x}_i - \mathbf{x}_j) \right), \quad (7)$$

$$\mathbf{K}(\mathbf{x}_i, \mathbf{x}_j, \mathbf{W}^l) = \left(1 + \frac{(\mathbf{x}_i - \mathbf{x}_j)^\top \mathbf{W}^l (\mathbf{x}_i - \mathbf{x}_j)}{\alpha} \right)^{-\frac{\alpha+1}{2}}. \quad (8)$$

When $d' = 1$, $\mathbf{W}^l$ is a scalar variable, which means worker a_l performs consistently on the entire dataset. When $d' = d$, it potentially learns the rich representation of worker ability by interacting with each dimension in the object embeddings $\mathbf{x}_i$ when computing the probability of similarity relations among objects.

Object Difficulty Modeling. Besides the worker ability, the object difficulty is also an important factor that can influence the correctness of the judgments by workers. We thus also propose models that consider the object difficulty. In the existing work, methods for categorical labels, e.g., GLAD [12], leverage a scalar variable to represent object difficulty; methods for pairwise labels, e.g., CrowdBT [2], do not model the object difficulty which is required to consider the interactions of difficulties of two objects for pairwise preference comparisons. In this study that focuses on object triplet similarity comparisons, we define the difficulty based on an object, i.e., we utilize a d-dimensional vector $\mathbf{h}_i$ to represent the difficulty of an object o_i. To model the difficulty of a triplet, we need to interact the difficulties of the three objects in it. We thus use the dot product on the difficulties of two objects to compute a scalar for each object pair, to represent the difficulties of judging the similarity of the object pair. We propose the probabilistic model and candidate kernel functions as

$$p_{ijk}^l = \frac{\mathbf{K}(\mathbf{x}_i, \mathbf{x}_j, \mathbf{h_i}, \mathbf{h_j})}{\mathbf{K}(\mathbf{x}_i, \mathbf{x}_j, \mathbf{h_i}, \mathbf{h_j}) + \mathbf{K}(\mathbf{x}_i, \mathbf{x}_k, \mathbf{h_i}, \mathbf{h_k})}, \tag{9}$$

$$\mathbf{K}(\mathbf{x}_i, \mathbf{x}_j, \mathbf{h_i}, \mathbf{h_j}) = \exp\left(-(\mathbf{x}_i - \mathbf{x}_j)^\top (\mathbf{h}_i^\top \mathbf{h}_j)(\mathbf{x}_i - \mathbf{x}_j)\right), \tag{10}$$

$$\mathbf{K}(\mathbf{x}_i, \mathbf{x}_j, \mathbf{h_i}, \mathbf{h_j}) = \left(1 + \frac{(\mathbf{x}_i - \mathbf{x}_j)^\top (\mathbf{h}_i^\top \mathbf{h}_j)(\mathbf{x}_i - \mathbf{x}_j)}{\alpha}\right)^{-\frac{\alpha+1}{2}}. \tag{11}$$

Label Aggregation by Learning Object Embeddings. In summary, we propose a family of the crowdsourced stochastic triplet embedding models by incorporating worker ability and object difficulty. The generalized model is

$$p_{ijk}^l = \frac{\mathbf{K}(\mathbf{x}_i, \mathbf{x}_j, \mathbf{h}_i, \mathbf{h}_j, \mathbf{W}^l)}{\mathbf{K}(\mathbf{x}_i, \mathbf{x}_j, \mathbf{h}_i, \mathbf{h}_j, \mathbf{W}^l) + \mathbf{K}(\mathbf{x}_i, \mathbf{x}_k, \mathbf{h}_i, \mathbf{h}_k, \mathbf{W}^l)}. \tag{12}$$

$$\mathbf{K}(\mathbf{x}_i, \mathbf{x}_j, \mathbf{h_i}, \mathbf{h_j}, \mathbf{W}^l) = \exp\left(-(\mathbf{x}_i - \mathbf{x}_j)^\top (\mathbf{h}_i^\top \mathbf{h}_j)\mathbf{W}^l(\mathbf{x}_i - \mathbf{x}_j)\right), \tag{13}$$

$$\mathbf{K}(\mathbf{x}_i, \mathbf{x}_j, \mathbf{h_i}, \mathbf{h_j}, \mathbf{W}^l) = \left(1 + \frac{(\mathbf{x}_i - \mathbf{x}_j)^\top (\mathbf{h}_i^\top \mathbf{h}_j)\mathbf{W}^l(\mathbf{x}_i - \mathbf{x}_j)}{\alpha}\right)^{-\frac{\alpha+1}{2}}. \tag{14}$$

When $\mathbf{H} = \mathbf{1}$, it is equivalent to the model with Eqs. (6), (7), and (8); when $\mathbf{W} = \mathbf{1}$, it is equivalent to the model with Eqs. (9), (10), and (11). Note that although seemingly similar forms are utilized for two different factors of worker ability and object difficulty, they can be distinguished in the optimization because, when computing the loss, worker ability is aggregated by the labels of a worker and object difficulty is aggregated by the labels of an object. The loss function in Eq. (3) of (t)STE utilizes an aggregated label s_{ijk}. In contrast, because we individually consider the influences of triplet labels from different workers, we modify the loss function to differ these labels. The cross-entropy loss function of Crowd-(t)STE can be formulated as follows:

$$\mathcal{L} = -\sum_{y_{ijk}^l \in \mathcal{Y}_t} \left(y_{ijk}^l \log p_{ijk}^l + (1 - y_{ijk}^l) \log(1 - p_{ijk}^l)\right)$$
$$+ \lambda_0 ||\mathbf{X}||_2^2 + \lambda_1 ||\mathbf{W}||_2^2 + \lambda_2 ||\mathbf{H}||_2^2. \tag{15}$$

With the combinations of two types of worker ability, one type of object difficulty, and two types of kernel functions (Gaussian and Student-t), there are 10 variants of the proposed model in total. The combinations only without worker ability (or object difficulty) are included. Because of the diverse properties of real datasets, certain variants are more appropriate for certain cases. We thus automatically search the variants when utilizing our approach. Because the search space is small, we utilize a brute force search to select the variant with optimal performance on the validation subset.

Table 1. Statistics of the datasets. $|\mathcal{O}|$: number of objects, $|\mathcal{T}|$: number of triplets, $|\mathcal{Y}_{ijk}|$: number of workers for each triplet, $|\mathcal{A}|$: total number of workers, $|\mathcal{Y}|$: total number of labels; $|\mathcal{Y}^l|_{min}$: minimum label numbers of workers, $|\mathcal{Y}^l|_{max}$: maximum label numbers of workers, and $|\mathcal{Y}^l|_{avg}$: average label numbers of workers.

Data	$|\mathcal{O}|$	$|\mathcal{T}|$	$|\mathcal{Y}_{ijk}|$	$|\mathcal{A}|$	$|\mathcal{Y}|$	$|\mathcal{Y}^l|_{min}$	$|\mathcal{Y}^l|_{max}$	$|\mathcal{Y}^l|_{avg}$
Food	50	20,000	20	433	400,000	50	19,950	923.79
Scene	50	20,000	20	528	400,000	50	19,950	757.58

3   Experiments

3.1   Dataset Collection

In order to investigate the performance of the label aggregation approaches in the context of crowdsourced triplet similarity comparisons, we require real datasets that contain crowdsourced triplet similarity labels. However, to the best of our knowledge, no public datasets were available, thus we created two novel datasets[1] by using a real-world crowdsourcing platform Lancers. We first extracted sets of objects from existing image collections and then generated the triplets to publish them on the crowdsourcing platform. The questions we asked the crowd workers were "which image o_j and o_k is more similar to image o_i?".

The *food dataset* consists of images of five categories (bread, dessert, meat, soup, and vegetable/fruit) from the Food-11 image collection [9] (No Licence Required). For each category, we randomly selected ten images. The *scene dataset* consists of images of five categories (coast, forest, highway, open country, and street) from a collection of urban and natural scenes [8] (Licence CC BY 4.0). We also randomly selected ten images for each category. In each dataset, there are 50 images (objects) in total. We randomly sampled 20,000 triplets in each dataset and published them on the crowdsourcing platform to obtain comparison labels. Each crowd task includes 50 triplets. For each triplet, we collected labels from 20 workers. Each worker did not need to judge all of the triplets and only provided labels for a subset. Table 1 shows the statistics of the datasets. Although the number of objects is not large, there are 400,000 crowd labels in

---

[1] https://github.com/garfieldpigljy/CrowdTSC2021.

each dataset, which is large-scale. The numbers of objects and triplets are same for two datasets; the numbers of workers and average label numbers of workers are different.

3.2   Experimental Settings

We compared our approach to two typical baselines that extend existing methods that do not consider the factors of worker ability and object difficulty. We adapted and extended the vanilla STE and tSTE [3] for the crowdsourcing context as the baselines. Specifically, we extended the STE method using Eqs. (1), (2), and (15), and we extended tSTE method using Eqs. (1), (5), and (15), without using the regularization terms of worker ability and object difficulty in Eq. (15).

We define the names of the variants of our approach by using several suffixes to Crowd-(t)STE; '-s' denotes scalar worker ability, '-m' for matrix worker ability, '-d' for object difficulty. The detailed hyperparameter settings of our approach are as follows. We carried out experiments for each type of kernel function (Gaussian and Student-t) respectively. The degree of freedom α in all approaches using Student-t kernels is set to $d-1$. The regularization terms of all approaches are set to $\lambda_0, \lambda_1, \lambda_2 \in \{0.001, 0.005, 0.01, 0.05, 0.1\}$, $\lambda_0 = \lambda_1 = \lambda_2$. Although it is possible to tune different values for each λ ($\lambda_0 \neq \lambda_1 \neq \lambda_2$) to improve the performance, we utilized equal λ to show the performance in a general setting. We tuned the hyperparameters λ and search model variants based on their performance on the validation set.

3.3   Evaluation Methods

We verify the approaches on their capability to estimate the triplet comparison labels of all object triplets using only a small number of labeled object triplets. In one experimental trial, we first created a subset $\mathcal{Y}_T^u$ by only using $u \in \{3, 5, 10\}$ labels in all labels of each triplet in $\mathcal{Y}$. $\mathcal{Y}_T^u$ still contains all object triplets in $\mathcal{T}$. We then randomly selected a subset $\mathcal{T}_t$ of all object triplets in $\mathcal{T}$ with the sampling rate $r \in \{0.05, 0.1, 0.2\}$. This triplet subset is defined as $\mathcal{Y}_t^u$ and was used as the training set. A subset $\mathcal{Y}_t^{u'}$ with the same size and settings was also created and used as the validation set. d is not tuned so that the proposed approaches and baselines are compared using the same $d = 10$. We evaluated the average performance of ten trials for each (u, r) group.

The objects in the real datasets we create have the category labels in the raw collections that they are from. We can use this category information to verify the performance of object embeddings by using the estimated object similarities. We utilized two object o_i and o_j from the same category and an object o_k from another category to create a triplet (o_i, o_j, o_k); then, we utilized all the triplet combinations from the objects in $\mathcal{O}$ that satisfy the above condition as the triplets in ground truth. We computed the estimated similarity comparisons of these triplets using the estimated object embeddings and evaluated the accuracy of the estimated triplet comparisons. For an object triplet (o_i, o_j, o_k) in ground truth, if the estimated similarity of (o_i, o_j) is higher than that of (o_i, o_k), we judge the estimated similarity comparison of this object triplet to be correct.

3.4 Experimental Results

We show the results with representative hyperparameter setting and data properties as the conditions to compare the approaches: $d = 10$, which is a moderate number of dimensions for representing an object; $r = 0.1$ because we want to verify the performance when there are not many labels available; and $u = 5$ which is a moderate number of workers for annotating a triplet. The columns of $r = 0.10$ in Table 2 lists the results. We organize our methods and the baselines into two groups: Gaussian kernel-based group and Student-t kernel-based group. First, our proposed approach has better performance than the baselines in all of the cases in the columns of $r = 0.10$ in Table 2, regardless of which of the kernels (Gaussian or Student-t) being used. This shows that modeling crowdsourced factors such as worker ability and object difficulty is crucial for the task of label aggregation from crowdsourced triplet similarity comparisons. Secondly, the selected optimal variant of our approach is diverse. All two factors of worker ability and object difficulty have ever been selected in some cases. This shows that all these factors are effective for improving the overall performance and automatically search the optimal variant is important because certain variants

Table 2. Results for different sampling rates r. The number of dimensions $d = 10$. The number of labels (workers) per triplet $u = 5$.

Data	$r = 0.05$		$r = 0.10$		$r = 0.20$	
	STE	Crowd-STE	STE	Crowd-STE	STE	Crowd-STE
Food	0.8700	**0.8927** -s-d	0.9023	**0.9155** -s-d	0.9179	**0.9127** -s-d
Scene	0.8531	**0.9083** -s-d	0.8978	**0.9174** -s	0.9219	**0.9312** -s
	tSTE	Crowd-tSTE	tSTE	Crowd-tSTE	tSTE	Crowd-tSTE
Food	0.8397	**0.8833** -s-d	0.8943	**0.9116** -s-d	0.9187	**0.9175** -s-d
Scene	0.8166	**0.8904** -s	0.8828	**0.9203** -s-d	0.9184	**0.9268** -s-d

Table 3. Results for different numbers of labels (workers) per triplet u. The number of dimensions $d = 10$. The sampling rate $r = 0.10$.

Data	$u = 3$		$u = 5$		$u = 10$	
	STE	Crowd-STE	STE	Crowd-STE	STE	Crowd-STE
Food	0.8911	**0.9132** -s-d	0.9023	**0.9155** -s-d	0.9097	**0.9109** -s
Scene	0.8732	**0.9167** -s-d	0.8978	**0.9174** -s	0.9176	**0.9364** -s-d
	tSTE	Crowd-tSTE	tSTE	Crowd-tSTE	tSTE	Crowd-tSTE
Food	0.8824	**0.9066** -s-d	0.8943	**0.9116** -s-d	0.9001	**0.9108** -s-d
Scene	0.8672	**0.9078** -s	0.8828	**0.9203** -s-d	0.9076	**0.9299** -s-d

are appropriate for certain data properties. Furthermore, because the variants modeling worker ability are always selected, it shows that worker ability is the required crowdsourced factor which needs to be considered in the label aggregation approaches.

We investigated the influences of two data properties, i.e., the label (worker) number per triplet u and triplet sampling rate r. We changed one factor and fixed the others ($u = 5$ and $r = 0.10$ as default), and verified the changes in the performance. Table 2 and Table 3 list the results. First, the family of the proposed approaches always outperforms the baselines in all these cases. Secondly, when u and r increase, the amount of training data increases. The performances on the two accuracy metrics generally increase. Thirdly, when the data are very few and sparse, i.e., $r = 0.05$ in Table 2 and $u = 3$ in Table 3, our approach still performs well. The performance difference between the baselines and our approach when the data are relatively few (e.g., $u = 3$ in Table 3) is larger than that when the data are relatively abundant (e.g., $u = 10$ in Table 3). This shows that our approach is very efficient when the number of collected labels is small. It also shows that although collecting more labels can improve the performance, the improvement may be small. As shown in Table 3, $u = 10$ doubles the number of collected labels from $u = 5$, but the performance only increases by approximately 1%. Therefore, cares must be taken in the trade-off between budget cost and accuracy. Fourthly, the selected variants are different for each dataset with the same u and r, which also shows the effectiveness of the automatic variant search.

4   Conclusion

We considered the label aggregation from crowdsourced triplet similarity comparisons, i.e., the stochastic triplet embedding in the crowdsourcing context. We created two novel real datasets for investigating this research topic. We proposed a family of models by incorporating worker ability and object difficulty with different similarity kernels as well as automatically searching the optimal model from possible model variants. A limitation of these datasets is that the objects are only images, other types of objects will be considered in future work.

Acknowledgments. This work was partially supported by JSPS KAKENHI Grant Number 19K20277 and JST CREST Grant Number JPMJCR21D1.

References

1. Agarwal, S., Wills, J., Cayton, L., Lanckriet, G., Kriegman, D., Belongie, S.: Generalized non-metric multidimensional scaling. In: AISTATS, pp. 11–18 (2007)
2. Chen, X., Bennett, P.N., Collins-Thompson, K., Horvitz, E.: Pairwise ranking aggregation in a crowdsourced setting. In: WSDM, pp. 193–202 (2013)
3. van Der Maaten, L., Weinberger, K.: Stochastic triplet embedding. In: MLSP, pp. 1–6 (2012)
4. Gomes, R.G., Welinder, P., Krause, A., Perona, P.: Crowdclustering. In: NIPS, pp. 558–566 (2011)

5. Li, J., Baba, Y., Kashima, H.: Hyper questions: unsupervised targeting of a few experts in crowdsourcing. In: CIKM, pp. 1069–1078 (2017)
6. Li, J., Baba, Y., Kashima, H.: Incorporating worker similarity for label aggregation in crowdsourcing. In: ICANN, pp. 596–606 (2018)
7. Li, J., Baba, Y., Kashima, H.: Simultaneous clustering and ranking from pairwise comparisons. In: IJCAI, pp. 1554–1560 (2018)
8. Oliva, A., Torralba, A.: Modeling the shape of the scene: a holistic representation of the spatial envelope. Int. J. Comput. Vis. **42**(3), 145–175 (2001)
9. Singla, A., Yuan, L., Ebrahimi, T.: Food/non-food image classification and food categorization using pre-trained GoogLeNet model. In: MADiMa, pp. 3–11 (2016)
10. Tamuz, O., Liu, C., Belongie, S., Shamir, O., Kalai, A.T.: Adaptively learning the crowd kernel. In: ICML, pp. 673–680 (2011)
11. Ukkonen, A., Derakhshan, B., Heikinheimo, H.: Crowdsourced nonparametric density estimation using relative distances. In: HCOMP (2015)
12. Whitehill, J., fan Wu, T., Bergsma, J., Movellan, J.R., Ruvolo, P.L.: Whose vote should count more: Optimal integration of labels from labelers of unknown expertise. In: NIPS, pp. 2035–2043 (2009)

Relation-Aware Attribute Network for Fine-Grained Clothing Recognition

Mingjian Yang, Yixin Li, Zhuo Su$^{(\boxtimes)}$ (iD), and Fan Zhou

School of Computer Science and Engineering, National Engineering Research Center of Digital Life, Sun Yat-sen University, Guangzhou 510006, China
`suzhuo3@mail.sysu.edu.cn`

Abstract. In recent years, clothing attribute recognition made significant progress in the development of fine-grained clothing datasets. However, most existing methods treat some related attributes as different categories for attribute recognition in these fine-grained datasets, which ignores the intrinsic relations between clothing attributes. To describe the relations between clothing attributes and quantify the influence of attribute relation on attribute recognition tasks, we propose a novel Relation-Aware Attribute Network (RAAN). The relations between clothing attributes can be characterized by the Relation Graph Attention Network (RGAT) constructed for each attribute. Moreover, with the combination of visual features and relational features of attribute values, the influence of attribute relations on the attribute recognition task can be quantified. Extensive experiments show the effectiveness of RAAN in clothing attribute recognition.

Keywords: Attribute recognition · Fashion clothing attribute · Graph embedding · Relation modeling

1 Introduction

As an essential fashion image analysis tool, clothing attribute recognition [11–13] can usually improve other fashion-related tasks, such as clothing retrieval [8], clothing recommendation, clothing compatibility analysis, and fashion trend prediction. In recent years, with the appearance of large-scale fine-grained clothing datasets [3,7], the research on clothing attribute recognition has a rapid development and derives a few emerging applications.

At present, studies on clothing attribute recognition have made good progress. Some current works focus on the areas concerned by clothing attributes due to the different areas of attributes in a clothing image [1,8,12]. And a few studies made an effort to establish the transfer learning about clothing attribute recognition tasks [3,4]. In addition, Several works focused on the concatenation of different types of clothing features [7,13].

The development of GNNs also drives the research on clothing attribute recognition. The GNNs proposed in the early stage are basically designed based

ⓒ Springer Nature Switzerland AG 2021
T. Mantoro et al. (Eds.): ICONIP 2021, CCIS 1517, pp. 186–193, 2021.
https://doi.org/10.1007/978-3-030-92310-5_22

on graph propagation algorithm, but the computational cost of propagation operator is extremely high. So many researchers are devoted to introducing the convolution operation into GNN [2,5,6] and many new models such as GCN are produced. After that, many methods were derived based on GCN such as GAT [10] and RGAT [9].

However, there are still many challenges in fine-grained attribute recognition. At present, the typical way to recognize clothing attributes is to define the recognition as an image classification problem. In these fine-grained clothing datasets, the original attribute values belonging to the same class are divided into more detailed attribute values. For example, for the "color" attribute, "red" is divided into a series of attribute values that can be classified as red such as "rose-red" and "claret". Most of the existing works regard these attribute values, which belong to the same category as different categories, for classification and recognition. However, it may lead to a poor result ignored the internal relations between the related attributes.

To address this limitation, we focus on the complicated relationships between clothing attributes. We propose a new modeling method of attribute relation called Relation Graph Attention Network (RGAT). In this model, we use an undirected graph to represent the relations between attribute values of attributes. Furthermore, we design our Relation-Aware Attribute Network that combines the relational features extracted from RGAT and visual features from the pre-trained ResNet for the fine-grained attribute recognition.

The main contributions are summarized as follows. (1) Propose a novel modeling method of attribute relation based on GNN. Through this modeling method, the relations between attribute values can be characterized. (2) Design a Relation-Aware Attribute Network that combines the visual features and relational features of attribute values for attribute recognition. It quantifies the influence of the relations between attributes on the task of attribute recognition. (3) The influences of different attribute relations on attribute recognition are explored. Finally, we established both similar and subordinate relations for the relations between attribute values. Experimental results show the feasibility and effectiveness of our RAAN in clothing attribute recognition.

2 The Proposed Method

As shown in Fig. 1, given a clothing image, the visual features are extracted through ResNet. And then after segmentation, resize and other operations, the visual features are assigned to each clothing attribute. After that, the visual features are input to the relation-aware model to generate the relational features between each attribute. Finally, the visual features and relational features are fed into the classifier to get the output.

2.1 Relation-Wise Graph Embedding

In this section, we will explore how to represent the relations between the clothing attribute values. According to our observations, we believe that specific cloth-

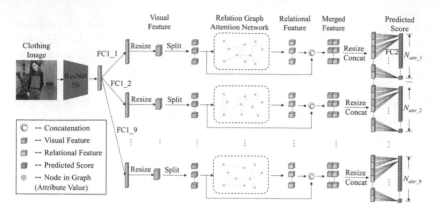

Fig. 1. Overview of our RAAN for clothing attribute recognition. Each branch is an attribute recognition task.

ing attributes will not affect the prediction of other attributes. Therefore, our method does not focus on the relations between different attributes. By contrast, it emphasizes the relations between attribute values, a.k.a. inter-attribute relation. A graph attention network [10], RGAT, is constructed to model the inter-attribute relation. Specifically, we build an undirected graph for each clothing attribute such as "color" and "category". In the undirected graph of the attribute relation, each node represents an attribute value such as "V-neck" and "round-neck". Moreover, the value of a node represents the visual feature of the attribute value. If there is some relation between two nodes, they are adjacent in the undirected graph. As for the relations between attribute values, we establish a similar relation and a subordinate relation.

The similar relation can be expressed as:

$$\{\forall v_i \in V, \forall u_j \in U, \text{s.t.} V = TU\}, \tag{1}$$

where v_i, u_j denote different attribute values, and T represents the coefficient of similarity transformation. For example, both "bright red" and "claret" are classified as "red", so there is a similar relation between "bright red" and "claret".

And the subordinate relation can be described as:

$$\{\forall v_i \in V, \forall u_j \in U, \text{s.t.} V \subseteq U\}. \tag{2}$$

After the attribute relation graph is constructed, the graph convolution operation is carried out in the spatial domain. Then each node will output a new feature. This new feature is related to the visual features of all other nodes connected to this node, so we define this feature as a relational feature. It represents the relationships between the current attribute value and other relevant attribute values:

$$R_i = \overset{K}{\underset{k=1}{\|}} \sigma(\sum_{j \in N_i} a_{ij}^k W^k V_j). \tag{3}$$

Here R_i represents the relational feature, $\|$ represents the concatenation, σ is the sigmoid activation function. N_i is the set of nodes that adjacent with the i-th node, W^k is the parameter matrix of the linear connected network, and V_j represents the j-th visual feature that is connected to the current node. In addition, a_{ij}^k denotes k-th attention function between the i-th node and the j-th node, and it can be obtained as follows:

$$a_{ij} = \frac{exp(LeakyReLU(W'[WV_i \| WV_j]))}{\sum_{k \in N_i} exp(LeakyReLU(W'[WV_i \| WV_k]))}, \tag{4}$$

where W and W' represents the different parameter in the model, respectively.

2.2   Network Structure

The RGAT proposed in the previous section obtains the representation of the relations between the clothing attributes. The key point of RGAT is that the input of the node in RAGT must be the visual feature of the attribute value. To get the visual feature of each attribute, we build a parallel branch for each clothing attribute. To reduce the training time, we adopt a pre-trained ResNet-50 as the backbone network. After the visual features $F \in R^{2048 \times 1}$ for images I is obtained, we deploy an attribute-independent fully connected layer FC_i to learn the visual features of each attribute $V_i \in R^{n_i \times N}$, where N denotes the feature dimension of the node in RGAT. Then, we derive the output of $FC1_i$:

$$V_i = relu(FC1_i(ResNet(I))). \tag{5}$$

Next, to obtain the visual feature of attribute value from each attribute's primary visual feature, a dimension transformation is carried out. Then we get a new visual feature $V_i \in R^{n_i \times N}$. Furthermore, the following slice operation is deployed to get a visual representation of the attribute value $V_{i,j} \in R^{1 \times N}$, which can be described as:

$$V_i = [V_{i,1}, V_{i,2}, V_{i,3}, ..., V_{i,n_i}]. \tag{6}$$

It is apparent that through dimension transformation and slicing operation, the features of an attribute alone do not output a representation of the visual feature of each attribute value. Additional operation is required to associate these characteristics with the corresponding attribute values. In order to do that, we design a local fully connected network for attribute values in the last layer of the attribute recognition classifier. Compared with the full connection of the general classifier, the predicted score of a particular attribute value is only associated with the visual features of the attribute value, but not with the visual features of other attributes. In this way, the visual features associated with the output of the attribute value in the classifier do represent the visual features of the corresponding attribute value.

For the visual feature $V_{i,j}$ of each attribute value, we input it as the node of RGAT and obtain the relational feature $R_{i,j}$ of the attribute value after the operation of the graph convolution in the spatial domain. In order to quantify the specific influence of clothing attribute relation on clothing attribute recognition task, we carried out the following operations. First, we concatenate $V_{i,j}$ and $R_{i,j}$ to get the merged features of each attribute value. Then the merged features are imported into the respective full connection layer $FC2_{i,j}$ to identify different clothing attributes. The predicted score is calculated as follows:

$$s_{i,j} = \sigma\big(FC2_{i,j}(V_{i,j} \parallel R_{i,j})\big). \tag{7}$$

Specifically, $FC2_{i,j}$ represents the local fully connected network for each attribute value, $s_{i,j}$ denotes the predicted score of the attribute value.

2.3 Loss Function

For the multi-task classification problem of clothing attribute prediction, we deploy the cross-entropy loss function of each branch to learn the model's parameters. Suppose given a batch of images $\{I^{(m)}\}_{m=1}^{n_{bs}}$, where n_{bs} is the batch size; and given the corresponding ground truth $\{\hat{y}^{(m)}\}_{m=1}^{n_{bs}}$, then the posterior probability that the i-th attribute being classified as $v_i^{(m)}$ is,

$$P_i^{(m)} = \frac{exp\big(s_{i,j}^{(m)}\big)}{\sum\limits_{k=1}^{n_i} exp(s_{i,k}^{(m)})}. \tag{8}$$

After obtaining the posterior probability of each attribute, the average cross-entropy loss of this batch of images can be calculated by the following formula.

$$l = \frac{1}{n_{bs}}\left[\sum_{m=1}^{n_{bs}}\sum_{i=1}^{n_{attr}} \delta(y_i^{(m)} = \hat{y}_i^{(m)})log P_i^{(m)}\right], \tag{9}$$

where δ is an indicator function and $y_i^{(m)}$ denotes the value of the i-th attributes of the m-th sample.

3 Experiments

We test our model on the task of clothing attribute recognition and compare it with state-of-the-art methods. And we adopt the Cross-domain Clothing Attributes Dataset [3] to train, evaluate, and test the model proposed in this paper. This dataset includes two different image source domains: the shop and the street. Only the shop domain is selected in ours. The authors provided 245,467 clothing images in the shop domain, but only 166,875 images were collected due to the download link failure from some URLs.

Table 1. Compare ours with the stare-of-the-arts clothing recognition methods on the Cross-domain Clothing Attribute Dataset. The evaluation metrics are the AP of each attribute and the mAP of all attributes.

Method	Category	Button	Color	Clo-length	Pattern	Clo-shape	Col-shape	Slv-length	Slv-shape	mAP
Baseline	33.78	40.59	29.63	48.24	9.81	44.35	25.88	32.14	23.07	31.94
MTN [4]	**57.19**	55.93	20.10	60.05	8.07	34.21	46.23	15.57	**39.66**	37.39
ASEN [8]	44.53	**59.21**	36.14	**66.99**	43.42	**58.97**	46.68	**66.02**	37.39	**51.13**
RAAN	55.84	50.01	**36.91**	62.91	**44.79**	47.39	**47.45**	56.09	34.35	48.59

3.1   Parameter Settings

For training our RAAN model, the learning rate is set at 1×10^{-4} and the weight-decay is set at 5×10^{-3}. Adam was adopted as the optimizer. Limited by the memory of the GPU, the batch-size is set at 80. The training epoch is set at 200. The feature dimension N of a node in RGAT is set at 10. For training other comparable models, we use the corresponding parameters given by the authors. Moreover, other parameters are determined as same as RAAN.

3.2   Comparison with the State-of-the-Art Methods

Two state-of-the-art models, MTN [4] and ASEN [8], are used as the compared models. And we adopt CNN with FC layers as the baseline method.

The comparisons are summarized in Table 1. Compared with baseline and MTN, our proposed method achieves the best performance in almost all attributes. Especially, the mean average precision is improved by 16.65% compared with the benchmark method and 11.2% compared with MTN. This is a great improvement, because these performances are the average of dozens of attributes. And there are data imbalance in clothing datasets, which makes it difficult to improve the accuracy of attribute recognition. Compared with ASEN, the performance of our proposed method on mAP is inferior to ASEN, which is 2.54% behind. The reason may be that our proposed method may not be applicable to all attributes.

3.3   Effects of Different Inter-attribute Relation

We intend to conduct further ablation experiments on the network structure of RGAT to prove the influence of the relations between clothing attributes and the feasibility and effectiveness of our RAAN model on the task of clothing attribute recognition. The undirected graph used to characterize the relations between attribute values in RGAT is constructed based on prior knowledge. As long as we input different adjacency matrices when constructing RGAT, we can characterize the different attribute values' relations. Specifically, we compare five different variants of our RAAN model.

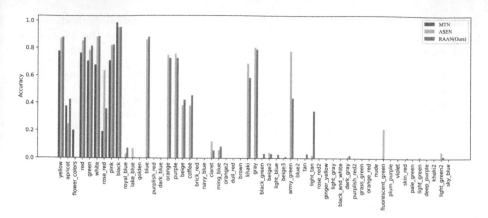

Fig. 2. The comparison results of each class for "color" attribute on the Cross-domain Clothing Attributes Dataset. The vertical axis is the acuuracy of each class. And there are 55 categories in total for "color" attribute.

Table 2. Performance of different relations between attribute values on the Cross-domain Clothing Attribute Dataset.

Method	Category	Button	Color	Clo-length	Pattern	Clo-shape	Col-shape	Slv-length	Slv-shape	mAP
RAAN (w/o RGAT)	20.17	36.85	9.51	43.33	8.70	17.82	31.36	16.86	24.65	23.08
RAAN (FC)	**57.43**	**58.81**	15.94	61.74	8.92	58.54	45.93	16.44	16.65	37.75
RAAN (Sub)	53.84	52.25	36.48	64.04	18.38	**59.85**	**47.50**	18.35	**41.60**	43.83
RAAN (Similar)	56.13	43.20	35.36	**68.07**	40.69	46.97	46.84	42.37	39.62	46.57
RAAN	55.84	50.01	**36.91**	62.91	**44.79**	47.39	47.45	**56.09**	34.35	**48.59**

RAAN (w/o RGAT). We removed RGAT directly. The visual features are directly imported into the classifier after resizing and splitting to recognize the clothing attributes. **RAAN (FC).** We established a full connection between every two attribute values. **RAAN (Sub).** We constructed the subordinate relation between attribute values. If there is no apparent subordinate relation in an attribute, we use the full connection instead. That is, every attribute value is connected in pairs in RGAT. **RAAN (Similar).** We presented the similar relation between attribute values. Similarly, if there is no apparent similar relation in an attribute, we also use full connection instead. **RAAN.** The relationship between attribute values contains the subordinate and similar relation.

Table 2 demonstrates the comparison of different variants. We can find that when RGAT is removed from the model, the model's performance is limited. This result proves the importance of internal attribute relations in clothing attribute recognition task. In addition, the experimental results show that the overall performance of subordinate and similar relations is better than that of full connection. It may be because the connection mode of full connection will connect some semantically unrelated attribute values. At last, although our RAAN is not superior to independent subordinate or similar in all indexes, its performance has achieved the best results, which is 2.02% higher than RAAN (similar) in mAP. Comparison fully demonstrates the feasibility of combining subordinate and similar relations.

4   Conclusions

In this paper, we analyze the importance of clothing attribute relations on the task of fine-grained attribute recognition. We find that mining the potential connections of clothing attributes can significantly improve the accuracy of fine-grained attribute recognition. From this discovery, we propose a novel Attribute Relation-Aware Network (RAAN) to characterize the relations between clothing attribute values and quantify the influence of clothing attribute relations on the attribute recognition task. Our RAAN model is evaluated on the Cross-domain Clothing Attribute Dataset, and it is superior to the previous state-of-the-art method in AP of each attribute and mAP. In addition, we also study the influence of different attribute relations on the task of attribute recognition.

Acknowledgment. This research is supported by the National Natural Science Foundation of China (No. 61872394, 61772140).

References

1. Ak, K., Kassim, A., Lim, J., Tham, J.: Learning attribute representations with localization for flexible fashion search. In: CVPR, pp. 7708–7717 (2018)
2. Bruna, J., Zaremba, W., Szlam, A., Lecun, Y.: Spectral networks and locally connected networks on graphs. In: ICLR (2014)
3. Chen, Q., Huang, J., Feris, R., Brown, L., Dong, J., Yan, S.: Deep domain adaptation for describing people based on fine-grained clothing attributes. In: CVPR, pp. 5315–5324 (2015)
4. Dong, Q., Gong, S., Zhu, X.: Multi-task curriculum transfer deep learning of clothing attributes. In: WACV, pp. 520–529 (2017)
5. Hamilton, W.L., Ying, R., Leskovec, J.: Inductive representation learning on large graphs. In: NIPS, pp. 1025–1035 (2017)
6. Kipf, T.N., Welling, M.: Semi-supervised classification with graph convolutional networks. In: ICLR, pp. 1–14 (2017)
7. Liu, Z., Luo, P., Qiu, S., Wang, X., Tang, X.: Deepfashion: Powering robust clothes recognition and retrieval with rich annotations. In: CVPR, pp. 1096–1104 (2016)
8. Ma, Z., et al.: Fine-grained fashion similarity learning by attribute-specific embedding network. In: AAAI, pp. 11741–11748 (2020)
9. Schlichtkrull, M., Kipf, T.N., Bloem, P., van den Berg, R., Titov, I., Welling, M.: Modeling relational data with graph convolutional networks. In: The Semantic Web, pp. 593–607 (2018)
10. Veličković, P., Cucurull, G., Casanova, A., Romero, A., Liò, P., Bengio, Y.: Graph attention networks. In: ICLR, pp. 1–12 (2018)
11. Zhan, H., Shi, B., Kot, A.C.: Fashion analysis with a subordinate attribute classification network. In: ICME, pp. 1506–1511 (2017)
12. Zhang, S., Song, Z., Cao, X., Zhang, H., Zhou, J.: Task-aware attention model for clothing attribute prediction. T-CSVT **30**(4), 1051–1064 (2020)
13. Zhang, Y., Zhang, P., Yuan, C., Wang, Z.: Texture and shape biased two-stream networks for clothing classification and attribute recognition. In: CVPR, pp. 13538–13547 (2020)

Skeletons on the Stairs: Are They Deceptive?

Yiran Li[1]([✉]), Yang Liu[1,2], Zhenyue Qin[1], Xuanying Zhu[1], Sabrina Caldwell[1], and Tom Gedeon[1]

[1] Australian National University, Canberra, Australia
u6920084@anu.edu.au
[2] Data61-CSIRO, Canberra, Australia

Abstract. Physiological signals have been widely applied for deception detection. However, these signals are usually collected by devices attached to subjects. Such attachments can cause discomfort and unexpected anxiety, and thus will be noticed. Alternatively, skeleton-based gait data collected in a non-contact setting can be a solution to detect deception. Therefore, in this paper, we aim to investigate whether liars can be recognized using their skeletal motion trajectories. We extract skeletal gait data from videos of participants going up and downstairs after they conduct a mock crime. With the extracted skeletal gait data, a simplified version of Multi-Scale Graph 3D (MS-G3D) network is able to recognise participants' deceptive behaviour with an average accuracy of 70.9%. This result is higher than those obtained from traditional classifiers such as neural networks, support vector machines and decision trees, which are trained on hand-crafted features calculated from the gait data.

Keywords: Skeleton-based gait data · GCN · Deception detection

1 Introduction

Deception is defined as an attempt to purposely mislead people [1]. Using non-contact signals such as facial expression [8] and voice [3], deception can be identified with a satisfactory accuracy. However, little research has been conducted using skeleton-based gait movements to recognize liars. This paper explores deception detection with skeleton-based gait on the stairs. Compared with RGB videos, skeletal data better indicate movement characteristics without being influenced by extraneous factors such as external environment and clothing [7]. They also protect privacy of the test subjects and have a smaller data volume, making them memory-saving and easier to process [10].

One of the similar tasks of our topic is action recognition, which has gained rapid progress in recent years [10]. Earlier skeleton-based action recognition is achieved by manually extracting features which are passed to machine learning models such as support vector machine (SVM) [11] for classification. More recently, deep learning methods are used for action recognition. For example, convolutional neural networks (CNN) [4] and recurrent neural network

© Springer Nature Switzerland AG 2021
T. Mantoro et al. (Eds.): ICONIP 2021, CCIS 1517, pp. 194–202, 2021.
https://doi.org/10.1007/978-3-030-92310-5_23

(RNN) [13] models can recognise gait, outperforming features-based machine learning models.

However, CNN and RNN models are limited in extracting associations between joints or bones. Alternatively, graph convolutional neural networks (GCN) [6,9] can learn the structural information with feature information of skeletal data, thus playing an important role in action recognition in recent years [14].

Based on some improved GCN models such as spatial temporal graph convolutional network (ST-GCN) [14] and dynamic multiscale graph neural network(DMGNN) [5], a relatively new and effective GCN model for action classification is proposed, which is called Multi-Scale Graph 3D (MS-G3D) model [7]. It measures complex connections between skeletal joints across time, and proposes a multi-scale aggregation in spatial features [7]. In this work, we use a simplified version of MS-G3D for deception detection. Our contributions are:

- We validate the feasibility of deception recognition using skeletal-based gait data of people going down and up stairs.
- We are the first to use a graph neural network for deception detection. Compared to previous methods which use hand-crafted features, a simplified version of MS-G3D can directly extract deception features from skeletons.
- Using skeletons of people both going down and up stairs, we achieve an average prediction accuracy of 70.9% with three-fold cross validation. This recognition rate can be further enhanced to 79.2% when only the movements of going down-stairs are included. We also find that skeletons captured from lower angles contribute to higher accuracy than those from higher angles. Similarly, skeletons captured from the front views of participants contain more deception information than those recorded from the back views.

2   Method

2.1   Graphs and Graph Convolutional Neural Networks

We use $\mathcal{G} = (\mathcal{V}, \mathcal{E})$ to represent the graph, where $\mathcal{V} = \{v_1, \dots, v_N\}$ denotes the set containing all the joint points, and $\mathcal{E}$ denotes the set of edges of the skeleton. An undirected graph is used to represent skeletal structure, so for adjacency matrix $\mathbf{A}$, if joint v_i is connected to v_j, then $\mathbf{A}_{ij} = 1$, otherwise, $\mathbf{A}_{ij} = 0$.

For skeletal actions, there exists a set of spatio-temporal features containing all joints $\mathcal{X} = \{x_{t,n} \in \mathbb{R}^C \mid t, n \in \mathbb{Z}, 1 \leq t \leq T, 1 \leq n \leq N\}$, which can be represented as $\mathbf{X} \in \mathbb{R}^{T \times N \times C}$. $x_{t,n}$ represents the coordinates of the joint v_n in frame t and it is a C dimensional vector. The adjacency matrix A identifies the neighbourhood relationships between the joints, and $\mathbf{X}_t \in \mathbb{R}^{N \times C}$ is the joint coordinates at frame t. The combination of these two can be used as the joint features with aggregated neighbourhood information. $\Theta^{(l)} \in \mathbb{R}^{C_l \times C_{l+1}}$ represents the weight matrix of the l-th layer of the neural network.

For GCN, the joint features on frame t of layer $l + 1$ are updated as:

$$\mathbf{X}_t^{(l+1)} = \sigma \left(\tilde{\mathbf{D}}^{-\frac{1}{2}} \tilde{\mathbf{A}} \tilde{\mathbf{D}}^{-\frac{1}{2}} \mathbf{X}_t^{(l)} \Theta^{(l)} \right) \tag{1}$$

where $\tilde{\mathbf{A}} = \mathbf{A} + \mathbf{I}$, meaning adding joint itself into the adjacency matrix. $\tilde{\mathbf{D}}$ is the diagonal matrix of $\tilde{\mathbf{A}}$. $\tilde{\mathbf{D}}^{-\frac{1}{2}}\tilde{\mathbf{A}}\tilde{\mathbf{D}}^{-\frac{1}{2}}\mathbf{X}_t^{(l)}$ denotes spatial averaged features obtained by aggregating the information of first-order neighbourhood with joint itself.

2.2 Disentangled Multi-scale Aggregation

In skeleton data, some non-adjacent joints are also closely related to each other (e.g. the left ankle joint and the right ankle joint when walking), so it is necessary to consider multi-scale aggregation of spatial information.

In other models, the k-scale neighbourhood information is represented by directly applying k powers to the adjacent matrix. Using this method, the added self-loop will result in more distant k order neighbouring joints of the central joint having smaller weights. So joints further away from each other will still share only a little information after aggregation, making it difficult to extract correlations between distant joints. Therefore a new expression for the k-order adjacency matrix [7] is proposed to disentangle the restriction on the neighbourhood relation:

$$\left[\tilde{\mathbf{A}}_{(k)}\right]_{i,j} = \begin{cases} 1 & \text{if } d\left(v_i, v_j\right) = k, \\ 1 & \text{if } \quad i = j, \\ 0 & \text{otherwise}, \end{cases} \tag{2}$$

where (v_i, v_j) denotes the shortest hop between v_i and v_j. It means that if v_i and v_j are k_{th} order neighbours, the value will be 1 and otherwise it will be 0. The k scale feature of the joint on frame t in the $l+1$ layer of the network will be as:

$$\mathbf{X}_t^{(l+1)} = \sigma\left(\sum_{k=0}^{n} \tilde{\mathbf{D}}_{(k)}^{-\frac{1}{2}}\tilde{\mathbf{A}}_{(k)}\tilde{\mathbf{D}}_{(k)}^{-\frac{1}{2}}\mathbf{X}_t^{(l)}\Theta_{(k)}^{(l)}\right) \tag{3}$$

where $\tilde{\mathbf{D}}_{(k)}^{-\frac{1}{2}}\tilde{\mathbf{A}}_{(k)}\tilde{\mathbf{D}}_{(k)}^{-\frac{1}{2}}$ is the normalized k order adjacency matrices.

This new expression eliminates the problem of biased weights. To aggregate information from multiple scales, we summarize the extracted features of various scales so that the neighbouring information of different scales are represented with equal importance, meanwhile alleviating the oversmoothing problem [10].

2.3 The Overall Model Architecture

As shown in Fig. 1, we use a simplified version of MS-G3D [7] to detect deception. The model contains three spatio-temporal graph convolution blocks (STB), a global average pooling layer and a softmax classifier. The three STBs are used to extract spatio-temporal features at multiple scales. The G3D module is excluded due to heavy computational cost [10] and less effectiveness in our task.

Each STB consists of a multiscale graph convolutional network (MS-GCN) and three multiscale temporal convolutional networks (MS-TCN). The MS-GCN module extracts the spatial dependence between a joint and its neighbours at

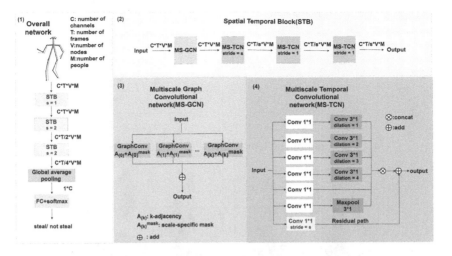

Fig. 1. The architecture of the simplified version of MS-G3D model

different scales and aggregates them. Different self-learning residual masks are used for $A_{(k)}$ to enable the graph convolution layer to be slightly self-adjusting.

The MS-TCN module aggregates temporal features at different scales with dilated convolutional layers. A larger temporal receptive field is achieved by using different dilation rates in different branches, which helps to improve computational efficiency. A maxpooling layer is also used to dispose the redundant information in the convolved features. Residual paths are also included to facilitate training.

3   Experiment

3.1   Dataset

The skeleton data is extracted from videos in the Whodunit dataset. The dataset collects responses of participants in a mock theft situation. Participants are directed to a room individually to read an instruction note. A phone is left near the note. Based on the instruction, participants are asked to either steal a phone, or leave the room without knowing anything about the phone. Upon leaving the room, participants are instructed to go downstairs to put down their signatures and returned, where four cameras are placed at the stairs to capture their movements, as shown in Fig (2a) and Fig (2b).

The Whodunit dataset contains videos of 30 participants going down and up stairs after being either instructed to steal the phone or stayed innocent. Due to technical failure of the camera, the final dataset contains videos for 24, 28, 28, and 23 participants from camera 1, 2, 3 and 4, respectively.

Since the collected data are RGB videos, we first extract skeletons with Alphapose [2], which can estimate 2D coordinates as well as the confidence scores of human joints in each frame. We choose 18 joints to represent the skeleton.

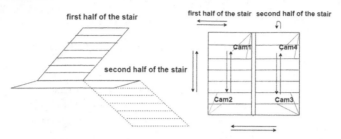

(a) A diagram of the four cameras' positions on the stairs

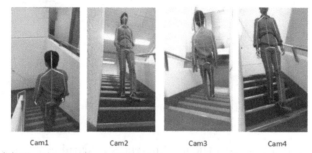

(b) Capture angles of four cameras during downstairs phase

Fig. 2. Camera placements at the stairs

To obtain clean skeleton data of participants, we use a limited range of motion as well as setting a threshold of $5e^{-6}$ for the confidence score to remove the noisy data. Also, we set different thresholds for different cameras for time intervals when participants disappear to segment out the downstairs and upstairs segments.

3.2 Training Details

We use the stratified 3-fold cross-validation to evaluate the performance. We use the average accuracy on the validation sets when tuning the hyperparameters. Data that are not in the test set are employed to train a model with chosen optimal hyperparameters. The reported accuracy is obtained on the test set.

Models are trained on NVIDIA GeForce 940MX GPU with SGD as the optimizer. We set the initial learning rate to $1e^{-3}$ and decrease it to 0.1 times are epoch 30 and 40. Weight decay is set to $5e^{-4}$ and epoch number is 50.

3.3 Baselines: SVM, Decision Tree and Neural Network

Machine learning models such as SVM, Decision Tree and Neural Network (2 layers) are used as baselines. For these classifiers, we first manually extract features from skeletal data. Features are extracted separately from joints and bones. Joints are represented by their x and y coordinates while bones are represented by the lengths and angles which can be derived from the coordinates of corresponding joints. For each joint (or bone), we calculate maximum, minimum, mean, median and standard deviation of x and y coordinates (or lengths and angles) in all frames of a video clip. These features indicate the movement of joints and bones. We get 10 features for each of the 18 joints and 17 bones, resulting in 180 joint features and 170 bone features for each video clip.

To avoid overfitting, we standardize the data first and use principal component analysis (PCA) to reduce the number of features. We also use 3-fold cross-validation and the same test set for fair comparison. Grid search is employed for tuning the hyperparameters.

Table 1. The accuracies of different cameras in different stages

Model		Accuracy								Both
		Downstairs				Upstairs				
		cam1	cam2	cam3	cam4	cam1	cam2	cam3	cam4	
Simplified MSG3D		66.7	100	66.7	83.3	66.7	50	66.7	66.7	**70.9**
NN	Bone	66.7	66.7	100	50	50	33.3	83.3	50	62.5
	Joint	16.7	50	66.7	50	50	33.3	100	50	52.1
	Joint+Bone	83.3	33.3	50	50	66.7	33.3	83.3	50	56.2
SVM	Bone	50	33.3	83.3	33.3	33.3	83.3	66.7	50	54.2
	Joint	66.7	66.7	16.7	50	83.3	33.3	83.3	83.3	60.4
	Joint+Bone	83.3	33.3	83.3	66.7	33.3	33.3	66.7	50	56.2
DT	Bone	50	50	83.3	50	33.3	50	50	50	52.1
	Joint	33.3	66.7	50	33.3	50	83.3	50	33.3	50
	Joint+Bone	66.7	50	66.7	100	66.7	50	66.7	16.7	60.4

NN: Neural network, SVM: Support vector machine, DT: Decision tree

Table 2. The accuracies of up and down stair stages; front and back views; and four different cameras

Model	Accuracy							
	Down	Up	Front	Back	Cam1	Cam2	Cam3	Cam4
Simplified MSG3D	79.2	62.5	79.2	62.5	66.7	75.0	66.7	75.0

3.4 Results and Discussion

The results are presented in Table 1. Using videos of participants going downstairs and upstairs, the simplified MS-G3D model is able to detect deception with an average accuracy of 70.9%. This suggests that the skeletal movements of liars exhibit different characteristics compared to movements of truth tellers.

The accuracy of GCN-based model is at least 8.3% higher than the traditional models, suggesting that the GCN-based model can extract better deceptive temporal and spatial features than the examined hand-crafted features. In many cases the baseline models contribute to accuracy lower than 50%. This may be because the examined features cannot reliably indicate deception, and therefore the results vary greatly when using different features.

We also compare the average accuracy of MSG3D using skeleton data taken from 1) participants going down and up stairs, 2) participants' front and back views and 3) four different cameras. The results are shown in Table 2. We highlight the following observations which can guide the collection of data in real life for gait-based deception detection.

The Behaviours Right After Lying Disclose more Deceptive Information. Table 2 shows that the accuracy of the downstairs phase is much higher than the upstairs phase. This may be because participants were more nervous and more influenced by the theft when going downstairs since they walked directly to the downstairs phase after performing the mock theft. By contrast, the upstairs phase was conducted after the downstairs phase when some unrelated actions had been completed. The participants might have been distracted by these irrelevant actions and thus less affected by the theft. Therefore, the recognition results of skeletons of walking upstairs are lower than those of walking downstairs. This suggests that the gait captured right after theft is more indicative of deception.

The Front Views of Gait Reveal more Clues for Deceit than the Back Views. Table 2 also demonstrates that the accuracy of the front views (79.2%) is higher than the back views (62.5%). As shown in Fig. 2b, the down stairs stage of cameras 2 and 4 and upstairs stage of cameras 1 and 3 captured front views of gait, while the remainder are back views. This suggests that when performing future data extraction for this field, front-side data could be used as much as possible to obtain more information and improve prediction accuracy.

The Movements of Legs are Better Deception Indicators than Arms. Table 2 also shows that the prediction accuracy of data taken from camera 2 and 4 is higher than those taken with camera 1 and 3. As demonstrated in Fig. 2b, cameras 2 and 4 captured video from a low angle, which allows for more pronounced visible movements of the legs, while cameras 1 and 3 capture from a high angle, allowing for clearer shots of the upper body movements. The results presented in this table illustrate that the lower body movements are more distinguishable than the upper body movements to detect liars.

4   Conclusion

In this study, we explore whether skeletal-based gait data could be used for deception detection. Firstly, we obtain the skeleton-based gait data extracted by Alphapose [2] and preprocess it. Then we input this data into a simplified version of MS-G3D model for classification. During this process, traditional classification methods such as SVM, Decision Tree and a two-layer Neural Network are chosen as baselines to compare with the simplified MS-G3D model. The experimental results show that the simplified MS-G3D model obtained better results than the baselines. This means that the skeleton-based gait data correlates to whether or not deception was committed. We also find that the accuracy of the down-stairs stage is better than the up-stairs stage, probably because the down-stairs stage is closer to the time of the deception action. Moreover, the results of cameras 2 and 4 are better than cameras 1 and 3, indicating that the lower angles of the gait recordings disclose more deception related information. In addition, the accuracy from the front views is higher than from the back views. All of these results can serve as suggestions for collecting data and setting up camera positions for deception detection using remotely collected skeletal data in situations where it is important to identify possible deception.

References

1. DePaulo, B.M., Lindsay, J.J., Malone, B.E., Muhlenbruck, L., Charlton, K., Cooper, H.: Cues to deception. Psychol. Bull. **129**(1), 74 (2003)
2. Fang, H.S., Xie, S., Tai, Y.W., Lu, C.: Rmpe: regional multi-person pose estimation. In: Proceedings of the IEEE International Conference on Computer Vision (2017)
3. Hollien, H., Geison, L., Hicks, J.: Voice stress evaluators and lie detection. J. Forensic Sci. **32**(2), 405–418 (1987)
4. Li, C., Zhong, Q., Xie, D., Pu, S.: Skeleton-based action recognition with convolutional neural networks. In: 2017 IEEE International Conference on Multimedia & Expo Workshops (ICMEW), pp. 597–600. IEEE (2017)
5. Li, M., Chen, S., Zhao, Y., Zhang, Y., Wang, Y., Tian, Q.: Dynamic multiscale graph neural networks for 3D skeleton based human motion prediction. In: Proceedings of the IEEE/CVF Conference on Computer Vision and Pattern Recognition, pp. 214–223 (2020)
6. Li, S., Wang, K., Fung, C., Zhu, D.: Improving question answering over knowledge graphs using graph summarization. In: International Conference on Neural Information Processing (2021)
7. Liu, Z., Zhang, H., Chen, Z., Wang, Z., Ouyang, W.: Disentangling and unifying graph convolutions for skeleton-based action recognition. In: Proceedings of the IEEE/CVF Conference on Computer Vision and Pattern Recognition, pp. 143–152 (2020)
8. Owayjan, M., Kashour, A., Al Haddad, N., Fadel, M., Al Souki, G.: The design and development of a lie detection system using facial micro-expressions. In: 2012 2nd International Conference on Advances in Computational Tools for Engineering Applications (ACTEA), pp. 33–38. IEEE (2012)
9. Qin, Z., Anwar, S., Kim, D., Liu, Y., Ji, P., Gedeon, T.: Position-Sensing Graph Neural Networks: Proactively Learning Nodes Relative Positions. arXiv preprint arXiv:2105.11346 (2021)
10. Qin, Z., et al.: Leveraging third-order features in skeleton-based action recognition. arXiv preprint arXiv:2105.01563 (2021)
11. Schuldt, C., Laptev, I., Caputo, B.: Recognizing human actions: a local svm approach. In: Proceedings of the 17th International Conference on Pattern Recognition, 2004. ICPR 2004, vol. 3, pp. 32–36. IEEE (2004)

12. Shi, L., Zhang, Y., Cheng, J., Lu, H.: Two-stream adaptive graph convolutional networks for skeleton-based action recognition. In: Proceedings of the IEEE/CVF Conference on Computer Vision and Pattern Recognition, pp. 12026–12035 (2019)
13. Wang, H., Wang, L.: Modeling temporal dynamics and spatial configurations of actions using two-stream recurrent neural networks. In: Proceedings of the IEEE Conference on Computer Vision and Pattern Recognition, pp. 499–508 (2017)
14. Yan, S., Xiong, Y., Lin, D.: Spatial temporal graph convolutional networks for skeleton-based action recognition. In: Proceedings of the AAAI Conference on Artificial Intelligence, vol. 32 (2018)

A Cross-subject and Cross-modal Model for Multimodal Emotion Recognition

Jian-Ming Zhang[1], Xu Yan[6], Zi-Yi Li[1], Li-Ming Zhao[1], Yu-Zhong Liu[7], Hua-Liang Li[7], and Bao-Liang Lu[1,2,3,4,5]([⊠])

[1] Department of Computer Science and Engineering, Shanghai Jiao Tong University, Shanghai 200240, China
{jmzhang98,liziyi,lm_zhao,bllu}@sjtu.edu.cn
[2] Center for Brain-Machine Interface and Neuromodulation, RuiJin Hospital Shanghai Jiao Tong University School of Medicine, Shanghai 200020, China
[3] RuiJin-Mihoyo Laboratory, RuiJin Hospital, Shanghai Jiao Tong University School of Medicine, Shanghai 200020, China
[4] Key Laboratory of Shanghai Commission for Intelligent Interaction and Cognitive Engineering, Shanghai Jiao Tong University, Shanghai 200240, China
[5] Qing Yuan Research Institute, Shanghai Jiao Tong University, Shanghai 200240, China
[6] Department of Linguistics, University of Washington, Seattle, WA 98195, USA
xyan3@uw.edu
[7] Key Laboratory of Occupational Health and Safety of Guangdong, Power Grid Co., Ltd, Electric Power Research Institute of Guangdong Power Grid Co., Ltd., Guangdong, China

Abstract. The combination of eye movements and electroencephalography (EEG) signals, representing the external subconscious behaviors and internal physiological responses, respectively, has been proved to be a dependable approach with high interpretability. However, EEG is unfeasible to be put into practical applications due to the inconvenience of data acquisition and inter-subject variability. To take advantage of EEG without being restricted by its limitations, we propose a cross-subject and cross-modal (CSCM) model with a specially designed structure called gradient reversal layer to bridge the modality differences and eliminate the subject variation, so that the CSCM model only requires eye movements and avoids using EEG in real applications. We verify our proposed model on two classic public emotion recognition datasets, SEED and SEED-IV. The competitive performance not only illustrates the efficacy of CSCM model but also sheds light on possible solutions to dealing with cross-subject variations and cross-modal differences simultaneously which help make effective emotion recognition practicable.

Keywords: Cross subject · Cross modality · EEG · Eye movements · Multimodal emotion recognition · Transfer learning

© Springer Nature Switzerland AG 2021
T. Mantoro et al. (Eds.): ICONIP 2021, CCIS 1517, pp. 203–211, 2021.
https://doi.org/10.1007/978-3-030-92310-5_24

1   Introduction

Emotional intelligence (EI) has become the spotlight in artificial intelligence since it is a promising way to perfect user experience in human-computer interfaces. EI contains three phases, namely emotion recognition, emotion understanding, and emotion regulation, among which the first step is the most critical [1] for its huge potential to be applied in broad scenarios such as entertainment, smart gadgets, education, and even medical treatment.

Researchers have dived into various modalities to seek an effective way to measure emotions. It has been proved that the combination of eye movements and EEG signals, representing the external subconscious behaviors and internal physiological responses, respectively, is a more dependable approach with high interpretability [12]. However, although this complementary collocation delivers decent performance, it is unfeasible to put it into real-life practice due to the restrictions of EEG in both extrinsic and intrinsic sides. The extrinsic obstacles are unavoidably caused by the equipment like injecting conductive gel, which leads to high cost and operational difficulty when using in daily life. Comparatively, the intrinsic limitation is related to the property of physiological signals. EEG data is highly subject-dependent and susceptible to the structural and functional differences between subjects [7], which brings great challenges to the construction of practical EEG-involved affective models.

To overcome the impediments raised by EEG, scholars have attempted to find solutions from diverse aspects, such as cross-modal transfer. Palazzo et al. [6] combined GAN with RNN to generate corresponding images from EEG signals recorded when subjects were watching images. Our previous work has verified the complementary characteristics of EEG and eye movements [5], supporting that eye movement analysis can be an accessible, simple, and effective method to study the brain mechanism behind cognition. As for subject dependency, transfer learning provides a practical solution to diminish the variability of data distribution between individuals. Zheng et al. [11] first applied several basic domain adaptation (DA) methods to EEG-based emotion recognition task, including transfer component analysis (TCA) [8], etc. Furthermore, combining DA with deep networks is an alternative way. Ganin et al. [3] proposed the domain-adversarial neural network (DANN) to extract the shared representations between the source domain and the target domain. Li et al. [4] first applied deep adaptation network (DAN) to EEG-based cross-subject emotion recognition. To reduce the huge demand of the target domain data in the test stage, Zhao et al. [9] proposed a plug-and-play domain adaptation (PPDA) method and achieved a trade-off between performances and user experience by using only a few target data to calibrate the model.

However, all these models are either cross-subject or cross-modal. The CSCM model that we propose eliminates the structural variability between individuals while learning the shared features of EEG and eye movements so that the latter can be an alternative modality to their combination. As a consequence, the test phase only requires data from the single eye movement modality with no need for data from the new subject in advance. In this way, we guarantee the model with both maximum generalization ability and good feasibility in real applications.

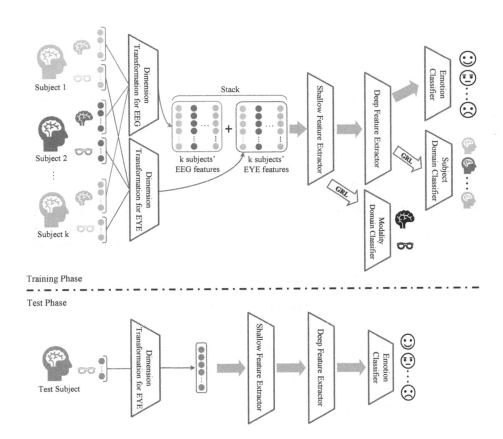

Fig. 1. The framework of our proposed CSCM model. The whole structure contains the training phase and the test phase. The training phase has a main chain in blue and two subchains to bridge the modality differences and eliminate the subject variation, respectively. The test phase only requires eye movement signals as input to predict emotions.

2   Methods

2.1   Overview

To make emotion recognition more generalizable and practicable, we propose a cross-subject and cross-modal model called CSCM model that gets over the inter-subject variability and modal restrictions caused by EEG signals. The framework of CSCM model is depicted in Fig. 1. The whole process can be divided into the training phase and the test phase. In the training phase, both eye movements and EEG signals from source subjects are required as input. There is a main chain together with two subchains aiming to bridge modality differences and eliminate subject variation, respectively. In the main chain, dimension transformation layers are applied first to both types of signals separately to unify the dimensions. Then they are fed to a shallow feature extractor where the first subchain stretches out. A gradient reversal layer [3] connects the modality domain classifier in the subchain to the shallow feature extractor in order to generate domain-invariant features. The deep feature extractor follows the shallow one with the second subchain to make subject domains indistinguishable. An emotion classifier ends the training phase at last. For the test phase, our model only demands eye movement signals from the target subject.

2.2   Training Phase

Dimension Transformation. We use $X'_{EEG} \in \mathbb{R}^p$ to annotate EEG feature vectors, where p is the feature dimension. Each dimension represents information from a specific channel of a frequency band. Similarly, $X'_{EYE} \in \mathbb{R}^q$ stands for eye movement feature vectors with dimension q. Since p is much larger than q due to the information sufficiency of EEG, we conduct dimension transformation via a specific layer separately first to unify the feature dimensions so that $X_{EEG}, X_{EYE} \in \mathbb{R}^r$ where r is the dimension of mapped features.

Modality Reduction. After dimension transformation, we feed the mapped features to the shallow feature extractor E_s with parameters θ_s where s represents shallow. It is connected to the modality domain classifier C_{md} via a specially designed layer called Gradient Reversal Layer (GRL) L_{md}, where md represents a modality domain. In the forward propagation, L_{md} functions in the typical way but in the backpropagation period it takes the gradient from C_{md} and multiplies by a certain negative number before passing back to E_s, i.e. reversing the sign of the gradient. Optimization process is integrated as follows:

$$
\begin{aligned}
(\hat{\theta}_s, \hat{\theta}_y) &= arg\min_{\theta_s, \theta_y} E(\theta_s, \theta_y, \hat{\theta}_{md}) \\
(\hat{\theta}_{md}) &= arg\max_{\theta_{md}} E(\hat{\theta}_s, \hat{\theta}_y, \theta_{md}),
\end{aligned}
\tag{1}
$$

where y stands for a label, i.e. a modality of EEG or eye movements. By this ingenious gradient reversal mechanism, features from EEG and eye movement modalities are gradually indistinguishable until C_{md} cannot tell them apart. Thus, modality-invariant features have been extracted out.

Inter-subject Variability Elimination. Since subject differences are determined by more factors and vary a lot, it is harder to minimize this variability than those between modalities. Hence, deep features are generated by E_d, where d means deep, from the output of E_s. We adopt the same structure with L_{md} to build $\boldsymbol{L}_{sd}$ where sd is a subject domain linking $\boldsymbol{E}_d$ to the subject domain classifier $\boldsymbol{C}_{sd}$. Different from $\boldsymbol{L}_{md}$, $\boldsymbol{L}_{sd}$ tries to obtain subject-invariant features guided by the reversed gradient. Features after this step are expected to no longer contain modal or subject information. The prediction given by the emotion classifier $\boldsymbol{C}_e$ is based on both modality-invariant and subject-invariant features.

Learning Loss. In the training phase, EEG data and eye movement data from source subjects are utilized to train the model to minimize the following loss:

$$\mathcal{L} = \alpha\mathcal{L}_{\boldsymbol{C}_e} + \beta\mathcal{L}_{\boldsymbol{L}_{md}} + \gamma\mathcal{L}_{\boldsymbol{L}_{sd}}, \tag{2}$$

where α, β and γ are trade-offs that control the synergy of the three loss terms. We minimize the cross-entropy loss of the emotion classifier as:

$$\mathcal{L}_{\boldsymbol{C}_e} = -\sum_i y_i \log \hat{y}_i, \tag{3}$$

where $\hat{y}_i$ is the prediction of $\boldsymbol{C}_e$, and y_i is the ground truth label for the input x_i. $\boldsymbol{C}_{md}$ and $\boldsymbol{C}_{sd}$ also use cross-entropy as the loss.

2.3   Test Phase

Since two pre-trained feature extractors $\boldsymbol{E}_s$ and $\boldsymbol{E}_d$ have learned the knowledge from EEG signals and subject-invariant components, the whole model does not need any calibration by the new data and only needs the eye movement signals of the new subject as input in this phase.

3   Experiments

3.1   Datasets and Protocols

We verify the performance of our model on two public datasets, SEED [13] and SEED-IV[1] [10]. For SEED, we take data from 9 subjects who have multimodal signals while all 15 subjects in SEED-IV are qualified to be tested. Each subject participated in the experiments three times to watch videos that evenly cover every emotion in each experiment on different days. The EEG signals and the eye movement signals were recorded with a 62-channel electrode cap together in ESI Neuroscan system and SMI wearable eye-tracking glasses, respectively.

The recorded EEG signals are downsampled 200 Hz and then processed with a bandpass filter of 0–75 Hz and baseline correction as well. After the preprocessing, different entropy (DE) [2] features are extracted with non-overlapping 1-second and 4-second time windows for SEED and SEED-IV, respectively, in the five frequency bands (δ: 1–3 Hz, θ: 4–7 Hz, α: 8–13 Hz, β: 14–30 Hz, and γ: 31–50 Hz) from every sample. The eye movement signals are extracted by SMI BeGaze software, including pupil diameter, dispersion, etc. [5]

---

[1] The SEED and SEED-IV are available at https://bcmi.sjtu.edu.cn/home/seed/index.html.

Table 1. Results of different methods running on SEED and SEED-IV.

Methods	Training modalities	Test modality	SEED		SEED-IV	
			Avg.	Std.	Avg.	Std.
SVM	EYE	EYE	0.5223	0.0724	0.5231	0.1088
SVM	EEG	EEG	0.5690	**0.0594**	0.5567	0.0899
MLP	EYE	EYE	0.6646	0.0762	0.5508	0.0951
MLP	EEG & EYE	EYE	0.6837	0.0975	0.6110	0.1243
CSCM-SM	EYE	EYE	0.7030	0.1316	0.6836	**0.0590**
CSCM	EEG & EYE	EYE	**0.7618**	0.0761	**0.7222**	0.1123

3.2   Experimental Results

We select two popular methods, namely support vector machine (SVM) and multilayer perceptron (MLP), to make comparisons. The average accuracies (avg.) and standard deviations (std.) are reported in Table 1. Results for each subject of each method on SEED and SEED-IV are depicted in Fig. 2.

Comparison Under Single Modality. To examine the performance of CSCM model, we first compare models all trained and tested with a single modality. Since our motivation is to avoid using EEG in the test stage, here we mainly focus on the eye movement modality. It is necessary to mention that CSCM-SM model on line 5 refers to a transformed model of CSCM model that does not have the modality domain classifier, allowing it to be trained with a single modality (SM) in the cross-subject emotion recognition task.

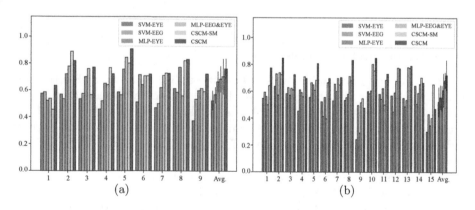

Fig. 2. The accuracies for each subject of each method and the averages on SEED (a) and SEED-IV (b).

Line 1, 3, and 5 display the results of training and testing with only the eye movement modality. We tested on data from 1 subject and used all remained data as training sets for each dataset. SVM is taken as the baseline. For three-class emotion recognition on SEED, CSCM model slightly outperforms MLP by 4%, and these performances are drastically higher than the baseline ranging from 14% to 18% as shown above. For SEED-IV when the number of emotion categories increases, CSCM model surpasses both SVM and MLP for at least 13% with a quite decent standard deviation around 0.06, which demonstrates that our proposed method is solid and has great potential to perform better when complicated emotional states are involved.

Previous studies have confirmed that EEG signals contain much more useful information than eye movement signals [5,10]. In other words, for the same method to be working on a single modality, the EEG modality is supposed to have better performance than the eye movement modality which has been proved by the comparison between the first two lines in Table 1. However, our model with eye movement modality acts much better than SVM with EEG modality as presented in line 2. This surprising fact convinces us that the utilization of information in CSCM model is of high efficiency.

Verification of Two GRL Layers. We corroborate the effect of the two specially designed GRL separately as follows. The first GRL L_{md} is set to minimize the modality differences. However, whether it really employs the knowledge from EEG remains a question. Therefore, we compare the standard CSCM model with CSCM-SM model. Specifically, these two differ from modalities used in the training phase that CSCM model takes both while the other only uses eye movement modality. The comparable results are listed on the last two lines in Table 1. The CSCM model shows great superiority over CSCM-SM model, especially in three-label classification about 6% with outstanding stability, proving that L_{md} works well in helping capture useful information from EEG and further provides a solid foundation for disposing of EEG in real applications.

The second GRL L_{sd} aims to reduce the subject discrepancies. For line 1, 3, and 5 in Table 1, all can be regarded as cross-subject methods with different implementation ways as mentioned in the previous subsection above. The better results on both datasets indicate that using L_{sd} to diminish subject variation is more reliable and effective than the traditional ways. This evidence supports the idea that CSCM model provides a new solution to tackle subject variability.

Comparison with Multimodal Models. Few existing models are cross-modal and cross-subject at the same time in the emotion recognition task. In order to examine our model, we adapt a classic model MLP to the same task as our baseline, i.e. training with multimodalities and testing with only eye movement signals. Particularly, in order to be consistent with CSCM model, we also transform the dimensions of EEG and eye movement features at first. Compared with MLP, it is evident that our model fits the properties of data well from the significantly higher accuracies and less standard deviations, especially on SEED-IV. Our proposed CSCM model affords researchers a novel idea to realize cross-subject and cross-modal simultaneously with respectable performances and more state-of-the-art methods need to be further explored in the future.

4   Conclusions

In this paper, we have devised a novel multimodal learning model, CSCM model, to make emotion recognition as practicable as possible beyond lab environment by applying cross-subject and cross-modal techniques simultaneously. It successfully outperforms baselines and is substantiated from both sides individually according to the comprehensive experiment results. Besides the effective model itself, this pioneering thought sheds light on further attempts at making affective computing systems more practicable and bringing tangible benefits to daily life.

Acknowledgments. This work was supported in part by grants from the National Natural Science Foundation of China (Grant No. 61976135), SJTU Trans-Med Awards Research (WF540162605), the Fundamental Research Funds for the Central Universities, the 111 Project, and the China Southern Power Grid (Grant No. GDKJXM20185761).

References

1. Brunner, C., et al.: Bnci horizon 2020: Towards a roadmap for the BCI community. Brain-Comput. Interf. **1**, 1–10 (2015)
2. Duan, R.N., Zhu, J.Y., Lu, B.L.: Differential entropy feature for EEG-based emotion classification. In: 6th International IEEE/EMBS Conference on Neural Engineering, pp. 81–84. IEEE (2013)
3. Ganin, Y., et al.: Domain-adversarial training of neural networks. J. Mach. Learn. Res. **17**(1), 2096–2030 (2017)
4. Li, H., Jin, Y.M., Zheng, W.-L., Lu, B.-L.: Cross-subject emotion recognition using deep adaptation networks. In: Cheng, L., Leung, A.C.S., Ozawa, S. (eds.) ICONIP 2018. LNCS, vol. 11305, pp. 403–413. Springer, Cham (2018). https://doi.org/10.1007/978-3-030-04221-9_36
5. Lu, Y.F., Zheng, W.L., Li, B., Lu, B.L.: Combining eye movements and EEG to enhance emotion recognition. In: Yang, Q., Wooldridge, M.J. (eds.) Proceedings of the Twenty-Fourth International Joint Conference on Artificial Intelligence, pp. 1170–1176. AAAI Press (2015)
6. Palazzo, S., Spampinato, C., Kavasidis, I., Giordano, D., Shah, M.: Generative adversarial networks conditioned by brain signals. In: Proceedings of the IEEE International Conference on Computer Vision, pp. 3410–3418 (2017)
7. Samek, W., Meinecke, F.C., Müller, K.R.: Transferring subspaces between subjects in brain-computer interfacing. IEEE Trans. Biomed. Eng. **60**(8), 2289–2298 (2013)
8. Pan, S.J., Tsang, I.W., Kwok, J.T., Yang, Q.: Domain adaptation via transfer component analysis. IEEE Trans. Neural Netw. **22**(2), 199–210 (2010)
9. Zhao, L.M., Yan, X., Lu, B.L.: Plug-and-play domain adaptation for cross-subject EEG-based emotion recognition. In: Proceedings of the 35th AAAI Conference on Artificial Intelligence (2021)
10. Zheng, W.L., Liu, W., Lu, Y.F., Lu, B.L., Cichocki, A.: Emotionmeter: a multimodal framework for recognizing human emotions. IEEE Trans. Cybern. **49**(3), 1–13 (2018)
11. Zheng, W.L., Lu, B.L.: Personalizing EEG-based affective models with transfer learning. In: Kambhampati, S. (ed.) Proceedings of the Twenty-Fifth International Joint Conference on Artificial Intelligence, 2016, pp. 2732–2739. IJCAI/AAAI Press (2016)

12. Zheng, W.L., Dong, B.N., Lu, B.L.: Multimodal emotion recognition using EEG and eye tracking data. In: 2014 36th Annual International Conference of the IEEE Engineering in Medicine and Biology Society, pp. 5040–5043. IEEE (2014)
13. Zheng, W.L., Lu, B.L.: Investigating critical frequency bands and channels for EEG-based emotion recognition with deep neural networks. IEEE Trans. Auton. Mental Dev. **7**(3), 162–175 (2015)

EEG Feature Significance Analysis

Yuhao Zhang[1(✉)], Yue Yao[1], Md Zakir Hossain[1,2], Shafin Rahman[3], and Tom Gedeon[4]

[1] The Australian National University, Canberra, ACT 2601, Australia
{yuhao.zhang,yue.yao,zakir.hossain}@anu.edu.au
[2] CSIRO Agriculture and Food, Black Mountain, Canberra, ACT 2601, Australia
[3] North South University, Dhaka, Bangladesh
shafin.rahman@northsouth.edu
[4] Curtin University, Perth, WA 6102, Australia
tom.gedeon@curtin.edu.au

Abstract. Electroencephalography (EEG), a recording of brain activities, is usually feature fused. Although such feature fusion characteristic makes many brain-computer interfaces (BCI) possible, it makes it hard to distinguish task-specific features. As a result, current works usually use the whole EEG signal or features for a specific task like classification, regardless of the fact that many of the features are not task-related. In this paper, we aim to analyze the task-specific significance of EEG features. Specifically, we extract the frequency domain features and perform classification on them. To ensure a generalized conclusion, we use various classification architectures like Multilayer Perceptron (MLP) and 2D convolutional neural network (Conv2D). Extensive experiments are conducted on the UCI EEG dataset. We find that the front part of the brain, namely channel Fpz, AFz, Fp1, and Fp2 contains the general distinct features. Besides, the beta frequency band of the EEG signal is the most significant in the alcoholism classification task.

Keywords: EEG · Significance analysis · Alcoholism · Deep learning

1 Introduction

Brain-computer interfaces (BCIs) have a wide range of applications in the medical, education, and gaming fields. Electroencephalogram (EEG), as an important physiological signal in BCIs, has attracted more attention from researchers in recent years. EEG is able to reflect the brain activities of human beings directly and convey much mental information such as emotion and intention [5]. So, it is widely used in pattern recognition/classification tasks with various machine learning techniques [6].

However, EEG data contains a huge amount of elements and it is hard to say which of them is more significant, and it is very computationally expensive if we use all of the EEG signals as input to some machine learning models such as decision tree or SVM [14]. Thus some feature extraction methods are

© Springer Nature Switzerland AG 2021
T. Mantoro et al. (Eds.): ICONIP 2021, CCIS 1517, pp. 212–220, 2021.
https://doi.org/10.1007/978-3-030-92310-5_25

applied on EEG signals to generate more salient features with smaller sizes. Two common EEG feature extraction methods are *(1)* calculating the spectral power of different frequency bands and different electrodes and *(2)* converting EEG signals to images and applying convolutional neural networks (CNNs) to extract high-level features automatically. Although the size of EEG features reduces significantly by these approaches, it is still difficult to decide which part of EEG features are more significant in the classification tasks. Feature distinctiveness analysis is useful in many aspects. It can help to improve the model efficiency by pruning the less significant features and make the model more explainable.

In summary, the major contributions of our work are:

- We are among the first to visualize and analyze the EEG feature significance with deep learning structure. Among many fused features, we aim to find task-related ones.
- Various models include simple neural network and CNN are tested as well as their feature significance analysis method. A consistent analysis result across methods is found.

2   Related Work

Feature Significance Analysis. In machine learning tasks including EEG classification, salient and effective features can significantly improve the model performance and efficiency. Particularly for deep learning, model-based feature significance analysis also optimizes the networks and makes them more explainable. So, it is very important to analyze and evaluate the feature significance.

For multi-layer perceptron (MLP), Garson [2] proposed an input contribution measure based on the weight matrix, however, it does not consider the neutralization of positive and negative weights; Gedeon [3] used the absolute value of neuron weights to calculate the contribution of an input neuron to an output neuron. It overcame the effect of the weight sign on the contribution and demonstrated its stability during training. Gedeon and Harris [4] proposed a distinctiveness analysis technique for hidden neurons based on the angle of two vectors (one for each hidden neuron) consisting of the activation for various patterns. This is extended to input analysis by replacing the activation values with normalized neuron weights.

CNN performs well in processing images but it is not very self-explaining [15]. Many visual explanation methods have been proposed which can analyze the significance of input features such as Class Activation Map (CAM) [13], which can identify the most relevant regions given a certain class. However, CAM has a limitation in model generalization since it requires a global pooling layer. Grad-CAM [8] uses the gradient to calculate the weight of each channel without a global pooling layer, so it can be widely used for models of different architectures. However, Grad-CAM also has some issues such as gradient noise and vanishing, and Wang *et al.*. proposed Score-CAM [10] to utilize an increase of confidence to represent the importance of each channel. It gets rid of the dependence on gradients and achieved state-of-the-art visualization explanation performance. This study adopts Score-CAM to visualize activation areas and analyze the significance of EEG feature maps.

3 Methodology

3.1 Dataset

This paper uses a public UCI EEG dataset[1], to perform the classification task and feature significance analysis. The dataset includes EEG signals of 122 subjects, 77 of which are diagnosed with alcoholism and the other 45 are control subjects. The 64-channel EEG signals of the subjects are recorded 256 Hz while seeing the pictures from the Snodgrass and Vanderwart picture set. Each subject has about 120 one-second trials, and the dataset size is proper to perform the feature significance analysis. For each trial, the EEG data has the shape of 64×256. All the trials of a subject share the same label which can be 1 for alcoholism and 0 for control. For the alcoholism classification task, we randomly split each subject's data into training, testing, and validation sets by 8:1:1.

3.2 EEG Feature Extraction

EEG Spectral Power Feature Extraction. Firstly, we apply Fast Fourier Transform (FFT) on EEG data to transfer them into the frequency domain. Since theta (4–7 Hz), alpha (8–13 Hz) and beta (13–30 Hz) frequency bands contain the most salient information of EEG when people are awake [1], the mean values for these three frequency bands of each electrode are calculated as the hand-crafted features (so-called spectral power feature).

EEG Image-Based Feature Extraction. Multi-channel EEG signals have spatial information based on the measuring electrodes. We transform 64-channel EEG signals to 2D images based on the electrode locations [11] and apply a 3-layer CNN to extract high-level spatial EEG features. The kernel number of three convolutional layers are 4, 8, 16 respectively with the same kernel size of 3×3. The first two convolutional layers are followed by 2×2 maxpooling layers.

3.3 EEG Alcoholism Classification

EEG spectral power and image-based features then flow into a 2-linear-layer network classifier and predict alcoholism labels separately. A 0.5 dropout is applied after the first layer to avoid overfitting. The number of hidden neurons in the first layer λ is regarded as a hyper-parameter determined as 16 by validation experiments. A ReLu activator follows the first layer and a Softmax activator follows the second layer. For the model training phase, we utilize the cross-entropy loss function and Adam optimizer. The epoch number, batch size and learning rate are 50, 8, and 5e−5.

---

[1] https://kdd.ics.uci.edu/databases/eeg/eeg.html.

3.4   EEG Feature Significance Analysis

EEG Spectral Power Significance Analysis. In this study, we apply Gedeon Method [3] to analyze the significance of the EEG spectral power features by the magnitude and functional measures. Firstly, we use a magnitude measure $P_{ij} = \frac{|W_{ij}|}{\sum_{p=1}^{N} |W_{pj}|}$, to represent the contribution of the last layer neuron i to a next layer neuron j, where N denotes the total neuron number in the last layer.

Our model is a 3-layer network, so the contribution of an input neuron i to the output neuron o can be calculated by $Q_{io} = \sum_{h=1}^{M} (P_{ih} \times P_{ho})$, where h and M denote a hidden neuron and the total number of hidden neurons. The contribution magnitude measure Q_{io} determines the significance of a certain EEG feature given a certain class. When the value is larger, the corresponding EEG feature is more important to this class; vice versa.

Secondly, we use the weight vector angle between input neurons as a functional measure to represent the distinctiveness of the input neuron. It is extended from the hidden neuron distinctiveness analysis technique proposed in [4]. The vector angle of the neurons i and j can represent how different between two neurons. If the angle is small, one of these neurons may be redundant and can be removed. In this study, we calculate the average angle of one input neuron to other 191 neurons as the functional measure, and the angle is calculated by Eq. 1, where $sact(p, h) = norm(weight(h)) - 0.5$.

$$angle(i,j) = tan^{-1}\left(\sqrt{\frac{\sum_{p}^{pats} sact(p, i)^2 * \sum_{p}^{pats} sact(p, j)^2}{\sum_{p}^{pats} (sact(p, i) * sact(p, j))^2}} - 1\right) \qquad (1)$$

Table 1. Mean alcoholism classification accuracy

Feature	Accuracy
Spectral power features	70.02%
Image-based features	71.80%

EEG Image-Based Feature Analysis. We apply Score-CAM [10] to analyze our EEG image-based features by visualizing the upsampled activation maps. It utilizes an increase of Confidence as the weight of each channel. The contribution of the activation of a CNN layer l of k-th channel is defined as $C(A_l^k) = f(X \cdot s(Up(A_l^k))) - f(X_b)$, where X and Xb denote an input and a known baseline input; f, $Up()$ and $s()$ denote CNN model, upsample (to input size) operation and normalization function. Then, we can calculate the Score-CAM using the activation maps and also the corresponding contributions as $S = ReLU(\sum_k C(A_l^k)A_l^k)$.

We select the last convolutional layer of our trained EEG image-based feature extractor and use its activation to generate the CAM. In order to explore the distinguishing parts between the control and the alcoholism subjects, we visualize the Score-CAMs for subjects of two classes separately and compare the differences. Meanwhile, we split each class into samples that are correctly classified and misclassified, and this can help us analyze the significant features more accurately and understand why the model makes a certain prediction.

Table 2. EEG features distinctiveness analysis using magnitude measure and functionality; alpha47 means the mean value of theta frequency band from 47th channel.

Measure	Top 5 most significant				
Magnitude-control	Theta FT7	Theta F4	Beta P7	Beta AFz	Theta POz
Magnitude-alcoholism	Beta P7	Theta F4	Theta FT7	Beta AFz	Theta POz
Magnitude-average	Theta F4	Beta P7	Theta FT7	Beta AFz	Theta POz
Functionality	Theta P7	Alpha AF4	Theta FT7	Beta FT10	Theta F4
Measure	Top 5 least significant				
Magnitude-control	Theta C2	Beta FC5	Alpha C5	Alpha PO4	Theta FC2
Magnitude-alcoholism	Theta C2	Theta F2	Beta FC5	Theta FC2	Alpha C5
Magnitude-average	Theta C2	Alpha PO4	Beta FC5	Alpha C5	Theta FC2
Functionality	Beta CP3	Theta C2	Theta TP8	Alpha P2	Alpha FT8

4   Results and Discussions

4.1   Classification Results

We use classification accuracy as the evaluation metric. Table 1 reports the experiment results using spectral power and image-based EEG features on the UCI EEG dataset. Both two features achieve satisfied classification accuracy above 70%. Image-based features perform better than spectral power features, and we believe this is because they extract spatial information from EEG signals.

4.2   EEG Feature Significance Analysis

EEG Spectral Power Feature Significance Analysis. Although EEG image-based features perform better in alcoholism classification, spectral power features are meaningful and explainable. We utilize magnitude and functional measures proposed in [3] to evaluate the EEG spectral power features significance based on our trained model (i.e. 2-linear-layer network classifier). Table 2 reports the top 5 most and least significant features using both two measurements. It notable that, theta F4 and theta FT7 appear in the 5 most significant features for both two measures demonstrating the consistency of two measures.

We visualize the spectral power feature significance by the EEG image generation method described in Sect. 3.2 and replacing the spectral power with the corresponding significance measures (Fig. 1). From Table 2 and Fig. 1, we get several findings: *(1)* For magnitude measurement, the feature significance distributions of the control and the alcoholism classes are similar. Specifically, AFz, AF8, TF7, P7, P4 and AF7 channels are more significant in magnitude measurement. *(2)* For functionality measurement, TF7, P7, AF8, TP10, F7 and Fp1 channels are more significant. And there are some common significant channels, namely TF7, P7, AF8, which can be regarded as general significant features in the alcoholism classification task. *(3)* Different frequency bands have different contributions in the classification. The average magnitude/functional measures of theta, alpha, and beta frequency bands are 5.25e−3/1.239, 5.01e−3/1.241 and 5.36e−3/1.251, respectively. So, the beta frequency band features are most significant and contribute the most to the alcoholism classification output.

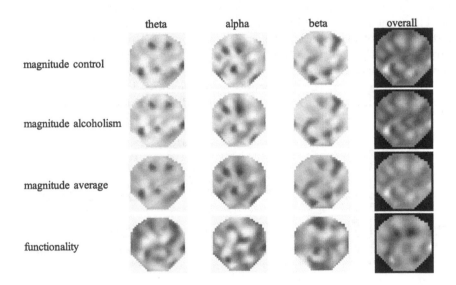

Fig. 1. EEG spectral power feature significance visualisation.

EEG Image Feature Significance Analysis. EEG image features are more salient and achieve better classification performance because they remain the 2D spatial information of EEG signals. We want to explore which parts of EEG images are more significant. To this end, we use Score-CAM [10] to visualize the EEG image feature maps. Figure 2(a) shows visualization results of two subjects. The first row is for alcoholism and the second row is for control. We find that, for both the alcoholism and the control, the activation areas are located at the front and the back parts of the brain, namely EEG electrodes of Fp1, Fp2, Fpz, AF3, AF4, AFz, PO3, PO4, POz, P1, P2, P3, P4, P5 P6 and Pz. Contrast to the control, the left middle part of the brain is more significant for alcoholism, namely the EEG electrodes of FC1, FC3, C1, C3, CP1 and CP3. We believe this is the distinct area of EEG images to distinguish the alcoholism and the control.

In order to obtain the general significant features, we generate Score-CAMs using the whole samples of classes as Fig. 2(b). The left column is for samples that are classified correctly, while the right column is for the misclassified samples. We find that the Score-CAMs with the same predictions (no matter correct or wrong) are quite similar. For samples that are predicted as alcoholism (left top and right bottom), the CNN feature extractor focuses on the left middle part (FC1, C1, CP1) and back part (PO3, POz, PO4, Pz, P1, P2) of brain; however, for samples predicted as control (left bottom and right top), the network focuses on the left front part (F7, AF7) and the right front part (F8, FT8) of the brain. By this way, we can analyze and explain the reason why our CNN-based classifier predicts a certain label.

Consistency Between Methods. Furthermore, we find that there is some consistency between spectral power and image-based feature significance analysis. The front part of the brain, namely channel Fpz, AFz, Fp1, and Fp2, is significant for both two kinds of features. However, we also notice that the significance visualizations of these two features are quite different in many regions, we believe this is because our image-based features remain the spatial attribution of EEG data, however, the 1D spectral power features lose this characteristic, leading to the difference of feature significance distribution.

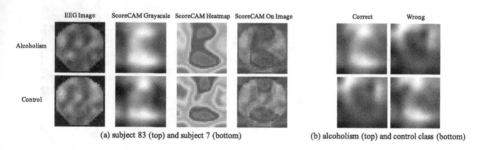

(a) subject 83 (top) and subject 7 (bottom)   (b) alcoholism (top) and control class (bottom)

Fig. 2. EEG image feature visualization using Score-CAM

5   Conclusion and Future Work

This study extracts EEG spectral power and image-based features from 64-channel EEG signals. We perform an alcoholism classification on UCI EEG dataset, and both methods achieve good accuracy above 70%. Gedeon method and Score-CAM technique are used to analyse the two kinds of EEG features respectively. We find that EEG channels in the front part of the brain, namely Fpz, AFz, Fp1 and Fp2 channels, are generally significant features. Besides, the beta frequency (13–30 Hz) contributes the most to EEG classification task.

In the future, we plan to analyze more EEG feature extraction methods, such as LSTM and transformer, to find if there is some consistency with spectral power and image-based features. Furthermore, more EEG classification tasks will be considered to enhance the generalisation of our analysis that will useful for emotion recognition [7,12], caffeine intake classification [9], and many more.

References

1. Abhang, P.A., Gawali, B.W.: Correlation of eeg images and speech signals for emotion analysis. Curr. J. Appl. Sci. Technol. **10**(5), 1–13 (2015)
2. Garson, D.G.: Interpreting neural network connection weights. AI Expert, pp. 47–51 (1991)
3. Gedeon, T.D.: Data mining of inputs: analysing magnitude and functional measures. Int. J. Neural Syst. **8**(02), 209–218 (1997)
4. Gedeon, T., Harris, D.: Network reduction techniques. In: Proceedings International Conference on Neural Networks Methodologies and Applications, pp. 119–126. AMSE (1991)
5. Lebedev, M.A., Nicolelis, M.A.: Brain-machine interfaces: past, present and future. TRENDS Neurosci. **29**(9), 536–546 (2006)
6. Lotte, F., Congedo, M., Lécuyer, A., Lamarche, F., Arnaldi, B.: A review of classification algorithms for eeg-based brain-computer interfaces. J. Neural Eng. **4**(2), R1 (2007)
7. Rostov, M., Hossain, M.Z., Rahman, J.S.: Robotic emotion monitoring for mental health applications: preliminary outcomes of a survey. In: Ardito, C., et al. (eds.) INTERACT 2021. LNCS, vol. 12936, pp. 481–485. Springer, Cham (2021). https://doi.org/10.1007/978-3-030-85607-6_62
8. Selvaraju, R.R., Cogswell, M., Das, A., Vedantam, R., Parikh, D., Batra, D.: Gradcam: visual explanations from deep networks via gradient-based localization. In: Proceedings of the IEEE International Conference on Computer Vision, pp. 618–626 (2017)
9. Uddin, M.B., Hossain, M., Ahmad, M., Ahmed, N., Rashid, M.A.: Effects of caffeinated beverage consumption on electrocardiographic parameters among healthy adults. Modern Appl. Sci. **8**(2), 69 (2014)
10. Wang, H., et al.: Score-cam: Score-weighted visual explanations for convolutional neural networks. In: Proceedings of the IEEE/CVF Conference on Computer Vision and Pattern Recognition (CVPR) Workshops, June 2020
11. Yao, Y., Plested, J., Gedeon, T.: Deep feature learning and visualization for EEG recording using autoencoders. In: Cheng, L., Leung, A.C.S., Ozawa, S. (eds.) ICONIP 2018. LNCS, vol. 11307, pp. 554–566. Springer, Cham (2018). https://doi.org/10.1007/978-3-030-04239-4_50
12. Zhang, Y., Hossain, M.Z., Rahman, S.: DeepVANet: a deep end-to-end network for multi-modal emotion recognition. In: Ardito, C., et al. (eds.) INTERACT 2021. LNCS, vol. 12934, pp. 227–237. Springer, Cham (2021). https://doi.org/10.1007/978-3-030-85613-7_16
13. Zhou, B., Khosla, A., Lapedriza, A., Oliva, A., Torralba, A.: Learning deep features for discriminative localization. In: Proceedings of the IEEE Conference on Computer Vision and Pattern Recognition, pp. 2921–2929 (2016)

14. Yao, Y., Plested, J., Gedeon, T.: Information-preserving feature filter for short-term EEG signals. Neurocomputing **408**, 91–99 (2020)
15. Yao, Y., Zheng, L., Yang, X., Naphade, M., Gedeon, T.: Simulating content consistent vehicle datasets with attribute Descent. In: Vedaldi, A., Bischof, H., Brox, T., Frahm, J.-M. (eds.) ECCV 2020. LNCS, vol. 12351, pp. 775–791. Springer, Cham (2020). https://doi.org/10.1007/978-3-030-58539-6_46

Quantitative Taxonomy of Hand Kinematics Based on Long Short-Term Memory Neural Network

Chenguang Li[1,2], Hongjun Yang[1], Shiying Sun[1], and Long Cheng[1,2(✉)]

[1] State Key Laboratory for Control and Management of Complex Systems, Institute of Automation, Chinese Academy of Sciences, Beijing 100190, China
[2] School of Artificial Intelligence, University of Chinese Academy of Sciences, Beijing 100049, China
{lichenguang2017,hongjun.yang,shiying.sun,long.cheng}@ia.ac.cn

Abstract. Assessment of hand motor function is crucial to stroke patients. However, the commonly used Fugl-Meyer assessment (FMA) scale requires 11 hand and wrist movements. To simplify these movements, this study proposes a hand motion classification framework based on deep learning to achieve the quantitative taxonomy of hand kinematics. To the best of our knowledge, this is the first study to use deep learning for the quantitative taxonomy of the hand kinematics. First, we use the Long Short-Term Memory (LSTM) neural network to extract deep features of 20 hand movements (including 11 FMA movements) from 37 healthy subjects, and rank the LSTM neural network output value (predicted probability) of each sample. The similarity between the movements obtained by the nonlinear transformation can be used to draw the confusion matrix. Then the confusion matrix is taken as the category feature to obtain the clustering dendrogram to show the similarity between different hand movements intuitively. Next, the 20 hand movements are divided into four groups by hierarchical clustering. The silhouette coefficient of the clustering results is 0.81, which is close to the ideal value of 1, indicating the validity of the clustering result. Finally, the clustering center is calculated to find the corresponding movement as the representative movement for motor function assessment. As a result, we reduced the 20 movements to 5 movements, allowing for a faster quantitative assessment of hand motor function than the FMA scale. This also lays the foundation of the assessment paradigm for our follow-up research on evaluation algorithm.

Keywords: Hand kinematics · Hand motor function assessment · Deep learning · LSTM · Hierarchical clustering

Project supported by the Beijing Municipal Natural Science Foundation under Grant JQ19020, National Natural Science Foundation of China under Grant 62025307, Grant U1913209, Grant62073319, Grant62103412 and China Postdoctoral Science Foundation under Grant 2021M693403.

T. Mantoro et al. (Eds.): ICONIP 2021, CCIS 1517, pp. 221–229, 2021.
https://doi.org/10.1007/978-3-030-92310-5_26

1   Introduction

Hand motor function is usually evaluated and judged by the hand's performance in fine grasp and strong grasp. However, these two aspects are obviously not enough to fully assess the complex functions of the hand. Fugl-Meyer assessment (FMA) scale is one of the most common subjective assessment methods, which can comprehensively evaluate the hand motor function of stroke patients. However, it is time consuming to evaluate so many movements. Can we simplify and optimize these movements? In order to better understand the law of hand movement, it is necessary to analyze the hand kinematics.

Santello et al. proposed an early method by applying principal component analysis (PCA) to the finger joint angles under a set of significant grasping movements [1]. Many other works that followed [2–4], were inspired by the grasp of taxonomy to select the correct hand movements. Until the past two years, the analysis of hand kinematics still continued. In [5], the hand kinematics in activities of daily living was characterized by PCA, and five synergistic effects were obtained. The 20 human hand grasping movements are classified, and the Mahalanobis distance between different movements is quantitatively analyzed in [6]. After PCA dimensionality reduction and hierarchical clustering of the finger joint movement data of 20 hand grasping movements, three synergistic effect modes were obtained [7]. There are also some studies introducing methods for analyzing hand kinematics based on sEMG signals [6,8].

Although there have been some studies on the analysis of hand kinematics, the movement of the wrist joints was ignored. The wide range of wrist movement enhances the functions of the hands and fingers, while providing sufficient stability. Therefore, the analysis of the hand kinematics cannot be separated from the wrist joint.

In [6], the use of manually extracted features for kinematics analysis is inferior in the ability of generalization and robustness. It is well known that deep learning can automatically extract appropriate deep features based on the tasks by using neural networks, which has been widely confirmed in convolutional neural networks. Therefore, long short-term memory (LSTM) is applied in this study. In addition, although the clustering result of hand kinematics was provided in [6], it did not give the evaluation metrics of the result, we thus do not know how effective the clustering was. This concern is addressed in this study. The contributions of this paper are summarized as follows:

1) Currently, most researchers have only studied the kinematics of the hand grasping movements, but we also analyze four wrist movements and two other finger movements, including wrist flexion, wrist extension, wrist supination, wrist pronation, thumb adduction and abduction of all fingers, facilitating a comprehensive quantitative taxonomy of hand kinematics.

2) A novel framework for the quantitative taxonomy of hand kinematics is proposed. It mainly includes the LSTM neural network to automatically extract the hand motion features and the nonlinear transformation to calculate the hand motion similarity. LSTM neural network can effectively extract deep

features with significant differences between categories. To the best of our knowledge, this is the first study using deep learning to perform quantitative taxonomy of hand kinematics.

3) The 20 hand movements are divided into four groups by the method of hierarchical clustering, and then the hand movements corresponding to the cluster centers are found. The silhouette coefficient of the clustering results is 0.81, which demonstrates the more effective performance than the result in [6]. As a result, we reduced the 20 movements to 5 movements, allowing for a faster quantitative assessment of hand motor function than the FMA scale.

2   Methodology

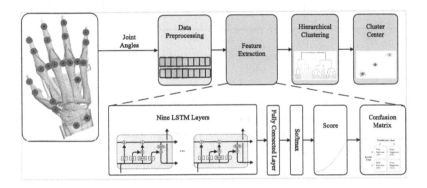

Fig. 1. The overall framework of the study

The proposed method mainly includes three parts: data capturing and preprocessing, feature extraction and hierarchical clustering. The overall framework of the study is shown in Fig. 1.

2.1   Data Capturing and Preprocessing

Data Capturing. The data were recorded from 22 finger joint angles of 37 intact subjects. There are more details about the experiment in [9]. In our study, the selected hand movements refer to the movements in the FMA scale, and are appropriately extended on this basis. All the 20 hand movements analyzed in this study are shown in Fig. 2. It should be noted that wrists and finger movements are crucial to the assessment of hand motor function, so they are added in the 20 hand movements.

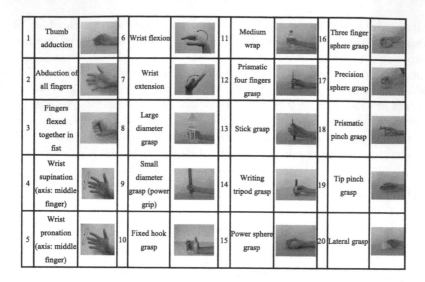

Fig. 2. Twenty different hand movements

Data Preprocessing. Since the data in two data sets (DB1 and DB5) are measured at different sampling rates (100 Hz 200 Hz respectively), a uniform sampling rate is required before data analysis. In this study, the resampling method [10] is used to unify the sampling rate. As the joint angles of the hand movements does not change very quickly, the sampling rate of the two data sets is unified 100 Hz. DB1 contains 20 types of hand movement data from 27 subjects, each of which is repeated 10 times; DB5 contains 20 types of hand movement data from 10 subjects, each of which is repeated 6 times. So the total number of movement repetitions is 27 * 20 * 10 + 10 * 20 * 6 = 6600, which make up the entire data set. The data set is randomly shuffled, 70% of which is used for training and 30% for testing. To increase the sample size, this study performs the sliding window method, and the window size and sliding distance are consistent with those in [6]. So each movement repetition has a window of 200 ms (20 sampling points), with an overlap of 100 ms (10 sampling points). The whole data preprocessing is performed with MATLAB R2019a, and the followed work is achieved by the Python language (version 3.6) based on the Tensorflow framework.

2.2 Feature Extraction

LSTM Neural Network. In this study, multi-layer LSTM network is introduced to extract the deep features of hand motion, which improves the generalization and robustness of the model, compared with manually feature extraction [6]. The network includes nine LSTM layers and one fully connected layer. The input size of the first LSTM layer is 22. The data of each time window is input to the LSTM in batches. The output size of each LSTM layer is 32, 64, 128,

256, 256, 128, 64, 32, 16 respectively and the output size of the fully connected layer is 20, which is activated by the algorithm of softmax. Sparse categorical cross entropy is used as the loss function. The Adams algorithm is used as an optimization method for network training.

Category Feature. The LSTM neural network is used to calculate the probability value of each sample, and the value is used to obtain the category feature. All data (including the training set and the test set) are input to the neural network, and the full connection layer outputs N (the total number of samples) vectors of 20 dimensions, where each movement contains $N/20$ vectors. The n-th sample vector of the m-th movement is represented by $p_{m,n} \in R^{20}$, where $m = 1, ..., 20; n = 1, ..., N/20$. The 20 elements in the vector represent the probabilities that this movement is respectively classified as the 20 movements. The elements in each vector are sorted from smallest to largest, and the sequence numbers are used to replace the corresponding elements in $p_{m,n}$ to form a new vector $p'_{m,n} \in R^{20}$. To maximize the distinction between the previous categories, each element in $p'_{m,n}$ is squared to get $p''_{m,n} \in R^{20}$, and then $N/20$ vectors $p''_{m,n}$ of each movement are summed to get the final score vector $S_m \in R^{20}$. Therefore, the score for 20 movements can be written as $Score = (S_1^T, S_2^T ..., S_{20}^T) \in R^{20*20}$. $Score$ is actually an initial confusion matrix, and the value of each element in the matrix describes the distance or similarity between the two movements represented by the abscissa and ordinate. A smaller value indicates that the two movements are more similar. It requires further normalization and diagonalization to obtain the final confusion matrix A as follows:

$$A = \left| \left(\frac{(Norm(Score) + Norm(Score)^T) * 100}{2} \right)^\star \right|, \tag{1}$$

where $Norm$ is the normalization operation, $\star$ is an operation that the rows and columns of the matrix are subtracted from the diagonal value, $||$ means take the absolute value. Confusion matrix A obtained by the above nonlinear transformation is used as the category feature of hierarchical clustering.

2.3 Hierarchical Clustering

Each column of the confusion matrix A is taken as the category feature, and the clustering dendrogram is obtained by the hierarchical clustering method. To judge the quality of the clustering results, the silhouette coefficient (SC) is used as a metric calculated by:

$$s(i) = \frac{b(i) - a(i)}{max(a(i), b(i))} \tag{2}$$

$$SC = \frac{1}{M} \sum_{i=1}^{M} s(i), \tag{3}$$

where $a(i)$ is the average distance between a movement i and other movements in the same cluster, $b(i)$ is the average distance between movement i and the movements of the other cluster, and $M = 20$ means the total number of movements, $SC \in [-1, 1]$. The clustering effect is better if SC is closer to 1.

Finally, we need to find the movement corresponding to the cluster center that has the minimum distance sum between the other movements in the same cluster, which could be calculated as follows:

$$SN(j) = arg \min_{i}(a_j(i)), \tag{4}$$

where $SN(j)$ represents the sequence number of the movement of the j-th cluster center, i is the movement in the j-th cluster, $a_j(i)$ is the average distance between a movement i and other movements in the j-th cluster. The cluster center movements will be used to evaluate the hand motor function of stroke patients.

3 Results and Discussion

3.1 LSTM Neural Network

After 15 epochs of training, the classification accuracy of LSTM neural network can reach 94.43%. If all the samples (train set and test set) are put into the network to obtain the category probability for each movement, we get that the accuracy of Top-1 classification is 94.69%, and the accuracy of Top-5 classification is 99.90%. The results show the deep feature extracted by the LSTM neural network leads to a high classification accuracy through the basic softmax classifier, indicating it can appropriately represent the characteristics of the corresponding category.

3.2 Confusion Matrix

The confusion matrix including 20 hand movements is shown in Fig. 3(a). The horizontal and vertical coordinates represent 20 movements, respectively. The labels 1–20 are consistent with the movement labels in Fig. 2. A smaller value (darker background color) of elements in the matrix indicates a greater similarity between the two movements represented by the abscissa and the ordinate.

3.3 Hierarchical Tree

The confusion matrix is transformed into a hierarchical tree by the single algorithm, as shown in Fig. 3(b). The abscissa in the Fig. 3(b) shows 20 hand movements, and the ordinate designates the distance between the movements, which builds the relationship between different hand movements intuitively. For the taxonomy of hand movements and decreasing the number of them as much as possible, three dashed lines of different colors are drawn. Their ordinates are approximately 34, 33, and 30, respectively.

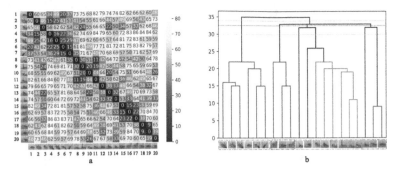

Fig. 3. Clustering results. (a) Cluster Confusion matrix of 20 movements. (b) Hierarchical tree of 20 movements (Color figure online)

- If the blue dashed line is used as the threshold line, the 20 movements can be divided into two categories. The movements on the left part are wrist movements and finger extension movements, and the ones on the right part are grabbing movements. The result of this classification is rough.
- If the red dashed line is used as the threshold line, the 20 movements can be divided into four groups. Counting from left to right, the icons below the abscissa are respectively framed by green, red, blue and purple dot-dash line. The first two groups represent movements of wrist and finger extension and movements of sphere grasp. The characteristic of the third group is that, except the thumb, the other four fingers all present the columnar grip posture, but the bending angles of the four fingers are different. In the forth group, the first movement (prismatic four fingers grasp) is the pinch between the thumb and the other four fingers, and the next two movements (prismatic pinch grasp and tip pinch grasp) are the pinch of thumb and index finger.
- If the yellow dashed line is used as the threshold line, the 20 movements can be divided into six groups. The reason is that on the basis of the above four groups, the writing tripod grasping in the third group and the lateral grasping in the fourth group are separately classified to form two new groups.

Considering the rapidity and accuracy of the assessment, we choose the second grouping way (divided into four groups) for the further research.

3.4   Metric of Clustering Result

We calculate that the SC of the confusion matrix obtained by the artificial feature method in [6] was 0.22. And if the framework of our study was used in [6], movements would be divided into six categories and the SC is $0.77 > 0.22$. It indicates that the features extracted by the LSTM neural network are more effective. In addition, the LSTM neural network is used to cluster 20 movements in this study, and the result of SC is 0.81, which also verified the validity of clustering results. More detailed information on the comparison of clustering is summarized in Table 1.

Table 1. Comparison of clustering results

Characteristic	Method in [6]	Method of our study in[6]	This study
Number of movements	20	20	20
Characteristic	Hand grasp	Hand grasp	Wrist movement finger extension and grasp
Data sources	DB2	DB2	DB1 and DB5
Number of subjects	40	40	37
Feature extraction	Artificial features	LSTM	LSTM
Clustering method	Hierarchical clustering	Hierarchical clustering	Hierarchical clustering
Number of clusters	five	six	four
SC	0.22	0.77	0.81

3.5   Cluster Center

Although we have classified the 20 movements into 4 groups, we still need to select 1 movement from each group as the representative one of this group to simplify and optimize the process for hand motor function assessment. After calculation, there are five cluster centers in the four groups, of which there are two in the first group (two points having the same minimum distance sum) and one in each of the remaining groups. The five movements are shown in Fig. 4.

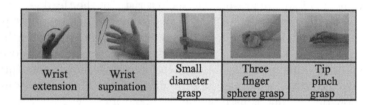

Fig. 4. Five representative hand movements

4   Conclusion

In this study, 20 hand movements involving wrist and finger extension are selected to comprehensively analyze the hand kinematics and serve the assessment of hand motor function of stroke patients. A novel framework for quantitative taxonomy of hand kinematics is proposed to extract the feature using LSTM neural network. A good classification effect is achieved to verify this feature has the common characteristics of this category. Then, the 20 behaviors are divided into four categories by using the nonlinear transformation, with a SC of 0.81. Finally, the cluster center of each group movement is calculated, and the hand movement corresponding to each cluster center is obtained. In the future work, we will collect the information of the 5 hand movements of a large number of stroke patients to replace the FMA scale, and propose an assessment algorithm to evaluate the hand motor function of stroke patients.

References

1. Santello, M., Flanders, M., Soechting, J.F.: Postural hand synergies for tool use. J. Neurosci. **18**(23), 10105–10115 (1998)
2. Charlotte, H.R., Schieber, M.H.: Quantifying the independence of human finger movements: comparisons of digits, hands, and movement frequencies. J. Neurosci. **20**(22), 8542–8550 (2000)
3. Veber, M., Bajd, T.: Assessment of human hand kinematics. In: 2006 IEEE International Conference on Robotics and Automation (ICRA), pp. 2966–2971 (2006)
4. Jarrass, N., Ribeiro, A.T., Sahbani, A., Bachta, W., Roby-Brami, A.: Analysis of hand synergies in healthy subjects during bimanual manipulation of various objects. J. Neuroeng. Rehabil. **11**(113), 1–11 (2014)
5. Jarque-Bou, N.J., Vergara, M., Sancho-Bru, J.L., Gracia-Ibanez, V., Roda-Sales, A.: Hand kinematics characterization while performing activities of daily living through kinematics reduction. IEEE Trans. Neural Syst. Rehabil. Eng. **28**(7), 1556–1565 (2020)
6. Stival, F., Michieletto, S., Cognolato, M., Pagello, E., Mller, H., Atzori, M.: A quantitative taxonomy of human hand grasps. J. Neuroeng. Rehabil. **16**(28), 1–17 (2019)
7. Jarque-Bou, N.J., Scano, A., Atzori, M., Mller, H.: Kinematic synergies of hand grasps: a comprehensive study on a large publicly available dataset. J. Neuroeng. Rehabil. **16**(63), 1–14 (2019)
8. Bao, T., Zaidi, S., Xie, S., Yang, P., Zhang, Z.: A deep kalman filter network for hand kinematics estimation using semg. Pattern Recogn. Lett. **143**(1), 88–94 (2021)
9. Jarque-Bou, N.J., Atzori, M., Mller, H.: A large calibrated database of hand movements and grasps kinematics. Sci. Data **7**(12), 1–10 (2020)
10. Richard, G.L.: Streamlining Digital Signal Processing. John Wiley & Sons, Hoboken (2012)

Evolving Deep Neural Networks for Collaborative Filtering

Yuhan Fang, Yuqiao Liu, and Yanan Sun(✉)

College of Computer Science, Sichuan University, Chengdu, China
ysun@scu.edu.cn

Abstract. Collaborative Filtering (CF) is widely used in recommender systems to model user-item interactions. With the great success of Deep Neural Networks (DNNs) in various fields, advanced works recently have proposed several DNN-based models for CF, which have been proven effective. However, the neural networks are all designed manually. As a consequence, it requires the designers to develop expertise in both CF and DNNs, which limits the application of deep learning methods in CF and the accuracy of recommended results. In this paper, we introduce the genetic algorithm into the process of designing DNNs. By means of genetic operations like crossover, mutation, and environmental selection strategy, the architectures and the connection weights initialization of the DNNs can be designed automatically. We conduct extensive experiments on two benchmark datasets. The results demonstrate the proposed algorithm outperforms several manually designed state-of-the-art neural networks.

Keywords: Deep neural networks · Genetic algorithm · Collaborative filtering

1 Introduction

Collaborative Filtering (CF) is a prevalent technique used by recommender systems [21]. The fundamental assumption of CF is that people with similar tastes tend to show similar preferences on items. Therefore, the purpose of CF is to match people with similar interests and make recommendations, by modeling people's preferences on items based on their past interactions. Generally, CF algorithms can be divided into two following different categories.

1) **Matrix Factorization (MF) Algorithms:** MF works by modeling the user's interaction on items [17]. Researchers have devoted much effort to enhancing MF and proposed various models such as the Funk MF [1] and the Singular Value Decomposition++ (SVD++) [4], *etc.* Funk MF factorizes the user-item rating matrix as the product of two lower dimensional matrices. SVD++ has the capability of predicting item ranking with both explicit and implicit feedback. Unfortunately, the cold start problem, causing by insufficient data, constitutes a limitation for MF algorithm [3].

© Springer Nature Switzerland AG 2021
T. Mantoro et al. (Eds.): ICONIP 2021, CCIS 1517, pp. 230–238, 2021.
https://doi.org/10.1007/978-3-030-92310-5_27

2) **Deep Learning Algorithms:** The introduction of deep learning and neural methods into CF tasks has been proven effective by various models, for example, the DeepFM [11] and the NeuMF [14]. Combining DNN with Factorization Machines (FM), DeepFM has the ability to model both the high-order and low-order feature interactions. In addition, NeuMF generalized the traditional MF with the neural network methods and constructed a nonlinear network architecture. Both these two models can maximize the feature of the finite interaction data and improve the recommendation precision.

Although deep learning methods have shown promising results, designing the network architecture is a challenging and time-consuming task for most inexperienced developers. Therefore, it is worthwhile to extend the automatic method to the network architecture design, ensuring that people who have no domain knowledge of DNNs can benefit from deep learning methods. To this end, we provide an algorithm based on Genetic Algorithm (GA) [2], to automatically design a competitive neural network with efficient weight initialization approaches.

To sum up, the contributions of the proposed Evolve-CF are summarized as follows: **1) Variable-length encoding strategy:** To represent DNNs in GA, we design a variable-length encoding strategy, which is more suitable to automatically determine the optimal depth of neural networks than traditional fixed-length encoding strategy. **2) Weights encoding strategy:** To automatically choose the appropriate weights initialization methods, we investigate the weights encoding strategy to optimize the weights efficiently during evolution. **3) Effective genetic operators:** To simulate the evolution process and increase population diversity, we propose effective genetic operators like crossover and mutation which can cope with the proposed gene encoding strategy. **4) Improved slack binary tournament selection:** To increase the overall fitness of the whole population during evolution, we improve the slack binary tournament selection to choose promising individuals from the parent population.

2   Background

2.1   Skeleton of DNNs

The skeleton of DNNs for CF consists of the embedding layer, the hidden part, and the output layer. To begin with, the embedding layer is fixed as the first layer to take effect in dimensionality reduction and learn the similarity between words [19]. Multiple sequential blocks, which are widely used in DNNs for CF, make up the hidden part. Each block contains a full connection layer, a Rectified Linear Unit (ReLU) [10] and a dropout layer. A full connection layer is capable of learning an offset and an average rate of correlation between the output and the input. Meanwhile, both the ReLU and the dropout layer can make the model less likely to cause overfitting [10].

Besides the arrangement of the blocks, the parameters of each layer affect the performance of DNNs as well, such as the number of neurons in the full connection layer, the dimension of embedding vectors in the embedding layer and the dropout rate in the dropout layer. Both the architecture and the parameters of each layer can be designed automatically.

2.2 Weights Initialization

In deep learning tasks, weights initialization plays a significant role in model convergence rate and model quality, allowing the loss function to be optimized easily [22]. Generally, there are three common categories of initialization methods that are widely used now: **1) Random Initialization. (R)** This method uses the probability distribution as the initializer. Nevertheless, without experience and repeated tries, it's hard for the designers to select the hyper-parameters in the probability model. **2) Xavier Initialization** [9]. (**X**) This method presents a range for uniform sampling based on neuron saturation. While the applicable activation function is limited, which should be a linear function. **3) Kaiming Initialization** [16]. (**K**) This method proposes an initialization works on ReLU, which is a more prevalent activation function in DNNs. However, its effectiveness highly relies on the architectures of DNNs.

Taking all the advantages and disadvantages into consideration, the designers may have trouble in deciding which weights initialization approaches to choose when designing the neural network for a specific CF task. As a consequence, incorporating searching for weights initialization approaches into GA is needed. Thus the weights initialization approaches can be designed automatically.

3 The Proposed Algorithm

Algorithm 1 displays the framework of the proposed Evolve-CF. Firstly, a population is randomly initialized with the predefined population size, and each individual in the population is randomly generated according to the proposed encoding strategy. Then the evolution begins to work until the generation number exceeds the maximal value defined ahead. In the course of evolution, the fitness of each individual is estimated through a specific method which is selected based on the dataset. After that, by means of the improved slack binary tournament selection method, parent individuals are selected from the population to further conduct the genetic operations consisting of crossover and mutation. Thereafter the offspring is generated. Next, environmental selection takes effect to choose individuals from both the parent population and the generated offspring population, and thereby create the next generation. Then the next round of evolution begins to work. When the whole evolution process is over, the expected best individual is selected, and then we build the DNN decoded from the individual for the final training.

3.1 Gene Encoding Strategy

Since the genetic operators in GA take effect based on encoding individuals, we present an encoding strategy to encode the DNNs. The architectures of the neural networks, especially the depths [8], play decisive roles in the performance of DNNs and the applicable depths are various. Because the encoding information contains the depth of the DNNs and the hyper-parameters of each layer, and the

---

Algorithm 1: Framework of the Proposed Algorithm

Input: The population size, the maximal generation number s
Output: The best individual

1 $P_0 \leftarrow$ Randomly initialize the population using the proposed gene encoding strategy;
2 $t \leftarrow 0$;
3 **while** $t < s$ **do**
4   Evaluate the fitness of each individual in P_t;
5       $Q_t \leftarrow$ Choose offspring from the selected parent individuals using the proposed genetic operations;
6       $P_{t+1} \leftarrow$ Environmental selection from $P_t \cup Q_t$;
7       $t \leftarrow t + 1$;
8 **end**
9 **return** The individual having the best fitness in P_t;

---

depth of the neural network is uncertain, the length of encoding should be variational correspondingly. As a result, we propose a variable-length gene encoding strategy being able to find the optimization automatically, freeing designers from constantly adjusting the length.

Via our strategy, the embedding layer and multiple sequential blocks make up the whole DNN. Each block consists of a full connection layer, a ReLU, and a dropout layer. Considering that the last layer determines the prediction results, we set the last block as only a full connection layer. In particular, an example of the proposed strategy representing a DNN is illustrated by Fig. 1.

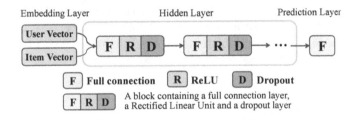

Fig. 1. An example of the proposed encoding strategy representing a DNN

To efficiently initialize the connection weights, we propose a new method, in which the weights initialization information is explicitly represented as the initialization type of each full connection layer. Simply put, the initialization types are randomly chosen from six types in three categories mentioned in Subsect. 2.2 (R with normal distribution R_n and uniform distribution R_u, X with normal distribution X_n and uniform distribution X_u, K with normal distribution K_n and uniform distribution K_u) and will be optimized during the evolution.

As for the initialization of each individual, we first choose an integer randomly within the range and use it as the length of the current individual. Second, the embedding layer with a predefined input size and a random embedding vector dimension is set as the head of the individual. After that, several blocks are added in sequence to the individual until it meets its predefined length. Finally, the last prediction layer is fixed to make sure the prediction results of each DNN are comparable.

3.2   Offspring Generation

In GA, the fitness function is usually set based on the task. As for CF, there is no doubt that the fitness function should be able to evaluate the accuracy of recommendations. Because the Normalized Discounted Cumulation Gain (NDCG) [13] can assign higher importance to results at higher ranks on the list, we use it as the fitness evaluation criterion for the task investigated in this work. Specifically, the NDCG is calculated by Eq. (1)

$$NDCG@K = \frac{1}{N}[\frac{1}{D_k}\sum_{i=1}^{K}\frac{2^{r(i)}-1}{\log_2(i+1)}] \tag{1}$$

where N denotes the total number of involving users, K denotes the length of the top-ranking list, and $r(i)$ refers to the correlation score for the item at position i. Respectively, $\sum(\cdot)$ and D_k denote the discounted cumulative gain of the predicted and real ranking list. For NDCG, larger values indicate better performance.

Completing all the fitness evaluations, several individuals are selected as parents in the way mentioned in Subsect. 3.3. After that, genetic operations like crossover and mutation are performed on the chosen parents. There are two main steps in the mutation operation. The individual is firstly mutated by the Polynomial Mutation (PM) [7] in a given probability. Next, the length of the DNN is randomly changed. This change happens in a random position, causing either an increase or decrease in the length of the DNN. As for the proposed crossover operation, we use the Simulated Binary Crossover (SBX) [6] for its good performance in local optimization. We first align the heads of two selected individuals and then exchange some of their corresponding blocks according to predefined the crossover rate.

3.3   Environmental Selection

In the proposed algorithm, we use a developed selection method which is described as Slack Binary Tournament Selection [22]. We add an elite mechanism to the traditional binary tournament selection to maintain the diversity and convergence of a population and avoid the premature phenomenon [18]. In the course of the environmental selection, firstly, several individuals with the best fitness are directly chosen for the next generation. Secondly, we randomly select two from the rest individuals in the current population using the binary tournament selection, the individuals with larger NDCG are placed into the next population until the population size meets the predefined number. Then, the next iteration starts to work.

4   Experiments

4.1   Experimental Settings

Consistent with previous CF tasks, we use the MovieLens dataset [12] and Pinterest dataset[1] as the benchmark datasets.

---

[1] https://sites.google.com/site/xueatalphabeta/academic-projects.

Table 1. Encoded information

Length of DNN	4–10
Number of neurons in each full connection layer	16–256
Dropout rate	0–0.5
Types of weights initialization approaches	R_n, R_u X_n, X_u K_n, K_u

Table 2. Parameters of GA

Population size	16
Total generation number	20
Distribution index of SBX and PM	1
Probability of SBX	0.9
Probability of PM	0.2
Elitism rate	0.2

The settings of the encoded information of each layer in DNN are listed in Table 1. Besides, all the parameter settings of the evolution are specified following the conventions of GA community [2], which are listed in Table 2. To evaluate the performance of item recommendation, we adopt the *leave-one-out* evaluation [14], which has been widely used in CF models. As mentioned in Sect. 3.2, the NDCG is used as the fitness criterion.

4.2 Experimental Results

To show the effectiveness of the proposed algorithm, the following state-of-the-art algorithms are selected as the peer competitors, including deep learning models: NeuMF, MLP [14], and MF models: GMF [14], eALS [15], BPR [20].

The performance of the ranked recommendation list is evaluated by Hit Ratio (HR), which intuitively measures whether the test item is present on the top-k list, and Normalized Discounted Cumulation Gain (NDCG) [13] mentioned in Subsect. 3.2. For both metrics, larger values indicate better performance.

Figure 2 shows the performance of Top-K recommended lists with respect to the number of ranking position K ranges from 1 to 10. As can be seen, Evolve-CF demonstrates consistent improvements over other methods across positions.

Table 3. The best performance of HR@10 and NDCG@10 on the two datasets

Measure	Method					
	BPR	eALS	GMF	MLP	NeuMF	Evolve-CF
Deep Learning Method	×	×	×	√	√	√
MovieLens						
HR@10	0.628	0.627	0.645	0.683	0.684	**0.694**
NDCG@10	0.364	0.367	0.372	0.408	0.411	**0.416**
Pinterest						
HR@10	0.856	0.861	0.864	0.862	0.868	**0.871**
NDCG@10	0.536	0.522	0.541	0.535	0.546	**0.551**

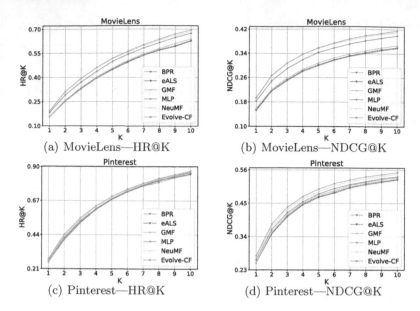

Fig. 2. Evaluation of Top-K item recommendation where K ranges from 1 to 10 on the two datasets

We further focus on the performance of the top 10 recommendation lists. Table 3 shows the best performance of HR@10 and NDCG@10. Obviously, Evolve-CF significantly outperforms both the traditional MF methods and the previous neural network models on two datasets. These experimental results intuitively indicate the effectiveness and generalization of the proposed Evolve-CF.

5   Conclusions

In this work, we explored the evolving strategy to automatically design an appropriate DNN for CF. Our proposed algorithm Evolve-CF provided an improved genetic encoding strategy for encoding the DNN architectures and the weights initialization approaches. Moreover, the genetic operators we selected can effectively find the optimal DNN architecture during the evolution process and the improved binary tournament selection is capable of selecting promising individuals. The results of several experiments on two benchmark datasets demonstrate the effectiveness of the automated DNN over the other CF algorithms. In the future, further researches will be conducted on finding out whether there are new components that contribute more to the performance of DNNs for CF tasks.

References

1. Agarwal, D., Chen, B.C.: Regression-based latent factor models. In: Proceedings of the 15th ACM SIGKDD International Conference on Knowledge Discovery and Data Mining, pp. 19–28 (2009)
2. Ashlock, D.: Evolutionary Computation for Modeling and Optimization. Springer, New York (2006). https://doi.org/10.1007/0-387-31909-3
3. Bobadilla, J., Ortega, F., Hernando, A., Bernal, J.: A collaborative filtering approach to mitigate the new user cold start problem. Knowl.-Based syst. **26**, 225–238 (2012)
4. Cao, J., et al.: Distributed design and implementation of SVD++ algorithm for e-commerce personalized recommender system. In: Zhang, X., Wu, Z., Sha, X. (eds.) Embedded System Technology. CCIS, vol. 572, pp. 30–44. Springer, Singapore (2015). https://doi.org/10.1007/978-981-10-0421-6_4
5. Covington, P., Adams, J., Sargin, E.: Deep neural networks for YouTube recommendations. In: Proceedings of the 10th ACM Conference on Recommender Systems, pp. 191–198 (2016)
6. Deb, K., Agrawal, R.B., et al.: Simulated binary crossover for continuous search space. Complex Syst. **9**(2), 115–148 (1995)
7. Deb, K., Sundar, J.: Reference point based multi-objective optimization using evolutionary algorithms. In: Proceedings of the 8th Annual Conference on Genetic and Evolutionary Computation, pp. 635–642 (2006)
8. Delalleau, O., Bengio, Y.: Shallow vs. deep sum-product networks. In: Advances in Neural Information Processing Systems, vol. 24, pp. 666–674 (2011)
9. Glorot, X., Bengio, Y.: Understanding the difficulty of training deep feedforward neural networks. In: Proceedings of the Thirteenth International Conference on Artificial Intelligence and Statistics, pp. 249–256. JMLR Workshop and Conference Proceedings (2010)
10. Glorot, X., Bordes, A., Bengio, Y.: Deep sparse rectifier neural networks. In: Proceedings of the Fourteenth International Conference on Artificial Intelligence and Statistics, pp. 315–323. JMLR Workshop and Conference Proceedings (2011)
11. Guo, H., Tang, R., Ye, Y., Li, Z., He, X.: DeepFM: a factorization-machine based neural network for CTR prediction. arXiv preprint arXiv:1703.04247 (2017)
12. Harper, F.M., Konstan, J.A.: The MovieLens datasets: history and context. ACM Trans. Interact. Intell. Syst. (TIIS) **5**(4), 1–19 (2015)
13. He, X., Chen, T., Kan, M.Y., Chen, X.: TriRank: review-aware explainable recommendation by modeling aspects. In: Proceedings of the 24th ACM International on Conference on Information and Knowledge Management, pp. 1661–1670 (2015)
14. He, X., Liao, L., Zhang, H., Nie, L., Hu, X., Chua, T.S.: Neural collaborative filtering. In: Proceedings of the 26th International Conference on World Wide Web, pp. 173–182 (2017)
15. He, X., Zhang, H., Kan, M.Y., Chua, T.S.: Fast matrix factorization for online recommendation with implicit feedback. In: Proceedings of the 39th International ACM SIGIR Conference on Research and Development in Information Retrieval, pp. 549–558 (2016)
16. He, K., Zhang X, R.S.: Delving deep into rectifiers: surpassing human-level performance on ImageNet classification. In: Proceedings of the IEEE International Conference on Computer Vision, pp. 1026–1034 (2015)
17. Koren, Y., Bell, R., Volinsky, C.: Matrix factorization techniques for recommender systems. Computer **42**(8), 30–37 (2009)

18. Michalewicz, Z.: Genetic Algorithms + Data Structures = Evolution Programs. Springer, Cham (2013). https://doi.org/10.1007/978-3-662-03315-9
19. Mikolov, T., Chen, K., Corrado, G., Dean, J.: Efficient estimation of word representations in vector space. arXiv preprint arXiv:1301.3781 (2013)
20. Rendle, S., Freudenthaler, C., Gantner, Z., Schmidt-Thieme, L.: BPR: Bayesian personalized ranking from implicit feedback. arXiv preprint arXiv:1205.2618 (2012)
21. Saleem, M.: Collaborative filtering: lifeblood of the social web (2008)
22. Sun, Y., Xue, B., Zhang, M., Yen, G.G.: Evolving deep convolutional neural networks for image classification. IEEE Trans. Evol. Comput. **24**(2), 394–407 (2019)

DocNER: A Deep Learning System for Named Entity Recognition in Handwritten Document Images

Marwa Dhiaf[1(✉)], Sana Khamekhem Jemni[2], and Yousri Kessentini[1]

[1] Digital Research Center of Sfax, SM@RTS: Laboratory of Signals, systeMs, aRtificial Intelligence and neTworkS, Sfax, Tunisia
marwa.dhiaf.doc@enetcom.usf.tn, yousri.kessentini@crns.rnrt.tn
[2] Digital Research Center of Sfax, MIR@CL: Multimedia, InfoRmation systems and Advanced Computing Laboratory, Sfax, Tunisia
sana.khamekhemjemni@enis.tn

Abstract. The extraction of relevant information from handwritten document images is still a challenging task. In this paper, we introduce a framework for named entities recognition from a collection of real handwritten marriage records. For this purpose, we perform an extensive evaluation of two different information extraction approaches to locate and recognize named entities from unstructured handwritten documents. The first one is based on an end-to-end neural network model that jointly performs transcription and semantic annotation of handwritten document images. While the second relies on two stages, the first one focuses on Handwritten Text Recognition (HTR) to transcribe documents into electronic texts, while the second seeks to identify semantic named entities using a state-of-the-art Natural Language Processing (NLP) model. This work is evaluated on a collection of real French handwritten marriage records, discussing the advantages and drawbacks of the explored approaches. The achieved results show the efficiency of the proposed framework even though it does not use any post-processing stage. Additional experiments are conducted using the Esposalles database to compare our methods to the participated systems in the ICDAR 2017 Information Extraction competition.

Keywords: Handwriting text recognition · Named entity recognition · Bidirectional Long Short Term Memory network · Bidirectional Encoder Representations from Transformers

1 Introduction

Handwritten documents contain a huge amount of data stored during the last decade. The extraction of information from those documents is a necessary step. In the one hand it makes these manuscripts available for access and research, in the other hand it allows the development of data. In this context, NER or Named Entity Recognition, is an effective alternative. NER consists in recognizing named entities (NE) in a corpus of texts and assigning to the different words

© Springer Nature Switzerland AG 2021
T. Mantoro et al. (Eds.): ICONIP 2021, CCIS 1517, pp. 239–246, 2021.
https://doi.org/10.1007/978-3-030-92310-5_28

a label such as «name», «place», «date», etc. There are several approaches dealing with named entity recognition. Those approaches can be classified into two main categories. The first adopts a two-stages processing to extract information from document images. It firstly transcribes the text using a Handwritten Text Recognition (HTR) system and sequentially applies a Named Entity Recognition (NER) mechanism using NLP tools in order to generate tag's candidates. The second aims to directly detect NE from images without an intermediate transcription step. We pass in review with state-of-the-art approaches of both categories. Regarding the first category, several methods make use of neural networks architectures (ANNs) [1], that transcribe handwritten text line images and then parse the transcribed text with NER models. Those methods have brought interesting improvements but not yet achieving human level accuracy. In [2] authors introduced their evaluation of a custom rule-based NER system [3] for person and place names on two sets of British Parliamentary records from the 17th and 19th centuries. The input of the NER system is the output of an OCR. They describe many of the problems encountered by NER systems that result from both OCR artefacts and the archaic nature of the sources themselves, such as conflation of marginal notes with body text, multi-line quoting rules, and capitalization of common nouns. In [4], authors evaluated the performance of existing NER tools (OpenNLP,[1] Stanford NER, AlchemyAPI and opencalais) on the output of an open-source OCR system (Tesseract). The test data was collected from the Wiener Library, London, and King's College London's Serving Soldier archive. The performance of NER was on overall lower than those reported in the literature due to the difference of the data sets generally used to train and test NER systems. The authors suggested to use controlled vocabularies or other kinds of domain knowledge in order to circumvent the variability in spelling these entities in general. Recent work in ANNs [5], suggested that using models that solve tasks as general as possible, might give better performance than concatenating sub-processes due to error propagation in the different steps. For instance, authors in [6] proposed a single convolutional-sequential model to jointly perform transcription and semantic annotation. The contribution of this work [6] is to show the improvement when joining a sequence of processes in a single one, and thus, avoiding to commit accumulation of errors and achieving generalization to emulate human-like intelligence. An interesting work introduced in [7], in which authors presented an end-to-end deep neural model combining three branches. The model jointly performs handwritten text detection, transcription, and named entity recognition at page level with a single feed forward step. Results prove the benefits of using triple task neural models, nevertheless it is limited in performance in cases where one specific task is much harder and unrelated to the others.

We propose in this paper a framework for named entities recognition from a collection of handwritten marriage records. For this aim, we explore two processing strategies, the first is based on an end-to-end neural network model that jointly performs transcription and named entity recognition. While the second relies on two stages, the first one focuses on handwritten text recognition to

---

[1] https://opennlp.apache.org/.

transcribe documents into electronic texts, while the second seeks to identify semantic named entities using a state-of-the-art NLP model. In order to cope with the lack of annotated training data, we exploit text data augmentation and synthetic data generation techniques. We have conducted extensive experiments using two datasets with two languages (French and Spanish) and compared our results to participating systems in IEHHR competition [13].

This paper is organized as follows. First, we present the joint HTR-NER approach in Sect. 2. Second, the two-stage approach is described in Sect. 3. Then, experimental results are given in Sect. 4. Finally, concluding remarks are provided in Sect. 5.

2   Joint HTR and Named Entity Recognition Approach

The joint model performs handwriting text recognition and NE localization jointly. First, a pre-processing stage is performed to extract textual blocs from handwritten document images. Second, text blocs were segmented into lines to be processed using Convolutional Neural Network (CNN) to extract relevant features. Third, an end-to-end deep Bidirectional Long Short Term Memory (BLSTM) model with Connectionist Temporal Classification stage (CTC) jointly performs transcription and NER task.

2.1   Handwriting Recognition System Design

The designed HTR system includes a preprocessing stage to extract relevant bloc texts. The input image is segmented into lines. So that a list of lines images is fed to the HTR system. In this way, documents are recognized at line level using the segmentation-free approach [8], overcoming the segmentation problems of lines into words and words into letters.

Document Layout Analysis. In order to process the full pages of handwritten text, we firstly extract the main textual bloc using the projection profile method. Then, a segmentation step of these blocs into separated lines is required. The used segmentation method relies on the A* path planning algorithm presented in [9].

Model Architecture. The used architecture consists of five convolutional layers with max pooling. On the top of the convolutional layers, two BLSTM layers are built which naturally renders the features spatially-context aware due to the BLSTM capacity to capture long-range correlations. The convolutional layers, designed for feature extraction, make use of a kernel of 3 * 3 and a stride of 1 * 1. We use also five filters whose sizes are 16, 32, 48, 64 and 80, respectively. Moreover, we apply max-pooling operations to reduce the size of the input sequence. After the feature extraction stage, we add two BLSTM recurrent layers of 256 units. In this way, we have 256 features for each direction. So, a depth-wise concatenation is carried out to adapt the input of the subsequent layer, in overall size of 512.

Data Collection and Encoding. In order to cope with the lack of annotated training data, we exploit data augmentation and synthetic data generation techniques. First, we trained our model using the RIMES database [10] since it includes French lines whose writing styles are close to those used in the documents that we process. This first stage is performed to train the model for HTR only, i.e. named entity tags are not included to the ground-truth. The second stage consists in generating synthetic data using a RNN model as described in [15]. In order to exploit the semantic correlation that exists between named entities, the ground truth text and the named entity tags are jointly encoded.

Curriculum Learning. We believe that training the model on different image levels (line then paragraph) allows it to exploit larger context information to identify the semantic NE tags. In the curriculum learning scenario, our model starts with learning easy examples (line text images) then progressively increases the difficulty of learning. In particular, the strategy consists of starting by learning to transcribe text lines and when the training is finished, continue with learning to transcribe text of the full page.

Language Models and Recognition. The marriage records contains many named entities including persons names, city names, etc. So, it is difficult to build a lexicon including all these words. For this reason, a word lexicon driven approach for the recognition of marriage records is not suitable as it will face the Out Of Vocabulary (OOV) problem. As an alternative, we propose to deal with different sub-word modeling strategies including character, syllabic and hybrid Language Models (LM). Here, the main idea consists of using word LM for non named entity words and substituting named entities in the LM by their corresponding sub-lexical entities.

3   Two-Stage Named Entity Recognition Approach

The NER approach adopts two stages to detect named entities. The first stage is the recognition step, where we applied the same HTR model introduced previously. The second consists of assigning to each word a semantic annotation: person and category. The transcribed text is parsed using the French duplication of BERT model [11]. Due to the lack of annotated data, we have generated a large sets of marriage records texts. The generated data follows the same structure as the ground truth. For token labeling, we used BIO-scheme, in which tokens are annotated with three types of labels for each named entity category: named entity beginning, named entity continuation and not a named entity. The transcribed text is processed using a replication of BERT model, known as CamemBERT [12], to extract named entities. BERT stands for (Bidirectional Encoder Representations from Transformer) is a language model representation based on self-attention blocks.

To perform the NER task, we fine tuned the CamemBERT model using the following configuration: 12 layers, 768 hidden dimensions, 12 attention heads, and

110M parameters. In order to identify the semantic entities, we adjust the pre-trained model, using texts generated in addition to the data annotated manually (from the French documents).

4 Experimental Results and Discussion

4.1 Datasets and Metrics

We have conducted our experiments using two different datasets. The first consists of French Handwritten Marriage Records (FHMR). FHMR is a private dataset that provides a collection of French handwritten marriage records. Each record contains several text lines giving information of the wife, husband and their parents' names, occupations, locations and dates. The text images are provided at paragraph level. The second is the public dataset proposed in ICDAR 2017 Information Extraction from Historical Handwritten Records (IEHHR) competition [13]. This dataset is composed of 125 handwritten pages, containing 1221 marriage records (paragraphs). Each record is composed of several text lines giving information of the persons. We have used 872, 96, 253 records training, validation and evaluation, respectively.

In these experiments, we used the Character Recognition Rate (CRR), the Word Recognition Rate (WRR) metrics based on the edit distance algorithm [14], NER IEHHR metrics for HTR and NER evaluations, respectively.

4.2 Baseline HTR System Results

The main goal of these experiments is to evaluate the different language modelling techniques to deal with the out of vocabulary word problem. Indeed, as it is quasi impossible to cover the whole lexicon of named entities in French language, we have performed the HTR task using different sub-lexical language models including character, syllabus and hybrid (word-character or word-syllabus). In this work, we used 5K lines for training and 900 lines for validation. The transfer learning is performed using 18 document images from the handwritten marriage records, corresponding to 500 lines for fine-tuning and 100 images for validation. The fine-tuning is stopped when there is no improvement on the character error rate.

As illustrated in Table 1, the use of a 3-gram hybrid character-word language model provides the best recognition results over the use of only character language model and the use of hybrid word and syllabus language model. A CRR of 88.95% is reached using the hybrid word-character n-gram model. This result can be explained by the ability of hybrid character-word LM to recover out of vocabulary words.

4.3 Named Entity Recognition Results

For the joint HTR-NER task, we have performed five series of experiments regarding the used data for training. All these models are firstly trained for HTR task only, i.e. named entity tags are not included to the ground-truth.

Table 1. Recognition results of the baseline HTR system using different n-gram language models.

N-gram order	Character level		Word-character level		Word-syllabic level	
	WRR%	CRR%	WRR%	CRR%	WRR%	CRR%
1	65.58	88.96	68.41	89.58	66.86	86.70
2	66 65	88.81	69.70	89.41	68.31	86. 73
3	67.89	88.39	70.48	88.95	68.41	86. 58
4	70.04	88.38	70.63	88.70	68.60	86.51
5	70.64	88.56	70.75	88.69	68.62	86.53
6	70.60	88.54	70.63	88.68	68.62	86.53

- **A:** The first model is fine-tuned using a dataset composed of 540 line images extracted from the real marriage record and manually annotated.
- **B:** The second model is fine-tuned using the same dataset used in A but at record level where the lines composing a record are concatenated.
- **C:** The third model is fine-tuned using 6000 synthetic handwritten line. Then a curriculum learning is conducted at record level.
- **D:** This model is firstly fine-tuned with synthetic data as in C, then a second fine-tuning is performed using a dataset of real records.
- **E:** This model is based on a pre-trained CamemBERT that we fine-tune using a labeled text corpus extracted from the marriage records.

It should be noted that we are using curriculum learning for the series of experiments (C) and (D). The above detailed experiments were conducted in order to evaluate the influence of the used data size and the incorporation of synthetic data on the system's performance for the HTR-NER joint task.

Table 2 summarizes the obtained results of the NER task using the different model presented previously. Considering the joint HTR-NER task, we notice that fine-tuning the model at record level (model B) gives a better result than fine-tuning it at line level (model A). Nevertheless, as the dataset of real marriage records is very small, the obtained performance is not satisfactory. For this reason, by augmenting the dataset by synthetic data, the performance is significantly improved and a CRR of 73.22% is achieved (model D). We note that the curriculum learning (training the model first on text lines and then on records) improves considerably the NE extraction results as it integrates a larger context to identify the semantic categories. We notice that the fine-tuning of the model using only synthetic data (model C) does not give good results as the generated samples present a different writing style compared to the real data. Finally, an interesting result was obtained using the sequential HTR and NLP approach (two-stage). A CRR of 71% was reached, while this rate was equal to 73.22% when using the joint HTR-NER approach. This can be explained by the fact that recognition errors in the HTR stage can affect the performance NER stage. We compared also our proposed approach with other methods from the literature

Table 2. Results of the different NER models.

System	Training level	CRR%
A: Joint HTR-NER	Line	23.25
B: Joint HTR-NER	Record	55.32
C: Joint HTR-NER	Record	48.30
D: Joint HTR-NER	**Record**	**73.22**
E: Two-stages HTR and NLP	Record	71.00

that participated in the IEHHR competition. The comparison is straightforward as we use the same experimental protocol used in the competition to evaluate our system. Table 3 shows the performance results of some methods from the literature and our best results on record level. As reported in Table 3, our joint model presents the best performance.

Table 3. Comparison with the participant systems in the IEHHR competition (Complete Task).

System	Score
Hitsz-ICRC-1	85.72
Hitsz-ICRC-2	91.97
CITlab-ARGUS-1	89.16
CITlab-ARGUS-2	91.56
Joint HTR-NER (ours)	**92.00**

5   Conclusion

In this paper, we introduced a framework for named entities recognition from French handwritten document records. Thus, we have carried out an extensive evaluation of two different approaches dealing with information extraction task. It can be concluded that information extraction using a joint HTR-NER approach is more efficient than using two subsequent tasks (HTR task followed by a NLP processing stage). We have also discussed the importance of synthetic data generation to cope with the lack of annotated training data. Also, we demonstrated that curriculum learning can improve the model performance by integrating a larger context to identify the semantic categories. In our future works, we propose to combine the two proposed approaches and to inject linguistic information in the end-to-end neural architecture to improve the accuracy of the prediction. Exploring new deep learning architecture based on Transformers is also an interesting perspective.

References

1. Romero, V., Fornés, A., Vidal, E., Sánchez, J.: Using the MGGI methodology for category-based language modeling in handwritten marriage licenses books. In: 201615th International Conference on Frontiers in Handwriting Recognition (ICFHR), pp. 331–336. IEEE (2016)
2. Grover, C., Givon, S., Tobin, R., Ball, J.: Named entity recognition for digitised historical texts. In: LREC (2008)
3. Grover, C., Matheson, C., Mikheev, A., Moens, M.: LT TTT-a flexible tokenisation tool. In: LREC, vol. 2000, p. 2nd (2000)
4. Rodriquez, K., Bryant, M., Blanke, T., Luszczynska, M.: Comparison of named entity recognition tools for raw OCR text. In: Konvens, pp. 410–414 (2012)
5. Liu, H., Feng, J., Qi, M., Jiang, J., Yan, S.: End-to-end comparative attention networks for person re-identification. IEEE Trans. Image Process. **26**, 3492–3506 (2017)
6. Carbonell, M., Villegas, M., Fornés, A., Lladós, J.: Joint recognition of handwritten text and named entities with a neural end-to-end model. In: 2018 13th IAPR International Workshop on Document Analysis Systems (DAS), pp. 399–404. IEEE (2018)
7. Carbonell, M., Fornés, A., Villegas, M., Lladós, J.: A neural model for text localization, transcription and named entity recognition in full pages. Pattern Recogn. Lett. **136**, 219–227 (2020)
8. Kessentini, Y., Paquet, T., Hamadou, A.: Off-line handwritten word recognition using multi-stream hidden Markov models. Pattern Recogn. Lett. **31**, 60–70 (2010)
9. Surinta, O., Holtkamp, M., Karabaa, F., Vanoosten, J., Schomaker, L., Wiering, M.: A path planning for line segmentation of handwritten documents. In: 2014 14th International Conference on Frontiers in Handwriting Recognition, pp. 175–180. IEEE (2014)
10. Augustin, E., Carré, M., Grosicki, E., Brodin, J., Geoffrois, E., Prêteux, F.: RIMES evaluation campaign for handwritten mail processing. In: International Workshop on Frontiers in Handwriting Recognition (IWFHR 2006), pp. 231–235 (2006)
11. Devlin, J., Chang, M., Lee, K., Toutanova, K.: BERT: pre-training of deep bidirectional transformers for language understanding. arXiv Preprint arXiv:1810.04805 (2018)
12. Martin, L., et al.: CamemBERT: a tasty French language model. arXiv Preprint arXiv:1911.03894 (2019)
13. Fornés, A., et al.: Competition on information extraction in historical handwritten records. In: 2013 12th International Conference on Document Analysis and Recognition. IEEE (2017)
14. Levenshtein, V.I.: Binary codes capable of correcting deletions, insertions, andreversals. In: Soviet physics doklady, vol. 10, pp. 707–710. Soviet Union (1966)
15. Graves, A.: Generating sequences with recurrent neural networks. arXiv preprint arXiv:1308.0850 (2013)

Advances in Deep and Shallow Machine Learning Algorithms for Biomedical Data and Imaging

OADA: An Online Data Augmentation Method for Raw Histopathology Images

Zhiyue Wu[1], Yijie Wang[1(✉)], Haibo Mi[1], Hongzuo Xu[1]📀, Wei Zhang[2],
and Lanlan Feng[2]

[1] Science and Technology on Parallel and Distributed Processing Laboratory, College
of Computer, National University of Defense Technology, Changsha, China
{wuzhiyue,wangyijie,xuhongzuo13}@nudt.edu.cn
[2] Department of Pathology, Tangdu Hospital, Airforce Military Medical University,
Xi'an, China

Abstract. Deep learning-based automatic medical diagnosis is intensively studied in recent years. Abundant clinical raw records can be
utilized, but we demonstrate that mixed and unknown magnification
scales and staining conditions of raw histopathology images greatly hinder many successful deep models in this task. To address this problem,
this paper proposes an Online Adaptive Data Augmentation method
(OADA). In each training epoch, OADA adaptively selects base images
and determines the personalized augmentation size of each image based
on the current training status. The chosen images are augmented
to update the training set. Extensive experiments show that OADA-
empowered deep models obtain significant improvement compared to
their bare versions, and OADA outperforms a suite of data augmentation baselines and state-of-the-art competitors.

Keywords: Histopathology image · Online data augmentation · Deep
learning

1 Introduction

Histopathology image analysis can discriminate benign or malignant tumors to
diagnose cancer and further classify cancer subtype to tailor treatment. With
the emergence and development of deep learning, the past decade has witnessed
the great potentials of deep learning in histopathology image analysis.

Many deep learning-based methods have been proposed to handle
histopathology images, but most of them are designed for high-definition
histopathology slides, i.e., whole slide image (WSI). Researchers use sliding windows to generate patches and perform patch-level classification. The magnifying
factors of these patches are fixed and known, and the staining of patches from
the same WSI is similar. However, in practical scenarios, each patient's record
normally contains several captured images from histopathological examinations,
which are originally saved as evidence of diagnoses. As pathologists often change

T. Mantoro et al. (Eds.): ICONIP 2021, CCIS 1517, pp. 249–256, 2021.
https://doi.org/10.1007/978-3-030-92310-5_29

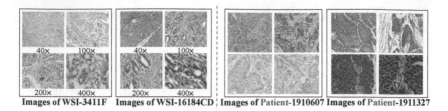

Fig. 1. Images from Public WSIs and Real Hospital Records. We choose images of four magnifying factors from two breast tissue biopsy slides in BreakHis [10]. The images of two patients in real hospital records are presented.

the magnifying factor of histopathology slides to check different shapes of tissues, these images are with mixed magnification scales. Besides, staining conditions of these images highly vary depending on specimen conditions. Thus, these methods may only obtain suboptimal results when processing raw medical records due to the difficulties caused by complex distributions of magnification scales and staining conditions. Figure 1 shows the difference between patches from WSIs in a public dataset and images from real-world medical records.

In this paper, to fully leverage raw histopathology images with mixed scales and staining conditions, we propose an Online Adaptive Data Augmentation method (termed OADA). OADA can adaptively augment selected images according to the model status in the training stage. Specifically, after each training epoch, we propose a selection function and an augmentation size calculation function to choose base images and determine personalized augmentation sizes. OADA then generates novel pseudo samples to update the training set.

Our main contributions are summarized as follows: (i) We demonstrate that one of the key barriers of training deep models on real-world medical records is mixed and unknown magnification scales and staining conditions. This finding can foster more studies to fully leverage existing plentiful medical records by considering this problem; (ii) We propose an online data augmentation method OADA. OADA-empowered deep models can be more robust by consistently augmenting data to cover unexplored input space in the original training data; and (iii) OADA can adaptively select base images, determine the personalized augmentation size of each base image, and choose suitable augmentation techniques to heuristically generate pseudo data samples according to training status.

2   Related Work

There are many deep models that analyze histopathology images to distinguish tumor type [1,14]. Most tumor classification methods train deep models using patches in a few magnification scales, and the patches from one WSI are with the same color space. For example, Wang et al. [13] use patches in an individual magnification, the latest work [2] extracts patches in 10x- and 20x-magnification. These methods can achieve good performance on datasets derived from WSIs because of high-quality training data (i.e., each magnification or color space has abundant training samples), but they may fail to effectively handle low-quality data with unknown, mixed, and jumbled magnifications and staining conditions.

Data Augmentation is a common solution when only limited and/or low-quality data are available [8]. There are many basic image manipulations like flipping and rotation that can be applied as augmentation techniques. Several geometric augmentation methods and photometric methods are evaluated in [12]. More complex data augmentation, e.g., mixing images [5], adversarial training [6], and GAN-based data augmentation [15], are further proposed. These data augmentation methods are performed before the training phase, but it is hard to know what kind of images should be augmented. There are only limited works considering online data augmentation. Tang et al. [11] propose an online data augmentation scheme based on a meta-learned augmentation network. A bilevel optimization-based method is proposed to automatically learn the optimal transformations in each iteration [7].

3   Methodology

This paper focuses on histopathology image classification as our target task of the proposed online data augmentation method. It is easy to transfer the proposed method to other related tasks. Let $\mathcal{X} = \{(X^{(i)}, y^{(i)})\}_{i=1}^N$ denote a dataset with N histopathology images. $X^{(i)} \in \mathbb{R}^{h \times w \times z}$ is a sample in $\mathcal{X}$ consisting of $h \times w$ pixels in z color channels. $y^{(i)}$ indicates the class of histopathology image X_i.

The framework of OADA is shown in Fig. 2. Firstly, OADA separates a candidate set $\mathcal{R}$ from the original training set $\mathcal{X}$. After each training epoch, the selection function f is employed to select base images from $\mathcal{R}$ according to the classification performance of the current model. Function g further determines the augmentation size, which is also based on the current training status. A set of generated pseudo samples $\mathcal{Q}$ is finally derived by two chosen augmentation techniques $\rho \circ \delta$ and is used to update the training set. The above process is repeatedly performed per training epoch. Following [2], we train classification model on the basis of deep networks pre-trained with ImageNet. Many successful models are proposed, e.g., VGG16 [9], ResNet50 [3], and DenseNet121 [4]. We use Φ to represent the deep classification network. We then detailedly introduce three key components in OADA, i.e., selection of base images, size of augmented samples, and data augmentation techniques.

Selection of Base Images. To achieve online adaptive data augmentation, one important problem is how to select base images from the original dataset to augment during the training period. The selection of base data greatly determines the effectiveness of data augmentation. Due to the stochastic distribution of magnification scales and staining conditions, deep models might be well trained on some specific scales and staining conditions that are with abundant training data, which means networks do not need similar augmented training data anymore. Therefore, OADA needs to consistently supervise the training process and select more valuable data samples as base images to feed into the augmentation stage. We specifically introduce the selection of augmentation images below.

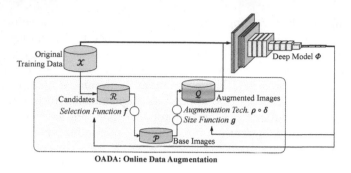

OADA: Online Data Augmentation

Fig. 2. OADA framework

We first initialize a candidate set $\mathcal{R}$, which is a randomly sampled subset of the original training data $\mathcal{X}$, to select base images to augment. The cardinality of $\mathcal{R}$ is a hyper-parameter, and a quarter of the original set is recommended in practical usage. A simple selection function $f(y^{(i)}, \hat{y}_t^{(i)})$ is further defined in OADA to determine whether to select image $X^{(i)}$ from the candidate set $\mathcal{R}$ in epoch t according to the predicted result $\hat{y}_t^{(i)}$ and the ground-truth label $y^{(i)}$.

$$f(y^{(i)}, \hat{y}_t^{(i)}) = \begin{cases} 1, & y^{(i)} \neq \hat{y}_t^{(i)} \\ 0, & y^{(i)} = \hat{y}_t^{(i)} \end{cases} \tag{1}$$

Essentially, function f is to choose images that are incorrectly classified in epoch t. Note that it is also possible to employ a heuristic way in function f to explore deeper insights about the data distribution and current training status.

After each training epoch t, OADA obtains a set $\mathcal{P}_t = \{X^{(i)} | f(y^{(i)}, \hat{y}_t^{(i)}) = 0\}$ that consists of base images to augment.

Size of Augmented Samples. A function g is proposed in OADA to calculate the size of augmented samples.

$$g(\{\Phi_c^t(X^{(i)})\}) = e^{|\max\{\Phi_c^t(X^{(i)})\} - \Phi_{y^{(i)}}^t(X^{(i)})|} \tag{2}$$

where $\{\Phi_c^t(X^i)\}$ is the output prediction probability vector of network Φ in epoch t, $\max\{\Phi_c^t(X^{(i)})\}$ is the maximum predicted probability, and $\Phi_{y^{(i)}}^t(X^{(i)})$ is the probability of the ground-truth class. We use the prediction probability difference between the incorrectly predicted class and the ground-truth class to describe the learning bias on each image. More augmented pseudo samples are required to rectify the network if the learning bias is large.

The augmentation size $k_t^{(i)}$ of base image $X^{(i)} \in \mathcal{P}$ can be derived as follows:

$$k_t^{(i)} = \theta g(\{\Phi_c^t(X^{(i)})\}) \tag{3}$$

where θ is a reinforcement factor. It is calculated as $\theta = 1 + \sum_{j=1}^{m} \alpha f_{t-j}$, where m is the number of rollback epochs and α is the strength. If the network consistently gives $X^{(i)}$ an incorrect prediction, the augmentation size is further reinforced.

Data Augmentation Techniques. After specifying the set of selected base images and the augmentation size of each base image, OADA manipulates these images to yield augmented pseudo samples. Recall that OADA is proposed to target training data containing real images with very different magnification scales and staining conditions. The network fails to perform satisfactorily on these selected base images in $\mathcal{P}$ mainly due to the sparsity of training data in particular magnifying factors and color spaces of these images. Therefore, one naive solution is to repeat these images by oversampling and feed into the network. However, simple repetition could cause the overfitting problem on some specific magnifications or color spaces so that the network cannot even identify images in adjacent magnifying factors or similar staining conditions.

In light of these limitations, OADA employs random cropping δ and color space manipulation ρ to generate new pseudo samples. Random cropping δ is essentially used to pose minor disturbances on the magnification scales of images. Additionally, color space can be easily manipulated via matrix operations to change the brightness, contrast, saturation, and hue of original images. Altering color spaces of training images ρ provides chances for the network to gain more insight on different staining conditions. Hence, the network can be trained on these particular scales and different staining conditions more robustly after these two data augmentation techniques.

Finally, OADA can dynamically and adaptively generate augmented pseudo samples during the training process, and the set of generated samples after epoch t is obtained as follows:

$$\mathcal{Q}_t = \bigcup_{\forall X^{(i)} \in \mathcal{P}_t} \left\{ (\rho \circ \delta)(X^{(i)}) \right\}_{k_t^{(i)}} \tag{4}$$

where $k_t^{(i)}$ is the augmentation size of image $X^{(i)}$, and $\rho \circ \delta$ is the combination of two augmentation techniques.

4   Experiments

4.1   Experimental Setup

Dataset. Our experiments are based on two datasets. One is a private Lung cancer Histopathology image dataset (termed as LungHis), which is collected from raw medial records from our cooperative hospital in Xi'an, China, and the other is a publicly available breast cancer histopathology dataset BreakHis [10]. The images in LungHis are screenshots that are originally saved as attached evidence of diagnoses, pathologists may choose very different magnifying factors. Moreover, the staining conditions of images from different biopsy samples are various. Different from our private datasets, the images in BreakHis are with four kinds of fixed magnification scales ($400\times$, $200\times$, $100\times$, and $40\times$).

Performance Evaluation Metrics. Four popular metrics, i.e., accuracy (Acc), precision (P), recall (R), and F1-score (F_1), are used to evaluate the classification performance. We use macro-averaged P, R, and F_1 as overall performance.

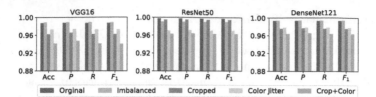

Fig. 3. Acc, P, R, and F_1 results of VGG16, ResNet50, and DenseNet121 on dataset BreakHis with different distributions of magnification scales and staining conditions simulated by four preprocessing methods.

4.2   Results and Analysis

Effect of Mixed Magnifying Factors and Staining Conditions. This experiment is to validate whether diversified scales and staining conditions really affect the performance of deep models. Dataset BreakHis is with four fixed magnification scales. The quantities of images in 400×, 200×, 100×, and 40× magnification are 267, 303, 320, and 305, respectively. We impose four preprocessing methods to simulate different distributions of magnification scales and staining conditions. (i) *Imbalanced*: We obtain an imbalanced distribution of magnification scales by randomly removing different numbers of images in each scale; (ii) *Cropped*: Each image in BreakHis is cropped to a random size. The dataset preprocessed by random cropping is with randomly distributed magnification scales; (iii) *Color Jitter*: We employ color jitter to randomly change the brightness, contrast, saturation, and hue of images to imitate different staining conditions; and (iv) *Crop+Color*: Random cropping and color jitter are simultaneously performed. Each dataset is divided into a training set (80%) and a testing set (20%). We utilize three popular deep Convolutional Neural Networks (CNNs), i.e., VGG16, ResNet50, and DenseNet121, on BreakHis and its preprocessed variants.

Figure 3 shows the classification results of three popular deep networks on histopathology dataset BreakHis and its variants. All models can obtain good performance in original BreakHis and the imbalanced BreakHis. This illustrates that these advanced CNN models can handle the histopathology dataset with a few limited magnification scales, even if the distribution of these scales is relatively imbalanced. However, these deep models can only obtain suboptimal results on the datasets preprocessed by random cropping or color jitter. The performance is further downgraded when the dataset suffers from both mixed magnification scales and complicated staining conditions simultaneously. This experiment validates that complex situations of magnification scales and staining conditions do hinder the performance of these successful deep networks.

Effectiveness of OADA. This experiment is to validate the effectiveness of OADA on datasets with practical challenges. We employ BreakHis* (preprocessed by *Crop+Color*) and our private dataset LungHis in this experiment.

Four existing augmentation strategies are used as competitors: (i) Traditional transformation-based Data Augmentation (TDA): the original dataset is augmented by four basic conventional transformation operations (horizontal flipping, rotation, resized cropping, and color jitter) [8]; (ii) Style transformation-based Data Augmentation (SDA): CycleGAN [15] is an image-to-image style transformation to augment the original dataset; (iii) STDA denotes the combination of the above two kinds of augmentation; and (iv) OADA$_{\text{offline}}$ is a variant of OADA. This method performs the same data transformation process before the training stage instead of online updating. We measure the performance of VGG16 empowered by the above data augmentation methods.

Table 1. VGG16 performance empowered by different data augmentation methods

	BreakHis*				LungHis			
	Acc	P	R	$F1$	Acc	P	R	F_1
OADA	**0.9434**	**0.9474**	**0.9434**	**0.9432**	**0.9271**	**0.9289**	**0.9271**	**0.9269**
TDA	0.9108	0.9133	0.9108	0.9105	0.8942	0.8969	0.8942	0.8942
SDA	0.9102	0.9184	0.9102	0.9097	0.9147	0.9159	0.9147	0.9145
STDA	0.8747	0.8808	0.8747	0.8745	0.8733	0.8841	0.8733	0.8730
OADA$_{\text{offline}}$	0.9024	0.9162	0.9024	0.9002	0.8489	0.8795	0.8489	0.8454
Bare Version	0.9036	0.9187	0.9036	0.9024	0.9120	0.9169	0.9120	0.9115

Table 1 illustrates the classification performance of VGG16 empowered by OADA and its four data augmentation contenders. We also report the bare version of VGG16 (without any data augmentation method) in Table 1. OADA-empowered VGG16 outperforms its four competitors on both BreakHis* and LungHis. Compared to the bare version of VGG16 and competitors, OADA-empowered VGG16 averagely achieves 4.8% accuracy improvement on BreakHis* and 4.4% on LungHis. Note that dataset LungHis is directly collected from real medical records in a hospital and is not cleaned by professional domain experts, and thus the quality of LungHis is relatively low. It is very challenging for data augmentation methods to produce significant improvements on this dataset, but our method OADA still obtains more superior performance over other data augmentation competitors.

5   Conclusion

In this paper, we demonstrate and validate that a key problem of leveraging real-world raw medical records is mixed and complex magnification scales and staining conditions of these histopathology images "in the wild". We propose an online adaptive data augmentation method OADA to address this problem. OADA improves the robustness of deep models by adaptively and dynamically augmenting images to update the training set according to the training status of models. Extensive experiments show the effectiveness of OADA on datasets with mixed magnifying factors and color spaces. We hope that our findings can promote future research on histopathology image analysis by fully leveraging these existing numerous real-world medical records.

Acknowledgements. This work is supported by the National Key Research and Development Program of China (2016YFB1000101), the National Natural Science Foundation of China (No. 61379052), the Science Foundation of Ministry of Education of China (No. 2018A02002), and the Natural Science Foundation for Distinguished Young Scholars of Hunan Province (No. 14JJ1026).

References

1. Coudray, N., Moreira, A.L., Sakellaropoulos, T., Feny, D., Tsirigos, A.: Classification and mutation prediction from non-small cell lung cancer histopathology images using deep learning. Nat. Med. **24**, 1559–1567 (2018)
2. Hashimoto, N., et al.: Multi-scale domain-adversarial multiple-instance CNN for cancer subtype classification with unannotated histopathological images. In: CVPR, pp. 3851–3860. IEEE (2020)
3. He, K., Zhang, X., Ren, S., Sun, J.: Deep residual learning for image recognition. In: CVPR, pp. 770–778. IEEE (2016)
4. Huang, G., Liu, Z., Van Der Maaten, L., Weinberger, K.Q.: Densely connected convolutional networks. In: CVPR, pp. 4700–4708 (2017)
5. Inoue, H.: Data augmentation by pairing samples for images classification. arXiv preprint arXiv:1801.02929 (2018)
6. Li, S., Chen, Y., Peng, Y., Bai, L.: Learning more robust features with adversarial training. arXiv preprint arXiv:1804.07757 (2018)
7. Mounsaveng, S., Laradji, I.H., Ayed, I.B., Vázquez, D., Pedersoli, M.: Learning data augmentation with online bilevel optimization for image classification. In: WACV, pp. 1690–1699. IEEE (2021)
8. Shorten, C., Khoshgoftaar, T.M.: A survey on image data augmentation for deep learning. J. Big Data **6**(1), 1–48 (2019)
9. Simonyan, K., Zisserman, A.: Very deep convolutional networks for large-scale image recognition. In: Bengio, Y., LeCun, Y. (eds.) ICLR (2015)
10. Spanhol, F.A., Oliveira, L.S., Petitjean, C., Heutte, L.: A dataset for breast cancer histopathological image classification. IEEE Trans. Biomed. Eng. **63**(7), 1455–1462 (2016)
11. Tang, Z., Gao, Y., Karlinsky, L., Sattigeri, P., Feris, R., Metaxas, D.: OnlineAugment: online data augmentation with less domain knowledge. In: Vedaldi, A., Bischof, H., Brox, T., Frahm, J.-M. (eds.) ECCV 2020. LNCS, vol. 12352, pp. 313–329. Springer, Cham (2020). https://doi.org/10.1007/978-3-030-58571-6_19
12. Taylor, L., Nitschke, G.: Improving deep learning using generic data augmentation. arXiv preprint arXiv:1708.06020 (2017)
13. Wang, D., Khosla, A., Gargeya, R., Irshad, H., Beck, A.H.: Deep learning for identifying metastatic breast cancer. arXiv preprint arXiv:1606.05718 (2016)
14. Wei, J.W., Tafe, L.J., Linnik, Y.A., Vaickus, L.J., Tomita, N., Hassanpour, S.: Pathologist-level classification of histologic patterns on resected lung adenocarcinoma slides with deep neural networks. Sci. Rep. **9**(1), 1–8 (2019)
15. Zhu, J.Y., Park, T., Isola, P., Efros, A.A.: Unpaired image-to-image translation using cycle-consistent adversarial networks. In: ICCV, pp. 2223–2232 (2017)

FetalNet: Multi-task Deep Learning Framework for Fetal Ultrasound Biometric Measurements

Szymon Płotka[1,2,4(✉)], Tomasz Włodarczyk[2,4], Adam Klasa[4], Michał Lipa[3],
Arkadiusz Sitek[1(✉)], and Tomasz Trzciński[2,5]

[1] Sano Centre for Computational Medicine, Nawojki 11, Cracow, Poland
{s.plotka,a.sitek}@sanoscience.org
[2] Warsaw University of Technology, Nowowiejska 15/19, Warsaw, Poland
[3] Medical University of Warsaw, pl. S. Starynkiewicza 1/3, Warsaw, Poland
[4] Fetai Health Ltd., pl. J. Kilinskiego 2, Rzeszow, Poland
[5] Tooploox, Teczowa 7, Wroclaw, Poland

Abstract. Fetal biometric measurements are routinely done during pregnancy for the fetus growth monitoring and estimation of gestational age and fetal weight. The main goal in fetal ultrasound scan video analysis is to find standard planes to measure the fetal head, abdomen and femur. In this paper, we propose an end-to-end multi-task neural network called FetalNet with an attention mechanism and stacked module for spatio-temporal fetal ultrasound scan video analysis to simultaneously localize, classify and measure the fetal body parts. We employ an attention mechanism with a stacked module to learn salient maps to suppress irrelevant ultrasound regions and efficient scan plane localization. We train on the fetal ultrasound video from routine examinations of 700 different patients. Our method called FetalNet outperforms existing state-of-the-art methods in both classification and segmentation in fetal ultrasound video recordings. The source code and pre-trained weights are publicly available (https://github.com/SanoScience/FetalNet).

Keywords: Deep learning · Fetal biometry · Video ultrasound

1 Introduction

Fetal organ measurement using ultrasound (US) is currently the most popular way of assessing the state of the fetus' growth and the safety of the pregnancy [8]. It enables the operator to perform an array of measurements during a single imaging session. Clinically, the most important are the measurements of biparietal diameter (BPD), head circumference (HC), femur length (FL) and abdominal circumference (AC). Fetal measurements enable obstetricians to evaluate fetal' growth and estimate the following parameters: gestational age (GA) and fetal weight (FW) [4].

© Springer Nature Switzerland AG 2021
T. Mantoro et al. (Eds.): ICONIP 2021, CCIS 1517, pp. 257–265, 2021.
https://doi.org/10.1007/978-3-030-92310-5_30

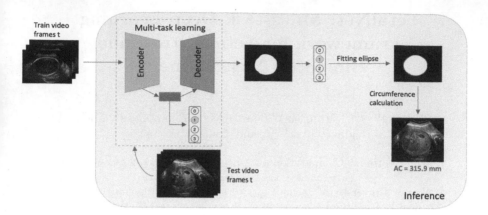

Fig. 1. Overview of the proposed framework for simultaneous segmentation and classification using fetal US video sequences. Our encoder part extract high-level US features to 1) classify the fetal body parts and background, 2) to predict binary mask of fetal head, abdomen and femur. During inference, our method localizes and classifies each image at the frame level, and performs measurements respective to the predicted class.

To automate the fetal body part measurements, researchers used computer-aided diagnosis, including the most advanced offered by deep learning. The problem of finding suitable views that meet the criteria of a standard measurement plane has been investigated [1]. Substantial research has been done to find the best algorithms that segment single fetal body parts. Encouraging results were achieved for the segmentation of fetal heads [16] and abdomens [12]. Jang et al. [6] proposed to use simultaneous segmentation and classification of the abdomen, [2] of the head, and [15] both. Unlike ours, the large majority of algorithms developed to date focus on solving only one task at a time. Some address the task of choosing a good plane for fetal measurement, while others focus on segmenting a single fetal body part [7].

In this paper, we propose an end-to-end pipeline called FetalNet that is designed to jointly localize, classify and measure the fetal body parts at the frame level. We examine the impact of temporal information extracted from frame sequence connected to the attention mechanism and stacked module on the fetal body parts measurement in the fetal US video recordings. The main contributions of our work are as follows: (i) we propose an end-to-end multi-task method called FetalNet for comprehensive $2D+t$ spatio-temporal fetal US video analysis to localize, classify and measure the fetal body parts simultaneously, (ii) we extend an attention gate mechanism by aggregating multi-scale feature maps of each decoder output to learn the local and global context of the fetal body structures that help to outperform both segmentation and classification state-of-the-art results.

2   Method

In this section, we describe a multi-task learning neural network for spatio-temporal fetal US video analysis. Next, we describe how to automatically obtain measurements of each fetal body part. Figure 1 shows an overview of our method called FetalNet for the automatic evaluation of fetal biometric measurement on fetal US scan video using a multi-task deep learning framework.

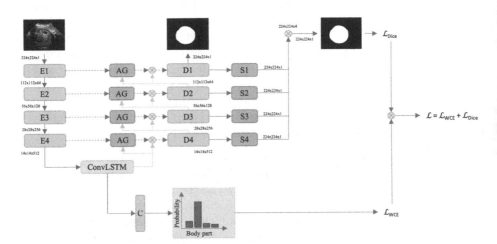

Fig. 2. Overview of the proposed multi-task neural network. We base on an encoder-decoder U-Net neural network. As a bottleneck, we use the ConvLSTM module to learn image sequences. To focus on a region-of-interest (ROI) in the segmentation task, we concatenate encoders (E1-E4) by attention gates (AG) to decoders (D1-D4) via skip connections. To improve the performance of the segmentation and smooth our binary predicted masks, we use stacked multi-scale probability maps via up-sample convolutional outputs of the sides (S1-S4) probability maps to the input image size. For the classification task, we use ConvLSTM output features and a fully connected layer (C) with 4 outputs.

Multi-task Neural Network: Inspired by [10, 14], we use an encoder-decoder based convolutional neural network (CNN) for simultaneous segmentation and classification of the fetal body parts on the fetal US video sequences. We use an encoder part to extract high-level US image features. The output of an encoder is forward to the ConvLSTM-based bottleneck. The ConvLSTM cells are able to retain spatial-temporal US image features in memory, which can effectively improve the performance precision and accuracy of both classification and segmentation. Due to various shapes and sizes in our dataset, we employ an attention gate mechanism to essentially learn to suppress inappropriate areas in an input video sequence, while highlighting the salient features of the target region-of-interest. Attention gate mechanism helps to better exploit local information to efficient object localize (i.e. fetal body parts) and improve prediction performance. Each block of decoder forwards its output feature maps and concatenates them with an attention gate to the decoder part. In fetal examinations, fetal body parts are hardly visible, and the sonographer's manual examination relies profoundly on low-level semantic information to draw boundaries. To improve the performance of binary prediction feature maps, we employ deep supervision to connect multi-scale lower and higher-level of each decoder features together [5] called stacked module. Multi-scale feature maps help to encode both global and local contexts. We employ a set of 3×3 2D convolutional layers to up-sample the feature maps after each convolutional block. Then, we combine the previous high-level feature maps to aggregated binary segmentation map. As our ablation study demonstrates, a stacked module with an attention gate can significantly impact segmentation and reduce the measurement error of the fetal body parts over both attention U-Net and stacked module U-Net. For the classification branch, we use spatial-temporal ConvLSTM-output features to classify each of the following classes: fetal head, abdomen, femur or background at the frame level. Figure 2 shows the proposed multi-task learning method called FetalNet for spatio-temporal video analysis of fetal ultrasound.

Biometric Measurement: First, we resize the segmentation output of our multi-task neural network, which comes in the form of a binary mask to the size of the input image. Next, we apply binary thresholding $p = 0.6$ and perform erosion followed by dilation, using a 5×5 cross-shaped structuring element. This ensures that the predicted masks are sufficiently denoised. Finally, we use a median blur filter to smooth the edges of the predicted masks. Depending on the classification results, we use different methods to obtain adequate measurements. For HC and AC, firstly, we use a function to find contours of segmentation output. Next, we use the Ramer-Douglas-Peucker approximation to enhance the accuracy of the subsequent ellipse fitting, for which perimeter is calculated and stored. Additionally, to acquire the measurement of BPD, we store the length of the short axis of the ellipse fitted to the head. To obtain FL, we precisely fit a rectangular bounding box to the contours of the predicted binary mask found by using the same function as in the case of head and abdomen. Next, we store the length of the fitted rectangle. Finally, we convert all of the obtained pixel-valued measurements to centimetres by multiplying them by pixel spacing, an attribute that encodes the physical distance between centres of the pixels, stored in DICOM files metadata.

3   Experiments and Results

In this section, we introduce a novel Fetal dataset and show the performance of our method called FetalNet on this dataset.

Fetal Dataset: Our dataset consists of 700 two-dimensional (2D) fetal US video sequences examinations of head, abdomen and femur and comes from 700 different patients. Each 2D fetal US video sequence consists of between 250 and 460 frames. Overall, our dataset consists of over 274,000 frames. The data comes from volunteer pregnant women with pregnancies between 15th and 38th weeks of gestation, acquired during a routine clinical screening examination. Data was acquired using five different GE Voluson ultrasound scanners (E8, E10, S6, S8, P8) at two different resolutions: 975 × 742 pixels or 1100 × 960 pixels. From video sequences sonographers identified standard views that are suitable to perform the measurement and annotated them. Overall, our annotated dataset consists of 62324 standard views and 211951 background views. We used the number of samples for each class for training and validation: 32215 heads, 26403 abdomens, 3706 femurs and 211951 backgrounds. The background class shows indistinguishable structures around standard view plane frames. The data come from six different research institutes and were anonymized before use in this study. Six sonographers with experience (40, 25, 20, 20, 15, 8 years, respectively) provided ground truths for the dataset in the form of annotations drawn on the anonymized images and values of the performed measurements. The annotations of heads and abdomens were ellipses similar to those that were used for manual measurements typically done at the ultrasound scanner. We create femurs annotations by free-hand drawings of theirs outlines.

Preprocessing: First of all, we transform 2D fetal US video sequences (between 17–36 FPS) into separate ordered frames. Then, we anonymize raw 2D US images by removing personal data displayed on the top of the images. Next, we remove unnecessary text burned in images like device settings. In the next step, we convert raw DICOM data into PNG files. Finally, we randomly split our dataset into 60% training (420 cases), 20% validation (140 cases) and 20% test (140 cases) sets.

Data Augmentation: During training, to prevent overfitting and make the neural network more robust, we apply various data augmentation techniques: random (i) rotation between −15 and 15°, (ii) brightness, (iii) contrast, (iv) horizontal and (v) vertical flip. We also use a shuffled sampler.

Implementation Details: We base our network on U-Net [13], our encoder-decoder includes eight convolutional blocks, four in the encoder part and four in the decoder part. We concatenate encoders with attention gates [11] to decoders via skip-connections. We use an attention gate mechanism to focus on certain parts of images. To improve the performance of the segmentation and smooth our binary predicted masks, we use stacked probability multi-scale feature maps via up-sample convolutional outputs of the side feature maps to the input image size. For the classification branch, we apply Adaptive Average Pooling 2D and Dropout2D with $p = 0.4$ as ConvLSTM output before Fully Connected layer with $14 \times 14 \times 16n$ feature maps on the output. We use Adam as an optimizer with a learning rate of 10^{-4}, weight decay of 10^{-5} and batch size of 16 for 80 epochs.

Segmentation Results: We evaluate our model on 57001 test images of fetal head (7250 images), abdomen (6580 images), femur (720 images) and background (42451 images) class. For segmentation, we use Jaccard Index, also known as Intersection over Union (IoU) and the Dice similarity coefficient (DSC) as the evaluation metrics. We obtain the following results: 0.905 and 0.962 for IoU and DSC, respectively. Figure 3 shows the qualitative results of our proposed network. It shows that our method was able to localise fetal head, abdomen and femur, which are subject to variability in scale and appearance.

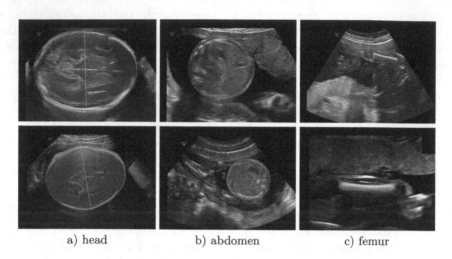

a) head   b) abdomen   c) femur

Fig. 3. We show two examples per class on test data. From the left to right: a) HC and BPD b) AC and c) FL measurement obtained by our multi-task deep learning framework. The red line represents a ground truth, while the green line our predictions. (Color figure online)

Classification Results: For classification as the evaluation metrics, we use accuracy, precision, recall and F1 score. We obtained the following results: 0.96, 0.97 and 0.96 for precision, recall and F1 score, respectively. Table 1 demonstrates FetalNet classification results against base U-Net, Deeplabv3 [3], FCN-8s and FCN-32s [9]. The proposed system outperforms the state-of-the-art neural networks in terms of head, abdomen and femur in segmentation and classification accuracy. Our method outperforms the current state-of-the-art methods in both classification and segmentation (Table 1), and the fetal body part measurement (Table 2). As shown in Fig. 3, our segmentation results of standard view scans are comparable to the ground-truths provided by experienced sonographers.

Measurement Results: Table 2 reports results of the fetal head, abdomen and femur error measurement (in mm) against state-of-the-art neural networks measured as the mean and standard deviation.

Ablation Study: We conduct the ablation study to show the effectiveness of the proposed method called FetalNet in terms of both segmentation and classification. We use the same dataset and hyperparameters of the neural network for each experiment, if not mentioned. Table 3 shows the experiments for the proposed method with different combinations of modules. As we can see, multi-task learning improves segmentation results to compare with the U-Net base

Table 1. Comparison of segmentation and classification of fetal body parts: head, abdomen, femur and background with the state-of-the-art neural networks and Fetal-Net.

Method	IoU	Dice	Accuracy	Precision	Recall	F1
U-Net (base)	0.862	0.921	–	–	–	–
DeepLabv3	0.851	0.912	0.922	0.91	0.89	0.90
FCN-8s	0.865	0.924	0.933	0.93	0.91	0.92
FCN-32s	0.872	0.932	0.935	0.93	0.91	0.92
FetalNet (ours)	**0.905**	**0.962**	**0.975**	**0.96**	**0.97**	**0.96**

Table 2. Comparison of measurement error (in mm) of fetal body parts: head, abdomen, femur with the state-of-the-art neural networks and FetalNet.

Method	Head	Abdomen	Femur
U-Net (base)	4.5 ± 3.2	5.4 ± 3.1	1.5 ± 1.4
DeepLabv3	4.8 ± 3.4	5.5 ± 3.4	1.5 ± 1.3
FCN-8s	4.7 ± 3.1	5.3 ± 3.3	1.6 ± 1.2
FCN-32s	$3.9 + 2.8$	4.9 ± 3.2	1.2 ± 0.8
FetalNet (ours)	**2.9 ± 1.2**	**3.8 ± 3.0**	**0.8 ± 1.2**

model. For the segmentation, combining the proposed $\mathcal{L}_{WCE}$ performed better than only using Dice loss. The results were further improved after introducing the attention gate mechanism and stacked modules separately. Finally, our model trained with each of the proposed extensions, resulting in a significant performance increase across all the metrics.

Table 3. Evaluation of different components of neural network on our dataset.

Method	Segmentation	Classification	IoU	Dice	Accuracy
U-Net (base)	✓	–	0.862	0.921	–
U-Net+cls	✓	✓	0.872	0.945	0.961
U-Net+cls+AG	✓	✓	0.891	0.951	0.971
U-Net+cls+SM	✓	✓	0.893	0.954	0.972
U-Net+cls+AG+SM (ours)	✓	✓	**0.905**	**0.962**	**0.975**

In this paper, we propose an end-to-end multi-task method called FetalNet for spatio-temporal full-length routine fetal US scan video analysis. In particular, we consider the attention mechanism and present how to incorporate it into fetal biometric measurement to better exploit local structures. We introduce aggregation of multi-scale feature maps as a stacked module making our approach more robust to spatio-temporal fetal US scan video analysis, where the previous methods fail. This allows for accurate and precise simultaneous localization and classification of the fetal body parts in freehand fetal US video recordings. Our method incorporates a classification branch to the U-Net-based encoder-decoder neural network. To learn temporal features, we employ the ConvLSTM layer as a bottleneck. To make our method more robust on ultrasound noise and shadow, we exploit an attention gate mechanism to focus on relevant ROIs at the frame level. We introduce a stacked module, aggregating the multi-scale feature maps of the decoder to learn the local and global context of the target. The ablation study shows that using both additional modules, our methods obtain better outcomes in the segmentation and classification of the fetal body parts.

4   Conclusions

In this paper, we proposed an end-to-end multi-task method called FetalNet for spatio-temporal fetal US scan video analysis. FetalNet is designed to jointly localize, classify and measure the fetal body parts during routine freehand fetal US examinations. The proposed method has the potential as a fetal biometry assistance tool for clinical use by non-experienced personnel. Usage of our approach in a clinical environment requires real-time feedback for a sonographer during routine fetal US examinations. Due to the large size of model parameters, we will implement a more efficient neural network to work on computationally low-cost devices. Additionally, we will improve and make our model more robust by adding to the training set data generated on a larger variety of devices as well as low-quality data to simulate data acquisitions made by non-expert personnel. We will also extend our method to automatically detect abnormalities of the fetus and perform a direct estimation of gestational age and fetal weight.

Acknowledgements. We would like to thank the following medical sonographers for data, annotations and clinical expertise: Jan Klasa, MD; Bogusław Marinković, MD; Wojciech Górczewski, MD; Norbert Majewski, MD; Anita Smal-Obarska, MD. This paper is supported by the European Union's Horizon 2020 research and innovation programme under grant agreement Sano No 857533 and the International Research Agendas programme of the Foundation for Polish Science, co-financed by the European Union under the European Regional Development Fund and by Warsaw University of Technology (grant of the Scientific Discipline of Computer Science and Telecommunications agreement of 18/06/2020).

References

1. Baumgartner, C.F., et al.: SonoNet: real-time detection and localisation of fetal standard scan planes in freehand ultrasound. IEEE Trans. Med. Imaging **36**, 2204–2215 (2017)
2. Budd, S., et al.: Confident head circumference measurement from ultrasound with real-time feedback for sonographers. In: Shen, D., et al. (eds.) MICCAI 2019. LNCS, vol. 11767, pp. 683–691. Springer, Cham (2019). https://doi.org/10.1007/978-3-030-32251-9_75

3. Chen, L.-C., Papandreou, G., Schroff, F., Adam, H.: Rethinking Atrous Convolution for Semantic Image Segmentation. arXiv:1706.05587 [cs] (2017)
4. Hadlock, F.P., Harrist, R.B., Sharman, R.S., Deter, R.L., Park, S.K.: Estimation of fetal weight with the use of head, body, and femur measurements-a prospective study. Am. J. Obstet. Gynecol. **151**, 333–337 (1985)
5. Harrison, A.P., Xu, Z., George, K., Lu, L., Summers, R.M., Mollura, D.J.: Progressive and multi-path holistically nested neural networks for pathological lung segmentation from CT images. In: Descoteaux, M., Maier-Hein, L., Franz, A., Jannin, P., Collins, D.L., Duchesne, S. (eds.) MICCAI 2017. LNCS, vol. 10435, pp. 621–629. Springer, Cham (2017). https://doi.org/10.1007/978-3-319-66179-7_71
6. Jang, J., Park, Y., Kim, B., Lee, S.M., Kwon, J.-Y., Seo, J.K.: Automatic estimation of fetal abdominal circumference from ultrasound images. IEEE J. Biomed. Health Inform. **22**, 1512–1520 (2018)
7. Liu, P., Zhao, H., Li, P., Cao, F.: Automated classification and measurement of fetal ultrasound images with attention feature pyramid network. In: Wang, T., Chai, T., Fan, H., Yu, Q. (eds.) Second Target Recognition and Artificial Intelligence Summit Forum, p. 116. SPIE, Changchun (2020)
8. Liu, S., et al.: Deep learning in medical ultrasound analysis: a review. Engineering **5**, 261–275 (2019)
9. Long, J., Shelhamer, E., Darrell, T.: Fully convolutional networks for semantic segmentation. In: 2015 IEEE Conference on Computer Vision and Pattern Recognition (CVPR), pp. 3431–3440. IEEE, Boston (2015)
10. Mehta, S., Mercan, E., Bartlett, J., Weaver, D., Elmore, J.G., Shapiro, L.: Y-net: joint segmentation and classification for diagnosis of breast biopsy images. In: Frangi, A.F., Schnabel, J.A., Davatzikos, C., Alberola-López, C., Fichtinger, G. (eds.) MICCAI 2018. LNCS, vol. 11071, pp. 893–901. Springer, Cham (2018). https://doi.org/10.1007/978-3-030-00934-2_99
11. Oktay, O., et al.: Attention U-net: learning where to look for the pancreas. arXiv:1804.03999 [cs] (2018)
12. Ravishankar, H., Prabhu, S.M., Vaidya, V., Singhal, N.: Hybrid approach for automatic segmentation of fetal abdomen from ultrasound images using deep learning. In: 2016 IEEE 13th International Symposium on Biomedical Imaging (ISBI), pp. 779–782. IEEE, Prague (2016)
13. Ronneberger, O., Fischer, P., Brox, T.: U-net: convolutional networks for biomedical image segmentation. In: Navab, N., Hornegger, J., Wells, W.M., Frangi, A.F. (eds.) MICCAI 2015. LNCS, vol. 9351, pp. 234–241. Springer, Cham (2015). https://doi.org/10.1007/978-3-319-24574-4_28
14. Wang, P., Patel, V.M., Hacihaliloglu, I.: Simultaneous segmentation and classification of bone surfaces from ultrasound using a multi-feature guided CNN. In: Frangi, A.F., Schnabel, J.A., Davatzikos, C., Alberola-López, C., Fichtinger, G. (eds.) MICCAI 2018. LNCS, vol. 11073, pp. 134–142. Springer, Cham (2018). https://doi.org/10.1007/978-3-030-00937-3_16
15. Wu, L., Xin, Y., Li, S., Wang, T., Heng, P.-A., Ni, D.: Cascaded fully convolutional networks for automatic prenatal ultrasound image segmentation. In: 2017 IEEE 14th International Symposium on Biomedical Imaging (ISBI 2017), pp. 663–666. IEEE, Melbourne (2017)
16. Zeng, Y., Tsui, P.-H., Wu, W., Zhou, Z., Wu, S.: Fetal ultrasound image segmentation for automatic head circumference biometry using deeply supervised attention-gated V-net. J. Digit. Imaging **34**(1), 134–148 (2021). https://doi.org/10.1007/s10278-020-00410-5

PoseGate-Former: Transformer Encoder with Trainable Gate for 3D Human Pose Estimation Using Weakly Supervised Learning

Shannan Guan[1(✉)], Haiyan Lu[1(✉)], Linchao Zhu[1(✉)], and Gengfa Fang[2(✉)]

[1] Australia Artificial Intelligence Institute, University of Technology Sydney, Ultimo, Australia
shannan.guan@uts.student.edu.au, {haiyan.lu,linchao.zhu}@uts.edu.au
[2] Global Big Data Technologies Centre, University of Technology Sydney, Ultimo, Australia
gengfa.fang@uts.edu.au

Abstract. Weakly supervised learning for 3D human pose estimation can learn a real human structure, but it generally has lower accuracy on reconstructing 3D poses. In this work, we present a 3D pose estimation model using a Transformer encoder based architecture with a trainable gate, **PoseGate-Former**. The model is trained using individual images from a weakly supervised learning approach. It can reduce possibility of overfitting on some action categories due to the addition of a trainable gate to the Transformer encoder. We evaluated this model on two benchmark datasets: *Human3.6M* and *HumanEva-I*. The experimental results show that this model can obtain substantially better accuracy in all action categories of 3D human poses in the datasets compared with some fully-supervised 3D pose estimation approaches.

Keywords: 3D pose estimation · Transformer · Weakly-supervised learning

1 Introduction

3D human pose estimation from individual monocular images aims to predict the (x, y, z) coordinates of each key joint of a human body in the camera coordinate system. It is a challenging problem in the computer vision area as the relationship between 2D and 3D human poses can be one-to-many. There are two main approaches to estimate 3D human pose from monocular images: supervised approach and a weakly-supervised approach [4–6,8,11,12]. Although it can learn a real human structure, the weakly-supervised approach generally has a lower accuracy in predicting the 3D joint coordinates. Therefore, it is highly desirable to develop a new method to improve the accuracy of 3D human pose estimation from the weakly supervised learning approach.

© Springer Nature Switzerland AG 2021
T. Mantoro et al. (Eds.): ICONIP 2021, CCIS 1517, pp. 266–274, 2021.
https://doi.org/10.1007/978-3-030-92310-5_31

With the inspiration of the success of Transformer architecture in Computer Vision, we proposed a new 3D pose estimation models using a modified transformer encoder with a trainable gate, referred to as **PoseGate-Former**, and this model is trained by using a weakly supervised learning approach. Compared with fully connected neural networks, self-attention mechanism in a transformer architecture could learn the relations among human key joints and improve the accuracy of 3D human pose estimation using a weakly supervised learning approach.

We evaluate our model on two benchmark datasets: 1) Human3.6M [2], and 2) HumanEva-I [10]. It has been observed that the **PoseGate-Former** can improve the estimation accuracy significantly in all action categories and improve the performance in a few specific action categories. It can reduce 30% in average MPJPE compared with RepNet [11], and can outperform most of supervised learning approaches.

Our contributions are twofold: 1) Introduced the self-attention architecture of a Transformer in 3D human pose estimation with significantly improved performance by using a weakly supervised training approach and 2) Proposed the PoseGate-Former by adding a trainable gate to the self-attention architecture of a Transformer to reduce the possibility of overfitting on some specific action categories, evidenced by our experimental results on Human3.6M and HumanEva-I.

2   Related Work

Two approaches in the literature are relevant to this study: One is 2D to 3D human pose conversion approaches based on individual images using a weakly supervised learning. For example, Wandt et al. [11] proposed a weakly supervised adversarial learning structure to lift human pose from 2D to 3D. The other one is the Transformer learning architecture. It is promising to use a Transformer architecture in the Computer Vision area. For examples, work in [4,12] use a Transformer encoder architecture to map 2D human poses to 3D poses by using a sequence of 2D key joints extracted from videos.

3   Method

In this section, we first present our new design of a 3D pose estimator, the PoseGate-Former, then present the weakly supervised learning structure and lastly explain the learning procedure.

3.1   PoseGate-Former Architecture for 3D Pose Estimation

As shown in Fig. 1 (a), the PoseGate-Former includes a trainable gate module, there are two branches feed to the multi-head self-attention module: The left branch is used for providing matrices $Q = (q_1, q_2, \ldots, q_h)$, $K = (k_1, k_2, \ldots, k_h)$, and $V = (v_1, v_2, \ldots, v_h)$, where q_i, k_i, and v_i is the i_{th} element in the matrices

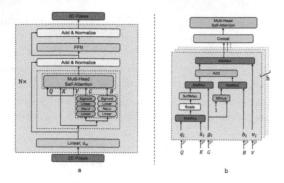

Fig. 1. Part (a) shows the structure of PoseGate-Former which is the 3D pose estimator. Part (b) illustrates the calculation procedure of a single head and the logic of how h heads of self-attention scores are concatenated to multi-head self-attention scores.

Q,K and V, respectively, $i = 1, 2, \ldots, h$. The right branch is split into two paths, one path outputs a h dimensional gate vector $G = (g_1, g_2, \ldots, g_h)$, and the other path outputs a h dimensional bias vector $B = (b_1, b_2, \ldots, b_h)$. In each path, two fully connected layers of 100 neurons with sigmoid activation function are used. The sigmoid activation function is used to limit the output value ranging from zero to one. From Fig. 1 (b), the self-attention score of the head i can be calculated by:

$$\text{head}_i = \left(\text{softmax} \left(\frac{q_i k_i^T}{\sqrt{d_k}} \right) g_i + (1 - b_i) g_i \right) v_i \tag{1}$$

where g_i is a gate value from gate vector G and b_i is a bias value from bias vector B. Then, the multi-head self-attention score can be obtained by concatenating the scores of all heads: MultiHead $(Q, K, V, G, B) = \text{Concat}(\text{head}_1, \ldots, \text{head}_h)$. Based on Eq. 1, the multi-head self-attention can be expressed as:

$$\begin{aligned} \text{Self-Attention}(Q, K, V, G, B) = &(\text{softmax} \left(\frac{QK^T}{\sqrt{d_k}} \right) \text{diag}(G) \\ &+ \text{diag}(I - B) \cdot \text{diag}(G))V \end{aligned} \tag{2}$$

where I is a h dimensional vector which only consists of one, and $diag$ is a diagonal matrix. This structure can output corresponding gate and bias values based on different poses and effectively reduce the possibility of overfitting in some specific action categories by correcting the multi-head self-attention scores.

3.2 Weakly Supervised Learning Structure

The weakly supervised learning structure for training the PoseGate-Former is developed based on the training structure in [11], and shown in Fig. 2. In this structure, a 2D pose is fed into the PostGate-Former to generate an estimated 3D pose. Meanwhile, this 2D pose is also fed into the camera module which outputs a projection matrix M for simulating the camera projection. Then, 3D pose and the generated projection matrix M are fed into a projection module for projecting the corresponding 2D pose. During the training process, a critic module will judge whether the generated 3D pose corresponds to a real human shape.

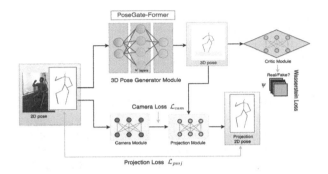

Fig. 2. The weakly supervised adversarial learning structure used in this work, which consists of four modules: 1) a 3D pose generator module, 2) a camera estimation module, 3) a projection module, and 4) a critic module.

3D Pose Generator Module. This module implements the PoseGate-Former. It's input is the extracted 2D key joints expressed as a matrix W, where $W \in \mathbb{R}^{2 \times n}$ and its output is a $3n$ dimensional vector that consists of (x, y, z)-coordinates of each key joint and is reshaped to X. In following expression, $X \in \mathbb{R}^{3 \times n}$ donates the 3D pose and the (x, y, z)-coordinates of each key joint are recorded in n columns that correspond to the inputs of this module, respectively.

Critic Module. This module is used to ensure that the generated 3D pose corresponds to a real human shape. The estimated 3D pose from the 3D pose generator will be transformed by a kinematic chain space (KCS) matrix [11] and fed into a fully connected neural networks to output a single critic value for calculating the Wasserstein loss ψ through a Wasserstein loss function [11].

Camera Module. In most instances, we do not know camera parameters to project 3D poses, therefore, we need to build a camera module to regress camera parameters to project 3D poses. The camera module regresses a vector with six parameters, and the vector is reshaped to the projection matrix $M \in \mathbb{R}^{2 \times 3}$.

Projection Module. This module is used to transfer the output X from 3D pose generator network to a 2D pose matrix W' by multiplying the 3D pose matrix X with the projection matrix M from camera estimation network: $W' = MX$.

3.3 Training Procedure

In order to train the PoseGate-Former, we apply three losses to guide the training from the weakly supervised learning approach: 1) Wasserstein Loss ψ in the last layer of critic network, 2) Camera Loss $\mathcal{L}_{cam}$ to calculate the camera loss in the camera network, and 3) Projection Loss $\mathcal{L}_{proj}$ to minimize the errors between the ground-truth and the estimated poses. In the training procedure, we implemented the Improved Wasserstein GAN training method [1]. We group different modules into two models: 1) adversarial model and 2) discriminator model and train them separately. The adversarial model contains a complete learning structure as shown in Fig. 2, but the critic module only implements the feed forward inference propagation without training the parameters. The discriminator model consists of the 3D pose generator module and the critic module, and only the critic module will be trained.

4   Model Evaluation and Discussion

There are two main evaluation protocols for evaluating the proposed methods, both of them use the mean per joint positioning error (MPJPE), which calculates the average Euclidean distance between the estimated joint and the corresponding ground truth joint coordinates. Protocol-I directly calculates the MPJPE. Protocol-II applies a rigid alignment between the ground truth and the estimated poses and calculates the P-MPJPE.

4.1   Quantitative Evaluation on Human3.6M

Human3.6M is the largest public 3D human pose estimation dataset. This dataset contains 15 categories of daily activities of 7 professional subjects. In this work, we used 5 subjects (1, 5, 6, 7, 8) for training and 2 subjects (9, 11) for evaluating. Table 1 shows the evaluation results on Human3.6M dataset using Protocol-I.

Table 1. Comparisons of MPJPE error from PoseGate-Former along with other state-of-the-art 3D post estimation methods. The column WS indicates whether this approach used a weakly-supervised method. The best are shown in bold, second-best are underlined.

Protocol-I	WS	Direct.	Disc.	Eat	Greet	Phone	Photo	Pose	Purch.	Sit	SitD	Smoke	Wait	Walk	WalkD	WalkT	Avg.
Park et al. [7]		100.3	116.2	90.0	116.5	115.3	149.5	117.6	106.9	137.2	190.8	105.8	125.1	131.9	62.6	96.2	117.3
Zhou et al. [14]		91.8	102.4	96.7	98.8	113.4	125.2	90.0	93.8	132.2	159.0	107.0	94.4	126.0	79.0	99.0	107.3
Luo et al. [5]		68.4	77.3	70.2	71.4	75.1	86.5	69.0	76.7	88.2	103.4	73.8	72.1	83.9	58.1	65.4	76.0
Pavlakos et al. [8]		67.4	71.9	66.7	69.1	72.0	77.0	65.0	68.3	83.7	96.5	71.7	65.8	74.9	59.1	63.2	71.9
Zhou et al. [13]		54.8	60.7	58.2	71.4	62.0	65.5	53.8	55.6	75.2	111.6	64.2	66.1	63.2	51.4	55.3	64.9
Martinez et al. [6]	✓	53.3	60.8	62.9	62.7	86.4	82.4	57.8	58.7	81.9	99.8	69.1	63.9	50.9	67.1	54.8	67.5
Wandt et al. [11]	✓	50.0	53.5	44.7	51.6	49.0	58.7	48.8	51.3	51.1	66.0	46.6	50.6	42.5	38.8	60.4	50.9
PoseGate-Former (Ours)	✓	32.0	34.3	26.9	34.6	37.8	35.7	27.8	38.2	34.9	38.7	31.4	39.8	38.5	37.0	40.2	35.2

It can be seen from Table 1 that the proposed PoseGate-Former shows a significant improvement compared with other benchmark methods. For each action category, the PoseGate-Former is able to mitigate the overfitting problem and the errors in each category are rapidly reduced or remain the same. The average error reduced is 30% compared with the one from RepNet [11]. Figure 3 shows the comparisons of reconstructed 3D poses by our PostGate-Former and the ground truth 3D poses in the validation dataset in Human3.6M. It can be seen from Fig. 3 that all the poses were well reconstructed, even complex poses, such as Sitting on the ground, Phoning, and Crossing legs.

4.2   Quantitative Evaluation on HumanEVA-I

Compared with Human3.6M, HumanEVA-I is a smaller dataset which contains three action categories (Walk, Jog, Box) performed by subjects (S1, S2, S3).

Table 2 shows the comparison results of P-MPJPE between our structure and other few state-of-the-art approaches on HumanEva-I. It can be seen that our PostGate-Former achieved promising performance. Compared with individual images based fully supervised approaches, our PoseGate-Former has a better performance across all action categories, including complex action categories (e.g. Walk S3 subject, Box action category). Compared with video based approach [4], our PoseGate-Former also achieved a comparable performance.

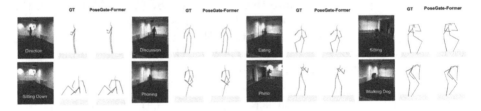

Fig. 3. Visualization examples of 3D pose reconstruction for some action categories from the validation dataset of Human3.6M. The GT columns show the ground truth poses and PoseGate-Former columns show the reconstructed 3D poses.

Table 2. Quantitative results for reconstructing 3D pose of HumanEva-I dataset following *Protocol-II*. Video means the approach is video based, and the best in bold, second-best underlined. Our results show P-MPJPE by using ground truth 2D labels.

HumanEVA-I	Walk			Jog			Box			Avg.
	S1	S2	S3	S1	S2	S3	S1	S2	S3	
Martinez et al. [6]	19.7	17.4	46.8	26.9	18.2	18.6	–	–	–	–
Pavlakos et al. [8]	22.3	19.5	29.7	28.9	21.9	23.8	–	–	–	–
Lee et al. [3]	18.6	19.9	30.5	25.7	16.8	17.7	42.8	48.1	53.4	30.3
Pavllo et al. [9]	13.9	10.2	46.6	20.9	13.1	13.8	23.8	33.7	32	23.1
Li et al. [4] (Video)	**9.7**	**7.6**	<u>15.8</u>	<u>12.3</u>	**9.4**	<u>11.2</u>	<u>14.8</u>	**12.9**	<u>16.5</u>	**12.2**
PoseGate-Former (Ours)	<u>13.0</u>	<u>9.9</u>	**15.7**	**11.9**	<u>12.1</u>	**10.23**	**12.4**	<u>13.4</u>	**12.1**	<u>12.3</u>

4.3 Ablation Study

To validate the contribution of key components of PoseGate-Former, e.g., the self-attention layer and the trainable gate, and the impact of hyperparameters on performance, we carried out an ablation study on Human3.6M dataset. This study is to verify the contributions made by the self-attention layer and the trainable gate to the performance of PoseGate-Former. In this study, we set the dimension of the Transformer architecture d_m to 256, and evaluate the contributions in each action category based on MPJPE. We implemented the structure/model under three conditions: 1) We fixed all self-attention scores to $1/n(n = 16)$. Because we take 16 key joints in Human3.6M and the sum of self-attention scores is one, thus the average value is $1/16$; 2) We use a naive Transformer self-attention architecture; and 3) We only used one trainable value in the gate and used a constant value $1/n(n = 16)$ as the bias.

It can be seen from Table 3 that the attention scores have significant impact on the performance of our pose generator, PostGate-Former. Compared with the naive Transformer model, a fixed self-attention score leads MPJPE to increase by 15%. The PoseGate-Former with a Fixed-bias column shows that one trainable value in the gate can enhance the performance by 9% compared with the naive Transformer model. It shows the best results in some action categories, such as Direction, Discussion, and Sitting. However, the overall performance under PoseGate-Former with a fixed bias is worse than PoseGate-Former due to overfitting in some specific action categories.

Table 3. Ablation study on different self-attention layers in the Transformer architecture. The results show MPJPE which are implemented on Human3.6M using *Protocol-I* with the ground-truth 2D poses as the inputs. Fix-attn is fixing all self-attention scores, Fix-bias is using one trainable value as gate and use a constant value as bias.

Ablation study 1	Direct.	Disc.	Eat	Greet	Phone	Photo	Pose	Purch.	Sit	SitD	Smoke	Wait	Walk	WalkD	WalkT	Avg. (↓)
Transformer (Fix-attn)	42.0	42.1	41.3	54.2	46.6	51.1	43.8	49.3	46.0	48.6	53.5	57.7	50.2	55.7	53.1	48.7
Naive Transformer	31.5	35.5	33.3	41.7	39.5	43.5	33.6	37.8	37.8	66.6	35.2	47.5	46.8	41.7	50.0	41.5
PoseGate-Former (Fix-bias)	28.9	33.5	30.9	37.3	40.4	38.5	33.7	37.9	34.5	43.5	33.9	45.5	41.5	46.6	41.6	37.9
PoseGate-Former	32.0	34.3	26.9	34.6	37.8	35.7	27.8	38.2	34.9	38.7	31.4	39.8	38.5	37.0	40.2	35.2

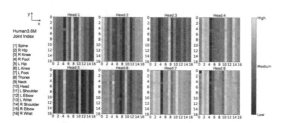

Fig. 4. Visualization of multi-head self-attentions in PoseGate-Former, the x-axis indicates input queries and y-axis show the predicted outputs. Yellow color indicates a stronger attention. (Color figure online)

4.4   Self-attention Visualization

To illustrate the multi-head self-attention mechanism, we visualized the self-attention scores of PoseGate-Former. As shown in Fig. 4, we can find that the Head 1 focuses on Thorax joint, Head 2 focuses Spine joint. Head 4 builds the connection among joints (11, 12, 13) and (14, 15, 16) which are grouped as left arm and right arm. For Head 8, it connects joints (2, 3, 4) which belong to right leg. These attention maps show that the PoseGate-Former successfully finds the relationship between key joints, and these relationships are hard to learn by fully-connect neural networks. This could explain why a Transformer architecture can significantly improve the performance of 3D pose estimation model.

5   Conclusions

In this work, we develop a Transformer based PoseGate-Former to lift 2D poses to 3D domain by using a weakly supervised learning approach. We found that the multi-head self-attention architecture in Transformer can easily learn the relationship among human key joints, which can significantly improve the performance of 3D human pose estimator. More importantly, our trainable gate mechanism can effectively reduce the possibility of overfitting in some specific action categories compared with the naive Transformer architecture and further improve the performance of PoseGate-Former.

References

1. Gulrajani, I., Ahmed, F., Arjovsky, M., Dumoulin, V., Courville, A.C.: Improved training of Wasserstein GANs. CoRR abs/1704.00028 (2017). http://arxiv.org/abs/1704.00028
2. Ionescu, C., Papava, D., Olaru, V., Sminchisescu, C.: Human3.6m: large scale datasets and predictive methods for 3D human sensing in natural environments. IEEE Trans. Pattern Anal. Mach. Intell. **36**(7), 1325–1339 (2014). https://doi.org/10.1109/TPAMI.2013.248
3. Lee, K., Lee, I., Lee, S.: Propagating LSTM: 3D pose estimation based on joint interdependency. In: Ferrari, V., Hebert, M., Sminchisescu, C., Weiss, Y. (eds.) ECCV 2018. LNCS, vol. 11211, pp. 123–141. Springer, Cham (2018). https://doi.org/10.1007/978-3-030-01234-2_8
4. Li, W., Liu, H., Ding, R., Liu, M., Wang, P.: Lifting transformer for 3D human pose estimation in video. CoRR abs/2103.14304 (2021). https://arxiv.org/abs/2103.14304
5. Luo, C., Chu, X., Yuille, A.L.: OriNet: a fully convolutional network for 3D human pose estimation. vol. abs/1811.04989 (2018). http://arxiv.org/abs/1811.04989
6. Martinez, J., Hossain, R., Romero, J., Little, J.J.: A simple yet effective baseline for 3D human pose estimation. In: Proceedings of the IEEE International Conference on Computer Vision (ICCV), October 2017
7. Park, S., Hwang, J., Kwak, N.: 3D human pose estimation using convolutional neural networks with 2D pose information. In: Hua, G., Jégou, H. (eds.) ECCV 2016. LNCS, vol. 9915, pp. 156–169. Springer, Cham (2016). https://doi.org/10.1007/978-3-319-49409-8_15

8. Pavlakos, G., Zhou, X., Derpanis, K.G., Daniilidis, K.: Coarse-to-fine volumetric prediction for single-image 3D human pose. In: Proceedings of the IEEE Conference on Computer Vision and Pattern Recognition (CVPR), July 2017

9. Pavllo, D., Feichtenhofer, C., Grangier, D., Auli, M.: 3D human pose estimation in video with temporal convolutions and semi-supervised training. In: Proceedings of the IEEE/CVF Conference on Computer Vision and Pattern Recognition (CVPR), June 2019

10. Sigal, L., Balan, A.O., Black, M.J.: HumanEva: synchronized video and motion capture dataset and baseline algorithm for evaluation of articulated human motion. Int. J. Comput. Vis. **87**, 4–27 (2009). https://doi.org/10.1007/s11263-009-0273-6

11. Wandt, B., Rosenhahn, B.: RepNet: weakly supervised training of an adversarial reprojection network for 3D human pose estimation, June 2019

12. Zheng, C., Zhu, S., Mendieta, M., Yang, T., Chen, C., Ding, Z.: 3D human pose estimation with spatial and temporal transformers. CoRR abs/2103.10455 (2021). https://arxiv.org/abs/2103.10455

13. Zhou, X., Huang, Q., Sun, X., Xue, X., Wei, Y.: Towards 3D human pose estimation in the wild: a weakly-supervised approach. In: Proceedings of the IEEE International Conference on Computer Vision (ICCV), October 2017

14. Zhou, X., Sun, X., Zhang, W., Liang, S., Wei, Y.: Deep kinematic pose regression. In: Hua, G., Jégou, H. (eds.) ECCV 2016. LNCS, vol. 9915, pp. 186–201. Springer, Cham (2016). https://doi.org/10.1007/978-3-319-49409-8_17

Pancreatic Neoplasm Image Translation Based on Feature Correlation Analysis of Cross-Phase Image

Yizhou Chen[1], Zihan Wei[1], Xu-Hua Yang[1], Zhicheng Li[2], Qiu Guan[1(✉)], and Feng Chen[3(✉)]

[1] College of Computer Science and Technology, Zhejiang University of Technology, Hangzhou, China
gq@zjut.edu.cn
[2] Shenzhen Institutes of Advanced Technology, Chinese Academy of Sciences, Shenzhen, China
[3] The First Affiliated Hospital, Zhejiang University School of Medicine, Hangzhou, China
chenfenghz@zju.edu.cn

Abstract. CT arterial phase images can provide a powerful auxiliary to formulate pancreatic neoplasm diagnosis and treatment plans. In the absence of such images, we can use the image translation model convert CT images of other phases into CT arterial phase synthetic images. Under the supervision of manual labeling by experts or pixel-level labeling, the model can achieve better performance. However, for pancreatic neoplasm image translation, such labels are usually scarce. In this regard, we use the easily obtained paired but unaligned cross-phase real pancreatic neoplasm images as labels and constructs a cross-phase image feature correlation analysis-based image translation method (CFCA-IT). This method analyzes the image feature correlation between the synthetic images and real images and takes it as the training constraint of the translation model. Simulation experiments show that CFCA-IT can further improve the translation performance of the five state-of-the-art translation models.

Keywords: Pancreatic neoplasm images · Image translation · Correlation analysis

1 Introduction

CT arterial phase images are significant for highlighting the anatomical structure content of pancreatic neoplasms, providing important reference information

This work is supported in part by the National Natural Science Foundation of China (61802347, 61972347, 61773348, U20A20171), and the Natural Science Foundation of Zhejiang Province (LGF20H180002, LY21F020027, LSD19H180003).

T. Mantoro et al. (Eds.): ICONIP 2021, CCIS 1517, pp. 275–282, 2021.
https://doi.org/10.1007/978-3-030-92310-5_32

for doctors to formulate diagnosis and treatment plans. However, due to the limitation of medical image acquisition methods, CT arterial phase images of some patients are not acquired.

The image translation model [1] can convert real CT images of other phases into CT arterial phase synthetic images. Ideally, the anatomical structure content of the synthetic image is consistent with the original image. Generally, the more accurate the content of the anatomical structure of the synthetic image, the more accurate the lesion information contained in the image. It is worth noting that when the label supervises the training of the image translation model, the performance of the model can usually be improved.

The annotation of doctor can be used as a label of medical image translation training [2,3]. However, expert annotation is usually expensive [4]. For example, the benign/malignant category label of pancreatic neoplasms is usually obtained by puncture diagnosis.

Medical images with consistent anatomical structure content (i.e., aligned images) can provide pixel-level labels for image translation training [5–7]. However, the anatomical structure of the abdomen is prone to deformation. Even if the interval between two image acquisitions is short, the pancreatic neoplasm anatomy of the paired images from the same patient and the same site is usually unaligned. Meanwhile, the performance of the existing image registration technology is limited, and it is difficult for these pancreatic neoplasm images to be manually aligned [8]. Therefore, this type of label is difficult to obtain.

In summary, it is important to search for more readily available labels and use them for training pancreatic neoplasm image translation. Usually, paired but unaligned pancreatic images can be obtained through image acquisition. Experts can select the region of interest (ROI) for pancreatic neoplasms by visual observation. In other words, paired but unaligned pancreatic neoplasm images without category labels are relatively easy to obtain.

As far as we know, paired but unaligned brain images have provided constraints for translation training. However, in previous research, many aligned images are used to construct the constraint mechanism (note: since the anatomical structure of brain is not easily deformed, the aligned images can be obtained). It is difficult to achieve this mechanism for pancreatic neoplasms because of the lack of aligned images.

In order to construct a constraint mechanism suitable for pancreatic neoplasm images, we utilize the Canonical Correlation Analysis (CCA) [9]. CCA has powerful cross-domain sample feature analysis capabilities, which can accurately analyze their feature correlation even for images and text that do not have a pixel-level alignment relationship [9]. In the case of unaligned images, we use CCA to construct a cross-phase feature correlation analysis module (i.e., CFCAM) to assist the training of pancreatic neoplasm image translation module (i.e., ITM). Our contribution is as follows.

1) Constructed a cross-phase image feature correlation analysis-based image translation method (CFCA-IT), which can make paired but unaligned pancreatic neoplasm image provide constraints for translation training;

2) Constructed an iterative training mechanism between the feature correlation analysis module and the translation module so that the two modules can be trained better;

3) The existing translation model can be freely embedded in the proposed method, and compared with the original model before embedding, the translation performance has been improved.

2   Proposed Method

As shown in Fig. 1, CFCA-IT consists of the existing translation models ITM and CFCAM. According to the real image batch X_{S_i} in the source phase S_i, the synthetic image batch Y^* and the real image batch Y in the target phase T, L_{CFCAM} and L_{ITMsup} are calculated. We constructed training based on adversarial learning [10].

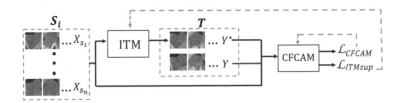

Fig. 1. Framework diagram of CFCA-IT. X_{S_i} is the source phase real image batch, Y/Y^* is the target phase real/synthetic image batch; X_{S_i}/Y is pair but not aligned.

2.1   Optimization of the CFCAM

The CFCAM consists of feature extractor f and CCA, and its training process is shown in Fig. 2.

1) Feature matrix extraction. Each corresponding f extracts the feature matrix H of each phase batch.

$$H_{S_1}, H_{S_2}, ..., H_{S_n} = f_{S_1}(X_{S_1}), f_{S_2}(X_{s_2}), ..., f_{S_n}(X_{S_n})$$
$$H_T, H_T^* = f_T(Y), f_T(G(X_{S_1}, X_{S_2}, ..., X_{S_n}))$$

(1)

Where, G is the image translation operation of ITM, $Y^* = G(X_{S_1}, X_{S_2}, ..., X_{S_n})$. The mainstream ResNet [11] is adopted as f in this research.

2) Feature matrix matching. "Group-i" obtained from H_{S_i}, H_T, and H_T^* is used for SLM_i training. Where, the image features in the same column of H_{S_i}/H_T come from paired but unaligned cross-phase images (i.e., the labels of this study). The images corresponding to the features of the same column of $\widetilde{H_{S_i}}/H_T$ are unpaired (Note: the sequence of the vector columns in H_{S_i} is randomized to obtain $\widetilde{H_{S_i}}$).

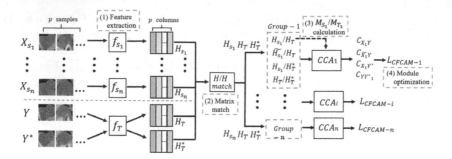

Fig. 2. The illustration of the CFCAM optimization. Y^* is converted from the source phase image, f is the feature extraction network, H is the feature matrix, and M_S/M_T is the mapping function.

3) Mapping function calculation. We calculate the mappings M_{S_i} and M_{T_i} of the S_i and T features to the shared subspace according to the H_{S_i}/H_T.

$$\underset{(M_{S_i}, M_{T_i})}{argmax}\ corr(M_{S_i}(H_{S_i}), M_{T_i}(H_T)) \tag{2}$$

Where, corr(.) is the correlation calculation operation of the mapped features. This process does not involve parameter learning [9].

4) Module optimization. The feature correlation C is calculated.

$$
\begin{aligned}
C_{X_iY} &= corr\left(M_{S_i}(H_{S_i}), M_{T_i}(H_T)\right); C_{\widetilde{X_i}Y} = corr(M_{S_i}(\widetilde{H_{S_i}}), M_{T_i}(H_T)) \\
C_{X_iY^*} &= corr(M_{S_i}(H_{S_i}), M_{T_i}(H_T^*)); C_{YY^*_i} = corr(M_{T_i}(H_T), M_{T_i}(H_T^*))
\end{aligned}
\tag{3}
$$

Because the correlation of the paired image is higher than that of the unpaired image, C_{X_iY} should be larger, and $C_{\widetilde{X_i}Y}$ should be smaller. Furthermore, in the CFCAM training phase, we expect this module can find the structure content deviation between Y^* and Y. Therefore, $C_{X_iY^*}$ and $C_{YY^*_i}$ should also be smaller.

$$\mathcal{L}_{CFCAM\text{-}i} = |log(\frac{C_{X_iY}}{k}) + log(1 - \frac{C_{\widetilde{X_i}Y}}{k}) + log(1 - \frac{C_{X_iY^*}}{k}) + log(1 - \frac{C_{YY^*_i}}{k})| \tag{4}$$

Where, k is a constant used for normalization, which can make $\frac{c}{k} \in [0, 1]$ [9]. By minimizing $\mathcal{L}_{CFCAM\text{-}i}$, the parameter of f_{S_i} can be updated. For f_T, the parameter update process is subject to all $\mathcal{L}_{CFCAM\text{-}i}$ feedback.

$$\mathcal{L}_{CFCAM} = \frac{\sum_1^n \mathcal{L}_{CFCAM\text{-}i}}{n} \tag{5}$$

2.2   Optimization of the ITM

As shown in Fig. 3, when both f_{S_i}/f_T and M_{X_i}/M_{T_i} of CFCAM are fixed, we expect through ITM training, the output Y^* has accurate structural content. In other words, both $C_{X_iY^*}$ and $C_{YY^*_i}$ should be as large as possible in this phase.

$$\mathcal{L}_{ITMsup} = |\sum_1^n (log(\frac{C_{X_iY^*}}{k}) + log(\frac{C_{YY^*_i}}{k}))|/n \qquad (6)$$

The loss term can constrain ITM training.

$$\mathcal{L}_{ITM} = \mathcal{L}_{ITMself} + \lambda \times \mathcal{L}_{ITMsup} \qquad (7)$$

Where, $\mathcal{L}_{ITMself}$ is the optimization item that comes with ITM; λ is the super parameter. For testing the performance of CFCA-IT, we set λ to 1. By minimizing $\mathcal{L}_{ITM}$, ITM is optimized.

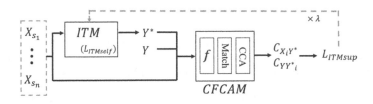

Fig. 3. The illustration of the ITM optimization. $\mathcal{L}_{ITMself}$ is the optimization item that comes with ITM.

3   Experiments

3.1   Datasets and Implementation Details

We used 1066 pairs of CT venous/plain/arterial (i.e., CTV/CTP/CTA) ROIs from 79 patients in a partner hospital. Each pair of ROI images is paired but not aligned, and both images are resized to 64 ∗ 64 pixels. CycleGAN [1], MUNIT [12], and SC-CycleGAN [13] are adopted as One to One; mmGAN [5] and Hi-Net [6] are adopted as Many-to-One in turn.

Five-fold cross-validation experiments are performed on a gtx2080TI GPU with 11 GB of memory, the epoch of training is 200, and the batch size is 16. We use the classification results to evaluate the synthesis performance indirectly. ResNet18 [11] is adopted as the classifier, which is trained by CTA real samples and tests the classification accuracy of CTA synthetic samples. Because the accuracy of the classifier in this paper on the CTA real benign/malignant neoplasms is 539/611 and 412/455, respectively, we only count the classification accuracy of the synthetic image corresponding to 948 correctly classified samples.

3.2   Comparison Analysis

1) One-to-One Experiment. The qualitative results of the experiment are shown in Fig. 4. Each CTV/CTP/CTA real images are paired but unaligned. It can be seen from this image that when the ITM is embedded in the CFCA-IT, the texture detail clarity of the CTA synthetic image is improved.

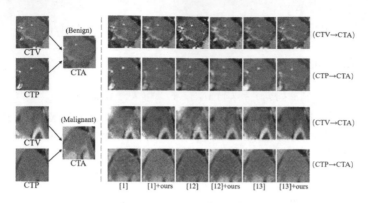

Fig. 4. The synthetic image obtained from the One-to-One experiment. The CTV/CTP on the left of the dotted line are respectively used as the input of ITM to obtain the CTA synthetic image. Where, "+ours" represents ITM is embedded in the CFCA-IT.

Table 1. The accuracy of the CTA synthetic image obtained by One-to-One ITM in the trained classifier.

	CTV → CTA			CTP → CTA		
	Ben.	Mal.	Total	Ben.	Mal.	Total
CycleGAN [1]	83.96%	84.22%	84.07%	81.16%	80.83%	81.01%
[1] + Ours	**87.69%**	**88.25%**	**87.97%**	**84.33%**	**86.41%**	**85.23%**
MUNIT [12]	74.06%	76.21%	75.00%	75.56%	77.67%	76.48%
[12] + Ours	**78.36%**	**79.37%**	**78.80%**	**79.85%**	**81.55%**	**80.59%**
SC-CycleGAN [13]	85.45%	87.62%	86.39%	82.46%	83.01%	82.70%
[13] + Ours	**89.55%**	**90.53%**	**89.98%**	**87.31%**	**87.14%**	**87.24%**

As shown in Table 1, the accuracy is improved when ITM is embedded in the CFCA-IT (in this experiment, the accuracy is improved by at least 3.59%). It proved that with the help of the CFCA-IT, the anatomical content of the pancreatic neoplasm image is better preserved.

For SC-CycleGAN [13], this model integrates the structural consistency loss based on unsupervised learning into the training of CycleGAN. By comparing with "[1]+ours" and "SC-CycleGAN [13]", it can be obtained that the CFCA-IT has more substantial constraints on ITM than those based on unsupervised learning.

2) Many-to-One experiment. As shown in Fig. 5, when the pixel-level supervision item constrains the ITM, the obtained CTA synthetic image will be blurred, as shown in the images of the "Ori." and "Ori.+ours" columns. It proved that when the images are not aligned, the pixel-level supervision used will negatively impact ITM training.

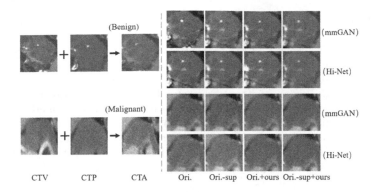

Fig. 5. The synthetic image obtained from the Many-to-One experiment. "Ori.", and "-sup" represent the original ITM, and the loss based on supervised learning is ablated, respectively.

Table 2. The quantitative classification results of the CTV synthetic image obtained by Many-to-One ITM in the trained classifier.

	mmGAN [5]			Hi-Net [6]		
	Ben.	Mal.	Total	Ben.	Mal.	Total
Ori.	79.29%	82.28%	80.59%	78.73%	81.31%	79.85%
Ori.+ours	85.26%	86.89%	85.97%	85.45%	86.41%	85.86%
Ori.-sup	87.13%	88.35%	87.66%	88.99%	89.81%	89.35%
Ori.-sup+ours	**90.86%**	**91.75%**	**91.24%**	**92.35%**	**93.45%**	**92.83%**

The indirect quantitative results are shown in Table 2. By comparing the accuracy of "Ori."/"Ori.-sup" and "Ori.+ours"/"Ori.-sup+ours", it can be obtained that when the pixel-level supervision item of ITM is ablated, the performance of ITM is improved.

4 Conclusion

Because the pancreatic neoplasm image translation model is challenging to achieve the ideal performance due to the lack of label supervision, this research uses the relatively easy-to-obtain paired but unaligned images as labels and constructs the CFCA-IT. The simulation experiment on the pancreatic neoplasm dataset from the cooperative hospital shows that the CFCA-IT can further improve the performances of the five state-of-the-art image translation models. As a result, the accuracy of the obtained CTA synthetic image in the classifier is improved by at least 3.48%.

References

1. Zhu, J., Park, T., Isola, P., Efros, A.A.: Unpaired image-to-image translation using cycle-consistent adversarial networks. In: IEEE International Conference on Computer Vision (ICCV), pp. 2242–2251 (2017)
2. Cai, J., Zhang, Z., Cui, L., Zheng, Y., Yang, L.: Towards cross-modal organ translation and segmentation: a cycle-and shape-consistent generative adversarial network. Med. Image Anal. **52**, 174–184 (2019)
3. Wang, C.J., Rost, N.S., Golland, P.: Spatial-intensity transform GANs for high fidelity medical image-to-image translation. In: Martel, A.L., et al. (eds.) MICCAI 2020. LNCS, vol. 12262, pp. 749–759. Springer, Cham (2020). https://doi.org/10.1007/978-3-030-59713-9_72
4. Xing, F., Bennett, T., Ghosh, D.: Adversarial domain adaptation and pseudo-labeling for cross-modality microscopy image quantification. In: Shen, D., et al. (eds.) MICCAI 2019. LNCS, vol. 11764, pp. 740–749. Springer, Cham (2019). https://doi.org/10.1007/978-3-030-32239-7_82
5. Chartsias, A., Joyce, T., Giuffrida, M.V., Tsaftaris, S.A.: Multimodal MR synthesis via modality-invariant latent representation. IEEE Trans. Med. Imaging **37**, 803–814 (2018)
6. Zhou, T., Fu, H., Chen, G., Shen, J., Shao, L.: Hi-Net: hybrid-fusion network for multi-modal MR image synthesis. IEEE Trans. Med. Imaging **39**, 2772–2781 (2020)
7. Shen, L., et al.: Multi-Domain image completion for random missing input data. IEEE Trans. Med. Imaging **40**, 1113–1122 (2021)
8. Wang, M., Li, P.: A review of deformation models in medical image registration. J. Med. Biol. Eng. **39**, 1C17 (2019)
9. Hardoon, D.R., Szedmak, S., Shawe-Taylor, J.: Canonical correlation analysis: an overview with application to learning methods. Neural Comput. **16**, 2639–2664 (2004)
10. Goodfellow, I.J., et al.: Generative adversarial nets. In: Neural Information Processing System, vol. 2, p. 2672C2680 (2014)
11. He, K., Zhang, X., Ren, S., Sun, J.: Deep residual learning for image recognition. In: IEEE Conference on Computer Vision and Pattern Recognition (CVPR), pp. 770–778 (2016)
12. Huang, X., Liu, M.-Y., Belongie, S., Kautz, J.: Multimodal unsupervised image-to-image translation. In: Ferrari, V., Hebert, M., Sminchisescu, C., Weiss, Y. (eds.) ECCV 2018. LNCS, vol. 11207, pp. 179–196. Springer, Cham (2018). https://doi.org/10.1007/978-3-030-01219-9_11
13. Yang, H., et al.: Unsupervised MR-to-CT synthesis using structure-constrained CycleGAN. In: IEEE Transactions on Medical Imaging, vol. 39, pp. 4249–4261 (2020)

Deformable Convolution and Semi-supervised Learning in Point Clouds for Aneurysm Classification and Segmentation

Yan Hu[1], Erik Meijering[1], Yong Xia[2], and Yang Song[1(✉)]

[1] School of Computer Science and Engineering, The University of New South Wales, Sydney, NSW 2052, Australia
yang.song1@unsw.edu.au
[2] School of Computer Science, Northwestern Polytechnical University, Xi'an, China

Abstract. Intracranial aneurysm is a life-threatening and high-risk abnormality. In practice, both aneurysm classification and segmentation are very important for diagnosis and treatment planning. There have been various studies of automatic diagnosis of aneurysms based on medical images with 2D image processing methods. However, the diagnosis of an aneurysm based on 3D models is potentially much more accurate than on 2D images. The edge of an aneurysm is much clearer with 3D visualization, and the complicated and time-consuming annotation on 2D images can be avoided. Here we propose a deep neural network incorporating deformable point convolution and self-attention to improve the classification and segmentation performance for 3D point clouds. In addition, we introduce semi-supervised learning to address the problem of class imbalance. Our experimental results on a public 3D point clouds dataset show that our model outperforms several state-of-the-art deep learning models.

Keywords: Point clouds · Aneurysm · Deformable convolution · Self-attention · Semi-supervised learning

1 Introduction

Despite decades of advanced medical research, the incidence and mortality rates of intracranial aneurysms are still high. The prevalence of intracranial aneurysm in the general population ranges from 0.4% to 3% [10]. Increased availability and widespread access to medical imaging such as Magnetic Resonance Imaging (MRI) and Computerized Tomography (CT) make it easier to screen and detect asymptomatic and unruptured cerebral aneurysms at early stages. However, the heavy workload and subjectiveness of doctors may lead to misdiagnosis when reading medical images. Thus it would be advantageous to develop computer-aided approaches to automatically analyze aneurysm cases from large scale medical images.

Intuitively, classification and segmentation results of 3D models can be better and more reliable than 2D models because 3D models are able to learn more

T. Mantoro et al. (Eds.): ICONIP 2021, CCIS 1517, pp. 283–290, 2021.
https://doi.org/10.1007/978-3-030-92310-5_33

comprehensive spatial context information. However, time complexity and computing resources of voxel-based 3D models can be very high. Point clouds provide a new approach to describe 3D information. With successful applications in natural scenes, point clouds have been introduced in medical image analysis area as well [3,5]. For the topic of aneurysm analysis, IntrA is the first public point clouds dataset [14]. Compared with other natural point clouds datasets, IntrA is small and highly imbalanced, thus adding further challenges. The IntrA dataset contains 2025 cases for classification and 116 cases for segmentation. Furthermore, it also exhibits high class imbalance with ratio about 5:1 for classification and 3:1 for segmentation.

As for point clouds, a major challenge is that they exhibit an irregular structure. Standard convolution operations are designed to operate on regular grid structures which naturally contain a spatial ordering among image pixels. Point clouds, however, are unordered data and the ordering of points or geometric transformations on the points should not affect the global category or segmentation of the points. To achieve rotation invariance, Chen et al. proposed PointNet [8], using learnable transformation matrix and symmetrical function, global pooing to maintain invariance to orientation changes. To enhance the learning of local feature presentation, Chen et al. proposed PointNet++ [9], in which the point set is divided into overlapping local areas and global features are learned hierarchically based on the features extracted from small geometric structures. Yang et al. [7] designed χ-transformations modules, helping simultaneously weight and permute the input features. Zhang et al. [16] proposed an RIConv operator, which takes low-level rotation invariant geometric features as input and then turns the convolution into 1D by a simple binning approach. In PointConv [13], convolution is defined as a Monte Carlo estimation of the continuous 3D convolution with respect to an importance sampling, making the network work on irregular structures point clouds and realizes the invariance of displacement. These approaches, however, are still not fully invariant and this has limited the network performance. To address this challenge better, we design a *deformable point convolution* as the basic components of our model, in which we predict an offset for each convolution operation within the filter window to transform the input. In addition, we incorporate the self-attention mechanism into the network so that the model would further exploit the spatial contexts.

In summary, our main contributions are: 1) We design a Deformable Point Convolution Network (DPCNet) for 3D point clouds classification and segmentation. 2) We develop a deformable point convolution module, in which the convolution operations are performed with an adaptive, irregularly shaped filter to better achieve ordering invariance. 3) We design a semi-supervised learning framework with pseudo cases to improve the network performance for small and imbalanced point clouds dataset. The proposed method is evaluated using the IntrA dataset with 5-fold cross validation and shows improved performance over several other state-of-the-art models. Through ablation experiments, we also demonstrate that semi-supervised training brings performance gain for both classification and segmentation of aneurysms.

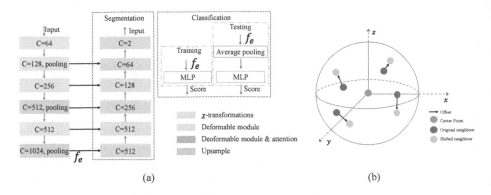

(a)   (b)

Fig. 1. Architecture of the proposed network (a) and illustration of deformable convolution (b). In (b), the red point is the center, similarly to the central pixel in 2D convolutions. Blue points are the searched four nearest neighbors. Deformable convolution generates various transformations for scale, (anisotropic) aspect ratio and rotation through offset (shown as black arrows). (Color figure online)

2 Method

In this work, we develop a Deformable Point Convolution Network (DPC-Net), which takes a collection of randomly sorted points as inputs and outputs aneurysm classification or segmentation results. The key component of this network is the deformable convolution operation which is extended from 2D image models. For each convolutional layer, the deformable convolution first predicts an offset for each point within the filter window, and then performs the convolution based on the deformed filter rather than the regular grid-based convolution. Self-attention is also adopted into the network to further improve the feature representation learning. Overall, the network model is embedded in a semi-supervised learning framework, by incorporating additional data with pseudo labels to address the class imbalance problem.

2.1 Network Architecture

Figure 1(a) depicts the architecture of our proposed network. The classification network and segmentation network share the same encoder. The encoder comprises a stack of interleaving layers, including χ-transformations, deformable convolution, and deformable convolution with self-attention. This encoder design is motivated by our objective of achieving invariance in feature learning. Specifically, we consider that a natural solution to invariance is to build additional branches to predict a transformation matrix and involve this matrix into the feature extraction. To do this, we first utilize the χ-transformations [7], which has been proposed specifically for point clouds for improving the invariance handling. However, we notice that while χ-transformations permute input points for order invariance, they lacks the ability to model rotation invariance. Therefore, we further incorporate deformable convolutions (Sect. 2.2) to introduce more flexibility in the convolution operation. On the other hand, there are interpolation steps in deformable convolution, which means high computational cost. To reduce the complexity, we thus alternate χ-transformations and deformable convolutions in the encoder. Moreover, to further exploit the high-level contextual information, we incorporate self-attention (Sect. 2.3) in the later layers of the encoder.

Following the encoder, the classification head includes multiple fully connected layers with 256, 128, 32 and 2 nodes. The segmentation network has an encoder-decoder architecture, which has the same encoder as the classification network. The decoder contains a stack of upsampling modules, composed of interpolation and convolution layers. Also, skip-connections are added between the encoder and decoder.

2.2   Deformable Point Convolution

In CNNs for 2D images, convolutional filter is restricted to a small local region, in which the relative position between different pixels is fixed, and the convolution operation lacks the capability to handle geometric transformations. Deformable convolution on 2D images [4] adds an offset to each pixel, allowing the relative position for each sampling location to vary. Intuitively, the extension of deformable convolution to 3D point clouds help improve invarance in the network model.

Specifically, point clouds are represented as a set of 3D points $\{p_i | i = 1, ..., n\}$, where each point p_i is represented by its coordinates (x, y, z) and features such as color. With this irregular structure, the filter window of a point is constructed based on its neighbors, as shown in Fig. 1(b). With deformable convolution, an offset $\Delta p = (\Delta x, \Delta y, \Delta z)$ would be predicted for each neighboring point to enable free-form deformation of the original sampling space. The offsets are learned from the preceding feature maps, via additional convolution layers.

Let F^l denote the input feature of layer l, a central point's coordinate is represented by $p_0 = (x_0, y_0, z_0)$. The coordinates of the center's neighbors are $P = \{(x_1, y_1, z_1), (x_2, y_2, z_2), ..., (x_k, y_k, z_k)\}$, where k means the number of neighbors used. For the point $\{F_0^l, p_0\}$, its output after a standard convolution is defined as:

$$F_0^{(l+1)} = activation(\sum_{p_n \in P} w(p_n) F_0^l(p_n)) \tag{1}$$

where p_n enumerates the neighbors in P and $w(p_n)$ denotes the weights of convolution at location p_n. With deformable convolutions, the sampled locations can shift, and with a shifting vector Δp_n, Eq. (1) becomes:

$$F_0^{(l+1)} = activation(\sum_{p_n \in P} w(p_n) F_0^l(p_n + \Delta p_n)) \tag{2}$$

When organizing the new input feature $F(p_n + \Delta p_n)$, three nearest neighbours are searched in the space P and then bilinear interpolation is used to obtain the shifted feature. The details of deformable convolution are described in Table 1.

Table 1. Algorithm of deformable point convolution.

Input	Coordinates $\{p_1, p_2, \ldots, p_N\}$ and corresponding features $\{F_1, F_2, \ldots, F_N\}$, N is the number of input points
Step 1	Sample a subset with N' points from input $\{p_1, p_2, \ldots, p_N\}$ and $\{F_1, F_2, \ldots, F_N\}$, representing as P_C and F_C
Step 2	MLP on N' central points. $F_C = MLP(F_C)$
Step 3	MLP on N' central points' nearest neighbors: $F_K = MLP(F_K)$, F_K is feature collection of KNN
Step 4	Concatenate. $F = \{F_C, F_K\}$
Step 5	$Output = conv(F)$

2.3 Self-attention

Our self-attention module is designed based on the Transformer model [11]. The dimension of the input is $B \times N \times C$, where B is the batch size, N is the number of input points and C is the number of feature maps (channels). Three MLPs with the same hyper-parameters are operated on the input and the outputs are called Q, K, V, respectively and they are split into groups by channel axis. Then we use scaled dot-product attention over the split feature maps following the definition (Eq. 3) in [11], where d_k is dimension of K. Finally, all feature maps are concatenated together as the output.

$$Attention(Q, K, V) = softmax(\frac{QK^T}{\sqrt{d_k}})V \qquad (3)$$

2.4 Semi-supervised Training

The IntrA dataset is small and imbalanced as described in Sect. 1. Some studies have demonstrated that using synthetic training data with pseudo labels can be useful to improve network performance when the training data is small and imbalanced [12,15]. Inspired by these studies, we design a semi-supervised learning approach to train our classification and segmentation network.

Generating Training Case. For image data, we can generate new cases through transforming source images and averaging pixel values to get new images such as MixMatch [2]. However, with point data represented by coordinates, we cannot simply add coordinates to generate new data. Therefore, we design a technique to fuse two cases in a geometrically meaningful way. Specifically, to address the problem of different scales in two sets of point clouds, the coordinates of points are first normalized to distribute on the surface of a sphere through dividing by the modulus length $(x', y', z') = \left(\frac{x}{\rho}, \frac{y}{\rho}, \frac{z}{\rho}, \right)$. Points of two cases are then concatenated using the new coordinates. Then for classification, we randomly sample a fixed number of points from the fused data as the newly generated case. For segmentation, since the network can work on inputs with various numbers of points, we directly use the fused data as the generated case.

Semi-supervised Learning. To apply semi-supervised learning, we first train a model f using the original labeled data D_l, and apply it to predict pseudo labels y' for unlabeled generated cases D_U. Here, we suppose when the predicted probability of an unlabeled data is larger than a threshold γ for class i, the pseudo label y' will be set to i. Otherwise, the generated case is discarded. In segmentation, we select points with the predicted probability higher than the threshold γ and assign labels for these points based on probability. Finally, the labeled data D_l and unlabeled data D_U with pseudo labels are combined as the training data to update the model f.

During the training, we use cross-entropy as the loss function and Adam as the optimizer. The batch size is 64, the learning rate starts at 0.01 and decays to 10^{-6}, and the threshold of generating pseudo labels is 0.90.

3   Experiment

3.1   Dataset and Preprocessing

We use the public 3D point clouds dataset IntrA [14] in this study. The original data was generated from 103 3D models of blood vessels in the brain reconstructed from 2D MRA images. In this dataset, 1909 blood vessel segments are generated automatically from the complete models, including 1694 healthy vessel segments and 215 aneurysm segments for the classification task. In addition, 116 aneurysm segments were annotated manually by medical experts for the segmentation task. The number of points in each case ranges from 500 to 4000. We randomly re-sample each case to 1024 points, that is, some points are duplicated in the input of the model if the total number of points is less than 1024. We also performed data augmentation, including oversampling for the minority class, and rotation and scaling for all cases.

3.2   Setup and Results

The proposed method is evaluated by five-fold cross validation following the dataset splits provided by [14], and we follow the benchmark in [14] for performance comparison. Specifically, for classification, we use F1-score and accuracy as the evaluation metrics; for segmentation, we evaluated Intersection-Over-Union (IOU) and Dice Similarity Coefficient (DSC). Segmentation and classification models are firstly trained on the dataset ModelNet40 [1] for initialization except for the last classification layer and the decoder for segmentation.

As shown in Table 2, our model achieves the highest accuracy on aneurysm classification compared with other top-performing methods reported in [14]. Especially for the minority class, aneurysm, the accuracy improves by 3.79 % compared to the previous state-of-the-art achieved by PointNet++. Though the highest accuracy of vessel is achieved by SO-Net with 98.88%, our model has the best overall performance since the F1-Score is much higher than the other methods. Table 2 shows the results of segmentation task and our method achieves the

Table 2. Comparison of the proposed method with other top-performing methods in classification and segmentation, respectively.

Method	Classification			Segmentation			
	Ves	Ane	F1-score	IOU		Dice	
				Ves	Ane	Ves	Ane
PointCNN [7]	98.79	81.28	0.9044	93.47	74.11	96.53	81.74
PointNet++ [9]	98.85	88.51	0.9029	93.28	76.53	96.43	84.82
SO-Net [6]	**98.88**	81.21	0.8684	94.42	80.99	97.06	88.41
w/o attention	95.28	87.69	0.8410	92.51	80.92	97.02	86.51
w/o deformable	95.83	88.05	0.8512	93.55	80.45	97.31	85.96
DPCNet	95.87	89.23	0.8551	94.88	80.45	93.71	85.96
DPCNet + semi	98.82	**92.30**	**0.9253**	**95.51**	**82.33**	**98.25**	**90.27**

state-of-the-art performance. For the aneurysm class, DSC and IOU are 90.27% and 82.33%, respectively, improved by 1.51% and 0.93% compared to SO-Net. Similarly, DSC and IOU are improved as well for the vessel class.

To better understand the usefulness of the different components in our model, various ablation studies were conducted using the same setup for training.

Deformable Convolution. We first explored the benefits of deformable convolutions. We substituted all deformable convolutions by χ- transformations (χ-conv) in DPCNet (w/o deformable), and the results are illustrated in Table 2. Improvements achieved by the complete DPCNet suggest that deformable convolution can learn more flexible representations and make the network more invariant to the order and rotation of point clouds.

Self-attention. We then analyzed the advantages of the self-attention module. As illustrated by w/o attention (DPCNet without attention modules) and DPCNet in Table 2, performance gain by DPCNet suggests that self-attention can effectively utilize the internal relationship of points and improve the performance of both classification and segmentation.

Semi-supervised Learning. We also investigated semi-supervised learning for addressing the issues with small sample size and imbalanced distribution. The last two rows of Table 2 show that semi-supervised learning by generating cases with pseudo labels of high confidence is highly effective to improve the model overall performance. Specifically, since we generate more cases of the aneurysm class (minority class), the large improvements also indicate our semi-supervised framework is beneficial for handling class imbalance.

4   Conclusion

In this paper, we propose a deep learning model called DPCNet for classification and segmentation in 3D medical point clouds. We designed deformable convolutions to make the network invariant to the order and rotation of input points.

Also, considering the context information of points in one set, we introduce self-attention into our model to learn representation of internal relations. Furthermore, aiming at small and imbalanced datasets, a semi-supervised approach is proposed. Our proposed model is evaluated on IntrA with 5-fold cross validation. Evaluation results show large improvement in the classification accuracy of aneurysm, reaching 92.30%. Moreover, our model achieves the highest performance on DSC and IOU in segmentation compared to current state-of-the-art point clouds networks.

References

1. ModelNet homepage. https://modelnet.cs.princeton.edu/
2. Berthelot, D., Carlini, N., Goodfellow, I., Papernot, N., Oliver, A., Raffel, C.A.: MixMatch: a holistic approach to semi-supervised learning. In: NeurIPS (2019)
3. Bizjak, Ž, Likar, B., Pernuš, F., Špiclin, Ž.: Vascular surface segmentation for intracranial aneurysm isolation and quantification. In: Martel, A.L., et al. (eds.) MICCAI 2020. LNCS, vol. 12266, pp. 128–137. Springer, Cham (2020). https://doi.org/10.1007/978-3-030-59725-2_13
4. Dai, J., et al.: Deformable convolutional networks. In: CVPR, pp. 764–773 (2017)
5. He, J., et al.: Learning hybrid representations for automatic 3D vessel centerline extraction. In: Martel, A.L., et al. (eds.) MICCAI 2020. LNCS, vol. 12266, pp. 24–34. Springer, Cham (2020). https://doi.org/10.1007/978-3-030-59725-2_3
6. Li, J., Chen, B.M., Lee, G.H.: SO-Net: self-organizing network for point cloud analysis. In: CVPR, pp. 9397–9406 (2018)
7. Li, Y., Bu, R., Sun, M., Wu, W., Di, X., Chen, B.: PointCNN: convolution on x-transformed points. In: NeurIPS (2018)
8. Qi, C.R., Su, H., Mo, K., Guibas, L.J.: PointNet: deep learning on point sets for 3D classification and segmentation. In: CVPR, pp. 652–660 (2017)
9. Qi, C.R., Yi, L., Su, H., Guibas, L.J.: PointNet++: deep hierarchical feature learning on point sets in a metric space. In: NeurIPS (2017)
10. Song, J., Lim, Y.C., Ko, I., Kim, J.Y., Kim, D.K.: Prevalence of intracranial aneurysms in patients with systemic vessel aneurysms: A nationwide cohort study. Stroke **51**(1), 115–120 (2020)
11. Vaswani, A., et al.: Attention is all you need. In: NeurIPS (2017)
12. Wei, C., Sohn, K., Mellina, C., Yuille, A., Yang, F.: CReST: a class-rebalancing self-training framework for imbalanced semi-supervised learning. In: CVPR, pp. 10857–10866 (2021)
13. Wu, W., Qi, Z., Fuxin, L.: PointConv: deep convolutional networks on 3D point clouds. In: CVPR, pp. 9621–9630 (2019)
14. Yang, X., Xia, D., Kin, T., Igarashi, T.: IntrA: 3D intracranial aneurysm dataset for deep learning. In: CVPR (2020)
15. Yang, Y., Xu, Z.: Rethinking the value of labels for improving class-imbalanced learning. In: NeurIPS (2020)
16. Zhang, Z., Hua, B.S., Rosen, D.W., Yeung, S.K.: Rotation invariant convolutions for 3D point clouds deep learning. In: 2019 International Conference on 3D Vision (3DV), pp. 204–213. IEEE (2019)

EEG-Based Human Decision Confidence Measurement Using Graph Neural Networks

Le-Dian Liu[1], Rui Li[1], Yu-Zhong Liu[6], Hua-Liang Li[6],
and Bao-Liang Lu[1,2,3,4,5(✉)]

[1] Center for Brain-Like Computing and Machine Intelligence,
Department of Computer Science and Engineering, Shanghai Jiao Tong University,
Shanghai 200240, China
{liuledian,realee,bllu}@sjtu.edu.cn
[2] Center for Brain-Machine Interface and Neuromodulation, RuiJin Hospital,
Shanghai Jiao Tong University School of Medicine, Shanghai 200020, China
[3] RuiJin-Mihoyo Laboratory, RuiJin Hospital, Shanghai Jiao Tong University School
of Medicine, Shanghai 200020, China
[4] Key Laboratory of Shanghai Commission for Intelligent Interaction and Cognitive
Engineering, Shanghai Jiao Tong University, Shanghai 200240, China
[5] Qing Yuan Research Institute, Shanghai Jiao Tong University,
Shanghai 200240, China
[6] Key Laboratory of Occupational Health and Safety of Guangdong, Power Grid Co.,
Ltd., Electric Power Research Institute of Guangdong Power Grid Co., Ltd.,
Guangzhou, China

Abstract. Most of the studies on decision confidence are from the fields
of neuroscience and cognitive science, and existing studies based on deep
neural networks do not exploit the topology of multi-channel EEG signals. In this paper, we propose an attentive simple graph convolutional
network (ASGC) for EEG-based human decision confidence measurement. ASGC captures both coarse-grained and fine-grained inter-channel
relationship by learning a shared adjacency matrix and utilizing self-
attention mechanism, respectively. In addition, we propose a confidence
distribution learning (CDL) loss based on a natural intuition to alleviate
two problems: lack of training samples and label ambiguity. We conduct
experiments on a dataset built for the confidence measurement in a visual
perception task. The experimental results demonstrate advanced performance of our model, achieving an accuracy of 68.83% and F1-score of
66.9%. Finally, we investigate the critical channels for decision confidence
measurement with the attention matrix of EEG channels.

Keywords: EEG · Graph neural network · Decision confidence

1 Introduction

Nowadays, with the development of deep learning algorithms, human participation
is no longer needed in some well-structured problems. Nevertheless, professionals

ⓒ Springer Nature Switzerland AG 2021
T. Mantoro et al. (Eds.): ICONIP 2021, CCIS 1517, pp. 291–298, 2021.
https://doi.org/10.1007/978-3-030-92310-5_34

are still indispensable in complex tasks with high risk, such as business decision making and military remote sensing images interpreting. Unfortunately, it is impossible to always make decisions with honesty and certainty. Hence, developing an objective and stable method to measure human decision confidence is of great practical value.

Human decision confidence is defined as the probability of an overt or covert decision, given the evidence, being correct [11]. Most of the studies on decision confidence are from the fields of neuroscience and cognitive science. They can be broadly divided into two categories depending on the techniques used to acquire data from brains: functional magnetic resonance imaging (fMRI) and electroencephalography (EEG). The studies based on fMRI [1,5,10] indicate that anterior cingulate cortex, prefrontal cortex, posterior parietal cortex, superior parietal lobule, and ventral striatum may be the brain regions closely related to human decision confidence. On the other hand, there are some works that use EEG and event-related potentials (ERPs) to investigate neural patterns of human decision confidence [2,4]. These works have shown that EEG signals recorded in decision-making process can be used to discriminate different degrees of human decision confidence. However, ERP experiments require rapid presentation of the stimulus in a laboratory environment, so they are not feasible to real-world one-trial applications.

In the field of machine learning, there have been some attempts to handle the strict requirements of ERP experiments and improve discrimination performance [7,8]. They leveraged the power of deep learning models to measure human decision confidence from multi-channel EEG recorded in decision-making process. Their experimental results show that EEG signals are capable of measuring different levels of decision confidence and the differential entropy (DE) feature using all 5 bands achieves the best performance. However, their approaches ignore the topological structure of multi-channel EEG. Moreover, their approaches suffer from the limited number of training samples and the label ambiguity of 5-level confidence categorization caused by the huge costs of collecting EEG data and the difficulty of acquiring accurate labels.

Graph neural networks (GNNs) are deep learning approaches applied in the graph domain. In GNNs, convolution operations are the most popular propagation operations, which aims to generalize the classical signal processing operation to the graph domain. Kipf and Welling [6] proposed graph convolutional network (GCN), which simplifies the convolution operation and handles gradient exploding/vanishing problem by introducing a renormalization trick. To reduce the excess complexity of GCNs, SGC [13] removes nonlinearities and merges weight matrices between consecutive layers. All of the models mentioned before use the fixed original adjacency matrices to represent relations between nodes. To capture implicit relations between nodes, Li et al. [9] proposed an Adaptive Graph Convolution Network(AGCN). The residual graph Laplacian is learned by AGCN and added to the original Laplacian matrix. In addition, many advanced works [14,15] in affective computing have successfully adopted GNN to exploit the topology of EEG signals.

In this paper, inspired by biological topology of human brains, we propose an attentive simple graph convolutional network (ASGC) to capture both the coarse-grained and fine-grained topological structure of multi-channel EEG. Specifically, inspired by [12], we use a learnable adjacency matrix to capture coarse-grained inter-channel relations shared among all samples. Furthermore, we use an attention score matrix to capture fine-grained inter-channel relations for each sample in runtime. In addition, we propose a confidence distribution learning (CDL) loss to solve two problems: inadequate training samples and ambiguous labels. Inspired by [3], our CDL loss enforce our model to learn a discrete class distribution rather than a single class for each sample, leading to a better performance of the trained model. We conduct experiments on the dataset built for the confidence measurement in a visual perception task developed in [8]. Our experimental results demonstrate the superior performance of our proposed ASGC compared to other baseline models. Finally, critical channels are explored for decision confidence measurement in the visual perception task.

2 Methodology

In this section, we formulate the confidence classification problem and our attentive simple graph convolutional network (ASGC). Then, we detail the confidence distribution loss (CDL) designed for this specific problem.

2.1 Attentive Simple Graph Convolutional Network

We consider each EEG channel as a graph node, so the input can be represented by a feature matrix $\mathbf{X} \in \mathbb{R}^{n \times d}$, where n denotes the number of channels and d denotes the feature dimension of each channel. For each training sample, a label $\mathbf{Y} \in \{1, 2, ..., C\}$ is given, where C denotes the number of categories.

The overall architecture of ASGC is illustrated in Fig. 1. The SGC is used to exploit the coarse-grained inter-channel relationship. Let $\mathbf{A} \in \mathbb{R}^{n \times n}$ be the learnable adjacency matrix in SGC. We define $\mathbf{S}$ as follows

$$\mathbf{S} = \tilde{\mathbf{D}}^{-\frac{1}{2}} \tilde{\mathbf{A}} \tilde{\mathbf{D}}^{-\frac{1}{2}}, \tag{1}$$

where $\tilde{\mathbf{A}} = \mathbf{A} + \mathbf{I}_n$, and $\tilde{\mathbf{D}}_{ii} = \sum_j \tilde{\mathbf{A}}_{ij}$. This is a renormalization trick introduced by [6] to solve the exploding and vanishing gradient problem. Then, the simple graph convolution network (SGC) can be formulated as follows

$$\mathbf{Z} = \mathbf{S}^K \mathbf{X} \mathbf{W} = \tilde{\mathbf{X}} \mathbf{W}, \tag{2}$$

where $\mathbf{W} \in \mathbb{R}^d \times h$, and h denotes the hidden size. In the graph convolution operation defined in (2), K implies that each node can aggregate information from the nodes that are $K-$hops away. Although $\tilde{\mathbf{X}}$ is still in the same feature space as $\mathbf{X}$, it incorporates the topological information of EEG channels. The final output of SGC $\mathbf{Z}$, linearly transformed from $\tilde{\mathbf{X}}$, is a feature matrix in a high-dimensional feature space. L1 regularization is applied on $\mathbf{A}$ to improve the sparsity of the adjacency matrix.

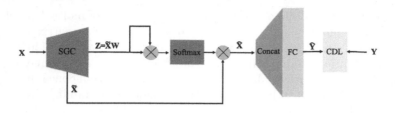

Fig. 1. The overall architecture of our ASGC model.

To further capture the fine-grained topological structure of EEG channels in runtime, we introduce a self-attention module as follows

$$\mathbf{M} = (m_{ij}) = softmax(\mathbf{Z}\mathbf{Z}^T), \tag{3}$$

$$\hat{\mathbf{X}} = \mathbf{M}\tilde{\mathbf{X}}, \tag{4}$$

where $\mathbf{M} \in \mathbb{R}^{n \times n}$ is the attention matrix, and softmax is employed in self-attention to normalize the attention matrix so that $\sum_j m_{ij} = 1$. Essentially, self-attention mechanism can be viewed as the refinement of the input feature using a linear combination of self-values. It worth noting that attention matrix is dynamically calculated for each sample, compared to the fixed adjacency matrix in the SGC.

Finally, rather than use global pooling, we concatenate the feature of all nodes into a vector. Then, the vector is fed into a fully-connected layer with softmax activation function. The output distribution over all classes is computed as follows

$$\hat{\mathbf{Y}} = softmax(\hat{\mathbf{X}}\mathbf{W}^o), \tag{5}$$

where $\mathbf{W}^o \in \mathbb{R}^{h \times C}$, and $\hat{\mathbf{Y}} \in \mathbb{R}^C$.

2.2 Confidence Distribution Loss

The works in [7,8] simply use the one-hot encoding of 5-level confidence labels to calculate the training loss. However, the distance between each pair of classes should not be considered as equal due to the intuition that the confidence level is a continuous state. For example, the distance between level 1 and level 5 should be greater than the distance between level 1 and level 2. Inspired by [3], we propose a confidence distribution loss to address this problem. Specifically, we convert each label $\mathbf{Y} \in \{1, 2, .., C\}$ to a distribution $\tilde{\mathbf{Y}} \in \mathbb{R}^C$. We assume that the distribution should concentrate around the ground-truth label $\mathbf{Y}$ and the distance between the adjacent confidence levels is equal. Thus, it is nature to use the normal distribution with $\mu = \mathbf{Y}$ and σ to construct the target distribution:

$$\tilde{\mathbf{Y}}_c = \frac{p(c|\mu, \sigma)}{\sum_{l=1}^{C} p(l|\mu, \sigma))}, \tag{6}$$

$$p(l|\mu, \sigma) = \frac{1}{\sqrt{2\pi}\sigma} exp\left(-\frac{(l-\mu)^2}{2\sigma^2}\right), \tag{7}$$

where $c = 1, 2, ..., C$, σ is a hyper-parameter that can be tuned, and the distribution requirement $\sum_{l=1}^{C} \tilde{\mathbf{Y}}_l = 1$ is satisfied.

Then, the confidence distribution loss can be calculated as the Kullback-Leibler (KL) divergence between the predicted distribution $\hat{\mathbf{Y}}$ and target distribution $\tilde{\mathbf{Y}}$:

$$CDL = -\tilde{\mathbf{Y}}_c \sum_{l=1}^{C} \hat{\mathbf{Y}}_c \tag{8}$$

3   Experiments

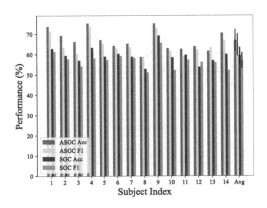

Fig. 2. The accuracy and F1-score (%) of ASGC and SGC for 14 subjects and their average.

3.1   Dataset

We conduct experiments on the dataset developed in [8]. When participants were performing visual perceptual decision-making task, the EEG data is recorded in 62 channels using an active AgCl electrode cap at a sampling rate 1000 Hz. The dataset comprises 14 subjects and each subject has 135 trials, where each trial corresponds to one decision process. For data preprocessing, a bandpass filter between 0.3 50 Hz is applied to each channel to filter the noise and linear dynamic system (LDS) method is adopted to smooth feature. We use the differential entropy (DE) feature on all five bands, since it achieves the best performance in [7,8]. We follow the subject-dependent classification setting in their works and train a model for each subject.

Table 1. The classification accuracy and F1-score (%) (mean/std) of SVM, DNNS, SGC, SGC with CDL and our ASGC model.

Metric	Model				
	SVM [8]	DNNS [8]	SGC	SGC+CDL	ASGC
Accuracy	40.93/ -	49.14/-	59.32/4.03	63.41/5.46	**68.83**/5.25
F1-score	37.43/ -	45.07/-	56.87/3.84	59.85/5.24	**66.90**/5.33

3.2   Performance Evaluations

The mean accuracy and F1-scores of SVM, DNNS, SGC, SGC with CDL and our final model ASGC are presented in Table 1. The performance of SVM and DNNS are quoted from [8]. We can find that SGC performs better than DNNS and SVM, which justifies the idea of capturing inter-channel topological relationship. Moreover, SGC with CDL performs better than SGC only, indicating the effectiveness of our proposed CDL. Finally, our ASGC model achieves the best accuracy and F1-score compared to all other baselines, showing the superior performance in this task.

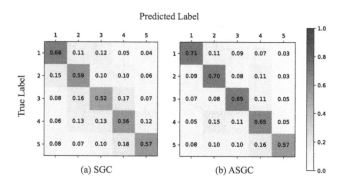

Fig. 3. The confusion matrices of SGC and ASGC. The rows of the confusion matrix represent the target class and the columns represent the predicted class.

The classification results of each subject (14 in total) and their average are shown in Fig. 2. We can find that our ASGC model achieves better accuracy and F1-score than SGC for all subjects. It shows that our ASGC model has consistent performance across different subjects, indicating the robustness of ASGC. The confusion matrices of SGC and ASGC averaged on all 14 subjects are shown in Fig. 3. We can find that both SGC and ASGC perform relatively better on the lowest confidence level, and that the intermediate levels are more difficult to classify. It may indicate that participants in the lowest confidence level may have similar EEG patterns. In addition, our model gets relatively

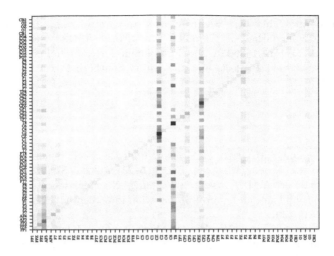

Fig. 4. The heatmap visualization of the attention matrix averaged on all subjects in the dataset.

worse at recognizing the highest confidence level, but still performs better than SGC does. Moreover, ASGC is better than SGC in discriminating intermediate confidence levels, showing a more fine-grained discrimination ability.

3.3 Analysis of Critical Channels

We further investigate the critical channels associated with confidence measurement in the visual perception decision-making task. Figure 4 visualizes the attention matrix averaged on all subjects in the dataset. Note that the sum of each row is equal 1 due to the softmax operation along each row. The diagonal values represent the attention paid to itself by each channel. We can find that the attention matrix is sparse and some of the channels are of greater importance than others. It is clear form Fig. 4 that FP2, CZ, C6, and CPZ may be the important channels to discriminate the decision confidence in the visual perception task.

4 Conclusion

In this paper, we have proposed an attentive simple graph convolutional network (ASGC) for capturing fine-grained topology structure of EEG channels compared to SGC. In addition, we used a concatenate operation instead of global pooling to preserve the structure of channels. Moreover, we have proposed a confidence distribution loss based on the intuition that samples with closer confidence levels are more similar, alleviating the problems of lacking training samples and label ambiguity. The experimental results demonstrate the superior performance of our ASGC model compared to other baseline models, and the effectiveness of the CDL designed for the confidence level classification problem. Finally, the analysis on the attention matrix suggests that FP2, CZ, C6, and CPZ may be the important channels for measuring decision confidence in the visual perception task.

Acknowledgments. This work was supported in part by grants from the National Natural Science Foundation of China (Grant No. 61976135), SJTU Trans-Med Awards Research (WF540162605), the Fundamental Research Funds for the Central Universities, the 111 Project, and the China Southern Power Grid (Grant No. GDKJXM20185761).

References

1. Bang, D., Fleming, S.M.: Distinct encoding of decision confidence in human medial prefrontal cortex. Proc. Natl. Acad. Sci. **115**(23), 6082–6087 (2018)
2. Boldt, A., Schiffer, A.M., Waszak, F., Yeung, N.: Confidence predictions affect performance confidence and neural preparation in perceptual decision making. Sci. Rep. **9**(1), 1–17 (2019)
3. Gao, B.B., Xing, C., Xie, C.W., Wu, J., Geng, X.: Deep label distribution learning with label ambiguity. IEEE Trans. Image Process. **26**(6), 2825–2838 (2017)
4. Gherman, S., Philiastides, M.G.: Neural representations of confidence emerge from the process of decision formation during perceptual choices. Neuroimage **106**, 134–143 (2015)
5. Hebart, M.N., Schriever, Y., Donner, T.H., Haynes, J.D.: The relationship between perceptual decision variables and confidence in the human brain. Cereb. Cortex **26**(1), 118–130 (2016)
6. Kipf, T.N., Welling, M.: Semi-supervised classification with graph convolutional networks. arXiv preprint arXiv:1609.02907 (2016)
7. Li, R., Liu, L.D., Lu, B.L.: Measuring human decision confidence from EEG signals in an object detection task. In: 2021 10th International IEEE/EMBS Conference on Neural Engineering (NER), pp. 942–945. IEEE (2021)
8. Li, R., Liu, L.D., Lu, B.L.: Discrimination of decision confidence levels from EEG signals. In: 2021 10th International IEEE/EMBS Conference on Neural Engineering (NER), pp. 946–949. IEEE (2021)
9. Li, R., Wang, S., Zhu, F., Huang, J.: Adaptive graph convolutional neural networks. In: Proceedings of the AAAI Conference on Artificial Intelligence, vol. 32 (2018)
10. Molenberghs, P., Trautwein, F.M., Böckler, A., Singer, T., Kanske, P.: Neural correlates of metacognitive ability and of feeling confident: a large-scale fMRI study. Soc. Cogn. Affect. Neurosci. **11**(12), 1942–1951 (2016)
11. Pouget, A., Drugowitsch, J., Kepecs, A.: Confidence and certainty: distinct probabilistic quantities for different goals. Nat. Neurosci. **19**(3), 366 (2016)
12. Song, T., Zheng, W., Song, P., Cui, Z.: EEG emotion recognition using dynamical graph convolutional neural networks. IEEE Trans. Affect. Comput. **11**(3), 532–541 (2018)
13. Wu, F., Souza, A., Zhang, T., Fifty, C., Yu, T., Weinberger, K.: Simplifying graph convolutional networks. In: International Conference on Machine Learning, pp. 6861–6871. PMLR (2019)
14. Zhang, G., Yu, M., Liu, Y.J., Zhao, G., Zhang, D., Zheng, W.: SparseDGCNN: recognizing emotion from multichannel EEG signals. IEEE Trans. Affect. Comput. (2021)
15. Zhong, P., Wang, D., Miao, C.: EEG-based emotion recognition using regularized graph neural networks. IEEE Trans. Affect. Comput. (2020)

Marginal Spectrum Modulated Hilbert-Huang Transform: Application to Time Courses Extracted by Independent Vector Analysis of Resting-State fMRI Data

Wei-Xing Li[1], Chao-Ying Zhang[1], Li-Dan Kuang[2], Yue Han[1], Huan-Jie Li[3], Qiu-Hua Lin[1(✉)], and Vince D. Calhoun[4]

[1] School of Information and Communication Engineering, Dalian University of Technology, Dalian 116024, China
qhlin@dlut.edu.cn
[2] School of Computer and Communication Engineering, Changsha University of Science and Technology, Changsha 410114, China
[3] School of Biomedical Engineering, Dalian University of Technology, Dalian 116024, China
[4] Tri-institutional Center for Translational Research in Neuroimaging and Data Science (TReNDS), Georgia State University, Georgia Institute of Technology, Emory University, Atlanta, GA, USA

Abstract. Hilbert-Huang transform (HHT) can reveal abnormal activations impacted by mental disorders from regions of interest (ROIs) based functional magnetic resonance imaging (fMRI) data with high temporal and frequency resolutions. However, this advantage has not been extended to the time courses extracted by data-driven methods such as independent vector analysis (IVA) from fMRI data. This study explores HHT to analyze IVA separated time courses and improves HHT via multiplying the HHT spectrum with the marginal HHT spectrum (named as marginal spectrum modulated HHT) to enhance the difference between patients and controls. We evaluated the proposed HHT using resting-state fMRI data collected from patients with schizophrenia and healthy controls, and compared with time series of ROIs defined according to Brodmann areas. Experimental results showed that the proposed HHT improved inter-group differences compared to HHT, in terms of the clustering precision, e.g., 7.7% higher (81.2% vs. 73.5%) for the temporal lobe, providing new evidence for potential imaging biomarkers for schizophrenia in the time-frequency domain.

Keywords: Time-frequency analysis · fMRI data · Hilbert-Huang transform spectrum · Independent vector analysis · Schizophrenia

1 Introduction

Blood oxygenation level-dependent (BOLD)-related functional magnetic resonance imaging (fMRI) has been widely used to study brain activity and mental

© Springer Nature Switzerland AG 2021
T. Mantoro et al. (Eds.): ICONIP 2021, CCIS 1517, pp. 299–306, 2021.
https://doi.org/10.1007/978-3-030-92310-5_35

disorders such as schizophrenia. Some approaches focus on BOLD-related fluctuations in the lower frequency band (<0.1 Hz) [1–3]. Biswal et al. studied low-frequency oscillation via Fourier transform analysis on time series of regions of interest (ROIs) for resting-state fMRI data [1]; Anand et al. found that patients with depression had increased correlation between anterior cingulate cortex and limbic regions after treatment in the frequency domain [2]. However, it is hard for such frequency analyses to simultaneously preserve the high resolution in the time domain [3]. Given that, time-frequency analyses enable us to study a signal in both time and frequency domains with high resolution. Among time-frequency analyses, Hilbert-Huang Transform (HHT), an adaptive time-frequency analytic method, has been proven not only suitable for the nonlinear and non-stationary signals, but also applicable to feature extraction from biomedical signals with high resolutions [4]. Recently, HHT has been utilized to explore the time-frequency characteristics of brain activity by decomposing fMRI data into several frequency signals adaptively and to study the underlying mechanisms of mental disorders.

To our best knowledge, HHT has only been applied to time series of ROIs. Considering that denoised data can better reflect the real time-frequency features, some studies proposed improved HHT algorithms to reduce effects of noise [5–7]. Since empirical mode decomposition (EMD) is the essential process in HHT, studies have focused on improving EMD. Wu et al. added different white noise series to the original data and decomposed the noisy data into intrinsic mode functions (IMFs) at each time [5]. As such, the means of IMFs of all the times were regarded as the denoised IMFs. Peng et al. proposed an improved EMD method using wavelet packet transform, which was proved to be efficient to eliminate pseudo-IMFs caused by noise [6]. Li et al. eliminated noise effects by introducing a time varying filter technique [7]. They fully facilitated the instantaneous amplitude and frequency information, which was proved robust against to the noise interference. Since the knowledge of the brain is limited, we choose to reduce noise before performing HHT to the fMRI data without using any prior knowledge. Independent vector analysis (IVA), a multi-subject extension of independent component analysis (ICA), has been widely used in fMRI analyses to separate a mixture of components [8]. Considering IVA captures the inter-subject variability within the same source component vector (SCV), it is beneficial to capture patterns of schizophrenia by exploiting IVA [8]. Compared with noisy time series of ROIs, the source temporal components are clear and meaningful. Motivated by this, we proposed to perform time-frequency analysis by HHT to time courses (TCs) extracted by IVA from fMRI data. Since the marginal HHT spectrum represents the cumulative amplitude of each frequency point of the whole data, the signals occupy the main part of energy with high amplitude, while noise accounts for a small percentage of whole energy especially for the TC components extracted by IVA. Therefore, we proposed an improved HHT named marginal spectrum modulated HHT by multiplying the HHT spectrum with the amplitude of marginal HHT spectrum. Resting-state fMRI datasets including 24 patients with schizophrenia (SZs) and 24 HCs were used to evaluate the proposed method.

The main contributions are three-fold: (1) We propose an improved HHT named marginal spectrum modulated HHT to improve the robustness to noise; (2) We propose to perform time-frequency analysis to TCs extracted by IVA rather than time series of ROIs; (3) We define evaluation indexes to quantify abilities of the proposed method in differentiating schizophrenia patients from controls. Results showed that the proposed HHT exhibited higher time-frequency intergroup differences and higher clustering precision than using ROI time series, indicating the potential for identifying imaging biomarkers for schizophrenia.

2   The Proposed Method

2.1   IVA Model

Given K subjects of fMRI data $\mathbf{X}^{(k)} \in \mathbb{R}^{J \times V}$, $k = 1, \ldots, K$, J and V are the number of time points and in-brain voxels, respectively. We first perform principal component analysis (PCA) to reduce $\mathbf{X}^{(k)}$ as follows:

$$\mathbf{Z}^{(k)} = \mathbf{F}^{(k)} \mathbf{X}^{(k)}, \tag{1}$$

where $\mathbf{F}^{(k)} \in \mathbb{R}^{N \times J}$ is a compression matrix, $\mathbf{Z}^{(k)} \in \mathbb{R}^{N \times V}$ is reduced fMRI data. The aim of IVA is to obtain a demixing matrix $\mathbf{W}^{(k)} \in \mathbb{R}^{N \times N}$ to estimate spatial maps (SMs) as follows:

$$\hat{\mathbf{y}}^{(k)} = \mathbf{W}^{(k)} \mathbf{Z}^{(k)}, \tag{2}$$

where $\hat{\mathbf{y}}^{(k)} \in \mathbb{R}^{N \times V}$ is the estimated SMs of the kth subject. IVA model is realized by maximizing the mutual information among estimated SCVs $\hat{\mathbf{y}}_n = [\hat{\mathbf{y}}_n^{(1)}, \ldots, \hat{\mathbf{y}}_n^{(K)}]^{\text{T}}, n = 1, \ldots, N$, i.e., similar SMs from different subjects were concatenated into a vector. The cost function of IVA denoted as $\mathcal{J}_{\text{IVA}}$ can be calculated as follows [8]:

$$\mathcal{J}_{\text{IVA}} = -\sum_{n=1}^{N} \mathrm{E}\left(\log p\left(\hat{\mathbf{y}}_n\right)\right) - \sum_{k=1}^{K} \log\left|\det\left(\mathbf{W}^{(k)}\right)\right| - C, \tag{3}$$

where $p\left(\hat{\mathbf{y}}_n\right)$ is a multivariate probability density distributions, "$|\cdot|$" represents modulus operation, "det" is the determinant and C is a constant item to be ignored. As such, the TCs of kth subject can be represented as:

$$\mathbf{a}^{(k)} = \left[\left(\mathbf{F}^{(k)}\right)^{\dagger}(\mathbf{W}\,(k))^{-1}\right]^{\text{T}}, \tag{4}$$

where $\left(\mathbf{F}^{(k)}\right)^{\dagger}$ denotes the pseudo-inverse matrix of $\mathbf{F}^{(k)}$, $\mathbf{a}^{(k)} = [\mathbf{a}_1^{(k)}, \ldots, \mathbf{a}_N^{(k)}]^{\text{T}}$ and similar TCs of different subjects can be formed into a vector as $\mathbf{a}_n = [\mathbf{a}_n^{(1)}, \ldots, \mathbf{a}_n^{(K)}]^{\text{T}}$.

2.2   The Proposed HHT

Assuming we obtain L IMFs $\mathbf{c}_l, 1 \leqslant l \leqslant L$ from an average TC component $\mathbf{a}_n$ using EMD [5], we perform Hilbert transform for each IMF as follows:

$$\mathbf{H}_l(t) = \frac{1}{\pi} \int_{-\infty}^{\infty} \frac{\mathbf{c}_l(\tau)}{t-\tau} d\tau. \tag{5}$$

Then, we obtain an analytical signal $\mathbf{U}_l(t, f)$ as follows:

$$\mathbf{U}_l(t, f) = \mathbf{b}_l(t)\exp\{ i\varphi_l(f)\} , \tag{6}$$

where $\mathbf{b}_l(t) = \sqrt{(\mathbf{c}_l)^2 + (\mathbf{H}_l)^2}$, $\varphi_l(f) = \arctan\left(\frac{\mathbf{H}_l}{\mathbf{c}_l}\right)$ and $i = \sqrt{-1}$. The instantaneous frequency of each IMF is defined as:

$$\mathbf{f}_l(f, t) = \frac{d\varphi_l(f)}{dt}. \tag{7}$$

Thus, we can simultaneously analyze instantaneous amplitude and frequency of the analytical signal $\mathbf{U}_l(t, f)$ of $\mathbf{a}_n$, by using HHT.

The HHT marginal spectrum can be obtained by integrating $\mathbf{U}_l(t, f)$ in the time domain as follows:

$$\widehat{\mathbf{H}}_l(f) = \int_{t=1}^{T} \mathbf{U}_l(f, t) \, dt, \tag{8}$$

The proposed method improves HHT by multiplying the analytical signal $\mathbf{U}_l(t, f)$ by the marginal HHT $\tilde{\mathbf{H}}_l(f)$ as follows:

$$\mathbf{MH}(t, f) = \sum_{l=1}^{L} \tilde{\mathbf{H}}_l(f) \cdot \mathbf{U}_l(t, f), \tag{9}$$

where $\mathbf{MH}(t, f)$ represents the proposed HHT in the time-frequency domain, and we focus on the amplitude of $\mathbf{MH}(t, f)$. Since signals have higher amplitudes than noise in the marginal HHT spectrum, the amplitude of $\mathbf{MH}(t, f)$ is more robust than the HHT spectrum $\mathbf{U}_l(t, f)$.

2.3   Evaluation Indexes

We define nonzero amplitudes of the proposed HHT spectrum as follows:

$$\mathbf{G}(m) = \begin{cases} |\mathbf{MH}(t, f)|, & if \ |\mathbf{MH}(t, f)| > 0 \\ 0, & \text{otherwise} \end{cases}, \ 1 \leqslant m \leqslant T \cdot F, \tag{10}$$

where T is the total length of time, F is the highest frequency. Then, the vector of nonzero points can be represented as $\mathbf{G} = [\mathbf{G}(1), \ldots, \mathbf{G}(M)]^{\mathrm{T}}$, where M is the number of nonzero amplitudes of the proposed HHT spectrum. We utilize two evaluation indexes to quantify the characteristics of the proposed HHT spectrum: (1) the number of nonzero points (denoted as M) and (2) the kurtosis of $\mathbf{G}$ (denoted as $\mathcal{K}$).

2.4   Validation

We perform bootstrapping to evaluate the repeatability of the proposed method. First, we generated 1000 bootstrapping samples for the HC and SZ groups. Then, the average indexes in each bootstrap sample are computed. Finally, one sample t-test on the average values in each bootstrapping sample is performed to determine whether the average evaluation indexes can represent the group characteristics.

3   Experiments and Results

3.1   Resting-State fMRI Data and Components Selection

Resting-state fMRI data were collected from 24 HCs and 24 SZs ($K = 24$) with written subject consent overseen by the University of New Mexico Institutional Review Board. More details are described in a previous study [9]. We run IVA 10 times and select the temporal lobe (TEM) as a component of interest from the total 50 SCV estimates from the best run [9].

3.2   Experimental Results

Figure 1 shows the results of TCs for TEM and time series of BA 48 (a large ROI of TEM) averaged across each group. For TCs, the waveform of HCs showed periodic changes across time while the waveform of SZs had more random changes. By contrast, the BA 48 ROI time series did not show obvious intergroup differences (e.g., the periodic changes is slight for HCs). Figure 2 shows the normalized marginal HHT of TCs for TEM. The energy mainly gathered in the lower frequency domain (<0.1 Hz). HCs had higher percentage gathering in lower frequency domain (<0.1 Hz) compared to SZs (73.7% vs. 57.6%). Since the marginal HHT spectrum represents the cumulative amplitude of the HHT spectrum, the

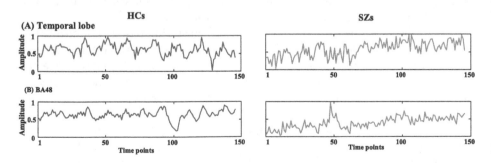

Fig. 1. Waveforms of (A) TCs and (B) BA 48 time series averaged across HCs and SZs. HCs showed periodic TC changes while SZs had random changes.

signals with high amplitude occupied the main part of energy, while noise with low amplitude accounts for a small percentage of whole energy. Therefore, HHT multiplied by the marginal HHT spectrum can improve the robustness to noise.

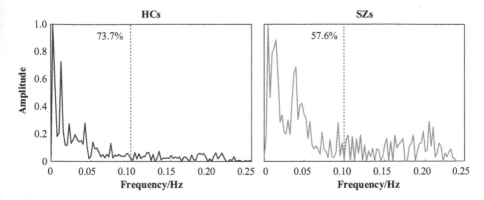

Fig. 2. The normalized marginal HHT spectrums of TCs for TEM. The main energy of marginal HHT spectrums gathered in the frequency range lower than 0.1 Hz. HCs showed higher percentage of energy within the frequency range lower than 0.1 Hz compared to SZs (73.7% vs. 57.6%).

Figure 3 displays a comparison of spectrums determined by the proposed HHT and the original HHT for TEM of HCs and SZs. The non-zero points were sequentially obtained ranging in 0–292 s with 2 s interval and ranging in 0–0.25 Hz with 0.01 Hz interval for time and frequency domain, respectively. While SZs showed more points with higher amplitudes gathering in frequencies lower than 0.1 Hz, compared to HCs for both methods, the proposed HHT exhibited larger intergroup differences in terms of the number of nonzero points M (107 vs. 70) and the kurtosis of nonzero points vector $\mathcal{K}$ (27 vs. 12) than HHT. Additionally, the proposed HHT increased the amplitude in frequencies lower than 0.1Hz and decreased the amplitude in frequencies higher than 0.2 Hz.

Table 1 displays precision results of k-means clustering based on multiple features extracted from amplitudes of HHT and the proposed HHT for TEM and four TEM-related ROIs including BA 6, 21, 22, 48. The four ROIs were selected due to larger activation voxels (>600). The features include the mean and variance in addition to the number of nonzero points and kurtosis values. These four features were used to cluster 48 subjects into two groups corresponding to HCs and SZs. TCs of TEM showed the highest clustering precision than ROI time series from any single BA. Compared with HHT, the proposed HHT obtained 7.7% increase (81.2% vs. 73.5%) for TCs of TEM than HHT and a maximal 3.4% increase (66.7% vs. 63.3%) for BA6. We also computed the clustering precision using the combined features extracted from four ROIs, the proposed method yielded an improved precision by 4.7% as well.

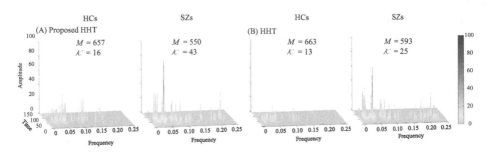

Fig. 3. The spectrums of TEM for (A) the proposed HHT and (B) HHT. The proposed HHT improved the intergroup differences in terms of the number of nonzero points M (107 vs. 70) and the kurtosis of nonzero point vector $\mathcal{K}$ (27 vs. 12).

Table 1. The precision (%) of k-means clustering for HHT and the proposed HHT.

	TCs			ROIs		
	TEM	BA6	BA21	BA22	BA48	4 BAs
HHT	73.5	63.3	63.2	61.9	58.8	63.9
Proposed	**81.2**	66.7	64.6	62.5	60.4	68.6

4 Conclusion

In this study, we propose an improved HHT via multiplying the HHT spectrum by the marginal HHT spectrum for analyzing the time-frequency characteristics of TCs extracted from fMRI data by IVA. We compared with time series of ROIs from observed fMRI data. The proposed HHT highlighted two main intergroup differences by analyzing TEM in the time-frequency range: (1) HCs showed more concentrated distributions in the lower frequency range (<0.1 Hz); (2) clustering precision improved 7.7% (81.2% vs. 73.5%) for TCs of TEM than HHT, and increased 12.6% (81.2% vs. 68.6%) compared to the highest precision case using time series of four BAs.

The higher amplitude in the low frequency domain (<0.1 Hz) for HCs is a previously noted intergroup difference between HCs and SZs [10–12]: Turner et al. proved that the stability of low-frequency activation in chronically treated SZs by twice assessments over a median interval of 2.5 months [10]; Yu et al. measured low-frequency activation in three different frequency bands and found that HCs had higher low-frequency activation in the range of 0.01–0.08 Hz [11]; Calhoun et al. used ICA to study brain networks decomposed from fMRI data and proved that HCs had more spectral power at lower frequencies than SZs [12]. These differences in low frequency bands may be informative and useful as a marker of the disorder.

In the future, the classification based on the proposed HHT spectrums is worth further investigation. Extending the proposed HHT to the analysis of complex-valued fMRI data is also promising in the use of additional phase fMRI data.

Acknowledgement. This work was supported in part by the National Natural Science Foundation of China under Grants 61871067, 61901061, 81601484; in part by the NSF under Grants 1539067, 0840895, 1539067, and 0715022, in part by NIH Grants R01MH104680, R01MH107354, R01EB005846, and R01MH117107, in part by the Fundamental Research Funds for the Central Universities, China, under Grant DUT20ZD220, and in part by the Supercomputing Center of Dalian University of Technology.

References

1. Biswal, B., Zerrin Yetkin, F., Haughton, V.M., Hyde, J.S.: Functional connectivity in the motor cortex of resting human brain using echo-planar MRI. Magn. Reson. Med. **34**(4), 537–541 (1995)
2. Anand, A., et al.: Antidepressant effect on connectivity of the mood-regulating circuit: an fMRI study. Neuropsychopharmacology **30**(7), 1334–1344 (2005)
3. Sartipi, S., Kalbkhani, H., Ghasemzadeh, P., Shayesteh, M.G.: Stockwell transform of time-series of fMRI data for diagnoses of attention deficit hyperactive disorder. Appl. Soft Comput. J. **86**, 105905 (2020)
4. Huang, N.E., Wu, M.L., Qu, W., Long, S.R., Shen, S.S.P.: Applications of Hilbert-Huang transform to non-stationary financial time series analysis. Appl. Stoch. Models Bus. Ind. **19**(3), 245–268 (2010)
5. Wu, Z., Huang, N.E.: Ensemble empirical mode decomposition: a noise-assisted data analysis method. Adv. Adapt. Data Anal. **1**(1), 1–41 (2009)
6. Peng, Z.K., Tse, P.W., Chu, F.L.: A comparison study of improved Hilbert-Huang trans-form and wavelet transform: application to fault diagnosis for rolling bearing. Mech. Syst. Signal Process. **19**(5), 974–988 (2005)
7. Li, H., Li, Z., Mo, W.: A time varying filter approach for empirical mode decomposition. Signal Process. **138**, 146–158 (2017)
8. Anderson, M., Adalı, T., Li, X.-L.: Joint blind source separation with multivariate Gaussian model: algorithms and performance analysis. IEEE Trans. Signal Process. **60**(4), 1672–1683 (2012). Author, F.: Article title. Journal **2**(5), 99–110 (2016)
9. Kuang, L.D., Lin, Q.H., Gong, X.F., Cong, F., Sui, J., Calhoun, V.D.: Model order effects on ICA of resting-state complex-valued fMRI data: application to schizophrenia. J. Neurosci. Methods **304**, 24–38 (2018)
10. Turner, J.A., et al.: Reliability of the amplitude of low-frequency fluctuations in resting state fMRI in chronic schizophrenia. Psychiatry Res. - Neuroimaging **201**(3), 253–255 (2012)
11. Yu, R., et al.: Frequency-specific alternations in the amplitude of low-frequency fluctuations in schizophrenia. Hum. Brain Mapp. **35**(2), 627–637 (2014)
12. Calhoun, V.D., Sui, J., Kiehl, K., Turner, J., Allen, E., Pearlson, G.: Exploring the psychosis functional connectome: aberrant intrinsic networks in schizophrenia and bipolar disorder. Front. Psychiatry **2**(1), 75 (2012)

Deep Learning Models with Time Delay Embedding for EEG-Based Attentive State Classification

Huan Cai, Min Xia, Li Nie, Yihan Wu, and Yangsong Zhang$^{(\boxtimes)}$

School of Computer Science and Technology,
Southwest University of Science and Technology, Mianyang, China

Abstract. Deep learning (DL) methods for attention detection based on electroencephalography (EEG) have received increasing interest in recent years. To improve the performance of the existing state-of-the-art (SOTA) DL models, we proposed to utilize time delay embedding method to construct new input for DL model which can yield better results on EEG classification task. To verify the effectiveness of the proposed strategy, the evaluation experiments were conducted on a public EEG dataset. Experimental results demonstrated the DL models with time delay embedding extension could outperform the counterpart original models. The findings indicate the improving DL models based on time delay embedding method could be a prospective methodology for EEG classification, especially for attention detection task.

Keywords: EEG · Brain-computer interface · Deep learning · Attention detection

1 Introduction

Brain Computer Interface (BCI) could provide a direct connection between brain and external devices to realize the information exchange [1]. Electroencephalography (EEG) has gained widespread use in recent years as a method of recording brain activity in BCI field since it provides a non-invasive, safe and low-cost way to measure neural activity compared to other implantable electrodes technologies [2]. There are a number of BCI-based tasks such as attention detection [3], motor imagery [4,5], steady-state visual evoked potentials (SSVEPs) [6,7], P300 [8,9] and emotion recognition [10,11], etc. In recent years, attention detection task has been paid increasing concern by researchers.

Attention is important for memory, learning and cognition, which can affect our daily life. Besides, effective methods to detect attention level (attentive state or non-attentive state) are important in the application of driving vigilance detection, improving learning efficiency and rehabilitation, especially in attention training for Attention Deficit Hyperactivity Disorder (ADHD) children [12].

Attention is a complex neuropsychological phenomenon involving a variety of brain areas and complicated mechanisms, and a number of studies have been

© Springer Nature Switzerland AG 2021
T. Mantoro et al. (Eds.): ICONIP 2021, CCIS 1517, pp. 307–314, 2021.
https://doi.org/10.1007/978-3-030-92310-5_36

investigated by researchers [13]. Some effective traditional methods were applied on the attention detection task in the early years. For instance, Liu et al. first extract the power spectral density (PSD) and energy value of different frequency bands, then use a support vector machine (SVM) classifier with polynomial kernel to classify the attention level [14]. Similarly, Fahimi et al. extracted the common features such as frequency band powers or their ratios [12]. Mutual information (MI) was used for feature selection, which were also input into a SVM classifier.

In recent years, DL algorithms became more popular in numerous EEG studies, including attentive level classification. For instance, Fahimi et al. [3] introduced an end-to-end DeepCNN model to improve the performance of attention detection task in case of subject-independent(see Sect. 2.4 for details). Another work [15] combined convolution and recurrent neural network to efficiently extract the context characteristics of EEG series, finally achieved better accuracy compared to other baselines. Although deep learning algorithms perform better than traditional methods in most cases, there are still some room for improvement based on DL models.

For the end-to-end models, original EEG signals instead of hand-crafted features are input into the DL models directly, which increase the performance of BCI device without the complicated feature extraction process required by traditional methods. However, proper manipulation and reorganization based on original signals could further improve the performance of original models. Inspired by previous studies [16,17], this paper proposed an effective framework based time delay embedding method to improve the existing popular DL methods, and evaluated the idea on attentive state detection task. Each extended DL model was termed as E- plus the original model name. For instance, the extension of EEGNet [18] was denoted as E-EEGNet. To validate the effectiveness of the proposed framework, these extended DL models will be compared with the original DL models on a public datasets recorded from 26 subjects. Experimental results demonstrated that these DL algorithm with the time delay embedding extension could yield better performance.

This paper is organized as follows: Sect. 2 introduces the datasets and the proposed methods based on existing DL models. Experimental results on a public dataset are presented in Sect. 3, and the concluding was presented in the end.

2 Materials and Methods

2.1 Dataset Description

The EEG signals were recorded from 26 right-handed healthy subjects (nine males and seventeen females, aged from 17 to 33 years) performing a discrimination/selection response task (DSR). EEG data in the task period and rest period are adopted as attention and non-attention data respectively. The sampling rate of EEG data was 1,000 Hz and 30 EEG electrodes were recorded according to the international 10–5 system [21]. More details of recording paradigm about the data description was presented in the reference [20].

In current paper, the EEG signals were downsampled 200 Hz, bandpassed between 0.5 40 Hz, and referred to average reference. Only 28 electrodes were used, i.e., Fp1, Fp2, AFF5h, AFF6h, AFz, F1, F2, FC1, FC2, FC5, FC6, Cz, C3, C4, T7, T8, CP1, CP2, CP5, CP6, Pz, P3, P4, P7, P8, POz, O1 and O2 (2 ground electrodes are removed). Then, the 20 s task and rest period EEG data were segmented using a 2 s sliding window and 1 s overlap. Finally, 684 samples were obtained for every subject and each sample had a dimension of 28 × 400 (channels × time points).

2.2 Temporal Delayed Representation

In the work [16], the author applied the delay embedding to the common spatial pattern (CSP) algorithm. Morover, another work utilized this extension trick to multivariate synchronization index (MSI) [17]. Both studies demonstrate that combining the time embedding method could improve the original CSP and MSI algorithms. Inspired by these studies, we proposed to enhance the performance of the existing popular deep learning models by incorporating time embedding method for the EEG data. Denote the $x \in \mathbf{R}^{C \times T}$ as the multichannel EEG samples. Then, the first-order time delay version of sample x with D number of samples is denoted as x^D, which can be acquired by moving the first D points of each channel to the end of the sample. Then, the new input for DL models with time delayed embedding on the original x is denoted as $\hat{x}$, which can be obtained by following formula:

$$\hat{x} = \begin{pmatrix} x \\ x^D \end{pmatrix} \tag{1}$$

The EEG signals after the time delayed embedding could be regarded as concatenating additional multichannel EEG data to the original EEG data. The schematic diagram of the operation was given in Fig. 1. Hence, there is an extra hyper-parameter D which indicates the number of delayed samples points. Then the $\hat{x}$ will be input into these SOTA DL models. In current paper, D ranges from 20 to 200 with a time step of 20. The optimal D may be different for various models and the analysis will be shown in the results section.

2.3 State-of-the-Art Deep Learning Models

To demonstrate the efficiency of this proposed framework, several state-of-the-art DL models are adopted as baselines and described as follows.

First, the DeepCNN introduced by Fahimi et al. was used as the baseline model which was specially designed for attentive detection task [3]. Besides, some popular DL models in EEG-based BCI, such as EEGNet [18], ShallowNet and DeepNet [19], were also selected as baseline algorithms. Concretely, EEGNet is a compact CNN composed of a convention convolution to extract temporal

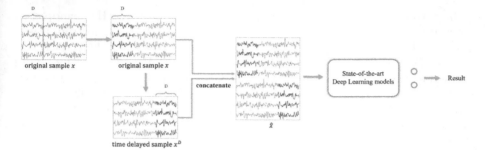

Fig. 1. The schematic diagram of the proposed framework. x denotes the original EEG sample which shaped as channels×time points. The first D points of the sample are moved to the end to generate time delayed embedding sample x^D. Then, x and x^D are concatenated as the input of the existing SOTA DL models to get the final prediction, namely, attentive state or non-attentive state.

features, a depthwise convolution to obtain spatial features and then followed by a separable convolution layer. Other details of EEGNet can be found in the reference [18]. ShallowNet and DeepNet were proposed by Schirrmeister et al. [19]. The structure of the first block of these two models is the same, while the kernel length is different. Besides, DeepNet is deeper than ShallowNet and followed by three convolution blocks which could extract more details of input signals. After the first block, ShallowNet is followed by a squaring nonlinearity activation, a mean pooling operation and a log activation step. The above three models are all excellent algorithms in BCI field and can be used in a variety of BCI tasks.

2.4   Experiment Implementation

Leave-one-subject-Out (LOSO) evaluation strategy was used in our study [24], where the data from one target subject were used as test dataset, and the data from remaining subjects were used as training data. The average accuracies of all these subjects were served as evaluation metric of the model performance.

For model implementation, the hyper-parameter of DL models was set the same as in the original studies [3,18,19], except for the DeepNet. We decrease the kernel size and pooling size of DeepNet to make it more suitable for our shorter EEG data length. All the DL models were implemented based on keras [23] and Adam optimizer was used.

The number of epochs was set to 30 and the learning rate is initialized to 0.001. A phased decaying learning rate was applied which multiplied by 0.4 each ten epochs. For the loss function, binary cross-entropy was used. Methods for faster convergence such as Batch Normalization and Dropout were performed in all of these models. In order to avoid huge random varieties, we trained each model for 3 times and took its average value as the final results.

3 Experimental Results

As described in Sect. 2, we evaluated the extended DL models under different values of D. Results are presented in Fig. 2, the horizontal axis denotes the D value and the vertical axis represent the accuracy. We can see that almost all extended versions of DeepCNN and ShallowNet performs better than the original model, the highest improvement is 1.98% for E-DeepCNN and 2.62% for E-ShallowNet. As can be seen in the two subgraphs on the right, though the accuracy is relatively lower when D range from 100 to 160 for E-EEGNet and 80 to 120 for E-DeepNet, other results are improved, among which the highest improvement is 1.24% and 2.75% for E-EEGNet and E-DeepNet respectively. Besides, various extended DL models show different regularity. For instance, the accuracy decreases as the D increases on DeepCNN while the performance improves in the same condition on ShallowNet. Moreover, all the four extended models improved at D values of 20, 60, 180 and 200. Accordingly, the experimental results indicate that the time delay embedding method on DL models is effective for attentive detection task. To clearly display the results, the maximal improvement of each extended DL model and the corresponding D value are listed in Table 1. It is worth noting that this optimal parameter D may vary for different tasks and various models, and should be adjusted in other BCI practical application.

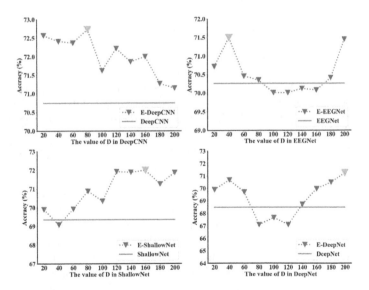

Fig. 2. The accuracies of original models and their extended models on different D value. The horizontal axis denotes the D value, and the vertical axis represent the accuracy. The red triangle represents the highest improvement.

Table 1. The maximum improvement of each DL model with time delay embedding method and the corresponding D value.

DL Models	DeepCNN	EEGNet	ShallowNet	DeepNet
Original model accuracy (%)	70.75	70.26	69.36	68.48
Extended model Accuracy (%)	72.73	71.50	71.99	71.23
Improvement (%)	1.98	1.24	2.63	2.75
Corresponding value of D	80	40	160	200

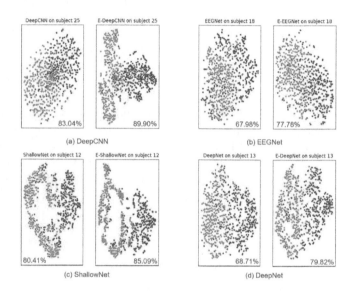

Fig. 3. A t-SNE visualization comparison on SOTA DL models and the extended models on specific subjects whose accuracy were highly promoted. The subgraph on the right shows a better categorization trend than the one on the left, especially for the E-DeepCNN in subfigure (a). The numbers in the lower right or left corner of the image indicate the accuracies of the corresponding subjects.

In order to better display the results, we also visualized the last full connection layer of each model using t-distributed stochastic neighbor embedding (t-SNE) as shown in Fig. 3. By comparing with original models, we could find that the classification results of extended models were slightly better. It should be noted that it is feasible to extend the time delay embedding by combining more than one temporal delay, which may lead to further improvement. But this will result in more computationally complexity and longer training process. We will conduct further research in the future.

4   Conclusion

In this paper, we proposed a framework to improve the performance of existing SOTA DL models with the time delay embedding method. To the best of our knowledge, this method has not been applied in DL models for the attentive detection task and other BCI paradigms. The effectiveness of the proposed method was evaluated on a public dataset, and the experimental results demonstrated that the performance of original DL models can further be improved with new input constructed with time delay embedding method. The proposed framework has a great potential in improving the performance of DL models for attentive detection task, and could be implemented in other DL models for EEG data analysis.

References

1. Li, Y., et al.: Multimodal BCIs: target detection, multidimensional control, and awareness evaluation in patients with disorder of consciousness. Proc. IEEE **104**(2), 332–352 (2016)
2. Roy, Y., Banville, H., Albuquerque, I., et al.: Deep learning-based electroencephalography analysis: a systematic review. J. Neural Eng. **16**(5), 051001 (2019)
3. Fahimi, F., Zhang, Z., Goh, W.B., et al.: Inter-subject transfer learning with an end-to-end deep convolutional neural network for EEG-based BCI. J. Neural Eng. **16**(2), 026007 (2019)
4. Liu, T., Yang, D.: A three-branch 3D convolutional neural network for EEG-based different hand movement stages classification. Sci. Rep. **11**(1), 1–13 (2021)
5. Yu, Y., Liu, Y., Jiang, J., et al.: An asynchronous control paradigm based on sequential motor imagery and its application in wheelchair navigation. IEEE Trans. Neural Syst. Rehabil. Eng. **26**(12), 2367–2375 (2018)
6. Waytowich, N., et al.: Compact convolutional neural networks for classification of asynchronous steady-state visual evoked potentials. J. Neural Eng. **15**(6), 066031 (2018)
7. Zhang, Y., et al.: Hierarchical feature fusion framework for frequency recognition in ssvep-based bcis. Neural Netw. **119**, 1–9 (2019)
8. Zhou, Z., Yin, E., Liu, Y., et al.: A novel task-oriented optimal design for P300-based brain-ccomputer interfaces. J. Neural Eng. **11**(5), 056003 (2014)
9. Jin, J., Zhang, H., Daly, I., et al.: An improved P300 pattern in BCI to catch user's attention. J. Neural Eng. **14**(3), 036001 (2017)
10. Ding, Y., Robinson, N., Zeng, Q., et al.: LGGNet: learning from local-global-graph representations for brain-computer interface. arXiv preprint arXiv:2105.02786 (2021)
11. Ding, Y., Robinson, N,. Zeng, Q., et al.: TSception: capturing temporal dynamics and spatial asymmetry from EEG for emotion recognition. arXiv preprint arXiv:2104.02935 (2021)
12. Fahimi, F., Guan, C., Goh, W.B., et al.: Personalized features for attention detection in children with attention deficit hyperactivity disorder. In: 2017 39th Annual International Conference of the IEEE Engineering in Medicine and Biology Society (EMBC), pp. 414–417. IEEE (2017)

13. Wai, A.A.P., Dou, M., Guan, C.: Generalizability of EEG-based mental attention modeling with multiple cognitive tasks. In: 2020 42nd Annual International Conference of the IEEE Engineering in Medicine & Biology Society (EMBC), pp. 2959–2962. IEEE (2020)

14. Liu, N.H., Chiang, C.Y., Chu, H.C.: Recognizing the degree of human attention using EEG signals from mobile sensors. Sensors **13**(8), 10273–10286 (2013)

15. Cai, H., Tang, J., Wu, Y., et al.: The detection of attentive mental state using a mixed neural network model. In: 2021 IEEE International Symposium on Circuits and Systems (ISCAS), pp. 1–5. IEEE (2021)

16. Lemm, S., Blankertz, B., Curio, G., et al.: Spatio-spectral filters for improving the classification of single trial EEG. IEEE Trans. Biomed. Eng. **52**(9), 1541–1548 (2005)

17. Zhang, Y., Guo, D., Yao, D., et al.: The extension of multivariate synchronization index method for SSVEP-based BCI. Neurocomputing **269**, 226–231 (2017)

18. Lawhern, V.J., Solon, A.J., Waytowich, N.R., et al.: EEGNet: a compact convolutional neural network for EEG-based brain-computer interfaces. J. Neural Eng. **15**(5), 056013 (2018)

19. Schirrmeister, R.T., Springenberg, J.T., Fiederer, L.D.J., et al.: Deep learning with convolutional neural networks for EEG decoding and visualization. Hum. Brain Mapp. **38**(11), 5391–5420 (2017)

20. Shin, J., Von Lhmann, A., Kim, D.W., et al.: Simultaneous acquisition of EEG and NIRS during cognitive tasks for an open access dataset. Sci. Data **5**(1), 1–16 (2018)

21. Oostenveld, R., Praamstra, P.: The five percent electrode system for high-resolution EEG and ERP measurements. Clin. Neurophysiol. **112**(4), 713–719 (2001)

22. Zhang, Y., Xu, P., Cheng, K., et al.: Multivariate synchronization index for frequency recognition of SSVEP-based brain-computer interface. J. Neurosci. Methods **221**, 32–40 (2014)

23. Gulli, A., Pal, S.: Deep Learning with Keras. Packt Publishing Ltd, Birmingham (2017)

24. Kwon, O.Y., Lee, M.H., Guan, C., et al.: Subject-independent brain-computer interfaces based on deep convolutional neural networks. IEEE Trans. Neural Netw. Learn. Syst. **31**(10), 3839–3852 (2019)

Neural Network Pruning Based on Improved Constrained Particle Swarm Optimization

Jihene Tmamna[1]($\boxtimes$), Emna Ben Ayed[1], and Mounir Ben Ayed[2]

[1] REGIM-Lab.: REsearch Groups in Intelligent Machines, National Engineering School of Sfax (ENIS), University of Sfax, BP 1173, 3038 Sfax, Tunisia
`jihen.tmamna@enis.tn, emna.benayed.b@ieee.org`
[2] Faculty of Science of Sfax, University of Sfax, BP 1171, 3000 Sfax, Tunisia
`mounir.benayed@ieee.org`

Abstract. Pruning has recently become ever-important research to compress deep neural networks. Previous pruning methods focus on removing filters, channels, or weights to reduce the large layer width of the models. Therefore, constrained by the dense model's depth, these methods often cannot achieve a high latency reduction. Another line of work focuses on reducing the model's depth by removing the irrelevant layers/blocks to guarantee a reduction in prediction time and resource usage. The weakness of these methods is that they used handcrafted rules to select the irrelevant layers/blocks that can lead to sub-optimal pruning. In this work, a novel method named IPSOPruner is proposed to automatically search the optimal pruned model that satisfies the resource constraint. IPSOPruner is based on improved particle swarm optimization (PSO). The main two improvements adopted into the original PSO to solve the layer/block pruning problem are: (1) the use of chaotic map and opposition based learning to speed up the convergence and avoid being trapped in a locally optimal solution and (2) the incorporation with the constrained handling method to lead the search to the feasible region. Finally, to recover the accuracy, the obtained pruned model will be fine-tuned. Experimental results on CIFAR-10 demonstrate that our IPSOPruner achieves superior results in depth and FLOPs reduction and also in an accuracy improvement.

Keywords: Neural network pruning · Constrained particle swarm optimization · Opposition based learning · Chaotic map

1 Introduction

The deep convolutional neural networks (CNNs) become accompanied by a significant demand in memory and computing power that is the major problem for real-time application deployment in resource-constrained devices [1]. Recently, neural network pruning [2] is recognized as the most predominant method to decrease the complexity of these models in terms of storage and computational requirements.

© Springer Nature Switzerland AG 2021
T. Mantoro et al. (Eds.): ICONIP 2021, CCIS 1517, pp. 315–322, 2021.
https://doi.org/10.1007/978-3-030-92310-5_37

Pruning methods are mainly pursued to remove weights, filters, or channels across different layers such as presented in [3–5]. The limitation of these methods is that they cannot achieve a high latency reduction.

The motivation of our proposed method inspires by the deduction of the three pioneering works. First, Liu et al. [6] showed that instead of selecting irrelevant parameters, the essence of pruning is performing implicit architecture search and finding effective structures. Second, He et al. [7] proved that the efficiency of applying the automatic method to neural network pruning alleviates human efforts. Third, Jordao et al. [8] showed that the reduction of model depth by layer achieved high latency reduction than filter or weight pruning. Based on these three deductions, we want to prune the model's layers/blocks to reduce the latency by automatically searching for the effective structure using the automatic method.

In this paper, we introduce a novel method for layer/block pruning named IPSOPruner. Particularly, we formulate the layer/block pruning as an optimization problem and, we adopt an automatic approach using PSO to address it. The main contributions of this study are:

1. We formulate the layer/block pruning as an optimization problem to automatically determine the irrelevant layers/blocks instead of using handcrafted rules to minimize the human intervention.
2. We attend to skip the more sensitive layers during the pruning process where their deletion can more damage the accuracy.
3. We improve the basic PSO by combining the PSO algorithm with opposition-based learning (OBL) and a chaotic map to enhance the population diversity. In addition, the constrained handling method is incorporated with the PSO to guide the search to a feasible region.
4. We demonstrate the effectiveness of our IPSOPruner by conducting experiments with different CNN models on CIFAR-10 dataset.

2   Related Works

Existing methods are mainly divided into two types: fine-grained pruning and coarse-grained pruning. The first aims to prune weights, filters, or channels from different layers. Some works use handcrafted criteria to judge the importance such as presented in [2,9]. However, these works rely on handcrafted rules. Another group focuses on AutoML methods to search automatically the pruned model such as published in [7,10]. However, these methods are focused only on pruning filters, channels, or weights to reduce FLOPs which are not directly correlated with latency consumption. This is due to that the latency reduction depends not only on the number of filters in each layer but also on other various aspects such as deployment devices. Thus, there is a non-linearity between the latency and the number of filters in each layer. To overcome the limitation of the latency reduction of the previous works, we need to focus on the depth reduction by removing the whole layer/block.

Coarse-grained pruning aims to reduce the depth of the model by removing the entire layer/block. In pruning literature, few works such as [8,11] support layer/block pruning. Elkerdawy et al. [11] used a one-shot proxy classifier for each layer to estimate their importance and the least important one will be removed from the model. However, these existing layer/block pruning methods are usually based on handcrafted rules which can lead to a sub-optimal solution. Different from the prior layer/block pruning methods, our proposed approach focuses on eliminating the need to use handcrafted rules to estimate the layer/block importance by searching the optimal pruned model automatically using our improved PSO algorithm.

3 Proposed Method

In this section, we introduce a new pruning method, IPOSPruner, that removes a portion of layers/blocks to meet resource constraints while keeping the original model accuracy or improving it.

3.1 Problem Formulation

Given a pre-trained CNN model with N convolutional layers/blocks, our problem can be regarded as finding the optimal pruned model that has the best accuracy and satisfies the resource constraint. For any pruned model M', we can present its structure by a set of decision variables where each variable is set to 0 if its corresponding layer/block is pruned or 1 otherwise. This set of variables can be presented as follow: $L = (l_1, l_2, ...l_N), l \in \{0, 1\}$

To that effect, our layer/block pruning problem can be formulated as follow:

$$\text{Max} \quad accuracy(M'(L))$$
$$\text{s.t.} \quad budget(M') \leq constraint \tag{1}$$

Where budget () computes the computational resources required by the model while the constraint is the predefined resource constraint.

3.2 Proposed IPSOPruner

Conventional PSO. Each individual in the PSO algorithm [12] is regarded as a particle that flies in the decision space towards the best solution. Each particle P_i has two main properties velocity $v_i = (v_{i1}, v_{i2}, ..., v_{iD})$ and position $x_i = (x_{i1}; x_{i2}, ..., x_{iD})$. The P_i can be updated as:

$$v_i^{(t+1)} = w.v_i^t + c_1.r_1.(P_{best,i}^t - x_i^t) + c_2.r_2.(G_{best}^t - x_i^t) \tag{2}$$

$$x_i^{t+1} = x_i^t + v_i^{t+1} \tag{3}$$

Where t is the number of iteration, $P_{best,i}$ is the personal best position, G_{best} is the global best position found by the swarm. w is the inertia coefficient. c_1 and c_2 are two acceleration coefficients to control the effects of $P_{best,i}$ and G_{best} on the new velocity. r_1 and r_2 are random numbers within $[0, 1]$.

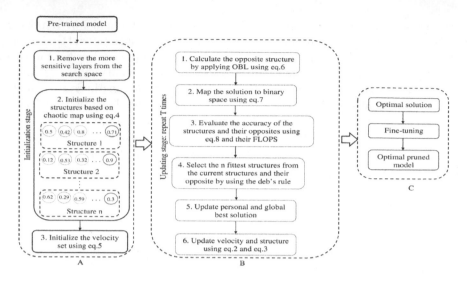

Fig. 1. Pipeline of our IPSOPruner

IPSOPruner. The conventional PSO may have some limits such as population diversity and fall into local optima. To overcome these limits, an improved PSO based on constraint handling method, chaotic map and OBL is proposed. Furthermore, layer/block pruning is a binary optimization problem, so an encoding strategy is introduced to map the solutions from the continuous space to the discrete space. Figure 1 presents the pipeline of our IPSOPruner. Taking a pretrained model as inputs, the optimal pruned model has achieved by a constraint improved PSO (see Fig. 1A, B). Once the search is achieved, the obtained pruned model will be fine-tuned until convergence (see Fig. 1C). The fine-tuning will be discussed in more detail in the Sect. 4.1. The improved PSO can be divided into two stages which are initialization stage and updating stage described in more detail below.

Initialization Stage. Li et al. [2] proved that there is a set of critical layers that shouldn't be removed during the pruning process as they affect directly the accuracy. So, in this stage (see Fig. 1A), we firstly remove the more critical layers from the search space. Secondly, the chaotic map is used to initialize the structures replacing the random initialization in the basic PSO. We apply a Logistic map [13] to generate initial values in the range [0, 1] which involve regularity and non-repetitiveness. The utility of this function is to improve population diversity. Generated chaotic structure values are as follow:

$$s_{i+1,j}^0 = a * s_{ij}^0 (1 - s_{ij}^0), a = 4, i = 1...N, j = 1...n \tag{4}$$

Where s_{ij}^0 is the chaotic variable of jth dimension of ith structure. These variables represent the probability of the layers being pruned.

Then, we initialize the searching velocity set V_i^0 of particle P_i randomly where $V_i^0 = (v_{i1}^0; v_{i2}^0; ...; v_{iN}^0)$ using Eq. 5:

$$v_{ij}^0 = rand[0, 1] \tag{5}$$

Updating Stage. At this stage, iterative searching is performed to find the optimal pruned model. The different steps of updating stage (see Fig. 1B) are as follow:

1. Apply Opposition Based Learning: In this step, the OBL [14] is used to calculate the opposite of each structure in order to enhance the diversity of the population and search in both directions using the following equation: let $S_i = (s_{i1}, s_{i2}, ...s_{iN})$ be a structure in N-dimension space, where $s_{ij} \in [a, b]$, the opposite point $\overline{S_i} = (\overline{s_{i1}}, \overline{s_{i2}}, ...\overline{s_{iN}})$ defined by its components:

$$\overline{s_{ij}} = a + b - s_{ij} \tag{6}$$

2. Encoding strategy: In this step, an encoding function applied to different structures and their opposites is introduced to map the structure vector to a binary one. The detail of this function is as follows:

$$l_{ij}^{binary} = \begin{cases} 1 \text{ if } s_{ij} > 0.5 \\ 0 \quad \text{otherwise} \end{cases} \tag{7}$$

where l_{ij}^{binary} is the binary converted value, 1 means that the layer/block has remained in the sub-model, otherwise, the layer/block is pruned.

3. Accuracy and FLOPs evaluation: In this step, IPSOPruner determines the FLOPs and the accuracy of each structure and its opposite. To measure the accuracy, we assign the filter weights of the preserved layers to initialize each structure and then we fine-tune these structures for a given number of epochs. The accuracy value will be determined using Eq. 8:

$$acc(S_i) = acc((D_{Train}, W_i', S_i), D_{Test}) \tag{8}$$

4. Apply the deb's rule: In this step, the deb's rule [15] as constraint handling method will be incorporated with PSO to choose the n fittest solutions from the set of structures and their opposites that satisfy the resource constraint which is the FLOPs in this work. The main principle of the deb's rule is as follows: (i) when we have two feasible solutions, the one with the best accuracy is selected, (ii) when we have one infeasible and one feasible solution, the feasible one is selected, and (iii) when we have two infeasible solutions, the one with smaller constraint violation is selected. The deb's rule algorithm used to select the best structure by comparing the current structures and their opposites based on their constrained value and their accuracy.

5. Update personal and global best structure: In the beginning, the personal best structures P_{best} are initialized by N initial structures respectively and the feasible structure with the greatest accuracy that satisfies the resource constraint regarded as the global best structure G_{best}. In this fifth step, P_{best} and G_{best} are updated using the deb's rule algorithm which compare the current structure S_i with $P_{best,i}$ and G_{best} based on their accuracy and FLOPs consumption values. Deb's rule is then used to determine if the current structure S_i can replace $P_{best,i}$ and G_{best}.

6. Update structure and velocity: In this step, the structure and the velocity of each particle will be updated using Eqs. 2 and 3.

When the search is finished, the feasible structure with the maximal accuracy in the population is returned as the optimal solution.

4   Experiments

We evaluate our IPSOPruner for representative models and standard datasets and we compare it with the traditional layer/block pruning methods.

4.1   Experiments Setting

Models and Datasets. To evaluate our IPSOPruner, we adopt the mainstream CNN models: ResNet and VGG on the dataset: CIFAR-10.

Fine-Tuning Setting. In our experiments, the fine-tuning is performed using SGD algorithm with a momentum of 0.9 and the batch size of 256. During the search, we fine-tune each solution candidate with a learning rate of 0.01 for 2 epochs to recover accuracy. Once the search is achieved, the final obtained structure will be fine-tuned with a 0.01 learning rate for 150 epochs. Every 50 epochs, the learning rate divided by 10.

4.2   Results

For pruning on CIFAR-10, we perform our experiments with ResNet and VGGNet. As can be observed in the Table 1, the performance of all the pruned models has improved compared with the original models.

VGGNet. We use the modified version of the VGG16 model with 13 convolutional layers. Under 40% constraint, our method prunes 6 layers and reduces up to 37.5% depth, 45.11% FLOPs and 84.16% parameters while improving the accuracy with 0.93% compared to the original model. During the layer pruning, we found that the last layers are the most pruned.

ResNet. We adopt two depths 110 and 56. For Resnet-56, we remove 8 blocks, 30.10% FLOPs, 19.02% parameters while the accuracy improved by 0.44%. For Resnet-110, we prune 22 blocks, 41.06% FLOPs and 33.24% parameters with an accuracy of 94.31%. With an increase of the constraint ratio, for ResNet-56, we achieve to remove 11 blocks, 41.38% FLOPs and 30.42% parameters with an accuracy of 93.4% which still better than the baseline model. On ResNet-110, we remove 27 blocks, 50.43% FLOPs and 35.39% parameters with accuracy enhanced by 0.48%.

These results show that there are irrelevant blocks in CNN models and their pruning will not affect the accuracy. In addition, we noticed that the blocks in the first stages of ResNet-56 and ResNet-110 are the most removed.

Table 1. Results on cifar-10, Acc and Para represent the accuracy and the parameters respectively

Model	Constraint ratio	Depth	Acc.	↓↑	Flops (M)	Pruned	Para (M)	Pruned
VGG16	0	16	93.02%	0.00%	314.03	0.0%	14.73	0.00%
	30%	11	94.19%	↑1.17%	210.16	33.08%	2.92	80.15%
	40%	10	93.95%	↑0.93%	172.36	45.11%	2.33	84.16%
ResNet-56	0	56	93,26%	0.00%	126.55	0.00%	0.85	0.00%
	30%	40	93.7%	↑0.44%	88.46	30.10%	0.69	19.02%
	40%	34	93,4%	↑0,14%	74.19	41.38%	0.59	30.42%
Resnet-110	0	110	93.50%	0.00%	254.99	0.00%	1.73	0.00%
	40%	66	94.31%	↑0.81%	150.28	41.06%	1.15	33.24%
	50%	56	93.98	↑0.48%	126.39	50.43%	1.12	35.39%

4.3 Comparison with Other Methods

We compare the performance of our IPSOPruner on CIFAR-10, with existing layer/block pruning methods. The superiority of our IPSOPruner compared with the traditional layer/block pruning methods is the adaptation of an automatic structure search to find the optimal structure. Therefore, as it can be observed in Table 2, our IPSOPruner produces many superior results in terms of depth reduction, FLOPs, parameters and accuracy. The results further manifest the effectiveness of our IPSOPruner for pruning CNN.

Table 2. Comparison of our IPSOPruner with the existing layer/block pruning methods

Model	Method	Baseline Acc.	↓↑	Flops	Para	Depth
Resnet-56 CIFAR-10	[8]	–	↓0.98%	30.01%	30.16%	40
	IPSOPruner	93.26%	**↑0.14%**	**41.38%**	**30.42%**	**34**
Resnet-110 CIFAR-10	[8]	–	↓0.18%	31.68%	32.32%	76
	IPSOPruner	**93.5%**	**↑0.48%**	**50.43%**	**35.39%**	**56**

5 Conclusion

This work introduces a new layer/block pruning approach, IPSOPruner, regarding pruning as a constrained optimization problem. To solve this problem, we first propose to improve the search space by removing the more critical layers/blocks from the search space during the pruning process, where their deletion can more damage the accuracy. Then, to find the optimal pruned model, we propose an improved particle swarm algorithm using OBL and a chaotic map to enhance the population diversity and avoid falling into local optima, and using the constraint handling method to guide the search to feasible region. We demonstrate that our IPSOPruner reaches promising results compared to traditional layer pruning and filter pruning methods. In the future, we intend to combine our IPSOPruner with the filter pruning method to reduce more FLOPs and latency.

References

1. Tmamna, J., Ayed, E.B., Ayed, M.B.: Deep learning for internet of things in fog computing: survey and open issues. In: International Conference on Advanced Technologies for Signal and Image Processing (ATSIP), pp. 1–6 (2020). https://doi.org/10.1109/ATSIP49331.2020.9231685
2. Li, H., Kadav, A., Durdanovic, I., Samet, H., Graf, H.P.: Pruning filters for efficient convnets. In: International Conference on Learning Representations (ICLR) (2017)
3. Li, H., Ma, C., Xu, W., Liu, X.: Feature statistics guided efficient filter pruning. In: International Joint Conference on Artificial Intelligence (IJCAI), pp. 2619–2625 (2020)
4. Xiao, X., Wang, Z., Rajasekaran, S.: Autoprune: automatic network pruning by regularizing auxiliary parameters. In: Advances in Neural Information Processing Systems, pp. 13681–13691. Vancouver Canada (2019)
5. Wang, Z., Li, C., Wang, X.: Convolutional neural network pruning with structural redundancy reduction. In: Proceedings of the IEEE/CVF Conference on Computer Vision and Pattern Recognition, pp. 14913–14922 (2021)
6. Liu, Z., Sun, M., Zhou, T., Huang, G., Darrell, T.: Rethinking the value of network pruning. In: International Conference on Learning Representations (ICLR) (2019)
7. He, Y., Lin, J., Liu, Z., Wang, H., Li, L.J., Han, S.: Amc: automl for model compression and acceleration on mobile devices. In: Proceedings of the European Conference on Computer Vision, Munich, Germany, pp. 784–800 (2018)
8. Jordao, A., Lie, M., Schwartz, W.R.: Discriminative layer pruning for convolutional neural networks. IEEE J. Sel. Top. Sig. Process. **14**(4), 828–837 (2020)
9. He, Y., Liu, P., Wang, Z., Hu, Z., Yang, Y.: Filter pruning via geometric median for deep convolutional neural networks acceleration. In: Proceedings of the IEEE/CVF Conference on Computer Vision and Pattern Recognition, Long Beach, CA, USA, pp. 4340–4349 (2019)
10. Liu, Z., et al.: MetaPruning: meta learning for automatic neural network channel pruning. In: Proceedings of IEEE/CVF International Conference on Computer Vision, pp. 3296–3305 (2019)
11. Elkerdawy, S., Elhoushi, M., Singh, A., Zhang, H., Ray, N.: One-shot layer-wise accuracy approximation for layer pruning. In: IEEE International Conference on Image Processing, pp. 2940–2944. IEEE, Abu Dhabi (2020). https://doi.org/10.1109/ICIP40778.2020.9191238
12. Kennedy, J., Eberhart, R.: Particle swarm optimization. In: Proceedings of ICNN 1995-International Conference on Neural Networks, vol. 4, pp. 1942–1948. IEEE, Perth (1995). https://doi.org/10.1109/ICNN.1995.488968
13. Zhenyu, G., Bo, C., Min, Y., Binggang, C.: Self-adaptive chaos differential evolution. In: Jiao, L., Wang, L., Gao, X., Liu, J., Wu, F. (eds.) ICNC 2006. LNCS, vol. 4221, pp. 972–975. Springer, Heidelberg (2006). https://doi.org/10.1007/11881070_128
14. Tizhoosh, H.R.: Opposition-based learning: a new scheme for machine intelligence. In: International Conference on Computational Intelligence for Modelling, Control and Automation and International Conference on Intelligent Agents, Web Technologies and Internet Commerce (CIMCA-IAWTIC 2006), vol. 1, pp. 695–701. IEEE, Vienna (2005). https://doi.org/10.1109/CIMCA.2005.1631345
15. Deb, K.: An efficient constraint handling method for genetic algorithms. Comput. Methods Appl. Mech. Eng. **186**(2–4), 311–338 (2000)

Reliable, Robust, and Secure Machine Learning Algorithms

On Robustness of Generative Representations Against Catastrophic Forgetting

Wojciech Masarczyk[1]($\boxtimes$) (iD), Kamil Deja[1] (iD), and Tomasz Trzcinski[1,2,3] (iD)

[1] Warsaw University of Technology, Warsaw, Poland
{wojciech.masarczyk.dokt,kamil.deja.dokt,tomasz.trzcinski}@pw.edu.pl
[2] Jagiellonian University, Kraków, Poland
[3] Tooploox, Wrocław, Poland

Abstract. Catastrophic forgetting of previously learned knowledge while learning new tasks is a widely observed limitation of contemporary neural networks. Although many continual learning methods are proposed to mitigate this drawback, the main question remains unanswered: what is the root cause of catastrophic forgetting? In this work, we aim at answering this question by posing and validating a set of research hypotheses related to the specificity of representations built internally by neural models. More specifically, we design a set of empirical evaluations that compare the robustness of representations in discriminative and generative models against catastrophic forgetting. We observe that representations learned by discriminative models are more prone to catastrophic forgetting than their generative counterparts, which sheds new light on the advantages of developing generative models for continual learning. Finally, our work opens new research pathways and possibilities to adopt generative models in continual learning beyond mere replay mechanisms.

1 Introduction

Neural networks are widely used across many real-life applications, ranging from image recognition [11] to natural language processing [14]. Nevertheless, neural models used in those applications assume identical and independently distributed training data - the assumption rarely met in practice. As a result, contemporary neural network models are prone to catastrophic forgetting [2] - a well-known limitation of neural networks that erode previously learned knowledge. Continual learning is a field of machine learning that aims at addressing this pitfall of neural models by constant adaption to new data. The majority of works in this field focus on developing methods for mitigating the effects of catastrophic forgetting [7]. Nevertheless, recent findings [8,13] show that it is possible to surpass well-established continual learning methods across popular benchmarks with simplistic, heuristic-based methods. The surprising effectiveness of these baselines indicates that the root cause of catastrophic forgetting is yet to be discovered, and we follow this intuition in our work (Fig. 1).

K. Deja—Work done prior joining Amazon.

© Springer Nature Switzerland AG 2021
T. Mantoro et al. (Eds.): ICONIP 2021, CCIS 1517, pp. 325–333, 2021.
https://doi.org/10.1007/978-3-030-92310-5_38

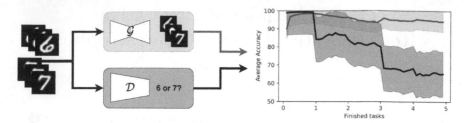

Fig. 1. A schematic overview of our main experiment. Representations learned by the generative model are less susceptible to catastrophic forgetting than discriminative ones.

We investigate the catastrophic forgetting with methodological rigor; we state and empirically validate research hypotheses that shed new light on this phenomenon. We build upon the works of [1,9] where the roots of catastrophic forgetting are investigated. Contrary to previous works, we postulate to look at the continual learning from the perspective of internal representations of neural networks and analyze their impact on the final performance of the continually learned model.

To summarize, the main contribution of our work is the statement of the following research hypotheses, along with their empirical validation:

Hypothesis 1 – *Representations learned by autoencoders and variational autoencoders are less prone to catastrophic forgetting than representations of discriminative models.*

Hypothesis 2 – *Autoencoders and variational autoencoders learn more transferable features than discriminative models.*

Moreover, based on our results, we explain the effect observed in [13], where the authors attribute the lack of catastrophic forgetting to the reconstruction task. We show this is not the case, and one can explain the effect through the differences in building model representations.

This result shows that the lack of catastrophic forgetting is not an artifact of reconstruction task but rather a phenomenon linked to the nature of generative representations.

In Sect. 3.2 we show that it is possible to achieve surprisingly good performance on continual learning benchmarks without any specific mechanism to overcome catastrophic forgetting. These results undermine the validity of commonly used continual learning benchmarks.

2   Related Works

Following [7], we group continual learning methods into three categories. *Regularization methods* typically train a single model and penalize the change of essential parameters of the model on subsequent tasks [3,18]. *Growing architecture methods* train separate substructures in isolation for specific tasks. Then an independent mechanism decides which substructure to use during evaluation [12,17]. *Rehearsal methods* prevent forgetting by retraining the model with a combination of new and previous data examples stored either in buffer [10] or generative model [15].

While most of the works develop new methods that are more robust to catastrophic forgetting, only several works investigate the actual phenomenon [1,6,9]. Specifically, in [9] authors analyze the relationship between semantic similarity of tasks and magnitude of catastrophic forgetting. In [1] authors show that the effect of catastrophic forgetting diminishes with prolonged exposure to the domain, which suggests that catastrophic forgetting could be an artifact of immature systems. Another approach [6] investigates the problem with Explainable Artificial Intelligence (XAI) tools, comparing the effects of catastrophic forgetting for different layers of CNN.

Our work builds upon Thai et al. [13], where authors claim that networks trained in continual reconstruction tasks do not suffer from catastrophic forgetting. We show that different dynamics of catastrophic forgetting in generative and classification tasks are linked to the representations of the data constructed by the neural networks. Specifically, we argue that learning representations through generative modeling is naturally more aligned with continual learning.

3   Methodology

To examine and compare representations from different models, we consider three types of models: discriminative – $\mathcal{D}$, Autoencoder – $\mathcal{G}_{AE}$ and Variational Autonecoder [4] – $\mathcal{G}_{VAE}$. The networks share the same architecture, except for the last layer, to minimize the impact of different architectures on catastrophic forgetting. The networks' objective defines the last layers.

As shown in Fig. 2, we train all models on the same training sequence T_N but with different aims (generation or classification). The index of particular task is denoted by k, where $k = 1, \ldots, N$. To obtain the representations of data for a particular model, we feed the data to the model and collect the representations from the penultimate layer of the model. We use $\mathcal{A}_{\mathcal{D}}^t(\mathbf{x}^k)$, to denote activations from penultimate layer of the model $\mathcal{D}$ after finishing task t for input data $\langle \mathbf{x}^k \rangle$ from task k.

Datasets. We use three commonly used continual learning benchmarks to create a continuous sequence of tasks: splitMNIST, splitFashionMNIST, splitCIFAR-10. We follow the typical formulation of the continual learning task and split the datasets to 5 disjoint subsets with two classes for each task.

Architectures. We use simple six-layer MLP architectures. ReLU activations follow each layer except for the last layer. The last layers of generative models map activation vectors from penultimate layers to images of equal size as the input images. In the case of classification, we use a multi-head output layer with two neurons per task.

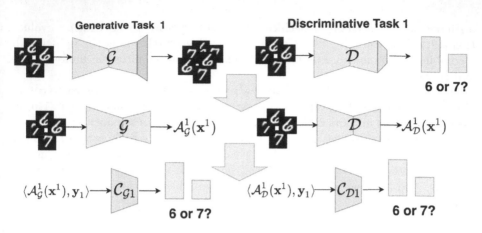

Fig. 2. A schematic overview describing the process of learning and collecting discriminative and generative representations.

3.1 Hypothesis 1

Discriminative Abilities of Representations.
First, to test our hypothesis, we look at the problem of catastrophic forgetting from the perspective of models' accuracy. To measure the robustness of representations to the catastrophic forgetting, we train all models on identical data sequences T_N and for each task, we collect their representations from the penultimate layer. These representations serve as data for a particular linear classifier, *i.e.*, we train only the first linear classifier on representations of the first task. After finishing the first task, we freeze the first classifier for the rest of the training. This way, the degradation of its performance can be attributed exclusively to forgetting the representations for the first task, and we can directly measure the amount of forgetting in the model. The same procedure applies to the remaining tasks. More precisely, after each epoch of training on task k with data $\langle \mathbf{x}^k, \mathbf{y}^k \rangle$, we collect the representations for model $\mathcal{D}$ from its penultimate layer $A_\mathcal{D}^k(\mathbf{x}^j)$ for $j = k$ and train linear classifier $C_{\mathcal{D}j}$ on dataset $\langle A_\mathcal{D}^k(\mathbf{x}^k), \mathbf{y}^k \rangle$. The rest of the classifiers $C_{\mathcal{D}j}$ for $j > k$, remain untrained. Next, all classifiers $C_{\mathcal{D}j}$, $j = 1, \ldots, 5$ are evaluated on the validation dataset.

Since all the classifiers $C_{\mathcal{D}j}$ are trained only during j-th task, the loss of performance may only be attributed to the drift of representations from the penultimate layer. Therefore, the smaller the degradation of the classifier's performance, the more resilient the features are to the catastrophic forgetting. We apply the same procedure to the models $\mathcal{G}_{AE}$ and $\mathcal{G}_{VAE}$ as shown in Fig. 2.

The left column of Fig. 3 shows that across all benchmarks, the classifier's performance trained with representations of discriminative model suddenly drops down to the level of random guessing. In contrast, the performance of $\mathcal{G}_{AE}$ or $\mathcal{G}_{VAE}$ is stable throughout the whole sequence of training. This suggests that the representations of tested generative models are almost immune to the problem of catastrophic forgetting, especially in the case of less complex datasets as

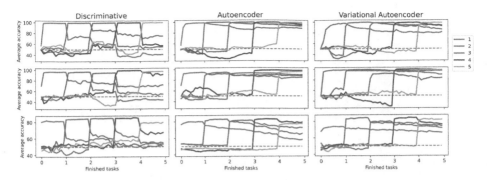

Fig. 3. Each curve represents the average accuracy of a specific task. The dashed line is for the reference presenting the performance of a random classifier. Columns represent results for representations of $\mathcal{D}$, $\mathcal{G}_{AE}$ and $\mathcal{G}_{VAE}$ respectively. Top row – MNIST, middle - FashionMNIST, bottom – CIFAR-10.

MNIST and FashionMNIST. In the case of CIFAR-10, the amount of forgetting is considerable for $\mathcal{G}_{AE}$, yet still less severe than in the discriminative models. The gradual and monotonic deterioration of the performance suggests that forgetting in generative models has a different nature than in discriminative models. The above experiment proves the validity of the first hypothesis through the lenses of accuracy. To investigate this phenomenon further, we propose to measure catastrophic forgetting through the index of representations similarity.

Centered Kernel Alignment (CKA). To further examine the validity of our hypothesis that representations learned by generative models are less susceptible to catastrophic forgetting, we investigate the evolution of network representations in time. To that end, we use a task-agnostic measure to estimate the relative drift of the representations, known as Centered Kernel Alignment (CKA) [5]:

$$CKA(X,Y) = \frac{\left\|X^T Y\right\|_F^2}{\left\|X^T X\right\|_F \left\|Y^T Y\right\|_F}, \tag{1}$$

where $X \in \mathbb{R}^{n \times m_x}$, $Y \in \mathbb{R}^{n \times m_y}$, and $\|\|_F$ is a Frobenius norm. We measure the similarity between representations of the same network collected at different moments of the training of the neural network. To analyze the evolution of representations from model $\mathcal{D}$, we collect the reference representations $\mathcal{A}_{\mathcal{D}}^k(\mathbf{x}^k)$ at the end of task k. Then, to measure the relative drift of representations of model $\mathcal{D}$ on task k, we compute the CKA index between the reference and current representations $CKA(\mathcal{A}_{\mathcal{D}}^k(\mathbf{x}^k), \mathcal{A}_{\mathcal{D}}^j(\mathbf{x}^k))$, for $j \geq k$. We follow this procedure for each task in training sequence T_N. The analogous procedure is applied to the representations of models $\mathcal{G}_{AE}$ and $\mathcal{G}_{VAE}$.

Figure 4 presents the results of the experiment. In the case of discriminative representations (top row), we can see an abrupt change of representations across all datasets, which is in line with the results from the previous experiment. The results from the middle row of Fig. 4 show that representations from $\mathcal{G}_{AE}$ only

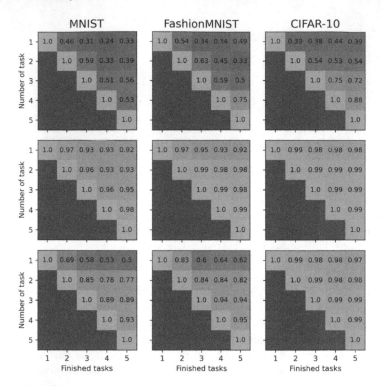

Fig. 4. Illustration of the evolution of representations similarity measure with CKA index. The rows (top to bottom) represent results of different models: $\mathcal{D}$, $\mathcal{G}_{AE}$ and $\mathcal{G}_{VAE}$ respectively. Columns (from left to right) – MNIST, FashionMNIST, CIFAR-10.

slightly evolve during the training on consecutive tasks and remain similar to the reference representations. The representations of $\mathcal{G}_{VAE}$ changes significantly on the first two tasks of less complex datasets (MNIST and FashionMNIST). However, this is not the case for CIFAR-10, where forgetting on VAE representations is unnoticeable. This may suggest that the complexity of the data impacts the learning process of generative representations.

3.2 Hypothesis 2

To validate the second hypothesis, which states that *autoencoders and variational autoencoders learn more transferable features than discriminative models*, we train all the models only on the first task in the learning sequence T_N. We adopt this approach as we are interested in measuring the transferability of learned features in the context of future tasks.

After finishing the first task, we collect representations for all data splits and train all classifiers on respective data splits. Then, we evaluate these classifiers on the validation datasets. Because the backbone of the neural network is trained

Table 1. Average accuracy (in %± std) across all tasks ("Split") and on the joint dataset ("All") after finishing the first task.

Model	MNIST		FashionMNIST		CIFAR-10	
	Split	All	Split	All	Split	All
$\mathcal{D}$	$76.8_{\pm12.0}$	$31.4_{\pm3.1}$	$74.3_{\pm11.5}$	$36.0_{\pm3.0}$	$69.2_{\pm6.4}$	$23.3_{\pm2.3}$
$\mathcal{G}_{AE}$	$\mathbf{96.8}_{\pm5.4}$	$\mathbf{82.9}_{\pm2.4}$	$92.1_{\pm7.2}$	$\mathbf{74.6}_{\pm1.6}$	$\mathbf{80.5}_{\pm2.0}$	$\mathbf{44.4}_{\pm1.0}$
$\mathcal{G}_{VAE}$	$88.9_{\pm6.7}$	$58.6_{\pm5.2}$	$\mathbf{94.2}_{\pm5.5}$	$61.1_{\pm0.9}$	$78.9_{\pm3.0}$	$37.4_{\pm0.2}$

only for the first task, we measure the transferability of the features learned during the first task to other tasks ("Split" in Table 1). To gain further insights, we train a single classifier on all collected representations. This way, for each dataset, the task is a 10-way classification. The results of this experiment tell us how general the features learned during the first task are in classifying the whole dataset ("All" in Table 1).

The superiority of the generative representations in terms of transferability is undeniable across all benchmarks. Although classifiers learned on $\mathcal{G}_{VAE}$ representations from the VAE model performs worse than classifiers trained on $\mathcal{G}_{AE}$ representations, both of these approaches obtain significantly better results than classifiers trained of model $\mathcal{D}$ representations. In the case of the model $\mathcal{G}_{AE}$ for MNIST and FashionMNIST datasets, the classifiers have a nearly perfect average accuracy of 96.8% and 92.1%, respectively. The results of the classifiers trained on joint datasets ("All") are even more surprising. It turns out that a linear classifier using representations from the model trained on a single task achieves an average accuracy of 82.9%, 74.6%, and 44.36% in 10-way classification tasks on MNIST, FashionMNIST, and CIFAR-10, respectively. On the other hand, the poor performance of classifiers trained with the representations learned by the discriminative model confirms that representations learned this way do not generalize beyond the current task.

Guided by the above results, we create an additional experiment to analyze how the training on the first task impacts the reconstruction quality on other tasks. To that end, we carry out experiments only with the generative models $\mathcal{G}_{AE}$ and $\mathcal{G}_{VAE}$. We evaluate the model with data samples from other tasks while training the network on the first task.

Figure 5 presents the results of this experiment. In each plot, the blue curve represents the loss on the first task, the one that the model is trained. All the plots have the same tendency – the reconstruction loss on all tasks decreases proportionally with the loss of the first task. This proves the point that unvisited tasks directly benefit from the training on the first task. In other words, the representations learned during the first task are helpful for the following tasks. In MNIST and FashionMNIST, there is a significant gap between the loss on the current task (blue curve) and other tasks. The gap is more significant in the case of $\mathcal{G}_{VAE}$, which is in line with the results from previous experiments suggesting that VAE based models need more complex datasets to develop general features.

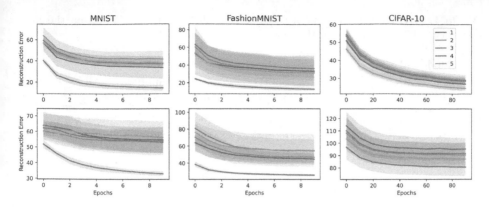

Fig. 5. Reconstruction loss on different tasks for SplitMNIST (left), FashionMNIST (middle), and CIFAR-10 (right) with respect to training epochs on the first task. Top – $\mathcal{G}_{AE}$, bottom – $\mathcal{G}_{VAE}$. The solid line is the mean of 5 runs, shaded area – standard dev.

With these experiments, we provide an intuitive explanation to the phenomenon observed by Thai et al. [13], where authors suggest that the continual reconstruction task does not suffer from catastrophic forgetting. We argue that the transferability of generative features contributes to the diminished impact of catastrophic forgetting. As the results in Fig. 5 show, future tasks benefit from the features learned during the first task, and therefore they are not forgotten by the model.

4 Discussion

In this work, we stated two hypotheses concerning different representations and their impact on catastrophic forgetting. We carried out experiments to empirically validate our hypotheses. The performed experiments show that the dynamics of the catastrophic forgetting for discriminative and generative representations are different. In particular, results from Fig. 4 show that the amount of forgetting in generative models is significantly smaller than in discriminative models. Additionally, the forgetting of generative representations is gradual and monotonic in contrast to the chaotic behavior of discriminative representations. Since it becomes more evident that catastrophic forgetting is not a homogeneous phenomenon and its character depends on the task or learning paradigm, we foresee the need for task-agnostic measures of catastrophic forgetting.

This work is the first step towards understanding the relationship between generative and discriminative representations in the context of continual learning. While several papers discuss this relation, *e.g.*, [16] many questions remain unanswered, especially in the context of continual learning. How can one use the mechanisms of generative learning to obtain better representations for discrimination tasks? Is the generic nature of generative representations the only explanation for the lack of catastrophic forgetting? Answering these and other questions, we left as future work.

Acknowledgment. This research was funded by National Science Centre, Poland (grant no 2020/39/ B/ST6/01511 and 2018/31/N/ST6/02374), Foundation for Polish Science (grant no POIR.04.04.00-00-14DE/ 18-00 carried out within the Team-Net program co-financed by the European Union under the European Regional Development Fund) and Warsaw University of Technology (POB Research Centre for Artificial Intelligence and Robotics within the Excellence Initiative Program - Research University). For the purpose of Open Access, the author has applied a CC-BY public copyright license to any Author Accepted Manuscript (AAM) version arising from this submission.

References

1. Davidson, G., Mozer, M.C.: Sequential mastery of multiple visual tasks: networks naturally learn to learn and forget to forget. In: CVPR (2020)
2. French, R.M.: Catastrophic forgetting in connectionist networks. TiCS **3**, 128–135 (1999)
3. Kirkpatrick, J., et al.: Overcoming catastrophic forgetting in neural networks. PNAS **114**, 3521–3526 (2017)
4. Kingma, D.P., Welling, M.: Auto-encoding variational Bayes. In: ICLR (2014)
5. Kornblith, S., et al.: Similarity of neural network representations revisited. In: ICML(2019)
6. Nguyen, G., et al.: Dissecting catastrophic forgetting in continual learning by deep visualization. arXiv (2020)
7. Parisi, G.I., et al.: Continual lifelong learning with neural networks: a review. Neural Netw. **113**, 54–71 (2019)
8. Prabhu, A., Torr, P.H.S., Dokania, P.K.: GDumb: a simple approach that questions our progress in continual learning. In: Vedaldi, A., Bischof, H., Brox, T., Frahm, J.-M. (eds.) ECCV 2020. LNCS, vol. 12347, pp. 524–540. Springer, Cham (2020). https://doi.org/10.1007/978-3-030-58536-5_31
9. Ramasesh, V., et al.: Anatomy of catastrophic forgetting: hidden representations and task semantics. In: ICLR (2021)
10. Rolnick, D., et al.: Experience Replay for Continual Learning. In: NeurIPS (2019)
11. Russakovsky, O., et al.: ImageNet large scale visual recognition challenge. IJCV (2015)
12. Rusu, A., et al.: Progressive neural networks. arXiv (2016)
13. Thai, A., et al.: Does continual learning = catastrophic forgetting? arXiv (2021)
14. Vaswani, A., et al.: Attention is all you need. In: NeurIPS (2017)
15. van de Ven, G.M., Tolias, A.S.: Generative replay with feedback connections as a general strategy for continual learning. arXiv (2018)
16. Wu, Y.N., et al.: A tale of three probabilistic families: discriminative, descriptive and generative models (2018)
17. Yoon, J., et al.: Lifelong learning with dynamically expandable networks. In: ICLR (2018)
18. Zenke, F., et al.: Continual learning through synaptic intelligence. In: ICML (2017)

Continual Learning with Differential Privacy

Pradnya Desai[1], Phung Lai[1], NhatHai Phan[1(✉)], and My T. Thai[2]

[1] New Jersey Institute of Technology, Newark, USA
{pnd26,tl353,phan}@njit.edu
[2] University of Florida, Gainesville, USA
mythai@cise.ufl.edu

Abstract. In this paper, we focus on preserving differential privacy (DP) in continual learning (CL), in which we train ML models to learn a sequence of new tasks while memorizing previous tasks. We first introduce a notion of continual adjacent databases to bound the sensitivity of any data record participating in the training process of CL. Based upon that, we develop a new DP-preserving algorithm for CL with a data sampling strategy to quantify the privacy risk of training data in the well-known Averaged Gradient Episodic Memory (A-GEM) approach by applying a moments accountant. Our algorithm provides formal guarantees of privacy for data records across tasks in CL. Preliminary theoretical analysis and evaluations show that our mechanism tightens the privacy loss while maintaining a promising model utility.

Keywords: Continual learning · Differential privacy · Deep learning

1 Introduction

The ability to acquire new knowledge over time while retaining previously learned experiences, referred to as continual learning (CL), brings machine learning (ML) closer to human learning [17]. More specifically, given a stream of tasks, CL focuses on training a ML model to quickly learn a new task by leveraging the acquired knowledge after learning previous tasks under a limited amount of computation and memory resources [10]. As a result, the main challenge of existing CL algorithms is that they can be quickly suffered by catastrophic forgetting.

Also, memorizing previous tasks while learning new tasks further exposes CL models to adversarial attacks [7,18]. CL models can disclose private information in the training set, such as healthcare and financial data [9]. Continuously accessing the data from the previously learned tasks, either stored in episodic memories [3] or produced from generative memories [11], incurs additional privacy risk compared to a ML model trained on a single task. However, there is still a lack of scientific study to protect private training data in CL algorithms.

Motivated by this, we propose to preserve differential privacy (DP) [4], offering rigorous privacy protection as probabilistic terms for the training data in CL.

P. Desai and P. Lai—These two authors contributed equally.

© Springer Nature Switzerland AG 2021
T. Mantoro et al. (Eds.): ICONIP 2021, CCIS 1517, pp. 334–343, 2021.
https://doi.org/10.1007/978-3-030-92310-5_39

Merely employing existing DP-preserving mechanisms can either cause a significantly large privacy loss or quickly exhaust the limited computation and memory resources in learning new tasks while memorizing previous tasks through either episodic or generative memories. Thus, effectively and efficiently preserving DP in CL remains a mostly open problem.

Key Contributions. To effectively bound the DP privacy loss in CL, we first define continual adjacent databases (Definition 2) to capture the impact of the current task's data and the episodic memory on the privacy loss and model utility. From that, we incorporate a moments accountant [1] into the A-GEM algorithm [3] in a new **DP-CL** algorithm to preserve DP in CL.

Our idea is to configure the episodic memory $\mathcal{M}$ in A-GEM as independent mini-memory blocks. We store a subset of training data of the current task in a mini-memory block with an associated task index in $\mathcal{M}$ for each task. At each training step, we compute reference gradients on the mini-memory blocks independently. The reference gradients will be used to optimize the process of memorizing previously learned tasks as in A-GEM. Importantly, by keep tracking of the task and mini-memory block index, we can leverage a moments accountant to estimate the privacy cost spent on each mini-memory block. Based upon this, we derive a new strategy (Lemma 2) to bound DP loss in the whole CL process while maintaining the computation efficiency of the A-GEM algorithm.

To our knowledge, our proposed mechanism establishes the first formal connection between DP and CL. Experiments conducted on the permuted MNIST dataset [8] and the Split CIFAR [19] show promising results in preserving DP in CL, compared with baseline approaches.

2 Background

In this section, we revisit continual learning, differential privacy, and introduce our problem statement. The goal of CL is to learn a model through a sequence of tasks $T = [t_i]_{i \in [1,N]}$ such that the learning of each new task will not cause forgetting of the previously learned tasks. Let $\mathcal{D}_T$ be the dataset at task T consisting of S_T samples, each of which is a sample $x \in \mathbb{R}^d$ associated with a label y. Each y is a one-hot vector of C categories: $y = [y_c]_{c \in [1,C]}$. A classifier outputs class scores $f : \mathbb{R}^d \to \mathbb{R}^C$ mapping an input x to a vector of scores $f(x) = [f_c(x)]_{c \in [1,C]}$ s.t. $\forall c \in [1,C] : f_c(x) \in [0,1]$ and $\sum_{c=1}^{C} f_c(x) = 1$. The class with the highest score is selected as the predicted label for the sample. The classifier f is trained by minimizing a loss function $\mathcal{L}(f(x), y)$ that penalizes mismatching between the prediction $f(x)$ and the original value y.

Averaged Gradient Episodic Memory (A-GEM) [3]. There is a sequence of tasks $[t_i]_{i \in [1,T-1]}$ that have been learnt, where $T < N$. The goal is to train the model at the current task T so that it minimizes the loss on the task T and does not forget previous learned tasks $i < T$. The key feature of A-GEM is to store a subset of data from task i, denoted as $\mathcal{M}_i$, in an episodic memory $\mathcal{M}$. Then the algorithm ensures that the loss on an average episodic memory across all the previously learned tasks, i.e., $\mathcal{M} = \cup_{i < \mathcal{T}} \mathcal{M}_i$, does not increase at every step. In A-GEM, the objective function of learning the current task $\mathcal{T}$ is:

$$\theta^{\mathcal{T}} = \min_{\theta} \mathcal{L}\big(f(\theta^{\mathcal{T}-1}, \mathcal{D}_{\mathcal{T}})\big) \text{ s.t. } \mathcal{L}\big(f(\theta^{\mathcal{T}}, \mathcal{M})\big) \leq \mathcal{L}\big(f(\theta^{\mathcal{T}-1}, \mathcal{M})\big) \tag{1}$$

where $\theta^{\mathcal{T}-1}$ is the values of model parameters θ learned after training the task $\mathcal{T} - 1$, and $\mathcal{L}\big(f(\theta^{\mathcal{T}-1}, \mathcal{D}_{\mathcal{T}})\big) = \frac{1}{|\mathcal{D}_{\mathcal{T}}|} \sum_{x \in \mathcal{D}_{\mathcal{T}}} \mathcal{L}\big(f(\theta^{\mathcal{T}-1}, x)\big)$.

The constrained optimization problem of Eq. 1 can be approximated quickly and the updated gradient $\tilde{g}$ is as follows:

$$\tilde{g} = g - \frac{g^T g_{ref}}{g_{ref}^T g_{ref}} g_{ref} \tag{2}$$

where g is the proposed gradient update on $\mathcal{T}$ and g_{ref} is the reference gradient computed from the episodic memory $\mathcal{M}$ from previous tasks.

Differential Privacy [4,5]. To avoid the training data leakage, DP guarantees to restrict what the adversaries can learn from the training data given the model parameters by ensuring similar model outcomes with and without any single data sample in the dataset. The definition of DP is as follows:

Definition 1 (ϵ, δ)-*DP* [4]. *A randomized algorithm A fulfills (ϵ, δ)-DP, if for any two adjacent databases D and D' differ at most one sample, and for all outcomes $\mathcal{O} \subseteq Range(A)$, we have: $Pr[A(D) = \mathcal{O}] \leq e^{\epsilon} Pr[A(D') = \mathcal{O}] + \delta$, where ϵ is the privacy budget and δ is the broken probability.*

DP in Continual Learning. There are several works of DP in CL [6,13]. In [6], the authors train a DP-GAN to approximate the distribution of the past datasets. They leverage a small portion of public data (i.e., the data that does not need to keep private) to initialize and train the GAN in the first few iterations of each task, then continue training the GAN model under DP constraint. The trained generator produces adversarial examples imitating real examples of past tasks. Then, the adversarial examples are employed to supplement the actual data of the current training task. DPL2M [13] perturbs the objective functions using a DPAL mechanism [12,14] and applies A-GEM to optimize the perturbed objective function. However, there is a lack of a concrete definition of adjacent databases with unclear or not well-justified DP protection in [6,13]. Different from existing works, we provide a formal DP protection for CL models.

3 Continual Learning with DP

This section establishes a connection between differential privacy and continual learning. We first propose a definition of continual adjacent databases in CL, as follows: Two databases D and D' are continual adjacent if they differ in a single sample of the training data and differ in a single sample of the episodic memory across all the tasks. The definition is presented as follows:

Definition 2 *Continual Adjacent Databases. Two databases $D = (\mathcal{D}, \mathcal{M})$ and $D' = (\mathcal{D}', \mathcal{M}')$, where $\mathcal{D} = \cup_{i=1}^{N} \mathcal{D}_i$, $\mathcal{D}' = \cup_{i=1}^{N} \mathcal{D}'_i$, $\mathcal{M} = \cup_{i=1}^{N} \mathcal{M}_i$, and $\mathcal{M}' = \cup_{i=1}^{N} \mathcal{M}'_i$, are called continual adjacent if: $\|\mathcal{D} - \mathcal{D}'\|_1 \leq 1$ and $\|\mathcal{M} - \mathcal{M}'\|_1 \leq 1$.*

A Naive Algorithm. Based upon Definition 2, a straightforward approach, called DP-AGEM, is to simply apply a moments accountant [1] into A-GEM [3], to preserve DP in CL. At each task $\mathcal{T}$, we divide the dataset $D_{\mathcal{T}}$ into $D_{\mathcal{T}}^{train}$ and $D_{\mathcal{T}}^{ref}$ such that $D_{\mathcal{T}}^{train}$ and $D_{\mathcal{T}}^{ref}$ are disjoint: $D_{\mathcal{T}}^{train} \cap D_{\mathcal{T}}^{ref} = \emptyset$. By using the training data $\mathcal{D}_{\mathcal{T}}^{train}$ with a sampling rate p, DP-AGEM computes a proposed gradient g, which is bounded by a predefined l_2-norm clipping bound β. It is beneficial in real-world to keep track of the privacy budget spent on each task independently,

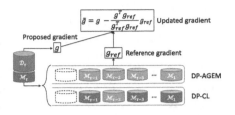

Fig. 1. DP in CL protects privacy for a stream of different tasks. Here, blue box indicates training data of task $\mathcal{T}$, orange and green boxes indicate mini-memory blocks in $\mathcal{M}$, and the orange ones are for computing g_{ref}. (Color figure online)

and the total privacy budget used in the entire training process. To achieve this, in computing the reference gradients g_{ref}, the algorithm first randomly samples data from all the data samples in the episodic memory $\mathcal{M}$ with a sampling probability q. Given a particular D_i^{ref} ($i \in [1, \mathcal{T} - 1]$) in the episodic memory, the sampled data is used to compute a reference gradient g_{ref}^i, which is clipped with the l_2-norm bound β. Then Gaussian mechanism is employed to inject random Gaussian noise $\mathcal{N}(0, \sigma^2 \beta^2 I)$ with a predefined hyper-parameter σ into both g and g_{ref}^i. The reference gradient g_{ref} is the average of all the reference gradients computed on each D_i^{ref}, as follows: $g_{ref} = \frac{1}{\mathcal{T}-1} \sum_{i \in [1, \mathcal{T}-1]} g_{ref}^i$. Finally, the updated gradient $\tilde{g}$ computed using Eq. 2 with g_{ref} and g can be used to update the model parameters. After training the task $\mathcal{T}$, $D_{\mathcal{T}}^{ref}$ is added into the episodic memory $\mathcal{M}$. The training process will continue until the model is trained on all the tasks.

Since the l_2-norms of g and g_{ref}^i are bounded, we can leverage a moments accountant to bound the privacy loss for a single task $\mathcal{T}$ and for accumulation across all tasks. Let $\epsilon_{\mathcal{T}}$ be the privacy budget used to compute g on $\mathcal{D}_{\mathcal{T}}^{train}$, and ϵ'_i is the privacy budget spent on computing the reference gradient g_{ref}^i at each training task. The privacy budget used for a specific task $i \in [1, \mathcal{T})$, denoted as $\epsilon_i(\mathcal{T})$ and the total privacy budgets $\epsilon_{\mathcal{T}}^{all}$ of DP-AGEM accumulated until the task $\mathcal{T}$ can be computed in the following lemma.

Lemma 1. *Until the task $\mathcal{T}$, 1) the privacy budget used for a specific and previously learned task $i \in [1, \mathcal{T}]$ is: $\epsilon_i(\mathcal{T}) = \epsilon_i + (\mathcal{T} - i)\epsilon'_i$, and 2) the total privacy budget $\epsilon_{\mathcal{T}}^{all}$ of DP-AGEM is: $\epsilon_{\mathcal{T}}^{all} = \sum_{i=1}^{\mathcal{T}} \epsilon_i(\mathcal{T})$.*

Proof. We use induction to prove Lemma 1. When $\mathcal{T} = 1$, $\mathcal{M}$ is empty; therefore, $\epsilon_1^{all} = \epsilon_1 = \epsilon_1(1)$. Hence, Lemma 1 is true for $\mathcal{T} = 1$. Assuming that it is true for $\mathcal{T} = k$, so $\epsilon_i(k) = \epsilon_i + (k-i)\epsilon_i'$ and $\epsilon_k^{all} = \sum_{i=1}^{k} \epsilon_i(k)$. We need to show that Lemma 1 is true for $\mathcal{T} = k+1$. We have: $\epsilon_i(k+1) = \epsilon_i(k) + \epsilon_i' = \epsilon_i + (k+1-i)\epsilon_i'$, and $\epsilon_{k+1}^{all} = \sum_{i=1}^{k} \epsilon_i(k) + \epsilon_{k+1} + \sum_{i=1}^{k} \epsilon_i' = \sum_{i=1}^{k+1} \epsilon_i(k+1)$. Thus, Lemma 1 holds.

Two Levels of DP Protection. In Lemma 1, based on our definition of continual adjacent databases (Definition 2), it is essential that there are two levels of DP protection provided to an arbitrary data sample, as follows. Until the task $\mathcal{T} \in [1, N]$: **(1)** Given the DP budget $\epsilon_i(\mathcal{T})$ for a specific task $i \in [1, \mathcal{T}]$, the participation information of an arbitrary data sample in the task i is protected under a $(\epsilon_i(\mathcal{T}), \delta)$-DP given the released parameters θ. This can be presented as: $Pr[\text{DP-AGEM}(\mathcal{D}_i) = \theta] \le e^{\epsilon_i(\mathcal{T})} Pr[\text{DP-AGEM}(\mathcal{D}_i') = \theta] + \delta$, for any adjacent databases $\mathcal{D}_i$ and $\mathcal{D}_i'$; and **(2)** The participation information of an arbitrary data sample in the whole training data $(\mathcal{D} = \cup_{i=1}^{\mathcal{T}} \mathcal{D}_i^{train}, \mathcal{M} = \cup_{i=1}^{\mathcal{T}} \mathcal{D}_i^{ref})$ is protected under a $(\epsilon_{\mathcal{T}}^{all}, \delta)$-DP given the released parameters θ. This can be presented as: $Pr[\text{DP-AGEM}(\mathcal{D}, \mathcal{M}) = \theta] \le e^{\epsilon_{\mathcal{T}}^{all}} Pr[\text{DP-AGEM}(\mathcal{D}', \mathcal{M}') = \theta] + \delta$, for any continual adjacent databases $(\mathcal{D}, \mathcal{M})$ and $(\mathcal{D}', \mathcal{M}')$. This is fundamentally different from existing works [6,13], which do not provide any formal DP in CL.

Although DP-AGEM can preserve DP in CL, it suffers from a large privacy budget accumulation across tasks with an $O(\mathcal{T}^2)$ for $\epsilon_{\mathcal{T}}^{all}$. To address this impractical issue, we present an algorithm to tighten the DP loss.

DP-CL Algorithm. Our DP-CL (Algorithm 1 and Fig. 1) takes a sequence of tasks $\mathcal{T} = [t_i]_{i \in [1, N]}$ and dataset $\mathcal{D} = \cup_{i=1}^{N} \mathcal{D}_i$ as inputs. All samples in $D_{\mathcal{T}}^{train}$ are used to compute the proposed gradient update g on task $\mathcal{T}$ with a sampling rate p (Line 6). We clip g so that its l_2-norm is bounded by a predefined gradient clipping bound β. Then we add a random Gaussian noise $\mathcal{N}(0, \sigma^2 \beta^2 I)$ into g with a predefined noise scale σ (Line 9). Note that after training the task $\mathcal{T}$, samples in $D_{\mathcal{T}}^{ref}$ are added to the episodic memory $\mathcal{M}$ as a mini-memory block $\mathcal{M}_{\mathcal{T}}$ (Lines 17, 24–26). To reduce the privacy budget accumulated over the number of tasks, we limit the access to seen data of previous tasks by using a randomly selected mini-memory block $\mathcal{M}_i$ $(i < \mathcal{T})$ from $\mathcal{M}$ to compute g_{ref} (Lines 20–23). We clip g_{ref} by the gradient clipping bound β and then add a random Gaussian noise $\mathcal{N}(0, \sigma^2 \beta^2 I)$ to g_{ref} (Line 14). The updated gradient $\tilde{g}$ is computed by Eq. 2 (Line 15). Then $\tilde{g}$ is used to update the model parameters θ (Line 16). The privacy budgets in our DP-CL can be bounded in the following lemma.

Lemma 2. *Until the task $\mathcal{T}$, 1) the privacy budget used for a specific and previously learned task $i \in [1, \mathcal{T}]$ is: $\epsilon_i(\mathcal{T}) = \epsilon_i + \epsilon_i'$, where ϵ_i' is the privacy budget used for a randomly chosen mini-memory block from $\mathcal{M}$ to compute g_{ref} at task i, and 2) the total privacy budget $\epsilon_{\mathcal{T}}^{all}$ of DP-CL is: $\epsilon_{\mathcal{T}}^{all} = \sum_{i=1}^{\mathcal{T}} \epsilon_i(\mathcal{T})$.*

Proof. Similar to the proof of Lemma 1 with using induction. Here, we need to show that it is true for $\mathcal{T} = k+1$. We have: $\epsilon_i(k+1) = \epsilon_i + \epsilon_i'$, and $\epsilon_{k+1}^{all} = \sum_{i=1}^{k} \epsilon_i(k) + \epsilon_{k+1} + \epsilon_{k+1}' = \sum_{i=1}^{k+1} \epsilon_i(k+1)$. Consequently, Lemma 2 hold.

It is obvious that our DP-CL algorithm significantly reduces the privacy consumption to $O(\mathcal{T})$, which is linear to the number of training tasks. In addition, our sampling approach to compute g_{ref} is unbiased, since the expectation for any data sample selected to compute g_{ref} is the same: $\forall x \in \mathcal{M}, \mathbb{E}(x \in \mathcal{M}_i) = q/(\mathcal{T}-1)$. In our experiment, we will show that DP-CL outperforms DP-AGEM.

Algorithm 1. DP in Continual Learning (DP-CL) Algorithm

1: **Input:** Number of tasks N, dataset $\mathcal{D} = \cup_{i=1}^{N}\mathcal{D}_i$, gradient clipping bound β
2: Initialize model θ, episodic memory $\mathcal{M} = \emptyset$, moments accountant $\mathbb{M}$
3: **for** $\mathcal{T} = \{1,...,N\}$ **do**
4:     $D_{\mathcal{T}}^{train} \sim \mathcal{D}_{\mathcal{T}}, D_{\mathcal{T}}^{ref} \sim \mathcal{D}_{\mathcal{T}}$ s.t. $D_{\mathcal{T}}^{train} \cup D_{\mathcal{T}}^{ref} = \mathcal{D}_{\mathcal{T}}, D_{\mathcal{T}}^{train} \cap D_{\mathcal{T}}^{ref} = \emptyset$
5:     **for** each iteration $e = 0, 1, 2, ...$ **do**
6:         $\mathcal{D}_{\mathcal{T}}^{e} \leftarrow$ Take random samples in $\mathcal{D}_{\mathcal{T}}^{train}$ with a sampling rate p
7:         **for** $(x, y) \in D_{\mathcal{T}}^{e}$ **do**
8:             $g \leftarrow \text{ClipGrad}(\nabla_\theta \mathcal{L}(f_\theta(x), y), \beta) + \mathcal{N}(0, \sigma^2\beta^2 I)$
9:             **if** $\mathcal{T} = 1$ **then**
10:                 $\tilde{g} \leftarrow g$
11:             **else**
12:                 $g_{ref} \leftarrow \text{ClipGrad}(\text{CalGref}(\mathcal{M}, \mathcal{T}), \beta) + \mathcal{N}(0, \sigma^2\beta^2 I)$
13:                 Compute $\tilde{g}$ with Eq. 2
14:         $\theta \leftarrow \theta - \alpha\tilde{g}$
15:     $\mathcal{M} \leftarrow \textbf{UpdateEpsMem}(\mathcal{M}, D_{\mathcal{T}}^{ref}, \mathcal{T})$
16: **Output:** (ϵ, δ)-DP-CL θ, $\mathbb{M}$ (from $\mathbb{M}.\texttt{get\_priv\_spent}()$)
17: **CalGref**$(\mathcal{M}, \mathcal{T})$:
18:     Randomly choose $\mathcal{M}_i$ from $\mathcal{M}$, where $i < \mathcal{T}$
19:     $(x^{ref}, y^{ref}) \sim \mathcal{M}_i$ ($\mathcal{M}_i$ is randomly chosen from $\mathcal{M}$, where $i < \mathcal{T}$)
20:     return $g_{ref} = \nabla_\theta \mathcal{L}(f_\theta(x^{ref}), y^{ref})$
21: **UpdateEpsMem**$(\mathcal{M}, D_{\mathcal{T}}^{ref}, \mathcal{T})$:
22:     $\mathcal{M}_{\mathcal{T}} \leftarrow D_{\mathcal{T}}^{ref}$
23:     return $\mathcal{M} \cup \mathcal{M}_{\mathcal{T}}$
24: **ClipGrad**(g, β): return $\pi(g, \beta) = g \cdot \min\left(1, \frac{\beta}{\|g\|}\right)$

---

4 Experimental Results

We have conducted experiments on the permuted MNIST dataset [8] and the Split CIFAR dataset [19]. Our validation focuses on shedding light on the interplay between model utility and privacy loss of preserving DP in CL. Our code, datasets, and model configurations are available on Github[1].

Baseline Approaches. We evaluate our DP-CL algorithm and compare it with A-GEM [3], one of the state-of-the-art CL algorithms. Since A-GEM does not preserve DP, we only use A-GEM to show the upper-bound performance. We use the *average accuracy*, the *average forgetting* (F), the *worst-case forgetting* (worst-case F), and the *learning curve area* (LCA) [3] for evaluation.

---

[1] https://github.com/PhungLai728/DP-CL.

- **Comparing Privacy Accumulation.** Since the number of data samples and the sampling rate remain the same for every task, ϵ_i and ϵ_i' can be the same for every task. Therefore, for the sake of clarity without loss of generality, we draw different random Gaussian values (mean $= 1$, std $= 0.02$) and assign the generated values as the privacy budget ϵ_i and ϵ_i' for 17 tasks.

Figure 2a illustrates how privacy loss accumulates over 17 tasks in DP-AGEM and our DP-CL. Our algorithm achieves a notably tighter privacy budget compared with DP-AGEM, which accesses data samples from the whole episodic memory to compute g_{ref}. When the number of tasks increases, DP-AGEM's privacy budget exponentially increases. In contrast, our approach's privacy budget slightly increases and is linear to the number of tasks or training steps.

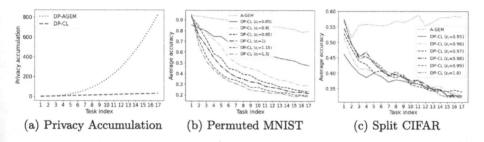

(a) Privacy Accumulation   (b) Permuted MNIST   (c) Split CIFAR

Fig. 2. Theoretical analysis for privacy accumulation (a); and Average accuracy over 17 tasks of A-GEM and DP-CL algorithms with varying ϵ_i.

- **Privacy Loss and Model Utility.** From our theoretical analysis, DP-AGEM suffers from a huge privacy budget accumulation over tasks. Therefore, we only compare our DP-CL and A-GEM for the sake of simplicity.

As shown in Fig. 2b and 2c, our proposed method achieves a comparable average accuracy with the noiseless A-GEM model at the first task. In the permuted MNIST dataset, when the number of tasks increases, the average accuracy of our DP-CL drops faster than the average accuracy of the A-GEM model. For example, at task 17-th, A-GEM's average accuracy drops to 79.3%, while DP-CL's average accuracy drops to 47.5% with a tight privacy budget $\epsilon_i = 0.85$. When the privacy budget increases, the average accuracy gap between our model and the noiseless A-GEM is larger, indicating that preserving DP in CL may increase the catastrophic forgetting. This phenomenon is further clarified by F, worst-case F, and LCA (Table 1). At $\epsilon_i = 0.85$, the values of F, worst-case F, and LCA are 0.401, 0.586, and 0.146 respectively in DP-CL. After that, the F and worst-case F significantly increase, and LCA moderately decreases in DP-CL.

In the Split CIFAR dataset, when the number of tasks increases, the average accuracy of DP-CL drops quickly while the average accuracy of the A-GEM model fluctuates. For instances, A-GEM's average accuracy is 57.5% at the first task, drops to 51.5% at the second task, and is 58.1% at the last task. Meanwhile, DP-CL's average accuracy is 56.8% at the first task, and gradually drops to

Table 1. Forgetting measure (F), worst-case F, and LCA results for the MNIST dataset. The lower F, worst-case F, and the higher LCA the better.

			Forgetting (F)	Worst-case F	LCA
MNIST	**A-GEM**		0.166 ± 0.0070	0.272 ± 0.0086	0.481 ± 0.0051
	DP-CL	$\epsilon_i = 0.85$	0.401 ± 0.0070	0.586 ± 0.0191	0.146 ± 0.0077
	($\epsilon_i' = 1.47$ and	$\epsilon_i = 0.9$	0.657 ± 0.0099	0.809 ± 0.0110	0.123 ± 0.0039
	$\delta = 10^{-4}$ for	$\epsilon_i = 0.95$	0.713 ± 0.0060	0.840 ± 0.0186	0.120 ± 0.0038
	all tasks)	$\epsilon_i = 1.0$	0.750 ± 0.0017	0.851 ± 0.0081	0.119 ± 0.0115
		$\epsilon_i = 1.15$	0.782 ± 0.0017	0.863 ± 0.0061	0.124 ± 0.0013
		$\epsilon_i = 1.30$	0.796 ± 0.0023	0.864 ± 0.0077	0.121 ± 0.0021
CIFAR	**A-GEM**		0.089 ± 0.0163	0.188 ± 0.0317	0.348 ± 0.0111
	DP-CL	$\epsilon_i = 0.95$	0.149 ± 0.0123	0.314 ± 0.0057	0.262 ± 0.0058
	($\epsilon_i' = 1.47$ and	$\epsilon_i = 0.96$	0.181 ± 0.0193	0.335 ± 0.0421	0.259 ± 0.0130
	$\delta = 10^{-4}$ for	$\epsilon_i = 0.97$	0.196 ± 0.0194	0.377 ± 0.0174	0.266 ± 0.0111
	all tasks)	$\epsilon_i = 0.98$	0.239 ± 0.0162	0.428 ± 0.0701	0.266 ± 0.0008
		$\epsilon_i = 0.99$	0.249 ± 0.0097	0.435 ± 0.0432	0.259 ± 0.0053
		$\epsilon_i = 1.0$	0.262 ± 0.031	0.455 ± 0.0452	0.263 ± 0.0096

31.9% at the last task with a tight privacy budget $\epsilon_i = 1.0$. The fluctuation phenomenon in the A-GEM model is probably due to the curse of dimension in which there are $2,500$ training examples, which is much smaller than the number of trainable parameters in the ResNet-18, i.e., 11 million. Different from the permuted MNIST dataset, in the Split CIFAR dataset, when the privacy budget increases, the average accuracy gap between DP-CL and the noiseless A-GEM is smaller, especially at the first task. For instance, at the first task, the gaps are 11.4%, 6.3%, 4.7%, 3.1%, 0.3%, and 0.7% when the values of $\epsilon_i \in [0.95, 1.0]$. This shows the trade-off between privacy budget and model utility in which when we spend more privacy budget, the model accuracy improves. The gap between DP-CL's and A-GEM's average accuracy are significantly bigger when the number of tasks increases, but the difference among different privacy budgets decreases. For instance, at the last task, the gaps are $[24.2\%, 26.2\%]$ when $\epsilon_i \in [0.95, 1.0]$. As shown in Table 1, when the privacy budget increases, the F and worst-case F significantly increase, while the LCA slightly fluctuates around $[0.259, 0.266]$.

Key Observations. From our experiments, we obtain the following observations. **(1)** Merely incorporating the moments accountant into A-GEM causes a large privacy budget accumulation. **(2)** Although our DP-CL algorithm preserves DP in CL, optimizing the trade-off between model utility and privacy loss is an open problem as the privacy noise can worsen the catastrophic forgetting.

5   Conclusion and Future Work

In this paper, we established the first formal connection between DP and CL. We combine the moments accountant and A-GEM in a holistic approach to preserve DP in CL in a tightly accumulated privacy budget. Our model shows promising results under strong DP guarantees in CL and opens a new research line to optimize the model utility and privacy loss trade-off. One of the immediate questions is how to align the privacy noise with the catastrophic forgetting under the same privacy protection. We will examine our approach to a broader range of models and datasets, especially under attacks [2,18], and heterogeneous privacy-preserving mechanisms [15,16]. Our work further highlights an open direction of quantifying the privacy risk given a diverse correlation among tasks.

Acknowledgment. The authors gratefully acknowledge the support from the National Science Foundation grants NSF CNS-1935928/1935923, CNS-1850094, IIS-2041096/2041065.

References

1. Abadi, M., et al.: Deep learning with differential privacy. In: ACM SIGSAC, pp. 308–318 (2016)
2. Carlini, N., et al.: Extracting training data from large language models. In: USENIX Security Symposium (2021)
3. Chaudhry, A., Ranzato, M., Rohrbach, M., Elhoseiny, M.: Efficient lifelong learning with a-GEM. In: ICLR (2019)
4. Dwork, C., McSherry, F., Nissim, K., Smith, A.: Calibrating noise to sensitivity in private data analysis. In: Theory of Cryptography Conference, pp. 265–284 (2006)
5. Dwork, C., Roth, A., et al.: The algorithmic foundations of differential privacy. Found. Trends Theor. Comput. Sci. **9**(3–4), 211–407 (2014)
6. Farquhar, S., Gal, Y.: Differentially private continual learning. In: Privacy in Machine Learning and AI workshop at ICML (2018)
7. Fredrikson, M., Jha, S., Ristenpart, T.: Model inversion attacks that exploit confidence information and basic countermeasures. In: ACM SIGSAC (2015)
8. Goodfellow, I., Mirza, M., Xiao, D., Courville, A., Bengio, Y.: An empirical investigation of catastrophic forgetting in gradient-based neural networks. In: ICLR (2014)
9. Kartal, H., Liu, X., Li, X.: Differential privacy for the vast majority. ACM Trans. Manag. Inf. Syst. (TMIS) **10**(2), 1–15 (2019)
10. Lopez-Paz, D., Ranzato, M.: Gradient episodic memory for continual learning. In: Neural Information Processing Systems (NeurIPS) (2017)
11. Ostapenko, O., Puscas, M., Klein, T., Jahnichen, P., Nabi, M.: Learning to remember: a synaptic plasticity driven framework for continual learning. In: CVPR (2019)
12. Phan, H., Thai, M.T., Hu, H., Jin, R., Sun, T., Dou, D.: Scalable differential privacy with certified robustness in adversarial learning. In: ICML (2020)
13. Phan, N., Thai, M., Devu, M., Jin, R.: Differentially private lifelong learning. In: Privacy in Machine Learning (NeurIPS 2019 Workshop) (2019)
14. Phan, N., Jin, R., Thai, M.T., Hu, H., Dou, D.: Preserving differential privacy in adversarial learning with provable robustness. CoRR abs/1903.09822 (2019). http://arxiv.org/abs/1903.09822

15. Phan, N., et al.: Heterogeneous gaussian mechanism: preserving differential privacy in deep learning with provable robustness. In: IJCAI, pp. 4753–4759 (2019)
16. Phan, N., Wu, X., Hu, H., Dou, D.: Adaptive laplace mechanism: differential privacy preservation in deep learning. In: ICDM, pp. 385–394 (2017)
17. Schwarz, J., et al.: Progress & compress: a scalable framework for continual learning. In: ICML, pp. 4528–4537 (2018)
18. Shokri, R., Stronati, M., Song, C., Shmatikov, V.: Membership inference attacks against machine learning models. In: 2017 IEEE SP, pp. 3–18 (2017)
19. Zenke, F., Poole, B., Ganguli, S.: Continual learning through synaptic intelligence. In: International Conference on Machine Learning, pp. 3987–3995 (2017)

Combat Unit Selection Based on Hybrid Neural Network in Real-Time Strategy Games

Hongcun Guo[1,2], Zhaoxiang Zang[1,2(✉)], Zhen Zhang[1,2], and Pei Tian[1,2]

[1] Hubei Key Laboratory of Intelligent Vision Based Monitoring for Hydroelectric Engineering, China Three Gorges University, Yichang 443002, Hubei, China
zhaoxiang.zang@ctgu.edu.cn
[2] College of Computer and Information Technology, China Three Gorges University, Yichang 443002, China

Abstract. Real-Time Strategy (RTS) games are one of the most complex and challenging areas from the perspective of artificial intelligence. Besides, some real-time wargaming platforms not only have the characteristics of large state-action space, incomplete information, and instantaneity but also have not many decision-making in the whole game. In this paper, we propose a data augmentation method and a hybrid neural network model combining Gated Recurrent Unit(GRU) network and Pointer network, which can select an action unit to execute the decision and a target unit to be attacked at a few time points in the game. The hybrid neural network model and data augmentation method are evaluated in a war simulation platform. Experimental results show that in the unit selection of real-time strategy games, the hybrid network model and data augmentation method outperform the hybrid neural network without data augmentation or simply using pointer network model.

Keywords: Real-time strategy games · Intelligent decision making · Unit selection · Incomplete information game

1 Introduction

Real-time strategy games can be seen as a simulation of the real world, which has the characteristics of incomplete information, coordination between long-term strategy and short-term goal, huge action-state space and immediacy of decision-making, etc. So many scholars began to pay more attention to this field. In recent years, RTS games have become one of the excellent test platforms to studying artificial intelligence [12]. Many researchers use RTS games as tests platform in case-based reasoning and planning, machine learning [2], deep learning [7], heuristic, and adversarial search [1].

War simulation is a type of real-time strategy game. In war simulation an important issue is that the battlefield information is not completely visible, so the agent can get the enemy information until it's detected. Another problem is that there are a few decision-makings on the experimental platform rather than many decision-makings. Recently, in unit selection, researchers mainly use Alpha-Beta search [5], UTC [13], and Portfolio [4]. Such methods can lead to inaccurate actions, lower intelligence, and poor adaptability to the environment. The Cluster-based Alpha-Beta (CABCD) was proposed by

© Springer Nature Switzerland AG 2021
T. Mantoro et al. (Eds.): ICONIP 2021, CCIS 1517, pp. 344–352, 2021.
https://doi.org/10.1007/978-3-030-92310-5_40

X Han is based on the clustering method to select the target unit action. Moreover, it can consider the execution time of the command [9]. So far, Dota2 AI developed by OpenAI using reinforcement learning, i.e., OpenAI Five, has made the great advanced progress (OpenAI 2018a) [10]. OpenAI Five was trained directly on micro-level action space using proximal policy optimization algorithms along with team rewards (Schulman et al. 2017) [11]. Tencent has proposed a novel learning-based Hierarchical Macro Strategy model for mastering Multiplayer Online Battle Arena (MOBA) games [16]. Deep Mind has proposed a multi-agent reinforcement learning algorithm that uses data from both human and agent games in StarCraft II [14].

The common characteristic of Dota2, MOBA, and StarCraftII is that their state-action pairs are very dense. However, the platform we use in our experiment belongs to the special war simulation platform, which not only has common characteristics of real-time strategic game, but also has the feature of very sparse decision-making. In the experimental platform, decision-making is to provide an instruction to execute. We put forward a term called null instruction, also called dummy instruction, which means that null instruction will appear when there is no command moment. This method can alleviate the difficulty caused by sparse instructions. We also propose a method of data augmentation, which makes the model improve the ability of learning unit features.

The major contributions of this paper are as follows:

1. We propose a hybrid neural network model combining GRU network and Pointer network, which can select the action unit and the target unit in RTS games with sparse decision-making.
2. A data augmentation method is proposed to improve the performance of the model.

2   Background

The section briefly summarizes the game characteristics of the simulation platform and describes its environment. The platform used in our experiment is an open-access simulation platform created to test the theoretical algorithms of researchers [6].

2.1   Features of the Platform

The experimental platform is a real-time strategy game platform. It has the characteristics of incomplete information, huge action-state space. In addition, the experimental platform has the feature of sparse decision-making. The whole game lasts for about 2 h and the interval between the two time steps is about 10 s, the agent will issue some instruction in the game, but not every time point. Less than 10% of the time points the agent will issue the instructions, which leads to the sparse decision-making.

2.2   Rules of the Platform

1. The game scene is divided into red and blue sides, namely attackers and defenders.
2. The goal of the game is that the red side must capture the two island guarded by the blue side within the specified time range and the blue side will protect its two islands within the specified time range.
3. Different units must cooperate with each other, use resources rationally, and use clever tactics to defeat opponents.

2.3   Settings of the Platform

The battle map of the game is a space range of 350 km * 350 km. The game can be run under visual conditions or in the background, and the results can be viewed on the visual interface or console windows. The Fig. 1 shonws the simulation platform is running under visual mode. The units number of the red and blue sides is shown in Table 1 and Table 2, including Airborne Warning And Control System (AWACS), Unmanned Aerial Vehicle (UAV), Air Defense Ship (ADS) and Surface-to-air missile (SAM), etc. It can be seen that the strength of the two sides is balanced.

Table 1. The red side's military setup

Bomber	AWACS	UAV	Jammer
16	1	3	1
Fighter	ADS	Radar	Airport
20	2	1	1

Table 2. The blue side's military setup

Bomber	AWACS	Radar	ADS
8	1	2	2
Fighter	SAM	Command Post	Airport
12	2	1	1

3   The Neural Network Model

In this section, the architecture of the hybrid network and their components were introduced respectively.

3.1   A Hybrid Neural Network Model Composed of GRU Network and Pointer Network

First, we get the observation state S from the platform, and then input S to the GRU network and get the output h. h has the historical state information at this time. Then h is combined with the action entity list, and the combined result is input into the Pointer network. Finally, we can get the predicted value of the action unit. Similarly, the combination of h and the target entities can be input into the Pointer network to get the selected target unit. Its network structure is shown in Fig. 1(a). In order to better learn the characteristics of each unit and increase the amount of training data, we propose a data augmentation method, which is used before the data input into the pointer network. Its specific operation is to randomly swap positions of units in the action entity list and target entity list at each time point.

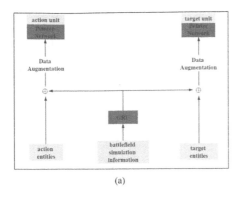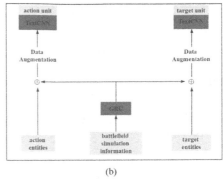

(a)   (b)

Fig. 1. (a) GRU+Pointer Network. (b) GRU+TextCNN Network.

Data Augmentation Method. Firstly, the entity list information of each time step is obtained, and then the positions of each entity unit in the list are randomly exchanged. For example, there are two units A and B in the current time step entity list where A at the first position in the entity list and B at the second position. After the exchange, B at the first position in the list and A at the second position.

GRU Network. The GRU network model is an improvement of the standard recurrent neural network. Given an input sequence $(x_1, ..., x_n)$, we can get the hidden layer h through the following iteration formula of the GRU [3].

$$R_t = \sigma(X_t W_{xr} + H_{t-1} W_{hr} + b_r), \tag{1}$$

$$Z_t = \sigma(X_t W_{xz} + H_{t-1} W_{hz} + b_z), \tag{2}$$

$$\hat{H}_t = tanh(x_t W_{xh} + R_t \odot H_{t-1} W_{hh}), \tag{3}$$

$$H_t = Z_t \odot H_{t-1} + (1 - Z_t) \odot \hat{H}_t. \tag{4}$$

Where t represents the time step, X represents the input, W_{xr}, W_{hr}, W_{xz}, W_{hh} and W_{hz} are weight parameters, b_r, b_z and b_h are bias parameters, H_{t-1} represents the state of the hidden layer at the previous time, Z represents the update gate, R represents the reset gate, the candidate's hidden state is $\hat{H}_t$, H is the hidden state of the current time step and $\odot$ represents element-wise product.

Because the output of each hidden layer takes the previous historical information into account, this model can capture the dependence of long-distance better in the time series.

Pointer Network. Given an input sequence $(x_1, ..., x_n)$ through the following pointer network calculations, the output y can be obtained, where the output y is selected from the input sequence $(x_1, ..., x_n)$ [15].

$$u_j^i = v^T tanh(W_1 e_j + W_2 d_i) \quad j \in (1, ...n), \tag{5}$$

$$p(C_i|C_1, ...C_{i-1}, P) = softmax(u^i). \tag{6}$$

Where $(e_1, e_2, ..., e_n)$ and $(d_1, d_2, ..., d_{m(p)})$ are defined as encoder hidden state and decoder hidden state. v, W_1 and W_2 are learnable parameters of the model, $p(C_i|C_1, ..., C_{i-1}, P)$ represents conditional probability, and u^i_j is the pointer of the input elements.

3.2 A Hybrid Neural Network Model Composed of GRU Network and TextCNN Network

The network structure of the GRU+TextCNN model is the same as the hybrid model GRU+Pointer network. Its structure is shown in Fig. 1(b).

TextCNN Model: The TextCNN network is a three-layer convolutional neural network based on multiple convolution kernels proposed by Kim [8]. This network is an improvement of CNN and first used in the classification problem of natural language processing, where this model is used for unit selection. Here we input the feature representation of each action unit or target unit into the TextCNN network. The input layer is a matrix. Where, the column represents the unit in each unit entity, and the row represents the dimension of the corresponding unit. After the convolution kernel pooling and softmax operation, the action unit and target unit is finally selected.

4 Experiments

We describe the experimental setup firstly, including the introduction of data preparation, model settings and introduction of evaluation criteria, and then give the results of each network model under different conditions.

4.1 Experimental Setup

First, the platform needs to be run to generate a lot of data for the model training. The training data in this paper are generated by the competition between two agents. One agent is generated by a hard-coded bot built in this platform, and the other is generated by a hard-coded bot we wrote. A total of 180 pieces of data were generated through the competition. Then, we get the data and process it. There are two problems here. One is that at each time point, the number of units in the entity list for candidate is different. We can fill them up manually. In addition, the position of the same action unit or the same target unit in the entity list may be different.

In order to evaluate the performance of the model, we propose a simple approach, which is based on statistics. The operation of this method are as follows. First, find the position where the label appears in the entity list. Then calculate the times when each position appears at all time points in a game. Next, sum up the times of the positions in the training data. Finally, calculate the proportion of the times of each location, and then use this proportion to predict the action unit or target unit.

In this experiment, the evaluation indicator is the accuracy of model selection, which refers to how close the test result is to the real value. Before introducing the calculation formula, we first explain the meaning of each term in the formula.

$inst$: Ground truth instruction set.
$pred$: Predicted instruction set.

The following formula is the calculation of accuracy, n represents the size of the set and f is the indicator function.

$$Accuracy = \frac{\sum_{i=1}^{n} f(pred_i, inst_i)}{n} \tag{7}$$

$$f(x, y) = \begin{cases} 1, & if \quad x = y \\ 0, & else \end{cases}. \tag{8}$$

We use the TextCNN model, the Pointer network model, the GRU + Pointer network model, the GRU + TextCNN model, and statistical method to calculate the accuracy in the selection of action units and target units with data augmentation method and without data augmentation method.

Dataset division: training set 70%, validation set 10%, test set 20%.

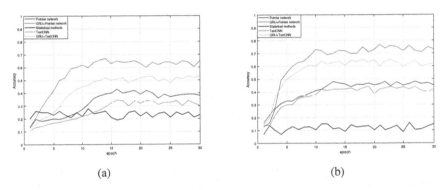

(a)   (b)

Fig. 2. (a) The accuracy of action unit selection before data augmentation. (b) The accuracy of action unit selection after data augmentation.

4.2 Experimental Result and Analysis

As shown in Fig. 2 and Fig. 3, the accuracy of the models includes GRU+Pointer network model, GRU+TextCNN model, Pointer network model and TextCNN model, which tends to be stable at about 10 epochs of training. Besides, the accuracy of GRU+Pointer network model is much higher than other models. There is, in addition, the accuracy of simple statistical methods has been stable with the increase of training times, and the fluctuation is not large.

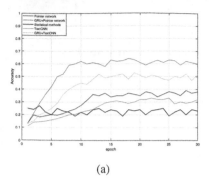
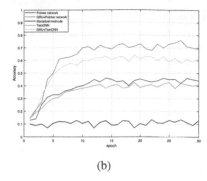

(a)	(b)

Fig. 3. (a) The accuracy of target unit selection before data augmentation. (b) The accuracy of target unit selection after data augmentation.

Table 3. The accuracy of unit selection with data enhancement

Model	Accuracy	
	Combat unit	Target unit
Simple statistics	15.18%	16.23%
TextCNN	41.24%	42.47%
Pointer Network	50.91%	52.69%
GRU+TextCNN	69.67%	65.33%
GRU+Pointer Network	78.85%	77.20%

To highlight the potential of our method, we compare with other models on the dataset. Results of the models are shown in Table 3. We employ accuracy as measurements. It is obvious that other methods are inferior to our method in choosing action units and target units. As shown in Tabel 3 the accuracy of GRU+Pointer network with data augmentation method reaches 78.85% and 77.20% respectively, which is higher than 69.67% and 65.33% of GRU+TextCNN model. Compared with the simple statistical method, the accuracy of our model is increased by 60%.

4.3 Ablation Study

To verify the effectiveness of each major module of the GRU+Pointer network model, we conducted ablation experiments on the dataset and evaluated them with accuracy. The results are shown in Table 4. Obviously, when the model does not use the data augmentation method, the accuracy of the GRU+Pointer network has decreased by 11.21% and 11.82% respectively in the selection of action unit and target unit. In addition, we also verify the influence of data augmentation method on GRU+TextCNN model. It can be seen from Table 4 that the accuracy of GRU+TextCNN model is reduced by 16.05% and 11.49% without data augmentation method. Therefore, we conclude that the data augmentation method is effective and is an important part of the whole network.

Besides, we verify the influence of GRU network on the model. Table 4 shows that the accuracy of the model has decreased by about 20% without GRU model in selection of action units and target units. This shows that the problem encountered in this experiment is partially observable. Furthermore, we verify that the performance of the model when the two methods of GRU model and data augmentation method are not used at the same time, that is, only using pointer network structure or TextCNN network. The accuracy rate is reduced by about 40%. Therefore, in our proposed network model GRU network and data augmentation method are indispensable parts.

Table 4. The accuracy of unit selection without data enhancement

Model	Accuracy	
	Combat unit	Target unit
TextCNN	34.23%	32.39%
Pointer Network	40.37%	39.45%
GRU+TextCNN	53.62%	53.84%
GRU+Pointer Network	67.64%	65.38%

5   Conclusion

This paper proposes a method of selecting action unit and target unit based on deep learning, and a method of augmentation data in RTS game. This deep learning method is a hybrid neural network model Combining with GRU and Pointer network. In the unit selection problem of intelligent decision-making, the information of the enemy is not perfect, and the decision-making are very sparse. We use the GRU model to deal with the problem of imperfect information. So historical information can be taken into account when we make decisions at the current time step. We propose the data augmentation method so that the model can learn the characteristics of unit better than the model without the data augmentation method. The experimental results show that the hybrid model and data augmentation method proposed in this paper can effectively select action unit and target unit, with an accuracy rate of about 78%.

As part of our future work, we will to combine reinforcement learning methods to adapt the combat model to the current opponent.

Acknowledgement. This work was supported by National Natural Science Foundation of China (Grant No. 61502274), Natural Science Foundation of Hubei (Grant No. 2015CFB336), and Open Fund of Hubei Key Laboratory of Intelligent Vision Based Monitoring for Hydroelectric Engineering (CTGU)(Grant No. 2015KLA08)

References

1. Barriga, N., Stanescu, M., Buro, M.: Puppet search: enhancing scripted behavior by lookahead search with applications to real-time strategy games. In: Proceedings of the AAAI Conference on Artificial Intelligence and Interactive Digital Entertainment, vol. 11, pp. 9–15 (2015)

2. Barriga, N., Stanescu, M., Buro, M.: Combining strategic learning with tactical search in real-time strategy games. In: Proceedings of the AAAI Conference on Artificial Intelligence and Interactive Digital Entertainment, vol. 13, pp. 9–15 (2017)

3. Che, Z., Purushotham, S., Cho, K., Sontag, D., Liu, Y.: Recurrent neural networks for multivariate time series with missing values. Sci. Rep. **8**(1), 1–12 (2018)

4. Churchill, D., Buro, M.: Portfolio greedy search and simulation for large-scale combat in StarCraft. In: 2013 IEEE Conference on Computational Intelligence in Games (CIG), pp. 1–8. IEEE (2013)

5. Churchill, D., Saffidine, A., Buro, M.: Fast heuristic search for RTS game combat scenarios. In: Proceedings of the AAAI Conference on Artificial Intelligence and Interactive Digital Entertainment, vol. 8 (2012)

6. DataCastle: Intelligent game confrontation competition of joint operation (2020). https://encourage.dcjingsai.com/WarGame.html

7. Foerster, J., et al.: Stabilising experience replay for deep multi-agent reinforcement learning. In: International Conference on Machine Learning, pp. 1146–1155. PMLR (2017)

8. Guo, B., Zhang, C., Liu, J., Ma, X.: Improving text classification with weighted word embeddings via a multi-channel TextCNN model. Neurocomputing **363**, 366–374 (2019)

9. Han, X., Yan, H., Zhang, J., Wang, L.: Cluster-based alpha-beta search for real-time strategy games. In: IOP Conference Series: Materials Science and Engineering, vol. 435, pp. 1–10 (2018)

10. OpenAI.: Openai blog: Dota 2, 17 April 2018. https://blog.openai.com/dota-2/

11. Schulman, J., Wolski, F., Dhariwal, P., Radford, A., Klimov, O.: Proximal policy optimization algorithms. arXiv preprint arXiv:1707.06347 (2017)

12. Shafi, K., Abbass, H.A.: A survey of learning classifier systems in games. IEEE Comput. Intell. Mag. **12**(1), 42–55 (2017)

13. Silver, D., Huang, A., Maddison, C.J., Guez, A., Sifre, L., Van Den Driessche, G., Schrittwieser, J., Antonoglou, I., Panneershelvam, V., Lanctot, M., et al.: Mastering the game of go with deep neural networks and tree search. Nature **529**(7587), 484–489 (2016)

14. Vinyals, O., et al.: Grandmaster level in StarCraft ii using multi-agent reinforcement learning. Nature **575**(7782), 350–354 (2019)

15. Vinyals, O., Fortunato, M., Jaitly, N.: Pointer networks. In: International Conference on Neural Information Processing Systems, pp. 2692–2700 (2015)

16. Wu, B.: Hierarchical macro strategy model for MOBA game AI. In: Proceedings of the AAAI Conference on Artificial Intelligence, vol. 33, pp. 1206–1213 (2019)

A Scan-to-Locality Map Strategy for 2D LiDAR and RGB-D Data Fusion

Jiaqing Zhang[1,2], Minghao Yang[1(✉)], Yuanhao Qu[2], Jinlong Chen[2], Baohua Qiang[2], and Hong Shi[1]

[1] Research Center for Brain-Inspired Intelligence (BII), Institute of Automation, Chinese Academy of Sciences (CASIA), Beijing 100190, China
mhyang@nlpr.ia.ac.cn
[2] School of Computer Science and Information Security, Guilin University of Electronic Technology, Guilin 541004, China

Abstract. 2D LiDAR and RGB-D camera are two widely used sensors in the task of simultaneous localization and mapping (SLAM). In spite of various map methods for SLAM, an effective strategy which is able to fuse 2D-LiDAR and RGB-D data in a uniform style is still expected. This work proposes a novel map strategy for 2D-LiDAR and RGB-D data. Different from traditional maps where the map information for different views is stored separately in their original two-dimensional (2D) grids or three-dimensional (3D) voxels, in the proposed map strategy, the data obtained by multiple sensors for current view are fused as feature vectors and stored in the current grids. We call this as Scan-to-Locality (STL) map strategy. In re-localization phase, the fusion vector obtained at the current view is used to find the similar ones from the STL map using distance based similarity evaluation and Siamese-network image matching technique. In this way, the re-localization strategy is optimized as a coarse-to-fine schema in the proposed STL map strategy. We validate the proposed method on the widely recognized in-door navigation database Robot@Home. The experiments indicate the proposed method own the abilities of accurate re-localization in nearly real time.

Keywords: Map construction · Deep learning · Loop detection

1 Introduction

Map is the foundation and key component of indoors simultaneous localization and mapping (SLAM) and various map methods have been proposed in history. According to their generation and storage styles, these maps could be divided into 2D grid map [1,2] and 3D voxel map [3–7], etc. The 2D map has the advantage of fast localization and re-localization and obstacle avoidance in a given horizontal level. However, the contextual information is absent in 2D map presentations. In contrast to 2D map, 3D map contains abundant contextual information in its voxels. However, it is time-consuming for 3D map in the task of localization and re-localization since it contains multiple high time cost steps,

© Springer Nature Switzerland AG 2021
T. Mantoro et al. (Eds.): ICONIP 2021, CCIS 1517, pp. 353–360, 2021.
https://doi.org/10.1007/978-3-030-92310-5_41

such as feature points extraction, points' matching between current view and the existed feature points in map database, etc.

This work proposes a new map strategy. Different from traditional 2D grid or 3D maps where the map information for different views is stored separately in their original grids or voxels, in the phase of map generation stage of the proposed method, the data obtained by multiple sensors for current view are compressed and stored as feature vectors in local grid. We call this as Scan-to-Locality (STL) map strategy. While in the re-localization phase, a coarse-to-fine strategy is adopted to accelerate the relocalization process using the distance based similarity evaluation between the current view vector and the vectors stored in map. In this way, the re-localization task is converted to a nearest vector retrieving problem, which could be optimized using a coarse-to-fine schema in the proposed STL map strategy. We validate the STL map strategy on a widely recognized in-door navigation database. The experiments indicate that the performance of the proposed method.

2   Related Work

Robot's autonomous navigation includes the techniques such as the map generation, localization/re-localization, loop closure detection, routine, environment recognition, etc. Among them, map generation and localization/re-localization are two basic and important functionalities of them. There are some differences between localization and re-localization. Re-localization is more challenge than that of localization. In this work, we mainly focus on the discussion of map generation and re-localization.

2D LiDAR is essentially widely used in the 2D map. The device uses laser to measure the distance between robot and obstacles in front views. 2D LIDAR is able to obtain the contours' information in the environments with relatively high data frequency, and the contours contribute to the 2D map with robots' movements frame by frame. However, with the cumulative errors and possible noises caused by possible strong light absorption for laser projection and reflections in 2D LiDAR [8], the contours have motion distortion in a long time. To this end, iterative closest point methods [9], particle filer [10], GMapping [11], are used to contour points registration. These methods contribute to 2D map generation from the coarse 2D contours obtained by 2D LiDAR devices.

RGB-D camera is widely used devices in 3D map generation. Different from 2D map generation, where the points' distances or contours' shapes are used for similarity measurement in point generation, robust 3D point are depended on the points' features, such as scale invariant feature transform (SIFT) [12], speeded up robust features (SURF) [13], Deep Learning based feature point (FP) [14], etc., to their 3D positions. However, SIFT, SURF, Deep Learning based FP feature extraction and matching are very time- consuming. Therefore, traditional 3D points map generation methods have the disadvantages on time cost since a large number of points exists on the rays in the front sight of view frustum.

For the re-localization task in 2D map, various methods, such as scan-to-submap [15,16], GMapping [11] etc., have been widely discussed to match the ranges and locations of eye's view from full 2D LiDAR map. However, for 3D map, it still a challenge to achieve re-localization accurately and fast because it is time-consuming to find the good match points from huge number of possible candidates since a large number of candidates exist in the map database for the front sight of view.

3   The Proposed Map Strategy

In this section, we first present the map structure and then introduce how we use the proposed map in map generation and re-localization.

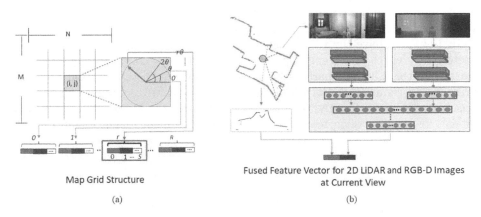

Map Grid Structure

(a)

Fused Feature Vector for 2D LiDAR and RGB-D Images at Current View

(b)

Fig. 1. The outline of the generation and storage scheme for the proposed Scan-to-Locality (STL) map strategy.

3.1   Map Structure

In the proposed STL map strategy, all the information from multiple sensors are converted to 1D vector and stored in local grid according to their view-sight position and angles. Let the current grid be (i, j) with $1 \leq i \leq M$, where M and N are the number of rows and columns for the map. The current view angle in horizontal level is $r\theta$, where θ is the minimal angle unit, $r(1 \leq r \leq R)$ is the index for view orientation, $R = 360/\theta$ is the maxima index number of view angles. Supposing that there are total S kinds of sensors on robot and each sensors' data could be compressed into 1D vector, then a storage example for the scenario information at grid (i, j) for all possible $r\theta$ $(1 \leq r \leq R)$ observation angles is given at the bottom of Fig. 1(a), where a combination of S sensors' features for the view of current position and angle is given as the 1D vector in red rectangle.

The 2D LiDAR device determines its relative localization in the environment based on the laser measurement technology. It has the advantages of wide detection range which presents obstacle avoidance information in the horizontal level [17]. The left-up part of Fig. 1(b) presents an example of a robot navigation in a room, where the grey circle is robot, the lines in red are the room contours in ground truth. The right part of room contour could be obtained by 2D LiDAR and the lines in green are the observation contours of robot in sight-view. Supposing there are C points in 2D LiDAR contour, then the points x_c $(1 \leq c \leq C)$ given by 2D LiDAR are taken as 1D feature vector directly. The green part of the box in the bottom of Fig. 1(a) and Fig. 1(b) presents an example of 2D LiDAR feature vector for the current position and angle.

In our method, we store the compressed RGB image and depth image after they are converted into 1D feature vectors using deep learning techniques. In this work, we use Convolutional Neural Network (CNN) based Auto-encoder to convert RGB and depth images into 1D vector simultaneously [18]. The blue arrow lines in the right part of Fig. 1(b) present an example of the work flow of RGB-D images coded into 1D vector using CNN Auto-encoder. Supposing the RGB-D images have the resolution ratio of $I_w \times I_h$, and they are coded into a vector with length of D items, then the data y_d $(1 \leq d \leq D)$ are taken as RGB-D feature vector. The blue part of the box in the bottom of Fig. 1(a) and Fig. 1(b) presents an example of RGB and depth image feature vector for the current position and angle. Finally, the fused 1D vector of the 2D LiDAR and RGB-D images for the view of current position and angle are presented as a vector which consist of x_c and y_d.

$$X = [R \quad T]X^{t-1}, R = \begin{bmatrix} cos\alpha & -sin\alpha \\ sin\alpha & cos\alpha \end{bmatrix} \text{ and } T = \begin{bmatrix} t_x \\ t_y \end{bmatrix} \qquad (1)$$

3.2   Map Generation

The first step of map generation is to construct the 2D map contour from the 2D LiDAR points frame by frame. This task could be view as 2D LiDAR contours register between frames. The target of map generation is to match the continuous multiple local 2D contours from the rotation and translation parameters, which could be written as Eq. (1). In Eq. (1), R and T are initial rotation and translation matrix, α represents the rotation angle offset of the 2D map contour point between the adjacent two frames, and t_x, t_y represents the distance offset of the 2D map contour point along the x and y axis direction in the 2D map in the adjacent two frames. X^{t-1} is homogeneous coordinate value for the contour points in t−1 frame with size of 3 × C and X^t is coordinate value for the contour points in t−1 frame with size of 2 × C, where C is number of the contour points. In practical navigation environment, the solution of Eq. (1) relies on the relationship between at least four points in the overlapped view-insight. With the near global optimal solution, we could continually obtain more precise values of R and T using Newton-Raphson method. In addition, other methods, such as iterative close point (ICP) [19] and iterative point curves matching [20] are well suitable for resolution of Eq. (1).

Equation (2) gives an evaluation formula between the view feature vector and the vectors in map, where f_{view} is the fused feature vector for current view and $F_{(i,j,\theta)}$ is the feature vectors stored in map around location (i, j) and view angle θ. The function dist(.) is a distance measure function between two 1D vector f_{view} and $F_{(i,j,\theta)}$. $\hat{I}$, $\hat{J}$, $\hat{\theta}$ are the index values for the position and view angle when the minimal distance is found between f_{view} and $F_{(i,j,\theta)}$.

$$\hat{I}, \hat{J}, \hat{\theta} = arg_{1 \le i < u, 1 \le \theta < R} min[dist(f_{view}, F_{(i,j,\theta)})] \tag{2}$$

3.3 Map Parameters

Six parameters are tightly related to the map structure: M, N, R, u, v, S. In these parameters, S indicates the types of sensors. u, v are the sample ratio between layers of pyramid, which could be empirically set between 2 and 5 from small environment to large environment. M, N, R are the range of environment, which are determined by the size of grid and the interval value of θ. Equation (3) Eq. (5) give three formulas to calculate the values of M, N, R. In Eq. (3) Eq. (5), C_x, C_y are the values of map in its x-coordinate and y-coordinate respectively. G_x, G_y are the width and height of map gird and G_θ is interval angle with anti-clockwise rotation.

$$M = (max(C_x) - min(C_x))/G_x \tag{3}$$

$$N = (max(C_y) - min(C_y))/G_y \tag{4}$$

$$R = 360/G_\theta \tag{5}$$

4 Experiments

In the experiments, we validate the proposed map strategy in a widely recognized indoor navigation dataset Robot@Home [21]. The dataset contains 87,000+ time-stamped observations gathered by a mobile robot endowed with a rig of 4 RGB-D(Kinect V2) cameras and a 2D laser scanner (HOKUYO UST-10LX) for 42 rooms in 6 apartments. We used VGG16 structure as the backbone of autoencoder and the VGG16 autoencoder runs on the MindSpore AI framework deployed on Ascend 910 [22].

4.1 Re-localization

We validate the task of re-localization by random picking 32 2D LiDAR data, RGB and depth image in each room. The picked view data are coded as 1194 dimensional feature vector f_{view}, and is used to find the most similar vector stored in map grids. According to the Eq. (2), once the most similar stored vector is found, then the re-localization position of $\hat{I}$, $\hat{J}$, $\hat{\theta}$ for X, Y and θ are obtained.

The values in the W, H columns of Table 1 list the actual size of room measured in metre (m) in its width and height. The values in the columns of G_x, G_y

Table 1. The structure and the re-localization performance of STL map for the 5 rooms of the "alma-s1" apartment in Robot@Home.

Map												Re-localization							
Room		Grid				Map Size			Pyramid			SN		KNN (Autoencoder)+SN					
$W(m)$	$H(m)$	$G_x(m)$	$G_y(m)$	$G_\theta(°)$	M	N	R	L	u	v	$T(s)$	$A(\%)$	$\tau = 1$		$\tau = 2$		$\tau = 3$	
														T(s)	A(%)	T(s)	A(%)	T(s)	A(%)
Bathroom1	2.3	3	0.5	0.5	20	5	6	18	2	2	2	15.9	93.2	0.38	72.3	0.79	79.5	1	91.9
Bedroom1	5.2	2.6	0.7	0.4	30	8	7	12	2	2	2	18.4	94.1	0.44	74.7	0.89	81.3	1.1	93.7
Kitchenroom1	2.8	2.6	0.5	0.5	30	6	6	12	2	2	2	11.6	94.6	0.27	76.2	0.69	83.4	0.9	94.3
Livingroom1	5.2	4.8	0.4	0.4	15	13	12	24	2	2	2	85	92.8	2.07	70.6	2.48	78.7	2.6	93.1
Masterroom1	2.6	3.6	0.5	0.6	20	6	6	18	2	2	2	15.9	93.7	0.38	71.9	0.79	79.1	1	93.4
Average	3.6	3.3	0.5	0.5	23	7.6	7.4	17	2	2	2	29.3	93.7	0.71	73.1	1.13	80.4	1.3	93.3

of Table 1 are the grid size along x, y coordinate respectively measured in metre (m), and G_θ is the interval values of along anti-clockwise rotation measured in degree (°). Then the map parameters M, N and R are determined according to Eq. (3) Eq. (4). We can see from Table 1 that the livingroom1 are relatively larger than other rooms in size, and at the same time, the livingroom1 has the related small values of G_x, G_y and G_θ than those values of other rooms, especially for bedroom and bathroom. The reason for this phenomenon is that the scenes in livingroom1 are relatively complex than those of bathroom and bedroom.

In the re-localization column of Table 1, the numbers in L column are the layer number of map pyramid, and u, v columns are the downsample ratio along x and y coordinates. We can see from Table 1 that all the rooms in have the downsample ratio with u = 2 and v = 2 for all rooms in "alma-s1" apartment. The item "SN" in re-localization column means that we use Siamese network in the matching process between f_{view} and $F_{(i,j,\theta)}$. The item "KNN (Autoencoder)+SM" in re-localization column means that we first use KNN to find the top τ candidates, and then use Siamese network to find the best matching one from the top τ candidates. In experiments, the time cost for making a comparison using Siamese network is about 0.102 s and that for Autoencoded KNN is about 0.002 s, then the time cost of "SN" and "KNN (Autoencoder)+SN" for livingroom1 are 85.0 s and 2.278 s. The numbers in column T of Table 1 list the re-localization cost time in second for each room. We can see from Table 1 that the proposed map method could retrieve robot's position in about 2.0 s for a random given position using "KNN (Autoencoder)+SN".

4.2   Discussions

In experiments, we first analyze the map generation parameters using KNN similarity calculation based objective evaluations and subjective evaluations from 34 volunteers. It was found that objective and subjective evaluations obtain similar parameters' setting results. It is found that "KNN (Autoencoder)+SN" combined with STL map pyramid obtain satisfied performance using low time cost. We did not use traditional point register technique, such as ICP method, to accelerate the matching processing for initial position and angle locations.

We think this helps to analyze the performance of the 2D LiDAR and RGB-D data fusion in the STL map strategy.

5   Conclusions

In this work, we take the data obtained by 2D LiDAR and RGB-D camera as examples to introduce how the multiple sensors' information are fused and stored in the map. It is noticeable that the map itself supports more kinds of sensors' data fusion so long as the sensors' data could be presented or compressed in 1D feature vector. The future work includes the performance of the proposed method validated with more kinds of sensors in its map structure and in re-localization task. In addition, in spite of high performances obtained on Robot@Home dataset, the propose map strategy should be validated on more datasets and in practical navigation environments.

Acknowledgments. This work is supported by the National Key Research & Development Program of China (No. 2018AAA0102902), the National Natural Science Foundation of China (NSFC) (No. 61873269), the Beijing Natural Science Foundation (No: L192005), the CAAI-Huawei MindSpore Open Fund (CAAIXSJLJJ-20202-027A), the Guangxi Key Research and Development Program (AB18221011, AB21075004, AD18281002, AD19110137), the Natural Science Foundation of Guangxi of China (No: 2020GXNSFAA297061, 2019GXNSFDA185006, 2019GXN SFDA185007), Guangxi Key Laboratory of Intelligent Processing of Computer Images and Graphics (No GIIP201702) and Guangxi Key Laboratory of Trusted Software (NO kx201621, kx201715).

References

1. Zlot, R., Bosse, M.: Place recognition using keypoint similarities in 2D lidar maps. In: Springer Tracts in Advanced Robotics, vol. 54, pp. 363–372 (2009)
2. Olson, E.B.: Real-time correlative scan matching. In: IEEE International Conference on Robotics & Automation. IEEE (2009)
3. Manasi Muglikar, Z.Z., Scaramuzza, D.: Voxel map for visual SLAM. Presented at the IEEE Conference on Robotics and Automation (ICRA), Paris (2020)
4. Endres, F., Hess, J., Sturm, J., et al.: 3-D mapping with an RGB-D camera. IEEE Trans. Rob. **30**(1), 177–187 (2014)
5. Endres, F., Hess, J., Sturm, J.: 3-D mapping with an RGB-D camera. IEEE Trans. Rob. **30**(1), 177–187 (2014)
6. Bo, T., et al.: RGB-D based cognitive map building and navigation. In: 2013 IEEE/RSJ International Conference on IEEE Intelligent Robots and Systems (IROS) (2014)
7. Ylimaki, M., Heikkil, J., Kannala, J.: Accurate 3-D reconstruction with RGB-D cameras using depth map fusion and pose refinement. Presented at the 2018 24th International Conference on Pattern Recognition (ICPR) Beijing, China (2018)
8. Kuan, Y.W., Ee, N.O., Wei, L.S.: Comparative study of Intel R200, Kinect v2, and Primesense RGB-D sensors performance outdoors. IEEE Sens. J. **19**(19), 8741–8750 (2019)

9. François Pomerleau, F.C., Siegwart, R., Magnenat, S.: Comparing ICP variants on real-world data sets. Auton. Rob. **34**, 133–148 (2013)
10. Ji-Hua, Z., Nan-Ning, Z., Ze-Jian, Y., Qiang, Z.: A SLAM algorithm based on central difference particle filter. Acta Automatica Sinica **36**(2), 249–57 (2010)
11. Zhang, J., Singh, S.: LOAM: lidar odometry and mapping in real-time. In: Robotics: Science and Systems Conference (2014)
12. Lowe, D.G.: Distinctive image features from scale-invariant keypoints. Int. J. Comput. Vis. **60**, 91–110 (2004)
13. Bay, H., Tuytelaars, T., Van Gool, L.: SURF: speeded up robust features. In: Leonardis, A., Bischof, H., Pinz, A. (eds.) ECCV 2006. LNCS, vol. 3951, pp. 404–417. Springer, Heidelberg (2006). https://doi.org/10.1007/11744023_32
14. Edgar Simo-Serra, E.T., Ferraz, L., Kokkinos, I., Fua, P., Moreno-Noguer, F.: Discriminative learning of deep convolutional feature point descriptors. Presented at the 2015 IEEE International Conference on Computer Vision (CVPR) (2015)
15. Besl, P.J., McKay, N.D.: A method for registration of 3-D shapes. In: Sensor Fusion IV: Control Paradigms and Data Structures, vol. 1611, pp. 586–606 (1992)
16. Himstedt, M., et al.: Large scale place recognition in 2D LIDAR scans using Geometrical landmark relations. In: 2014 IEEE/RSJ International Conference on Intelligent Robots and Systems IEEE (2014)
17. Debeunne, C., Vivet, D.: A review of visual-LiDAR fusion based simultaneous localization and mapping. Sensors **20**(7) (2020)
18. Bo, D., Wei, X., Jia, W., et al.: Stacked convolutional denoising auto-encoders for feature representation. IEEE Trans. Cybern. **47**(4), 1017–1027 (2017)
19. Paul, N.D.M., Besl, J.: A method for registration of 3-D shapes. IEEE T. Pattern Anal. **14**(2), 239–256 (1992)
20. Zhang, Z.: Iterative point matching for registration of free-form curves and surfaces. Int. J. Comput. Vision **13**(2), 119–152 (1994)
21. Ruiz-Sarmiento, J.R, Galindo, C., et al.: Robot@Home, a robotic dataset for semantic mapping of home environments. Int. J. Rob. Res. **36**, 131–141 (2017)
22. Mindspore: VGG16. Website (2020). https://gitee.com/mindspore/mindspore/blob/r1.1/model_zoo/official/cv/vgg16/src/vgg.py

On the Importance of Regularisation and Auxiliary Information in OOD Detection

John Mitros[(✉)] [iD] and Brian Mac Namee[iD]

School of Computer Science, University College Dublin, Dublin, Ireland
ioanni.mitro@ucdconnect.ie, brian.macnamee@ucd.ie

Abstract. Neural networks are often utilised in critical domain applications, even though they exhibit overconfident predictions for ambiguous inputs. This deficiency demonstrates a fundamental flaw: that neural networks often overfit on spurious correlations. We address this limitation by presenting two novel objectives that improve out-of-distribution (OOD) detection. We empirically demonstrate that our methods outperform the baseline while still maintaining a competitive performance against the rest. Additionally, we empirically demonstrate the robustness of our approach against common corruptions and the importance of regularisation and auxiliary information in OOD detection.

Keywords: Out-of-distribution detection · Neural networks · Robust predictions · Stability · Anomaly detection · Open set recognition

1 Introduction

Out of distribution (OOD) detection is becoming an integral part in evaluating the robustness of deployed machine learning models developed for critical applications. The main goal of OOD detection is to equip a classifier with the ability to provide stable, consistent and low confidence predictions for ambiguous data different from in-distribution (ID) training data. A central assumption in statistical learning theory [14] states that the train and test set are generated independent and identically distributed (IID) from an unknown joint distribution P. Unfortunately, this assumption fails to assess whether the model has learned to properly generalise to new unseen data or simply overfits to irrelevant factors (e.g., backgrounds, texture, etc.) spuriously correlated with the correct labels.

Inspired by recent progress in contrastive learning [2] we propose two novel objectives for OOD detection and demonstrate empirically that our method is not only competitive with existing approaches, but also outperforms the majority on most occasions. The main contributions of this work are:

Research conducted with financial support of Science Foundation Ireland under Grant number 15/CDA/3520. For Open Access, the author has applied a CC BY public copyright licence to any Author Accepted Manuscript submission.

© Springer Nature Switzerland AG 2021
T. Mantoro et al. (Eds.): ICONIP 2021, CCIS 1517, pp. 361–368, 2021.
https://doi.org/10.1007/978-3-030-92310-5_42

– A novel objective function based on the cosine similarity between ID and OOD data.
– A novel objective function inspired by prior work on margin and ranking objectives utilising the cosine similarity between ID and OOD data, as well as additional explicit regularisation.

2   Related Work

Early attempts at OOD detection [4] utilised the maximum softmax probability (MSP) as an indicator to identify OOD samples, while alternative approaches such as ODIN [9] use adversarially perturbed samples when computing the softmax with high temperature during training. Furthermore, the Mahalanobis detector [8] fits a Gaussian distribution to the activation of the last layer of a neural network and performs OOD by measuring the Mahalanobis distance from the inputs to the ID data. In addition, methods explicitly trained to output uniform distributions over perturbed ID samples usually resemble techniques simulating OOD inputs from a GAN [7], or utilise auxiliary information as outliers [5]. Finally, existing approaches rely on averaging predictions of randomly initialised, independently trained, neural networks.

Most objectives adopted today in machine learning have a single goal: to induce a cost for an underlying model to learn an input/output relationship. In contrast, ranking objectives strive to compute relative distances between inputs, thus the underlying task is often referred to as metric learning. The key idea is to employ a metric function in order to obtain a similarity score between inputs embedded in a latent feature space $\mathbf{z}$. One such example is SimCLR [1] that maximises the agreement in latent representations via a contrastive objective between pairs of inputs.

3   Objective Functions for OOD Detection

The first contribution that this article makes to OOD detection is a novel objective based on the cosine similarity between ID and OOD predictions. Let $(\mathbf{x}_{id}, y_{id}) \sim S_{ID}$ and $(\mathbf{x}_{ood}, y_{ood}) \sim S_{OOD}$ represent two data points sampled from ID and OOD datasets respectively, and, define $\mathbf{p}_{id} = \max_{y_{id}} p(y_{id}|f_\theta(\mathbf{x}_{id}))$ to be the MSP for $\mathbf{x}_{id} \in S_{ID}$, and, $\mathbf{p}_{ood} = \max_{y_{id}} p(y_{id}|f_\theta(\mathbf{x}_{ood}))$ for $\mathbf{x}_{ood} \in S_{OOD}$. Finally, let $\cos(\mathbf{p}_{id}, \mathbf{p}_{ood})$ be the cosine between two vectors. Then, our objective is formulated as:

$$L(\mathbf{x}_{id}, \mathbf{x}_{ood}, y_{id}) = \underbrace{-\mathbb{E}\left[\log p(y_{id}|\mathbf{x}_{id})\right]}_{\text{cross-entropy loss}} + \underbrace{\lambda \cos(\mathbf{p}_{id}, \mathbf{p}_{ood})}_{\text{cosine-regularisation}} \tag{1}$$

The regularisation strength λ is obtained using the validation set, whenever $\lambda = -1$ then the underlying objective becomes a minimax optimisation formulation, but faster to train since it avoids computing gradients for worst-case

---

Algorithm 1. Cosine regularised objective

---

procedure REGULARISED-OBJECTIVE($\mathbf{x}_{id}, \mathbf{x}_{ood}, y_{id}$)

    $f_\theta \leftarrow \theta$ ▷ initialise model

    $\mathbf{z}_{id}, \mathbf{z}_{ood} \leftarrow f_\theta(\mathbf{x}_{id}), f_\theta(\mathbf{x}_{ood})$ ▷ compute logits for $\mathbf{x}_{id} \in S_{ID}, \mathbf{x}_{ood} \in S_{OOD}$

    $\widehat{\mathbf{p}}_{id}, \widehat{\mathbf{p}}_{ood} \leftarrow softmax(\mathbf{z}_{id}), softmax(\mathbf{z}_{ood})$ ▷ probs. for logits $\in (S_{ID}, S_{OOD})$

    $CE \leftarrow -\mathbb{E}[\log p(y_{id}|\mathbf{x}_{id})]$ ▷ compute cross-entropy for $(\mathbf{x}_{id}, y_{id}) \in S_{ID}$

    $\cos \leftarrow \frac{\mathbf{p}_{id}{}^\top \mathbf{p}_{ood}}{\|\mathbf{p}_{id}\| \|\mathbf{p}_{ood}\|}$ ▷ compute cosine for probabilities $\widehat{\mathbf{p}}_{id}, \widehat{\mathbf{p}}_{ood}$

    $L \leftarrow CE + \lambda \cos$ ▷ compute final regularised loss

    $\theta_{t+1} = \theta_t - \eta \nabla_\theta L$ ▷ compute gradient w.r.t params θ and backprop errors

end procedure

---

perturbations on the inputs. The goal is to lower the cross-entropy error on S_{ID} while at the same time increasing the cosine angle between S_{ID} and S_{OOD}. This approach is described in Algorithm 1.

The second contribution is a novel ranking objective for OOD detection. We utilise cosine similarity as a metric learning function in addition to explicit regularisation. We use $\ell_2 = \lambda_2 \sum_n \|y_{id} \mathbf{p}_{id}, \alpha\|$ and $\ell_1 = \lambda_1 \sum_n |\mathbf{p}_{ood} - 1/k|$ for S_{ID} and S_{OOD} respectively. This results in the following objective:

$$L(\mathbf{x}_{id}, \mathbf{x}_{ood}, y_{id}) = \underbrace{\max(0, \gamma + \cos(\mathbf{p}_{id}, \mathbf{p}_{ood}))}_{\text{ranking objective}} + \ell_1 + \ell_2 \qquad (2)$$

Notice, $k \in \mathbb{Z}$ refers to the number of ID classes in S_{ID}; y_{id} represents a one-hot encoding of the labels; and $\alpha \in \mathbb{R}$ is a user defined scalar that indicates the desired ID accuracy. There are a number of hyperpameters $\{\gamma, \lambda_1, \lambda_2\}$ that can be tuned on the validation set. γ defines the margin; and λ_1 and λ_2 refer to regularisation strength. This approach is depicted in Algorithm 2.

Algorithm 2. Cosine ranking objective

---

procedure RANKING-OBJECTIVE($\mathbf{x}_{id}, \mathbf{x}_{ood}, y_{id}$)

    $f_\theta \leftarrow \theta$ ▷ initialise model

    $\mathbf{z}_{id}, \mathbf{z}_{ood} \leftarrow f_\theta(\mathbf{x}_{id}), f_\theta(\mathbf{x}_{ood})$ ▷ compute logits for $\mathbf{x}_{id} \in S_{ID}, \mathbf{x}_{ood} \in S_{OOD}$

    $\widehat{\mathbf{p}}_{id}, \widehat{\mathbf{p}}_{ood} \leftarrow softmax(\mathbf{z}_{id}), softmax(\mathbf{z}_{ood})$ ▷ probs. for logits $\in (S_{ID}, S_{OOD})$

    $\ell_1 \leftarrow \lambda_1 \sum_n |\mathbf{p}_{ood} - 1/k|$ ▷ compute ℓ_1-regularisation for $\widehat{\mathbf{p}}_{ood} \in S_{OOD}$

    $\ell_2 \leftarrow \lambda_2 \sum_n \|y_{id} \mathbf{p}_{id}, \alpha\|$ ▷ compute ℓ_2-regularisation for $\widehat{\mathbf{p}}_{id} \in S_{ID}$

    $\cos \leftarrow \frac{\mathbf{p}_{id}{}^\top \mathbf{p}_{out}}{\|\mathbf{p}_{id}\| \|\mathbf{p}_{ood}\|}$ ▷ compute cosine for probabilities $\widehat{\mathbf{p}}_{id}, \widehat{\mathbf{p}}_{ood}$

    $L \leftarrow \max(0, \gamma + \cos)) + \ell_1 + \ell_2$ ▷ compute the final ranking loss

    $\theta_{t+1} = \theta_t - \eta \nabla_\theta L$ ▷ compute gradient w.r.t params θ and backprop errors

end procedure

---

4 Artificial Data Experiments

To validate the efficacy of the proposed objectives we designed a controlled experiment utilising synthetic data. The ID training data, S_{ID}, is comprised of

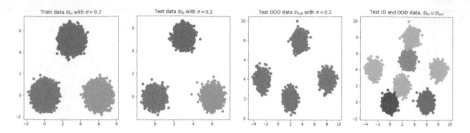

Fig. 1. Synthetic dataset. From left to right ID train data, ID test data, OOD test data, and $S_{ID} \cup S_{OOD}$ (yellow) test data. (Color figure online)

3 Gaussian clusters with standard deviation σ representing different classes in a multi-class classification setting. The different subset splits $train \sim S_{ID}^{train}$, $test \sim S_{ID}^{test}$ and $ood \sim S_{OOD}$ over the synthetic dataset are shown in Fig. 1. The underlying model is a 3-layer MLP, trained on the synthetic data, S_{ID}^{train}. During inference we test each objective on the OOD test data, S_{OOD}, constructed of 4-Gaussian clusters displaced at different locations. To measure performance at OOD detection we measure AUC based on three OOD metrics on the models' logits: *confidence*, *entropy*, and *mutual information*.

4.1   Results and Discussion

Table 1 shows OOD detection for the different objectives, while Fig. 2 shows the decision boundaries learned by two objectives.

As suggested in Table 1 our proposed methods achieve near optimal OOD detection when presented with ambiguous test data. Notice, explicit regularisation (e.g. MC-Dropout) does indeed provide additional benefit in OOD detection which confirms prior work on the impact of regularisation [6]. Regularisation improves OOD detection because it acts as boundary thickness [15].

5   Real Data Experiment

Five well-known image classification datasets are used in this experiment: *CIFAR-10*, *CIFAR-100*, *SVHN*, *FashionMNIST*, and *LSUN*. Every dataset was

Table 1. Classification accuracy and OOD detection for different objectives & metrics.

Objective	Classification	OOD Detection (AUC-ROC)		
	Accuracy	Confidence	Entropy	Mutual information
CrossEntropy	100	61.64	61.61	63.62
CrossEntropy+MC-Dropout	100	75.14	73.63	73.56
CrossEntropy+Cosine (ours)	100	99.99	99.99	99.99
Ranking Objective (ours)	100	99.99	99.99	99.99

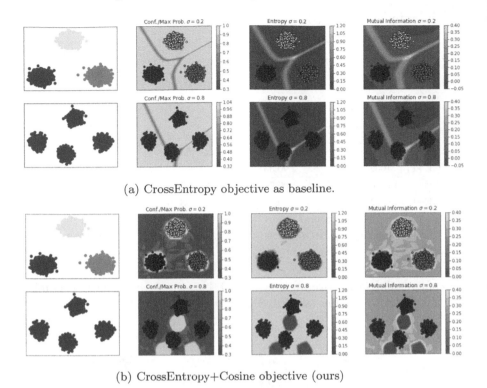

(a) CrossEntropy objective as baseline.

(b) CrossEntropy+Cosine objective (ours)

Fig. 2. Decision boundaries across objective functions for ID (1st row) and OOD (2nd row) test data.

split into three distinct sets {*train, validation, test*} with random mirroring and cropping augmentations. We utilised WideResNet28x10 as the DNN model trained for 300 epochs using a validation set for hyper-parameter tuning, and rolling back to the best checkpoint to avoid overfitting. The optimiser was Stochastic Gradient Descent (SGD) with momentum set to 0.9 and weight decay $5e^{-4}$. We utilised classification accuracy to measure the performance on the clean ID test data. We measure the separation between ID and OOD data using the area under the curve (AUC-ROC). We also compare the proposed objective with the following OOD detection methods: Mahalanobis [8], ODIN [9], MSRep [12], OE [5], EnergyOOD [10], CSI [13], and DoSE [11].

5.1   Results and Discussion

Tables 2 and 3 compares our proposed objectives with existing OOD approaches. In Table 2 we show classification accuracies for the different methods compared. In Table 3 we report confidence-based AUC-ROC scores matching our experimental setting. Our methods outperform *MSP, ODIN, EnergyOOD*, and provide comparable results with *Mahalanobis, MSRep*, and *OE*. These results also

Table 2. Accuracy of models on ID dataset classification tasks.

Model	CIFAR-10	SVHN	FashionMNIST	CIFAR-100
DNN	95.06	96.67	95.27	77.44
DPN	88.10	90.10	93.20	79.34
MC-Dropout	96.22	96.90	95.40	78.39
SWAG	96.53	97.06	93.80	78.61
JEM	92.83	96.13	83.21	77.86
CE+ℓ_1	90.66	95.34	93.89	62.30
CE+ℓ_1+MCD	90.33	94.85	91.37	60.35
CE+Cosine (ours)	90.76	95.25	93.68	72.78
CE+Cosine+MCD	90.31	94.75	93.01	64.04
CosineMargin+ℓ_1+ℓ_2 (ours)	89.01	94.97	93.40	64.32
CosineMargin+ℓ_1+ℓ_2+MCD	91.96	82.34	93.13	60.43

show that regularisation overall is beneficial, but excessive regularisation might deteriorate OOD detection (see Fig. 3).

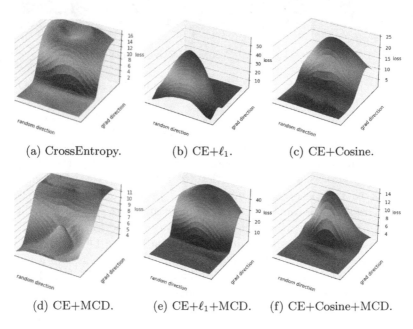

(a) CrossEntropy.   (b) CE+ℓ_1.   (c) CE+Cosine.

(d) CE+MCD.   (e) CE+ℓ_1+MCD.   (f) CE+Cosine+MCD.

Fig. 3. Comparison of objective functions with (1st row) & without (2nd row) explicit regularisation (MCD: Monte-Carlo Dropout); trained on S_{ID} CIFAR-10 and tested on S_{OOD} CIFAR-100.

To evaluate whether our method is robust against common corruptions we utilised *CIFAR10-C* and *CIFAR100-C*. Similar to [3] we report the mean

Table 3. Comparison of our methods with related work based on published results in the literature corresponding with our setting.

Data		OOD Detection (AUC-ROC)							
S_{ID}	S_{OOD}	MSP	Mahalanobis	ODIN	MSRep	OE	EnergyOOD	Cos(ours)	RankCos(ours)
CIFAR-10	CIFAR-100*	86.15	93.90	85.59	91.23	93.30	92.60	92.23	94.23
	SVHN	89.60	97.62	91.96	99.48	98.40	90.96	99.18	95.40
	LSUN	88.54	96.30	90.35	96.05	97.60	94.24	92.44	94.77
CIFAR-100	CIFAR-10	73.41	81.34	74.54	81.49	75.70	76.61	72.94	68.89
	SVHN*	71.44	86.01	67.26	87.42	86.66	73.99	99.68	99.95
	LSUN	75.38	93.9	78.94	79.05	79.71	79.23	70.50	62.17

corruption error (mCE) in Table 4. Our objective attains the smallest mCE on *CIFAR10-C* indicating that it is indeed robust against common corruptions. On *CIFAR100-C* cross-entropy + ℓ_1 attains the smallest error with ours second best.

Table 4. Evaluating objective functions across common corruptions against *CIFAR10-C* and *CIFAR100-C* measured in average corruption error (mCE).

Objectives	mCE	
	CIFAR10-C	CIFAR100-C
CrossEntropy	161.14	717.04
CrossEntropy+MCD	120.91	536.63
CrossEntropy+ℓ_1	144.02	247.78
CrossEntropy+ℓ_1+MCD	140.96	285.04
CrossEntropy+Cosine (ours)	119.98	337.94
CrossEntropy+Cosine+MCD	129.20	269.52
CosineMargin+ℓ_1+ℓ_2 (ours)	149.46	258.73
CosineMargin+ℓ_1+ℓ_2+MCD	167.30	306.42

6   Conclusion

In this work we presented two novel objective functions designed to be used in regular classification settings while at the same time exhibiting some robustness properties against common corruptions and ambiguous inputs when evaluated in OOD detection. We demonstrated that our approach outperforms half of the competitive methods and performs comparably to the remaining ones. Furthermore, we presented the efficacy of our method against common corruptions measured in mCE compared to competitive alternative methods. Finally, we identified the importance of auxiliary information as well as the role of regularisation in OOD detection, followed by questions in identifying the role of bias in the choice of objective function, family class, and algorithm when considering OOD detection.

References

1. Chen, T., Kornblith, S., Norouzi, M., Hinton, G.: A simple framework for contrastive learning of visual representations. In: Proceedings of the 37th International Conference on Machine Learning. Proceedings of Machine Learning Research, vol. 119, pp. 1597–1607. PMLR (2020)
2. Henaff, O.: Data-efficient image recognition with contrastive predictive coding. In: Proceedings of the 37th International Conference on Machine Learning. Proceedings of Machine Learning Research, vol. 119, pp. 4182–4192. PMLR (2020)
3. Hendrycks, D., Dietterich, T.: Benchmarking neural network robustness to common corruptions and perturbations. In: International Conference on Learning Representations (2019)
4. Hendrycks, D., Gimpel, K.: A baseline for detecting misclassified and out-of-distribution examples in neural networks. ICLR (2017)
5. Hendrycks, D., Mazeika, M., Dietterich, T.: Deep anomaly detection with outlier exposure. In: International Conference on Learning Representations (2019)
6. Khani, F., Liang, P.: Removing spurious features can hurt accuracy and affect groups disproportionately. In: Proceedings of the 2021 ACM Conference on Fairness, Accountability, and Transparency, FAccT 2021. Association for Computing Machinery (2021). https://doi.org/10.1145/3442188.3445883
7. Lee, K., Lee, H., Lee, K., Shin, J.: Training confidence-calibrated classifiers for detecting out-of-distribution samples. ArXiv:1711.09325 [cs, stat] (2017)
8. Lee, K., Lee, K., Lee, H., Shin, J.: A simple unified framework for detecting out-of-distribution samples and adversarial attacks. In: Advances in Neural Information Processing Systems, vol. 31. Curran Associates, Inc. (2018)
9. Liang, S., Li, Y., Srikant, R.: Enhancing the reliability of out-of-distribution image detection in neural networks. In: International Conference on Learning Representations (2018)
10. Liu, W., Wang, X., Owens, J., Li, Y.: Energy-based out-of-distribution detection. In: Advances in Neural Information Processing Systems, vol. 33, pp. 21464–21475 (2020)
11. Morningstar, W., Ham, C., Gallagher, A., Lakshminarayanan, B., Alemi, A., Dillon, J.: Density of states estimation for out of distribution detection. In: Proceedings of The 24th International Conference on Artificial Intelligence and Statistics. Proceedings of Machine Learning Research, vol. 130. PMLR (2021)
12. Shalev, G., Adi, Y., Keshet, J.: Out-of-distribution detection using multiple semantic label representations. In: Advances in Neural Information Processing Systems, vol. 31. Curran Associates, Inc. (2018)
13. Tack, J., Mo, S., Jeong, J., Shin, J.: CSI: novelty detection via contrastive learning on distributionally shifted instances. In: Larochelle, H., Ranzato, M., Hadsell, R., Balcan, M.F., Lin, H. (eds.) Advances in Neural Information Processing Systems, vol. 33. Curran Associates, Inc. (2020)
14. Vapnik, V.N.: An overview of statistical learning theory. IEEE Trans. Neural Networks **10**(5), 988–999 (1999)
15. Yang, Y., et al.: Boundary thickness and robustness in learning models. In: Advances in Neural Information Processing Systems, vol. 33, pp. 6223–6234. Curran Associates, Inc. (2020)

Developing GCN: Graph Convolutional Network with Evolving Parameters for Dynamic Graphs

Lin Lan[iD], Jin Li, and Yang-Geng Fu[(✉)][iD]

College of Computer and Data Science, Fuzhou University, Fuzhou, China
fu@fzu.edu.cn

Abstract. Dynamic graph representation learning has caused much attention in many practical applications. There is an interesting method that uses RNNS (e.g., LSTM, GRU) to update the GCN's weights dynamically with weights from the previous time step. However, it only uses one time-step weights, which eventually leads to the lack of sufficient historical information. In this work, we focus on this method for the developing parameters and propose a developing GCN model, which adapts an attention mechanism to get richer historical information so that the RNNs will decode better fused historical representations to capture the temporal correlation of weights in the GCN, which not only can learn those dynamic graphs with fewer features, but also can extract richer historical information to learn. We evaluate our method on the task for link prediction and the result shows a better performance in most data sets we test.

Keywords: Dynamic graphs · Attention mechanism · Developing parameters

1 Introduction

The graph representation is a kind of data mining task which aims at the graph data. It has been more and more practical in our real life and there are some related studies. In [1–5], these papers proposed a series of conventional and effective methods, which learned the graph representation on both the node and the graph level. There also exist models combining with deep neural networks. Detail can be seen from [6–15], and [16].

However, the models mentioned above are mainly about the static graphs with ignorance of the dynamic ones which will change their attributes (such as the existence of edges and nodes, node features). The similar work includes [17–19]. The primary idea of these methods use the GNNs for extracting the features of nodes and put them into the RNNs to build sequence learning, expecting to predict the developing trend of graphs.

This research was supported by the National Natural Science Foundation of China (No. 61773123) and the Natural Science Foundation of Fujian Province, China (No. 2019J01647).

T. Mantoro et al. (Eds.): ICONIP 2021, CCIS 1517, pp. 369–376, 2021.
https://doi.org/10.1007/978-3-030-92310-5_43

In this work, we focus on the dynamics of GCN parameters which can deal with graphs under different conditions overtimes. We consider more time steps' GCN parameters for aggregating into richer historical information. The model we adopt is the graph convolutional network (GCN, [11]). Its parameters which are used for the linear transformation of the node embeddings in each layer are what we consider to update. We design an Encoder-Decoder architecture that takes several time steps' parameters as inputs and updates the next time's GCN parameters we need to predict.

The reason why we consider the dynamics of GCN parameters is that sometimes we have to process some data with fewer node features, and finally the result may be bad in the models aiming at the dynamics of features. So we need to develop models to solve the problem of lack of features.

2   Related Work

The research of dynamic graphs usually develops from the static one by adding a temporal updating module. The conventional methods of matrix factorization-based [20–22] and the random walk-based [1,5,23,24] are common ones.

There are also approaches combined with deep learning. For example, the DynGEM [26] is an auto encoder based one. The most relevant to our works are those with the combination of GNNs and temporal module(e.g., RNNs, attention), such as [11,17–19,25,27], and [28].

3   Method

In this section, we present a novel model for graph representation learning, which will capture the temporal developing trend of the GCN model's weights in each layer to update them for the next time step so that the GCN can steadily adapt to the changing graphs. It includes two modules: one is the GCN module used for extracting the helpful feature information from the input graphs and the other is the Encoder-Decoder architecture comprising Attention Mechanism and GRU which is used for modeling the temporal relations of different historical GCN weights and predict the next one. Its entire structure is in Fig. 1. Please note that all named mathematical notations(such as X_t, H_t) are just local variables and what they stand for is not different in each section.

3.1   Graph Convolutional Network(GCN)

We select the GCN model proposed by ([11]) which comprises multiple graph convolution layers and it belongs to the spectral convolution. The graph convolution layers are primarily to aggregate the neighborhood's information for the nodes. At time t the l-th layer input is the adjacency matrix A_t and the node embedding matrix $H_t^{(l)}$. After the updating with the help of weight matrix $W_t^{(l)}$, the node embedding matrix updated to $H_t^{(l+1)}$. It is written:

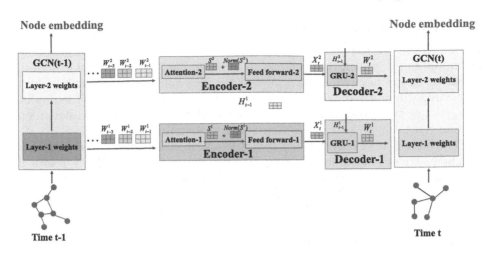

Fig. 1. A comprehensive architecture of the model we propose.

$$H_t^{(l+1)} = \text{GCONV}\left(A_t, H_t^{(l)}, W_t^{(l)}\right) = \sigma\left(\widehat{A}_t H_t^{(l)} W_t^{(l)}\right) \tag{1}$$

The $\widehat{A}_t$ is a normalization of A_t defined as:

$$\widehat{A} = \widetilde{D}^{-\frac{1}{2}} \widetilde{A} \widetilde{D}^{-\frac{1}{2}}, \quad \widetilde{A} = A + I, \quad \widetilde{D} = \text{diag}\left(\sum_j \widetilde{A}_{ij}\right) \tag{2}$$

The initial embedding matrix usually adapts node features (The definitions of these variables like H_t, W_t are only valid in this section).

3.2 The Encoder-Decoder Architecture

Because of that, the weights in GCN are no longer the trained parameters and we treat them as the feature vectors to learn their temporal evolution. Under this situation, we may view the problem as long sequence learning. So the "Encoder-Decoder" architecture coming from [29] will work well. On the other hand, the relative methods focusing on developing parameters just use an RNN module to update them without sufficient historical information. So we should add an encoder module to fuse more historical information so that the long sequence problem of information extraction will be effectively solved. We use the attention mechanism being expert in solving long sequence problems as an encoder to learn how the historical time steps' information affects the unknown time step and the RNNs to decode the fused historical information for new weights. We write the whole formula:

$$W_t^l = EncoderDecoder(W_{t-1}^l, W_{t-2}^l, ..., W_{t-k}^l) \tag{3}$$

The $W_t^l \in R^{r \times c}$ denotes the l-th layer weights in GCN at the t-th time step. The k is the scale of time steps considered by us.

3.3   Key-Value Pair Attention with Mult-Heads

In Self-Attention, the snapshot takes itself into computing when aggregating attention. In our model, the "self one" is what we need to update and unknown, so the attention mechanism we choose is the Key-Value Pair Attention, which transforms the input data ($W_{t-1}^l, W_{t-2}^l, ..., W_{t-k}^l$) into the form of key-value pair. Among them, the "keys" are used for calculating the attention distribution α_n and the "Values" for calculating the aggregating information.

The basic unit we compute now is matrices instead of vectors. Here we denote weight matrices from different time steps as ($W_1^{r \times c}, W_2^{r \times c}, ..., W_n^{r \times c}$) with n denoted the size of time steps we consider and the r and c denoted rows and columns respectively. Then we define three parameter matrices to be trained: $K \in R^{r \times r}$, $V \in R^{r \times r}$, $q \in R^{r \times c}$. These weight matrices will be transformed to $(K, v) = [(k_1, v_1), ..., (k_n, v_n)]$ with $k_n, v_n \in R^{r \times c}$ by the mapping of matrices K and V. The q is called query matrice used to calculate the scores with each key. We wrote the score function as:

$$s(k_n, q) = \frac{< k_n, q >}{\sqrt{r \times c}} \tag{4}$$

$< k_n, q >$ denotes the inner product between two matrices.

Then the final fused historical weights from different time steps can be computed by

$$att((K, V), q) = \sum_{n=1}^N \alpha_n v_n = \sum_{n=1}^N \frac{\exp\left(s\left(k_n, q\right)\right)}{\sum_j \exp\left(s\left(k_j, q\right)\right)} v_n, \tag{5}$$

In addition, we also introduce the Mult-Head Attention Mechanism, which defines multiple query matrices $Q = [q_1, ..., q_M]$ to obtain more information from the input data. The calculation formula as follows:

$$att((K, V), Q) = Concat(att\left((K, V), q_1\right) \cdots att\left((K, V), q_M\right)) \tag{6}$$

The function $Concat(.)$ means the operation of splicing those matrices horizontally. After the computation of function $Concat(.)$, the output of att$((K, V), Q) \in R^{r \times Mc}$ should be additionally transformed by a matrice $O \in R^{Mc \times c}$ to a new fused matrice $X \in R^{r \times c}$. The matrice O also need to be trained.

We can assume that the multi-head may pay attention to different aspects from inputs so that we can capture richer information.

3.4   Residual Connection and Normalization

After the computation of attention, we get a fused matrice $X^{r \times c}$(means different from other sections). Then we further calculate the all elements' mean value(m) and standard deviation(std). We define two trainable parameters named a and b, two constant matrices $M \in R^{r \times c}$ with all elements m and $B \in R^{r \times c}$ with all elements 1. The normalization is computed:

$$Norm(X) = a(\frac{X - M}{std}) + Bb \tag{7}$$

The motivation for what we calculate like this is that we expect the fused matrice X will adaptively adjust its mean value and standard deviation for better representation to extract the historical information.

Sometimes the information in $Norm(X)$ may not be represented well. We should combine the original X to put them in the feed-forward network(FNN). Therefore, the final output of the encoder is that:

$$Encode(W_1, W_2, ..., W_n) = FFN(X + Norm(X)) \tag{8}$$

3.5 Gated Recurrent Unit(GRU)

The decoding part is the GRU, one of RNNs. Compared to LSTM, it has advantages of simpler computation and faster convergence. Its input come from two parts: one is the final output of the encoder and the other is the output itself from its previous time step used as the hidden state(H_{t-1}) at this time step. The output $H_t \in R^{r \times c}$ of GRU will act as two roles: one is used as weights in the corresponding layer for GCN and the other is the hidden state for the next time step's GRU.

4 Experiments

In this section, we present an experiment to show the effectiveness of our Developing GCN. It mainly includes the datasets we use, the task we perform, the evaluation metrics, and the results.

4.1 Data Sets

The data sets include Stochastic Block Model (SBM), Bitcoin OTC(BC-OTC), Bitcoin Alpha(BC-Alpha), UC Irvine messages(UCI), and Autonomous Systems (AS).

4.2 Task and Evaluation Metrics

Our proposed developing GCN can perform the dynamic graph link prediction. That is to predict the existence of an edge at time t according to the state of historical time. The computed probability 0 means this edge disappears and 1 stands for existing. Thus, the task can be analogous to a binary classification task and we use the cross-entropy loss function. The evaluation metrics include mean average precision (MAP) and mean reciprocal rank (MRR)

4.3 Compared Methods

We compare our model with some other methods similar to the architecture of ours, such as GCN-GRU [17], DynGEM [26], dyngraph2vec [30] with a few variants: dyngraph2vecAE, dyngraph2vecRNN, and dyngraph2vecAERNN, EvolveGCN-H and EvolveGCN-O [28]. Besides, we take the GCN into account to see how much these dynamic methods improve.

4.4   Results

From Table 1 and Table 2, our methods achieve the best performance in SBM, BC-OTC, and UCI, which outperform much better than any others, especially in BC-OTC and UCI under both MAP and MRR baselines, proving that our Encoder-Decoder architecture is quite effective for modeling time dependency. As for the BC-Alpha, dyngraph2vecAERNN performs the best in MAP, because this method differs from others in the getting of node embedding in an unsupervised manner, causing the related evaluation metrics about precision may perform better. For the AS, the EvolveGCN-H achieves the best result in both MAP and MRR. It is because that this method takes not only the previous weights, but the node embeddings into account, which makes it have better performance in the data sets with more features.

Table 1. Performance of link prediction. (MAP)

	SBM	BC-OTC	BC-Alpha	UCI	AS
GCN	0.1987	0.0003	0.0003	0.0251	0.0003
GCN-GRU	0.1898	0.0001	0.0001	0.0114	0.0713
DynGEM	0.1680	0.0134	0.0525	0.0209	0.0529
dyngraph2vecAE	0.0983	0.0090	0.0507	0.0044	0.0331
dyngraph2vecAERNN	0.1593	0.0220	**0.1100**	0.0205	0.0711
EvolveGCN-H	0.1947	0.0026	0.0049	0.0126	**0.1534**
EvolveGCN-O	0.1989	0.0028	0.0036	0.0270	0.1139
Developing GCN	**0.2057**	**0.0482**	0.0941	**0.0370**	0.0582

Table 2. Performance of link prediction.(MRR)

	SBM	BC-OTC	BC-Alpha	UCI	AS
GCN	0.0138	0.0025	0.0031	0.1141	0.0555
GCN-GRU	0.0119	0.0003	0.0004	0.0985	0.3388
DynGEM	0.0139	0.0921	0.1287	0.1055	0.1028
dyngraph2vecAE	0.0079	0.0916	0.1478	0.0540	0.0698
dyngraph2vecAERNN	0.0120	0.1268	0.1945	0.0713	0.0493
EvolveGCN-H	0.0141	0.0690	0.1104	0.0899	**0.3632**
EvolveGCN-O	0.0138	0.0968	0.1185	0.1379	0.2746
Developing GCN	**0.0147**	**0.2307**	**0.2833**	**0.2543**	0.1924

5   Conclusions

A series of models were proposed for graph learning. But we often inevitably encounter some graphs with dynamic features. To solve this problem, some methods combining GNN and RNN enter our vision. Instead of using RNN to update the node features, we just make the attention to capture the richer historical information and the GRU to decode the fused message for updating GCN weights. The experimental results show that our work is significant and performs better in most data sets.

References

1. Perozzi, B., Al-Rfou, R., Skiena, S.: DeepWalk: online learning of social representations. In Proceedings of the 20th ACM SIGKDD International Conference on Knowledge Discovery and Data Mining, pp. 701–710 (2014)
2. Tang, J., Qu, M., Wang, M., Zhang, M., Yan, J., Mei, Q.: Line: large-scale information network embedding. In: Proceedings of the 24th International Conference on World Wide Web, pp. 1067–1077 (2015)
3. Ou, M., Cui, P., Pei, J., Zhang, Z., Zhu, W.: Asymmetric transitivity preserving graph embedding. In: Proceedings of the 22nd ACM SIGKDD International Conference on Knowledge Discovery and Data Mining, pp. 1105–1114 (2016)
4. Cao, S., Lu, W., Xu, Q.: GraRep: learning graph representations with global structural information. In: Proceedings of the 24th ACM International on Conference on Information and Knowledge Management, pp. 891–900 (2015)
5. Grover, A., Leskovec, J.: node2vec: scalable feature learning for networks. In: Proceedings of the 22nd ACM SIGKDD International Conference on Knowledge Discovery and Data Mining, pp. 855–864 (2016)
6. Bruna, J., Zaremba, W., Szlam, A., LeCun, Y.: Spectral networks and locally connected networks on graphs. arXiv preprint arXiv:1312.6203 (2013)
7. Duvenaud, D., et al.: Convolutional networks on graphs for learning molecular fingerprints. arXiv preprint arXiv:1509.09292 (2015)
8. Defferrard, M., Bresson, X., Vandergheynst, P.: Convolutional neural networks on graphs with fast localized spectral filtering. In: Advances in Neural Information Processing Systems, vol. 29, pp. 3844–3852 (2016)
9. Li, Y., Tarlow, D., Brockschmidt, M., Zemel, R.: Gated graph sequence neural networks. arXiv preprint arXiv:1511.05493 (2015)
10. Gilmer, J., Schoenholz, S.S., Riley, P.F., Vinyals, O., Dahl, G.E.: Neural message passing for quantum chemistry. In: International Conference on Machine Learning, pp. 1263–1272. PMLR (2017)
11. Kipf, T.N., Welling, M.: Semi-supervised classification with graph convolutional networks. arXiv preprint arXiv:1609.02907 (2016)
12. Hamilton, W.L., Ying, R., Leskovec, J.: Inductive representation learning on large graphs. In: Proceedings of the 31st International Conference on Neural Information Processing Systems, pp. 1025–1035 (2017)
13. Jin, W., Coley, C.W., Barzilay, R., Jaakkola, T.: Predicting organic reaction outcomes with Weisfeiler-Lehman network. arXiv preprint arXiv:1709.04555 (2017)
14. Chen, J., Ma, T., Xiao, C.: FastGCN: fast learning with graph convolutional networks via importance sampling. arXiv preprint arXiv:1801.10247 (2018)

15. Veličković, P., Cucurull, G., Casanova, A., Romero, A., Lio, P., Bengio, Y.: Graph attention networks. arXiv preprint arXiv:1710.10903 (2017)
16. Gao, H., Ji, S.: Graph U-Nets. In: International Conference on Machine Learning, pp. 2083–2092. PMLR (2019)
17. Seo, Y., Defferrard, M., Vandergheynst, P., Bresson, X.: Structured sequence modeling with graph convolutional recurrent networks. In: Cheng, L., Leung, A.C.S., Ozawa, S. (eds.) ICONIP 2018. LNCS, vol. 11301, pp. 362–373. Springer, Cham (2018). https://doi.org/10.1007/978-3-030-04167-0_33
18. Manessi, F., Rozza, A., Manzo, M.: Dynamic graph convolutional networks. Pattern Recogn. **97**, 107000 (2020)
19. Narayan, A., HO'N Roe, P.: Learning graph dynamics using deep neural networks. IFAC-PapersOnLine **51**(2), 433–438 (2018)
20. Roweis, S.T., Saul, L.K.: Nonlinear dimensionality reduction by locally linear embedding. Science **290**(5500), 2323–2326 (2000)
21. Belkin, M., Niyogi, P.: Laplacian eigenmaps and spectral techniques for embedding and clustering. In: NIPS, vol. 14, pp. 585–591 (2001)
22. Li, J., Dani, H., Hu, X., Tang, J., Chang, Y., Liu, H.: Attributed network embedding for learning in a dynamic environment. In: Proceedings of the 2017 ACM on Conference on Information and Knowledge Management, pp. 387–396 (2017)
23. Nguyen, G.H., Lee, J.B., Rossi, R.A., Ahmed, N.K., Koh, E., Kim, S.: Continuous-time dynamic network embeddings. In: Companion Proceedings of the The Web Conference 2018, pp. 969–976 (2018)
24. Yu, W., Cheng, W., Aggarwal, C.C., Zhang, K., Chen, H., Wang, W.: Netwalk: a flexible deep embedding approach for anomaly detection in dynamic networks. In: Proceedings of the 24th ACM SIGKDD International Conference on Knowledge Discovery & Data Mining, pp. 2672–2681 (2018)
25. Skardinga, J., Gabrys, B., Musial, K.: Foundations and modelling of dynamic networks using dynamic graph neural networks: a survey (2021)
26. Goyal, P., Kamra, N., He, X., Liu, Y.: DynGEM: deep embedding method for dynamic graphs. arXiv preprint arXiv:1805.11273 (2018)
27. Yu, B., Yin, H., Zhu, Z.: Spatio-temporal graph convolutional networks: a deep learning framework for traffic forecasting. arXiv preprint arXiv:1709.04875 (2017)
28. Pareja, A., et al.: EvolveGCN: evolving graph convolutional networks for dynamic graphs. In: Proceedings of the AAAI Conference on Artificial Intelligence, vol. 34, pp. 5363–5370 (2020)
29. Vaswani, A., et al.: Attention is all you need. In: Advances in Neural Information Processing Systems, pp. 5998–6008 (2017)
30. Goyal, P., Rokka Chhetri, S., Canedo, A.: dyngraph2vec: Capturing network dynamics using dynamic graph representation learning. Knowl. Based Syst. **187**, 104816 (2020)

Dual Feature Distributional Regularization for Defending Against Adversarial Attacks

Mingyang Li, Xiangxiang Xu, Shao-Lun Huang$^{(\boxtimes)}$, and Lin Zhang

Tsinghua-Berkeley Shenzhen Institute (TBSI), Tsinghua University, Shenzhen, China
lmy17@mails.tsinghua.edu.cn, shaolun.huang@sz.tsinghua.edu.cn,
linzhang@tsinghua.edu.cn

Abstract. In recent years, the security of widely used deep learning models has been threatened by adversarial attacks. In this paper, we aim to incorporate a newly proposed metric H-score with the adversarial training framework to further improve model robustness on classification tasks. Specifically, we propose a novel defense method called Dual Feature Distributional Regularization (DFDR) to give dual-level regularization on feature distribution of both normal and adversarial examples, achieving maximal inter-class and minimal intra-class feature distance in a normalized feature space. The experimental results show that our DFDR can not only outperform many other defense methods against adversarial attacks but also improve the adversarial detection results effectively.

Keywords: Adversarial defense · Model robustness · Deep learning

1 Introduction

With the fast development of deep learning in past decades, deep neural network (DNN) models have achieved unprecedented performance in many machine learning tasks. However, it has been shown that DNN models are vulnerable to adversarial examples [11], which are maliciously crafted by adversarial attack methods to cause DNN models to make mistakes. Such a phenomenon hinders the future development of deep learning in the real world, especially in the areas closely related to security and privacy. So that defending against and detecting such adversarial examples are of great significance for the applications of deep learning.

In recent years, numerous methods are proposed to defend against adversarial attacks from various aspects. However, many of them can be broken when they are known to the attacker [4], and some of them may cause obfuscated gradients [1], which gives a false sense of security. Among all the defense methods, adversarial training based defense methods are proved to be effective, which do not suffer from the above problems. Some representative methods include adversarial training with projected gradient descent (Madry) [7] and TRADES [12]. Although these methods can achieve good defense results, there is still space for further improvement, since they neglect the robustness on the feature distribution level.

In this paper, we aim to incorporate H-score [5], a recently proposed information-theoretical metric, for achieving the robustness on the feature distributional level in the adversarial training framework to further improve model robustness. We propose to

T. Mantoro et al. (Eds.): ICONIP 2021, CCIS 1517, pp. 377–386, 2021.
https://doi.org/10.1007/978-3-030-92310-5_44

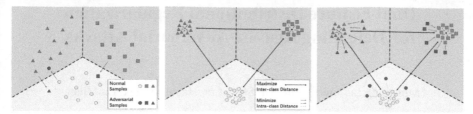

(a) Common feature distribu-(b) Feature distribution regular-(c) Dual feature distributional
tion   ized with H-score   regularization

Fig. 1. In (a), some of the features trained with cross-entropy loss may lie close to the decision boundary (dashed lines) and can be easily attacked (marked as red). In (b), the feature distribution regularized with H-score achieves larger inter-class and smaller intra-class feature distance, making adversarial attack difficult. In (c), our proposed method DFDR generates adversarial samples and adds regularization on both normal and adversarial samples during training. (Color figure online)

optimize H-score as a novel regularizer on the feature distribution to achieve the minimal intra-class and maximal inter-class feature distance in a normalized feature space. To further improve model robustness, we propose a novel training method called **Dual Feature Distributional Regularization (DFDR)**, in which a dual-level regularization is applied to the feature distributions of both normal and adversarial examples. In extensive experiments, the result shows our method not only achieves higher classification accuracy than other defense methods against adversarial attacks, but also benefits adversarial detection tasks, which verifies the efficacy of our proposed method (Fig. 1).

2 Methodology

2.1 Learning Distributional Robust Features Using H-Score

H-score metric is originally proposed in [5] for measuring feature distribution quality from an information-theoretical perspective. According to [8], a feature distribution with higher inter-class separation and intra-class compactness is more robust since each feature lies far from the decision boundary. Here we extend the meaning of H-score from the aspect of feature distance and show that it can evaluate feature distributional robustness.

Theorem 1. *For each feature distribution $f(X)$, the following three formulations are equivalent:*

1. **Original H-score formulation**

$$H(f(X)) = \mathbb{E}_{P_Y}[\|\mathbb{E}_{P_{X|Y}}[\widehat{f}(X)|Y]\|_2^2] \tag{1}$$

2. **Inter-class distance formulation**

$$H(f(X)) = \frac{1}{2}\mathbb{E}_{P_{YY'}}[\|\mathbb{E}_{P_{X|Y}}[\widehat{f}(X)|Y] - \mathbb{E}_{P_{X|Y'}}[\widehat{f}(X)|Y']\|_2^2]$$
$$= \frac{1}{2}\mathbb{E}_{P_{YY'}}[d_{i,j}^{inter}] \tag{2}$$

3. Intra-class distance formulation

$$H(f(X)) = \text{Const} - \mathbb{E}_{P_Y}[\mathbb{E}_{P_{X|Y}}[\|\widehat{f}(X) - \mathbb{E}_{P_{X|Y}}[\widehat{f}(X)|Y]\|_2^2]]$$

$$= \text{Const} - \mathbb{E}_{P_Y}[d_i^{intra}] \tag{3}$$

where $\widehat{f}(X)$ is normalized $f(X)$ with $\mathbb{E}[\widehat{f}(X)] = 0$ and $\text{cov}(\widehat{f}(X)) = \mathbf{I}$, Y and Y' are i.i.d. label variables, inter-class distance $d_{i,j}^{inter} = \|\mathbb{E}_{X|Y}[\widehat{f}(X)|Y = i] - \mathbb{E}_{X|Y'}[\widehat{f}(X)|Y' = j]\|_2^2$ is defined as the ℓ_2 distance between the feature centroid of class i and j, and intra-class distance $d_i^{intra} = \mathbb{E}_{X|Y}[\|\widehat{f}(X) - \mathbb{E}_{X|Y}[\widehat{f}(X)|Y = i]\|_2^2|Y = i]$ is defined as the mean ℓ_2 distance between each feature of class i to their centroid.

In the inter-class distance formulation, the H-score metric can be interpreted as the mean distance between feature centroids by randomly picking two classes. As for the intra-class distance formulation, it is a constant value minus the mean distance of each feature to the feature centroid of its corresponding class. The higher the H-score metric value, the larger inter-class and the lower the intra-class distance. So that the H-score can be used for evaluating feature distribution robustness in a normalized feature space.

However, the H-score metric is hard to be optimized directly since the inverse of the covariance matrix may cause training unstable. So that we propose to use the dual-sided H-score [5] as a loss term for regularizing feature distribution, which is proved to be a lower bound of the above H-score metric. The definition of the H-score loss is as follows:

$$\mathcal{L}_H(X, Y) = -\frac{1}{m}\sum_{i=1}^{m}\widetilde{f}(x_i)^{\mathrm{T}}\widetilde{g}(y_i) + \frac{1}{2}\text{tr}(\text{cov}(\widetilde{\mathbf{f}})\,\text{cov}(\widetilde{\mathbf{g}})) \tag{4}$$

where m is batch size, $\widetilde{f}(x)$ and $\widetilde{g}(y)$ are the normalized features of data and labels with zero-mean, $\text{cov}(\cdot)$ represents the covariance matrix.

The calculation of this H-score loss does not involve matrix inversion and can be trained with common stochastic gradient descent methods. We embeds one-hot label variable as $g(Y)$ in the same feature space to interact with $f(X)$ for calculating H-score loss. In this way, we can maximize H-score metric by efficiently optimizing with this achievable lower bound instead. By optimizing with such loss function, the maximum inter-class distance and the minimum intra-class distance can be achieved simultaneously.

2.2 Dual Feature Distributional Regularization

To incorporate with adversarial training framework, we propose a novel training method called **Dual Feature Distributional Regularization (DFDR)**. Our method gives dual regularization on the feature distribution of both normal samples and adversarial examples to further improve the model robustness. Now we introduce our method in detail.

At first, we use standard cross-entropy loss for normal samples to assure a high normal classification accuracy. Then, we add regularization on the feature distribution of normal samples to increase its inter-class separation and intra-class compression. In this way, the features of normal samples have a larger margin to the decision boundary, which means each normal data becomes harder to be perturbed by the adversarial attack.

For generating adversarial examples, we consider perturbation on both model prediction and feature distribution. For model prediction level, we adopt KL divergence between the predictions of normal and adversarial examples as regularization term from [12]. It has been shown to be effective for achieving high classification accuracy under attacks. Then, we further improve the model robustness by involving perturbation on the feature distribution level during adversarial training process. We combine H-score loss on feature distribution level and KL divergence on prediction level altogether as $\mathcal{L}_{KL}(x + \delta, x) + \lambda \cdot \mathcal{L}_H(x + \delta, y)$ for generating adversarial examples in adversarial training, where λ is the hyper-parameter for balancing two loss terms. In this way, the generated adversarial examples not only threat model prediction but also feature distribution, which are more detrimental to the model. After getting adversarial examples, we minimize the same formulation to update model parameters. The robustness of the model can be further improved since the model is trained to not only give correct predictions for adversarial examples but also regularize the features to the centroid of the correct class, diminishing their harmfulness.

Final Formulation. The formulation of the total training loss function is as follows:

$$\min_{\theta} \frac{1}{N} \sum_{(x,y) \in D} \mathcal{L}_{CE}(x,y) + \alpha \cdot \mathcal{L}_H(x,y) + \max_{\delta \in [-\epsilon, \epsilon]^N} [\beta \cdot \mathcal{L}_{KL}(x + \delta, x) + \gamma \cdot \mathcal{L}_H(x + \delta, y)] \quad (5)$$

where $\mathcal{L}_{CE}$ is the cross-entropy loss, $\mathcal{L}_H$ is the H-score loss, and $\mathcal{L}_{KL}$ is the KL divergence. Such loss function combines model prediction and feature distributional regularization of both normal and adversarial examples. Except for the standard cross-entropy loss, the other three terms can be all viewed as regularizers. We use α, β, γ as hyper-parameters to control the influence of each term in the loss function. We implement feature extraction function $f(\cdot)$ using deep neural network with parameter θ. For label embedding function $g(\cdot)$ used in H-score loss, we find using a linear layer with parameter θ_g is enough since labels are simple one-hot categorical variables.

3 Experiments

3.1 Defense Against Adversarial Attack

Setup. In experiments, we choose MNIST, Fashion-MNIST (F-MNIST), CIFAR-10, CIFAR-100 and Tiny-ImageNet datasets for classification tasks. For MNIST and F-MNIST, We use a small CNN model with 4 convolutional layers and 3 linear layers. For CIFAR-10, CIFAR-100 and Tiny-ImageNet, we use ResNet-18 as base model. We use stochastic gradient descent (SGD) optimizer for each dataset. For our and other methods, we set the maximum ℓ_∞ perturbation value ϵ used in adversarial training to 0.3 (for MNIST and F-MNIST) and 0.031 (8/255, for other datasets). The hyper-parameters α, β and γ in our method are set to 0.2, 1, 0.2 by grid search.

Comparison with Other Defense Methods. We evaluate model robustness under several mainstream white-box adversarial attack methods including FGSM, MIM, PGD, DeepFool, C&W, and Autoattack (AA). We set maximum perturbation value ϵ the same with the value used in adversarial training. For DeepFool and C&W attack which do not involve perturbation constraint, we just clip their adversarial perturbation to satisfy the constraint. Due to the high computation cost of the C&W and AA method, we only evaluate the same randomly selected 1000 images for each model on CIFAR-10, CIFAR-100 and Tiny-ImageNet.

We compare our method with several adversarial training defense methods: FGSM adversarial training (AdvTrain) [3], PGD adversarial training (Madry) [7], TRADES [12] and PCL [9]. We also select some other regularization-based methods, such as Stability Training (StbTrain) [13] and Input Gradient Regularization (IGR) [10], and use a model trained with cross-entropy loss only (No Defense) as baseline. We use the same model architecture and training process for each method. For TRADES, we set the hyper-parameter $1/\lambda$ as 1. For PCL, we pre-train the model as in [9] and only adds regularization on the final feature layer as ours.

The classification results are demonstrated in Table 1. Each row represents a adversarial attack used for evaluating model robustness and each column represents a defense method. The column on the leftmost shows the dataset and L_∞ perturbation size ϵ used in the experiments. As can be seen from the table, our method (the rightmost column in the table) outperforms other defense methods under most attacks in each dataset. On MNIST and F-MNIST, our method achieves the best performance almost under each attack. On CIFAR-10, our method achieves higher classification accuracy under most attacks but lower than AdvTrain under FGSM attack, whose robustness is not convincing due to overfitting on FGSM attack only during training. On CIFAR-100, the improvement of our method under attacks is more obvious and consistent. In addition, our method achieves highest normal classification accuracy 64.32 on CIFAR-100. It shows that our dual regularization scheme can also benefit the classification of normal samples on relatively complex datasets. On Tiny-ImageNet, all the methods show relatively low classification accuracy under each attack, while our method still outperforms other comparing methods on most mainstream attacks. These experiments result proves the superiority of our proposed feature distributional regularizer using H-score and dual regularization scheme.

Table 1. The classification accuracy under different white-box adversarial attacks of different defense methods. Each column (from the third to the last) represents a different defense method. The highest accuracy result under each attack (in each row) is shown with **bold** text. Our method (rightmost column) performs better under most attacks on each dataset.

Dataset	Attack	No defense	StbTrain	AdvTrain	IGR	PCL	Madry	TRADES	Ours
MNIST ($\epsilon = 0.3$)	No Attack	99.43	99.50	99.47	99.54	99.24	99.22	99.30	99.28
	FGSM	49.57	57.07	74.67	26.7	**97.75**	97.17	96.59	97.51
	MIM	20.08	26.11	37.79	2.23	96.20	95.69	95.55	**96.43**
	DeepFool	36.04	33.98	53.42	40.33	96.39	95.90	96.19	**96.78**
	C&W	79.59	86.52	93.36	93.85	96.88	97.85	97.95	**98.05**
	PGD	5.03	8.57	14.02	0.17	96.49	96.23	96.1	**96.74**
	AA	0	0	0	0	90.93	92.69	92.53	**93.72**
FMNIST ($\epsilon = 0.3$)	No Attack	99.10	99.12	99.26	99.15	99.05	98.88	99.01	98.98
	FGSM	48.17	55.47	74.60	29.42	95.68	95.45	96.35	**96.36**
	MIM	18.71	23.75	39.02	1.97	94.04	93.86	94.47	**94.95**
	DeepFool	35.30	36.40	54.00	40.90	94.30	94.00	95.60	**95.80**
	C&W	75.60	83.60	93.40	90.40	96.60	96.30	96.90	**97.40**
	PGD	4.90	6.45	13.50	0.15	94.64	94.49	95.30	**95.47**
	AA	0	0	0	0	89.59	89.69	90.68	**91.54**
CIFAR-10 ($\epsilon = 0.03$)	No Attack	94.53	92.04	92.86	86.64	81.56	85.26	87.57	86.73
	FGSM	20.56	26.02	**64.14**	23.24	50.08	56.80	54.85	56.97
	MIM	0	16.54	0.25	34.88	46.58	53.53	51.53	**53.80**
	DeepFool	0.59	18.95	0.98	15.23	47.44	50.00	49.61	**53.20**
	C&W	4.20	73.80	15.10	64.90	75.20	80.40	80.90	**82.60**
	PGD	0	8.35	0.03	9.87	41.79	48.87	46.24	**49.63**
	AA	0	3.90	0	8.40	40.80	45.30	44.80	**45.80**
CIFAR-100 ($\epsilon = 0.03$)	No Attack	62.32	59.83	55.87	47.27	48.01	57.76	59.98	64.32
	FGSM	6.94	8.41	24.85	3.91	21.62	27.09	26.83	**29.66**
	MIM	1.43	5.75	1.99	2.12	20.03	25.20	24.92	**26.97**
	DeepFool	2.48	5.68	2.61	3.69	18.34	23.83	23.54	**25.34**
	C&W	1.80	31.80	6.40	21.40	39.40	48.00	47.50	**57.10**
	PGD	0.54	3.52	1.21	1.14	18.18	22.73	21.98	**23.48**
	AA	0	0.9	0	0.5	14.10	19.80	19.40	**21.00**
Tiny-ImageNet ($\epsilon = 0.03$)	No Attack	51.64	52.96	43.35	50.75	35.91	39.60	42.10	44.61
	FGSM	5.04	7.12	10.53	1.56	11.63	11.45	10.28	**12.82**
	MIM	0.62	2.59	9.27	0.93	10.26	10.47	9.08	**11.10**
	DeepFool	1.22	1.63	8.59	1.69	8.61	9.28	8.34	**9.48**
	C&W	0.30	15.50	32.20	19.80	29.30	33.30	32.40	**34.90**
	PGD	0.14	0.82	7.45	0.40	8.62	**8.86**	7.28	8.86
	AA	0	0	5.90	0.20	7.10	**7.40**	5.90	6.40

3.2   Feature Distribution Analysis

Feature Visualization. We give a visualization comparison between feature distribution under models trained with TRADES and our DFDR respectively. We use t-SNE to map high dimension features into the 2-D plane in Fig. 2. It is obvious that the features with the same label (shown with same color in the figure) trained with DFDR are

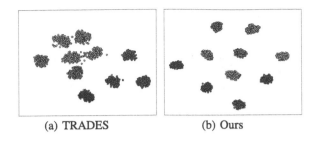

| | (a) TRADES | (b) Ours |

Fig. 2. The t-SNE visualization of feature distribution on CIFAR-10 trained with TRADES (left) and our method DFDR (right).

Table 2. The normalized feature distance comparison. For inter-class distance (Inter) and inter-/intra- distance ratio (Ratio), the larger value is better. For intra-class distance (Intra), the smaller value is better. Our method achieves larger inter-class and smaller intra-class distance compared with other methods.

Methods	MNIST			FMNIST			CIFAR-10			CIFAR-100		
	Inter	Intra	Ratio	Inter	Intra	Ratio	Inter	Intra	Ratio	Inter	Intra	Ratio
Madry	21.32	14.73	1.45	20.99	15.34	1.37	20.21	13.37	1.51	16.29	17.23	0.94
TRADES	22.07	14.23	1.55	21.94	14.36	1.53	21.64	12.66	1.71	17.01	17.05	1.00
Ours	**24.67**	**11.91**	**2.07**	**23.93**	**12.66**	**1.89**	**27.87**	**9.41**	**2.96**	**25.85**	**9.66**	**2.68**

gathered more close into clusters and these clusters are more scattered in feature space with a clear margin, which represents the smaller intra-class distance and larger inter-class distance. On the contrary, the features trained with TRADES can also be gathered into clusters but some of them lie very close to each other, which means some features are more likely to be perturbed to cross decision boundary. Such difference visually shows stronger robustness achieved by our method on feature space.

Numerical Feature Distance. We further calculate numerical results of inter-class and intra-class feature distance and their ratio. We compare our method with Madry and TRADES. We use the definition of inter-class and intra-class distance in (2) and (3). The features of test data are taken out from each model and then we normalize them to zero-mean and unit-variance on each dimension for a fair comparison. As shown in Table 2, the model trained with our method has larger inter-class and smaller intra-class feature distance and larger ratio value compared with the other two methods on each dataset. Such a result is consistent with the t-SNE visualization with larger margin between different clusters. For our method, the features with different labels are more distant from each other in feature space so that the robustness can be improved. These results verify the effectiveness of the regularization on feature distribution of our method.

3.3   Further Detection of Adversarial Examples

In recent years, many adversarial detection methods are proposed to detect adversarial examples. These methods are usually based on the assumption that features of normal

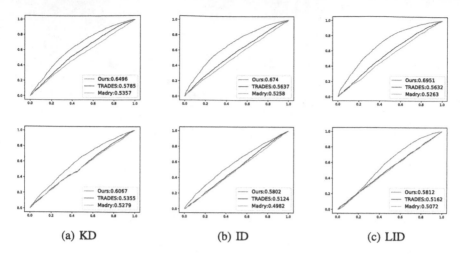

Fig. 3. The ROC curves (higher is better) of detection results on the feature distributions of Madry (green), TRADES (blue) and ours (red). The AUC values (larger value is better) are listed in the figure legend. Each row represents a different dataset: CIFAR-10 (top row) and CIFAR-100 (bottom row). Each column represents a different detection method: KD (left column), ID (middle column) and LID (right column). Our method (red) achieves a higher ROC curve and larger AUC value, which shows the feature distributions regularized by H-score can benefit many different adversarial detection methods. (Color figure online)

and adversarial examples lie in different manifolds and they use some statistical characteristics for detection. Since our method regularizes feature distribution for higher inter-class separation and inter-class compression, the manifold of normal samples in feature space could be easier to fit so that the detection result can be improved. To verify our intuition, we take out the features of adversarial examples that can successfully mistake defense models and their corresponding normal samples to train the following detectors. We choose Kernel Density Estimation (KDE) [2], I-defender (ID) [14] and Local Intrinsic Dimensionality (LID) [6], which are effective adversarial detection methods proposed in recent years. We do experiments on CIFAR-10 and CIFAR-100 datasets because there are still many adversarial examples that can successfully break the defense models for training detectors. The ROC curves and AUC values of the detection results are shown in Fig. 3 (higher is better). Each row represents a different dataset: CIFAR-10 (top row) and CIFAR-100 (bottom row). Each column represents a different detection method: KD (left column), ID (middle column) and LID (right column). For each detection method on each dataset, the ROC curve on our model (red in the figure) are always above those of the compared methods and the AUC values on our model are the highest. It shows that our dual feature distributional regularization scheme can not only improve model robustness but also enlarge the difference between feature manifolds of normal and adversarial examples for improving further adversarial detection performance.

4 Conclusions

In this paper, we address the security problem of deep learning models against adversarial attacks and propose a novel defense method called DFDR to improve model robustness by incorporating the regularization on the feature distribution in the adversarial training framework. Our method is based on the H-score metric and aims to achieve a feature distribution with high intra-class compactness and inter-class separability. We propose a dual regularization scheme to give dual-level feature distributional regularization on both normal and adversarial examples. Extensive experiments show that our method outperforms many other adversarial defense methods for defending against adversarial attacks and it can also benefit the adversarial detection tasks. Our method indicates the importance of the robustness on feature distribution and can effectively improve the robustness of the deep learning model to a higher level.

Acknowledgement. The research of Shao-Lun Huang was supported in part by the Natural Science Foundation of China under Grant 61807021, in part by the Shenzhen Science and Technology Program under Grant KQTD20170810150821146, and in part by the Innovation and Entrepreneurship Project for Overseas High-Level Talents of Shenzhen under Grant KQJSCX20180327144037831.

References

1. Athalye, A., Carlini, N., Wagner, D.: Obfuscated gradients give a false sense of security: circumventing defenses to adversarial examples. arXiv preprint arXiv:1802.00420 (2018)
2. Feinman, R., Curtin, R.R., Shintre, S., Gardner, A.B.: Detecting adversarial samples from artifacts. arXiv preprint arXiv:1703.00410 (2017)
3. Goodfellow, I.J., Shlens, J., Szegedy, C.: Explaining and harnessing adversarial examples. arXiv preprint arXiv:1412.6572 (2014)
4. He, W., Wei, J., Chen, X., Carlini, N., Song, D.: Adversarial example defense: ensembles of weak defenses are not strong. In: 11th {USENIX} Workshop on Offensive Technologies ({WOOT} 17) (2017)
5. Huang, S.L., Xu, X., Zheng, L., Wornell, G.W.: An information theoretic interpretation to deep neural networks. arXiv preprint arXiv:1905.06600 (2019)
6. Ma, X., et al.: Characterizing adversarial subspaces using local intrinsic dimensionality. arXiv preprint arXiv:1801.02613 (2018)
7. Madry, A., Makelov, A., Schmidt, L., Tsipras, D., Vladu, A.: Towards deep learning models resistant to adversarial attacks. arXiv preprint arXiv:1706.06083 (2017)
8. Moosavi-Dezfooli, S.M., Fawzi, A., Frossard, P.: DeepFool: a simple and accurate method to fool deep neural networks. In: Proceedings of the IEEE Conference on Computer Vision and Pattern Recognition, pp. 2574–2582 (2016)
9. Mustafa, A., Khan, S., Hayat, M., Goecke, R., Shen, J., Shao, L.: Adversarial defense by restricting the hidden space of deep neural networks. arXiv preprint arXiv:1904.00887 (2019)
10. Ross, A.S., Doshi-Velez, F.: Improving the adversarial robustness and interpretability of deep neural networks by regularizing their input gradients. In: Thirty-second AAAI Conference on Artificial Intelligence (2018)
11. Szegedy, C., et al.: Intriguing properties of neural networks. arXiv preprint arXiv:1312.6199 (2013)

12. Zhang, H., Yu, Y., Jiao, J., Xing, E.P., Ghaoui, L.E., Jordan, M.I.: Theoretically principled trade-off between robustness and accuracy. arXiv preprint arXiv:1901.08573 (2019)

13. Zheng, S., Song, Y., Leung, T., Goodfellow, I.: Improving the robustness of deep neural networks via stability training. In: Proceedings of the IEEE Conference on Computer Vision and Pattern Recognition, pp. 4480–4488 (2016)

14. Zheng, Z., Hong, P.: Robust detection of adversarial attacks by modeling the intrinsic properties of deep neural networks. In: Advances in Neural Information Processing Systems, pp. 7913–7922 (2018)

Theory and Applications of Natural Computing Paradigms

Compositional Committees of Tiny Networks

Goh Howe Seng[1], Tomas Maul[1(✉)], and Manav Nitin Kapadnis[2]

[1] University of Nottingham Malaysia, Semenyih, Malaysia
Tomas.Maul@nottingham.edu.my
[2] Indian Institute of Technology Kharagpur, Kharagpur, India

Abstract. Deep neural networks tend to be accurate but computationally expensive, whereas ensembles tend to be fast but do not capitalize on hierarchical representations. This paper proposes an approach that attempts to combine the advantages of both approaches. Hierarchical ensembles represent an effort in this direction, however they are not compositional in a representational sense, since they only combine classifier decisions and/or outputs. We propose to take this effort one step further in the form of compositional ensembles, which exploit the composition of the hidden representations of classifiers, here defined as tiny networks on account of being neural networks of significantly limited scale. As such, our particular instance of compositional ensembles is called Compositional Committee of Tiny Networks (CoCoTiNe). We experimented with different CoCoTiNe variants involving different types of composition, input usage, and ensemble decisions. The best variant demonstrated that CoCoTiNe is more accurate than standard hierarchical committees, and is relatable to the accuracy of vanilla Convolutional Neural Networks, whilst being 25.7 times faster in a standard CPU setup. In conclusion, the paper demonstrates that compositional ensembles, especially in the context of tiny networks, are a viable and efficient approach for combining the advantages of deep networks and ensembles.

Keywords: Neural networks · Ensembles · Compositionality · Hierarchical representations

1 Introduction

Deep learning or deep neural networks (DNNs) are important engines underlying current artificial intelligence applications. DNNs have many advantages, chief among them being the levels of accuracy attained, frequently surpassing human levels of performance. However, they do also have disadvantages, such as memory and computational cost, and the fact that they can be hard to design and train. On the other hand, we have ensembles, with strengths such as the fact that they can be very simple, predictable, and fast to train, especially when using small classifiers. On the downside, ensembles do not generally achieve the same levels of accuracy as DNNs.

© Springer Nature Switzerland AG 2021
T. Mantoro et al. (Eds.): ICONIP 2021, CCIS 1517, pp. 389–396, 2021.
https://doi.org/10.1007/978-3-030-92310-5_45

This paper is concerned with the question: can we combine the advantages of both DNNs and ensembles, whilst avoiding their disadvantages? So far, it seems this combination has been done primarily by inserting the key concept of ensembles (i.e. committee of classifiers) into DNNs, i.e. ensembles of DNNs [2]. In spite of improving accuracy further, this does not solve the computational cost problem of DNNs. The opposite idea, i.e. inserting the key concept of DNNs (i.e. hierarchical feature composition) into ensembles, does not seem to have been explored so far in the literature. The literature on hierarchical ensembles is very close to this concept, however, typically only decisions and/or outputs are combined in a hierarchical manner, which is not strictly feature composition [3–5, 7–10, 12–14]. Thus we propose to imbue ensembles with feature compositionality and propose to call this approach Compositional Committee of Tiny Networks (CoCoTiNe). We use the term *tiny networks* (TNs) to denote networks with a small number of narrow layers. In order to simplify the experimental design we restrict ourselves to data belonging to the image domain, although the approach can easily be extended to any type of data.

The main contribution of this research is to provide an alternative solution to DNNs by designing a compositional ensemble that exploits and combines the best attributes of both deep learning and ensemble methods. The proposed approach aims to get realistically close to the accuracy levels of deep learning networks, whilst affording better speed and consistency.

2   Related Works

This section focuses on the research works most closely related to CoCoTiNe, i.e.: hierarchical ensembles. As outlined in [12], hierarchical ensembles can be classified into the following five categories: (1) top-down ensemble methods, (2) Bayesian ensemble methods, (3) Reconciliation methods, (4) true path rule ensembles, and (5) decision tree-based ensembles. We propose that CoCoTiNe is an instantiation of an additional category within this taxonomy, i.e. compositional ensembles, which are essentially hierarchical ensembles that implement some form of feature compositionality across the ensemble's hierarchical layers.

In [9] a hierarchical ensemble of convolutional neural networks was proposed for diagnosing Diabetic Macular Edema which is an advanced state of diabetic retinopathy and can lead to permanent vision loss. This approach outperformed the existing state-of-the-art methods on publicly available Diabetic Macular Edema databases, and uses a flexible hierarchical ensemble of CNNs (large networks) rather than tiny networks proposed in this research. Moreover, the hierarchy is built from the outputs of previous layers, rather than hidden representation as proposed in this research.

Similarly, in [3] a hierarchical ensemble was proposed for the task of Indian Language identification. This approach uses 2 layers of ensembles, with the first layer consisting of two ensembles which train on different feature sets. The final classification is computed using a majority vote from the classification outputs of these ensembles. This method differs from our approach as it does not put emphasis on the use of tiny networks and has a fixed hierarchical structure of two layers, with the first layer having two separate ensembles. Moreover, the composition of this approach is also based on the outputs of the networks rather than hidden representations.

In [8] a hierarchical long short term memory (LSTM) ensemble was proposed for short-term forecasting of wind speed. Similar to [3], this approach adopts a fixed 2-layer structure, uses LSTMs as compared to tiny (feedforward) networks, and implements the hierarchy based on previous-layer outputs (rather than hidden representations), all of which are distinct from our approach.

As the examples above illustrate the single most important differentiating factor compared to our work consists of the fact that these works do not implement feature compositions. Apart from lacking feature compositions, most hierarchical ensemble studies, are also based on a fixed/rigid number of layers, and do not intentionally involve tiny networks. Other examples of such studies include [5,7,10,13,14]. However, some hierarchical approaches do allow for an unconstrained number of hierarchical layers, e.g. [4,9]. The key conclusion of this brief survey is that, so far, there do not seem to be other systematic studies of feature compositionality in hierarchical ensembles.

3   Methodology

3.1   CoCoTiNe

A CoCoTiNe consists of a multi-layer architecture with an ensemble of tiny networks (TNs) at each layer that generally receive as input the combined hidden representations of a subset of tiny networks from the previous layer. In theory, this connectivity structure should provide good compositionality properties to the model as TNs can build from hidden representations from previous Compositional Committee (CoCo) layers. The use of ensembles also means that the final classification is based on a committee decision which in turn decreases prediction variance. Furthermore, the use of TNs (i.e. fully-connected networks with 1–3 narrow hidden-layers) in each layer also encourages fast and predictable training processes, compared to large networks. Figure 1 provides a simplified representation of our general approach to compositional ensembles.

CoCoTiNe classifies images based on local receptive fields (image sub-regions) that can vary in terms of scale and position. Based on this, one of the assumptions currently adopted in this work is that target objects are reasonably centered and scaled, as in the MNIST handwritten digits dataset.

During the training of CoCoTiNe, each tiny network in the first CoCo layer takes in the pre-processed sub-region of a training image and its class label. Each CoCo layer 1 TN is assigned to one random sub-region, and this association is fixed for the lifetime of the model. The hidden representations generated in TNs in COCO layer 1 and associated target class labels (for inputted images) are then fed into TNs in CoCo layer 2 for further training. Each TN in CoCo layer 2 may take in multiple hidden representations produced by multiple tiny networks in CoCo layer 1. Connections with TNs in the previous CoCo layer are

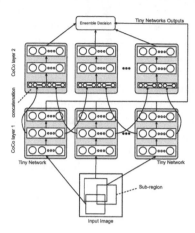

Fig. 1. Simplified diagram of a CoCoTiNe architecture

randomly determined, and are again fixed for the lifetime of the model. The tiny networks in subsequent layers are implemented in exactly the same way as CoCo layer 2. Each CoCo layer is trained independently and only after the training of its previous layer. All of our CoCoTiNe experiments were implemented using Python, Tensorflow 2.0, Keras, NumPy, SciPy, Scikit-learn and Pickle, and all experiments were run in the Google Colab environment.

4   Experimental Design

4.1   Datasets

Three datasets were used in this work, namely MNIST [1], Fashion MNIST [15], and CIFAR-10 [6]. All the target objects in all three datasets are reasonably well centered and scaled, complying with one of the key assumptions of the current CoCoTiNe implementation. Due to space constraints, and since these datasets are well-known, we refrain from describing them further here.

4.2   Experimental Variants

As the general CoCoTiNe concept allows for multiple variants, we experimented with variations along different dimensions in order to find the most effective implementation, namely: (1) the method for combining hidden representations from previous CoCo layers, (2) how/whether the input information is allowed to influence multiple layers, and (3) the method for making the committee decision. We abbreviate these dimensions to *hidden*, *input*, and *decision*, respectively. Unfortunately, due to space constraints, we can't outline all of the variations here, however we summarize our main findings in the results/discussion section.

4.3   Baseline Conditions

In this experiment, a total of seven baseline conditions (BCs) were implemented and tested along with the final implementation of CoCoTiNe. Since to the best of our knowledge there are no other comparable compositional ensemble approaches, we used standard ensemble and hierarchical ensemble techniques for comparison purposes. The baseline conditions are summarized below:

1. **(CNN)** We implemented a vanilla convolutional neural network (CNN) as a deep learning baseline.
2. **(MLP-Mixer)** We chose MLP-Mixer [11] as a recent and strong baseline representative of recent efforts to re-invent multilayer perceptron (MLP) based architectures such that they can be competitive with CNNs.
3. **(tiny-whole)** This condition implements a single TN that takes in the whole image instead of an image sub-region as input.
4. **(tiny-sub)** This condition uses a single TN that takes in a random image sub-region as input. During prediction, it takes a few random sub-regions of the same image and performs classification by taking the max of the summed logits.
5. **(flat-whole)** This condition implements a flat ensemble of TNs that take in the whole image instead of image sub-regions as input, whereby each TN is associated with a random subset of 60% of training instances, as a simple form of bagging.
6. **(flat-sub)** This condition implements a flat ensemble of TNs that take in random image sub-regions as input.
7. **(hierarchical)** This condition is similar to the final implementation of CoCo-TiNe, except that the inputs to TNs in CoCo layers 2 and above, are based only on the output logits of TNs in the previous layer (i.e. no hidden representation composition occurs).
   (a) **(hierarch-concat)** The output logits from the previous layer are combined via concatenation.
   (b) **(hierarch-sum)** The output logits from the previous layer are combined by summation.

In order to maximize comparative fairness between BCs and CoCoTiNe, the number of TNs in BCs with flat ensembles was set to 30, which is inline with the number of TNs used in the final implementation of CoCoTiNe. The number of network parameters in the CNN condition was also set to match as closely as possible that of CoCoTiNe. Finally, training was conducted for five epochs per dataset across all conditions.

5   Results and Discussion

5.1   Experimental Variants

Our experiments on how to incorporate hidden representations showed that concatenation is a better approach for combining hidden representations, compared for example to summation. Similarly, our experiments suggest that output logits seem to be best combined via concatenation. With regards to input information, our experiments show that adding additional raw input information to TNs in deeper CoCo layers provides no clear advantage to the model, even reducing its accuracy. Finally, with regards to ensemble decisions, our experiments showed that computing decision weights via the number of TNs in each CoCo layer, relative to the CoCo layer with the most TNs, and using this to weight votes, yields a better accuracy. The results of these experiments informed our final CoCoTiNe variant which was used in the comparative study below.

5.2   Baselines vs. CoCoTiNe

Table 1. Average test accuracy (across 10 trials) for all main conditions (Values in bold refer to the best conditions, and values with an asterisk refer to the second-best conditions.)

Condition	MNIST	Fashion-MNIST	CIFAR-10
CoCoTiNe	98.71 (0.04)*	86.43 (0.07)*	53.47 (0.08)*
MLP-Mixer	96.89 (0.24)	86.10 (0.57)	40.26 (1.39)
CNN	**98.82 (0.96)**	**90.33 (1.2)**	**70.86 (5.32)**
tiny-whole	97.07 (0.16)	86.29 (0.09)	42.7 (0.62)
tiny-sub	82.48 (0.85)	70.06 (0.13)	31.9 (0.98)
flat-whole	97.08 (0.02)	86.43 (0.07)	44.18 (0.46)
flat-sub	91.06 (0.05)	73.56 (0.08)	34.04 (0.51)
hierarch-concat	97.87 (0.04)	84.13 (0.07)	47.9 (0.17)
hierarch-sum	97.32 (0.19)	82.87 (0.21)	46.28 (0.16)

Table 2. Average training times (across 10 trials) in seconds (Values in brackets correspond to standard deviations.)

Condition	MNIST	Fashion-MNIST	CIFAR-10
CoCoTiNe	**180 (0.04)**	**184 (0.07)**	**182 (0.08)**
MLP-Mixer	300 (1.59)	305 (0.7)	290 (0.9)
CNN	4665 (0.96)	4838 (1.2)	4533 (5.32)

Based on the results obtained in Table 1, CoCoTiNe has a better accuracy compared across all conditions which take image sub-regions as input, either as only a single tiny network or a flat ensemble of tiny networks (*tiny-sub* and *flat-sub*). This demonstrates the effectiveness of enhancing ensembles with the architectural feature of compositionality, obtained via the hierarchical composition of hidden representations. However, the accuracy advantage of CoCoTiNe, while present, is somewhat less significant when compared to conditions which take in the whole image as input (*tiny-whole* and *flat-whole*). This suggests that future work should look into new ways of exploiting and combining local/global image information in the context of compositional ensembles.

When comparing conditions of single tiny networks vs. flat ensembles of tiny networks with their respective input types, i.e. (*tiny-whole* vs. *flat-whole*) and (*tiny-sub* vs. *flat-sub*), conditions that use an ensemble of tiny networks (*flat-whole* and *flat-sub*) significantly improve the accuracy compared to their single tiny network peers, as expected.

When comparing CoCoTiNe against non-compositional hierarchical baselines (similar to CoCoTiNe but without the compositionality of hidden representations), CoCoTiNe consistently achieves better results. This further demonstrates the importance of the use of hidden representations to achieve useful compositional properties and supports the view that compositionality of hidden representations is an important architectural feature for further research in the domain of hierarchical ensembles.

When comparing CoCoTiNe to the CNN baseline using the MNIST dataset, CoCoTiNe exhibits similar average accuracy. This proves that CoCoTiNe's first aim of obtaining comparable accuracy to DNNs is achievable. However, the accuracy gap widens when using the Fashion MNIST and CIFAR-10 datasets, which is likely to be due to the fact that these datasets are more challenging. It is likely that future extensions of CoCoTiNe, as discussed below, can bridge this gap.

The second and third aims of CoCoTiNe, which were affording significantly better speed and consistency compared to DNNs, were also achieved as CoCoTiNe showed significant training time reduction and lower standard deviations across multiple trials when compared to CNN, as depicted in Table 2, in a classic central processing unit (CPU) setup. Overall CoCoTiNe was found to be 25.7 times faster than the corresponding CNN condition. We have omitted a speed comparison in a hardware setup with graphics processing units (GPUs) since this is deemed to be an unfair comparison, given that GPUs and deep learning frameworks have to an extent co-evolved in order to optimize the training and inference time of DNNs, whereas this process has not yet occurred for compositional ensembles. The overall stability and consistency of CoCoTiNe can also be seen in the standard deviations of accuracy measures as depicted in Table 1, which are small for CoCoTiNe, especially when compared to the CNN and MLP-Mixer conditions.

6   Conclusion

The key finding of this paper is that compositional ensembles are a viable machine learning approach. A particular instance of a compositional ensemble was proposed (i.e. CoCoTiNe) and multiple variations were experimented with in order to find the best variant. The accuracy of this compositional ensemble was found to be better than standard hierarchical ensembles (that do not exploit the composition of hidden representations) and was found to be relatively close to vanilla DNNs. Moreover, the speed properties were found to be significantly better than those of DNNs in the context of standard CPU setups. Future work is recommended in terms of: (1) exploring other strategies for representational composition and architectural tuning (e.g. architecture of TNs and CoCo layers), (2) experimenting with different ways to exploit local/global image information, including learnt or adaptive approaches for patch extraction, (3) exploiting hardware parallelization, (4) exploring compositional ensembles in the context of continual learning. We hope that in the future other authors will explore the idea of compositional ensembles further, in order to maximize the variance reduction and speed advantages of ensembles, whilst capitalizing on the representational advantages of DNNs.

References

1. Deng, L.: The MNIST database of handwritten digit images for machine learning research. IEEE Signal Process. Mag. **29**(6), 141–142 (2012)
2. Ganaie, M., Hu, M., et al.: Ensemble deep learning: a review. arXiv preprint arXiv:2104.02395 (2021)
3. Jain, R., Duppada, V., Hiray, S.: Seernet@ INLI-FIRE-2017: hierarchical ensemble for Indian native language identification. In: FIRE (Working Notes), pp. 127–129 (2017)
4. Kim, B.-K., Roh, J., Dong, S.-Y., Lee, S.-Y.: Hierarchical committee of deep convolutional neural networks for robust facial expression recognition. J. Multimodal User Interfaces **10**(2), 173–189 (2016). https://doi.org/10.1007/s12193-015-0209-0
5. Kim, K., Lin, H., Choi, J.Y., Choi, K.: A design framework for hierarchical ensemble of multiple feature extractors and multiple classifiers. Pattern Recognit. **52**, 1–16 (2016)
6. Krizhevsky, A., Hinton, G., et al.: Learning multiple layers of features from tiny images (2009)
7. Liang, X., Ma, Y., Xu, M.: THU-HCSI at SemEval-2019 task 3: hierarchical ensemble classification of contextual emotion in conversation. In: Proceedings of the 13th International Workshop on Semantic Evaluation, pp. 345–349 (2019)
8. Marndi, A., Patra, G.K., Gouda, K.C.: Short-term forecasting of wind speed using time division ensemble of hierarchical deep neural networks. Bull. Atmos. Sci. Technol. **1**(1), 91–108 (2020). https://doi.org/10.1007/s42865-020-00009-2
9. Singh, R.K., Gorantla, R.: Dmenet: diabetic macular edema diagnosis using hierarchical ensemble of CNNs. Plos One **15**(2), e0220677 (2020)
10. Sudderth, E., Freeman, W.: Hierarchical ensemble of global and local classifiers for face recognition. IEEE Signal Process. Mag. **25**(2), 114–141 (2008)
11. Tolstikhin, I., et al.: MLP-Mixer: an all-MLP architecture for vision. arXiv preprint arXiv:2105.01601 (2021)
12. Valentini, G.: Hierarchical ensemble methods for protein function prediction. International Scholarly Research Notices 2014 (2014)
13. Wang, H., Li, J., He, K.: Hierarchical ensemble reduction and learning for resource-constrained computing. ACM Trans. Des. Autom. Electron. Syst. (TODAES) **25**(1), 1–21 (2019)
14. Wang, R., Li, H., Lan, R., Luo, S., Luo, X.: Hierarchical ensemble learning for Alzheimer's disease classification. In: 2018 7th International Conference on Digital Home (ICDH), pp. 224–229. IEEE (2018)
15. Xiao, H., Rasul, K., Vollgraf, R.: Fashion-MNIST: a novel image dataset for benchmarking machine learning algorithms. arXiv preprint arXiv:1708.07747 (2017)

EEG-Based Classification of Lower Limb Motor Imagery with STFT and CNN

Boyang Lu[1], Sheng Ge[1], and Haixian Wang[1,2(✉)]

[1] Key Laboratory of Child Development and Learning Science of Ministry of Education, School of Biological Science and Medical Engineering, Southeast University, Nanjing 210096, Jiangsu, People's Republic of China
hxwang@seu.edu.cn
[2] Institute of Artificial Intelligence of Hefei Comprehensive National Science Center, Hefei 230094, Anhui, People's Republic of China

Abstract. In order to classify the brain signals of lower limb motor imagery, we used the method of short-time fourier transform (STFT) to transform the signals into time spectrum, and then processed the size and gray scale of the obtained time spectrum. Thus we constructed a neural network model called pragmatic convolutional neural network (pCNN), and the processed 128 * 128 pixel grayscale time spectrums were used as the input for classification. The classification effect was good on all 10 subjects, with the highest accuracy reaching 76%, while the comparison model was only 66.88% (shallow CNN), 52% (recurrent CNN) and 68.62 (common spatial pattern + support vector machines). The research results show that STFT is very effective in transforming the EEG input of CNN, and due to the difference of the activated regions between lower limbs and upper limbs, many models with good performance for upper limbs cannot be simply copied to lower limbs.

Keywords: Short-time Fourier transform · Lower limb · Convolutional neural network

1 Introduction

Brain Computer Interface (BCI) recognizes people's intentions by collecting and extracting the electroencephalogram (EEG) signals and completes the tasks of transferring information and controlling between external devices and brain based on the EEG signals. This way can help restoring or even enhancing people's physical movement and cognitive ability [1]. In recent years, researches related to BCI have made rapid progress [2,3]. Motor imagery with BCI (MI-BCI) represents the electrical signals generated by the mental activity of a person imagining an action, e.g., raise or lower the right or left hand without doing it. Most of the studies have been focused on the upper limb [4–6]. With regard to lower limb, the results of classification based on traditional method were mostly unsatisfactory [7,8].

T. Mantoro et al. (Eds.): ICONIP 2021, CCIS 1517, pp. 397–404, 2021.
https://doi.org/10.1007/978-3-030-92310-5_46

Recently, Deep Learning (DL) techniques performed well in analyzing large-scale datasets [9]. However, DL method have not been applied to lower limb motor imagery classification. The main contribution of this study is to combine STFT and CNN in lower limb motor imagery EEG classification. Aiming at the difficulty of lower limb motor imagery EEG classification, a comparative experiment was conducted on lower limb motor imagery EEG signals by combining some upper limb classification methods. Based on the characteristics that STFT can transform signals into time-spectrum images and CNN has better effect on image classification, we achieved results in the classification of lower limb motion imagery. In order to confirm the role played by STFT in the classification, we also made a comparison with CNN method and traditional machine learning method.

2   Materials and Method

2.1   Subjects

This study contains ten individuals who are healthy and right-handed (4 males, 6 females; aged 22–27 years, mean ± SD: 24.09 ± 1.14). The study has complied with ethical standards formulated in the 1964 Declaration of Helsinki. Meanwhile, The ethics committee of Southeast University (Nanjing, China) has approved this study. All subjects agreed to participated and never suffered from neuromuscular disease. Before the experiments, the procedure has been explained in detail. Six of the subjects had previously participated in neurophysiological experiments.

2.2   Experimental Preparation

During EEG data collection, all subjects did the task of Imagery Foot movements (IF task) according to requirements. Five session make up the entire task which contains stimulation. Each session contains 15 trials of the right foot and 15 trials of the left foot in a random order. There was no feedback from the experiment. Between every session, the subject had three minutes to rest. During imagery movement, the subject only needed to image the movement ceaselessly, but not to implement any concrete operations. Figure 1 describes the experimental paradigm of one session. Those tasks were divided into left and right foot of imagery movement.

In this study, the equipment used to record the EEG is a 64-channel Synamps amplifier (NeuroScan, version 4.3). The 10-10 international electrode system was used to place the electrodes. The ground reference is the right ear mastoid. The impedances of the electrode were below 5 kΩ during the recording process. The sampling rate of the EEG data 1000 Hz. Meanwhile, a bandpass filter was used which is 0.3 to 70 Hz. We also recorded the horizontal electro-oculogram signals and vertical electro-oculogram signals.

The independent component analysis (ICA) was used to reject the ocular artifacts with EEGLAB 14.0 [10]. Meanwhile, we found a strong correlation between action evoked potentials and mastoid reference. Therefore, we used bilateral

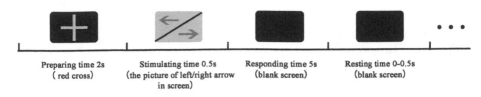

Preparing time 2s   Stimulating time 0.5s   Responding time 5s   Resting time 0-0.5s
(red cross)   (the picture of left/right arrow   (blank screen)   (blank screen)
in screen)

Fig. 1. The time sequence of one session in the experiment. In the stimuli, a red symbol '+' is first presented on the screen with 2 s. Then, a picture of left/right arrow is shown for 0.5 s. The subject has to imagine the movement of the left and right foot according to the direction of the arrow. During this time, the screen remains blank for 5 s. Finally, the subject is given a short rest for 0–0.5 s. (Color figure online)

mastoid reference (M1, M2) instead of unilateral mastoid reference (M1). The processing EEG recording were filtered 1 Hz to 30 Hz with the Basic FIR filter in the EEGLAB.

The original EEG recordings were divided according to the period from 1 s before stimulation to 1 s after stimulation, using the cue to determine stimulus onset. All trials with a maximum mean absolute value greater than $+75\,\mu V$ in the data were rejected. In this way, the ten participants produced a total of two artificial data sets (left foot and right foot). Every set had 750 trials for further study.

2.3 Model Structure

In neural network model, we referred to the pCNN [11], which contains three convolution blocks. Each block contains one convolutional layer, one batch normalization layer and one max-pooling layer. The activation function is the rectified linear unit (ReLU). The batch normalization layer can ensure the robustness of the model. The downsampling factor of max-pooling layer is 2 between each layer. The final probability of each class is computed by a fully connected layer with a softmax activation. To prevent overfitting, we added a dropout layer after the full connection layer, which temporarily dropped neurons from the network according to a certain probability. Weights are learned by the Adam optimizer. The network architecture is shown in Fig. 2.

For the input of neural network, the EEG data have a time series structure, STFT can be used to transform it into time spectrum. STFT, also known as window Fourier Transform, is an effective time-frequency analysis method. It is applied to the signal in the window to obtain the time-varying spectrum of the signal. The time-varying spectrum of the whole signal can be obtained by continually sliding the time window and Fourier transform to the end of the signal. The calculation formula as follows:

$$STFT_x(t, f) = \sum_{n=0}^{L-1} x(n)\, m(n-t)\, e^{-j2\pi f n} \tag{1}$$

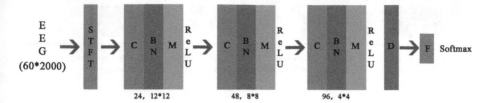

Fig. 2. The architecture of the pragmatic conventional neural network (pCNN) model, where C is the 2D convolution layer, BN is the batch Normalization layer, M is the 2D max pooling layer, D is the dropout layer, and F is the flatten layer. The number at the bottom represents the number and size of the convolution kernel.

where $x(n)$ denotes the original signal at time n, $m(n)$ denotes the sliding window function of the original signal at time n, and L denotes the length of the window function.

However, there will be more interference information when the original time-spectrum image is directly used as input. After some experiments, we set the original time-spectrum image as 128 * 128 pixels and extracted the grayscale image features as the input of the neural network. In this way, not only network parameters were greatly reduced, resource consumption was reduced and computing efficiency was improved, but also classification accuracy was increased.

3   Results

3.1   Models Parameter and STFT Image

The EEG recordings of 10 subjects (S1–S10) were used in this study, and 150 data were collected for each subject. Parameter setting has a great influence on the effect of CNN model. Two subjects S1 and S2 were selected to adjust the parameters of the model. The pCNN model was used to train the two subjects with 150 epochs. During training, the value of the dropout layer was set to 0.5 and the weight was updated in real time. Combined with the experience of upper limb experiment, the batch size was 8. We got the minimum validation loss around 35 epoch through experiments.

Then we performed the STFT on the original EEG signal to obtain the time spectrum characteristics. The characteristic of the time spectrum image obtained was converted into a 128 * 128 pixel grayscale time spectrum image. Figure 3 shows the time-domain image of the original size of the left and right foot EEG signal and the time spectrum image after short-time Fourier transform. Figure 4 shows the 128 * 128 pixel time-spectrum image and grayscale time spectrum image of the left and right foot EEG signal. The 128 * 128 pixel grayscale time spectrum would be used as the input of the pCNN model. In order to avoid possible errors, we performed 100 times of 5-fold cross-validation and calculated the average of all experiments as the final result.

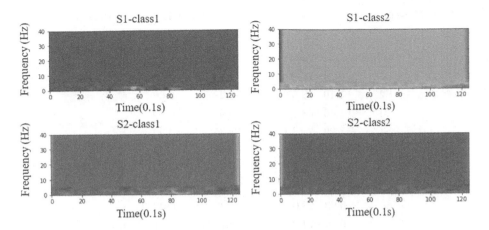

Fig. 3. Example of the generated spectrum image from S1 and S2 during left (class1) and right (class2) foot movements imagery.

Fig. 4. A: The left and right figure represent the S1 left (class1) foot movements imagery 128 * 128 pixel 60 channel time spectrum and gray-scale time spectrum, respectively; B: the left and right figure represent the S1 right (class2) foot movements imagery 128 * 128 pixel 60 channel time spectrum and gray-scale time spectrum, respectively.

3.2   Classification Results

In this part, we used pCNN to classify the EEG recording of the lower limb motor imagery. Table 1 displays the average loss, average classification accuracy and standard deviation of S1–S10. The lowest accuracy rate is over 68%, and the highest accuracy rate is over 75% from the table. For loss, the minimum loss is not more than 0.65, and the maximum loss is not more than 1.52. In terms of standard deviation, the standard deviation of classification accuracy is not more than 0.12, but the maximum standard deviation of loss is more than 0.95.

Table 1. Classification results of the experiment. The S.D. denotes the standard deviation.

subject	Loss	Accuracy(%)	Loss S.D.	Accuracy S.D.
S1	0.86	76.00	0.42	0.08
S2	1.19	72.67	0.28	0.06
S3	1.46	68.00	0.95	0.09
S4	1.09	71.33	0.35	0.09
S5	0.63	74.00	0.08	0.06
S6	0.70	69.33	0.12	0.11
S7	1.30	72.67	0.20	0.08
S8	0.93	68.00	0.38	0.03
S9	0.73	74.00	0.17	0.11
S10	1.21	75.33	0.56	0.13
Mean	1.01	72.13	0.35	0.08

In order to further verify the classification performance of the proposed method in lower limbs, we referred to the sCNN method and the RCNN method [12,13], which performed well in upper limb classification. We inputted the same data set into these two models. The method of data input was the original method without STFT. At the same time, we also used the traditional machine learning method (CSP+SVM) [14] to classify the dataset. The kernel type of SVM is redial basis kernel and we achieved the λ and the C is 2^{-3} by grid search method. The comparison results of these four methods are shown in Fig. 5. The achieved mean accuracy with the sCNN model is 66.88 % ($\pm6.23\%$) and the mean accuracy with RCNN is 52.00% ($\pm10.24\%$). The performance of these two models is barely lower than pCNN. Finally, a mean accuracy of 68.62% ($\pm5.98\%$) is obtained with the traditional machine learning method (CSP+SVM).

4   Discussion

We can draw some conclusions from the results and do some thinking with them. Then, we will elaborate on this part of the relevant content.

As can be seen from STFT figure, there is a significant difference in the time spectrum of the left and right lower limb motor imagery. Such differences can be distinguished by proper model learning. When the spectrum graph is converted to size and gray scale, some differences will become more obvious. Changing the size of the image can highlight features and remove unwanted parts. Grayscale images can remove some of the noise and enhance the useful parts. It will be easier for the convolutional neural network to learn, thus improving the classification accuracy.

The classification results of pCNN displays that S1 has the highest accuracy of 76%, while S3 and S8 have the lowest accuracy of 68%, indicating that pCNN model can achieve effective classification results on the motor imagery of lower limbs, and it may have a better effect for certain subjects. It is worth noting that the average standard deviation of accuracy is only 8%. It indicates that the model can show good results for different subjects, which also indicates that the pCNN model has good robustness and will not be affected by different noises from different subjects. The comparison results display that sCNN and RCNN models with better performance in upper limbs can't achieve a high accuracy in lower limbs, even lower than the classification accuracy of traditional machine learning methods (CSP+SVM). This situation can explain that there is a big difference between upper limb motor imagery classification and lower limb motor imagery classification. It maybe because the activated regions of right and left lower limb motor imagery is closer than that of upper limb, so more time domain information need to be extracted to assist classification. The common CNN method mainly convolves with spatial information, which may lose part of the time domain information, thus leading to a low classification accuracy. After STFT is added into pCNN model, time-domain information is well integrated, so better results can be obtained.

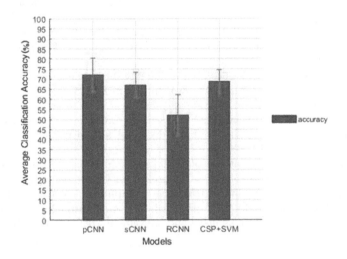

Fig. 5. Average classification accuracies on four models. The red line denotes the standard deviation. The datasets use the same one. (Color figure online)

Acknowledgments. This work was supported by the National Natural Science Foundation of China under Grants 62176054 and 61773114, and the University Synergy Innovation Program of Anhui Province under Grant GXXT-2020-015.

References

1. Rao, R.P.N.: Brain-Computer Interfacing: An Introduction, 1st edn., pp. 109–148. Cambridge University Press, Cambridge (2013)

2. Pfurtscheller, G., Brunner, C., Schlogl, A., et al.: Mu rhythm (de)synchronization and EEG single-trial classification of different motor imagery tasks. Neuroimage **31**(1), 153–159 (2006)

3. Sun, H., Fu, Y., Xiong, X., et al.: Study on EEG pattern recognition based on HHT motor imagery. Acta Automatica Sinica **41**(9), 1686–1692 (2015)

4. Heo, J., Yoon, G.: EEG studies on physical discomforts induced by virtual reality gaming. J. Electr. Eng. Technol. **15**(3), 1323–1329 (2020)

5. Czeszumski, A., Eustergerling, S., Lang, A., et al.: Hyperscanning: a valid method to study neural inter-brain underpinnings of social interaction. Front. Hum. Neurosci. **14**, 39 (2020)

6. Meng, J., Zhang, S., Bekyo, A., et al.: Noninvasive electroencephalogram based control of a robotic arm for reach and grasp tasks. Sci. Rep. **6**(1), 38565 (2016)

7. Stippich, C., Heiland, S., Tronnier, V., et al.: Functional magnetic resonance imaging: physiological background, technical aspects and prerequisites for clinical use. Rofo Fortschr Geb Rontgenstr Neuen Bildgeb Verfahr **174**(2), 242 (2002)

8. Hsu, W., Fong, L., Wei, C., et al.: EEG classification of imaginary lower limb stepping movements based on fuzzy support vector machine with kernel-induced membership function. Int. J. Fuzzy Syst. **19**(2), 1–14 (2017)

9. Padfield, N., Zabalza, J., Zhao, H., et al.: EEG-based brain-computer interfaces using motor-imagery: techniques and challenges. Sensors (Switzerland) **19**(6), 1–34 (2019)

10. Arnaud, D., Scott, M.: EEGLAB: an open source toolbox for analysis of single-trial EEG dynamics including independent component analysis. J. Neurosci. Methods **134**(1), 9–21 (2004)

11. Tayeb, Z., Fedjaev, J., Ghaboosi, N., et al.: Validating deep neural networks for online decoding of motor imagery movements from EEG signals. Sensors **19**(210), 1–17 (2019)

12. Schirrmeister, R.T., Springenberg, J.T., Fiederer, L.D.J., et al.: Deep learning with convolutional neural networks for EEG decoding and visualization. Hum. Brain Mapp. **38**(11), 5391–5420 (2017)

13. Liang, M., Hu, X.: Recurrent convolutional neural network for object recognition. In: Proceedings of the 2015 IEEE Conference on Computer Vision and Pattern Recognition (CVPR), pp. 3367–3375. IEEE Computer Society, Boston (2015)

14. Ramoser, H., Muller-Gerking, J., Pfurtscheller, G.: Optimal spatial filtering of single trial EEG during imagined hand movement. IEEE Trans. Rehabil. Eng. **8**(4), 441–446 (2000)

Recurrent Neural Network with Adaptive Gating Timescales Mechanisms for Language and Action Learning

Libo Zhao[1]([✉]) and Junpei Zhong[2]

[1] S.M.Wu School of Intelligent Engineering, South China University of Technology, Guangzhou, China
`wilbzhao@mail.scut.edu.cn`
[2] Department of Rehabilitation Sciences, The Hong Kong Polytechnic University, Hong Kong, China
`joni.zhong@polyu.edu.hk`

Abstract. Inspired by the neurons' differences in membrane time-scales, the multiple timescale recurrent neural network model (MTRNN) adopts the hierarchical architecture with increasing time-scales from bottom to top layers. Based on this idea, the recent adaptive and continuous time recurrent neural networks (ACTRNN) and the gated adaptive continuous time recurrent neural network (GACTRNN) develop the novel learning mechanism on the time-scales. In this paper, we test the performance of GACTRNN using the dataset obtained from a real-world humanoid robot's object manipulation experiment. By using trainable timescale parameters with the gating mechanism, it can be observed that the GACTRNN can better learn the temporal characteristics of the sequences. Besides, to eliminate the effects of parameters' overgrowing with a large data-set, we improve the GACTRNN model and propose the MATRNN model. In this model, the *sigmoid* function is used instead of *exponential* function. We compare the performances of the CTRNN, GACTRNN and MATRNN models, and find that the GACTRNN and MATRNN models perform better than the CTRNN model with the large-scale dataset. By visualizing the timescales adapting in the training process, we also qualitatively show that the MATRNN model performs better than the GACTRNN model in terms of stability with the dataset.

Keywords: Recurrent neural network · Adaptive timescale · Membrane time constants · Developmental robotics

1 Introduction

Neurons process information with adaptively converting complex entities (e.g. information comes from motor actions to semantic meanings) into smaller elements in the sequential sequences. Such elements, when learnt in the neural populations, can be further reused to form new complex entities or to understand the sensory information when needed. The idea underlying this process

© Springer Nature Switzerland AG 2021
T. Mantoro et al. (Eds.): ICONIP 2021, CCIS 1517, pp. 405–413, 2021.
https://doi.org/10.1007/978-3-030-92310-5_47

was proposed by Arbib called "schema theory" [1], and based on the above capability, a brain system can divide any complex information entity into primitives and reuse them is broadly defined as functional hierarchy [2,5,6,11]. The functional hierarchy in the large-scale brain networks allows the human brain to cope with sequential processes with different levels of granularity of sensorimotor sequences. However, how this mechanism could be implemented in artificial neural system is not clear. Furthermore, another related challenge is that how can the brain system determine the levels of granularity of such primitives in the sequences, in order to make the encoding in the most efficient way.

The Recurrent Neural Network (RNN) models may be useful to model the recurrent and feedback connections which contribute a lot of the connections in the hierarchical brain [20]. The Long Short-Term Memory (LSTM) [12] and the Gated Recurrent Unit (GRU) [3] are two of the most common RNN variants with gating mechanisms in the state-of-the-art machine learning community. Both of them use particular architectural constraints called gating mechanisms which can alleviate the vanishing gradient problem of original RNNs and help the recurrent networks to learn both the short-term dependencies and long-term dependencies of the data. Nevertheless, with the lack of modeling the critical mechanisms of the neural dynamics in the biological brain, the above RNN variants are not sufficient to build biologically inspired neural systems. To mimic the mechanism of functional hierarchy in neural system at the level of neural dynamics, multiple timescale recurrent neural network (MTRNN) [19] model was proposed. Adopting the concept of time-scale, it can capture the information of sequential data on different timescales by manually-set time-scales. Besides, inspired by the idea that time constants in the brain are subjects to change during development [8], Heinrich et al. proposed the adaptive and continuous time recurrent neural networks (ACTRNN) [10], and its improved version, the gated and adaptive continuous time recurrent neural networks (GACTRNN) [9].

In the original paper of GACTRNN, the proposed model has shown its potential to learn the temporal characteristics on multiple timescales from sequential data, but the paper did not involve an experiment with larger data sets that show distinct and highly complex multi-timescale dependencies such as sensorimotor sequences from robot behavioral data. On the other hand, interaction of a humanoid robot with a physical embodiment is important if we would like to use the neural network to model certain cognitive functions [15,18]. In this paper, we will fill such a gap using a set of multi-modal data containing sensorimotor sequences of a robotic manipulation experiment as training data. We use CTRNN model as the baseline, compare the performance of the CTRNN model, the GACTRNN model and the MATRNN model. The adaptive process of the timescales is also visualized to investigate what the models learn from the sequential data with complex temporal characteristics. By this way, we prove that the MATRNN model performs better than the GACTRNN model in terms of timescale adaptation in more challenging cases.

2   Models

2.1   Continuous Time Recurrent Neural Network Model

Continuous time recurrent neural network (CTRNN) is the main component of the MTRNN model. It is derived from the leaky integrate-and-fire model and thus from a simplification of the Hodgkin-Huxley model. Afterwards, the network architecture was initially developed by Hopfield and Tank [13] as a nonlinear graded-response neural network. Later Doya and Yoshizawa [4] developed an adaptive neural oscillator based on previous work. The transformation and activation functions for the CTRNN units are as below:

$$z_t = \left(1 - \frac{1}{\tau_t}\right) z_{t-1} + \frac{1}{\tau_t} \left(Wx + Vy_{t-1} + b\right) \tag{1}$$

$$y_t = f\left(z_t\right) \tag{2}$$

where x is the input, z_{t-1} is the previous internal state, W and V are the weights, b is the bias and $f(\cdot)$ is the activation function. The timescale parameter τ_t expresses the leakage within a certain time, which is biologically plausible. When the value of τ_t is large, the activation will change slowly. Conversely the activation will change quickly when the value of τ_t is small [19].

2.2   Gated Adaptive Continuous Time Recurrent Neural Network Model

Compared with the CTRNN model, in the gated adaptive continuous time recurrent neural network (GACTRNN), the timescales are no longer hyperparameters that are determined by means of empiricism. Instead they are trainable parameter determined by the learning mechanism. The adaptive and gating timescales mechanisms of the GACTRNN model are implemented by the computation of the timescale parameter as follows:

$$\tau_t = 1 + \exp\left(Hx + Gy_{t-1} + a + \tau_0\right) \tag{3}$$

where x and y are defined the same as the CTRNN, τ_t is the timescale parameter at time t, H and G are the weights which simulates the gating on the neuron's leakage characteristic, a is the bias, τ_0 is a vector that can be defined as initial values of the timescales.

2.3   Multiple Adaptive Timescale Recurrent Neural Network Model

It can be noticed that the value range of the timescale parameter in the GACTRNN model is $[1, +\infty]$. The infinity timescale is not we expect in most cases. Therefore, in this paper, we propose a novel model called the multiple adaptive timescale recurrent neuron network (MATRNN), to eliminate this problem by changing the activation function so that the timescale parameter can hierarchically adapt and will not obtain any unexpected values during the training process. The computation for the timescale parameter of the MATRNN model is as follows:

$$\tau_t = 1 + \tau_0 \otimes sigmoid\left(\mathbf{Hx} + \mathbf{Gy}_{t-1} + \mathbf{a}\right) \tag{4}$$

Where $\otimes$ indicates the element-wise multiplication and the other parameters are similar to the GACTRNN model.

3   Experiment

3.1   Experiment Dataset

The dataset we use is from the object manipulation experiment on the iCub robot [14], recorded by Zhong et al. [21]. The iCub robot is a child sized humanoid robot, built as an open humanoid platform for cognitive and neuroscience research [17]. This training data includes two parts of information: semantic commands and sensorimotor information. The semantic command part is composed of two discrete words: 9 actions and 9 objects are used to form 81 possible combinations, which are represented by discrete values, as shown in Table 1. The sensorimotor information part of training data, which includes object location (neck and eyes) and torso joints of the iCub robot, is the recording of a complete movement sequence of the corresponding semantic command.

Table 1. Look-up table of verbs and nouns for the data sets: the instructor showed the robot with different combinations of the 9 actions and 9 objects

Actions	Slide left	Slide right	Torch	Reach	Push	Pull	Point	Grasp	Lift
Verb values	0.0	0.1	0.2	0.3	0.4	0.5	0.6	0.7	0.8
Objects	Tractor	Hammer	Ball	Bus	Modi	Car	Cup	Cubes	Spiky
Noun values	0.0	0.1	0.2	0.3	0.4	0.5	0.6	0.7	0.8

3.2   Case 1: Basic Mode

The purpose of this case is to enable the models to learn specific semantic commands and corresponding action sequences through training process. The input data and ground truth of our experiment are both training data.

To get a fair comparison, the same architecture with the same parameters are used for the three models. We selected the hyperparameters that perform well in the model after a brief hyperparameter search experiment. In our experiments, we defined networks with one hidden layer, which consists of $(43, 30, 20, 10)$ neurons (4 modules) where recurrent connections are only connected to neighboring modules (adjacent connectivity [9]). All hidden neurons were densely (fully) connected to the input and activated with a tanh function. Besides, our experiment has the initial timescales of $(1, 35, 70, 125)$, and a learning rate of 0.001 using Adam optimization algorithm for training over $5,000$ epochs. During training, the loss was calculated by the Mean Squared Error (MSE).

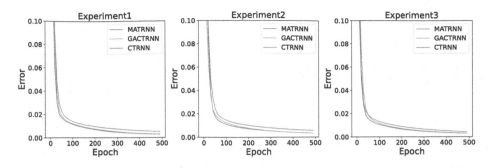

Fig. 1. Training curves of the three models. The three training curves are from three experiments with the same hyperparameters. In order to better show the details, we only select the data of the first 500 epochs for illustration.

Table 2. Performance of the three models

	Experiment1	Experiment2	Experiment3	Average
CTRNN	3.12E−04	3.49E−04	2.72E−0.4	3.11E−04
GACTRNN	1.78E−04	1.81E−04	1.60E−04	1.73E−04
MATRNN	1.76E−04	1.93E−04	1.71E−04	1.80E−04

To eliminate the effect of randomness, three experiments were done with the same parameters. The performance of these three models is shown in Table 2, and the training curves of the models are illustrated in Fig. 1. In the above experiments on the multi-modal data, the GACTRNN and MATRNN model perform a bit better in terms of error, although each model generates a low error. Next, the adaptive process of the timescale parameters is visualized to explore more information during the training process, as shown in Fig. 2 and Fig. 3. We can see that compared with the CTRNN model using pre-determined timescales, the timescale parameters in GACTRNN and MATRNN are constantly changing with the increasing of epoch and finally have a tendency to converge to a certain distribution. So in this basic mode, the adaptation of the timescale parameters in the GACTRNN and MATRNN models performs well, which has the potential to simulate the adaptation process of the timescale in the neuron.

3.3 Case 2: Trajectory Generation Mode

In the basic mode, the mixed signal, which includes the output of the previous step (y_{t-1}) and the original input (x_t), is used for training of the model. While in the trajectory generation mode, we explored the situation where the input of each step only includes the output of the previous step (y_{t-1}). This is a mode of automatically generating trajectories, which is more challenging for the models, in which a neural system may exhibit its instability due to small error. For the generation model, we expect that after training, the models can generate corresponding sensorimotor sequences based on the semantic commands and

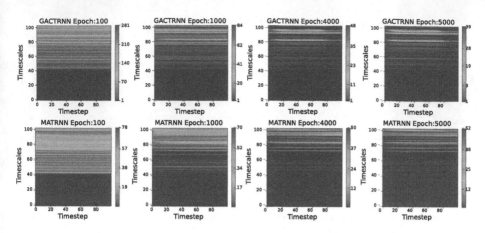

Fig. 2. Distribution diagram of the timescale parameters of a certain action sequence in GACTRNN and MATRNN. The figure shows the timescale parameters distribution of four epochs during a training process of a certain action sequence.

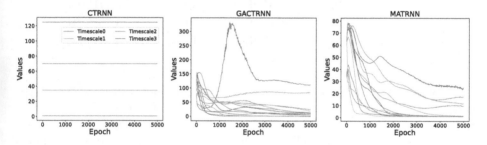

Fig. 3. Adaptive process of part of the timescale parameters of the three models.

information of object location and torso joints at the first timestep and the initial condition.

To realize the generation mode, the computation for activation $\mathbf{y}$ in the new mode is as below:

$$\mathbf{z}_t = \left(1 - \frac{1}{\tau_t}\right)\mathbf{z}_{t-1} + \frac{1}{\tau_t}\left(\mathbf{V}\mathbf{y}_{t-1} + \mathbf{b}\right) \tag{5}$$

$$\mathbf{y}_t = f\left(\mathbf{z}_t\right) \tag{6}$$

$$For\ GACTRNN : \boldsymbol{\tau}_t = 1 + \exp\left(\mathbf{G}\mathbf{y}_{t-1} + \mathbf{a} + \boldsymbol{\tau}_0\right) \tag{7}$$

$$For\ MATRNN : \boldsymbol{\tau}_t = 1 + \boldsymbol{\tau}_0 \otimes sigmoid\left(\mathbf{G}\mathbf{y}_{t-1} + \mathbf{a}\right) \tag{8}$$

In addition, by visualizing the timescale parameters, we investigated the adaptive process of timescales in these two models. The hyperparameters of the model were set to be the same as in the Case 1. The results are shown in Table 3, Fig. 4, and Fig. 5. From the perspective of the error curve shown in Table 3 and Fig. 4, the performances in the training of two models look similar. However, the adaptive process of timescale parameters of these two models is quite different. From Fig. 5 we can see that in the later stage of the training process of this challenging task, only the timescale parameters of a small area in GACTRNN achieve abnormally large values, while the distribution of timescale parameters in MATRNN is more normal and capable of simulating the adaptivity in neuron's timescales. Therefore, in this challenging trajectory generation mode, as a cognitive neural network model, the MATRNN model performs better than the GACTRNN model in terms of timescales' stability.

Table 3. Performance of the two models

	Experiment1	Experiment2	Experiment3	Average
GACTRNN	3.25E−03	4.04E−03	4.05E−03	3.78E−03
MATRNN	4.46E−03	3.52E−03	3.26E−03	3.75E−03

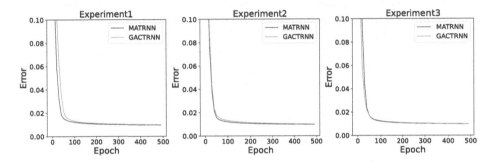

Fig. 4. Training curves of the two models. The three training curves are from three experiments with the same hyperparameters.

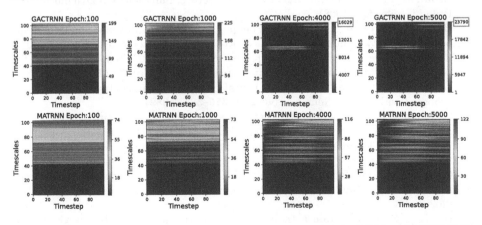

Fig. 5. Adaptive process of the timescale parameters in GACTRNN and MATRNN. As shown in the red-boxes, timescale parameters of a small area in GACTRNN achieve abnormally large values. (Color figure online)

4   Conclusion and Future Work

In this study, using the large-scale sensorimotor dataset based on a humanoid robot, we compared the performance of CTRNN, GACTRNN, and MATRNN, and visualized adaptive process of the timescale parameters. Through the experiment, the following conclusions can be drawn:

1. The GACTRNN and MATRNN models perform a little better than the CTRNN model in our basic mode experiment.
2. During the training process, the timescale parameters in GACTRNN and MATRNN are constantly adapting and have a tendency to converge to a certain distribution which can simulate the adaptivity in neuron's timescales.
3. In the challenging trajectory generation mode, as a cognitive neural network model, the MATRNN model performs better than the GACTRNN model in terms of timescale adaptation.

Neurons' timescales seem to be quite dynamic in prefrontal cortex while neurons in other regions seem quite stable over a short period of time [7,16]. Using the MATRNN model or GACTRNN model, we have interest to apply them in computational psychiatry where the neural dysfunctional mechanisms related to abnormal timescales can be simulated. The artificial model can also make the computational psychiatry embodiment be feasible.

Acknowledgments. This work is partially supported by PolyU Start-up Grant (ZVUY-P0035417).

References

1. Arbib, M.A., et al.: Neural Organization: Structure, Function, and Dynamics. MIT Press, Cambridge (1998)
2. Boemio, A., Fromm, S., Braun, A., Poeppel, D.: Hierarchical and asymmetric temporal sensitivity in human auditory cortices. Nat. Neurosci. **8**(3), 389–395 (2005)
3. Cho, K., et al.: Learning phrase representations using RNN encoder-decoder for statistical machine translation. arXiv preprint arXiv:1406.1078 (2014)
4. Doya, K., Yoshizawa, S.: Adaptive neural oscillator using continuous-time back-propagation learning. Neural Netw. **2**(5), 375–385 (1989)
5. Felleman, D.J., Van Essen, D.C.: Distributed hierarchical processing in the primate cerebral cortex. Cereb. Cortex (New York, NY: 1991) **1**(1), 1–47 (1991)
6. Fuster, J.M.: The prefrontal cortex-an update: time is of the essence. Neuron **30**(2), 319–333 (2001)
7. Gao, R., van den Brink, R.L., Pfeffer, T., Voytek, B.: Neuronal timescales are functionally dynamic and shaped by cortical microarchitecture. Elife **9**, e61277 (2020)
8. He, B.J.: Scale-free brain activity: past, present, and future. Trends Cogn. Sci. **18**(9), 480–487 (2014)
9. Heinrich, S., Alpay, T., Nagai, Y.: Learning timescales in gated and adaptive continuous time recurrent neural networks. In: 2020 IEEE International Conference on Systems, Man, and Cybernetics (SMC), pp. 2662–2667. IEEE (2020)

10. Heinrich, S., Alpay, T., Wermter, S.: Adaptive and variational continuous time recurrent neural networks. In: 2018 Joint IEEE 8th International Conference on Development and Learning and Epigenetic Robotics (ICDL-EpiRob), pp. 13–18. IEEE (2018)

11. Hilgetag, C.C., O'Neill, M.A., Young, M.P.: Hierarchical organization of macaque and cat cortical sensory systems explored with a novel network processor. Philos. Trans. R. Soc. Lond. Ser. B: Biol. Sci. **355**(1393), 71–89 (2000)

12. Hochreiter, S., Schmidhuber, J.: Long short-term memory. Neural Comput. **9**(8), 1735–1780 (1997)

13. Hopfield, J.J., Tank, D.W.: Computing with neural circuits: a model. Science **233**(4764), 625–633 (1986)

14. Metta, G., Sandini, G., Vernon, D., Natale, L., Nori, F.: The iCub humanoid robot: an open platform for research in embodied cognition. In: Proceedings of the 8th Workshop on Performance Metrics for Intelligent Systems, pp. 50–56. Association for Computing Machinery (2008)

15. Pfeifer, R., Lungarella, M., Iida, F.: Self-organization, embodiment, and biologically inspired robotics. Science **318**, 1088–1093 (2007)

16. Spitmaan, M., Seo, H., Lee, D., Soltani, A.: Multiple timescales of neural dynamics and integration of task-relevant signals across cortex. Proc. Natl. Acad. Sci. **117**(36), 22522–22531 (2020)

17. Tsagarakis, N.G., et al.: iCub: the design and realization of an open humanoid platform for cognitive and neuroscience research. Adv. Robot. **21**(10), 1151–1175 (2007)

18. Varela, F.J., Thompson, E., Rosch, E.: The Embodied Mind, Revised Edition: Cognitive Science and Human Experience. MIT Press, Cambridge (2017)

19. Yamashita, Y., Tani, J.: Emergence of functional hierarchy in a multiple timescale neural network model: a humanoid robot experiment. PLoS Comput. Biol. **4**(11), e1000220 (2008)

20. Zhong, J.: Artificial neural models for feedback pathways for sensorimotor integration. Ph.D. thesis, Staats-und Universitätsbibliothek Hamburg Carl von Ossietzky (2015)

21. Zhong, J., Peniak, M., Tani, J., Ogata, T., Cangelosi, A.: Sensorimotor input as a language generalisation tool: a neurorobotics model for generation and generalisation of noun-verb combinations with sensorimotor inputs. Auton. Robot. **43**(5), 1271–1290 (2019)

Applications

Bottom-Up Progressive Semantic Alignment for Image-Text Retrieval

Zheng Cui[1], Yongli Hu[1(✉)], Yanfeng Sun[1], Junbin Gao[2], and Baocai Yin[1]

[1] Beijing Key Laboratory of Multimedia and Intelligent Software Technology, Beijing Institute of Artificial Intelligence, Faculty of Information Technology, Beijing University of Technology, Beijing, China
CuiZ@emails.bjut.edu.cn, {huyongli,yfsun,ybc}@bjut.edu.cn
[2] Discipline of Business Analytics, The University of Sydney Business School, The University of Sydney, Sydney, NSW, Australia
junbin.gao@sydney.edu.au

Abstract. Image-text retrieval is a challenging task due to image and text are heterogeneous cross-modal data, which possess semantic gap. The key issue of image-text retrieval is how to learn a common feature space while semantic correspondence between image and text remains. Some existing works extract region feature in image and word feature in text to implement cross-modal alignment between local elements, the other works integrate relation-aware information to local elements to compute cross-modal similarity, while these methods not utilize the semantic information in different semantic-level. In order to address this issue, we propose a Bottom-up Progressive Semantic Alignment (BPSA) network, in which precise fine-grained alignment is carried out on diverse semantic-levels progressively. Specifically, the feature of the cross-modal data are extracted from bottom element to local-group, and global-representation by graph convolution and attention mechanism. We conduct extensive experiments on Flickr30K and MS-COCO datasets, compared with the related state-of-the-art methods. The results show that our network achieves competitive performance.

Keywords: Image-text retrieval · Cross-modal similarity · Bottom-up progressive semantic alignment

1 Introduction

The image-text retrieval task is one of the hottest topic receiving a lot of interest, in which given an image or text, the algorithm can seek out the semantic close samples in another modal in the database. The cores of this task are semantic understanding and cross-modal alignment for the data from diverse modal. In recent years, extensive methods have been proposed to achieve the bidirectional retrieval of image and text. Early methods [5–7,9,15,16] learn global feature for data in each modality and project these features into a common feature space where semantic correspondence between image and text is remained to measure

© Springer Nature Switzerland AG 2021
T. Mantoro et al. (Eds.): ICONIP 2021, CCIS 1517, pp. 417–424, 2021.
https://doi.org/10.1007/978-3-030-92310-5_48

their similarity. These methods achieve preliminary successes, while the details of data are ignored since the rough feature representation. Since the global feature is extremely summarized description of image, much useful fine-grained information is unavoidably lost, resulting in the lack of precise alignment of cross-modal local elements. To preserve specific information, local representation based methods [3,4,10,12,13,17] have been developed, which focus on the local alignment between images and texts. For example, stacked cross attention model [10] uses the region-level feature of salient regions in image and the word-level feature to compute similarity score. This method takes advantage of cross-attention mechanism to achieve fine-grained cross-modal alignment on element-level.

However, the existing methods not utilize the semantic information in different semantic-level and consider the relation between different levels. In this paper, we propose a bottom-up progressive semantic alignment network. Our network implements text-to-image and image-to-text alignment at element, local-group and global-representation semantic level to get discriminative similarity scores between images and texts. We conduct extensive experiments on several benchmark datasets for cross-modal image-text retrieval, including Flickr30K and MS-COCO datasets. Our contributions are summarized as follows:

1. The bottom-up progressive semantic alignment network is proposed to handle the alignment of cross-modal data, which extracts multi-level of semantics and thus get precise similarity score.
2. We utilize the consistency constraint at multiple semantic levels to achieve precise similarity calculation.
3. Extensive cross-modal retrieval experiments on Flickr30K and MS-COCO dataset show that our network achieves competitive results.

2   Bottom-Up Progressive Semantic Alignment Network

In this section, we will elaborate on the details of our proposed Bottom-up Progressive Semantic Alignment (BPSA) network. The overall architecture of the proposed network is shown in Fig. 1.

2.1   Element Alignment

Preparing for cross-modal alignment, we represent an image as a set of features of several salient regions like [1]. Then a fully-connect layer is applied to transform these features to d-dimensional vectors, denoted by $V = \{v_1, v_2, ..., v_m\}, v_i \in \mathbb{R}^d$. For a sentence that captions corresponding image, we project each word into a contiguous embedding space and use bidirectional GRU [14] to encode embedding features. Eventually, we can obtain word-level features for each sentence, $T = \{t_1, t_2, ..., t_n\}, t_j \in \mathbb{R}^d$.

In the element alignment, the similarity between the image features $V \in \mathbb{R}^{m \times d}$ and text features $T \in \mathbb{R}^{n \times d}$ should be firstly considered. Simply, the similarity between each pair (v_i, t_j) is computed by:

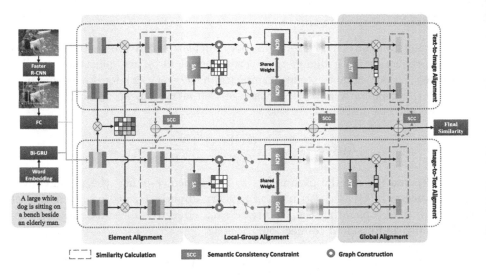

Fig. 1. Framework of the proposed bottom-up progressive semantic alignment network.

$$C_{ij} = \frac{v_i \cdot t_j^T}{\|v_i\|\|t_j\|}, i \in [1, m], j \in [1, n], \tag{1}$$

Then we obtain the text attended image features as follows:

$$\hat{V} = AT, \tag{2}$$

$$A_{ij} = \frac{exp(\lambda C_{ij})}{\sum_{j=1}^{n} exp(\lambda C_{ij})}, \tag{3}$$

where λ is the temperature parameter. Through setting a larger temperature parameter, we can obtain a sparse similarity matrix A. Similarly, image attended text features $\hat{T}$ are also calculated. After learning the attended features, $\hat{T}$ and $\hat{V}$, we perform element level alignment at text-to-image (tti) and image-to-text (itt) direction. The similarity score at element level is computed as follows:

$$S_e = S_e(tti) + S_e(itt), \tag{4}$$

$$S_e(tti) = \frac{\sum_{i=1}^{m} cosine(v_i, \hat{v}_i)}{m}, \tag{5}$$

$$S_e(itt) = \frac{\sum_{i=1}^{n} cosine(t_i, \hat{t}_i)}{n}, \tag{6}$$

where $cosine(x, y) = (x \cdot y)/(\|x\|\|y\|)$. Ultimately, considering that the semantic consistency between text-to-image and image-to-text direction, we use the consistency loss to restrain similarity calculation inspired by [2]:

$$l_e = (S_e(tti) - S_e(itt))^2. \tag{7}$$

2.2 Local-Group Alignment

Considering that the complex relations between features are crucial to the semantic comprehension and alignment of cross-modal data, we construct a fully-connected visual semantic relationship graph $G = (V, E)$ for image features to learn their semantic relations. Based on self-attention, an adjacency matrix R can be used to describe edge set:

$$R(v_i, v_j) = \frac{exp((W_1 v_i)^T (W_2 v_j))}{\sum_{j=1}^{m} exp((W_1 v_i)^T (W_2 v_j))}, \tag{8}$$

where W_1 and W_2 are the parameters to be learned. Further, the graph convolutional network (GCN) [8] is utilized to learn abundant feature information of the graph via propagating the feature of each node to adjacent nodes, and we additionally add residual connection:

$$V^l = W_g(\sum_j R(v_i, v_j) \cdot V) + V, \tag{9}$$

where $W_g \in \mathbb{R}^{d \times d}$ is the weight matrix of the graph convolutional layer, $V^l \in \mathbb{R}^{m \times d}$ is a new set of features that contains abundant local semantic relations information. Based on the features $\hat{V}$ that are aligned at element level, we use the shared adjacency matrix R and graph convolution weight matrix W_g to obtain $\hat{V}^l \in \mathbb{R}^{m \times d}$ to perform text-to-image alignment at local-group level:

$$\hat{V}^l = W_g(\sum_j R(v_i, v_j) \cdot \hat{V}) + \hat{V}, \tag{10}$$

$$S_l(tti) = \frac{\sum_{i=1}^{m} cosine(v_i^l, \hat{v}_i^l)}{m}, \tag{11}$$

where s_l is the text-to-image similarity score at local-group level. Next, the image-to-text alignment is conducted in the same way and $S_l(itt)$ can be obtained. Finally, the similarity score and the consistency loss at local-group level can be gained:

$$S_l = S_l(tti) + S_l(itt), \tag{12}$$

$$l_l = (S_l(tti) - S_l(itt))^2. \tag{13}$$

2.3 Global-Representation Alignment

Aiming to remove redundant information and obtain more summary feature representation, attention mechanism is used to learn global-representation for cross-modal data.

$$V^g = \sum_{i=1}^{m} p_i \cdot v_i^l, \tag{14}$$

$$p_i = \frac{exp(W_6 \cdot \sigma(W_5 v_i^l))}{\sum_{i=1}^{m} exp(W_6 \cdot \sigma(W_5 v_i^l))}, \tag{15}$$

where $W_5 \in \mathbb{R}^{(d/2) \times d}, W_6 \in \mathbb{R}^{1 \times (d_x/2)}$ are parameters, $\sigma()$ is a nonlinear activation function and V^g is the global-representation feature. Supposing that $\hat{V}^l$ is aligned to V^l, the two set of features ought to possess the same attention weights distribution. So, we employ the constraint of shared weights to get the global-representation feature $\hat{V}^g$:

$$\hat{V}^g = \sum_{i=1}^{m} p_i \cdot \hat{v}_i^l. \tag{16}$$

Then, we perform text-to-image alignment at global-representation level:

$$S_g(tti) = cosine(V^g, \hat{V}^g). \tag{17}$$

Similarly, the image-to-text alignment can be conducted and $S_g(itt)$ can be obtained. The similarity score and the consistency loss at global-representation level can be computed as follows:

$$S_g = S_g(tti) + S_g(itt), \tag{18}$$

$$l_g = (S_g(tti) - S_g(itt))^2. \tag{19}$$

2.4   Objective Function

After computing the similarity score at three semantic levels, we define the final similarity score function as follows:

$$S = \beta_1 S_e + \beta_2 S_l + \beta_3 S_g, \tag{20}$$

where β_1, β_2 and β_3 are coefficients. To make matched image-text pairs have high similarity value and decrease similarity value among unmatched image-text pairs, triplet loss is used in our work inspired by the previous method [6]:

$$L_{hard} = \sum_{T^-} [\alpha - S(I,T) + S(I,T_h^-)]_+ + \sum_{I^-} [\alpha - S(I,T) + S(I_h^-,T)]_+, \tag{21}$$

where α is a margin parameter, $[x]_+ = max(x,0)$, T_h^- and I_h^- are the hardest negatives in the mini-batch, and $S()$ is the similarity score function that computes the similarity value among an image and a sentence. According to the above definitions, the final objective function of our proposed network can be formulated as:

$$Loss = L_{hard} + \beta_4 \cdot \frac{\sum_{(I,T)} l_e + l_l + l_g}{bs}, \tag{22}$$

where bs is the batch size and β_4 is coefficient.

3   Experiments

3.1   Experiments Setting

We conduct our network on Flickr30k [18] and MS-COCO [11] datasets, which are commonly used in image-text retrieval task. Concerning image representation, we use Faster R-CNN to extract a 36×2048 dimensional object features for each image and then transform to 512 dimension. For text representation, we embed each word to 300-dimension vector and feed embedded vector into bidirectional GRUs with 512 hidden state dimension. The temperature parameter λ is set to 20. The coefficients β_1, β_2 and β_3 are set to 1, 1.5 and 1.8, respectively. The β_4 is set to 1.0 for MS-COCO and 0.3 for Flickr30k. The margin of triplet loss α is set to 0.6. We train the network with the batch size bs of 90. The initial learning rate is set to 0.0005 for MS-COCO and 0.0002 for Flickr30k.

3.2   Experimental Results and Analysis

The experimental results on the Flickr30k and MS-COCO dataset are shown in Table 1. From the results on Flickr30k, it can be found that the BPSA network outperforms the recent state-of-the-art methods. Compared to IMRAM, our method improves R@1 from 74.1 to 75.2 for text retrieval and from 53.9 to 55.4 for image retrieval. From the results on MS-COCO, compared to the recent state-of-the-art methods, BPSA network achieves the competitive results and gets the value of 520.6 in R@sum.

3.3   Ablation Study

For the sake of demonstrating the effectiveness of bottom-up progressive semantic alignment, bidirectional alignment of image and text and semantic consistency constraint, we implement compared experiments on the Flickr30k dataset. As shown in Table 2, "element" denotes alignment at element level, "local" denotes alignment at local-group level, "global" denotes alignment at global-representation level. "image-text" denotes that model implements image-to-text alignment. "text-image" denotes that model implements text-to-image alignment. "SCC" denotes the semantic consistency constraint. It is obvious that the network possessing complete compositions achieves the best results. This ablation study proves the effectiveness of our network.

Table 1. Cross-modal retrieval results of different methods on Flickr30K test set and MS-COCO 1K test set.

Method	Flickr30K							MS-COCO						
	Text retrieval			Image retrieval			R@sum	Text retrieval			Image retrieval			R@sum
	R@1	R@5	R@10	R@1	R@5	R@10		R@1	R@5	R@10	R@1	R@5	R@10	
HM-LSTM [13]	38.1	–	76.5	27.7	–	68.8	–	43.9	–	87.8	36.1	–	86.7	–
VSE++ [6]	52.9	–	87.2	39.6	–	79.5	–	64.6	–	95.7	52.0	–	92.0	–
SCAN [10]	67.4	90.3	95.8	48.6	77.7	85.2	465.0	72.7	94.8	98.4	58.8	88.4	94.8	507.9
MDM [12]	44.9	75.4	84.4	34.4	67.0	77.7	383.8	54.7	84.1	91.9	44.6	79.6	90.5	445.4
CAMP [17]	68.1	89.7	95.2	51.5	77.1	85.3	466.9	72.3	94.8	98.3	58.5	87.9	95.0	506.8
DP-RNN [4]	70.2	91.6	95.8	**55.5**	81.3	88.2	482.6	75.3	95.8	98.6	62.5	89.7	95.1	517
IMRAM [3]	74.1	93.0	96.6	53.9	79.4	87.2	484.2	76.7	95.6	98.5	61.7	89.1	95.0	516.6
BPSA (ours)	**75.2**	**93.7**	**97.5**	55.4	**82.1**	**88.9**	**492.8**	**77.1**	**96.8**	**98.8**	**62.6**	**90.1**	**95.2**	**520.6**

Table 2. The results of ablation experiment on the Flickr30k dataset.

Element	Local	Global	Image-text	Text-image	scc	Text Retrieval		Image Retrieval	
						R@1	R@10	R@1	R@10
✓			✓	✓		69.5	93.1	50.0	85.0
✓	✓		✓	✓		71.2	94.6	51.7	86.8
✓	✓	✓		✓		71.5	94.5	51.0	86.5
✓	✓	✓	✓			72.5	94.9	52.3	86.8
✓	✓	✓	✓	✓		73.8	95.8	54.0	87.3
✓	✓	✓	✓	✓	✓	**75.2**	**97.5**	**55.4**	**88.9**

4 Conclusion

In this paper, we propose a Bottom-up Progressive Semantic Alignment (BPSA) network for cross-modal image-text retrieval task. We consider the semantic similarity between image and text at three semantic levels to achieve fine-grained bi-directional alignment. Extensive experiments on Flickr30K and MS-COCO datasets show that our model achieves the competitive results. In the future work, we will research the common learning method for cross-modal data and resolve the problem of lack of accurate semantic understanding for image and text.

Acknowledgments. This work is supported by National Natural Science Foundation of China under Grant No. 61772048, 61672071, U1811463, U19B2039, Beijing Talents Project (20 17A24).

References

1. Anderson, P., et al.: Bottom-up and top-down attention for image captioning and visual question answering. In: Proceedings of the IEEE Conference on Computer Vision and Pattern Recognition, pp. 6077–6086 (2018)

2. Chen, H., Ding, G., Lin, Z., Zhao, S., Han, J.: Cross-modal image-text retrieval with semantic consistency. In: Proceedings of the 27th ACM International Conference on Multimedia, pp. 1749–1757 (2019)
3. Chen, H., Ding, G., Liu, X., Lin, Z., Liu, J., Han, J.: IMRAM: iterative matching with recurrent attention memory for cross-modal image-text retrieval. In: Proceedings of the IEEE/CVF Conference on Computer Vision and Pattern Recognition, pp. 12655–12663 (2020)
4. Chen, T., Luo, J.: Expressing objects just like words: recurrent visual embedding for image-text matching. In: Proceedings of the AAAI Conference on Artificial Intelligence, vol. 34, pp. 10583–10590 (2020)
5. Eisenschtat, A., Wolf, L.: Linking image and text with 2-way nets. In: Proceedings of the IEEE Conference on Computer Vision and Pattern Recognition, pp. 4601–4611(2017)
6. Faghri, F., Fleet, D.J., Kiros, J.R., Fidler, S.: VSE++: improving visual-semantic embeddings with hard negatives. arXiv preprint arXiv:1707.05612 (2017)
7. Frome, A., et al.: Devise: a deep visual-semantic embedding model. In: Advances in Neural Information Processing Systems, pp. 2121–2129 (2013)
8. Kipf, T.N., Welling, M.: Semi-supervised classification with graph convolutional networks. arXiv preprint arXiv:1609.02907 (2016)
9. Klein, B., Lev, G., Sadeh, G., Wolf, L.: Associating neural word embeddings with deep image representations using fisher vectors. In: 2015 IEEE Conference on Computer Vision and Pattern Recognition (CVPR) (2015)
10. Lee, K.-H., Chen, X., Hua, G., Hu, H., He, X.: Stacked cross attention for image-text matching. In: Ferrari, V., Hebert, M., Sminchisescu, C., Weiss, Y. (eds.) ECCV 2018, Part IV. LNCS, vol. 11208, pp. 212–228. Springer, Cham (2018). https://doi.org/10.1007/978-3-030-01225-0_13
11. Lin, T.-Y., et al.: Microsoft COCO: common objects in context. In: Fleet, D., Pajdla, T., Schiele, B., Tuytelaars, T. (eds.) ECCV 2014, Part V. LNCS, vol. 8693, pp. 740–755. Springer, Cham (2014). https://doi.org/10.1007/978-3-319-10602-1_48
12. Ma, L., Jiang, W., Jie, Z., Wang, X.: Bidirectional image-sentence retrieval by local and global deep matching. Neurocomputing 345, 36–44 (2019)
13. Niu, Z., Zhou, M., Wang, L., Gao, X., Hua, G.: Hierarchical multimodal LSTM for dense visual-semantic embedding. In: Proceedings of the IEEE International Conference on Computer Vision, pp. 1881–1889 (2017)
14. Schuster, M., Paliwal, K.K.: Bidirectional recurrent neural networks. IEEE Trans. Signal Process. 45(11), 2673–2681 (1997)
15. Wang, B., Yang, Y., Xu, X., Hanjalic, A., Shen, H.T.: Adversarial cross-modal retrieval. In: Proceedings of the 25th ACM International Conference on Multimedia, pp. 154–162 (2017)
16. Wang, J.J., He, Y., Kang, C., Xiang, S., Pan, C.: Image-text cross-modal retrieval via modality-specific feature learning. In: Proceedings of the 5th ACM on International Conference on Multimedia Retrieval (2015)
17. Wang, Z., et al.: Camp: cross-modal adaptive message passing for text-image retrieval. In: Proceedings of the IEEE International Conference on Computer Vision, pp. 5764–5773 (2019)
18. Young, P., Lai, A., Hodosh, M., Hockenmaier, J.: From image descriptions to visual denotations: new similarity metrics for semantic inference over event descriptions. Trans. Assoc. Comput. Linguist. 2, 67–78 (2014)

Multi-loss Siamese Convolutional Neural Network for Chinese Calligraphy Style Classification

Li Liu[1(✉)], Wenyan Cheng[1], Taorong Qiu[1], Chengying Tao[2], Qiu Chen[3], Yue Lu[4], and Ching Y. Suen[5]

[1] School of Information Engineering, Nanchang University, Nanchang 330031, China
[2] Experimental Primary School of Beijing Normal University, Beijing 100875, China
[3] Major of Electrical Engineering and Electronics, Graduate School of Engineering, Kogakuin University, Tokyo 163-8677, Japan
[4] School of Communication and Electronic Engineering, East China Normal University, Shanghai 200241, China
[5] Centre for Pattern Recognition and Machine Intelligence, Concordia University, Montreal H3G 1M8, Canada

Abstract. We tackle the problem of Chinese calligraphy style classification in this paper, which is an important concern in the field of calligraphy art. The subtle difference among different calligraphy styles makes style classification a very challenging problem. To solve this problem, we propose a multi-loss siamese convolutional neural network, which is composed of two streams sharing weights. Each stream accepts a distinct image and then employs a convolutional neural network for feature extraction. We adopt the contrastive loss to explicitly enforce that the distance between the features of the images from the same category is smaller than that between the features of the images from different categories. Moreover, each stream of the siamese network is extended with a classification subnetwork to fully exploit the supervised information of an individual image. The cross-entropy loss is then employed for the classification subnetwork. By jointly optimizing the two types of loss, the proposed network has obtained remarkable performance according to the extensive experiments, achieving an accuracy in excess of 98%.

Keywords: Chinese calligraphy style classification · Multi-loss siamese convolutional neural network · Contrastive loss · Cross-entropy loss

1 Introduction

Chinese calligraphy plays a vital role in Chinese culture. Many Chinese calligraphers and their works are famous around the world. For the purpose of preservation, more and more calligraphy works have been digitalized. For example, a lot of calligraphy works can be found in CADAL (China Academic Digital Associate Library) [1], which is the largest digital library in China. In this way, the

© Springer Nature Switzerland AG 2021
T. Mantoro et al. (Eds.): ICONIP 2021, CCIS 1517, pp. 425–432, 2021.
https://doi.org/10.1007/978-3-030-92310-5_49

computer-aided calligraphy research has been greatly facilitated, which involves font and style classification [2,3], calligraphy synthesis [4], etc.

In this paper, we aim at Chinese calligraphy style classification, which is an important concern in the field of calligraphy art. As pointed out in [3], calligraphy style differs from font. More specifically, font refers to a broad taxonomy of the scripts. The popular Chinese fonts involve regular, clerical, cursive or semi-cursive, etc. Yet, the calligraphy styles are closely related to the calligraphers. Each calligrapher possesses his own unique style. We are mainly concerned with the style classification of four ancient calligraphers: Ouyang Xun, Yan Zhenqing, Zhao Mengfu and Liu Gongquan, who are considered as the top four great regular script calligraphers in China. In Fig. 1, several sample characters from the four calligraphers are shown. All the characters belong to regular font but with subtle differences, consequently making style classification a very challenging problem.

(a)   Ouyang (b) Yan Zhen- (c)   Liu (d)   Zhao
Xun   qing   Gongquan   Mengfu

Fig. 1. Sample character images from the four calligraphers.

There has been only a few works in the literature that are devoted to Chinese calligraphy style classification. For example, in [5], some handcrafted features like the aspect ratio of the characters, thickness of horizontal and vertical strokes were first extracted and then two simple Bayesian classifiers were employed for Chinese calligraphy style classification. With the compelling success of deep learning [6] in many fields, convolutional neural networks have also been employed to attack the issue of Chinese calligraphy style classification. In [3], a convolutional neural network with squeeze-and-excitation (SE) blocks and Haar wavelet modules embedded was proposed for Chinese calligraphy style classification. A problem closely related to Chinese calligraphy style classification is Chinese font classification, which has been extensively investigated [2,7,8]. Yet, style classification is more challenging compared with font classification as stated above. It is mainly due to that the difference among different styles is small compared with that among different fonts.

In this paper, we propose a novel multi-loss siamese convolutional network to cope with the issue of Chinese calligraphy style classification. The siamese network is composed of two streams which share weights. Each stream consists of a convolutional network which can extract features from the input image. We adopt the contrastive loss [9] to explicitly enforce that the distance between the features of the two input images from the same category is smaller than that between the features of the images from different categories. Moreover, we extend each stream of the network with a classification subnetwork. The cross-entropy loss is used for the classification subnetwork. By simultaneously optimizing the two types of loss, viz. contrastive loss and cross-entropy loss, we can make use of the relations between two images on one hand; on the other hand, the supervised information of each single image is fully exploited. With the trained multi-loss siamese convolutional network, the category of an arbitrary image can be determined by feeding it to the classification subnetwork in either stream of the siamese network. In the experiments, the proposed multi-loss siamese convolutional network is thoroughly evaluated, which has shown superior performance to the state-of-the-art methods.

2   Proposed Methodology

Figure 2(a) demonstrates the overall architecture of our proposed siamese network. It is composed of two streams. Besides, each stream of the network is extended with a classification subnetwork.

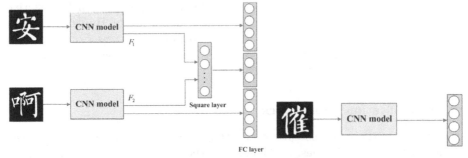

(a) Architecture of our proposed network.   (b) Classification of an arbitrary image.

Fig. 2. Our proposed multi-loss siamese convolutional neural network.

2.1   Siamese Convolutional Network

Siamese network typically consists of two identical streams sharing weights. It has been widely applied in various tasks such as signature verification [9] or person re-identification [10], etc. Inspired by the work [10], we employ the siamese convolutional network to address the issue of Chinese calligraphy style classification. As shown in Fig. 2(a), each stream accepts a distinct image. Then a convolutional neural network (CNN) is employed to extract features from the image. Various convolutional neural networks may be employed, e.g. VGG-16 [11]. Note the final fully-connected layer of the convolutional neural network is removed, and we adopt the penultimate layer as the feature of the image. Given the features F_1 and F_2 of the two input images, they are joined by a non-parametric square layer F_{square} as in [10], which is defined by subtracting F_2 from F_1 and then squaring elementwisely, viz. $F_{square} = (F_2 - F_1)^2$. So the dimension of F_{square} is the same as that of F_1 and F_2. The square layer is finally followed by a fully-connected layer composed of two neurons n_1 and n_2. The softmax function is applied in the fully-connected layer. Consequently, the output of the last fully-connected layer represents a probability distribution, with $n_1 = 1, n_2 = 0$ ($n_1 = 0, n_2 = 1$) indicating the two images from the same category and $n_1 = 0, n_2 = 1$ ($n_1 = 1, n_2 = 0$) denoting the two images from different categories.

In order to train the siamese convolutional network, we employ the contrastive loss as defined in the following:

$$L_{contra} = \frac{1}{2N} \sum_{n=1}^{N} y d^2 + (1 - y) \max(m - d, 0)^2 \tag{1}$$

where N denotes the training set size and d represents the Euclidean distance between the features F_1 and F_2 of the two input images. $y = 1$ indicates that the two input images are from the same category, viz. positive pair, while $y = 0$ means that the two input images are from different categories, namely, negative pair. m is the margin and is empirically set as 1 in our study. By using the loss defined above, the distance between the features of the images from the same category will be smaller than that between the features of images from different categories, which is very reasonable.

2.2   Classification Subnetwork

As depicted in the previous subsection, the siamese network only exploits the relations between two images, which discards the supervised information of each individual image. To overcome this issue, we extend each stream of the siamese network with a classification subnetwork. As shown in Fig. 2(a), the extracted feature representation F_1 or F_2 is fed to a fully connected layer for classification, with the number of neurons in the fully connected layer being equal to the number of possible classes.

To train the classification subnetwork, the cross-entropy loss is employed as defined below:

$$L_{cross} = -\frac{1}{N} \sum_{i=1}^{N} \sum_{k=1}^{K} y_{i,k} \log p_{i,k} \tag{2}$$

where N is the training set size and K denotes the number of possible classes. So $K = 4$ in our study, since we aim at style classification of four calligraphers as stated in Sect. 1. $p_{i,k}$ represents the predicted probability that the ith training sample belongs to the kth class. $y_{i,k} = 1$ if the groundtruth label of the ith training sample is k; otherwise, $y_{i,k} = 0$.

2.3   Multi-loss Training

Overall, our proposed network is trained to minimize three losses simultaneously, which include a contrastive loss and two cross-entropy losses. In greater details, the total loss is formally defined as follows:

$$L_{total} = L_{contra} + \lambda(L_{cross_1} + L_{cross_2})   \tag{3}$$

where L_{contra} represents the contrastive loss. L_{cross_1} and L_{cross_2} denote the cross-entropy losses for the two streams, respectively. The coefficient λ balances the weight assigned to the two different types of loss.

With the trained network, we may feed forward an arbitrary image to the classification subnetwork in either stream of the network to determine its category as depicted in Fig. 2(b).

3   Experiments

3.1   Dataset

Since there are no public datasets for Chinese calligraphy style classification, we collect $3,000$ character images for each of the four calligraphers. Therefore, the dataset is composed of $12,000$ character images. The size of the character image is 96×96. All the character images are in grayscale and JPEG format. Sample character images from the four calligraphers are illustrated in Fig. 1. The dataset is further split into the training set and test set with a ratio of $6 : 4$. Furthermore, 20% of the images in the training set is employed for validation, and the remaining images are used for training. Various configurations of the proposed approach are compared on the validation set, with the best configuration selected and then applied to the test set. We conduct five random training set and test set splits, and the average classification accuracy is reported.

3.2   Implementation Details

As shown in Fig. 2(a), the input of our proposed network is a pair of images. Regarding the positive pair, it is composed of two character images from the same calligrapher. For the negative pair, it consists of two character images from different calligraphers. We employ $5,500$ positive and $5,500$ negative pairs for network training. The network is trained with stochastic gradient descent with the size of minibatch set at 64. The momentum is set as 0.9. The learning rate is initially set as 0.0001, and is then reduced by a factor of 10 when the loss on the validation set plateaus. The network is trained for a maximum number of 100 epochs.

3.3   Configurations

We compare various configurations of the proposed approach on the validation set. The details are given in the following:

Comparison Among Different Convolutional Neural Networks. As demonstrated in Fig. 2(a), a convolutional neural network is employed to extract features from the image in each stream of the network. We compare four popular convolutional neural networks, which include AlexNet [6], VGG-16 [11], ResNet-50 [12] and Xception [13]. The comparison results are shown in Table 1. We can see that VGG-16 greatly outperforms the other three networks. Hence we employ VGG-16 in our study.

Table 1. Comparison among four convolutional neural networks.

	AlexNet	VGG-16	ResNet-50	Xception
Accuracy (%)	86.63	**98.12**	84.85	86.02

Effect of the Weight Coefficient λ. In Eq. (3), we employ a coefficient λ to balance the weight assigned to the two types of losses, viz. contrastive loss and cross-entropy loss. In Fig. 3, we compare the classification accuracy with different values of λ. One can observe that the highest accuracy is obtained when $\lambda = 1$, indicating that the two types of loss are equally important. Thus we set λ as 1 in our study.

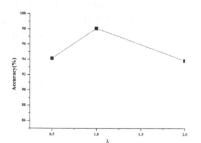

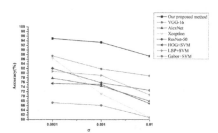

Fig. 3. Performance w.r.t. different values of λ.

Fig. 4. Performance comparison under various levels of noise.

3.4   Comparison with the Literature

In order to demonstrate the validity of the proposed approach, we further compare it with several state-of-the-art methods on the test set. Both hand-crafted feature-based methods and CNN-based methods are considered. Regarding handcrafted feature-based methods, HOG+SVM [3], Gabor+SVM [3] and LBP+SVM [8] are employed. For CNN-based methods, four popular baseline convolutional neural networks, namely, VGG-16, AlexNet, Xception and ResNet-50, are employed. These convolutional neural networks have demonstrated great power in image classification. The results are shown in Table 2.

Table 2. Comparison of the proposed method with state-of-the-art methods.

	Methods	Accuracy(%)
Handcrafted feature-based methods	HOG + SVM	78.87
	LBP + SVM	75.87
	Gabor + SVM	72.37
CNN-based methods	AlexNet	75.50
	VGG-16	84.87
	Xception	74.50
	ResNet-50	69.88
	Our proposed method	**98.08**

We can see that HOG+SVM performs the best among the handcrafted feature-based methods. Regarding CNN-based methods, only a single type of loss, e.g. cross-entropy loss, is considered in the four baseline convolutional neural networks. Yet, our proposed network adopts a siamese architecture and jointly optimizes two types of loss, viz. cross-entropy loss and contrastive loss. By employing the cross-entropy loss, the supervised information of each single image can be exploited just as in the baseline convolutional neural networks. Besides, we also employ the contrastive loss to explicitly force that the distance between the features of images from the same category is smaller than that between the features of images from different categories. Consequently, the two types of information provide complementary information, which is beneficial. According to the table, our proposed method achieves an accuracy of 98.08%, greatly outperforming the other methods.

Performance Comparison Under Various Levels of Noise. We further compare the performance of different methods under various levels of noise. More specifically, the images in the test set are contaminated with Gaussian noise with mean 0 and different standard deviations σ, viz. 0.001, 0.01 and 0.1. The results are illustrated in Fig. 4. One can observe that the performance of all the methods deteriorates with the increase of the noise levels. However, the proposed method still consistently surpasses the other methods across all the noise levels.

4   Conclusion

The issue of Chinese calligraphy style classification is addressed in this paper. We are mainly concerned with the style classification of four famous Chinese ancient calligraphers, which is challenging due to the subtle difference among them. In order to solve this problem, we propose a novel multi-loss siamese convolutional neural network which optimizes two types of loss simultaneously. By employing the contrastive loss, the distance between the features of the images from the same category is explicitly forced to be smaller than that between the features of images from different categories. In addition, each stream of the siamese network is extended with a classification subnetwork to fully exploit the supervised information of a single image. The cross-entropy loss is employed for the classification subnetwork. The proposed network shows promising results in the extensive experiments, which compares favorably to the state-of-the-art methods.

Acknowledgments. This work is supported by National Natural Science Foundation of China under Grant 61603256 and the Natural Sciences and Engineering Research Council of Canada.

References

1. https://cadal.edu.cn/index/home
2. Dai, F., Tang, C., Lv, J.: Classification of calligraphy style based on convolutional neural network. In: International Conference on Neural Information Processing, pp. 359–370 (2018)
3. Zhang, J., Guo, M., Fan, J.: A novel CNN structure for fine-grained classification of Chinese calligraphy styles. Int. J. Doc. Anal. Recogn. **22**(2), 177–188 (2019)
4. Lyu, P., Bai, X., Yao, C., Zhu, Z., Huang, T., Liu, W.: Auto-encoder guided GAN for Chinese calligraphy synthesis. In: International Conference on Document Analysis and Recognition, pp. 1095–1100 (2017)
5. Zhang, X., Nagy, G.: Style comparisons in calligraphy. In: Document Recognition and Retrieval XIX, vol. 8297, p. 82970O. International Society for Optics and Photonics (2012)
6. Krizhevsky, A., Sutskever, I., Hinton, G.E.: Imagenet classification with deep convolutional neural networks. Adv. Neural. Inf. Process. Syst. **25**, 1097–1105 (2012)
7. Song, W., Lian, Z., Tang, Y., Xiao, J.: Content-independent font recognition on a single Chinese character using sparse representation. In: International Conference on Document Analysis and Recognition, pp. 376–380 (2015)
8. Huang, S., Zhong, Z., Jin, L., Zhang, S., Wang, H.: DropRegion training of inception font network for high-performance Chinese font recognition. Pattern Recognit. **77**, 395–411 (2018)
9. Dey, S., Dutta, A., Toledo, J.I., Ghosh, S.K., Llads, J., Pal, U.: Signet: convolutional siamese network for writer independent offline signature verification. arXiv preprint arXiv:1707.02131 (2017)
10. Zheng, Z., Zheng, L., Yang, Y.: A discriminatively learned CNN embedding for person reidentification. ACM Trans. Multimedia Comput. Commun. Appl. **14**(1), 1–20 (2017)
11. Simonyan, K., Zisserman, A.: Very deep convolutional networks for large-scale image recognition. arXiv preprint arXiv:1409.1556 (2014)
12. He, K., Zhang, X., Ren, S., Sun, J.: Deep residual learning for image recognition. In: International Conference on Computer Vision and Pattern Recognition, pp. 770–778 (2016)
13. Chollet, F.: Xception: deep learning with depthwise separable convolutions. In: International Conference on Computer Vision and Pattern Recognition, pp. 1251–1258 (2017)

Malingering Scraper: A Novel Framework to Reconstruct Honest Profiles from Malingerer Psychopathological Tests

Matteo Cardaioli[1,4]($\boxtimes$), Stefano Cecconello[1], Merylin Monaro[2], Giuseppe Sartori[2], Mauro Conti[1], and Graziella Orrù[3]

[1] Department of Mathematics, University of Padua, Padua, Italy
matteo.cardaioli@phd.unipd.it
[2] Department of General Psychology, University of Padua, Padua, Italy
[3] Department of Surgical, Medical, Molecular and Critical Area Pathology, University of Pisa, Pisa, Italy
[4] GFT Italy, Milan, Italy

Abstract. Malingered responses to psychological testing are frequent when monetary incentives or other forms of rewards are at stake. Psychological symptoms are usually identified through clinical questionnaires which, however, may be easily inflated by malingered responses (fake-bad). A fake-bad response style is usually identified through specialized scales embedded in the personality questionnaires, but no procedure is currently available that reconstructs honest responses from malingered responses.

In this paper, we present a technique for the Millon (MCMI-III) questionnaire a widely used test for investigating psychopathology. This technique detects malingered MCMI-III profiles (malingering detector) and removes the intentionally inflated test results (malingering remover). We demonstrate that by applying machine learning to the validity scales of MCMI-III we can discriminate between malingerer and honest profiles with 90% accuracy. Moreover, our results show that by applying regression models to malingerer tests, we are able to well reconstruct the original honest profile. Our models decrease the RMSE (Root Mean Square Error) of the reconstruction up to 19% compared to base correction procedures. Finally, applying the malingering detector to the reconstructed scales, we show that only 9% were classified as malingerers, demonstrating the validity of the proposed approach.

Keywords: Malingering remover · Millon · Machine learning

1 Introduction

Deception to direct questions may take two different forms: faking-bad and faking-good. Faking-bad characterizes some forensic settings (e.g., criminal, insurance claims) in which the examinee is likely to exaggerate or make up his psychological disorder [11]. Clinical interviews generally yield low detection rates of malingerers, meaning that many cases will be misclassified if clinicians rely solely on

© Springer Nature Switzerland AG 2021
T. Mantoro et al. (Eds.): ICONIP 2021, CCIS 1517, pp. 433–440, 2021.
https://doi.org/10.1007/978-3-030-92310-5_50

their subjective judgement [10]. Indeed, intuitive clinical judgment yields detection rates of faking-bad that are comparable to the disappointingly low hit rates (i.e., 60%) found for intuitive judgment in the broader deception–detection literature [15]. Malingering is the dishonest and intentional production or exaggeration of physical or psychological symptoms to obtain external gain [13]. Despite it being categorically coded by both ICD10 [8] and DSM5 [1], malingering is not a binary "present" or "absent" phenomenon: it must be considered within specific domains (e.g., psychological, cognitive, and medical), often coexists with genuine disorders and can be classified into different types. Due to these considerable variations, appraising the prevalence of malingering in clinical and forensic populations is difficult.

Usually, psychological symptoms are identified, in psychopathological inventories, through responses to direct questions where the examinee is required to respond YES/NO to sentences targeting relevant symptoms. However, the evaluation based only on responses to direct questions is failing miserably in some contexts. Specifically, the responder has an incentive to aggravate his symptoms to gain economic advantage or any other form of gain. To counter this problem, a wide array of tests has been developed that provide scores on the credibility level of the endorsed symptoms. When employing these instruments, empirically-based cut-offs aid in determining whether symptoms are likely to be genuine or not [6]. As regards the detection of malingering, several detection techniques for psychological testing are based on validity scales embedded in general psychopathological questionnaires (e.g., MCMI-III [7]) or specific tests (e.g., SIMS [12]) as reported by [9] and [5]. Such detection strategies usually evaluate the endorsement of very atypical symptoms. For example, the SIMS may distinguish malingerers from honest responding with good accuracy [14], collecting responses to questions that cover a broad spectrum of pseudo-psychopathology (e.g., items indexing atypical depression, improbable memory problems, pseudoneurological symptoms, hyperbolic signs of mental retardation).

Malingering is a continuous variable and the level of malingering is modulated by the stake and by the strategy under the implicit or explicit control of the malingerer. For this reason, efforts have been made to develop specific tests that flag the responder as a faker. Such tests may be specific (e.g., SIMS) or may take the form of a validity scale embedded in a psychopathological questionnaire (e.g., MCMI-III). While such procedures may spot the faker with decent accuracy, to the best of our knowledge, no procedure has been proposed to reconstruct the honest response profile once a faker has been identified and only the faked profile is available. In short, a non-depressed subject who wants to appear depressed may be spotted as a faker. However, there is no valid procedure that may be used to uncover his true level of depression resulting from honest responses.

Main Contributions

- We propose a new framework for detecting malingered MCMI-III profiles and removing the intentionally inflated test results.
- We demonstrate our approach with an extensive data collection on 100 volunteers participating in the MCMI-III questionnaire.

- We make our dataset publicly available (at this link) to the research community. We hope this is beneficial to investigate the problem further and propose new possible solutions.

2   Method

The MCMI-III format requires the examinee to respond to sentences that index psychopathological symptoms. Malingerers can easily alter their true response from non-pathological to pathological, thus inflating the pathological significance of the resulting score. To highlight the effect of such intentional (and unintentional) distortions, the MCMI-III is equipped with a number of validity scales. As with other modern psychological tests, the MCMI-III has three validity scales devised to capture exaggeration (X scale) and symptoms denial, also called social desirability (Y scale). It has been shown that from scores at these two scales, the faker can be identified with an accuracy that depends on several factors [3]. Apart from the three validity scales reported above, the MCMI-III has 11 scales indexing personality patterns, three scales indexing severe personality disorders, three severe clinical syndromes, and finally, seven clinical syndromes for a total of 24 clinical scales.

Our work aims to reconstruct honest MCMI-III profiles starting from dishonest malingered profiles. The procedure we propose consists of two steps: the Malingerer Detection and the Malingerer Removing. The malingerer detector takes in input the 24 clinical and the three validity scales of the MCMI-III questionnaire. This first step consists of a binary classifier that labels the input in honest or malingerer. If the profile is classified as honest, no further elaborations are needed, and the final output corresponds to the original output of clinical and validity scales. On the contrary, the original scales are processed by the malingering remover if a malingerer profile is identified. The malingering remover consists of a regression algorithm that filters the input, removing the malingering distortion and providing a reconstructed honest profile as output.

2.1   Data Collection

One hundred healthy participants (60 females and 40 males, age mean = 27.45, sd = 7.87) were required to respond to the Italian MCMI-III [16] honestly and also to respond faking depression in order to sustain an insurance compensation seeking claim. All the subjects did not report previous psychological or psychiatric assessments. Half of them responded in the honest condition first and half in the honest condition second. The responses were collected using a computer presentation of the MCMI-III with one of the experimenters supervising in the room. Instructions for the condition requiring malingering were the following: *"You are now asked to fake a severe depression due to a family mourning. Please, respond to the questionnaire pretending to be depressed. The final goal is to obtain insurance compensation for the psychological damage you had after the mourning. Be careful to respond in a way that the depression is credible".*

At the end, for each participant, two MCMI-III raw results were available. The first with standard instructions was regarded as honest responding and was used as ground truth in the development of the malingering remover. The second collected with fake-bad instructions was regarded as the malingered MCMI-III to be corrected by the model.

3   Experimental Results

In this section we evaluate the results of different malingerer detection classifiers. Further, we report and compare the performance of different approaches for the malingering remover.

3.1   Malingering Detection

The discrimination of honest and malingerer profiles represents the first step of our method. To perform this task, five machine learning (ML) algorithms were tested using leave-one-out cross-validation (LOOCV) on the collected dataset: decision tree (DT), logistic regression (LR), Support Vector Machine (SVM), random forest (RF), and KNN. Further, an inner 5-fold cross-validation was used on the training set to tune the hyper-parameters using grid search. In particular, for DT max_depth was set in $[2, 3, 4]$, for LR $penalty$ was set in $[l1, l2]$, for SVM C was set in $\{10^{-3}, 10^{-2}, \ldots, 10^2\}$ and γ in $\{10^{-4}, 10^{-3}, \ldots, 10^1\}$, for RF max_depth was set in $[3, 4, 5]$ and $n\_estimators$ in $[5, 10, 20, 50, 100]$, and finally, for KNN $n\_neighbors$ was set in $\{3, \ldots, 12\}$. Malingering detector was trained using only the three validity scales X, Y, and Z. Our results show that honest-malingerer discrimination is a simple task for the considered ML classifiers. Indeed, all the models achieved an accuracy higher than 87%. In particular, decision tree and SVM (kernel RBF) classifiers showed the best performance, achieving 90% of accuracy. Similar performance is also achieved in validation for the two models. Because of its simplicity and intelligibility, we have chosen to use the decision tree for our framework.

3.2   Malingering Remover

In clinical and forensic evaluations, good accuracy at the single-subject level is required. This objective is essential given that it has been shown, in many datasets, that the number of single cases that behave differently from the trend observed in the group is high [4]. As already mentioned, an important but unaddressed issue in malingering research is the reconstruction of the honest test profile on the sole basis of the malingered test profile. To deal with this problem, we introduced two malingering removing algorithms: average removing and multi-output regressor. We applied the LOOCV procedure in all the reported analyses. One honest and one malingerer test of the same participant were excluded iteratively from the training set. The malingerer trial was used as test while honest as the ground truth. The training set consisted of the remaining 99 malingering trials and the corresponding 99 honest trials. In the following, we describe the two proposed malingering removing techniques.

Average Removing. A simple malingering removing technique consists of correcting each malingered profile by subtracting the average score of the honest responses for each scale. To avoid inconsistency, values that were out of their specific scale range were set to the closer scale bound (i.e., values lower than 0 were set to 0). Consider, for example, how Scale 1 for subject one is corrected with the average removing. Subject one had a score of 11 on Scale 1, and the average of malingered responses of this same scale is 15.6. The average for honest responses is 5.7. The estimated corrected score for subject one is 1.1 (11-(15.6–5.7)). In short, this method assumes that, on each specific scale, malingering has the same effect for all the participants. Moreover, possible correlations between scales are not considered using this method. The average Root Mean Square Error (RMSE) achieved by this trivial technique is 4.05 ± 1.78.

Multi-output Regressor. A multi-output regressor was developed to predict all the honest scales based on the malingered test results of the same participant. The multi-output regressor estimates the honest scale scores one by one. As reported in Table 1, we tested different regression models using a grid-search with an inner 5-fold cross-validation on the training set to tune the hyper-parameters. The best model resulted a Support Vector Regressor (SVR) with Radial Basis Function (RBF) kernel, achieving in test an average RMSE of 3.27 ± 1.51.

Table 1. Performance and hyper-parameters ranges for the tested regression models.

Model	Parameters	Values	AVG RMSE on test
Random forest	n_estimators	$[10, 20, 30]$	3.41
	max_depth	$[4, \ldots, 7]$	
Ridge	α	$[200, 225, \ldots, 500]$	3.38
SVR RBF	c	$[10^{-3}, 10^{-1}, 1, 10^{2}]$	**3.27**
	γ	$[10^{-4}, 10^{-3}, 10^{-1}, 10^{0}, 10^{1}]$	
KNN Regressor	n_neighbors	$[2, \ldots, 12]$	3.34

3.3 Reconstruction Performance Analysis

In Table 2 we compare the reconstruction performance of average removing and SVM RBF, considering several metrics. Firstly, we compared the average RMSEs between the reconstructed profiles and the honest profiles. In particular, the SVR RBF showed an improvement of 19% in the RMSE metric compared to the average remover. Another method to evaluate the quality of the reconstruction is to perform the malingering detection to the reconstructed honest profile. If a malinger removing technique succeeds, the malingering detector should classify the reconstructed profile as honest. Our results show that 78% of reconstructed profiles with average removing were classified as honest, while 91% of reconstructed profiles with SVR were classified as honest.

Finally, in evaluating the MCMI-III questionnaires, one factor that is commonly considered is the order of the scales when rearranged by increasing value. Based on this consideration, we developed a metric that evaluates the capacity of our malingerer removing algorithms to reproduce the order of the honest profile scales. This metric uses the Top N accuracy defined in [2]. Firstly, we normalized the scales on their upper-bound value in the MCMI-III questionnaire. Then, we calculated the Top N accuracy as the percentage of common Top N scales between honest and reconstructed profiles. In Fig. 1, we show the Top N accuracy results for the two proposed malingerer removing algorithms. The metric has been calculated for values of N ranging from 1 to 5. This choice is motivated by the consideration that, among the ordered scales. We also report the Top N accuracy values obtained by directly comparing the honest profiles with the malingerer profiles (without using any malingering remover). The results obtained show that the Top N accuracy calculated on the malingerer profiles is significantly lower than those calculated for the two malingering removing methods. This result confirms that the order of the scales changes significantly between the honest and malingerer tests. Regarding the methods of malingering removing, we can see how SVR always obtains better performance when compared with the average remover. For values of N up to 3 (which are the most interesting), SVR performs significantly better than average removal (18% improvement).

Figure 2 depicts our average accuracy in reconstructing the honest profile.

Table 2. Performance comparison of malingerer removing techniques.

Model	Average RMSE	Reconstuction Accuracy (%)	Top 3 scales Accuracy (%)
Average	4.05	78	54
SVR RBF	**3.27**	**91**	**72**

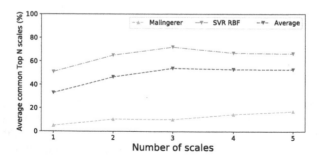

Fig. 1. Percentage of average common Top N scales between honest/reconstructed profiles and honest/malingerer profiles.

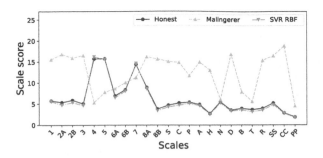

Fig. 2. Average values of the 24 clinical scales for honest, malingerer and reconstructed profiles with SVR.

4   Conclusion

In this paper, we presented a proof-of-concept using the MCMI-III, a widely used test for investigating psychopathology that is complemented with validity scales used to detect malingering. We demonstrate that using decision tree as a malingerer detector, we achieve an accuracy of 90% in discriminating between honest and malingerer profiles. Further, the main results regarding the malingering removal procedures were:

- The malingered profile, after malingering removal, is identified by a classifier as an honest profile with high accuracy (91% for SVM regressor);
- ML models were very good at group level in removing malingering and approximating the honest test results;
- In predicting individual responses, ML-based models were better than a simple correction strategy (average removing) consisting of subtracting to the subjects' scale score the average difference between the group score in the honest and malingerer condition. In short, ML models succeeded in personalizing the process of malingering removal;
- The scales' ranking in the honest condition was mostly maintained after malingering removal, identifying the highest three scales 72% of the times.

It is relevant to stress that the malingering removers proposed here permit individualized modulation of the prediction. This is relevant to the current debate about the lack of group-to-individual generalizability that has been shown to undermine the validity of scientific research in many fields [4]. In short, the ML models used for malingering removal have shown extremely good reconstruction accuracy at the group level and good reconstruction accuracy at the individual level. Given the correction of the ML models, SVR reduces the error by 19% with respect to the correction using the average remover (i.e., correcting all the subjects with the same procedure), we can say that this strategy gives the desired individualized predictions. It is worth noting that the personalization of results is not a trivial task, given that different subjects may fake with different levels of intensity and on different symptoms for a variety of reasons.

References

1. American Psychiatric Association: Diagnostic and statistical manual of mental disorders (DSM-5®). American Psychiatric Pub (2013)
2. Boyd, S., Cortes, C., Mohri, M., Radovanovic, A.: Accuracy at the top. In: Advances in Neural Information Processing Systems, pp. 953–961 (2012)
3. Daubert, S.D., Metzler, A.E.: The detection of fake-bad and fake-good responding on the millon clinical multiaxial inventory III. Psychol. Assess. 12(4), 418 (2000)
4. Fisher, A.J., Medaglia, J.D., Jeronimus, B.F.: Lack of group-to-individual generalizability is a threat to human subjects research. Proc. Natl. Acad. Sci. 115(27), E6106–E6115 (2018)
5. Mazza, C., et al.: Indicators to distinguish symptom accentuators from symptom producers in individuals with a diagnosed adjustment disorder: A pilot study on inconsistency subtypes using sims and MMPI-2-RF. PLoS ONE 14(12), e0227113 (2019)
6. Merten, T., Merckelbach, H.: Symptom validity testing in somatoform and dissociative disorders: a critical review. Psychol. Injury Law 6(2), 122–137 (2013)
7. Millon, T., Davis, R.D.: The mcmi-iii: present and future directions. J. Pers. Assess. 68(1), 69–85 (1997)
8. Organization, W.H., et al.: The ICD-10 classification of mental and behavioural disorders: clinical descriptions and diagnostic guidelines. Weekly Epidemiol. Rec. = Relevé épidémiologique hebdomadaire 67(30), 227–227 (1992)
9. Orrù, G., Mazza, C., Monaro, M., Ferracuti, S., Sartori, G., Roma, P.: The development of a short version of the sims using machine learning to detect feigning in forensic assessment. Psychol. Injury Law 14, 1–12 (2020). https://doi.org/10.1007/s12207-020-09389-4
10. Rosen, G.M., Phillips, W.R.: A cautionary lesson from simulated patients. J. Am. Acad. Psychiatry Law 32(2), 132–133 (2004)
11. Sartori, G., Zangrossi, A., Orrù, G., Monaro, M.: Detection of malingering in psychic damage ascertainment. In: Ferrara, S.D. (ed.) P5 Medicine and Justice, pp. 330–341. Springer, Cham (2017). https://doi.org/10.1007/978-3-319-67092-8_21
12. Smith, G.P., Burger, G.K.: Detection of malingering: validation of the structured inventory of malingered symptomatology (SIMS). J. Am. Acad. Psychiatry Law 25(2), 183–189 (1997)
13. Tracy, D.K., Rix, K.J.: Malingering mental disorders: clinical assessment. BJPsych Adv. 23(1), 27–35 (2017)
14. Van Impelen, A., Merckelbach, H., Jelicic, M., Merten, T.: The structured inventory of malingered symptomatology (SIMS): a systematic review and meta-analysis. Clin. Neuropsychol. 28(8), 1336–1365 (2014)
15. Vrij, A.: Detecting Lies and Deceit: The Psychology of Lying and Implications for Professional Practice. Wiley, Hoboken (2000)
16. Zennaro, A., Ferracuti, S., Lang, M., Sanavio, E.: Millon Clinical Multiaxial Inventory-III [MCMI-III Italian Adaptation]. Giunti OS, Firenze (2008)

Aspect-Based Sentiment Analysis Using Graph Convolutional Networks and Co-attention Mechanism

Zhaowei Chen[1], Yun Xue[1(✉)], Luwei Xiao[1], Jinpeng Chen[1], and Haolan Zhang[2]

[1] School of Physics and Telecommunication Engineering, South China Normal University, Guangzhou, China
`xueyun@m.scnu.edu.cn`
[2] The Center for SCDM, NIT, Zhejiang University, Ningbo, China
`haolan.zhang@nit.zju.edu.cn`

Abstract. Aspect-based sentiment analysis (ABSA) refers to classifying the sentiment polarity of a specific aspect in a sentence. Recently, attention-based deep learning approaches are proposed to capture the semantic information and achieve satisfying results. However, due to the significance of syntactic structure, syntactic information is also analyzed for ABSA. As such, this work proposes a model that integrates the graph convolution network (GCN) and the co-attention mechanism to deal with the aspect-based information and remove the noise from unrelated context words. Both the semantic information and the syntactic information are conveyed by the representation for sentiment analysis. Experimental results show our model achieves a better working performance, which establishes a strong evidence of the capability.

Keywords: Aspect-based sentiment analysis · Co-attention · GCN

1 Introduction

Aspect-based sentiment analysis (ABSA) is currently applied a variety of natural language processing domains, especially where a large amount of text data on the Internet are collected for sentiment analysis [1]. As an example, in the sentence "The food was delicious, but the service was terrible", the sentiment polarities for aspects "food" and "service" are classified as positive and negative respectively. Thereby, the ABSA identifies its distinctiveness in sentiment classification [2].

The flourishing of NLP are largely driven by the advances of deep learning methods [3]. Recent publications report that both recurrent neural networks and convolutional neural networks have their distinctiveness in ABSA tasks. Specifically, two commonly used recurrent neural networks, namely long short-term memory (LSTM) [4] and gated recurrent unit (GRU) [5], are widely applied to capture the semantic and sentiment information from sequence. In this context, attention mechanisms show the superiority in precisely capturing aspect sentiment within of either simple or complex sentence structure [6]. So much is

© Springer Nature Switzerland AG 2021
T. Mantoro et al. (Eds.): ICONIP 2021, CCIS 1517, pp. 441–448, 2021.
https://doi.org/10.1007/978-3-030-92310-5_51

its significance in learning aspect-specific representations that integrating attention mechanisms into RNN is highlighted. More recently, researchers propose to apply graph convolutional network (GCN) into ABSA tasks [7]. By using syntactic dependency tree, a GCN model not only captures the relation among different words, but also links specific aspects to syntax-related words. Thus, we obtain syntactic information of sentence and more accurate representations of aspects.

Whereas, there still exist limits for the syntactic dependency tree. For one thing, since the layers in GCN models are not devised distinctively for processing the aspect, irrelevant information can be integrated into the representation. Hence, the suboptimal aspect representation will result in an accuracy drop. For another, texts in various cases have distinguishing dependencies on syntactic information. Specifically, colloquial expressions are typically of irregular syntax structure, which is difficult to extract their syntactic information.

This work aims to devise a model that is capable of addressing the aforementioned issues. To explicitly regulate each layer in GCN, the gate vectors involving with aspects are generated to extract relevant information from contexts and remove the noise. As such, the aspect representations with more related information are established. Considering the colloquial texts, both syntax structure and semantic information are captured and utilized in the sentiment delivery of specific aspects. That is, the sentiment analysis performance is optimized by integrating aspect-related semantic and syntactic information.

2   Related Works

2.1   Attention Mechanism

Attention mechanisms, due to its focusing on specific aspect and its related information, are most pronounced in RNN-based models [8]. Wang et al. propose attention-based LSTM with aspect embedding (ATAE-LSTM) to precisely compute attention weights [6]. Ma et al. establish an Interactive attention networks (IAN) to interactively learn the attention weights of the aspect and its contexts [9]. Li et al. devise a co-attentive-based network to obtain the precise and essential presentations, which presents a high accuracy in ABSA tasks [3].

2.2   Graph Convolutional Network

The popularity of GCN is due to its capable of processing the graph-based data [10]. Advances in NLP significantly promote the rapid spread of GCN in various fields [11]. Each text, each sentence or each word can be considered as a single node in the graph. Recent publications show that the GCN model is effective in capturing the relation between nodes within a graph. Moreover, dependency tree establishment within GCN model is verified as both creative and practical in comprehensively understanding the node relation. In the context of ABSA, this method has profound effects and give rise to new opportunities to improve the working performance.

3 Model

Figure 1 show the architecture our proposed model. Each components of our model are described below.

3.1 Word Embedding and GRU Layer

Supposing that an n-word sentence $c = \{ w_1^c, w_2^c, \cdots, w_{\tau+1}^c, \cdots, w_{\tau+m}^c, \cdots, w_{n-1}^c, w_n^c \}$ with an m-word aspect $a = \{ w_1^a, w_2^a, \cdots, w_m^a \}$, we embed each word token into a vector space with embedding matrix $E \in R^{|V| \times d_e}$ where $(\tau + 1)$ is start token of the aspect, $|V|$ is the size of vocabulary and d_e is the word vector dimension. The word vectors of aspect and contexts are sent to the GRUs to generate the hidden states. The hidden representation of c is $H^c = \{ h_1^c, h_2^c, \cdots, h_{\tau+1}^c, \cdots, h_{\tau+m}^c, \cdots, h_{n-1}^c, h_n^c \}$ and that of a as $H^a = \{ h_1^a, h_2^a, \cdots, h_m^a \}$. $h_t^c, h_t^a \in R^{d_h}$ indicates the hidden state of GRU at time step t and the dimensionality of hidden state vector output by GRU is d_h.

3.2 Syntactical Feature Establishing

At this stage, the syntactic information, in line with the syntactic dependency tree, is encoded within the GCN module (Fig. 2). The gate mechanism is carried out, based on which hidden state representation of the aspect is generated.

A position decay function (Eq. (1)) is set prior to GCN, aiming to assign more importance to the context words of a shorter distance.

$$q_i = \begin{cases} \left(1 - \frac{\tau+1-i}{n}\right)^\gamma & 1 \le i \le \tau + 1 \\ 1 & \tau + 1 \le i \le \tau + m \\ \left(1 - \frac{i-\tau-m}{n}\right)^\gamma & \tau + m \le i \le n \end{cases} \tag{1}$$

where $q_i \in R$ is the position weight of the i-th word, γ is a hyperparameter. The decayed contextual word representation is expressed as:

$$s_i^l = F\left(h_i^l\right) = q_i h_i^l \tag{2}$$

The GCN model aims to deal with the syntactic dependency tree and to further generate the context representation containing syntactic information. For the sentence c of n words, we construct the syntactic dependency tree to obtain its adjacency matrix $A \in R^{n \times n}$. Supposing that the GCN is of L layers and $l \in 1, 2, \cdots, L$, we define h_i^l as the hidden state of node i in the l layer. The graph convolution of node i can be described as:

$$\widetilde{h_l^i} = \sigma\left(\sum_{j=1}^n A_{ij} W^l s_j^{l-1}\right) \tag{3}$$

$$h_l^i = ReLU\left(\frac{\widetilde{h_l^i}}{(d_i + 1)} + b^l\right) \tag{4}$$

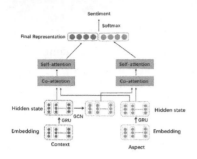

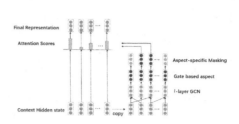

Fig. 1. Model architecture   **Fig. 2.** GCN module

σ refers to the activation function and $d_i = \sum_{j=1}^{n} A_{ij}$ represents the degree of the node i in the syntactic dependency tree.

During the graph convolution, the context hidden state is generated without identifying the aspect beforehand, which can result in preserving irrelevant information within the context representation. For this reason, the hidden state of each GCN layer is adjusted to focus more on the specific aspect. The gate mechanism, which is performed via point-by-point multiplication, is applied to the hidden state of each layer. The finetuned hidden state of l-th layer can be:

$$g_l = \sigma \left(W_g^l H^a + b \right) \tag{5}$$

$$\overline{h_i^l} = g_l \circ h_i^l \tag{6}$$

Then a mask layer is applied to the aspects for extracting aspect-oriented features. In this layer, we preserve the hidden states of the aspects and mask out those of other context words. $h_t^L = 0, 1 \le t < \tau+1, \tau+m < t \le n$, $H_{mask}^L = \{0, \cdots h_{\tau+1}^L, \cdots, h_{\tau+m}^L, \cdots, 0 \}$. The outcome H_{mask}^L is involved with both the syntactic dependency and the long-range multi-word relation. Hereafter, aspect-oriented features are sent to the attention module for generating an accurate representation of the context hidden state H^g. The syntactic information-based context representation, in relation to the aspect, is established.

$$\beta_t = \sum_{i=1}^{n} (h_t^c)^T h_i^L = \sum_{i=\tau+1}^{\tau+m} (h_t^c)^T h_i^L \tag{7}$$

$$\alpha_t = \frac{exp(\beta_t)}{\sum_{i=1}^{n} exp(\beta_i)} \tag{8}$$

$$h_t^g = \alpha_t h_t^c \tag{9}$$

Thus, the context hidden state is $H^g = \{ h_1^g, h_2^g, \cdots, h_n^g \}$.

3.3 Information Interaction

Two co-attention modules are employed for interactive learning between aspect and its contexts. The attention weight between hidden representations H^a and H^g is:

$$H^{ga} = \sigma(H^g W^{ga} H^{aT} + b^{ga}) \tag{10}$$

where $W^{ga} \in R^{d_h \times d_h}$ is the trainable parameter matrix, $b^{ga} \in R^{m \times n}$ is the bias and σ is the activation function. Thus the context representation R^{ga} containing syntactic information is:

$$R^{ga} = \sigma\left(W^g H^g + W^a H^{ga} H^a + b\right) \tag{11}$$

where $W^g \in R^{d_h \times d_h}$ and $W^a \in R^{d_h \times d_h}$ are trainable parameter matrices, $b \in R^{m \times d_h}$ is the bias.

The output context representation $r^g \in R^n$ via self-attention mechanism is obtained by the attention weight $\alpha \in R^n$, then

$$\alpha = softmax\left(w^g R^{ga} + b\right) \tag{12}$$

$$r^g = \sum_{i=1}^{n} \alpha_i R_i^{ga} \tag{13}$$

The basic hidden representation H^c is also sent to the co-attention module for interactive learning with H^a and to eliminate the noise from irregular syntactic structure. Similarly, the co-attention weight between H^c and H^a is:

$$H^{ca} = \sigma(H^c W^{ca} H^{aT} + b^{ca}) \tag{14}$$

The context representation R^{ca} is obtained as:

$$R^{ca} = \sigma(W^c H^c + W^a H^{ca} H^a + b) \tag{15}$$

Similar to Eq. (15) and Eq. (16), the context representation with basic semantic information $r^c \in R^n$ is computed through a self-attention module:

$$\beta = softmax(w^c R^{ca} + b) \tag{16}$$

$$r^c = \sum_{i=1}^{n} \beta_i R_i^{ca} \tag{17}$$

where β refers to the self-attention weight. The context representation for ABSA is obtained by concatenating r^c and r^g as $r = [r^c; r^g]$.

3.4 Output Layer

The final representation r is sent to a Softmax classifier for the purpose of aspect sentiment classification.

$$x = tanh(W_r r + b_r) \tag{18}$$

$$y = softmax(x) = \frac{exp(x_i)}{\sum_{i=1}^{C} exp(x_i)} \tag{19}$$

3.5   Model Training

Training is performed by using the cross entropy and L_2 regularization as the loss function, which is:

$$L = -\sum_i \sum_{j=1}^c y_i^j log \widehat{y}_i^j + \lambda \|\theta\|^2 \tag{20}$$

where i is the indicator of ith sample while j is that of jth sentiment class; C is the number of sentiment classes; y is the real sentiment while $\widehat{y}$ is the predicted one; θ is the trainable parameter collection; and the coefficient of L_2 regularization is λ.

4   Experiments

We conducted experiments on five public datasets, i.e. Twitter [12], Rest14 and lap14 from SemEval 2014 task4 [13], Rest15 from SemEval 2015 task 12 [14] and Rest16 from SemEval 2016 task 5 [15].

4.1   Baselines

The following baseline methods are taken to evaluate our proposed model. AOA-LSTM [16] takes bi-LSTMs and attention over attention networks for sentiment analysis. IAN [9] establishes LSTM based interactive attention networks to obtain the representation and relation. TNet-LF [17] employs a CNN layer to extract salient features from the transformed word representations originated from a bi-directional RNN layer. ASGCN [7] is established on the GCN structure, which aims to capture the syntactic information and long-range word dependencies. G-ATT [18] learns the weights of different edges in GCN to prevent the propagation of irrelevant words. BiGCN [19] employs syntactic graphs and lexical graphs to work in a collaborative manner.

4.2   Results

Experimental results of our model compared to the baseline methods are shown in Fig. 3. Our model is the best-performing method on Lap14, Rest14, Rest15 and Rest16. For these four datasets, there exist considerable performance gaps between our model and the baselines.

Generally, the syntactic-based models are more competitive than the attention-based models, indicating the syntactic dependency tree can be applied to capture the relation and eliminate the impacts from irrelevant words. In contrast, the GCN-attention integration methods perform significantly better, which provides a more accurate way to identify the sentiment. Among all these models, our model shows it superiority by improving the GCN module and using the multi-attention network. Clearly, the exploiting of syntactical features efficiently filters the noise from unrelated context words and focuses more on the

Model	TWITTER		LAP14		REST14		REST15		REST16	
	Acc	F1	Acc	F1	Acc	F1	Acc	F1	Acc	F1
AOA	72.30	70.20	72.62	67.52	79.97	70.42	78.17	57.02	87.50	66.21
IAN	72.50	70.81	72.05	67.38	79.26	70.09	78.54	52.65	84.74	55.21
TNet-LF	72.98	71.43	74.61	70.14	80.42	71.03	78.47	59.47	89.07	70.43
ASGCN-DT	71.53	69.68	74.14	69.24	80.86	72.19	79.34	60.78	88.69	66.64
ASGCN-DG	72.15	70.40	75.55	71.05	80.77	72.02	79.89	61.89	88.99	67.48
G-ATT-U	73.60	72.12	76.18	72.23	81.59	72.65	81.18	64.07	89.06	71.97
G-ATT-D	73.89	71.82	75.75	71.52	80.89	71.68	80.93	64.03	88.81	**72.36**
BiGCN	**74.16**	**73.35**	74.59	71.84	81.97	73.48	81.16	64.79	88.96	70.84
Ours	73.55	71.34	**76.96**	**72.85**	**82.41**	**73.81**	**81.55**	**66.14**	**89.94**	71.80

Fig. 3. Sentiment classification results (%)

related words. Besides, the processing via attention mechanisms enhance the interactive learning between the aspect and its contexts. In this way, a better working performance in ABSA tasks can be expected. Whereas, our model fails to overperform QG-ATT and BiGCN on the dataset Twitter. We speculate the possible reason is that colloquial expressions are widely-used in Twitter.

5 Conclusion

In this work, a model integrates GCN and co-attention networks is dedicatedly devised for ABSA tasks. To exploit the syntactic information of sentences, the aspect-based GCN is carried out to remove the noise from unrelated contexts words. Besides, the co-attention mechanism that captures the relation among different words, is performed for interactive learning of semantic and syntactic information between aspect and its contexts. The final representation delivering the syntactic and semantic information is taken for sentiment classification. Experiments on a variety of datasets are carried out to verify that our model is a best alternative with high accuracy comparing to baseline methods. An even better sentiment classification performance is thus obtained.

Acknowledgments. This work was supported by Humanity and Social Science Foundation of the Ministry of Education of China (21A13022003), Zhejiang Provincial Natural Science Fund (LY19F030010), Zhejiang Provincial Social Science Fund (20NDJC216YB), Zhejiang Educational Science Fund (GH2021642), the Science and Technology Plan Project of Guangzhou under Grant Nos. 202102080258 and 201903010013.

References

1. Liu, B.: Sentiment analysis and opinion mining. Synth. Lect. Hum. Lang. Technol. **5**(1), 1–167 (2012)
2. Xianghua, F., Yang, J., Li, J., Fang, M., Wang, H.: Lexicon-enhanced LSTM with attention for general sentiment analysis. IEEE Access **6**, 71884–71891 (2018)

3. Li, H., Xue, Y., Zhao, H., Hu, X., Peng, S.: Co-attention networks for aspect-level sentiment analysis. In: Tang, J., Kan, M.-Y., Zhao, D., Li, S., Zan, H. (eds.) NLPCC 2019. LNCS (LNAI), vol. 11839, pp. 200–209. Springer, Cham (2019). https://doi.org/10.1007/978-3-030-32236-6_17

4. Zeng, J., Ma, X., Zhou, K.: Enhancing attention-based LSTM with position context for aspect-level sentiment classification. IEEE Access **7**, 20462–20471 (2019)

5. Minh, D.L., Sadeghi-Niaraki, A., Huy, H.D., Min, K., Moon, H.: Deep learning approach for short-term stock trends prediction based on two-stream gated recurrent unit network. IEEE Access **6**, 55392–55404 (2018)

6. Wang, Y., Huang, M., Zhu, X., Zhao, L.: Attention-based LSTM for aspect-level sentiment classification. In: EMNLP, pp. 606–615 (2016)

7. Zhang, C., Li, Q., Song, D.: Aspect-based sentiment classification with aspect-specific graph convolutional networks. arXiv preprint arXiv:1909.03477 (2019)

8. Ma, X., Zeng, J., Peng, L., Fortino, G., Zhang, Y.: Modeling multi-aspects within one opinionated sentence simultaneously for aspect-level sentiment analysis. Futur. Gener. Comput. Syst. **93**, 304–311 (2019)

9. Ma, D., Li, S., Zhang, X., Wang, H.: Interactive attention networks for aspect-level sentiment classification. arXiv preprint arXiv:1709.00893 (2017)

10. Bruna, J., Zaremba, W., Szlam, A., LeCun, Y.: Spectral networks and locally connected networks on graphs. arXiv preprint arXiv:1312.6203 (2013)

11. Bastings, J., Titov, I., Aziz, W., Marcheggiani, D., Sima'an, K.: Graph convolutional encoders for syntax-aware neural machine translation. arXiv preprint arXiv:1704.04675 (2017)

12. Dong, L., Wei, F., Tan, C., Tang, D., Zhou, M., Xu, K.: Adaptive recursive neural network for target-dependent twitter sentiment classification. In: ACL (vol. 2: Short papers), pp. 49–54 (2014)

13. Maria Pontiki, D.G., John Pavlopoulos, H.P., Ion Androutsopoulos, S.M.: Semeval-2014 task 4: Semeval-2014 task 4: aspect based sentiment analysis. In: SemEval 2014, Dublin, Ireland, pp. 23–24 (2014)

14. Pontiki, M., Galanis, D., Papageorgiou, H., Manandhar, S., Androutsopoulos, I.: Semeval-2015 task 12: aspect based sentiment analysis. In: SemEval 2015, pp. 486–495 (2015)

15. Pontiki, M., et al.: Semeval- 2016 task 5: aspect based sentiment analysis. In: International Workshop on Semantic Evaluation, pp. 19–30 (2016)

16. Huang, B., Ou, Y., Carley, K.M.: Aspect level sentiment classification with attention-over-attention neural networks. In: Thomson, R., Dancy, C., Hyder, A., Bisgin, H. (eds.) SBP-BRiMS 2018. LNCS, vol. 10899, pp. 197–206. Springer, Cham (2018). https://doi.org/10.1007/978-3-319-93372-6_22

17. Li, X., Bing, L., Lam, W., Shi, B.: Transformation networks for target-oriented sentiment classification. arXiv preprint arXiv:1805.01086 (2018)

18. Yuan, L., Wang, J., Yu, L.C., Zhang, X.: Graph attention network with memory fusion for aspect-level sentiment analysis. In: AACL and the IJCNLP, pp. 27–36 (2020)

19. Zhang, M., Qian, T.: Convolution over hierarchical syntactic and lexical graphs for aspect level sentiment analysis. In: EMNLP, pp. 3540–3549 (2020)

Pre-trained Models and Evaluation Data for the Myanmar Language

Shengyi Jiang[1,2], Xiuwen Huang[1], Xiaonan Cai[3], and Nankai Lin[1(✉)]

[1] School of Information Science and Technology, Guangdong University of Foreign Studies, Guangzhou, Guangdong, China
[2] Guangzhou Key Laboratory of Multilingual Intelligent Processing, Guangdong University of Foreign Studies, Guangzhou, Guangdong, China
[3] School of Mathematics and Statistics, Guangdong University of Foreign Studies, Guangzhou, Guangdong, China

Abstract. Pre-trained language models (PLMs), which working for downstream natural language processing (NLP) tasks with the large corpus ubiquitously and favorably, have outstanding effectiveness due to their ability to learn universal language contexts as well as representations. Despite their success, most available models have trained on universal language, especially English. This phenomenon brings restriction to practical use of other low-resource languages, like Myanmar which is a language with underdeveloped electric resources and the previous work for it have been hampered by. Our aims in this paper are to train a monolingual pre-trained model for the Myanmar language and improve the state-of-the-art in its NLP tasks including Part-of-speech tagging and news classification. We presented transformer-based PTMs with four versions: BERT-small, BERT-base, ELECTRA-small and ELECTRA-base. Also we are the first to public large-scale Myanmar-specific models. Experimental results demonstrate the outperforms of our models. Our models and datasets will be available at the community to facilitate future research and downstream application for Myanmar NLP.

Keywords: Pre-trained language model · Myanmar · Part-of-speech tagging · Text classification

1 Introduction

In these years, BERT (Bidirectional Encoder Representations from Transformers) [1], the current state-of-the-art of the pre-trained language model (PLM), has been proven the effectiveness in the natural language processing (NLP) tasks. PLMs are qualified to capture contextual representations dynamically from substantial unlabeled text optimized by self-supervised. Pre-trained BERT-based language models are in two forms: (1) Multilingual models [1, 2], which are trained in datasets of different language and have shown high performance on zero-shot cross-lingual task. (2) Monolingual models [1, 3], the series of models trained in specific language that mostly outstrip the multilingual models in NLP tasks.

© Springer Nature Switzerland AG 2021
T. Mantoro et al. (Eds.): ICONIP 2021, CCIS 1517, pp. 449–458, 2021.
https://doi.org/10.1007/978-3-030-92310-5_52

In terms of Myanmar language modeling, to the best of our knowledge, there are some concerns as follows:

(1) Among all the existing monolingual pre-trained models, there are no PLMs for Myanmar language, impeding the practical use in Myanmar NLP systems.

(2) While multilingual and monolingual models have achieved great successes in NLP areas, their performances on datasets containing social media texts are difficult to estimate, because they are mainly trained and tested in Wikipedia corpus.

(3) As Myanmar is a language written from left to right and there are mostly no spaces between words, the valid of pre-trained may become worse if the Byte-Pair encoding (BPE) approaches [1] are straightly applied to. It is vital to use a feasible segmentation to improve the performance of monolingual downstream tasks for Myanmar's NLP.

To handle the three concerns above, our empirical exploration is performed on eight datasets in Myanmar language in this paper. We pre-trained two kinds of transformer-based models: BERT and ELECTRA, each of them has two versions, namely BERT-base, BERT-small, ELECTRA-base and ELECTRA-small. Instead of directly adopting BPE method, we take sentence-piece segmentation on Myanmar pre-training models and then evaluate the models on two NLP tasks, including part-of speech (POS) tagging and text classification.

Our contributions of this work are as follows:

- We train the first four BERT-based pre-trained models for Myanmar language using a large size of corpus.
- The competitive performances of two downstream Myanmar's NLP tasks: POS tagging and text classification prove the effectiveness of large-scale transformer-based monolingual language models for Myanmar.
- We publicly release our pre-trained models and datasets for future Myanmar's NLP research and applications.

2 Related Work

2.1 Text Classification for Myanmar

Based on having read a large amount of documents about text classification for Myanamar concerned, we found that Khine et al. [4] made a comparative study between k-Nearest Neighbors (KNN) and Naïve Bayes Classifier on Myanmar news classification. Then Nwet [5], drew a conclusion that very high-dimensional spaces led Support Vector Machines (SVM) to perform better than Naïve Bayes and KNN in the same task. Phyu et al. [6], compared the performance of Convolutional Neural Networks (CNN) and Recurrent Neural Networks (RNN) for both syllable and word level on Myanmar articles classification. According to the empirical exploration on six news datasets, CNN performed better. After that, Phyu et al. [7], presented a joint CNN and Bi-LSTM model and discussed most of the baseline deep learning models and their combination models on five datasets.

2.2 POS Tagging for Myanmar

Myanmar POS tagging could achieve by implementing a blend of measurable and principle-based technique. Zin et al. [8], proposed an approach for POS tagging of Myanmar using HMM with rule-based approach. The work of Khin et al. [9], compared six POS tagging methods on 11000 sentences and found that RDR approach was the best which achieved an accuracy 97.05% on open data set contained 1000 sentences. Ding et al. [10], displayed the efficiency of joint Myanmar tokenization and POS-tagging on their annotated corpus of 20000 sentences using the standard sequence-labeling approach of CRFs and a LSTM-based RNN approach. Cing and Soe [11] presented a joint word segmentation and POS tagging using HMM with morphological rules which had a significant improvement with 39716 sentences covering 690258 words.

2.3 Transformers-Based Language Model for Myanmar

There is no open-source monolingual pre-trained model for Myanmar right now. Open-source multilingual pre-trained models represented by mBERT [1], XLM-100 [2] and mT5 [12] are trained in a large-scale multilingual dataset aiming to support various downstream NLP tasks for multiple languages by learning independent knowledge. Among them, XLM 100 and mT5 include Myanmar language while mBERT excludes Myanmar. Because of huge language discrepancy between Myanmar and other languages, multilingual pre-trained models do not perform well in Myanmar downstream tasks.

3   Model

We pre-trained two types of transformer-based models, namely BERT [1] and ELECTRA [13].

3.1 Bert

BERT is a language model using the encoder of transformer [14] as the main framework of the algorithm. It demonstrates the outstanding performance of bidirectional pre-training for language representation with a large unsupervised dataset. While pre-training, there are two subtasks, Masked Language Model (MLM) and Next Sentence Prediction (NSP). With fine-tuning procedure, BERT advances the state-of-the-art for NLP tasks.

In this paper, there are two versions of our pre-trained Myanmar-BERT, namely BERT-base (12 layers, 768 hidden units, 12 attention heads) and BERT-small (4 layers, 512 hidden units, 8 attention heads) follow the same architecture respectively. The maximum sequence length is accepted by all our models, which are set 512.

3.2 Electra

ELECTRA (Efficiently Learning an Encoder that Classifies Token Replacements Accurately) is essentially to train the parameters of BERT in another way. The combination of generator and discriminator is adopted.

ELECTRA proposes replaced token detection (RTD), a new self-supervised task for language representation in order to solve the problem about data inefficiency of BERT because only 15% of tokens are predicted per epoch. The pre-training of ELECTRA can be divided into two parts. The generator part is MLM, whose structure is similar to that of BERT. Then the masked words of original input sequence are replaced by the trusted substitutes sampled in it. The discriminator part is to detect whether each word of the result of generator is the original word or not. When predicting, we only used the discriminator part in order to decrease the computational complexity.

We propose two ELECTRA models, one is in the base size (12 layers, 768 hidden units, 12 attention heads) called ELECTRA-base, and the other is in the small size (4 layers, 512 hidden units, 8 attention heads) called ELECTRA-small. Each of their maximum sequence length is adopted 512.

4 Downstream Tasks

4.1 POS Tagging

Table 1. Statistics of the POS tagging dataset.

Data	Num. of sentence	Num. of token
Train	9000	195361
Dev	1000	22272
Test	1000	21415
Total	11000	239048

Part-of-speech tagging is a process of confirming the grammatical class of a word in a text by its definition and context. Part-of-speech tagging is always considered as a sequence labeling task, and all given input sequences are allotted to a part of speech label.

In this task, the dataset we used comes from Htike et al. [9]. They first collected 10,000 sentences from some Myanmar websites. We divided 10000 sentences into two parts, 9000 for train set and 1000 for validation set. On top of that, they collected 1,000 Myanmar sentences to build a test set. 16 Myanmar POS are used in the tag set. Some statistics about this corpus are presented in Table 1. The performance of POS tagging is evaluated using accuracy, precision, recall and F1 score, provided by the seqeval[1] module.

4.2 Classification

In the tasks of classification, we respectively evaluated two types of tasks, one is news category classification and the other is e-commerce comment sentiment classification.

---

[1] https://github.com/chakki-works/seqeval.

Table 2. Statistics of the classification dataset.

Dataset	Category	Num. of articles	Num. of training data	Num. of validation data	Num. of test data
7 Days Daily	–	14512	10154	1455	2903
DVB	–	10934	7649	1095	2190
Htoo Lwin	–	16398	11474	1642	3282
The Voice	–	10346	7238	1036	2072
Miscellaneous	–	48150	33699	4818	9633
Myanmar Wiki	–	15065	10541	1508	3016
Product Sentiment	Negative	346	241	35	70
	Neural	405	282	41	82
	Positive	2815	1969	282	564
	Total	3566	2492	358	716

For the task of news category classification, we used six news classification datasets constructed by PHYU et al. [6], which were from 7 Day Daily news website, DVB news website, Voice news website, Htoo Lwin news website and Myanmar Wikipedia website. The last one is the collection of common topics from five datasets that contains five classes including art, education, health, sport and crime.

During PHYU's experiment, they only divided the data into the train set and the test set. And there was no validation set to help select the best model in the training process. Therefore, we optimized the method and divided the data set into training set, verification set and test set, and the proportion was 7:1:2.

What is more, e-commerce comment sentiment classification is a hot task in natural language processing. However, due to the difficulty of data acquisition and data set construction, there is still no e-commerce comment sentiment classification data set in Myanmar.

Therefore, we crawler a set of comments (total of 3566 comments) on electronic products of shopping[2] website. Similar to Lin et al.'s method [15], we labeled the samples with positive, neutral and negative emotions by using website information. The detailed information of all classification data is shown in Table 2.

5 Results

5.1 Pre-training

To train our models, we tried to collect texts from different sources. On the one hand, we utilized all the Myanmar data from the OSCAR corpus[3], a humongous multilingual corpus whose texts all come from the Common Crawl corpus[4]. In addition, articles on

---

[2] https://www.shop.com.mm/.
[3] https://oscar-corpus.com/.
[4] https://commoncrawl.org/.

Table 3. Statistics of the pre-trained dataset.

Source	Num. of sentences	Size
Oscar	3517762	1.14G
CC100	1984183	0.47G
Wiki	750912	0.19G
All	6252857	1.8G

CC-100 [16] were also used as part of our corpus for pre-training. This corpus was constructed for training XLM-R and consisted of monolingual data for 100+ languages and also include data for Romanized languages. Apart from these, we used the data from Wikipedia for pre-training. The corpus statistics for pre-training are shown in Table 3.

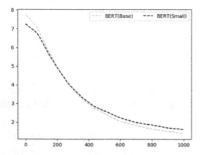

Fig. 1. Pre-training losses for BERT over the steps.

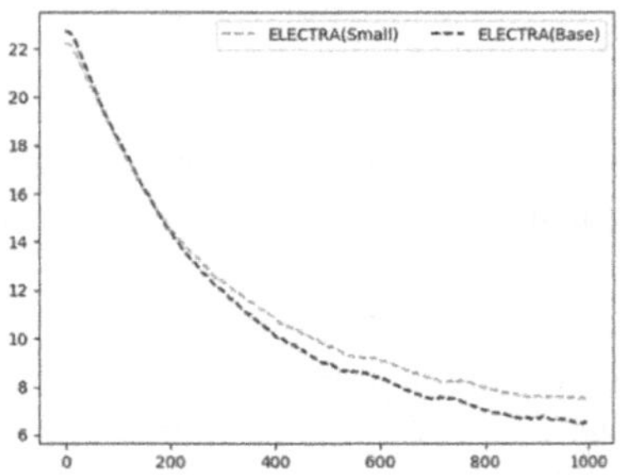

Fig. 2. Pre-training losses for ELECTRA over the steps.

The batch size for pre-training was set as 8. All the models were trained on the pre-training data for 1,000,000 steps. The learning rate of BERT (Small) and ELECTRA (Base) were all warmed up over the first 5,000 steps to a peak value of 1e−4, and then decayed linearly. The learning rate of BERT (Base) is 5e−5, and the learning rate of ELECTRA (Small) was 2e−4. The weights were initialized randomly from a normal distribution with a mean of 0.0 and a standard deviation of 0.02. Instead of directly adopting BPE method, we utilized sentence-piece segmentation on Myanmar pre-training data to tackle the problem of no explicit delimiters between words. We directly adopted the sentence-piece segmentation model[5] trained by Heinzerling and Strube [17], which had the vocabulary size of 25,000. Figures 1 and 2 illustrated the pre-training loss for each model. It could be observed that given the same training time, the deeper and wider models could greatly help to achieve lower training loss than shallower models.

---

[5] https://github.com/bheinzerling/bpemb.

5.2 POS Tagging

Apart from developing the Myanmar POS corpus, Htike et al. [9] also evaluated several POS tagging approaches. To better assess the performance of our models, we attempted to run their released codes to reproduce the results reported in their paper, as our baseline. In their codes, they provided the implementation of 4 approaches, which were Support Vector Machine (SVM), Hidden Markov Model (HMM), Maximum Entropy (MAX-Ent) and Ripple-Down Rules (RDR). For the previous three methods, the features they adopted include the label of the current word and its neighboring words. Their paper only reported the accuracy of these methods; however, we also presented the micro precisions, recalls and F1 scores for a more comprehensive comparison. Table 4 demonstrated the results of our models on this task.

Table 4. The result of POS tagging.

Model	Acc	P	R	F1
RDR	96.98%	95.85%	95.80%	95.92%
MaxEnt	95.01%	93.62%	92.42%	93.01%
HMM	95.91%	94.30%	94.29%	94.30%
SVM	93.18%	89.94%	91.33%	90.58%
ELECTRA (Small)	95.23%	93.50%	93.23%	93.37%
ELECTRA (Base)	95.56%	93.88%	94.13%	94.00%
BERT (Small)	97.42%	96.34%	96.24%	96.29%
BERT (Base)	**97.49%**	**96.40%**	**96.60%**	**96.50%**

5.3 Classification

Table 5. The result of news classification.

Model	F1	Acc
BERT (Small)	93.05	94.08
BERT (Base)	**93.22%**	**94.35%**
ELECTRA (Small)	92.42%	93.87%
ELECTRA (Base)	92.76%	94.03

The average results of our model on six news classification datasets were shown in Table 5. During the fine-tune process, we set the maximum length to 128. For two small models, we fine-tuned for 5 epochs with a learning rate of 1e−4. For BERT (Base) model, we fine-tuned for 5 epochs with a learning rate of 5e−5. For ELECTRA (BASE) model, we fine-tuned for 10 epochs with a learning rate of 3e−5 because it needed a longer training time and a smaller learning rate to converge. In general, the performances of those four models were all excellent, and the BERT (Base) model was the best. From the average results, BERT (BASE) also reached the optimal value, the F1 and the Acc value 93.22% and 94.35% respectively. In addition, we could also know that in the news classification task, the two models of BERT are better than the two models of ELECTRA.

In the task of e-commerce comment sentiment classification, we conducted experiments on the self-constructed dataset. Due to the difficulty of data acquisition, corpus construction and the small scale of the dataset, we particularly tried the Upsampling strategy to augment the data. In normal experiment, our training parameters were the same as the news classification task. But, when integrating the Upsampling strategy with the experiment, we expanded the category with less samples (negative data and neutral data) by three times. Because of the increase of the data amount, the epoch of fine-tuning was reduced from five times to three times. The experimental results were shown in Table 6. And the results dedicated that:

- In the scale of base pre-training model, Upsampling strategy had a significant improvement effect, while in the small-scale model, the strategy did not play a significant improvement.
- The performance of the pre-trained model was still poor in small-scale dataset. How to use data augmentation strategy to assist training was still an important research direction of low resource languages such as Myanmar.
- Each pre-trained model was higher in acc index and lower in F1 index, so the unbalanced data had a great influence on the pre-trained model.
- On a small-scale dataset, the small-scale pre-trained model could converge better.

Table 6. The result of e-commerce comment sentiment classification.

Model	F1	Acc
BERT (Small)	51.77%	84.22%
BERT (Small) + Upsampling	46.44%	84.64%
BERT (Base)	47.57%	83.52%
BERT (Base) + Upsampling	49.98%	84.78%
ELECTRA (Small)	**57.22%**	84.78%
ELECTRA (Small) + Upsampling	51.49%	**84.92%**
ELECTRA (Base)	45.16%	83.80%
ELECTRA (Base) + Upsampling	52.38%	81.84%

6 Conclusion

In this work, we pre-trained four Myanmar-specific monolingual models and investigated the feasibility of them for two NLP tasks: part-of-speech tagging and text classification, which advance the development of Myanmar NLP application. The transformer-based language models and all of the datasets introduced in this paper will be released to the community, hoping to be a hands-on guide or starting point for using and developing PLMs for various Myanmar NLP tasks. In future researches, we would expand the size of the corpus and solve the problem of data categories which is lack of balance.

Acknowledgements. This work was supported by the Key Field Project for Universities of Guangdong Province (No. 2019KZDZX1016), the National Natural Science Foundation of China (No. 61572145) and the National Social Science Foundation of China (No. 17CTQ045).

References

1. Devlin, J., Chang, M., Lee, K., Toutanova, K.: BERT: Pre-training of deep bidirectional transformers for language understanding. In: Proceedings of NAACL, Minneapolis, Minnesota, pp. 4171–4186 (2019)
2. Conneau, A., Lample, G.: Cross-lingual language model pretraining (2019)
3. Cui, Y., et al.: Pre-training with whole word masking for chinese bert (2019)
4. Khine, A.H., Nwet, K.T., Soc, K.M.: Automatic Myanmar news classification. In: International Conference on Computer Applications, ICCA-2017 (2017)
5. Nwet, K.T.: Machine learning algorithms for Myanmar news classification. In: International Journal on Natural Language Computing (IJNLC) (2019)
6. Phyu, M.S., Nwet, K.T.: Articles classification in Myanmar language. In: 2019 International Conference on Advanced Information Technologies (ICAIT), November 2019, pp. 188–193. IEEE (2019)
7. Phyu, M.S., Nwet, K.T.: Comparative analysis of deep learning models for Myanmar text classification. In: Nguyen, N.T., Jearanaitanakij, K., Selamat, A., Trawiński, B., Chittayasothorn, S. (eds.) ACIIDS 2020. LNCS (LNAI), vol. 12033, pp. 76–85. Springer, Cham (2020). https://doi.org/10.1007/978-3-030-41964-6_7
8. Zin, K.K., Thein, N.L.: Hidden Markov model with rule based approach for part of speech tagging of Myanmar language. In: Proceedings of 3rd International Conference on Communications and Information, December 2009, pp. 123–128 (2009)
9. Htike, K.W.W., Thu, Y.K., Zuping Zhang, W.P.P., Sagisaka, Y., Iwahashi, N.: Comparison of six POS tagging methods on 10K sentences Myanmar language (Burmese) POS tagged corpus. In Proceedings of the CICLING, April 2017 (2017)
10. Ding, C., et al.: Towards Burmese (Myanmar) morphological analysis: syllable-based tokenization and part-of-speech tagging. In: ACM Transactions on Asian and Low-Resource Language Information Processing (TALLIP), vol. 19, no. 1, pp. 1–34 (2019)
11. Cing, D.L., Soe, K.M.: Improving accuracy of Part-of-Speech (POS) tagging using hidden Markov model and morphological analysis for Myanmar Language. Int. J. Electr. Comput. Eng. **10**(2), 2023 (2020)
12. Xue, L., et al.: mT5: A massively multilingual pre-trained text-to-text transformer. In: CORR (2021)
13. Clark, K., Luong, M.T., Le, Q.V., Manning, C.D.: ELECTRA: pre-training text encoders as discriminators rather than generators. In: Proceedings of ICLR. Online (2020)

14. Vaswani, A., et al.: Attention is all you need. In: Proceedings of NeurIPS, Long Beach, California, pp. 5998–6008 (2017)
15. Lin, N., Chen, B., Fu, S., Lin, X., Jiang, S.: Multi-domain sentiment classification on self-constructed indonesian dataset. In: Zhu, X., Zhang, M., Hong, Y., He, R. (eds.) NLPCC 2020. LNCS (LNAI), vol. 12430, pp. 789–801. Springer, Cham (2020). https://doi.org/10.1007/978-3-030-60450-9_62
16. Wenzek, G., et al.: CCNet: extracting high quality monolingual datasets from web crawl data. In: CORR (2019)
17. Heinzerling, B., Strube, M.: BPEmb: tokenization-free pre-trained subword embeddings in 275 languages. In: Proceedings of the Eleventh International Conference on Language Resources and Evaluation, European Language Resources Association (ELRA) (2018)

MOOC Student Dropout Rate Prediction via Separating and Conquering Micro and Macro Information

Jiayin Lin[1]($\boxtimes$), Geng Sun[1]($\boxtimes$), Jun Shen[1]($\boxtimes$), David Pritchard[2]($\boxtimes$),
Ping Yu[1]($\boxtimes$), Tingru Cui[3]($\boxtimes$), Li Li[4]($\boxtimes$), and Ghassan Beydoun[5]($\boxtimes$)

[1] School of Computing and Information Technology, University of Wollongong,
Wollongong, Australia
jl461@uowmail.edu.au, {gsun,jshen,ping}@uow.edu.au
[2] Research Lab of Electronics, Massachusetts Institute of Technology,
Cambridge, MA, USA
dpritch@mit.edu
[3] University of Melbourne, Melbourne, Australia
tingru.cui@unimelb.edu.au
[4] Faculty of Computer and Information Science, Southwest University,
Chongqing, China
lily@swu.edu.cn
[5] School of Information System and Modelling, University of Technology Sydney,
Sydney, Australia
ghassan.beydoun@uts.edu.au

Abstract. With the increasing availability of ubiquitous and intelligent mobile devices, MOOC (Massive Open Online Courses) has become a popular choice for people who want to learn in a more flexible manner. However, compared to traditional in-class face-to-face learning, the MOOC platforms always suffer from a high learner dropout rate. Hence, correctly predicting the dropout rate at the early stage of a learning activity is significant for the MOOC adaptors and developers, who can conduct effective intervention strategies to improve the online course's quality and increase the retention rate. In this paper, we designed a double-tower-based framework for dropout rate prediction. The framework separately models the different types of information, namely the macro and the micro information. Our work also leads to the design of a Convolutional Neural Network (CNN)-based model for effectively mining time-series information from the learners' successive activity records. The experimental results demonstrated that the proposed double-tower-based framework also clearly outperformed the various baselines.

Keywords: Deep learning · Data mining · Dropout rate prediction · Neural network

© Springer Nature Switzerland AG 2021
T. Mantoro et al. (Eds.): ICONIP 2021, CCIS 1517, pp. 459–467, 2021.
https://doi.org/10.1007/978-3-030-92310-5_53

1   Introduction

Famous MOOC platforms, such as Coursera, EdX, and Udacity, provide high-quality learning resources to learners globally every day. Despite this advancement, a high dropout rate for MOOC courses persists [1]. The causes for dropout rates have been difficult to precisely pin down or predict. It could be the quality issue of the quiz question, or the unsatisfactory presentation of the course material, or maybe even just some personal issues. As highlighted in the prior research, dropout prediction can be an effective precursor for early intervention [2]; it can also be used as a pedagogy enhancement method to decide whether an online course needs adjustment or modification [3].

In general, an online course is composed of several instructional videos, and each video contains a certain number of complete knowledge points. Such course structure can offer two types of information for the dropout prediction task, micro information and macro information. The coarse-grained macro information refers to the overall profile of a course, like a discipline area it belongs to and the difficulty level of the course. The micro information is fine-grained information, which refers to the interaction detail between a user and a certain video, such as duration and the start time of video watching. Both types of information offer valuable information about the course itself and how a user interacted with this course historically. However, to the best of our knowledge, the research about how to properly handle these two types of information still remains untouched. A double tow-er-based deep learning framework with a carefully designed CNN-based micro component is proposed in this paper to tackle the above research motivation.

2   Related Work

With growing interest in applying the machine learning technique to e-learning problems in the multi-disciplinary research community, learner dropout prediction models have been generated using various techniques [4,5]. They include logistic regression and its variants [6], support vector machine [1,7], and decision trees [8,9]. Deep learning-based models have also shown great potential in mining complex latent information for the task of dropout prediction in more recent years. For example, multi-layer perceptron (MLP) was used with an in-depth comparison concerning various evaluation metrics [10]. Model ConRec was proposed by [4], which combined the merits of the RNN and the CNN. A context-aware feature interaction model was proposed in [11], which utilised context-smoothing to smooth feature with different contexts and combine user and course information by the attention mechanism. However, to the best of our knowledge, for the task of learner dropout prediction, none of the prior studies have tried to distinguish and model the micro and macro information separately.

3   Model Design

3.1   The Architecture of the Double-Tower Framework

Inspired by the prior exceptional work in the recommender systems [12], the proposed framework is in a double-tower structure containing two intelligent components, one for modelling the macro information and another for modelling the micro information (see Fig. 1). The design of the framework structure is based on the idea of 'separate and conquer', which aims to separate different types of information and use the most suitable model to conquer each type of information. The raw input comes from the user's interaction logs and the courses' profile, which contain a mixture of both micro and macro information (indicated in blue and red colour in Fig. 1, respectively). Each component takes and handles different information and produces an intermediate result solely bases on one type of information (micro or macro). At last, two intermediate results are summarized through a regression function and used to produce the final prediction.

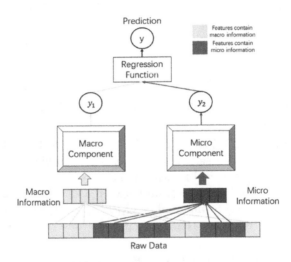

Fig. 1. The overall network structure of the proposed double-tower framework

3.2   Problem Formulation

Objective. Given the input with different types and granularities of information, the goal of the proposed framework is to predict whether a learner will drop a given online course. Defining the ground truth as $y \in \{0,1\}$ (where 1 stands for dropout and 0 for not dropout), and the prior knowledge of course profile and user's historical learning records as x. Given the input signal x and the target output y.

Micro Information. In this study, the term of micro information refers to the interaction details of a certain user u_i with a course c; it is formulated as $L_i(u_i, c)$. As one course may contain several instruction videos, the above definition can be further notated as $L_i(u_i, c) \in R^{n \cdot m}$, $c = v_1, v_2, \ldots, v_n$; where n is the number of the videos (belonging to the course c) that the user u_i has already interacted with, m is the dimensionality of the feature space. The features notated as f_1 f_m represent the interaction detail between the user u_i and a video v_j. Specifically, given a course c, $L_{i,j}$ is the interaction record between a certain user u_i and a certain video v_j, and $L_{i,j}(u_i, v_j) \in L_i(u_i, c)$. Inspired by the research of pattern recognition from computer vision, in this study, the interaction between a user and a course is organized and represented in the form of a 'figure'. The organization and relationships between the user-video interaction and the user-course interaction are thus shown in Fig. 2.

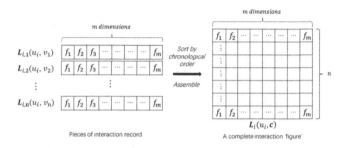

Fig. 2. The organization detail of an interaction 'figure'

Macro Information. The macro information refers to the high-level, general information of a certain course. This includes basic profile information of this course and descriptive statistical information about all learners' interaction history with the course. For the interaction between a certain user u_i and a course c, the macro information is formulated as $G_i(u_i, c) \in R^h$, where h is the dimensionality that used to represent the macro information.

Convolutional Network with Fixed Kernel Width. Inspired by the network structure proposed in the prior work reported in [13], we have also carefully designed a CNN-based network to capture the micro information, which may contain valuable time-series patterns. The interaction 'figure' is scanned by multiple kernels with a fixed-width m, which equals to the feature size (the dimension size). Hence, each convolutional operation summarises k_i pieces of successive learning activities where k_i equals to the kernel height.

3.3   Separate and Joint Training Strategies

As shown in Fig. 1, the intermediate results produced by the micro component and the macro component are combined using a weighted sum before the final prediction. This processing step is formulated as Eq. (1).

$$P\left(Y = 1|x\right) = \sigma(W_{micro}r_{micro} + W_{macro}r_{macro} + b) \tag{1}$$

where r_{micro} and r_{macro} are the intermediate results from micro and macro components, respectively; W_{micro} and W_{macro} are two different weights; b is the bias value; and σ represents regression function.

Note that in this framework, the micro and macro components can be trained in two different ways: joint mode or separate mode. As its name implies, in the joint mode, two components are trained jointly. Conversely, in the separate mode, two components are trained separately without knowing each other.

4   Experiments

4.1   Dataset

The dataset used in this experiment was collected from XuetangX. The data used in the experiment was extracted from the public data repository MOOCCube, which hosted 706 online courses, more than 30 thousand videos, and about 200 thousand users. For details of the statistic information about MOOCCube and the explanation of the dataset, please refer to the original work reported in [14].

4.2   Evaluation Metrics

Accuracy (ACC), F1-score, and Area Under Curve (AUC) score were used in the experiment to comprehensively evaluate the proposed solution.

4.3   Baselines

In the experiments, to comprehensively investigate the learner dropout prediction problem for the MOOC learning environment and demonstrate the effectiveness of our proposed solution, different models were used to construct the proposed double-tower framework. For the macro component, we applied: Logistic Regression (LR) and Gradient Boosting Decision Tree (GBDT). For the micro component, we implemented and compared the following models: 1. the proposed CNN-based model, 2. (Bi-)GRU, 3. (Bi-)LSTM, and 4. Multilayer Perceptron (MLP).

4.4   Experiment Setup

All neural networks were implemented using the PyTorch framework [15]. The dimension number of the hidden layer for GRU and LSTM was set to 64, and 32 for Bi-GRU and Bi-LSTM. For the CNN model, three different kernels (height 3, 4, and 5) were used with 32 output channels. The input of the MLP was the concatenation of shuffled interaction records. We used the shuffled data in MLP to verify the existence of the time-series pattern in the micro information. ReLU was used as the activation function for all non-linear transformation layers except for the output layer, which was activated by a Sigmoid function.

4.5   Experimental Results and Discussions

The Existence of the Time-Series Pattern. To find out whether the interaction log contains any latent time-series information, in the experiment, we firstly applied several models with/without time-series modelling mechanisms to handle the micro and macro information. Specifically, LR, GBDT and MLP are the models that do not involve any specialised time-series modelling mechanisms. The GRU, LSTM and the proposed CNN-based network are the ones that contain time-series modelling mechanisms. Ac-cording to the comparison results (see Table 1), it is comfortable to find that the models with time-series modelling mechanism outperform the ones without it. This finding suggests the existence of the latent time-series pattern in the online learning interaction log. As the macro information only contains the category and demographic information (such as subject popularity, number of courses involved, and subject discipline), we can further conclude that the time-series pattern exists in the micro information. Hence, to achieve better performance, we should use the model with time-series pattern modelling ability when handling the micro information.

Table 1. Comparison of single model

Models	ACC	F1	AUC
LR	0.7727	0.7037	0.8382
GBDT	0.7967	0.7293	0.8619
Proposed	0.8292	0.7859	0.8948
GRU	0.8211	0.773	0.8918
LSTM	0.8142	0.756	0.8892
MLP	0.8032	0.7462	0.8739

Effectiveness of Double-Tower Framework. By comparing the results from Table 1 and Table 2, we can conclude that the double-tower framework in either joint mode or separate mode outperformed the single model. Using different components to handle different types of information, respectively, could further improve the model performance. Solely using a single model to process all types of information is difficult to find the optimal solution. The diversity of the information in an online learning platform like MOOC requires us involving different models for better system performance. Moreover, when closely looking at the results in Table 2, we can also find out that the effectiveness of the double-tower framework is determined by the model used in each component and the training mode. The analysis of this result will be discussed in the remainder of this section.

Comparison of Effectiveness and Efficiency Between Two Training Modes. When comparing the left part of the first five results with the right part

Table 2. Comparison of the separate mode and joint mode

	Separate mode			Joint mode		
Model	ACC	F1	AUC	ACC	F1	AUC
LR + Proposed	0.8363	0.7875	0.9004	0.8566	0.8223	0.9194
LR + GRU	0.8259	0.7755	0.894	0.8449	0.8109	0.9143
LR + Bi-GRU	0.822	0.7694	0.8915	0.8472	0.812	0.9178
LR + LSTM	0.8187	0.7601	0.8895	0.8377	0.7908	0.8972
LR + Bi-LSTM	0.8172	0.7639	0.8858	0.8396	0.7928	0.9013
GBDT + Proposed	0.8423	0.8016	0.9093			
GBDT + GRU	0.8395	0.7988	0.9095			
GBDT + Bi-GRU	0.8386	0.7962	0.9084			

in Table 2, we can see that training micro and macro components jointly produces better results than training them separately. We ascribe this improvement to sufficient information exploring in the joint mode. As an end-to-end framework, all the information is exposed to the framework and exchanged between two components at the same time. In the experiments, we also monitored the training time in order to compare the efficiency of the proposed framework in different settings. Table 3 records the running time (seconds) per training epoch and the number of epochs a training process needs to reach the optimal point. It is worth mentioning that when using the separate mode, two components can be trained simultaneously. In addition, the macro component requires much less training time than the micro component as it has a simpler structure. Hence, we had merely measured the running time of micro component for the separate mode.

The frameworks with the proposed CNN-based component requires the least time for both joint mode and separate mode (see Table 3, the first and fourth row). The frameworks with LSTM component took longer time in each training epoch comparing to the ones with GRU. Notably, such result corresponds with the mathematical definitions [17] of these two models, where GRU is much simpler and lightweight than LSTM. Furthermore, the joint mode required a little more time for each training epoch but less training epoch to reach the optimal point. This also corresponds to the mathematical derivation from which the joint mode has involved more parameters in the training process and has higher time complexity.

The Implication of Two Training Modes. As for the implications, the joint mode is an end-to-end training process, which is a more efficient training strategy. Compared to the separate mode. However, in some cases, these two components cannot be trained in an end-to-end manner. For example, in some high-performance conventional models, such as the random forest, they are very difficult to be trained together with a neural network. To better demonstrate such

Table 3. Comparison of the framework efficiency

Models	Epoch number	Time (s/epoch)
LR + Proposed (J)	15	287.12
LR + GRU (J)	15	320.35
LR + LSTM (J)	15	345.04
LR + Proposed (S)	25	286.36
LR + GRU (S)	25	294.97
LR + LSTM (S)	25	327.27

a situation, GBDT was also used as another type of macro component, which was difficult to implement under the PyTorch framework. According to Table 2, the framework using GBDT as the macro component outperformed those having used LR as the macro component. Empirically, one of the two components may reuse an existing trained model. This will allow us to only train one new model for another component. Undoubtedly, in these situations, the separate mode is more efficient than the joint mode. In summary, the joint is more efficient, but the separate mode is more flexible.

5   Conclusions and Future Work

In this study, we investigated and analysed the learner dropout prediction problem for the MOOC platform. In order to deal with different types of information, we proposed a double-tower framework. A CNN-based network is designed to model the time-series information from users' successive learning records. The results have shown that the proposed framework with a CNN-based micro component outperforms all baseline models. The experiments demonstrated that, both the proposed double-tower framework and the CNN-based neural network are entitled with high effectiveness. This novel work also provided empirical implications for the practical usage of different training modes. Moreover, the proposed model showed effectiveness in both the joint mode and the separate mode. In our future research, to ensure the model to be more robust, we will seek to integrate other state-of-the-art techniques.

Acknowledgments. This research is supported by the Australian Research Council Discovery Project, DP180101051, and Natural Science Foundation of China, no. 61877051.

References

1. Kloft, M., Stiehler, F., Zheng, Z., Pinkwart, N.: Predicting MOOC dropout over weeks using machine learning methods. In: Proceedings of the EMNLP 2014 Workshop on Analysis of Large Scale Social Interaction in MOOCs, pp. 60–65 (2014)

2. Whitehill, J., Williams, J., Lopez, G., Coleman, C., Reich, J.: Beyond prediction: first steps toward automatic intervention in MOOC student stopout. Available at SSRN 26117502015

3. Tang, C., Ouyang, Y., Rong, W., Zhang, J., Xiong, Z.: Time series model for predicting dropout in massive open online courses. In: Penstein Rosé, C., et al. (eds.) AIED 2018. LNCS (LNAI), vol. 10948, pp. 353–357. Springer, Cham (2018). https://doi.org/10.1007/978-3-319-93846-2_66

4. Wang, W., Yu, H., Miao, C.: Deep model for dropout prediction in MOOCs. In: Proceedings of the 2nd International Conference on Crowd Science and Engineering, pp. 26–32 (2017)

5. Dalipi, F., Imran, A.S., Kastrati, Z.: MOOC dropout prediction using machine learning techniques: review and research challenges. In: 2018 IEEE Global Engineering Education Conference (EDUCON), pp. 1007–1014. IEEE (2018)

6. He, J., Bailey, J., Rubinstein, B.I., Zhang, R.: Identifying at-risk students in massive open online courses. In: Twenty-Ninth AAAI Conference on Artificial Intelligence (2015)

7. Amnueypornsakul, B., Bhat, S., Chinprutthiwong, P.: Predicting attrition along the way: the UIUC model. In: Proceedings of the EMNLP 2014 Workshop on Analysis of Large Scale Social Interaction in MOOCs, pp. 55–59 (2014)

8. Al-Shabandar, R., Hussain, A., Laws, A., Keight, R., Lunn, J., Radi, N.: Machine learning approaches to predict learning outcomes in Massive open online courses. In: 2017 International Joint Conference on Neural Networks (IJCNN), pp. 713–720, IEEE (2017)

9. Al-Shabandar, R., Hussain, A., Laws, A., Keight, R., Lunn, J.: Towards the differentiation of initial and final retention in massive open online courses. In: Huang, D.-S., Bevilacqua, V., Premaratne, P., Gupta, P. (eds.) ICIC 2017. LNCS, vol. 10361, pp. 26–36. Springer, Cham (2017). https://doi.org/10.1007/978-3-319-63309-1_3

10. Imran, A.S., Dalipi, F., Kastrati, Z.: Predicting student dropout in a MOOC: an evaluation of a deep neural network model. In: Proceedings of the 2019 5th International Conference on Computing and Artificial Intelligence, pp. 190–195 (2019)

11. Feng, W., Tang, J., Liu, T.X.: Understanding dropouts in MOOCs. In: Proceedings of the AAAI Conference on Artificial Intelligence, pp. 517–524 (2019)

12. Cheng, H.-T., et al.: Wide & deep learning for recommender systems. In: Proceedings of the 1st Workshop on Deep Learning for Recommender Systems, pp. 7–10 (2016)

13. Kim, Y.: Convolutional neural networks for sentence classification. arXiv preprint arXiv:1408.58822014

14. Yu, J., et al.: MOOCCube: a large-scale data repository for NLP applications in MOOCs. In: Proceedings of the 58th Annual Meeting of the Association for Computational Linguistics, pp. 3135–3142 (2020)

15. Paszke, A., et al.: Pytorch: an imperative style, high-performance deep learning library. In: Advances in Neural Information Processing Systems, pp. 8026–8037 (2019)

16. Gers, F.A., Schmidhuber, J., Cummins, F.: Learning to forget: continual prediction with LSTM (1999)

17. Cho, K., et al.: Learning phrase representations using RNN encoder-decoder for statistical machine translation. arXiv preprint arXiv:1406.10782014

SEOVER: Sentence-Level Emotion Orientation Vector Based Conversation Emotion Recognition Model

Zaijing Li[1], Fengxiao Tang[1(✉)], Tieyu Sun[3], Yusen Zhu[2], and Ming Zhao[1(✉)]

[1] School of Computer Science, Central South University, Changsha, China
{lizaijing,tangfengxiao,meanzhao}@csu.edu.cn
[2] School of Mathematics, Hunan University, Changsha, China
[3] Prevision Technology Limited, Hong Kong, China

Abstract. In this paper, we propose a new expression paradigm of sentence-level emotion orientation vector to model the potential correlation of emotions between sentence vectors. Based on it, we design an emotion recognition model referred to as SEOVER, which extracts the sentence-level emotion orientation vectors from the pre-trained language model and jointly learns from the dialogue sentiment analysis model and extracted sentence-level emotion orientation vectors to identify the speaker's emotional orientation during the conversation. We conduct experiments on two benchmark datasets and compare them with the five baseline models. The experimental results show that our model has better performance on all data sets.

Keywords: Conversation emotion recognition · Pre-trained language model · Emotion vector

1 Introduction

Conversation emotion recognition (CER) refers to the process of identifying the speaker's emotions through text, audio, and visual information in the process of two or more persons' conversations. Nowadays, conversation emotion recognition tasks are widely used in social media such as Twitter and Facebook.

Recent work of conversation emotion recognition mainly focuses on speaker identification and conversation relationship modeling (Majumder et al. 2019; Ghosal et al. 2019). However, these proposals use CNN (Kim 2014) to encode the utterances, which can not express the grammatical and semantic features of the utterance well and lead to inaccurate emotion identification. To mitigate this issue, some works try to employ the BERT (Devlin et al. 2019) model with improved semantic features extraction ability to encode the sentences (Mao et al. 2020; Li et al. 2020). The proposal achieves good results, however, the proposed BERT-based CER does not fully extract the correlation of emotional tendency between sentences especially when the emotion turns in sudden. As shown in

© Springer Nature Switzerland AG 2021
T. Mantoro et al. (Eds.): ICONIP 2021, CCIS 1517, pp. 468–475, 2021.
https://doi.org/10.1007/978-3-030-92310-5_54

Fig. 1, we encode the first sentence of the first dialogue of the MELD dataset with CNN and BERT models respectively to obtain a 600-dimensional vector, and normalize the data of each dimension so that its value is a continuous number within (0,1). Then, a hot zone map is leveraged to show the difference between the feature maps encoded with the two models. It is obvious that trends of the feature maps are totally opposite. It seems that those encoding methods and corresponding feature maps lose some important features of the sentences and can't represent the emotional tendency of the utterance well.

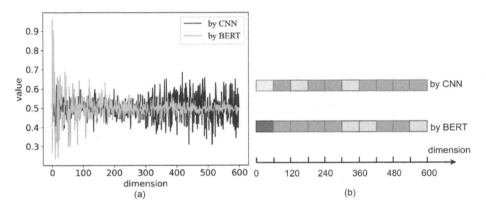

Fig. 1. (a) Comparison of the value of each dimension of the sentence vector get by CNN and BERT. (b) Hot zone map of features. The shade of the color indicates the size of the value, the larger the value, the darker the color. (Color figure online)

So, we propose a new utterance representation vector referred to as the sentence-level emotion orientation vector (SEOV) to further represent the potential emotion correlation of sentences. The SEOV represents the emotional intensity of sentence encoding vector with its "size", and models the emotion tendency between vectors with its "direction", which is as shown in Fig. 2.

Based on the proposed SEOV, we further propose a sentence-level emotion orientation vector based conversation emotion recognition model (SEOVER) to encode and decode the utterances of dialogue, and get the emotions of each speaker. In the model, we employ an improved transformer called as transformer-emo to extract the SEOV and then jointly use the SEOV and dialogue sentiment analysis model (DSAM) to obtain the contextual semantic information. With continuous fine-tune, we finally get the speaker's emotion classification result.

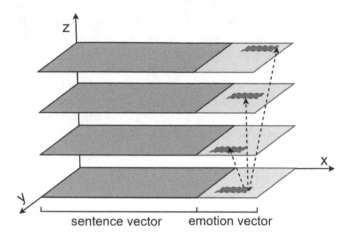

Fig. 2. The schematic diagram of SEOV, where the x-axis represents the dimension of the vector, y-axis represents the value of each dimension of the vector, and z-axis represents different sentence-level emotion orientation vectors. There is a correlation between different emotion vectors, indicating the "direction" of the SEOV.

2 Methodology

2.1 Problem Definition

Given a conversation U: $U_1, U_2, U_3, ...U_n$, N is the number of conversations, the speaker's utterance is represented by the function $P_t(U_i)$, where t is the t-th speaker. Our task is to input each utterance U_i and to get its correct classification result in the emotional label set L: $l_1, l_2, l_3, ...l_m$, where M is the number of types of emotional label.

2.2 Model

As shown in the Fig. 3, our model is divided into three parts: Sentence-level encoder, emotion-level encoder and context modeling.

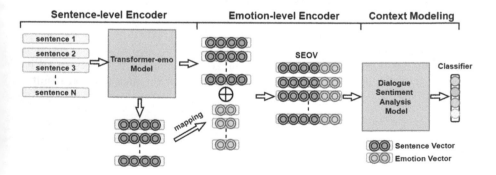

Fig. 3. Our model's structure.

Sentence-Level Encoder: Since the pre-trained language model can't directly encode the dialogue, we at first split the conversation U_n into a series of single sentences: $s_1, s_2, s_3...s_n$. Then, we input them into an improved pre-trained language model called transformer-emo model, which can map the representation of utterance to the sentence vectors Q:

$$Q = Transformer - emo(s_1, s_2, s_3 \ldots s_n) \tag{1}$$

where Q is a series of sentence vectors: $q_1, q_2, q_3...q_n$, the length of each sentence vector is set as d (d is set to 786 in our experiment). The classical pre-trained language model BERT is proposed with transformer structure to train the general text corpus (Devlin et al., 2019). Compared with the CNN model (Kim,2014), transformer can obtain more syntactic and semantic information. In order to better adapting to our model, we improve the transformer model by adjusting the output form (referred to as transformer-emo) to obtain the sentence vectors of the utterance.

Emotion-Level Encoder: As for sentence vectors, the length of the sentence itself, semantic information, symbols, etc. are the "size" of the vector, and its classification attributes are the "direction" of the vector. The sentence representation obtained by encoding the sentence in the existing method is not a "vector" in the true sense, because it only contains the "size" without the "direction". So we propose a new expression paradigm, SEOV, which represents the emotional intensity of sentence vector with its "size", and models the emotion tendency between emotion vectors with its "direction".

We map the vector q from the k-dim space to the k*-dim space to obtain the emotion vector $q*$, to achieve emotions representation:

$$q* = q[w_1, w_2, ...w_{k*}] \tag{2}$$

where $w_1, w_2, \ldots, w_{k*}$ is the weight parameter.

In theory, when the spatial dimension after the mapping is equal to the number of categories, we can regard it as the classification result. The elements in the emotion vector $q*$ represent the probabilities of classified emotions in each sentence.

Then we merge the original vector q and the obtained emotion vector $q*$ to obtain the sentence-level emotion orientation vector e:

$$e = q \oplus q^* \tag{3}$$

The e is called as SEOV, in which, the emotion's direction is represented in the collection of SEOVs as shown in Fig. 2. With the final DSAM, the "direction" of the emotion tendencies can be efficiently extracted and achieves better emotion recognition performance.

Context Modeling: Finally, we reassemble SEOVs into dialogue lists, and input them into the DSAM. The existing DSAMs can distinguish the speaker and obtain the speaker state, so it can fully obtain the context information and context. We choose DialogueRNN, DialogueGCN, and bc-LSTM models as the benchmark version of the dialogue emotion analysis models to compare the test results.

3   Experimental Setting

3.1   Datasets

IEMOCAP (Busso et al. 2008): IEMOCAP dataset contains the conversation data of ten actors in the emotional interaction process, including video, voice, facial expression capture, and conversation text. The emotions are classified into six types of emotions: happy, sad, neutral, angry, excited, frustrated.

MELD (Poria et al. 2019): MELD dataset selects 1432 conversations from the TV series "Friends", with a total of 13,708 sentences, including video, text, voice and other data content. Emotions are classified into seven emotions: neutral, surprise, fear, sadness, joy, disgust, and angry.

3.2   State-of-the-Art Baselines

DialogueRNN (Majumder et al. 2019): DialogueRNN uses different GRU units to obtain contextual information and speaker relationships. It is the first conversation sentiment analysis model to distinguish between speakers.

DialogueGCN (Ghosal et al. 2019): DialogueGCN constructs a conversation into a graph, transforms the speech emotion classification problem into a node classification problem of the graph, and uses the graph convolutional neural network to classify the results.

DialogXL (Shen et al. 2020): DialogXL use XLNet model for conversation emotion recognition to obtain longer-term contextual information.

Bc-LSTM (Poria et al. 2017): Bc-LSTM uses a two-way LSTM structure to obtain contextual semantic information, but does not distinguish between speaker states.

TRMSM (Li et al. 2020): TRMSM uses the transformer structure to simplify the conversation relationship into Intra-Speaker and Inter-Speaker, which can solve the problem of long-distance context dependence.

BERT (Devlin et al. 2019): BERT is a pre-trained language model that can be fine-tuned to achieve good results in downstream tasks. In this article, we use BERT to classify the sentiment of a single sentence text and compare it with our model.

4   Results and Analysis

We compare our model with all baselines on the MELD and IEMOCAP datasets and get the experimental results in Tables 1. As expected, our proposal outperforms other baseline models.

Table 1. Experimental results (F1 score) on the IEMOCAP dataset and MELD dataset. SEOVER-RNN represents the result of using DialogueRNN as the fine-tuning model, SEOVER-GCN represents the result of using DialogueGCN as the fine-tuning model, and SEOVER-LSTM represents the result of using bc-LSTM as the fine-tuning model.

Model	IEMOCAP							MELD
	Happy	Sad	Neutral	Angry	Excited	Frustrated	Average	Average
DialogueRNN	33.18	78.80	59.21	65.28	71.86	58.91	62.75	55.90
DialogueGCN	42.75	84.54	63.54	64.19	63.08	**66.99**	64.18	-
DialogXL	-	-	-	-	-	-	65.95	62.41
TRMSM	50.22	75.82	64.15	60.97	72.70	63.45	65.74	62.36
bc-LSTM	43.40	69.82	55.84	61.80	59.33	60.20	59.19	55.90
BERT	-	-	-	-	-	-	54.01	60.34
SEOVER-RNN	69.47	83.57	**66.67**	67.46	**82.46**	55.36	69.86	**65.66**
SEOVER-GCN	53.85	80.40	58.77	62.09	79.22	56.87	65.29	-
SEOVER-LSTM	**70.38**	**85.65**	65.40	**69.45**	80.98	64.96	**72.07**	63.82

4.1 Comparison with Baseline Models

Compared with the state-of-the-art conversation emotion recognition models, our proposal achieves better performance. This is cause by two reasons. Firstly, our model can obtain more syntactic and semantic features of utterances' presentation by using transformer-emo which is a transformer based pretraining model. Secondly, the proposed SEOV can efficiently map the emotion orientations between sentence vectors.

4.2 Ablation Study

In order to study the influence of the fusion of SEOV on the experimental results, we remove the emotion vectors in the SEOVER to compare the emotion recognition performance with benchmark model of DialogueRNN on the MELD dataset. As shown in Table 2, unsurprisingly, the accuracy and F1 score of the model without emotion vectors are much lower. The comparison illustrates the importance of the emotion tendency encoding in SEOV for the conversation emotion recognition.

Table 2. Results of ablation experiments, where accuracy and F1 score are both weighted results.

Model	Accuracy	F1 score
DialogueRNN	56.10	55.90
DialogueRNN-BERT	58.59	59.40
SEOVER-RNN	**65.33**	**65.66**

4.3 Error Analysis

We analyze the confusion matrix on the MELD data set. As shown in Table 3, assuming "sad" and "joy" are oppose emotions, the count of the misjudge between "sad" an "joy" is relatively small. On the other hand, the "sad" and "angry" are a pair of adjacent emotions. The misjudge count of this pair adjacent is relatively high. It is not difficult to find that the fusion of emotion vectors is a double-edged sword, which improves the classification accuracy of flipped emotions, but slightly reduced the classification accuracy of adjacent emotions. Therefore, in future research, we will focus on improving the performance of the adjacent emotions classification.

Table 3. Confusion matrix obtained on the test set using the MELD dataset and DialogueRNN as the benchmark model

Confusion matrix							
	Neutral	Surprise	Fear	Sad	Joy	Disgust	Anger
Neutral	3781	164	30	176	428	33	135
Surprise	28	134	1	20	52	4	41
Fear	14	6	1	6	8	5	10
Sad	44	20	3	68	28	7	38
Joy	71	27	2	14	272	2	14
Disgust	17	6	4	12	9	9	11
Anger	55	36	5	29	30	18	165

5 Conclusion

In this work, we propose a new paradigm of sentence-level emotion orientation vector (SEOV) to assist the emotion recognition, which solves the discourse representation information loss problem of conventional methods in the CER. Then, we designed a conversation emotion recognition model based on the SEOV called as SEOVER. It uses the Transformer-emo model to encode sentence vectors and emotion vectors containing emotion tendency information and fuses them as SEOV. Then, the SEOV is leveraged as input to active the final dialogue emotion analysis model to classify the speaker's emotions. We conducted comparative experiments of the proposal with several benchmarks on both the MELD and IEMOCAP dataset. The experimental results prove that the proposed SEOVER outperforms the state-of-the-art methods.

References

Bahdanau, D., Cho, K., Bengio, Y.: Neural machine translation by jointly learning to align and translate. Computer Science (2014)

Busso, C., et al.: Iemocap: interactive emotional dyadic motion capture database. Lang. Resou. Eval. **42**(4), 335–359 (2008)

Devlin, J., Chang, M.W., Lee, K., Toutanova, K.: Bert: pre-training of deep bidirectional transformers for language understanding. In: NAACL-HLT (2019)

Ghosal, D., Majumder, N., Gelbukh, A., Mihalcea, R., Poria, S.: Cosmic: commonsense knowledge for emotion identification in conversations. In: Findings of the Association for Computational Linguistics: EMNLP 2020 (2020)

Ghosal, D., Majumder, N., Poria, S., Chhaya, N., Gelbukh, A.: Dialoguegcn: A graph convolutional neural network for emotion recognition in conversation. In: Proceedings of the 2019 Conference on Empirical Methods in Natural Language Processing and the 9th International Joint Conference on Natural Language Processing (EMNLP-IJCNLP) (2019)

Hazarika, D., Poria, S., Mihalcea, R., Cambria, E., Zimmermann, R.: Icon: interactive conversational memory network for multimodal emotion detection. In: Proceedings of the 2018 Conference on Empirical Methods in Natural Language Processing, pp. 2594–2604 (2018)

Hazarika, D., Poria, S., Zadeh, A., Cambria, E., Morency, L.P., Zimmermann, R.: Conversational memory network for emotion recognition in dyadic dialogue videos. In: Proceedings of the Conference Association for Computational Linguistics North American Chapter Meeting, vol. 2018, p. 2122. NIH Public Access (2018)

Hazarika, D., Poria, S., Zimmermann, R., Mihalcea, R.: Conversational transfer learning for emotion recognition. Inf. Fusion **65**, 1–12 (2021)

Kim, Y.: Convolutional neural networks for sentence classification. preprint arXiv:1408.5882 (2014)

Li, J., Lin, Z., Fu, P., Si, Q., Wang, W.: A hierarchical transformer with speaker modeling for emotion recognition in conversation. arXiv preprint arXiv:2012.14781 (2020)

Majumder, N., Poria, S., Hazarika, D., Mihalcea, R., Gelbukh, A., Cambria, E.: Dialoguernn: an attentive rnn for emotion detection in conversations. In: Proceedings of the AAAI Conference on Artificial Intelligence, vol. 33, pp. 6818–6825 (2019)

Mao, Y., et al.: Dialoguetrm: exploring the intra-and inter-modal emotional behaviors in the conversation. arXiv preprint arXiv:2010.07637 (2020)

Poria, S., Cambria, E., Hazarika, D., Majumder, N., Zadeh, A., Morency, L.P.: Context-dependent sentiment analysis in user-generated videos. In: Proceedings of the 55th Annual Meeting of the Association for Computational Linguistics (volume 1: Long papers), pp. 873–883 (2017)

Poria, S., Hazarika, D., Majumder, N., Naik, G., Cambria, E., Mihalcea, R.: Meld: a multimodal multi-party dataset for emotion recognition in conversations. In: Proceedings of the 57th Annual Meeting of the Association for Computational Linguistics (2019)

Shen, W., Chen, J., Quan, X., Xie, Z.: Dialogxl: All-in-one xlnet for multi-party conversation emotion recognition. In: Proceedings of the AAAI Conference on Artificial Intelligence (2020)

Vaswani, A., et al.: Attention is all you need. In: 31st Conference on Neural Information Processing Systems (NIPS 2017), Long Beach, CA (2017). abs/1706.03762

A Multi-interaction Model with Cross-Branch Feature Fusion for Video-Text Retrieval

Junting Li, Dehao Wu, Yuesheng Zhu$^{(\boxtimes)}$, and Zhiqiang Bai

Shenzhen Graduate School, Peking University, Beijing, China
juntingli@stu.pku.edu.cn, {wudehao,zhuys,baizq}@pku.edu.cn

Abstract. With the explosive growth of videos on the internet, video-text retrieval is receiving increasing attention. Most of the existing approaches map videos and texts into a shared latent vector space and then measure their similarities. However, for video encoding, most methods ignore the interactions of frames in a video. In addition, many works obtain features of various aspects but lack a proper module to fuse them. They use simple concatenation, gate unit, or average pooling, which possibly can not fully exploit the interactions of different features. To solve these problems, we propose the Multi-Interaction Model (MIM). Concretely, we propose a well-designed multi-scale interaction module to exploit interactions among frames. Besides, a fusion module is designed to combine representations from different branches by encoding them into various subspaces and capturing interactions among them. Furthermore, to learn more discriminative representations, we propose an improved loss function. And we design a new mining strategy, which selectively reserves informative pairs. Extensive experiments conducted on MSR-VTT, TGIF, and VATEX datasets demonstrate the effectiveness of the proposed video-text retrieval model.

Keywords: Video-text retrieval · Feature interactions · Feature fusion · Loss function

1 Introduction

Since natural language texts contain richer content than keywords, video retrieval with natural language queries has received more attention. Usually, both texts and videos are projected into a latent space via different methods, which still have some limitations. First, most methods do not exploit sufficient inter-frame interactions. HGR [1] uses a weighted sum to get video embeddings, ignoring exploring more inter-frame interactions. Second, many works obtain

---

This work was supported in part by the National Innovation 2030 Major S&T Project of China under Grant 2020AAA0104203, and in part by the Nature Science Foundation of China under Grant 62006007.

© Springer Nature Switzerland AG 2021
T. Mantoro et al. (Eds.): ICONIP 2021, CCIS 1517, pp. 476–484, 2021.
https://doi.org/10.1007/978-3-030-92310-5_55

features of various aspects but fuse them with simple methods. CE [5] fuses the results of multiple experts by average pooling and gate unit. Third, most loss functions for video retrieval are not flexible enough. The hinge-based triplet ranking loss [7–9] treats all samples equally, ignoring the effect of different samples on optimization. And most loss functions either focus on the hardest negative pair or average all negative pairs. [10,12] The former may cause model affected by outliers, while the latter brings lots of redundancy.

To address the above limitations, we propose the Multi-Interaction Model (MIM). First, we propose a multi-scale inter-frame interactions module (MSIFI) to encode videos. It is implemented by a well-designed convolutional module. It regards each frame feature as a channel and performs 1-D convolution along the feature axis. Through MSIFI, each element of output embeddings comes from all the elements of inputs. Second, a fusion method is designed to merge features from MSIFI, bi-GRU, and global branches sufficiently. It maps the outputs of MSIFI and bi-GRU into different subspaces. Features from all subspaces will interact with each other. Then it is combined with global features via an adaptive gate unit. Third, we propose an improved loss function. It assigns weights to each pair with non-linear functions, whose value changes with the similarity score. Pairs whose similarity scores are far from the optimum will get larger weights and converge faster. Moreover, an adaptive mining strategy is designed to reserve informative samples with different weights. The main contributions of this work are as follows:

- To fully exploit interactions among frames in multi scales, we propose a novel MSIFI module. It utilizes a well-designed convolution operation to learn more accurate and significant information from multi-scale interactions.
- We design a novel fusion module to merge different features. Through sufficient interactions among features from multiple latent subspaces, we integrate features of various aspects and get an accurate video representation.
- Considering the influence of different samples on optimization, we propose an improved loss with a new mining strategy.
- Extensive experiments on several datasets validate the effectiveness of MIM.

2   Related Work

Frame Aggregations for Video-Text Retrieval. HGR [1] decomposes videos to match with texts in different levels and JSFusion [4] encodes all frames of videos with texts and directly predicts the video-text similarities. They both ignore exploring more inter-frame interactions.

Fusion Methods for Video-Text Retrieval. Dual Encoding [9] concatenates the results of multiple encoders. Howto100m [6] aggregates different features by max pooling and concatenation. CE [5] aggregates various information with a gate unit and average pooling.

Loss Functions for Video-Text Retrieval. Most methods [7–9] adopt hinge-based triplet ranking loss or bi-directional max-margin ranking loss [5,6]. However, they treat all samples equally. Circle loss [12] assigns weights to different

pairs with a linear function and Polynomial Loss [10] just considers the hardest
negative sample or averages all negative samples, which are not flexible enough.

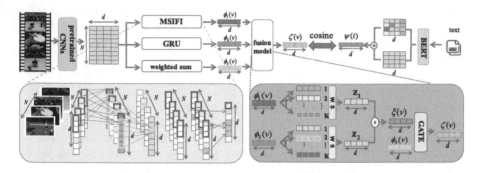

Fig. 1. The architecture of MIM. The video encoder has three branches. The Text
encoder contains a multi-dimensional attention module. The MSIFI module captures
multi-scaled interactions among frames. The fusion module merges three branches features. N is the number of video frames and the dimension of features is unchanged by
proper padding. Details are in Sect. 3. *WS* denotes weighted sum and $\odot$ is Hadamard
product.

3   Methodology

Given a video v and a text t, our model encodes them into fixed d-dimensional
vectors in a common space. We use the features extracted by pre-trained
CNNs [19–21] and BERT [11]. As illustrated in Fig. 1, the video encoder has
three branches, whose outputs are denoted as $\phi_1(v)$, $\phi_2(v)$, $\phi_3(v)$. Then they are
integrated into $\zeta(v)$ by the fusion module. Text encoder handles text features
with a multi-dimensional attention mechanism to get the result $\psi(t)$.

3.1   Multi-scale Inter-frame Interactions (MSIFI) Branch

As shown in the upper-left part of Fig. 1, a video is projected into a matrix
$I \in \mathbb{R}^{N \times d}$ by pre-trained CNNs. I is the input of MSIFI and N is the number of
frames. Specifically, each element of the feature corresponds to a channel of the
last layer in pre-trained CNNs. We treat each frame as one channel of MSIFI and
perform the convolution along the feature axis. This actually combines different
channels of pre-trained CNNs when sliding our convolutional kernels. As the
number of layers increases, the receptive field of each layer is enlarged and it
completely covers I in the last layer. In this way, we achieve multi-scale inter-
frame interactions and merge significant information from all frames. They are
aggregated into $\phi_1(v) \in \mathbb{R}^d$ by max pooling, reserving the most informative
features. Each element of $\phi_1(v)$ is derived from the interactions among all frames.

3.2   Temporal Branch and Global Branch

Since temporal information plays an important role in video encoding, we employ the bi-GRU network to capture temporal information. The input is $I \in \mathbb{R}^{N \times d}$ and the output is aggregated into $\phi_2(v) \in \mathbb{R}^d$ by max pooling.

To obtain a more comprehensive video embedding, we also extract the global features. As the significance of frames in a video are different, we assign weights to them based on significance. Each frame $v_i \in \mathbb{R}^d$ is mapped into $\tau_i \in \mathbb{R}$ by a FC layer. The global embedding of the video is the weighted sum of all frames:

$$\phi_3(v) = \sum_{i=1}^{N} \gamma_i v_i, \quad \gamma_i = \frac{exp(\tau_i)}{\sum_{i=1}^{N} exp(\tau_i)}, \tag{1}$$

where $\gamma_i \in \mathbb{R}$ is the weight of the i-th frame and $\phi_3(v)$ represents relatively primitive video information.

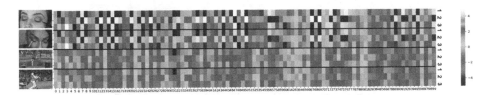

Fig. 2. Visualization of attentions of different videos to K subspaces. Each row denotes the attention of a subspace, and every K rows correspond to a video. We set K = 3. Semantic similar videos have similar attentions. The content of the first two and last two videos are different, so they have different attentions. This indicates different subspaces represent different aspects of video features.

3.3   Fusion Module

To fuse information from three branches, we conduct another kind of interaction between $\phi_1(v)$ and $\phi_2(v)$ and then merge the result with $\phi_3(v)$. As illustrated in the lower-right part of Fig. 1, we first map $\phi_1(v)$ and $\phi_2(v)$ into K subspaces respectively. They are denoted as $\{h^{(k)}\}$ and $\{e^{(k)}\}$, where k represents the k-th subspace. Different subspaces represent different aspects of video features. Figure 2 shows the representations of several videos in K subspaces. Semantic similar videos pay similar attention to certain subspaces, and unrelated videos have different dependencies on each subspace. After that, the representations from all subspaces are aggregated by weighted sum to obtain $\mathbf{z_1} \in \mathbb{R}^d$ and $\mathbf{z_2} \in \mathbb{R}^d$. They are fused into $\xi(v)$ by Hadamard product. The q-th element of $\xi(v)$ is as follow, where $\alpha^{(i)} \in \mathbb{R}$ and $\beta^{(i)} \in \mathbb{R}$ are trainable parameters.

$$\mathbf{z_1} = \sum_{i=1}^{K} \alpha^{(i)} h^{(i)}, \quad \mathbf{z_2} = \sum_{j=1}^{K} \beta^{(j)} e^{(j)}, \quad \xi(v)_q = \sum_{i=1}^{K} \alpha^{(i)} h_q^{(i)} \sum_{j=1}^{K} \beta^{(j)} e_q^{(j)}. \tag{2}$$

It can be seen that the representation from each subspace interacts with representations from all subspaces of another branch. As $\phi_3(v)$ contains global information, an adaptive fusion gate is uesd to mix $\xi(v)$ and $\phi_3(v)$ into $\zeta(v) \in \mathbb{R}^d$:

$$\zeta(v) = \lambda \cdot \xi(v) + (1 - \lambda) \cdot \phi_3(v), \quad \lambda = \sigma(\mathbf{FC_1}(\xi(v))), \tag{3}$$

where $\lambda \in \mathbb{R}^d$ denotes the gating weight, $\mathbf{FC_1}$ represents a fully connected layer and σ is the sigmoid function.

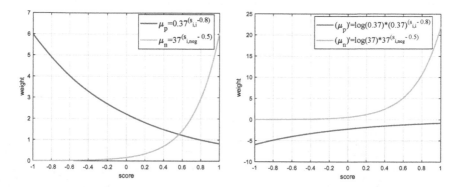

Fig. 3. The weight function curves (left) and their derivative curves (right) of pairs in loss function. Blue curves are for positive pairs and red curves are for negative pairs.

3.4   Text Encoder with Multi-dimensional Attention

Inspired by MAGP [14], we believe that different dimensions attend to different properties and we adopt the text encoder of MAGP. The difference is that we add up the output of every 2 adjacent layers of BERT, and concatenate the results of 6 groups. Then the multi-dimensional attention module obtains attention weights for every word and aggregates them into a vector $\psi(t) \in \mathbb{R}^d$.

3.5   Video-Text Matching

The cosine similarity of $\zeta(v)$ and $\psi(t)$ is their similarity score: $s_{i,j} = \frac{\zeta(v)_i^T \psi(t)_j}{||\zeta(v)_i|| ||\psi(t)_j||}$. $s_{i,i}$ is a positive pair and $s_{i,j}$ is a negative pair, where $i \neq j$. An adaptive mining strategy is used to reserve informative pairs. We select and assign weights to informative pairs while discarding other pairs. All negative samples are sorted based on similarity scores. Harder samples rank higher. Then we save top $\frac{U}{r}$ samples, assign weights, and aggregate them to get the negative pairs representative $s_{i,neg}$ for the i-th query. r is a hyper-parameter, U is the size of one batch.

$$s_{i,neg} = \sum_{j=1, j \neq i}^{\frac{U}{r}} \eta_j s_{ij}, \quad \eta_j = \frac{exp(s_{ij})}{\sum_{j=1, j \neq i}^{\frac{U}{r}} exp(s_{ij})}, \tag{4}$$

Our loss function is as follow, where μ_n and μ_p are the weight functions of negative and positive pairs. Δ is the margin and $[\cdot]_+ = max(\cdot, 0)$, a, b_0 and b_1 are hyper-parameters.

$$L = log\left[1 + \sum_{i=1}^{U}\sum_{q=1}^{U} exp(\mu_n s_{i,neg} - \mu_p(s_{q,q} - \Delta))\sum_{j=1}^{U}\sum_{k=1}^{U} exp(\mu_n s_{neg,j} - \mu_p(s_{k,k} - \Delta))\right],$$
(5)

$$\mu_p = \left[a^{s_{i,i}-\Delta}\right]_+, \quad \mu_n = \left[b_0^{s_{i,neg}-b_1}\right]_+,$$
(6)

Table 1. Comparison with state-of-the-arts on MSR-VTT, TGIF and VATEX dataset.

Dataset	Methods	Text-to-Video				Video-to-Text				rsum
		R@1	R@5	R@10	MedR	R@1	R@5	R@10	MedR	
MSR-VTT	VSE++ [8]	8.7	24.3	34.1	28	15.6	36.6	48.6	11	167.9
	W2VV++ [7]	11.1	29.6	40.5	18	17.5	40.2	52.5	9	191.4
	HGR [1]	11.1	30.5	42.1	16	18.7	44.3	57.6	7	204.4
	Dual Encoding [9]	11.6	30.3	41.3	17	22.5	47.1	58.9	7	211.7
	MAGP [14]	13.0	34.7	47.0	12	22.2	48.6	59.8	6	225.3
	Ours	**13.6**	**36.0**	**48.3**	11	**23.8**	**49.2**	**62.1**	6	**233.0**
TGIF	VSE++ [8]	1.6	5.9	9.8	220	1.4	5.6	9.6	192	33.9
	Corr-AE [13]	2.1	7.4	11.9	148	2.2	7.3	11.5	158	42.4
	PVSE [2]	3.0	9.7	14.9	109	3.3	9.9	15.6	115	56.4
	HGR [1]	5.0	13.6	19.4	110	7.2	18.0	24.8	66	88
	MAGP [14]	6.0	15.6	22.1	85	9.1	21.0	28.6	49	102.4
	Ours	**6.8**	**17.3**	**24.2**	68	**9.3**	21.1	**29.1**	46	**107.8**
VATEX	VSE++ [8]	31.3	65.8	76.4	-	42.9	73.9	83.6	-	373.9
	CE [5]	31.1	68.7	80.2	-	41.3	71.0	82.3	-	374.6
	HGR [1]	35.2	73.5	83.4	2	45.8	**76.9**	**85.4**	2	400.2
	MAGP [14]	34.1	74.6	85.1	2	-	-	-	-	-
	Dual Encoding [9]	**36.8**	73.6	83.7	-	46.8	75.7	85.1	-	401.7
	Ours	36.0	**75.4**	**85.2**	2	**48.5**	74.7	82.7	2	**402.5**

The curves of weight functions and their derivative functions are shown in Fig. 3. Our loss functions satisfy the following characteristics. When the similarity score is far from its optimum, this pair is more informative. The value and derivative value of its weight function will be greater. It means that this pair gets a bigger weight in the loss function and updates at a faster pace, and vice versa.

4   Experiments

4.1   Experimental Settings

Datasets and Metrics. We conduct experiments on MSR-VTT [15], VATEX [16], and TGIF [17]. We use the official partition of MSR-VTT. For

VATEX and TGIF, we follow the experimental setup of HGR [1].The performance is evaluated with common retrieval metrics, namely R@K (Recall at rank K), MedR (Median Rank), MnR (Mean Rank), and rsum (the sum of all recall scores).

Implementation Details. For MSR-VTT, the visual features are extracted by ResNet-152 and ResNeXt-101 pre-trained on ImageNet [9]. For TGIF and VATEX, we use the pre-trained ResNet-152 visual feature and the officially provided I3D [19] visual feature respectively. The MSIFI module has 5 convolutional layers with kernel size = 3,5,5,7,9. The number of subspaces K is 3. The dimension d is 4096. For loss function, we choose hyper-parameters by grid search. We set $r = 20$, $a = 0.37$, $\Delta = 0.8$, $b_0 = 37$, and $b_1 = 0.5$. The model is trained for 20 epochs using Adam optmizer [18] with batch size of 64 and learning rate is 1e−4.

Table 2. Ablation studies on MSR-VTT dataset.

Methods	Text-to-Video Retrieval					Video-to-Text Retrieval					rsum
	R@1	R@5	R@10	MedR	MnR	R@1	R@5	R@10	MedR	MnR	
Ours w/o MSIFI	10.7	30.5	42.6	15	91.6	14.7	37.2	49.9	11	63.4	185.6
Ours-transformer	13.5	35.4	48.0	12	84.8	22.8	47.0	59.7	6	44.6	226.4
Ours-gate	13.3	35.7	48.2	**11**	90.8	21.4	46.2	58.8	7	51.7	223.6
Ours-concat	11.9	32.6	44.9	14	94.9	19.7	43.6	56.8	7	53.3	209.5
Ours-CircleLoss	12.7	33.9	46.2	13	94.2	20.2	45.1	58.0	7	51.3	216.1
Ours-MaxPolyLoss	13.0	34.3	46.6	13	97.3	21.9	47.8	60.7	6	47.9	224.3
Ours-TripleLoss [8]	11.8	32.5	44.7	14	**84.0**	16.0	39.8	52.6	9	73.9	197.4
Ours-hard	13.4	34.5	46.8	13	92.3	21.7	48.0	61.3	6	45.9	225.7
Ours-avg	9.1	26.2	37.3	20	92.1	12.8	33.5	46.7	12	95.8	165.6
Full model	**13.6**	**36.0**	**48.3**	**11**	87.4	**23.8**	**49.2**	**62.1**	6	**43.8**	**233.0**

4.2   Comparisons with State-of-the-Arts (SOTAs)

As shown in Table 1. On all datasets, MIM has the highest rsum, demonstrating the advantages of MIM. Specifically, MIM outperforms MAGP. As they have the same text encoder, it proves that our video encoder is more effective. As the features of VATEX are not frame-level features, it is hard to implement interframe interactions as sufficiently as on MSR-VTT or TGIF. Our performance on VATEX degrades slightly. Nevertheless, our rsum is still the highest, proving the superiority of our fusion module and loss function.

4.3   Ablation Studies

We conduct ablation studies on MRS-VTT and results are displayed in Table 2.

Effectiveness of MSIFI. We remove MSIFI and compare it with Transformer [3]. To maintain similar number of parameters, we use 1 layer Transformer with 4096 hidden dimensions and 8 attention heads. Results show that MSIFI is effective.

Effectiveness of Fusion Module. We replace the fusion module with gate unit and concatenation respectively. And rsum decreases by 9.4 and 23.5, which proves that our fusion strategy can integrate different features more effectively.

Effectiveness of Loss Function. We compare our loss function with other loss functions and replace the mining strategy with hard mining and average operation. Results confirm the superiority of our loss function and mining strategy.

5   Conclusions

This paper introduces a multi-interaction model for video-text retrieval, with an MSIFI branch to capture multi-scale interactions among videos frames and a fusion method to exploit multiple complementary information between different video features. Moreover, a loss function and a mining strategy are proposed. Extensive experiments show the effectiveness of this approach.

References

1. Chen, S., Zhao, Y., Jin, Q., et al.: Fine-grained video-text retrieval with hierarchical graph reasoning. In: CVPR, pp. 10638–10647 (2020)
2. Song, Y., Soleymani, M.: Polysemous Visual-semantic embedding for cross-modal retrieval. arXiv preprint arXiv:1906.04402 (2019)
3. Vaswani, A., et al.: Attention is all you need. In: NIPS, pp. 5998–6008 (2017)
4. Yu, Y., Kim, J., Kim, G.: A joint sequence fusion model for video question answering and retrieval. In: ECCV, pp. 471–487 (2018)
5. Liu, Y., et al.: Use what you have: video retrieval using representations from collaborative experts. In: BMVC (2019)
6. Miech, A., Zhukov, D., et al.: Howto100m: learning a text-video embedding by watching hundred million narrated video clips. In: ICCV, pp. 2630–2640 (2019)
7. Loko, J., et al.: A W2VV++ case study with automated and interactive text-to-video retrieval. In: MM, pp. 2553–2561 (2020)
8. Faghri, F., et al.: VSE++: improving visual-semantic embeddings with hard negatives. In: BMVC (2018)
9. Dong, J., et al.: Dual encoding for video retrieval by text. In: TPAMI (2021)
10. Wei, J., et al.: Universal weighting metric learning for cross-modal matching. In: CVPR, pp. 13005–13014 (2020)
11. Devlin, J., et al.: Bert: pre-training of deep bidirectional transformers for language understanding. In: NAACL-HLT, pp. 4171–4186 (2019)
12. Sun, Y., et al.: Circle loss: a unified perspective of pair similarity optimization. In: CVPR, pp. 6398–6407 (2020)
13. Feng, F., et al.: Cross-modal retrieval with correspondence autoencoder. In: MM, pp. 7–16 (2014)
14. Wu, D., et al.: Multi-dimensional attentive hierarchical graph pooling network for video-text retrieval. In: ICME (2021)
15. Xu, J., et al.: MSR-VTT: a large video description dataset for bridging video and language. In: CVPR, pp. 5288–5296 (2016)
16. Wang, X., et al.: Vatex: a large-scale, high-quality multilingual dataset for video-and-language research. In: CVPR, pp. 4581–4591 (2019)

17. Li, Y., et al.: TGIF: a new dataset and benchmark on animated GIF description. In: CVPR, pp. 4641–4650 (2016)
18. Kingma, DP., Ba, J.: Adam: a method for stochastic optimization. In: ICLR (2015)
19. Carreira, J., Zisserman, A.: Quo vadis, action recognition? a new model and the kinetics dataset. In: CVPR, pp. 6299–6308 (2017)
20. Xie, S., et al.: Aggregated residual transformations for deep neural networks. In: CVPR, pp. 1492–1500. (2017)
21. He, K., et al.: Deep residual learning for image recognition. In: CVPR, pp: 770–778 (2016)

Detection of Retinal Vascular Bifurcation and Crossover Points in Optical Coherence Tomography Angiography Images Based on CenterNet

Chengliang Wang[1(✉)], Shitong Xiao[1], Chao Liao[1], Xing Wu[1], and Shiying Li[2,3]

[1] College of Computer Science, Chongqing University, Chongqing, China
{wangcl,stxiao,wuxing}@cqu.edu.cn
[2] Department of Ophthalmology, Xiang'an Hospital of Xiamen University, Medical Center of Xiamen University, School of Medicine, Xiamen University, Xiamen, China
[3] Eye Institute of Xiamen University, Xiamen, China

Abstract. Optical coherence tomography angiography (OCTA) is a non-invasive imaging technique developed in recent years and has been used in ophthalmology to assist clinical diagnosis and treatment. Detecting the retinal vascular bifurcation and crossover points (feature points) in OCTA images is helpful for disease prediction, image registration and some other biomedical applications. In this paper, we construct an OCTA dataset with manually annotated vascular bifurcation and crossover points. In order to detect and classify these feature points, we first propose a method based on CenterNet, which adds attention gates (AGs) to the skip connection of the Stacked Hourglass Network. AGs can highlight valuable features in the input image to improve detection performance. Moreover, since we focus more on the coordinates of vascular feature points, we modify the traditional average precision (AP) and mean average precision (mAP) by calculating the Euclidean distance between two points rather than the intersection over union (IOU) of two bounding boxes. Experiments indicate that our method can achieve 80.81% AP for bifurcation points, 85.86% AP for crossover points and 83.34% mAP.

Keywords: Optical coherence tomography angiography · Bifurcation points · Crossover points · CenterNet · Object detection

1 Introduction

The retinal vasculature is a significant part of clinical pathology and is associated with many ocular diseases. Optical coherence tomography angiography (OCTA) is a novel and safe tool for ophthalmologic examinations. It can both produce data of multiple retinal and choroidal layers, and display structure and blood flow information [1].

© Springer Nature Switzerland AG 2021
T. Mantoro et al. (Eds.): ICONIP 2021, CCIS 1517, pp. 485–493, 2021.
https://doi.org/10.1007/978-3-030-92310-5_56

A vessel bifurcation is where one vessel divides into two vessels, and a vessel crossover is where two vessels cross each other. As special landmarks of retinal vessels, the vascular bifurcation and crossover points are valuable features for disease prediction, image registration, mosaicing and biometric security applications [2]. At present, there are a few methods [3–5] to detect retinal vascular bifurcation and crossover points in OCTA images. In these methods, vascular segmentation and skeleton directly affect the detection results. Due to the complexity of the vascular network and the ambiguous contrast between blood vessels and background, achieving accurate segmentation for OCTA images is a great challenge. Therefore, we aim to detect and classify the bifurcation and crossover points in OCTA images without blood vessel segmentation.

Object detection based on deep learning can complete detection and classification at the same time, which satisfies our requirements. We choose the keypoint-based anchor-free CenterNet [10] from a number of object detectors for the following reasons. First, CenterNet eliminates the elaborate and complicated anchor design, and uses a larger output resolution than other traditional detectors [6], which is beneficial to the detection of small and dense points. Second, CenterNet models an object as the center point of its bounding box, and directly predicts the coordinates of center points (vascular feature points). Third, CenterNet does not need keypoint grouping or post-processing compared with other keypoint-based detectors [8,9].

According to the above mentioned, we propose a method based on CenterNet [10] to detect and classify the vascular bifurcation and crossover points in OCTA images. As far as we know, this is the first time that keypoint-based anchor-free object detection has been applied to OCTA images. We add attention gates (AGs) [12] to the skip connections of the Stacked Hourglass Network [10,11] to enhance the valuable features in complex and ambiguous vascular network of OCTA images. CenterNet is a supervised deep learning algorithm which needs ground-truth labels. Consequently, we construct an OCTA dataset where each image is manually annotated with retinal vascular bifurcation and crossover points. To evaluate the accuracy of our method, especially in the coordinates of vascular feature points, we modify the traditional average precision (AP) and mean average precision (mAP) using the Euclidean distance between two points to replace the intersection over union (IOU) of two bounding boxes. We evaluate the proposed method on the constructed OCTA dataset. The experimental results show the effectiveness of our method.

The rest of this paper is organized as follows. In Sect. 2, we introduce our elaborate OCTA dataset. In Sect. 3, we describe the details of the proposed detection method. Section 4 shows the experimental details and results. Finally, Sect. 5 presents some conclusions.

2   Dataset

All the OCTA images in our work were collected from the Department of Ophthalmology, Southwest Hospital, Army Medical University, Chongqing, China.

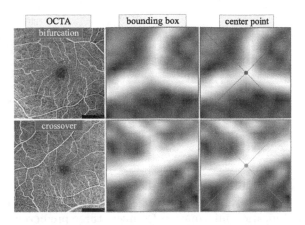

Fig. 1. The example of manual annotations. Column 1 shows the OCTA images whose ZEISS AngioPlex logo at the bottom-right corner were removed. Columns 2 and 3 respectively show the zoomed bounding box patches and their center points.

Our dataset contains a total of 151 OCTA images acquired from March 2017 to July 2020, captured by Zeiss Cirrus HD-OCT with AngioPlex. All the images are en face angiographs of the superficial vascular plexuses (SVP) and have a $6 \times 6\,\text{mm}^2$ field of view. In addition to normal eyes, these images were from eyes with diabetic retinopathy and age-related macular degeneration. The resolution of each image was resized to 512×512.

The retinal vascular bifurcation and crossover points were annotated with the format of PASCAL VOC [13]. As shown in Fig. 1, each bifurcation point or crossover point was located at the center of its bounding box. The coordinates of the top-left and bottom-right corners are (x_{min}, y_{min}) and (x_{max}, y_{max}) respectively, then the location of the center point is $\left(\frac{x_{min}+x_{max}}{2}, \frac{y_{min}+y_{max}}{2}\right)$.

The objects to be detected are in three sizes: small (area smaller than 32^2 pixels), medium (area between 32^2 and 96^2 pixels) and large (area greater than 96^2 pixels) [14,15]. On the basis of these three size definitions, almost all of the vascular bifurcation and crossover points are small objects. In 151 OCTA images, a total of 9,548 manually annotated objects consist of 9,542 small objects and only 6 medium objects. On average each image contains 63 objects, which is denser than PASCAL VOC [13] and MS COCO [14]. The number of objects in each image is more than 20, and the maximum is 110.

3 Proposed Method

Our method extracts the center point of each object using keypoint estimation and takes each peak keypoint as a bifurcation point or a crossover point. The overall framework of the proposed method is shown in Fig. 2. First, we extract and fuse the features of input images using the modified Stacked Hourglass Network, which generally achieves the best keypoint estimation performance [10].

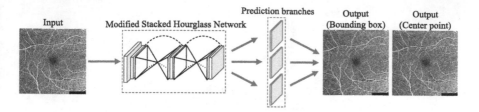

Fig. 2. The framework of our proposed method.

Second, we set up three branches to predict the center point heatmap, the local offset for center points, and the object size. At last we can obtain the classification results and location information from the three prediction branches. The Stacked Hourglass Network is composed of two successive hourglass modules, but each module is modified with AGs [12], which is different from CenterNet. In our method, we use the loss functions in CenterNet. However, it should be noted that we set a fixed Gaussian kernel radius of 5 for calculating the loss of keypoint heatmap because the objects are similar small points.

3.1 Attention Gates

In an encoder-decoder network, skip connections are usually used to fuse the features generated in the encoding and decoding stages. However, the low-level features in initial layers express insufficiently and some are redundant for the final task. Considering this problem, adding AGs to skip connections can enhance useful features and suppress irrelevant features for our task.

Attention gate (AG) differs from general attention modules in that it takes two inputs whereas other modules usually have only one input. We illustrate the 2D AG used in this paper with Fig. 3. Let $x^l \in \mathcal{R}^{F_l \times H_x \times W_x}$ and $g \in \mathcal{R}^{F_g \times H_g \times W_g}$ be the inputs of AG, where F, H and W are the number, height and width of feature maps respectively. The input x^l denotes the output feature maps of layer l, and g is a gating signal upsampled from a deeper layer. Channel-wise 1×1 convolutions are used to map x^l and g to a $\mathcal{R}^{F_{int}}$ dimensional intermediate space. The additive operation is followed by a rectified linear unit (ReLU). To obtain the attention coefficients α^l, a sigmoid activation function is applied after another 1×1 convolution. For each pixel i, the attention coefficient $\alpha_i^l \in [0,1]$ can be formulated as:

$$\alpha_i^l = \sigma_2 \left(\psi^T \left(\sigma_1 \left(\Theta_x^T x_i^l + \Phi_g^T g_i + b_g \right) \right) + b_\psi \right), \tag{1}$$

where $x_i^l \in \mathcal{R}^{F_l}$ and $g_i \in \mathcal{R}^{F_g}$ are vectors of the pixel i, $\Theta_x \in \mathcal{R}^{F_l \times F_{int}}$, $\Phi_g \in \mathcal{R}^{F_g \times F_{int}}$ and $\psi \in \mathcal{R}^{F_{int} \times 1}$ are linear transformations, $b_g \in \mathcal{R}^{F_{int}}$ and $b_\psi \in \mathcal{R}$ are bias terms, and $\sigma_2(x) = \frac{1}{1+\exp(-x)}$ denotes a sigmoid activation function. Finally, the input x^l and attention coefficients α^l are multiplied by element to get the output $\hat{x}^l$: $\hat{x}_{i,c}^l = x_{i,c}^l \cdot \alpha_i^l$, where c represents a channel.

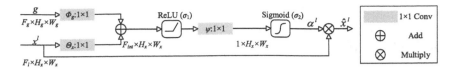

Fig. 3. The schematic of the 2D attention gate. The input x^l is multiplied by attention coefficients α^l computed in attention gate. The other input g is a gating signal for determining salient regions.

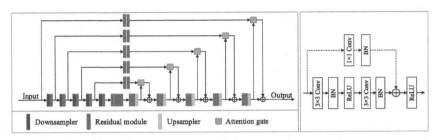

Fig. 4. Left: the illustration of a modified hourglass module. **Right:** the composition of a residual module in the left hourglass module.

3.2 Hourglass Module with Attention Gates

Each hourglass module is a symmetric 5-stage bottom-up, top-down convolutional network. There are two branches in each stage. One of the branches downsamples the features using convolutional layers. The other branch makes the features pass through more convolutions and keep the original resolution. If the features are downsampled to the lowest resolution, the network begins its top-down processing of upsampling and feature fusion. For the features across two adjacent scales, the features with lower resolution are processed by nearest neighbor upsampling and then the two sets of features are fed into an AG. To integrate the information of different scales, the upsampled features and the output of AG are added by element. Figure 4 shows a modified hourglass module.

4 Experiments

4.1 Experimental Details

In this paper, our constructed OCTA dataset is divided into 91 images for training, 30 images for validating and 30 images for testing. Due to the limited data available, offline data augmentation is performed on the training set. We randomly apply multiple augmentation operations to each training image, including adding noise, scaling, rotation, translation and so on.

The proposed method is implemented on a local machine with NVIDIA GeForce GTX 1080 Ti GPU and PyTorch 1.1.0. For the Stacked Hourglass Network with AGs (Hourglass-AG), we train it for 80 epochs with a batch size of 4.

We set the initial learning rate of Adam optimizer to 1.25e−4, but it will drop by a factor of 10 at 25 and 50 epochs. For testing, we set a confidence score threshold of 0.5 to select valid detections.

4.2   Evaluation Metrics

In most object detection challenges, the IOU is compared with a given threshold t to decide whether a detection is true positive (TP) or false positive (FP). If $IOU \geq t$, the detection is TP, otherwise it is FP. In our detection task, we focus on the coordinates of the vascular feature points, but using the IOU may lead to misjudgment of the detection results. As illustrated in Fig. 5, when the center points of the two bounding boxes are at the same location, we think that the detected point is correct. The given threshold t is usually 50%, but the IOU in Fig. 5 is less than 50%, which indicates that the detection is incorrect. Therefore, we use the Euclidean distance between the center points of two bounding boxes instead of the IOU.

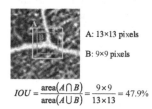

$$IOU = \frac{\text{area}(A \cap B)}{\text{area}(A \cup B)} = \frac{9 \times 9}{13 \times 13} = 47.9\%$$

Fig. 5. The red point is the common center point of the two bounding boxes A (prediction) and B (ground truth). The IOU of A and B is 47.9%. (Color figure online)

Let (x_p, y_p) be a predicted point, and (x_g, y_g) be a ground-truth point. The Euclidean distance between the two point is

$$d = \sqrt{(x_p - x_g)^2 + (y_p - y_g)^2}. \qquad (2)$$

For each class, the detection results are sorted in descending order by their confidence values. The minimum Euclidean distance between each predicted point and all the ground-truth points in the corresponding image is recorded as d_{min}. We give a distance threshold d_t. If $d_{min} \leq d_t$, the predicted point is TP, or else it is FP. In our work, we set $d_t = 3.0$ unless otherwise stated.

The precision (P) and recall (R) are defined as $P = \frac{TP}{TP+FP} = \frac{TP}{all\ detections}$ and $R = \frac{TP}{TP+FN} = \frac{TP}{all\ ground\ truths}$, respectively. We can further calculate the AP according to the Precision-Recall curve. We use the all-point interpolation in [15], and the AP for each class is denoted as:

$$AP = \sum_n (R_{n+1} - R_n) P_{interp}(R_{n+1}), \qquad (3)$$

where $P_{interp}(R_{n+1})$ is the precision value to be interpolated, which takes the maximum precision corresponding to the recall value greater than or equal to R_{n+1} [15].

The mAP measures the accuracy for all classes, formulated as:

$$mAP = \frac{1}{N_c} \sum_{j=1}^{N_c} AP_j, \qquad (4)$$

where N_c is the number of all classes and AP_j is the average precision of class j.

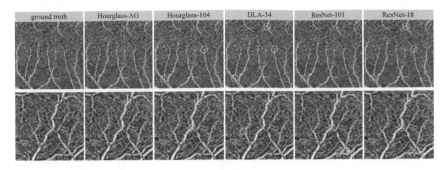

Fig. 6. Output patches indicating vascular bifurcation points (marked with red points) and crossover points (marked with green points). Note that yellow circles present undetected vascular feature points, and blue circles present incorrect detections. (Color figure online)

Table 1. Detection results of different backbones.

Backbone	AP (bifurcation)	AP (crossover)	mAP
Hourglass-AG	**80.81**	**85.86**	**83.34**
Hourglass-104	78.09	85.00	81.55
DLA-34	75.67	82.99	79.33
ResNet-101	66.13	68.25	67.19
ResNet-18	50.44	59.81	55.13

4.3 Experimental Results and Comparisons

We evaluate our proposed method on the test set which contains 30 OCTA images. In order to demonstrate the improvement of the proposed Hourglass-AG, we compare it with different backbones in CenterNet [10]. Figure 6 presents the output patches of center points produced by Hourglass-AG, Hourglass-104, DLA-34, ResNet-101 and ResNet-18. We can see that Hourglass-AG yields the best localization and classification. In addition, Table 1 reports AP and mAP at the Euclidean distance threshold of 3.0. Hourglass-AG achieves the best performance with 80.81% AP for bifurcation points, 85.86% AP for crossover points and 83.34% mAP, which indicates that AGs are effective for our task.

We compare our method with other object detectors and the results are shown in Table 2. Our method achieves the highest mAP because of its simple architecture design and effective feature extraction. Faster R-CNN [6] is an anchor-based two-stage detector without multi-scale feature fusion so that it is unable to perform well on small object detection. We add level P_2 to the pyramid of RetinaNet [7] to improve its detection ability of small objects. The modified RetinaNet with backbone ResNet-101-FPN achieves a respectable mAP of 78.17%. CornerNet [8] (65.62% mAP) and another CenterNet [9] (70.48% mAP) are anchor-free detectors with corner detection and keypoint grouping. Whereas, grouping errors can affect the detection results.

Table 2. Comparison between different detectors.

	Backbone	AP (bifurcation)	AP (crossover)	mAP
Faster R-CNN [6]	ResNet-50	50.62	51.93	51.28
Faster R-CNN [6]	ResNet-101	55.56	60.82	58.19
RetinaNet [7]	ResNet-50	76.16	78.81	77.49
RetinaNet [7]	ResNet-101	76.07	80.26	78.17
CornerNet [8]	Hourglass-104	65.95	65.29	65.62
CenterNet [9]	Hourglass-104	70.70	70.25	70.48
Ours	Hourglass-AG	**80.81**	**85.86**	**83.34**

5   Conclusions

In this paper, we construct an OCTA dataset for detection of retinal vascular bifurcation and crossover points. Each OCTA image is manually annotated with vascular bifurcation and crossover points. We propose a method based on CenterNet to detect vascular feature points in OCTA images. We combine the Stacked Hourglass Network with AGs to improve the detection performance. To our knowledge, this is the first time that keypoint-based anchor-free object detection has been used for this specific task. To evaluate the accuracy of the coordinates of the detected vascular feature points, we calculate the AP and mAP based on Euclidean distance rather than IOU. Compared with other object detectors, our proposed detection method achieves better performance.

Our work provides a new idea to analyze retinal vascular features in OCTA images. In the future work, we can make more analysis based on the detected bifurcation and crossover points, such as vessel width and bifurcation angle.

Acknowledgments. This work is supported by the National Natural Science Foundation of China (Grant No. 61672115); the Chongqing Technology & Application Development Project (No. cstc2019jscx-gksbX0038 and No. cstc2019jscx-zdztzxX0037) and the Fundamental Research Funds for the Central Universities, China (No. 2020CDCGJSJ040). We thank the Southwest Hospital of Army Medical University for providing the OCTA dataset.

References

1. Chalam, K., Sambhav, K.: Optical coherence tomography angiography in retinal diseases. J. Ophthalmic Vis. Res. **11**(1), 84–92 (2016)
2. Bhuiyan, A., Nath, B., Ramamohanarao, K.: Detection and classification of bifurcation and branch points on retinal vascular network. In: 2012 International Conference on Digital Image Computing Techniques and Applications (DICTA), pp. 1–8 (2012)
3. Eladawi, N., et al.: An octa based diagnosis system based on a comprehensive local features analysis for early diabetic retinopathy detection. In: 2018 IEEE International Conference on Imaging Systems and Techniques (IST), pp. 1–6 (2018)

4. Eladawi, N., et al.: Diabetic retinopathy early detection based on oct and octa feature fusion. In: 2019 IEEE 16th International Symposium on Biomedical Imaging (ISBI 2019), pp. 587–591 (2019)
5. Le, D., Alam, M., Miao, B.A., Lim, J.I., Yao, X.: Fully automated geometric feature analysis in optical coherence tomography angiography for objective classification of diabetic retinopathy. Biomed. Opt. Express **10**(5), 2493–2503 (2019)
6. Ren, S., He, K., Girshick, R., Sun, J.: Faster R-CNN: towards real-time object detection with region proposal networks. IEEE Trans. Pattern Anal. Mach. Intell. **39**(6), 1137–1149 (2017)
7. Lin, T.Y., Goyal, P., Girshick, R., He, K., Dollár, P.: Focal loss for dense object detection. In: 2017 IEEE International Conference on Computer Vision (ICCV), pp. 2999–3007 (2017)
8. Law, H., Deng, J.: CornerNet: detecting objects as paired keypoints. In: Ferrari, V., Hebert, M., Sminchisescu, C., Weiss, Y. (eds.) Computer Vision – ECCV 2018. LNCS, vol. 11218, pp. 765–781. Springer, Cham (2018). https://doi.org/10.1007/978-3-030-01264-9_45
9. Duan, K., Bai, S., Xie, L., Qi, H., Huang, Q., Tian, Q.: CenterNet: keypoint triplets for object detection. In: 2019 IEEE/CVF International Conference on Computer Vision (ICCV), pp. 6568–6577 (2019)
10. Zhou, X., Wang, D., Krähenbühl, P.: Objects as points. arXiv preprint arXiv:1904.07850 (2019)
11. Newell, A., Yang, K., Deng, J.: Stacked hourglass networks for human pose estimation. In: Leibe, B., Matas, J., Sebe, N., Welling, M. (eds.) ECCV 2016. LNCS, vol. 9912, pp. 483–499. Springer, Cham (2016). https://doi.org/10.1007/978-3-319-46484-8_29
12. Oktay, O., et al.: Attention U-Net: learning where to look for the pancreas. arXiv preprint arXiv:1804.03999 (2018)
13. Everingham, M., Van Gool, L., Williams, C.K., Winn, J., Zisserman, A.: The pascal visual object classes (VOC) challenge. Int. J. Comput. Vision **88**(2), 303–338 (2010)
14. Lin, T.-Y., et al.: Microsoft COCO: common objects in context. In: Fleet, D., Pajdla, T., Schiele, B., Tuytelaars, T. (eds.) ECCV 2014. LNCS, vol. 8693, pp. 740–755. Springer, Cham (2014). https://doi.org/10.1007/978-3-319-10602-1_48
15. Padilla, R., Netto, S.L., da Silva, E.A.B.: A survey on performance metrics for object-detection algorithms. In: 2020 International Conference on Systems, Signals and Image Processing (IWSSIP), pp. 237–242 (2020)

A Large-Scale Hierarchical Structure Knowledge Enhanced Pre-training Framework for Automatic ICD Coding

Shi Wang[1(✉)], Daniel Tang[1], and Luchen Zhang[2]

[1] Key Laboratory of Intelligent Information Processing, Institute of Computing Technology, Chinese Academy of Sciences, Beijing, China
`wangshi@ict.ac.cn`
[2] National Computer Network Emergency Response Technical Team/Coordination Center of China, Beijing, China
`zlc@cert.org.cn`

Abstract. ICD coding is usually considered as a multi-label prediction task, which assigns accurate multiple ICD codes to clinical texts. In this paper, we present a novel way of injecting prior knowledge of hierarchical structures into BERT (HieBERT) to predict ICD codes automatically. Hierarchical structures consist of code tree positions and code tree sequence LSTM embeddings. We generate them as hierarchical representations of ICD codes. Besides, we train a clinical BERT model on millions of clinical texts to capture contextual and co-occurrence information. Then, we propose an aligning method to map the hierarchical representations into BERT vector space. We implement HieBERT on a widely used dataset: MIMIC-III. And the experimental results indicate that our proposed model achieves great performance compared with previous works.

Keywords: Structural and co-occurrence embedding · Automatic ICD coding · Hierarchical BERT

1 Introduction

The International Classification of Diseases (ICD) have been a focus of healthcare community in recent years. ICD codes have been widely used in reimbursement and monitoring health issues [9].

Some automatic ICD coding methods [8] have been proposed to address the problems above. These methods explore some special characteristics in ICD codes: First, ICD codes can be organized in hierarchical tree structure and siblings in the tree cannot appear in one clinical text, since the descriptions of siblings are extremely similar. Second, some diseases have strong co-occurrence relationships. For example, a patient with hypertension usually suffers from headache at the same time. In terms of clinical texts, we get that the average length on random 30,000 samples of them is 1,762, which is too long for the normal neural network methods.

S. Wang and D. Tang—Represents equal contribution to this work.

T. Mantoro et al. (Eds.): ICONIP 2021, CCIS 1517, pp. 494–502, 2021.
https://doi.org/10.1007/978-3-030-92310-5_57

Some previous methods [16] have been proposed to extract the hierarchy information and co-occurrence relationships. These prior methods achieve the state-of-the art performance on MIMIC-II and MIMIC-III [4,6]. However, they just directly add or aggregate two or more different kinds of vector space as the input to feed into the deep learning architecture. In terms of the long text issue, [19] proposed the BERT-XML to capture the long input sequence.

Pre-training BERT: Recently, there has been interest in fine-tuning pre-trained BERT [19] on Electronic Health Records (EHR) to extract relevant disease documentation. As a result, the fine-tuned BERT with clinical texts have the ability to capture semantic over longer span of clinical texts.

Code Hierarchy: As stated above, siblings cannot occur in the same clinical text, some codes have strong co-occurrence relationships. Methods with Tree-LSTM encoder [16] has been proposed to encode the code hierarchy representations. However, they cannot deal with long input clinical sequences and ignore the difference of different kinds vector space. Thus, it is a challenging problem to align all the embeddings into one vector space.

In this paper, we present a novel method **HieBERT** to address the above issues. HieBERT obtains code hierarchical embeddings by aggregating code tree-position encoding and code Tree-LSTM encoding.

In summary, the contributions of this paper are threefold.

- This is the first work to integrate hierarchical structures into a large scale pre-trained BERT.
- We propose a new normalization method transforming different embeddings into one vector space, including hierarchical vector space and wordpiece vector space in BERT.
- The experimental results on widely used MIMIC-III illustrate that our model HieBERT outperforms the previous methods.

2   Related Work

2.1   For Non-transformer Methods

Extensive previous and efficient works have been done to automatic ICD coding. Some CNN and attention methods are proposed to capture the key information in clinical texts, including [1,8,12,18]. Another study [16] proposes a tree-sequence LSTM architecture to simultaneously extract the hierarchical relationship among ICD codes and the semantics of each code. In addition, some researchers [20] employ Graph Neural Network (GNN) to capture the parent-child relations between ICD codes and obtain representations of these codes. Similarly, [17] employs GNNs to encode the ICD hierarchy and incorporate multi-scale feature attention for ICD coding.

2.2   For Transformer-Based Methods

Several works have employed BERT models for medical tasks. [13] uses a BERT-like method for medicine recommendation by learning representations for ICD codes.

BioBERT [11] employs BERT as base model for ICD prediction. Similarly, Clinical BERT and BERT-XML [2, 19] use BERT models fine-tuned on millions of EHR notes and MIMIC-MIMIC-III [4] notes and apply to downstream tasks.

Transformer-based methods have led to a large increase performance on clinical tasks. However, many of previous methods rely on off-the-shelf pre-trained BERT models and do not fine-tune on clinical notes to capture the contextual features of clinical information. Moreover, some works take fine-tuning clinical corpus [2, 19] into consideration, but they miss the hierarchical features among codes that can be captured by some structural methods, for example, tree-lstm.

Inspired by these methods, we propose HieBERT that fine-tunes BERT on millions of clinical texts to obtain code co-occurrence information and merge hierarchical information by being fed with hierarchical code-wise document representations.

3   Method

We propose a hierarchical code-wise method with fine-tuned BERT on millions of clinical texts for automatic ICD coding. Firstly, to capture the hierarchical representations in healthcare diagnoses, we utilize tree-lstm encoder and tree-position encoder. Secondly, to capture the code co-occurrence, we employ large scale pre-trained BERT as our initial semantic encoder and train it on millions of clinical notes. Thirdly, we employ hierarchical code-wise attention to learn relevant document representations for each hierarchical code. Finally, we feed the hierarchical code-wise document representations into fine-tuned clinical BERT and evaluate the HieBERT on code prediction task. The overview of our model HieBERT is shown in Fig. 1.

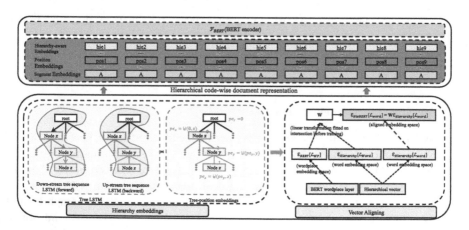

Fig. 1. The architecture of HieBERT

3.1   Hierarchical Representations

This section introduces the progress of generation of hierarchical representations by Tree-position encoder

Tree-Position Encoder: The distance of two tree nodes is a path. We can arrive one node from another node by some steps of length-1 paths. The progress above can be seen as an affine transforming operation A_ϕ [14] in Eq. 1.

$$PE_\beta = A_\phi PE_\alpha \tag{1}$$

In Eq. 1, given a position α, we can get the target position β with affine transform operation A_ϕ. Some directions of these path refer to the parents, and others refer to the children. We take the step up to the parent as operation U and step down to children as D. Thus, for any path ϕ, we can obtain the transform A_ϕ by some combinations of U and D. For example, the position encoding of the second child of node x's grandpa can described path $\phi = \langle$parent, parent, child-2$\rangle$, which can also be represented as $D_2 U^2 PE_x$.

Given a n-ary tree, we set the position embedding of the root as zero vector ($\mathbf{0} \in R^{d_e}$), which is shown in the Tree-position embeddings part of Fig. 1. Every down-step length-1 path is seen as operation D and every up-step length-1 path is seen as operation U. Thus, every node embedding can be obtained by some combinations of multiple D operations from the root. Given a position x, then $x = D_{b_L} D_{b_{L-1}} ... D_{b_1}$, where L means which layer the node is located, and b_i represents the chosen path in the i-th layer.

We treat tree position encoding as a stack of length-1 component parts. Every D operation pushes a length-1 path onto the stack, while U pops a length-1 path which is described as Eq. 2:

$$
\begin{aligned}
D_i x &= e_i^n \oplus (x \ominus x[n+1:]) \\
Ux &= (x \ominus x[:(n-1)]) \oplus \mathbf{0}_n
\end{aligned}
\tag{2}
$$

where $\ominus$ means pop operation or truncation, and $\oplus$ indicates pull or concatenate operation.

In addition, if y is the child of x, then we can get that $y = \uplus(0, x)$ (if x in the first layer in code tree), where *uplus* the D operation in Eq. 2.

After tree-position encoding, we obtain tree-position embedding ($Vp \in R^{d_e * N}$) of each code.

Tree-LSTM Encoder: We utilize an up-stream tree LSTM (TLSTM) [15, 16] and a down-stream TLSTM to capture the structure relationships among clinical codes. Inspired by Tree-LSTM method [16], we employ sequence LSTM to generate the initial Tree-LSTM code embeddings since each code has a description. Then, we feed the hidden states of individual codes produced by the sequence LSTM into Tree-LSTM Encoder.

3.2 Pre-training BERT

We employ BERT to represent input text. Specially, We trained BERT model on clinical texts including diagnosis descriptions and admission records with mask language model (MLM) to capture the co-occurrence relationship of some diseases. Before training, we address two major issues. Firstly, we extend the vocabulary words of origin BERT with special medical words in clinical texts. Secondly, the origin BERT model only support sequence lengths up to 512, while the average length of clinical texts is 1,762. Thus, we pop the first layer of BERT and add a new full neural layer, which supports 1024 sequence length. Meanwhile, other parameters in the origin BERT remains as the initial of our clinical BERT. Finally, we trained the clinical BERT on millions of clinical texts with MLM method.

3.3 Aligning Hierarchy and Wordpiece Vectors

To keep the consistency of input vector space in HieBERT, we train an aligning model in this section. Specially, we transform the vectors of hierarchical vector space $\varepsilon_H [L_{word}]$ into BERT native wordpiece vector space $\varepsilon_{BERT} [L_{word}]$.

We model the transformation as unconstrained linear mapping $W \in R^{d_B * d_H}$. We take 80% words as training set, and the 20% as test set. The goal of aligning method is to minimize the Eq. 3.

$$\Sigma_x \| W\varepsilon_{Hierarchy}(x) - \varepsilon_{BERT}(x) \|_2^2 \tag{3}$$

Similar to the hierarchy aligning method, we align clinical document representations into BERT vector space and get $H = \{h_1, h_2, ..., h_N\}$, where h_i is the vector of the i-th word in H and N is the length of H. After hierarchy aligning, we obtain new Hierarchy vectors Vpt^{BERT}.

3.4 Hierarchical Code-Wise Attention

We generate the hierarchical code-wise attention embedding via the *softmax* function:

$$\alpha_i = softmax(H^T Vpt_i^{BERT}) \tag{4}$$

Then, we use attention α and document embedding H to generate hierarchical code-wise document representation $C = \{c_1, c_2, ..., c_L\} \in R^{d_e * L}$, where $c_i = H \alpha_i$ and L is the number of clinical codes.

3.5 Training

ICD prediction can be seemed as multiple binary prediction, which means for each code, the prediction value $\hat{y}_i = \sigma(u_i)$, where $i = 1, ... , L$. Thus, the loss of ICD coding is expressed in Eq. 5:

$$\mathcal{L} = \Sigma_{i=1}^{L}[-y_i \log(\hat{y}_i) - (1 - y_i) \log(1 - \hat{y}_i)] \tag{5}$$

where y_i equals 0 or 1.

4   Experiments

4.1   Datasets and Metrics

MIMIC-III [4] is one of the most widely open-access datasets. MIMIC-III includes two versions: MIMIC-III full and MIMIC-III 50.

In addition, the corpus of pre-training models are extracted from medical notes and diagnoses in ICD-9/10 codes mainly in MIMIC-II and MIMIC-III. The resulting data set of pre-training contains a total of 6.3 million notes. The data is then randomly split by patient number into train, dev, test sets respectively with 7:1:2.

We use macro-averaged F1, micro-averaged F1, macro-averaged and micro-average area under the ROC curve (AUC), and P@N (the accuracy of the first N results, and here, N = 8, 15) as the main metrics to evaluate the efficiency of our model and baselines.

4.2 Baselines

For Non-transformers:

- Logistic Regression: Logistic regression is a bag-of-words logistic regression model.
- Flat SVMs: Flat SVMs [10] use 10,000 tf-idf unigram features and train 8,929 binary SVMs for flat SVMs.
- CNN: A widely applied method in NLP [3,5,7]. [8] employed CNN as the baseline.
- CAML & DRCAML: CAML [8] employs convolutional attention network for multi-label ICD prediction. DR-CAML is a updated version of CAML with code description.
- Bi-GRU: Bi-GRU uses bidirectional gated recurrent unit for document representation, we take it as our baseline.

For Transformers:

- BioBERT: Inspired by the success of BERT, BioBERT [11] was proposed by using BERT model for medicine recommendation by learning embeddings for ICD codes.
- Clinical BERT: Clinical BERT [2] employs a BERT model fine-tuned on MIMIC-III notes, charge summaries and apply it to downstream tasks.
- EHR BERT + XML: BERT-XML [19] trained a BERT model from scratch on millions of EHR notes and adapted the BERT architecture for ICD coding with multi-label attention.

4.3 Experimental Results

The comparisons between our model and non-transformer and transformer-based methods on MIMIC-III is given in Table 1 and Table 2, respectively.

Compared with Non-transformer Methods: For MIMIC-III full: Compared with baselines, our method HieBERT achieves the best performance in Macro-F1, Micro-F1, and Macro-AUC. Since clinical codes are in uneven distribution and Macro-F1 emphasizes the performance of rare label, it is difficult to obtain high Macro-F1 score. Even in this case, $HieBERT_{big,length=1024}$ performs better and achieves 26.67% improvement compared to the latest state-of-the-art Hypercore method. In recall@8 and recall@15, $HieBERT_{max}$ obtains 21.1% and 39.4% improvement compared with CAML, respectively. This demonstrates the effectiveness of HieBERT.

For MIMIC-III 50: We also evaluate our model and baselines on the most common 50 codes set of MIMIC-III. MIMIC-III 50 has a relatively even distribution, which leads to the possibility of achieving higher Macro-F1 scores. Our method (max version) obtains the highest score 0.675 on the Macro-F1 metric.

Compared with Transformer-Based Methods: We compare transformer-based methods with different size in the metric of AUC (micro and macro), which is shown in Table 2. We find that transformer-based methods with max length of 1024 performs better than those of 512. Clinical notes tend to be long and methods with max length of 1024 have more ability to capture the features of those long sequences. However, training 1024-length models costs roughly more than 3 times than the 512-length ones. In order to train methods for long sequences, it is necessary to develop a faster transformer models.

Table 1. Results of the comparison of our model and other baselines on the MIMIC-III full and MIMIC-III 50 labels. In all tables, the bold number with * indicates the best result compared to the other methods. LR represents logistic regression and w/o-t represents without tree-lstm model.

Model	MIMIC-III full								MIMIC-III 50				
	AUC		F1		R@N		P@N		AUC		F1		P@5
	Macro	Micro	Macro	Micro	8	15	8	15	Macro	Micro	Macro	Micro	
LR	56.1	93.7	1.1	27.2	–	–	54.2	41.1	82.9	86.4	47.7	53.3	54.6
Flat-SVMs	–	–	–	39.7	–	–	–	–	–	–	–	–	–
CNN	80.6	96.9	4.2	41.9	–	–	40.2	49.1	87.6	90.7	57.6	62.5	62.0
CAML	88.8	98.4	7.2	51.9	36.5	51.2	69.7	54.9	87.5	90.9	53.2	61.4	60.9
DR-CAML	92.4	96.3	9.0	54.7	–	–	70.1	65.3	88.2	90.7	60.7	66.4	62.5
Bi-GRU	82.2	97.1	3.8	41.7	–	–	58.5	44.5	82.8	86.8	48.4	54.9	59.1
HieBERT(w/o-t)	89.7	96.0	8.6	52.9	–	–	69.0	54.8	88.4	91.6	57.6	63.3	61.8
HieBERT$_{min}$	91.7 ± 0.4	96.5 ± 0.7	9.7 ± 0.3	61.3 ± 0.5	39.0 ± 0.1	62.0 ± 0.4	78.8 ± 0.5	71.4 ± 0.1	92.4 ± 0.1	93.7 ± 0.5	64.3 ± 0.4	66.9 ± 0.3	64.8 ± 0.5
HieBERT$_{max}$	94.0* ± 0.4	98.9* ± 0.2	11.4* ± 0.5	65.2* ± 0.3	44.2* ± 0.5	71.4* ± 0.5	79.5* ± 0.1	75.3* ± 0.3	93.5* ± 0.3	94.5* ± 0.5	67.5* ± 0.7	68.5* ± 0.6	65.3* ± 0.3

Table 2. The compared results of test set performance of transformer-used methods.

Methods	AUC	
	Micro	Macro
BERT (max length = 1024)	95.5	89.8
Fine-tuned BERT (max length = 1024)	95.8	90.3
BioBERT	96.0	90.8
Clinical BERT	96.1	90.4
EHR BERT (small, max length = 1024)	96.5	91.8
EHR BERT + XML (small, max length = 1024)	96.8	92.4
EHR BERT + XML (big, max length = 512)	97.0	92.7
HieBERT (small, max length = 512)	96.5	91.7
HieBERT (small, max length = 1024)	96.8	92.7
HieBERT (big, max length = 512)	97.1	93.4
HieBERT (big, max length = 1024)	98.9	94.0

Acknowledgements. We thank the reviewers and colleagues for their valuable feedback. This research was supported by the Chinese National 242 Information Security Program (2021A008), Beijing NOVA Program (Cross-discipline, Z191100001119014), the National Key Research and Development Program of China (2017YFB1002300, 2017YFC1700300), National Natural Science Foundation of China (61702234).

References

1. Allamanis, M., Peng, H., Sutton, C.: A convolutional attention network for extreme summarization of source code. In: Balcan, M., Weinberger, K.Q. (eds.) Proceedings of the 33nd International Conference on Machine Learning, ICML 2016, New York City, NY, USA, 19–24 June 2016. JMLR Workshop and Conference Proceedings, vol. 48, pp. 2091–2100. JMLR.org (2016)
2. Alsentzer, E., et al.: Publicly available clinical BERT embeddings. arXiv preprint arXiv:1904.03323 (2019)
3. Dauphin, Y.N., Fan, A., Auli, M., Grangier, D.: Language modeling with gated convolutional networks. In: Precup, D., Teh, Y.W. (eds.) ICML 2017. Proceedings of Machine Learning Research, vol. 70, pp. 933–941. PMLR (2017)
4. Johnson, A.E., et al.: MIMIC-III, a freely accessible critical care database. Sci. Data **3**(1), 1–9 (2016)
5. Johnson, R., Zhang, T.: Deep pyramid convolutional neural networks for text categorization. In: Barzilay, R., Kan, M. (eds.) ACL 2017, pp. 562–570. ACL (2017)
6. Jouhet, V., et al.: Automated classification of free-text pathology reports for registration of incident cases of cancer. Methods Inf. Med. **51**(3), 242 (2012)
7. Kim, Y.: Convolutional neural networks for sentence classification. In: Moschitti, A., Pang, B., Daelemans, W. (eds.) ACL 2014. pp. 1746–1751. ACL (2014)
8. Mullenbach, J., Wiegreffe, S., Duke, J., Sun, J., Eisenstein, J.: Explainable prediction of medical codes from clinical text. In: NAACL 2018, June 2018
9. Nadathur, S.G.: Maximising the value of hospital administrative datasets. Aust. Health Rev. **34**(2), 216–223 (2010)
10. Perotte, A., Pivovarov, R., Natarajan, K., Weiskopf, N., Wood, F., Elhadad, N.: Diagnosis code assignment: models and evaluation metrics. J. Am. Med. Inform. Assoc. **21**(2), 231–237 (2014)
11. Sänger, M., Weber, L., Kittner, M., Leser, U.: Classifying German animal experiment summaries with multi-lingual BERT at CLEF eHealth 2019 task 1. In: CLEF (Working Notes) (2019)
12. dos Santos, C.N., Tan, M., Xiang, B., Zhou, B.: Attentive pooling networks. CoRR (2016). http://arxiv.org/abs/1602.03609
13. Shang, J., Ma, T., Xiao, C., Sun, J.: Pre-training of graph augmented transformers for medication recommendation. arXiv preprint arXiv:1906.00346 (2019)
14. Shiv, V.L., Quirk, C.: Novel positional encodings to enable tree-based transformers. In: Wallach, H.M., Larochelle, H., Beygelzimer, A., d'Alché-Buc, F., Fox, E.B., Garnett, R. (eds.) NeurIPS 2019, pp. 12058–12068 (2019)
15. Tai, K.S., Socher, R., Manning, C.D.: Improved semantic representations from tree-structured long short-term memory networks. In: ACL, July 2015
16. Xie, P., Xing, E.: A neural architecture for automated ICD coding. In: ACL 2018, July 2018
17. Xie, X., Xiong, Y., Yu, P.S., Zhu, Y.: EHR coding with multi-scale feature attention and structured knowledge graph propagation. In: Proceedings of the 28th ACM International Conference on Information and Knowledge Management, pp. 649–658 (2019)

18. Yin, W., Schütze, H.: Attentive convolution. CoRR abs/1710.00519 (2017)
19. Zhang, Z., Liu, J., Razavian, N.: BERT-XML: large scale automated ICD coding using BERT pretraining. In: Proceedings of the 3rd Clinical Natural Language Processing Workshop, November 2020
20. Zhou, J., et al.: Graph neural networks: a review of methods and applications. AI Open **1**, 57–81 (2020)

Triple Tag Network for Aspect-Level Sentiment Classification

Guangtao Xu[1], Peiyu Liu[1(✉)], Zhenfang Zhu[2], Ru Wang[1], Fuyong Xu[1], and Dun Jin[1]

[1] Shandong Normal University, Jinan, China
liupy@sdnu.edu.cn
[2] Shandong JiaoTong University, Jinan, China
zhuzf@sdjtu.edu.cn

Abstract. The purpose of aspect-level sentiment classification is to determine the sentiment polarity of specific aspects in a sentence. Since the attention-based neural network model cannot accurately capture the connection between aspects and opinion words, many studies have adopted graph neural networks (GNN) to capture the structural information in the dependency tree of sentences, establish the relationship between aspects and opinion words. However, the sentence structure information used by these models when making sentiment polarity prediction is not comprehensive enough. Therefore, we propose a triple tag network (TTN) to imitate the operation of humans when judging the sentiment polarity. Specifically, when people determine the sentiment polarity of a certain aspect in a sentence, they generally consider the two tags of part-of-speech and dependency. On this basis, we add an additional distance tag to fit our model. We have conducted many experiments on three benchmark datasets. The experimental results show that our method can well capture the connection between aspects and opinion words, and further improve the performance of the graph attention networks (GAT).

Keywords: Aspect-level sentiment classification · Graph neural networks · Dependency tree · Syntactic information

1 Introduction

Aspect-level sentiment classification (ALSC) is a subtask under sentiment analysis, whose purpose is to identify the sentiment polarity (positive, neutral, negative) of the given aspect in a sentence. For example, in a restaurant review "The environment of this restaurant is good, but the dishes taste bad", the sentiment polarity of the aspect "environment" and "dishes" are respectively "positive" and "negative". In our research, the aspects are usually nouns or noun phrases.

In view of the advantages of the attention mechanism in capturing the semantic association of aspects and context, many studies consider using attention for ALSC [1–4]. However, these models still cannot accurately capture the relationship between aspects and opinion words.

© Springer Nature Switzerland AG 2021
T. Mantoro et al. (Eds.): ICONIP 2021, CCIS 1517, pp. 503–510, 2021.
https://doi.org/10.1007/978-3-030-92310-5_58

Recently, many studies have tried to use graph neural networks (GNN) and dependency tree to re-encode the hidden state vector to capture the grammatical information of the sentence [5–8]. It is undeniable that these works have achieved very good results, but they are not comprehensive enough in using the structural information in the dependency tree. Specifically, here we simply divide the structure information contained in the dependency tree into three types: part-of-speech, dependency, and distance. Usually these GNN-based models use one or two of the above structural information. In addition, because GNN is a hierarchical structure network, the network must be deepened to capture more distant dependent information. But this inevitably leads to the introduction of too much noise information.

In this paper, we propose a triple tag network (TTN) to make full use of the structural information and mitigate the impact of noise information. TTN is divided into two parts. In the first part, we propose a relational graph attention network (RGAT). It aims to solve the problem that the graph attention network may pay attention to the wrong neighboring nodes when updating node information. Specifically, we calculate the attention coefficient through the dependency relationship labels between adjacent nodes when updating node information. Intuitively, this calculation method is more logical than using hidden state vectors to calculate the implicit relationship between neighboring nodes. In the second part, we propose a part-of-speech-distance network (POSDN), which purpose is to solve the problem of noise information from another angle. Due to the limitations of the GNN itself, it cannot accurately capture the long-distance dependency relationship. Therefore, we propose the POSDN to obtain the global structure information related to the aspects. First, we believe that part-of-speech information can have a positive impact on ALSC. Because usually aspects are nouns or noun phrases, and opinion words are mostly adjectives. Second, we introduce distance tags to make the model focus on words that are closer to the aspect, prevent the model from paying attention to the wrong opinion words when the sentence contains multiple aspects and multiple opinion words.

2   Model

2.1   Aspect-Based Encoder

Figure 1 gives an overview of TTN for a given sentence $W^c = \{w_1^c, w_2^c, \cdots, w_n^c\}$ and its aspect $W^a = \{w_1^a, w_2^a, \cdots, w_m^a\}$, we connect them and input them into the pre-trained BERT[1] model to obtain an aspect-based contextual output. Where n and m represent sentence length and aspect length, respectively. That is, the input of BERT is "[CLS] + W^c + [SEP] + W^a + [SEP]". We use the output of the BERT encoder corresponding to W^c as the contextual representation of the sentence. We denote the final output of the aspect-based encoder layer as $H^c = \{h_1^c, h_2^c, \cdots, h_n^c\} \in \mathbb{R}^{n \times d}$, where d represents the hidden state dimension.

---

[1] https://github.com/huggingface/transformers.

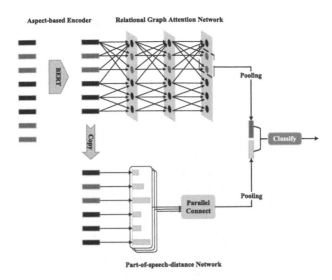

Fig. 1. The structure of proposed triple tag network (TTN). Aspect words are shown in red. (Color figure online)

2.2 Relational Graph Attention Network

Before inputting the output H^c of the aspect-based encoder layer to RGAT for re-encoding, we need to construct a relational adjacency matrix $A^r \in \mathbb{R}^{n \times n}$. We use SpaCy[2] to obtain the dependency tree of each sentence, and then construct a relational adjacency matrix for each sentence based on the dependency tree. Figure 2 shows an example of three types of tags. The element a_{ij}^r in A^r represents the dependency between the i-th word and the j-th word in the sentence. If two words are not adjacent on the dependency tree, we use "pad" to indicate. Particularly, we use "root" to indicate diagonal elements.

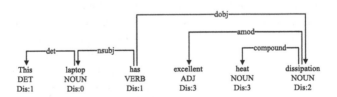

Fig. 2. An example of part-of-speech, dependency and distance tags. The aspect is highlighted in red. (Color figure online)

Then we convert all the tag elements a_{ij}^r in the relational adjacency matrix A^r into a vector $e_{ij}^r \in \mathbb{R}^{1 \times d}$ via the embedding matrix $E^r \in \mathbb{R}^{|V_r| \times d}$. Where $|V_r|$

---

[2] https://spacy.io.

represents the size of the dependency tag vocabulary. After non-linear transformation and softmax operation, we convert each tag vector into relational coefficient a_{ij}^l.

$$\hat{a}_{ij}^l = relu\left(e_{ij}^r W_1^{rl} + b_1^{rl}\right) W_2^{rl} + b_2^{rl} \tag{1}$$

$$a_{ij}^l = \frac{\exp\left(\hat{a}_{ij}^l\right)}{\sum_{j=1}^{n} \exp\left(\hat{a}_{ij}^l\right)} \tag{2}$$

Among them, W_1^{rl} and W_2^{rl} are the weight matrices that need to be learned, and b_1^{rl} and b_2^{rl} are biases. l represents the number of layers of RGAT.

To facilitate understanding, we denote the output of the l-th layer in RGAT as $H^l = \{h_1^l, h_2^l, \cdots, h_n^l\} \in \mathbb{R}^{n \times d}$, where $l \in [1, 2, \cdots, L]$. Then the output of node i at the l-th layer of RGAT can be expressed as:

$$h_i^l = \sum_{j=1}^{n} a_{ij}^l W^l h_j^l + b^l \tag{3}$$

Where W^l and b^l are the weights and biases that need to be learned, respectively. We denote the aspect output of the last layer of RGAT as $H^a = \{h_1^a, h_2^a, \cdots, h_m^a\} \in \mathbb{R}^{m \times d}$.

2.3 Part-of-Speech-Distance Network

Before introducing the POSDN, we first construct part-of-speech and distance tags for each sentence. First, we use the dependency parser to obtain the part-of-speech tags and dependency tree. Secondly, we construct the distance tag from each word to the aspect according to the dependency tree. Specifically, first we put a distance tag "Dis:0" for the aspect, and then we traverse the words adjacent to the aspect and label them "Dis:1". Then we traverse the words adjacent to the word with the tag "Dis:1", and if they are not aspect, we label them with the tag "Dis:2", and so on. Here we use "Dis:5" as the farthest distance. When the distance between a word and the aspect exceeds 5, we label them as "Dis:∞". We use $P = \{p_1, p_2, \cdots, p_n\}$ to represent the list of part-of-speech tags of the sentence, use $D = \{d_1, d_2, \cdots, d_n\}$ to represent the list of distance tags of the sentence. Figure 2 shows an example of distance and part-of-speech tags.

After getting the two tag lists P and D of the sentence, we use two embedding matrices $E^p \in \mathbb{R}^{|V_p| \times d}$ and $E^d \in \mathbb{R}^{|V_d| \times d}$ to convert the tags p_i and d_i into vectors $e_i^p \in \mathbb{R}^{1 \times d}$ and $e_i^d \in \mathbb{R}^{1 \times d}$. Where $|V_p|$ and $|V_d|$ represent the size of the part of speech and distance vocabulary, respectively. Then the output $H^p = \{h_1^p, h_2^p, \cdots, h_K^p\}$ of POSDN can be obtained as follows:

$$\beta_i^k = relu\left(e_i^p W_1^{pk} + b_1^{pk}\right) W_2^{pk} + b_2^{pk} \tag{4}$$

$$\gamma_i^k = relu\left(e_i^d W_1^{dk} + b_1^{dk}\right) W_2^{dk} + b_2^{dk} \tag{5}$$

$$\delta_i^k = \frac{\exp\left(\beta_i^k \gamma_i^k\right)}{\sum_{j=1}^{n} \exp\left(\beta_j^k \gamma_j^k\right)} \tag{6}$$

$$H^p = \|_{k=1}^{K} \sum_{i=1}^{n} \delta_i^k h_i^c \tag{7}$$

Among them, β_i^k and γ_i^k represent the part-of-speech tag score and distance tag score of the k-th head node i of POSDN, respectively. δ_i^k is the relational coefficient of the k-th head node i. $\|_{k=1}^{K} x_i$ denotes the parallel connection of vectors from x_1 to x_K. $W_1^{pk}, W_2^{pk}, W_1^{dk}, W_2^{dk}$ and $b_1^{pk}, b_2^{pk}, b_1^{dk}, b_2^{dk}$ are the weights and biases that need to be learned, respectively.

2.4   Sentiment Classification

We combine the aspect average pooling output h^{gat} of RGAT with the average pooling output h^{pos} of POSDN to obtain the final feature representation h^f. After sending h^f to a fully connected softmax layer, the probability distribution of each sentiment polarity is obtained:

$$h^{gat} = \frac{1}{m} \sum_{i=1}^{m} h_i^a \tag{8}$$

$$h^{pos} = \frac{1}{K} \sum_{i=1}^{K} h_i^p \tag{9}$$

$$h^f = h^{gat} \oplus h^{pos} \tag{10}$$

$$p = \text{softmax}\left(W_p h^f + b_p\right) \tag{11}$$

Where $\oplus$ denotes vector concatenation, and W_p and b_p are the weights and biases that need to be learned, respectively.

2.5   Training

The proposed triple tag network is optimized using a standard gradient descent algorithm with cross-entropy loss and L_2-regularization:

$$\text{Loss} = -\sum_{(c,\tilde{p}) \in C} \log\left(p_{\tilde{p}}\right) + \lambda \|\theta\|_2 \tag{12}$$

Among them, C represents the set of training samples, $\hat{p}$ represents the truth label, θ represents all the parameters that need to be learned, and λ is the L_2-regularization term coefficient.

Table 1. Detailed statistical of the three datasets in our experiments.

Dataset	Category	Positive	Neural	Negtivate
Twitter	Train	1561	3127	1560
	Test	173	346	173
Laptop	Train	994	464	870
	Test	341	169	128
Restaurant	Train	2164	637	807
	Test	728	196	196

3   Experiments

3.1   Datasets and Experiment Settings

We conducted experiments on three datasets, among which the Restaurant and Laptop datasets are from SemEval 2014 Task 4 [9], and the Twitter dataset is constructed by Dong et al. [10]. Each sample data is composed of three parts: sentence, aspect, and sentiment polarity. The sentiment polarity is divided into three categories: positive, negative, and neutral. Table 1 shows the detailed statistics of each dataset.

To be consistent with the BERT embedding dimension, we set the embedding dimension of all tags to 768. According to different dataset, the learning rate is $1 \times e^{-5}$ or $3 \times e^{-5}$, the value of the maximum distance tag is 4 or 5. The drop rate is 0.3, RGAT layers is 3 and batch size is 16. We use Adam as the optimizer, and the coefficient of the L_2-regularization term is $1 \times e^{-3}$. The evaluation metrics are Accuracy and Macro-F1. All experimental results are the average of three random initialization runs.

3.2   Results and Analysis

Table 2. Model comparison results of Accuracy and Macro-F1 (%) on three datasets. The best results are shown in bold.

Category	Model	Twitter		Laptop		Restaurant	
		Acc	F1	Acc	F1	Acc	F1
w/o Syn	MGAN [3]	72.54	70.81	75.39	72.47	81.25	71.94
	AEN [4]	72.83	69.81	73.51	69.04	80.98	72.14
	AEN-BERT [4]	74.71	73.13	79.93	76.31	83.12	73.769
Syn	ASGCN [5]	72.15	70.40	75.55	71.05	80.77	72.02
	CDT [6]	74.66	73.66	77.19	72.99	82.30	74.02
	RGAT [7]	75.57	73.82	77.42	73.76	83.30	76.08
	RGAT-BERT [7]	76.15	74.88	78.21	74.07	86.60	81.35
	DGEDT [8]	74.8	73.4	76.8	72.3	83.9	75.1
	DGEDT-BERT [8]	**77.9**	**75.4**	79.8	75.6	86.3	80.0
Ours	TTN-BERT	76.16	74.8	**80.41**	**76.31**	**87.68**	**82.39**

Table 2 shows the experimental results of our model and all comparison models on three benchmark datasets. We divide the models into two categories according to their different categories, one is syntactically related models, and the other is syntactically unrelated models.

According to the results in Table 2, we can draw the following conclusions. First, our model performs better than all comparison models on most datasets. Second, the performance of the BERT-based models are significantly better than the models based on GloVe embedding, which further illustrates the advantages of the large-scale pre-training models in this task. Third, the sentence syntactic-based model can indeed capture valuable structural information to further improve the accuracy of sentiment polarity prediction. The performance of our model on the Twitter dataset is slightly worse than that of RAGAT-BERT and DGEDT-BERT. We think this is because the sentence structure of the Twitter dataset is complex and contains some colloquial expressions.

3.3 Ablation Study

To verify the influence of each component in our model on the experimental results, we designed several ablation experiments. The experimental results are shown in Table 3.

Table 3. Ablation study results of Accuracy (%) on three datasets.

Model	Twitter	Laptop	Restaurant
	Accuracy	Accuracy	Accuracy
TTN-BERT	76.16	80.41	87.68
–POSDN	75.38	78.13	86.11
–RGAT	75.21	78.38	85.10
–RGAT(+GAT)	75.87	79.36	86.32

In Table 3, "–POSD" means removing the POSDN, and "–RGAT" means removing the RGAT. The impact of these two components on the Twitter dataset is basically the same and the impact is small, both less than one percent. On the Laptop and Restaurant datasets, these two components have a greater impact on the experimental results, ranging from one to two percent. This shows that these two components produce better results on datasets with clearer sentence structure. "–RGAT (+GAT)" indicates that the GAT is used instead of the RGAT. This change has the least impact on the model, and the experimental results have a slight drop. This shows that the method of assigning attention coefficients to GAT through relationship tags can slightly improve the performance of GAT.

4 Conclusion

Recently, models based on dependency trees and graph neural networks have been widely used in ALSC to establish connections between aspects and opinion words. But they only use part of the syntactic information in the dependency tree, and do not consider the influence of noise information on the graph neural network. To this end, we propose a triple tag network. First, we reduce the influence of noise information on GAT through dependency tags. Secondly, to capture the global syntactic dependency information, we propose a POSDN to establish the connection between aspects and context through part of speech and distance tags. The experimental results on three benchmark datasets prove the effectiveness of our model and confirm that the tag information can be used as guidance information for ALSC.

References

1. Wang, Y., Huang, M., Zhu, X., Zhao, L.: Attention-based LSTM for aspect-level sentiment classification. In: Proceedings of the 2016 Conference on Empirical Methods in Natural Language Processing, pp. 606–615, November 2016
2. Ma, D., Li, S., Zhang, X., Wang, H.: Interactive attention networks for aspect-level sentiment classification. In: Proceedings of the 26th International Joint Conference on Artificial Intelligence, pp. 4068–4074, August 2017
3. Fan, F., Feng, Y., Zhao, D.: Multi-grained attention network for aspect-level sentiment classification. In: Proceedings of the 2018 Conference on Empirical Methods in Natural Language Processing, pp. 3433–3442 (2018)
4. Song, Y., Wang, J., Jiang, T., Liu, Z., Rao, Y.: Attentional encoder network for targeted sentiment classification. arXiv preprint arXiv:1902.09314 (2019)
5. Zhang, C., Li, Q., Song, D.: Aspect-based sentiment classification with aspect-specific graph convolutional networks. In: Proceedings of the 2019 Conference on Empirical Methods in Natural Language Processing and the 9th International Joint Conference on Natural Language Processing (EMNLP-IJCNLP), pp. 4560–4570, November 2019
6. Sun, K., Zhang, R., Mensah, S., Mao, Y., Liu, X.: Aspect-level sentiment analysis via convolution over dependency tree. In: Proceedings of the 2019 Conference on Empirical Methods in Natural Language Processing and the 9th International Joint Conference on Natural Language Processing (EMNLP-IJCNLP), pp. 5683–5692, November 2019
7. Wang, K., Shen, W., Yang, Y., Quan, X., Wang, R.: Relational graph attention network for aspect-based sentiment analysis. In: Proceedings of the 58th Annual Meeting of the Association for Computational Linguistics, pp. 3229–3238, July 2020
8. Tang, H., Ji, D., Li, C., Zhou, Q.: Dependency graph enhanced dual-transformer structure for aspect-based sentiment classification. In: Proceedings of the 58th Annual Meeting of the Association for Computational Linguistics, pp. 6578–6588, July 2020
9. Pontiki, M., Papageorgiou, H., Galanis, D., Androutsopoulos, I., Pavlopoulos, J., Manandhar, S.: Semeval-2014 task 4: aspect based sentiment analysis. In: Proceedings of the 8th International Workshop on Semantic Evaluation (SemEval 2014), pp. 27–35 (2014)
10. Dong, L., Wei, F., Tan, C., Tang, D., Zhou, M., Xu, K.: Adaptive recursive neural network for target-dependent twitter sentiment classification. In: Proceedings of the 52nd Annual Meeting of the Association for Computational Linguistics (volume 2: Short papers), pp. 49–54, June 2014

CMAT: Column-Mask-Augmented Training for Text-to-SQL Parsers

Chen Chang[1,2]($\boxtimes$)

[1] Peking University, Beijing, China
leon_chang@pku.edu.cn
[2] Center for Data Science of Peking University, Beijing, China

Abstract. When it comes to text-to-SQL tasks, the model needs to learn context-based representations of schema along with natural language utterances. We present a simple and effective method for text-to-SQL tasks, Column-Mask-Augmented Training (CMAT), to make up for the insufficiency of training data. To exploit the synthesized data, we propose the clause prediction (CP) object for multi-task learning, which forces the model to capture contextual features of the schema items. Besides, we add the fuzzy match and subword match to the schema linking strategy in RAT-SQL. As a result, our method significantly increases the recall and F1 value of schema linking and achieves a competitive result with RAT-SQL and GraPPa on Spider.

Keywords: Text-to-SQL · Multi-task learning · Data augmentation

1 Introduction

Tabular data serve an essential role in many domains, such as finance and medicine. However, non-technical users are not familiar with the structured query language (SQL) required to access tabular data efficiently. Thus the text-to-SQL parser that converts natural language utterances into SQL queries has drawn significant attention recently.

In contrast to the prior semantic parsing datasets, Spider [15] contains complex and cross-domain examples, which proposes a more realistic and challenging task. Each example is based on a schema with multi tables. Besides, SQL queries in Spider have complicated structures with clauses such as `HAVING`, `GROUPBY`, and `ORDERBY`. Therefore, a text-to-SQL parser should overcome the following two difficulties.

Firstly, schema linking is critical to the performance of the model. The model will know that there may be a relationship between a word and a column (or table) in advance. Based on the error analysis from some text-to-SQL parsers, we find schema linking with exact or partial match sometimes misses the correct link, as shown in Table 1. This example indicates that the linking strategy affects the final result to some extent.

© Springer Nature Switzerland AG 2021
T. Mantoro et al. (Eds.): ICONIP 2021, CCIS 1517, pp. 511–518, 2021.
https://doi.org/10.1007/978-3-030-92310-5_59

Secondly, the lack of labeled data is another challenge. Semantic parsing tasks [16], including text-to-SQL, rely on sufficient training data. However, data annotation of text-to-SQL is a complex task and needs experts in SQL.

In this paper, we develop a two-stage training strategy. In the first training stage, we apply data augmentation by generating masked examples from training data and use the synthesis data for multi-task training. While in the second stage, we only use the origin data for training. In addition, we enhance the schema linking by fuzzy match and subword match, which significantly increases the recall of schema linking.

Experiments on Spider show that our model achieves competitive results in exact match accuracy and has a slighter decrease in accuracy when the labeled data is limited.

Table 1. An error example from RAT-SQL on Spider. The prediction misses a column and its value in the WHERE clause. The schema linking fails because the word *republics* neither matches Republic exactly nor is a part of it.

NL Utterance: Give the average life expectancy for countries in Africa which are republics?
Prediction: SELECT Avg(LifeExpectancy) FROM country WHERE Continent = 'Africa'
Gold SQL: SELECT Avg(LifeExpectancy) FROM country WHERE Continent = 'Africa' AND GovernmentForm = 'Republic'

2 Related Works

2.1 Multi-task Learning

In order to make full use of the labeled data, multi-task learning has been proved successful in many NLP tasks [7,10]. It forces the model to focus on the final output and generate appropriate hidden states as well. For example, Shao et al. [10] propose multi-task learning consisting of classification and mention detection for semantic parsing. All these tasks share the same encoder, and the training target is the combination of each task's loss function. Concerning other models such as pre-trained models, multi-task learning enables them to be capable of various downstream tasks. Specifically, the MLM object used in BERT [4] helps give a comprehensive understanding of natural language texts.

2.2 Data Augmentation

Data Augmentation in semantic parsing has evolved into two main streams. The first method is to generate data by word substitution [2]. Replacing entities or predicates is a simple and effective way to deal with the lack of labeled data.

The second one is to synthesize data through grammar rules or trained models [11,14]. This approach requires to design generation rules conditioned on grammar and the dataset or train a model converting SQL queries (or other logical forms) into natural language. Thus the synthesized data is likely to be of high quality, but the process is complex and dataset-specific.

Our model randomly replaces the column names with mask tokens and uses multi-task learning to exploit the generated data.

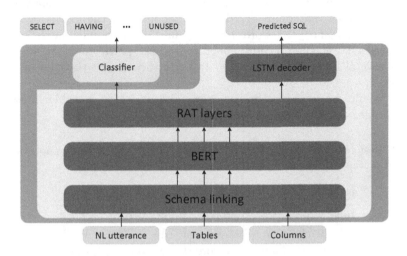

Fig. 1. An overview of our multi-task learning model. The green part is the RAT-SQL+BERT model, transferring natural language utterances and schema items to SQL queries. We use a classifier to classify schema items from ten classes: SELECT, HAVING, WHERE, FROM, GROUPBY, OERDERBY, INTERSECT, UNION, EXCEPT, UNUSED. (Color figure online)

3   Model

3.1   Text-to-SQL Parser

A text-to-SQL parser aims to convert an utterance $\mathcal{X} = \{x_1, x_2, ..., x_n\}$ into a SQL query $\mathcal{Y} = \{y_1, y_2, ..., y_m\}$ conditioned on schema $\mathcal{S} = \{c_1, c_2, ..., c_k\} \cup \{t_1, t_2, ..., t_l\}$, where c_i, t_j denote the column and table respectively. We follow the implementation of RAT-SQL [13] based on the encoder-decoder architecture. First, the relational Transformer encoder maps $\mathcal{X}$ and $\mathcal{S}$ to fixed-dimensional vectors Z. Then, we obtain the distribution $P(\mathcal{Y}|\mathcal{X}, \mathcal{S})$ over SQL queries from Z by the treelike LSTM [5] decoder. The green part of Fig. 1 illustrates this structure.

3.2   Schema Linking

The goal of schema linking is to construct a relational graph $\mathcal{G}$ on $\mathcal{X} \cup \mathcal{S}$. Recent models divide the schema linking into two types: *name-based linking* and *value-based linking*. The previous approaches of name-based linking focus on exact match and partial match [13]. In addition, our model proposes the fuzzy match, which uses Levenshtein Distance [6] to calculate the similarity between two strings. The similarity is a real number between 0 and 1. We consider two strings match if the similarity is greater than 0.7.

With regard to value-based linking, prior models rely on the exact match between phrases in $\mathcal{X}$ and database contents. However, after analyzing the dataset, we notice that many words do not appear in the exact form in the database. For instance, the word *republics* in Table 1 should match Republic in GovernmentForm column, but *republics* is in the plural form. So we cut the word by several letters in the head or tail and then search the subword in the database.

As a result, we improve the recall by 35% and 15% in table linking and column linking respectively, as Table 2 shows.

Table 2. Results of schema linking. We take whether a table/column appears in SQL as ground truth.

Type	Recall	Precision	F1
Table w/o fuzzy & subword	0.409	**0.753**	0.512
Table w/ fuzzy & subword	**0.753**	0.720	**0.736**
Column w/o fuzzy & subword	0.711	0.158	0.259
Column w/ fuzzy & subword	**0.861**	**0.164**	**0.276**

3.3   Masked Data Generation

Our Column-Mask-Augmented Training (CMAT) method is inspired by the successful implementation of duplicating masked data for training in BERT. However, instead of masking words in $\mathcal{X}$, we only substitute 15% of the column names with mask tokens and duplicate training examples several times so that each example is masked in different ways.

Bogin et al. [1] have proved that using the oracle schema as input can significantly improve performance. Moreover, from Table 2, we can infer that about 17% of the columns are used in SQL on average. So the chances are that many unused schema items are masked, which may let the model focus on the used schema items.

3.4   Training

In the first stage of training, we propose a clause predict (CP) loss. We define nine types of clauses, and the object of CP is to predict which clause each schema item is in. Take Fig. 2 as an example, there are three tables (the third line) in this database. According to the SQL query, only head is used and in the FROM clause, while others should be labeled UNUSED. Specifically, a two-layer MLP and a sigmoid function afterward are applied to calculate the distribution over nine

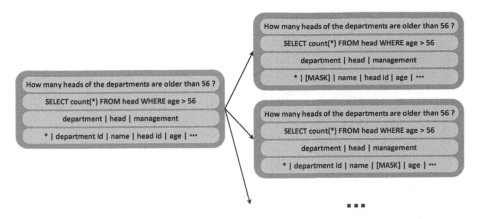

Fig. 2. An example of our data augmentation strategy. We randomly mask the column names and create different duplicates.

types of clauses and an UNUSED tag, based on the output of the encoder's last layer.[1] Like SQL generation loss, CP loss is also a cross-entropy loss. The model then minimizes both CP loss and SQL generation loss. So the final loss is

$$loss = \lambda \cdot loss_{CP} + (1 - \lambda) \cdot loss_{SQL},$$

where $\lambda \in (0, 1)$ is a hyperparameter.

The second stage is simple, where the model focuses on the origin training data and minimizes the SQL generation loss.

4   Experiments

4.1   Dataset

Spider is a text-to-SQL dataset with 9,693 annotated utterance-queries-schema triples split into 8,659 training and 1,034 development examples.

4.2   Model Configuration

We choose the same hyperparameters with RAT-SQL+BERT except for batch size and learning rate. We set the batch size to 4 because of the limited GPU memory and set the accumulated batch number to 4, equivalent to the batch size of 16. When generating masked data, we make five duplicates for each origin training example. We use AdamW [8] optimizer and apply the same warmup strategy as Vaswani et al. [12] with the beginning learning rate 6.44e−4 for non-BERT parameters. While for BERT parameters, the learning rate is 2.5e−6. The hyperparameter λ balancing two loss functions is set to 0.5.

---

[1] A schema item may have multiple classes. In this case, the target distribution follows the discrete uniform distribution.

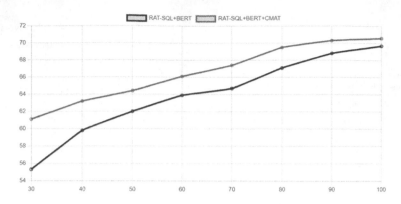

Fig. 3. The ratio-accuracy graph of two models. X axis stands for the ratio of data used, and Y axis stands for the accuracy on dev set.

4.3   Main Results

Table 3. Accuracy on Spider dev set.

Models	Accuracy
RAT-SQL+STRUG [3]	72.6
RAT-SQL+GAP [11]	71.8
SmBoP+GraPPa [9]	**74.7**
RAT-SQL+BERT [13]	69.7
RAT-SQL+BERT+CMAT	70.6
RAT-SQL+GraPPa [14]	73.4
RAT-SQL+GraPPa+CMAT	73.5

Table 3 shows the exact match accuracy on the Spider development set. Compared to the RAT-SQL+BERT model, our method achieves a 0.9% improvement. However, compared to the RAT-SQL+GraPPa model, our method has only a slight improvement. One possible reason is that Grappa is a model pre-trained on data augmented from Spider, weakening the effectiveness of the first stage training. Concerning the highly structure-aware models like SmBoP, we still achieve a competitive result, 1.2% lower in exact match accuracy.

Furthermore, we investigate the efficiency of our method, varying the ratio of the origin training data we use. From Fig. 3, we can see that our CMAT strategy enhances the baseline model over all the ratios. Moreover, the gap with the baseline model increases when the ratio goes down, implying text-to-SQL task needs sufficient training data.

4.4   Ablation Study

To determine how much the two components in our method affect the result, we conduct experiments with each component separately. From Table 4 we find that fuzzy match has a regular contribution to the model, while the improvement of CMAT greatly changes by the amount of data.

Table 4. Ablation study using 100% and 50% of training data.

Models	Accuracy
RAT-SQL+BERT	69.7
RAT-SQL+BERT w/ fuzzy match	70.0
RAT-SQL+BERT w/ masked data	70.4
RAT-SQL+BERT w/ both	70.6
RAT-SQL+BERT (50% data)	62.0
RAT-SQL+BERT w/ fuzzy match (50% data)	62.9
RAT-SQL+BERT w/ masked data (50% data)	63.8
RAT-SQL+BERT w/ both (50% data)	64.4

5   Conclusion

In this paper, we propose a novel and effective way of data augmentation for text-to-SQL. Unused schema items are likely to be masked by our CMAT strategy and thus allows the model to pay more attention to used schema items. Moreover, experiments show that the lower the ratio of training data is, the more improvement the model will achieve. Thanks to multi-task learning with clause prediction, we can fully use the labeled data. Qualitatively, we present a non-dataset-specific method that can be applied to any schema-based text-to-SQL dataset. Since the masked data has already been implemented successfully in pre-trained models, it will be beneficial to NLP tasks beyond text-to-SQL.

Acknowledgements. This research was supported by Peking University Education Big Data Project, grant number 2020ZDB04.

References

1. Bogin, B., Berant, J., Gardner, M.: Representing schema structure with graph neural networks for text-to-SQL parsing. In: Proceedings of the 57th Annual Meeting of the Association for Computational Linguistics, pp. 4560–4565 (2019)
2. Cao, R., Zhu, S., Liu, C., Li, J., Yu, K.: Semantic parsing with dual learning. In: Proceedings of the 57th Annual Meeting of the Association for Computational Linguistics, pp. 51–64 (2019)

3. Deng, X., Hassan, A., Meek, C., Polozov, O., Sun, H., Richardson, M.: Structure-grounded pretraining for text-to-SQL. In: Proceedings of the 2021 Conference of the North American Chapter of the Association for Computational Linguistics: Human Language Technologies, pp. 1337–1350 (2021)

4. Devlin, J., Chang, M.W., Lee, K., Toutanova, K.: BERT: pre-training of deep bidirectional transformers for language understanding. arXiv preprint arXiv:1810.04805 (2018)

5. Hochreiter, S., Schmidhuber, J.: Long short-term memory. Neural Comput. **9**(8), 1735–1780 (1997)

6. Levenshtein, V.I., et al.: Binary codes capable of correcting deletions, insertions, and reversals. In: Soviet physics doklady, vol. 10, pp. 707–710. Soviet Union (1966)

7. Lin, Y., Yang, S., Stoyanov, V., Ji, H.: A multi-lingual multi-task architecture for low-resource sequence labeling. In: Proceedings of the 56th Annual Meeting of the Association for Computational Linguistics (Volume 1: Long Papers), pp. 799–809 (2018)

8. Loshchilov, I., Hutter, F.: Fixing weight decay regularization in adam (2018)

9. Rubin, O., Berant, J.: SmBoP: semi-autoregressive bottom-up semantic parsing. In: Proceedings of the 2021 Conference of the North American Chapter of the Association for Computational Linguistics: Human Language Technologies, pp. 311–324 (2021)

10. Shao, B., et al.: Weakly supervised multi-task learning for semantic parsing. In: IJCAI, pp. 3375–3381 (2019)

11. Shi, P., et al.: Learning contextual representations for semantic parsing with generation-augmented pre-training. In: Proceedings of the AAAI Conference on Artificial Intelligence, vol. 35, pp. 13806–13814 (2021)

12. Vaswani, A., et al.: Attention is all you need. In: Advances in Neural Information Processing Systems, pp. 5998–6008 (2017)

13. Wang, B., Shin, R., Liu, X., Polozov, O., Richardson, M.: RAT-SQL: relation-aware schema encoding and linking for text-to-SQL parsers. In: Proceedings of the 58th Annual Meeting of the Association for Computational Linguistics, pp. 7567–7578 (2020)

14. Yu, T., et al.: GraPPa: grammar-augmented pre-training for table semantic parsing. arXiv preprint arXiv:2009.13845 (2020)

15. Yu, T., et al.: Spider: a large-scale human-labeled dataset for complex and cross-domain semantic parsing and text-to-SQL task. In: Proceedings of the 2018 Conference on Empirical Methods in Natural Language Processing, pp. 3911–3921 (2018)

16. Zettlemoyer, L.S., Collins, M.: Learning to map sentences to logical form: structured classification with probabilistic categorial grammars. In: Proceedings of the Twenty-First Conference on Uncertainty in Artificial Intelligence, pp. 658–666 (2005)

MeTGAN: Memory Efficient Tabular GAN for High Cardinality Categorical Datasets

Shreyansh Singh[✉], Kanishka Kayathwal, Hardik Wadhwa,
and Gaurav Dhama

AI Garage, Mastercard, Gurugram, India
{shreyansh.singh,kanishka.kayathwal,hardik.wadhwa,
gaurav.dhama}@mastercard.com

Abstract. Generative Adversarial Networks (GANs) have seen their use for generating synthetic data expand, from unstructured data like images to structured tabular data. One of the recently proposed models in the field of tabular data generation, CTGAN, demonstrated state-of-the-art performance on this task even in the presence of a high class imbalance in categorical columns or multiple modes in continuous columns. Many of the recently proposed methods have also derived ideas from CTGAN. However, training CTGAN requires a high memory footprint while dealing with high cardinality categorical columns in the dataset. In this paper, we propose MeTGAN, a memory-efficient version of CTGAN, which reduces memory usage by roughly 80%, with a minimal effect on performance. MeTGAN uses sparse linear layers to overcome the memory bottlenecks of CTGAN. We compare the performance of MeTGAN with the other models on publicly available datasets. Quality of data generation, memory requirements, and the privacy guarantees of the models are the metrics considered in this study. The goal of this paper is also to draw the attention of the research community on the issue of the computational footprint of tabular data generation methods to enable them on larger datasets especially ones with high cardinality categorical variables.

Keywords: Synthetic data generation · Generative Adversarial Networks · Tabular data · Privacy

1 Introduction

Despite the growing interest in areas like natural language processing and computer vision, the type of datasets have diversified considerably. However, tabular datasets remain prominent for a number of scenarios like patient records, banking records, census data, etc. Often, due to privacy concerns, these datasets cannot be used to train machine learning models as that would make it easy for attackers to extract details about the original data. Furthermore, the lack of sufficient real data for training the machine learning models also creates a need for synthetic data generation methods.

© Springer Nature Switzerland AG 2021
T. Mantoro et al. (Eds.): ICONIP 2021, CCIS 1517, pp. 519–527, 2021.
https://doi.org/10.1007/978-3-030-92310-5_60

Tabular data usually consists of both numerical and categorical columns. Real-world numerical data is typically multi-modal and categorical columns are often imbalanced. These two issues make synthetic tabular data generation a difficult task. GANs have shown a promising ability to model arbitrary distributions in the data for a variety of datasets. In this paper, we focus primarily on the GAN-based methods for tabular data generation. Some of the recently proposed and well known models in the synthetic tabular data generation domain include medGAN [2], tableGAN [10], TGAN [20], CTGAN [19] and cWGAN [4]. We compare the performance of these models on two publicly available datasets from the UCI Machine Learning repository namely the Adult [7] (classification data) and News [15] (regression data) datasets. CTGAN was found to be the best performer among these models. The Adult and News datasets although widely used in synthetic data generation papers like [10,19], do no have high cardinality categorical columns and hence are not very close to what large datasets would look like. CTGAN creates a one-hot encoded representation for all the categorical columns in the conditional vector and uses a residual connection in the first layer of the generator. This creates a memory bottleneck, mainly while dealing with a large number of categories in the dataset.

As demonstrated in the experiments section, it was observed that for the Loan [18] dataset, CTGAN has a very high memory footprint. To overcome this, we propose a new architecture MeTGAN, wherein we use a sparse linear layer for the conditional vector in both the generator and discriminator. Additionally, we remove residual connections in the first layer of the generator. This helps to get an 80% reduction in memory usage that makes it easy to generate synthetic data for large datasets. The proposed model performs at par with CTGAN across all the datasets. To summarise, the paper's contributions are:

- Propose a memory-efficient tabular GAN architecture to handle datasets with high cardinality categorical columns with at par performance as compared to the current state of the art algorithms
- A thorough comparison of the current existing GAN-based tabular data generation methods with MeTGAN on several metrics, machine learning efficacy, distribution similarity, privacy guarantees, and the memory requirements.
- Draw the attention of the research community to the computational requirements of such models and motivate researchers to work towards solutions.
- Additional details regarding the paper are available at: https://github.com/shreyansh26/MeTGAN-Paper.

2   Related Work

Initial contributions in the field of tabular data generation treated each column in the table as a distinct random variable and their distributions were modeled separately. [14] used decision trees to model the categorical variables while [21] used Bayesian networks. In [3] spatial data was modeled using trees. Continuous variables that were non-linearly related were modeled using copulas in [11].

Later, the use of GANs [5] started to emerge in the domain of synthetic tabular data generation. medGAN [2] uses an autoencoder with a GAN model to generate medical patient records with heterogeneous non-time-series continuous and/or binary data. tableGAN [10] uses a DCGAN [13] based architecture for synthetic data generation. TGAN [20] uses an LSTM based generator and an MLP based discriminator while CTGAN [19] uses a conditional generator and training-by-sampling to deal with the imbalanced categorical columns. CTGAN also uses mode-specific normalization to handle the non-Gaussian and multimodal distribution of continuous data. The architecture integrates PacGAN [8] and uses Wasserstein loss with gradient penalty [6]. cWGAN [4] models the data using self-conditioning in the generator and uses crosslayers for both the generator and the discriminator to explicitly calculate the feature interactions. Additionally embedding layers are used for dimensionality reduction and better representative power. In [19], in addition to CTGAN, the authors also propose a variational autoencoder-based approach, TVAE for synthetic tabular data generation. CrGAN-Cnet [9] uses GAN to perform synthetic airline passenger name record generation. CTAB-GAN [22] is a very recent paper that can effectively model columns that have a mix of continuous and categorical data. It introduces the information loss and classification loss to the conditional GAN. We were not able to reproduce the CTAB-GAN paper ourselves correctly and hence we do not include the results in our paper. However, from their paper, we understand that, architecturally, CTAB-GAN will not be more memory efficient than CTGAN, so not including the model in this paper will not affect the goal of our study.

3 Proposed Model

In this section, we present the MeTGAN architecture, which is designed to overcome the shortcomings of CTGAN on datasets with high cardinality. The conditional vector in CTGAN is sparse, most of its values are zero, ones being only at the places corresponding to the conditioned columns of the real data. This conditional vector is concatenated with a noise vector before passing it as an input to the generator. Similarly, in the case of the discriminator, the input is the concatenation of the conditional vector with either the generated data or with the real data. For datasets with high cardinality, this concatenated vector becomes large and leads to a memory bottleneck. Moreover, in the generator, an addition of a residual layer over this large vector further escalates the memory requirements.

In MeTGAN (architecture shown in Fig. 1), we address the above-mentioned issues as follows: First, we do not concatenate the conditional vector, neither with the noise vector in the case of the generator nor with real/generated data in the case of the discriminator. Second, we remove the first residual layer of the generator. In the case of the generator, the noise vector is passed through a linear layer and the conditional vector is passed through a separate sparse linear layer. The outputs from these layers are concatenated before passing it to the next layer. For discriminator, the real/generated data is passed through a fully connected layer with LeakyReLU activation and Dropout, whereas for the conditional vector the

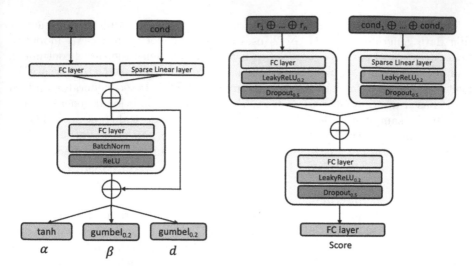

Fig. 1. Architecture of the generator (left) and discriminator (right) of MeTGAN. $\oplus$ indicates concatenation. The input z to the generator is the noise vector sampled from a standard multivariate normal distribution. *cond* is the conditional vector that represents the column name and value that the generator conditions upon. For the discriminator, a PacGAN [8] framework with n samples in each pac is used. $r_1, ..., r_n$ is the real or generated data which is passed through the discriminator, and $cond_1, ..., cond_n$ is used for the conditional vector. The outputs β, α indicate the one-hot vector of the mode and the value within the mode for continuous columns and d is the one-hot vector of the discrete values for categorical columns. The *Score* from the discriminator is the critic score indicating the realness of the input data given the conditional vector.

fully connected layer is replaced by a sparse linear layer. The outputs of these layers are also concatenated before passing it to the next layer.

4   Datasets

For the comparison of the models, two publicly available datasets were considered. The Adult dataset and the News dataset. The objective of taking these two datasets is that 1) They are widely used in synthetic tabular data literature [10,19,20] and 2) the Adult dataset poses a classification problem and the News dataset presents a regression problem, which can help to better analyze the performance of the models on the two major facets of machine learning on tabular data - regression and classification. The statistics associated with the datasets are shown in Table 1.

To compare the performance of CTGAN and MeTGAN on a dataset with high cardinality, we used the Loan dataset. A sample size of 150k data points was selected from the Loan dataset such that it had a sufficiently large number of total distinct categories across columns (21k) to test the memory efficacy of MeTGAN. The statistics of the Loan dataset are also shown in Table 1.

Table 1. Dataset statistics. #N and #C represent the number of continuous (numerical) and categorical columns in the dataset respectively. #Categories is the total number of categories across all the categorical columns.

Name	Train/test	#N	#C	#Categories
Adult	26k/6.5k	6	9	104
News	31k/8k	45	14	28
Loan	120k/30k	11	10	21k

Additional details of the features from each dataset used in our experiments and the target feature used for the Machine Learning Efficacy tests are described in our Github repository.

5 Metrics

5.1 Non-privacy Metrics

Memory Requirements - The GPU memory requirements of the MeTGAN and CTGAN models on the Loan dataset is one of the key metrics.

Machine Learning Efficacy - As defined in [19]. For the Adult dataset, we used Logistic Regression (LR) and Random Forest Classifier (RFC) and for News and Loan we used Random Forest Regressor (RFR) and ElasticNet (ENet). In both cases, we reported the difference ($\Delta F1$ or ΔMSE) of the ML model. The smaller the difference, the better the ML efficacy.

Statistical Similarity - The statistical closeness between the two datasets is shown using the Chi-squared (CS) test and the Kolmogorov–Smirnov (KS) test.

5.2 Privacy Metrics

DCR - [10] introduced a metric - Distance to Closest Record (DCR) which we use in this paper as well to measure privacy.

CategoricalCAP (CCAP) - This is based on the Correct Attribution Probability privacy method. It requires a set of key columns and a sensitive column for a dataset. We use the [1] package for the implementation. The closer the CCAP score is to one, the better is the privacy. CCAP was used for the Adult data.

NumericalLR (NLR) - This method also requires a set of key columns and a sensitive column. We use the [1] package for the implementation. Again, here higher the score (closer to 1), the better is the model performance. NumericalLR was used for the News and Loan datasets.

6   Results and Discussion

We study five GAN baselines, on Adult and News datasets, to compare the performance of the proposed MeTGAN model. Additionally, MeTGAN and CTGAN were studied on the Loan dataset keeping a focus on memory usage. We used an NVIDIA Quadro RTX 6000 for all our experiments. The training parameters for all the models and the key and sensitive columns required for CCAP and NLR metrics are mentioned in our Github repository.

The performance of the models on the Adult dataset is reported in Table 2. In terms of ML Efficacy, except medGAN, all models have a reasonably good performance. The MeTGAN model stands out in this test among all the models. TGAN performs well particularly in the CS and KS tests while MeTGAN and CTGAN have the next best performance. MeTGAN has a good CategoricalCAP score and is comparable to CTGAN. Overall, CTGAN and MeTGAN are the most balanced methods across all the metrics for synthetic data generation on this dataset, with MeTGAN performing slightly better on ML Efficacy than CTGAN.

Table 3 shows the performance of the models on the News dataset. On this dataset, CTGAN has the best ML Efficacy performance. MeTGAN and medGAN are next with reasonably good performance as well. cWGAN does not support regression tasks so it is not evaluated on the News dataset. medGAN has a good KS test score on this dataset. MeTGAN has a higher DCR-mean, and the relatively good NumericalLR score confirms that the higher DCR-mean is a positive sign. Although medGAN has a high KS test score, the low NumericalLR score indicates that it somehow leaks information. Overall, again both CTGAN and MeTGAN have a stable performance.

Table 4 shows the results of CTGAN and MeTGAN on the Loan dataset. It can be seen from the ΔMSE score that both CTGAN and MeTGAN do not perform well on this dataset in terms of ML Efficacy score. In the ML Efficacy metrics, MeTGAN outperforms CTGAN on the Random Forest regressor test and marginally loses out on the ElasticNet test. CTGAN has a slightly better performance on the CS and KS tests. In the privacy metrics, the performance of CTGAN and MeTGAN are very close to each other.

The main thing to note however is that for this high cardinality categorical dataset, the MeTGAN model requires 80% less memory (from Table 5) to give a similar performance as CTGAN. The use of the sparse layers for the model resulted in memory-efficient matrix operations over the sparse conditional vector. Additionally, removing the first residual layer from the generator helped to reduce the size of the input to the next layer. These two reasons primarily caused the reduction in GPU memory usage while not hampering the performance of the model significantly. Overall, MeTGAN performed at par or even marginally better than other models across different metrics on all the datasets.

Table 2. Results on the Adult dataset

Dataset	Model	ΔF1-LR	ΔF1-RFC	CS test	KS test	DCR-mean	DCR-std	CCAP
Adult	MeTGAN	**0.013**	**0.028**	0.987	0.813	1.711	0.706	0.300
	CTGAN	0.030	0.035	0.970	0.773	1.782	0.732	**0.310**
	TGAN	0.085	0.087	**0.990**	**0.917**	1.742	0.727	0.304
	cWGAN	0.051	0.030	0.906	0.596	1.890	0.619	0.232
	medGAN	0.719	0.725	0.872	0.109	**2.246**	0.975	0.035
	tableGAN	0.036	0.052	0.976	0.610	1.826	**0.537**	0.303

Table 3. Results on the News dataset

Dataset	Model	ΔMSE-RFR	ΔMSE-ENet	CS test	KS test	DCR-mean	DCR-std	NLR
News	MeTGAN	154	125	NA	0.915	**3.041**	5.433	0.263
	CTGAN	**87**	**106**	NA	0.910	2.903	5.430	**0.279**
	TGAN	408	2491	NA	0.902	2.787	5.389	0.267
	medGAN	128	126	NA	**0.965**	2.026	5.436	0.182
	tableGAN	540	262	NA	0.585	2.741	**5.235**	0.217

Table 4. Results on the Loan dataset

Dataset	Model	ΔMSE-RFR	ΔMSE-ENet	CS test	KS test	DCR-mean	DCR-std	NLR
Loan	MeTGAN	**64015**	23320	0.632	0.716	**3.007**	1.234	0.093
	CTGAN	74323	**23082**	**0.656**	**0.755**	2.746	2.626	**0.115**

Table 5. GPU Memory usage on the Loan dataset

Dataset	Model	GPU Mem.
Loan	MeTGAN	**3.2 GB**
	CTGAN	16.3 GB

7   Conclusion and Future Work

In this paper, we propose MeTGAN, a memory-efficient approach of synthetic tabular data generation, that performs at par with other recent GAN approaches. In addition, for large datasets, MeTGAN considerably reduces the memory consumption without any significant degradation in performance. Reducing memory footprint of models has recently gained popularity, like [16] for large pre-trained language models, [12] for speech recognition, [17] for computer vision, but not much work has been done in the domain of synthetic tabular data generation. As per our knowledge, MeTGAN is the first work in this direction. Additionally, for future work, it can be seen that on a high cardinality categorical dataset like the Loan dataset, both CTGAN and MeTGAN models have limited efficacy. With the current architecture of these models, they are not yet capable of capturing the distribution well when there are a large number of columns and categories. Certain architectural changes are required that can better capture the nuances in variance. Future work directions could include the intersection of these aspects i.e., improving the memory footprint of such algorithms and/or making more real-world usable models.

References

1. Data to AI Lab, at MIT: Sdmetrics (2020). https://github.com/sdv-dev/SDMetrics
2. Choi, E., Biswal, S., Malin, B., Duke, J., Stewart, W.F., Sun, J.: Generating multi-label discrete patient records using generative adversarial networks. In: Proceedings of the 2nd Machine Learning for Healthcare Conference, vol. 68. PMLR (2017)
3. Cormode, G., Procopiuc, C., Srivastava, D., Shen, E., Yu, T.: Differentially private spatial decompositions. In: 2012 IEEE 28th International Conference on Data Engineering, pp. 20–31 (2012). https://doi.org/10.1109/ICDE.2012.16
4. Engelmann, J., Lessmann, S.: Conditional wasserstein GAN-based oversampling of tabular data for imbalanced learning. Expert Syst. Appl. **174**, 114582 (2021). https://doi.org/10.1016/j.eswa.2021.114582
5. Goodfellow, I.J., et al.: Generative adversarial networks (2014)
6. Gulrajani, I., Ahmed, F., Arjovsky, M., Dumoulin, V., Courville, A.: Improved training of wasserstein GANs. In: Proceedings of the 31st International Conference on Neural Information Processing Systems, NIPS 2017, pp. 5769–5779. Curran Associates Inc., Red Hook (2017)
7. Kohavi, R., Becker, B.: Adult data set, May 1996. https://bit.ly/3v3VDIj
8. Lin, Z., Khetan, A., Fanti, G., Oh, S.: PacGAN: the power of two samples in generative adversarial networks. IEEE J. Sel. Areas Inf. Theory **1**, 324–335 (2020)
9. Mottini, A., Lheritier, A., Acuna-Agost, R.: Airline passenger name record generation using generative adversarial networks. CoRR abs/1807.06657 (2018)
10. Park, N., Mohammadi, M., Gorde, K., Jajodia, S., Park, H., Kim, Y.: Data synthesis based on generative adversarial networks. Proc. VLDB Endow. **11**(10), 1071–1083 (2018). https://doi.org/10.14778/3231751.3231757
11. Patki, N., Wedge, R., Veeramachaneni, K.: The synthetic data vault, pp. 399–410, October 2016. https://doi.org/10.1109/DSAA.2016.49
12. Peng, Z., et al.: Shrinking bigfoot: reducing wav2vec 2.0 footprint (2021)
13. Radford, A., Metz, L., Chintala, S.: Unsupervised representation learning with deep convolutional generative adversarial networks (2016)
14. Reiter, J.: Using cart to generate partially synthetic, public use microdata. J. Off. Stat. **21**, 441–462 (2005)
15. Fernandes, K., Vinagre, P., Cortez, P.: A proactive intelligent decision support system for predicting the popularity of online news. In: Pereira, F., Machado, P., Costa, E., Cardoso, A. (eds.) EPIA 2015. LNCS (LNAI), vol. 9273, pp. 535–546. Springer, Cham (2015). https://doi.org/10.1007/978-3-319-23485-4_53
16. Sanh, V., Debut, L., Chaumond, J., Wolf, T.: DistilBERT, a distilled version of BERT: smaller, faster, cheaper and lighter. ArXiv abs/1910.01108 (2019)
17. Tan, M., Le, Q.V.: EfficientNetV2: smaller models and faster training (2021)
18. Toktogaraev, M.: Should this loan be approved or denied? https://bit.ly/3AptJaW
19. Xu, L., Skoularidou, M., Cuesta-Infante, A., Veeramachaneni, K.: Modeling tabular data using conditional GAN. In: NIPS (2019)
20. Xu, L., Veeramachaneni, K.: Synthesizing tabular data using generative adversarial networks. arXiv preprint arXiv:1811.11264 (2018)

21. Zhang, J., Cormode, G., Procopiuc, C.M., Srivastava, D., Xiao, X.: PrivBayes: private data release via Bayesian networks. ACM Trans. Database Syst. **42**(4), 1–41 (2017)
22. Zhao, Z., Kunar, A., der Scheer, H.V., Birke, R., Chen, L.Y.: CTAB-GAN: effective table data synthesizing (2021)

Vehicle Taillight Detection Based on Semantic Information Fusion

Le Chang and Chongyang Zhang[✉]

School of Computer Science and Engineering, Nanjing University of Science and Technology, Nanjing, China

Abstract. The detection of the vehicle taillights is important for predicting the driving intention of the vehicle in front. The YOLOv4 target detection algorithm has problems such as insufficient detection capabilities for small targets and inaccurate bounding box positioning. In response to this problem, a front vehicle taillight detection algorithm combining high-level semantics and low-level features is proposed. Based on the improved CSPResNeXt model to extract features, the algorithm uses the mask image containing semantic information and the corresponding feature map to fuse and enhance distinguishability of vehicle taillights and background. At the same time, BiFPN model is used for further multi-scale feature fusion to extract more detailed information. The experimental results show that our proposed algorithm can improve the mAP of object detection without affecting the real-time performance of the YOLOv4 algorithm. Our algorithm achieves 90.55% mAP (IoU = 0.5) on the test set, which is 14.42% mAP (IoU [0.5:0.95]) higher than the original YOLOv4 algorithm.

Keywords: Assistant and autonomous driving · Taillight detection · Semantic segmentation · Feature fusion

1 Introduction

According to the front vehicle taillights on and off and the color of light, the driver of the following vehicle is reminded to predict the behavior of the vehicle in front in advance and take effective actions to avoid rear-end collisions and other traffic accidents. Therefore, the accurate recognition of vehicle taillight signals is closely related to driving safety. In real road conditions, different weather and illumination factors will have a great impact on the quality of collected images. How to obtain high-precision recognition effects in real-time has always been the research focus.

With the improvement of computing power and the emergence of large-scale labeled samples, deep neural networks have been widely used, which has made people have a breakthrough on vehicle taillight detection. Guangyu Zhong et al. [1] use the temporal coherence and smooth motion between two frames to identify

© Springer Nature Switzerland AG 2021
T. Mantoro et al. (Eds.): ICONIP 2021, CCIS 1517, pp. 528–536, 2021.
https://doi.org/10.1007/978-3-030-92310-5_61

the taillight region through the fine-tuned FCN (full convolutional network). F. I. Vancea et al. [2] use an improved FCN to segment the taillights. Then extracted candidates were paired by comparing their sizes and centroid locations. F. I. Vancea and S. Nedevschi [3] use Faster RCNN to detect vehicles and improve the ERFNet model to segment the taillight pixels to identify the signal state of the taillights. D. Nava et al. [4] use lane detection algorithm and YOLO model to detect the forward vehicle and recognize the brake lights status through SVMs classifiers. Xiang Li [5] use the YOLOv3-tiny model to improve the accuracy of identifying the semantics of taillights. H. Hsu et al. [6] input a short sequence into the CNN-LSTM model to determine the state of the rear lights. Two separate classifiers are learned to recognize the static brake signals and the dynamic turn signals. Subsequently, K. Lee et al. [7] extend this method and propose a network framework based on the end-to-end CNN-LSTM framework. This method integrated attention models in both spatial and temporal domains.

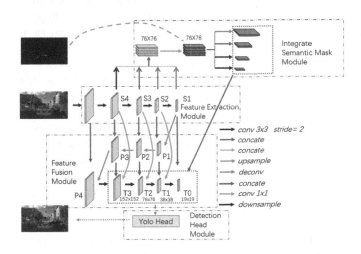

Fig. 1. Overall architecture of our model

2   Proposed Algorithm

2.1   CSPResNeXt-40 Feature Extraction Module

Based on the small size of the taillight, this section optimizes the CSPResNeXt-34 feature extraction network and names it CSPResNeXt-40. At the same time, the SE attention mechanism module [8] is added to enhance the representational power of the network.

The structure of CSPResNeXt-40 increases the number of network layers, from the original $3\times$, $4\times$, $6\times$, and $3\times$ to $3\times$, $4\times$, $6\times$, $3\times$, $3\times$, respectively. The main network of the original CSPResNeXt-34 is 34 layers, and the improved main network is $1 + 1 + (3 \times 2) + (4 \times 2) + (6 \times 2) + (3 \times 2) + (3 \times 2) = 40$ layers which increase the network depth on the large-scale feature map, and reduce the network depth on the small-scale feature map. Thereby enhancing the network's feature extraction ability for small targets without affecting the real-time performance of the network. At the same time, the SE module is added to the small-scale feature extraction module. By processing the convolved feature map, a one-dimensional vector with the same number of channels as the evaluation score of each channel is obtained, and then the scores are respectively applied to the corresponding channel. In this study, SEnet is added after the Conv2-3 layer, Conv3-2 layer, Conv4-2 layer, Conv5-2 layer, and Conv6-2 layer, respectively. Without changing the output dimension, the nonlinear characteristics of the network are enhanced and the model is improved generalization ability.

2.2   Multi-scale Feature Fusion Module

In this paper, the 152×152 feature layer is used as a new feature fusion layer to integrate with the other three fusion layers, so that the high-level features have stronger location information, and the bottom-level features have stronger semantic information. This does not only strengthen the accuracy of positioning, and can enhance the accuracy of small target detection.

At the same time, the improved YOLOv4 model uses four down-sampling layers as BiFPN that the 32-fold down-sampled feature map is up-sampled twice, and the scale is matched with the 16-fold down-sampled feature map and spliced. The spliced 16-fold down-sampled feature map is merged with the 8-fold down-sampled feature map in the same way, and then the 8-fold down-sampled feature map is also subjected to this operation and merged with the 4-fold down-sampled image to obtain a size of 19×19, 38×38, 76×76, 152×152 feature maps are named P1, P2, P3, P4, respectively. Then P4 is down-sampling and P3 is fused to obtain T3, T3 is also down-sampling and fused with P2 to get T2, T2 is down-sampling and fused with P1 to get T1, T1 is down-sampling and S1 is fused to get T0. Finally obtained T3, T2, T1, and T0 are high-level feature maps, as shown in Fig. 1.

2.3   Integrate High-Level Semantic Mask Module

The feature maps generated by different convolutional layers represent taillights of different scales. The deeper the convolutional layer, the smaller the size of the feature map. The high-level semantic Mask module uses the last four layers of the feature extraction module to extract high-level semantic features. The specific method is: keeping the size of the feature map of the Conv4-3 layer unchanged (76×76), adding a 2×2 and 4×4 deconvolution on the Conv5-3 and Conv6-3 layers to upsample the feature map, denoted as Dconv5-3 and Dconv6-3. Add a 2×2 convolution on the Conv3-3 layer to downsample the feature map, which is denoted as Conv3-4. Then, the feature maps output by Dconv5-3, Dconv6-3, Conv3-4, and Conv4-3 are concatenated and recorded as the fusion layer. To obtain better semantic feature mapping, a semantic segmentation branch composed of 1×1 convolution is added to the fusion layer, which is used to predict the category of each pixel of the input image at the sampling resolution.

The pixel-by-pixel segmentation method is based on the target box in this paper. The label information (coordinates, width, height) of the taillights in the training data set is used to form a segmented area based on the target box, as the label for the taillight segmentation.

Figure 2 is the comparison of the Conv5-3 layer before and after adding the semantic mask module. The first line is part images of test set. The second line is the feature maps of the Conv5-3 layer. The third line is the feature maps of the semantic segmentation branch merged in the Conv5-3 layer after fusing multi-layer features. The highlighted area in the image indicates the location of the taillight.

Through the comparison, it can be seen that due to factors such as dense taillights and small taillight targets, the features of the taillights after fusing multi-layer features in the Conv5-3 layer are not obvious. After adding the semantic segmentation branch, the taillight features are significantly enhanced, which verifies that the fusion of high-level semantic masks can better distinguish the taillight from the background area.

Fig. 2. Comparison of feature maps before and after adding semantic mask module

2.4   The Loss Functions

The loss function L of the network consists of four parts: target confidence loss L_{conf}, target class loss L_{cls}, target location loss L_{loc} and segmentation loss L_{mask}. The target confidence loss, target class loss, and target location loss are consistent with the loss functions of the common target detector, and the segmentation loss adopts CE (cross entropy) loss. The total loss function is as follows:

$$L = L_{conf} + L_{cls} + L_{loc} + \lambda_m * L_{mask} \qquad (1)$$

where λ_m is the loss weight of the mask, in the experiment, $\lambda_m = 0.05$.

L_{mask} represents the segmentation loss, and the loss function is:

$$L_{mask} = -\sum_{i=0}^{k \times k} I_{ij}^{obj} \sum_{c \in class} [\hat{t}_i(c)log(t_i(c)) \\ + (1 - \hat{t}_i(c))log(1 - t_i(c))]$$ (2)

In the formula, t represents the segmented tail light mask, and t_i represents the probability that the i-th anchor box is the target. When the generated t represents the target, the target area is marked as $\hat{t}_i = 1$; if the generated t represents the background, the target area is marked as $\hat{t}_i = 0$.

3 Experiments

3.1 Dataset

Based on the BDD100K automatic driving data set [9], the experimental data set was re-labeled with the taillight samples of the vehicle in front, and 3,504 representative pictures were selected as the training set and test set of this experiment. Factors such as weather, the distance of the vehicle in front, and the state of the taillights were fully considered, as shown in Fig. 3.

Table 1. Quantity of each class of data set structure

	Weather condition	brake	mid_brake	turn
Train	All	4318	1700	2901
Test		1133	439	732
Train	Sunny	2510	988	1700
Test		661	252	420
Train	Rainy	794	309	512
Test		197	79	127
Train	Cloudy or dark environment	1014	403	689
Test		275	108	185

Fig. 3. Sample images from the vehicle light detection dataset

The experimental data set is labeled and classified into brake lights, high-position brake lights (mid_brake), and turn signals. According to the labeled image coordinate informat ion, the image is transformed into a per-pixel segmented image based on the boundary of the target box, and then it is randomly divided into the training set and test set in a 4:1 ratio. The specific information of taillights is shown in Table 1.

3.2   Experimental Results and Analysis

Comparison of Other Nets. To verify the performance of this algorithm, five detection algorithms are selected and compared with the detection results in this paper. The overall performance is shown in Table 2. YOLO-SMF can achieve the best detection performance in all classes of taillights. In particular, compared with the second-best network, EfficientDet-D3 [10], the detection accuracy of the Brake class is close to saturation, so it is difficult to improve the detection effect. However, YOLO-SMF improves 3.26% and 7.26% compared with the EfficientDet-D3 network for the smaller target as mid_brake and turn class, respectively. The main reason is that YOLO-SMF combines the low-level features which are beneficial to the target location and the high-level features which are beneficial to target recognition to obtain high-quality semantic features and improve the overall performance.

Table 2. Comparison of algorithm performance

Method	Backbone	Class	F1	Recall	Precision	AP	mAP
YOLO-SMF (ours)	SE-CSPResNeXt-40	break	0.89	88.26%	90.42%	90.75%	90.55%
		mid_brake	0.91	88.38%	94.17%	90.19%	
		turn	0.90	88.68%	91.81%	90.71%	
RetinaNet [11]	ResNet50	break	0.78	70.59%	87.14%	75.49%	64.35%
		mid_brake	0.56	52.86%	60.21%	57.21%	
		turn	0.62	56.58%	67.71%	60.36%	
Faster RCNN	ResNet50+ FPN [12]	break	0.83	80.68%	85.56%	79.68%	71.53%
		mid_brake	0.64	60.26%	68.08%	65.57%	
		turn	0.68	65.43%	71.46%	69.34%	
CenterNet [13]	ResNet50	break	0.86	82.19%	90.14%	89.18%	78.60%
		mid_brake	0.73	70.51%	76.56%	71.13%	
		turn	0.77	74.54%	80.28%	75.49%	
FCOS [14]	ResNet101	break	0.85	79.1%	91.6%	87.47%	82.52%
		mid_brake	0.86	81.62%	91.36%	84.25%	
		turn	0.78	72.18%	84.36%	75.85%	
EfficientDet-D3 [10]	EfficientNet-B3	break	0.88	84.55%	92.47%	86.60%	85.66%
		mid_brake	0.88	86.56%	90.48%	86.93%	
		turn	0.86	84.72%	87.46%	83.45%	

Ablation Experiment. Figure 4 shows the comparison of the detection results of the YOLOv4 baseline network (line 1) and YOLO-SMF (line 2), where the true bounding box is red and the predicted bounding box is green. It can be seen from the figure that YOLO-SMF makes full use of the image details of the low-level feature map and has less missed detection for small target taillight detection.

In this paper, CSPResNeXt-40 is used as the backbone. To verify the improvement of the proposed feature extraction method on the detection of the front vehicle taillight, the detection results of CSPDarkNet-53, CSPResNeXt-50, and CSPResNeXt-40 are compared. It can be seen from Table 3 that CSPResNeXt-40 has the best detection performance in the test set.

Fig. 4. Detection results of baseline network and our network (Color figure online)

Table 3. Detection results of CSPResNeXt-40, CSPResNeXt-50 and CSPDarkNet-53

Backbone	Class	F1	Recall	Precision	AP	mAP
CSPDarkNet-53 [15]	brake	0.88	85.44%	90.81%	90.02%	87.56%
	mid_brake	0.87	84.74%	88.78%	86.59%	
	turn	0.87	83.77%	90.69%	86.06%	
CSPResNeXt-50 [16]	brake	0.86	82.08%	91.27%	86.64%	85.82%
	mid_brake	0.87	84.05%	90.89%	84.33%	
	turn	0.86	84.58%	87.69%	88.10%	
CSPResNeXt-40	brake	0.89	88.26%	90.42%	90.75%	90.55%
	mid_brake	0.91	88.38%	94.17%	90.19%	
	turn	0.90	88.68%	91.81%	90.71%	

4   Conclusion

We propose a real-time detection method of vehicle taillights based on the improved YOLOv4 model. Firstly, increasing the number of prediction layers with an attention mechanism, which makes extracted feature maps with more detailed location information of some small objects as the semantic mask fusion brach inputs. Secondly, the BiFPN module is used to enrich the receptive fields in multi-scale feature maps to benefit the positioning and discrimination of the detector. Finally, a high-level semantic mask module is introduced to reduce the interference of useless features which reduce the possibility of undetected. This model provides a significant improvement on YOLOV4 and can be easily embedded into the existing detection framework.

References

1. Zhong, G., et al.: Learning to tell brake lights with convolutional features. In: 2016 IEEE 19th International Conference on Intelligent Transportation Systems (ITSC), pp. 1558–1563. IEEE (2016)
2. Vancea, F.I., Costea, A.D., Nedevschi, S.: Vehicle taillight detection and tracking using deep learning and thresholding for candidate generation. In: 2017 13th IEEE International Conference on Intelligent Computer Communication and Processing (ICCP), pp. 267–272. IEEE (2017)
3. Vancea, F.I., Nedevschi, S.: Semantic information based vehicle relative orientation and taillight detection. In: 2018 IEEE 14th International Conference on Intelligent Computer Communication and Processing (ICCP), pp. 259–264. IEEE (2018)
4. Nava, D., Panzani, G., Savaresi, S.M.: A collision warning oriented brake lights detection and classification algorithm based on a mono camera sensor. In: 2019 IEEE Intelligent Transportation Systems Conference (ITSC), pp. 319–324. IEEE (2019)
5. Li, X.: Recognition of the vehicle and rear light videos based on deep learning. Master's thesis, Guangdong University of Technology (2019)
6. Hsu, H.K., et al.: Learning to tell brake and turn signals in videos using CNN-LSTM structure. In: 2017 IEEE 20th International Conference on Intelligent Transportation Systems (ITSC), pp. 1–6. IEEE (2017)
7. Lee, K.H., Tagawa, T., Pan, J.E.M., Gaidon, A., Douillard, B.: An attention-based recurrent convolutional network for vehicle taillight recognition. In: 2019 IEEE Intelligent Vehicles Symposium (IV), pp. 2365–2370. IEEE (2019)
8. Hu, J., Shen, L., Sun, G.: Squeeze-and-excitation networks. In: Proceedings of the IEEE Conference on Computer Vision and Pattern Recognition, pp. 7132–7141 (2018)
9. Yu, F., et al.: BDD100K: a diverse driving video database with scalable annotation tooling, vol. 2, no. 5, p. 6. arXiv preprint arXiv http://arxiv.org/abs/1805.04687 (2018)
10. Tan, M., Pang, R., Le, Q.V.: EfficientDet: scalable and efficient object detection. In: Proceedings of the IEEE/CVF Conference on Computer Vision and Pattern Recognition, pp. 10781–10790 (2020)
11. Lin, T.Y., Goyal, P., Girshick, R., He, K., Dollár, P.: Focal loss for dense object detection. In: Proceedings of the IEEE International Conference on Computer Vision, pp. 2980–2988 (2017)
12. Lin, T.Y., Dollár, P., Girshick, R., He, K., Hariharan, B., Belongie, S.: Feature pyramid networks for object detection. In: Proceedings of the IEEE Conference on Computer Vision and Pattern Recognition, pp. 2117–2125 (2017)

13. Zhou, X., Wang, D., Krähenbühl, P.: Objects as points. arXiv preprint arXiv http://arxiv.org/abs/1904.07850 (2019)
14. Tian, Z., Shen, C., Chen, H., He, T.: FCOS: fully convolutional one-stage object detection. In: Proceedings of the IEEE/CVF International Conference on Computer Vision, pp. 9627–9636 (2019)
15. Bochkovskiy, A., Wang, C.Y., Liao, H.Y.M.: YOLOv4: optimal speed and accuracy of object detection. arXiv preprint arXiv http://arxiv.org/abs/2004.10934 (2020)
16. Xie, S., Girshick, R., Dollár, P., Tu, Z., He, K.: Aggregated residual transformations for deep neural networks. In: Proceedings of the IEEE Conference on Computer Vision and Pattern Recognition, pp. 1492–1500 (2017)

Less Is Better: Fooling Scene Text Recognition with Minimal Perturbations

Yikun Xu[1,2(✉)], Pengwen Dai[1,2], and Xiaochun Cao[1,2(✉)]

[1] State Key Laboratory of Information Security, The Institute of Information Engineering, The Chinese Academy of Sciences, Beijing, China
{xuyikun,daipengwen,caoxiaochun}@iie.ac.cn
[2] School of Cyber Security, University of Chinese Academy of Sciences, Beijing, China

Abstract. Scene text recognition (STR) has made tremendous progress in the era of deep learning. However, the attack of the sequential STR does not attract sufficient scholarly attention. The very few existing researches to fool STR belong to white-box attacks and thus would have limitations in practical applications. In this paper, we propose a novel black-box attack on STR models, only using the probability distribution of the model output. Instead of disturbing most pixels like existing STR attack methods, our proposed approach only disturbs very few pixels and utilizes own characteristics of recurrent neural networks (RNNs) to propagate perturbations. Experiments validate the effectiveness and superiority of our attack approach.

Keywords: Scene text recognition · Adversarial examples · Black-box

1 Introduction

Scene text recognition (STR) aims to read texts in natural images. It plays significant roles in a lot of practical applications [1,2]. In the past few years, numerous STR algorithms using deep neural networks (DNNs) have been proposed. These methods usually regard the STR task as a sequence recognition problem, which can be divided into two mainstreams, namely, CTC-based methods [3,4] and attention-based methods [5,6].

Adversarial examples on non-sequential tasks have been hotly studied for many years [8–10]. However, adversarial threats of sequential task, i.e. scene text recognition, do not attract obvious scholarly attention. Actually, attacking the STR models involves more challenges. Firstly, the sequential model owns inherent varied-length labels, instead of the single label in non-sequential tasks, which

---

Y. Xu and P. Dai—Equal contribution.

This research work has been funded by the Guangdong United Fund (Grant No. E010061112), the Xinjiang Fund (Grant No. Y910071112) and the Key Fund of the Institute of Computing Technology of the Chinese Academy of Sciences (Grant No. Y950421112).

T. Mantoro et al. (Eds.): ICONIP 2021, CCIS 1517, pp. 537–544, 2021.
https://doi.org/10.1007/978-3-030-92310-5_62

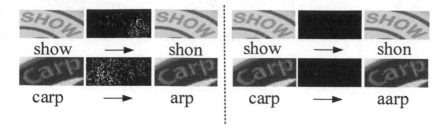

Fig. 1. Qualitative results. The left part denotes the results from [7]. The right part means our results. In both parts, the first column denotes the clean image; the second column denotes the perturbation; the third column denotes the adversarial image. Note that we magnify the perturbation for better visualization by multiplying a value of 100.

hence would increase the difficulties of simultaneously altering multiple labels. Secondly, the sequential model usually utilizes recurrent neural networks (RNNs) or their variants to encode sequential contexts, which would generate more robust feature representations, hence resulting in more attacking difficulties. Although several works [7,11–13] have been proposed to fool the text image recognition in recent years, they all belong to white-box attacks. These approaches need to have complete knowledge of the target model, that is, to access the architecture, the parameters and the gradients, which limit their applications in real life.

In this paper, we propose a novel and efficient black-box attack on STR models by disturbing minimal pixels with the differential evolution algorithm (DEA). As shown in Fig. 1, we can successfully attack the images with less knowledge of the model and disturb much fewer pixels than the existing white-box attack (there are no existing works for black-box attacks on STR). Especially, our work has the following advantages and contributions: we only need black-box partial feedback information (probability output of the model) without the information of the STR target model such as the architecture, parameters, and gradients. We can modify very few pixels to achieve the successful rate, while the previous works need to disturb much more pixels.

2   Related Work

Attacks on Sequential Tasks of STR. In [12], the authors introduced a practical adversarial attack against deep license plate recognition, termed Robust LightMask Attacks (RoLMA), which adopted illumination technologies to create several light spots as noises and achieves good performance. Chen *et al.* [15] proposed a targeted attack method, named Fast Adversarial Watermark Attack (FAWA). FAWA added perturbations as watermarks to achieve a perfect attack success rate. Moreover, the authors in [11] proposed an adaptive approach to speed up the attack on sequential tasks. Meanwhile, the authors in [7,16] made comprehensive attempts on crafting adversarial examples to fool the state-of-the-art CTC-based and attention-based STR models, by exploiting an optimization-based attack approach. Furthermore, researchers in [17] proposed a novel and

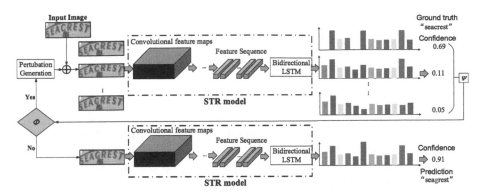

Fig. 2. Overview of crafting adversarial examples by minimal perturbations. Given an input clear image that can be correctly recognized by the STR model, we first alter it with randomly different initial perturbations. Then, we feed these dirty images into the model to obtain the probability distribution of predictions. Next, we choose the best one according to function Ψ. After that, we choose a validation process which is denoted as ϕ. If the prediction is equal to the ground truth, we iteratively use DEA to craft a new perturbation generation and estimate Ψ. Otherwise, we obtain the adversarial image successfully.

effective objective function to achieve a higher attack success rate with less $L2$ perturbation.

Different from existing white-box attacks for STR models and the optimization objective of $L2$ perturbation, we conduct a black-box attack in the perspective of the extremely limited conditions to modify as few pixels as possible ($L0$ norm). It should be pointed out that, for black-box attacks, scholars in [14] showed that a few pixels could successfully attack the classification models. We show that the phenomena also exit for STR models.

3 Methodology

3.1 Problem Setup

As shown in Fig. 2, given an image $I \in \mathbb{R}^{H \times W \times 3}$ (H and W are the height and width of the image) that can be corrected read by the STR model, we first convert it to the grayscale image and normalize it to $x \in [-1, 1]$. Then, the normalized image is fed into the STR model to output the probability $O \in \mathbb{R}^{T \times C}$ of the prediction (T is the number of sequence features; C denotes the character classes plus one blank). The problem of attacking STR is to disturb the image, letting it lead to a wrong label. Previous works often disturb most pixels in the high-dimensional space whose dimension is the number of all the pixels of the input image. We attempt to find a disturbance path in an extremely low dimensional subspace, i.e., along the direction parallel to one or a very few pixels. That is we constraint the L_0 distance of the perturbations as small as possible. Mathematically, it formulates the solution as:

$$argmin||\boldsymbol{I} - \boldsymbol{I'}||_0, \ s.t. \ \mathcal{F}(\boldsymbol{I'}) \neq \mathcal{F}(\boldsymbol{I}). \tag{1}$$

Equation 1 represents the number of different pixels between the clean image $\boldsymbol{I}$ and the adversarial example $\boldsymbol{I'}$ to be as small as possible.

3.2   Optimization

To solve the above-mentioned formulation in Eq. 1, we employ the differential evolution algorithm (DEA), as it makes few or no assumptions about the optimization problem. It also needs no knowledge of gradient information, and can search high dimensional spaces of candidate solutions. Besides, DEA is a parallel direct search method by iteratively trying to find better candidate solutions compared with the previous populations (parents) [18,19]. Specifically, DEA includes three main steps: mutation, crossover, and selection. The mutation and crossover are designed to explore the search space, while the selection process ensures that promising individuals can be further utilized.

In our work, we perform on the grayscale image and encode the perturbations $P \in R^{N_p \times N_d}$ as a candidate solution, i.e., each chromosome (pixel perturbation) $p^j (j \in [1, N_p])$ holds $N_d = 3$ elements: x-y coordinates and the gray value of the perturbation, N_p is the number of pixels to be attacked. The initial number N_s of candidate solutions is set as a fixed scale by using uniform distributions $\mathcal{U}(0, H)$, $\mathcal{U}(0, W)$ and Gaussian distributions $\mathcal{N}(\mu = 128, \delta = 127)$ for every attacked pixel p^j to generate x-y coordinate and gray value.

Mutation: At each iteration, another N_s candidate solutions will be produced by using DEA. The i-th individual in the g-th generation could be written as:

$$P_i(g) = (p_i^1(g), p_i^2(g), ..., p_i^{N_p}(g)), \tag{2}$$

where $i \in [1, N_s]$; $p_i^j(g)$ is the j-th attacked pixel; N_p represents the number of the attacked pixels; g is the current index of generation.

Then we use the default "best1bin" mutation strategy method. Specifically, it selects two individuals $P_{c1}(g)$ and $P_{c2}(g)$ from the population $\{P_1(g), P_2(g), ..., P_{N_s}(g)\}$ randomly. The generated mutation vector could be written as follows:

$$H_i(g) = P_{best}(g) + \alpha(P_{c1}(g) - P_{c2}(g)), \tag{3}$$

where $c1 \neq c2 \neq i$; $P_{best}(g)$ represents the best individual chosen from the population by a fitness function f, which is simply the probabilistic label of the ground truth sequence; α is set as 0.5 in the experiment.

Crossover: This operation can increase the population diversity, which is formulated as:

$$v_i^j(g) = \begin{cases} h_i^j(g), \ if \ rand(0,1) \leq \epsilon, \\ p_i^j(g), \ else, \end{cases} \tag{4}$$

where $\epsilon \in [0, 1]$ denotes the probability of crossover; $rand(0, 1)$ represents the random number chosen from the uniform distribution of $[0, 1]$; $h_i^j(g)$ means the j-th chromosome (pixel perturbation) for the individual $H_i(g)$ we calculate in

Eq. 3; $p_i^j(g)$ represents the j-th chromosome (pixel perturbation) for the individual $P_i(g)$ in Eq. 2. The crossover probability ϵ is set as 1, which means we allow all mutation individual to replace the last generation and no crossover is included.

Selection: This operation aims to guarantee that $P_i(g+1)$ for each individual is better than or equal to $P_i(g)$. It is formulated as follows:

$$P_i(g + 1) = \begin{cases} V_i(g), & if \ f(V_i(g)) < f(P_i(g)), \\ P_i(g), & else, \end{cases} \tag{5}$$

where f is the target function to be minimized. $V_i(g)$ is comprised by N_p chromosomes $v_i^j(g)$ in Eq. 4.

The early-stop criterion will be triggered when the prediction sequence is not equal to ground truth anymore. The algorithm is summarized in Algorithm 1.

Algorithm 1: Attack on STR

Input : {I: input image; S_{gt}: the ground truth label sequence; N_{iter}: the maximum number of iterations; N_s: the number of population; N_p: the number of pixels to be disturbed; ϵ: the crossover probability.}

Output: {I^{adv}: adversarial image.}

1   $p_i^k(0) = [\mathcal{U}(0, H), \mathcal{U}(0, W), \mathcal{N}(\mu, \delta)], \forall i \in [1, N_o], \forall k \in [1, N_p]$ //**Initialization**;

2   $g = 0$ // **Starting attacking by DEA**;

3   **while** $g < N_{iter}$ and $S_{predict} == S_{gt}$ **do**

4   **for** $i = 1$ to N_s **do**

5       $H_i(g) = Mutation(P_i(g))$, using Eq. 3;

6       $V_i(g) = Crossover(P_i(g), H_i(g))$, using Eq. 4;

7       $P_i(g + 1) = Selection(P_i(g), V_i(g))$, using Eq. 5;

8   **end**

9     $g = g + 1$;

10 **end**

11 $I^{adv} = perbturb(I, P_{i(adv)})$ // **Modify clean image by solution**

---

4   Experiments

4.1   Experimental Settings

In this paper, we attack the CTC-based STR models (e.g., CRNN [4], Rosetta [3], and STAR [20]) and the attention-based STR models (e.g., TRBA [5]). Following [7], we validate our attack model on four datasets (e.g., IC13, IC15, IIIT5K and CUTE) with the evaluation metrics success rate (**SR**), **L2** and **L0**. In experiments, we set H, W, and N_s to 100, 32 and 600 by default, respectively. The maximum number N_{iter} of iteration is set as 300.

Table 1. Quantitative comparisons of untargeted STR attack approaches. * means our implementation which is a little different from [7]. ↑ means the higher is better and ↓ means the lower is better.

Method		IC13			IC15			IIIT5K			CUTE		
		SR ↑	L2 ↓	L0 ↓	SR ↑	L2 ↓	L0 ↓	SR ↑	L2 ↓	L0 ↓	SR ↑	L2 ↓	L0 ↓
White-box	Basic_0.1 [11]	–	–	–	–	–	–	99.7	2.9	–	–	–	–
	Basic_1 [11]	–	–	–	–	–	–	95.4	1.77	–	–	–	–
	Basic_10 [11]	–	–	–	–	–	–	39.1	0.39	–	–	–	–
	BasicBinary_3 [11]	–	–	–	–	–	–	100	2.01	–	–	–	–
	BasicBinary_5 [11]	–	–	–	–	–	–	100	1.96	–	–	–	–
	BasicBinary_10 [11]	–	–	–	–	–	–	100	1.94	–	–	–	–
	Adaptive (CRNN) [11]	–	–	–	–	–	–	100	2.68	–	–	–	–
	Yang et al. (ASTER) [17]	100	0.71	–	100	0.45	–	100	0.69	–	100	0.5	–
	Xu et al. (CRNN) * [7]	99.5	1.33	2319	99.9	0.54	1850	99.9	1.01	2238	100	0.73	2148
	Xu et al. (Rosetta) * [7]	99.7	0.76	2073	100	0.39	1741	100	0.66	2037	100	0.52	1981
	Xu et al. (STAR) * [7]	96.2	1.83	2374	99.7	0.73	1929	98.1	1.41	2243	100	0.82	2157
	Xu et al. (TRBA) * [7]	93.5	2.25	2413	99.6	0.72	1924	97.1	1.53	2245	99.06	1.02	2248
Black-box	Ours (CRNN)	97.5	2.22	7	99.4	2.22	7	98.3	2.57	7	98.9	2.09	5
	Ours (Rosetta)	99.5	2.15	7	100	2.18	7	98.8	2.41	7	100	2.08	5
	Ours (STAR)	96.7	2.15	7	97.6	2.13	7	96.7	2.36	7	99	1.93	4
	Ours (TRBA)	96	2.18	7	97.2	2.15	7	94.7	2.38	7	98.1	2.22	6

4.2   Comparison with State-of-the-Art Methods

Quantitative comparisons between our proposed approach and previous related STR attack methods are illustrated in Table 1. We can observe that our method can achieve similar performance with fewer perturbations. Specially, when compared with the adaptive adversarial attack (termed as "Adaptive") [11], our method achieves the comparable success rate (**SR**), i.e., 100% vs. 98.3% on IIIT5K, while our method obtains lower **L2** distances (2.57 vs. 2.68). When compared with the attack method in [17], although **SR** and **L2** distance are lower than [17], the comparison is not convincing as they attack different STR models. When compared with the attack method proposed in [7], our method also achieves the comparable **SR** and **L2** on different models (e.g., CRNN [4], Rosetta [3], STAR [20], and TRBA [5]). However, the **L0** distance of our attack approach is obviously much lower than [7], as the adversarial perturbations in [7] involve most pixels in the input image.

Some qualitative results are shown in Fig. 1. It is easy to perceive that the adversarial perturbations in [7] cover large connected components while our method only influences several pixels. The adversarial examples generated by our method are also hard to be perceived by humans in complicated scenarios.

4.3   Ablation Studies

The Influence of the Number of Perturbed Pixels. As shown in Fig. 3(a), with the increase in the number of perturbed pixels, the success rate (**SR**) of our attack method is becoming better and better, until it is stable. Experimental

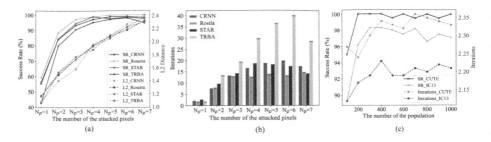

Fig. 3. (a) denotes the effect of the number of perturbed pixels on SR and L2 for the dataset CUTE. (b) denotes the average number of iterations against the number of attacked pixels for the dataset CUTE. (c) denotes the SR and iterations against the number of the population. The experiments are conducted with the STR model Rosetta [3] for datasets CUTE and IC13.

results show that when only altering one pixel, the **SR** of our method on multiple datasets is satisfactory. In effect, **SR** can nearly achieve 100% on all models, after the number of perturbed pixels is increased to 6. It is because 6 pixels perturbations can be sufficient to generate decent adversarial examples. When only altering one pixel, it is easier to attack CUTE by over 40% with complicated backgrounds or layouts. Figure 3(b) also shows that with the change of the number of the population, the average numbers of **iterations** for the successful attack are also different. It indicates that the number of perturbed pixels in DEA can influence the optimization, and thus results in different iterations. Although the average number of iterations is the lowest when $N_p = 1$, most adversarial examples generated by the maximum iterations can not fool the STR model. It indicates that few pixels attack is efficient for some simple texts while is insufficient for complicated scene texts (e.g., IC13, IC15, CUTE, etc.). The reason lies that the STR model is robust to these simple text images in IC13.

The Influence of the Number of the Population. In the process of optimization, the number of the population N_s plays an important role. As shown in Fig. 3(c), experimental results indicate that the **SR** of our attack method can be promoted with the increase of the population, until it achieves a stable **SR**. For the influence of iterations, we can find it is quite stable after the population increase to 400 for the datasets.

5   Conclusion

In this paper, we propose a novel black-box attack method for STR. This attack approach does not require the network configurations, and only employs the probability distribution of the network output to perform the sequential vision attack via very few pixel perturbations. Experiments have demonstrated the effectiveness and superiority of our proposed method, where our attack method achieves over 98% success rate on almost all datasets.

References

1. Karaoglu, S., Tao, R., Gevers, T., Smeulders, A.W.M.: Words matter: scene text for image classification and retrieval. IEEE Trans. Multimedia **19**(5), 1063–1076 (2017)
2. Wang, J., Tang, J., Luo, J. : Multimodal attention with image text spatial relationship for OCR-based image captioning. In: MM, pp. 4337–4345 (2020)
3. Borisyuk, F., Gordo, A., Sivakumar, V.: Rosetta: large scale system for text detection and recognition in images. In: SIGKDD, pp. 71–79 (2018)
4. Shi, B., Bai, X., Yao, C.: An end-to-end trainable neural network for image-based sequence recognition and its application to scene text recognition. IEEE Trans. Pattern Anal. Mach. Intell. **39**(11), 2298–2304 (2017)
5. Baek, J., et al.: What is wrong with scene text recognition model comparisons? dataset and model analysis. In: ICCV, pp. 4714–4722 (2019)
6. Dai, P., Zhang, H., Cao, X.: SLOAN: scale-adaptive orientation attention network for scene text recognition. IEEE Trans. Image Process. **30**, 1687–1701 (2021)
7. Xu, X., Chen, J., Xiao, J., Gao, L., Shen, F., Shen, H.T.: What machines see is not what they get: fooling scene text recognition models with adversarial text images. In: CVPR, vol. 311, pp. 12 301–12 (2020)
8. Sharif, M., Bhagavatula, S., Bauer, L., Reiter, M.K.: Accessorize to a crime: real and stealthy attacks on state-of-the-art face recognition. In: CCS, pp. 1528–1540 (2016)
9. Goswami, G., Ratha, N.K. Agarwal, A., Singh, R., Vatsa, M.: Unravelling robustness of deep learning based face recognition against adversarial attacks. In: AAAI, pp. 6829–6836 (2018)
10. Goodfellow, I.J., Shlens, J., Szegedy, C.: Explaining and harnessing adversarial examples. In: ICLR (2015)
11. Yuan, X., He, P., Li, X., Wu, D.: Adaptive adversarial attack on scene text recognition. In: INFOCOM Workshops, pp. 358–363 (2020)
12. Zha, M., Meng, G., Lin, C., Zhou, Z., Chen, K.: RoLMA: a practical adversarial attack against deep learning-based LPR systems. In: Inscrypt, pp. 101–117 (2019)
13. Song, C., Shmatikov, V.: Fooling OCR systems with adversarial text images. In: CoRR, vol. abs/1802.05385 (2018)
14. Su, J., Vargas, D.V., Kouichi, S.: One pixel attack for fooling deep neural networks. IEEE Trans. Evol. Comp. (2017)
15. Chen, I., Sun, J., Xu, W.: FAWA: fast adversarial watermark attack on optical character recognition (OCR) systems. In: ECML-PKDD, pp. 547–563 (2020)
16. Xu, X., Chen, J., Xiao, J., Wang, Z., Yang, Y., Shen, H.T.: Learning optimization-based adversarial perturbations for attacking sequential recognition models. In: MM, pp. 2802–2822 (2020)
17. Yang, M., Zheng, H., Bai, X., Luo, J.: Cost-effective adversarial attacks against scene text recognition. In: ICPR, pp. 2368–2374 (2021)
18. Storn, R., Price, K.: Differential evolution-a simple and efficient heuristic for global optimization over continuous spaces. J. Gob. Optim. **11**(4), 341–359 (1997)
19. Das, S., Suganthan, P.N.: Differential evolution: a survey of the state-of-the-art. IEEE Trans. Evol. Comp. **15**(1), 4–31 (2010)
20. Liu, W., Chen, C., Wong, K.-Y.K., Su, Z., Han, J.: STAR-Net: a spatial attention residue network for scene text recognition. In: BMVC, vol. 2, p. 7 (2016)

Solving the N-Queens and Golomb Ruler Problems Using DQN and an Approximation of the Convergence

Patnala Prudhvi Raj[1], Snehanshu Saha[2], and Gowri Srinivasa[1(✉)]

[1] PES Center for Pattern Recognition and Department of Computer Science and Engineering, PES University, Bengaluru, India
gsrinivasa@pes.edu
[2] Department of Computer Science and Information Systems and APPCAIR, BITS Pilani, K K Birla Goa Campus, Goa, India
snehanshu.saha@ieee.org

Abstract. We build on the Deep Q-Learning Network (DQN) to solve the N-Queens problem to propose a solution to the Golomb Ruler problem, a popular example of a one dimensional constraint satisfaction problem. A comparison of the DQN approach with standard solution approaches to solve constraint satisfaction problems, such as backtracking and branch-and-bound, demonstrates the efficacy of the DQN approach, with significant computational savings as the order of the problem increases. The convergence behavior of the DQN model has been approximated using Locally Weighted Regression and Cybenko Approximation, demonstrating an improvement in the performance of the DQN with episodes, regardless of the order of the problem.

Keywords: N-Queens problem · Golomb Ruler problem · Reinforcement learning · Deep Q-learning · Locally weighted regression · Cybenko approximation

1 Introduction

A Constraint Satisfaction Problem (CSP) consists of a set of constraints that restricts the values that a set of variables can take on. Solving a CSP, i.e., finding a global map between the variables and values in a manner that satisfies all the constraints, is nontrivial. A traditional approach to solving a CSP is through recursive or search based approaches such as backtracking, constraint propagation or tree decomposition methods. We consider two popular problems: the N-Queens problem, an example of a two dimensional CSP and the Golomb Ruler problem, as an example of a one dimensional CSP that poses a significant computational challenge as the order of the problem increases.

© Springer Nature Switzerland AG 2021
T. Mantoro et al. (Eds.): ICONIP 2021, CCIS 1517, pp. 545–553, 2021.
https://doi.org/10.1007/978-3-030-92310-5_63

1.1   N-Queens Problem

The N-Queens problem requires n queens to be placed in an $n \times n$ chess board such that a conflict between any two queens is avoided. A conflict occurs when two queens cross each others' paths. Hence, placing two or more queens along the same row, column or diagonal must be avoided to reach a solution. With an increase in the value of n, we see a significant increase in computation to converge to a solution owing to huge permutations of board configurations. It has wide applications in multiple fields and has been extensively studied.

N-Queens as a Constraint Satisfaction Problem

For the N-Queens problem, all the constraints should collectively imply that no queen can attack any other queen. Suppose i, j are row numbers and Q_i and Q_j are the column numbers for queens on rows i and j respectively. The constraints that apply to every pair of (Q_i, Q_j) would be: (1) $i \neq j$, (2) $Q_i \neq Q_j$ and (3) $|Q_i - Q_j| \neq |i - j|$.

1.2   Golomb Ruler Problem

A Golomb ruler is a set of distinct non-negative integers with the difference between every pair of integers being unique. This is akin to an imaginary ruler with markings such that no two pairs of marks are apart by the same distance. The number of marks on the ruler is called the order of the ruler. A Golomb Ruler is *perfect* if it can measure all distances up to its length. It is *optimal* if no ruler of shorter length exists for the given order. Optimal or near optimal solutions are often sought after for applications such as finding multicurrent transformer tap points in the placement of radio antennae, selection of radio frequency to avoid the effects of intermodulation frequency and in generating self-modulation codes [1, 13]. Since the computational complexity increases exponentially as the order of the ruler increases, traditional search based algorithms like backtracking and branch-and-bound would not scale to large orders. A mathematical model to construct a Golomb Ruler would be difficult to arrive at as compared to using a model that learns to generate the solution set based on constraints.

Golomb Ruler as a Constraint Satisfaction Problem

This problem is posed as an optimization problem by keeping M, the markings, constant and reducing the length, L, until no solution is possible. The constraint would have M variables whose domain is between 0 and $L-1$ such that distances between each pair is unique. That is,

(1) $P = \{x_i | 1 <= i <= M, 0 =< x_i <= L - 1\}$

(2) $|x_i - x_j| \neq |x_p - x_q| \, \forall ((x_i, x_j), (x_p, x_q)) \in P | (i, j) \neq (p, q)$

1.3   Deep Q-Learning Learning

Reinforcement Learning (RL) algorithms aim to find a mapping from a state (or a representation of the environment at a particular time) to an action that maximizes the expected cumulative reward (or the value function). Q-learning is an RL approach that does not require a model of the environment. Deep Q-learning (DQN) uses a neural network with multiple hidden layers to expedite the learning of the map in a manner that maximizes the expected cumulative reward. Q-learning and DQN have shown promising success in solving the N-Queens problem [11]. We recapitulate the solution here to set the context for using DQN to solve the Golomb Ruler problem. Further, we compare the convergence rate of DQN for the the N-Queens and Golomb Ruler problems with the convergence rates of traditional solution approaches (the Backtracking and Branch and Bound algorithms) for these problems. Finally, we present approximations of the convergence behavior of DQN. Thus, The contributions of this paper are twofold:

(1) A DQN solution to the Golomb Ruler problem with significant computational savings over traditional solution approaches and

(2) An approximation of the convergence behavior of the DQN models for the N-Queens and the Golomb Ruler problem using locally weighted regression and Cybenko approach.

2   Literature Survey

Backtracking is one of the classic approaches to solving the N-Queens problem [6]. An improvement over the backtracking solution came in the form of a dynamic programming to solve an 8×8 board problem [12]. While multiple other solution approaches exist with varying degrees of improvement, a simple way for agents to learn to act optimally in controlled Markovian domains shows that Q-learning converges to the optimum action-values with a probability of 1, provided all actions are repeatedly sampled in all states and the action-values are represented discreetly [15]. DQN - has shown to outperform the best RL methods at various games and to find an approximate global optimum for non-linear hypothesis classes [7,8]. Further, approaches to quickly stabilize the model with a better choice of hyperparameters has shown potential [10]. This forms the inspiration for exploring a DQN based solution to the Golomb Ruler problem and to approximate the convergence behavior of the DQN solution to both the N-Queens and Golomb Ruler problems.

The earliest solutions to Golomb Rulers for orders 1 to 4 that were both perfect and optimal were proved by W.C. Babcock [1]. When it was proved that perfect rulers do not exist for orders ≥ 5, the search for optimal rulers ensued. Multiple optimal solutions to rulers of orders 5, 6 and 7 were found in a study related to error propagation in information theory [13]. Later, computational search methods were explored to find optimal solutions to higher order Golomb rulers (14 to 16) [14]. Genetic Algorithms (GA) and their variants have been shown to generate near optimal and optimal solutions [2].

Mathematical models have been used to find solutions to or to set upper and lower bounds to the Golomb Ruler problem [4]. The work on constraint based search for optimal rulers with better bounds provides various approaches to obtain optimal solutions to Golomb Ruler problem [9]. The efficacy of reinforcement learning, particularly, DQN, in trying to obtain solutions to this problem is yet to be explored and the present work is an effort in this direction.

3   Methodology

A neural network with multiple hidden layers is used to approximate the Q-value function—the rewards for an action taken in a given state. For each state input to the system, the Q-value of all possible actions is generated as the output. The experience is stored as a sequence of previous actions and the corresponding rewards. The maximum output of the Q-network determines the next action. The loss function that is minimized is the mean squared error of the predicted Q-value from the target. This is a regression problem. The network updates its gradient using back-propagation to eventually converge.

3.1   Solving the N-Queens Problem Using Deep Q-Learning

A sequential neural network that takes the state of the chessboard as input and predicts the best action as output is used. The state is represented as a $n * n + 1$ sized vector, where the last bit is used to represent the queen whose action has to be predicted. The output of the network is a set of Q-values from which the action corresponding to the highest Q-value is chosen. The reward is calculated as the negative of the number of conflicts on the board. The sequence of actions and their rewards are saved in memory and used to train the neural network to better approximate Q-values to eventually converge to optimal action sequences. The reward is optimal if an action leads to the solution. Else, the target is updated as the sum of the reward and the argmax of the prediction of the next state. With every update, the model is re-trained to approximate the new target. The effect of hyperparameters on the convergence has been reported previously [11].

3.2   Solving the Golomb Ruler Problem Using Deep Q-Learning

The network architecture remained the same as in the case of N-Queens. The state was represented by an array of -1s of length equal to the order of the ruler. The number of actions for the agent were chosen based on known solutions for a given order of the ruler. The agent outputs a set of Q-values and the number (action) with the highest Q-value is selected and the state modified such that the first -1 would be replaced by the latest action. The reward is calculated based on the violation score of the current state of the ruler [9]. Given the values of all markings for the current ruler, G, the violation $V_G(d)$ of a distance d is the number of times distance d appears between two marks in excess of its permissible occurrences,

$$V_G(d) = max(0, |\{d_{ij} = d : 1 \le j < i \le m\}| - 1).$$

The violation $V(G)$ of the current ruler is the sum of $V_G(d)$s: $V(G) = \sum_{d=1}^{n} V_G(d)$. Given a state of the ruler, the reward is simply the negative of violation score. So, a violation score of 0 would imply that we have a valid Golomb Ruler. The agent repeatedly takes actions until all the markings are predicted and the violation score is 0. This would mark the end of one episode and the agent is trained over a total of 100 episodes. The replay phase trains the agent to better predict the markings of a ruler. The exploration rate ϵ and discount rate γ remain the same from the N-queens implementation.

4   Approximating the Convergence of DQN for CSP

Two forms of approximations, namely Locally Weighted Regression and Cybenko Approximation, have been presented to gain an understanding of the convergence behavior of the DQN approach.

4.1   Approximation Using Locally Weighted Regression

The convergence behavior of the Deep Q-Learning approach was approximated using locally weighted regression [5]. The cost function incorporates a weight for each neighboring point: $J(\theta) = \sum_{i=1}^{m} w^{(i)} \left(y^{(i)} - (\theta_0 + \theta_1 x^{(i)}) \right)^2$. The weight for a neighboring point is a function of its proximity to the point to be estimated; a point that is closer has a higher weight, while a point that is farther away is weighed less. The typical choice for the weight is the radial basis function: $w^{(i)} = \exp\left(-\frac{(x^{(i)} - x)^2}{2\tau^2} \right)$. The plot of the approximation for N-queens (with n = 4) is shown in Fig. 1a. It is observed that the estimates are fairly accurate after a few episodes. The results are similar for the Golomb Ruler problem. To prevent overfitting, $\tau = 1.5$ was used for the estimation. Even though locally weighted regression is seen to approximate the iterations per episode quite well, it is computationally expensive as a regression model is computed for each point. Further, there is no closed form description of the graph that limits its use to estimate iterations for episodes beyond the training data.

4.2   Approximation Using the Cybenko Approach

To mitigate the issue with scalability of the Locally Weighted Regression model, a neural network has been used to estimate the iterations per episode. Cybenko proved that a "linear combination of univariate functions can approximate any continuous function" [3]. With mild conditions on the univariate function, the work demonstrates that a simple feed forward neural network with a single hidden layer using continuous sigmoidal non-linearity has universal approximation properties. Let the original function be $f(x)$. The approximated function by Cybenko Approximation is of the form: $G(x) = \sum_{j=1}^{N} \alpha_j \sigma(w_j^T x + b_i)$. If the error ϵ is measured as the absolute difference between the actual function and the approximated one such that $|G(x) - f(x)| < \epsilon$, where $\epsilon > 0$. The objective of the neural network is to minimize this error.

Experiments: A Multilayer Perceptron Regressor with an adaptive learning rate was used to obtain an approximation model for different n values. From Fig. 1b, we observe that the error for each estimate reduces gradually, much akin to the Locally Weighted Regression model. However, it is noteworthy that the Cybenko Approximation does a better job at estimating the iterations per episode when compared to Locally Weighted Regression model (see Table 1).

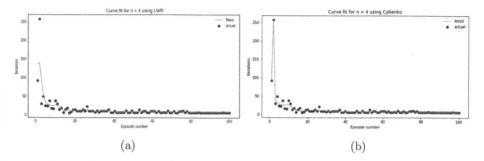

(a)   (b)

Fig. 1. A plot of iterations versus episode for N-Queens with $n = 4$ using (a) Locally Weighted Regression and (b) Cybenko Approximation.

Table 1. A comparison of approximation methods: Cybenko performs better than Locally Weighted Regression for both the (a) N-Queens and (b) Golomb Ruler.

N-	LWR		Cyebnko	
Value	MSE	MAE	MSE	MAE
4	213.04	4.34	14.87	2.66
5	7178.79	18.31	87.66	3.50
6	395593.94	113.91	360.30	12.03
7	302073.16	97.29	61.93	5.43
8	550790.72	131.32	79129.79	64.68

(a)

N-	LWR		Cyebnko	
Value	MSE	MAE	MSE	MAE
4	27.63	2.28	5.69	1.60
5	1218.93	7.99	11.07	2.67
6	198732.05	83.08	97.86	6.02
7	558654.10	136.56	187.03	9.19

(b)

5 Conclusions

The convergence of iterations for the DQN approach is compared with the number of iterations taken by traditional algorithms like Backtracking and Branch and Bound for a given order of the problem. The iterations corresponding to the 22nd episode of training are considered for results. The wall clock time for each iteration corresponding to different algorithms varies with the DQN approach taking slightly higher time due many matrix operations in the neural network. However, the wall clock time to reach a solution remained lowest for the DQN approach because of lesser number of iterations. The number of iterations for the Deep Q-learning approach to converge to a solution is plotted against the episode number for two different values of n in Fig. 2. From the convergence graphs in Fig. 2(a) and 2(b), we observe that the agent improves over episodes across different values of n for both problems. It is noteworthy that (1) Deep Q-Learning typically arrives at a solution in less than 50% of the iterations required by the traditional methods like Backtracking and Branch and Bound. The computational savings offered by Reinforcement Learning is particularly evident with the Golomb Ruler problem as n increases. (2) The convergence behavior of DQN for CSP can be approximated fairly accurately using Locally Weighted Regression and Cybenko Approximation.

In the spirit of reproducible research the code used to obtain the tables and graphs in this study has been made publicly available.

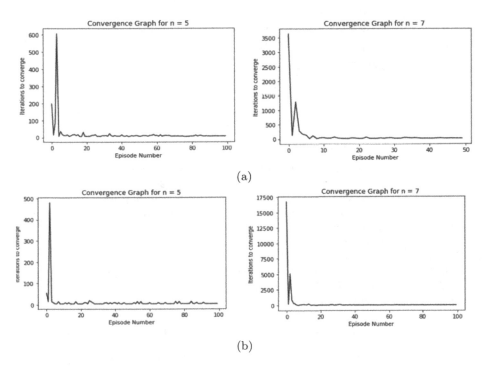

Fig. 2. Convergence for n = 5 and n = 7 of the DQN for (a) the N-Queens Problem and (b) the Golomb Ruler Problem.

Table 2. Iterations to converge to a solution by various algorithms: DQN shows a significant improvement compared to other algorithms for both the (a) N-Queens Problem and (b) Golomb Ruler Problem.

N-Value	Back Tracking	Branch and Bound	DQN	LWR(22)	Cybenko(22)
4	26	9	9	9.75	10.41
5	15	10	7	19.88	12.8
6	171	27	7	25.43	8.01
7	42	10	15	22.48	15.28
8	876	114	14	20.06	16.14

(a)

N-Value	Back Tracking	Branch and Bound	DQN	LWR(22)	Cybenko(22)
4	6	6	4	5.41	5.27
5	3615	13	5	6.63	7.56
6	170294	48	6	19.26	12.95
7	10095777	268	7	12.16	10.49

(b)

References

1. Babcock, W.C.: Intermodulation interference in radio systems frequency of occurrence and control by channel selection. Bell Syst J. **32**(1), 63–73 (1953)
2. Bansal, S., Singh, A.K., Gupta, N.: Optimal golomb ruler sequences generation for optical WDM systems: a novel parallel hybrid multi-objective bat algorithm. J. Inst. Eng. India Ser. B **98**(1), 43–64 (2017)
3. Cybenko, G.: Approximation by superpositions of a sigmoidal function. Math. Control Signal. Syst. **2**(4), 303–314 (1989)
4. Drakakis, K.: A review of the available construction methods for Golomb rulers. Adv. Math. Commun. **3**(3), 235 (2009)
5. Englert, P.: Locally weighted learning. In: Seminar Class on Autonomous Learning Systems (2012)
6. Kumar, V.: Algorithms for constraint-satisfaction problems: a survey. AI Mag. **13**(1), 32–32 (1992)
7. Mnih, V., et al.: Human-level control through deep reinforcement learning. Nature **518**(7540), 529 (2015)
8. Papavassiliou, V.A., Russell, S.: Convergence of reinforcement learning with general function approximators. In: IJCAI, pp. 748–757 (1999)
9. Polash, M.A., Newton, M.H., Sattar, A.: Constraint-based search for optimal Golomb rulers. J. Heur. **23**(6), 501–532 (2017)
10. Potapov, A., Ali, M.: Convergence of reinforcement learning algorithms and acceleration of learning. Phys. Rev. E **67**(2), 026706 (2003)
11. Prudhvi Raj, P., Shah, P., Suresh, P.: Faster convergence to N-queens problem using reinforcement learning. In: Saha, S., Nagaraj, N., Tripathi, S. (eds.) MMLA 2019. CCIS, vol. 1290, pp. 66–77. Springer, Singapore (2020). https://doi.org/10.1007/978-981-33-6463-9_6

12. Rivin, I., Zabih, R.: A dynamic programming solution to the N-Queens problem. Inf. Proces. Lett. **41**(5), 253–256 (1992)
13. Robinson, J.p., Bernstein, A.: A class of binary recurrent codes with limited error propagation. IEEE Trans. Inf. Theory **13**(1), 106–113 (1967)
14. Shearer, J.B.: Some new optimum golomb rulers. IEEE Transactions on Information Theory **36**(1), 183–184 (1990)
15. Watkins, C.J.C.H., Dayan, P.: Q-learning. Mach. Learn. **8**(3), 279–292 (1992). https://doi.org/10.1007/BF00992698, https://doi.org/10.1007/BF00992698

List Recommendation via Co-attentive User Preference Fine-Tuning

Beibei Li[1,2], Beihong Jin[1,2(✉)], Xinzhou Dong[1,2], and Wei Zhuo[3]

[1] State Key Laboratory of Computer Science, Institute of Software,
Chinese Academy of Science, Beijing, China
Beihong@iscas.ac.cn
[2] University of Chinese Academy of Sciences, Beijing, China
[3] MX Media Co., Ltd., Singapore, Singapore

Abstract. Most existing recommendation models focus on individual items. However, in many real-world scenarios, items are organized into lists (also called bundles) composed of multiple items with certain common correlations, e.g., video lists containing videos in the same genres, which makes list recommendation a significant task. In this paper, we propose a model named **CAPLE** which learns coarse-grained and fine-grained user preferences from user-list and user-item interactions respectively to achieve list recommendation. In particular, CAPLE develops a co-attention module, which fine-tunes user preferences by learning collaborative relations between user preferences of different granularities via jointly modeling tangled interactions of two different granularities. We conduct extensive experiments on real-world datasets. The performance enhancement on recall@K and NDCG@K verifies the effectiveness of the model.

Keywords: Recommender system · List recommendation · Attention

1 Introduction

Nowadays, recommender systems have become an indispensable part of many online services. Existing recommendation models mostly focus on individual items [4], which are referred to as item recommendation models. Recently, some online services organize multiple items with certain correlations into lists/bundles [8], such as music lists [2,6], commodity bundles [1] and video lists. Naturally, two list-related categories of tasks, i.e., list generation [11] and list recommendation are spawned. List generation aims to construct lists that conform to user preferences from candidate items. Next-basket [7] and product bundle generation [15] fall into this category of task. List recommendation is to recommend previously constructed lists. This paper focuses on list recommendation.

List recommendation, similar to item recommendation, can be carried out by analyzing user preferences from historical interactions. User preferences for lists

---

This work was supported by the National Natural Science Foundation of China (No. 62072450) and the 2019 joint project with MX Media.

T. Mantoro et al. (Eds.): ICONIP 2021, CCIS 1517, pp. 554–562, 2021.
https://doi.org/10.1007/978-3-030-92310-5_64

can be either on the overall intrinsic quality of lists, such as themes of lists, or on one or a few constituent items. If we ignore the list-item hierarchical structure and treat lists as generalized items, then list recommendation can be solved by existing item recommendation models, such as collaborative filtering models [5, 12], or sequential recommendation models [13], etc. However, such a solution totally ignores whether items in lists conform to the user preferences. Currently, there emerge some models for the list recommendation [3,6,11], however, these models are far from being perfect. The main reason is that their understandings of user preferences are not complete. Besides, most of the existing models have not exploited the sequential information of user interactions.

Considering that, in list recommendation scenarios, lists and items are objects of two different granularities, we can first model user preferences of two different granularities (i.e., coarse-grained and fine-grained preferences) from interactions of two different granularities (i.e., user-list and user-item interactions), respectively. Furthermore, since user-list and user-item interactions are always entangled, the coarse-grained and the fine-grained user preferences in a period might show collaborative relations. For example, for a user who interacted with the movie "Frozen" and the movie "Titanic", if he/she also interacted with the list "Disney Movies", then he/she may be inferred to prefer the movie "Frozen" and have strong preferences on Disney animations, while if he/she interacted with the list "Top Romantic Movies", then he/she is more likely to prefer the movie "Titanic" and romantic movies. By generalizing this example, whether and to what extent each item in user-item interactions matches coarse-grained user preferences essentially can be used to fine-tune fine-grained preferences. Similarly, considering that user preferences for lists sometimes depend on the user preferences on some constituent items, whether each constituent item meets the fine-grained preferences assesses the degree that the constituent item is important to the list personally and can be used to fine-tune the coarse-grained user preferences.

In this paper, we present a list recommendation model **CAPLE** (Co-Attentive Preference LEarning), which models and fine-tunes coarse-grained and fine-grained user preferences. In addition, CAPLE also mines sequential information of interactions. Our contributions are summarized as follows.

1. We highlight that user preferences of two different granularities have the collaborative relations and can be fine-tuned if jointly learning from tangled interactions of two different granularities.
2. We design a co-attention module to learn the collaborative relations between coarse-grained and fine-grained user preferences from list-item hierarchical structure, user-list and user-item interactions.
3. We conduct extensive experiments on real-world datasets to evaluate and analyze CAPLE, whose results demonstrate the effectiveness of CAPLE via improvement in different metrics and also verify the rationality of user preferences fine-tuning and sequential information modeling.

2   Problem Formulation

We denote the user, item and list sets as $\mathcal{U}$, $\mathcal{V}$ and $\mathcal{C}$, respectively. For each user, we have item sequence $r = [v_1, v_2, \ldots, v_{|r|}]^T$, where $v_i \in \mathcal{V}$ and list sequence $s = [c_1, c_2, \ldots, c_{|s|}]^T$, where $c_i \in \mathcal{C}$. They contain items and lists that the user has interacted and are sorted by interaction timestamp in ascending order, respectively. Further, items in list c_i can be expressed as an item list l_i according to their displaying order, i.e., $l_i = [v_1^{li}, v_2^{li}, \ldots, v_f^{li}]^T$, where $v_i^{li} \in \mathcal{V}$ and f is the maximum number of items in a single list. If a list contains less than f items, then we fill it with padding items. Thus, items in all the interacted lists form a matrix $[l_1, l_2, \ldots, l_{|s|}]$. Our goal is to build a model to predict the next list the user will interact with.

3   The CAPLE Model

In this section, we first give an overview of the procedure for learning user preferences. Then, we describe the carefully designed co-attention module. Finally, we elaborate on prediction and the loss function.

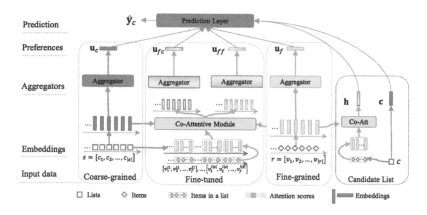

Fig. 1. The architecture of CAPLE

3.1   User Preference Learning

Figure 1 gives the architecture of CAPLE. The model learns coarse-grained and fine-grained user preferences from user-list and user-item interactions, respectively, and fine-tunes these user preferences based on interaction sequences and list-item hierarchical structure.

The process of learning user preferences from interaction sequences can be divided into two steps. First, we generate embedding matrices of sequences, that is, learn an embedding for each element in a sequence, and stack them into an embedding matrix. Second, we aggregate each sequence embedding matrix into an embedding vector, that is to learn user preferences from sequence embedding matrices via aggregators.

Sequence Embedding Matrix Generation. For coarse-grained and fined-grained preferences, the corresponding sequence embedding matrices are generated via list and item ID embeddings. Specifically, let the ID embedding matrix of lists be $\mathbf{C} \in \mathbb{R}^{d \times |\mathcal{C}|}$, where d is the dimension of embedding, as for a user-list interaction sequence $s = [c_1, c_2, \ldots, c_{|s|}]$, ID embeddings of each item in s form a sequence embedding matrix $\mathbf{S}_{id}$, where $\mathbf{S}_{id} = [\mathbf{c}_1, \mathbf{c}_2, \ldots, \mathbf{c}_{|s|}]$, $\mathbf{c}_i$ is the ID embedding of c_i. Similarly, let the ID embedding matrix of items be $\mathbf{V} \in \mathbb{R}^{d \times |\mathcal{V}|}$. We get the sequence embedding matrix $\mathbf{R}_{id} = [\mathbf{v}_1, \mathbf{v}_2, \ldots, \mathbf{v}_{|r|}]$ of the user-item interaction sequence $r = [v_1, v_2, \ldots, v_{|r|}]$, where $\mathbf{v}_i$ is the ID embedding of item v_i.

For fine-tuning preferences, we design a co-attention module which takes interaction data and list-item hierarchical information as input and outputs fine-tuned embedding matrices of user-list and user-item sequences. In detail, apart from $\mathbf{S}_{id}$ and $\mathbf{R}_{id}$, we generate list content embedding matrix of list c_i as $\mathbf{L}_i = [\mathbf{v}_1^{li}, \mathbf{v}_2^{li}, \ldots, \mathbf{v}_f^{li}]$, where $\mathbf{L}_i \in \mathbb{R}^{d \times f}$, $\mathbf{v}_i^{li}$ is the ID embedding of i-th item in list c_i. The content embedding matrices of each list in the sequence s form a content embedding tensor $[\mathbf{L}_1, \mathbf{L}_2, \ldots, \mathbf{L}_{|s|}]$. Then, we obtain the fine-tuned embedding matrices as shown in Eq. (1).

$$\begin{aligned}
\mathbf{S}_d &= \mathrm{COATT}([\mathbf{L}_1, \mathbf{L}_2, \ldots, \mathbf{L}_{|s|}], \mathbf{R}_{id}) \\
\mathbf{R}_d &= \mathrm{COATT}(\mathbf{S}_{id}, \mathbf{R}_{id})
\end{aligned} \tag{1}$$

In Eq. (1), $\mathbf{S}_d$ and $\mathbf{R}_d$ denote the fine-tuned sequence embedding matrices for user-list and user-item interaction sequences, respectively. $\mathrm{COATT}(\cdot)$ represents the co-attention module, which will be explained specifically in Sect. 3.2. Up to now, we have four sequence matrices ready for aggregation, i.e., $\mathbf{S}_{id}$, $\mathbf{R}_{id}$, $\mathbf{S}_d$ and $\mathbf{R}_d$.

Sequence Embedding Matrix Aggregation. Sequence aggregators are to aggregate the sequence embedding matrix into a single embedding, which combines the sequence information [9,14]. Here, we adopt an aggregator similar to SR-GNN which is simple but effective and widely used. Note that we tried to add the same GNN module as SR-GNN, but it achieves little performance improvement, so we remove it for Occam's razor. The four sequence embedding matrices are aggregated analogously. Here, we take $\mathbf{S}_{id}$ as an example to describe the procedure.

First, the embedding of the last interacted list, $\mathbf{c}_{|s|}$, is used to portray short-term user interest $\mathbf{s}_l$, i.e., $\mathbf{s}_l = c_{|s|}$. Second, we calculate the soft attention scores between $\mathbf{s}_l$ and each interacted list $\mathbf{c}_i$ by $\theta_i = \mathbf{q}^\top \sigma \left(\mathbf{H}_1 \mathbf{c}_{|s|} + \mathbf{H}_2 \mathbf{c}_i + \mathbf{b} \right)$, where $\mathbf{q}, \mathbf{b} \in \mathbb{R}^{d \times 1}$, and $\mathbf{H}_* \in \mathbb{R}^{d \times d}$ are parameters, $\sigma(\cdot)$ is the sigmoid function. Third, we weighted aggregate each column of $\mathbf{S}_{id}$ with θ_* to obtain the long-term interest embedding $\mathbf{s}_g$. Finally, the coarse-grained user preferences $\mathbf{u}_c$ is obtained by $\mathbf{u}_c = \mathbf{H}_3 [\mathbf{s}_l \| \mathbf{s}_g]$, where $\|$ represents the concatenation, $\mathbf{H}_3 \in \mathbb{R}^{d \times d}$ is the parameter to learn.

By adopting aggregators with different parameters on $\mathbf{R}_{id}$, $\mathbf{S}_d$ and $\mathbf{R}_d$ successively, we obtain the fine-grained user preferences $\mathbf{u}_f$, the fine-tuned coarse-grained user preferences $\mathbf{u}_{fc}$, the fine-tuned fine-grained user preferences $\mathbf{u}_{ff}$.

3.2   Co-attention Module

The co-attention module consists of two main components: the component for coarse-grained preference fine-tuning and the component for fine-grained preference fine-tuning. The two components take sequence embedding matrices and list content embedding tensor as input.

Before being inputted into the fine-tuning components, $\mathbf{L}_*$, $\mathbf{S}_{id}$, $\mathbf{R}_{id}$ are performed non-linear transformations as Eq. (2) to generate the key matrices and value matrices, where $\mathbf{W}_* \in \mathbb{R}^{d \times d}$ and $\mathbf{b}_* \in \mathbb{R}^{d \times 1}$ are all parameters.

$$\mathbf{K}_{l*} = \tanh\left(\mathbf{W}_1 \mathbf{L}_* + \mathbf{b}_1\right), \mathbf{V}_{l*} = \tanh\left(\mathbf{W}_2 \mathbf{L}_* + \mathbf{b}_2\right)$$
$$\mathbf{K}_s = \tanh\left(\mathbf{W}_3 \mathbf{S}_{id} + \mathbf{b}_3\right), \mathbf{V}_s = \tanh\left(\mathbf{W}_4 \mathbf{S}_{id} + \mathbf{b}_4\right) \qquad (2)$$
$$\mathbf{K}_r = \tanh\left(\mathbf{W}_5 \mathbf{R}_{id} + \mathbf{b}_5\right), \mathbf{V}_r = \tanh\left(\mathbf{W}_6 \mathbf{R}_{id} + \mathbf{b}_6\right)$$

Component for Coarse-Grained Preference Fine-Tuning. Aggregating embeddings of constituent items can form list content embeddings, which is a common operation [3,6]. However, existing aggregations are all in non-personalized styles. We argue that constituent items in line with fine-grained user preferences are supposed to play a more important role.

Since user-item interaction sequences imply fine-grained user preferences, the correlation between interacted items and each constituent item of a list can be used to measure the user preferences on the constituent item and how important it is. So, as for the i-th list the user interacted with, we calculate the correlation coefficients as $\mathbf{A} = \frac{\mathbf{K}_{li}^{\top} \mathbf{K}_r}{\sqrt{d}}$, where $\sqrt{d}$ scales the scores. $\mathbf{a}_{ij}$ in $\mathbf{A} \in \mathbb{R}^{f \times |r|}$ measures the correlation between the i-th item in the list and the j-th interacted item.

Then, we calculate the important factor of each constituent item, i.e., the attention score by $\alpha = (\text{mean}_{row}(\text{softmax}_{col}(\mathbf{A})))^T$, where $\alpha \in \mathbb{R}^{f \times 1}$. Finally, the weighted aggregation of constituent item embeddings yields a personalized list embedding $\mathbf{h}_i$ of list c_i, where $\mathbf{h}_i = \mathbf{V}_{li}\alpha$.

We perform the above procedure on each list in s successively, and form the fine-tuned embedding matrix of user-list interaction sequence $\mathbf{S}_d$, where $\mathbf{S}_d = [\mathbf{h}_1, \mathbf{h}_2, \ldots, \mathbf{h}_{|s|}]$.

Component for Fine-Grained Preference Fine-Tuning. User-list interaction sequences reflect coarse-grained user preferences, therefore, the correlation between the user-list interaction sequence and each item in the user-item interaction sequence is able to measure how well each interacted item matches the coarse-grained user taste. By exploring this correlation, we can get the embedding matrices of user-item interaction sequences fine-tuned by coarse-grained user preferences. So, we use $\mathbf{K}_s$ and $\mathbf{K}_r$ to calculate the correlation matrix $\mathbf{B}$ as $\mathbf{B} = \frac{\mathbf{K}_s^{\top} \mathbf{K}_r}{\sqrt{d}}$, where b_{ij} in $\mathbf{B} \in \mathbb{R}^{|s| \times |r|}$ measures the relation between the i-th interacted list and the j-th interacted item.

Then, we calculate the attention score $\beta \in \mathbb{R}^{|r| \times 1}$ by $\beta = \text{mean}_{col}(\text{softmax}_{row}(\mathbf{B}))$. Finally, we weight each item embedding in $\mathbf{V}_r$ with β and obtain the fine-tuned embedding matrix of user-item interaction sequence denoted as $\mathbf{R}_d$, $\mathbf{R}_d = [\mathbf{z}_1, \mathbf{z}_2, \ldots, \mathbf{z}_{|r|}]$, where $\mathbf{z}_i = \beta_i \mathbf{V}_{ri}$, β_i is the i-th element of β, $\mathbf{V}_{ri}$ is the i-th column in $\mathbf{V}_r$.

3.3 Prediction and Loss

For a target user, we firstly calculate his/her preference embeddings $\mathbf{u}_c$, $\mathbf{u}_f$, $\mathbf{u}_{fc}$, $\mathbf{u}_{ff}$. Then, for each candidate list $c \in \mathcal{C}$, we can obtain two embeddings, i.e., the ID embedding $\mathbf{c}$ and the list content embedding matrix $\mathbf{h}$ fine-tuned by the user-item interaction sequence. Next, we predict the interaction scores between the user and list c by $\hat{\mathbf{x}}_c^1 = \mathbf{u}_c^T \mathbf{c}$, $\hat{\mathbf{x}}_c^2 = \mathbf{u}_f^T \mathbf{h}$, $\hat{\mathbf{x}}_c^3 = \mathbf{u}_{fc}^T \mathbf{h}$, $\hat{\mathbf{x}}_c^4 = \mathbf{u}_{ff}^T \mathbf{h}$. Finally, we combine interaction scores to get the final predicted interaction probability by $\hat{\mathbf{y}}_c = \text{softmax}(\hat{\mathbf{x}}_c^1 + \hat{\mathbf{x}}_c^2 + \hat{\mathbf{x}}_c^3 + \hat{\mathbf{x}}_c^4)$.

To train the model, we define the loss function as the cross-entropy of the prediction $\hat{\mathbf{y}}_c$ and the ground truth $\mathbf{y}_c$ as $\mathcal{L}(\hat{\mathbf{y}}_c) = -\sum_{c \in \mathcal{C}} \mathbf{y}_c \log(\hat{\mathbf{y}}_c)$, where $\mathbf{y}_c = 1$ if list c is the ground-truth next interacted list, otherwise, $\mathbf{y}_c = 0$.

4 Experiments and Analyses

4.1 Experimental Setup

Datasets. Since there are no public datasets that provide comprehensive information required by our CAPLE, we collect data from MX Player, one of the largest streaming services in India that organizes and exposes videos via lists. We collect the user interactions between Sept. 1. 2020 and Sept. 7. 2020 on MX Player and construct three datasets of different sizes, named MX_Weekly_5K, MX_Weekly_10K, and MX_Weekly_20K. The statistics of these three datasets are listed in Table 1. The number of lists, which is counted by the different list names, is not large, but since the lists are personally constructed, different users have the lists with the same name but different list contents. For example, a personalized list named 'Hindi Films for You' will contain different Hindi movies when exposed to different users. As a result, total number of lists with different contents are in the order of millions.

Table 1. Statistics of the three datasets, where #Lists-DN denotes the number of lists with different names and #Lists-DC denotes the number of lists with different contents.

Datasets	#User	#Item	#Lists-DN	#Lists-DC	#User-item	#User-list
MX_Weekly_5K	5211	5994	209	870279	126598	43417
MX_Weekly_10K	9825	6460	209	1640817	236954	81268
MX_Weekly_20K	18087	7095	222	3201431	435840	149937

We group the interactions into user-list and user-item interaction sequences, filter out the sequences less than 5 in length and preprocess user-list interactions by splitting sequences. In detail, given a list sequence $s = [c_1, c_2, \ldots, c_{|s|}]$, we generate the following sequences and corresponding labels $([c_1, c_2, \ldots, c_4], c_5)$, $([c_1, c_2, \ldots, c_5], c_6), \ldots, ([c_1, c_2, \ldots, c_{n-2}], c_{n-1}), ([c_1, c_2, \ldots, c_{n-1}], c_n)$, where the last one is used for testing, the second last one is used for validation, and the others are used for training.

Metrics. We adopt Recall@K and NDCG@K as metrics, where $K \in \{5, 10, 20\}$.

4.2   Performance Evaluation

In order to evaluate the performance of CAPLE, we choose both item and list recommendation models as competitors, where we regard lists as generalized items when applying item recommendation models. The competitors includes (1) **BprMF** [10]: a collaborative filtering item recommendation model using matrix factorization with a pairwise loss, (2) **NCF** [5]: a collaborative filtering item recommendation model based on MLP, (3) **SR-GNN** [14]: a sequential item recommendation model using a GNN, (4) **DAM** [3]: a list recommendation model based on MLP neural networks and factorized attention networks and (5) **AttList** [6]: a list recommendation model based on hierarchical attention networks.

Table 2. Performance comparison, where the best performance in a row is in bold and the second best performance is underlined. The last column shows the improvement rate between CAPLE and the best competitor.

Datasets	Metrics (%)	BprMF	NCF	SRGNN	DAM	AttList	CAPLE	Impr (%)
MX_Weekly_5K	Recall@5	31.169	33.815	34.000	_41.015_	40.708	**47.015**	14.629
	Recall@10	47.631	47.754	48.708	55.662	_56.985_	**63.754**	11.879
	Recall@20	63.969	64.031	66.985	72.277	_74.123_	**80.462**	8.551
	NDCG@5	19.786	22.390	22.839	26.744	_27.130_	**31.812**	17.259
	NDCG@10	25.089	26.907	27.554	31.218	_32.417_	**37.230**	14.847
	NDCG@20	29.214	31.016	32.154	35.358	_36.740_	**41.457**	12.838
MX_Weekly_10K	Recall@5	28.974	29.247	34.039	_39.231_	38.622	**47.564**	21.242
	Recall@10	45.160	44.151	49.327	52.901	_56.058_	**64.760**	15.523
	Recall@20	62.532	61.699	67.612	69.904	_75.401_	**82.019**	8.778
	NDCG@5	17.790	18.550	23.218	25.674	_25.899_	**32.800**	26.645
	NDCG@10	23.008	23.356	28.146	29.889	_31.524_	**38.363**	21.696
	NDCG@20	27.392	27.770	32.742	34.090	_36.405_	**42.737**	17.395
MX_Weekly_20K	Recall@5	28.337	30.015	35.866	_40.918_	39.988	**50.013**	22.227
	Recall@10	45.274	45.144	51.778	53.961	_58.091_	**67.881**	16.854
	Recall@20	63.795	62.273	70.116	70.411	_78.211_	**84.427**	7.949
	NDCG@5	16.940	19.428	24.225	26.073	_26.326_	**35.096**	33.311
	NDCG@10	22.400	24.318	29.333	30.067	_32.177_	**40.882**	27.054
	NDCG@20	27.071	28.635	33.955	34.145	_37.266_	**45.076**	20.958

As listed in Table 2, the two collaborative filtering models for item recommendation, i.e., BprMF and NCF perform worse than the sequential model SR-GNN. The list recommendation models all perform better than the item recommendation models, and CAPLE outperforms all the competitors significantly, which reaches about 8% improvement in Recall@20 and about 12.8%–20.9% improvement in NDCG@20. The reason is that compared with BprMF and NCF, SR-GNN integrates the sequential information of user interactions. Compared with DAM and AttList, BprMF, NCF, and SR-GNN take lists as generalized items and ignore the fine-grained information. Compared with the competitors, CAPLE not only models both coarse-grained and fine-grained user preferences but also exploits the sequential information of interaction behaviors. Besides, AttList which does not exploit user-item interactions outperforms DAM, which implies that learning user embeddings by aggregating the embeddings of interacted items is more efficient than setting user embeddings as parameters and training them directly. Note that we tried BGCN [2], but it leads to even worse performance than BprMF, the reason might be it constructs the graph according to global list-item hierarchical relations, which does not fit personalized lists.

5   Conclusion

In this paper, we present a list recommendation model. The model can capture coarse-grained and fine-grained user preferences and learn collaborative relations between them via a co-attention module. The experimental results show that different user preferences make more or fewer contributions to the improvement of the recommendation performance, demonstrating the effectiveness of different user preferences. Further, our solution for list recommendation provides a reference framework, and a similar idea and implementation can be applied to bundle recommendation in other scenarios.

References

1. Bai, J., et al.: Personalized bundle list recommendation. In: The World Wide Web Conference, pp. 60–71 (2019)
2. Chang, J., Gao, C., He, X., Jin, D., Li, Y.: Bundle recommendation with graph convolutional networks. In: Proceedings of the 43rd International ACM Conference on Research and Development in Information Retrieval, pp. 1673–1676 (2020)
3. Chen, L., Liu, Y., He, X., Gao, L., Zheng, Z.: Matching user with item set: collaborative bundle recommendation with deep attention network. In: Proceedings of the 28th International Joint Conference on Artificial Intelligence, pp. 2095–2101 (2019)
4. Covington, P., Adams, J., Sargin, E.: Deep neural networks for YouTube recommendations. In: Proceedings of the 10th ACM Conference on Recommender Systems, pp. 191–198 (2016)
5. He, X., Liao, L., Zhang, H., Nie, L., Hu, X., Chua, T.S.: Neural collaborative filtering. In: Proceedings of the 26th International Conference on World Wide Web, pp. 173–182 (2017)

6. He, Y., Wang, J., Niu, W., Caverlee, J.: A hierarchical self-attentive model for recommending user-generated item lists. In: Proceedings of the 28th ACM International Conference on Information and Knowledge Management, pp. 1481–1490 (2019)

7. Le, D.T., Lauw, H.W., Fang, Y.: Correlation-sensitive next-basket recommendation. In: Proceedings of the 28th International Joint Conference on Artificial Intelligence, pp. 2808–2814 (2019)

8. Liu, G., Fu, Y., Chen, G., Xiong, H., Chen, C.: Modeling buying motives for personalized product bundle recommendation. ACM Trans. Knowl. Discov. Data (TKDD) **11**(3), 28 (2017)

9. Liu, Q., Zeng, Y., Mokhosi, R., Zhang, H.: STAMP: short-term attention/memory priority model for session-based recommendation. In: Proceedings of the 24th ACM International Conference on Knowledge Discovery & Data Mining, pp. 1831–1839 (2018)

10. Rendle, S., Freudenthaler, C., Gantner, Z., Schmidt-Thieme, L.: BPR: Bayesian personalized ranking from implicit feedback. In Proceedings of the Twenty-Fifth Conference on Uncertainty in Artificial Intelligence, pp. 452–461 (2009)

11. Sar Shalom, O., Koenigstein, N., Paquet, U., Vanchinathan, H.P.: Beyond collaborative filtering: the list recommendation problem. In: Proceedings of the 25th International Conference on World Wide Web, pp. 63–72 (2016)

12. Wang, X., He, X., Wang, M., Feng, F., Chua, T.S.: Neural graph collaborative filtering. In: Proceedings of the 42nd International ACM Conference on Research and Development in Information Retrieval, pp. 165–174 (2019)

13. Wu, C., Wu, F., An, M., Huang, J., Huang, Y., Xie, X.: NPA: neural news recommendation with personalized attention. In: Proceedings of the 25th ACM International Conference on Knowledge Discovery & Data Mining, pp. 2576–2584 (2019)

14. Wu, S., Tang, Y., Zhu, Y., Wang, L., Xie, X., Tan, T.: Session-based recommendation with graph neural networks. In: Proceedings of the AAAI Conference on Artificial Intelligence, vol. 33, pp. 346–353 (2019)

15. Zhu, T., Harrington, P., Li, J., Tang, L.: Bundle recommendation in ecommerce. In: Proceedings of the 37th ACM International Conference on Research & Development in Information Retrieval, pp. 657–666 (2014)

End-to-End Multiple Object Tracking with Siamese Networks

Jinyu Qin[1], Chenhui Huang[2], and Jinhua Xu[1(✉)]

[1] School of Computer Science and Technology, East China Normal University,
Shanghai, China
51194506030@stu.ecnu.edu.cn, jhxu@cs.ecnu.edu.cn
[2] Mindnova Brain Technology Limited Co., Shanghai, China

Abstract. Multiple Object Tracking (MOT) consists of two components: detection and data association. In the popular tracking-by-detection models, these two components are separate: all objects of interest in a frame are detected first, and then associated with the objects in tracked queues using intersection-over-union (IOU) of bounding box and/or appearance matching. Appearance feature (ID embedding) can be extracted from a separate re-identification model or from a joint model with the detection network. In this paper, a joint detection and tracking model with Siamese structure is proposed for MOT. We apply Center-Net, an anchor free object detector for detection. Motion prediction and appearance matching are implemented with the network for association. Experimental results demonstrate the effectiveness of our model. State-of-the-art MOTA of 69.9% on MOT20 is achieved.

Keywords: Multiple Object Tracking · Object tracking · Correlation filter · Anchor free object detection · Re-identification

1 Introduction

Multiple Object Tracking (MOT) aims to estimate the trajectories of multiple objects of interest in videos. It has attracted an increasing attention due to its applications in automatic driving, public security, sport videos analysis, elderly care and so on. The task usually consists of two components: detection and data association. In the popular tracking-by-detection models [1–3, 5, 10, 16], these two components are separate: all objects in a frame are detected first, and then associated with the objects in tracked queues using intersection-over-union (IOU) of bounding boxes and/or appearance matching. There are two issues for the tracking-by-detection models. First, detection and association are separate and cannot benefit from each other. If the detector misses an object, it will be impossible to track it in the association stage. Second, separate sub-models are needed

This work is supported by the National Natural Science Foundation of China under Project 61175116.

T. Mantoro et al. (Eds.): ICONIP 2021, CCIS 1517, pp. 563–570, 2021.
https://doi.org/10.1007/978-3-030-92310-5_65

for detection, motion prediction and re-identification, leading to duplicate computation. To address these issues, joint detection and tracking approaches are proposed, in which different tasks share the same backbone network.

Most MOT works [1–3, 16] represent objects with bounding boxes. However, when occlusion happens, which is quite common in crowded scenes, using IOU of the bounding boxes is not reliable for tracking. Therefore, appearance matching and motion prediction are used [1, 6, 14, 16, 18].

In this paper, we propose a joint detection and tracking model with Siamese structure for MOT, in which two branches are applied to two consecutive frames. Each branch includes an anchor-free object detector [20]. Correlation module is integrated into the network for motion prediction. In addition, a novel similarity matching module is proposed to improve the discrimination of the ID embedding. We find that our method is superior in crowded scenes. We conduct experiments on MOT20 and achieve the state-of-the-art results.

2   Related Works

2.1   Multiple Object Tracking

Multiple Object Tracking (MOT) can be categorized as tracking-by-detection (TBD) method [1–3, 10, 16] and joint-detection-and-embedding (JDE) method [6, 12, 13, 17–19]. The former (TBD) views MOT as two separate pipelined tasks and has been the mainstream for a long time due to the huge progress in object detection and Re-ID field. They find objects in frames first and then conduct data association based on the ID features and/or geometry information. For example, Tracktor++ [1] utilizes Faster-RCNN [11] to localize objects and crops them to train an identity embedding network. The latter (JDE) shares backbone features between detection and Re-ID model. Track-RCNN [12] directly adds a Re-ID branch in Mask-RCNN [7]. FairMOT [18] adds an identification head to the anchor-free detector to balance the detection and Re-ID task. CenterTrack [19] uses two images as input, together with the previous heatmap. Its outputs include the offset of objects in the successive frames.

Siamese Networks have been used for re-identification and MOT. In DAN [14], a pair of video frames is processed by two extended VGG-like networks with shared parameters and the appearances of the two frames are fed into an affinity estimator to compute similarity. In D&T [6], motion prediction is applied for data association. In [4], a joint detection and tracking model named DEFT is proposed, which relies on an appearance-based object matching network jointly-learned with an underlying object detection network.

Our model is based on the JDE paradigm with Siamese structure, in which motion prediction and similarity matching can be integrated straightly. Therefore, we can train our model in an end-to-end fashion. Different from the previous models with Siamese structure, no affinity estimator or matching head is needed in our model. With the proposed matching loss and tracking loss, motion prediction and appearance matching is implemented effectively.

2.2 Correlation Filter

Correlation is a term in digital signal processing and describes the mutual relationship which exists between two or more signals. The correlation-filter-based methods have become the mainstream for Single Object Tracking (SOT). Correlation filter is also widely used in optical flow estimation [8]. D&T [6] introduces it into MOT for motion prediction. They construct a Region of Interest(RoI) tracking branch and use correlation to estimate the offset of the same object in successive frames. Inspired by the success of correlation filter in these works, we integrate a correlation module in our model to assist the tracking.

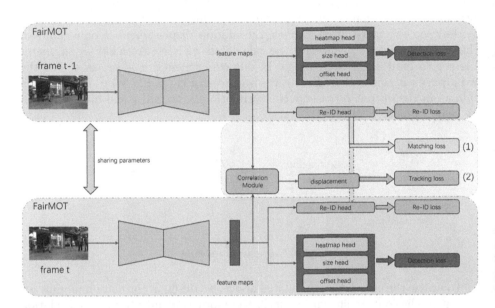

Fig. 1. The architecture of our model. The frame t and the frame $t-1$ go through the same backbone. The grey parts are just FairMOT [18]. The green part is our contribution: (1) **ID Matching.** Thanks to the Siamese architecture, we can design matching loss straightly to obtain more discriminative identity embeddings. (2) **Motion prediction.** We add a correlation module to learn offset of the same person in two successive frames. (Color figure online)

3 Methods

We mainly focus on how to integrate the detection and association within a unified model. For this purpose, we propose a Siamese network, in which the motion prediction and similarity matching can be implemented effectively. The architecture of our model is illustrated in the Fig. 1. The upper (lower) branch is just the FairMOT [18], which consists of a detection head and a Re-ID head.

3.1   Correlation Module

We propose a correlation module to describe the pixel-wise relationship of the two inputs and predict object motion. A tracking loss is exploited to supervise its output. The correlation between two points in two continuous frames can be calculated as follows:

$$c(x_1, x_2) = \sum_{o \in [-k,k] \times [-k,k]} <f_t(x_1 + o), f_{t-1}(x_2 + o)> \tag{1}$$

where f_t, f_{t-1} mean the feature maps of the frames and x_1, x_2 represent the coordinates in the feature maps. For each pair of (x_1, x_2), the patch size for correlation calculation is $(2k + 1)$. In our experiments, k is set as 4.

Between two consecutive frames, the motion displacement is quite limited. Therefore, not every x_2 needs to be calculated with x_1. Actually, a parameter d is set to limit the search range. In our experiments, d is set as 4. For the two inputs with size (B, C, H, W), the output size is $(B, (2d + 1)^2, H, W)$. Each channel in the output represents the correlation between x_1 and different x_2 in the search range.

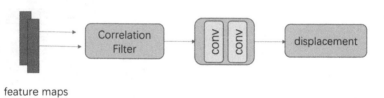

feature maps

Fig. 2. Correlation module.

To utilize the correlation calculated above, we design a correlation module for motion prediction. As shown in Fig. 2, the module mainly contains correlation filter and two stacked convolutional layers, and finally outputs the displacements estimation. An up-sampling operation is used to recover the size.

Tracking Loss. We simply view it as a regression task and utilize L_1 loss. The ground-truth of this task is the center offset of the same person between two frames, $y_{t,t-1}$. Therefore, the tracking loss can be formulated as Eq. (2):

$$L_{tracking}(pred_{t,t-1}, y_{t,t-1}) = \frac{1}{O} \sum_{o=1}^{O} |y_{t,t-1}^o - pred_{t,t-1}^o|, \tag{2}$$

here, $pred_{t,t-1}^o$ is the predicted displacement for the o-th object and O is the number of objects in the two frames.

3.2   Matching Loss

In FairMOT, Re-ID is tackled as a classification task with the cross entropy loss. Suppose the number of persons in the dataset is N, then the Re-ID task is a $(N + 1)$-class classification problem. The embeddings of objects are finally used to compute cosine similarity during association. This makes great demands on datasets and ignores the characteristics inherent in videos. In our proposed Siamese network, we detect the objects in two consecutive frames. It is straightforward to collect positive pairs and negative pairs for metric learning. Therefore, a matching loss is added to improve the discriminative of the ID embeddings. We propose the loss to pull the positive pairs closer and push the negative pairs further away.

$$L_{matching^+}(f_t, f_{t-1}) = \frac{\sum_{f_t^i.id=f_{t-1}^j.id} 1 - \cos <f_t^i, f_{t-1}^j>}{K^+} \tag{3}$$

$$L_{matching^-}(f_t, f_{t-1}) = \frac{\sum_{f_t^i.id \neq f_{t-1}^j.id} 1 + \cos <f_t^i, f_{t-1}^j>}{K^-} \tag{4}$$

$$L_{matching} = \sum L_{matching^+} + \sum L_{matching^-} \tag{5}$$

in which, f_t^i and f_{t-1}^j are features of objects belonging to two consecutive frames respectively. $L_{matching^+}$ is applied to positive pairs, that is $f_t^i.id = f_{t-1}^j.id$ and $L_{matching^-}$ to negative pairs, that is $f_t^i.id \neq f_{t-1}^j.id$. K^+ (K^-) is the number of positive (negative) pairs in the consecutive frames. The overall matching loss is combined with $L_{matching^+}$ and $L_{matching^+}$.

3.3   Training Loss

The training loss of our model includes detection loss, Re-ID loss as well as our matching loss and tracking loss. The detection loss and Re-ID loss follow the FairMOT [18]. The loss of the whole model is written as:

$$L_{whole} = e^{\theta_{det}} L_{det} + e^{\theta_{id}}(L_{re-ID} + L_{matching}) + L_{tracking} \tag{6}$$

4   Experiments

4.1   Datasets and Experimental Settings

We mainly conduct our experiments on MOT20. Its test set contains 1501 trajectories distributed in 4479 frames. It is the latest MOT dataset released by MOT Challenge. MOT20 is more challenging due to more occluded and smaller objects than MOT16 and MOT17. We pre-train our method on extra datasets as FairMOT to obtain more robust representations. Then, we train our model for 30 epochs on MOT series datasets. In our loss function, θ_{det} is 1.85 and θ_{id} is 1.05.

4.2 Inference

We evaluate our method under private detections. The tracking process is roughly the same as FairMOT. We associate the detected objects with tracked ones with ID embedding similarity and IOU. A new track is born when the detection is unmatched. An old track will be discarded if it has been left aside for τ frames. τ is set as 30 in our experiments.

Table 1. Results on MOT20.

Method	MOTA↑	MOTP↑	IDF1↑	IDS↓
TransTrack [13]	64.5	**80.0**	59.2	3,565
TrackCenter [17]	61.9	79.9	50.4	4,653
GSDT [15]	67.1	79.1	67.5	3,230
CSTrack [9]	66.6	78.8	68.6	**3,196**
FairMOT [18]	61.8	78.6	67.3	5,243
Ours	**69.9**	79.1	**69.0**	4,053

4.3 Results

We report our results on the MOT20 dataset and compare with other recent methods on Table 1. It shows that our model achieved a significant improvement (+8.1% MOTA, +1.7% IDF1) compared with FairMOT. We also see a large drop in IDS. We attribute the improvement to the application of our correlation module and two well-designed loss. We will prove it with ablation experiments.

We also give qualitative tracking results in Fig. 3. The frames are from MOT20-04. The top row contains results of FairMOT and the bottom is ours. Let's pay attention to the man on the right-bottom corner marked by semitransparent yellow box. In frame 749, FairMOT gives the person two boxes and its ID number is changed in frame 752. While our method keeps the ID unchanged and unique. Then take notice of the man on the top marked by red box, who is walking out of the frame. The person in the frames is cropped and it is challenging to track it. Its ID number is changed in frame 749 with FairMOT. Although our method misses it in frame 749, it recovers the person in frame 752 with the same ID number in frame 746 (Table 2).

Table 2. Ablation experiments.

Method	MOTA↑	MOTP↑	IDF1↑	IDS↓
FairMOT [18]	61.8	78.6	67.3	5,243
Baseline	63.3	78.3	69.6	5,185
+matching loss	68.3	78.7	70.1	3,944
+corr	69.2	**79.1**	**72.0**	**3,916**
+matching loss, +corr	**69.9**	**79.1**	69.0	4,053

Ablation Experiments. We remove the matching loss and tracking loss when optimizing the model to form our baseline. The difference between our baseline and FairMOT is that we finetune our model with all MOT datasets (MOT15, MOT16, MOT17 and MOT20). Comparing our baseline with FairMOT, it can be seen that more data could facilitate improvement to a certain extent. We observe a significant improvement with MOTA of $+5\%$ and IDS of -1241 when the matching loss is added. The correlation module brings improvement from 63.3% to 69.2% with MOTA, from 78.3% to 79.1% with MOTP, from 69.6% to 72.0% with IDF1 and from 5185 to 3916 with IDS. Furthermore, when the correlation module and matching loss are both applied, the MOTA achieves the best result 69.9, but the IDF1 and IDS deteriorate slightly. We think it is due to super parameters in the loss (6).

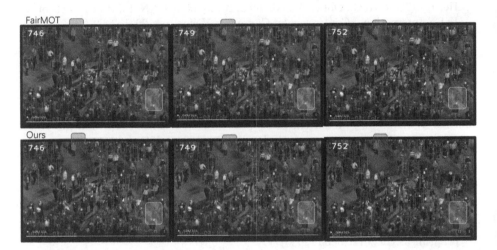

Fig. 3. Qualitative tracking results on the test sequence MOT20-04. (Color figure online)

5   Conclusions

In this paper, we propose an end-to-end MOT model with Siamese network. A correlation module with tracking loss and a Re-ID assisted matching loss was integrated into our model. The experiments illustrate that our model could extract more discriminative features and finally achieves more competitive results.

References

1. Bergmann, P., Meinhardt, T., Leal-Taixe, L.: Tracking without bells and whistles. In: Proceedings of the IEEE/CVF International Conference on Computer Vision, pp. 941–951 (2019)

2. Bewley, A., Ge, Z., Ott, L., Ramos, F., Upcroft, B.: Simple online and realtime tracking. In: 2016 IEEE International Conference on Image Processing (ICIP), pp. 3464–3468. IEEE (2016)
3. Bochinski, E., Eiselein, V., Sikora, T.: High-speed tracking-by-detection without using image information. In: 2017 14th IEEE International Conference on Advanced Video and Signal Based Surveillance (AVSS), pp. 1–6. IEEE (2017)
4. Chaabane, M., Zhang, P., Beveridge, J.R., et al.: DEFT: detection embeddings for tracking. arXiv:2102.02267v2 (2021)
5. Ciaparrone, G., Sánchez, F.L., Tabik, S., Troiano, L., Tagliaferri, R., Herrera, F.: Deep learning in video multi-object tracking: a survey. Neurocomputing **381**, 61–88 (2020)
6. Feichtenhofer, C., Pinz, A., Zisserman, A.: Detect to track and track to detect. In: Proceedings of the IEEE International Conference on Computer Vision, pp. 3038–3046 (2017)
7. He, K., Gkioxari, G., Dollár, P., Girshick, R.: Mask R-CNN. In: Proceedings of the IEEE International Conference on Computer Vision, pp. 2961–2969 (2017)
8. Ilg, E., Mayer, N., Saikia, T., Keuper, M., Dosovitskiy, A., Brox, T.: FlowNet 2.0: evolution of optical flow estimation with deep networks. In: Proceedings of the IEEE Conference on Computer Vision and Pattern Recognition, pp. 2462–2470 (2017)
9. Liang, C., et al.: Rethinking the competition between detection and ReID in multi-object tracking. arXiv preprint arXiv:2010.12138 (2020)
10. Luo, W., Xing, J., Milan, A., Zhang, X., Liu, W., Kim, T.K.: Multiple object tracking: a literature review. Artif. Intell. **293**, 103448 (2020)
11. Ren, S., He, K., Girshick, R., Sun, J.: Faster R-CNN: towards real-time object detection with region proposal networks. Adv. Neural. Inf. Process. Syst. **28**, 91–99 (2015)
12. Shuai, B., Berneshawi, A.G., Modolo, D., Tighe, J.: Multi-object tracking with siamese track-RCNN. arXiv preprint arXiv:2004.07786 (2020)
13. Sun, P., et al.: TransTrack: multiple-object tracking with transformer. arXiv preprint arXiv:2012.15460 (2020)
14. Sun, S., Akhtar, N., Song, H., Mian, A., Shah, M.: Deep affinity network for multiple object tracking. IEEE Trans. Pattern Anal. Mach. Intell. **43**(1), 104–119 (2019)
15. Wang, Y., Kitani, K., Weng, X.: Joint object detection and multi-object tracking with graph neural networks. arXiv preprint arXiv:2006.13164 (2020)
16. Wojke, N., Bewley, A., Paulus, D.: Simple online and realtime tracking with a deep association metric. In: 2017 IEEE International Conference on Image Processing (ICIP), pp. 3645–3649. IEEE (2017)
17. Xu, Y., Ban, Y., Delorme, G., Gan, C., Rus, D., Alameda-Pineda, X.: TransCenter: transformers with dense queries for multiple-object tracking. arXiv preprint arXiv:2103.15145 (2021)
18. Zhang, Y., Wang, C., Wang, X., Zeng, W., Liu, W.: FairMOT: on the fairness of detection and re-identification in multiple object tracking. Int. J. Comput. Vis. **129**, 3069–3087 (2021). https://doi.org/10.1007/s11263-021-01513-4
19. Zhou, X., Koltun, V., Krähenbühl, P.: Tracking objects as points. In: Vedaldi, A., Bischof, H., Brox, T., Frahm, J.-M. (eds.) ECCV 2020. LNCS, vol. 12349, pp. 474–490. Springer, Cham (2020). https://doi.org/10.1007/978-3-030-58548-8_28
20. Zhou, X., Wang, D., Krähenbühl, P.: Objects as points. arXiv preprint arXiv:1904.07850 (2019)

HIANet: Hierarchical Interweaved Aggregation Network for Crowd Counting

Jinyang Xie[1], Jinfang Zheng[1], Lingyu Gu[1], Chen Lyu[1,2], and Lei Lyu[1,2(✉)]

[1] School of Information Science and Engineering, Shandong Normal University,
Jinan 250358, China
lvlei@sdnu.edu.cn

[2] Shandong Provincial Key Laboratory for Distributed Computer Software Novel
Technology, Jinan 250358, China

Abstract. Aiming at scale variation in crowd counting, we consider that an optimal solution is to take full advantage of the complementarity between multi-scale features. To implement this idea, we devise a Hierarchical Interweaved Aggregation Network (HIANet) in this paper. Instead of directly using the traditional concatenation method to aggregate multi-level features, our Hierarchical Interweaved Aggregation Module (HIAM) utilizes an innovative multiplication aggregation strategy to facilitate sufficient multi-scale feature fusion, which can help HIANet recover more structural and detail information. Furthermore, our HIANet employs a Gated Passing Mechanism (GPM) to selectively control the passing of feature information on each level, thus further to suppress the useless background information. Extensive experiments in different crowd scenes well demonstrate that our method has clear advantages under different evaluation metrics.

Keywords: Crowd counting · Multi-level feature · Computer vision · Deep learning

1 Introduction

Crowd counting is designed for counting the amount of individuals in unconstrained scenes and has gained increasingly attention. Due to its huge application potential, crowd counting is widely used in some basic fields, such as data analysis [12], traffic guidance [15], and city management [8]. In particular, during the time COVID-19 swept the world, crowd counting is widely used for social distance monitoring to prevent crowd mass gatherings [13].

As an intractable problem in the crowd counting field, scale variation has attracted wide research interests. Scale variation means that the scales of individuals in image vary as the distance from the camera and it is difficult to be encoded effectively [1]. To address scale variation, it is necessary to adequately exploit the advantages of complementarity between multi-scale features. This because features at different scales contain different scale information and they

T. Mantoro et al. (Eds.): ICONIP 2021, CCIS 1517, pp. 571–578, 2021.
https://doi.org/10.1007/978-3-030-92310-5_66

are complementary to each other, the combination of these features can enhance the performance of the method in handling complex scenes [8].

With the purpose of better combining multi-scale features, we devise a novel Hierarchical Interweaved Aggregation Network (HIANet). Specifically, we first design a Gated Passing Mechanism that uses a gate function to control the passing of feature information at each level. After that, we design a Hierarchical Interweaved Aggregation Module (HIAM), which uses the multiplication operation to hierarchically and progressively aggregate feature information at different levels. With this module, multiple levels of feature information can collaborate with each other to recover more structural and detail information.

In summary, this paper is innovative in three ways:

- We propose a Hierarchical Interweaved Aggregation Network (HIANet), which can fully exert the complementary advantages between multi-level features.
- We design a Hierarchical Interweaved Aggregation Module (HIAM), which can facilitate sufficient multi-scale feature fusions.
- We introduce a Gated Passing Mechanism, which can suppress the influence of useless information.

2   Related Works

2.1   Multi-column Based Methods

Multi-column based methods generally adopt multiple sub-columns with different convolutional kernels to capture crowds on different scales. MCNN [16] uses three branches with different sized kernels to accurately capture multi-scale features on different sizes of receptive fields. CP-CNN [10] employs two branches to extract different contextual information respectively, and efficiently fuses them to cope with scale variation. DADNet [2] uses multiple columns of dilation-CNNs with different rates to capture wider contextual information, so that the location of the crowd can be accurately located.

2.2   Multi-level Based Methods

Multi-level based methods aim to learn multi-scale representations hierarchically from different internal layers of the backbone network, thus adapting to different scale spaces. SaCNN [15] extracts multi-level features from the FCN and further resizes them to have the same size. TEDnet [6] utilizes an innovative multi-path decoder architecture to gradually fuse multi-level features. In addition, it also deploys surveillance mechanisms at each level to optimize the performance of the network. SASNet [11] achieves accurate crowd counts by automatically learning the internal correspondence between scales and feature levels.

3   Our Method

3.1   Overview

We present a Hierarchical Interweaved Aggregation Network (HIANet) in this paper, as shown in Fig. 1, it comprises an encoding stage and a decoding stage. During the encoding stage, we feed the crowd images into VGG-16 to generate multi-level feature representations $(F_1, F_2, F_3, F_4, F_5)$ that capture the contextual information at different scale spaces.

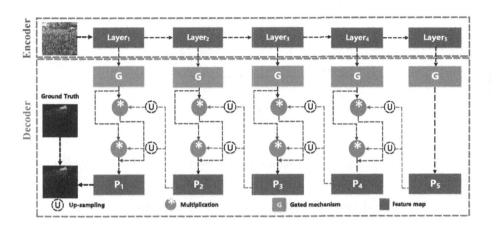

Fig. 1. The details of Hierarchical Interweaved Aggregation Network (HIANet).

In the decoding stage, a Gated Passing Mechanism (GPM) is used to control whether the feature information in the F_i should be passed to the next stage. After that, a Hierarchical Interweaved Aggregation Module (HIAM) is further used to aggregate feature information from higher to lower levels. Finally, the aggregated features is regressed to output the crowd density map.

3.2   Gated Passing Mechanism

Since there is a certain degree of noise information in multi-level features F_i, to abandon these superfluous noisy, we design a Gated Passing Mechanism (GPM) to adaptively filter multi-level features F_i and generate adaptive features G_i.

Our GPM includes a set of convolutional layers and a sigmoid activation function, which can generate information passing rate in the range $[0, 1]$. The specific process is:

$$G(F_i) = Sig(Conv(F_i)) \tag{1}$$

where $Sig()$ denotes the Sigmoid activation function, $Conv()$ denotes the 1×1 convolutional layer.

After that, the GPM controls the passing of feature information at each level based on this rate and generates adaptive features G_i. Thus, the adaptive features G_i can be expressed as:

$$G_i = \varphi \left(Conv \left(G \left(F_i \right) \right) \otimes \varphi \left(Conv \left(F_i \right) \right) \right) \tag{2}$$

where $\otimes$ is element multiplication operation, φ is a ReLU activation function.

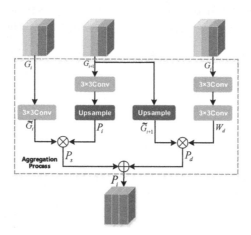

Fig. 2. The architecture of Hierarchical Interweaved Aggregation Module (HIAM).

3.3   Hierarchical Interweaved Aggregation Module

Since the effective combination of features at different levels can generate complementary information, which helps to enhance the expression capacity of multilevel features. Therefore, we design the HIAM to aggregate features from higher to lower levels. In our implementation, we employ multiplication operations to facilitate sufficient multi-level feature fusion, which contributes to retain more detailed information and suppress background noise.

As shown in Fig. 2, for each level of adaptive features $G_{i\,(1 \leq i \leq 4)}$, we first compress them to have the same number of channels as the high-level features G_{i+1} by utilizing a 1×1 convolution, so that we can obtain features $\widetilde{G}_i$. For high-level features G_{i+1}, we perform two operations. 1) G_{i+1} is passed through a 3×3 convolution, then it is up-sampled to have the same size as G_i for obtaining semantic weights W_s. After that, we combine the weights W_s and the features $\widetilde{G}_i$ by utilizing the multiplication operation. Thus, we can obtain the semantic features P_s.

2) G_{i+1} is up-sampled directly to obtain features $\widetilde{G_{i+1}}$, and the $\widetilde{G}_i$ is applied a 3×3 convolution to generate the detail weights W_d. After that they are both performed a multiplication operation to generate detail features P_d.

Finally, we employ a 3×3 convolution to concatenate these two features to obtain the aggregated features P_i:

$$P_i = Conv \left(Concat \left(P_s, P_d \right) \right) \tag{3}$$

where $Concat()$ denotes the concatenation operation, $Conv()$ denotes the 3×3 convolution.

Table 1. Comparison of different selection strategies.

Version	MAE	MSE
Backbone	66.7	114.7
Backbone+GPM	61.9	102.3
Backbone+HIAM	59.4	99.6
Backbone+GPM+HIAM (HIANet)	**52.8**	**87.2**

3.4 Loss Function

We use MSE loss to define the difference between the ground-truth and the estimated density map:

$$L(\theta) = \frac{1}{2N} \sum_{i=1}^{N} \left\| Z(X_i; \theta) - Z_i^{GT} \right\|_2^2 \tag{4}$$

where N represents batch size, X_i represents experimental image, Z_i^{GT} denotes the ground-truth, and $Z(X_i; \theta)$ denotes the estimated density map, respectively.

4 Experiments

4.1 Experiment Details

Ground Truth Generation. To generate the ground-truth density map, we blur each head annotation in the crowd image by utilizing a Gaussian kernel (normalized to 1). The specific implementation process is based on CSRNet [7].

Evaluation Criteria. MAE [13] and MSE [13] are adopted to evaluate the counting accuracy and the robustness of the method, respectively.

4.2 Ablation Study

To verify the performance of different modules, we first conduct several ablation studies on the ShanghaiTech dataset [16]. Specifically, in our implementation, we adopt a VGG-16 encoder as the Backbone. After that, we gradually add the corresponding modules to verify the effectiveness of these modules.

As shown in the second row of Table 1, compared with Backbone individually, Backbone+GPM improves MAE by 7% and MSE by 10%. As shown in Fig. 3(a), since GPM further abandons useless information, so that our method can effectively avoid the influence of background and accurately locate foreground regions.

As shown in the third row of Table 1, compared with Backbone individually, Backbone+HIAM achieves MAE of 59.4 and MSE of 99.6, which substantially improves the counting accuracy. As shown in Fig. 3(b), due to the HIAM recovering structure and detail information to some extent, so that our method can accurately capture the crowd on different scale spaces.

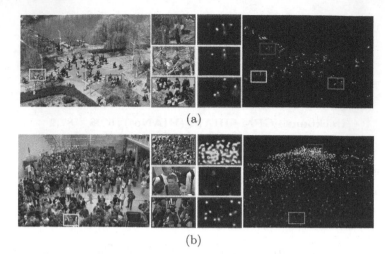

Fig. 3. Density map visualization of different scenes. (a) Visualization of complex background scenes. (b) Visualization of scale variation scenes.

Table 2. Comparisons of HIANet and existing methods on three datasets.

Dataset	Part A		Part B		UCF_CC_50		UCF-QNRF	
Method	MAE	MSE	MAE	MSE	MAE	MSE	MAE	MSE
MCNN [16]	110.2	173.2	26.4	41.3	377.6	509.1	277.0	426.0
CSRNet [7]	68.2	115.0	10.6	16.0	266.1	397.5	120.3	208.5
TEDNet [6]	64.2	109.1	8.2	12.8	249.4	354.5	113.0	188.0
CANNet [9]	62.3	100.0	7.8	12.2	212.2	243.7	107.0	183.0
M-SFANet [12]	59.7	95.7	6.8	11.9	162.3	276.8	85.6	151.2
SASNet [11]	53.6	88.5	6.4	9.9	161.4	234.5	85.2	147.3
HIANet	**52.8**	**87.2**	**6.2**	**9.7**	**160.9**	**235.8**	**84.6**	**146.2**

4.3   Comparison of Counting Performance

To analyze the performance of our method in different scenes, we verify the proposed method on four datasets: Shanghai Tech dataset [16], UCF_CCF_50 dataset [3], UCF-QNRF dataset [4] and WorldExpo'10 dataset [14].

As can be seen from the Table 2, in Part A, our method compares with SAS-Net that has the best performance, MAE improves by 1.4% and MSE improves by 1.4%. In Part B, our method compares with the SASNet, MAE improves by 3.1% and MSE improves by 2%, respectively. For UCF_CC_50 dataset, our method obtains suboptimal results in the robustness, which is still 0.6% away from the best-performing SASNet. However, in terms of counting accuracy, comparing with the second place, our method improves 0.3% in MAE. Similarly, for the UCF-QNRF dataset, our method consistently and significantly outperforms other methods.

Table 3. Performance comparison on WorldExpo'10 dataset.

Method	Scene1	Scene2	Scene3	Scene4	Scene5	Average
MCNN [16]	3.4	14.1	14.3	22.2	3.7	12.9
CSRNet [7]	2.9	11.5	8.6	16.6	3.4	8.6
HSRNet [17]	2.3	9.6	12.7	9.4	3.2	7.44
CANNet [9]	2.9	12.0	10.0	7.9	4.3	7.4
ASNet [5]	2.22	10.1	8.9	7.1	4.9	6.7
HIANet	**2.3**	**9.4**	**10.2**	**7.3**	**3.5**	**6.54**

As can be seen from the Table 3, for the scenes with relatively dense crowds in WorldExpo'10 dataset, such as in scene 2, our method with still outperforms the other methods and leads the second best in MAE by 2%. In Scene 4, our method leads ASNet by 7%. In addition, our method reaches the optimal average performance, which is 11% ahead of the second best.

5 Conclusion

We propose a novel Hierarchical Interweaved Aggregation Network (HIANet) in this work, which can effectively adapt to complex crowd scenes with rapid scale variation. With the proposed Gated Passing Mechanism (GPM), our HIANet can refine the features at each level and enhance their robustness. After that, the Hierarchical Interweaved Aggregation Module (HIAM) adopts multiplication operations to aggregate semantic and detail information from different levels, so that it can recover more structural and detail information and take full advantage of the complementarity between multi-scale features. Extensive experiments in different crowd scenes have shown the clear advantages of our method.

Acknowledgments. This work is supported by the National Natural Science Foundation of China under Grant 61976127.

References

1. Gao, J., Wang, Q., Li, X.: PCC Net: perspective crowd counting via spatial convolutional network. IEEE Trans. Circ. Syst. Video Technol. **30**(10), 3486–3498 (2019)
2. Guo, D., Li, K., Zha, Z.J., Wang, M.: DADNet: dilated-attention-deformable convnet for crowd counting. In: Proceedings of the 27th ACM International Conference on Multimedia, pp. 1823–1832 (2019)
3. Idrees, H., Saleemi, I., Seibert, C., Shah, M.: Multi-source multi-scale counting in extremely dense crowd images. In: Proceedings of the IEEE Conference on Computer Vision and Pattern Recognition, pp. 2547–2554 (2013)

4. Idrees, H., et al.: Composition loss for counting, density map estimation and localization in dense crowds. In: Ferrari, V., Hebert, M., Sminchisescu, C., Weiss, Y. (eds.) ECCV 2018. LNCS, vol. 11206, pp. 544–559. Springer, Cham (2018). https://doi.org/10.1007/978-3-030-01216-8_33

5. Jiang, X., et al.: Attention scaling for crowd counting. In: Proceedings of the IEEE/CVF Conference on Computer Vision and Pattern Recognition, pp. 4706–4715 (2020)

6. Jiang, X., et al.: Crowd counting and density estimation by trellis encoder-decoder networks. In: Proceedings of the IEEE/CVF Conference on Computer Vision and Pattern Recognition, pp. 6133–6142 (2019)

7. Li, Y., Zhang, X., Chen, D.: CSRNet: dilated convolutional neural networks for understanding the highly congested scenes. In: Proceedings of the IEEE Conference on Computer Vision and Pattern Recognition, pp. 1091–1100 (2018)

8. Liu, L., Qiu, Z., Li, G., Liu, S., Ouyang, W., Lin, L.: Crowd counting with deep structured scale integration network. In: Proceedings of the IEEE/CVF International Conference on Computer Vision, pp. 1774–1783 (2019)

9. Liu, W., Salzmann, M., Fua, P.: Context-aware crowd counting. In: Proceedings of the IEEE/CVF Conference on Computer Vision and Pattern Recognition, pp. 5099–5108 (2019)

10. Sindagi, V.A., Patel, V.M.: Generating high-quality crowd density maps using contextual pyramid CNNs. In: Proceedings of the IEEE International Conference on Computer Vision, pp. 1861–1870 (2017)

11. Song, Q., et al.: To choose or to fuse? Scale selection for crowd counting. In: Proceedings of the AAAI Conference on Artificial Intelligence, vol. 35, pp. 2576–2583 (2021)

12. Thanasutives, P., Fukui, K.I., Numao, M., Kijsirikul, B.: Encoder-decoder based convolutional neural networks with multi-scale-aware modules for crowd counting. In: 2020 25th International Conference on Pattern Recognition (ICPR), pp. 2382–2389. IEEE (2021)

13. Wang, Q., Han, T., Gao, J., Yuan, Y.: Neuron linear transformation: modeling the domain shift for crowd counting. IEEE Trans. Neural Netw. Learn. Syst. (2021)

14. Zhang, C., Li, H., Wang, X., Yang, X.: Cross-scene crowd counting via deep convolutional neural networks. In: Proceedings of the IEEE Conference on Computer Vision and Pattern Recognition, pp. 833–841 (2015)

15. Zhang, L., Shi, M., Chen, Q.: Crowd counting via scale-adaptive convolutional neural network. In: 2018 IEEE Winter Conference on Applications of Computer Vision (WACV), pp. 1113–1121. IEEE (2018)

16. Zhang, Y., Zhou, D., Chen, S., Gao, S., Ma, Y.: Single-image crowd counting via multi-column convolutional neural network. In: Proceedings of the IEEE Conference on Computer Vision and Pattern Recognition, pp. 589–597 (2016)

17. Zou, Z., Liu, Y., Xu, S., Wei, W., Wen, S., Zhou, P.: Crowd counting via hierarchical scale recalibration network. In: 24th European Conference on Artificial Intelligence (ECAI), pp. 2864–2871 (2020)

Associated Lattice-BERT for Spoken Language Understanding

Ye Zou$^{(\boxtimes)}$, Huiping Sun$^{(\boxtimes)}$, and Zhong Chen

School of Software and Microelectronics, Peking University, Beijing 100080, China
zouye19@pku.edu.cn, {sunhp,chen}@ss.pku.edu.cn

Abstract. Lattices are compact representations that can encode multiple speech recognition hypotheses in spoken language understanding tasks. Previous work has extended the pre-trained transformer to model lattice inputs and achieved significant improvements in natural language processing tasks. However, these models do not consider the global probability distribution of lattices path and the correlation among multiple speech recognition hypotheses. In this paper, we propose an associated Lattice-BERT, an extension of BERT that is tailored for spoken language understanding (SLU). Associated Lattice-BERT augments self-attention with positional relation representations and lattice scores to incorporate lattice structure. We further design a lattice confusion-aware attention mechanism in the prediction layer to push the model to learn from the association information between the lattice confusion paths, which mitigates the impact of the Automatic Speech Recognizer (ASR) errors on the model. We apply the proposed model to a spoken language understanding task, the experiments on the datasets of intention detection recognition show that our proposed method outperforms the strong baselines when evaluated on spoken inputs.

Keywords: Spoken language understanding · BERT · Lattice · Attention mechanism

1 Introduction

SLU plays an important role in the spoken dialogue system, which aims to extract useful information from spoken utterances and provides structured information for downstream tasks. SLU usually consists of two parts. Namely, the input spoken is transcribed into texts by the ASR system, and then the transcribed texts are used as input to the language model to complete the target task. However, this kind of two-stage language understanding system is based on manual transcripts [1] may transmit the wrong recognition results of ASR to a later stage of the dialogue system and yield a wrong output.

Inspired by earlier works [2–5] proposes LatticeRNN to model lattices for addressing the above problem. However, this method prevents convenient use of batched computation and leads to low computational efficiency. In addition, this method cannot exploit lattice structural information.

© Springer Nature Switzerland AG 2021
T. Mantoro et al. (Eds.): ICONIP 2021, CCIS 1517, pp. 579–586, 2021.
https://doi.org/10.1007/978-3-030-92310-5_67

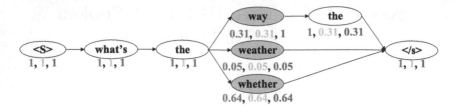

Fig. 1. Example of a lattice. The blue score is the forward probability, the orange score is the marginal probability, the red score is the backward probability. (Color figure online)

To mitigate this problem, [6] extends the previously purely sequential self-attentional models to lattice inputs, which also incorporates the lattice structure information into the model. Although this method is effective, it doesn't consider the correlation information among competitive words on the lattice confusion path. Take the sentence in Fig. 1 as an example, the word "the" has three successors: "way", "weather" and "whether", and we define the successors as competitive words. If the high-confidence words are incorrect competition words, which will cause the influence of incorrect words to be greater than the influence of correct words and lead to a wrong recognition result.

Lattice-BERT [7] has been exploited in Chinese NER, [8] exploits the lattice positional structures in self-attention layers. However, this model doesn't consider the lattice scores [9] information from lattice graphs and the correlation information between competitive words.

In this paper, we propose an associated Lattice-BERT for SLU. We evaluate our model on three datasets. Compared with the baseline with lattice as input, our proposed model brings an average increase of 2.43% in the spoken language understanding task. Our contributions can be summarized as:

1. To our knowledge, we first designed associated Lattice-BERT for SLU.
2. We design a lattice joint-aware self-attention to account for the lattice scores to capture lattice structure and path probability distribution information.
3. We propose a lattice confusion-aware attention (LCA) in the prediction layer, which incorporates the association information of the competitive words on the confusion path to improve the effectiveness of the model by capturing the global information and reduce the impact of ASR errors on the model.
4. The proposed approach achieves better performance on the SLU tasks.

2   Background

2.1   Lattice

The lattice is the output of ASR which is a directed acyclic graph that stores multiple decoding hypotheses. Each possible hypothesis represents a path, as shown in Fig. 1. More formally, let $G = (V, E)$ be a directed acyclic graph containing node set V and edge set E. For arbitrary node $i \in V$, let $S^+(i)$ denotes all successors (reachable nodes) of node i, and let $N^+(i)$ denote the neighborhood, defined as the set of all adjacent successors. $S^-(i)$, $N^-(i)$ are defined analogously for predecessors. i→j means that there is at least one common path between node i and node j. We define the forward probability of node i as $f(i)$, the backward transition of node i as $b(i)$, and the marginal probability of node i as $m(i)$. According to the conditional probability, we can deduce the forward transition probability P_G^+ and the backward transition probability P_G^-.

3 Model

The structure of our model is shown in Fig. 2, which consists of 3 main components, lattice input layer, associated Lattice-BERT encoder and Decoding layer.

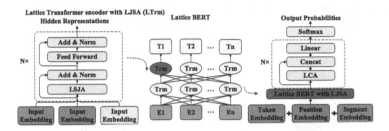

Fig. 2. Left: The architecture of Lattice Transformer encoder with LJSA (LTrm). Middle: The architecture of Lattice-BERT with LJSA, which uses a bidirectional LTrm. Right: The overall model architecture of our proposed an associated Lattice-BERT.

3.1 Lattice Input Layer

The input layer aims to embed both semantic information and positional information of tokens into their token embeddings. We use the longest-path distances between lattice nodes to encode positional information.

3.2 Associated Lattice-BERT Encoder

Our primary goal is to adapt the standard BERT to the task of SLU with lattice inputs. To this end, we propose lattice joint-aware self-attention to consume the lattice scores and the positional information of lattice structure.

Lattice Embedding. We exploit the longest-path distance from the start node to construct the lattice positional matrix $Z^P \in R^{N \times N}$. For unreachable nodes and the node itself, we set the value to 0. In addition, we add a positive number k to every entry of Z^P to ensure the uniqueness of the lattice embedding. In order to make Z^P learnable, we represent Z^P as the relation positional embedding, a 3D tensor $Z \in R^{N \times N \times d}$ by looking up a trainable embedding matrix $Z^A \in R^{(2k+1) \times d}$, where N is the number of lattice nodes.

Lattice Reachability Masks. The lattice is a directed acyclic graph, and the input of the language model is generally a sequential sequence. To extend the language model to handle lattices, [9] proposes lattice reachability masks to prevent the self-attention mechanism from attending to unreachable nodes.

$$M_{ij}^f = \begin{cases} \log P_G^+ (i \to j \mid i), j \in S^+(i) \text{ or } i = j \\ -\infty, \text{ else} \end{cases} \tag{1}$$

$$M_{ij}^b = \begin{cases} \log P_G^- (i \to j \mid i), j \in S^-(i) \text{ or } i = j \\ -\infty, \text{ else} \end{cases} \tag{2}$$

$$\alpha_{ij} = \text{softmax}\left(\frac{(x_i W^Q)(x_j W^K)^T}{\sqrt{d}} + M_{ij} \right) \tag{3}$$

Lattice Joint-Aware Self-attention. Our proposed Lattice Joint-aware Self-Attention (LJSA) mechanism is depicted in Fig. 3.

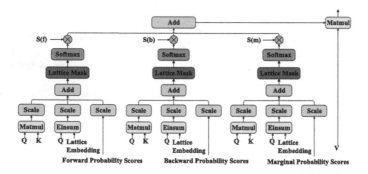

Fig. 3. Lattice joint-aware self-attention, where $s(f), s(b), s(m)$ are learnable scalars, and $s(f) + s(b) + s(m) = 1$

The original Lattice-BERT proposed by [8] cannot account for lattice scores, which will cause the influence of low-confidence regions on computed representations to be greater than the influence of high-confidence regions. To accurately incorporate the probability scores from lattice into the interactions between tokens, we propose lattice joint-aware self-attention, which also incorporates positional information into the model. Inspired by [10], we take the weighted average of the three attention vectors and use the new attention vector to represent the value of V, where the three weights are all scalars that can be learned.

$$\alpha_{ij}^f = \text{softmax} \left(\frac{(x_i W^Q)(x_j W^K)^T + \sum_k Q_{ij} Z_{ijk}}{\sqrt{d}} + M_{ij}^f \right) \tag{4}$$

$$\alpha_{ij} = s(f)\alpha_{ij}^f + s(b)\alpha_{ij}^b + s(m)\alpha_{ij}^m \tag{5}$$

$$\mu_i = \sum_{j=1}^{M} \alpha_{ij} \left(x_j W^V \right) \tag{6}$$

Where $Z \in R^{N \times N \times d}$ are lattice positional embeddings and w_m is a learnable scalar. $Q \in R^{N \times d}$ is a 2D matrix, but Z is a 3D matrix. The result is a 2D matrix of shape $[N \times N]$ whose i-th row and j-th column have elements $\sum_k Q_{ij} E_{ijk}$. We achieved this operation through Einstein summation convention.

3.3   Decoding Layer

After extracting the semantic information by the encoder layer, we feed the sequence representations into a lattice confusion-aware attention layer to make intent recognition. The overall architecture of the model is shown in Fig. 2.

Fig. 4. Example of a lattice competition words matrix.

Lattice Competitive Words Matrix. As shown in Fig. 1, We construct a lattice competitive words matrix $L \in R^{N \times N}$. The matrix generation details are as follows: (1) Initialize the matrix L to the identity matrix E; (2) We define C as a set of competitive words, and traverse lattice, when the number of successors is greater than 1, we generate a set of competitive words for this node and store it in set C; (3) Traverse the set C, for arbitrary node $i \in C(k)$, and node $j \in C(k), L(i,j) = L(j,i) = 1$. Finally, the lattice competitive words matrix we get is shown in Fig. 4. After extracting the semantic information by the encoder layer, we feed the sequence representations into a lattice confusion-aware attention layer to make intent recognition. The overall architecture of the model is shown in Fig. 2.

Lattice Confusion-Aware Attention. Our proposed LCA mechanism is a multi-head attention model, which summarizes the attention scores among confusion paths, and integrates the associated information among into the prediction layer of the model. The calculation process of single attention is as follows:

$$e_{ij}^1 = \frac{\left(o_i W^Q\right)\left(o_j W^K\right)^T}{\sqrt{d}} \tag{7}$$

$$\alpha_{ij}^1 = \text{softmax}_j\left(e_{ij}^1\right) = \frac{\exp\left(e_{ij}^1\right)}{\sum_{k \in N_i} \exp\left(e_{ik}^1\right)} \tag{8}$$

$$\mu_i^1 = \sum_{j \in N_i} \alpha_{ij}^1\left(x_j W^V\right) \tag{9}$$

Where $O_{1:M}$ represents the output vector of associated Lattice-BERT, which is also the input vector of the LCA model. N_i represents the set of node pairs with a value greater than 0 in the confusion path matrix. For arbitrary $(i,j) \in N_i$, there is $L(j,i) > 0$. As shown in Eq. 8, LCA only pay attention to competitive nodes to improve the confusion-aware ability of the model.

4   Experiments

4.1   Datasets

The three benchmark datasets used for intent detection are as follows:

1. Snips Smartlights [11] contains spoken commands for the smart light assistant. The dataset has two microphone settings: close field and far field.
2. The SNIPS [12] corpus only contains written text, so we use the text-to-speech system to synthesize the spoken version of the dataset.
3. SLURP [13] contains the spoken commands of the home robot. The dataset has two microphone settings: close field and far field.

4.2   Results

Table 2 presents the results of intent detection. All experimental results are the average of at least three training sessions. Lines (a)–(c) are the upper limit of the model, and we use manual transcripts as input to the model. The experimental results show that our proposed model achieves significant improvement on all datasets. The baseline model with ASR lattice as input always performs better

Table 1. Dataset statistics (Wer is words error rate of ASR system).

		Train	Test	Valid	Intents	Wer (%)
SNIPS		13084	700	700	7	45.61
SmartLights	Close	1328	166	166	6	32.83
	Far	1328	166	166	6	83.36
SLURP	Close	11514	2033	2974	46	43.13
	Far	11514	2033	2974	46	58.81

than the baseline model with ASR 1-best as input, which shows that lattices are important in the model. Compared with baseline biLatticeLSTM+ELMO [14] (row(i)) and baseline Lattice-BERT (row(h)), our proposed model yield 8.2%–40% relative error reduction, and 6.7%–23.4% relative error reduction. These results demonstrate that our proposed model yields clear and consistent improvement for SLU (Table 2).

Table 2. Results of our experiments in terms of accuracy (%).

			SNIPS	SmartLights		SLURP	
				Close	Far	Close	Far
Manual	a	biLSTM	97.00	90.34	77.57	84.49	72.92
	b	(a)+ELMO	96.83	90.61	77.17	85.72	72.63
	c	BERT	96.92	91.03	78.32	86.42	73.11
ASR 1-best	d	biLSTM	91.89	73.45	39.08	74.93	58.86
	e	(d)+ELMO	91.98	75.56	40.45	75.11	61.52
	f	BERT	93.29	77.12	41.43	75.58	62.91
ASR lattice	g	biLatticeLSTM	91.69	75.44	40.33	74.16	62.38
	h	Lattice-BERT	94.43	78.51	42.35	76.74	63.27
	i	(g)+ELMO	95.37	79.17	43.14	77.23	64.52
	j	(h)+ LJSA	95.28	82.56	44.83	79.27	65.32
	k	(h)+ LCA	95.09	81.08	43.92	78.69	64.83
	l	**We proposed**	**95.70**	**83.13**	**46.22**	**80.11**	**66.46**

4.3   Model Ablation Study

We perform an ablation study to examine the effectiveness of every module in the associated Lattice-BERT. The results show that the ablation of either module LJSA or module LCA will lead to a decrease in model performance.

Our LJSA method can capture lattice structure information which prevents the low-confidence regions from having a greater influence on the calculated representation. When the probability of the correct competition word "weather" is very small (see Fig. 1), the LJSA model can not capture enough information to understand the intention of this utterance. Our proposed model, a complement of the two methods, can accurately understand that users are asking about the weather, even though the word has the lowest probability among competitive words. It proves the validity of our model.

5   Conclusion

In this paper, we propose an associated Lattice-BERT architecture for SLU, with lattice joint-aware self-attention mechanism and lattice confusion-aware attention mechanism. Associated Lattice-BERT can account for lattice scores to exploit the lattice structure. It also learns the correlation between multiple speech recognition hypotheses to enhance the ability of modeling. Experiments in the tasks of SLU prove the effectiveness of our method.

References

1. Goo, C., et al.: Slot-gated modeling for joint slot filling and intent prediction. In: NAACL-HLT (2), pp. 753–757 (2018)
2. Socher, R., et al.: Recursive deep models for semantic compositionality over a sentiment treebank. In: Proceedings of EMNLP, pp. 1631–1642. ACL (2013)
3. Tai, K., et al.: Improved semantic representations from tree-structured long short-term memory networks. In: Proceedings of ACL, pp. 1556–1566. ACL (2015)
4. Zhu, X., Sobhani, P., Guo, H.: Long short-term memory over recursive structures. In: Proceedings of ICML, pp. 1604–1612. ICML (2015)
5. Ladhak, F., et al.: LatticeRnn: recurrent neural networks over lattices. In: Interspeech 2016 (2016)
6. Sperber, M., et al.: Self-attentional models for lattice inputs. In: Proceedings of ACL, pp. 1185–1197. ACL (2019)
7. Devlin, J., et al.: BERT: pre-training of deep bidirectional transformers for language understanding. In: Proceedings of NAACL, pp. 4171–4186. ACL (2019)
8. Lai, Y., et al.: Lattice-BERT: leveraging multi-granularity representations in Chinese pre-trained language models. In: Proceedings of NAACL, pp. 1716–1731. ACL (2021)
9. Rabiner, L.: A tutorial on hidden Markov models and selected applications in speech recognition. Proc. IEEE **77**(2), 257–286 (1989)
10. Zhang, P., et al.: Lattice transformer for speech translation. In: Proceedings of ACL, pp. 6475–6484. ACL (2019)
11. Saade, A., et al.: Spoken language understanding on the edge. In: 2019 Fifth Workshop on Energy Efficient Machine Learning and Cognitive Computing - NeurIPS Edition (EMC2-NIPS), pp. 57–61 (2019)
12. Coucke, A., et al.: Snips voice platform: an embedded spoken language understanding system for private-by-design voice interfaces. CoRR abs/1805.10190 (2018)
13. Bastianelli, E., et al.: SLURP: a spoken language understanding resource package. In: Proceedings of EMNLP, pp. 7252–7262. ACL (2020)
14. Huang, C., Chen, Y.: Learning spoken language representations with neural lattice language modeling. In: Proceedings of ACL, pp. 3764–3769. ACL (2020)

An Improved Time-Series Forecasting Model Using Time Series Decomposition and GRU Architecture

Hyun Jae Jo⬤, Won Joong Kim⬤, Hyo Kyung Goh⬤,
and Chi-Hyuck Jun$^{(\boxtimes)}$⬤

POSTECH, Pohang 37673, Republic of Korea
{present,wjkim0229,hyokyung,chjun}@postech.ac.kr

Abstract. In this paper, we proposed an improved a time series forecasting method using time series decomposition and a deep learning model. The proposed method combined Seasonal-Trend decomposition using Loess (STL) and Gated Recurrent Units (GRU) architecture to forecast time series data. We used trend, seasonality and the remainder as input in GRU model simultaneously. In proposed model, it does not assume independence between the components differently from other papers. According to the experiments for several data in various fields, our model outperforms other traditional methods such as Seasonal ARIMA, Holt-Winters and GRU without decomposition. Furthermore, we also demonstrated that the proposed model decrease MSE comparing with the GRU model assuming independence.

Keywords: Time-series forecasting · Time-series decomposition · STL decomposition · Deep learning · GRU

1 Introduction

Importance of analyzing time-series data cannot be overemphasized nowadays, especially in forecasting. Future uncertainty can be predicted with historical data. However, as data became bigger and more complicated, it is hard to forecast precisely with traditional methods like ARIMA because most of them are based on a linear relationship. For this reason, a lot of recent papers have been using deep learning models to handle a complicate pattern in a time series. However, there is still a problem in deep learning models, which may have high variability and are very sensitive to input data. In order to solve this problem, several studies tried to combine time series decomposition and deep learning. Time series decomposition is a method that decompose time series data into three components usually, which are trend, seasonality and a noise (remainder) subseries, respectively. Huo et al. used LSTM and STL decomposition to predict network passengers [9].

H. J. Jo, W. J. Kim and H. K. Goh—Equal contribution.

ⓒ Springer Nature Switzerland AG 2021
T. Mantoro et al. (Eds.): ICONIP 2021, CCIS 1517, pp. 587–596, 2021.
https://doi.org/10.1007/978-3-030-92310-5_68

Most of recent studies, however, set up a precondition that there is independence between trend, seasonality and the remainder to make covariance zero. For example, Zhang et al. [15] assumed that components after decomposition are completely independent of each other to reduce forecasting variance. This independence assumption may not be reasonable in general because the correlation between components still exists after decomposition.

For these reasons, we proposed a model which does not need to assume independence. We assumed decomposed subseries could offer refined information to predict more than original time-series. Since time series decomposition smooths the original time series with some prior and later values, it enables a forecasting model to estimate each component much lower variance than to handle the original time series. Thus, combining decomposition and deep learning has advantages over deep learning model which uses only original time series in forecasting future series. We adopted both STL decomposition [5] as a time series decomposition method and GRU model [3] together and we present some reasons why we used STL decomposition and GRU model in Sect. 3. Our main contribution is as following; the proposed model does not lose any generalization from assuming independence, comparing with other papers. Nevertheless, we confirmed that our model can reduce Mean Squared Error (MSE) of forecasting values comparing with model assuming independence. Especially, our model outperforms with data that has a stable pattern of seasonality but fluctuating trend.

In this paper, we used several time series datasets from various fields to confirm performance of our model in general. We set a time lag of input that enables model to train sufficiently. In most cases, our proposed model outperformed other methods.

The remaining of this paper is organized as follows; Sect. 2 describes the latest related works done in forecasting time series data with decomposition and deep learning model. In Sect. 3, we explore the proposed model framework in detail including STL decomposition and GRU architecture. Our numerical experiment and the results are presented in Sect. 4. Finally, we conclude the paper and offer a brief summary in Sect. 5.

2   Literature Review

Recently, there have been researches to predict complex time series data by combining decomposition and deep-learning.

There are several methods to decompose a time-series data. Some papers [10, 14] used Seasonal and Trend decomposition using Loess, STL. STL is proposed by Cleveland et al. [5] which is widely applied for time-series decomposition. A detailed algorithm will be explained at Sect. 3. Huo et al. suggested a improved STL which can obtain multiple seasonal components to extract strong periodic characteristics of long-term passengers data [9]. Bandara et al. [1] used a series of decomposition techniques such as Multiple STL Decomposition (MSTL), Seasonal-Trend decomposition by Regression (STR) and Trigonometric, Box-Cox, ARMA, Trend and Seasonal (TBATS) [6,7]. Through these methods, they could accommodate repeating patterns that change slowly over time. Zhang et al. proposed Filter Cycle Decomposition (FCD) [15], simplified version of X-11 proposed by Shiskin [12].

On the other hands, research adopted deep-learning models to forecast time-series data effectively and showed that a method combining decomposition and deep-learning model achieves higher prediction accuracy than traditional time-series forecasting model or a single deep-learning model. Some papers adopted Gated Recurrent Unit [11,15], Zhang et al. combines FCD and GRU Neural Network [15], variable length time lag sampling and multi-lag ensemble forecasting. A difference between our proposed model and [11] is assuming independence. Sebastian et al. put decomposed components into GRU respectively comparing to our model reflected them simultaneously. Long-Short Term Memory (LSTM) which instituted by Hochreiter and Juregn [8] is widely used [1,9,14] and Mendez-Jimenez and Miguel applied both Convolutional Neural Network (CNN) and LSTM [10]. Huo et al. proposed that decomposed components become input into the Seq2Seq model based on the LSTM added with the improved attention mechanism for prediction [9]. A paper showed LSTM-MSNet, Long Short-Term Memory Multi-Seasonal Net, a decomposition-based, unified prediction framework to forecast time series with multiple seasonal patterns [1], while another one suggested the STL-ATTLSTM (STL-Attention-based LSTM) model [14], which integrated the seasonal trend decomposition using the Loess preprocessing method and attention mechanism based on long short-term memory. Mendez-Jimenez and Miguel also suggested the improvement of the forecasting capacity of CNN and RNN s evaluated when using the STL components as input [10]. A summary of papers we mentioned above is presented in Table 1.

Table 1. Recent research using decomposition and deep learning

Reference	Decomposition method	Deep learning model
[15]	FCD	GRU
[10]	STL	CNN, LSTM
[9]	Improved STL	Seq2Seq model based on LSTM
[1]	M-STL, STR, TBATS, Prophet	LSTM-MSNet
[14]	STL	ATTLSTM
[11]	STL	GRU

3 Proposed Method

We decomposed the original time-series into trend, seasonal and remainder subseries using STL decomposition. A time series is represented as X_t and this can be decomposed into $X_t = S_t + T_t + R_t$ for $t = 1, \ldots, N$, where $S_t, T_t,$ and R_t are the seasonal, trend-cycle, and remainder components respectively. In the proposed method, model is trained by existing decomposed subseries and forecast future subseries. Thus, existing time series at each time should be decomposed by trend, seasonal, and remainder component. However, we cannot obtain seasonality of some first and last subseries when using traditional decomposition method. Thus, in this paper, we used STL decomposition which can decompose time series at every time t. STL decomposition analyze three components respectively using some prior and later values, so it offers refined information to estimate each component and enables model to predict the future time series more precisely. Another advantage of this method over other decomposition methods is being robust to outliers because of its characteristics that use local regression. STL decomposition has 6 main hyperparameters as follows: n_p is the number of observations in each cycle of the seasonal component, n_i is the number of passes through the inner loop, n_o is the number of robustness iterations of the outer loop, n_l is the smoothing parameter for the low pass filter, n_t is the smoothing parameter for the trend component, and n_s is the smoothing parameter for the seasonal component.

Then, we used GRU model to predict future time series. GRU model is variant of a Recurrent Neural Network (RNN), and a lot of studies on time series analysis using the RNN have been conducted. The RNN have an advantage to learn the patterns of the data over the time flow. However, since general RNN structure cannot fully utilize the information of the past due to long-term dependency problem [2], we used GRU architecture in this paper. It also has the advantage of improving past memory with a small number of parameters in the state compared to other variants [4]. In proposed model, we trained GRU model using trend, seasonal and remainder subseries after STL decomposition. Namely, input vector of time lag t is $x_t = (T_t, S_t, R_t)$ and GRU learns weights of model W and hidden state h_t at time t using input vectors of each time lags. They are trained by two gates u_t, and r_t. Parameters we mentioned can be formulated as follows:

$$r_t = \sigma(W_{hr}h_{t-1} + W_{xr}x_t)$$
$$u_t = \sigma(W_{hu}h_{t-1} + W_{xu}x_t)$$
$$h_t = (1 - u_t) * h_{t-1} + u_t * \bar{h}_t$$
$$\bar{h}_t = \tau(W h_{t-1} * r_t + U x_t)$$

where σ means sigmoid function, τ means tangent hyperbolic, and $*$ means point-wise operation.

The process of proposed model is as follows. Firstly, we transform original time series to decomposed subseries using STL decomposition. Secondly, we train GRU architecture through normalized subseries as input, and forecast future decomposed subseries as output. Lastly, model calculates future time series using subseries of each time lag.

In time series decomposition, original time series from X_{t-k+1} to X_t decomposes into trend, seasonality and remainder from T_{t-k+1}, S_{t-k+1} and R_{t-k+1} to T_t, S_t and R_t. The hyperparameters of STL was set in the way as Cleveland et al. suggested [5]. Then, in GRU model, GRU cell takes input vectors time sequentially. Input vectors from x_{t-k+1} to x_t contain normalized trend, seasonality and remainder at each time lag. At time t, cell takes hidden state h_{t-1} and input vector x_t, then calculate hidden state h_t. We used k lags of past decomposed time subseries as input vectors and forecast output vector which contain p decomposed subseries. In other words, input vectors contain subseries from time $t - k + 1$ to t, and output vector contains subseries from time $t + 1$ to $t + p$. After forecasting decomposed p subseries, time series X_{t+1} to X_{t+p} are derived by adding three components at each time lag. In model architecture, we adopted many-to-one structure, which has many input vectors and forecasts one output vector. In addition, model had only one hidden layer to learn the characteristics of the time series. The reason why we used one hidden layer is to prevent overfitting from stacking hidden layers with quite simple data. The architecture of proposed model is presented in Fig. 1.

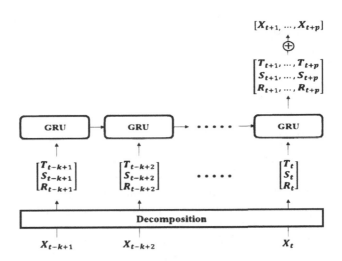

Fig. 1. Architecture of proposed model

Figure 2 compares the construction of model proposed by Sebastian et al. [11] and our model. Sebastian et al. proposed method combining STL decomposition and GRU model considering trend, seasonality and remainder respectively. It used three GRU models for each subseries. However, in this paper, we used only one GRU model considering three subseries simultaneously because we thought trend, seasonality and remainder are dependent and they affect each other. Through constructing model this way, we could use less computation power than using three GRU model for each subseries respectively. Moreover, we tried to reduce MSE without assuming independence between three subseries. For example, some time series data which have high variance but small number of series, deep learning model may overfit to the training data which occurs high MSE. To prevent overfitting, some regularizations like dropout should be added to model, which increase the number of hyperparameters. Thus, it might expand search time to find optimal hyperparameters. However, if time series could be decomposed well by remainder and trend and seasonality which has lower variance, deep learning model may fit well to trend and seasonality without regularization, which would reduce MSE. Even though model does not predict remainder well, MSE of the model could be lower than deep learning model which takes original time series as input if variance of remainder is lower than original time series variance.

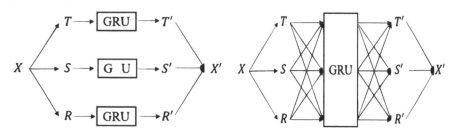

Fig. 2. Model construction comparison (left: proposed by Sebastian et al., right: our proposed model)

4   Numerical Experiment

4.1   Data Description

We evaluated our method on three datasets: daily temperature of Delhi, level of Ozone in Los Angeles and the number of journeys on the public bus in London. We varied the time series interval depending on the characteristics and length of the data. The value of each data is the average value within time interval. For Delhi temperature, we made weekly data, also we made montly data for Ozone data and London passengers, respectively. The adjusted data of time length is from 164 to 226 and standard deviation for each data is quite high. A detailed description is provided in Table 2. In addition, plots of our data are presented in Fig. 3 and they also show that these datasets have characteristics such as seasonality and varing trend.

Table 2. Summary on statistics for time series data

Dataset	Date	Time Interval	Time Length	Average	Standard Deviation
Delhi temperature	2013-01–2017-04	Weekly	226	25.246	7.203
LA ozone	1955-01–1972-12	Monthly	216	3.666	1.416
London passengers	2008-01–2020-08	Monthly	164	174.999	12.003

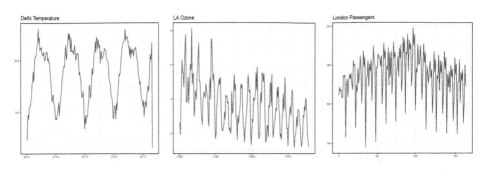

Fig. 3. Time-series diagrams of datasets

4.2   Experimental Design

The performance of our proposed model was compared with that of Seasonal-ARIMA, additive Holt-Winters, GRU model without decomposition and GRU model assuming independence between components. For all GRU models, we set same hyperparameters. Through using same hyperparameters, we could focus on analyzing the effect of combining decomposition and deep learning model while not assuming independence. Diagrams of three subseries after decomposition for each dataset is presented in Fig. 4. The performance of each model was measured by Root Mean Squared Error (RMSE) and Mean Absolute Percentage Error (MAPE). Each dataset is divided into a test set and a training set. We used the last one year of time series as the test set, and the rest of them are the training set. Each data has a different time interval, so the length of each test and training set is also different. For example, in case of weekly data, the lag of test data was set as $p = 52$. Due to the different learning processes of time series models and GRU models, we compared them as follows; In time-series model such as Seasonal-ARIMA and additive Holt-Winters, we predicted each test data by k-step forecasting formula. In Seasonal-ARIMA, we searched and selected hyperparameters according to lowest information criteria such as AIC, AICc, and BIC value. In additive Holt-Winters, we set period hyperparameter as one year. In GRU model, we set a hyperparameter k as double length of test data. For example, in case of weekly data, the lag of input data was set as $k = 104$.

4.3   Results

Our main findings can be summarized as follows. Table 3 and 4 presents error statistics of forecasting three datasets for each method. As we can see in Table 3, the proposed model predicted on three datasets with the lowest RMSE. Seasonal ARIMA model showed the worst performance among all methods. Holt-Winters forecast future data quite precisely comparing with Seasonal ARIMA. Especially, it highly outperformed Seasonal ARIMA for Delhi Temperature and London Passengers because those datasets are relatively more stable than LA ozone. On the other hand, traditional methods, both of Seasonal ARIMA and Holt-Winters poorly predicted for LA Ozone and we thought it is because the data has a lot of noise as we can see in Fig. 3. Deep learning models, however, outperformed traditional data for most cases. GRU assuming independence often showed lower accuracy than GRU without decomposition. For our proposed model, the performance of predicting for LA Ozone showed with 78% lower RMSE compared with Seasonal ARIMA. In addition, we could confirm our assumption that decomposition would decrease Mean Squared Error comparing the results of GRU without decomposition. Furthermore, we confirmed that our model outperformed the model assuming independence between components. Similar with this result, our proposed model outperformed in forecasting for all datasets except for London passengers with the lowest MAPE and the result is presented in Table 4. The forecasting results of each method for every dataset are showed in Fig. 5. Especially in some periods with high variance, our proposed model showed a quite precise prediction while other methods seemed to be inaccurate (Fig. 5).

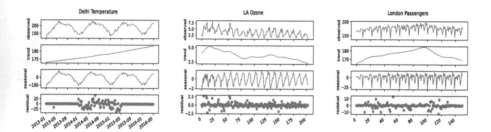

Fig. 4. Components after decomposition of each Dataset

Table 3. RMSE for each method (* denotes best performance method)

Dataset	Seasonal ARIMA	Holt-Winters	GRU	GRU (independent)	Proposed model
Delhi temperature	5.257	2.038	2.201	2.221	**1.892***
LA ozone	1.746	0.683	0.421	0.475	**0.38***
London passengers	8.948	3.141	5.143	3.506	**3.101***

Table 4. MAPE for each method (* denotes best performance method)

Dataset	Seasonal ARIMA	Holt-Winters	GRU	GRU (independent)	Proposed model
Delhi temperature	0.201	0.069	0.076	0.075	**0.062***
LA ozone	0.47	0.215	0.125	0.137	**0.106***
London passengers	0.043	**0.013***	0.025	0.018	0.015

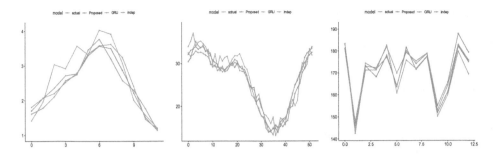

Fig. 5. Forecasting result of proposed method and GRU models (left: LA ozone, middle: Delhi temperature, right: London passengers)

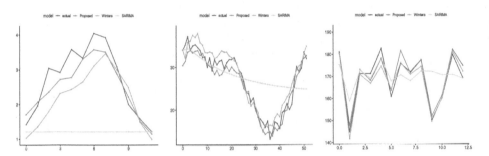

Fig. 6. Forecasting result of proposed method and traditional models (left: LA ozone, middle: Delhi temperature, right: London passengers)

5   Summary and Concluding Remarks

The purpose of this study is to propose time series forecasting model with lower MSE and without the loss of generalization. We used STL decomposition and GRU together. Existing studies on prediction of time series data using decomposition and deep learning model focused on specific data and assumed independence between trend, seasonality and remainder in order to reduce variance after decomposition. In contrast to other papers, our proposed model does not need to assume the independence while the forecasting error decreases. In addition, we confirmed that our method generally outperforms other methods through applying it to three time series data in various fields. This paper is significant because it demonstrated that using three components after decomposing as input data simultaneously for GRU model dramatically decreases MSE when forecasting data has fluctuating trend.

Several experiments can be considered as future research. We predicted the time series data with fixed time lags, but the time lag is very significant to forecasting which means a model is highly dependent on it, so a robust model for various time lags will be able to be studied as Zhang et al. proposed [15]. The multivariate time series data also could be analyzed with our proposed method.

The proposed method will be able to consider trend, seasonality and remainder of multiple time series that affected by each other [13] and we can find out casual relationship using proposed architecture.

References

1. Bandara, K., Bergmeir, C., Hewamalage, H.: LSTM-MSNet: leveraging forecasts on sets of related time series with multiple seasonal patterns. IEEE Trans. Neural Netw. Learn. Syst. **32**(4), 1586–1599 (2020)
2. Bengio, Y., Simard, P., Frasconi, P.: Learning long-term dependencies with gradient descent is difficult. IEEE Trans. Neural Netw. **5**(2), 157–166 (1994)
3. Cho, K., et al.: Learning phrase representations using RNN encoder-decoder for statistical machine translation. arXiv preprint arXiv:1406.1078 (2014)
4. Chung, J., et al.: Empirical evaluation of gated recurrent neural networks on sequence modeling. arXiv preprint arXiv:1412.3555 (2014)
5. Cleveland, R.B., et al.: STL: a seasonal-trend decomposition. J. Off. Stat. **6**(1), 3–73 (1990)
6. De Livera, A.M., Hyndman, R.J., Snyder, R.D.: Forecasting time series with complex seasonal patterns using exponential smoothing. J. Am. Stat. Assoc. **106**(496), 1513–1527 (2011)
7. Dokumentov, A., Hyndman, R.J.: STR: a seasonal-trend decomposition procedure based on regression. arXiv preprint arXiv:2009.05894 (2020)
8. Hochreiter, S., Schmidhuber, J.: Long short-term memory. Neural Comput. **9**(8), 1735–1780 (1997)
9. Huo, Y., et al.: Long-term span passengers prediction model based on STL decomposition and LSTM. In: 2019 20th Asia-Pacific Network Operations and Management Symposium (APNOMS), pp. 1–4. IEEE (2019)
10. Méndez-Jiménez, I., Cárdenas-Montes, M.: Time series decomposition for improving the forecasting performance of convolutional neural networks. In: Herrera, F., et al. (eds.) CAEPIA 2018. LNCS (LNAI), vol. 11160, pp. 87–97. Springer, Cham (2018). https://doi.org/10.1007/978-3-030-00374-6_9
11. Sebastian, K., Gao, H., Xing, X.: Utilizing an ensemble STL decomposition and GRU model for base station traffic forecasting. In: 2020 59th Annual Conference of the Society of Instrument and Control Engineers of Japan (SICE), pp. 314–319. IEEE (2020)
12. Shiskin, J.: The X-11 variant of the census method II seasonal adjustment program. No. 15. US Department of Commerce, Bureau of the Census (1967)
13. Peng, W.: DLI: a deep learning-based granger causality inference. Complexity **2020**, article ID 5960171, 6 p. (2020)
14. Yin, H., et al.: STL-ATTLSTM: vegetable price forecasting using STL and attention mechanism-based LSTM. Agriculture **10**(12), 612 (2020)
15. Zhang, X., Shen, F., Zhao, J., Yang, G.H.: Time series forecasting using GRU neural network with multi-lag after decomposition. In: Liu, D., Xie, S., Li, Y., Zhao, D., El-Alfy, E.-S.M. (eds.) ICONIP 2017. LNCS, vol. 10638, pp. 523–532. Springer, Cham (2017). https://doi.org/10.1007/978-3-319-70139-4_53

Robust Deep Reinforcement Learning for Extractive Legal Summarization

Duy-Hung Nguyen[1($\boxtimes$)], Bao-Sinh Nguyen[1], Nguyen Viet Dung Nghiem[1],
Dung Tien Le[1], Mim Amina Khatun[1], Minh-Tien Nguyen[1,3], and Hung Le[2]

[1] Cinnamon AI, 10th Floor, Geleximco Building, 36 Hoang Cau, Dong Da,
Hanoi, Vietnam
{hector,simon,henry93,nathan,amim,ryan.nguyen}@cinnamon.is
[2] Deakin University, Burwood, Australia
thai.le@deakin.edu.au
[3] Hung Yen University of Technology and Education, Hai Duong, Vietnam
tiennm@utehy.edu.vn

Abstract. Automatic summarization of legal texts is an important
and still a challenging task since legal documents are often long and
complicated with unusual structures and styles. Recent advances of deep
models trained end-to-end with differentiable losses can well-summarize
natural text, yet when applied to the legal domain, they show limited
results. In this paper, we propose to use reinforcement learning to train
current deep summarization models to improve their performance in
the legal domain. To this end, we adopt proximal policy optimization
methods and introduce novel reward functions that encourage the
generation of candidate summaries satisfying both lexical and semantic
criteria. We apply our method to training different summarization
backbones and observe a consistent and significant performance gain
across three public legal datasets.

Keywords: Legal document · Summarization · Reinforcement learning

1 Introduction

Legal documents are long and hard to understand. These documents, either in
the form court orders, contracts or terms of service, involve elaborative sentences,
formal grammars and dense texts with free-flowing legal jargon [1,2]. Reading
legal texts is thus challenging for both ordinary people and legal experts and
thus, there is an urgent need for automating legal text summarization.

For legal data analysis, classical summarization methods usually use
handcrafted features and simple statistics designed for specific types of case
judgments. CaseSummarizer [3], as an example, extract keywords using word
frequency enhanced with domain-specific words to find a candidate summary.

With the rise of deep learning and available public legal documents, there
have been various attempts to train automated end-to-end legal summarization

© Springer Nature Switzerland AG 2021
T. Mantoro et al. (Eds.): ICONIP 2021, CCIS 1517, pp. 597–604, 2021.
https://doi.org/10.1007/978-3-030-92310-5_69

systems [2]. One straightforward way is to adopt powerful domain-independent summarization models, which fall into two categories: abstraction and extraction. Extractive summarization allows the model to create a summary by selecting some sentences from the original document. One typical study in this field is BERTSUM [4] that obtains state-of-the-art results on news datasets. Whereas, an abstractive summarizer aims to interpret the main concepts of a document and create a summary in another format. The abstractive summarizers are usually trained by using the differentiable loss (i.e. cross-entropy) to maximize the likelihood of the ground-truth summaries, showing better results compared to classical methods on some legal datasets [5–7].

However, the performance of general summarization methods is still limited and does not satisfy the requirement of the law industry[2]. This is attributed to a well-known problem in text summarization [8]: the mismatch between the learning objective and the evaluation criterion, namely Recall-Oriented Understudy for Gisting Evaluation (ROUGE) [9]. To fix this problem, many works use reinforcement learning (RL), where they design complementary reward schemes that guide the learning, employing discrete functions like ROUGE as a part of reward [10, 11]. [10] introduced a novel salient reward that gives high weight to the important words in summary. In the same vein, [11] proposed distributional semantic reward to capture semantic relation between similar words.

In this paper, we propose to use keyword-level semantics for the reward function to generate summaries which contain critical legal terms and phrases in the document. Our method is illustrated as Fig. 1. We first train an extractive summarization backbone model using normal supervised training. Then, we finetune the backbone by using RL with a novel reward model that smoothly integrates lexical, sentence and keyword-level semantics into one reward function, unifying different perspectives constituting a good legal summary. Moreover, to ensure a stable finetuning process, we use proximal policy optimization (PPO) and enforce the exploring policy to be close to the supervised model by using Kullback-Leibler (KL) divergence as the additional intermediate rewards.

Our contributions are three-fold: (1) we pioneer employing reinforcement learning to train summarization models for the legal domain; (2) we construct a new training objective in the form of RL rewards to facilitate both semantics and lexical requirements; (3) we evaluate the proposed method in diverse legal document types. The proposed method gains significant improvement over other baselines across three public legal datasets.

2   Method

2.1   Supervised Summarization Backbone Model

Document Encoder. We follow BERTSUM [4] to encode input sentences of a document. To do that, a special [CLS] token (short for "classification") was inserted at the start position of every sentence. We also modify the interval segment embeddings by assigning embedding E_A or E_B for the i-th sentence, depending on its odd or even position. This way, both tokens' relations and inter-relations among sentences are learned simultaneously through different layers of the Transformer encoder. The encoder of BERT returns representations

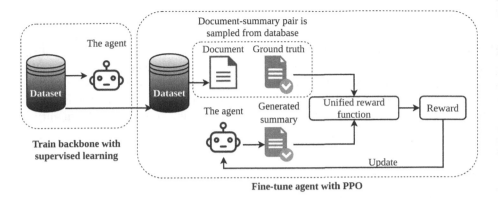

Fig. 1. Our summarization framework.

of each token, where the embedding of the i-th [CLS] token from the top layer of the encoder (denoted as h_i^L) is used as the sentence representation of s_i.

Sentence Selector. Given the sentence representation, neural networks are used to predict whether to select the sentence as part of the summary. We examine three architectures: linear, LSTM, and Transformer to create three different summarization backbones. A sigmoid function follows the output of each backbone to compute the score for each sentence as follows.

- a linear layer: $y_i = sigmoid(W_0 h_i^L + b_0)$
- an LSTM layer [12]: $y_i = sigmoid(W_0 \overrightarrow{\mathrm{LSTM}}(h_i^L) + b_0)$
- a Transformer encoder block with multi-head attention followed by two fully-connected feed-forward network (FFN) [13]. The attention is: $Attention(Q, K, V) = softmax\left(\frac{QK^T}{\sqrt{d_k}}\right) V$ where Q, K, V are matrices from the embeddings of all tokens in the i-th sentence.

2.2   Finetuning with Proximal Policy Optimization

PPO. After training the backbone model by using cross-entropy, we consider the trained backbone model as the initial policy. Then we employ PPO [14] as our RL algorithm to optimize the policy. PPO controls changes in the policy being updated at each iteration so that the policy does not move too far. We hypothesize that it can give benefit to our policy for extracting better summaries.

KL Reward. We follow [10,11] to define the reward scheme for RL. Let π^{SL} denotes the supervised trained backbone model and π^{RL} is the one that we optimize with RL. We calculate the reward at the time step i as:

$$r_i = -\beta_{KL} * \log\left[\frac{\pi^{\mathrm{RL}}(y_i|s_i, D, \theta)}{\pi^{\mathrm{SL}}(y_i|s_i, D, \theta)}\right] + 1(i = n) \times R_{\mathrm{unified}}(S) \qquad (1)$$

where β_{KL} is the KL coefficient, n is the final time step corresponding to the total number of sentences in the document D. For the intermediate time step i ($i < n$), the reward is the negative KL divergence between the output distribution of the backbone model and the current policy. It ensures to prevent the current policy from generating outputs which are too different from the outputs of the backbone model. For the final time step i ($i = n$), when the model obtains the complete summary S, a reward term $R_{unified}(S)$ that we design to measure the quality of the extracted summary as a whole.

2.3   The Unified Reward

As mentioned, the reward using ROUGE-scores only considers n-grams overlapping between an extracted summary and the ground-truth reference. It ignores the semantic aspect of word and sentence levels. We argue that the reward function should encode the semantics to guide the summarization model to output a good summary, that can reach the human level. To exploit the semantic aspect, we introduce a unified reward function in Eq. (2), which considers different vital aspects of a good summary.

$$R_{unified} = \alpha_1 R_{ROUGE} + \alpha_2 R_{kw} + \alpha_3 R_{seq} \tag{2}$$

where α_1, α_2, and α_3 are the control coefficients; R_{ROUGE} is the ROUGE-score function; R_{kw} considers the semantics of keywords; and R_{seq} captures the semantics of a sequence.

The R_{ROUGE} Function. The ROUGE metrics encode the word overlapping between an extracted summary and the gold reference. We use this function to directly force the backbone model to extract important sentences which tend to be similar to the gold reference [8].

Algorithm 1. Algorithm for Get_Keywords.

Require: A document: D and number of keywords n_k;
Ensure: Keyword set $\mathbb{K}$;
1: $\mathbb{S} \leftarrow$ Top $2 * n_k$ keywords from D ▷ *Select based on* $\|emb(phrase)\|$
2: $\mathbb{K} \leftarrow \{\mathbb{S}[1]\}$ ▷ *Take the first element of* $\mathbb{S}$
3: **while** $|\mathbb{K}| < n_k$ **do**
4:     $best\_kw \leftarrow \arg\min_{kw \in \mathbb{S} \setminus \mathbb{K}} (\max_{kw' \in \mathbb{K}} cosine(kw, kw'))$
        ▷ *Find the least similarity keyword to the current keyword set* $\mathbb{K}$
5:     $\mathbb{K} \leftarrow \mathbb{K} \cup \{best\_kw\}$
6: **end while**
7: Return $\mathbb{K}$;

The R_{kw} Function. Opposed to DSR [11], we select the list of keywords before comparing them. Keywords play a vital role in the legal text's meaning and amplify its effect on the reward function. In addition, several terms used in the legal domain can have the same meaning. Therefore, to reduce the redundancy and inaccuracy, we take a phrase that is the most different from the current set of keywords when choosing keywords. To produce R_{kw}, we first use BERT to embed phrases and utilize the cosine function to compute the similarity among embedded vectors. Then, the method shown in Algorithm 1 is used to produce two sets of keywords $\mathbb{K}_D, \mathbb{K}_S$ from the original document D and the summary S. For each keyword in $\mathbb{K}_D$, we find the most similar keywords in $\mathbb{K}_S$. Finally, the keyword reward is computed by the average of all similarities.

$$R_{kw} = \frac{\sum_{kw \in \mathbb{K}_D} \max_{kw' \in \mathbb{K}_S} consine(kw, kw')}{|\mathbb{K}_D|} \tag{3}$$

The R_{seq} Function. Since R_{kw} only encourages similar keywords appearing in the summary. It does not guarantee the coherence of the whole summary. Thus, we define R_{seq} to enforce the semantic similarity between the final summary S and the gold reference $S*$. Initially, Moverscore [15] is used to measure the translating distance between the two texts $d(S, S*)$. Concretely, the reward is defined as $R_{seq} = \frac{1}{d(S,S*)+\epsilon}$ where $\epsilon = 10^{-2}$.

3 Experimental Setup

3.1 Datasets

We used three legal datasets for evaluation as follows.

Plain English Summarization of Contracts (PESC) is a legal dataset written in plain English, in which a text snippet is paired with an abstractive summary [7]. Each legal snippet contains approximately 595 characters. The length of a summary is around 202 characters.

BillSum consists of 22,218 US Congressional bills with human-written reference summaries collected from United States Government Publishing Office [6]. The data was split into 18,949 training bills and 3,269 testing bills. Each document contains around 46 sentences and each summary includes around 6 sentences.

Legal Case Reports Dataset (LCR) contains 3,890 Australian legal cases from the Federal Court of Australia [5]. Each case contains around 221 sentences and 8.3 catchphrases which is considered as a summary. We divided the data into three sets: training (2,590), validation (800), and testing (500 samples).

3.2 Settings and Evaluation Metrics

The summarization model is based on BERT-base with 12 Transformer blocks, the hidden size of h_i^L from BERT is 768. We used one layer for the backbone of LSTM and two linear layers for the backbone of transformers with the output vector of 768. All models were trained with a batch size of 256 on a single Tesla T4 GPU. In our experiment, we set $\alpha_1 = 0.3$, $\alpha_2 = 0.4$, and $\alpha_3 = 0.3$ for $R_{unified}$ by using random search tuning on the validation set. We set $\beta_{KL} = 0.05$ for the KL coefficient. At the testing time, the number of selected sentences was set as 3 for PESC, 6 for BillSum, and 8 for LCR datasets. We used ROUGE-scores[1] to measure the quality of summaries. We report the F-score of ROUGE-1, ROUGE-2, and ROUGE-L as the main metrics.

---

[1] The parameter: -c 95 -m -r 1000 -n 2.

4   Experimental Results

4.1   Legal Cases: Working with Different Summarization Backbones

In Table 1, we report quantitative improvement over the backbone baselines on two formal and complicated legal datasets: BillSum and LCR. Here, The **backbone** is the BERTSum model with three different sentence selectors: Linear, LSTM, and Transformer. In addition, we also compare the backbone to other classical legal summarization baselines: CaseSummarizer [3] and Restricted Boltzmann Machine (RBM) [16].

Table 1. Evaluation scores for all backbones. Column R-* represents ROUGE.

Model	BillSum			LCR		
	R-1	R-2	R-L	R-1	R-2	R-L
CaseSummarizer [3]	27.32	15.65	25.98	1.49	0.59	1.31
RBM [16]	27.86	13.58	25.18	1.66	0.83	1.44
The backbone						
Linear	31.87	11.46	28.77	21.79	5.96	20.42
LSTM	33.56	12.67	30.42	22.76	6.34	21.29
Transformer	32.58	11.68	29.44	23.09	6.59	21.59
RL with $R_{unified}$						
Linear+$R_{unified}$	33.31	12.62	30.30	21.81	6.00	20.43
LSTM+$R_{unified}$	**33.57**	12.68	**30.42**	22.8	6.33	21.31
Transformer+$R_{unified}$	33.33	**12.70**	30.21	**23.21**	**6.92**	**21.72**

Notably, our backbones significantly outperform traditional legal summarizers. In this case, classical methods use handcrafted features and only work for certain types of legal documents, thus showing poor results on the datasets. We observe that after training with our reward function, the backbones' performance improves by a substantial amount. The improvements indicate that the proposed method can effectively improve all types of the pretrained-supervised model. The new reward function in Eq. (2) forces the summarization model to select salient sentences which are good in terms of lexical and semantic aspects on the word and sentence levels. Overall, the Transformer backbone gives the best results. The possible reason is that this backbone uses a more complicated architecture than Linear and LSTM. Due to the high accuracy, we use the Transformer as the main backbone in other experiments.

4.2   Terms of Service: State-of-the-Art Results on PESC

In this section, we compare our method to strong baselines from the literature on the PESC dataset. **Lead-m** extracts m first sentences of a document to form a summary [7]. **ROUGE** [9] uses the ROUGE-L as the final reward to optimize the policy [10,11]. **DSR** [11] is a strong reward method that boost the performance of backbone [11]. **BLANC** [17] is also a metric to estimate the quality of summaries of documents. This metric will be used to provide a reward signal when optimizing the policy. **REFRESH** [8] uses an encoder-decoder to select top-ranked sentences as a summary. The model was updated using REINFORCE algorithm.

Table 2. Best results on PESC dataset. Column R-* represents ROUGE

Model	R-1	R-2	R-L
Lead-m [7]	24.38	7.52	17.63
REFRESH [8]	23.47	8.23	20.83
Backbone	24.67	8.91	20.76
ROUGE [9]	25.52	9.50	21.50
DSR [11]	25.53	9.35	21.76
BLANC [17]	25.56	9.51	21.96
$R_{unified}$	**25.70**	**9.53**	**22.30**

Table 3. Effect of ablating components of our model on PESC dataset. Column R-* represents ROUGE

Model	R-1	R-2	R-L
Ours w/o KL	24.83	8.95	21.36
Ours w/o PPO	24.79	9.13	21.17
Ours w/o R_{kw}	25.65	9.52	21.92
Ours w/o R_{seq}	25.61	9.48	21.85
Ours full	**25.70**	**9.53**	**22.3**

Table 2 describes the best results on the PESC dataset. We note that for reward-based methods, all models in this experiment are in the same configuration except for the final reward. It is noticeable that all these models improve the supervised backbone (Transformer). Our model with $R_{unified}$ achieves SOTA result on the dataset. There is also a large performance gap between our method and baselines: REFRESH and Lead-m. Our method achieves 2.23%, 1.3%, and 1.45% higher than REFRESH on ROUGE-1, ROUGE-2, and ROUGE-L respectively. In comparison with Lead-m, which is the best model reported in [7], our approach performs nearly 5 ROUGE-L points higher.

4.3   Ablation Studies

We conduct more evaluations to assess the impact of KL reward and PPO on the proposed method. We also validate components of our $R_{unified}$ including R_{kw} and R_{seq}. Table 3 shows that the proposed approach obtains significant benefits from KL rewards. Without the KL rewards, ROUGE-scores drop approximately 1%. We also observe similar drops in performance when we replace PPO with the classical REINFORCE, which stresses the importance of using proximal policy optimization. Training without R_{seq} and R_{kw} also reduces the performance of the baselines. Since the ROUGE-score is our objective, combining the R_{ROUGE} with our R_{seq} and R_{kw} will provide a sufficient training signal to the backbone. As our expectation, the $R_{unified}$ model performs the best.

5   Conclusion

In this paper, we have presented a new method for summarizing various types of legal documents.

Our approach for training the summarization model with a novel reward scheme has reached a ROUGE-score of 25.70% for the PESC dataset, achieving the SOTA result. To further validate our approach, we extensively experiment on different datasets with different configurations. Experimental results show that the method is consistently better than the strong baselines on additional BillSum and Legal Case Reports datasets.

Future work will expand our research to tasks such as case entailment: using reinforcement learning with novel reward designs to find precedents from the law database given a query case to achieve expert-level results.

References

1. Bhattacharya, P., et al.: A comparative study of summarization algorithms applied to legal case judgments. In: European Conference on Information Retrieval, pp. 413–428 (2019)
2. Jain, D., Borah, M.D., Biswas, A.: Summarization of legal documents: where are we now and the way forward. Comput. Sci. Rev. **40**, 100388 (2021)
3. Polsley, S., Jhunjhunwala, P., Huang, R.: Casesummarizer: a system for automated summarization of legal texts. In: Proceedings of COLING 2016, The 26th International Conference on Computational Linguistics: System Demonstrations, pp. 258–262 (2016)
4. Liu, Y.: Fine-tune BERT for extractive summarization. arXiv preprint arXiv:1903.10318 (2019)
5. Galgani, F., Compton, P., Hoffmann, A.: Combining different summarization techniques for legal text. In: Proceedings of the Workshop on Innovative Hybrid Approaches to the Processing of Textual Data, pp. 115–123 (2012)
6. Kornilova, A., Eidelman, V.: BillSum: a corpus for automatic summarization of US legislation. arXiv preprint arXiv:1910.00523 (2019)
7. Manor, L., Li, J.J.: Plain English summarization of contracts. arXiv preprint arXiv:1906.00424 (2019)
8. Narayan, S., Cohen, S.B., Lapata, M.: Ranking sentences for extractive summarization with reinforcement learning. arXiv preprint arXiv:1802.08636 (2018)
9. Lin, C.-Y.: ROUGE: a package for automatic evaluation of summaries. In: Text Summarization Branches Out, pp. 74–81 (2004)
10. Pasunuru, R., Bansal, M.: Multi-reward reinforced summarization with saliency and entailment. arXiv preprint arXiv:1804.06451 (2018)
11. Li, S., Lei, D., Qin, P., Wang, W.Y.: Deep reinforcement learning with distributional semantic rewards for abstractive summarization. arXiv preprint arXiv:1909.00141 (2019)
12. Hochreiter, S., Schmidhuber, J.: Long short-term memory. Neural Comput. **9**, 1735–1780 (1997)
13. Vaswani, A., et al.: Attention is all you need. In: Proceedings of the 31st Conference on Neural Information Processing Systems, pp. 6000–6010 (2017)
14. Schulman, J., Wolski, F., Dhariwal, P., Radford, A., Klimov, O.: Proximal policy optimization algorithms. arXiv preprint arXiv:1707.06347 (2017)
15. Kusner, M., Sun, Y., Kolkin, N., Weinberger, K.: From word embeddings to document distances. In: International Conference on Machine Learning, pp. 957–966 (2015)
16. Verma, S., Nidhi, V.: Extractive summarization using deep learning. Res. Comput. Sci. **147**, 107–117 (2018)
17. Vasilyev, O., Dharnidharka, V., Bohannon, J.: Fill in the BLANC: human-free quality estimation of document summaries. arXiv preprint arXiv:2002.09836 (2020)

Video Summarization
by DiffPointer-GAN

Fangyuan Ke, Pengcheng Li, and Wenlian Lu[(✉)]

Fudan University, Shanghai 200082, China
{20110180036,wenlian}@fudan.edu.cn

Abstract. Recent years have witnessed the explosive growth of video and clips with the popularization of mobile devices that are deeply shaping people's life. Video summarization is an important approach to highlight and label the videos. Since the requirement of video summarization in practice is diverse due to the consumer majority and videos themselves, it is difficult for a neural network that extracts specific features to be adapted according to the changing requirements. In this paper, we propose a novel method of video summarization that employs the characteristics of the bullet-screen comments as a reference and train a novel neural network to generate a short clip as the video summary. First, we propose a method to select candidate clips for video summarization based on the distribution of the bullet-screen comments and these candidates are annotated manually to construct our labelled dataset from the Bilibili video library. Second, we propose and train a novel network combined with the pointer network and the General Adversarial Networks, named by diffPointer-GAN, to directly identify the start and end of the summary clip, other than the previous process composed of scoring, segmentation and selecting. Finally, we demonstrate that the proposed method has a definite priority to two baseline methods that are implemented on our dataset.

Keywords: Dynamic video summarization · Dataset of video summarization · Pointer Network · Generative Adversarial Network

1 Introduction

Video summarization is to select some clips in the video to form a new relatively short video file, which has been widely studied in many research institutions and companies [6,7], with many applications, including improving the efficiency in the security field, making the highlight collection in sports field, displaying to draw audiences in the commercial field. In this field static video summarization is a basic problem, which is solved by using the sampling methods [2,12], the clustering algorithms [5,17], the MSR algorithm [10], the methods of machine learning [9,16] or other feasible methods [1,8].

At present, dynamic video summarization has arisen from the static video summarization [16]: First building a model to give each frame an importance score, then using some shot segmentation algorithms to divide the video frames

© Springer Nature Switzerland AG 2021
T. Mantoro et al. (Eds.): ICONIP 2021, CCIS 1517, pp. 605–614, 2021.
https://doi.org/10.1007/978-3-030-92310-5_70

into disjoint segments, finally using knapsack algorithm to decide the final segments. To have a unified measurement result, some standard datasets have emerged, such as SumMe [4], TVSun [13], Youtube [3].

On the one hand, the content of current video summary data set is not rich enough, the average time length is short, and its label principle based on restoration does not match the purpose of display and sharing. On the other hand, the current algorithm usually are affected in the process of finding keyframes due to the existence of the middle layer. To solve these problems, first we construct a richer dataset composed of 1200 labelled videos with the help of the bullet-screens in videos. Then we propose an algorithm of getting a dynamic video summary to avoid the disadvantages of the traditional process. We use the idea of Pointer Network [11] and the structure of the Generative Adversarial Network (GAN) [9] to build the diffPointer-GAN Network model. In this way, not only our result is never affected by frame scores and shot segmentation operation, but also the problem of unbalanced length of video summary in training and testing is overcome. Finally, we apply the model to the dataset, analyze the results of training and testing, and compare it with the results of other models. At the same time, we also discuss some problems of the baseline models.

2   Dateset

In the present paper, we propose a video dataset based on the Bilibili video website. First some candidate video summaries are decided with the help of the bullet-screens, which can reflect the wonderful degree of videos. Then we select some senior users of the Bilibili video website to vote for the best one from those candidate video summaries. Finally, we construct the dataset composed of 1200 labelled videos with their bullet-screens, including six categories: dance, vlog, film, food, daily life and TV play. The original video length is between 20 s and 20 min and the summary one is between 3 and 6 s.

Specifically, we first obtain the bullet-screen comments density data, choose all the peak time points, and then add some randomness to choose the candidate summaries as follows:

1. Take time as a variable and the bullet-screen density as its probability distribution, a segment V_1 is selected as the first segment according to the probability distribution;
2. Before the selected V_1 time, keep the density unchanged, after the time double the density. Then the new density is regarded as the new distribution, and randomly take out the second segment V_2 as before. If V_2 is less than V_1, then delete V_2; The selection of V_1 and V_2 is shown in Fig. 1(a)–1(c).
3. Before and after the max (V_1, V_2) time, change the density as we have done in (b), and randomly take out the third segment V_3. If V_3 is less than V_1 or V_2, delete V_3;
4. Repeat the process of (b) and (c) until 6 segments V_1, V_2, V_3, V_4, V_5 and V_6 are taken.

5. By splicing V_1, V_2, V_3, V_4, V_5 and V_6, a GIF is obtained;
6. Repeat (a)–(e) and randomly select for 20 times to get 20 candidate GIFs;

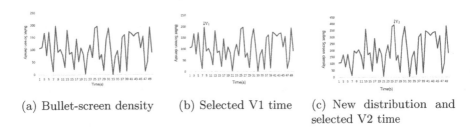

(a) Bullet-screen density   (b) Selected V1 time   (c) New distribution and selected V2 time

Fig. 1. Bullet-screen density distribution

3   Method

We combine the structures of Pointer network [11] and GAN [9] to build the diffPointer-GAN Network model (diffPotinter), in which we neither give importance score to each frame nor carry out the shot segmentation. Instead the starting point and ending point of the summary are learned directly to reduce the impact of the intermediate steps on the results.

3.1   Network Diagram and Workflow

Our model, diffPointer-GAN, as shown in Fig. 2(a)–2(c) consists of a generator and a discriminator. We use the Pointer Network [11] as the generator, taking frame difference into considerations. It consists of an encoder receiving the video features and the frame difference and a decoder generating the start and endpoints of the summary. Meanwhile, we use the 3D convolution network as the discriminator to judge whether the input segment is the real summary or the generated summary.

(a) Generator   (b) Discriminator   (c) DiffPointer

Fig. 2. Structure of the model.

Set the frames of the video as T, and the input video frame vector is $v = \{v_t : t = 1, ..., T\}$. To unify the visual features of the frames, we use the output of the pool-5 layer in pretrained GoogleNet [14] as the features of the image (The output dimension is 1024). Denote the features of the frames as $X = \{x_t : t = 1, ..., T\}$. The frame k-difference is denoted as $D^k = \{d_t^k : t = 1, ..., T - k\}$, where $d_t^k = |x_{t+k} - x_t|$. We introduce the features and k-difference into the encoder respectively. The features are encoded by a bidirectional LSTM structure network. For x_t, the forward hidden state h_t^f and the backward hidden state h_t^b are calculated by the LSTM neural units. Then, we obtain the forward hidden state $H^f = \{h_t^f : t = 1, ..., T\}$ and the backward hidden state $H^b = \{h_t^b : t = 1, ..., T\}$.

For frame difference, we use 1-difference, 2-difference and 3-difference, and pass them into FC layer respectively as $D'^1 = FC(D^1), D'^2 = FC(D^2), D'^3 = FC(D^3)$. Then they are spliced as a representative of frame difference as $D = [D'^1, D'^2, D'^3]$. We utilize the unidirectional LSTM as the decoder. Since a summary contains at least one segment, which means at least two points, thus the decoder needs to be a sequence structure of at least 2. Assuming the length of a decoder is M. At decoding time $i = 1$, the LSTM accepts the last hidden layer of the encoder $h_T = [h_T^f, h_T^b]$ as input, and generates the hidden state s_1. The softmax function represents the probability distribution in the original sequence of length T. The position with the largest probability value is the position selected for this decoding.

$$s_1 = LSTM(h_T)$$
$$e_j^1 = v^T \tanh(W_1(h_j^f, h_j^b) + W_2 \cdot D + W_3 \cdot s_1), j \in \{1, 2, ..., T\}$$
$$a^1 = softmax(e^1) = P(o_1|H^f, H^b), \quad \hat{y}_1 = argmax(a^1)$$

Here, $\hat{y}_1$ is an integer, which represents the starting point of the first segment learned from the model. y_1 is its label, which represents the starting point of the real first segment. Then, the hidden state s_{i-1} generated by the last LSTM unit is successively operated as follows:

$$s_i = LSTM(x_{y_{i-1}}, s_{i-1}) \quad i \in \{1, 2, ..., M\}$$
$$e_j^i = f_G(h_j^f, h_j^b, D, s_i)$$
$$= v^T \tanh(W_1(h_j^f, h_j^b) + W_2 \cdot D + W_3 \cdot s_i), \quad i, j \in \{1, 2, ..., T\}$$
$$a^i = softmax(e^i) = P(o_i|H^f, H^b, o_1, ..., o_{i-1}) \quad i \in \{1, 2, ..., M\}$$
$$\hat{y}_i = argmax(a^i), \quad i \in \{1, 2, ..., M\}$$

To prevent the accumulated errors from the prediction inaccuracy of the LSTM in training, the input frame feature of decoding time i is from the real label, i.e. $x_{y_{i-1}}$. While in predicting, the input frame feature is from the output position of last time, i.e. $x_{\hat{y}_{i-1}}$. Through the above process, we can get a sequence pointing to the positions of the original video in the decoding stage and select the summary segment according to the form of starting and ending points.

To make the output positions close to the positions indicated by the label in each decoding process, we use the distance between $\hat{y}_i$ and y_i as the loss function at the generator stage as $L_1 = \frac{1}{M}\sum_{i=1}^{M}(y_i - \hat{y}_i)^2$. We use a 3D convolution network as our discriminator, which is actually a 0–1 binary classifier to determine whether the input segment is the real summary. And the loss function of our discriminator is defined as:

$$L_2 = -correct = -\mathbb{E}_{x \sim gt}[\log(D(x))] - \mathbb{E}_{\hat{x} \sim generator}[\log(1 - D(\hat{x}))]$$

3.2   Training Method

Considering the influence of the discriminator output on the generator, we use the Policy Gradient [15] to train the parameters. Let θ and ϕ represent the parameter space in the generator and the discriminator. Given input X and generator G_θ, we can output $\hat{Y}_{1:T} = (\hat{y}_1, ..., \hat{y}_t, ...\hat{y}_T)$. Then $D_\phi(\hat{Y}_{1:T})$ represents the probability of which $\hat{Y}_{1:T}$ is the real summary. Our generator G_θ is updated with the MC search and a gradient based on the expected return from the discriminant model D_ϕ. Expected return is defined as $reward = \mathbb{E}_{P(o_{1:M})}[R|\theta]$, where, R is the output of the discriminator. Define: $P(o_{1:M}) = \prod_i P(o_i|o_{1:i-1})$, where $P(o_i|o_{1:i-1})$ represents the position probability distribution of the i-th decoding. We use Monte Carlo algorithm (MC) to estimate the gradient. If we sample for N times, then:

$$\nabla\mathbb{E}[R|P(o_{1:M}),\theta] = \sum_{i=1}^{M}\mathbb{E}_{P(o_{1:M})}[\nabla\log P(o_i|o_{1:i-1},\theta)R]$$

$$\approx \frac{1}{N}\sum_{n=1}^{N}\sum_{i=1}^{M}[\nabla\log P(o_i^n|o_{1:i-1}^n,\theta)R^n]$$

Therefore, we have the following objective functions respectively when learning network parameters: *generator*: $L_1 - reward$ and *discriminator*: L_2. In conclusion, we use the following algorithm to summarize the steps in the training:

4   Numerical Examples

4.1   Experiment Setup

As mentioned, we construct a new dataset of 6 categories. Then we use this dataset to train and test our model and the vsLSTM and the SUM-GAN baseline models in [9,16]. Total dataset are divided into training set, testing set and validation set according to the ratio of 2:1:1. In addition, we use the F-score to measure the results, which is the harmonic mean of the precision and recall.

In the model, we downsample the video at the rate of one frame per second (1 PFS), input them to a pre-trained GoogleNet [14] and extract the pool-5

Algorithm 1. Train the diffPointer-GAN model

Input: Training video v
Output: learning parameters$\{\theta, \phi\}$
1: Initialize all parameters$\{\theta, \phi\}$
2: **while** Iterations less than the max **do**
3:     $X \leftarrow$ feature sequence obtained from v after GoogleNet pool-5
4:     $D^k \leftarrow$ Frame difference of X
5:     $D'^k = \text{FC}(D^k)$
6:     $H^f, H^b, h_T = \text{BiLSTM}(X)$
7:     **if** less than the maximum decoding length M **then**
8:         $s_i = LSTM(x_{y_{i-1}}, s_{i-1}), i \leq M$(obtain hidden state)
9:         $e_j^i = f_G(h_j^f, h_j^b, D, s_i)$(obtain corresponding pointer)
10:        $\hat{y}_i = argmax(softmax(e^i))$(obtain selected positions)
11:    $D(\hat{x}) \leftarrow$ The segment learned in step 10
12:    Use gradient descent method and strategy gradient descent method to update parameters:

$$\{\theta\} \xleftarrow{+} -\nabla(L_1 - reward)$$

$$\{\phi\} \xleftarrow{+} -\nabla L_2$$

return

---

output as the feature representation. By zero-padding, we can fix the number of memory units denoted as N.

We use Python 3.6 with Tensorflow 1.8.0 and Pytorch 1.1.0 for this experiment, via four GPU graphics cards. And the values of M and N are set as 12 and 8 separately after a pre-experiment.

4.2 Results

For comparison, we consider the loss of generator and discriminator separately. The loss function has been defined before. Here, we train a generator and a discriminator at the same time for a total of 600 epochs. Their change trend is shown in Fig. 3(a)–3(b):

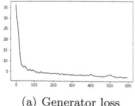
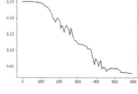
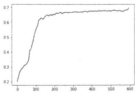

(a) Generator loss   (b) Discriminator loss   (c) Accuracy to the test set

Fig. 3. Performance of the model.

It can be seen that in the training stage, the loss function is continuously decreasing and finally fluctuating near a value. For the generator, the loss in the first 100 epochs drops faster and then tends to be stable. However the loss of the discriminator in the first 100–400 epochs drops faster and tends to be stable after 550 epochs.

Then we consider the change of accuracy on the test set. First, we consider 6 categories together to test and see the recognition ability of the model on the overall test set; then we test each category separately and list the final accuracy in Table 2.

Table 1. The final accuracy on test set of diffPointer-GAN for each category

Category	1	2	3	4	5	6
Accuracy (%)	73.18	71.52	67.49	70.85	69.13	66.87

We can see that the overall accuracy is steadily increasing and tends to be stable near 0.7. And for a specific category, the model performs well in category 1, 2 and 4, which are dance, food and film categories, all of which have certain rules on the change of frames. Introducing frame difference in the generator, our model is naturally more sensitive to the obvious changes between frames and thus more accurate on videos with such characteristic.

In addition, although our network belongs to supervised learning, we can apply the model to a video without a label to generate its summary directly, to achieve the video display requirements even if the video has not got many bullet-screen comments.

4.3 Model Comparison

We compare the results of diffPointer-GAN model and two baseline models and get their F-scores of each categories on the dataset and time required for 600 epochs of training. From Table 2 and Table 3, we can see that our model has

Table 2. F-scores of different models

Model	vsLSTM	SUM-GAN	diffPointer-GAN
Category 1	54.2	71.9	73.4
Category 2	54.7	70.7	71.6
Category 3	53.7	68.2	67.5
Category 4	55.1	69.7	69.9
Category 5	53.6	68.8	69.1
Category 6	52.3	68.1	67.2

Table 3. Time consumed for training

Model	Time(h)
vsLSTM	4.5
SUM-GAN	50
diffPointer-GAN	25

achieved better results than SUM-GAN in categories 1, 2, 4 and 5, and better results than vsLSTM in all categories. Because of the simple structure, the training time of vsLSTM is relatively shorter. In contrast, the training time of SUM-GAN with a complex structure is significantly longer than that of our model. Our diffPointer-GAN network synthesizes the recognition ability and training time and achieves relatively better recognition ability when the training time is not very long, Which means our model is more in line with the needs of application.

As shown in the following Figs. 4(a) and 4(b), which is frame scores given by vsLSTM and SUM-GAN. When the score is relatively flat, the result of the summary will depend heavily on the segmentation algorithm. However, our model can learn the starting point and the ending point of the summary directly without assigning importance score and segmentation, thus reducing the impact of the intermediate steps.

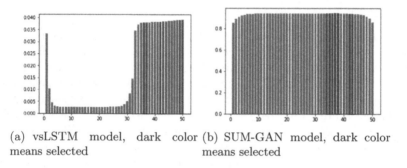

(a) vsLSTM model, dark color means selected   (b) SUM-GAN model, dark color means selected

Fig. 4. Frame scores

5   Conclusions

In conclusion, we establish a new private dataset composed of 1200 labelled videos of six categories and propose the diffPointer-GAN, a new model of dynamic video summarization, which takes advantage of GAN and 3D convolution network, using pointer network to directly learn the starting and ending points of the summary. On the private dataset, the numerical examples show that our model is superior to the baseline model when the accuracy and training time are both taken into considerations and thus has more practical application value. We also discuss the feature of the frame importance scores in the baseline models, which further shows the effectiveness of our model. Of course, there are still many works left to optimize our model, including how to improve the accuracy of the segmentation algorithm, how to remove the occasional high repetition phenomenon of pointer network, and how to add more video features beyond the image vision.

References

1. Aradhye, H., Toderici, G., Yagnik, J.: Video2text: learning to annotate video content. In: 2009 IEEE International Conference on Data Mining Workshops, pp. 144–151. IEEE (2009)
2. Calic, J., Thomas, B.: Spatial analysis in key-frame extraction using video segmentation. In: Workshop on Image Analysis for Multimedia Interactive Services (2004)
3. De Avila, S.E.F., Lopes, A.P.B., da Luz, A., Jr., de Albuquerque Araújo, A.: Vsumm a mechanism designed to produce static video summaries and a novel evaluation method. Pattern Recogn. Lett. **32**(1), 56–68 (2011)
4. Gygli, M., Grabner, H., Riemenschneider, H., Van Gool, L.: Creating summaries from user videos. In: Fleet, D., Pajdla, T., Schiele, B., Tuytelaars, T. (eds.) ECCV 2014. LNCS, vol. 8695, pp. 505–520. Springer, Cham (2014). https://doi.org/10. 1007/978-3-319-10584-0_33
5. Gygli, M., Grabner, H., Van Gool, L.: Video summarization by learning submodular mixtures of objectives. In: Proceedings of the IEEE Conference on Computer Vision and Pattern Recognition, pp. 3090–3098 (2015)
6. Kawashima, T., Tateyama, K., Iijima, T., Aoki, Y.: Indexing of baseball telecast for content-based video retrieval. In: Proceedings 1998 International Conference on Image Processing. ICIP98 (Cat. No. 98CB36269), vol. 1, pp. 871–874. IEEE (1998)
7. Kuramoto, M., Masaki, T., Kitamura, Y., Kishino, F.: Video database retrieval based on gestures and its application. IEEE Trans. Multimedia **4**(4), 500–508 (2002)
8. Li, G., Ma, S., Han, Y.: Summarization-based video caption via deep neural networks. In: Proceedings of the 23rd ACM International Conference on Multimedia, pp. 1191–1194 (2015)
9. Mahasseni, B., Lam, M., Todorovic, S.: Unsupervised video summarization with adversarial LSTM networks. In: Proceedings of the IEEE Conference on Computer Vision and Pattern Recognition, pp. 202–211 (2017)
10. Mei, S., Guan, G., Wang, Z., Wan, S., He, M., Feng, D.D.: Video summarization via minimum sparse reconstruction. Pattern Recogn. **48**(2), 522–533 (2015)
11. See, A., Liu, P.J., Manning, C.D.: Get to the point: summarization with pointer-generator networks. arXiv preprint arXiv:1704.04368 (2017)
12. Song, W., Yongguo, H., Yadong, W., Zhang, S.: Video key frame extraction method based on image dominant color (in Chinese). Comput. Appl. **33**(09), 2631–2635 (2013)
13. Song, Y., Vallmitjana, J., Stent, A., Jaimes, A.: Tvsum: summarizing web videos using titles. In: Proceedings of the IEEE Conference on Computer Vision and Pattern Recognition, pp. 5179–5187 (2015)
14. Szegedy, C., et al.: Going deeper with convolutions. In: Proceedings of the IEEE Conference on Computer Vision and Pattern Recognition, pp. 1–9 (2015)
15. Yu, L., Zhang, W., Wang, J., SeqGAN, Y.Y.: Sequence generative adversarial nets with policy gradient. arxiv e-prints, arXiv preprint arXiv:1609.05473 (2016)

16. Zhang, K., Chao, W.-L., Sha, F., Grauman, K.: Video summarization with long short-term memory. In: Leibe, B., Matas, J., Sebe, N., Welling, M. (eds.) ECCV 2016. LNCS, vol. 9911, pp. 766–782. Springer, Cham (2016). https://doi.org/10.1007/978-3-319-46478-7_47
17. Zhuang, Y., Rui, Y., Huang, T.S., Mehrotra, S.: Adaptive key frame extraction using unsupervised clustering. In: Proceedings 1998 International Conference on Image Processing. ICIP98 (Cat. No. 98cb36269), vol. 1, pp. 866–870. IEEE (1998)

A No-Reference Perception Based Metric for Detection of Packet Loss Induced Artifacts in Videos

Shreyan Sanyal[ID] and Sarbani Palit[✉][ID]

Indian Statistical Institute, 203, B.T. Road, Kolkata 700108, India
sarbanip@isical.ac.in
http://www.isical.ac.in

Abstract. Objective quality measures are usually concerned with overall degradation in quality, disregarding impairments and artifacts such as those due to packet loss error concealment. Unfortunately, it is particularly hard to model due to its unpredictable nature and content-dependency. We propose a human perception based no-reference framework utilizing motion-compensated frame interpolation and colour gradients to identify and localize packet loss impaired regions in video frames. The unique and principal contribution of this work is the attempt to mimic the human visual system throughout the process instead of the traditional approach of trying to replicate the mean opinion score.

Keywords: Packet loss · Error concealment · Perception based metric

1 Introduction

The world today cannot be imagined without video sequences transmitted over communication networks, as seen in popular services such as Youtube, Netflix and Twitch. Transmission often involves dropping of packets of information and when the video is decoded, it affects the users quality of experience (QoE). These channel artefacts are usually detected and corrected in the transport layer or the video syntax layer itself [1]. Other methods include error resilient encoding and error concealment [2,3]. However, each of these algorithms have their own disadvantages and traces of impairment remain in the video.

In this paper, we deal with error concealment, which essentially means that the macroblock areas whose information was in the dropped packets are 'concealed'. Error concealment can be temporal, where the affected area is filled in by information from the previous frame or spatial, where pixels from neighbouring regions are used for interpolation. Packet loss artifacts are particularly hard to model since, (1) It is extremely unpredictable, not having have any kind of temporal linearity, (2) Its visibility is dependent on a multitude of factors, and

---

Supported by Indian Statistical Institute.

T. Mantoro et al. (Eds.): ICONIP 2021, CCIS 1517, pp. 615–623, 2021.
https://doi.org/10.1007/978-3-030-92310-5_71

concealment methods often give decent results, thereby not affecting the QoE and (3) The human visual system (HVS) is too complex to model accurately.

Objective quality measures are designed to quantify image and video distortions, but rarely incorporate network impairments into their model. Popular methods such as peak signal-to-noise ratio (PSNR) and mean squared error (MSE) are fairly simple but they have been seen to not correlate well with QoE. More complex models such as video BLIINDS [4] return decent results but still are generic and not specifically modelled to include distortions due to packet loss (PL). Currently, PL is tackled by two main classes of algorithms: bit-stream based [5] and pixel-based, employing a variety of techniques such as natural scene statistics [6], slice-boundary mismatch [7], block-based correlation [8] etc.

Manasa K. et al. [9] propose a spatio-temporal approach where the spatial and temporal distortions are quantified separately and then combined using a specific pooling method. However, the assumptions made regarding optical flow are not very realistic, leaving much to be desired. The approach of Shabtay et al. [1] has a sequential method for labelling spatially concealed macroblocks which are PL affected as 'suspicious' using variance and average vertical gradient. Assumptions including zero-motion vector temporal concealment, row-based impairment etc. adversely affect performance. Much work has been done focusing on blockiness artefact detection metrics, which have been extended to work on packet loss [8,10]. Though efficient, they are not sophisticated enough to deal with the different kinds of packet loss that occur [11]. The main drawbacks include the assumption that video content is rarely aligned horizontally with the macroblock row boundary as well as the fact that packet loss occurs horizontally.

This article proposes a no-reference approach for packet loss error concealment estimation based on human perception. This method requires only the decoded video, and takes into consideration contrast, colour, as well as, motion. It further includes the after-effect of spatial and temporal concealment to estimate the loss in video quality due to packet loss. The proposed approach is thereby able to achieve a degree of correlation with subjective ratings that is far above those obtained by standard techniques. The paper is organized as follows. In Sect. 2, we describe the different stages of the proposed algorithm. Section 3 elaborates on the experiments conducted and discusses their results. Section 4 concludes the article.

2   The Proposed Algorithm

The proposed algorithm is based on human perception, and every stage is based on specific traits of the artefact in question as well as the characteristics of the human visual system. It is, in essence, a two-stage, no-reference quality assessment metric for packet loss error concealment. A primary identification stage is followed by a quantification stage, as illustrated in Fig. 1.

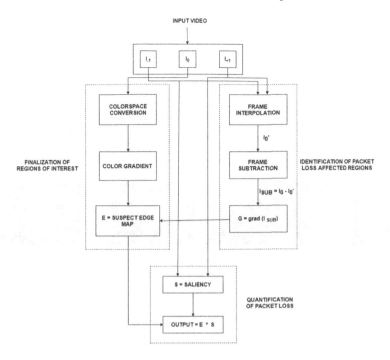

Fig. 1. A block diagram of the proposed scheme. I_0 refers to the current video frame while I_{-1} and I_{+1} refer to the frames immediately before and after

2.1 Identification of Packet Loss Affected Regions

The identification of packet loss affected regions involves two main steps, namely, intra-frame segmentation and finalization of the regions of interest. Intra-frame segmentation, which uses motion-compensated frame interpolation to remove the redundant areas in the frames, followed by gradient filtering to increase the difference of these areas in comparison to the redundant areas of the frame. Finalization of regions of interest also involves two sub-stages, color gradient formation and edge checking. Color gradients are more in tune with how the human visual system notices differences in comparison to just noticing the edge strength. Edge checking is the final step of the quantification stage, which uses all the information of the previous stages in tandem to find the noticeable edges.

2.1.1 Intra-frame Segmentation

Motion Compensated Frame Interpolation. We use phase-based frame interpolation between alternate frames as proposed by Meyer et al. [12]. Frame interpolation is primarily used to increase the frame rate of a video by interpolating in-between frames. However, we exploit this accuracy in predicting inter-frames to capture the 'sudden appearance' of spatial packet loss. Theoretically, the interpolated frame would be an exact copy of the actual frame sparing only the packet loss affected region. The only thing that remains is to localize the impaired region by taking the frame difference between the predicted frame and the actual frame as shown in Figs. 2(a), 2(b) and 2(c).

(a)   (b)   (c)   (d)

(e)   (f)   (g)   (h)

Fig. 2. (a) The same frame after gradient filtering (b) Suspect edges (c) Saliency map of frame number 118 of BQMall (d) Output of the Hadamard product of the saliency map S, and edge map E (e) Example of a Video Frame I_{-1} (f) Example of a video frame I_{+1} (g) Difference of predicted frame I_0' & actual frame I_0 (h) Motion subtracted frame

In practical situations, the interpolated frame has motion errors and the end product is a frame which contains imperfect areas which are made up of areas of high motion as well as packet loss impaired regions. As we can see from Figs. 2(a), 2(b) and 2(c) the packet loss regions are in fact captured in the image obtained as a result of the difference between the actual and interpolated frames. However, there is a significant amount of noise in the image, consisting of the inaccuracies of the motion interpolation. The areas of high motion present as blurry regions, which is one of the limitations of [12] while frame subtraction yields regions of low motion but similar pixel intensities. This is addressed subsequently.

Gradient Filtering. The result of the frame subtraction is converted from the RGB colorspace to grayscale. We do this, to proceed to gradient filtering. Gradient filtering acts as a method to enhance the contrast of the frame. Representing the result of frame subtraction by I_{SUB}, gradient filtering is mathematically defined as,

$$G = \frac{\partial I_{SUB}}{\partial x} + \frac{\partial I_{SUB}}{\partial y} \tag{1}$$

The areas of highest intensity are the regions of packet loss and very high motion (areas where motion interpolation is most inaccurate). However, the smaller errors in motion interpolation as well as normal differences result in a lot of areas with similar intensities. Gradient filtering helps suppress these areas with lower intensity. The increased contrast implies that the difference between the two classes is more prominent, thereby making it easier to consider only the areas of interest. Figures 2(d) and 2(e) show an illustration of this idea.

2.1.2   Finalization of Regions of Interest

In an ideal situation, Sect. 2.1.1 would remove all the areas in the frame which does not have packet loss, and we would be left with a frame where all the packet loss affected regions are marked. The result of Sect. 2.1.2 contains only areas containing packet loss and the inaccuracies of motion interpolation. However, without any idea about the video content, it is hard to segregate these two. We attempt to make this distinction using the formation of a color gradient image, followed by edge checking to determine the blocks which are affected by packet loss.

Color Gradient. The most popular color space is obviously the RGB color space. However, it is well established that the delta equation or the color similarity measure is more sensitive for the CIELAB color space. La*b* is closer in similarity to the non-linear response of the eye and that is what we have used to form the color gradient of the image. The relative perceptual difference measure or the delta equation for image I is defined as,

$$\Delta_p = \sqrt{(L_1 - L_2)^2 + (a_1^* - a_2^*)^2 + (b_1^* - b_2^*)^2} \tag{2}$$

where, $p \in \{x, y\}$, the pixel $I(x, y)$ has the values (L_1, a_1^*, b_1^*) , for $p = x$, the pixel $I(x + 1, y)$ has the values (L_2, a_2^*, b_2^*), while for $p = y$, pixel $I(x, y + 1)$ has the values (L_2, a_2^*, b_2^*).

The color gradient image is formed as $M = \Delta_x + \Delta_y$

A grayscale gradient condenses the chrominance and the luminance information thereby reducing the individual differences. Moreover, packet loss often present as a slight change in colour information, which would not be detected accurately by a grayscale gradient image.

Edge Checking. This is the basis on which the algorithm stands. It combines the packet loss candidate regions from Sect. 2.1 and the colour gradient from Sect. 2.1.2 to give us the edges which will be detected by the human visual system. Considering the video being discussed is H.264/AVC compressed, the encoding is usually into 16×16 blocks or higher. We approach this in a non-overlapping block-based manner. Given the color gradient image M, and the original image I, let the lowermost row of the kth block $I(k, x, y)$ be R_1, the top-most row of the next block $I(k+1, x, y)$ be R_2 and the corresponding row in the color gradient be the top-row of $M(k+1, x, y)$. Then the map E of suspected edges becomes,

$$E_{vertical}(k, x, y) = \begin{cases} 1, & \text{if } C = 1 \\ 0, & \text{otherwise} \end{cases} \tag{3}$$

Note that $C = 1$ only if, each of the following conditions are true:
(1) $\sum_{k=1}^{N_B} M(k, x, y) \geq 75$,   (2) $|\sum R_1 - \sum R_2| \leq \xi$,   (3) $DR_1 \leq \beta$, and   (4)
$DR_2 \leq \beta$

Here, $\beta = 3$ and $\xi = 75$, N_B is the total number of blocks and is computed as $N_B = \frac{\text{image size}}{16 \times 16}$, DR_1 and DR_2 are the 4×4 reshaped 2D discrete cosine transform(DCT) of rows R_1 and R_2 respectively. (It is worth noting that reshaping is not essential, and the process can be replaced by 1-D DCT alongside a suitable threshold as well.) Moreover, β and ξ are heuristically assigned thresholds, where β is the threshold which limits the summation of the highest quarter of values in the 2D-DCT transform of the individual rows, while ξ represents the threshold for sum of the differences of the pixels of the adjacent rows R_1 and R_2. The thresholds are used to prevent false positives during the edge checking process. If the magnitude of the high frequencies of the row is higher than the threshold β then we discard that edge, since it is noisy and would almost always give a false positive. The other threshold ξ is used to calculate the edge strength so that weak edges can be eliminated.

The same process is followed in the horizontal direction giving $E_{horizontal}$, and the two resulting suspect edge maps are pooled together to form the output of this stage, $E = E_{vertical} + E_{horizontal}$.

As Fig. 2(f) clearly demonstrates, the suspect edges are marked, and they do not always form blocks. Trying to detect block formation is particularly tricky because oftentimes, the only thing that can be perceived is one edge, or even two edges, and trying to reconstruct the extent of the other two sides would lead to a high number of false positives.

2.2   Quantification of Packet Loss

The identification part of the algorithm sets the stage for quantification which uses the Suspect Edges as well as the ROIs, along with saliency to help us quantify the degradation as close to the human visual system as possible, ensuring that the model includes human attention. The use of saliency maps to augment packet loss detection is not new [15], where the use of conventional algorithms such as SSIM and MSE when appropriately weighted according to a saliency map, significantly boost the results.

2.2.1   Saliency

Saliency determines the likelihood of the observer noticing something because it stands out from the surroundings, which in this case is packet loss error concealment. The simple presence of an edge or PL concealed area does not guarantee that it will contribute to visual degradation but the user's attention would get drawn to the most salient regions, thereby missing the artefacts not present in those locations. The saliency map of the given frame comes from the works of Harel et al. [13]. Graph-based visual saliency presented in [13] works by extracting relevant feature vectors from the image plane, creates an activation map using the feature vectors and then normalizes the activation map. The output is a saliency map, similar to a weight map where higher weights correspond to areas where the human attention is most likely to go to, as illustrated in Fig. 2(g). The Hadamard product of this map with image E which is essentially the image containing the relevant edges, is computed. Hence, the image containing the edges according to the likelihood of them being noticed can be formulated as $F = E^\circ S$, where, S is the saliency map of image I. Figure 2(g) shows the saliency map corresponding to Fig. 2(f). Figure 2(h) shows the final output computed from the edge and saliency maps.

2.2.2 Formulation of Packet Loss Error Score

The proposed Packet Loss Error Score (PLES) is the culmination of all the different stages of the algorithm representing a singular score, $PLES = \frac{\sum_i \sum_j F(i,j)}{N_E}$, where $N_E =$ Total number of possible edges. The PLES for the entire video is simply the mean of the individual scores for the entire video.

3   Simulations and Results

The algorithm was tested on the CSIQ Video Quality Database [14]. The CSIQ database contains 12 reference videos, each of spatial resolution 832×480 pixels, but with differing frame rates, specifically, 24 frames per second (fps), 25 fps, 30 fps, 50 fps and 60 fps. It has 3 different levels of packet loss which we determine to be low, medium and high.

Table 1. Comparison of metrics for competing methods

Algorithm	PCC	SROCC	RMSE
MSE	0.3214	0.3214	35.6754
Babu et al. [10]	0.2571	0.2571	44.2158
Morais et al. [8]	0.5909	0.5909	10.6500
Proposed algorithm	0.7917	0.7917	35.7172

There are several ways in which the efficacy of packet loss metrics has been determined in the past. [1] uses apriori knowledge of the affected area and compares that with the algorithmic output, while the standard practice is to correlate the quantified result with the MOS value as seen in [8,9] etc. We have followed the standard approach and chosen the gold standard of MSE, only as a benchmark as well as the works of [8,10] which are both no-reference metrics and therefore are more apt comparisons. The comparison is done taking into account Pearson's Correlation Coefficient (PCC), Spearman's Rank Correlation Coefficient (SROCC) and Root Mean Squared Error (RMSE), as seen in Table 1.

It is evident that the proposed method outperforms all the existing approaches. It should however be mentioned that the values were taken across videos with low, medium and high packet loss. The final value for each method is the mean of the entire database. This is the reason for the equal PCC and SROCC values. The high RMSE for the proposed algorithm on the other hand is due to the scale we have employed. Since PLES is calculated by dividing by the total number of possible edges, the resulting values are very low, thereby causing the differences between the MOS value and the PLES score to be higher.

It is to be emphasized that the motion interpolation stage is one the most crucial steps of the algorithm and as its accuracy increases, so does the accuracy of our algorithm. A block size of 16×16 was selected because smaller block sizes are too trivial, and larger sizes will be a multiple of the given block size and hence included anyway.

4   Conclusion

In this paper, a novel no reference metric is presented for packet loss error concealment detection. This technique is able to detect as well as localize the presence of packet loss impairments, and quantify the loss in quality. Testing on a wide variety of video content proves its efficiency and robustness as compared to existing approaches. The technique derives its power from the fact that it is chiefly based on human perception. In the future, we intend to factor even more aspects of the HVS into our model, as well as making it robust for situations containing very high motion.

References

1. Shabtay, D. et al.: Video packet loss concealment detection based on image content. In: EUSIPCO 2008, Lausanne, Switzerland, pp. 1–5, 25–29 August 2008
2. Farrugia, R.A., et al.: A support vector machine approach for detection and localization of transmission errors within standard H.263++ decoders. IEEE Trans. Multimedia 11(7), 1323–1330 (2009)
3. Chen, J., et al.: An effective error concealment method based on abrupt scene change detection algorithm. In: ICISCE 2012, pp. 1–4 (2012)
4. Saad, M.A., et al.: Blind prediction of natural video quality. IEEE Trans. Image Process. 23(3), 1352–1365 (2014)
5. Argyropoulos, S., et al.: No reference bit stream model for video quality assessment of H.264/AVC video based on packet loss visibility. In: ICASSP-2011, pp. 1169–1172 (2011)
6. Goodall, T.R., et al.: Detecting and mapping video impairments. IEEE Trans. Image Process. 28(6), 2680–2691 (2019)
7. Reibman, A.R., et al.: Characterizing packet-loss impairments in compressed video. In: ICIP 2007, pp. V-77–V-80 (2007)
8. Morais, D., et al.: A Correlation-Based No-Reference Packet-Loss Metric. Anais de XXXIV Simpósio Brasileiro de Telecomunicações (2016)
9. Manasa, K., et al.: A perceptually motivated no-reference video quality assessment algorithm for packet loss artefacts. In: QOMEX 2014, pp. 67–68, Singapore, 18–20 September 2014
10. Babu, R.V., et al.: No-Reference metrics for video streaming applications. In: Proceedings International Workshop on Packet Video (2004)
11. Glavota, I. et al.: Pixel-based statistical analysis of packet loss artefact features. In: ZINC, pp. 16–19 (2016)

12. Meyer, S. et al.: Phase-Based frame interpolation for video. In: CVPR 2015, pp. 1410–1418 (2016)
13. Harel, J., et al.: Graph-Based visual saliency. In: NIPS, pp. 545–552 (2006)
14. Vu, P.V., et al.: ViS3: an algorithm for video quality assessment via analysis of spatial and spatiotemporal slices. J. Elect. Imag. **23**(1), 013016 (2014)
15. Feng, X., et al.: Saliency based objective quality assessment of decoded video affected by packet losses. In: ICIP, pp. 2560–2563 (2008)

A Context-Aware Model with Flow Mechanism for Conversational Question Answering

Daomiao Song[✉], Yan Yang, and Ailian Fang[✉]

School of Computer Science, East China Normal University, Shanghai, China
{yanyang,alfang}@cs.ecnu.edu.cn

Abstract. Conversational Question Answering (ConvQA) requires a deep understanding of conversation history to answer the current question. However, most existing works ignore the sequential dependencies among history turns and treat all history indiscriminately. We propose a Flow based Context-Aware Question Answering model to alleviate the above problems. In specific, we first use a hierarchical history selector to filter out irrelated history turns according to the features of word level, utterance level and dialogue level. Then we introduce a FlowRNN to model the sequential dependencies between history turns along dialog direction. Finally we incorporate these hidden dependencies to BERT for answer predictions. Experiments on a large-scale conversational question answering dataset QuAC show that our proposed method can use conversation history effectively and outperforms most of the recent ConvQA models.

Keywords: Conversational Question Answering · Hierarchical history selector · Flow-based machine

1 Introduction

A conversational question answering system aims to read a given passage and answer a series of interrelated questions [2,6]. Dialogue history is helpful for good understanding questions, but also brings the noise. How to better utilize conversation contextual information is a critical challenge on the ConvQA task.

Various methods have been proposed to model conversation history in ConvQA. One method is to append the immediate N-turn history to current questions [7]. Another approach is to use flow-based [3] models in ConvQA. FlowQA [3], FlowDelta [9], GraphFlow [1] introduced Integration-Flow(IF) mechanism integrating hidden representations generated from previous reasoning processes to answer the current question. However, the concept of IF does not mimic a human's style of conversation, which performs reasoning in parallel for each question without modeling the sequential dependencies along dialog direction.

© Springer Nature Switzerland AG 2021
T. Mantoro et al. (Eds.): ICONIP 2021, CCIS 1517, pp. 624–631, 2021.
https://doi.org/10.1007/978-3-030-92310-5_72

There have been several attempts to apply pre-trained language models to conversational question answering, such as HAE [4], HAM [5], Env-ConvQA [11] and achieve state-of-the-art performance.

To model history more deeply, we propose a Flow based Context-Aware Question Answering model to capture the dependencies of history turns along the dialog direction and incorporate the dependencies into BERT. In specific, we first use a hierarchical history selector to filter out irrelated history turns. Then, we use a FlowRNN to model sequential dependencies along the direction of the dialog. Finally, we incorporate these dependencies into BERT for answer predictions. We evaluate our approach on a large-scale ConvQA dataset QuAC. Experiments show that our model outperforms most exist models.

2   Model

2.1   Task Definition and Overview

In ConvQA task, the model need to read the passage P, and conversation history $H_k = \{Q_0, A_0, \ldots, Q_i, A_i, \ldots, Q_{k-1}, A_{k-1}\}$, and then give the answer of Q_k, the answer A_k is an text span in P.

As shown in Fig. 1, our model consists of Hierarchical History Selector, Reasoning Layer, and Prediction Layer. The History Selector is used to find the most relevant history turns. The Reasoning Layer applies a FlowRNN to model the selected history. Finally, the Prediction Layer predicts the answer of the question.

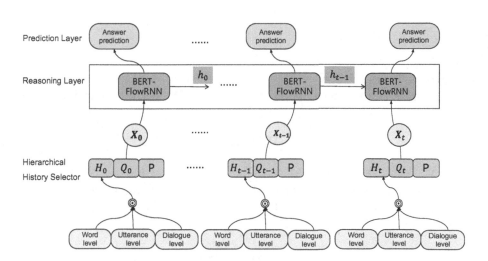

Fig. 1. Overview of the our proposed model.

2.2 Hierarchical History Selector

Given the conversation history H_k, inspired by recent work Yuan et al. [10], We built a hierarchical history selector to select the most relevant history turns based on word-level, utterance-level, and Dialogue-level.

Word Level. At word level, we first use an Attentive Module to learn word representations of conversation history and current question, get H_k' and Q_k'. And then we utilize cross attention to obtain a matching feature map between history utterances $\mathbf{H_k}'$ and key $\mathbf{K_1} = \mathbf{Q_k}'$, which is formulated as:

$$A = v^T \tanh \left(\mathbf{K_1}^T \mathbf{W} \mathbf{H_k}' + \mathbf{b} \right) \tag{1}$$

where $\mathbf{W} \in R^{d \times d \times N}, \mathbf{b} \in R^N$ and $\mathbf{v} \in R^{N \times 1}$, N is the maximum number of history turns. The word alignment matrix between history turns and the current question is A, w is the maximum number of words in each utterance. We apply max pooling on A from row and column direction to get the most prominent matching features, finally we concat these features:

$$m\left(\mathbf{K_1}, \mathbf{H_k}'\right) = \left[\max_{dim=2} \mathbf{A}; \max_{dim=3} \mathbf{A} \right] \tag{2}$$

where $m\left(\mathbf{K_1}, \mathbf{H_k}'\right) \in R^{N \times 2w}$, indicates history turns and the current question is similar at word-level. The relevance score is formulated as:

$$\mathbf{s_1} = \mathbf{softmax}(m(\mathbf{K_1}, \mathbf{H_k}')\mathbf{c} + b) \tag{3}$$

where $\mathbf{c} \in R^{2w \times 1}$ and $b \in R^{N \times 1}$.

Utterance Level. The word-level representations of history and question are $\mathbf{H_k}'$ and $\mathbf{Q_k}'$, we apply mean pooling on $\mathbf{H_k}'$ and $\mathbf{Q_k}'$ get utterance-level representations:

$$\widetilde{\mathbf{H_k}} = mean(\mathbf{H_k}'), \widetilde{\mathbf{Q_k}} = mean(\mathbf{Q_k}') \tag{4}$$

where $\widetilde{\mathbf{H_k}}, \widetilde{\mathbf{Q_k}} \in R^{N \times d}$, N is the maximum number of history turns, d is the dimension of the word embedding. The utterance level similarity between key $\mathbf{K_2} = \widetilde{\mathbf{Q_k}}$ and history utterances $\widetilde{\mathbf{H_k}}$ is measured by cosine similarity, which is formulated as:

$$s_2 = \frac{\widetilde{\mathbf{H_k}} \mathbf{K_2^T}}{\left\| \widetilde{\mathbf{H_k}} \right\|_2 \|\mathbf{K_2}\|_2} \tag{5}$$

where $\mathbf{s_2} \in R^{N \times 1}$ is the relevance score at utterance level.

Dialogue Level. We use relative distance between history turns and the current question to represent the dialogue-level relevance. There are 55.3% of the questions in the QuAC dataset are along with the original topic, and a closer history turn may be more helpful in this type of question. Therefore, we introduce relative distances, which can moderate the errors caused by purely semantic matching.

Given the current question Q_k and a history QA pairs Q_i, A_i, we compute the relative distance at turn level as $k - i$, the score at dialogue level is formulated as:

$$s_3 = softmax(e^{i-k}) \tag{6}$$

word-level score, utterance-level score, and dialogue-level score are all essential to measure the relevance of history utterances and the current question. To make full use of the these parts, we design a combined strategy to fuse the three scores. Specifically, we use the weighted sum of three scores for selection:

$$\mathbf{s} = \alpha * \mathbf{s}_1 + \beta * \mathbf{s}_2 + (1 - \alpha - \beta) * \mathbf{s}_3 \tag{7}$$

where α, β is hyper-parameters and $\mathbf{s}$ is the final score produced by the hierarchical history selector. The default value of α is set to 0.5, β is set to 0.2. Finally, we select the highest scoring K rounds of historical information. We append all history question-answer pairs separated by some special symbols [Q] or [A], the format of selected history is:

$$\hat{\mathbf{H}}_\mathbf{k} = \{Q_0, [Q], A_0, [A] \ldots Q_i, [Q], A_i, [A] \ldots\} \tag{8}$$

2.3   Reasoning Layer

Given the selected conversation history $\hat{H}_k$, the current question Q_k and the given passage P, tokens are packed into a sequence:

$$\mathbf{X}_\mathbf{k} = \left\{ [CLS]\hat{\mathbf{H}}_\mathbf{k}\mathbf{Q}_\mathbf{k}[SEP]\mathbf{P}[SEP] \right\} \tag{9}$$

where [CLS] and [SEP] are special tokens, X_k is then fed into a BERT-FlowRNN model for contextual reasoning. We first use BERT to model the input sequence and then incorporate FlowRNN in the last layer of BERT to generate the final representations for answer predictions.

BERT. Each layer of BERT is a Transformer block [8]:

$$C_k^{l+1} = \text{Transformer} \left(C_k^l \right) \tag{10}$$

where C_k^l is the hidden representation of the *l-th* layer for *k-th* question.

FlowRNN. In this paper, we use a FlowRNN to model sequential dependencies of these hidden representations along dialog direction. These sequential dependencies preserve the variation of conversation topics, which is helpful for later answer prediction.

We incorporate FlowRNN to the last layer of BERT. The hidden representation from $(k$-$1)$-th question is h_{k-1}, the intermediate vector generated from the $(L$-$1)$-th BERT layer is C_k^{L-1}. Then, A GRU is used to update the reasoning representation of k-th question by incorporating the hidden vectors h_{k-1}. The update process formulated as:

$$
\begin{aligned}
z_k &= \sigma \left(W_z C_k^{L-1} + U_z\, h_{k-1} \right) \\
r_k &= \sigma \left(W_r C_k^{L-1} + U_r\, h_{k-1} \right) \\
\tilde{h}_k &= \tanh \left(W_s C_k^{L-1} + U_s \left(r_k \circ h_{k-1} \right) \right) \\
h_k &= \left(1 - z_k \right) \circ h_{k-1} + z_k \circ \tilde{h}_k
\end{aligned}
\tag{11}
$$

where $\mathbf{W}_z, \mathbf{W}_r, \mathbf{W}_s, \mathbf{U}_z, \mathbf{U}_r, \mathbf{U}_s$ are parameters. When answering the first question in a dialog, the history hidden representation is None.

The h_k is going to be passed to the next question as an intermediate expression of the k-th question. In this way, our model can capture long-distance dependencies at dialog level. The FlowRNN is formulated as:

$$
FlowRNN(C_k^{L-1}) = h_k
\tag{12}
$$

Finally, the output of BERT-FlowRNN module is formulated as:

$$
C_k^L = Concat(\text{ Transformer } (C_k^{L-1}), FlowRNN(C_k^{L-1}))
\tag{13}
$$

where $concat(\cdot, \cdot)$ is an operation for concat two elements.

2.4   Prediction Layer

The hidden representations from last layer for k-th question C_k^L are feed to a fully-connected layer (NN) for answer predictions, which is formulated as:

$$
P^B, P^E = NN(C_k^L)
\tag{14}
$$

where P^B and P^E are span start and span end vector respectively. The probabilities of m-th token in the given passage to be the begin token is p_m^B and to be end token is p_m^E. The loss function of begin and end vector are $\mathcal{L}_B$ and $\mathcal{L}_E$, formulated as:

$$
\mathcal{L}_B = - \sum_M 1\{m = m_B\} \log p_m^B, \mathcal{L}_E = - \sum_M 1\{m = m_E\} \log p_m^E
$$

$$
\mathcal{L}_{ans} = \frac{1}{2} \left(\mathcal{L}_B + \mathcal{L}_E \right)
\tag{15}
$$

where m_B and m_E are the start and end token of the grouth answer respectively, $1\{\cdot\}$ is an indicator function, and M is the maximum number of tokens in the given passage. $\mathcal{L}_{ans}$ is the final loss for answer predictions.

3   Experiments

3.1   Datasets and Evaluation Metrics

We conduct experiments on a large-scale ConvQA dataset QuAC [2]. This dataset is more challenging than other datasets because most of the questions do not exist independently, and only by using the conversation history can understand the current question correctly.

The QuAC dataset has two challenge evaluation metrics, F1 and HEQ. F1 evaluates the overlap between the prediction and the grouth truth at the word level. HEQ evaluates whether the system can equal or exceed an average human at the correct rate of prediction. HEQ can be further divided into question level (HEQQ) and dialog level (HEQD).

3.2   Baselines

We consider all methods with published papers on the QuAC leaderboard as baselines. Note that those methods that consider transfer learning or data augmentation are not compared here as they used external data.

– **BiDAF++** [7] is a classic ConvQA model without history.
– **FlowQA** [3] introduces the hidden representation generated in the reasoning of the previous questions.
– **BERT+HAE** [4] embeds the history anwer marker into BERT.
– **BERT+PosHAE** [4] adds the information of the relative position between history turns and the current question based on BERT+HAE [4].
– **HAM** [5] uses a history attention module to weigh the history turns based on their contributions to answer the current question.
– **Env-ConvQA** [11] uses reinforcement learning to select history turns.

3.3   Main Evaluation Results

As shown in Table 1, our method can obtain the best performance in F1, HEQQ, and HEQD wins first place in the total score. Our method can exceed a recent history attended model called Env-ConvQA method 4.0 scores in F1 (from 66.1% to 70.1%). Given that the task is very challenging, this improvement is not tiny. The experimental results demonstrate the effectiveness of our history selection and history modeling approaches.

At the same time, compared with FlowQA [3], which is also based on Flow Machine, our training time is much shorter, with FlowQA taking 56.8 h and ours taking 11 h.

3.4   Ablation Analysis

Table 1 demonstrates the overall validity of our model, but this effect is the result of several parts combined, so we conduct an ablation experiment to further

Table 1. Comparison between our method and ConvQA baselines

Methods	F1	HEQQ	HEQD	Total
BiDAF++	51.8	45.3	2.0	99.1
FlowQA	64.6	59.6	5.8	130.0
Bert+HAE	63.9	59.7	5.9	129.5
Bert+PosHAE	64.7	60.7	6.0	131.4
HAM	65.7	62.1	7.3	135.1
Env-ConvQA	66.1	62.2	7.3	135.6
Our method	**70.1**	**65.7**	**11.6**	**147.4**

Table 2. Results for ablation analysis

Methods	F1	HEQQ	HEQD	Total
Our method	70.1	65.7	11.6	147.4
w/o PreQA	66.1	61.4	8.4	135.9
w/o History Selector	65.6	61.0	8.3	134.9
w/o FlowRNN	68.1	63.9	9.6	141.6

analyze the indispensability of each part. The results of the ablation experiment are shown in Table 2.

Specifically, we have three settings as follows: -PreQA means do not prepend any previous question-answer pairs, -History Selector removed the History Selector in the model, treat all history indiscriminately.-FlowRNN means do not incorporate hidden representation from previous answering reasoning. From Table 2, we can see that the effect of the model decreases the most after removing the History Selector, and even decreases 0.5% than not using any history, which indicates that the indiscriminate processing of all the history information will introduce much noise and further affects the performance. Meanwhile, the model's effectiveness decreases by 2% after removing the FlowRNN, which illustrates the importance of the hidden representation. All of this verifies the superiority of our proposed model in the selection and modeling of conversation history.

4   Conclusion

In this paper, we propose a Flow based Context-Aware Question Answering model for ConvQA. First, we employ a hierarchical history selector to filter out redundant history turns from different granularity. In addition, We naturally incorporate the hidden representation of previous answering reasoning into the pre-trained model Bert for answer prediction. We empirically evaluate our approach on the ConvQA dataset QuAC. Extensive experiments show that our proposed model outperformed most ConvQA models in F1 values. Ablation analysis show the good interpretability of our model. In the future, we will further explore the dependencies transmission in long-distance conversations.

References

1. Chen, Y., Wu, L., Zaki, M.J.: GraphFlow: exploiting conversation flow with graph neural networks for conversational machine comprehension. In: Proceedings of the Twenty-Ninth International Joint Conference on Artificial Intelligence, IJCAI 2020, pp. 1230–1236. ijcai.org (2020)
2. Choi, E., et al.: QuAC: question answering in context. In: Proceedings of the 2018 Conference on Empirical Methods in Natural Language Processing, Brussels, Belgium, 31 October–4 November 2018, pp. 2174–2184. Association for Computational Linguistics (2018)
3. Huang, H., Choi, E., Yih, W.: FlowQA: grasping flow in history for conversational machine comprehension. In: 7th International Conference on Learning Representations, ICLR 2019, New Orleans, LA, USA, 6–9 May 2019. OpenReview.net (2019)
4. Qu, C., Yang, L., Qiu, M., Croft, W.B., Zhang, Y., Iyyer, M.: BERT with history answer embedding for conversational question answering. In: Proceedings of the 42nd International ACM SIGIR Conference on Research and Development in Information Retrieval, SIGIR 2019, Paris, France, 21–25 July 2019, pp. 1133–1136. ACM (2019)
5. Qu, C., et al.: Attentive history selection for conversational question answering. In: Proceedings of the 28th ACM International Conference on Information and Knowledge Management, CIKM 2019, Beijing, China, 3–7 November 2019, pp. 1391–1400. ACM (2019)
6. Reddy, S., Chen, D., Manning, C.D.: CoQA: a conversational question answering challenge. CoRR abs/1808.07042 (2018)
7. Seo, M.J., Kembhavi, A., Farhadi, A., Hajishirzi, H.: Bidirectional attention flow for machine comprehension. In: 5th International Conference on Learning Representations, ICLR 2017, Toulon, France, 24–26 April 2017, Conference Track Proceedings. OpenReview.net (2017)
8. Vaswani, A., et al.: Attention is all you need. In: Advances in Neural Information Processing Systems 30: Annual Conference on Neural Information Processing Systems 2017, 4–9 December 2017, Long Beach, CA, USA, pp. 5998–6008 (2017)
9. Yeh, Y.T., Chen, Y.: FlowDelta: modeling flow information gain in reasoning for conversational machine comprehension. CoRR abs/1908.05117 (2019)
10. Yuan, C., et al.: Multi-hop selector network for multi-turn response selection in retrieval-based chatbots. In: Proceedings of the 2019 Conference on Empirical Methods in Natural Language Processing and the 9th International Joint Conference on Natural Language Processing, EMNLP-IJCNLP 2019, Hong Kong, China, 3–7 November 2019, pp. 111–120. Association for Computational Linguistics (2019)
11. Qiu, M., et al.: Reinforced history backtracking for conversational question answering. In: Thirty-Fifth AAAI Conference on Artificial Intelligence, AAAI 2021, pp. 13718–13726. AAAI Press (2021)

Homography Estimation Network Based on Dense Correspondence

Xiaohang Yang, Lingtong Kong, Ziyun Liang, and Jie Yang[✉]

Institute of Image Processing and Pattern Recognition, Shanghai Jiao Tong University, Shanghai, China
{yang_xh,ltkong,ziyunliang,jieyang}@sjtu.edu.cn

Abstract. Reliable homography estimation is essential for plenty of computer vision tasks. However, the ground truth of homography is difficult to obtain. Moreover, it is relatively hard for ordinary convolutional neural networks to model correspondence, which leads to the difficulty for optimization. In this paper, we propose a novel framework based on unsupervised dense correspondence. We extract feature pyramid for each image and estimate the dense correspondence map in a coarse-to-fine manner. Relying on correlation layers and photometric loss, we can get rid of the deficiency of ordinary networks and estimate reliable dense correspondence for each image pair, which facilitates the later prediction of homography matrix. To achieve the homography training on both synthetic dataset and realistic dataset, we apply different losses for different tasks respectively being supervised loss and triplet loss, to regulate the training procedure. Qualitative and quantitative evaluations illustrate the effectiveness of the dense correspondence map, and shows the competitive performance of our method compared with traditional feature-based algorithms and deep learning methods.

Keywords: Homography estimation · Dense correspondence · Unsupervised learning · Image alignment

1 Introduction

Homography is an important correspondence mapping between two images in multiple computer vision tasks. For these tasks, calculating the correspondence between two images is the first step and the foundation of later processes. The accuracy of matching can influence the final performances of these algorithms.

Traditional methods are mainly feature-based. They generally use feature descriptors like Scale-Invariant Feature Transform (SIFT) [1], and the quality of features would have a large impact on their performance. As deep learning has shown its potential in multiple tasks in recent years, researchers have developed various methods for matching tasks using convolutional neural networks (CNN). [2] is the first approach estimating homography matrix directly

This research is partly supported by NSFC, China (No: 61876107, U1803261).

T. Mantoro et al. (Eds.): ICONIP 2021, CCIS 1517, pp. 632–639, 2021.
https://doi.org/10.1007/978-3-030-92310-5_73

with one CNN end-to-end. Like dense or sparse matching methods, homography estimation lacks supervision since it is difficult to obtain the ground truth of correspondence between two frames. To overcome this shortage, researchers propose various algorithms, including supervised methods and unsupervised ones. For the supervised approaches, the network is trained with generated dataset [2]. For unsupervised approaches, photometric loss [3] or triplet loss [4] are applied to guide the training on realistic image pairs. While for both supervised and unsupervised methods, obtaining reliable correspondence information directly from two stacked images with CNN is relatively difficult, as the ordinary network is not good at learning correlation between different patches of two images.

To obtain the homography matrix directly and accurately, we propose a novel unsupervised, end-to-end homography estimation framework named Homography-from-Flow Network (HfF-Net). We use cross-correlation layer which is extensively used in optical flow estimation methods [5]. The cross-correlation layer can densely calculate the correlation between different patches from two images, then the dense correspondence can be estimated much more easier based on the cost volume produced by cross-correlation layer. Although the correspondence map cannot be accurate for each pixel, with the help of it, we do not need a deep and powerful network to select reliable information and estimate the homography matrix. The dense correspondence is trained by minimizing the pixel-wise photometric similarity and smooth regularization, and the homography matrix is trained in different ways depending on the dataset. For generated dataset, we sample a homography matrix randomly like [2], then warp one image according to the homography matrix to create a new image, which forms a pair of images with the ground truth, then we can train the network with Mean Squared Error (MSE). For realistic dataset, such as the image pairs sampled from video clips, if we have two consecutive frames, we optimize the homography estimation between two frames by minimizing the difference between the warped second image and the first one at the feature space. Both qualitative visualization of the learned dense correspondence and quantitative evaluations demonstrate the effectiveness of our proposed techniques. The main contributions of our method are as follows:

1. We propose a novel end-to-end framework, which enhances the homography estimation by predicting a dense correspondence map first, and then regressing a reliable homography based on it.
2. We apply photometric loss and smoothness loss to restrain the training of dense correspondence, which is the intermediate result and reliable hints for later estimation, and we use MSE or feature similarity loss to restrain the training of alignment.

2 Method

2.1 Network Architecture

Our framework, as illustrated in Fig. 1, consists of three stages, feature extraction $f(\cdot)$, dense matching $m(\cdot)$ and homography estimation $h(\cdot)$. It takes two images

I_a, I_b as input, produces a dense correspondence map as an intermediate result and finally outputs the 4-point homography.

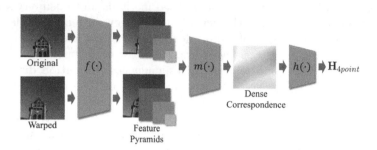

Original

$f(\cdot)$

$m(\cdot)$

$h(\cdot)$ $\mathbf{H}_{4point}$

Dense
Correspondence

Warped

Feature
Pyramids

Fig. 1. Architecture of our proposed method.

Feature Pyramid Extractor. Given image I_a and I_b, our network extracts feature maps from different layers of the feature extractor and forms 7-layer pyramids, among which the zeroth level of the pyramid is the input image. In the pyramid, each feature map is downsampled from the last feature map with a factor of 2. For image I_a, the feature pyramid is as follows:

$$\{F_a^0, F_a^1, ..., F_a^6\} = f(I_a) \tag{1}$$

Dense Matching and Refinement. The dense correspondence is estimated in a coarse-to-fine manner. At l-level, dense correspondence U^l is constructed based on the feature map F_a^l, the upsampled correspondence of last level up(U^{l+1}), and the cost volume between F_a^l and the warped $\hat{F}_b^l$ according to up(U^{l+1}), in which the up($\cdot$) stands for upsampling operator. The warping operation for pixel $\mathbf{x}$ is formulated as:

$$\hat{F}_b^l(\mathbf{x}) = F_b^l(\mathbf{x} + \text{up}(U^{l+1})(\mathbf{x})) \tag{2}$$

and the cost volume between pixel $\mathbf{x}_a$ from F_a^l and pixel $\mathbf{x}_b$ from $\hat{F}_b^l$ within a local search patch is:

$$\text{cv}^l(\mathbf{x}_a, \mathbf{x}_b) = \frac{1}{N} F_a^l(\mathbf{x}_a)^{\mathsf{T}} \hat{F}_b^l(\mathbf{x}_b) \tag{3}$$

where N is the length of $F_a^l(\mathbf{x}_a)$, and T is the transpose operator. For l-level, we estimate a residual correspondence u^l on the basis of the upsampled coarse correspondence map up(U^{l+1}) to refine the matching map, where the cat($\cdot$) represents the concatenation operator:

$$u^l = m^l \left(\text{cat}(F_a^l, \text{up}(U^{l+1}), \text{cv}^l) \right) \tag{4}$$

$$U^l = \text{up}(U^{l+1}) + u^l \tag{5}$$

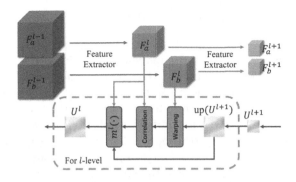

Fig. 2. Dense correspondence estimation for one level.

Homography Estimation. The homography matrix regression pipeline could be simplified with the help of dense correspondence. In our approach, given a coarse dense correspondence map, we can build a simple CNN to predict the displacement vectors of 4 corners. Then the homography $\mathbf{H}_{4point}$ is solved from the 4 vectors. Let $h(\cdot)$ represent the pipeline:

$$\mathbf{H}_{4point} = h(U^0) \tag{6}$$

2.2 Unsupervised Dense Correspondence Learning

Inspired by the advancement of optical flow estimation [5] and unsupervised homography network [3], we adopt the photometric loss and smoothness loss to optimize the result to deal with the lacking of labeled data. Given the pyramid of predicted dense correspondence map U^l between image I_a and I_b, we use Mean Absolute Error (MAE) and census loss [6] as the unsupervised photometric loss. For l-level, original image I_a and I_b are interpolated according to size of U^l, and the losses of this level can be defined as:

$$\mathcal{L}_{\text{diff}}^l = \sum_{i,j}^{M} \left\| p_a^l(i,j) - \hat{p}_b^l(i,j) \right\|_1 \tag{7}$$

$$\mathcal{L}_{\text{census}}^l = \sum_{i,j}^{M} d(c_a^l(i,j), c_b^l(i,j)) \tag{8}$$

where M is the number of pixels of the image at l-level, $p_a^l(i,j)$ is the small patch of 3×3 from I_a^l at coordinate (i,j), $d(\cdot)$ denotes the Hamming Distance, and $c_a^i(i,j)$ is the census code at (i,j). The smoothness loss is calculated with the gradient and can be formulated as:

$$\mathcal{L}_{\text{smooth}}^l = \sum_{d=x,y} \sum_{i,j}^{M} \left\| \nabla_d U^l \right\|_1 e^{-\left\| \nabla_d I_a^l \right\|_1}. \tag{9}$$

2.3   Homography Estimation Based on Dense Correspondence

The 3×3 homography is not suitable for regression as it combines different transformation components, and these components have different scales. An effective way to solve the homography matrix is to estimate the homogeneous correspondences of four corner points. The dense matching has already included disparity information of correspondent points, based on which the target of homography estimation is transferred to regressing four reliable offset vectors [2]. For corner $p_i : (u_i, v_i), i \in \{1, 2, 3, 4\}$, its correspondent point is $p_i' : (u_i', v_i')$, and its offset is $\Delta u_i = u_i' - u_i$, $\Delta v_i = v_i' - v_i$. The 4-point homography has an one-to-one mapping to the 3×3 matrix and can be parameterized as follows:

$$\mathbf{H}_{4point} = \begin{pmatrix} \Delta u_1 \; \Delta v_1 \\ \Delta u_2 \; \Delta v_2 \\ \Delta u_3 \; \Delta v_3 \\ \Delta u_4 \; \Delta v_4 \end{pmatrix} \tag{10}$$

For synthetic data, we use MSE loss as the homography loss. Let $\mathcal{L}_{\mathbf{H}}$ denote the similarity of estimated homography $\mathbf{H}_{4point}$ and the ground truth $\mathbf{H}_{4point}^{gt}$:

$$\mathcal{L}_{\mathbf{H}} = \left\| \mathbf{H}_{4point} - \mathbf{H}_{4point}^{gt} \right\|_2 \tag{11}$$

While for realistic data, since there is no ground truth, and the objects at different depth cannot align well with the same homography, using the same training approach would lead to suboptimal result, therefore, we adopt the triplet loss which is similar to [4]. I_a is warped to I_a' according to the estimated homography, and the feature maps of I_a, I_b and I_a' are denoted as F_a, F_b, F_a' respectively. Then the loss $\mathcal{L}_f$ between the three feature maps is formulated as follows:

$$\mathcal{L}_f = \max \left(\left\| F_a' - F_b \right\|_1 - \left\| F_a' - F_a \right\|_1 + margin, \; 0 \right) \tag{12}$$

3   Experiments

3.1   Evaluation Setup

Dataset. We evaluate our method on both synthetic and real-world dataset. For synthetic one, we follow the setting of [2] on MS-COCO [7]. For real-world one, we choose the dataset from [4], and follow the same training and testing split. To fit the data in our network, we slightly enlarge the patch size to 576×320.

Training Details. We train the dense correspondence from scratch. The network is trained by Adam optimizer for $100k$ iterations, the parameter settings are $l_r^1 = 1.0 \times 10^{-4}$, $\beta_1^1 = 0.9$, $\beta_2^1 = 0.999$, $\epsilon^1 = 1.0 \times 10^{-7}$. The batch size is set to 16. 2 NVIDIA 1080Ti GPUs are used for the training process, and the training takes $\sim$24 h for synthetic dataset, and $\sim$48 h for realistic dataset.

Table 1. Evaluation on synthetic dataset.

Methods	Error
ORB [8] + RANSAC [9]	11.70
SURF [10] + RANSAC [9]	8.97
HomographyNet [2]	9.2
Ours (w/. pre-train only)	2.85
Ours (scratch)	2.56

3.2   Performance Comparisons

Quantitative Comparison. As illustrated in Table 1, we first compare our methods with traditional feature-based methods and the supervised method [2] on synthetic dataset. For feature-based methods, we choose ORB [8] and SURF [10] as the feature extractors and RANSAC [9] as the outlier rejection method. The error evaluates the MSE loss between predicted vectors of 4 corners with the ground truth H_{4point}. The HomographyNet [2] can achieve better performance than the feature-based methods, and our HfF-Net outperforms both the feature-based methods and the supervised one. We also implemented a version whose dense correspondence is trained on Sintel dataset [11] and frozen during homography training. The images from MS-COCO [7] have rich texture, and the dense correspondence estimation network without fine-tuning can perform as well as the one trained from scratch on the synthetic dataset.

Table 2. Evaluation on realistic dataset.

Methods	RE	LT	LL	SF	LF	Avg
ORB [8] + RANSAC [9]	1.85	3.76	2.56	2.00	2.29	2.49
SIFT [1] + RANSAC [9]	1.72	2.56	4.97	1.82	1.84	2.58
HomographyNet [2]	7.12	7.53	6.86	7.83	4.46	6.76
Unsupervised [3]	1.88	3.21	2.27	1.93	1.97	2.25
DeepHomography [4]	1.81	1.90	1.94	1.75	1.72	1.82
Ours (w/. pre-train only)	4.12	5.02	4.89	4.56	4.35	4.50
Ours (scratch)	3.00	3.99	3.95	3.04	3.05	3.41
Ours (Triplet Loss & scratch)	1.90	2.65	2.36	1.98	2.29	2.24

The performance of our method on the real-world dataset [4] is demonstrated in Table 2, the real-world dataset is split into different scenes: regular (**RE**), low-texture (**LT**), low-light (**LL**), small-foreground (**SF**) and large-foreground (**LF**). There are 6–8 matching points for each image pair [4], and the evaluation is the MSE error between warped points and target points. Our method achieve better performance than supervised method [2], however, our method cannot outperform the [4]. The reason could be that our matching part cannot predict well on the low-textual and low-light scenes, and the unreliable correspondence influences the performance of the final homography estimation.

Qualitative Comparison. We also qualitatively compare our method with supervised method [2], as displayed in Fig. 3. The left two columns are the input image pairs, the middle column is the result of [2], and the right two columns are the result of our network and the dense correspondence respectively. From the dense correspondence, we can observe clear warping field, and thanks to the correspondence map, our method can produce more reliable homography than [2]. Also, the results show that our method can align two images more precisely.

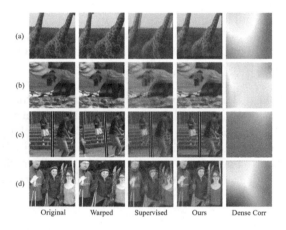

Original   Warped   Supervised   Ours   Dense Corr

Fig. 3. Visualization of the results of our method and the supervised method.

Ablation Study. As displayed at the bottom of Table 1 and Table 2, the dense correspondence map trained from scratch on the target dataset is essential and effective. On synthetic data, the dense matching pre-trained on Sintel [11] can work as well as the dense correspondence trained from scratch. However, the result on real-world data is not satisfying, because the pre-trained model cannot adapt to the new scenes and the dense correspondence is inaccurate and misleading for later homography estimation. It results from the domain variance between the Sintel and realistic dataset. The improvement of accuracy after we train the network on realistic dataset from scratch demonstrates the effectiveness of dense correspondence training. For loss function on real-world dataset, as shown at the bottom of Table 2, triplet loss is more suitable for homography task and can benefit all scenes. The triplet loss can evaluate the performance of final alignment and fit with all kinds of dataset, while the MSE loss can only work on synthetic data. The results also show the in-feasibility of directly transferring training method and loss function from synthetic dataset to realistic dataset.

4   Conclusions

In this paper, we design a new framework for deep homography estimation based on unsupervised dense correspondence, distinguished from existing methods which are mainly based on RGB images. To learn a reliable dense correspondence map, we utilize photometric loss and smoothness loss to restrain the training process, and then the dense correspondence facilitates the homography estimation. In order to obtain credible homography on both synthetic and realistic dataset, we apply supervised loss for generated data and triplet loss for real-world data. The evaluation and visualization results reveal the competitive performance of our methods and the effectiveness of dense correspondence map. Benefited from the coarse-to-fine architecture, our network can deal with large displacements. The ablation study also demonstrates the importance of the training of dense correspondence on target dataset due to the domain variance.

References

1. Lowe, D.G.: Distinctive image features from scale-invariant keypoints. Int. J. Comput. Vis. 91–110 (2004)
2. DeTone, D., Malisiewicz, T., Rabinovich, A.: Deep image homography estimation (2016)
3. Nguyen, T., Chen, S.W., Shivakumar, S.S., Taylor, C.J., Kumar, V.: Unsupervised deep homography: a fast and robust homography estimation model. IEEE Robot. Autom. Lett. 3(3), 2346–2353 (2018)
4. Zhang, J., et al.: Content-Aware unsupervised deep homography estimation. In: Vedaldi, A., Bischof, H., Brox, T., Frahm, J.-M. (eds.) ECCV 2020. LNCS, vol. 12346, pp. 653–669. Springer, Cham (2020). https://doi.org/10.1007/978-3-030-58452-8_38
5. Liu, L., et al.: Learning by analogy: Reliable supervision from transformations for unsupervised optical flow estimation. In: Proceedings of the IEEE/CVF Conference on Computer Vision and Pattern Recognition (CVPR), June 2020
6. Meister, S., Hur, J., Roth, S.: Unsupervised learning of optical flow with a bidirectional census loss. CoRR Unflow (2017)
7. Lin, T.-Y.: Microsoft COCO: common objects in context. CoRR (2014)
8. Rublee, E., Rabaud, V., Konolige, K., Bradski, G.: ORB: an efficient alternative to sift or surf. In: 2011 International Conference on Computer Vision, pp. 2564–2571 (2011)
9. Fischler, M.A., Bolles, R.C.: Random sample consensus: a paradigm for model fitting with applications to image analysis and automated cartography. Commun. ACM 24(6), 381–395 (1981)
10. Bay, H., Ess, A., Tuytelaars, T., Van Gool, L.: Speeded-up robust features (surf). In: Computer Vision and Image Understanding, pp. 346–359 (2008)
11. Butler, D.J., Wulff, J., Stanley, G.B., Black, M.J.: A naturalistic open source movie for optical flow evaluation. In: Fitzgibbon, A., Lazebnik, S., Perona, P., Sato, Y., Schmid, C. (eds.) ECCV 2012. LNCS, vol. 7577, pp. 611–625. Springer, Heidelberg (2012). https://doi.org/10.1007/978-3-642-33783-3_44

Progressive Inpainting Strategy with Partial Convolutions Generative Networks (PPCGN)

Liang Nie[1], Wenxin Yu[1(✉)], Siyuan Li[1], Zhiqiang Zhang[2], Ning Jiang[1], Xuewen Zhang[1], and Jun Gong[3]

[1] Southwest University of Science and Technology, Mianyang, Sichuan, China
yuwenxin@swust.edu.cn
[2] Hosei University, Tokyo, Japan
[3] Beijing Institute of Technology, Beijing, China

Abstract. Recently, there have been great advances in many one-stage image inpainting methods. They may have a slight advantage in computation time but lack sufficient context information for inpainting. These inpainting approaches can not inpaint large holes naturalist. This paper proposes a progressive image inpainting algorithm with partial convolution generative networks for solving the above problem. It consists of a generator with partial convolution layers, a fully convolutional discriminative network, and a long short-term memory (LSTM) module. PPCGN has four steps to inpaint the image. Each Step will concentrate on a specific area for inpainting. The final generation results are completed by the cooperation of these four steps, which are connected through the LSTM module. Due to the partial convolution module and LSTM structure characteristics, our method has a good advantage in restoring the images with large holes and achieves better objective results, increasing 1.46 dB and 0.44 dB on the Paris Street View dataset, and CelebA dataset, respectively.

Keywords: Partial convolution · LSTM · Progressive image inpainting · Generative adversarial networks

1 Introduction

Historically, traditional image restoration tasks can be roughly summarized into two types. The first class is based on diffusion [2] as the high redundancy of image information. However, pixel diffusion will lead the inpainting results blurry, so this method does not work with richly textured images. Another is the sample-based approach proposed by the assumption of spatial correlation [1]. This method copies the patches from the general area and filling them in the appropriate stations. However, seeking similar patches needs much calculation. Consequently, it unsuitable for repairing super-resolution pictures.

© Springer Nature Switzerland AG 2021
T. Mantoro et al. (Eds.): ICONIP 2021, CCIS 1517, pp. 640–647, 2021.
https://doi.org/10.1007/978-3-030-92310-5_74

In recent years, more and more researchers begin to use deep learning-based methods. In 2016, Pathak et al. [9] first proposed Context Encoders for image reconstruction, which adopted a encoder-decoder structure. The experimental results show that the learning-based methods can better build the image's semantic information to deal with the large missing areas. After that, Iizuka et al. [5] proposed some different learning-based image inpainting schemes in other scenarios. Unfortunately, these approaches still have some problems, such as artifact, ambiguity, and incoherent semantic information, which needs to be continuously improved.

Therefore, this paper proposes a partial convolution [8] generative adversarial network based on the progressive repair strategy (see Fig. 1).

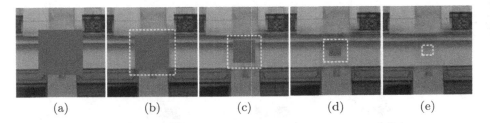

$$(a) \qquad\qquad (b) \qquad\qquad (c) \qquad\qquad (d) \qquad\qquad (e)$$

Fig. 1. PPCGN' inpainting result in different phase. (a) is the input of phase 1. (b) is the result from phase 1, and the next phase's input. (c) is generated by phase 2 and will send to phase 3. (d) is from phase 3. (e) is the final inpainting result from phase 4 with d as the input. As shown in the pictures, in each image, the missing area will shrink at the outside.

2   Related Work

2.1   Deep Learning

In deep learning, the convolution method plays a vital role. The dilated convolution [1] applies the adjacent elements in the convolution kernel to separated a certain distance to increase the receptive field while keeping the parameters constant. Depthwise convolution [3] divides a convolution operation into several smaller convolution operations to increase computing speed. However, none of these convolution methods can reasonably use the image's useful information.

The invalid pixels in the missing region will interfere with the inpainting results to produce artifacts. We slove this problem by utilizing partial convolution [8]. Partial convolution can dynamically decide the diverse contributions to loss with the mask in different layers. This strategy makes the training process appear that shrink the hole from the edge to the center gradually.

2.2   Image Inpainting

To inpaint large holes, Zhang et al. [11], and Li et al. [7] suggested progressive inpainting tactics, which fill from the invalid region's boundary and gradually approaching its center area. They believe that the boundary is more relaxed to imagine than the center area. Although this strategy decreases the difficulty of semantic image inpainting successfully. It still involves invalid pixels in the restoration process, resulting in inconsistencies between the filled and known regions.

Although the above semantic image inpainting methods can produce visually satisfy content, they sometimes fail to produce satisfactory structure, especially when the object layout is complicated.

3   Proposed Approach

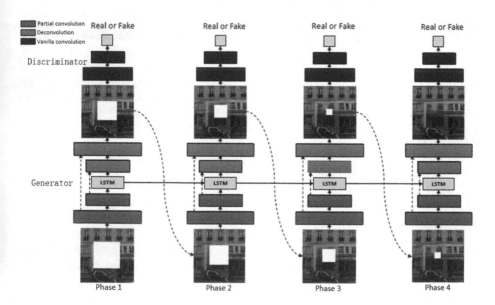

Fig. 2. Here is the whole networks proposed in this paper.

3.1   Network Structure

Generator Network. An excellent generator, which can directly affect image generation's quality, plays a vital role in image inpainting. Unlike Context-Enconder's streamlined pipeline design, the PPCGN's generator uses a codec similar to the U-NET architecture.

Besides, partial convolution is introduced into the encoder for image feature extraction. The partial convolution formula is as follows:

$$x'_{(i,j)} = \begin{cases} \mathbf{W}^T \left(\mathbf{X}_{(i,j)} \odot \mathbf{M}_{(i,j)} \right) r_{(i,j)}, & \left\| \mathbf{M}_{(i,j)} \right\|_1 > 0 \\ 0, & \text{otherwise} \end{cases} \qquad (1)$$

$$r_{(i,j)} = \frac{\left\| \mathbf{1}_{(i,j)} \right\|_1}{\left\| \mathbf{M}_{(i,j)} \right\|_1} \qquad (2)$$

where $\odot$ denotes element-wise multiplication. $\mathbf{1}_{(i,j)}$ has all elements with 1 and the same shape as $M_{(i,j)}$. M is the mask which 0 for holes and 1 for others. Subscripts i and j are the coordinate in the center of the current window of the raw image. As can be seen, $x'_{(i,j)}$ depend only on the unmasked inputs. The scaling factor $r_{(i,j)}$ applies appropriate scaling to adjust for the varying amount of valid (unmasked) inputs. As we can see, only the valid pixels can fill holes. The whole generator network is shown in Fig. 2.

Discriminator Network. Because of the adversarial training strategy, the discriminator is also significant. The discriminator is used to decide whether an image is real or generated by the generator. A simple generator can also get good convergence. However, it cannot guarantee that the generated image looks natural. Discriminator can be regarded as another guide to the adversarial training process. Similar to the previous work, in this paper, fully convolutional discriminative networks (PatchGAN) is used, which can judge whether a small patch is real or not.

Long and Short Term Memory Modules. We divide the semantic image inpainting task into several subtasks. We connect them through the LSTM module. The structure of the LSTM network is shown in Fig. 3.

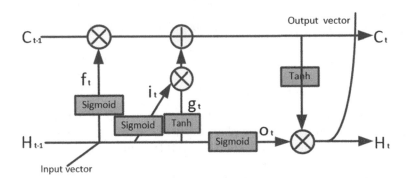

Fig. 3. This is the LSTM module.

At time t, C_t is the LSTM cell state, and H_t is its hidden state. Besides, i_t, f_t, g_t, and o_t are input, forget, cell, and output gates, respectively. The output data is a 2048-dimensional vector, which is generated by the hidden state of LSTM.

We combine the 2048-dimensional vector with the 512-dimensional vector to form a 2560-dimensional feature map sent to the decoder.

3.2 Loss Function

Reconstruction Loss. For generator, we use the L_1 loss as reconstruction loss, which has been proved to be effective in previous-generation models. Suppose the input of each stage is X_i (obviously X_1 is the original image to be repaired), then

$$x_{i+1} = G(x_i) \tag{3}$$

$$L_{rec}^{(i)} = \|G(x_i) - \hat{x} \odot M_{i+1}\|_1 \tag{4}$$

G is the generator. $\hat{x}$ represents the ground truth image.

Adversarial Loss. Adversarial loss comes from the generative adversarial network (GAN) proposed by Goodfellow et al. [4]. Adversarial loss is defined as:

$$L_{adv}^{(i)} = \max_D E\left[\log\left(D\left(\hat{x} \odot M_{i+1}\right)\right) + \log\left(1 - D\left(G\left(x_i\right)\right)\right)\right] \tag{5}$$

The adversarial loss function jointly optimizes the generator (G) and discriminator (D).

Total Variation Loss. Total variation (TV) loss is quite common in denoising and deblurring. As it can help spread image intensity smoothly, it is also widely used in image inpainting tasks. Similarly, this paper also adds a TV loss in PPCGN, as follows:

$$L_{tv} = \sum_{m,n} \left((x_{m,n+1} - x_{m,n})^2 + (x_{m+1,n} - x_{m,n})^2\right) \tag{6}$$

Subscripts m and n are the relative positions of pixels in the image.

4 Experiment

4.1 Quantitative Comparison

We compare PPCGN with GMCNN [10] (Image inpainting via generative multi-column convolutional neural networks), CA + lid [6] (Generative image inpainting with submanifold alignment), and PGN [11] (Semantic image inpainting with progressive generative networks).

Our method has dramatically improved image generation quality and the quantization results shown in Table 1. As we can see, on the Paris Street View dataset, our method improves 1.46 dB on PSNR compared to the previous method, which is a considerable improvement. In Celeba's face dataset, the PSNR value was improved by 0.44 dB. This is attributed to the full utilization of effective information in damaged images by LSTM network architecture and partial convolution module.

Table 1. Quantitative results on Paris StreetView and CelebA testing datasets.

Method	Pairs StreetView PSNR	CelebA PSNR
GMCNN	23.78	24.56
PGN	24.65	22.38
LID (CA)	23.86	24.35
Ours	**25.32**	**24.79**

4.2 Qualitative Comparison

We randomly selected two groups of repair results from two datasets for comparison. On the dataset of pairs street view, the restoration results (as show in Fig. 4) of the method in this paper are more abundant in texture. At the same time, the method in this paper significantly reduces artifacts and makes the results look realistic.

On the Celeba dataset (as show in Fig. 5), this method can generate more reasonable semantic content. As you can see, when the face is almost completely be covered, the other methods either produce a bunch of blurry patches of color or no distinct features (eyes, mouth, and nose). However, our method can generate a full face, and the result looks very natural.

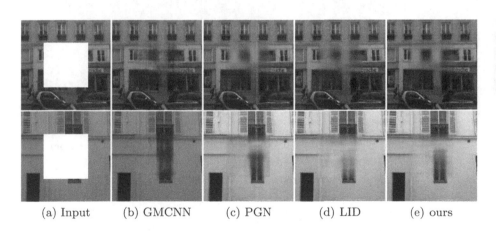

(a) Input   (b) GMCNN   (c) PGN   (d) LID   (e) ours

Fig. 4. Here is the PPCGN' inpainting result on Paris StreetView.

4.3 Ablation Study

With or Without Partial Convolution. We replace the full convolution layer with the partial convolution layer without changing the network structure. Then the two networks are trained respectively, and the results are shown in

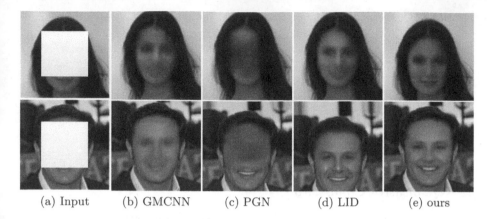

(a) Input   (b) GMCNN   (c) PGN   (d) LID   (e) ours

Fig. 5. Here is the PPCGN' inpainting result on CelebA.

Fig. 6. Using partial convolution is more comfortable to generate meaningful semantic content. Compared with without the addition of partial convolution, the artifacts of the restoration results are reduced to a certain extent after the addition of partial convolution.

(a) Input   (b) With PConv.   (c) Without PConv.

Fig. 6. Results of different phases.

5   Conclusion

We present a novel progressive image inpainting method. It is divided into four stages. Every stage is consists of a codec with partial convolution. Moreover, the corresponding discriminator is used for adversarial training. Our method can gradually reduce the area of damage step by step. Finally, we use an LSTM module to connect the four phases for gaining promising inpainting results. Especially in the dataset of Paris Street View, due to the more complex structure of the dataset, the previous methods can not effectively complete the inpainting task with missing large holes. However, the method in this paper can use partial convolution and LSTM network to gradually acquire the effective information of the image and discard the invalid information. As a result, a significant increase of 1.46 dB (PSNR) was achieved on the paris street view dataset. Celeba also improved by 0.44 dB (PSNR) over previous approaches and generated richer semantic information.

Acknowledgement. This research is supported by Sichuan Science and Technology Program (No. 2020YFS0307, No. 2020YFG0430, No. 2019YFS0146), Mianyang Science and Technology Program (No. 2020YFZJ016).

References

1. Bengio, S., Vinyals, O., Jaitly, N., Shazeer, N.: Scheduled sampling for sequence prediction with recurrent neural networks. In: Advances in Neural Information Processing Systems, pp. 1171–1179 (2015)
2. Bertalmio, M., Vese, L., Sapiro, G., Osher, S.: Simultaneous structure and texture image inpainting. IEEE Trans. Image Process. **8**, 882–889 (2003)
3. Chollet, F.: Xception: Deep learning with depthwise separable convolutions. In: Proceedings of the IEEE conference on computer vision and pattern recognition. pp. 1251–1258 (2017)
4. Goodfellow, I., et al.: Generative adversarial nets. In: Ghahramani, Z., Welling, M., Cortes, C., Lawrence, N., Weinberger, K.Q. (eds.) Advances in Neural Information Processing Systems, vol. 27, pp. 2672–2680. Curran Associates, Inc. (2014)
5. Iizuka, S., Simo-Serra, E., Ishikawa, H.: Globally and locally consistent image completion. ACM Trans.n Graph. (ToG) **4**, 1–14 (2017)
6. Li, A., Qi, J., Zhang, R., Ma, X., Ramamohanarao, K.: Generative image inpainting with submanifold alignment. arXiv preprint arXiv:1908.00211 (2019)
7. Li, J., He, F., Zhang, L., Du, B., Tao, D.: Progressive reconstruction of visual structure for image inpainting. In: Proceedings of the IEEE International Conference on Computer Vision, pp. 5962–5971 (2019)
8. Liu, G., Reda, F.A., Shih, K.J., Wang, T.C., Tao, A., Catanzaro, B.: Image inpainting for irregular holes using partial convolutions. In: Proceedings of the European Conference on Computer Vision (ECCV), pp. 85–100 (2018)
9. Pathak, D., Krahenbuhl, P., Donahue, J., Darrell, T., Efros, A.A.: Context encoders: feature learning by inpainting. In: Proceedings of the IEEE Conference on Computer Vision and Pattern Recognition, pp. 2536–2544 (2016)
10. Wang, Y., Tao, X., Qi, X., Shen, X., Jia, J.: Image inpainting via generative multi-column convolutional neural networks. In: Advances in Neural Information Processing Systems, pp. 331–340 (2018)
11. Zhang, H., Hu, Z., Luo, C., Zuo, W., Wang, M.: Semantic image inpainting with progressive generative networks. In: Proceedings of the 26th ACM International Conference on Multimedia, pp. 1939–1947 (2018)

Investigating Depression Semantics on Reddit

Swati Agarwal$^{(\boxtimes)}$, Keertan M, Parantak Singh, Jahanvi Shah,
and Nishanth Sanjeev

BITS Pilani, Goa Campus, Goa, India
agrswati@ieee.org, {f20160122,f20170109,f20160439,
f20170970}@goa.bits-pilani.ac.in

Abstract. Major depression is a challenging issue affecting individuals
and those of the people around them. This paper investigates the Reddit
comments for the automated identification of comments being indicative
of depressive behaviour. We measure the socio-psycho-linguistic attributes
as useful indicators and their importance for characterising the depression
content. We tested content-level classifiers on Reddit data. The proposed
BERT and BiLSTM with attention model outperform baseline machine
learning (ML) and deep learning (DL) models and achieve a weighted F1-
score of 0.81 and 0.84 respectively. Our results reveal that while semi-
supervised BERT underperform a few ML models, it still gives non-zero
classification and high class-wise precision for non-depressed class.

Keywords: Depression semantics · Psycho-linguistics · Word
embedding · Classification · Reddit

1 Introduction

Major Depressive Disorder (MDD), more commonly known as depression, exists
as a global illness that negatively affects upwards of 300 million people worldwide
[3]. The vast majority of individuals with MDD characteristics also endure indications of anxiety, troubled sleep and appetite, as well as manifestations that cannot
be explained by a medical examination [1]. Additionally, MDD has been established to be associated with a spectrum of chronic physical disorders, which, when
combined with a high risk of suicide, leads to the likelihood of early death. To diagnose an individual with the condition, an evaluation from a medical or psychological standpoint proves necessary [4]. However, this brings to light the issue of individuals who prefer to make their presence on online social media (OSM), compared
to an in-person admission of having symptoms of depression [5]. The content, language, emotions, and semantics in OSM posts can reveal feelings and mental state
of the user. Thus, OSM is a vital resource to study the language associated with
depression, self-harm, and suicide, as well as to comprehend the narrator's reasons
for penning such posts and classifying at-risk individuals [2]. The assessment of
OSM posts can provide access to a more abundant amount of critical information

© Springer Nature Switzerland AG 2021
T. Mantoro et al. (Eds.): ICONIP 2021, CCIS 1517, pp. 648–656, 2021.
https://doi.org/10.1007/978-3-030-92310-5_75

to clinicians which could prove instrumental in the further diagnosis of depression in patients. Over the last decade, several ML models are developed and employed on social media texts (especially Twitter) to determine the users showing indications of depressed behaviour. Literature survey shows that majority of the studies utilises probabilistic support vector machine (SVM) [5,16], logistic regression, naive bayes, and tree-based models for the classification. Furthermore, n-gram, topic modelling, and bag-of-words are some of the most commonly used approach in text processing [11]. Additionally, sentiment analysis, mood, part-of-speech, statistics extracted from LIWC, ANEW, AFINN, and labMT are the common features for training the model [8,14].

Recently, deep learning techniques have also been used popularity for depression text classification. Literature shows that deep convolutional neural Network (CNN) model has been employed on audio, video, and text for learning depressed and non-depressed behaviour patterns [18]. Further, long short-term memory (LSTM) model has been used to learn emoticons and emojis as separate features from text to classify depressed users [15,17]. Based on our literature survey, we observe that the differences in the paradigm and lengths of the user-generated posts make it arduous for them to be analysed. Furthermore, the nature of the user-generated text is largely ignored in the previous studies; i.e., the presence of grammatical and spelling errors, usage of slangs, and emojis as an integral part of the text. This paper aims to address these shortcomings with supplemental pre-processing techniques and leverage the feature analysis and characterisation of depressed comments for developing an automated classifier.

2   Experimental Dataset

Depression is a subjective domain and requires either experts' annotation or self-declaration of diagnosis. We collected the comments from within the feed of a very expressive and largely answered question asked on the AskReddit subreddit. The selected discussion thread (https://bit.ly/3hjUBSf) consisted of comments where users have opened up about depression, self-declaration of clinical diagnoses of depression, and other mental health-related issues. We extracted 6224 comments using Python Reddit API Wrapper (PRAW). Even though the comments represent the self-declaration of users diagnosed with depression. This, however, does not confirm that the comments belong to depression category. For example, a user may be sharing his/her experience of recovering from depression and hence the post does not belong to depression class. Thus, instead of marking subreddit comments as depressed, we perform a manual annotation on them and label non-depressed comments. We additionally observe the lack of publicly available datasets that highlight depression ideation and we seek to resolve that with our dataset. Co-authors annotated the comments based on DSM-5 diagnostic criteria and a few other thought-streams that emerge as a common theme across many users that transcribe their depression. Below are these criterion.

1. Depressed mood most of the day (MoD), nearly every day (NED).
2. Markedly diminished interest or pleasure in all, or almost all, activities MoD, NED.

3. Significant weight loss when not dieting or weight gain, or decrease or increase in appetite NED.
4. A slowing down of thought and a reduction of physical movement (observable by others).
5. Fatigue or loss of energy nearly every day.
6. Feelings of worthlessness or excessive or inappropriate guilt nearly every day.
7. Diminished ability to think or concentrate, or indecisiveness, nearly every day.
8. Recurrent thoughts of death, recurrent suicidal ideation without a specific plan, or a suicide attempt or a specific plan for committing suicide.
9. Yearning for the existence of home, despite having one.
10. The constant entanglement of loneliness and emptiness; doesn't have to strictly mean being so in a physical space.

Based on the annotation results, the data consists of 4833 depressed (C1) and 1391 non-depressed (C0) comments revealing the class imbalance in the dataset.

2.1 Data Pre-processing

We divide data pre-processing into two steps - data cleaning and data enrichment. Data cleaning includes the steps to remove noisy content such as external URLs, along with any username mentions, and stopwords. We use regular expressions (RegEx) to expand the contractions and remove punctuation and special characters. Data enrichment includes making sense of emojis, spell error correction, and sequence generation. We propose to use emojis as an integral part of the post and identify hidden context from them. We used EmojiNet library that takes the Unicode value of an emoji as an input, and returns all possible textual representations. For example, U+1F604 is expanded as eye, smile, mouth, open, face. We used SymSpellPY to rectify misspelt words. Furthermore, spell check was employed after splitting contractions and removing punctuation, as it uses the edit distance algorithm to rectify misspelt words, which can otherwise lead to improper results. For example, the word "don't" could be changed to "done". Finally, we apply sequence generation and extract a vocabulary (34,693 unique tokens) from the training set prepared using (GloVe) embeddings. We provided a sequence of words (represented as tokens) to the network, such that, any arrangement, $A = [a_1, a_2, a_3, ..., a_k]$ where k denotes the length of said arrangement. We used the Keras tokeniser to tokenize the posts. Each sequence is assigned a fixed-length equal to the upper bound of average word length. After pre-processing, any posts with an empty set were removed, thus we had 6224 comments in the dataset after pre-processing. We split our dataset into three parts, i.e., training-validation-testing set in 70:15:15 (4356, 934, 934) ratio.

3   Features Extraction and Selection

We extract features using LIWC library which essentially quantifies the suggestive strengths of words in the document that could fall under various categories. While existing literature [5,7,14] uses all features extracted from LIWC, we selected the features that characterise the MDD on OSM. Inspired by the prior studies [6,9,10,13], we selected only six categories of attributes; i.e. affective, social, cognitive, perceptual, time, and self-addressal. From these categories, we select such attributes that represent social exclusion, inclusion, stressors, self-esteem, grievances, and personality traits. We use existing evidence-based mixed-method research to select these features from LIWC categories. We select all unique fields present in these six attributes and encompassing a feature set of 25 attributes (to see, to hear, to feel, past, present, future, I, we, insight, causation, discrepancy, tentative, certainty, differentiation). The subsequent columns represent psychological and emotional attributes, such as emotions polarity, sadness, anxiety, and more. We further included features that define social exclusion, inclusion, and stressors; represented using social category: "friend" and "family". We focus towards the socio and psycholinguistic features obtained from LIWC, as these features mainly help us differentiate between usual and MDD-indicative posts.

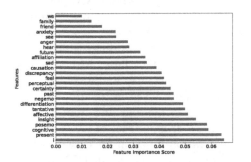

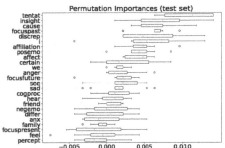

Fig. 1. Feature importance scores   **Fig. 2.** Permutation feature importance.

We employed the Extra Trees classifier to account for the variability of different trees and express the explanatory power of different features. We used permutation importance to cross check for overfitting and to allay the limitations if necessary. Figure 1 and 2 shows the feature importance and permutation importance score of 25 attributes. Since permuterm importance is calculated after a model has been fitted, Fig. 2 shows the importance score for test data. Boxplots in Fig. 2 reveal that the importance of features in different set (real or permuted) is similar to a negligible variation (swapped).

4   Classification

We employ the Bidirectional Encoder Representations from Transformers (**BERT**), given the overwhelming evidence of its success. We use the pre-trained bert-base-cased model as provided by huggingface. Inspired by [12], we set the batch size, learning rate, optimiser, and epochs to be respectively 32, 5e−5, Adam optimiser, and 3. We additionally try a semi-supervised approach **BERT-ss**, where we fine-tune our BERT model on 10% of the training data, perform label propagation on the other 90% data. We fine-tune BERT yet again on the entire training data assuming that dataset can be scarce and diffused. We observe that themes of depression are very recurrent; thus supporting our hypothesis and approach. We also employ Bidirectional LSTM (**BiLSTM**) with and without attention layer model. We utilise BiLSTM with 100 units, which can capture the temporal information of a sequence both forwardly and backwardly. We additionally use Keras Embedding layer, with pre-trained vectors (GloVe Common Crawl, 300 dimensions, 42 billion tokens and 'context-aware attention' as an effort to mimic the actions of the human brain and. The model consists of 3 dense layers - the first two layers are 128 units each, with ReLU activation, and the output layer uses a sigmoid activation function. Dropout layers are present between these, with values of 0.4 and 0.2 each. We applied mini-batch gradient descent with a batch size of 32 for five epochs, along with the use of an Adam optimiser.

For baseline models, we use several ML models, i.e., SVM, gaussian naive bayes (NB), multinominal NB, K-nearest neighbor, logistic regression, and random forest. Additionally, CNN with maxpooling, multichannel CNN, and BiLSTM CNN are used for benchmarking deep learning models used in prior studies. CNN model architecture consists of an input layer to which text as a sequence is fed. An embedding matrix is formed using the GloVe embeddings which is fed into the embedding layer with trainable parameter set as false. Five different sizes of filters (2, 3, 4, 5, 6) are applied to each Conv1D layer and a GlobalMaxPooling1D layer is applied to each of them. A Dropout layer with a dropout rate of 0.1 is applied followed by a Dense layer with 128 neurons and 'relu' activation function. An additional Dropout layer with a dropout rate of 0.2 is applied succeeded by a Dense layer with 'sigmoid' activation function for classification. The CNN model can be improvised by employing multiple parallel CNNs that interprets the text sequences using different kernel sizes. This gives rise to the multichannel CNN that evaluates text sequences with different n-gram sizes. The implemented model architecture consists of three channels thus giving rise to three input layers in each channel to which the text sequence is fed. Each channel consists of an embedding layer to which the embedding matrix formed using the GloVe embeddings is fed. The different kernel sizes used in this model are 4, 6 and 8. Every channel comprises of a Conv1D layer with three different kernel sizes followed by a Dropout layer with a dropout rate of 0.5 and a GlobalMaxPooling1D layer of pool_size 2. All the three channels are flattened using the Flatten layer and concatenated into a single layer. The concatenated single layer is then passed through two Dense layers with 'relu' and 'sigmoid' activation functions respectively. For both regular and multichannel CNN, we have surveilled Binary Cross-Entropy loss with the use of Adam optimiser. The model is trained with a batch size of 1000 tweets over 5 epochs.

Further, Bi-LSTM CNN is a combination of CNN and BiLSTM. We aim to capture the features extracted using CNN, and use them as an LSTM input. Therefore, we employ a model such that the vectors built in the word embedding part are used as CNN input. 128 filters of size 3 are applied and after that a layer of max pooling is applied to update and reduce the size of the data. Then the results of all max pooling layers are concatenated to build the BiLSTM input. The output of this step is the input to a Global Max pooling layer followed by 3 Dense layers, the first two with 128 units each using ReLU activation followed by the last layer using sigmoid activation function. We applied mini-batch gradient descent with a batch size of 32 for six epochs and used Adam optimiser.

5   Experimental Results

As discussed above, the distribution of C0 (1391) and C1 (4833) instances reveal the imbalance in the original data. The Reddit dataset was split into training-validation-testing set in 70:15:15 percentile ratio. Out of 6224 instances, 4356 (3386 C1, 970 C0) were used for training while 934 (716, 218) instances for validation and 934 (731, 203) instances were used for testing set. Table 1 shows the detailed performance results of all proposed and baseline models. The results reveal that majority of ML models have poor precision due to not learning enough about class C0. Since the model learns specifically from C1 class, it increases the overall recall of the model and results into a very high recall for C1 but affecting the recall of C0 going less than 10% for regression model. Eventually, the macro f1-score (based on number of instances) is very poor. Our results reveal that the proposed BiLSTM with attention model outperforms both ML and DL models. BERT model gives a high macro f1-score of 0.71 which is higher than all baseline ML models. It is observed that several time BERT is unable to capture longer sequences better, hence it underperforms BiLSTM with attention model. CNN, however, results into 0 classification when employed in multichannel architecture.

Table 1. Performance of proposed models benchmarked against baseline models

Model	Precision				Recall				F1 score			
	Macro	Weighted	C0	C1	Macro	Weighted	C0	C1	Macro	Weighted	C0	C1
BiLSTM	0.69	0.77	0.55	0.83	0.63	0.8	0.34	0.92	0.65	0.78	0.42	0.88
BiLSTM + attention	0.76	0.84	0.63	0.9	0.77	0.84	0.65	0.89	0.77	0.84	0.64	0.9
CNN + BiLSTM	0.72	0.8	0.56	0.87	0.71	0.81	0.54	0.88	0.71	0.81	0.55	0.88
CNN (maxpool)	0.87	0.83	0.94	0.8	0.54	0.8	0.08	1	0.52	0.73	0.15	0.89
Multichannel CNN	0.39	0.61	0	0.78	0.5	0.78	0	1	0.44	0.69	0	0.88
BERT	0.77	0.82	0.69	0.85	0.68	0.83	0.41	0.95	0.71	0.81	0.52	0.9
BERT SS	0.81	0.82	0.79	0.82	0.61	0.82	0.24	0.98	0.63	0.78	0.37	0.9
SVM	0.39	0.61	0	0.78	0.5	0.78	0	1	0.44	0.69	0	0.88
Gaussian NB	0.67	0.77	0.51	0.84	0.64	0.79	0.38	0.9	0.65	0.78	0.44	0.87
Random Forest	0.74	0.79	0.66	0.83	0.63	0.81	0.3	0.96	0.65	0.78	0.41	0.89
K-Nearest Neighbor	0.67	0.75	0.54	0.81	0.57	0.79	0.19	0.95	0.58	0.75	0.28	0.88
Multinominal NB	0.55	0.7	0.29	0.81	0.56	0.67	0.38	0.75	0.55	0.68	0.33	0.78
Logistic Regression	0.73	0.77	0.66	0.8	0.54	0.79	0.09	0.99	0.52	0.73	0.16	0.79

Additionally, Figs. 3 and 4 show the ROC curves for ML and DL models validated on Reddit data. Figure 3 reveals that except Gaussian NB model, all

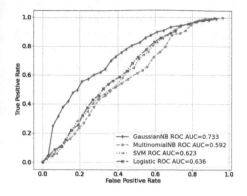

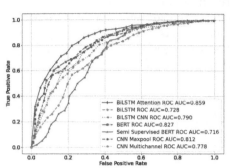

Fig. 3. ML classifiers results   **Fig. 4.** DL classifiers results

other ML models perform poorly (nearly baseline accuracy). Further, the TPR is fluctuating across the FPR values. Whereas, Fig. 4 shows that all DL models perform significant well as compared to ML models. BiLSTM with attention model has maximum AUC value of 0.859 which is significantly larger than CNN models and its variants. Furthermore, BERT gives second highest AUC after BiLSTM+attention model. Proposed BERT model even outperforms popularly used BiLSTM, BiLSTM CNN, and CNN maxpool models. Further, our results confirm that the proposed models are not being overfitted across LIWC features.

5.1   Characterisation of Depression Semantics

We divide each comment into sentences to make a segmented corpus and generate parsing dependencies. We extract entities along with their modifiers and compound entities so as to minimize the chance of abandoning a multi worded entity followed by extraction of ROOT (verb) of the dependency tree serving as a relation between two entities. We used these relations to analyse the context and words that are most often related to depressive symptoms such as "hate", "sucks", "sad", "tired", "feel", "abuse" etc. We map the association between words by computing the normalized eigenvector centrality of each word ranging between $[0, 1]$. We find that the entities "I", "me", and "it" are commonly present in C1 class comments. The relation R between two entities $< E1, R, E2 >$ reveals the emotional range, feeling, social relation, and context of the entities. For example, $<$it, feels like, crap$>$ and $<$depression, want, just emptiness$>$. This KG also helps to understand the word semantics and relationship between indirect entities in depression posts. These relations can further be used for pre-training purposes.

6   Conclusions and Future Work

This paper aimed to identify text-based indicatives of depression from Reddit comments. We extracted LIWC based socio-psycho-linguistic features and exploited emojis by mapping them to their respective textual meaning. Our results reveal that proposed BiLSTM with attention model outperformed all baseline DL and ML models with a significant margin. Further, transforming emojis to text proved instrumental towards improving the performance of our mdoels. The misclassification in the prediction is due to the variety in clinical diagnoses and user behaviour on OSM. The characterisation of subreddits reveals that the entity relationships are useful for learning the semantics in depression posts.

References

1. Alías-Ferri, M., et al.: Cocaine and depressive disorders: when standard clinical diagnosis is insufficient. Adicciones **33**(3), 1321 (2020)
2. Berryman, C., Ferguson, C.J., Negy, C.: Social media use and mental health among young adults. Psychiatr. Q. **89**(2), 307–314 (2018)
3. Cacheda, F., Fernandez, D., Novoa, F.J., Carneiro, V.: Early detection of depression: social network analysis and random forest techniques. J. Med. Internet Res. **21**(6), e12554 (2019)
4. Clark, L.A., Cuthbert, B., Lewis-Fernández, R., Narrow, W.E., Reed, G.M.: Three approaches to understanding and classifying mental disorder: Icd-11, dsm-5, and the national institute of mental health's research domain criteria (rdoc). Psychol. Sci. Public Interest **18**(2), 72–145 (2017)
5. De Choudhury, M., Counts, S., Horvitz, E.: Social media as a measurement tool of depression in populations. In: 5th ACM WebSci, pp. 47–56 (2013)
6. Dillon, A., Timulak, L., Greenberg, L.S.: Transforming core emotional pain in a course of emotion-focused therapy for depression: a case study. Psychother. Res. **28**(3), 406–422 (2018)
7. Islam, M.R., Kabir, M.A., Ahmed, A., Kamal, A.R.M., Wang, H., Ulhaq, A.: Depression detection from social network data using machine learning techniques. Health Inf. Sci. Syst. **6**(1), 1–12 (2018). https://doi.org/10.1007/s13755-018-0046-0
8. Jamil, Z., Inkpen, D., Buddhitha, P., White, K.: Monitoring tweets for depression to detect at-risk users. In: Fourth Workshop on CLPsych@ACL, pp. 32–40 (2017)
9. Krauss, S., Orth, U., Robins, R.W.: Family environment and self-esteem development: a longitudinal study from age 10 to 16. J. Pers. Soc. Psychol. **119**(2), 457 (2020)
10. Loula, R., Monteiro, L.: An individual-based model for predicting the prevalence of depression. Ecol. Complex. **38**, 168–172 (2019)
11. Nguyen, T., Phung, D., Dao, B., Venkatesh, S., Berk, M.: Affective and content analysis of online depression communities. IEEE Transactions on Affective Computing **5**(3), 217–226 (2014)
12. Orabi, A.H., Buddhitha, P., Orabi, M.H., Inkpen, D.: Deep learning for depression detection of twitter users. In: Proceedings of the Fifth Workshop on Computational Linguistics and Clinical Psychology: From Keyboard to Clinic, pp. 88–97 (2018)
13. Orth, U., Robins, R.W.: Development of self-esteem across the lifespan. Handbook of Personality Development, p. 328 (2018)
14. Reece, A.G., Reagan, A.J., Lix, K.L., Dodds, P.S., Danforth, C.M., Langer, E.J.: Forecasting the onset and course of mental illness with twitter data. Sci. Rep. **7**(1), 1–11 (2017)

15. Shetty, N.P., Muniyal, B., Anand, A., Kumar, S., Prabhu, S.: Predicting depression using deep learning and ensemble algorithms on raw twitter data. Int. J. Electr. Comput. Eng. **10**, 2088–8708 (2020)
16. Tsugawa, S., Kikuchi, Y., Kishino, F., Nakajima, K., Itoh, Y., Ohsaki, H.: Recognizing depression from twitter activity. In: Proceedings of the 33rd Annual ACM Conference on Human Factors in Computing Systems, pp. 3187–3196 (2015)
17. Vivek, D., Balasubramanie, P.: An ensemble learning model to predict mental depression disorder using tweets. J. Med. Imag. Health Inform. **10**(1), 143–151 (2020)
18. Yang, L., Jiang, D., Xia, X., Pei, E., Oveneke, M.C., Sahli, H.: Multimodal measurement of depression using deep learning models. In: Proceedings of the 7th Annual Workshop on Audio/Visual Emotion Challenge, pp. 53–59 (2017)

ViMQ: A Vietnamese Medical Question Dataset for Healthcare Dialogue System Development

Ta Duc Huy$^{(\boxtimes)}$ iD, Nguyen Anh Tu, Tran Hoang Vu, Nguyen Phuc Minh, Nguyen Phan, Trung H. Bui, and Steven Q. H. Truong

VinBrain, Hanoi, Vietnam
{v.huyta,v.tunguyen,v.vutran,v.minhng,v.nguyenphan,
v.brain01}@vinbrain.net

Abstract. Existing medical text datasets usually take the form of question and answer pairs that support the task of natural language generation, but lacking the composite annotations of the medical terms. In this study, we publish a Vietnamese dataset of medical questions from patients with sentence-level and entity-level annotations for the Intent Classification and Named Entity Recognition tasks. The tag sets for two tasks are in medical domain and can facilitate the development of task-oriented healthcare chatbots with better comprehension of queries from patients. We train baseline models for the two tasks and propose a simple self-supervised training strategy with span-noise modelling that substantially improves the performance. Dataset and code will be published at https://github.com/tadeephuy/ViMQ.

Keywords: NER · Intent classification · Medical question dataset · Self-supervised · Learning with noise

1 Introduction

Named Entity Recognition (NER) involves extracting certain entities in a sentence and classifying them into a defined set of tags such as organizations, locations, dates, time, or person names. In the medical domain, NER tag sets usually contain patient information and clinical terms. Intent Classification (IC) is the task of categorizing a sequence into a set of defined intentions. In the medical domain, IC classes could include the conversation objectives in interactions between patients and clinical experts. NER and IC are two major components of a task-oriented dialogue system. There exist several medical conversation datasets in English [2], German [6], and Chinese [2,9], while Vietnamese medical conversation datasets are not abundant. COVID-19 NER for Vietnamese [7] is a dataset for the named entity recognition task with generalized entity types that can extend its application to other future epidemics. The dataset is crawled from Vietnamese online news websites with the keyword "COVID" and filtered out irrelevant sentences, resulting in 34,984 entities and 10,027 sentences.

© Springer Nature Switzerland AG 2021
T. Mantoro et al. (Eds.): ICONIP 2021, CCIS 1517, pp. 657–664, 2021.
https://doi.org/10.1007/978-3-030-92310-5_76

To our knowledge, we are the first to publish a Vietnamese Medical Question dataset (ViMQ) that contains medical NER and IC tags set where the applications could be generalized to developing the Natural Language Understanding (NLU) module for healthcare chatbots.

NER annotation includes highlighting the span of a given entity and assigning an appropriate tag. Specifying the spans of the entities can raise consensus issues stemming from the subjectivity of different annotators while classifying entities into tags are far more compliant due to the distinctiveness of the tags. In this paper, we developed an annotation methodology that aims to minimize this effect. In addition, NER annotation tools with poor ergonomic design can contribute to the span-noise, where the start and end indexes of a given span are shifted from their correct ground truth. We propose a training strategy to learn the model with such noise. To summarize, our contributions are:

- We published a Vietnamese Medical Question dataset for healthcare chatbot development.
- We proposed a training strategy to learn the model with span-noise for the NER task.

2   ViMQ Dataset

2.1   Intent and Entity Types

The ViMQ dataset contains Vietnamese medical questions crawled from the consultation section online between patients and doctors from www.vinmec.com, a website of a Vietnamese general hospital. Each consultation consists of a question regarding a specific health issue of a patient and a detailed respond provided by a clinical expert. The dataset contains health issues that fall into a wide range of categories including common illness, cardiology, hematology, cancer, pediatrics, etc. We removed sections where users ask about information of the hospital and selected 9,000 questions for the dataset. We annotated the questions for the NER and IC tasks. The tag sets for two tasks could be applied to a dialogue system for medical consultation scenario, where the chatbot acts as a medical assistant that inquires queries from users for their health issues. Each question is annotated for both tasks. The statistics of the labels are shown in Table 1.

Entity Definition: The tag set for NER includes SYMPTOM&DISEASE, MEDICAL_PROCEDURES and MEDICINE:

- SYMPTOM&DISEASE: any symptom or disease that appears in the sentence, including disease that are mentioned as part of a medicine such as "rabies" in "rabies vaccine".
- MEDICAL_PROCEDURE: actions provided by clinical experts to address the health issue of the patient, including diagnosing, measuring, therapeutic or surgical procedures.
- MEDICINE: any medicine name that appears in the sentence.

Table 1. Statistics of ViMQ dataset.

Entity type	Train	Valid	Test	All
SYMPTOM&DISEASE	10,599	1,300	1,354	13,253
MEDICAL_PROCEDURE	1,583	204	213	2,000
MEDICINE	781	90	108	979
Intent type	Train	Valid	Test	All
Diagnosis	3,444	498	484	4,426
Severity	1,070	150	162	1,382
Treatment	1,998	264	265	2,527
Cause	488	88	89	625

Intent Definition: The tag sets for IC includes Diagnosis, Severity, Treatment and Cause:

- Diagnosis: questions relating to identification of symptoms or diseases.
- Severity: questions relating to the conditions or grade of an illness.
- Treatment: questions relating to the medical procedures for an illness.
- Cause: questions relating to factors of a symptom or disease.

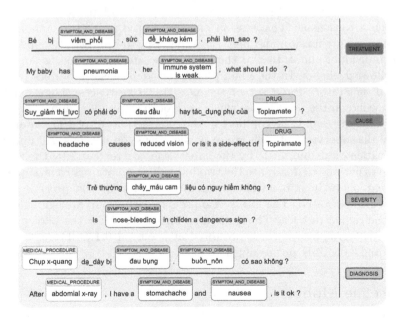

Fig. 1. Examples from ViMQ dataset. Each block includes the IC tag (right side) and the NER tags of an example from the dataset (above the horizontal line) and its English translation (below the horizontal line).

2.2 Annotation Process

We propose a novel method to manage the annotation process for the two tasks of NER and IC called Hierarchical Supervisors Seeding (HSS). The method circumvents around building a solid and consensual supervisor team which grows in size as the annotation process progresses. Leveraging a solid supervisor team mitigates the subjectivity and improves the task-oriented competency of individual annotators. Each supervisor, upon designated, does not only make mutual concessions for label disagreements of individual annotators but also acts as a seed to make way for them to become the next generation supervisors.

We first ran a pilot phase where 1,000 samples are selected for annotation, called the pilot set. The author of the annotation guideline is designated as the first supervisor, where two other NLP engineers are individual annotators. The two individual annotators follow the annotation guideline and annotate two overlapping sets of 600 sentences in the pilot set. The intersection of the two sets consisting of 100 sentences is also annotated by the supervisor and is used to measure the annotation quality of the two NLP engineers using F1-score. The intersection set is selected such that it covers a broad range of difficulties. Hard sentences contain rare diseases such as anxiety disorders, thalassemia. Easy sentences contain common diseases or symptoms such as flu, fever, and cold. Both individual annotators are required to achieve an F1-score of at least 0.9 on both tasks on the intersection set before discussing with the supervisor on the disagreement cases. The supervisor has to point out which parts of the annotation guideline could solve these conflicts and update the guideline until they reach a consensus. This session encourages the individual annotators to gain better comprehension and help the supervisor to improve the guideline.

Two individual annotators in the pilot phase are designated as supervisors in the following phases. In the main phase, each supervisor monitors two other individual annotators for a set of the next 1,000 sentences. They follow the same procedure in the pilot phase where each of the individual annotators works with 600 sentences, and the conflicts in the intersection set of 100 sentences are solved by the supervisor of each group in the discussion sessions. All updates to the annotation guideline made by the supervisors are reviewed by the guideline author. We continue to designate the two individual annotators to be supervisors in the next phase in a hierarchical manner. We repeat the process until all sentences are annotated. The intersection sets in each group are aggregated and used as the golden test set. The individual annotators after the pilot phase are medical under-graduates, which are hired at a rate of 0.1 USD per annotated sentence and 0.05 USD per resolved conflict.

3 Baseline Models

3.1 Intent Classification

For task intent classification, we follow a common strategy when fine tuning pretrained BERT [1] for sequence classification task, we use PhoBERT [4] to extract contextual features of sentences then take the hidden state of the first special token ([CLS]) denoted h_1, the intent is predicted as:

$$y^i = softmax(W^i h_1 + b^i) \qquad (1)$$

3.2   Named Entity Recognition

A standard approach for NER task is to formulate it as a sequence labeling problem with the Begin-Inside-Outside (BIO) tagging scheme. Similar to the intent classification task, we use PhoBERT to extract contextual embedding with a conditional random fields (CRF) [3] inference layer on top of our model to improve sequence labeling performance.

Sub-word Alignment: In our approach, because PhoBERT uses a Byte Pair Encoder (BPE) to segment the input sentence with sub-word units. A word is split into k sub-words. The original word label is assigned to the first sub-word and k-1 sub-words is marked with a special label (X). Final, the predicted label of original word based on the first label of sub-word, we keep a binary vector for active positions.

4   Method

As the annotators only agree on the intersection sets, the remaining sets, which were only labeled by single annotators, could be polluted with noise. We develop a training strategy to minimize the effect of remaining noisy labels in the training set. We empirically show that the method makes use of the potentially noisy samples and improves the performance substantially. We apply our training strategy on the ViMQ dataset and the COVID-19 NER Vietnamese dataset and achieve better performance using the standard settings.

Given a set of entities $\{E_i\}$ in a sentence, where E_i is a tuple of (s_i, e_i, c_i) where s_i and e_i is the start and end index of the named entity i^{th} and c_i is its category.

Span-Noise Modelling. We model the span-noise by adding δ to s_i and e_i with a probability of p during training. Span-noise modeling acts as a regularization method and possibly corrects the noisy span indexes during training model.

Online Self-supervised Training. The training progresses through N iterations, each consisting of T epochs. After training for the first iteration, we start to aggregate the predictions made by the model in each epoch in the jth iteration. Entities with correct predictions for the entity category c_i and have an $IoU > 0.4$ with the span ground truth (s_i, e_i) are saved. We then employ major voting for the start/end indices of the span of each entity to combine the aggregated predictions of T epochs in iteration j^{th} and use the result as labels for training the model in the next iteration.

Table 2. Confusion matrix of the IC task on the ViMQ dataset.

	Sev.	Cau.	Tre.	Dia.
Sev.	152	0	0	10
Cau.	0	85	0	4
Tre.	1	1	233	30
Dia.	19	2	27	436

Table 3. F1-score of IC task on ViMQ dataset.

	F1-score (%)	
Baseline	✓	✓
+ self-sup.	–	✓
Dia.	90.22 ± 0.05	**90.55 ± 0,09**
Sev.	90.22 ± 0.38	**91.02 ± 0,00**
Tre.	**89.04 ± 0,23**	88.97 ± 0.21
Cau.	95.15 ± 0.9	**96.05 ± 0.00**
Mic.F1	90.36 ± 0.05	**90.65 ± 0.15**
Mac.F1	91.17 ± 0.23	**91.65 ± 0.08**

5 Experiments

5.1 Experiments Setups

We conduct experiments on our dataset and the COVID-19 NER dataset to compare the performances of the baseline models and the online self-supervised training strategy for the IC and NER tasks which are presented in Sects. 3 and 4. It should be noted that we do not add noise in the IC task because span-noise is inapplicable. Our experimental models were implemented PyTorch [5] using Huggingface's Transformers [8], a huge library for pretrained Transformer-based models. We train both of the models for 5 iterations, each with 10 epochs. In the online self-supervised approach, the model starts using pseudo-labels from the second iteration. We set the noise injection probability p to 0.1 and the noise shifting offset δ to 1 in all of our experiments. We employ AdamW optimizer with learning rate at $5e^{-5}$. In this study, we ran each experiments 5 times with different random seeds and report the average values with their standard deviations.

5.2 Results

Intent Classification. Table 3 shows that the online self-supervised method improves baseline model from 90.36% to 90.65% Micro-F1 and from 91.17% to 91.65% Macro-F1. The confusion matrix in Table 2 shows that the IC model makes mistakes some of the sample having intent Diagnosis of intent Treatment and vice versa.

Named Entity Recognition. Tables 4 and 5 show the experiments results on the COVID-19 NER and ViMQ datasets for the NER task. Online self-supervised training consistently improves the F1-score compares to the baseline model. The injection of span-noise adds significant gain to the performance on both datasets with a margin of 1% on COVID-19 NER and 3% on ViMQ In ViMQ dataset, there are 389 sentences with wrong predictions. Boundary errors

Table 4. F1-score of NER task on COVID-19 Vietnamese dataset.

	F1-score (%)		
Baseline	✓	✓	✓
+ self-supervised	–	✓	✓
+ span-noise	—	–	✓
Mic.F1	93.34 ± 0.04	94.34 ± 0.52	**94.81 ± 0.33**
Mac.F1	91.15 ± 0.81	91.55 ± 0.81	**92.49 ± 0.22**

Table 5. F1-score of the NER task on the ViMQ dataset.

	F1-score (%)		
Baseline	✓	✓	✓
+ self-supervised	–	✓	✓
+ span-noise	–	–	✓
SYMP.&DIS.	73.44 ± 0.05	73.60 ± 0.29	**77,21 ± 0.09**
MEDICINE	58.14 ± 2.47	63.22 ± 0.47	**67,34 ± 0.51**
MED.PRO.	58.51 ± 0.41	59.01 ± 0.78	**61,73 ± 0.08**
Mic.F1	70.78 ± 0.20	71.22 ± 0.30	**74,78 ± 0.05**
Mac.F1	63.36 ± 0.70	65.28 ± 0.51	**68,76 ± 0.23**

exists in 295/389 sentences that contains 362 entities with correct categories but incorrect span indices. Most of them are from class SYMPTOM&DISEASE as labels sometimes contain the inflicted body parts of the patient.

6   Discussion

ViMQ dataset can be utilized to develop a NLU module for healthcare chatbots. We propose a standard use case where it is applicable. A model trained for NER and IC tasks on the dataset decomposes a question from user to the system into named entities and intent components. These components are used to retrieve a corresponding medical answer from a pre-installed database. If no respond can be retrieved, the system routes the question to a recommended doctor.

7   Conclusion

In this work, we published a Vietnamese dataset of medical questions for the two tasks of intent classification and named entity recognition. Additionally, we proposed a training strategy to learn the model with span-noise modeling. The training strategy demonstrates positive gains on our dataset and COVID-19 Vietnamese NER dataset. Our dataset can be leveraged to develop a NLU module for healthcare chatbots to reduce workload of Telehealth doctors.

References

1. Devlin, J., Chang, M.W., Lee, K., Toutanova, K.: BERT: Pre-training of deep bidirectional transformers for language understanding. In: Proceedings of the 2019 Conference of the North American Chapter of the Association for Computational Linguistics: Human Language Technologies, vol. 1 (Long and Short Papers), pp. 4171–4186. Association for Computational Linguistics, Minneapolis, Minnesota (2019). https://doi.org/10.18653/v1/N19-1423. https://www.aclweb.org/anthology/N19-1423
2. He, X., et al.: Meddialog: Two large-scale medical dialogue datasets (2020)
3. Lafferty, J.D., McCallum, A., Pereira, F.C.N.: Conditional random fields: Probabilistic models for segmenting and labeling sequence data. In: Proceedings of the Eighteenth International Conference on Machine Learning. p. 282–289. ICML 2001, Morgan Kaufmann Publishers Inc., San Francisco, CA, USA (2001)
4. Nguyen, D.Q., Nguyen, A.T.: PhoBERT: Pre-trained language models for Vietnamese. In: Findings of the Association for Computational Linguistics: EMNLP 2020, pp. 1037–1042 (2020)
5. Paszke, A., et al.: Pytorch: An imperative style, high-performance deep learning library. In: Wallach, H., Larochelle, H., Beygelzimer, A., d' Alché-Buc, F., Fox, E., Garnett, R. (eds.) Advances in Neural Information Processing Systems, vol. 32. Curran Associates Inc. (2019). https://proceedings.neurips.cc/paper/2019/file/bdbca288fee7f92f2bfa9f7012727740-Paper.pdf
6. Rojowiec, R., Roth, B., Fink, M.: Intent recognition in doctor-patient interviews. In: Proceedings of the 12th Language Resources and Evaluation Conference, pp. 702–709. European Language Resources Association, Marseille, France (2020). https://www.aclweb.org/anthology/2020.lrec-1.88
7. Truong, T.H., Dao, M.H., Nguyen, D.Q.: COVID-19 named entity recognition for Vietnamese. In: Proceedings of the 2021 Conference of the North American Chapter of the Association for Computational Linguistics: Human Language Technologies (2021)
8. Wolf, T., et al.: Transformers: State-of-the-art natural language processing. In: Proceedings of the 2020 Conference on Empirical Methods in Natural Language Processing: System Demonstrations, pp. 38–45. Association for Computational Linguistics, Online (2020). https://www.aclweb.org/anthology/2020.emnlp-demos.6
9. Zeng, G., et al.: MedDialog: Large-scale medical dialogue datasets. In: Proceedings of the 2020 Conference on Empirical Methods in Natural Language Processing, pp. 9241–9250. Association for Computational Linguistics, Online (2020). https://doi.org/10.18653/v1/2020.emnlp-main.743. https://www.aclweb.org/anthology/2020.emnlp-main.743

Prediction of the Facial Growth Direction is Challenging

Stanisław Kaźmierczak[1](✉)[iD], Zofia Juszka[2][iD], Vaska Vandevska-Radunovic[3][iD], Thomas J. J. Maal[4,5][iD], Piotr Fudalej[6,7,8][iD], and Jacek Mańdziuk[1][iD]

[1] Faculty of Mathematics and Information Science,
Warsaw University of Technology, Warsaw, Poland
{s.kazmierczak,mandziuk}@mini.pw.edu.pl
[2] Prof. Loster's Orthodontics, Krakow, Poland
[3] Institute of Clinical Dentistry, University of Oslo, Oslo, Norway
[4] Department of Oral and Maxillofacial Surgery 3D Lab, Radboud University
Medical Centre Nijmegen, Radboud Institute for Health Sciences,
Nijmegen, The Netherlands
[5] Department of Oral and Maxillofacial Surgery, Amsterdam UMC Location AMC
and Academic Centre for Dentistry Amsterdam (ACTA), University of Amsterdam,
Amsterdam, The Netherlands
[6] Department of Orthodontics, Jagiellonian University in Krakow, Krakow, Poland
[7] Department of Orthodontics, Institute of Dentistry and Oral Sciences,
Palacký University Olomouc, Olomouc, Czech Republic
[8] Department of Orthodontics and Dentofacial Orthopedics, University of Bern,
Bern, Switzerland

Abstract. Facial dysmorphology or malocclusion is frequently associated with abnormal growth of the face. The ability to predict facial growth (FG) direction would allow clinicians to prepare individualized therapy to increase the chance for successful treatment. Prediction of FG direction is a novel problem in the machine learning (ML) domain. In this paper, we perform feature selection and point the attribute that plays a central role in the abovementioned problem. Then we successfully apply data augmentation (DA) methods and improve the previously reported classification accuracy by 2.81%. Finally, we present the results of two experienced clinicians that were asked to solve a similar task to ours and show how tough is solving this problem for human experts.

Keywords: Orthodontics · Facial growth · Data augmentation

1 Introduction

Characteristics of FG are important during both facial development and treatment of possible developmental disturbances. For example, atypical FG in many types of malocclusion hinders achievement of optimal results of therapy. Irrespective of the form of pathology or its severity, the type of FG, i.e., its direction, intensity, and duration, can be favorable, neutral, or unfavorable when viewed

© Springer Nature Switzerland AG 2021
T. Mantoro et al. (Eds.): ICONIP 2021, CCIS 1517, pp. 665–673, 2021.
https://doi.org/10.1007/978-3-030-92310-5_77

from the clinical perspective. Favorable FG takes place when elements of the face grow in a direction or with intensity promoting advantageous treatment outcome, while unfavorable growth occurs when growth characteristics does not facilitate treatment. A typical example is mandibular hypoplasia (i.e., when lower jaw is too small) – in some patients, a hypoplastic mandible grows significantly forward (favorable growth), whereas in others it grows considerably downward (unfavorable growth). Clearly, direction of growth of the mandible is associated with clinical success or failure. Therefore, it seems obvious that the ability to predict FG is of paramount importance for both patients and clinicians. It would allow to select more individualized therapy or more appropriate orthodontic appliance for an individual patient to increase the chance for successful treatment.

The contribution of this work is fourfold: **(1)** addressing the problem of FG prediction with ML methods, which, to our knowledge, was analyzed only once before [11] and improving the prediction score by 2.81%; **(2)** showing that one feature – the difference between the values at the age of 12 and 9 of the same measurement whose change between the 9th and 18th year of age is prognosticated – plays a crucial role in the prediction process; **(3)** successfully applying DA techniques to the analyzed problem; **(4)** involving experienced clinicians to solve a similar problem and showing how difficult it is for human experts.

2   Related Literature

In our other article, we described in detail the attempts to date to predict craniofacial growth [11]. In summary, none of the methods to date have been sufficiently effective when validated on a sample other than the one used to develop the method. ML methods have not been used for craniofacial growth prediction to date, despite the fact that recent years are replete with publications describing the use of ML in orthodontics and related areas [3,7,14].

A recent scoping review [15] pointed out that artificial intelligence could assist in performing diagnostic assessments or determining treatment plans. Analysis of recent publications demonstrates that application of ML methods in orthodontics and related areas has been growing fast in recent years. However, few challenging "orthodontic" problems have been solved with ML so far.

3   Datasets

We utilized the same dataset as in our previous study [11], where it was described in detail. In our current experiments, we intended to predict the change of the value SN/MP angle between the age of 9 and 18, on the basis of the cephalometric measurements at 9 and 12 years. Thus, we collected data from subjects who had lateral cephalograms (LC) taken in timestamps as close as possible to 9, 12, and 18 years. The total number of samples included was 639. Characteristics of particular age groups are: (group name, average age, minimum and maximum age within a group, respectively) **9-year-olds** – 9.06 ± 0.45, 6.00, 10.92; **12-year-olds** – 12.07±0.39, 10.00, 13.75; **18-year-olds** – 17.41±1.71, 15.00, 28.42.

4   Experiments

To assess a subject, an orthodontic expert has to identify approximately 20 characteristic anatomic landmarks on LC. Some of them define angles which, from the clinical perspective, have special significance. As far as FG direction is concerned, there are no standardized measurements available in the literature to evaluate FG. In this paper, we focused on the prediction of the change of SN/MP, which is specified as the angle between Sella-Nasion and Menton-Gonion Inferior. The predicted variable is defined by subtracting the value of SN/MP at the age of 9 from SN/MP value at the age of 18. Categorization is conducted in the following way: first class, *horizontal growth*, is composed of samples whose predicted value is lower than a standard deviation from the mean; second, most frequent, class, *mixed growth*, contains instances that are in the scope of one standard deviation from the mean; third class, *vertical growth*, constitutes samples with a predicted value greater than a standard deviation from the mean.

As a result, 68.23% of instances belong to the most frequent class (MFC). Let us mark the categorized predicted variable as SN-MP(18-9). Figure 1a illustrates an LC with landmarks and SN/MP angle. Figure 1b and 1c present subjects with horizontal and vertical growth, respectively.

4.1   Task Complexity

Before moving to the experiment part, there are a couple of points worth noting that make solving the undertaken problem hard. The feature set is composed of either transformed landmarks or angles formed from these landmarks. Both approaches involve manual landmarking, which poses a source of noise since not every anatomical landmark location is unambiguous [17]. Additionally, the LC's included in this study were collected using different x-ray devices, which increases the non-uniformity of the data. Moreover, the image scale is diversified. Since it is impossible to determine the scaling factor, models may become confused when processing instances that do not reflect real growth properly. Further difficulties are related to the low number of dataset instances, which makes any deep architecture prone to overfitting and class imbalance. Lastly, due to the ethical issues described in [11], we are restricted to work with 2D LC's.

4.2   Models Parametrization

Let us introduce the following abbreviations for the sake of conciseness in the presentation: MLP, MLP(n), MLP(n_1, n_2) – perceptron with no hidden layer, one n-neuron hidden layer, and two hidden layers containing n_1 and n_2 neurons, respectively; NN(k) – nearest neighbors classifier that takes k neighbors into account; XGB(r) – XGBoost algorithm with r boosting iterations; RF(t) – random forest containing t trees; SVM – Support Vector Machine classifier; LR – logistic regression algorithm performing 2 000 iterations at the maximum; DT – decision tree.

As far as neural networks are concerned, the input and each hidden layer applied ReLU, whereas the last layer used softmax. 20% of training data were set aside and served as a validation set. The batch size was set to the number of training samples and the training could last no longer than 10 000 epochs. After 50 epochs with no decrease of the loss function on the validation set, the training was ceased and parameters from the best epoch were brought back. Adam [12] served as the cross-entropy loss function optimizer. The remaining hyperparameters were left at their default settings, which were utilized in Keras 2.3.1 in terms of neural networks and scikit-learn 0.23.2 for all other models. Stratified 5-fold cross-validation was performed 20 times for each configuration presented in Sect. 4.3 (generating 100 results) and 100 times for each setup provided in Sect. 4.4 (yielding 500 results). In all experimental configurations, the following models were experimented: MLP, MLP(20), MLP(50), MLP(100), MLP(50, 10), MLP(50, 20), MLP(50, 50), SVM, LR, DT, NN(3), NN(5), RF(100), RF(300), XGB(100), XGB(300).

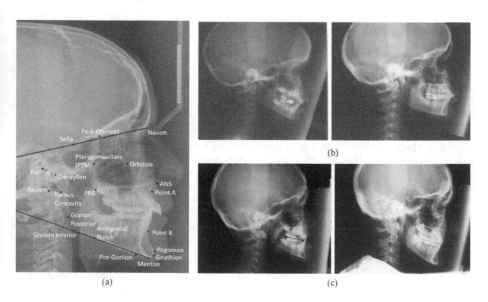

Fig. 1. Sample cephalograms. Figure (a) depicts marked landmarks, their names, as well as the measurement used to create the predicted variable – SN/MP angle. Figures (b) and (c) present horizontal and vertical growth, respectively. They illustrate the faces of two people in the age of 9 (left) and 18 (right).

4.3   Feature Selection

In our experiments, the features are in tabular form (we comment on images in Sect. 5). We analyze the following three types of attributes: *cephalometric* (ceph), *Procrustes* (proc), and *transformed* (trans). All of them are based on landmarks marked in LC's. Cephalometric features mainly consist of angles which are broadly used in the cephalometric analysis [13]. Images on which landmarking is based are in different scales. Moreover, the faces they depict are not centralized and are variously rotated. Thus, to create Procrustes features, we normalized the landmark coordinates so that they satisfy the following criteria for each face: (1) arithmetic mean position of all the landmarks is placed at (0, 0); (2) total distance between all converted coordinates and (0, 0) equals one; (3) a sum of squared distances between a specific landmark and its mean position over all images is minimized across all landmarks and images. The third set of features, transformed coordinates, is created by moving all raw landmarks so that the Sella point is positioned at (0, 0). Justification of such transformation and its visualization are presented in [11]. The total number of cephalometric features from one timestamp amounts to 15, Procrustes – 40, and transformed – 40. Besides, the subject's age is always incorporated in the attribute set. In our experiments, we consider the features being the above-mentioned values from the 9th (9) and 12th (12) year of age, as well as the difference between the respective values at the age of 12 and 9 (12-9).

As it was shown in [11], there is a couple of sources of noise that affect our dataset. Thus, we decided to perform feature selection to check which attributes are meaningful from the prediction perspective. Since SN/MP(12-9) (difference between the values at the age of 12 and 9 of the same measurement whose change between the 9th and 18th year of age is prognosticated) is noticeably correlated with the predicted variable [11], we supposed that a relatively small set of attributes containing SN/MP(12-9) could give positive results. We started with the empty feature set and operated in a similar way to forward feature selection [4].

Initially, we tested all types of models described in Sect. 4.2 built on any (but only one) attribute. The first group of rows in Table 1 shows three best configurations (model, feature, feature type), along with the obtained accuracy. All top models were built on SN/MP(12-9) attribute. MLP(100) outperformed the best model reported in [11] by 1.12%. Additionally, the best one-feature model which is not built on SN/MP(12-9), achieved only 68.87%. These two observations show, on the one hand how important SN/MP(12-9) attribute is, and on the other hand, how much noise is carried by many other features.

Second, we tested all model types built on two features, out of which one is SN/MP(12-9). In Table 1, the second group of rows depicts the three best configurations. Y Antegonial Notch(12-9) proved to be valuable. Obtained accuracy increased by 1.27% in comparison to the best one-feature model. However, only logistic regression was able to achieve such gain. It is also worth pointing out that nine out of the ten best models were built on the transformed coordinates, and in the case of the top five models, the second feature was the difference between the corresponding values at the age of 12 and 9.

Finally, all models were examined on all possible three-feature sets, out of which two, SN/MP(12-9) and Y Antegonial Notch(12-9), were fixed and established by the best two-feature score. Best configurations are shown in the last three rows of Table 1. Neither three-attribute model has obtained statistically significantly (*t*-Test, *p*-value equal to 0.05) higher accuracy than the best two-attribute model.

4.4 Data Augmentation

Having found a strong configuration, logistic regression built on SN/MP(12-9) and Y Antegonial Notch(12-9) attributes, we attempted to improve the classification accuracy further by applying DA methods. Since the analyzed problem is imbalanced and features are in tabular form, we focused on the SMOTE [5] technique and its extensions. When augmenting instances of class C, SMOTE randomly selects a sample s of class C and generates new instances in line segments connecting s and its k nearest neighbors of class C in the feature space.

Methods based on SMOTE but employing selective synthetic sample generation include Borderline-SMOTE [8], SVM-SMOTE [16], ADASYN [9], and K-means SMOTE [6]. They are all described in the extended version of the article [10].

SMOTE can create noisy instances when interpolating new points between marginal outliers and inliers. To deal with that issue, we employ two methods that clean a space resulting from DA: SMOTE-Tomek Links [2] and SMOTE-ENN [1]. Both techniques start with performing SMOTE, but they differ in the second phase. More details are provided in the extended version of this paper [10].

Table 1. Top models built on one, two, and three features.

No.	Model	$1^{st}/2^{nd}/3^{rd}$ feature and its type	Accuracy [%]
One-feature models			
1	MLP(100)	SN-MP(12-9), ceph	72.37 ± 1.87
2	MLP(50)	SN-MP(12-9), ceph	72.28 ± 2.00
3	MLP(50, 50)	SN-MP(12-9), ceph	72.25 ± 1.93
Two-feature models			
1	LR	Y Antegonial Notch(12-9), trans	73.64 ± 2.02
2	LR	Y Gonion Inferior(12-9), trans	72.64 ± 2.05
3	LR	X Gonion Inferior(12-9), trans	72.51 ± 2.14
Three-feature models			
1	LR	SN/PP(12), ceph	73.67 ± 2.18
2	LR	Y Post Ethmoid(12), proc	73.65 ± 2.02
3	LR	X Nasion(12), proc	72.65 ± 2.02

At the beginning of the experiments related to DA, we tried to enlarge the underrepresented class by a greater factor than the majority class. However, it turns out that when disturbing the original class proportion, the classification accuracy suffers. Thus, in further analysis, we stick to scenarios in which all three classes are augmented by the same factor.

All aforementioned DA methods are run on the original SN/MP(12-9) and Y Antegonial Notch(12-9) features, as well as their standardized values. In all experiments, we utilize logistic regression, which obtained the best results on the above attributes. Figure 2 shows classification accuracy as a function of the augmentation factor, which tells how many times the generated dataset is larger than the original one. The training dataset is composed of two parts – original and augmented instances.

The baseline for further analysis constitutes accuracies obtained on non-augmented datasets – 73.64% for original features and 73.45% on standardized. What can be observed in Fig. 2, only SMOTE and SMOTE with additional undersampling, SMOTE-Tomek and SMOTE-ENN, managed to outperform baseline. Moreover, the results achieved on standardized data are higher than those on raw data. Models built on standardized data reach a plateau slightly above 74.00% when the augmentation factor is about 20 and achieve the highest accuracy, 74.06%, for several larger values of the augmentation factor. Conversely, models constructed on the original data start to decrease very slightly then. Moreover, for most values of augmentation factor, SMOTE, SMOTE-TOMEK, and SMOTE-ENN applied to standardized data, achieve statistically significantly higher accuracy than the baseline (it is impossible to give the specific minimum value of accuracy to be viewed as statistically significantly different since the standard deviation varies a bit for different values of augmentation factor, but it oscillates about 73.90%). We regard two mean accuracies to be statistically significantly different if the p-value returned by t-Test is less than 0.05. Finally, we tested DA based on Gaussian noise injection. However, neither model obtained a statistically significantly higher result than the baseline.

4.5   Results of Experts

To our knowledge, [11] and this paper are the first studies investigating the prediction of FG with ML methods. Thus, we are unable to compare our outcome with any previous results. To check the level of difficulty of the problem and assess human-level performance, we asked two orthodontists with more than 10-year experience in cephalometric analysis to perform prediction. They were shown LC's taken at 9 years of age along with the results of cephalometric analysis as an input. Their task was to predict the growth category (categorized SN/MP(18-9) variable) for each subject. Experts obtained 40.33% and 40.88% of classification accuracy, respectively. Their prediction consistency (percentage of instances predicted as the same class) was 46.96%. Results revealed how difficult it is for humans to predict the FG direction having 9-year-olds' data as an input.

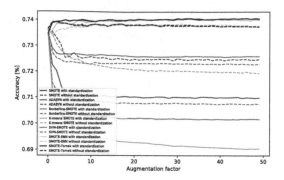

Fig. 2. Classification accuracy obtained by various SMOTE-related DA methods.

5   Conclusions and Future Work

This paper addresses FG prediction, which is a novel problem in the ML domain. The first interesting finding is that there is one feature, the difference between the values at the age of 12 and 9 of the same measurement whose change between the 9th and 18th year of age is prognosticated, that plays a crucial role in the prediction process. It is so important that models built solely on it outperform all other models tested in our previous work [11]. The feature selection process reveals that there are many attributes redundant from the prediction perspective, and just two features constitute a suboptimal or even optimal attribute set. The broad range of tabular DA methods was further applied, which allowed us to gain another 0.4% in classification accuracy. In all, the achieved score surpasses the previously reported classification accuracy by 2.81%. We also asked two experienced clinicians to perform predictions based on the data of 9-year-olds. Results unveiled how hard the problem is.

In further research, we think of the application of specific ensembling methods that would not combine models predicting the same variable but rather predictions of different measurements related to FG direction.

Acknowledgments. Studies were funded by BIOTECHMED-1 project granted by Warsaw University of Technology under the program Excellence Initiative: Research University (ID-UB). We would like to thank the custodian of AAOF Craniofacial Growth Legacy Collection for the possibility to use the lateral cephalograms from Craniofacial Growth Legacy Collection.

References

1. Batista, G.E., Bazzan, A.L., Monard, M.C., et al.: Balancing training data for automated annotation of keywords: a case study. In: WOB, pp. 10–18 (2003)
2. Batista, G.E., Prati, R.C., Monard, M.C.: A study of the behavior of several methods for balancing machine learning training data. ACM SIGKDD Explor. Newslett. **6**(1), 20–29 (2004)

3. Bianchi, J., et al.: Osteoarthritis of the Temporomandibular Joint can be diagnosed earlier using biomarkers and machine learning. Sci. Rep. **10**(1), 1–14 (2020)

4. Blanchet, F.G., Legendre, P., Borcard, D.: Forward selection of explanatory variables. Ecology **89**(9), 2623–2632 (2008)

5. Chawla, N.V., Bowyer, K.W., Hall, L.O., Kegelmeyer, W.P.: SMOTE: synthetic minority over-sampling technique. J. Artif. Intell. Res. **16**, 321–357 (2002)

6. Douzas, G., Bacao, F., Last, F.: Improving imbalanced learning through a heuristic oversampling method based on k-means and SMOTE. Inf. Sci. **465**, 1–20 (2018)

7. Etemad, L., et al.: Machine learning from clinical data sets of a contemporary decision for orthodontic tooth extraction. Orthod. Craniofac. Res. (2021, online). https://pubmed.ncbi.nlm.nih.gov/34031981/

8. Han, H., Wang, W.-Y., Mao, B.-H.: Borderline-SMOTE: a new over-sampling method in imbalanced data sets learning. In: Huang, D.-S., Zhang, X.-P., Huang, G.-B. (eds.) ICIC 2005. LNCS, vol. 3644, pp. 878–887. Springer, Heidelberg (2005). https://doi.org/10.1007/11538059_91

9. He, H., Bai, Y., Garcia, E.A., Li, S.: ADASYN: adaptive synthetic sampling approach for imbalanced learning. In: 2008 IEEE International Joint Conference on Neural Networks, pp. 1322–1328. IEEE (2008)

10. Kaźmierczak, S., Juszka, Z., Vandevska-Radunovic, V., Maal, T.J., Fudalej, P., Mańdziuk, J.: Prediction of the facial growth direction is challenging. arXiv preprint arXiv:2110.02316 (2021)

11. Kaźmierczak, S., Juszka, Z., Fudalej, P., Mańdziuk, J.: Prediction of the facial growth direction with machine learning methods. arXiv preprint arXiv:2106.10464 (2021)

12. Kingma, D.P., Ba, J.: Adam: a method for stochastic optimization. arXiv preprint arXiv:1412.6980 (2014)

13. Leonardi, R., Giordano, D., Maiorana, F., Spampinato, C.: Automatic cephalometric analysis: a systematic review. Angle Orthod. **78**(1), 145–151 (2008)

14. Lo, L.J., Yang, C.T., Ho, C.T., Liao, C.H., Lin, H.H.: Automatic assessment of 3-dimensional facial soft tissue symmetry before and after orthognathic surgery using a machine learning model: a preliminary experience. Ann. Plast. Surg. **86**(3S), S224–S228 (2021)

15. Mohammad-Rahimi, H., Nadimi, M., Rohban, M.H., Shamsoddin, E., Lee, V.Y., Motamedian, S.R.: Machine learning and orthodontics, current trends and the future opportunities: a scoping review. Am. J. Orthod. Dentofac. Orthop. **160**(2), 170–192.e4 (2021)

16. Nguyen, H.M., Cooper, E.W., Kamei, K.: Borderline over-sampling for imbalanced data classification. Int. J. Knowl. Eng. Soft Data Paradigms **3**(1), 4–21 (2011)

17. Perillo, M., et al.: Effect of landmark identification on cephalometric measurements: guidelines for cephalometric analyses. Clin. Orthod. Res. **3**(1), 29–36 (2000)

SCAN: Spatial and Channel Attention Normalization for Image Inpainting

Shiyu Chen[1], Wenxin Yu[1(✉)], Liang Nie[1], Xuewen Zhang[1], Siyuan Li[1], Zhiqiang Zhang[1], and Jun Gong[2]

[1] Southwest University of Science and Technology, Mianyang, China
yuwenxin@swust.edu.cn
[2] Beijing Institute of Technology, Beijing, China

Abstract. Image inpainting focuses on predicting contents with shape structure and consistent details in damaged regions. Recent approaches based on convolutional neural network (CNN) have shown promising results via adversarial learning, attention mechanism, and various loss functions. This paper introduces a novel module named Spatial and Channel Attention Normalization (SCAN), combining attention mechanisms in spatial and channel dimension and normalization to handle complex information of known regions while avoiding its misuse. Experiments on the varies datasets indicate that the performance of the proposed method outperforms the current state-of-the-art (SOTA) inpainting approaches.

Keywords: Image inpainting · Deep learning · Attention mechanism · Normalization

1 Introduction

Image inpainting task as a research hotspot in computer vision has many applications in photo editing, object removal, and image-based rendering. The attention mechanism is becoming increasingly popular as a plug-and-play module to encode where to emphasize or suppress. The attention mechanism [5,9] in spatial dimension explicitly constructs the long-range dependency between the pixels or regions inside and outside the hole via computing their similarity to tackle the ineffectiveness of basic convolutional neural networks in learning long-range information. Also, some approaches model the attention map in channel dimension to enhance those critical features. Feature normalization (FN) is an important technique to help neural network training, typically normalizing features across spatial-dimension, even though it can lead to the shift of mean and variance and mislead training due to the impact of information in damaged regions.

Motivated by these, we proposed a two-stage network with Spatial and Channel Attention Normalization (SCAN) module to handle these problems. The SCAN module we proposed comprises Spatial Attention Normalization (SAN) and Channel Attention Normalization (CAN). The idea of SAN, same as region normalization [11] and attentive normalization [6], is to improve instance normalization. The idea of CAN is to improve group normalization [8].

© Springer Nature Switzerland AG 2021
T. Mantoro et al. (Eds.): ICONIP 2021, CCIS 1517, pp. 674–682, 2021.
https://doi.org/10.1007/978-3-030-92310-5_78

The models we presented are evaluated on the test dataset of CelebA-HQ and Paris Street View. Compared with those SOTA, the produced results achieve significant improvement. Our main contributions are as follows:

- We propose a Spatial Attention Normalization method for image inpainting, which will not be disturbed by damaged information when normalization.
- We propose a Channel Attention Normalization method that can strengthen the connection between similar semantics and enable semantic separation.
- Experiments on the CelebA-HQ and Paris Street View datasets show the superiority of our approach compares to the existing advanced approaches.

2   Related Work

2.1   Learning-Based Image Inpainting

The methods based on convolutional neural networks [3,4] are introduced to help understand the semantic of images during inpainting in the last few years. Pathak et al. [4] first introduce Context Encoder, which uses an encoder-decoder architecture with adversarial training to analyse the high-level semantic information. Nazeri et al. [3] divide the training process into two parts, taking the outputs of the first stage as prior structure knowledge to guide image inpainting in the second stage.

However, these approaches let convolution kernels deal with the information inside and outside the hole regions in the same way, which will mislead the encoder. Liu et al. [2] take this issue via exploiting the partial convolutional layer and mask-update operation. After then, Yu et al. [10] present the Gated Convolutional that learns a dynamic mask-update mechanism to replace the hard mask-update.

2.2   Attention Mechanism

Yu et al. [9] propose a contextual attention layer to catch and borrow information of the related patches explicitly at distant spatial locations from the hole. Wang et al. [5] propose a multi-scale attention module to capture information in multiple scales via using attention module of different matching patch sizes.

Meanwhile, the interdependencies between channels of feature map in deep layers are also important for the model to understand the semantics of the image. Hu et al. [1] introduce a Squeeze-and-Excitation module to calculate the relationship between channels by exploiting the averages of each channel explicitly. Woo et al. [7] aggregate channel information of a feature map by using max and average pooling operations and then forward them to a shared MLP.

2.3   Normalization

In the inpainting task, Tao et al. [11] exploit Region Normalization to simply separates the feature map into only two regions, uncorrupted region, and corrupted region, according to region mask and normalize them separately to avoid the effect of error information in holes. Yi et al. [6] further propose Attentive Normalization (AN) to divide the feature map into different semantic regions by the learning semantic map and normalize them separately. AN cannot avoid the possibility of being misled by error information in damaged regions and invalid information in known regions because AN randomly selects n feature pixels from translated feature map as initial semantic filters to guide the learning of the semantic layout map.

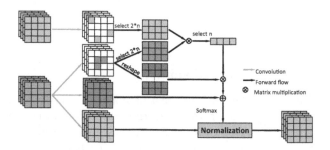

Fig. 1. The proposed SAN module. The selected patches' size is 3×3.

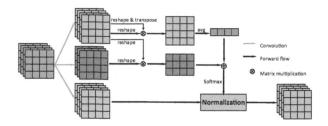

Fig. 2. The proposed CAN module.

3   Method

3.1   Spatial Attention Normalization (SAN)

The SAN can be divided into three steps, attention map learning, self-sampling regularization, and normalization, as shown in Fig. 1.

Attention Map Learning. For the given feature map $\mathbf{X} \in \mathbb{R}^{c \times h \times w}$ from decoder, we have filters $K_s \in \mathbb{R}^{n \times c \times 1 \times 1}$ to fit the semantic entities, where n denotes a predefined number of semantics entities.

We define the correlation between the feature map and these semantic entities as the raw attention map about these semantic entities $\mathbf{S}^{raw}$, of which the calculation could be implemented as a convolution calculation $\mathbf{S}^{raw} = K_s(\mathbf{X})$.

Further, to ensure that these filters learns diverse semantic entities, orthogonal regularization is employed to these entities as

$$\mathcal{L}_{so} = \lambda_{so} \| K_s K_s^T - I \|_F^2 \tag{1}$$

where $K_s \in \mathbb{R}^{n \times c}$ is a weight matrix squeezed to 2-dimension.

Self-sampling Regularization. We firstly randomly select 2*n patches from damaged regions of feature map $\mathbf{X}$ and known regions of $\mathbf{F}$, respectively, where $\mathbf{F}$ is the feature maps from the encoder located symmetrically to $\mathbf{X}$. We use partial convolution [2] to update the mask to distinguish the damaged regions from known regions and denote the selected patches from them as $s(\mathbf{X})^{2n}$ and $s(\mathbf{F})^{2n}$, respectively. Then the correlation between them could be calculated as

$$\varphi_{i,j} = < \frac{s(\mathbf{X})_i^{2n}}{\| s(\mathbf{X})_i^{2n} \|}, \frac{s(\mathbf{F})_j^{2n}}{\| s(\mathbf{F})_j^{2n} \|} > \tag{2}$$

where i and j denote index of patches.

Next, we select the n patches in $s(\mathbf{F})^{2n}$ with the highest similarity to the damaged regions as regularizing semantic filters $s(\mathbf{F})^n$, according to the relation-map φ, distinguishing helpful semantic information. Finally, the calculation of regularization term $\mathbf{S}^{re}$ could be implemented using $s(\mathbf{F})^n$ as kernels to perform convolution calculations on $\mathbf{X}$.

Normalization. Then, the semantics attention map $\mathbf{S}$ are computed as $\mathbf{S} = \mathbf{S}^{raw} + \alpha \mathbf{S}^{re}$, where $\alpha \in \mathbb{R}^{1 \times 1 \times n}$ is a learnable vector initialized as 0.1. It adjusts the effects of $\mathbf{S}^{re}$ adaptively, preventing some entities from learning useless semantics. In order to get attention score map $\mathbf{S}^*$, we apply the softmax operations in channel dimension. Each $\mathbf{S}_i^*$ (i is the index of channels) is a soft weight map, indicating the probability of every pixel belonging to semantic entity i.

According to the attention score map, we can divide the feature map into n regions and normalization them respectively as

$$\bar{\mathbf{X}} = \sum_{i=1}^{n} \frac{\mathbf{X} - \mu(\mathbf{X}_{\mathbf{S}_i^*})}{\sigma(\mathbf{X}_{\mathbf{S}_i^*}) + \epsilon} \odot \mathbf{S}_i^* \tag{3}$$

where $\mathbf{X}_{\mathbf{S}_i^*} = \mathbf{X} \odot \mathbf{S}_i^*$ and broadcast operations first broadcast $\mathbf{X}$ and $\mathbf{S}^*$ to $\mathbb{R}^{c \times n \times h \times w}$ to match the dimensions of the two matrices. $\mu(\cdot)$ and $\sigma(\cdot)$ compute the mean and standard deviation from instance respectively. Each region shares a mean and variance, strengthening the connection between internal pixels, even if they are far apart.

The final output of SAN computes the weighted sum of the original input feature map and the normalized one as $SAN(\mathbf{X}) = \gamma \bar{\mathbf{X}} + \mathbf{X}$, where γ is a learnable scalar initialized as 0.

3.2   Channel Attention Normalization (CAN)

The commonly used group normalization (GN) [8] only simply groups the channels. However, CAN groups these channels adaptively through semantic similarity and operate normalization within the group. Similar to SAN, CAN can be divided into three same steps, as shown in Fig. 2.

Attention Map Learning. Firstly, we calculate the attention map $\mathbf{C}$ by convolution calculation using K_c as filters, similar to $\mathbf{S}^{raw}$. We still have $\mathcal{L}_{co}$ to guide K_c, which is calculated similarly to Eq. (1). In order to divide the channels of the feature map into various groups according to their semantics, we continue to calculate the correlation between $\mathbf{X}$ and the attention map $\mathbf{C}$ as the raw grouping basis $\mathbf{R}^{raw}$. Specifically, we reshape $\mathbf{C}$ to $\mathbb{R}^{n \times hw}$ and $\mathbf{X}$ to $\mathbb{R}^{c \times hw}$, and then perform a matrix multiplication between $\mathbf{C}$ and the transpose of $\mathbf{X}$.

Self-attention Sampling. Different from SAN, we first calculate the correlation between channels and then calculate its average value as

$$\mathbf{R}_j^{re} = \frac{\sum_{i=0, i \neq j}^c \mathbf{X}_i(\mathbf{X}_j)^T}{c} \qquad (4)$$

$\mathbf{R}_j^{re}$ represents the average correlation between the j-th channels and other channels, $j \in [1, c]$. $\mathbf{R}^{re}$ is broadcasted to $\mathbb{R}^{n \times c}$ as the regularization term.

Normalization. Finally, we get the regularized grouping basis $\mathbf{R}$ by summing $\mathbf{R}^{raw}$ and $\mathbf{R}^{re}$ which is weighted with a learnable vector $\beta \in \mathbb{R}^{1 \times 1 \times n}$ initialized to 0.1. Then we apply softmax to obtain the soft grouping basis,

$$x_{i,j}^* = \frac{exp(x_{i,j})}{\sum_{i=1}^n exp(x_{i,j})} \qquad (5)$$

where $j \in [1, c]$. Each $x_{i,j}^*$ in $\mathbf{R}^* \in \mathbb{R}^{n \times c}$ measures the possibility that the i-th channel of the feature map belongs to the j-th group.

Then we divide the feature map into n groups in channel dimension and normalize them respectively similarly to Eq. (8). The final output of CAN compute the weighted sum of the original input feature map and the normalized one as $CAN(\mathbf{X}) = \eta \bar{\mathbf{X}} + \mathbf{X}$, where η is a learnable scalar initialized as 0.

3.3   Networks and Loss Functions

The overall network architecture is shown in Fig. 3. Formally, let $\mathbf{I}$ be the ground truth, $\mathbf{G}$ and $\mathbf{H}$ denote its gradient and high-frequency residual map.

The task of the first stage is to generate a rough result with good structure information but insufficient texture details. Thus, we take the masked image $\hat{\mathbf{I}} = \mathbf{I} \odot \mathbf{M}$ as the input, corresponding gradient map $\hat{\mathbf{G}} = \mathbf{G} \odot \mathbf{M}$ ($\mathbf{M}$ as the image mask with value 1 for known region otherwise 0). Here, $\odot$ denotes the Hadamard product. The generator produces a rough result $\mathbf{I}_{rough} = G_1(\hat{\mathbf{I}}, \hat{\mathbf{G}}, \mathbf{M})$

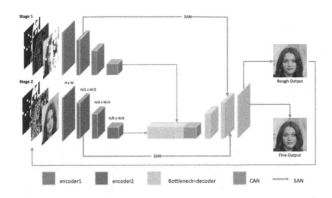

Fig. 3. The overview of our network architecture.

as part of the input of second stage, where G_1 represents the generator of the first stage, which is composed of enc_1 and dec.

The second-stage generator has its own independent encoder and a shared decoder with the first stage. Specifically, the masked high-frequency residual map $\hat{\mathbf{H}} = \mathbf{H} \odot \mathbf{M}$, instead of the gradient map, is another part of the input. In addition, smaller convolution kernels are used in the second stage's encoder than in the first stage's. We get the fine image $\mathbf{I}_{fine} = G_2(\hat{\mathbf{I}} + \mathbf{I}_{rough} \odot (1 - \mathbf{M}), \hat{\mathbf{H}}, \mathbf{M})$, where G_2 represents the generator of the second stage, which is composed of enc_2 and dec. The final predicted image is $\mathbf{I}_{pred} = \hat{\mathbf{I}} + \mathbf{I}_{fine} \odot (1 - \mathbf{M})$.

The Generator is trained over a joint loss, similar to the other methods, which consists of ℓ_1 loss ($\mathcal{L}_{\ell_1}$), perceptual loss ($\mathcal{L}_{perc}$), style loss ($\mathcal{L}_{style}$), and adversarial loss ($\mathcal{L}_G$). Besides, there is an orthogonal loss equal to the sum of $\mathcal{L}_{so}$ and $\mathcal{L}_{co}$ of two-stage, enabling attention map can learn various semantic attention. Therefore, the overall loss function of the proposed SCAN algorithm is as $\mathcal{L}_{total} = 10\mathcal{L}_o + \mathcal{L}_{\ell_1} + 0.1\mathcal{L}_{prec} + 250\mathcal{L}_{style} + 0.1\mathcal{L}_G$.

4   Experiments

All of the experiments in this paper are conducted in the dataset of CelebA-HQ and Paris Street View. The CelebA-HQ dataset is a high-quality version of CelebA that consists of 28000 train images and 2000 test images. The Paris Street View contains 14900 training images and 100 test images. We use Sobel filters to extract the gradient map and use the result after the image subtracting its Gaussian blur to get the high-frequency residual map. The irregular mask dataset used in this paper comes from the work of Liu [2]. We train the proposed model and the compared models on a single NVIDIA 2080Ti with a batch size of 8 until the generators converge, using Adam optimizer.

Table 1. The comparison of PSNR and SSIM over the CelebA-HQ and Paris Street View. Both quantitative evaluations are higher is better.

Dataset		CelebA-HQ			Paris street view		
Mask ratio		20%–30%	30%–40%	40%–50%	20%–30%	30%–40%	40%–50%
PSNR	EC [3]	27.18	25.29	23.33	27.28	25.80	24.10
	RN [11]	27.43	25.51	23.66	27.57	26.19	24.26
	Ours	**28.54**	**26.91**	**24.69**	**28.76**	**27.09**	**25.27**
SSIM	EC	0.917	0.902	0.862	0.875	0.851	0.804
	RN	0.929	0.912	0.871	0.887	0.864	0.812
	Ours	**0.953**	**0.933**	**0.894**	**0.918**	**0.873**	**0.840**

Table 2. The comparison of PSNR, SSIM, and MAE (Mean absolute error) over the Paris, in case of 30%–40% mask ratio. †Higher is better. △Lower is better.

	PC [2]	GC [10]	EC [3]	RN [11]	Ours
PSNR †	25.46	25.54	25.80	26.19	**27.09**
SSIM †	0.835	0.849	0.851	0.864	**0.873**
MAE (%) △	3.13	3.09	2.90	3.04	**2.53**

4.1   Quantitative Results

The Quantitative results in the test dataset of CelebA-HQ and Paris Street View are shown in Table 1, where some results produced by popular inpainting methods in comparison are also shown. In the case of different ratios of the damaged region, the table demonstrates the inpainting ability of our network, showing that our results are better than other results in PSNR (Peak Signal-to-Noise) and SSIM (Structural Similarity) metrics. In particular, Table 2 demonstrates our method has a more remarkable improvement in all metrics in detail when the mask ratio is 30%–40%. Compared with PC, GC, EC, RN, and RFR, our method can effectively use the correlation with the limited known regions information.

4.2   Qualitative Results

Figure 4 illustrates the visual inpainting results of different methods on the test set of CelebA-HQ and Paris Street View with mask ratios of 30%–40% and 40%–50%.

EC is misled by the edge information generated in the first stage when predicting the results. RN tends to produce smoother results and lacks texture details. Compared with EC and RN, the proposed method can better handle much larger damaged regions and achieves better subjective results, even houses with complex structural information on Paris Street View. Also, the visual

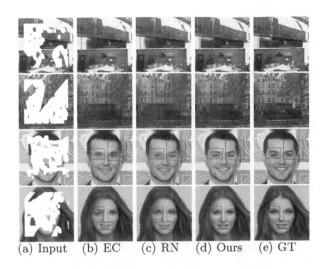

(a) Input   (b) EC   (c) RN   (d) Ours   (e) GT

Fig. 4. Qualitative comparisons with EC and RN on Paris Street View and CelebA-HQ with the mask ratio of 30%–40% and 40%–50%.

comparison on CelebA-HQ shows obvious enhancement of our method, such as sharp facial contours, crisp eyes and ears, and reason-able object boundaries.

5   Conclusions

This paper proposed a two-stage image inpainting approach with a SCAN module. The SAN and CAN module normalize feature map in spatial and channel dimensions, respectively. Various experiments show that the proposed SCAN generates promising images and achieves the state-of-the-art performance. In addition, the CAN module improving the group normalization could also be generalized to similar image restoration tasks, including image denoising, conditional image generation, and image segmentation.

References

1. Hu, J., Shen, L., Sun, G.: Squeeze-and-excitation networks. In: Proceedings of the IEEE Conference on Computer Vision and Pattern Recognition, pp. 7132–7141 (2018)
2. Liu, G., Reda, F.A., Shih, K.J., Wang, T.C., Tao, A., Catanzaro, B.: Image inpainting for irregular holes using partial convolutions. In: Proceedings of the European Conference on Computer Vision (ECCV), pp. 85–100 (2018)
3. Nazeri, K., Ng, E., Joseph, T., Qureshi, F.Z., Ebrahimi, M.: Edgeconnect: generative image inpainting with adversarial edge learning. arXiv preprint arXiv:1901.00212 (2019)
4. Pathak, D., Krahenbuhl, P., Donahue, J., Darrell, T., Efros, A.A.: Context encoders: feature learning by inpainting. In: Proceedings of the IEEE Conference on Computer Vision and Pattern Recognition, pp. 2536–2544 (2016)

5. Wang, N., Li, J., Zhang, L., Du, B.: Musical: multi-scale image contextual attention learning for inpainting. In: IJCAI, pp. 3748–3754 (2019)
6. Wang, Y., Chen, Y.C., Zhang, X., Sun, J., Jia, J.: Attentive normalization for conditional image generation. In: Proceedings of the IEEE/CVF Conference on Computer Vision and Pattern Recognition, pp. 5094–5103 (2020)
7. Woo, S., Park, J., Lee, J.Y., Kweon, I.S.: Cbam: convolutional block attention module. In: Proceedings of the European Conference on Computer Vision (ECCV), pp. 3–19 (2018)
8. Wu, Y., He, K.: Group normalization. In: Proceedings of the European Conference on Computer Vision (ECCV), pp. 3–19 (2018)
9. Yu, J., Lin, Z., Yang, J., Shen, X., Lu, X., Huang, T.S.: Generative image inpainting with contextual attention. In: Proceedings of the IEEE conference on computer vision and pattern recognition. pp. 5505–5514 (2018)
10. Yu, J., Lin, Z., Yang, J., Shen, X., Lu, X., Huang, T.S.: Free-form image inpainting with gated convolution. In: Proceedings of the IEEE/CVF International Conference on Computer Vision, pp. 4471–4480 (2019)
11. Yu, T., et al.: Region normalization for image inpainting. In: Proceedings of the AAAI Conference on Artificial Intelligence, pp. 12733–12740 (2020)

Designing Multiplier-Less JPEG Luminance Quantisation Matrix

Nabila Brahimi[1] [ID], Toufik Bouden[2] [ID], Larbi Boubchir[3(✉)] [ID], and Tahar Brahimi[4]

[1] NDT Laboratory, Electronic Department, University of Jijel, Jijel, Algeria
`nabila.brahimi@univ-jijel.dz`
[2] NDT Laboratory, Automatic Department, University of Jijel, Jijel, Algeria
`bouden_toufik@univ-jijel.dz`
[3] LIASD Research Laboratory, University of Paris 8, Saint-Denis, France
`larbi.boubchir@univ-paris8.fr`
[4] L2EI Laboratory, Electronic Department, University of Jijel, Jijel, Algeria
`t.brahimi@univ-jijel.dz`

Abstract. A novel approach for generating a multiplier-less approximate JPEG quantisation matrix has been proposed in this paper. It is based on energy distribution of integer DCTs coefficients and rounding to integer power-of-two matrix. No multiplications required during the encode and decode stages using the combination between an integer DCT and the proposed rounded quantisation matrix. An arithmetic operation savings about 44.8% using the proposed quantisation matrix with integer DCT against the JPEG. The proposed quantisation matrix has been successfully evaluated against the conventional JPEG quantisation matrix for all different type test images. The experimental results reveal that JPEG compression scheme base on integer DCT combined with our proposed quantisation matrix can provide significant improvement in PSNR values compared with other quantisation matrices.

Keywords: DCT energy distribution · Integer DCT approximation · Integer DTT · JPEG quantisation matrix

1 Introduction

Today, the standard Joint Photographic Expert Group (JPEG) [1] is widely accepted format for image compression, largely due to its simplicity of implementation and its rather trad-off between complexity and compression image quality. The Peak Signal to Noise Ratio (PSNR) of a JPEG image is just a few dB less than that of the same JPEG 2000 image, whereas the compression time of the former image is seven times smaller than that of the latter image [2].

In comparison, the noise resilience of a JPEG image is, in many cases, equivalent to that of a JPEG 2000 image [2], and the modern systems specified by the JPEG 2000 standard (i.e., scalability and region-of-interest) are also defined

© Springer Nature Switzerland AG 2021
T. Mantoro et al. (Eds.): ICONIP 2021, CCIS 1517, pp. 683–691, 2021.
https://doi.org/10.1007/978-3-030-92310-5_79

by the JPEG standard and its extensions. Although these extensions to the primary core of JPEG may be less successful, the low complexity of the JPEG can effectively offset this lower performance in many applications (especially battery driven ones) compared to those of the JPEG 2000.

The standard JPEG is, despite its age and multiple attempts to replace it by more modern technology, still the most prominent still image codec used today [2]. Most digital cameras export JPEG format and most image editing software supports JPEG compression operation. Hence, JPEG images are involved in many forensics issues, such as authenticity of JPEG compression history [3], image forgery detection [4,5] or steganalysis application [6,7] and the JPEG standard is also applicable to Computer generated holography [8].

The JPEG standard uses the Discrete Cosine Transform (DCT-II) as the core of the standard and three standard quantisation tables [9]. For grayscale images, only one quantisation matrix is used, while in color images, separate quantisation matrices are allowed for two-color components. It has been recognized in the field of image compression and mentioned in the CCITT recommendation documents that the JPEG quantisation matrix is strongly linked on image quality and compression rate. To this end, in recent decades, many researchers in literature have been carried out different approaches to generate image dependent/independent quantisation matrices. Wu in [10], based on Genetic algorithm (GA), proposed a quantisation matrix referred a slightly improvement quality decoded image compared with the conventional quantisation matrix of the baseline JPEG. A better image compression and quality trade-off technique is developed by Lazzerini et al. [11] utilizing Non-dominated Sorting Generic Algorithm II (NSGAII). A more efficient firefly algorithm has been proposed by Tuba and Bacanin in [12] using the Average Pixel Intensity Distance (APID) between the original and compressed image as an objective function. Noted that all of these algorithms have the parameter dependent nature, and they are intended for specific types of images.

Over the last decade, the researchers in the field of image compression, have been focused on reduction of computational complexity of integer approximation transforms such as Discrete Cosine Transform (DCT) [13] and Discrete Tchebichef Transform (DTT) [14]; whose they are suggested as solutions of DCT floating points multiplications problems [15–20], while the floating point calculations may consume too much energy compared with integer DCT approximations. These techniques accomplish a reduction in energy consumption for image compression at different levels (algorithmic, logic, transistor).

However, researchers of images and video compression field agree that in image and video compression standards, the DCT transformation is the most demanding step in terms of the number of operations. It alone consumes more than 60% of all of the encoder's calculation needs [21]. For the vector of 8 elements, the 1D-DCT of order 8, requires 64 floating-points multiplications and 56 additions. Consequently, a number of considerable studies have been carried out by researchers to overcome this problem by minimizing the number of arithmetic operations [16,19], and achieving a trade-off between number of arithmetic operations and reconstructed image quality. Hence, the integer transforms were widely adopted for image/video compression.

Newly, a novel matrix for DCT, which requires only 16 additions, is reported in [22]. It achieves a good compromise between computational cost and image compression performance. Besides, several studies have been carried out to improve the performance of the DCT module and then reduce the complexity of the treatment.

Hence, we show that the generation of quantisation matrices for the based-integer transforms JPEG baseline is a necessary task. In our best knowledge, the only approximate JPEG quantisation matrix required bit-shift operations only is introduced in 2017 by Oliveira et al. [23]. The reason is to reduce the complexity of the transform-quantisation pair of JPEG algorithm. The elements of the approximate quantisation matrix are power of two numbers and it provided almost the same performances compared it with its exact counterparts with arithmetic operation savings of 24.1% in additions.

This paper proposes an enhancement of baseline Jpeg compression standard based on integer DCT approximations.

– Regarding energy distribution of integer DCT coefficients an appropriate quantisation matrix has been proposed.
– This matrix is approximated to a power of two elements to reduce the complexity cost in image compression standard JPEG.

2   Default Luminance JPEG Quantisation Marix

The JPEG is the well-known standard for still grayscale and color images compression. It is based on DCT (or fast DCT/FDCT) whereas the quantisation is an important stage in this standard. Indeed, it is the part of the process that allows reducing the size of the images to be stored. However, it is also during this stage, the information losses are generated.

In JPEG standard, after preprocessing stage, the $M \times N$ input image is subdivided into blocs of 8×8 pixels $X_{i,j}$ whose DCT is applied. The resulting coefficients, $F_{u,v}$, are quantified afterwards, $F_{u,v}^{quant}$.

$$F_{u,v}^{quant} = round(F_{u,v} \oslash Q_{JPEG}) \qquad (1)$$

where $round(.)$ is the rounding function, and $\oslash$ denotes the elements-by-element division.

JPEG proposes luminance quantisation matrix where each of the 64 DCT coefficients is quantised by the uniform quantiser, Q_{JPEG} [1].

The dequantisation stage in decodage process is given by:

$$\hat{F}_{u,v}^{dequant} = (F_{u,v}^{quant} \odot Q_{JPEG}) \qquad (2)$$

where $\hat{F}_{u,v}^{dequant}$ is the dequantised coefficients, and $\odot$ denotes the element-wise multiplication.

3   Relaled Work and Motivation

In 2017, a JPEG quantisation table demands bit-shift operations only is introduced by Oliveira et al. in [23]. The approach consists to apply the nearest power of two functions named $np2$ to default luminance JPEG quantisation matrix.

$$np2(x) = 2^{round(\log_2 x)}, x \in \mathcal{R} \tag{3}$$

The approximate quatisation matrix obtained, denoted $\tilde{Q}_{oliveira}$, is given in [23].

Over the past decade, a successful alternative of the conventional DCT-II has been applied in image and video compression field, Integer DCT (InDCT) [18]. Using few numbers of integer arithmetic operations, several integer DCT approximations has been proposed in literature [15, 16, 18, 22, 24]. Thus, it is necessary to improve the compression ratio (CR) obtained by JPEG based on DCT approximations. Therefore, we have to adapt the quantification step with these DCT approximations.

As integer approximation DCT matrix $T_{8 \times 8}$ can be expressed as a multiplication of an 8×8 matrix $C_{8 \times 8}$ and a diagonal matrix $D_{8 \times 8}$.

$$T_{8 \times 8} = D_{8 \times 8} . C_{8 \times 8} \tag{4}$$

The $D_{8 \times 8}$ matrix can be integrated into the quantisation matrix for eliminating the multiplication operations resulting from it. Then, the modified forward and inverse quantisation matrices, $\hat{Q}_f$ and $\hat{Q}_i$, respectively, can be written as:

$$\hat{Q}_f = np2(Q_{JPEG} \oslash (d \times d^t)) \tag{5}$$

and

$$\hat{Q}_i = np2((d \times d^t) \odot Q_{JPEG}) \tag{6}$$

where d presents the column-vector with the element corresponding to main diagonal of $D_{8 \times 8}$. d^t is its transpose.

4   Proposed Approach for Generating the Quantisation Matrix

The quantisation of the DCT coefficients consists to divide all them by a factor. The method described by JPEG norm has an objective that invalidates the coefficients of low value that are only limited information in the image and reduce the dynamics of others. The caused degradation cannot be seen with the eye. However, it is important to note that all the coefficients have not the same quantity of information. However, this quantisation must take into account this quantity and the fact that DCT packing the image energy into few numbers of transformed coefficients associated with low frequencies. Then, they are the richest in information. The quantisation factor should therefore be different depending on the position of the coefficient in the block: it will be all the stronger as the coefficients will be poor in information. It will be larger at high frequency than at low frequency. Indeed, reducing the dynamic, view zeroing, a coefficient corresponding to high frequencies (often related to noise) will not cause as much degradation as a coefficient corresponding to low frequencies since the human eyes cannot sense the high frequency components in the image. Then, the energy of DCT coefficients plays a very important role to define the best suitable quantisation step for each coefficient. In this regard, using this strategy, we present a new approach to generate a quantisation matrix intended to integer DCT-based JPEG encoder.

Our approach is composed of two stages (stage 1 and stage 2):

Stage 1: It consists to generate a quantisation matrix based on energy distribution of integer DCT coefficients. Thus, two integer DCT approximations introduced in [22, 25] have been considered which they present the more efficient transforms that approximate the floating points DCT and they provide the best trade-off between coding performances and computation cost. Figure 1 shows an example of energy distribution of the 64 coefficients of the integer DCT approximations reported in [22] for test image Lena 512×512. Concerning the transform in [24], the results are not presented here due to the limited space. We can show from Fig. 1 that the energy of the coefficients differs from transform to other. The quantisation factor should depend on the position of the coefficient in the block as well as on its energy. A coefficient with low energy has poor information, so the corresponding quantisation step should be high and vice versa.

1	2	4	3	13	6	9	5
72.1db	25.1db	3.2db	16.0db	-18.5db	-5.5db	-12.1db	-0.1db
7	**8**	**11**	**10**	**53**	**30**	**17**	**12**
-8.5db	-11.2db	-15.7db	-15.3db	-37.3db	-29.0db	-23.8db	-18.0db
38	**20**	**31**	**16**	**50**	**34**	**37**	**22**
-31.0db	-25.3db	-29.3db	-21.3db	-35.9db	-30.3db	-30.7db	-26.1db
32	**26**	**39**	**28**	**63**	**55**	**52**	**36**
-29.9db	-28.4db	-31.5db	-28.5db	-47.6db	-39.1db	-37.1db	-30.6db
23	**18**	**19**	**14**	**44**	**25**	**24**	**15**
-27.7db	-25.2db	-25.3db	-19.4db	-32.9db	-28.1db	-28.1db	-20.8db
49	**35**	**41**	**21**	**61**	**51**	**46**	**27**
-35.2db	-30.6db	-31.8db	-25.3db	-43.0db	-36.2db	-33.4db	-28.4db
56	**40**	**42**	**33**	**59**	**47**	**43**	**29**
-39.4db	-31.8db	-32.8db	-29.9db	-40.4db	-33.7db	-32.9db	-28.9db
62	**54**	**58**	**48**	**64**	**60**	**57**	**45**
-43.2db	-38.3db	-40.4db	-34.4db	-51.3db	-42.9db	-40.2db	-33.3db

Fig. 1. Energy distribution of transform coefficients using the approximation in [22] on the test image Lena (512×512).

The implementation of this strategy, leads us to construct the following quantisation matrix for integer DC-based JPEG standard based on integer DCT approximations.

$$Q_{proposed} = \begin{bmatrix} 20 & 17 & 18 & 19 & 22 & 36 & 36 & 31 \\ 19 & 17 & 20 & 22 & 24 & 40 & 23 & 40 \\ 20 & 22 & 24 & 28 & 37 & 53 & 50 & 54 \\ 22 & 20 & 25 & 35 & 45 & 73 & 73 & 58 \\ 22 & 21 & 37 & 74 & 70 & 92 & 101 & 103 \\ 24 & 43 & 50 & 64 & 100 & 104 & 120 & 92 \\ 45 & 100 & 62 & 79 & 100 & 70 & 70 & 101 \\ 41 & 41 & 74 & 59 & 70 & 90 & 100 & 99 \end{bmatrix} \tag{7}$$

Then, as explain in Sect. 3, the diagonal matrix of an integer DCT approximation can be integrated in quantisation step. Then, $Q_{proposed}$ becomes:

$$Q_{f-proposed} = Q_{proposed} \oslash (d \times d^t) \tag{8}$$

$Q_{f-proposed}$ is the forward quantisation matrix appropriate to JPEG coder based on integer DCT approximations.

In dequantisation stage, the inverse quantization matrix can be delivered by the same method, we obtained:

$$Q_{i-proposed} = (d \times d^t) \odot Q_{proposed} \tag{9}$$

Stage 2: Although the integer DCT approximations require additions and/or bits shift operations only, the JPEG quantisation/dequantisation stages still require floating-point multiplications and call of rounding operations. However, we suggest an integer power-of-two approximation matrix for the proposed quantisation matrix, $Q_{f-proposed}$. The proposed approach ensures the multiplication-free of the matrices of quantisation/dequantisation stages.

The new proposed forward and inverse approximate quantisation matrices are expressed as:

$$\tilde{Q}_{f-proposed} = 2^{ceil(\log_2(Q_{f-proposed}))} \tag{10}$$

$$\tilde{Q}_{i-proposed} = 2^{ceil(\log_2(Q_{i-proposed}))} \tag{11}$$

where $ceil(x)$ rounds the elements of x, $x \in \mathcal{R}$, to the nearest integers. The resulting matrices required bit-shift operations only and it can be integrated directly in image compression standard JPEG based on integer DCT.

5   Arithmetic Cost Evaluation

The arithmetic cost of forward transformation/quantisation pair and inverse transformation/dequantisation pair stages for a single 8×8 image block is tabulated in Table 1.

If no approximations are applied to the standard JPEG standard and using only the fast scaled DCT (5 multiplications and 29 additions for a vector of 8 samples), the standard JPEG requires the greatest number of operations (1180). This number is reduced by Oliveira et al. in [23], an arithmetic operations savings of 24.1% in additions and no multiplication is needed in their implementation. An additional bit-shift operation is required; it can be implemented visually with no computation cost [7]. In all our five proposed scenarios mentioned in Table 1, the number of arithmetic operations is decreased compared with JPEG standard, it reaches to 640 operations only and no multiplication is required using the transform in [22] with 16 additions and the proposed quantisation matrix, $\tilde{Q}_{f-proposed}$, with bit-shift operations only. The reduction achieved to 512 additions, it means a saving of 44.8% compared with JPEG baseline and 27.3% compared with the quantisation matrix in [23].

Table 1. Arithmetic complexity comparison.

Approximation	Addition	Bits-shift	Multiplication	Round (.)	Total	Operation saving
Standard JPEG	928	0	188	64	1180	-
Transf. in [22] and Q_{JPEG}	512	0	128	64	704	40.34%
Transf. in [22] and $Q_{proposed}$	512	0	128	64	704	40.34%
Transf. in [22] and $\tilde{Q}_{proposed}$	512	128	0	0	640	45.8%
Transf. in [23] and $\tilde{Q}_{Oliveira}$	704	128	0	0	832	29.5%

6 Results and Discussion

For an appropriate assessment of our proposed quantisation matrix in image compression application, the simulation of the JPEG-like standard is considered. Four different scenarios summarized in Table 2 have been applied to the three well-known gray-scale test images of size 512×512: Lena, Boat and Bridge. These images are chosen for its different in the type of content and the amount of detail they contain, which is indicated by their Spatial Frequency Measure (SFM) [26] and Spectral Activity Measure (SAM) [27] parameters. Kipping the same values of CR for the different considered scenarios, the PSNR improvement is given in Table 2.

By analyzing the obtained results in Table 2, we can notice that the high PSNR values are achieved when we used the proposed bit-shift approximate quantization matrix combined with the integer DCT transform suggested in [22] for all considered test images. This can offer an average gain in PSNR until about 2 dB. A slight improvement can be shown using the approach suggested in [23], about 0.3 dB compared to the conventional JPEG approach.

Table 2. Image quality comparison in terms of PSNR for different test images.

Test image	CR	Quantisation matrix	PSNR (db)	PSNR improvement (db)
Lena	14.70	Q_{JPEG}	29.81	-
	14.56	$Q_{proposed}$	31.08	1.27
	14.65	$\tilde{Q}_{proposed}$	32.03	2.22
	14.86	$\tilde{Q}_{oliveira}$	29.84	0.03
Boat	12.16	Q_{JPEG}	28.76	-
	11.96	$Q_{proposed}$	29.83	1.07
	12.10	$\tilde{Q}_{proposed}$	31.14	2.38
	12.09	$\tilde{Q}_{oliveira}$	29.14	0.38
Bridge	7.72	Q_{JPEG}	25.70	-
	7.67	$Q_{proposed}$	26.31	0.61
	7.66	$\tilde{Q}_{proposed}$	27.29	1.59
	7.81	$\tilde{Q}_{oliveira}$	25.77	0.07

7   Conclusion

This paper proposes a new multiplier-less JPEG quantisation matrix based on energy distribution of existing 8×8 integer DCT approximations. On one hand, to assure efficient image compression and on the other hand, to eliminate and rounding operations due on quantisation stage. The proposed quantisation matrix improves their capability in image compression, whose it provides high PSNR improvement compared to the existing quantisation matrices.

References

1. Wallace, G.K.: The JPEG still picture compression standard. IEEE Trans. Consum. Electr. **38**(1), xviii–xxxiv (1992)
2. Richter, T., Clark, R.: Why JPEG is not JPEG -testing a 25 years old Standard. In: 2018 Picture Coding Symposium (PCS), pp. 1–5 (2018)
3. Fan, Z., de Queiroz, R.L.: Identification of bitmap compression history: JPEG detection and quantizer estimation. IEEE Trans. Image Process. **12**(2), 230–235 (2003)
4. Bianchi, T., Piva, A.: Image forgery localization via block-grained analysis of JPEG artifacts. IEEE Trans. Inf. Foren. Secur. **7**(3), 1003–1017 (2012)
5. Wang, Q., Zhang, R.: Double JPEG compression forensics based on a convolutional neural network. In: EURASIP J. Inf. Secur. **23** (2016)
6. Li, W., Zhou, W., Zhang, W., Qin, C., Hu, H., Yu, N.: Shortening the cover for fast JPEG steganography. IEEE Trans. Circuits Syst. Video Technol. **30**(6), 1745–1757 (2019)
7. Tao, J., Li, S., Zhang, X., Wang, Z.: Towards robust image steganography. IEEE Trans. Circuits Syst. Video Technol. **29**(2), 594–600 (2019)
8. Jiao, S., Jin, Z., Chang, C., Zhou, C., Zou, W., Li, X.: Compression of phase-only holograms with JPEG standard and deep learning. Appl. Sci. **8**(8), 1258 (2018)

9. Parker, M.: Digital Signal Processing 101: Everything You Need to Know to Get Started, 2nd edn, Elsevier, Pacific Grove (2017)
10. Wu, Y.-G.: GA-based DCT quantisation table design procedure for medical images. IEE-Vis. Image Sig. Process. **151**(5), 353–359 (2004)
11. Lazzerini, B., Marcelloni, F., Vecchio, M.: A multi-objective evolutionary approach to image quality/compression trade-off in JPEG baseline algorithm. Appl. Soft Comput. **10**(2), 548–561 (2010)
12. Tuba, M., Bacanin, N.: JPEG quantization tables selection by the firefly algorithm. In: International Conference on Multimedia Computing and Systems (ICMCS), pp. 153–158 (2014)
13. Ochoa-Domínguez, H., Rao, K.R.: Discrete Cosine Transform, 2nd edn, CRC Press, Boca Raton(2019)
14. Kouadria, N., Mechouek, K., Harize, S., Doghmane, N.: Region-of-interest based image compression using the discrete Tchebichef transform in wireless visual sensor networks. Comput. Electr. Eng. **73**, 194–208 (2019)
15. Jridi, M., Meher, P.K.: Scalable approximate DCT architectures for efficient HEVC-compliant video coding. IEEE Trans. Circuits Syst. Video Technol. **27**(8), 1815–1825 (2017)
16. de A. Coutinho, V., Cintra, R.J., Bayer, F.M.: Low-complexity multidimensional DCT approximations for high-order tensor data decorrelation. IEEE Trans. Image Process. **26**(5), 2296–2310 (2017)
17. Zhang, J., Shi, W., Zhou, L., Gong, R., Wang, L., Zhou, H.: A low-power and high-PSNR unified DCT/IDCT architecture based on EARC and enhanced scale factor approximation. IEEE Access **7**, 165684–165691 (2019)
18. Gassoumi, I., Touil, L., Ouni, B., Mtibaa, A.: An efficient design of DCT approximation based on quantum dot cellular automata (QCA) technology. J. Electr. Comput. Eng. **2019** (2019)
19. Oliveira, P.A.M., Cintra, R.J., Bayer, F.M., Kulasekera, S., Madanayake, A.: Low-complexity image and video coding based on an approximate discrete Tchebichef transform. IEEE Trans. Circuits Syst. Video Technol. **27**(5), 1066–1076 (2016)
20. Ezhilarasi, R., Venkatalakshmi, K., Pradeep Khanth, B.: Enhanced approximate discrete cosine transforms for image compression and multimedia applications. Multimedia Tools Appl. **79**, 8539–8552 (2020)
21. Taylor, C.N., Panigrahi, D., Dey, S.: Design of an adaptive architecture for energy efficient wireless image communication. In: International Workshop on Embedded Computer Systems (SAMOS), pp. 260–273 (2001)
22. Brahimi, M., Bouden, T., Brahimi, T., Boubchir, L.: A novel and efficient 8-point DCT approximation for image compression. Multimedia Tools Appl. **79**, 7615–7631 (2020)
23. Oliveira, P.A.M., Oliveira, R.S., Cintra, R.J., Bayer, F.M., Madanayake, A.: JPEG quantisation requires bit-shifts only. Electr. Lett. **53**(9), 588–590 (2017)
24. Cintra, R.J., Bayer, F.M., Tablada, C.J.: Low-complexity 8-point DCT approximations based on integer functions. Sig. Process. **99**, 201–214 (2014)
25. Cintra, R.J., Bayer, F.M.: A DCT approximation for image compression. IEEE Sig. Process. Lett. **18**(10), 579–582 (2011)
26. Eskicioglu, A.M., Fisher, P.S.: Image quality measures and their performance. IEEE Trans. Commun. **43**(12), 2959–2965 (1995)
27. Grgic, S., Mrak, M., Grgic, M.: Comparison of JPEG image coders. In: Proceedings of the 3rd International Symposium on Video Processing and Multimedia Communications, pp. 79–85 (2001)

Federated Learning Meets Fairness and Differential Privacy

Manisha Padala[✉], Sankarshan Damle, and Sujit Gujar

Machine Learning Lab, International Institute of Information Technology (IIIT),
Hyderabad, Hyderabad, India
{manisha.padala,sankarshan.damle}@research.iiit.ac.in,
sujit.gujar@iiit.ac.in

Abstract. Deep learning's unprecedented success raises several ethical concerns ranging from biased predictions to data privacy. Researchers tackle these issues by introducing fairness metrics, or federated learning, or differential privacy. A first, this work presents an ethical federated learning model, incorporating all three measures simultaneously. Experiments on the Adult, Bank and Dutch datasets highlight the resulting "empirical interplay" between accuracy, fairness, and privacy.

Keywords: Federated learning · Fairness · Differential privacy

1 Introduction

Deep Learning's success is made possible in part due to the availability of big datasets – distributed across several owners. To resolve this, researchers propose *Federated Learning* (FL), which enables parallel training of a unified model [9]. In FL, these respective owners are referred to as 'clients' (henceforth *agents*). The agents individually train a model on their private data. A 'central server,' referred henceforth as an *aggregator*, receives the individual models and computes a single overall model through different heuristics for achieving high performance on any test data [16].

The data available with each agent is often imbalanced or biased. Machine learning models may further amplify the bias present. More concretely, when trained only for achieving high accuracy, the model predictions become highly biased towards certain demographic groups like gender, age, or race [3]. Such groups are known as the *sensitive attributes*. Post the impossibility result on achieving a perfectly unbiased model [3]; researchers propose approaches that focus on minimizing the bias while maintaining high accuracy [13].

Invariably all these approaches require the knowledge of the sensitive attribute. These attributes often comprise the most critical information. The law regulations at various places prohibit using such attributes to develop ML models. E.g., the EU General Data Protection Regulation prevents the collection of sensitive user attributes [15]. Thus, it is imperative to address discrimination while preserving the leakage of sensitive attributes from the data samples.

© Springer Nature Switzerland AG 2021
T. Mantoro et al. (Eds.): ICONIP 2021, CCIS 1517, pp. 692–699, 2021.
https://doi.org/10.1007/978-3-030-92310-5_80

Observing that the aggregator in FL has no direct access to private data or sensitive attributes, prima facie preserves privacy. However, there exist several attacks that highlight the information leak in an FL setting [10]. To plug this information leak, researchers either use cryptographic solutions based mainly on complex *Partial Homomorphic Encryption* (PHE) or use Differential Privacy (DP). Private FL solutions using PHE (e,g., [17]) suffer from computational inefficiency and post-processing attacks. Thus, in this work, we focus on the strong privacy guarantees provided by a *differentially private* solution [12,14].

FPFL Framework. A first, we incorporate both fairness and privacy guarantees for an FL setting through our novel framework *FPFL*: Fair and Private Federated Learning. Our primary goal is to simultaneously preserve the privacy of the training data and the sensitive attribute while ensuring fairness. With FPFL, we achieve this goal by ingeniously decoupling the training process in two *phases*. In Phase 1, each agent trains a model, on its private dataset, for fair predictions. Then in Phase 2, the agents train a differentially private model to *mimic* the fair predictions from the previous model. At last, each agent communicates the private model from Phase 2 to the aggregator.

Fairness and Privacy Notions. The deliberate phase-wise training ensures an overall fair and accurate model which does not encode any information related to the sensitive attribute. Our framework is general and absorbs any fairness or DP metrics. It also allows any fairness guaranteeing technique in Phase 1. We demonstrate FPFL's efficacy w.r.t. the following.

1. Fairness: We consider *demographic parity* (DemP) and *equalized odds* (EO). DemP states that a model's predictions are independent of a sensitive attribute of the dataset [5]. EO states that the *false positive rates* and *false negative rates* of a model are equal across different groups or independent of the sensitive attribute [7].
2. Privacy: We quantify the privacy guarantees within the notion of (ϵ, δ)-*local differential privacy* [6]. In our setting, the aggregator acts as an adversary with access to each agent's model. We show that with local-DP, the privacy of each agent's training data and sensitive attribute is protected from the aggregator.

Empirical Interplay Between Accuracy, Fairness, and Privacy. The trade-off between fairness and privacy in ML is under-explored [2,4,11,15]. To the best of our knowledge, only [15] looks at the confidentiality of the sensitive attribute. However, in [15] the authors simultaneously train the model to achieve accuracy and fairness while ensuring DP; and only add noise to the gradients from the fairness loss. Thus, their approach only preserves the sensitive attribute and *not* the training data. Refer to our extended version [8, Table 1] for a detailed comparison.

2 Preliminaries

We consider a binary classification problem with $\mathcal{X}$ as our (d-dimensional) instance space, $\mathcal{X} \in \mathbb{R}^d$; and our output space as $\mathcal{Y} \in \{0, 1\}$. We consider a single sensitive attribute $\mathcal{A}$ associated with each instance. Such an attribute may represent sensitive information like age, gender, or caste. W.r.t $\mathcal{A}$, every $a \in \mathcal{A}$ represents a particular category of the sensitive attribute; e.g., like male or female.

Federated Learning Model. Federated Learning (FL) decentralizes the classical machine learning training process. FL comprises two type of actors: (i) a set of agents $\mathbb{A} = \{1, \ldots, m\}$ where each agent i owns a *private* dataset $\mathcal{X}_i{}^1$; and (ii) an *Aggregator*. Each agent provides its model, trained on its dataset, to the aggregator. The aggregator's job is to derive an overall model, then communicate it back to the agents. This back-and-forth process continues until a model with sufficient accuracy is derived.

At the start of an FL training, the aggregator communicates an initial, often random, set of model parameters to the agents. Let us refer to the initial parameters as θ_0. At each timestep t each agent updates their individual parameters denoted by $\theta_{(i,t)}$, using their private datasets. A random subset of agents then communicates the updated parameters to the aggregator, who derives an overall model through different heuristics [16]. In this paper, we focus on the weighted sum heuristics, i.e., the overall model parameters take the form $\theta_t = \sum_{j \in \mathbb{A}} \frac{|\mathcal{X}_j|}{\mathbf{X}} \cdot \theta_{(j,t)}$. To distinguish the final overall model, we refer to it as θ^*, calculated at a timestep T.

Fairness Metrics. We consider the following two fairness constraints.

Definition 1 (Demographic Parity (DemP)). *A classifier h satisfies Demographic Parity under a distribution over $(\mathcal{X}, \mathcal{A}, \mathcal{Y})$ if its predictions $h(\mathcal{X})$ is independent of the sensitive attribute $\mathcal{A}$. That is, $\forall a \in \mathcal{A}$ and $p \in \{0,1\}$,*

$$\Pr[h(\mathcal{X}) = p | \mathcal{A} = a] = \Pr[h(\mathcal{X}) = p]$$

Given that $p \in \{0,1\}$, we have, $\forall a\ \mathbb{E}[h(\mathcal{X})|\mathcal{A} = a] = \mathbb{E}[h(\mathcal{X})]$.

Definition 2 (Equalized Odds (EO)). *A classifier h satisfies Equalized Odds under a distribution over $(\mathcal{X}, \mathcal{A}, \mathcal{Y})$ if its predictions $h(\mathcal{X})$ are independent of the sensitive attribute $\mathcal{A}$ given the label $\mathcal{Y}$. That is, $\forall a \in \mathcal{A}$, $p \in \{0,1\}$ and $y \in \mathcal{Y}$*

$$\Pr[h(\mathcal{X}) = p | \mathcal{A} = a, \mathcal{Y} = y] = \Pr[h(\mathcal{X}) = p | \mathcal{Y} = y]$$

Given that $p \in \{0,1\}$, we can say $\forall a, y$, $\mathbb{E}[h(\mathcal{X})|\mathcal{A} = a, \mathcal{Y} = y] = \mathbb{E}[h(\mathcal{X})|\mathcal{Y} = y]$.

Local Differential Privacy (LDP).

Definition 3 (Local Differential Privacy (LDP) [6]). *For an input set $\mathcal{X}$ and the set of noisy outputs $\mathcal{Y}$, a randomized algorithm $\mathcal{M} : \mathcal{X} \to \mathcal{Y}$ is said to be (ϵ, δ)-LDP if $\forall x, x' \in \mathcal{X}$ and $\forall y \in \mathcal{Y}$ the following holds,*

$$\Pr[\mathcal{M}(x) = y] \leq \exp(\epsilon) \Pr[\mathcal{M}(x') = y] + \delta. \tag{1}$$

---

[1] Let $|\mathcal{X}_i|$ denote the cardinality of $\mathcal{X}_i$ with $\mathbf{X} = \sum_i |\mathcal{X}_i|$.

The privacy budget, ϵ, controls the trade-off between quality (or, in our case, the accuracy) of the output vis-a-vis the privacy guarantee. That is, lower the budget, better the privacy but at the cost of quality. The "δ" parameter in (1) allows for the violation of the upper-bound ϵ. However, with a small probability. We consider the "black-box" model for our *adversary*, i.e., the aggregator has access to the trained model and can interact with it via inputs and outputs.

3   FPFL: Fair and Private Federated Learning

In FPFL, we consider a classification problem. Each agent i deploys two multi-layer *neural networks* (NNs) to learn the model parameters in each phase. The training comprises of *two* phases. In Phase 1, each agent privately trains a model on its private dataset to learn a highly fair and accurate model. Then in Phase 2, each agent trains a second model to mimic the first, with DP guarantees. In FPFL, only the model trained in Phase 2 is sent to the aggregator.

To remain consistent with FL notations, we denote the model parameters learned for Phase 1 with ϕ and Phase 2 with θ. Likewise, we represent the total number of training steps in Phase 1 with T_1, and for Phase 2, we use T_2.

Phase 1: Fair-SGD. In this phase, we train the network to maximize accuracy while achieving the best possible fairness on each agent's private dataset. We adapt the *Lagrangian Multiplier method* [13] to achieve a fair and accurate model. We denote the model for agent i as h^{ϕ_i} with parameters ϕ_i. Briefly, the method trains a network with a unified loss that has two components. The first component of the loss maximizes accuracy, i.e., the cross-entropy loss,

$$l_{CE}(h^{\phi_i}, \mathcal{X}, \mathcal{Y}) = \mathop{\mathbb{E}}_{(x,y)\sim(\mathcal{X},\mathcal{Y})}[-y_i \log(h^{\phi_i}(x)) - (1-y)\log(1 - h^{\phi_i}(x))]$$

The second component of the loss is a specific fairness measure. For achieving DemP (Definition 1), the loss function is given by,

$$l_{DemP}(h^{\phi_i}, \mathcal{X}, \mathcal{A}) = |\mathbb{E}[h^{\phi_i}(x)|\mathcal{A} = a] - \mathbb{E}[h^{\phi_i}(x)]| \qquad (2)$$

For achieving EO (Definition 2), the corresponding loss function is,

$$l_{EO}(h^{\phi_i}, \mathcal{X}, \mathcal{A}, \mathcal{Y}) = |\mathbb{E}[h^{\phi_i}(x)|\mathcal{A} = a, y] - \mathbb{E}[h^{\phi_i}(x)|y]| \qquad (3)$$

Hence, the overall loss from the Lagrangian method is,

$$L_1(h^{\phi_i}, \mathcal{X}, \mathcal{A}, Y) = l_{CE} + \lambda l_k, \quad k \in \{DemP, EO\} \qquad (4)$$

In the equation above, $\lambda \in \mathbb{R}^+$ is the Lagrangian multiplier. The overall optimization is as follows: $\min_{\phi} \max_{\lambda} L_1(\cdot)$. Thus, each agent trains the Fair-SGD model h_i^{ϕ} to obtain the best accuracy w.r.t. a given fairness metric. We present it formally in [8, Algorithm 1].

Phase 2: DP-SGD. In this phase, the agents train a model and communicate it with the aggregator. This model denoted by h^{θ_i} is trained by each agent i to learn the predictions of its Fair-SGD model (h^{ϕ_i}). The loss function is given by,

$$L_2(h^{\theta_i}, h^{\phi_i}) = \mathop{\mathbb{E}}_{x\sim\mathcal{X}}[-h^{\phi_i}(x)\log(h^{\theta_i}(x)) - (1 - h^{\phi_i}(x))\log(1 - h^{\phi_i}(x))] \qquad (5)$$

Equation 5 is the cross-entropy loss between predictions from Phase 2's model and the labels given by the predictions from Fair-SGD model, i.e., $L_2(\cdot) \downarrow \Longrightarrow \theta_i \rightarrow \phi_i$.

To preserve the privacy of training data and sensitive attribute, we focus on (ϵ, δ)-LDP using DP-SGD [Algorithm 1][1]. In it, the privacy of the training data is preserved by sanitizing the gradients provided by SGD with *Gaussian* noise $(\mathcal{N}(0, \sigma^2))$. Given that the learned model h^{θ_i} mimics h^{ϕ_i}, the learned model is reasonably fair and accurate. [8, Algorithm 2] formally presents the training.

FPFL Framework. The θ_i's from each agent are communicated to the aggregator for further performance improvement. The aggregator takes a weighted sum of the individual θ_i's and broadcasts it to the agents. The agents further train on top of the aggregated model before sending it to the aggregator. This process gets repeated to achieve the following overall objective,

$$\theta^* = \arg\min_{\theta} \sum_{j \in [m]} \frac{|\mathcal{X}_j|}{\mathbf{X}} \cdot L_2(h^\theta, h^{\phi_j}). \tag{6}$$

The two phases are coupled and comprise the FPFL framework [8, Figure 2]. Observe that the framework presents itself as a *plug-and-play* system, i.e., a user can use any other loss function instead of L_1 and L_2, or change the underlying algorithms for fairness and DP, or do any other tweak it so desires.

FPFL: Differential Privacy Bounds. We remark that the model learned in Phase 1, h^ϕ, requires access to both the training data $(\mathcal{X})$ and the sensitive attribute $(\mathcal{A})$. Fortunately, this phase is entirely independent of the FL aggregation process. In contrast, the model learned in Phase 2, h^θ – trained to mimic the predictions of h^ϕ – is communicated to the aggregator.

Any information leak in FPFL may take place in the following two ways. Firstly, training data may get compromised through h^θ. Secondly, mimicking the predictions from h^ϕ may, in turn, leak information about the sensitive attribute. We observe that the DP guarantee for the training data follows from [1, Theorem 1] directly. In [8, Proposition 1], we formally prove that the training process in Phase 2 does not leak any additional information regarding $\mathcal{A}$ to the aggregator. Then, Corollary 1 uses the result with [1, Theorem 1] to provide the privacy bounds. The formal proof is available at [8].

Corollary 1. *For the FPFL framework, $\forall i \in \mathbb{A}$ there exists constants c_1 and c_2, with the sampling probability $q_i = B_i/\mathcal{X}_i$ and the total number of timesteps T in Phase 2, such that for any $\epsilon_i < c_1 q_i^2 T$, the framework satisfies (ϵ_i, δ_i)-LDP for $\delta_i > 0$ and for $\sigma_i \geq c_2 \frac{q_i\sqrt{T \ln(1/\delta_i)}}{\epsilon_i}$.*

4   FPFL: Experimental Results

Datasets. We conduct experiments on the following three datasets: Adult [13], Bank [13] and Dutch [18]. In the Adult dataset, the task is to predict if an individual's income is above or below USD 50000. The sensitive attribute is *gender*. In the Bank dataset, the task is to predict if an agent has subscribed to the term deposit or not. Here, *age* as the sensitive attribute grouped as 25 to 60 majority group, and those under 25 or over 60 form the minority group. In the Dutch dataset, *gender* is the sensitive attribute, and the task is to predict the occupation. For training an FL model, we split the datasets such that each agent has an equal number of samples. In order to do so, we duplicate the samples in the existing data – especially the minority group – to get exactly $50k$ samples for the first two datasets. Despite this, each agent ends with an uneven distribution of samples belonging to each attribute, maintaining the data heterogeneity. This results in heterogeneous data distribution among the agents. We hold 20% of the data from each dataset as the test set.

Hyperparameters. For each agent, we train two fully connected neural networks having the same architecture. Each network has two hidden layers with $(500, 100)$ neurons and ReLU activation. For DemP, we consider 5 agents in our experiments and split datasets accordingly. To estimate EO, we need sufficient samples for both sensitive groups such that each group has enough samples with both the possible outcomes. In the Adult dataset, we find only 3% female samples earning above USD 50000. Similarly, in the Bank dataset, the minority group that has subscribed to the term deposit forms only 1% of the entire data. Due to this, in our experiments for EO, we consider only 2 agents.

Training Fair-SGD (Phase 1). We use [8, Algorithm 1], with $\eta = 0.001$ and $B = 500$. The optimizer used is Adam for updating the loss using the Lagrangian multiplier method. For the Adult dataset, we initialize with $\lambda = 10$, and for Bank and Dutch, we initialize with $\lambda = 5$. The model is trained for 200 epochs.

Training DP-SGD (Phase 2). We use [8, Algorithm 2], with $\eta = 0.25$, $B = 500$, and the clipping norm $C = 1.5$. For the optimizer we use the Tensorflow-privacy library's Keras DP-SGD optimizer. We train the model in this phase for 5 epochs locally before aggregation. This process is repeated 4 times, i.e. $T = 20$.

Baselines. To compare the resultant interplay between accuracy, fairness, and privacy in FPFL, we create the following two baselines.

B1 In this, the agents train the model in an FL setting only for maximizing accuracy without any fairness constraints in the loss.

B2 To obtain B2, each agent trains the model in an FL setting for both accuracy and fairness using [8, Algorithm 1] with DemP loss (2) or EO loss (3).

(ϵ, δ)-*bounds.* We calculate the bounds for an agent from Corollary 1. We vary ϵ in the range $(0, 10]$ by appropriately selecting σ (noise multiplier). Observe that $\epsilon \to \infty$ for B1 and B2 as the sensitivity is unbounded. As standard $\forall i \in \mathbb{A}$, we keep $\delta = 10^{-4} < 1/|\mathcal{X}_i|$ for DemP and $\delta = 0.5 \times 10^{-4} < 1/|\mathcal{X}_i|$ for EO.

DemP and EO. When the loss for DemP (2) and EO (3) is exactly zero, the model is perfectly fair. As perfect fairness is impossible, we try to minimize the loss. In our results, to quantify the fairness guarantees, we plot l_{DemP} and l_{EO} on the test set. *Lower* the values, *better* is the guarantee. For readability we refer l_{DemP} and l_{EO} as DemP and EO in our results.

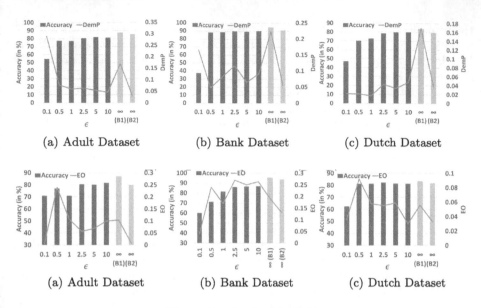

(a) Adult Dataset   (b) Bank Dataset   (c) Dutch Dataset

Fig. 2. Equalized odds (EO)

Demographic Parity: Figure 1. We consider an FL setting with 5 agents for ensuring DemP. For the Adult dataset, Fig. 1(a), we find that for B1, we get an accuracy of 87% and a DemP of 0.17. We observe that a model trained with fairness constraints, i.e., for B2, has a reduced accuracy of 85%, but DemP reduces to 0.029. We find similar trends in the baselines for the Bank (Fig. 1(b)) and the Dutch datasets (Fig. 1(c)). Introducing privacy guarantees with FPFL, we observe a further compromise in accuracy and fairness compared to our baselines. In general, with increasing ϵ, i.e., increasing privacy loss, there is an improvement in the trade-off of accuracy and DemP. For $\epsilon = 10$, the accuracy and DemP are similar to that in B2. While the drop in accuracy is consistent with the decrease in ϵ, DemP values do not always follow this trend.

Equalized Odds: Figure 2. For EO, we consider FL setting with only 2 agents. From Fig. 2(a), we find in B1 the accuracy is 87% for the Adult dataset with EO as 0.104. With B2, we obtain reduced accuracy of 80%, but EO reduces to 0.008. We find similar trends in the baselines for the Bank (Fig. 2(b)) and the Dutch datasets (Fig. 2(c)). When we compare the FPFL training, which also guarantees privacy, we observe a trade-off in fairness and accuracy. We note that ensuring EO, especially in the Bank dataset, is very challenging. Therefore, the trade-off is not as smooth. With the decrease in ϵ, the accuracy decreases, but the EO values do not follow any trend. We believe this is due to the lack of distinct samples for each category after splitting the data (despite duplication) for FL.

Conclusion. We presented FPFL: a framework that learns fair and accurate models while preserving privacy. A first, we provided a DP guarantee for the training data and sensitive attributes in an FL setting. We then applied FPFL on the Adult, Bank, and Dutch datasets to highlight the relation between accuracy, fairness, and privacy of an FL model.

References

1. Abadi, M., et al.: Deep learning with differential privacy. In: ACM SIGSAC CCS (2016)
2. Bagdasaryan, E., Poursaeed, O., Shmatikov, V.: Differential privacy has disparate impact on model accuracy. In: NeurIPS (2019)
3. Chouldechova, A.: Fair prediction with disparate impact: a study of bias in recidivism prediction instruments. Big Data **5**(2), 153–163 (2017)
4. Cummings, R., Gupta, V., Kimpara, D., Morgenstern, J.: On the compatibility of privacy and fairness. In: Adjunct Publication of the 27th Conference on User Modeling, Adaptation and Personalization (2019)
5. Dwork, C., Hardt, M., Pitassi, T., Reingold, O., Zemel, R.: Fairness through awareness. In: Proceedings of the 3rd Innovations in Theoretical Computer Science Conference, pp. 214–226 (2012)
6. Dwork, C., Roth, A., et al.: The algorithmic foundations of differential privacy. Found. Trends Theor. Comput. Sci. **9**(3–4), 211–407 (2014)
7. Hardt, M., Price, E., Srebro, N.: Equality of opportunity in supervised learning. In: NIPS (2016)
8. Manisha, P., Damle, S., Gujar, S.: Federated learning meets fairness and differential privacy. CoRR (2021). https://arxiv.org/abs/2108.09932
9. McMahan, B., Moore, E., Ramage, D., Hampson, S., y Arcas, B.A.: Communication-efficient learning of deep networks from decentralized data. In: Artificial Intelligence and Statistics, pp. 1273–1282. PMLR (2017)
10. Mothukuri, V., Parizi, R.M., Pouriyeh, S., Huang, Y., Dehghantanha, A., Srivastava, G.: A survey on security and privacy of federated learning. Futur. Gener. Comput. Syst. **115**, 619–640 (2021)
11. Mozannar, H., Ohannessian, M., Srebro, N.: Fair learning with private demographic data. In: International Conference on Machine Learning. PMLR (2020)
12. Naseri, M., Hayes, J., De Cristofaro, E.: Toward robustness and privacy in federated learning: experimenting with local and central differential privacy. arXiv preprint arXiv:2009.03561 (2020)
13. Padala, M., Gujar, S.: FNNC: achieving fairness through neural networks. In: IJCAI. International Joint Conferences on Artificial Intelligence Organization (2020)
14. Shokri, R., Shmatikov, V.: Privacy-preserving deep learning. In: Proceedings of the 22nd ACM SIGSAC Conference on Computer and Communications Security (2015)
15. Tran, C., Fioretto, F., Van Hentenryck, P.: Differentially private and fair deep learning: a Lagrangian dual approach. arXiv preprint arXiv:2009.12562 (2020)
16. Wahab, O.A., Mourad, A., Otrok, H., Taleb, T.: Federated machine learning: survey, multi-level classification, desirable criteria and future directions in communication and networking systems. IEEE Commun. Surv. Tutor. **23**(2), 1342–1397 (2021)
17. Zhang, C., Li, S., Xia, J., Wang, W., Yan, F., Liu, Y.: BatchCrypt: efficient homomorphic encryption for cross-silo federated learning. In: 2020 USENIX Annual Technical Conference (USENIX ATC 2020) (2020)
18. Žliobaite, I., Kamiran, F., Calders, T.: Handling conditional discrimination. In: 2011 IEEE 11th International Conference on Data Mining (2011)

Spark Deficient Gabor Frame Provides A Novel Analysis Operator For Compressed Sensing

Vasiliki Kouni[1,2(✉)] and Holger Rauhut[1]

[1] Chair for Mathematics of Information Processing, RWTH Aachen University,
Aachen, Germany
{kouni,rauhut}@mathc.rwth-aachen.de
[2] Department of Informatics and Telecommunications, National and Kapodistrian
University of Athens, Athens, Greece
vicky-kouni@di.uoa.gr

Abstract. The analysis sparsity model is a very effective approach in modern Compressed Sensing applications. Specifically, redundant analysis operators can lead to fewer measurements needed for reconstruction when employing the analysis l_1-minimization in Compressed Sensing. In this paper, we pick an eigenvector of the Zauner unitary matrix and –under certain assumptions on the ambient dimension– we build a spark deficient Gabor frame. The analysis operator associated with such a frame, is a new (highly) redundant Gabor transform, which we use as a sparsifier in Compressed Sensing. We conduct computational experiments –on both synthetic and real-world data– solving the analysis l_1-minimization problem of Compressed Sensing, with four different choices of analysis operators, including our Gabor analysis operator. The results show that our proposed redundant Gabor transform outperforms –in all cases– Gabor transforms generated by state-of-the-art window vectors of time-frequency analysis.

Keywords: Compressed sensing · Analysis sparsity · Gabor
transform · Window vector · Spark deficient gabor frame

1 Introduction

Compressed Sensing (CS) [1] is a modern technique to recover vectors $x \in \mathbb{V}^L$ ($\mathbb{V} = \mathbb{R}$ or $\mathbb{C}$) from few linear and possibly corrupted measurements

$$y = Ax + e \in \mathbb{V}^K, \tag{1}$$

$K < L$. The applications of CS vary among Radar Imaging [2], Cryptography [3], Telecommunications [4], Magnetic Resonance Imaging [5], Deep Learning [6].

Related Work: CS heavily relies on sparsity/compressibility of the signal of interest x. Sparse data models are split in synthesis and analysis sparsity. The former is by now very well studied [5,7–9]. On the other hand, significant research

© Springer Nature Switzerland AG 2021
T. Mantoro et al. (Eds.): ICONIP 2021, CCIS 1517, pp. 700–708, 2021.
https://doi.org/10.1007/978-3-030-92310-5_81

has also been conducted over the last years towards its analysis counterpart [10–12], (also known as co-sparse model [13,14]), due to the flexibility it provides in modelling sparse signals, since it leverages the redundancy of the involved analysis operators. Related work [10] has also demonstrated that it is computationally more appealing to solve the optimization algorithm of analysis CS since a) the actual optimization takes place in the ambient space b) the algorithm may need less measurements for perfect reconstruction, if one uses a redundant transform instead of an orthogonal one.

Motivation: Our work is inspired by the articles [10,11,15], which propose either analysis operators associated to redundant frames with atoms in general position, or a finite difference operator, in which many linear dependencies appear for large dimensions. In a similar spirit, we also deploy frames, but we differentiate our approach by using *spark deficient frames*, i.e. their elements are not in general linear position. Our intuition behind this choice is based on remarks of [14]. The authors of [14] refer to the union-of-subspaces model [16], according to which, it is desired to have analysis operators exhibiting high linear dependencies among their rows; this is a condition satisfied by spark deficient frames. To that end, we introduce a novel analysis operator associated with a spark deficient Gabor frame (SDGF). The latter can be generated by time-frequency shifts of any eigenvector of the Zauner unitary matrix [17], under certain assumptions. To the best of our knowledge, its efficiency when combined with CS has not yet been demonstrated. Moreover, since Gabor transforms are little explored in terms of CS [9,18,19], we compare our proposed Gabor transform to three other Gabor transforms, emerging from state-of-the-art window vectors in time-frequency analysis. Finally, we illustrate the practical importance of our method for synthetic and real-world data.

Key Contributions: Our novelty is twofold: (a) we generate a SDGF based on a window vector, associate this SDGF to a new Gabor analysis operator and use the latter as a sparsifier in analysis CS (b) we compare numerically our proposed method with three other Gabor analysis operators, based on common windows of time-frequency analysis, on synthetic data and real-world speech signals. Our experiments show that our method outperforms all others, consistently for synthetic and real-world signals.

2   Compressed Sensing Setup

Notation: For a set of indices $N = \{0, 1, \ldots, N-1\}$, we write $[N]$. The set of (column) vectors $|0\rangle, |1\rangle, \ldots, |L-1\rangle$ is the standard basis of $\mathbb{C}^L$. We write $\mathbb{Z}_L$ for the ring of residues $\mathrm{mod}L$, that is $\mathbb{Z}_L = \{0\mathrm{mod}L, 1\mathrm{mod}L, \ldots, (L-1)\mathrm{mod}L\}$ and $a \equiv b(\mathrm{mod}L)$ denotes the congruence modulo, $a, b \in \mathbb{Z}$. The support of a signal $x \in \mathbb{V}^L$ is denoted by $\mathrm{supp}(x) = \{i \in [L] : x_i \neq 0\}$. For its cardinality we write $|\mathrm{supp}(x)|$ and if $|\mathrm{supp}(x)| \leq s << L$, we call x s-sparse.

Analysis Compressed Sensing Formulation: As already described in Section I, the main idea of CS is to reconstruct a signal $x \in \mathbb{V}^L$ from

$y = Ax + e \in \mathbb{V}^K$, $K < L$, where A is the so-called measurement matrix and $e \in \mathbb{V}^K$, with $\|e\|_2 \leq \eta$, corresponds to noise. To do so, we first assume there exists a redundant sparsifying transform $\Phi \in \mathbb{V}^{P \times L}$ ($P > L$) called the analysis operator, such that Φx is (approximately) sparse. On the other hand, the choice of A is tailored to the application for which CS is employed. In this paper, we choose A to be a randomly subsampled identity operator, since this is considered a standard CS setup. Moreover, this type of measurement matrix has proven to work well [8], since it meets conditions ensuring exact or approximate reconstruction of x, i.e., the matrix has small *coherence* or satisfies the *restricted isometry property* [7]. Now, using analysis sparsity in CS, we wish to recover x from y. A common approach is the *analysis l_1-minimization* problem

$$\min_{x \in \mathbb{V}^L} \|\Phi x\|_1 \quad \text{subject to} \quad \|Ax - y\|_2 \leq \eta, \tag{2}$$

or a regularized[1] version [20] of it:

$$\min_{x \in \mathbb{V}^L} \|\Phi x\|_1 + \frac{\mu}{2}\|x - x_0\|_2^2 \quad \text{subject to} \quad \|Ax - y\|_2 \leq \eta, \tag{3}$$

with x_0 being an initial guess on x and $\mu > 0$ a smoothing parameter. We will devote the next Section to the construction of a suitable analysis operator Φ.

3   Gabor Frames

Gabor Systems: A *discrete Gabor system* (g, a, b) [21] is defined as a collection of time-frequency shifts of the so-called window vector $g \in \mathbb{C}^L$, expressed as

$$g_{n,m}(l) = e^{2\pi i m b l / L} g(l - na), \quad l \in [L], \tag{4}$$

where a, b denote time and frequency (lattice) parameters respectively, $n \in [N]$ chosen such that $N = L/a \in \mathbb{N}$ and $m \in [M]$ chosen such that $M = L/b \in \mathbb{N}$ denote time and frequency shift indices, respectively. If (4) spans $\mathbb{C}^L$, it is called a *Gabor frame*. The number of elements in (g, a, b) according to (4) is $P = MN = L^2/ab$ and if (g, a, b) is a frame, we have $ab < L$. Good time-frequency resolution of a signal with respect to a Gabor frame, depends on appropriately choosing a, b. This challenge can only be treated by numerically experimenting with different values of a, b with respect to L. Now, we associate to the Gabor frame (g, a, b) the following operator.

Definition 1. *Let $\Phi_g : \mathbb{C}^L \mapsto \mathbb{C}^{M \times N}$ denote the Gabor analysis operator –also known as digital Gabor transform (DGT)– whose action on a signal $x \in \mathbb{C}^L$ is defined as*

$$c_{m,n} = \sum_{l=0}^{L-1} x_l \overline{g(l - na)} e^{-2\pi i m b l / L}, \qquad m \in [M], n \in [N]. \tag{5}$$

---

[1] in terms of optimization, it is preferred to solve (2) instead of (3).

Spark Deficient Gabor Frames: Let us first introduce some basic notions.

Definition 2. *The symplectic group* $SL(2, \mathbb{Z}_L)$ *consists of all matrices*

$$G = \begin{pmatrix} \alpha & \beta \\ \gamma & \delta \end{pmatrix} \tag{6}$$

such that α, β, γ, $\delta \in \mathbb{Z}_L$ *and* $\alpha\delta - \beta\gamma \equiv 1(\mathrm{mod}L)$. *To each such matrix corresponds a unitary matrix given by the explicit formula [22]*

$$U_G = \frac{e^{i\theta}}{\sqrt{L}} \sum_{u,v=0}^{L-1} \tau^{\beta^{-1}(\alpha v^2 - 2uv + \delta u^2)} |u\rangle\langle v|, \tag{7}$$

where θ *is an arbitrary phase,* β^{-1} *is the inverse*[2] *of* $\beta\mathrm{mod}L$ *and* $\tau = -e^{\frac{i\pi}{L}}$.

Definition 3. *The spark of a set* F *–denoted by* $\mathrm{sp}(F)$– *of* P *vectors in* $\mathbb{C}^L$ *is the size of the smallest linearly dependent subset of* F. *A frame* F *is full spark if and only if every set of* L *elements of* F *is a basis, or equivalently* $\mathrm{sp}(F) = L+1$, *otherwise it is spark deficient.*

Based on the previous definition, a Gabor frame with $P = L^2/ab$ elements of the form (4) is full spark, if and only if every set of L of its elements is a basis. Now, as proven in [23], almost all window vectors generate full spark Gabor frames, so the SDGFs are generated by exceptional window vectors. Indeed, the following theorem was proven in [22] and informally stated in [24], for the *Zauner matrix* $\mathcal{Z} \in SL(2, \mathbb{Z}_L)$ given by

$$\mathcal{Z} = \begin{pmatrix} 0 & -1 \\ 1 & -1 \end{pmatrix} \equiv \begin{pmatrix} 0 & L-1 \\ 1 & L-1 \end{pmatrix}. \tag{8}$$

Theorem 1 ([22]). *Let* $L \in \mathbb{Z}$ *such that* $2 \nmid L$, $3 \mid L$ *and* L *is square-free. Then, any eigenvector of the Zauner unitary matrix* $U_{\mathcal{Z}}$ *(produced by combining (7) and (8)), generates a spark deficient Gabor frames for* $\mathbb{C}^L$.

According to Theorem 1, since all the eigenvectors of $U_{\mathcal{Z}}$ generate SDGFs, we may choose without loss of generality an arbitrary one, call it *star window vector* and denote it as g_*. We call *star-DGT* the analysis operator associated with a SDGF produced by g_*, and denote it Φ_{g_*}. We coin the term "star", due to the slight resemblance of this DGT to a star when plotted in MATLAB.

Remark 1. A simple way to choose L, is by considering its prime factorization: take k prime numbers $p_1^{\alpha_1}, \ldots, p_k^{\alpha_k}$, with $\alpha_1, \ldots, \alpha_k$ not all a multiple of 2 and $p_1 = 3, p_i \neq 2, i = 2, \ldots, k$, such that $L = 3^{\alpha_1} p_2^{\alpha_2} \cdots \cdots p_k^{\alpha_k}$. Since $a, b \mid L$, we may also choose $a = 1$ and $b = p_i^{\alpha_i}, i = 1, \ldots, k$. Otherwise, both a, b may be one, or a multiplication of more than one, prime numbers from the prime factorization of L. We have seen empirically that this method for fixing (L, a, b) produces satisfying results, as it is illustrated in the figures of the upcoming pages.

---

[2] $bb^{-1} \equiv 1(\mathrm{mod}L)$.

4 Numerical Experiments

Signals' Description and Preprocessing: We experiment with 3 synthetic data and 6 real-world speech signals, taken from Wavelab package [25] and TIMIT corpus [26], respectively. All signals are real-valued; the real-world data are sampled at 16 kHz. The true ambient dimension of each real-world signal does not usually match the conditions of Theorem 1. Hence, we use Remark 1 to cut-off each speech signal to a specific ambient dimension L, being as closer as it gets to its true dimension, in order to both capture a meaningful part of the signal and meet the conditions of Theorem 1. For the synthetic data, we use again Theorem 1 and Remark 1 to fix each signal's ambient dimension L.

Table 1. Signals' details and summary of parameters

Labels	Samples	(L, a, b)	x_0	μ_i, $i = 1, 2, 3, *$
Cusp	33	$(33, 1, 11)$	zero vector	$\|\Phi_i x\|_\infty$
Ramp	33	$(33, 1, 11)$	zero vector	$\|\Phi_i x\|_\infty$
Sing	45	$(45, 1, 9)$	zero vector	$\|\Phi_i x\|_\infty$
SI1899	22938	$(20349, 19, 21)$	$A^T A x$	$10^{-1}\|\Phi_i x\|_\infty$
SI1948	27680	$(27531, 19, 23)$	$A^T A x$	$10^{-1}\|\Phi_i x\|_\infty$
SI2141	42800	$(41769, 21, 17)$	$A^T A x$	$10^{-1}\|\Phi_i x\|_\infty$
SX5	24167	$(23205, 17, 13)$	$A^T A x$	$10^{-1}\|\Phi_i x\|_\infty$
SX224	25805	$(24633, 23, 21)$	$A^T A x$	$10^{-1}\|\Phi_i x\|_\infty$
SI1716	25908	$(24633, 23, 21)$	$A^T A x$	$\|\Phi_i x\|_\infty$

Proposed Framework for Each Signal: We choose a, b according to Remark 1. We consider a vector K of 1000 evenly spaced points in $[1, L]$ and use it as the measurements' interval. We use the power iteration method [27] which yields the largest in magnitude eigenvalue and corresponding eigenvector of $U_{\mathcal{Z}}$, then set this eigenvector to be the star window vector. We use the MATLAB package *LTFAT* [28], to generate four different Gabor frames, with their associated analysis operators/DGTs: Φ_{g_1}, Φ_{g_2}, Φ_{g_3} and Φ_{g_*}, corresponding to a Gaussian, a Hann, a Hamming [21] and the star window vector, respectively. Since we process real-valued signals, we alter the four analysis operators to compute only the DGT coefficients of positive frequencies. For each choice of K in the measurements' interval, we set up a randomly subsampled identity operator $A \in \mathbb{R}^{K \times L}$ and determine the noisy measurements $y = Ax + e$, with e being zero-mean Gaussian noise with standard deviation $\sigma = 0.001$. We employ the MATLAB package *TFOCS* [20] to solve four different instances of (3), one for each of the four DGTs. For each Φ_{g_i}, $i = 1, 2, 3, *$, we set $\mu_i = C\|\Phi_i x\|_\infty$, $C > 0$, since we noticed an improved performance of the algorithm when μ is a function of Φ_i (the constant C and the function $\|\cdot\|_\infty$ are simply chosen empirically). From the aforementioned procedure, we obtain four different estimators of x, namely $\hat{x}_1$, $\hat{x}_2$, $\hat{x}_3$, $\hat{x}_*$ and their corresponding relative errors $\|x - \hat{x}_i\|_2/\|x\|_2$, $i = 1, 2, 3, *$.

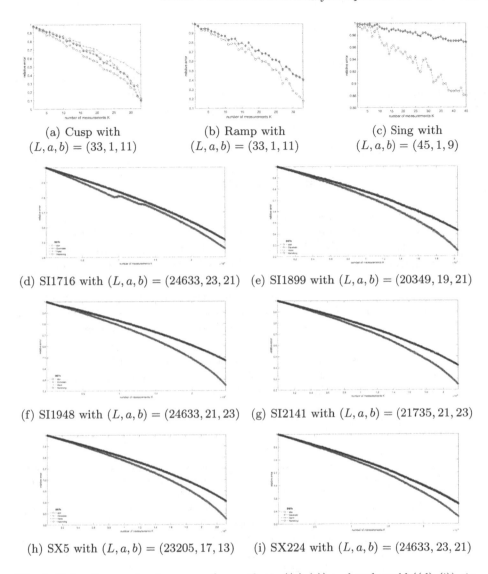

(a) Cusp with
$(L, a, b) = (33, 1, 11)$

(b) Ramp with
$(L, a, b) = (33, 1, 11)$

(c) Sing with
$(L, a, b) = (45, 1, 9)$

(d) SI1716 with $(L, a, b) = (24633, 23, 21)$ (e) SI1899 with $(L, a, b) = (20349, 19, 21)$

(f) SI1948 with $(L, a, b) = (24633, 21, 23)$ (g) SI2141 with $(L, a, b) = (21735, 21, 23)$

(h) SX5 with $(L, a, b) = (23205, 17, 13)$ (i) SX224 with $(L, a, b) = (24633, 23, 21)$

Fig. 1. Rate of approximate success for synthetic ((a)-(c)) and real-world ((d)-(i)) signals for different parameters (L, a, b). Red: gaussian, magenta: Hann, black: hamming, blue: proposed. (Color figure online)

Discussion of the Results: The labels of all signals, along with short description and some key characteristics of the application of our framework to all signals, can be found in Table 1. The resulting figures show the relative reconstruction error decay as the number of measurements increases. Figure 1a–1c demonstrate the success rate of our proposed DGT (blue line), outperforming the rest of DGTs for the synthetic data. Similarly, for the real-world speech signals, Fig. 1d–1i indicate that our method (again blue line) achieves state-of-the-art performance in the first 15–20% of the measurements and from this point on, star-DGT outperforms the rest of DGTs. Moreover, the TFOCS algorithm needed only one iteration to reconstruct the signal of interest when our proposed star-DGT was employed; for the rest 3 DGTs, the algorithm needed at least three iterations. This behaviour confirms improved performance when a DGT associated with a SDGF is applied to analysis CS.

5   Conclusion and Future Work

In the present paper, we took advantage of a window vector to generate a spark deficient Gabor frame and introduced a novel redundant analysis operator/DGT, namely the star DGT, associated with this SDGF. We then applied the star DGT to analysis Compressed Sensing, along with three other DGTs generated by state-of-the-art window vectors in the field of Gabor Analysis. Our experiments confirm improved performance: the increased amount of linear dependencies provided by this SDGF, yields in all cases lower relative reconstruction error for both synthetic and real-world data, as the number of measurements increases. Future directions will be the extension of the present framework to largescale problems (e.g. images or videos). Additionally, it would be interesting to compare this star-DGT to other similar choices of redundant analysis operators (e.g. redundant wavelet transform, shearlets [29] etc.).

References

1. Candès, E.J., Romberg, J., Tao, T.: Robust uncertainty principles: exact signal reconstruction from highly incomplete frequency information. IEEE Trans. Inf. Theor. **52**(2), 489–509 (2006)
2. Potter, L.C., Ertin, E., Parker, J.T., Cetin, M.: Sparsity and compressed sensing in radar imaging. Proc. IEEE **98**(6), 1006–1020 (2010)
3. Chen, J., Zhang, Y., Qi, L., Fu, C., Xu, L.: Exploiting chaos-based compressed sensing and cryptographic algorithm for image encryption and compression. Opt. Laser Technol. **99**, 238–248 (2018)
4. Alexandropoulos, G.C., Chouvardas, S.: Low complexity channel estimation for millimeter wave systems with hybrid A/D antenna processing. In: 2016 IEEE Globecom Workshops (GC Wkshps), pp. 1–6. IEEE (2016)
5. Pejoski, S., Kafedziski, V., Gleich, D.: Compressed sensing MRI using discrete non-separable shearlet transform and FISTA. IEEE Sig. Process. Lett. **22**(10), 1566–1570 (2015)
6. Wu, Y., Rosca, M., Lillicrap, T.: Deep compressed sensing. In: International Conference on Machine Learning, pp. 6850–6860. PMLR (2019)
7. Foucart S., Rauhut H.: An invitation to compressive sensing. In: A Mathematical Introduction to Compressive Sensing. Applied and Numerical Harmonic Analysis. Birkhäuser, New York (2013)

8. Li, C., Adcock, B.: Compressed sensing with local structure: uniform recovery guarantees for the sparsity in levels class. Appl. Comput. Harmonic Anal. **46**(3), 453–477 (2019)
9. Dao, P.T., Griffin, A., Li, X.J.: Compressed sensing of EEG with Gabor dictionary: Effect of time and frequency resolution. In: 2018 40th annual international conference of the IEEE engineering in medicine and biology society (EMBC), pp. 3108–3111. IEEE (2018)
10. Genzel, M., Kutyniok, G., März, M.: l_1-Analysis minimization and generalized (co-) sparsity: when does recovery succeed? Appl. Comput. Harmonic Anal. **52**, 82–140 (2021)
11. Kabanava, M., Rauhut, H.: Analysis l_1-recovery with frames and gaussian measurements. Acta Applicandae Mathematicae **140**(1), 173–195 (2015)
12. Candes, E.J., Eldar, Y.C., Needell, D., Randall, P.: Compressed sensing with coherent and redundant dictionaries. Appl. Comput. Harmonic Anal. **31**(1), 59–73 (2011)
13. Nam, S., Davies, M.E., Elad, M., Gribonval, R.: The cosparse analysis model and algorithms. Appl. Comput. Harmonic Anal. **34**(1), 30–56 (2013)
14. Kabanava, M., Rauhut, H.: Cosparsity in compressed sensing. In: Boche, H., Calderbank, R., Kutyniok, G., Vybíral, J. (eds.) Compressed Sensing and its Applications. ANHA, pp. 315–339. Springer, Cham (2015). https://doi.org/10.1007/978-3-319-16042-9_11
15. Krahmer, F., Kruschel, C., Sandbichler, M.: Total variation minimization in compressed sensing. In: Boche, H., Caire, G., Calderbank, R., März, M., Kutyniok, G., Mathar, R. (eds.) Compressed Sensing and its Applications. ANHA, pp. 333–358. Springer, Cham (2017). https://doi.org/10.1007/978-3-319-69802-1_11
16. Blumensath, T., Davies, M.E.: Sampling theorems for signals from the union of finite-dimensional linear subspaces. IEEE Trans. Inf. Theor. **55**(4), 1872–1882 (2009)
17. Zauner, G.: Quantum designs (Doctoral dissertation, University of Vienna, Vienna) (1999)
18. Pfander, G.E., Rauhut, H.: Sparsity in time-frequency representations. J. Fourier Anal. Appl. **16**(2), 233–260 (2010)
19. Rajbamshi, S., Tauböck, G., Balazs, P., Abreu, L.D.: Random gabor multipliers for compressive sensing: a simulation study. In: 2019 27th European Signal Processing Conference (EUSIPCO), pp. 1–5. IEEE (2019)
20. Becker, S.R., Candès, E.J., Grant, M.C.: Templates for convex cone problems with applications to sparse signal recovery. Math. Program. Comput. **3**(3), 165 (2011)
21. Søndergaard, P.L., Hansen, P.C., Christensen, O.: Finite discrete Gabor analysis (Doctoral dissertation, Institut for Matematik, DTU) (2007)
22. Dang, H.B., Blanchfield, K., Bengtsson, I., Appleby, D.M.: Linear dependencies in Weyl-Heisenberg orbits. Quantum Inf. Process. **12**(11), 3449–3475 (2013)
23. Malikiosis, R.D.: A note on Gabor frames in finite dimensions. Appl. Comput. Harmonic Anal. **38**(2), 318–330 (2015)
24. Malikiosis, R.D.: Spark deficient Gabor frames. Pacific J. Math. **294**(1), 159–180 (2018)
25. Buckheit J.B., Donoho D.L.: WaveLab and reproducible research. In: Antoniadis A., Oppenheim G. (eds.) Wavelets and Statistics. Lecture Notes in Statistics, vol. 103. Springer, New York (1995)
26. Garofolo, J.S., Lamel, L.F., Fisher, W.M., Fiscus, J.G. and Pallett, D.S.: DARPA TIMIT acoustic-phonetic continous speech corpus CD-ROM. NIST speech disc 1–1.1. NASA STI/Recon technical report n, 93, p. 27403 (1993)

27. Booth, T.E.: Power iteration method for the several largest eigenvalues and eigen-functions. Nuclear Sci. Eng. **154**(1), 48–62 (2006)
28. Pruša, Z., Søndergaard, P., Balazs, P., Holighaus, N.: LTFAT: A Matlab/Octave toolbox for sound processing. In: Proceedings 10th International Symposium on Computer Music Multidisciplinary Research (CMMR), pp. 299–314 (2013)
29. Yuan, M., Yang, B., Ma, Y., Zhang, J., Zhang, R., Zhang, C.: Compressed sensing MRI reconstruction from highly undersampled-space data using nonsubsampled shearlet transform sparsity prior. Mathematical Problems in Engineering **2015** (2015)

Enriching BERT With Knowledge Graph Embedding For Industry Classification

Shiyue Wang, Youcheng Pan, Zhenran Xu, Baotian Hu$^{(\boxtimes)}$, and Xiaolong Wang

Harbin Institute of Technology, Shenzhen, China
{19s151128,youcheng.pan,xuzhenran}@stu.hit.edu.cn,
{hubaotian,xlwangsz}@hit.edu.cn

Abstract. Industry classification for startup companies is meaningful not only to navigate investment strategies but also to find potential competitors. It is essentially a challenging domain-specific text classification task. Due to the lack of such dataset, in this paper, we first construct a dataset for industry classification based on the companies listed on the Chinese National Equities Exchange and Quotations (NEEQ), which consists of 17,604 annual business reports and their corresponding industry labels. Second, we introduce a novel Knowledge Graph Enriched BERT model (KGEB), which can understand a domain-specific text by enhancing the word representation with external knowledge and can take full use of the local knowledge graph without pre-training. Experimental results show the promising performance of the proposed model and demonstrate its effectiveness for tackling the domain-specific classification task.

Keywords: Industry classification · Knowledge graph · Graph convolutional network

1 Introduction

Industry classification is a primary problem to classify companies into specific industry category according to their primary business sectors, market performances and the major products [1]. It is essential to research in the financial field, as dividing the companies into homogeneous groups could help the academic researchers narrow down the scope of their investigation, identify comparable companies and set performance benchmarks [2]. It also can reflect the industry characteristics of companies and provide investors with market trends.

Unlike A-shares with persistent main business sectors, small-and-medium-sized enterprises (SMEs), especially new startup companies, usually react to the ever-evolving demand of the market by changing their main businesses frequently. For startup companies that aim at publicly trading, classification can help them catch up with the existing A-share companies and find potential competitors. There are already plenty of applications on industry classification on

© Springer Nature Switzerland AG 2021
T. Mantoro et al. (Eds.): ICONIP 2021, CCIS 1517, pp. 709–717, 2021.
https://doi.org/10.1007/978-3-030-92310-5_82

A-share companies like Global Industry Classification Standard (GICS), still, there is a lack of datasets on startup companies for further studies.

As industry classification can be attributed to financial text classification task, common deep neural networks do not perform well on domain-specific tasks. The text classification task is a fundamental task in neural language processing as numerous methods have been proposed, such as TextCNN [6] and BERT [4]. However, the professional terms stand for special meaning which needs an additional explanation when understanding. Recent studies have made attempts to integrate knowledge graphs into basic models. Zhang et al. [15] propose an enhanced language representation model, but the model ignores the relation between entities. W. Liu et al. [10] transform input sentence into a knowledge-rich sentence tree and introduce soft-position and visible matrix. Still, it only concerns relevant triples from the entities present in the sentence, dismissing expanding relations in the knowledge graphs.

Table 1. The annual business reports of one company and its corresponding classification label.

Year: 2015 **Label**: Industrials **Business model**: The abbreviation of the company's security name is "Daocong Technology". The company is mainly engaged in the research and development of traffic safety technology, technical consulting
Year: 2016 **Label**: Information Technology **Business model**: The company's security name is changed to "Gaiya Entertainment". The company has established a new strategic pattern with mobile game development and operation business as the core

For the problems mentioned above, in this work, we focus on solving the integration of word representation and knowledge. As an effort towards it, we first construct a dataset on startup companies for the industry classification task. The dataset contains the annual business reports of companies on NEEQ and their corresponding labels. These companies are typically SMEs, and their classifications could be wavering in years. For instance listed in Table 1, a firm renamed its security from Daocong Technology into Gaiya Entertainment, with the leading business sector changing from transportation to mobile games. Second, We propose a Knowledge Graph Enriched BERT (KGEB) which can load any pre-trained BERT models and be fine-tuned for classification. It makes full use of the structure of the knowledge graphs extracted from texts by entity linking and nodes expanding. Finally, experiments are conducted on the dataset, and results demonstrate that KGEB can get superior performances.

The contribution of this work is threefold: (1) A large dataset is constructed for industry classification based on the companies listed on NEEQ, consisting of companies' descriptions of business models and corresponding labels.

(2) A Knowledge Graph Enriched BERT (KGEB), which can understand domain-specific texts by integrating both word and knowledge representation, is proposed and is demonstrated beneficial. (3) The KGEB obtains the results of 0.9198 on Accuracy and 0.9089 on F1, which outperforms the competitive experiments and demonstrates that the proposed approach can improve the classification quality.

2   NEEQ Industry Classification Dataset

NEEQ is the third national securities' trading venue after the Shanghai Stock Exchange and Shenzhen Stock Exchange. We construct the industry classification dataset based on the NEEQ website, and the process is summarized as follows: 1) we acquire 20,040 descriptions of the business model from 2014 to 2017 from the open-source dataset [1]. 2) For each description of the business model, we acquire the releasing time of the report and check out the investment-based industry classification result which is rightly after the releasing time. 3) By filtering and cleaning repeated descriptions, we obtain the final dataset which consists of 17,604 pairs of descriptions of business models and their industry classification labels. We split the dataset into a training set (80%), a dev set (10%), and a test set (10%). Among the dataset, the maximum of descriptions of business model is 13,308, and the minimum is 38, and the median is 630. On average, each company contributes to 1.79 different business model descriptions, demonstrating the wavering features of startup companies. Table 2 summarizes the preliminary information about the dataset of industry classification. The dataset is freely available at https://github.com/theDyingofLight/neeq_dataset.

Table 2. Overview of the classification dataset NEEQ industry classification.

Label	Name	Train	Dev	Test
0	Materials (MT)	1726	200	213
1	Consumer Discretionary (CD)	1834	242	233
2	Industrials (ID)	4122	488	492
3	Information Technology (IT)	3793	494	490
4	Financials (FN)	198	20	26
5	Telecommunication Services (TS)	322	33	49
6	Consumer Staples (CS)	739	93	107
7	Health Care (HC)	894	115	108
8	Energy (EG)	298	27	29
9	Utilities (UT)	98	7	15
10	Real Estates (RE)	84	6	9
	Total	14108	1725	1771

3   Methodology

The text classification task can be defined as follows. Given a passage denoted as $X = \{x_1, x_2, ..., x_n\}$, n is the length of the passage. In this paper, Chinese tokens are at the character level. The model's target is to predict the classification label Y defined as $Y = argmaxP(Y|X, \theta)$, where θ denotes the model parameters. Our overall approach is depicted in Fig. 1.

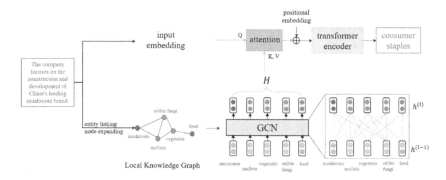

Fig. 1. The overview of our approach. It contains three steps: (1) Build the local knowledge graphs. (2) Transform the graphs into node representation. (3) Combine input passage representation with node representation for classification.

Local Knowledge Graph. Given an input passage, a set of triples can be retrieved from the knowledge base by linking the mentions parsed from the passage to the entities in the knowledge base and expanding relation paths. We define the set of triples as a Local Knowledge Graph. Formally, a Knowledge Base is represented as a $K = (V, E)$, where $V = \{v_j\}$ is the set of vertices and $E = \{e_j\}$ is the set of edges of the vertices, and each triple (head entity, relation, tail entity) in KB is denoted as $\tau = (e_h, v_{hs}, e_s)$. The local knowledge graph is assumed as $G = \{\tau_1, \tau_2, ..., \tau_g\}$, where g is the number of triples. The way to construct the local knowledge graph is as follows. Firstly, for each passage X, we conduct mention parsing to obtain mentions and entity disambiguation to get pairs of entities and nodes from the knowledge base called XLore [13] with the entity linking system XLink [5]. We rank all the candidate nodes by their cosine similarity with the word embedding [9] and select the entities by the threshold larger than 0.4 and top-10 entities if there are more than 10.

Node Representation. After obtaining the local knowledge graph G with g nodes, we feed G into the $L-$layer GCN model [14] for the representation of each node, where we denote $h_i^{(l-1)}$ as the input vector and $h_i^{(l)}$ as the output vector of node i at the $l-$layer. The process of calculation is: $h_i^{(l)} = \sigma(\sum_{j=1}^n \widetilde{A}_{ij} W^{(l)} h_j^{(l-1)}/d_i + b^{(l)})$ where $\widetilde{A} = A + I$ represents the matrix sum of adjacency matrix A and identity matrix I, $d_i = \sum_{j=1}^n \widetilde{A}_{ij}$ is the degree of entity i in the local knowledge graph, $W^{(l)}$ is a trainable linear transformation and σ is a nonlinear function. We initialize the node embedding with the output of a pre-trained model, which takes the whole words in the node as input and outputs a fixed length vector. The output of the GCN last layer is used as the node representation $H = \{h_1^{(L)}, h_2^{(L)}, ..., h_g^{(L)}\}$.

Knowledge Graph Enriched BERT. Knowledge Graph Enriched BERT is proposed to enrich the representation of long passage with node representation from local knowledge graphs. As a multi-layer bidirectional Transformer encoder, BERT maps an input sequence of characters X to a sequence of representations $Z = \{z_1, z_2, ..., z_n\}$. To fuse node representation into the word embedding layer, we utilize attention mechanism to integrate word embedding $W = \{w_1, w_2, ..., w_n\}$ and node representation $H = \{h_1^{(L)}, h_2^{(L)}, ..., h_g^{(L)}\}$ formulated as: $\alpha_t = softmax(H^T W^P w_t)$, $w_t' = H \cdot \alpha_t$ where W^P is the trainable parameters and $W' = \{w_1', w_2', ..., w_n'\}$ is the output of the fusion. Then we add a residual connection on the original word embedding to avoid vanishing gradient. We also adopt consistent position embedding and token type embedding with BERT and we sum up three layers of embedding as the output of the embedding layer. The output is then fed into a stack of identical layers which contains a multi-head self-attention mechanism and a position-wise fully connected feed-forward network [12]. We utilize the final hidden vector $z_1 \in \mathbb{R}^H$ corresponding to the first input token ($[CLS]$) to represent the entire sequence. We introduce classification layer weights $W \in \mathbb{R}^{K \times H}$, where K is the number of labels.

We compute a standard classification loss with z_1 and W, and I^* denotes the target category: $O = softmax(z_1 W^T)$, $\mathcal{L} = -log(O(I^*))$

4   Experiments

Our experiments study the proposed model on the NEEQ industry classification dataset, compare the model with existing approaches and analyze the results.

4.1   Experimental Settings

We have five models for comparison. The models are implemented on open source code. (1) GCN [8]: A fundamental GNN model for the classification task. (2) Logistic Regression [11]: A basic linear model for classification. (3) TextCNN [6]: A CNN with one convolution layer on top of word vectors. (4) BERT [4]: A language model pre-trained on a large scale of corpus to obtain deep bidirectional representations and renews the records on many downstream tasks. (5) K-BERT [10]: it enables language representation model with knowledge graphs by first injecting relevant triples into the input sentence and second being fed into the embedding layer, seeing layer and the mask-transformer.

In all our experiments, we initialize the word embedding with parameters of bert-base-chinese with a hidden size of 768 and 12 hidden layers. In the fine-tuning process, we use a batch size of 8, the number of gradient accumulation steps of 8, the learning rate of 5e−5. In the embedding layer, we use bert-as-service equipped with bert-base-chinese to get the initial node embedding whose dimension is 768, the threshold of similarity of entites in XLore is 0.4, and the layer size of GCN is 4. The dropout in GCN layers is 0.5. Models are trained with the Adam optimizer [7]. We select model based on the dev set.

We conduct the automatic evaluation with the following metrics: Accuracy measures the proportion of the number of samples that are correctly predicted to the total samples. F1 is the macro average of Precision and Recall, which measures the correctness of all categories.

4.2 Results and Analysis

Table 3 shows the experimental results against the competitor methods. GCN achieves the worst performance since it only utilizes the local knowledge graphs, missing information from the passages. Logistic Regression focuses much on the statistical information of words and can benefit from the long texts as in our dataset. TextCNN is a CNN model designed for text classification. It can represent text sequences with a deep neural network, but it doesn't model the long passage well and lacks domain-specific knowledge. Likewise, BERT is initialized with the pre-train parameters and has been significantly improved, but it still has problems understanding domain-specific texts. Although the result of K-BERT is worse than our model, it demonstrates the influence of knowledge graphs. Compared with CN-DBpedia [3] K-BERT extracts knowledge triples from, XLore contains 3.6 times the amount of entities, which contributes to the deeper comprehension of domain information.

Table 3. The experimental results (%) on the NEEQ industry classification dataset.

Model	Accuracy	Precision	Recall	F1
GCN	69.70	66.16	61.77	63.20
LR	89.21	91.95	85.99	88.63
TextCNN	89.16	90.98	84.32	87.18
BERT	91.41	91.71	88.46	89.95
K-BERT	90.97	89.26	86.55	87.88
KGEB	**91.98**	**92.55**	**89.45**	**90.89**

Compared with the competitor methods, our model takes advantage of the knowledge. Complementing words with node representation is helpful because it provides additional information and considers the structure of the graphs, making the word embedding select more helpful information from the nodes. The performance achieves absolute improvements by at least +0.5 in Accuracy and +0.94 in F1.

As Table 4 shows, the experimental results on each category support the effectiveness of KGEB. TextCNN performs worst on almost all of the classes. BERT performs better, but in most categories, KGEB achieves the highest Precision,

Table 4. The experimental results (%) on the NEEQ industry classification dataset on each category.

	Precision			Recall			F1		
	TextCNN	BERT	KGEB	TextCNN	BERT	KGEB	TextCNN	BERT	KGEB
MT	86.57	87.91	**88.69**	87.79	88.73	**92.02**	87.18	88.32	**90.32**
CD	83.12	88.16	**90.31**	84.55	86.27	**87.98**	83.83	87.20	**89.13**
ID	89.19	**91.52**	91.03	92.28	94.31	**94.92**	90.71	92.89	**92.94**
IT	90.69	93.69	**94.39**	91.43	**93.88**	92.65	91.06	**93.78**	93.51
FN	100	92.86	**100**	92.31	100	**100**	96.00	96.30	**100**
TS	87.88	**90.48**	84.09	59.18	**77.55**	75.51	70.73	**83.52**	79.57
CS	**94.06**	93.40	93.46	88.79	92.52	**93.46**	91.35	92.96	**93.46**
HC	91.96	93.40	**95.24**	**95.37**	91.67	92.59	93.64	92.52	**93.90**
EG	91.67	85.19	**92.00**	75.86	79.31	79.31	83.02	82.14	**85.19**
UT	100	92.31	**100**	**93.33**	80.00	86.67	**96.55**	85.71	92.86
RE	85.71	**100**	88.89	85.71	88.89	**88.89**	75.00	**94.12**	88.89

Recall and F1 score, demonstrating that the additional knowledge information can not only help distinguish terms and draw attention on domain-specific words but also understand the meaning of decisive words. However, since KGEB is still far from a perfect classifier, we also show that there are descriptions our current model cannot classify well. These labels could be predicted correctly if we had a better entity linking system and node expanding strategies. Taking a text labeled "Telecommunication Service" as an example, the local knowledge graph is constructed based on the entities containing "digital television", "health" and "care" from the text "In addition to retaining the original digital television business, the future will be based on the field of health care" and it is possible to bring noise interference.

4.3 Case Study

Comparing the predicted labels of TextCNN, BERT and KGEB, our model improves the recall of the labels with respect to the baselines. In the cases where all of them predict correctly, the keywords in the sentence can help the models increase the probability of correct labels. In the cases where BERT and TextCNN predict wrong labels, like the sentence "The company is committed to the production and sales of core equipment for water treatment and recycling of domestic sewage", BERT and TextCNN label the description "Industrials", but owing to the additional information about "sewage disposal", KGEB obtains the correct prediction. In some cases, all of the models classify the description with the wrong label. If we removed the noise when conducting entity linking system and node expanding strategies, we could obtain the correct classification results like in the last example.

5 Conclusions

In this paper, we construct a large dataset for industry classification task and propose a novel knowledge enriched BERT which can extract the local knowledge graph from the business sentences and integrate word and knowledge representation. The experimental results outperform the competitor methods and demonstrate the effectiveness of our proposed model. In the future, we will continue to improve this work and extend the method to more applications.

Acknowledgements. We appreciate the insightful feedback from the anonymous reviewers. This work is jointly supported by grants: Natural Science Foundation of China (No. 62006061), Strategic Emerging Industry Development Special Funds of Shenzhen (No. JCYJ20200109113441941) and Stable Support Program for Higher Education Institutions of Shenzhen (No. GXWD20201230155427003-20200824155011001).

References

1. Bai, H., Xing, F.Z., Cambria, E., Huang, W.B.: Business taxonomy construction using concept-level hierarchical clustering. Papers (2019)
2. Bhojraj, S., Lee, C., Oler, D.K.: What's my line? A comparison of industry classification schemes for capital market research. J. Acc. Res. **41**(5), 745–774 (2003)
3. Bo, X., et al.: CN-DBpedia: a never-ending Chinese knowledge extraction system. In: International Conference on Industrial, Engineering and Other Applications of Applied Intelligent Systems (2017)
4. Devlin, J., Chang, M.W., Lee, K., Toutanova, K.: Bert: Pre-training of deep bidirectional transformers for language understanding. arXiv preprint arXiv:1810.04805 (2018)
5. Zhang, J., Cao, Y., Hou, L., Li, J., Zheng, H.-T.: XLink: an unsupervised bilingual entity linking system. In: Sun, M., Wang, X., Chang, B., Xiong, D. (eds.) CCL/NLP-NABD -2017. LNCS (LNAI), vol. 10565, pp. 172–183. Springer, Cham (2017). https://doi.org/10.1007/978-3-319-69005-6_15
6. Kim, Y.: Convolutional neural networks for sentence classification. Eprint Arxiv (2014)
7. Kingma, D.P., Ba, J.: Adam: a method for stochastic optimization. arXiv preprint arXiv:1412.6980 (2014)
8. Kipf, T.N., Welling, M.: Semi-supervised classification with graph convolutional networks. arXiv preprint arXiv:1609.02907 (2016)
9. Li, S., Zhao, Z., Hu, R., Li, W., Liu, T., Du, X.: Analogical reasoning on Chinese morphological and semantic relations. In: Proceedings of the 56th Annual Meeting of the Association for Computational Linguistics, Vol. 2: Short Papers (2018)
10. Liu, W., Zhou, P., Zhao, Z., Wang, Z., Wang, P.: K-bert: enabling language representation with knowledge graph. In: Proceedings of the AAAI Conference on Artificial Intelligence (2020)
11. Menard, S.: Logistic regression. American Statistician (2004)
12. Vaswani, A., et al.: Attention is all you need. In: Advances in neural information processing systems, pp. 5998–6008 (2017)
13. Wang, Z., et al.: Xlore: a large-scale english-chinese bilingual knowledge graph. In: Proceedings of the 12th International Semantic Web Conference (2013)

14. Zhang, Y., Qi, P., Manning, C.D.: Graph convolution over pruned dependency trees improves relation extraction. In: Proceedings of the 2018 Conference on Empirical Methods in Natural Language Processing (2018)
15. Zhang, Z., Han, X., Liu, Z., Jiang, X., Sun, M., Liu, Q.: Ernie: enhanced language representation with informative entities. In: Proceedings of the 57th Annual Meeting of the Association for Computational Linguistics (2019)

Learning Multi-dimensional Parallax Prior for Stereo Image Super-Resolution

Changyu Li[1], Dongyang Zhang[1], Chunlin Jiang[2], Ning Xie[1], and Jie Shao[1,2(✉)]

[1] University of Electronic Science and Technology of China, Chengdu 611731, China
{changyulve,dyzhang}@std.uestc.edu.cn, shaojie@uestc.edu.cn
[2] Sichuan Artificial Intelligence Research Institute, Yibin 644000, China

Abstract. Recent years have witnessed great success in image super-resolution (SR). However, how to effectively exploit stereo information for the SR purpose is still challenging. This paper focuses on proposing a general solution to stereo image SR. We propose a novel module named Parallax Multi-Dimensional Attention (PMDA) that could not only be seamlessly integrated into most of existing SISR networks but also explore cross-view information from stereo images. Specifically, a pair of stereo images are fed into two identical SISR networks. The extracted middle features are transferred into PMDA to capture the inherent correlation within stereo image pairs. Finally, the internal-view and cross-view information is mixed by SISR network to generate the final output. We also introduce Self Multi-Dimensional Attention (SMDA) to effectively improve the feature representation capacity of a single image. Based on PMDA and SMDA, we design a stereo image SR model named Progressive Attention Stereo SR (PASR), which illustrates the flexibility of PMDA and performance-boosting guided by PMDA and SMDA. Extensive experiments show its superiority in the aspects of visual quality and quantitative comparison.

Keywords: Image super-resolution · Deep learning · Stereo image

1 Introduction

Recently with the development of optical imaging technology, binocular cameras have become ubiquitous in our daily life. For instance, almost all smart phones are equipped with binocular cameras, and autonomous vehicles use them for depth estimation [1]. Binocular cameras also have received attention in computer-assisted surgery [18]. Since the binocular imaging devices have advanced, the high-resolution stereo images are in increasingly high demand, and hence it is of great urgency to develop the stereo Super-Resolution (SR) technique, which targets at generating a High-Resolution (HR) image of a certain view from two Low-Resolution (LR) images with different viewpoints.

However, stereo images have higher pixel similarity and this parallax prior information could not be fully exploited along the single-dimensional attention

© Springer Nature Switzerland AG 2021
T. Mantoro et al. (Eds.): ICONIP 2021, CCIS 1517, pp. 718–727, 2021.
https://doi.org/10.1007/978-3-030-92310-5_83

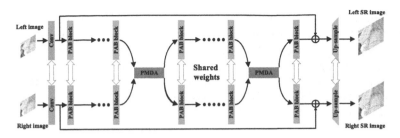

Fig. 1. Illustration of our proposed PASR equipped with PMDA. PAB can be referred to any reconstruction block in various SISR networks. The blue arrows indicate that pair modules are sharing parameters and all up-sample modules also share weights. (Color figure online)

block, which is used by previous stereo image SR methods [14]. To alleviate this issue and exploit the self-attention mechanism, we propose a novel Parallax Multi-Dimensional Attention (PMDA) module, which is used to capture the multi-dimensional parallax prior between two viewpoints. Specifically, except for the conventional dependency relationship which is calculated along channel dimension $(W \times C)$, PMDA also aggregates interactive features between the spatial dimensions (either $H \times C$ or $H \times W$).

Consequently, PMDA module could help SISR capture parallax prior information. As shown in Fig. 1, stereo images would be fed into two identical SISR networks to extract internal image-specific information. Then, PMDA helps transfer the proper parallax prior between two views. Finally, the internal-view and cross-view information would mix and generate the final output with the help of the subsequent part in the SISR networks. Since most recent SISR networks use several cascaded modules with final up-sample block [8,19], PMDAs could be easily inserted into these networks for leveraging cross-view information. Therefore, this module could be combined with different SISR networks flexibly to enhance the restoration quality of stereo SR.

PMDA captures the cross-view information between two views of the stereo images. However, the useful feature of an image should also be considered and the attention mechanism should be a solution to achieve this. Therefore, we propose a Self Multi-Dimensional Attention (SMDA) module which is a variant of PMDA. SMDA aims at capturing multi-dimensional dependencies of the single image itself. Finally, based on PMDA and SMDA, we design a new lightweight stereo image SR model named Progressive Attention Stereo SR (PASR). The performance of PASR not only demonstrates the superiority of PMDA and SMDA but also shows the ease of using PMDA. Overall, the main contributions of our work can be summarized as follows:

- We propose a generic module named PMDA to fully exploit the disparity information of stereo images introduced by different viewpoints. PMDA could be incorporated into various SISR networks at multiple stages to better model cross-view information interaction.

- Based on the idea of capturing multi-dimensional dependencies, we also propose SMDA which captures multi-dimensional features of an image. Experiments demonstrate that SMDA can adaptively learn more useful internal-view prior from a single view image.
- We design a lightweight stereo images SR network named PASR based on PMDA and SMDA, which achieves an excellent balance between model size and performance.

2   Related Work

Efforts have been made to solve the stereo SR problem. One of the exemplary methods that contributed to the incremental exploration of stereo SR is proposed by [6], which firstly developed a novel two-stage joint network to enhance the spatial resolution of stereo images using a parallax prior. Then, PASSR-net [14] introduced a parallax-attention mechanism with a global receptive field to deal with the disparity information between stereo images. Ying et al. [17] proposed a generic Stereo Attention Module (SAM) to exploit cross-view and intra-view information, which can be embedded into arbitrary SISR networks for stereo image SR. Song et al. [12] proposed a Self and Parallax Attention Mechanism (SPAM) to maintain the stereo-consistency. NNRANet [15] utilized the non-local operation to capture the long-range dependencies of sub-pixel shifts. Moreover, Yan et al. [16] proposed a unified stereo image restoration framework by transferring the knowledge of the disparity domain to the image domain.

3   Our Method

This section introduces the design of Progressive Attention Stereo SR (PASR) network. As shown in Fig. 1, our proposed PASR is composed of Parallax Multi-Dimensional Attention Module (PMDA) and Progressive Attention Block (PAB). The details of PMDA and PAB are introduced in the following.

3.1   Multi-Dimensional Attention (MDA) Module

Previous multi-head attention [13] only accounts for one-dimension interaction, resulting in inadequate feature exploration in image processing tasks. Therefore, in addition to the conventional dependency relationship which is calculated along channel dimension ($W \times C$), our proposed Multi-Dimensional Attention (MDA) module also aggregates interactive features between the spatial dimensions (either $H \times C$ or $H \times W$). Specifically, given the *query*, *key* and *value* tensors, *query* would be batch-wisely reshaped into three different shapes, which are $Q_1 \in \mathbb{R}^{H \times W \times C}, Q_2 \in \mathbb{R}^{W \times H \times C}, Q_3 \in \mathbb{R}^{C \times H \times W}$. *key* would also be reshaped into batch-wisely matrix multiplication format $K_1 \in \mathbb{R}^{H \times C \times W}, K_2 \in \mathbb{R}^{W \times C \times H}, K_3 \in \mathbb{R}^{C \times W \times H}$. Here the subscript denotes three different shapes the matrix multiplication performed on. We perform the matrix multiplication

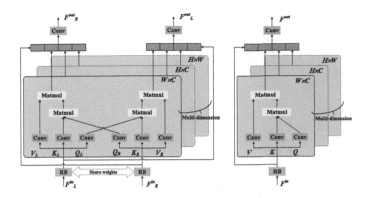

Fig. 2. Left: PMDA module with three sub-modules capturing multi-dimensional interaction for stereo inputs. Right: the proposed SMDA module.

among Q_1K_1, Q_2K_2 and Q_3K_3. Then, softmax operation is applied on them along the batch-wise column to generate a group of dependency maps A_1, A_2 and A_3. This can be formulated as:

$$A_i = softmax(Q_i \otimes K_i), i \in \{1, 2, 3\}, \tag{1}$$

where $A_1 \in \mathbb{R}^{H \times W \times W}$, $A_2 \in \mathbb{R}^{W \times H \times H}$ and $A_3 \in \mathbb{R}^{C \times H \times H}$. Next, to combine the attention feature maps into corresponding features, we perform matrix multiplication between $Value$ and dependency maps $A_i, i \in 1, 2, 3$. $Value$ would also be batch-wisely reshaped into three different shapes, which are $V_1 \in \mathbb{R}^{H \times W \times C}, V_2 \in \mathbb{R}^{W \times H \times C}, V_3 \in \mathbb{R}^{C \times H \times W}$. The operation between A and V can be represented as:

$$F_i = A_i \otimes V_i, i \in \{1, 2, 3\}. \tag{2}$$

Since the preceding operations repeat on $W \times C, H \times C$ and $H \times W$, this process generates three features F_1, F_2, F_3. They will be reshaped into proper dimension $F_i \in \mathbb{R}^{C \times H \times W}, i \in \{1, 2, 3\}$ and concatenated with residual features $value$. Finally, a 1×1 convolution layer helps to reduce the channel number of these concatenated features and get the final outputs F_{out}. Formally, it can be expressed as:

$$F_{out} = Conv(Concat(V, F_1, F_2, F_3)). \tag{3}$$

Consequently, attention operation is operated at three dimensions $W \times C, H \times C, H \times W$, and this is the reason why this module is called multi-dimensional.

3.2   Parallax Multi-Dimensional Attention (PMDA) Module

In the stereo image SR task, the parallax prior brought by the other viewpoint could enhance the reconstruction performance of super-resolution. Therefore, the transmission of cross-view information should be emphasized. The transmission process can be regarded as a process that given a specific *query*, search the corresponding *value* based on *key*. Here *query, key, value* are first fed to a project layer, then the Multi-Dimensional Attention (MDA) module computes the attention weights between *query* and *key*, which then are assigned to *value*. The process of the prior transmission from right view to left view $I_{RightToLeft}$ can be expressed as:

$$
\begin{cases}
Q_L = FE(Left), \\
K_R = FE(Right), \\
V_R = FE(Right), \\
I_{RightToLeft} = MDA(Q_L, K_R, V_R),
\end{cases}
\tag{4}
$$

where $FE(\cdot)$ denotes the residual block and 1×1 convolution layer. The transmission from left view to right view $I_{LeftToRight}$ shares the same idea. Finally the extracted features of Q_L, K_R, V_R will be further fed into the subsequent feature processing module in the Multi-Dimensional Attention (MDA) module. Since it aims at capturing the parallel dependencies between two views, we named it Parallax Multi-Dimensional Attention (PMDA) module.

3.3   Progressive Attention Stereo SR (PASR) Network

Compared with PMDA which receives different *key*, *value* and *query* from parallel view, Self Multi-Dimensional Attention (SMDA) module receives the identical input from one view. Finally, we design an effective stereo SR network named Progressive Attention Stereo SR (PASR) network. The backbone of PASR is Progressive Attention Block (PAB). The up-sample module consists of two sub-pixel layers [11]. The following are the definitions of SMDA and PAB.

Self Multi-Dimensional Attention (SMDA). Compared with PMDA, SMDA shares the same *query*, *key* and *value*. Therefore, it is designed to explore the dependency relationship from the same input. As shown in Fig. 2, it can be express as:

$$
\begin{cases}
Q = Conv(Input), \\
K = Conv(Input), \\
V = Conv(Input), \\
I_{output} = MDA(Q, K, V),
\end{cases}
\tag{5}
$$

where *Input* denotes the identical input feature map. It is first fed to different 1×1 convolution layers to have a diverse projection and generate Q, K and V. MDA will be performed on Q, K and V.

Progressive Attention Block (PAB). PAB is the combination of Res2Net [3] and SMDA. Specifically, Res2Net directly splits the feature map into *s* subsets and uses several paralleled but connected convolution layers to process these feature maps. Finally, a 1×1 convolution layer helps concatenate and reduce the channel size of these features. Our proposed SMDA is inserted after this 1×1 convolution layer. Since it aims at capturing the dependency from a single view, we name it Self Multi-Dimensional Attention (SMDA) module.

Table 1. Quantitative results by PASR with different locations of PMDA on three benchmark datasets ($\times 4$). Note that PASR+PMDA$_i$ represents PMDA module inserted after the i-th module of PASR (red/blue: best/second-best).

Model	PASR w/o PMDA	PASR+PMDA$_1$	PASR+PMDA$_3$	PASR+PMDA$_5$	PASR+PMDA$_7$	PASR+PMDA$_{10}$
KITTI 2012	26.21/0.870	26.26/0.870	26.30/0.871	26.36/0.874	26.39/0.874	26.30/0.872
KITTI 2015	25.40/0.859	25.45/0.860	25.45/0.861	25.51/0.863	25.59/0.864	25.41/0.861
Middlebury	28.75/0.893	28.83/0.894	28.92/0.896	28.98/0.898	28.98/0.898	28.91/0.897

Table 2. Quantitative results of PSNR/SSIM achieved by SRResNet with different dimensions of PMDA on three benchmark datasets ($\times 4$). PMDA is inserted after the 9-th module of SRResNet (red/blue: best/second-best).

	SRResNet	Vanilla 1	Vanilla 2	Vanilla 3	Vanilla 4	Vanilla 5	Vanilla 6	SRResNet+PMDA
W×C		✓			✓	✓		✓
H×W			✓		✓		✓	✓
H×C				✓		✓	✓	✓
KITTI 2012	26.28/0.871	26.40/0.873	26.28/0.871	26.30/0.871	26.41/0.874	26.40/0.874	26.30/0.871	26.43/0.874
KITTI 2015	25.48/0.861	25.58/0.864	25.47/0.861	25.50/0.861	25.58/0.864	25.57/0.864	25.45/0.861	25.60/0.864
Middlebury	28.87/0.895	28.97/0.898	28.89/0.895	28.90/0.895	28.96/0.898	28.97/0.898	28.86/0.895	29.00/0.898

4 Experimental Evaluation

4.1 Implementation Details

All the models in our comparison are trained on the Flickr1024 dataset [14] and 60 Middlebury images [10]. It is also evaluated on 20 images from the KITTI 2012 dataset [4], 20 images from the KITTI 2015 dataset [9] and 5 images from the Middlebury dataset. Before the training phase, the original training images are down-sampled by the scale factors of 2 and 4 to produce the LR images. Then, following [14], we cropped all the LR images into patch 90×30 with a stride of 20. Data augmentation only includes random horizontal and vertical flippings. Two widely used quantitative metrics, the average Peak Signal-to-Noise Ratio (PSNR) and Structural Similarity (SSIM) are used to measure model performance and calculated on RGB color space [6]. Besides, PSNR and SSIM are calculated on the left views with their left boundaries (64 pixels) being cropped [6]. We adopt Mean Absolute Error (MAE) as the loss function, with the help of Adam optimizer. The training will stop after 50 epochs for those SISR networks since more epoch will not lead to performance gain. The batch size is set to 32 stereo images, except RCAN and SAN which only contain 8 stereo images due to the hardware limitation. The number of parameters, mult-adds and running time are computed on $3 \times 256 \times 90$ stereo images. All networks are implemented by the PyTorch framework with an NVIDIA RTX 3090 GPU.

4.2 Ablation Study

Different Locations of PMDA. PMDA is inserted at the different stages of PASR to investigate whether PMDA really works and how the location of PMDA affects

Table 3. Effect of SMDA measured on three benchmark datasets (×4). The following experiments are conducted based on PASR+PMDA$_7$ (red/blue: best/second-best).

Model	KITTI 2012	KITTI 2015	Middlebury
PASR w/o SMDA	26.20/0.870	25.35/0.858	28.81/0.895
PASR with SMDA	26.39/0.874	25.59/0.864	28.98/0.898

Table 4. Quantitative results of SISR models combined with our proposed PMDA on three benchmark datasets (×4).

Model	IMDN		SRResNet		RCAN		SAN	
	w/o PMDA	with PMDA	w/o PMDA	with PMDA	w/o PMDA	with PMDA	w/o PMDA	with PMDA
KITTI 2012	26.15/0.868	26.25/0.870	26.24/0.870	26.39/0.873	26.18/0.870	26.53/0.877	26.27/0.872	26.40/0.875
KITTI 2015	25.33/0.857	25.45/0.860	25.41/0.860	25.59/0.864	25.32/0.860	25.67/0.868	25.42/0.862	25.54/0.865
Middlebury	28.53/0.890	28.68/0.893	28.76/0.894	28.98/0.898	28.87/0.897	29.13/0.902	28.92/0.896	29.04/0.900

the results. We report the results in Table 1. Comparing the results of PASR with PMDA and PASR, it is easy to find that the reconstruction performance can be significantly boosted. This is because, by adding the proposed PMDA, the network can exploit cross-view information while maintaining the superiority of intra-view information exploitation, leading to prominent performance gain to the SISR network. Meanwhile, there is no exact location preference for PMDA since PMDA could achieve superior results if it is inserted in the middle of the SISR network, which also shows the easy usage of PMDA.

Different Dimensions in PMDA. Table 2 shows how the choice of dimension affects the final results, where $W \times C$, $H \times C$ and $H \times W$ indicate on which axis the matrix multiplication is performed in PMDA. It is observed that the full module SRResNet+PMDA (full) which builds inter-dependencies among three dimensions obtains a considerable improvement on the three datasets. The result supports our intuition that PMDA with all three-dimensional features (denoted as full) outperforms other vanilla versions.

Effect of SMDA. To demonstrate the benefits introduced by SMDA, we directly removed SMDA and only retrained the original Res2Net module in our proposed network. The results are shown in Table 3. It demonstrates that the Multi-Dimensional Attention (MDA) mechanism is a benefit for the exploration of internal HR information. Thus, our proposed SMDA can improve the feature representation capacity and reconstruction performance.

4.3 Combinations with SISR Models

PMDA has been combined with various SISR models including IMDN [5], SRResNet [7], RCAN [19] and SAN [2]. Besides, to demonstrate the generality of PMDA, it is directly inserted into the middle stage of these SISR models. Quantitative results are shown in Table 4. It can be easily observed that with

Table 5. Quantitative comparisons of existing methods (red/blue: best/second-best). Here PMDA is inserted after the 7-*th* PAB of PASR.

Model	Scale	Param (M)	Mult-adds (G)	Running-time (s)	KITTI 2012	KITTI 2015	Middlebury
Bicubic	2×	–	–	–	28.64/0.929	28.01/0.928	30.67/0.940
IMDN		0.694	31.75	0.014	30.65/0.950	29.79/0.950	33.90/0.965
PASSRnet		1.368	55.65	0.013	30.68/0.916	29.78/0.919	34.05/0.960
SRResNet		1.399	66.44	0.019	30.57/0.950	29.74/0.950	33.95/0.965
PASR (ours)		1.193	55.97	0.053	30.77/0.951	29.85/0.950	34.32/0.968
Bicubic	4×	–	–	–	24.64/0.830	23.90/0.812	26.39/0.848
IMDN		0.715	32.71	0.012	26.15/0.868	25.33/0.857	28.53/0.890
PASSRnet		1.417	57.28	0.014	26.26/0.790	25.43/0.776	28.63/0.871
SRResNet		1.547	102.22	0.040	26.24/0.870	25.41/0.860	28.76/0.894
SRResNet+SAM		1.637	106.18	0.048	26.35/0.873	25.53/0.863	28.81/0.897
RCAN		15.592	1430.2	0.165	26.18/0.870	25.32/0.860	28.87/0.879
SAN		15.822	749.06	1.349	26.27/0.872	25.42/0.862	28.92/0.896
PASR (ours)		1.193	91.75	0.081	26.39/0.874	25.59/0.864	28.98/0.898

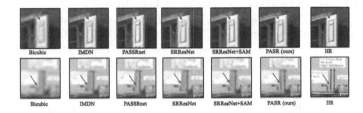

Fig. 3. Visual comparison of the ×4 stereo SR results of our PASR and other methods.

the help of PMDA, the SISR networks have a huge performance gain in three benchmark datasets. This is because the SISR model cannot take advantage of the cross-view information from another view, while PMDA can make up for this shortage.

4.4 Comparisons with State-of-the-Art Methods

We compare our proposed PASR with common SISR models, PASSRnet [14] and SAM [17]. Quantitative results are listed in Table 5. It can be observed that with the help of PMDA, PASR can obtain all the best performance on the three benchmarks with smaller number of parameters and mult-adds. We also analyze the quality of the obtained results qualitatively, as illustrated in Fig. 3. Note that, PASR performs better than others and accurately reconstructs different line patterns. Therefore, the proposed PMDA is indeed beneficial to generate much clearer images with high perceptual quality.

5 Conclusion

In this paper, we introduce Parallax Multi-Dimensional Attention (PMDA), a generic module for exploring inherent correlation within stereo image pairs.

PMDA can capture cross-dimensional dependencies of stereo input among channels or spatial locations. Existing SISR methods can be improved for stereo SR by directly inserting one PMDA into the network. Self Multi-Dimensional Attention (SMDA) is also proposed which captures multi-dimensional attention feature from one image. Finally, a new stereo SR network named PASR is proposed. Results demonstrate that our model not only achieves the best performance but also generates clear HR images perceptually closer to the HR counterparts.

Acknowledgments. This work is supported by Sichuan Science and Technology Program (No. 2021YFS0007).

References

1. Dai, F., Chen, X., Ma, Y., Jin, G., Zhao, Q.: Wide range depth estimation from binocular light field camera. In: BMVC, p. 107 (2018)
2. Dai, T., Cai, J., Zhang, Y., Xia, S., Zhang, L.: Second-order attention network for single image super-resolution. In: CVPR, pp. 11065–11074 (2019)
3. Gao, S., Cheng, M., Zhao, K., Zhang, X., Yang, M., Torr, P.H.S.: Res2Net: a new multi-scale backbone architecture. IEEE Trans. Pattern Anal. Mach. Intell. **43**(2), 652–662 (2021)
4. Geiger, A., Lenz, P., Urtasun, R.: Are we ready for autonomous driving? The KITTI vision benchmark suite. In: CVPR, pp. 3354–3361 (2012)
5. Hui, Z., Gao, X., Yang, Y., Wang, X.: Lightweight image super-resolution with information multi-distillation network. In: ACM MM, pp. 2024–2032 (2019)
6. Jeon, D.S., Baek, S., Choi, I., Kim, M.H.: Enhancing the spatial resolution of stereo images using a parallax prior. In: CVPR, pp. 1721–1730 (2018)
7. Ledig, C., et al.: Photo-realistic single image super-resolution using a generative adversarial network. In: CVPR, pp. 105–114 (2017)
8. Mei, Y., Fan, Y., Zhou, Y., Huang, L., Huang, T.S., Shi, H.: Image super-resolution with cross-scale non-local attention and exhaustive self-exemplars mining. In: CVPR, pp. 5689–5698 (2020)
9. Menze, M., Geiger, A.: Object scene flow for autonomous vehicles. In: CVPR, pp. 3061–3070 (2015)
10. Scharstein, D., et al.: High-resolution stereo datasets with subpixel-accurate ground truth. In: Jiang, X., Hornegger, J., Koch, R. (eds.) GCPR 2014. LNCS, vol. 8753, pp. 31–42. Springer, Cham (2014). https://doi.org/10.1007/978-3-319-11752-2_3
11. Shi, W., et al.: Real-time single image and video super-resolution using an efficient sub-pixel convolutional neural network. In: CVPR, pp. 1874–1883 (2016)
12. Song, W., Choi, S., Jeong, S., Sohn, K.: Stereoscopic image super-resolution with stereo consistent feature. In: AAAI, pp. 12031–12038 (2020)
13. Vaswani, A., et al.: Attention is all you need. In: NIPS, pp. 5998–6008 (2017)
14. Wang, L., et al.: Learning parallax attention for stereo image super-resolution. In: CVPR, pp. 12250–12259 (2019)
15. Xie, W., Zhang, J., Lu, Z., Cao, M., Zhao, Y.: Non-local nested residual attention network for stereo image super-resolution. In: ICASSP, pp. 2643–2647 (2020)
16. Yan, B., Ma, C., Bare, B., Tan, W., Hoi, S.C.H.: Disparity-aware domain adaptation in stereo image restoration. In: CVPR, pp. 13176–13184 (2020)

17. Ying, X., Wang, Y., Wang, L., Sheng, W., An, W., Guo, Y.: A stereo attention module for stereo image super-resolution. IEEE Signal Process. Lett. **27**, 496–500 (2020)
18. Zhang, T., Gu, Y., Huang, X., Tu, E., Yang, J.: Stereo endoscopic image super-resolution using disparity-constrained parallel attention. In: ICLR Workshop (2020)
19. Zhang, Y., Li, K., Li, K., Wang, L., Zhong, B., Fu, Y.: Image super-resolution using very deep residual channel attention networks. In: Ferrari, V., Hebert, M., Sminchisescu, C., Weiss, Y. (eds.) ECCV 2018. LNCS, vol. 11211, pp. 294–310. Springer, Cham (2018). https://doi.org/10.1007/978-3-030-01234-2_18

Fusing the Degree of Nodes in the Session Graph for Session-Based Recommendation

Xiang Huang[1], Yixin He[1], Bin Yan[2], and Wei Zeng[1(✉)]

[1] University of Electronic Science and Technology of China, Chengdu, Sichuan, China
huangxiang@std.uestc.edu.cn, zwei504@uestc.edu.cn
[2] China Southwest Geotechnical Investigation and Design Institute Co., Ltd., Chengdu, China

Abstract. With the increasing number of data appears in the form of session, it shows great importance to predict the future items based on the present ones in the session. By now, great progress has been made in the Graph Neural Network to build the session-based recommendation system. Nevertheless, the existing method of session-data modeling through the graph neural network ignores the degree of nodes which to some extent reflects the importance of the nodes in the graph. Intuitively, the possibility of the item to be clicked increases along with the degree of the node represents this item. Inspired by the aforementioned observation, we analyze the session data and propose to use the degree information of the nodes in the session graph to improve the effect of session recommendation. The experiments show that the proposed method outperforms the current mainstream approaches on a number of real-world data sets, such as Tmall and Diginetica.

Keywords: Degree information · Transition information · GNN · Session

1 Introduction

Since entering the era of big data, users are always faced with the problem of information overload. It is becoming increasingly difficult to obtain the expected information from the high volume of data, while the application of the recommendation system can alleviate this problem. In the existing real scenes, more and more data are presented in the form of session, such as music, movies, and goods clicked by a user, which constitute the session of this user.

Traditional recommendation systems often make recommendations based on the interaction between users and items, while users' information in session data is usually unknown. Compared with traditional recommendation systems, session-based recommendation systems can target at scenarios where the users' information is unknown. Therefore, the session-based recommendation system has become a hot spot in the research.

T. Mantoro et al. (Eds.): ICONIP 2021, CCIS 1517, pp. 728–735, 2021.
https://doi.org/10.1007/978-3-030-92310-5_84

In recent years, deep learning has gained significant development on the applications in various fields. A great progress has also been made on the application of deep learning in session-based recommendation systems. So far, the best way to apply deep learning to session recommendation is to model the session data through the graph neural network, which compared with ordinary neural networks, is able to obtain the complex transition information among items by constructing session graphs.

Although some progress has been made by previous work, the recommendation based on session data is still confronted with some challenges. One of the most intractable challenges is that high proportion of the data in the session-based recommendation tasks only provide the time series of items clicked by users, while the specific information of these users is unknown. The existing graph neural networks only take the simple session graph into consideration but ignore a lot of important information, such as the degrees of the nodes.

For example, when users browse yahoo.com to look through the news, they tend to click the one they are interested in from the multiple pieces of news in the homepage. After reading it, users will return to the homepage to choose another one they are interested in to click in and then read. In this session of reading news, the homepage will appear multiple times, which makes the homepage have a larger degree in the whole session graph compared to other pages. Therefore, in a session, items that appear more frequently are more likely to be clicked by users, and thus using the times they appear can help improve the effect of session recommendation.

Based on the analysis above, this paper proposes a method of combining the transition information with the degree information in session data to predict the next item in the session. The main contributions of this paper are as follows:

(1) The distribution of the degrees of nodes in the session is analyzed firstly and the practical cases are applied to analyze the impact of the degrees of nodes in the session.
(2) The out-degree matrix and the in-degree matrix are constructed to represent the degrees of the nodes in the session, which combined with the graph neural network can generate more accurate latent vectors of items.
(3) The effectiveness of the proposed method is verified by several ablation experiments on real world data.

2   Related Work

The session-based recommendation system mainly has two technological paths, one of which is Markov chain [1]. To be specific, the probability of the items to be clicked is calculated through the state transition probability matrix. The other path is related to deep learning. There are two mainstream methods of applying deep learning to session recommendation, based on recurrent neural network (RNN) and graph neural network (GNN) respectively.

The pioneer of combining the recurrent neural network with the session recommendation is GRU4Rec [2], verifying the effectiveness of this combination. It jointed different sessions together for training to compensate for the inefficiency of RNNs due to their inability to be parallel computed. Afterwards, much effort has been made to develop the GRU4Rec. HRNN [3] wielded Session-level GRU and User-level GRU to model the session information and user history information respectively. This hierarchical RNN model is helpful in characterizing the changes in the user's personal interest in the session. The phenomenon that the longer a user stays on an item in a session, the more interested the user is in it inspired Bogina et al. [4] to combine dwell time with RNN to improve the effectiveness of recommendations. Although this kind of methods which convert the transition relations of items into dependencies among nodes in RNNs have achieved good results, they still fail to obtain an accurate representation of the item vector and ignore the complex transition properties in items.

The relationship between items in a session can often be represented by different graphs and thus a large number of researchers have applied graph neural networks to session recommendation, achieving very significant results. The most classic work is SR-GNN [5], which first applied gated graph neural network [6] to session recommendation. It is SR-GNN that first represents session data as graph-structured data, then obtains node vectors by gated graph neural network, after which the attention network is used to acquire the combination of global preferences and current interests of users, and finally predicts the probability of the next item to be clicked in the session. GC-SAN [7] replaced soft-attention with self-attention layer on the basis of SR-GNN, utilizing the self-attention mechanism to enhance the session recommendation. Considering the diversity of target items and user interests, as well as the model's limited ability of representation in the case of the session represented as a fixed vector, adaptive target perception attention was proposed in TA-GNN [8] to learn the interest representation vector that can change with the different target objects based on SR-GNN. Although all of the above approaches can model the complex transition characteristics in a session by graph neural networks, they failed to fully consider the degree information other than transition information contained in a session. Therefore, this paper proposes to combine the degree information of nodes in the session graph with the transition information to improve the effect of the next item recommendation.

3   Method

This chapter first introduces the notations used in this paper, then introduces how to construct the degree matrix and how to use GGNN to learn item embedding, and finally describes the fusion of degree information and transformation information.

3.1   Notations

We define the set of all the sessions as $S = \{s_1, s_2, \ldots, s_i, \ldots, s_n\}$, among them, s_i is a specific session, $s_i = \{v_{si,1}, v_{si,2}, \ldots, v_{si,i}, \ldots, v_{si,n}\}$. $v_{si,i}$ is the item that the user clicked in the chronological order. The set of all item types incorporated in the session is defined as $V = \{v_1, v_2, \ldots, v_i, \ldots, v_m\}$. The task of this section is to predict the value of $v_{si,n+1}$ when given a session s_i.

3.2   GGNN with Degree Matrices

As for our degree matrix, because we deal with the out-of-degree and in-degree of nodes respectively through the gated graph neural network, compared with the original gated graph neural network, we need to change the dimension of the weight with dimension $\mathbb{R}^{2d \times d}$ in the network to $\mathbb{R}^{d \times d}$. The method proposed in this paper is shown in Fig. 1.

For the out-degree matrix, we modify Eq. (1) as follows:

$$d_{os,i}^t = D_{os,i:} \left[v_1^{t-1}, \ldots, v_n^{t-1} \right]^T H_o + b_o \tag{1}$$

For the in-degree matrix, we modify Eq. (1) as follows:

$$d_{is,i}^t = D_{is,i:} \left[v_1^{t-1}, \ldots, v_n^{t-1} \right]^T H_i + b_i \tag{2}$$

Where D_{os} is the out-degree matrix in the degree matrix, and D_{is} is the in-degree matrix in the degree matrix. Through the gated graph neural network, we can get the item embedding vectors $(d_1^o, d_i^o, \ldots, d_n^o)$ representing the out-degree information, the item embedding vectors $(d_1^i, d_i^i, \ldots, d_n^i)$ representing the in-degree information, and the item embedding vectors $(v_1, v_i, \ldots, v_n)$ representing the transition information.

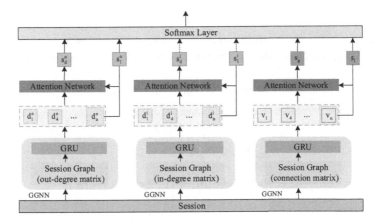

Fig. 1. The workflow of the proposed method. (1) Construct the connection matrix and the degree matrix to represent the transition information and the degree information respectively. (2) A gated graph neural network is utilized to model the transition information and degree information separately and thus a representation vector of the items in the session can be obtained. (3) In order to represent the degree information and the transition information in the form of the concrete vector, the soft attention mechanism is combine with each of the last items so that the session feature vectors s_d^o, s_d^i and s_g, and the feature vectors s_1^o, s_1^i and s_1 of the last item can be acquired. (4) s_d^o, s_1^o, s_d^i, s_1^i, s_g and s_1 are added up and then pass through the softmax layer for the prediction of the next item.

3.3 Generating Session Embeddings and Prediction

The soft attention mechanism is applied to combine the degree information and transition information with the last item to obtain a vector that accurately represents the session feature. Since the calculation process of out-degree and in-degree is the same, we only show the process of in-degree below. The specific calculation process is as follows:

$$\alpha_i^d = \mathbf{q}_d^T \sigma \left(\mathbf{W}_1^d \, d_n^i + \mathbf{W}_2^d \, d_i^i + c \right) \tag{3}$$

$$s_d^i = \sum_{i=1}^n \alpha_i^d \, d_i^i \tag{4}$$

$$s_1^i = d_n^i \tag{5}$$

where $\mathbf{W}_1^d \in \mathbb{R}^{d \times d}$, $\mathbf{W}_2^d \in \mathbb{R}^{d \times d}$, $\mathbf{q}_d \in \mathbb{R}^d$ is the parameter matrix. In addition, using the above three formulas, we can get s_d^o and s_1^o in Fig. 1.

$$s_1 = \sigma \left(\mathbf{W}_1^v v_n \right) \tag{6}$$

$$\alpha_i^v = \mathbf{q}_v^T \sigma \left(s_1 + \mathbf{W}_2^v v_i + c \right) \tag{7}$$

$$s_g = \sum_{i=1}^n \alpha_i^v \, v_i \tag{8}$$

where $\mathbf{W}_1^v \in \mathbb{R}^{d \times d}$, $\mathbf{W}_2^v \in \mathbb{R}^{d \times d}$, $\mathbf{q}_v \in \mathbb{R}^d$ is the parameter matrix. Finally, as shown in Fig. 1, multiple different feature vectors are added up to make the next prediction:

$$s_{\text{all}} = s_d^o + s_1^o + s_d^i + s_1^i + s_g + s_1 \tag{9}$$

$$y_{\text{pre}} = \text{softmax} \left(s_{\text{all}}^T \times v_i \right) \tag{10}$$

$$L \left(y_{\text{pre}} \right) = - \sum_{i=1}^m y^i \log \left(y_{\text{pre}}^i \right) + \left(1 - y^i \right) \log \left(1 - y_{\text{pre}}^i \right) \tag{11}$$

Where y is the one-hot encoding vector of the ground truth item.

4 Experiments

The experiments are designed to figure out the following three questions: (1) Can the processing and setting of the experiment data ensure fairness and persuasiveness? (2) From the aspect of effectiveness, can our method outperform the baseline? (3) Is the degree information capable of playing a significant role?

4.1 Dataset and Experimental Setup

To assure the fairness, the dataset was directly processed the by the code provided by the SR-GNN authors. The datasets we used are Diginetica, Nowplaying, and Tmall. The parameter settings in our model remain the same as SR-GNN. Batch size, embedding size, and hidden size in GRU are all 100, the initial learning rate is 0.001, and the learning rate decays to one-tenth of the original one for every three training epochs. L2 regularization is set to 10^{-5}.

4.2 Comparison with the Experiment Results of the Baseline

The performance of our method is evaluated by comparing it with the current classical methods. The baseline we use is as follows:

POP: Recommend the most frequent N items in the training set.

FPMC [1]: Recommend through the combination of first-order Markov chain and matrix decomposition.

Item-KNN [9]: Recommend the items which are similar to that have previously been clicked through calculating the cosine similarity.

GRU4REC [2]: The pioneer of applying a variant of RNN (gated recurrent unit) in session recommendation to model the user sequences.

NARM [10]: Use attention to capture the user's purpose to enhance the recommendation effect based on GRU4Rec.

STAMP [11]: The last click is taken as the current interest and the previous are the long-term preferences. A better recommendation effect is achieved by the combination of the two.

SR-GNN [5]: The gated graph neural network is used to obtain an accurate representation of the item vector and then combine the long-term preferences with current interests through a soft-attention mechanism to make recommendations.

The evaluation indicators used in this paper are P@n and MRR@n. P@n means the correct proportion of the n returned results. MRR@n refers to the mean of the reciprocal of the ranking of the correct recommendation results. Table 1 shows the comparison among the results of our method and that of the baseline on the three datasets.

From the results in Table 1, the neural network represented by GRU4REC and STAMP performs better in session-based recommendation systems than the traditional methods such as POP, FPMC, Item-KNN. However, the neural network-based method still have some shortcomings.

The technical path that GRU4REC and NARM model the sessions through recurrent neural networks ignores the interaction between items and STAMP neglects the chronological order of items. By means of GGNN and soft attention, SR-GNN not only obtains the interactions of items in the session, but also captures the changes in the short-term interest of users, and thus attains better results than the above methods. Nevertheless, compared with SR-GNN, our method combines the degree information with the transition information, which fully exploits the sessions with limited information. Therefore, our method is better than SR-GNN.

Table 1. Comparison of results with baseline.

Method	Tmall		Nowplaying		Diginetica	
	P@20	MRR@20	P@20	MRR@20	P@20	MRR@20
POP	2.00	0.90	2.28	0.86	0.89	0.20
FPMC	16.06	7.32	7.36	2.82	26.53	6.95
Item-KNN	9.15	3.31	15.94	4.91	35.75	11.57
GRU4REC	10.93	5.89	7.92	4.48	29.45	8.33
NARM	23.30	10.70	18.59	6.93	49.70	16.17
STAMP	26.47	13.36	17.66	6.88	45.64	14.32
SR-GNN	27.57	13.72	18.87	7.47	50.73	17.59
Ours	29.68	14.36	21.64	8.01	53.17	18.25

4.3 The Result of In-Degree and Out-Degree Information

Figure 2 show the results of in-degree information and out-degree information in the model. Compared with using both out-degree and in-degree information, singly using in-degree information or out-degree information will make the results of the model decline on all three data sets. This is because the in-degree matrix and the out-degree matrix respectively contain the in-degree information and out-degree information of the items in the session, and both of these two kinds of information is conducive to modeling the session data and generating more accurate latent vectors of items.

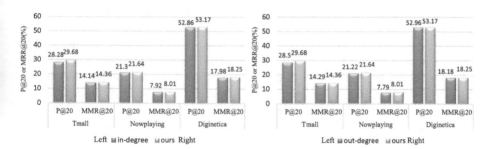

Fig. 2. Results with only in-degree information and out-degree information.

5 Conclusion

Nowadays, the world is full of various session data, which makes the application of graph neural networks in session-based recommender systems the future trend. Most of the existing methods based on recurrent neural networks and graph neural networks merely use the transition information of the items in the session, leading to the insufficient utilization of the session data. Based on the existing work, this paper fully exploits the limited information in the session and further improves the effectiveness of session recommendation by integrating transition information with degree information. In addition, this paper validates the effectiveness of the information fusion on multiple real-world datasets through several ablation experiments. In the future, we will further excavate the data in the sessions and dig more deeply into the information in the sessions.

Acknowledgments. The work is supported by the National Natural Science Foundation of China No. 61872062, the National High Technology Research and Development Program of China (No. 2018YFB1005100, 2018YFB1005104), special fund project of science and technology incubation and achievement transformation in Neijiang City (No. 2019KJFH005).

References

1. Rendle, S., Freudenthaler, C., Schmidt-Thieme, L.: Factorizing personalized Markov chains for next-basket recommendation. In: Proceedings of the 19th International Conference on World Wide Web, pp. 811–820 (2010)
2. Hidasi, B., Karatzoglou, A., Baltrunas, L., et al.: Session-based recommendations with recurrent neural networks. arXiv preprint arXiv:1511.06939 (2015)
3. Quadrana, M., Karatzoglou, A., Hidasi, B., et al.: Personalizing session-based recommendations with hierarchical recurrent neural networks. In: Proceedings of the Eleventh ACM Conference on Recommender Systems, pp. 130–137 (2017)
4. Bogina, V., Kuflik, T.: Incorporating dwell time in session-based recommendations with recurrent neural networks. In: RecTemp@ RecSys, pp. 57–59 (2017)
5. Wu, S., Tang, Y., Zhu, Y., et al.: Session-based recommendation with graph neural networks. In: Proceedings of the AAAI Conference on Artificial Intelligence, vol. 33, no. 01, pp. 346–353 (2019)
6. Li, Y., Tarlow, D., Brockschmidt, M., et al.: Gated graph sequence neural networks. arXiv preprint arXiv:1511.05493 (2015)
7. Xu, C., Zhao, P., Liu, Y., et al.: Graph contextualized self-attention network for session-based recommendation. In: IJCAI, vol. 19, pp. 3940–3946 (2019)
8. Yu, F., Zhu, Y., Liu, Q., et al.: TAGNN: target attentive graph neural networks for session-based recommendation. In: Proceedings of the 43rd International ACM SIGIR Conference on Research and Development in Information Retrieval, pp. 1921–1924 (2020)
9. Sarwar, B., Karypis, G., Konstan, J., et al.: Item-based collaborative filtering recommendation algorithms. In: Proceedings of the 10th International Conference on World Wide Web, pp. 285–295 (2001)
10. Li, J., Ren, P., Chen, Z., et al.: Neural attentive session-based recommendation. In: 2017 Proceedings of the ACM on Conference on Information and Knowledge Management, pp. 1419–1428 (2017)
11. Liu, Q., Zeng, Y., Mokhosi, R., et al.: STAMP: short-term attention memory priority model for session-based recommendation. In: Proceedings of the 24th ACM SIGKDD International Conference on Knowledge Discovery and Data Mining, pp. 1831–1839 (2018)

A Restriction Training Recipe for Speech Separation on Sparsely Mixed Speech

Shaoxiang Dang[1(✉)], Tetsuya Matsumoto[1], Hiroaki Kudo[1],
and Yoshinori Takeuchi[2]

[1] Graduate School of Informatics, Nagoya University, Furo-cho, Chikusa-ku,
Nagoya 464-8601, Japan
`dang.shaoxiang@i.mbox.nagoya-u.ac.jp`
[2] School of Informatics, Daido University, 10-3, Takiharu-cho, Minani-ku,
Nagoya 457-8530, Japan

Abstract. Techniques of speech separation have changed rapidly in the last few years. The traditional recurrent neural networks (RNNs) have been replaced by any other architecture like convolutional neural networks (CNNs) steadily. Although these models have improved the performance greatly in speed and accuracy, it is still inevitable to sacrifice some long-term dependency. As a result, the separated signals are vulnerable to be wrong assigned. This situation could be even common when the mixed speech is sparse, like the communication. In this paper, a two-stage training recipe with a restriction term based on scale-invariant signal-to-noise ratio (SISNR) is put forward to prevent wrong assignment problem on sparsely mixed speech. The experiment is conducted on the mixture of Japanese Newspaper Article Sentences (JNAS). According to the experiments, the proposed approach can work efficiently on sparse data (overlapping rate around 50%), and performances are improved consequently. In order to test the application of speech separation in actual situations, such as meeting transcription, the separation results are also evaluated by speech recognition. The results show that the character error rate is reduced by 10% compared to the baseline.

Keywords: Speech separation · Restricted training · Sparse speech

1 Introduction

Speech separation [1], a fundamental topic in speech processing, is originally proposed for tackling the cocktail party problem where many people are speaking simultaneously. The vast majority of recent supervised models have excellent performance, and can be roughly divided into two categories: recurrent neural networks (RNNs) models and convolutional neural networks (CNNs) models. RNNs-based models use RNNs to capture temporal and causal relationships of the entire utterance [1–6], and CNNs-based ones focus on the parallelized computations by splitting sequence data into chunks and adopting CNNs or local

© Springer Nature Switzerland AG 2021
T. Mantoro et al. (Eds.): ICONIP 2021, CCIS 1517, pp. 736–743, 2021.
https://doi.org/10.1007/978-3-030-92310-5_85

and global RNNs on chunks [7–10]. For the first category, the cost of computation is relatively higher. Another downside is that feature extraction is independent of the models, rendering those models too difficult to extract features by themselves and construct a true end-to-end structure [1]. By contrast, most CNNs-based models introduce an encoder-decoder structure that contains convolutional layers to learn a representation resembling short-term Fourier transform (STFT), and their performance exhibits great superiority.

The similarity of vectors is highly adopted as the loss function after the introduction of CNNs-based models, because the outputs which were time-frequency bins are simpler and more efficient to be processed as vectors. Scale-invariant signal-to-noise ratio (SISNR) [11], a simplified version of signal-to-distortion ratio (SDR) proposed in [12], is then picked to train the separation model. The essence of SISNR is a trigonometric function, so the target of the model of using SISNR is to try to minimize the angle between reference waveform and estimated waveform. By using permutation-invariant training (PIT) method [14], the original formula of both SISNR and SDR can directly measure the relationships between the separated signals and excepted supervised signals. However, for the sparsely mixed signals like those collected at the meeting, models are more likely to separate behave contrary to the expectations. One hypothesis put forward in [7] argues that separation on the batch-level seems weak to process sparsely mixed parts because the model seems hard to keep consistency in long term.

In view of the separation like this, a restricted term in loss function is taken into consideration to prevent the wrong assigned signals that usually appear in the sparse mixture in this paper. In this way, mixed speech with the more sparse parts which is a common situation in communication can be separated precisely, thus paving the way to improve the speech recognition of multi-speakers. In the context of automatic speech recognition (ASR), the character error rate (CER), a criterion for evaluating the phonetic content of characters, is used to test separated results. CER can tell the accuracy of recognition by calculating the deletions, insertions, and substitutions of estimations.

2   The Separation Model

2.1   Encoder-Decoder Separation Structure

The separation model is based on encoder-decoder separation structure [7–9] and consist of three parts: encoder, separator and decoder. The learnable encoder and decoder are convolutional layers and establish relationships between time-domain and learned-domain. The separator learns masks of each clean signal in the learned-domain. Temporal convolutional network (TCN) in [7] is adopted as the separator. The overall structure (Conv-TasNet)is shown in Fig. 1(a). One TCN stacks several convolutional blocks with exponentially increasing dilations, as shown in Fig. 1(b). The model has n TCNs totally, and the 1×1 convolutional layer at the end doubles the channels to generate masks. Each block in TCNs has a residual structure, and dialation factor is functioned at the middle layer circled with red in Fig. 1(c).

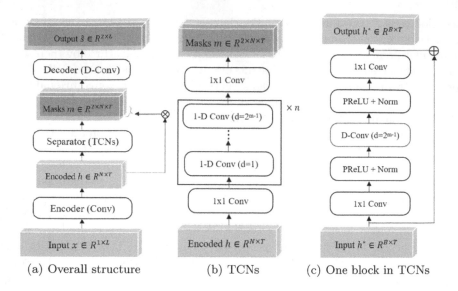

Fig. 1. Separation Network [7].

2.2 Proposed Training Recipe

The widely used simplified but powerful loss function: SISNR [12] is formulated below:

$$SISNR = 10 \log_{10} \frac{\| s_{target} \|^2}{\| \hat{s} - s_{target} \|^2} \qquad (1)$$

where

$$s_{target} = \frac{\langle \hat{s}, s \rangle s}{\| s \|^2} \qquad (2)$$

Here, s and $\hat{s}$ are reference and estimated waveform respectively. s_{target} is the projection of $\hat{s}$ onto s.

Utterance-level permutation-invariant training [6], a guidance that allow the model to make a correct back-propagation in speech separation, is based on the modeling of entire utterance, while inputs of the separation network used have fixed sizes. Thus permutation-invariant training is applied on batch-level (bPIT) in this work. Training with SISNR and bPIT is insufficient, as the long-term dependency cannot be accurately captured and consistency within a batch sometimes cannot be guaranteed. So some parts that are allocated incorrectly can often be observed: the signals originally belonging to speaker A are partly assigned to speaker B, especially for sparsely mixed parts of speech and those after noticeable pauses. As shown in Fig. 2, it is partly assigned to the wrong speaker in 4–6 s. Here, we call it wrong assignment.

In view of this, a two-stage training approach is developed to make an enhanced separation. In the first stage, the model is trained by using the loss functions of Eq. 1. The second stage is trained based on the model trained in the first stage by employing an extended loss function of SISNR and bPIT. In this stage, an additional term describing the relationships between the separated signals and opponent's supervised signals is added. The ideal situation is that the separated signals are as similar as possible to the corresponding supervised signals, and as different as possible from the opponent signals. For this reason, the first term in the second training stage ensures the separation of the main feature parts. The second term penalizes the similarity of signals under the wrong assignment. Based on the results of the first stage, the penalization term can increase the loss of the separation in the wrong assignment, thereby forcing the estimated signals away from the opponent's supervised signals and repairing the wrong assigned portions. The restriction cost function is formulated as:

$$L = \frac{1}{N} \sum_i (S(s_i, \hat{s}_{\overline{P}(i)}) - \alpha S(s_i, \hat{s}_{\underline{P}(i)})) \tag{3}$$

where $S(\cdot)$ is the operation of SISNR, i represents the speaker. N is the number of overall speakers. $\overline{P}$ and $\underline{P}$ are given by:

$$\overline{P} = \operatorname*{argmax}_P \sum_i S(s_i, \hat{s}_{P(i)}) \tag{4}$$

$$\underline{P} = \operatorname*{argmax}_P \sum_i S(s_i, \hat{s}_{P(i)}) \tag{5}$$

P contains all possible permutation functions, where every permutation function indicates a mapping from one index to the permutation of another index. The permutation function $\overline{P}$, a subset of P, lets SISNR achieve the maximum. For example, the function $\overline{P}$ returns another index for index i, so that the SISNR of them is able to take the maximum value among all possible pairs of i. Likewise, $\underline{P}$ of Eq. 5 represents the subset of P that allow SISNR get the minimum.

The hyper-parameter α in Eq. 3 controls the degree of influence of the second term to ensure that the model is optimized in the desired direction. With the proper limitation between separated signals and opponent supervised signals, the proposed method can effectively differentiate the estimated signals from the opponent's signals on the original basis. Accordingly, the situation of wrong assigned portions discussed above can be dramatically alleviated, so that the overall separation performance are expected to improve comprehensively.

3   Experiment Setup

3.1   Datasets

The default mixture dataset using Japanese Newspaper Article Sentences (JNAS) is named JNAS-2mix (80%) and is built by padding two selected utterances with 0 to the same length. The overlapping rate (the proportion of the part outside the padding) of the default mixing dataset is larger than 80%, so it actually is a completely overlapping status. Another dataset with more sparse parts based on the JNAS-2mix is created to testify the effectiveness of restriction training method: 0-padding is applied in the head of one speech and at the tail of another speech. In this manner, the proportion of overlapping portion in the middle of speech is set to be 50%, and this dataset is marked JNAS-2mix (50%). The arrangement of two datasets are same and shown in Table 1. The model is trained in speaker-independent situation [1,13]. Test subset has additional transcriptions for recognition.

Table 1. Statistic of datasets.

Datasets	Split	# Utterances	# Speakers
JNAS-2mix (80%&50%)	training	10,000	200
	validation	3,000	60
	test	800	16

3.2 Architecture and Training

The encoder contains 256 convolutional filters with a kernel size of 20 and a stride of 10, followed by a channel-wise layer normalization. As for the separation network, there are 8 convolutional blocks with different dilations, and the dilations are the values between 1 and 128 with an exponential increase of 2. The number of TCNs is 4, and results of 4 times are summed together to generate masks of estimated signals on the time domain. The decoder, a 1-dimension transposed convolution operation, is applied after masking the encoded mixture with generated masks. The kernel size and the stride distance of the decoder are consistent with the encoder.

The initial learn rate is set to 1×10^{-3}, and it will be annealed by cutting half if no improvement can be observed in successive 3 epochs. The training will have an early stop when the learning rate drops below 1×10^{-8}. Batch size and chunk size are 2 and 4s respectively. The data in one utterance is approximately the same as that in one batch actually. The optimizer is Adam. In the proposed restriction training step, the adjustable constant α is given by an empirical value $\alpha = 0.05$ [15] to conduct experiments on JNAS-2mix(80%) and JNAS-2mix(50%).

In the first stage, the model is trained with original loss function. The results of first trained are reported as the baseline. The second stage training with proposed loss function makes fine-tuning on the results of first trained model.

3.3 Evaluation Metrics

The SISNR used as plain loss function is going to be reported as first metric. In addition, the evaluation criteria of downstream topics of speech separation are also taken into consideration. The CER of ASR model is then picked. A transformer-based ASR model trained on cross-lingual representation is employed to evaluate the quality of the separated speech [16]. The outputs of ASR model is compared with the ground truths of transcription finally.

4 Results

Table 2. SISNR of the average separation results of two speakers.

Datasets	Original(dB)	Proposed(dB)
JNAS-2mix (80%)	12.81	**13.05**
JNAS-2mix (50%)	6.29	**10.49**

Table 2 shows the SISNR results. In the created sparse dataset JNAS-2mix (50%), the proposed training recipe gets a SISNR score of 10.49 (increased by 67%), which outperforms that of the original training manner. On the default mixing dataset JNAS-2mix (80%), proposed training method behaves slightly better than the original one. For the mixture with higher sparsity, the improvement is more significant. In all the separation results using the plain model, more than half of the data can be observed to have wrong assignment problem in some sparse portions. By contrast, the results of restriction training manner show that sparse parts are re-assigned correctly. In a nutshell, proposed loss function can impose an efficient restriction on sparsely mixed data.

Table 3. CER of the average separation results of two speakers.

Datasets	Original(%)	Proposed(%)
Ground-truth	31.7	
JNAS-2mix (80%)	50.2	**49.3**
JNAS-2mix (50%)	70.0	**59.5**

Likewise, the results of different methods plus the behavior of ground truth in the context of ASR are gathered in the Table 3. A quite similar conclusion that training with restriction is able to achieve an obviously better result on the sparse data can be drawn. The CER is reduced by 10%. As for the JNAS-2mix(80%), the proportion of sparse is heavily less, thus a relatively slight improvement is reported here. Based on the results above, we can conclude that loss function with a restriction term is highly efficient with the sparse data, since it improves greatly on sparse parts of mixture data.

At the end of this section, a typical separated example of JNAS-2mix(50%) is shown in Fig. 2. All the utterances are depicted in time-frequency domain, the difference between plain training and restriction training can be seen straightforward.

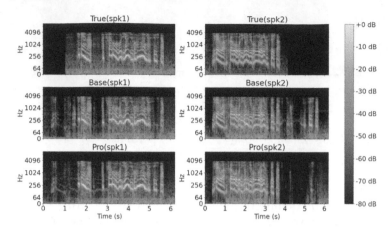

Fig. 2. Comparison of spectrograms of ground truths, results of baseline method and the proposed method.

Top two spectrograms in Fig. 2 are two ground truths before mixing. 0-padding is applied before the utterance of speaker 1 and after the utterance of speaker 2 to increase the sparsity. Two spectrograms at the middle are the results of two mixed speech of using traditional loss function as the baseline. The separation model behaves poorly to the parts that barely overlapped, like the part from 4s to 6s. We can observe that some information that originally belonging to the speaker 1 in the 4s-6s is assigned to speaker 2. However, this kind of ill-separated problem is largely settled using proposed training recipe. Two separated spectrograms using restriction training method are illustrated on the bottom of the figure. It depicts sparse parts are relatively greatly repaired.

5   Conclusion

In this paper, we talked about speech separation and focused on the separation on sparsely mixed speech. The results of traditional training methods suffer from long-term dependence and consistency, and wrong assignment appears frequently. A separation method with restriction based on the originally trained model is proposed to prevent sparse parts from losing consistency. We examined it on two subsets of JNAS, and results proved the efficiency of this training approach. SISNR is increased by 4.2 dB (67%), and CER in the downstream model is decreased by 10.5%.

Acknowledgments. We used "ASJ Japanese Newspaper Article Sentences Read Speech Corpus" provided by Speech Resources Consortium, National Institute of Informatics.

References

1. Wang, D., Chen, J.: Supervised speech separation based on deep learning: an overview. IEEE/ACM Trans. Audio Speech Lang. Process. **26**(10), 1702–1726 (2018)
2. Huang, P.S., Kim, M., Hasegawa-Johnson, M., Smaragdis, P.: Deep learning for monaural speech separation. In: Proceedings of ICASSP, pp. 1562–1566 (2014)
3. Hershey, J.R., Chen, Z., Le Roux, J., Watanabe, S.: Deep clustering: discriminative embeddings for segmentation and separation. In: Proceedings of ICASSP, pp. 31–35 (2016)
4. Chen, Z., Luo, Y., Mesgarani, N.: Deep attractor network for single-microphone speaker separation. In: Proceedings of ICASSP, pp. 246–250 (2017)
5. Chen, J., Wang, D.: Long short-term memory for speaker generalization in supervised speech separation. J. Acoust. Soc. Am. **141**(6), 4705–4714 (2017)
6. Kolbæk, M., Yu, D., Tan, Z.H., Jensen, J.: Multitalker speech separation with utterance-level permutation invariant training of deep recurrent neural networks. IEEE/ACM Trans. Audio Speech Lang. Process. **25**(10), 1901–1913 (2017)
7. Luo, Y., Mesgarani, N.: Conv-tasnet: surpassing ideal time-frequency magnitude masking for speech separation. IEEE/ACM Trans. Audio Speech Lang. Process. **27**(8), 1256–1266 (2019)
8. Yang, G.P., Tuan, C.I., Lee, H.Y., Lee, L.S.: Improved speech separation with time-and-frequency cross-domain joint embedding and clustering. arXiv preprint arXiv:1904.07845 (2019)
9. Luo, Y., Chen, Z., Yoshioka, T.: Dual-path RNN: efficient long sequence modeling for time-domain single-channel speech separation. In: Proceedings of ICASSP, pp. 46–50 (2020)
10. Pandey, A., Wang, D.: TCNN: Temporal convolutional neural network for real-time speech enhancement in the time domain. In: Proceedings of ICASSP, pp. 6875–6879 (2019)
11. Le Roux, J., Wisdom, S., Erdogan, H., Hershey, J.R.: SDR-half-baked or well done? In: Proceedings of ICASSP, pp. 626–630 (2019)
12. Vincent, E., Gribonval, R., Févotte, C.: Performance measurement in blind audio source separation. IEEE Trans. Audio Speech Lang. Process. **14**(4), 1462–1469 (2006)
13. Luo, Y., Chen, Z., Mesgarani, N.: Speaker-independent speech separation with deep attractor network. IEEE/ACM Trans. Audio Speech Lang. Process. **26**(4), 787–796 (2018)
14. Yu, D., Kolbæk, M., Tan, Z.H., Jensen, J.: Permutation invariant training of deep models for speaker-independent multi-talker speech separation. In: Proceedings of ICASSP, pp. 241–245 (2017)
15. Huang, P.S., Kim, M., Hasegawa-Johnson, M., Smaragdis, P.: Joint optimization of masks and deep recurrent neural networks for monaural source separation. IEEE/ACM Trans. Audio Speech Lang. Process. **23**(12), 2136–2147 (2015)
16. Conneau, A., Baevski, A., Collobert, R., Mohamed, A., Auli, M.: Unsupervised cross-lingual representation learning for speech recognition. arXiv preprint arXiv:2006.13979 (2020)

Predicting Software Defect Severity Level Using Deep-Learning Approach with Various Hidden Layers

Lov Kumar[1]([✉]), Triyasha Ghosh Dastidar[1], Anjali Goyal[3],
Lalita Bhanu Murthy[1], Sanjay Misra[2], Vipul Kocher[4],
and Srinivas Padmanabhuni[4]

[1] BITS-Pilani Hyderabad, Hyderabad, India
{lovkumar,f20170829,bhanu}@hyderabad.bits-pilani.ac.in
[2] Covenant University, Ota, Nigeria
sanjay.misra@covenantuniversity.edu.ng
[3] Amity University, Noida, India
Anjaligoyal19@yahoo.in
[4] Testaing.Com, Noida, India
{vipulkocher,srinivas}@testAing.com

Abstract. The severity value of the defect helps to decide how soon the defects needs to be fixed. The software used to handle defect reports gets more than ten thousands defects every week, and it is not feasible to assign severity value of the defect by manually reading defect reports. So, severity value prediction based on defect contents helps to find an appropriate severity value. These models have applications in appropriate scheduling of testing resources. The predictive power of severity value prediction models dependent on the input features computed from the description reports of defect. In this paper, we have applied eight different embedding techniques with an objective to compute n-dimensional numeric vector for defect report. Further, we have also applied feature selection techniques and data sampling technique to find relevant features and handle the unequal distribution of sample present in different classes. The predictive power of considered eight different embedding techniques have been assessed using eight different varieties of deep learning models. The experimental results on six projects highlight that the usage of feature selection techniques, embedding to extract feature from text, and SMOTE help in improving the predictive ability of defect severity level prediction models.

Keywords: Software defects · Data imbalnce · Severity prediction · Deep learning · Feature selection · Word embedding

1 Introduction

The primary objective of any software company to deliver fault free software to the user, however, a fault-free software in the domain of requirements fluctuation, immense complexity and expediting size is hardly practicable. It is observed from

© Springer Nature Switzerland AG 2021
T. Mantoro et al. (Eds.): ICONIP 2021, CCIS 1517, pp. 744–751, 2021.
https://doi.org/10.1007/978-3-030-92310-5_86

software survey that maintenance related tasks can consume more than 70% of the total software development cost [1]. It is also observed that the Defect tracking systems play vital role during the maintenance phase of software development process. This tracking systems used to organize, accumulate, and monitor the reported defects. However, it has been observed in the past studies that defect resolution is a time consuming and expensive process [2]. Defect severity prediction is a research area that has emerged recently in the past few years. This research area helps in the effective utilization of resources. Severity level prediction tries to identify or predict the overall impact of a newly reported defect on the complete software product. The impact analysis of newly reported bug is later used for the timely allocation of different types of resources to the high impact defects first as they often deteriorate the software quality in a fast manner.

In the past studies, severity level defect prediction is being considered as a classification problem where data mining techniques are used to obtain the features from the textual description data present in the defect report. The data mining techniques try to obtain various numerical features from the textual description data. Word embedding is another popular representation of document vocabulary and has been used in various recent studies. It is capable of capturing the context of a word in a document and hence often leads to better feature representation. In this work, we employed the usage of seven different word-embedding along with the SMOTE technique for class imbalance handling and three feature selection techniques. Finally, we applied eight deep learning models for defect severity model building. The performance of eight deep learning-based models have been analyzed using a five-fold cross-validation technique.

2   Study Design

We have presented the various design settings used for software severity level prediction.

2.1   Experimental Dataset

In this work, we utilized datasets from six different software projects, namely JDT, CDT, Platform, PDE, Bugzilla, and Thunderbird. The datasets have been gathered from msr2013-bug_dataset-master. The msr2013-bug_dataset-master is a huge collection of defect reports possessing data field ID, description, and severity level. The defect reports in the given dataset are marked with six different severity levels: Normal, Minor, Major, Trivial, Blocker, and Critical [3,4]. Figure 1 presents the details of the dataset employed in this work in terms of the number and percentage of defect reports in each software project corresponding to different severity levels.

2.2   Deep Learning Architecture

Traditional machine learning techniques not have ability to find good pattern after increasing certain amount of data. Deep learning based techniques have

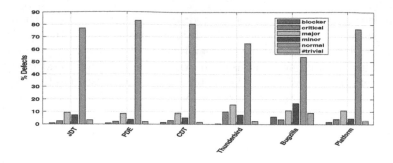

Fig. 1. Experimental data set description

ability to grasp complex perception tasks with good accuracy [5]. This work make the use of eight different architecture of deep learning techniques to train model for predicting value of severity based of defect contents. Table 1 shows the details of the deep learning architecture used to train the models to predict severity value. The above considered models are validated using 5-fold cross-validation with batch size = 30, epochs = 100, and Dropout = 0.2.

Table 1. Deep learning architecture

Model	Hidden layers	Dropout layer	Activation fun	Optimizer
DL1	1	0	ReLU	adam
DL2	1	1	ReLU	adam
DL3	2	1	ReLU	adam
DL4	2	2	ReLU	adam
DL5	3	2	ReLU	adam
DL6	3	3	ReLU	adam
DL7	4	3	ReLU	adam
DL8	4	4	ReLU	adam

3   Research Methodology

In this paper, we have applied different architecture of deep learning to train severity value prediction models by taking contents of defect report as an input. Figure 2 shows the research framework used to design severity level prediction models based on content of defect report. The information present in Fig. 2 suggested that the proposed methods have multiple steps:

Step 1: The initial step consists of features extraction from defect report using different word-embedding techniques. We have used eight different word-embedding techniques to represent the content of defect reports not just as a number but as a vector in n-dimensional space.

Step 2: After the successful transformation of the word to number, SMOTE technique has been applied on extracted features with an objective to make equal distribution of data samples across the different classes.

Step 3: The next step of the proposed method is to enhance the predictive power of the developed models by considering sets of relevant features as input. In this work, three feature selection techniques such as significant feature selection technique used to find sets of significant features [6], Correlation-analysis used to find the sets of un-correlated features, and Principal Component Analysis (PCA) used to extract new sets of un-correlated features [7].

Step 4: Finally, we have applied different architecture of deep learning to train severity value. The trained models are validated with help of 5-fold cross validation and compared using AUC, and Accuracy.

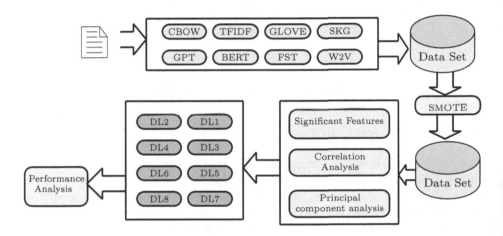

Fig. 2. Research framework

4   Results

This section present the predictive power of severity value prediction models in terms of AUC, and Accuracy. Figures 3 and 4 show the roc curve for the severity value prediction models trained using different architecture of deep learning on smote sampled data and original data. From Fig. 3 and 4, we can observed that the severity value prediction models trained on balanced data have good predictive power as compared to original data. The severity value prediction models achieved almost 1 AUC value after trained on sampled data while the same models trained on original data have 0.55 to 0.85 AUC value.

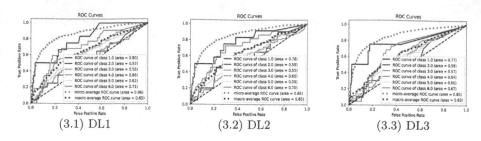

Fig. 3. ROC curve for CDT project: original data with PCA

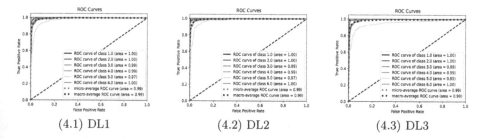

Fig. 4. ROC curve for CDT poject: SMOTE sampled data with PCA

5   Performance Comparison

This section describes the comparison of predictive power of severity value prediction models trained using different techniques like deep learning techniques, embedding techniques, smote, and feature selection techniques. The predictive power of severity value prediction models compared with the help of Box-Plot diagram. The Box-Plot diagram based comparison helps to find the min, mean, Q3, Q1, and max performance of models.

5.1   Word-Embedding Technique

In this study, eight different word-embedding techniques have been extracted features from defect reports. In the proposed framework, each word-embedding technique has been applied on six data-set (shown in Table 1) with eight deep learning models with 5-fold cross-validation, 2 sets of data such as original data and sampled data, and 4 sets of features such as all features, significant features, un-correlated significant features, and PCA features. Therefore, a combination of $8 * 6 * 2 * 4 * 5 = 1920$ models are assessed to compare the predictive power of different word-embedding and identify the best word-embedding technique for defect severity level prediction. Figure 5 shows the performance Box-Plot diagram in terms of F-measure, Accuracy, and AUC for the models trained by considering extracted features from defect report using different word-embedding. On analyzing the information present in Fig. 5, it has been observed that the models trained using different word-embedding techniques except GPT have more than 0.72 average AUC value. The high value of AUC showing that the models developed using embedding techniques have the ability to assign appropriate level of severity for defects.

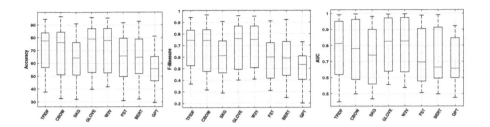

Fig. 5. Word embedding

5.2   Original Data and SMOTE Data

The data-set has highly imbalanced, which may lead to poor performance in predicting the minority class. In this study, the SMOTE technique has been used to convert imbalances data to balanced data by oversampling the minority classes. Figure 6 shows the performance Box-Plot diagram in terms of Accuracy, F-measure, and AUC for the models trained on original data and sampled data. On analyzing the information present in Fig. 6, it shows the higher average value for the SMOTE sampling technique. The Box-Plot in terms of AUC shows that the models trained using SMOTE data have the highest average value as compared to original data.

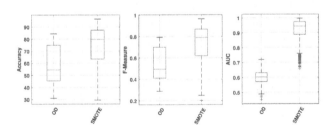

Fig. 6. Original data and SMOTE

5.3   Feature Selection

The considered research framework for severity value prediction models also used different types of techniques such as CCRA, PCA, and SIGF to remove irrelevant features and provide best sets of relevant features. Figure 7 shows the performance Box-Plot diagram in terms of area under curve, F-Measure, and accuracy for the severity value prediction models trained by considering extracted features from defect report using four different feature selection techniques. On analyzing the information present in Fig. 7, it has been seen that the models trained by considering un-correlated significant sets of features have a better ability to predict the severity level of the defects.

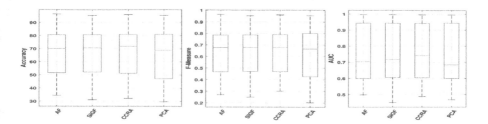

Fig. 7. Different sets of features

5.4   Classification Methods

In this paper, we have also considered deep learning with various hidden layers with an objective to improve the predictive power of defects severity level prediction models. In the proposed framework, eight different deep learning techniques have been applied on six data-sets (shown in Table 1) with 5-fold cross-validation, four feature selection techniques, eight types of word embedding techniques, and two sampling techniques. Therefore, a combination of $6 * 5 * 8 * 4 * 2 = 1920$ models are assessed to compare the predictive power of the different deep learning techniques and identify the best technique for defect severity level prediction. Figure 8 shows the performance Box-Plot diagram in terms of Accuracy, F-measure, and AUC for the models trained using eight different deep learning classification techniques. The information present in Fig. 8 suggested that the models trained using different deep learning have similar performance. The models trained using DLM1, which consists of only one hidden layer, has max AUC of 0.99, an average AUC of 0.76, and Q3 AUC value of 0.94 i.e., 25% of the models trained using DLM1 have AUC value of 0.94.

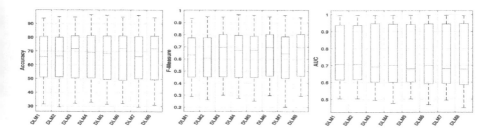

Fig. 8. Deep learning techniques

6   Conclusion

This work focus on development of severity value prediction models using different architecture of deep learning, embedding techniques, smote and feature selection techniques. The developed severity value prediction models have been verified using 5-fold cross validation and predictive power these verified models are compared using AUC and Accuracy. The high value of AUC on six different projects confirms that the trained models for severity value prediction have sufficient ability to estimate the right value of severity based on description reports of defects. From performance values in terms of AUC, and Accuracy, it has been concluded that the severity value prediction models trained using deep learning architecture with less number of hidden layers have better ability to estimate the right value of severity based on description reports of defects as compared to other architecture. The box-plot diagram of performance values in terms of Accuracy and area under curve indicate that the severity value prediction models trained on balanced data using SMOTE have better ability to estimate the right value of severity based on description reports as compared to original data. Finally, the trained models on small sets of feature have similar ability to estimate the right value of severity based on description reports as compared to all features.

Acknowledgments. This research is funded by TestAIng Solutions Pvt. Ltd.

References

1. Hooimeijer, P., Weimer, W.: Modeling bug report quality. In: Proceedings of the Twenty-Second IEEE/ACM International Conference on Automated Software Engineering, pp. 34–43 (2007)
2. Bhattacharya, P., Neamtiu, I.: Bug-fix time prediction models: can we do better? In: Proceedings of the 8th Working Conference on Mining Software Repositories, pp. 207–210 (2011)
3. Chaturvedi, K.K., Singh, V.B.: Determining bug severity using machine learning techniques. In: 2012 CSI Sixth International Conference on Software Engineering (CONSEG), pp. 1–6. IEEE (2012)
4. Jindal, R., Malhotra, R., Jain, A.: Software defect prediction using neural networks. In: Proceedings of 3rd International Conference on Reliability, Infocom Technologies and Optimization, pp. 1–6. IEEE (2014)
5. Dargan, S., Kumar, M., Ayyagari, M.R., Kumar, G.: A survey of deep learning and its applications: a new paradigm to machine learning. Arch. Comput. Methods Eng. **27**(4), 1071–1092 (2019). https://doi.org/10.1007/s11831-019-09344-w
6. de Barros, R.S.M., Hidalgo, J.I.G., de Lima Cabral, D.R.: Wilcoxon rank sum test drift detector. Neurocomputing **275**, 1954–1963 (2018)
7. Lever, J., Krzywinski, M., Altman, N.: Points of significance: principal component analysis. Nat. Methods **14**(7), 641–643 (2017)

Combining Reduction and Dense Blocks
for Music Genre Classification

Charbel El Achkar[1,2(✉)], Raphaël Couturier[2], Talar Atéchian[1],
and Abdallah Makhoul[2]

[1] TICKET Lab, Antonine University (UA), Baabda, Lebanon
{charbel.elachkar,talar.atechian}@ua.edu.lb
[2] FEMTO-ST Institute, CNRS, Université Bourgogne Franche-Comté (UBFC),
Belfort, France
{raphael.couturier,abdallah.makhoul}@univ-fcomte.fr

Abstract. Embedding music genre classifiers in music recommendation systems offers a satisfying user experience. It predicts music tracks depending on the user's taste in music. In this paper, we propose a preprocessing approach for generating STFT spectrograms and upgrades to a CNN-based music classifier named Bottom-up Broadcast Neural Network (BBNN). These upgrades concern the expansion of the number of inception and dense blocks, as well as the enhancement of the inception block through reduction block implementation. The proposed approach is able to outperform state-of-the-art music genre classifiers in terms of accuracy scores. It achieves an accuracy of 97.51% and 74.39% over the GTZAN and the FMA dataset respectively. Code is available at https://github.com/elachkarcharbel/music-genre-classifier.

Keywords: Music genre classification · STFT spectrogram · CNN · Music recommendation systems

1 Introduction

Modern studies found interest in building robust music classifiers to automate genre classification of unlabeled music tracks. There were diverse approaches in their feature engineering process as well as the neural network selection [1–5].

In this paper, we propose a custom approach for music genre classification. STFT spectrograms are generated and diversified by slicing each spectrogram into multiple slices to ensure a variety of visual representations among the same music track. Furthermore, upgrades to a state-of-the-art Convolutional Neural Network (CNN) network for music genre classification named BBNN [2] are proposed. **The contribution of this paper relies on two main improvements:** expanding the number of inception and dense blocks of the network and enhancing the inception block by implementing the reduction block B proposed in [6] instead of the existing block inspired by [7]. The proposition is evaluated through its application using the GTZAN [8] and the FMA [9] music datasets.

© Springer Nature Switzerland AG 2021
T. Mantoro et al. (Eds.): ICONIP 2021, CCIS 1517, pp. 752–760, 2021.
https://doi.org/10.1007/978-3-030-92310-5_87

The remainder of this paper is organized as follows: in Sect. 2, we discuss the recent music related classifiers used on the two datasets. In Sect. 3, we present the preprocessing process in addition to the contributed upgrades. Section 4 explores the experimental results of the proposed upgrades over competitive CNN networks, followed by a conclusion and future work thoughts in Sect. 5.

2   Related Work

Many studies took advantage of deep learning technologies to build efficient music genre classifiers. They adapted visual-related features (audio spectrogram) to build CNNs for audio classification tasks [1, 4, 11]. The audio data is converted to spectrograms and used as input features to CNN classifiers. These spectrograms are the visual representation of the spectrum of frequencies of the audio signal. As mentioned in Sect. 1, the proposed contribution is validated through experimental results. These experiments are applied using both the GTZAN dataset [8] and the FMA dataset [9]. Thus, the most recent and relevant publications over the two datasets are presented below.

Starting with GTZAN-related publications, a framework achieved an accuracy of 93.7% over the GTZAN dataset by producing a multilinear subspace analysis. It reduced the dimension of cortical representations of music signals [10]. Further studies took profit from DNNs and CNNs to try reaching higher accuracies over music datasets. Inspired by multilingual techniques for automatic speech recognition, a multilingual DNN was used in [4] for music genre classification purposes. It was able to achieve an accuracy of 93.4% through 10-fold cross-validation over the GTZAN dataset. Several approaches used CNN-based networks but were not able to exceed the accuracy of 91% such as [1, 11–13]. Others tried refining their results by overcoming the blurry classification of certain genres inside the GTZAN dataset. Their study did not surpass the accuracies mentioned previously [3]. After several attempts to outperform the accuracy reached in [10], three publications succeeded in using Mel spectrograms as input features to their DNNs. The use of convolutional long-short term memory-based neural networks (CNN LSTM) in combination with a transfer learning model helped in achieving an accuracy of 94.20% in [14]. As for the two remaining publications, the BBNN network proposed in [2] was able to achieve an accuracy of 93.90% by fully exploiting Mel spectrograms as a low-level feature for the music genre classification. The GIF generation method proposed in [5] was able to achieve the highest accuracy of 94.70% by providing efficient audio processing for animated GIF generation through acoustic features. Although this dataset has several faults [15], it is still the most dataset used in music genre classification use cases. These faults are taken into consideration in the preprocessing process that we will develop in later sections.

Concerning the FMA-related publications, a method of vertically slicing STFT spectrograms took place, in addition to applying oversampling and undersampling techniques for data augmentation purposes. This method achieved an F-score of 62.20% using an MLP classifier [16]. Another study trained a convolutional recurrent neural network (C-RNN) using raw audio to provide a real-time classification of FMA's music genres. It achieved an accuracy of 65.23% [17].

Motivated by FMA's challenges, an approach of two Deep Convolutional Neural Networks (DCNN) was proposed to classify music genres. The first DCNN was trained by the whole artist labels simultaneously, and the second was trained with a subset of the artist labels based on the artist's identity. This approach achieved an accuracy of 57.91% taking Mel spectrograms as input features to the DCNNs created [18]. Moreover, a method proposed in [13] took advantage of Densely Connected Convolutional Networks (DenseNet), found to be better than Residual Neural Network (ResNet) in music classification studies. It achieved an accuracy of 68.20% over the small subset of FMA.

3   Proposed Approach

In this section, the BBNN network proposed in [2] is briefly introduced. Later, the proposed approach is elaborated while mentioning the proposed upgrades to achieve higher accuracy results against the GTZAN and the FMA dataset.

As mentioned in the related work, the Bottom-up Broadcast Neural Network (BBNN) is a recent CNN architecture that fully exploits the low-level features of a spectrogram. It takes the multi-scale time-frequency information transferring suitable semantic features for the decision-making layers [2]. The BBNN network consists of inception blocks interconnected through dense blocks. The inception block is inspired by the inception v1 module proposed in [7] while adding a Batch Normalization (BN) operation and a Rectified Linear Unit activation (ReLU) before each convolution. This approach relied on generating coloured Mel spectrograms from the music tracks while providing the latter as input features to the CNN network. The spectrograms had the size of 647 × 128 and were used as-is for training purposes. This network was able to achieve the second-best accuracy over the GTZAN dataset (93.90%) by stacking three inception blocks with their corresponding dense connections.

3.1   Preprocessing

Spectrograms are the key to successful music genre classification using CNN-based networks. Based on the approaches mentioned in Sect. 2, greyscale STFT spectrograms are adopted instead of coloured Mel spectrograms. The majority of CNN-based music genre classifiers relied on Mel spectrograms since STFT spectrograms required greater GPU memory for their increased quantity of embedded features. Thus, we use STFT spectrograms in our experiments to leverage the latter increase on accuracy scores, in addition to the availability of efficient GPUs for experimental testing. Using the Sound eXchange (SOX) package, the greyscale spectrograms are generated with a size of 600 × 128. As expressed in Sect. 2, the GTZAN dataset has several faults [15]. For instance, three audio tracks were discarded while recursively generating the spectrograms using the SOX package. Each music track of the discarded ones was associated with a separate genre of the dataset. Therefore, we randomly removed a single audio track from the remaining genres to normalize the number of music tracks per genre.

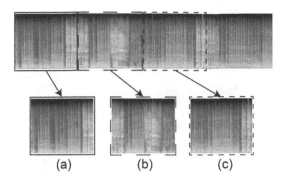

Fig. 1. Spectrogram slicing approach

Subsequently, the Python Imaging Libray (PIL) is used to slice the STFT spectrograms into multiple images. The spectrogram is divided into three to four separated slices. Each slice is a normalized 128 × 128 slice that represents a 6.4 s track out of the initial 30 s music tracks. Therefore, the last one and a half slices of the spectrogram are discarded, keeping only the first three slices (a, b and c in Fig. 1). This approach is mainly used for better data preparation for CNNs by normalizing the spectrogram's width and height. It also increases the diversity of the music genres, since spectrograms variate dependently on the time axis. Thus, this normalization does not accentuate overfitting due to the variety in every spectrogram's slices. It is important to mention that the discarded slices may hold useful data for our classification. However, we adopted this approach to limit the number of training/testing images as well as ensuring the obtention of the same number of slices per music track (music tracks length is not always consistent to 30 s).

3.2 Network Contribution

Inspired by the BBNN network [2], custom modifications are proposed to achieve higher accuracy results. Even though the BBNN stacks three inception blocks connected with dense blocks, the trained model possessed a tiny size (only 0.18 M). Using a small sample of both datasets, we performed a hyperparameter search taking the number of inception and dense blocks as the hyperparameter in question. The search result showed that the optimal number of blocks is equal to 6 for achieving the greatest accuracy. At this stage, the proposed network consisted of doubling the number of inception and dense blocks in the Broadcast Module (BM) of the BBNN, leaving the remaining layers (Shallow, Transition, and Decision) as proposed in [2].

Increasing the number of blocks reflected an increase in accuracy scores. On the other hand, it expanded the size of the training model and slowed the training process. Consequently, the architecture of the BBNN network was modified to reduce significant drawbacks due to overfitting and computation problems in the inception v1 block [6]. Many CNN related studies, in particular a music-related

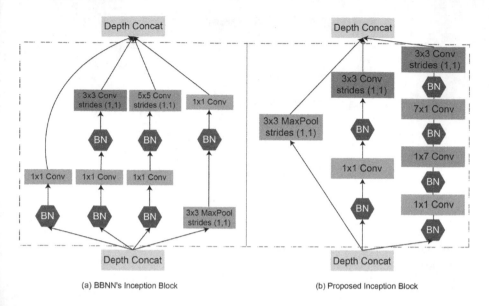

(a) BBNN's Inception Block   (b) Proposed Inception Block

Fig. 2. Proposed inception block modifications over the BBNN network

study in [13], proved that dense blocks are better than residual blocks. Thus, it was decided to keep the dense connection of the BBNN network intact. Moreover, the BBNN network relied on the inception v1 proposed in [7] while adding BN and ReLU operations before each convolution. The original inception v1 was found computationally expensive as well as prone to overfitting in many cases. At this stage, the next contribution was to replace the modified inception v1 blocks with modified inception v4 blocks in order to improve the computation efficiency and most importantly to increase the accuracy. As mentioned in [6], the earlier inception modules (v1, v2, v3) were found more complicated than necessary. They proposed specialized "Reduction Blocks" A and B to change the width and height of the grid. This change produces a performance boost by applying uniform and simplified operations to the network. Figure 2 presents the modified inception blocks in detail. The block on the left concerns the custom inception v1 block of BBNN, and the block on the right concerns our proposed inception v4 block. As previously mentioned, the left block is inspired by the inception v1 block in [7], while adding BN and ReLU operation before each convolution. On the other hand, the proposed inception block is inspired by the "Reduction Block B" introduced in [6]. Compared with BBNN's inception block in [2], the "Reduction Block B" of inception v4 [6] reduces the network complexity by mainly removing unnecessary 1×1 convolution operations and replacing the 5×5 convolution with a stack of 1×7, 7×1, and 3×3 convolution operations. Also, it accentuates memory optimization to backpropagation by implementing the factorization technique of inception v3. This technique is responsible to reduce the dimensionality of convolution layers, which reduce overfitting problems. In this matter, it was proposed to use the same architecture as the "Reduction Block B", while implementing BN and ReLU operations before each convolution.

4   Experimental Evaluation

In this section, the training hyperparameters are presented while evaluating the proposed contribution against state-of-the-art music genre classifiers. The training operations are performed using an NVIDIA Tesla V100 SXM2 GPU with 32 GB of memory.

4.1   Hyperparameters and Training Details

As mentioned in Sect. 3, the input images were prepared by generating a STFT spectrogram out of each music track of the GTZAN and the FMA dataset. Each spectrogram (600×128) was sliced into 128×128 slices, taking only the first three slices as a visual representation of each music track. At this stage, the input images for GTZAN classification were 297 slices of spectrograms per genre (99 music tracks per genre), and the input images for FMA classification were 3000 per genre (1000 music tracks per genre).

Inspired by BBNN [2], the proposed network upgrades were added as well as the hyperparameters to start the training. Considering that the BBNN network was initially tested against the GTZAN dataset [8], the same hyperparameters as the BBNN network were used for this case. The ADAM optimizer was selected to minimize the categorical cross-entropy between music genre labels, a batch size of 8 and an epoch size equal to 100. An initial learning rate of 0.01 was configured, while automatically decreasing its value by a factor of 0.5 once the loss stops improving after 3 epochs. The early stopping mechanism was implemented to prevent overfitting, and the GTZAN input spectrograms were fed to the classifier through 10-folds cross-validation training. Since all related publications used different dataset split ratios, the same ratio as BBNN's [2] is adopted to compare our results with BBNN in particular and with other publications in general. Thus, the training, testing and validation sets were randomly divided following an 8/1/1 proportion (80% for training, 10% for testing, and 10% for validation). The resulting training and testing accuracies were calculated by averaging all the accuracies concluded in the cross-validation folds.

Concerning the FMA dataset, the increase in the batch size revealed an accuracy increase. However, the same hyperparameters as GTZAN were used, in addition to keeping the same value of the batch size (8), to align our results with the existing ones.

Before initiating the training, the inception block's training parameters were calculated for both, the BBNN network and the proposed approach. This calculation showed that the proposed inception block uses less than 26.78 percentage points (pp) of BBNN's inception block parameters.

4.2   Testing Results

In the tables below (Table 1 and Table 2), the proposed approach is compared to the most recent and accurate methods. These methods either rely on deep learning models or hand-crafted feature descriptors to provide an efficient classification of the GTZAN and the FMA datasets.

Table 1. Comparative table for GTZAN classification methods in terms of accuracy (%)

GTZAN classification		
Methods	Preprocessing	Accuracy
AuDeep [1]	Mel spectrogram	85.40
NNet2 [11]	STFT	87.40
Hybrid model [3]	MFCC, SSD, etc.	88.30
Transform learning [12]	MFCC	89.80
DenseNet+Data augmentation [13]	STFT spectrogram	90.20
Multi-DNN [4]	MFCC	93.40
TPNTF[10]	MFCC	93.70
BBNN [2]	Mel spectrogram	93.90
DNN+Transfer learning [14]	Mel spectrogram	94.20
GIF generation framework [5]	MFCC spectrogram	94.70
Our approach	**STFT spectrogram**	**97.51**

Table 1 compares the music genre classifiers used on the GTZAN dataset. It shows the different methods used over this dataset, including its preprocessing features and the resulted accuracies. As mentioned in Sect. 2, each method relied on a different preprocessing and training approach to achieve the highest accuracy possible. The classification methods are enumerated in ascending order based on the accuracy score. As for the proposed approach, its related fields are displayed in bold in the table. The results show that the proposed method can outperform the accuracy of the BBNN network [2] specifically by 3.61 pp, and outperform the highest accuracy mentioned [5] by 2.81 pp.

Table 2. Comparative table for FMA classification methods in terms of accuracy (%)

FMA classification (fma-small subset)		
Methods	Preprocessing	Accuracy
Representation learning [18]	Mel spectrogram	57.91
BBNN [2]	Mel spectrogram	61.11
SongNet [17]	Raw audio	65.23
DenseNet+Data augmentation [13]	STFT spectrogram	68.20
Our approach	**STFT spectrogram**	**74.39**

As for the small subset of FMA, Table 2 presents the methods applied over the latter to provide accurate music genre classification. Similar to Table 1, this table shows the different methods used over this dataset, in addition to the preprocessing features used and the resulted accuracies. As for the proposed approach, it outperformed the highest accuracy over the FMA small subset [13] by 6.19 pp. Since the proposed approach was inspired by the BBNN network and the latter is not tested against the small subset of FMA, the BBNN Github code[1] was used as-is over this dataset for experimentation purposes. It resulted in an accuracy of 61.11%, found to be less than 13.28 pp of the proposed approach.

It is important to note that the outperformance against the related publications is not limited to the proposed network contribution only. The proposed preprocessing process assisted in this outperformance, especially with the GTZAN faults, where we reduced the number of music tracks per genre. Furthermore, the idea of slicing the generated spectrograms to obtain a diversity of visual representations among the same music track.

5 Conclusion and Future Work

In this paper, upgrades to a CNN-based music genre classifier named BBNN are proposed, in addition to a custom preprocessing process for generating STFT spectrograms out of the music tracks. The experiment results showed that the proposed approach was able to outperform existing methods in terms of accuracy. It achieved an accuracy of 97.51% and 74.39% over the GTZAN and the FMA datasets individually while outperforming the best GTZAN and FMA classification methods by 2.81 pp and 6.19 pp respectively. Also, the proposed approach was found to be better in terms of accuracy while relying on an optimized inception block that uses fewer training parameters to achieve greater results. Our future work should focus on leveraging recent technologies, such as audio and visual transformers, while focusing on reducing the model size and speeding the training process, to create greater music genre classifiers.

Acknowledgments. This work was funded by the "Agence universitaire de la Francophonie" (AUF) and supported by the EIPHI Graduate School (contract ANR-17-EURE-0002). Computations have been performed on the supercomputer facilities of the "Mésocentre de Franche-Comté".

References

1. Freitag, M., Amiriparian, S., Pugachevskiy, S., Cummins, N., Schuller, B.: auDeep: unsupervised learning of representations from audio with deep recurrent neural networks. J. Mach. Learn. Res. **18**, 12 (2017)
2. Liu, C., Feng, L., Liu, G., Wang, H., Liu, S.: Bottom-up broadcast neural network for music genre classification. Multimedia Tools Appl. **80**, 1–19 (2021)

---

[1] https://github.com/CaifengLiu/music-genre-classification.

3. Karunakaran, N., Arya, A.: A scalable hybrid classifier for music genre classification using machine learning concepts and spark. In: 2018 International Conference on Intelligent Autonomous Systems (ICoIAS), pp. 128–135 (2018)
4. Dai, J., Liu, W., Ni, C., Dong, L., Yang, H.: Multilingual deep neural network for music genre classification. In: INTERSPEECH (2015)
5. Mujtaba, G., Lee, S., Kim, J., et al.: Client-driven animated GIF generation framework using an acoustic feature. Multimedia Tools Appl. (2021). https://doi.org/10.1007/s11042-020-10236-6
6. Szegedy, C., Ioffe, S., Vanhoucke, V., Alemi, A.A.: Inception-v4, inception-ResNet and the impact of residual connections on learning. In: AAAI'17: Proceedings of the Thirty-First AAAI Conference on Artificial Intelligence Go to Proceedings of the Thirty-First AAAI Conference on Artificial Intelligence (2017)
7. Szegedy, C., et al.: Going deeper with convolutions. In: 2015 IEEE Conference on Computer Vision and Pattern Recognition (CVPR), pp. 1–9 (2015)
8. Tzanetakis, G., Essl, G., Cook, P.: Automatic musical genre classification of audio signals (2001).http://ismir2001.ismir.net/pdf/478tzanetakis.pdf
9. Defferrard, M., Benzi, K., Vandergheynst, P., Bresson, X.: FMA: a dataset for music analysis. In: 18th International Society for Music Information Retrieval Conference (ISMIR), (2017). ArXiv arXiv:1703.09179
10. Panagakis, Y., Kotropoulos, C.: Music genre classification via topology preserving non-negative tensor factorization and sparse representations. In: 2010 IEEE International Conference on Acoustics, Speech and Signal Processing, pp. 249–252 (2010)
11. Zhang, W., Lei, W., Xu, K., Xing, X.: Improved music genre classification with convolutional neural networks. In: INTERSPEECH (2016)
12. Choi, K., Fazekas, G., Sandler, M., Cho, K.: Transfer learning for music classification and regression tasks. ArXiv arXiv:1703.09179 (2017)
13. Bian, W., Wang, J., Zhuang, B., Yang, J., Wang, S., Xiao. J.: Audio-based music classification with DenseNet and data augmentation. In: PRICAI (2019)
14. Ghosal, D., Kolekar, M.: Music genre recognition using deep neural networks and transfer learning. In: INTERSPEECH (2018)
15. Sturm, B.L.: The GTZAN dataset: its contents, its faults, their effects on evaluation, and its future use. 11, 1–29 (2013). https://doi.org/10.1080/09298215.2014.894533
16. Valerio, V.D., Pereira, R.M., Costa, Y.M.G., Bertolini, D., Silla, N.: A resampling approach for Imbalanceness on music genre classification using spectrograms. In: FLAIRS Conference (2018)
17. Zhang, C., Zhang, Y.: SongNet: Real-time Music Classification. (2018)
18. Park, J., Lee, J., Park, J., Ha, J.-W., Nam, J.: Representation learning of music using artist labels. In: ISMIR (2018)

Attend to Your Review: A Deep Neural Network to Extract Aspects from Peer Reviews

Rajeev Verma[1], Kartik Shinde[2(✉)], Hardik Arora[2], and Tirthankar Ghosal[3]

[1] University of Amsterdam, Amsterdam, Netherlands
`rajeev.verma@student.uva.nl`
[2] Indian Institute of Technology Patna, Patna, India
`{kartik_1901ce16,hardik_1901ce15}@iitp.ac.in`
[3] Institute of Formal and Applied Linguistics, Faculty of Mathematics and Physics, Charles University, Prague, Czech Republic
`ghosal@ufal.mff.cuni.cz`

Abstract. Peer-review process is fraught with issues like bias, inconsistencies, arbitrariness, non-committal weak rejects, etc. However, it is anticipated that the peer reviews provide constructive feedback to the authors against some aspects of the paper such as *Motivation/Impact, Soundness/Correctness, Novelty, Substance*, etc. A good review is expected to evaluate a paper under the lens of these aspects. An automated system to extract these implicit aspects from the reviews would help determine the quality/goodness of the peer review. In this work, we propose a deep neural architecture to extract the aspects of the paper on which the reviewer commented in their review. Our automatic aspect-extraction model based on BERT and neural attention mechanism achieves superior performance over the standard baselines. We make our codes, analyses and other matrials available at https://github.com/cruxieu17/aspect-extraction-peer-reviews.

Keywords: Aspect extraction · Peer reviews · Deep neural networks

1 Introduction

Peer review is the central system of scientific research validation. However, several studies highlight the bias [1], inconsistencies [2,3], arbitrariness [4] of the peer-review process, thus, degrading the integrity and trust of the central system of research validation. Area chairs/Editors are responsible for mitigating such issues via assigning expert reviewers and evaluating reviewers' comments to generate informed decisions. However, the exponential rise in paper submissions has put the peer-review system under severe stress in recent years, leading to a dearth of experienced reviewers.

R. Verma and K. Shinde—Equal contribution.

The original version of this chapter was revised: The acknowledgement statement has been added to the chapter. The correction to this chapter is available at https://doi.org/10.1007/978-3-030-92310-5_89

More recently, the peer-review system has been shown to be suffering from the problem of Collusion Rings and Non-Committal Weak Rejects. Non-Committal Weak rejects are defined as paper rejects with no substantial feedback for the authors to act upon and have conflicting scores compared with the reviews with a good evaluation of the said manuscript. Sometimes the competitive venues have vested interests in controlling their acceptance rates. Coupled with the increasing submission rate, this makes the senior area chairs reject as many papers as possible in a bid to accept only perfect papers. Thus, the Non-Committal Weak Rejects reviews increase the probability that the said paper will eventually be rejected as the low review score deems the paper imperfect.

We believe that an essential step in the direction of re-establishing trust in the peer-review process should be an attempt to establish confidence in the peer-review reports.

As per the rubrics defined in [5], we expect the review to evaluate the work for indicators like novelty, theoretical and empirical soundness of the research methodology, writing, and clarity of the work, impact of the work in a broader academic context, etc. We call these indicators review-level aspects.

In this work, we propose a deep neural network architecture that takes the review text as input and extracts the review-level aspects from it. Our model is based on the simple Attention mechanism that can decompose the review text into aspect-level representations, thus, aiding the extraction. We get superior performance compared with the baselines. Such a system can help check the quality of the review reports, thus maintaining the peer-review integrity of the peer-review system.

2   Related Work

Some studies analyze the reviewing process for major ML conferences like Tran et al. [7], Shah et al. [2]. Researchers have also argued for changes in reviewing practices and proposed changes. Sculley et al. [5] proposed a rubric to hold reviewers to an objective standard for review quality. Rogers and Augenstein et al. [6] identifies challenges and problems in the reviewing system and suggests ways to tackle them. Yuan et al. [8] investigated if the writing of reviews could be automated. They also propose a review dataset with phrase-level annotations for the aspects present and present preliminary results on sentence-level aspect prediction. We use this dataset in our experiments. Our objective to judge the review reports is somewhat similar to Xiong and Litman et al. [9] who predict the helpfulness of a peer-review using manual features.

3   Dataset Statistics

We use the ASAP-Review dataset recently propose by [8]. ASAP-Review dataset is composed of review text, their annotated review-level annotations, and review meta-data. It contains ICLR (International Conference on Learning Representations (2017–2020) and NeurIPS (Neural Information Processing Systems

Table 1. Dataset statistics. Along with the standard review text, the dataset also includes as reviews the replies to the reviews and discussion on the OpenReview platform.

Venues	Papers	Acc/Rej	# Reviews
ICLR	5,192	1,859/3,333	15,728
NeurIPS	3,685	3,685/0	12,391
Total	8,877	5,244/3,333	28,119

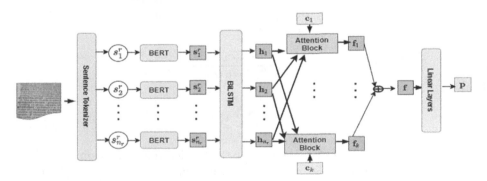

Fig. 1. Proportion of the present aspects in the dataset. As can be seen, the data is unbalanced and aspects like CMP and REP are very scarce.

(2016–2019) reviews from the open-access platform OpenReview[1] platform. We show the detailed dataset statistic in Table 1 and refer the reader to the original paper for more details. We further note that the dataset is unbalanced and show the percentage of each aspect in the whole dataset in Fig. 1.

4 Methodology

A visual schema of the architecture can be seen in Fig. 2. The input to the model is review text. We do not employ any special preprocessing so as to preserve the review structure. We describe the main components of the proposed model in the following subsections.

Fig. 2. Proposed Architecture for the review-level aspect extraction. As shown, we use the pretrained BERT model (specifically, RoBERTa) to get sentence representations. We then use BiLSTM to get the review representation. We use the simple attention mechanism using trainable codes $C_a = \{c_1, c_2, \ldots, c_k\}$ to decompose the review representation into aspect-level representation. We then concatenate them and pass into feedforward linear layers for final classification.

---

[1] https://openreview.net/.

4.1   Review Representation and Encoder

The input to our model are review sentences. Denote the review $R = (s_1^r, s_2^r, ..., s_{n_r}^r)$ as the sequence of their respective sentences. For a sentence s_i^p we get a d dimensional embedding vector $\mathbf{s}_i^p \in \mathbb{R}^d$ using RoBERTa [11] model. We specifically use Sentence Transformers [10] with stsb-RoBERTa-base as the encoder. We use the Sentence Embeddings with Sentence Transformers using pretrained model to get meaningful sentence embeddings. Pretrained language models incorporate rich representation power, as they are trained on large corpora. We get the review representation $\mathbf{R} \in \mathbb{R}^{n_r \times d}$ as $\mathbf{R} = \mathbf{s}_1^r \oplus \mathbf{s}_2^r \oplus ... \oplus \mathbf{s}_{n_r}^r$, $\mathbf{R} \in \mathbb{R}^{n_r \times d}$ We then pass the review representation $\mathbf{R}$ to the BiLSTM layers [12] $g_{\theta_1}(.)$ to model contextual inter dependencies between individual sentences, and we get output hidden representation $\mathbf{h}_i$ at each step i, i.e. $(\mathbf{h}_1, \mathbf{h}_2, ..., \mathbf{h}_{n_r}) = g_{\theta_1}(\mathbf{R})$

In this way, our encoding model is a hierarchical module which first models contextual dependencies between tokens to get sentence representations using Transformers based attention mechanism [13], and then uses BiLSTM to model sentence level dependencies.

4.2   Aspect-Level Feature Extractor

To extract aspect level information from the review representation, we use a simple attention mechanism. The goal is to decompose the review into aspect based representations. Given the review level aspects $R_a = \{a_1, a_2, ..., a_k\}$, we define codes $C_a = \{\mathbf{c}_1, \mathbf{c}_2, ..., \mathbf{c}_k\}$ where $|C_a| = |R_a|$ We extract the representation for the kth aspect as follows:

$$\alpha_k^i = \frac{\exp(\mathbf{c}_k \cdot \mathbf{h}_i)}{\sum_{j=1}^{n_r} \exp(\mathbf{c}_k \cdot \mathbf{h}_j)}$$

$$\mathbf{f}_k = \sum_{i=1}^{n_r} \alpha_k^i \mathbf{h}_i$$

Here, α_k^i denote the attention weight for the hidden representation $\mathbf{h}_i$ and for code $\mathbf{c}_k$. And $\mathbf{f}_k$ denote the output representation for the code $\mathbf{c}_k$. The C_a is learned during the training procedure.

4.3   Feedforward Prediction Layers

We concatenate the outputs from the aspect-level feature extractor together for the final classification. Thus, we obtain $\mathbf{f}$ as $\mathbf{f} = \mathbf{f}_1 \oplus \mathbf{f}_2 \oplus ... \oplus \mathbf{f}_k$ We pass $\mathbf{f}$ to the feedforward linear layers $l_{\theta_2}(.)$ as get the prediction $\mathbf{p}$ as

$$\mathbf{p} = \frac{1}{1 + \exp(-l_{\theta_2}(\mathbf{f}))}$$

5   Experimental Setup and Evaluation

We split our dataset into 80% train,5% validation and 15% test sets. We use the loss on validation set to monitor the training and employ early stopping when the loss won't improve for 10 epochs. We use a learning rate of $1e-3$, a batch size of 32 to train our main model. We use fixed set $\{1e-1, 1e-2, 1e-3, 3e-3\}$ to tune the learning rate, and find $1e-3$ works best. We used Adam optimizer with a weight_decay=1e-3 (for avoiding overfitting) for training.

5.1   Comparison Systems

Our task of review-level aspect extraction is a multi-label classification problem. We compare our method with common multi-label classification techniques. The comparison systems are described next. To highlight the difference with our method, we follow the same notation from Sect. 4.

1. **Average Sentence Embeddings (ASE)**: We use average of the sentence embeddings as review representation and pass it to the feedforward linear layers for prediction.
2. **BiLSTM**: We use BiLSTM model to do the multi-label classification. More specifically, we do not use our aspect-level feature extractor, and instead get the prediction $\mathbf{p}$ as $\mathbf{h} = \mathbf{h}_1 \oplus \mathbf{h}_2 \oplus \ldots \oplus \mathbf{h}_{n_r}$, $\mathbf{p} = l_{\theta_2}(\mathbf{h})$
3. **BERT**: We finetune the pretrained BERT model [14], specifically bert-base-large using Huggingface [15]. The model takes full review text as input (although, the input gets truncated to 512 tokens as the model has the maximum limit of 512 tokens). The review representation is taken from the [CLS] token, which is then passed to the feedforward linear layers for prediction.

6   Results and Analysis

We show the results for the proposed architecture and the baselines in Table 2. The table shows that our simple attention-based model outperforms other baselines consistently for all aspects. One interesting thing to note is that even the simple baseline like Average Sentence Embeddings (ASE) has decent performance on this task. We attribute this to the use of pretrained RoBERTa embeddings. Since the RoBERTa model is trained on a huge corpus, this model employs all its inductive biases and superior language representation capabilities to give good performance. However, the performance is not consistently good for all aspects. As can be seen, the F1 score on aspect Meaningful Comparison (CMP) is a mere 0.570, while on aspect Replicability (REP), it is abysmally low. The lower performance for these two aspects is due to the imbalance in the dataset. Replicability (REP) and Meaningful Comparison (CMP) are present in a small percentage of the reviews in the dataset.

BiLSTM baseline improves the numbers for all the aspects compared with the ASE baseline. However, the F1 for aspect Replicability (REP) is still low. BiLSTM improves over the ASE baseline as BiLSTM can better model the review

Table 2. Results for the review-level aspect extraction task for each of the aspect corresponding to the proposed model and the baselines. The task is multi-label classification. We report Accuracy(**ACC**) and F1 (**F1**) score.

Aspect	ASE		BiLSTM		BERT		Ours	
	ACC	F1	ACC	F1	ACC	F1	ACC	F1
Motivation (MOT)	0.712	0.714	**0.835**	0.809	0.72	0.716	**0.835**	**0.827**
Clarity (CLA)	0.878	0.907	0.913	0.935	0.838	0.889	**0.933**	**0.95**
Soundness/Correctness (SOU)	0.749	0.830	0.800	0.860	0.753	0.837	**0.829**	**0.877**
Substance (SUB)	0.720	0.720	0.747	0.749	0.748	0.739	**0.817**	**0.803**
Meaningful Comparison (CMP)	0.752	0.570	0.872	0.794	0.825	0.685	**0.893**	**0.824**
Originality (ORI)	0.808	0.839	**0.876**	**0.885**	0.741	0.787	**0.876**	**0.886**
Replicability (REP)	0.852	0.248	0.875	0.291	0.872	0.422	**0.916**	**0.691**

representation than the less informative average operation of the ASE baseline. Surprisingly, the BERT baseline performs poorer than the BiLSTM and the simple ASE baseline except for the Replicability (REP) aspect. This is contrary to the general knowledge in the NLP community where BERT models are state-of-the-art across many NLP tasks. However, we remark that the ASE and BiLSTM baselines are not independent of the significant performance gains that come with BERT. Both the ASE and BiLSTM model uses pretrained RoBERTa sentence embeddings and then build a review representation. As stated before, the representation obtained is hierarchical with utilizing token-level contextual information in a sentence to get sentence representation and then use sentence-level contextual information to get the review representation. We assert that this hierarchy is missing in the BERT baseline. The BERT model gets the review representation by using only token-level information. However, it models a longer-range context (by self-attention across the complete review), and we get the review representation from the [CLS] token. We hypothesize that the review representation obtained from BERT is not that richer as the reviews can be arbitrarily large. This can affect getting good informative representations.

Finally, we note that our proposed architecture gives good performance even for scarce aspects like Meaningful Comparison (CMP) and Replicability (REP). As stated before, our model is hierarchical in nature, and the aspect-level attention makes it more precise. The attention mechanism is designed to get fine-grained aspect-level representations that can better aid the classification. This lowers false positives and false negatives, thus, improving the F1 score.

We can see the effect of the attention mechanism for the representative review examples - Review 1[2] and Review 2[3] have their attention heatmaps in Fig. 3. We can see that, for each sentence, attention weight shows significant attention weight for some of the aspect c_i. For example, sentence 5 of Review 1, *"furthermore, the paper lacks in novelty aspect, as it uses mostly well-known techniques."*, which clearly has aspect "Originality (ORI)", shows the highest attention weight for aspect 3 (c_3). This means that c_3 is sensitive to the Originality aspect. This conclusion is drawn together with sentence 1 of Review 2, which again has the "Originality(ORI)" aspect and shows the highest attention weight for c_3. The same conclusions can be drawn for other aspects as well. Another thing to note is that the heatmaps are sparse, showing the distinctiveness of the attention mechanism. This means that the aggregate representation f_k that we get aspect k is representative of the aspect level information. This shows that our model is able to decompose the review representation into aspect-level representations resulting in better prediction.

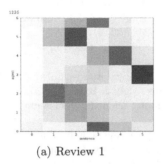
(a) Review 1

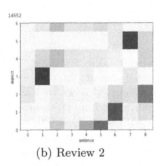
(b) Review 2

Fig. 3. Attention maps for each sentence (on x-axis) and c_k (k on y-axis) for Review-1:(https://openreview.net/forum?id=HkGJUXb0-&noteId=ry_11ijeM) and Review-2:(https://github.com/cruxieu17/aspect-extraction-peer-reviews/blob/main/review_2.txt) Darker color means high attention weight (α_k^i) for i_{th} review sentence. As can be observed, the attention weight is higher for the sentences having presence of the present aspect.

7 Conclusions

In this work, we propose attention-based deep-neural network architecture for aspect extraction from peer-review. The proposed model takes full review text as input. We also show the efficacy of the attention mechanism by demonstrating its distinctiveness quality. The attention mechanism works by decomposing the review representation into aspect-level representations. One major application of our work would be to detect the Non-Committal Weak rejects reviews which

---

[2] https://openreview.net/forum?id=HkGJUXb0-&noteId=ry_11ijeM.

[3] https://github.com/cruxieu17/aspect-extraction-peer-reviews/blob/main/review_2.txt.

do not provide actionable feedback. Having such an automated system can help detect the inferior quality reviews to penalize them, thereby alleviating some of the trust issues with the peer-review reports.

Acknowledgement. Tirthankar Ghosal is funded by Cactus Communications, India (Award # CAC-2021-01) to carry out this research.

References

1. Tomkins, A., Zhang, M., Heavlin, W.D.: Reviewer bias in single-versus double-blind peer review. Proc. Natl. Acad. Sci. **114**(48), 12708–12713 (2017)
2. Shah, N.B., Tabibian, B., Muandet, K., Guyon, I., Von Luxburg, U.: Design and analysis of the NIPS 2016 review process. J. Mach. Learn. Res. **19**(49), 1–34 (2018)
3. Langford, J., Guzdial, M.: The arbitrariness of reviews, and advice for school administrators. Commun. ACM **58**(4), 12–13 (2015)
4. Brezis, E.S., Birukou, A.: Arbitrariness in the peer review process. Scientometrics **123**(1), 393–411 (2020). https://doi.org/10.1007/s11192-020-03348-1
5. Sculley, D., Snoek, J., Wiltschko, A.: Avoiding a tragedy of the commons in the peer review process. arXiv preprint arXiv:1901.06246 (2018)
6. Rogers, A., Augenstein, I.: What can we do to improve peer review in NLP?. arXiv preprint arXiv:2010.03863 (2020)
7. Tran, D., et al.: An open review of OpenReview: a critical analysis of the machine learning conference review process. arXiv preprint arXiv:2010.05137 (2020)
8. Yuan, W., Liu, P., Neubig, G.: Can we automate scientific reviewing?. arXiv preprint arXiv:2102.00176 (2021)
9. Xiong, W., Litman, D.: Automatically predicting peer-review helpfulness. In: Proceedings of the 49th Annual Meeting of the Association for Computational Linguistics: Human Language Technologies, pp. 502–507, June 2011
10. Reimers, N., Gurevych, I.: Sentence-HERT: sentence embeddings using Siamese HERT-networks. arXiv preprint arXiv:1908.10084 (2019)
11. Liu, Y., et al.: Roberta: a robustly optimized HERT pretraining approach. arXiv preprint arXiv:1907.11692, (2019)
12. Hochreiter, S., Schmidhuber, J.: Long short-term memory. Neural Comput. **9**(8), 1735–1780 (1997)
13. Vaswani, A., et al.: Attention is all you need. In: Advances in Neural Information Processing Systems, pp. 5998–6008 (2017)
14. Devlin, J., Chang, M.W., Lee, K., Toutanova, K.: Bert: pre-training of deep bidirectional transformers for language understanding. arXiv preprint arXiv:1810.04805 (2018)
15. Wolf, T., et al.: Transformers: state-of-the-art natural language processing. In: Proceedings of the 2020 Conference on Empirical Methods in Natural Language Processing: System Demonstrations, pp. 38–45, October2020

Correction to: *Attend to Your Review*: A Deep Neural Network to Extract Aspects from Peer Reviews

Rajeev Verma, Kartik Shinde, Hardik Arora, and Tirthankar Ghosal

Correction to:
Chapter *"Attend to Your Review*: A Deep Neural Network to Extract Aspects from Peer Reviews"
in: T. Mantoro et al. (Eds.): *Neural Information Processing*, CCIS 1517, https://doi.org/10.1007/978-3-030-92310-5_88

In the originally published version of chapter 88 the acknowledgement statement was erroneously omitted. The acknowledgement statement has been added to the chapter.

The updated version of this chapter can be found at
https://doi.org/10.1007/978-3-030-92310-5_88

© Springer Nature Switzerland AG 2022
T. Mantoro et al. (Eds.): ICONIP 2021, CCIS 1517, p. C1, 2022.
https://doi.org/10.1007/978-3-030-92310-5_89

Author Index

Printed in the United States
by Baker & Taylor Publisher Services